The Enduring Vision

The Enduring Vision

A History of the American People

Volume 1: To 1877

Paul S. Boyer
University of Wisconsin, Madison

Clifford E. Clark, Jr.
Carleton College

Joseph F. Kett
University of Virginia

Thomas L. Purvis

Harvard Sitkoff
University of New Hampshire

Nancy Woloch
Barnard College

D. C. Heath and Company
Lexington, Massachusetts   Toronto

Acquisitions Editors: Linda Halvorson and James Miller
Developmental Editor: Sylvia Mallory
Production Editor: Rosemary R. Jaffe
Designer: Henry Rachlin
Production Coordinator: Michael O'Dea
Text Permissions Editor: Margaret Roll
Graphs: Boston Graphics, Inc.
Maps: Sanderson Associates
Photo Research: Martha Shethar with assistance from Sharon Donahue, Linda
            Finigan, Martha Friedman, Janet Goldman, Billie Ingram, and
            Sylvia Mallory

Cover: Summer Spread with Appliquéd Farm Scene (Detail), 1853. Sarah Ann
Gargis, Feasterville or Doylstown, Pennsylvania. Cotton front, muslin back. Gift
of Warner Communications Inc. Museum of American Folk Art, New York.

Published simultaneously in Canada.

Printed in the United States of America.

International Standard Book Number: 0−669−09799−3

Library of Congress Catalog Card Number: 89−83818

10 9 8 7 6 5 4 3 2 1

ABOUT THE AUTHORS

Paul S. Boyer, Merle Curti professor of history at the University of Wisconsin, Madison, earned his Ph.D. from Harvard University. An editor of *Notable American Women, 1607–1950* (1971), he also coauthored *Salem Possessed: The Social Origins of Witchcraft* (1974), for which, with Stephen Nissenbaum, he received the John H. Dunning Prize of the American Historical Association. His other published works include *Purity in Print: Book Censorship in America* (1968), *Urban Masses and Moral Order in America, 1820–1920* (1978), and *By the Bomb's Early Light: American Thought and Culture at the Dawn of the Atomic Age* (1985). Also a frequent contributor to journals such as *American Quarterly* and *The New Republic,* he is currently researching another work on contemporary American culture. He is an elected member of the American Antiquarian Society.

Clifford E. Clark, Jr., professor of history at Carleton College, earned his Ph.D. from Harvard University. He has served as both chair of the history department and director of the American Studies program at Carleton. Clark is the author of *Henry Ward Beecher: Spokesman for a Middle-Class America* (1978), *The American Family Home, 1800–1960* (1986), and *American and Canadian Intellectual History, 1789 to 1960,* a volume in the forthcoming *General History of the Americas.* He has also edited and contributed to *Minnesota in a Century of Change: The State and Its People Since 1900* (1989) and serves on the editorial board of the *Winterthur Portfolio, A Journal of American Material Culture.* At present he is researching a study of a midwestern community that began as a planned railroad town.

Joseph F. Kett, professor of history and department chair at the University of Virginia, received his Ph.D. from Harvard University. His works include *The Formation of the American Medical Profession, 1780–1860: The Role of Institutions* (1968), *Rites of Passage: Adolescence in America, 1790–Present* (1977), *The American Family, 1978* (1978), and *The Dictionary of Cultural Literacy* (1988), of which he is a coauthor. His current research project is on the diffusion of knowledge in the United States. He has participated on the Panel on Youth of the President's Science Advisory Committee, has served on the Board of Editors of the *History of Education Quarterly,* and is a past member of the Council of the American Studies Association.

Thomas L. Purvis, who has served as Editor of Publications at the Institute for Early American History and Culture and as adjunct associate professor of history at the College of William and Mary, received his Ph.D. from the Johns Hopkins University. He is the recipient of numerous academic honors and awards and a frequent contributor to journals such as the *William and Mary Quarterly* and *New Jersey History.* The author of *Proprietors, Patronage, and Paper Money: Legislative Politics in New Jersey, 1703–1776* (1986), for which he won the McCormick Prize, he is currently at work on a study of the Seven Years' War in America.

Harvard Sitkoff, professor of history at the University of New Hampshire and John Adams Professor of American Civilization in the Netherlands, earned his Ph.D. from Columbia University. He is the author of *A New Deal for Blacks* (1978) and *The Struggle for Black Equality* (1981); coeditor of *A History of Our Time* (1982, 1987); and editor of *Fifty Years Later: The New Deal Evaluated* (1985). A contributor to a number of edited collections, he has also published articles in many journals, among them *The Journal of American History, The Journal of Southern History,* and *The Wilson Quarterly.*

Nancy Woloch received her Ph.D. from Indiana University. She is the author of *Women and the American Experience* (1984), a coeditor of *Images of America: Selected Readings* (1978), and, with Walter LaFeber and Richard Polenberg, the coauthor of *The American Century: A History of the United States Since the 1890s* (1986). Currently working on a documentary history of early American women, she teaches American history at Barnard College.

PREFACE

The Enduring Vision

This is the story of America and of the visions that Americans have shared. The first vision was of the land itself. For the prehistoric adventurers who crossed the land bridge from Asia, for the Europeans who began to arrive in the sixteenth century, and for the later immigrants who poured in by the tens of millions, North America offered a haven for new beginnings. If life was hard in the Old World, it would be better in the New. And once here, the lure of the land continued—away from the crowded city, beyond the rim of settlement. If times were tough in the East, they would be better in the West. New Englanders migrated to Ohio; Ohioans migrated to Kansas; Kansans migrated to California. Southern blacks after the Civil War dreamed of new opportunities elsewhere:

> I got my ticket,
> Leaving the thicket,
> And I'm a-heading for the Golden Shore!

Even today, the land itself remains part of the vision. Indeed, it becomes more precious as we realize its vulnerability to pollution and exploitation. In this way, we share a link with those who went before us who also cherished this continent's forests, mountains, lakes, and rivers.

But the vision involves more than simply a love of the land. It also entails a commitment to an ongoing social and intellectual process: the process of creating a just social order. In pursuing this goal, we have experimented with new social forms and engaged in bitter debates. As the French immigrant Michel Crèvecoeur wrote in 1782: "The American is a new man, who acts upon new principles, . . . new ideas, and . . . new opinions."

Central to the American vision of the good society is the notion of individual freedom. To be sure, our commitment to freedom as frequently faltered in practice. The Puritans who sought freedom of worship for themselves often denied it to others. Southern whites who cheered the Declaration of Independence lived by the labor of black slaves. Many a capitalist tycoon conveniently forgot that economic exploitation can extinguish freedom as effectively as political tyranny or military force. And through much of our history, women—one-half the population—were relegated to second-class status. Yet the battered vision endured, prodding a sometimes reluctant nation to confront and explore its full meaning.

But freedom can be an empty and cheerless thing unless one is also part of a social group. The novelist O. E. Rolvaag, describing the emotions of a nineteenth-century Norwegian immigrant farm woman on the Great Plains, captured this feeling of social isolation:

> A sense of desolation so profound settled upon her that she seemed unable to think at all. . . . She threw herself back in the grass and looked up into the heavens. But darkness and infinitude lay there, also—the sense of utter desolation still remained. . . . Suddenly, for the first time, she realized the full extent of her loneliness. . . .

Thus the vision must also be one of community. John Winthrop, addressing a group of English immigrants aboard the *Arbella* on their way to America in 1630, eloquently summed up this dimension of the vision: "We must delight in each other, make others' conditions our own, rejoice together, mourn together, labor and suffer together: always having before our eyes our commission and community . . . as members of the same body."

The family, the town, the neighborhood, the church, and the nation itself have been ways by which Americans have woven into their lives a web of social meaning. And *community* is not just a high-sounding abstraction; it has political implications. If we are not just a fragmented collection of self-absorbed individuals but also a *people,* what obligations do we owe each other? What limitations on our freedom are we willing to accept in order to be part of a social group? In struggling with tough questions like these, we have further defined our vision of America.

Finally, this vision is one of renewal and new beginnings. The story of America is part of the human story, and thus it has its dark and shameful passages as well as its bright moments of achievement. Arrogance, injustice, callous blindness to suffering, and national self-delusion have all figured in our history. But balancing the times when we lost our way are the moments when we found our bearings and returned to the hard task of defining what America at its best might truly be.

This, then, is the essence of the vision: a vision not of a foreordained national destiny unfolding effortlessly but of a laborious, often frustrating struggle to define what our common life as a people shall be. For all the failures and the wrong turns, it remains a vision rooted in hope, not despair. In 1980 Jesse de la Cruz, a Mexican-American woman who had fought for years to improve conditions for California's migrant workers, summed up the philosophy that kept her going: "Is America progressing toward the better? . . . We're the ones that are gonna do it. We have to keep on struggling. . . . With us, there's a saying: *La esperanza muere al último.* Hope dies last. You can't lose hope. If you lose hope, that's losing everything."

No sentiment could better sum up the enduring vision of American history.

Introduction

In writing *The Enduring Vision,* our aim has been twofold: to do full justice to the history of public events, with maximum chronological clarity, and to bring into the story the rich findings of research into social and cultural history over the past few decades. In short, we set out to trace the interaction of public and private spheres in the American past. Times were ripe for such a venture. History is enjoying a long overdue resurgence in the undergraduate curriculum. Students come to American history eager for a compelling narrative, ready to encounter the grand sweep of the nation's past and to ponder America's identity as a nation. Their teachers reached intellectual maturity during and after the enormous expansion of history's domain that began in the 1960s with the absorption of social-science theory and a determination to study

previously neglected social groups. The dual purpose of inquiring rigorously into a problem and of telling a story with grace and conviction has always guided the greatest practitioners of the craft of history. We have made it our purpose as well.

Our book maintains a reasonable level of rigor. We have not hesitated to take up challenging topics. But we have *explained* these matters clearly and shown how they are essential to understanding American history. Every step of the way, we and our editors have asked hard questions: what do college students beginning the study of American history need to know, and how does *this* particular piece of evidence fit into the picture?

Throughout, we have sought to describe the experiences and perspectives of ordinary people as well as to account for the motivations of history's great figures. Our view of history is neither rigidly "top-down" nor "bottom-up"; rather, we see a constant interplay between communities, regions, and nation. As frequently as possible, we introduce students to real people from the past and allow these participants to speak for themselves. The revealing anecdote or pungent quotation can be worth many words of abstract explanation, and we have ransacked our sources to find fresh material that piquantly captures the mentality of the era. Above all, we realize the importance of encouraging students to judge historical events with the values of the past in mind. There is no better way to foster respect for history.

Every working historian knows how difficult is the challenge of combining analysis and narrative. Our solution has been to break the narrative down into manageable, chapter-length chunks and to "stop the music" where appropriate in order to analyze the forces underlying events. We have tried to ensure that the reader always knows how private social interactions fit into larger patterns of public events yet never sees those events merely as a random progression of "facts" without social or cultural context.

We have tried to give our book character, to avoid impersonal blandness of style, to employ humor where appropriate, to communicate a sense of drama, and to evoke sympathy for those who have suffered. We hope that students will find the book's brisk, lively style readable and engrossing. But we also recognize that a textbook must "work" in hundreds of different courses, whose teachers may vary tremendously in pedagogical approach or interpretation. Here again, we felt an obligation to be as inclusive as possible. We have advanced our own views of controversial questions in such a way that instructors who think otherwise can engage our textbook in constructive debate. By thus seeing that the study of history is an ongoing inquiry rather than a handing-down of revealed truth, students can only be the gainers.

Plan of the Book

Our approach should be apparent from the opening pages. The Prologue offers a unique survey of the geographical foundations of American history—landforms, river systems, natural regions, climate, and vegetation. The theme of human interaction with the environment first appears here as well, as we describe precontact native American life. Chapter 1, analyzing the encounter and contrasting the cultures and societies of native Americans, West Africans, and Europeans, allows each people to speak for itself and offers a detailed, integrated portrait of native American history and culture. Against this comparative backdrop, we then take up the narrative of the planting of North America's first colonies. Chapters 2 and 3 discuss colonial society and culture in narratives that interlace chronological, regional, and topical presentations. Chapter 2, for example, contrasts New England, the English Caribbean, and the Chesapeake colonies throughout the seventeenth century; Chapter 3 introduces the Restoration colonies and the French and Spanish experiences, brings colonial society to maturity in the era of the Great Awakening and the Enlightenment, and discusses everyday life through the prism of family experiences over the life cycle.

The forging of the American nation is the theme of Chapters 4–6, from the onset of the imperial crisis to the Revolution and the Federalist decade. Here we rely primarily on narrative interspersed at key points with social analysis. Our story is essentially one of American unity in resistance to perceived British encroachments, and of civil war when the issue became independence and the disruption of traditional loyalties. The treatment of the Federalist era (Chapter 6) goes well beyond the usual dry survey of partisan bickering by studying the new nation region-by-region and stressing that the Republic's very survival was a matter of serious doubt.

The antebellum section—Chapters 7–12—begins with a chronological overview of political history from Jefferson to the Monroe Doctrine (Chapter 7), followed by a comprehensive social and economic introduction to the age of Jackson (Chapter 8). In Chapter 9 we take an innovative approach by treating Jacksonian political and reform movements as interlocking public and private attacks on social ills. We turn to the Old South in Chapter 10, offering a comprehensive portrait of this distinctive, self-sufficient, and viable region whose white citizens were deeply convinced that they had built a society worth defending. Chapter 11 provides a unique treatment of antebellum culture (using the word in its broadest sense) and of the rhythms of pre–Civil War daily life. Finally, Chapter 12 ties together a dual theme: the social change resulting from the great wave of immigration in the 1840s, and the expansionism of Manifest Destiny.

In Chapters 13–15 we consider the crisis of the Union, spanning the 1850s, the Civil War, and Reconstruction. The presentation strives to maintain a sense of drama and contingency—never, for example, assuming that northern victory and southern defeat were foreordained. In Chapter 14 we consider at length the war's powerful impact on the home front and on American culture, and in Chapter 15 we show how persistent racist assumptions and a preoccupation with other national issues eventually caused the North to lose interest in defending southern blacks' rights against the "redeemers."

We cover the post–Civil War decades in Chapters 16–20, whose unifying theme is the extraordinary social and cultural change triggered by industrial capitalism. Chapters on the West (16), industrialization (17), urbanization and immigration (18), and daily life (19) precede Chapter 20's narrative of Gilded Age politics and turn-of-the-century expansionism. However, Chapter 20 can also be read first without loss of continuity. Throughout, we have spotlighted the cultural ramifications of social change; explored the ways in which public and private issues intertwined; and stressed the autonomy of immigrants, workers, rural people, women, blacks, and native Americans.

In Chapters 21–25 our theme is the consequences of industrialization and urbanization, from progressivism to the New Deal. Chapter 21 presents progressivism as a multistranded movement, offering a variety of responses (not all of them benevolent) to the new industrial order. The treatment of World War I (Chapter 22) and of the 1920s (Chapter 23) comments at some length on the nation's cultural response to war and perseverant social tension. Finally, two chapters on the 1930s (24 and 25) assess the Great Depression as the most serious crisis yet faced by American industrial capitalism. In Chapter 24 we discuss the New Deal not as an array of alphabetical agencies but as the cradle of the modern welfare state; and Chapter 25's treatment of daily life and culture in the 1930s continues the text's approach of emphasizing the influence of individuals and communities on national social and political change.

The final cluster of chapters (26–31) extends from World War II to the present. Chapter 26 deals extensively with the home-front experience during World War II, integrating it into the narrative of military campaigns and global politics. We see in the immediate postwar years (Chapter 27) the end of American isolationism, a preoccupation with communism, and the nation's not always successful attempt to assimilate the New Deal; and in the 1950s (Chapter 28), an era of mature industrial society in which daily life assumed its essentially contemporary form through suburbanization and the expansion of leisure. The discussion of the tumultuous years from Kennedy's inauguration to Nixon's downfall (Chapters 29 and 30) focuses on modern industrial society's entrapment in Vietnam and ability to absorb the civil-rights revolution. We end the book not with the usual miscellaneous catalogue of unresolved contemporary problems but with an interpretation of recent history as the nation's gradual coming-to-terms with a sense of limits: the rise of ecological consciousness, the waning of global dominance, and the challenge of competing technological societies. By striving to put the recent past into a longer perspective, we are also in a position to round off the coverage of modern America with a unique Epilogue—a brief summing-up of our view of the lessons of history, and an assessment of challenges that the nation's next generations will face.

Special Pedagogical Features

A range of useful and appealing study aids has been built into *The Enduring Vision*. Each chapter begins with a vivid vignette of a person or event that both swiftly draws the reader into the atmosphere and issues of the times and establishes the chapter's major themes. In every chapter there also appears an absorbing two-page illustrated essay, "A Place in Time," which explores in depth a single community's experiences in the era under consideration. Tables and chronological charts on special topics occur regularly throughout the text; and each chapter closes with a "Conclusion," an illustrated "Chronology" of pivotal events and developments, and a wealth of suggestions for further reading. The Appendix provides statistical tables; handy reference lists; and the text of the Declaration of Independence, the Articles of Confederation, and the Constitution (with its amendments).

The text's elegant full-color design features some 670 photographs and cartoons, over 100 maps, and 37 graphs. In the photographs we have taken care to avoid reproducing tired, overused images and have concentrated on historically accurate illustrations that, with rare exception, are contemporaneous with a chapter's time period. A special focus of the photographic selections has been material culture—the clothing, tools, housing, and other artifacts left by the peoples of the past. The strikingly beautiful quilts that grace *The Enduring Vision*'s covers reflect our fascination with this rich source of information about the daily lives of those gone before. The map and graph program encompasses exceptionally clear, accurate, and up-to-date illustrations, each accompanied by an explanatory caption.

Supplementary Program for The Enduring Vision

An extensive ancillary program accompanies *The Enduring Vision*. It has been designed not only to assist instructors, but to develop students' critical-thinking skills and to bolster readers' understanding of key topics and themes treated in the textbook.

The *Student Guide,* by Barbara Blumberg of Pace University, features (for each text chapter) review outlines, a statement of the central issues to understand, a vocabulary-building section, identifications, map exercises, sample test questions, and provocative exercises tracing the text authors' use of various historical sources. The *Instructor's Guide,* by Robert Grant of Framingham State College, offers innovative essays and handout masters centered on creative teaching techniques; summaries of each text chapter's main themes; and ideas for lecture, additional instruction, print and nonprint resources, and use of *Enduring Voices: Document Sets to Accompany The Enduring Vision.* In *Enduring Voices,* edited by James Lorence of the University of Wisconsin, Marathon Center, we provide a most unusual instructional resource. The package comprises sixty-two sets of primary-source documents for use with the text; the instructor may freely photocopy these materials for classroom discussions, course projects, or as parts of examinations. Each documentary set presents a variety of examples of primary documentary evidence—including excerpts from letters, diaries, contemporary fiction, speeches, and petitions, as well as song lyrics and advertisements—highlighting a topic or theme developed in the parallel text chapter. Rounding out the supplementary package are the *HeathTest Plus Computerized Testing Program,* which allows instructors to create customized problem sets for quizzes and examinations, and the accompanying *Test Item File,* in convenient printed format. Almost 3,000 questions, prepared by Kenneth Blume of Union College and the Albany College of Pharmacy, are available in the testing program. Finally, we have produced a large *Overhead-Transparency and Slide Package* comprising about 85 full-color illustrations based on text maps and graphs. In the supplements as in the textbook, our goal has been to make teaching and learning enjoyable and challenging.

Acknowledgments

Writing a textbook, especially one with multiple authors, is a team effort. *The Enduring Vision* has been five years in the making, and as we have planned the project, critiqued one anothers' chapters, responded to reviewers' suggestions, and watched our publisher produce the book, we have all felt a growing appreciation of the word *teamwork*. We want to take this opportunity to thank a number of individuals whose crucial role could never be appreciated by those who have not participated in such a project.

Sylvia Mallory, Senior Developmental Editor, has thrown heart and soul into the project since it was launched. She is a gifted stylist with a keen sense of how a chapter ought to flow and a realization (to quote Mark Twain) that the difference between the right word and an almost right word is like the difference between lightning and a lightning bug. She can put herself in the place of a student reader and spot where a passage will be obscure, while at the same time preserving the essence of a sophisticated idea. She worried about every detail, not only in the manuscript but also in the design, the illustration program, and the conceptualization of the supplementary materials. Through it all, she kept good humor, and we finish the job even better friends than when we began it. We also wish to thank Linda Halvorson and James Miller, successively Senior Acquisitions Editors. The first persuaded us to sign on (no mean feat), while the second cajoled us to get the job done on time. Rosemary Jaffe, Senior Production Editor, toiled with tremendous persistence—often long after closing hours—to shepherd the textbook through production, and meticulously kept track of innumerable details. In working with her during the year of actual production, we have greatly appreciated her enthusiasm and tact. Senior Designer Henry Rachlin contributed the book's clean, open, and arresting layout, whose excellence speaks for itself. Photo researcher Martha Shethar helped collect an array of fresh and intriguing illustrations—many of them real rarities—from which we had a hard time making final selections. Developmental Editor Patricia Wakeley worked with the supplements author team to produce what we believe is the fullest, most carefully executed set of ancillary materials available. Production Editor Cormac Morrissey contributed meticulous attention to the myriad details of producing the supplements. Permissions Editor Margaret Roll spent many a long day securing rights to reproduce copyrighted material. At the end of the production process, Michael O'Dea, Manager of Manufacturing, worked his customary miracles to get the bound books delivered on time. Marketing Manager James Hamann shared with us the insights of his many years' experience in selling history textbooks.

Special words of thanks go to our many colleagues around the country who read and commented on the chapters, often at great length and with great insight. Ours was the final responsibility for sifting through their (occasionally contradictory) suggestions, but we want each of them to know that we have deeply appreciated their work. Many of them will see the stamp of their ideas in the book.

Our thanks go first to the members of the Editorial Review Board that D. C. Heath assembled to advise us and the editors in an ongoing way as our chapters were written and revised. They were:

Robert Abzug, University of Texas, Austin
Charles Alexander, Ohio University
Michael Bellesiles, Emory University
Jane De Hart, University of North Carolina, Chapel Hill
Ellen DuBois, University of California, Los Angeles
Karen Halttunen, Northwestern University
Richard Kirkendall, University of Washington
Richard L. McCormick, Rutgers University
Eric Monkkonen, University of California, Los Angeles
Walter Nugent, University of Notre Dame
James Ronda, Youngstown State University
Ronald Walters, Johns Hopkins University

The following scholars reviewed chapters in various stages of draft: **Richard Abbott,** Eastern Michigan University; **W. Andrew Achenbaum,** University of Michigan; **John L. Allen,** University of Connecticut; **Ted Alsop,** Brigham Young University; **Sharon Alter,** William Rainey Harper College; **David L. Ammerman,** Florida State University; **James Axtell,** College of William and Mary; **Edward Ayers,** University of Virginia; **William Barney,** University of North Carolina, Chapel Hill; **Susan Benson,** University of Missouri; **Dennis Berge,** San Diego State University; **Robert Berkhofer,** University of Michigan; **Chuck Bishop,** Johnson County Community College; **Julia Blackwelder,** University of North Carolina, Charlotte; **Charmarie Blaisdell,** Northeastern University; **Sidney Bland,** James Madison University; **Barbara Blum-**berg, Pace University; **Kenneth Blume,** Union College and Albany College of Pharmacy; **Nancy Bowen,** Del Mar College; **Paul Bowers,** Ohio State University; **James Broussard,** Lebanon Valley College; **Richard Buel,** Wesleyan University; **Frank Byrne,** Kent State University; **Betty Caroli,** Kingsborough Community College; **Patricia Cohen,** University of California, Santa Barbara; **Linda Cross,** Tyler Junior College; **John Cumbler,** University of Louisville; **David Danbom,** North Dakota State University; **George Daniels,** University of South Alabama; **Douglas Deal,** State University College of New York, Oswego; **Don Doyle,** Vanderbilt University; **Robert Dykstra,** State University of New York, Albany; **R. David Edmunds,** Indiana University; **Richard Ellis,** State University of New York, Buffalo; **Gary Fink,** Georgia State University; **Eric Foner,** Columbia University; **Sharon Fritz,** Moraine Valley Community College; **Richard Frucht,** Northwest Missouri State University; **David Glassberg,** University of Massachusetts, Amherst; **David Goldfield,** University of North Carolina, Charlotte; **Robert Grant,** Framingham State College; **Maurine Greenwald,** University of Pittsburgh; **Robert Griffith,** University of Maryland, College Park; **Ira Gruber,** Rice University; **Richard Haan,** Hartwick College; **Susan Hartmann,** Ohio State University; **Ellis Hawley,** University of Iowa; and **Jim Heath,** Portland State University.

Also, **Joan Hoff-Wilson,** Indiana University; **William Hogan,** Southeastern Massachusetts University; **William Holmes,** University of Georgia; **Michael Holt,** University of Virginia; **Robert Ireland,** University of Kentucky; **Jesse Jennings,** University of Utah; **Susan E. Kennedy,** Virginia Commonwealth University; **Peter Kolchin,** University of Delaware; **Michael Kurtz,** Southeastern Louisiana University; **Walter LaFeber,** Cornell University; **Walter Licht,** University of Pennsylvania; **Barbara Lindemann,** Santa Barbara City College; **John McCardell,** Middlebury College; **Jim McClellan,** Northern Virginia Community College; **J. Sears McGee,** University of California, Santa Barbara; **James McGovern,** University of West Florida; **Murdo McLeod,** University of Florida; **James McPherson,** Princeton University; **C. Roland Marchand,** University of California, Davis; **Jack Marietta,** University of Arizona; **Cathy Matson,** University of Tennessee; **Michael Mayer,** University of Montana; **James Merrell,** Vassar College;

Robert Messer, University of Illinois, Chicago; Douglas Miller, Michigan State University; James Mohr, University of Maryland, Baltimore County; H. Wayne Morgan, University of Oklahoma; Joseph Morice, Duquesne University; Jerome Mushkat, University of Akron; Gerald Nash, University of New Mexico; Michael Parrish, University of California, San Diego; J'Nell Pate, Tarrant County Community College; Michael Perman, University of Illinois, Chicago; Edward Pessen, Baruch College; Ronald Petrin, Oklahoma State University; Howard Rabinowitz, University of New Mexico; Elizabeth Raymond, University of Nevada, Reno; James Reed, Rutgers University; Daniel Richter, Dickinson College; Jere Roberson, Central State University; David Robson, John Carroll University; Roy Rosenzweig, George Mason University; David Rowe, Middle Tennessee State University; Jeffrey J. Safford, Montana State University; Neal Salisbury, Smith College; Martin Schiesl, California State University, Los Angeles; Judith Sealander, Wright State University; Richard Selcoe, Union Community College; Howard Shorr, Downtown Business Magnet High School; Joel Silbey, Cornell University; Neil Stout, University of Vermont; Alan Taylor, Boston University; Emory Thomas, University of Georgia; Robert Twombly, City College of New York; David Walker, University of Northern Iowa; Lynn Westerkamp, University of California, Santa Cruz; William Bruce Wheeler, University of Tennessee; Major Wilson, Memphis State University; Raymond Wolters, University of Delaware; Donald Worster, Brandeis University; Donald Wright, State University of New York, Cortland; Gavin Wright, Stanford University; Bertram Wyatt-Brown, University of Florida; and Kathleen Xidis, Johnson County Community College.

P. S. B.   T. L. P.
C. E. C.   H. S.
J. F. K.   N. W.

CONTENTS

4 The Road to Revolution, 1748–1776 **126**

8

The Transformation of American Society, 1815–1840 276

10   The Old South and Slavery, 1800–1860   350

13

From Compromise to Secession,
1850–1861   **452**

14

Reforging the Union: Civil War, 1861–1865   486

MAPS

CHARTS, GRAPHS, AND TABLES

The Enduring Vision

American Land, Native Peoples

"The land was ours before we were the land's." So begins the poem "The Gift Outright," which the aged Robert Frost read at John F. Kennedy's inauguration in 1961. Frost's poem meditates on the interrelatedness of history, geography, and human consciousness. At first, wrote Frost, North American settlers merely possessed the land; but then, in a subtle spiritual process, they became possessed by it. Only by entering into this deep relationship with the land itself—"such as she was, such as she would become"—did their identity as a people fully take shape.

Frost's poem speaks of the encounter of English colonists with a strange new continent of mystery and promise; but of course, what the Europeans called the New World was in fact the homeland of the native American peoples whose ancestors had been "the land's" for at least fifteen thousand years. Native Americans had undergone an immensely long process of settling the continent, developing divergent cultures, discovering agriculture, and creating a rich spiritual life tightly interwoven with the physical environment that sustained them. Although the native Americans' story before the Europeans' incursion is recorded in archaeological relics rather than written documents, it is nonetheless fully a part of American history. Nor can we grasp the tragic conflict between Old and New World peoples that began soon after Columbus's arrival in 1492 without understanding the conti-nuities of native American history before and after contact with whites, or without appreciating the Indians' tenacious hold on their ancestral soil, forests, and waters.

This Prologue has a dual purpose. The first is to recount how the earliest Americans—the Indians—became "the land's." The second purpose is to tell the story of the land itself: its geological origins; its reshaping by eons of lifting, sinking, erosion, and glaciation; the opportunities and limitations that it presents to human endeavor. By weaving together the strands of geography and Indian experience, we shall consider as well the ultimate dependence of human beings on their environment.

To comprehend the American past we must first know the American land itself. The patterns of weather; the undulations of valley, plain, and mountain; the shifting mosaic of sand, soil, and rock; the intricate network of rivers, streams, and lakes—these have profoundly influenced United States history. North America's fundamental physical characteristics have shaped the course of human events from the earliest migrations from Asia to the later cycles of agricultural and industrial development, the rise of cities, the course of politics, and even the basic themes of American literature, art, and music. Geology, geography, and environment are among the fundamental building blocks of human history.

An Ancient Heritage

It is sobering to begin the study of American history by contrasting the recent rise of a rich, complex human society on this continent with the awesomely slow pace by which the North American environment took form. Geologists trace the oldest known rocks on the continent back some 3 billion years. The rocky "floor" known as the Canadian Shield first became visible on the surface of the northeastern United States and Canada during the earliest geologic era, the Precambrian, which ended 500 million years ago. Halfway between that remote age and the present, during the Paleozoic ("ancient life") era, forests covered much of what would eventually be the United States. From this organic matter, America's enormous coal reserves would be created, the largest yet discovered in the entire world. Only at the close of the Paleozoic, about 225 million years ago, did the continent become in a sense the "New World" by starting to split off from the single landmass that previously had encompassed all the earth's dry land surfaces. By a process known as plate tectonics—which continues today, at the rate of a few centimeters a year—the North American continent slowly began moving westward. At roughly the same time, the Appalachian Mountains arose in what is now the east-

200 million years ago

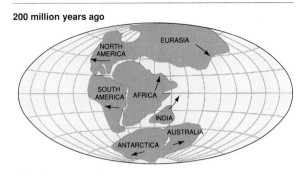

100 million years ago

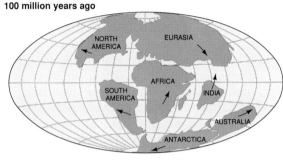

Present

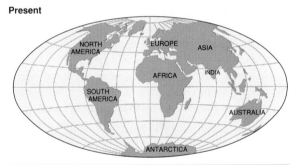

Movement of the Continents

(Top) The giant supercontinent of Pangaea; (center) continental positions 100 million years ago; (bottom) present position of the continents.

ern United States. Animal life had not as yet emerged from the sea. So enormous a gulf of time separates the origins of North America from the beginning of human history that, if those 225 million years were compressed into the space of a single twenty-four-hour day, everything that has happened since the Indians' ancestors first migrated here would flash by in the last half-second before midnight, and the New World's history since Columbus would occupy about five-thousandths of a second. In considering the sweep of geologic time, one inevitably

wonders how ephemeral human history itself may yet prove to be.

Many millions of years after North America's initial separation, during the Mesozoic ("middle life") era—the age of the dinosaurs—violent movements of the earth's crust thrust up the Pacific Coastal, Sierra Nevada, and Cascade ranges on the continent's western edge. As the dinosaurs were dying out, toward the end of the Mesozoic some 65–70 million years ago, the vast, shallow sea that washed over much of west-central North America disappeared, having been replaced by the Rocky Mountains. By then, the decay and fossilization of plant and animal life were creating North America's once great petroleum deposits, which even a generation ago seemed almost limitless. Within the last 50 million years, volcanic eruptions raised the cones that now form the Hawaiian Islands, twenty-five hundred miles southwest of California. Active Pacific-rim volcanoes and powerful earthquakes all over the continent dramatically demonstrate that the molding of the American landscape still continues.

Volcanic Eruption, Hawaii

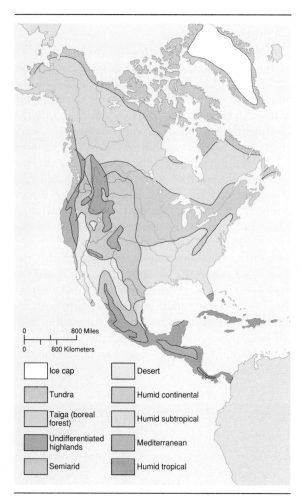

North American Climatic Regions

pockmarked the terrain over which the glaciers had spread, and areas adjacent to the ice sheets were covered with thick deposits of glacial outwash—sediment carried by streams from melting inland glaciers. Several thousand years passed before the Midwest and New England ceased to resemble present-day northern Alaska in climate and vegetation.

Like the slow but relentless shaping of land-forms, the origins of the human species extend back to the mists of prehistoric time. Some 5 million years ago, direct human ancestors first evolved in the temperate grasslands of Africa. Between three hundred thousand and one hundred thousand years ago, *Homo sapiens* evolved and began migrating throughout the Old World. Then, late in the Ice Age, hunting bands pursuing large game animals reached northeastern Asia and the Alaska-Siberia land bridge. As the glaciers retreated, small hunting bands followed a corridor southward along the mountain slopes of northwestern Canada. Some of this movement occurred perhaps as early as forty thousand years ago, but most migration into the heart of the Americas can be dated very roughly to 20,000–10,000 B.C.

Almost all native American peoples were descended from these original migrants who ventured across the Alaska-Siberia land bridge. A few, however, were the offspring of more recent arrivals. Some four thousand years ago, for example, Eskimos and Aleuts from Siberia began paddling their kayaks to North America. These hardy peoples settled the coasts of the Bering Sea and the Arctic Ocean. Around the polar seas, they established a way of life based on small communities of remarkable resourcefulness and endurance. Most Eskimo peoples traded extensively with the Indians dwelling inland, but a few were so isolated that, as recently as the early twentieth century, some learned to their astonishment that they were not the only human beings on earth. Far more inviting to migrants, but even more isolated, were the Hawaiian Islands. About A.D. 400 and again about 1000, Polynesians from the South Pacific reached Hawaii in giant outrigger canoes. Part of the vast migrations then peopling the Pacific Islands, the Hawaiians created a vigorous warrior society that flourished undisturbed by outsiders until the English sea captain James Cook found his way there in 1778.

Between 2 million and ten thousand years ago, four great glaciations left a tremendous imprint on the land. The Ice Age staggers the imagination. A carpet of ice as thick as thirteen thousand feet extended over most of Canada and crept southward into what is now New England, New York State, and much of the Midwest. As the last ice caps retreated, water formerly locked in the ice sheets flooded shallow offshore regions like the land bridge that linked Alaska and Siberia. The climatic changes triggered by the melting ice drastically affected North American plant and animal life and helped turn the Southwest into a desert. Glacial runoff filled the Great Lakes and the Mississippi River basin. Ice and rocky debris

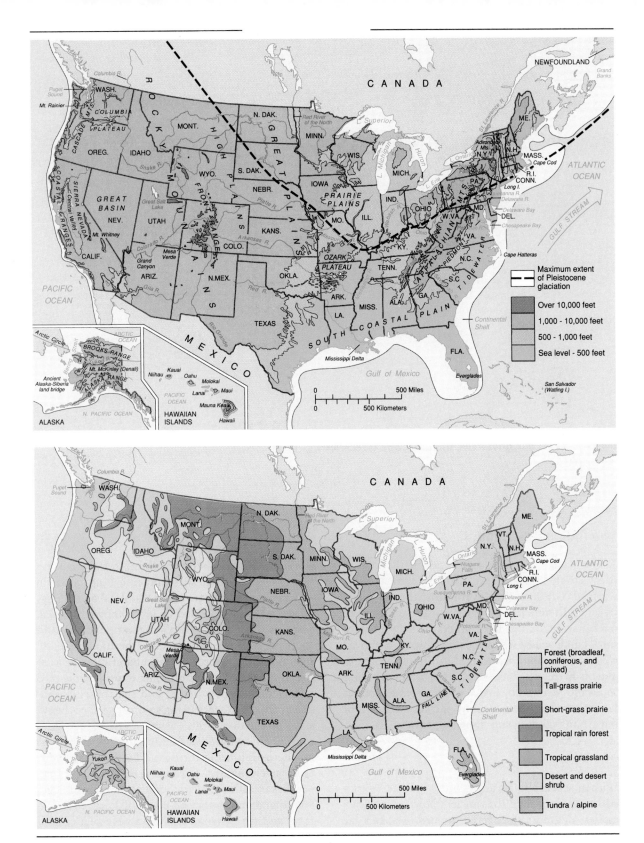

Above, **Physiographic Map of the United States**   Below, **Natural Vegetation of the United States**

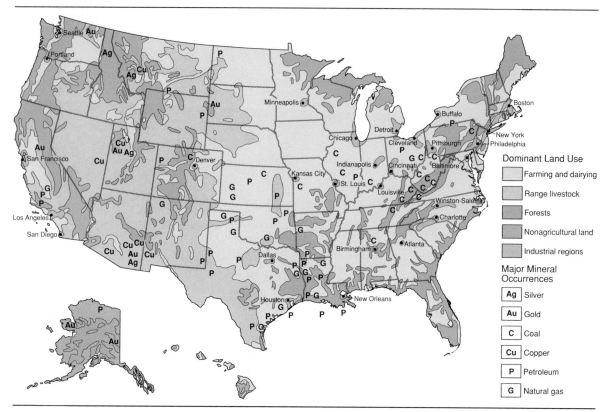

Present-Day U.S. Agriculture, Industry, and Resources

The Indians' Continent

As the glacial ice melted at last, raising the world's oceans to their present level, North America slowly warmed. Gradually the evergreens, the broadleaf trees, and temperate-zone animal life returned to once glaciated land. The hunters fanned out, too: small bands armed with flint-tipped weapons moved with the mammoths, mastodons, horses, camels, and bison that they stalked. Six thousand to twelve thousand years ago, many of these large species became extinct, destroyed by the combination of a warming climate and hunters' prowess.

The Northwest and the West

With its severe climate and profuse wildlife, Alaska still evokes the land that ancient North America's earliest migrants discovered. Indeed, Alaska's far north resembles a world from which ice caps have just retreated—a treeless tundra of grasses, lichens, and stunted shrubs. This region, the Arctic, is a

stark wilderness in winter, reborn in fleeting summers of colorful flowers and returning birds. In contrast, the subarctic of central Alaska and Canada is a heavily forested country known as taiga. Here rises North America's highest peak, 20,300-foot Mt. McKinley, or Denali (the Indian name). Average temperatures in the subarctic range from the fifties above zero in summer to well below zero in the long, dark winters, and the soil is permanently frozen except during summer surface thaws.

The expanse from Alaska's glacier-gouged and ruggedly mountainous Pacific shore southward to northern California forms the Pacific Northwest. Only a few natural harbors break the shoreline, but they include the magnificent anchorages of Puget Sound and San Francisco Bay. Offshore, cool currents and warm winds make possible rich coastal fisheries.

The Pacific coastal region is in some ways a world apart. Vegetation and animal life, isolated

Mendenhall Glacier, Alaska

from the rest of the continent by deserts and mountains, include many species unfamiliar farther east. Warm, wet westerly winds blowing off the Pacific create a climate more uniformly temperate than anywhere else in North America. From Anchorage and the Alaska panhandle to a little south of San Francisco Bay, winters are cool, humid, and foggy, and the coast's dense forest cover includes the largest living organisms on earth, the giant sequoia (redwood) trees. Along the southern California coast, winds and currents generate a warmer, "Mediterranean" climate, and vegetation includes a heavy growth of shrubs and short trees, scattered stands of oak, and grasses able to endure prolonged seasonal drought.

The rugged Sierra Nevada, Cascade, and coastal ranges stretch the length of British Columbia, Washington, Oregon, and California. Their majestic peaks trap abundant Pacific Ocean moisture that gigantic clockwise air currents carry eastward. Between the ranges nestle flat, fertile valleys—California's Central Valley (formed by the San Joa-

Coastal Farming, Northern California

quin and Sacramento rivers), Oregon's Willamette Valley, and the Puget Sound region in Washington—that have become major agricultural centers in recent times.

Well east of the Pacific coastal band lies the Great Basin, encompassing Nevada, western Utah, southern Idaho, and eastern Oregon. The few streams here have no outlet to the sea. Much of the Great Basin was once covered by an inland sea holding glacial meltwater, a remnant of which survives in Utah's Great Salt Lake. Today, however, the Great Basin is dry and severely eroded, a cold desert rich in minerals, imposing in its austere grandeur and lonely emptiness. North of the basin, the Columbia and Snake rivers, which drain the plateau country of Idaho and eastern Washington and Oregon, provide plentiful water for farming.

Western North America's "backbone" is the Rocky Mountains. In turn, the Rockies form part of the immense mountain system that reaches from

Joshua Tree, Western Nevada

Alaska to the Andes of South America. Elevations in the Rockies rise from a mile above sea level at Denver at the foot of the mountains to permanently snowcapped peaks more than fourteen thousand feet above sea level. Beyond the front range of the Rockies lies the Continental Divide, the watershed separating the rivers flowing eastward into the Atlantic from those draining westward into the Pacific. The climate and vegetation of the Rocky Mountain high country resemble Arctic and subarctic types.

The Indians who settled the North and West between ten thousand and twenty thousand years ago adapted to their often severely challenging environments in diverse ways. For sustenance they depended on hunting, fishing, and gathering wild vegetation. Many of the plants they ate had to be leached of toxins. California Indians ground acorns into flour from which they made bread. Population densities varied enormously with locale. For example, in the forbidding subarctic North and the Great Basin, only scattered, wandering bands that occasionally converged in large winter encampments peopled the land, whereas mild and resource-rich California and the sheltered inlets of the northwestern coast supported many diverse cultures and the densest Indian populations in what would later be the United States. Abundant marine life, roots, and berries kept them well fed, and they excelled in intricate basket making. A Spanish friar who reached California overland from Mexico in 1770 wrote, "This land exceeds all the preceding territory in fertility and abundance of things necessary for sustenance."

Isolated from cultivators elsewhere, none of the Pacific coast Indians ever developed agriculture. Nevertheless, the same Spanish padre's 1770 account of the Chumash Indians gives a glimpse of a hardy, self-sufficient native California society. The Chumash, he found, were "well-appearing, of good disposition, affable, liberal [generous], and friendly towards the Spanish." Their villages were governed by civil chiefs who took multiple wives so that they could maintain kinship links with as many families as possible. Other males took but a single wife. Kin lived together in "neatly built" houses large enough for four or five families. The women carried their swaddled babies on their backs, strapped to boards, and thus were left "unencum-

Maroon Bells of the Rocky Mountains, near Aspen, Colorado

bered for all their duties." Evidently, the Indians were exceedingly healthy before the sudden arrival of European peoples and their infectious diseases, which had a devastating effect.

The Southwest and the Origins of Agriculture

Arizona, southern Utah, western New Mexico, and southeastern California form America's southwestern desert. The climate is arid, searingly hot on summer days and cold on winter nights. Adapted to stringent environmental conditions, many plants and animals here could not survive elsewhere. Dust storms, cloudbursts, and flash floods have everywhere carved, abraded, and twisted the rocky landscape. Nature's fantastic sculpture appears on the most monumental scale in the Grand Canyon, where

for 20 million years the Colorado River has been cutting down to Precambrian bedrock.

In the face of such tremendous natural forces, human activity might well seem paltry and transitory. Yet here, sometime between 3000 and 2000 B.C., the first crop cultivation began on what is now United States soil. Agriculture probably originated when women noticed that wild seeds dropped to the ground could later sprout and bear new seeds, and when they realized that they might supplement their dwindling gatherings by reaping from what they had sown. For centuries crop cultivation remained a relatively minor source of food. But even as the Southwest slowly grew more arid, Indians preserved the precious water on which their corn, melons, and beans depended.

Agriculture supplied a major share of southwestern Indians' food after about 300 B.C., when new influxes of Indian peoples from Mexico brought more drought-resistant strains of corn to the Southwest. Within several centuries the possibility of more extensive crop cultivation nurtured several distinctive southwestern cultural traditions that live on today. One such tradition was the Hohokam culture of the peoples of Arizona's Gila River Valley, who diverted river water with networks of ditches. Another culture was the world of the pueblos—the massive "apartment-house" masonry villages that appeared in northern Arizona's and New Mexico's plateau country during the first millennium A.D.

Nothing in North America better embodies the human ability to thrive despite nature's inclemency than the enduring southwestern Indian cultures. By 1400 worsening desert conditions helped undermine the Hohokam culture. It yielded to the simpler but tenacious way of life of the Pima-Papago Indians who cultivated southern Arizona's river valleys using floodwater but not irrigation works. Meanwhile, the complex, tightly organized pueblo cultures also surmounted a prolonged crisis. By the late thirteenth century, increasing aridity forced the abandonment of many villages, particularly in the highlands (see "A Place in Time"). The center of pueblo life shifted to northeastern Arizona and to New Mexico's Rio Grande Valley. Pueblos grew even larger and more strongly fortified. Such precautions became necessary after the Southwest was invaded by marauding hunter-gatherer peoples from the Canadian subarctic, who formed the modern Navahos and Apaches. In the sixteenth century, an equally disruptive force would invade the region from the south: the Spanish.

The Heartland: Diffusion of Agriculture and Early Indian Civilization

North America's heartland comprises the area extending eastward from the Rockies to the Appalachians. This vast region forms one of the world's largest drainage systems. From it the Great Lakes empty into the North Atlantic through the St. Lawrence River, and the Mississippi-Missouri-Ohio river network flows southward into the Gulf of Mexico. Where the drainage system originates, at the northern and western reaches of the Great Lakes region, lie some of the world's richest deposits of iron and copper ore. In our own time, the heartland's waterways have offered a splendid means of carrying this mineral wealth to nearby coal-producing areas for processing, unfortunately also spawning widespread environmental pollution.

The Mississippi—the "Father of Waters" to the Indians, and one of the world's longest rivers—carries a prodigious volume of water and silt. It has changed course many times in geological history. The lower Mississippi (below the junction with the Ohio River) meanders constantly. In the process, the river deposits rich sediments throughout its broad, ancient floodplain. Indeed, the Mississippi has carried so much silt over the millennia that in its lower stretches, the river flows *above* the surrounding valley, which it catastrophically floods when its high banks (levees) are breached. Over millions of years, such riverborne sediment covered what was once the westward extension of the Appalachians in northern Mississippi and eastern Arkansas. Only the Ozark Plateau and Ouachita Mountains remain exposed, forming the hill country of southern Missouri, north-central Arkansas, and eastern Oklahoma. These uplands have evolved into an economically and culturally distinctive region—beautiful but isolated and impoverished.

Below New Orleans the Mississippi empties into the Gulf of Mexico through an enormous delta with an intricate network of grassy swamps known as bayous. The Mississippi Delta offers good farm soil, capable of supporting a large population. Swarming with waterfowl, insects, alligators, and marine plants and animals, this environment has nurtured a distinctive way of life for the Indian, white, and black peoples who have inhabited it.

North of the Ohio and Missouri rivers, themselves products of glacial runoff, Ice Age glaciation molded the American heartland. Because the local terrain was generally flat prior to glaciation, the ice sheets distributed glacial debris quite evenly. Spread even farther by wind and rivers, this fine-ground glacial dust slowly created the fertile farm soil of the Midwest. Glaciers also dug out the five Great Lakes (Superior, Huron, Michigan, Ontario, and Erie), collectively the world's largest body of fresh water. Water flowing from Lake Erie to the lower elevation of Lake Ontario created Niagara Falls, comparable only to the Grand Canyon as testimony to nature's power.

Confluence of the Mississippi and Ohio Rivers near Cairo, Illinois

Most of the heartland's eastern and northern sectors were once heavily forested. To the west thick, tall-grass prairie covered Illinois and parts of adjoining states, as well as much of the Missouri River basin and the middle Arkansas River basin (Oklahoma and central Texas). Beyond the Missouri the prairie gave way to short-grass steppe—the Great Plains, cold in winter, blazing hot in summer, and always dry. The great distances that separate the heartland's prairies and Great Plains from the moderating effects of the oceans have made this region's annual temperature range the most extreme in North America. As the traveler moves westward, elevations rise gradually, winds howl ceaselessly, trees grow only along streambeds, long droughts alternate with violent thunderstorms and tornadoes, and water and wood are ever scarcer.

From the Rockies to the wooded slopes of western Pennsylvania, the heartland was the habitat of the bison. Some twelve thousand years ago, Indian bands hunted a now extinct form of the

Cypress Pond in Bayou Country

Mesa Verde in the Thirteenth Century

Mesa Verde Panorama, Showing the Cliff Palace

North of the desert lands of Arizona and New Mexico, the elevation gradually rises to a high plateau in the present-day Four Corners area, where Arizona, New Mexico, Colorado, and Utah meet. Modern-day scientists' analysis of ancient tree rings and pollen levels shows that a thousand years ago the plateau was somewhat wetter and more heavily forested than today, although rainfall was still sparse. But the environment was hospitable enough to support the emergence of new Indian cultures. Archaeologists call the early plateau peoples the Basketmakers, a name derived from the tightly woven basketry that the women fashioned from yucca fibers. About A.D. 700, Basketmaker mothers began to strap their infants to hard cradleboards, producing the flattened skull that for centuries would be the distinguishing physical characteristic of the plateau peoples. At the same time, the population first gathered in pueblos. Small in the beginning, the pueblos mushroomed in size over the centuries. They were generally located on the flat-topped elevations that the later Spanish invaders of the Southwest called mesas (after the Spanish word for *table*).

In about the year 1200, pueblo peoples of the Four Corners began to move from the mesas to cliffside caves that faced south for maximum sunlight. Protection against marauders must have been the reason, for living space was tighter in the new location. So it was that set-

tlers came to the Cliff Palace at Mesa Verde ("Green Table") in southwestern Colorado.

In this large settlement of some two hundred rooms, as many as a thousand people dwelled in cramped quarters. These conditions demanded effective public authority. Male societies organized to conduct religious rituals were one such form of social organization. For example, the Cliff Palace residents probably relied on a warrior society to mediate charges of antisocial behavior, whether theft, adultery, homicide, or witchcraft. Depending on circumstances, the people most likely recognized the leadership of

The Cliff Palace

two chiefs: a "civil chief" in peacetime and a "war chief" when they had to fight raiders or unfriendly pueblos. But no single person exercised leadership. Rather, it resided in the community as a whole, as expressed in the people's collective sense of what was proper behavior and what would please the gods who sent precious rain and made crops grow.

The supernatural penetrated all aspects of the people's everyday affairs. Omens and other signs of spiritual influence in daily life were interpreted by the community's shamans—individuals trusted for their ability to communicate with the spirit world. Ceremonies to honor the gods and ensure their favor went on continuously, performed without the slightest deviation from ancient ritual by the men of the pueblo's various religious societies who assembled in the kivas (ceremonial chambers). Cliff Palace had twenty-three kivas, each one closed to all but members of a single society. The most awful offense that anyone could commit was to reveal kiva secrets.

Thus accustomed to conform strictly to community standards, the Cliff Palace people went about their routines. Every day, men descended long ladders to the valley floor, where they worked the community's corn fields. By coiling and firing clay, women produced the highly distinctive Mesa Verde pottery—plain gray-white cookware for ordinary use and intricate black-on-white geometrically patterned vessels for ceremonial occasions. Women also looked after the community's turkeys and wove cotton fabric on looms. Everyone had to collect scarce rainwater; people even preserved early-morning dew on the rocks. No matter how generous the

Balcony House with Kiva, Mesa Verde

gods, farming was still intensely risky.

But at the end of the thirteenth century, the gods forsook Mesa Verde. A century-long climatic drying trend culminated in a terrible drought between 1276 and 1299, which possibly combined with epidemics or attacks by hostile neighbors to break the people's spirit. No telltale signs of violence survived. By 1300 the dwellers of the Cliff Palace and other Mesa Verde sites abandoned their pueblos and silently moved away. They probably regrouped to form the modern Hopi and Zuñi pueblos of Arizona and New Mexico. We do not even know what they had called themselves, although the Navahos who replaced them in the plateau region gave them the name by which the entire culture has become known: the Anasazis, or "Ancient Ones." Slowly the Mesa Verde cliff pueblos crumbled, bereft of inhabitants who could maintain the structures and the way

of life that they embodied. Whites first saw the ruins only in 1888. That year, some ranchers hunting for lost cattle happened into the valley and beheld the Cliff Palace, suspended ghostlike in a winter snowstorm.

Ancient Mesa Verde–type Pottery

A Folsom Point

This Folsom point is shown just as it was found, imbedded between two ribs of the extinct Bison taylori.

bison. The discovery in 1926 of the beautifully crafted "Folsom points" (stone spear points) in the bones of these ancient animals first proved how long ago the Indians' settlement of North America had occurred. Until the nineteenth century, bison herds supplied the greater part of the sustenance of many heartland Indian peoples. A Spanish trooper who saw the Great Plains in 1541–1542 wrote of the Indian inhabitants:

With the [bison's] skins they build their houses; with the skins they clothe and shoe themselves; from the skins they make rope and also obtain wool. With the sinews they make thread, with which they sew clothes and also their tents. With the bones they shape awls. The dung they use for firewood, since there is no other fuel in that land. The bladders they use as jugs and drinking containers. They sustain themselves on their meat, eating it slightly roasted and heated over the dung. Some they eat raw.

Grain Harvesting in America's Heartland

Now much of this forested, grassy world is forever altered. The heartland has become open farming country. Gone are the flocks of migratory birds that once darkened the daytime skies of the plains; gone are the free-roaming bison. Forests now only fringe the heartland: in the lake country of northern Minnesota and Wisconsin, on Michigan's upper peninsula, and across the hilly uplands of the Appalachians, southern Indiana, and the Ozarks. The settlers who displaced the Indians have done most of the plowing up of prairie grass and felling of trees since the early nineteenth century, although Indians may have contributed to the deforestation, too, by burning large woodland areas centuries ago. Destruction of the forest and grassy cover has made the Midwest a "breadbasket" for the world market. But several times since the nineteenth century, inadequate irrigation and improper plowing have turned this matchless soil into a dustbowl.

Agriculture came to the heartland almost three millennia ago. Around 800 B.C. migrants from the Southwest or Mexico who were familiar with agriculture reached the Ohio Valley, where they created the Adena culture. Adena peoples buried their

Great Serpent Mound, Ohio

Embossed Copper Falcon, Hopewell Culture

This remarkable artifact was found in a mound at Mound City, Ohio. Predatory birds were a common motif among Hopewell peoples.

dead in earthen mounds. This custom, based on increasingly complex religious ideas, passed on to the Hopewell culture, which flourished between 100 B.C. and A.D. 550 in the same forested core of the Midwest. After about 550, the Hopewell culture faded away, but its place was taken about two centuries later by a similar religious cult whose surviving artifacts represent the Mississippian culture, which endured until about 1500. Mississippian settlements spread northward along the Mississippi-Missouri valleys and southward to Florida and Oklahoma, their denizens everywhere building extensive earthen mounds. Atop the mounds, Mississippians erected imposing temples and residences for their priest-kings, whose tombs they filled with a profusion of ceramic pottery and carved stone objects.

Encompassing more than fifteen hundred years before the coming of the Europeans, the Hopewell and Mississippian cultures marked the rise in North America of an early civilization. Possibly the people benefited from contact with the impressive empires in Mexico that had been developing since the first millennium B.C. and that culminated in the Maya and Aztec states. But archaeologists have not unearthed convincing evidence of direct Mexican influence. More likely, the Hopewell and Mississippian cultures were native North American developments, unfolding from an original religious impulse to provide for the afterlife and to appease the gods who ensured fertility. Archaeological findings suggest that in the Mississippian culture particularly, the priest-kings who organized religious ceremonials exercised strong, even despotic sway over their subjects. But their capacity for organizing society was formidable. The largest Mississippian community—Cahokia, which flourished near present-day St. Louis between about 1050 and 1250—was a city of up to thirty thousand inhabitants, a population as large as that of any medieval western European urban center. Moreover, the trade networks on which the Hopewell and Mississippian cultures depended were enormous, extending from the Gulf of Mexico to the upper Great Lakes and the Rockies.

Environmental change, primarily the long-term cyclic recurrence of a colder, drier climate, doubtless hastened the decline of the Hopewell world in the sixth century A.D. and the abandonment of Cahokia and other large Mississippian cities in the thirteenth century. Similar change adversely affected the pueblo peoples of the Southwest; in fact, the climatic shift had worldwide effects, contributing in the Old World to the decline of the Roman Empire and (a thousand years later) to a severe economic and demographic crisis in fourteenth-century Europe.

Civilizations and empires rise and fall, but life goes on. The decline of great religious centers such as Cahokia led to the diffusion of Mississippian cultural influence to tribal societies throughout the heartland and beyond. The way of life of the midwestern, southeastern, and eastern Indians who lived at some distance from the religious centers continued to take shape. Anthropologists call this way of life the Woodland culture. Woodland peoples formed tribal societies in small villages that shifted seasonally from corn fields and bean fields to hunting or fishing encampments. The Woodland culture eventually reached as far west as the Great Plains river valleys; and crossing the Appalachians, it also extended eastward to the Atlantic coast and New England.

The Atlantic Seaboard

The eastern edge of the heartland is marked by the ancient Appalachian Mountain chain, which over the course of 200 million years has been ground down to gentle ridges paralleling one another southwest to northeast. Between the ridges lie fertile valleys such as Virginia's Shenandoah. The Appalachian hill country's wealth is in thick timber and mineral beds—particularly the Paleozoic coal deposits—whose heavy exploitation since the nineteenth century has accelerated destructive soil erosion in this softly beautiful, mountainous land.

Descending gently from the Appalachians' eastern slope is the piedmont ("foot of the mountain"). In this broad, rolling upland extending from Alabama to Maryland, the rich red soil has been ravaged in modern times by excessive cotton and tobacco cultivation. The piedmont's modern piney-woods cover constitutes "secondary growth" replacing the sturdy hardwood trees that native Americans and pioneering whites and blacks once knew. The northward extension of the piedmont from Pennsylvania to New England has more broadleaf vegetation, a harsher winter climate, and (through the Hudson and Connecticut river valleys) somewhat better access to the piedmont itself. But unlike the piedmont, upstate New York and New England were shaped by glaciation: the terrain here comprises hills contoured by advancing and retreating ice, and numerous lakes scoured out by glaciers. Belts of debris remain, and in many

Cades Cove, Great Smoky Mountains; Tennessee Strip Mining

The impact of human hands is dramatically apparent in these two starkly contrasting Appalachian hill-country scenes.

places granite boulders shoulder their way up through the soil. Though picturesque, the land is the despair of anyone who has tried to plow it.

From southeastern Massachusetts and Rhode Island to south-central Alabama runs the fall line, the boundary between the relatively hard rock of the interior and the softer sediment of the coastal plain. Rivers crossing the fall line drop quickly to near sea level, thus making a series of rapids that block navigation upstream from the coast.

The character of the Atlantic coastal plain varies strikingly from south to north. In the extreme south, at the tip of the Florida peninsula, the climate and vegetation are subtropical. The southern coastal lands running north from Florida to Chesapeake Bay and the mouth of the Delaware River compose the tidewater region. This is a wide, rather flat lowland, heavily wooded with a mixture of

Boulders and Autumn Leaves, Washington, New Hampshire

Tidewater Wetlands, North Carolina

broadleaf and coniferous forests, ribboned with numerous small rivers, occasionally swampy, and often miserably hot and humid in summer. North of Delaware Bay, the coastal lowlands narrow and flatten to form the New Jersey Pine Barrens, Long Island, and Cape Cod—all of these created by the deposit of glacial debris. Here the climate is noticeably milder than in the interior. North of Massachusetts Bay, the land back of the immediate shoreline becomes increasingly mountainous.

Many large rivers drain into the Atlantic: the St. Lawrence, flowing out of the Great Lakes northeastward through eastern Canada; the Connecticut in New England; the Hudson, Delaware, Susquehanna, and Potomac in what are now the Middle Atlantic states; the Savannah in the South. Most of these originally carried glacial meltwater. The Susquehanna and the Potomac filled in the broad, shallow Chesapeake Bay, teeming with marine life and offering numerous anchorages for oceangoing ships.

North America's true eastern edge is not the coastline but the offshore continental shelf, whose relatively shallow waters extend as far as 250 miles into the Atlantic before plunging deeply. Along the rocky Canadian and Maine coasts, where at the end of the Ice Age the rising ocean half covered glaciated mountains and valleys, oceangoing craft may find numerous small anchorages. South of

Pemigewasset Wilderness, White Mountains, New Hampshire

The Tip of Cape Cod, Massachusetts

Massachusetts Bay, the Atlantic shore and the Gulf of Mexico coastline form a shoreline of sandy beaches and long barrier islands paralleling the mainland. Tropical storms boiling up from the open seas regularly lash North America's Atlantic shores, and at all times brisk winds make coastal navigation treacherous.

Crossing the Atlantic east to west can daunt even skilled mariners, particularly those battling against powerful winds by sail. Here, on one of the world's stormiest seas, the mighty Gulf Stream current sweeps from southwest to northeast. Winds off the North American mainland also trend steadily eastward, and dangerous icebergs floating south from Greenland's waters threaten every ship. Little wonder that in 1620 the *Mayflower* Pilgrims' first impulse on landing was to sink to their knees in thanks to God for having transported them safely across "the vast and furious ocean." Many a vessel went to the bottom.

But for millennia, the Atlantic coastal region of North America offered a welcoming haven to settlers. For example, ten thousand years ago, ancient Indian hunters followed a warming climate eastward across the Appalachians to the coast. Early in the first millennium A.D., eastern peoples began adopting the Woodland culture and agriculture from the heartland. Offshore, well within their reach, lay such productive fishing grounds as the Grand Banks and Cape Cod's coastal bays, where cool-water upwellings on the continental shelf have lured swarms of fish and crustaceans. "The abundance

of sea-fish are almost beyond believing," wrote a breathless English settler in 1630, "and sure I should scarce have believed it, except I had seen it with my own eyes."

Indian hands tended eastern North America's coastal lands with skill and care. From southern Maine to the Carolinas, great expanses of hardwood trees formed an open, parklike landscape, free of underbrush (which the Indians had systematically burned) but rich with grass and berry bushes that attracted a profusion of game. The Woodland peoples' "slash-and-burn" method of land management was environmentally sound and economically productive. Indians cleared the land by burning underbrush and destroying the larger trees' bark. Then, amid the leafless deadwood, they planted their corn, beans, and pumpkins in soil enriched by ash. After several years of abundant harvests, yields declined, and the Indians moved on to a new site to repeat the process. Soon groundcover reclaimed the abandoned clearing, restoring fertility naturally. Over time, rather than shifting their cultivation aimlessly through the wilderness, the Indians rotated their sowing around a series of fields.

The crop yields of Woodland Indians' agricultural lands, where corn, beans, and melons grew together in tangled plenty, astonished Europeans. "Small labor but great pleasure" was how New England's first white explorer described the Indians' supposedly carefree lives. His remark epitomized Europeans' misunderstanding of native American ways from the very outset. But Europeans also learned to benefit from the Indians' expertise in cultivating unfamiliar New World crops, and former Indian clearings were soon serving whites as farmsites as they advanced into the North American interior.

A Legacy and a Challenge

At least three thousand miles of open sea separates North America from Europe and Africa; and Asia, except for the subarctic region where Alaska and Siberia once joined, lies even more distant. Ever since the first human wanderers crossed over from Asia, geographical isolation and ecological variety

Rock-strewn Crystal River near Redstone, Colorado

have been the New World's most striking characteristics. Isolation made possible native Americans' social and cultural development untouched by alien influences and infectious diseases. Meanwhile, the great climatic and geographical variations among North American regions ensured that native cultures—all of them highly dependent on the natural environment—would be extremely diverse.

Yet despite North America's isolation, Indian history did not begin at Columbus's arrival, with everything before 1492 relegated to a dim, uneventful limbo of "prehistory." When Europeans "discovered" America in 1492, they did not enter an unchanging world of simple savages. To take but one example, during the fifteenth century, the five Iroquois tribes of western New York created their "Great League of Peace," a formidable confederacy with commercial and religious significance as well as growing military prowess. We can only guess what course native American cultural and social evolution might have taken had it remained untouched by alien influences. But there can be no doubt that native Americans in 1492 were caught up in long-range historical change rooted in thousands of years of prior development.

"A people come from under the world, to take their world from them"—thus an early-seventeenth-century Virginia Indian characterized the English invaders of his homeland. Indeed, the modern society that since the seventeenth century has arisen on the Indians' ancient continent bears little resemblance to the world that native Americans once knew. Only the land itself remains.

A lingering sense of isolation has stimulated European-descended Americans' hopes of keeping Old World problems away from the pristine New World, just as North America's fertile soil, virgin forests, and rich mineral resources have long conjured up visions of limitless wealth. But industrialization, urbanization, rapid mass transportation, and tremendous population growth stretched to the limits the American land's ability to maintain a modern society without irreversible ecological damage. And only in the twentieth century have Americans learned that global transportation networks and instantaneous communication make isolation impossible. At last, as ecologist Aldo Leopold put it, they have begun discovering that the earth's people "are only fellow voyagers in the odyssey of evolution." And that lesson has been hard learned. "It required 19 centuries to define decent man-to-man conduct and the process is only half-done," Leopold admonished; "it may take as long to evolve a code of decency for man-to-land conduct."

It is in evolving such a code, however, that the native American legacy may yet prove most enduring. Living in constant dependence on their environment, native Americans achieved a religious reverence for their land and all living beings that shared it. In recapturing a sense that the land—its life-sustaining bounty and its soul-sustaining beauty—is itself of inestimable value and not merely a means to the end of material growth, future American generations may reestablish a sense of historical and cultural continuity with their native American precursors. Thereby they can truly be possessed by their land instead of simply being its possessors.

CHRONOLOGY

c. 300,000– 100,000 B.C. Migration of modern human beings throughout the Old World.

c. 40,000– 10,000 B.C. Ancestors of New World's native population cross Alaska-Siberia land bridge.

c. 3000– 2000 B.C. Crop cultivation begins on what is now U.S. soil.

c. 800 B.C. Adena culture emerges in the Ohio Valley.

c. 300 B.C. Agriculture supplies a major part of southwestern Indians' food.

c. 100 B.C.– A.D. 550 Hopewell culture flourishes in the Midwest.

c. A.D. 700 Mississippian culture takes shape near the junction of the Mississippi, Missouri, and Ohio rivers.

c. A.D. 1000 Pueblo culture emerges in the Southwest.

c. 1400– 1500 Iroquois "Great League of Peace" created.

CHAPTER 1

The New and Old Worlds·

At ten o'clock on a moonlit night, the tense crew spotted a glimmering light. Then at two the next morning came the shout "Land! Land!" At daybreak they entered a shallow lagoon. The captain rowed ashore, the royal flag fluttering in the breeze. "And, all having rendered thanks to the Lord, kneeling on the ground, embracing it with tears of joy for the immeasurable mercy of having reached it, [he] rose and gave this island the name San Salvador." The date was October 12, 1492. The place was a tiny tropical island less than four hundred miles southeast of present-day Florida.

Besides his crew, the only witnesses to Christopher Columbus's landing were a band of Taino Indians peeking from the jungle as he claimed for his queen the island that they called Guanahaní. Soon curiosity overcame their fears. Gesturing and smiling, the Tainos walked down to the beach, where the newcomers quickly noticed the cigars they offered and the gold pendants in their noses.

The voyagers learned to savor the islanders' tobacco and to trade for golden ornaments as they sailed on among the West Indies, searching for the emperor of China's capital city. Although Columbus had found no Oriental potentates, he sensed that fabulous wealth lay within his grasp. He was sure that he had reached Asia—the Indies. Two months later, bringing with him some "Indians" and various souvenirs, he sailed home to tell of "a land to be desired and, once seen, never to be left."

Perhaps some Tainos would have agreed with the astonished Canadian Indian who saw his first shaggily bearded white man in 1632: "O, what an ugly man! Is it possible that any woman would look with favor on such a man?" Later Indians' accounts of their first sightings of Europeans also speak of wonder at seeing white-sailed "canoes" descending as from the sky and of fascination with the strangers' "magic"—their guns, gunpowder, durable metal pots and tools, woven cloth, glass beads, and alcohol. Because the white strangers were seldom prepared to survive unaided in the New World, the superbly adapted native people had ample opportunity to make themselves useful.

But the potential for deep misunderstanding was already present. From his first day in America, Columbus thought like a benevolent colonial master. "They should be good servants and of quick intelligence, . . . and I believe that they would easily be made Christians, for it appeared to me that they had no creed." The Europeans would soon realize that native Americans were neither gullible fools nor humble servants. Disillusioned, the newcomers would begin to see the Indians as lazy and deceitful "savages." Meanwhile, the native Americans found the Europeans' "magic"—which included their germs as well as their tools—very powerful. In much of what is now Latin America, the coming of the Europeans quickly turned into conquest. In the future United States and Canada, European mastery would come more slowly. But everywhere, the native Americans had to yield in the end.

Few stories in history are as familiar as Columbus's landing on San Salvador. And few dates are so truly epoch-making as October 12, 1492. From that moment, the American continents became the stage for the encounter of the Old and New Worlds.

New World Peoples

In 1492 the entire Western Hemisphere may have had a population of up to 80–100 million. Native Americans clustered most thickly in Mexico and Central America, the Caribbean islands, and Peru. Booty-seeking Spanish conquerors gravitated to these populous lands, especially to the highly organized Indian empires in Mexico and Peru.

North America—the future United States and Canada—seldom beckoned the first impatient European empire builders. Wealth was hard to find there, and no centralized states lay ready for European armies to conquer. For almost a century after 1492, Europeans therefore made few attempts to establish outposts in North America. Only between 1565 and 1630 did the first permanent European colonies appear in North America.

But North America was not an empty wasteland. In 1492 between 2 million and 10 million native Americans lived north of present-day Mexico, unevenly distributed. Sparse populations of nomads inhabited the Great Basin, the high plains, and the northern forests. Fairly dense concentrations, however, thrived along the Pacific coast, in the Southwest and Southeast, in the Mississippi Valley, and along the Atlantic coast. All these peoples grouped themselves in roughly 250 tribes, speaking many diverse languages and dialects. But the most important Indian social groups were the family, the village, and the clan. Within these spheres native Americans fed themselves well, reared their children, and tried to sort out the mysteries of life.

North American Indian Societies at the Moment of European Contact

Between the early sixteenth century and the 1630s, Europeans and Indians met in four regions of North America. These encounters took place along the East coast from the Arctic to the Carolinas; in the Southeast and the lower Mississippi Valley; fleetingly, on the edge of the Great Plains; and in the Southwest. Although Europeans' accounts were biased and confused, they help provide a vivid picture of native North American society on the eve of colonization, especially when they are combined with archaeological evidence and anthropologists' findings.

In the first zone of contact, eastern North America, early European explorers and settlers penned the most numerous reports of their impressions. Particularly with regard to social organization, these first white observers noted patterns of Indian life that were typical of native Americans throughout the continent. The European intruders' accounts also contained many telltale signs of their own Old World values.

For example, one of the early white visitors to travel far up the St. Lawrence Valley, about 1630, commented on a few features of Indian life that pleased him. This man, the French missionary Father Gabriel Sagard, happily reported an absence of "the vice" of kissing and otherwise publicly displaying affection, and he noted with satisfaction that marriage required the consent not only of parents but also of the bride. In other respects, however, Sagard was horrified. With parental connivance young Indians enjoyed premarital sex and entered into trial marriages. Divorce was casual, "it being sufficient for the husband to say to the wife's relatives and to herself that she is no good . . . [and] the wives also leave their husbands with ease when the latter do not please them. Hence it often happens that some . . . [women have] more than a dozen or fifteen husbands."

The French priest's initial observations in this Huron village in present-day Ontario, Canada, touched only the surface of the social system shared by native North Americans in many parts of the continent. Customs defining proper marriage partners varied greatly, but strict rules always prevailed. In most cultures young people married in their teens, after winning social acceptance as adults and generally following a period of sexual experimentation. Sometimes important men took multiple wives, but the nuclear families that married couples and their children formed never stood alone. Instead, strong ties of residence and deference bound each couple to one or both sets of parents, producing what scholars call extended families. The first European to sail very far along the coast of North America, Giovanni da Verrazano, in 1524 observed households of twenty-five to thirty persons in what is now Rhode Island.

Kinship cemented all Indian societies together. Ties to cousins, aunts, and uncles created complex

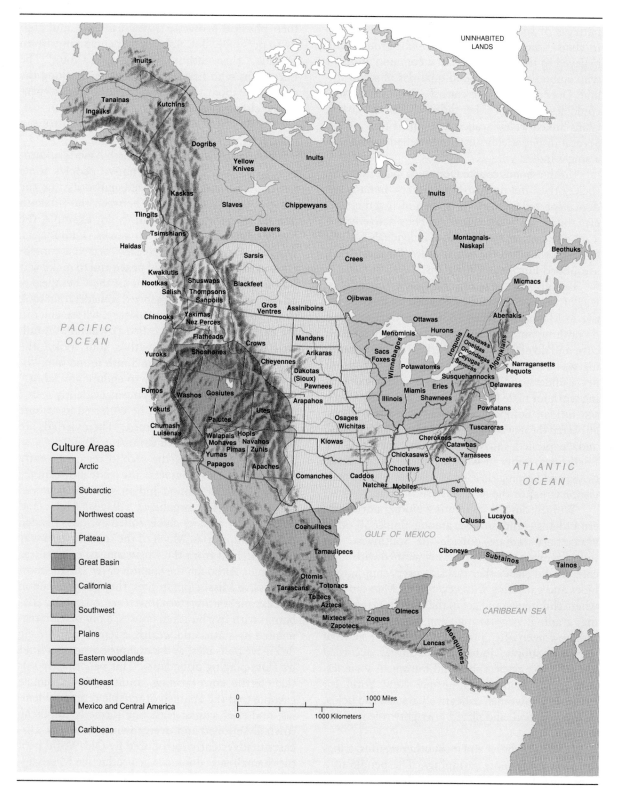

Cultural Divisions Among the Native Americans

By 1492 modern-day Canada and the United States may have had as many as 10 million Indian inhabitants, divided among more than fifty major linguistic groups and at least ten major cultural groups that had adapted to the local environment.

patterns of social obligation. So did membership in clans—the large networks of kin groups who believed in their descent from a common ancestor who embodied the admired qualities of some animal. Depending on the culture, clan membership could descend from either the mother or the father. Clans linked widely scattered groups within a tribe. Several different clans usually dwelled together in a single Indian village.

Kinship bonds counted for much more in Indian society than did nuclear-family units. Indians seldom expected spouses to be bound together forever, but kinship lasted for life. Thus native Americans could accept the divorce of individuals without feeling a threat to the social order. Such attitudes astounded European Christians.

Equally strange to Europeans was the Indians' way of work. "The men," recorded an English settler in Massachusetts in 1630, "for the most part do nothing but hunt and fish: their wives set their corn and do all their other work." In Europe hunting was an upper-class amusement, so Europeans never understood that it might constitute exhausting work for male Indians. Native Americans (who saw little of European women's housewifely labors) answered the newcomers' sneers about "lazy braves" and "exploited squaws" in kind: "they call the Englishmen fools in working themselves [in the fields] and keeping their wives idle," one white male visitor wrote of the northeastern Indians.

Women did the cultivating among northeastern Indians—and, indeed, among almost all other agricultural Indians outside the Southwest. For Indian women, field work easily meshed with child care, as did such other tasks as preparing animal hides and gathering wild vegetation. Men did jobs where children would get in the way: hunting, fishing, trading, negotiating, and fighting. Because Indian women often produced the greater share of the food supply, Indian communities accorded women more respect than did European societies. Among the Iroquois of upstate New York, for example, the women collectively owned the fields, distributed food, and played a weighty role in tribal councils.

In the Northeast and most other regions, tribes were generally loose groupings. The people of a tribe shared a common language and culture, and often they chose "civil chiefs" who mediated disputes between villages or clans, and "war chiefs" who led fights against outsiders. Chiefs had to prove

their physical prowess, trustworthiness, and ability to persuade. But, noted a Frenchman in eastern Canada, "their authority is most precarious." The Europeans who first encountered chiefs along the Atlantic seaboard (as well as in the Southeast) generally either overestimated their powers or disdained them for not measuring up to European monarchs.

Nevertheless, in eastern North America, Europeans did find among the native peoples some instances of more centralized authority. In the eastern Great Lakes region between the fifteenth and the mid-sixteenth centuries, for example, the five Iroquois tribes (the Mohawks, Onondagas, Oneidas, Cayugas, and Senacas) formed a confederation to maintain mutual peace and to make war on outsiders. About this time in the Chesapeake, an even more centrally organized confederation took shape: the Powhatan Confederacy, whose chief in the early 1600s was also called Powhatan. "A tall, well proportioned man, with a sour look," the English leader Captain John Smith found him, "of a very able and hardy body to endure any labor." Powhatan's life-and-death powers evidently rested on the stores of corn that he collected as tribute and redistributed in lean times. "Their victuals are their only riches," Smith commented.

In the Southeast, the second region of early European-Indian contacts, the sixteenth-century Spanish invaders found Indian societies centered on larger, highly organized villages. Male (and occasionally female) chiefs called caciques headed these communities. Much of the southeastern way of life derived from the Mississippian culture (see Prologue). Although the Spanish never saw the most impressive Mississippian sites, they did come upon at least one southeastern town (in modern-day Alabama) with five hundred houses, a population segmented by status and wealth, a temple and strong defensive palisades, and a cacique borne on a litter by flute-playing attendants. This was thickly settled, fertile corn-farming country. But a female cacique told the Spanish of terrible recent epidemics, and they saw at least one formerly imposing town abandoned and overgrown with weeds. Diseases inadvertently introduced by Old World peoples had already doomed the productive Mississippian culture and threatened all southeastern native Americans.

The third zone of contact was the Great Plains, where Spanish soldiers briefly visited both agri-

Wichita Chief, Two Daughters, and a Warrior

On the plains sixteenth-century Spanish explorers encountered river-valley peoples such as these members of the Wichita tribe of eastern Kansas.

cultural and nomadic, nonagricultural Indians. Hoping to find dazzling cities to conquer, Francisco Vásquez de Coronado was disappointed by the plains and their buffalo-hunting peoples, although he conceded that they had "the best physiques of any I have seen in the Indies." The settled river-valley people whom Coronado also met on

the plains, probably the Wichitas of eastern Kansas, seemed to him peaceful but poor. "The houses are of straw, and the people are savage. . . . They have no blankets, nor cotton with which to make them. All they have is the tanned skins of the cattle they kill. . . . They eat raw meat . . . [but] have the advantage over the others in their houses and in the growing of maize [corn]."

In the fourth region of European-Indian contact, the sunbaked Southwest, Coronado's quest for cities with gold-paved streets likewise ended in disillusionment. He reported little about the pueblo and river-valley peoples living there, and so modern scholars must rely on artifacts, ruins, and ecological evidence to piece together a picture of southwestern society at the moment of its first contact with Old World peoples.

Wresting a living from the severe southwestern environment demanded concentrated effort, but the native peoples succeeded remarkably well. The population was comparatively dense: a hundred thousand persons may have lived in the pueblos in the early sixteenth century, and intensive cultivation also supported large river-valley settlements. As in the rest of North America, extended families formed the foundation of southwestern village life in both the pueblos and the river valleys.

Stone Age Native American Culture

These laboriously made southwestern artifacts all date from before 1500. The photograph at the left includes a stone pick, mortar and pestle, drill, pipe, knife, and several axes and polishing stones, as well as a bone scraper and an awl. The painted figurine (right) was modeled from clay. Jewelry (center) made striking use of turquoise, a semiprecious stone traded as far as Mexico.

Southwestern patterns of property ownership and gender roles differed, not only from those of native Americans elsewhere but also among local cultures. Unlike Indians in other regions, here men and women shared agricultural labor. River-valley peoples of the Southwest owned land privately and passed it through the male line, and men dominated decision making. In pueblo society (which in this respect resembled societies in the Northeast and Southeast), land was communally owned, and women played an influential role in community affairs. A pueblo woman could end a marriage simply by tossing her husband's belongings out the door and sending him back to his kinfolk. Moreover, clan membership passed in the mother's line. Yet pueblo communities depended on secret male societies to perform the rituals that would secure the gods' blessing and ensure life-giving rain. In all respects, pueblo society strictly subordinated the individual to the group and demanded rigorous conformity. This cohesion would bolster the pueblo peoples when, after 1598, the Spanish conquered the Southwest and began imposing Christianity there.

Not only in the Southwest but throughout North America, almost every aspect of Indian life had some connection to the unseen world of spirits. Because many Indian peoples had no formal religious organizations, sixteenth-century Europeans such as Verrazano assumed "that they have no religion and that they live in absolute freedom, and that everything they do proceeds from Ignorance." Few more preposterous European misconceptions about the native Americans could be cited.

Indian Religion and Social Values

Most Indians explained the origin and destiny of the human race in deeply moving myths. In the beginning, said the Iroquois, was the sky world of unchanging perfection. From it fell a beautiful pregnant woman, whom the birds saved from plunging into the limitless ocean. On the back of a tortoise who rose from the sea, birds created the earth's soil, in which the woman planted seeds carried during her fall. From these seeds sprang all nature; from her womb, the human race.

Native American religion revolved around the conviction that all nature was alive, pulsating with a spiritual power—*manitou,* in the Algonkian lan-

guage of the northeastern Indians. A mysterious, awe-inspiring force that could affect human life for both good and evil, such power united all nature in an unbroken web. For most Indians, *manitou* was a far more vivid presence than the supreme, benevolent, but distant Good Spirit who they believed had created the universe. *Manitou* encompassed "every thing which they cannot comprehend," wrote the Puritan leader Roger Williams, one of the few European visitors who genuinely tried to understand the northeastern Indians' spiritual world. Their belief in *manitou* led most Indian peoples to seek constantly to conciliate all the spiritual forces in nature: living things, rocks and water, sun and moon, even ghosts and witches. For example, Indians were careful to pray to the spirits of the animals they hunted, justifying the killing of just enough game to sustain themselves. To the Indians, humanity was only one link in the great chain of living nature. The Judeo-Christian view that God had given humanity domination over nature was very strange to them.

Indians had many ways of gaining access to spiritual power. One was through dreaming: most native Americans took very seriously the visions that came to them in sleep. They also sought to link themselves to *manitou* by artificially altering their consciousness through difficult physical ordeals. Young men, for example, commonly endured a traumatic rite of passage before gaining recognition as adults. Such a rite often involved "questing"—going alone into a forest or up a mountain, fasting, sometimes taking a drug, and awaiting the mystical experience in which an animal spirit would reveal itself as a protective guide and offer a glimpse of the future. Girls went through comparable rituals at the onset of menstruation to initiate them into the spiritual world from which female reproductive power flowed. Moreover, entire communities often practiced collective power-seeking rituals such as the Plains Indians' Sun Dance, in which men tortured themselves not only to demonstrate indifference to pain but also to suffer on behalf of weaker members of their group (see Chapter 16).

Although on occasion all Indians tried to communicate directly with the spiritual world, they normally relied on shamans for help in understanding the unseen. The shamans ("medicine men" to whites) were healers who used both medicinal plants and magical chants, but their role in Indian society went further. They interpreted dreams, guided "questing" and other rituals, invoked war or peace spirits, and figured prominently in community councils. Chiefs had to maintain respectful relations with their people's shamans, and by the sixteenth century, shamans were forming organized priesthoods in the Southeast and Southwest.

Because most Indian cultures tried to maintain a sense of dependence among their people, native American communities demanded conformity and close cooperation. From early childhood Indians learned to be accommodating and reserved—slow to reveal their own feelings before they could sense others'. Although few native American peoples favored physical punishment in child rearing, Indian parents punished psychologically, by shaming. Throughout life the fear of becoming an isolated social outcast (a status that could mean death) forced individual Indians to maintain strict self-control. Communities took decisions by consensus, and leaders articulated slowly emerging agreements in memorable, persuasive, often passionate oratory. Shamans and chiefs therefore had to be dramatic orators. Noted John Smith, they spoke in public "with vehemency and so great passions that they sweat till they drop and are so out of breath they scarce can speak."

Because Indians highly valued consensus building in everyday life, their leaders' authority depended primarily on the respect that they invoked rather than what they could demand by compulsion. Distributing gifts was central to establishing and maintaining leadership with a native American community, as a Frenchman in early-seventeenth-century Canada clearly understood: "For the savages have that noble quality, that they give liberally, casting at the feet of him whom they will honor the present that they give him. But it is with hope to receive some reciprocal kindness, which is a kind of contract, which we call . . . 'I give thee, to the end thou shouldst give me.' "

Thus for Indians, trade was not merely an economic activity by which they acquired useful goods. It was also a means of ensuring goodwill with other peoples and of building their own prestige. European visitors almost always found native Americans eager to barter. For many centuries, trade among the Indians had spanned the continent. The Hurons of southern Ontario produced large agricultural surpluses for trade, and southwestern Indians' turquoise found its way to Mexico. Flint and other tool-making materials, salt, dyes, furs, and (in hard times) food and seeds were major objects of trade. So was tobacco, which Indians primarily regarded as a ceremonial drug, its fragrant smoke symbolizing the union of heaven and earth. Native Americans eagerly assimilated into their own way of life the new goods that European traders offered. Metal tools they valued for their practical, labor-saving benefits, while dyed cloth and glass objects quickly took on symbolic, prestige-enhancing qualities.

"They love not to be encumbered with too many utensils," remarked an early-seventeenth-century English visitor. Rather, prestige counted for everything in native American society. If Indians did accumulate possessions, it was primarily with the aim of giving them away, to win prestige. The most spectacular example of such gift-exchanging rituals was the Pacific Northwest potlatch ceremony. When a northwestern community's social hierarchy was shaken, an aspiring new leader would invite his neighbors to a potlatch, at which he would give away or destroy most of what he owned, all the while chanting about his own greatness and taunting his rivals. Those who received were expected later to give away even more. He who could give away the most gained the highest prestige and accumulated the greatest number of people obligated to him.

Scholars have used the word *reciprocity* to characterize native American religious and social values. Reciprocity involved mutual give-and-take, but its aim was not to confer equality. Instead, societies (like those of the Indians) based on reciprocity tried to maintain equilibrium and interdependence between individuals of unequal power and prestige. In their religious thinking, too, Indians applied the concept of reciprocity, in viewing nature as a web of interdependent power entities into which human beings had to fit. And in social organization, the Indians' principle of reciprocity required that communities be places of face-to-face, lifelong interaction. Trade and gift giving solidified such reciprocal bonds. The Indians' faith in social reciprocity also underlay their idea of property rights. They believed that the people of one area might agree to share with others the right to use the land for different but complementary pur-

Northwestern Totem Pole

The most famous symbol of northwestern Indian culture, totem poles served various purposes. Some advertised the genealogy and accomplishments of a clan, family, or individual. Others celebrated a successful potlatch. A few seem to have been intended to ridicule an enemy or simply to express the maker's whimsy and skill.

sessed a strong sense of order. Custom, the demands of social conformity, and the rigors of nature strictly regulated life, and the people's everyday affairs mingled with the spiritual world at every turn. Nature and the supernatural world could sometimes be frightening. For example, Indians feared ghosts and believed that nonconformists could invoke evil spirits by witchcraft—the most dreaded crime in Indian cultures. Much of Indian religion involved placating the evil spirits that caused sickness and death. The pueblo peoples, whose existence depended on carefully conserving a meager rainfall, relieved their constant anxiety by performing frequent rituals. And except in the Southwest, where stress on conformity minimized all competition, Indian life had an intensely competitive side. Individuals and communities eagerly strove to show physical prowess in ritualized games like football and lacrosse, and they bet enthusiastically on the outcome. "They are so bewitched with these . . . games, that they will lose sometimes all they have," said an Englishman of the Massachusett Indians about 1630. Such games served less as recreation than as a means of redistributing prestige.

The Mask of Death

In many Indian cultures, even individuals beloved in life could become malevolent ghosts after death. Rituals to placate the dead were common. This mask, representing the chief spirit of the dead, was made by the Kwakiutl people of the northwest coast.

poses: hunting, gathering, farming, trapping, or traveling. The notion (then emerging in Europe) that property ownership conferred perpetual and exclusive control of land was thus alien to Indians.

But native American society was hardly a simple, noncompetitive world. All Indian cultures pos-

The breakdown of order in Indian communities could bring fearful consequences: accusations of witchcraft, demands for revenge against wrongdoers, war against enemies. "They seldom make war for lands or goods," wrote Smith, "but for women and children [who would be adopted into the tribe], and principally for revenge." Going to war or exacting personal revenge was a ritualized way of restoring order that had broken down. A captured male could expect death after prolonged torture. Indian men learned from early childhood to inflict (and to bear) physical pain out of loyalty to kin and neighbors; they knew that they must withstand torture without flinching and death without fear. Endurance was central to Indian life.

"Many devilish gestures with a Hellish noise"—thus one Englishman dismissed native American religion. But at the same time, Europeans were apprehensive of shamans' power (they called them "priests of Satan") and feared Indian "savagery" as the evil influence of the devil, who was also a sinister figure in Christianity. As we shall see, the principle of social reciprocity also helped knit together Old World communities. But by 1492 reciprocity in Europe was starting to give way to a more impersonal social mentality, based on commercial exchange and an authoritarian chain of command. When Columbus encountered the Indians, Old and New World societies were moving apart, not converging.

Old World Peoples

The Old World gave birth to the human race. For several million years, early human beings went forth in waves from Africa's warm grasslands to people the globe. Then, over a span of at least five thousand years before 1492, a great range of societies arose, stretching from West Africa and Europe to Siberia and Polynesia. Complex networks of peaceful or aggressive interactions, cultural influences, and long-range trade linked many of these societies. Some Old World cultures were hunter-gatherer or simple agricultural communities. But throughout the Old World—as also in Mexico and Peru—there existed powerful states with armed forces, bureaucracies, religious institutions, proud aristocracies, and toiling common people.

West Africa

For almost five thousand years, the vast, barren Sahara Desert has lain between much of Africa and the rest of the world. In addition, West Africa was effectively isolated from the land to its north by the prevailing Atlantic winds, which could bring old-fashioned sailing ships south but hampered them from returning north. Moreover, the yellow fever rampant in the West African rain-forest coastline helped ward off outside intruders. If contracted in youth, yellow fever could be survived with lifelong immunity, but it generally killed adult newcomers lacking such defenses.

Nevertheless, between the formidable Sahara and the forbidding coast, a broad swath of grassland (savanna) offered a hospitable shelter. By about 3000 B.C., people here were growing grain and herding livestock. Late in the first millennium B.C., when knowledge of iron metallurgy reached the grasslands, the region's dark-skinned people began carrying their culture outward, eventually leaving their imprint on almost all of sub-Saharan Africa. By the sixteenth century, sub-Saharan Africa, twice the size of the United States, had a population of perhaps 20 million.

Despite its seeming isolation, West Africa looked northward. Camel caravans crossed the Sahara, and an important trade in gold and salt developed with North Africa's Mediterranean coast. From A.D. 600 to 1600, there arose in the grassland a series of West African empires—Ghana, Mali, and Songhai—that imposed tribute on their subject populations and taxed the merchant communities at the southern end of the caravan routes. Islam spread into West Africa from its Middle Eastern birthplace, and by the late eleventh century, the grassland empires became at least nominally Moslem. Their rulers kept records in Arabic and irregularly enforced Islamic law, but it was their wealth that made them famous throughout the Islamic world. By 1492 the last of the great West African empires, Songhai, stood at the height of its glory, with a bureaucracy and a vigorous army dominating much of the interior. Songhai's major city, Timbuktu, boasted flourishing markets and a famous Islamic university.

Compared with the grassland empires, coastal West Africa was relatively insignificant. In Senegambia at Africa's westernmost bulge, several small

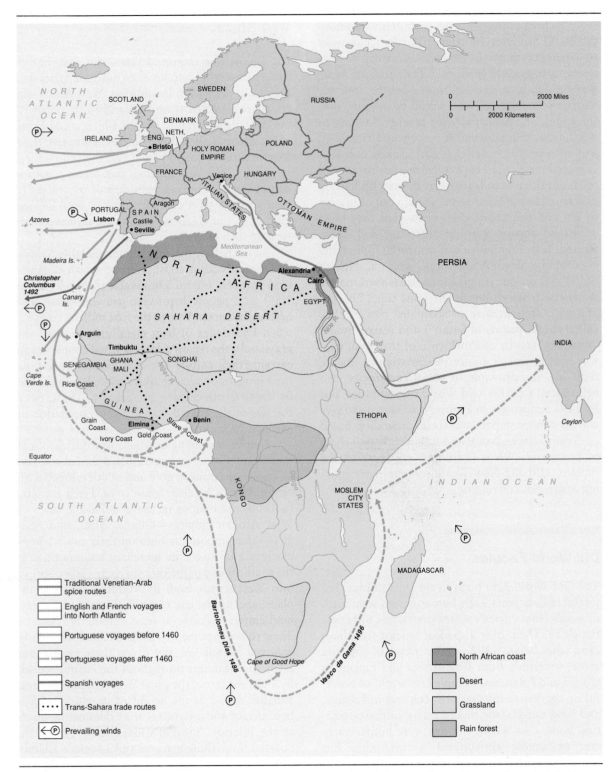

Europe, Africa, and the Near East in 1492

In 1492 Europeans had little knowledge of the outside world apart from the Mediterranean basin and Africa's west coast. Since the Azores and the Canary and Cape Verde Islands had been discovered recently in the eastern Atlantic, many Europeans were not surprised when Columbus found new islands farther west in 1492.

Bronze Head, Bini Tribe, Benin

Along with the Yoruba people of the city of Ife, the Bini tribe of Benin had by 1500 developed beautiful African art forms in their sculpture of human figures of ivory, terra cotta, and especially bronze.

Islamic states took root. Infestation by the tsetse fly, the carrier of sleeping sickness, kept livestock-herding peoples out of Guinea's coastal forests, but many small states arose here, too, during the first millennium A.D. Among these was Benin, where artisans had been fashioning magnificent iron-work for centuries.

Then in the fifteenth century, Guinea's population rose. Foreign demands for gold that Africans panned from streams or dug from the earth touched off the spurt. Grassland warriors and merchants poured into Guinea and Senegambia, seeking new opportunities and on occasion founding or expanding the region's tiny states. Similarly thirsting for fresh opportunities were the Portuguese, who in the mid-fifteenth century used new maritime techniques to sail up and down West Africa's coast in search of gold and slaves.

Parallels and contrasts between black African and native American societies before European contact are fascinating. Like the priest-kings who headed the complex Indian societies of the Mississippian culture, Mexico, and Peru, African grass-land emperors claimed semigodlike status, which they only thinly disguised when they adopted Islam. Small African kingdoms resembled the villages presided over by the caciques of southeastern North America. African kings' authority was primarily religious. Their power, like that of Indian chiefs, largely depended on their ability to persuade, to conform to custom, and sometimes to redistribute wealth justly among their people.

In Africa as in North America, the cohesiveness of kinship groups knitted society together. From childhood, Africans found themselves in a network of interlocking, mutual obligations to kinfolk. Not just parents but also aunts, uncles, distant cousins, and persons sharing clan ties formed an African's kin group and claimed his or her first loyalty. Africans held their grandparents in highest esteem and accorded village or clan elders great deference. In centuries to come, the tradition of strong extended families would help enslaved Africans in the New World to endure the breakup of nuclear families by sale.

Other aspects of family structure were also common to some native American and African societies. One was polygyny, the custom whereby a man married several wives and maintained numerous households. A second was bridewealth, a prospective husband's payment to his bride's kin before marriage. Christian Europeans wrongly interpreted both practices as demeaning to women and evidence of "barbarism." But an African man did not "buy" a wife; in effect, he posted bond for good behavior and acknowledged the relative prestige of his own and his bride's kin groups. Marrying several wives could cost a man heavily, so polygyny was largely confined to higher-status men who needed to establish marriage ties with more than one kin group. African and native American wives generally kept lifelong links with their own kin group, and in many societies children traced descent through the mother's, not the father's, bloodline. All this buttressed women's standing.

Still another parallel between the two cultures lay in their attitudes toward land and property. To Africans, kin groups not only enjoyed inalienable rights to the soil that their ancestors had always cultivated but also had a duty to honor ancestors and earth spirits by properly cultivating the land. Native Americans thought similarly, although their sense of proper land usage focused more on the village or tribe as a whole. Neither Africans nor native Americans treated land as a commodity to be bought and sold.

Cultivation was difficult in Africa and required the labor of both sexes. As in all tropical regions, scorching sunlight and frequent downpours prevented humus (slowly decaying vegetative matter) from accumulating in the African soil. Like Indians, Africans tried to maintain soil fertility by practicing slash-and-burn tillage (see Prologue). In the coastal rain forests, Africans grew root crops, primarily yams. On the grasslands the staff of life was grain, which in Senegambia meant rice. In the seventeenth and eighteenth centuries, both rice and the grain's enslaved Senegambian cultivators would be transplanted to the North American mainland.

Religion permeated African life. African, like native American, religion recognized spiritual presences pervading nature. The power of earth spirits and of agricultural ancestors reinforced the esteem that Africans accorded to cultivators. In the eighteenth century, Europeans got an authentic glimpse of African religion from Olaudah Equiano, a West African who eventually managed to purchase his freedom from slavery:

> The natives believe that there is one Creator of all things, and that he lives in the sun, [and] . . . that he governs events. . . . Some . . . believe in the transmigration of souls [reincarnation] to some degree. Those spirits, who are not transmigrated, such as their dear friends or relations, they believe always attend them, and guard them from the bad spirits of their foes. For this reason, they always, before eating . . . put some small portion of the meat and pour some of their drink, on the ground for them; and they often make oblations [offerings] of the blood of beasts or fowls at their graves.

Magic and the placating of spiritual powers were as important in African as in Indian life, and the responsibility for maintaining contact with the spirit world fell to shamans. Africans explained misfortunes in terms of witchcraft, much as did Indians and Europeans. But African religion differed from native American religion in its focus on ancestor worship. Indians often regarded the dead with uneasiness, lest they become harmful ghosts, whereas Africans commonly venerated departed forebears as spiritual guardians.

Africa's magnificent artistic traditions were also steeped in religion. The ivory, cast-iron, and wood sculpture of West Africa, whose bold design would help mold the twentieth-century Western world's modern art, was used in ceremonies reenacting creation myths and honoring spirits. A strong moralistic streak ran through African folk tales. Oral reciters transmitted these stories in dramatic public presentations with ritual masks, dance, and music of a highly complex rhythmic structure now appreciated as one of the foundations of jazz.

Much in traditional African culture seemed to clash with the great monotheistic religions, Islam and Christianity. Among Africans, Islam appealed primarily to merchants trading with Moslem North Africa and the Middle East and to the grassland rulers eager to consolidate their power. Even these ambitious emperors were incompletely Islamicized—some learned with dismay that Islam limited them to four wives. By the sixteenth century, Islam had only begun to affect the daily lives of grassland cultivators and artisans. Christianity, arriving in West Africa with the Portuguese in the fifteenth and sixteenth centuries, demanded that Africans break even more radically with their traditional culture and until the nineteenth century had little impact.

European Culture and Society

When Columbus landed on San Salvador in 1492, Europe was approaching the height of a mighty cultural revival, the Renaissance. Contemporary intellectuals and poets believed that their age was witnessing a return to the standards of ancient Greek and Roman civilization. After a century-long economic recession, money had accumulated to pay for magnificent architecture, and wealthy patrons commissioned master painters and sculptors to create works glowing with idealized human beauty. Renaissance scholars strove to reconcile ancient philosophy with Christian faith, to explore the mysteries of nature, to map the world, and to explain the motions of the heavens.

But European society was quivering with tension. The era's artistic and intellectual creativity was partly inspired by intense social and spiritual stress, as Renaissance Europeans groped for stability by glorifying order, hierarchy, and beauty. A concern for power and rank ("degree") dominated European life between the fifteenth and seventeenth centuries. William Shakespeare (1564–1616), who expressed Renaissance values with incomparable eloquence, wrote:

> *The heavens themselves, the planets and this*
> *center [earth]*
> *Observe degree, priority, and place . . .*
> *Take but degree away, untune that string,*
> *And hark, what discord follows!*

Gender, wealth, inherited position, and political power affected every European's status, and few lived outside the reach of some political authority's claim to tax and impose laws upon them. But this order was shaky. Conflicts between states, between religions, and between rich and poor constantly threatened the balance. All the more eagerly, then, did Europeans cling to their visions of order and hierarchy.

Atop the European hierarchy were enthroned the kings who governed most states. (Only a handful of republics existed, the most important of which were the two aristocratic city-states of Venice and Florence.) In 1492 the kingdoms of England, Scotland, France, Spain, and Portugal occupied roughly their present-day territories. Germany, Italy, and the Low Countries comprised a welter of smaller states. But the kings or the republican aristocrats of all these lands only occasionally pursued national goals. Sometimes rulers did not even speak their subjects' language. These complications sprang from the intricate networks of marriages that ruling families arranged among themselves, often sowing the seeds of future conflicts over dynastic claims. Monarchs sought above all to consolidate their power and to that end waged wars with mercenary armies that cost mountains of money. The kings' forces spread disease and misery everywhere; they were "an unchristian, cursed tribe whose trade consists of gouging, pillaging, burning, murdering, gambling, drinking, whoring, blaspheming, willfully killing husbands and fathers, persecuting peasants . . . , stripping fields, and demanding tribute," a German chronicler wrote in 1531.

Kings' power depended on gaining the cooperation of the upper classes, usually by consulting such representative institutions as Parliament in England. The men who dominated these institutions generally saw officeholding as a form of property owning and a legitimate way to improve their fortunes. Society expected these aristocrats to spend freely even if they could not afford it. No king could ride roughshod over such men, and by defending their own liberties, they were also pre-

Marriage Feast at Bermondsey,
by Joris Hoefnagel,
c. 1570 (Detail)

Hoefnagel's canvas richly illustrates the festivities surrounding an important event in sixteenth-century European society—the alliance of two aristocratic families in marriage. In the background, various ordinary people lend a hand.

serving the principle of limited government against encroaching despotism.

At the bottom of the social heap toiled the ordinary people. In the overwhelmingly rural Europe of the times, peasants composed between 70 percent and 80 percent of the population. Peasants ranged from a few prosperous families with a large holding, such as the English yeomen, to landless laborers who barely scraped by on odd jobs. Taxes, rents, and other dues to landlords and the Church were heavy, and poor harvests or war drove even well-to-do peasants to starvation.

Europe's population increased between the late fifteenth and early seventeenth centuries from about 55 million in 1450 to almost 100 million by 1600. But without corresponding improvements in technology and agriculture, output did not rise to meet growing demand. Northern European and English peasant families cultivated wheat or rye, barley, and oats on long strips scattered through the village's three or more fields; one field lay fallow every third year to restore fertility. Yields were pitifully low. Families had to cooperate in plowing, sowing, and harvesting, as well as in grazing their livestock on the fallow field and the jointly owned "commons," or pastureland and forest. With new land at a premium, the commons could be a tempting prize for landlords to "enclose"—that is, to convert to private property. Peasants who had no *written* title to their land were especially vulnerable, but those with strong titles could either keep their land or profit from joining the landlord in enclosing.

The problems of peasant tenure were particularly acute in England, where some landlords and peasants united to divide the commons among themselves, raise sheep, and grow rich selling wool. "Your sheep . . . even eat up men," wrote Sir Thomas More (with some exaggeration) in his passionate protest against greed, *Utopia* (1516). "They devastate and destroy fields, houses, and towns. For in whatever parts of the kingdom . . . wool is produced, there the nobles and gentlemen . . . are not content with the rents and annual profits that their predecessors used to get from their farms. . . . They leave nothing for arable land, enclose everything for pasture. . . ."

European towns were numerous but small, typically with several thousand inhabitants each. A great metropolis like London, whose population ballooned from fifty-five thousand in 1550 to two

European Peasants

This small illustration from a fifteenth-century French manuscript accurately illustrates northern European peasant life. Plowing, carried out with a clumsy, wheeled ox-drawn plow, often required cooperative effort, for not every household owned the necessary equipment. Once the field had been plowed, each household sowed and tended its own strips, but the entire community usually harvested together.

hundred thousand in 1600, was quite exceptional. But all towns were dirty and disease-ridden, and townspeople lived close-packed with their neighbors.

Unappealing as sixteenth-century towns might seem today, ambitious (or desperate) men and women of the time viewed them as growing, dynamic centers of opportunity. Immigration from the countryside—rather than an excess of urban births over deaths—accounted for towns' expansion. Most of the displaced country people who flocked into towns remained at the bottom of the social order, however, as servants or laborers who often failed to accumulate enough money to marry and live independently. Manufacturing took place in household workshops, where subordinate workers were dependent on an artisan master. Successful artisans and merchants formed guilds to control employment, prices, and the sale of goods. Dominated by the richest citizens, urban governments enforced social conformity by "sumptuary laws" that forbade dressing inappropriately to one's social rank. Thus the hopes and ambitions that drew thousands into towns usually ended in frustration. Commented the English writer Thomas Nashe on London's teeming populace in 1593:

> From the rich to the poor . . . there is ambition, or swelling above their states [proper place in society]; the rich citizen swells against the pride of the prodigal courtier; the prodigal courtier swells against the wealth of the citizen. One company swells against another. . . . The ancients [elderly], they oppose themselves against the younger, and suppress them and keep them down all that they may. The young men, they call [the elderly] dotards, and swell and rage. . . .

Conservative moralists like Nashe who thus condemned "overreaching" (individuals' attempts to rise in society) stoutly upheld the values of old-fashioned social reciprocity. As in the New World and Africa, in Europe traditional society rested on maintaining long-term, reciprocal relationships. Europeans' attempts to preserve reciprocity included their insistence on the joint use of common lands, their prohibitions against usury (charging interest on loans), and their bans on inappropriate dressing and "unjust" competition. Because its aim was the smooth functioning of social relationships between individuals of unequal status, reciprocity required the upper classes to act with self-restraint and dignity, while the lower classes had to show deference to their "betters." Finally, preserving reciprocity demanded strict economic regulation to ensure that sellers charged a "just price"—one that covered costs and allowed the seller a "reasonable" living standard but that barred him from taking advantage of buyers' and borrowers' misfortunes or of shortages to make "excessive" profits.

Yet for centuries Europeans had been compromising the ideals of traditional economic behavior. "In the Name of God and of Profit," thirteenth-century Italian merchants had written on their ledgers. By the sixteenth century, nothing could stop the charging of interest on borrowed money or sellers' price increases in response to demand. New forms of business organization slowly spread in the commercial world—especially the impersonal joint-stock company with many investors (see below), the ancestor of the modern corporation. Demand rose for capital investment, and so did the supply of accumulated wealth. Slowly a new economic outlook took form that justified both the unimpeded acquisition of wealth and unregulated economic competition, and insisted that individuals owed one another nothing but the money necessary to settle each market transaction. This new outlook, the central value system of capitalism or the "market economy," was the opposite of traditional demands for the strict regulation of economic activity to ensure social reciprocity and maintain "just prices."

In sixteenth- and seventeenth-century Europe, this new economic system was not yet dominant. Laws still sought to bolster the traditional goals of an unchanging, noncompetitive order of things, and peasants, artisans, and many small-scale merchants desperately supported these laws' enforcement. Even rich men tended to use their wealth to buy status rather than keep plowing profits back into production.

Sixteenth- and seventeenth-century Europeans therefore held conflicting attitudes toward economic enterprise and social change, and their ambivalence remained unresolved. In Europe itself and in transplanted Europeans' New World communities, a restless desire for fresh opportunity kept life simmering with competitive tension. But those who prospered still sought the security and pres-

The Banker and His Wife, *by Quentin Metsys, 1514*
Despite religious admonitions against excessive material gain, sixteenth-century Europeans were intensely money-conscious. In this portrait, a wealthy banker and his wife check their accounts and weigh gold coins to ensure their accurate value.

tige provided by traditional social distinctions, while the poor longed for the age-old values that they hoped would restrain irresponsible greed. Almost all intellectuals and clergymen defended traditional standards. When Europeans violated these standards, they did so with a bad conscience. Thus ideal and reality remained far apart.

Fundamental change in European society could also be seen in the growing importance of the nuclear family. The tradition of broad kinship networks did survive in the sense that nuclear families prudently tried to retain the goodwill of distant relatives, but these networks seldom overruled the male head of each nuclear family. In a common cliché of the age, the nuclear family was a "little commonwealth." The father's government within the family was supposed to mirror God's rule over Creation and kings' lordship over their subjects. Even grown sons and daughters regularly knelt for their father's blessing. The ideal, according to a German writer, was that "wives should obey their husbands and not seek to dominate them; they must manage the home efficiently. Husbands . . . should treat their wives with consideration and occasionally close an eye to their faults." In practice, the father's domination often had to make room for the wife's responsibility in managing family affairs and helping to run the farm or the workshop. And repeated male complaints (such as that of an English author in 1622) about wives "who think themselves every way as good as their husbands, and no way inferior to them," suggested that male domination had its limits.

Democracy had no place in Europe. A few late-medieval and sixteenth-century revolts had democratic overtones, but these uprisings were mercilessly suppressed. To Europeans of the era, democracy in practice meant mob rule and the destruction of social distinctions. Officials controlled crime, especially political and religious offenses by ordinary people, through brutal public punishments. Hierarchy implied subordination, strict rules, and the exercise of manly prowess.

Europeans and Their God

"In the beginning God created the heaven and the earth. . . . And God said, Let us make man in our image . . . and let them have dominion . . . over all the earth. . . . So God created man in his own image, . . . male and female he created them." Sixteenth-century Europeans firmly believed in this biblical explanation of the origins of the world and its peoples. Christianity, to which the vast majority of Europeans adhered, taught that Jesus Christ, God's Son, had redeemed sinners by suffering crucifixion and rising from the dead. Almost as vivid, perhaps, was Christians' belief in the devil, Satan, whom God had hurled from heaven soon after the Creation and who ceaselessly lured people to damnation by tempting them to do evil. The non-Christian European minority encompassed small Jewish communities, Moslem Turks, and descendants of medieval Spain's Arab conquerors. But all Europe's population—Christians, Jews, and Moslems—worshiped the same almighty Creator.

By the sixteenth century, Christianity (or Judaism or Islam) had sunk deep roots into the consciousness of most Europeans. But the people also retained beliefs in the supernatural that over the centuries had blended with their faith in Christ, the Christian saints, church ritual, and biblical teachings. Like native Americans and Africans, virtually all Europeans feared witches, and many thought that individuals could manipulate nature by invoking unseen spiritual powers—that is, by magic. (The most plausible alternative to magic was astrology, which insisted that a person's fate depended on the conjunction of various planets and stars.) Everyone envisioned nature as a "chain of being" infused by God with life and tingling with spiritual forces. Deeply embedded in European folklore, such supernaturalism also marked the "high culture" of educated medieval and Renaissance Europeans. Indeed, the sixteenth-century European "mentality" had more in common with Indian and African mind sets than any of these traditional belief systems have with the stereotypical "modern" world view.

Medieval churchmen asserted that Christ had founded the Church to save sinners from hell and lead them to heaven. All but a few heretics (religious dissenters) accepted the dictum "Outside the Church, no salvation." Christ's sacrifice was repeated every time a priest said Mass, and divine grace flowed to sinners through the sacraments that consecrated priests alone could administer—above all, baptism, confession, and the Eucharist (communion). In most of Europe in 1492, "the Church" was a huge network of clergymen, set apart from laypeople by the fact that they did not marry. At the top was the pope, God's "vicar" (representative), whose authority reached everywhere in Europe but Russia and the Balkan Peninsula.

The papacy wielded awesome spiritual power. Fifteenth- and early-sixteenth-century popes claimed the authority to dispense to repentant sinners extra blessings, or "indulgences," in return for such "good works" as donating money to the Church. Indulgences promised time off from future punishment in purgatory, where souls atoned for sins they had already confessed and been forgiven. (Hell, from which there was no escape, awaited those who died unforgiven.) The Church grew wealthy and corrupt by providing indulgences, which, given people's anxieties over "sinful" behavior, were enormously popular. The jingle of a successful indulgence seller in early-sixteenth-century Germany promised that

As soon as the coin in the cash box rings,
The soul from purgatory's fire springs.

The sale of indulgences, however, provoked a tremendous crisis for the Church. In 1517 the German monk Martin Luther (1483–1546) attacked the practice. When the papacy tried to silence him, Luther merely broadened his criticism to encompass the Mass, purgatory, priests, and the pope. Luther's revolt initiated the Protestant Reformation, which changed Christianity forever.

To Luther, indulgence-selling and similar examples of clerical corruption were evil not just because they bilked people. The Church, he charged, gave people false confidence that they could "earn" salvation by doing good works. His own agonizing search for salvation had convinced Luther that God alone chose whom to save from damnation and that believers could trust only God's love. Luther's spiritual struggle and experience of being "born again" constituted a classic conversion experience—the heart of Protestant religion as it would be preached and practiced for centuries in England and North America. "I did not love a just and angry God, but rather hated and murmured against him," recalled Luther. "Night and day I pondered until I saw the connection between the justice of God and the [New Testament] statement that 'the just shall live [be saved] by faith.' . . . Thereupon I felt myself to be reborn and to have gone through open doors into paradise."

A religious prophet of genius, Luther was socially conservative and politically naive. His assault on the Church's abuses won a fervent following among the German public, but Luther and his followers could carry out their program only with the aid of the German princes and city-states. Protestantism* thus had to allow civil governments broad control over reformed religion. Luther's dream of rallying all Christendom around God's Word soon crumbled.

Protestant reformers could not even agree on what God's Word really meant. Thus Luther and the great French reformer John Calvin (1509–1564) interpreted the spiritual meaning of the Eucharist—a vital issue in their day—quite differently. Calvin also focused more closely than Luther on the stark doctrine of predestination; that is, God's foreknowledge of who would be saved and who would be damned. But Calvinists and Lutherans, as the followers of the two Reformation leaders came to be called, were horrified when more radical Protestants questioned Christ's divinity. Moreover, Calvin and Luther soon had socially as well as religiously radical opponents. Among them were the Anabaptists, who appealed strongly to women and common people with their criticisms of the rich and powerful and sought to restrict baptism to "converted" adults. Most Anabaptists were pacifists, and some renounced private property and lived communally. Judging the Anabaptists a threat to the social order, governments and the mainstream churches persecuted them.

Still another disappointment for Protestants was the Catholic church's remarkable resilience. Catholic reform had begun in Spain even before Luther's revolt, and soon the papacy vigorously attacked corruption and combated Protestant viewpoints on major religious issues. The popes also sponsored a new religious order fervently committed to the papacy: the Jesuits, whose members would distinguish themselves for centuries as teachers, missionaries, and royal advisers. This Catholic revival, the Counter-Reformation, brought into existence the modern Roman Catholic church, which would endure little changed until the mid-twentieth century. But those in all camps who hoped that Christian concord would overcome religious quarrels were sadly disillusioned.

---

*The word *Protestant* comes from the *protest* of Luther's princely supporters against Holy Roman Emperor Charles V's anti-Lutheran policies.

John Calvin, *by Hans Holbein the Younger, Sixteenth Century*

Calvin was trained as a classical scholar before his religious conversion. He brought to Protestant theology a scholar's erudition, a lawyer's appreciation of the importance of God's sovereignty over Creation, and a religious zealot's intense faith.

The Reformation era left three great legacies. First, it created almost all the major Christian traditions that would eventually take root in American soil: Protestantism, modern Roman Catholicism, and many radical Protestant religious impulses that would later flower into dozens of denominations and visionary groups striving for human perfection. Second, Protestantism placed a high value on reading. Luther's own conversion had sprung from his long study of the Bible, and Protestants demanded that God's Word be read carefully by believers and preached by the minister. The new faith was spread best by the newly invented printing press; wherever Protestantism became established, basic education and religious indoctrination followed. Third, Protestantism denied that God had endowed priests with special powers. Clergymen, Luther and Calvin insisted, could claim no more dignity than followers of any other honest profession. Work itself was dignified, and Christians should feel confident that God asked them only to fulfill the obligations of their station in life, however humble. Protestant leaders did not teach that work would earn salvation (no human effort could do that), and it did not necessarily follow that those predestined for salvation could be identified by their hard work or material success.

Overall, the Reformation was a conservative movement. It yearned to bring back the simplicity and purity of the ancient Christian church. Protestantism condemned the replacement of traditional reciprocity by marketplace values; even more than Catholicism, it questioned the pursuit of excessive wealth. In a world of troubling change, it could forge individuals of strong moral determination and equip them with the fortitude to survive and prosper. Protestantism's greatest appeal was to all those—ordinary people, merchants, and aristocrats alike—who brooded over their chances for salvation and valued the steady performance of duty.

Tudor England

The instability, tensions, and artistic creativity of sixteenth-century European life all converged in England. Deeply committed to the hierarchical view of society, English people faced major challenges: achieving political stability, settling the religious issues raised by the Reformation, and controlling social disorder. All three challenges were tightly intertwined and helped shape England's eventual involvement in North America.

Political instability weighed heavily upon the English. The ruling Tudor family had only recently (1485) come to the throne after bloody civil wars. The Tudor dynasty's fragility left Henry VIII (ruled 1509–1547) obsessed with producing a legitimate male heir. When his queen, Catharine of Aragon, failed to bear a son, Henry in 1527 asked the pope to annul his marriage. After the pope denied Henry's request, the king had Parliament dissolve his marriage and proclaim him "supreme head" of the Church of England (or Anglican church). The royal government executed a few opponents of the new church, and it closed monasteries and sold the extensive monastic lands to private buyers. At last one of Henry's later wives produced a male heir, the intelligent but sickly Edward VI (ruled 1547–1553), upon whose premature death the crown passed to Henry VIII's daughters—first Mary (ruled 1553–1558) and next Elizabeth I (ruled 1558–1603).

Rule by a woman frightened sixteenth-century people. Not only did they consider governance a male responsibility, but they also knew that a queen's marriage would ultimately transfer the crown to either a foreign dynasty or some domestic noble family. In this dangerous situation, Mary blundered repeatedly and saved the day only by dying soon. Elizabeth I, however, took her nation's interests to heart. Remaining the unmarried "virgin queen," she artfully managed Parliament, which represented the nation's landowning upper class and merchants. Parliament flooded her with advice, usually trying to push her further than she thought it prudent to go in dealing with political and religious issues. But by cleverly managing patronage—the distribution of royal favors and political offices—and by choosing shrewd advisers, Elizabeth remained in control of the kingdom's intricate political system and guided England through a perilous half-century.

Religion remained a source of trouble in England for well over a century after Henry VIII's break with Rome. The sale of monastic lands created a vested interest against returning to the old order. But Henry never quite decided whether he was a Protestant. Under Edward VI the church veered sharply toward Protestantism; then Mary tried to restore Catholicism by burning several hundred Protestants at the stake.

Elizabeth's reign, however, marked a crucial watershed. After "Bloody Mary," most English people were ready to become Protestant; *how* Protestant was the divisive question. A militant but minority religious viewpoint had arisen, called Puritanism. Puritans demanded a wholesale "purification" of the Church of England from "popish [Catholic] abuses." As Calvinists, Puritans affirmed predestination, denied Christ's presence in the Eucharist, denounced the ornate ritual of the Catholic Mass, and believed that hearing God's Word was the heart of true worship. The Puritan ranks

Elizabeth I, *by Nicholas Hilliard, 1572*
This miniature (created for a jeweled locket) portrays Queen Elizabeth at age thirty-nine. Unlike the more stylized portraits that date from her later years, the painting conveys Elizabeth's shrewd, sharp-witted character.

included aristocrats and other landowning gentlemen, university-educated clergymen and intellectuals, merchants, and hard-working, Bible-reading artisans and yeomen—but not Elizabeth, who distrusted Puritan militancy and preferred traditional, dignified ceremony in worship. The queen demanded, for example, that the Anglican church retain distinctive ceremonial attire for the clergy. Elizabeth even tried to avoid breaking with the papacy—until in 1570 the pope declared her a heretic and urged Catholics to overthrow her. Thereafter, the crown regarded English Catholics as potential traitors, and Elizabeth became more openly Protestant. But although Puritan sentiment gained ground in Parliament, Elizabeth never embraced it.

A troubled society lay beneath this political and religious turmoil. At the upper end of the social scale, only eldest sons inherited aristocratic titles; aristocrats' younger sons normally had to shift for themselves in a world of shrinking opportunities. The stagnant economy also pinched the gentry—the "respectable" landowners without aristocratic titles who traditionally lived without doing manual labor and played a prominent role in local government and Parliament. Everyone felt that the nation's population had grown too fast. With technology largely unchanged, per capita output and real household income fell. In effect, more workers competed for fewer jobs in the face of diminishing European markets for English cloth and rising prices for food. Enclosures aggravated the nation's unemployment problems, forcing great numbers of people to wander the countryside or pour into towns in search of work and so making England's population highly mobile. These "sturdy beggars" seemed to threaten law and order. To control them, Parliament passed "Poor Laws" that ordered vagrants whipped and sent home, where hard-pressed taxpayers had to maintain them on the dole. But Puritan and Anglican clergymen agreed that England's root problem was the irresponsible greed of the well-to-do, whom they charged with raising prices, goading the poor to revolt, and giving too little to charity. "You that eat till you blow, and feed till your eyes swell with fatness," preached moderate Puritan Henry Smith, ". . . impart some of your superfluity unto the poor. . . ."

By thus describing contemporary problems in moral terms, Smith displayed a traditional mentality. He—like Shakespeare, Luther, and Calvin—attributed social problems to people's improper behavior. In this respect, conservative European thinking paralleled the characteristic outlook of Africans and native Americans. But in the encounter of Old and New Worlds in the 150 years after 1492, the peoples on both sides of the Atlantic would find that they had little else in common with one another.

The Age of Discovery and the Beginnings of European Dominance

Europeans' outward thrust began centuries before Columbus's first voyage in 1492. In the tenth century, Scandinavian Vikings had reached Iceland and Greenland. From there, about A.D. 1000, Vikings made their way to North America. They established a settlement at "Vinland" (probably in Newfoundland) and may have explored the New England coast. But the Scandinavians soon abandoned and eventually almost forgot Vinland, and

the direction of European expansion changed. A series of crusading armies after 1096 struggled (ultimately in vain) to wrest Palestine from the Moslems. A brisk trade with the Middle East began in these years as the Europeans sold cloth and bought silks and the spices that they needed to preserve food and spark up a monotonous diet. Thirteenth-century merchants like Marco Polo even traveled overland to East Asia to buy directly from the Chinese. By the fourteenth and fifteenth centuries, the highly profitable spice and silk trade had enriched well-placed Italian merchants despite the era's generally depressed economic conditions, financed the cultural flowering of the early Renaissance, and excited the envy of all Europe.

Seaborne Expansion

Around 1460 a century of depression and population decline ended in Europe. An era of renewed economic and population growth opened. As Europeans competed for commercial advantage, they projected their power overseas.

Important changes in maritime technology occurred at this dawn of European expansion. In the early fifteenth century, shipbuilders and mariners along Europe's stormy Atlantic coast added the triangular Arab sail to the heavy cargo ship that they used for voyaging between England and the Mediterranean. They created a more maneuverable vessel, the caravel, that could sail against the wind. Sailors also mastered the compass and astrolabe, by which they got their bearings on the open sea. Without this "maritime revolution," European exploration would have been impossible.

Renaissance scholars' search for more accurate readings of ancient texts forced fifteenth-century Europeans to look at their world with new eyes. The great ancient Greek authority on geography was Ptolemy, but Renaissance scholars had to correct his data when they tried to draw accurate maps. Thus Renaissance "new learning" combined with older Arabic and European advances in mathematics to sharpen Europeans' geographic sense.

The adventuring spirit to explore new worlds first burned in impoverished little Portugal. Here zeal for continuing the struggle against the Moslems who had slowly been driven out of Spain and Portugal combined with an anxious search for new markets. Prince Henry "the Navigator" of Portu-

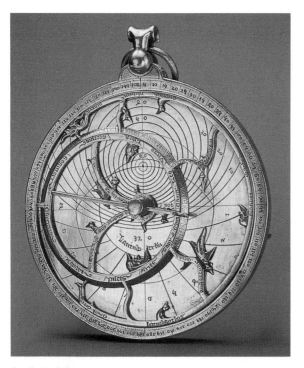

An Astrolabe

A device for calculating the position and altitude of the sun, stars, and planets, the astrolabe was one of the world's oldest scientific instruments. It was known to the ancient Greeks and perfected by the medieval Arabs. Ocean navigators found it indispensable. This brass English astrolabe, dating to 1326, may be the oldest such European instrument extant.

gal (1394–1460) embodied both urges. Henry encouraged Portuguese seamen to pilot the new caravels farther down the African coast searching for weak spots in the Moslem defenses and for opportunities to trade profitably. At the time of his death, the Portuguese had established a profitable slaving station at Arguin, and by the late fifteenth century, they had penetrated south of the equator. In 1488 Bartolomeu Días reached the Cape of Good Hope at Africa's southern tip. The Portuguese king John II seized the opportunity to open up direct contact with India, circumventing the Arabs and Venetians. In 1497 Vasco da Gama led a Portuguese fleet around the Cape of Good Hope and on to India.

Ultimately the Portuguese failed to destroy traditional Venetian-Arab commercial links, although for a century they remained an imperial presence in the Indian Ocean and present-day Indonesia. Already, however, they had brought Europeans face-to-face with black-skinned Africans.

The "New Slavery" and Racism

Slavery was well established in fifteenth-century West African life, as elsewhere. The grassland emperors, as well as individual families, depended heavily on slaves. Often, however, slaves or their children were absorbed into African families over time. The eighteenth-century West African Olaudah Equiano, who had suffered enslavement in the New World, thus explained the fate of war captives in his native society:

> *How different was their condition from that of the slaves in the West Indies! With us they do no more work than other members of the community, even their master. Their food, clothing, and lodging, were nearly the same as [free people's], except that they were not permitted to eat with those who were born free. . . . Some of these slaves even have slaves under them, as their own property, and for their own use.*

Outsiders—first Moslems, then Europeans—turned African slavery into an intercontinental business and tore slaves from their native society. A fifteenth-century Italian who witnessed Portuguese and Moslem slave trading reported that the Arabs "also have many Berber horses, which they trade, and take to the Land of the Blacks, exchanging them with the rulers for slaves. Ten or fifteen slaves are given for one of these horses, according to their quality. . . . These slaves are brought to the market town of Hoden; there they are divided. . . . [Some] are taken . . . and sold to the Portuguese leaseholders [of Arguin]. As a result every year the Portuguese carry away from [Arguin] a thousand slaves."

Equiano's eighteenth-century testimony paints a stark picture of slaves' experience in earlier centuries as well. Brought aboard a European slave ship, he wrote,

> *I was now persuaded that I had got into a world of bad spirits, and that they were going to kill me. Their complexions differing so much from ours, their long hair, and the languages they spoke . . . united to confirm me in this belief. . . . Quite overpowered with shock and horror,*

I . . . fainted. When I recovered a little, I found some black people around me, who I believed were some of those who brought me on board, and had been receiving their pay. . . . I asked them if we were not to be eaten by those white men with horrible looks, red faces, and long hair. They told me I was not. [But] soon after this the blacks who had brought me on board went off, and left me abandoned to despair. . . . I found some of my own nation [and] inquired . . . what was to be done with us? They gave me to understand that we were to be carried to these white people's country to work for them. I then was a little revived . . . but still I feared I should be put to death, the white people looked, as I thought, so savage. . . .

The Portuguese found slave trading lucrative and kept out competitors until about 1600. Although in 1482 they built an outpost, Elmina, on West Africa's Gold Coast, they exploited existing African commercial and social patterns. Often Portuguese merchants traded slaves and local products to other Africans for gold. The local African kingdoms were too strong for the Portuguese to attack, and black rulers traded—or chose not to trade—according to their own self-interest.

West African societies sometimes changed with the coming of Portuguese slavers. In Guinea and Senegambia, which supplied the bulk of sixteenth-century slaves, small kingdoms expanded to "service" the trade. Some of their rulers became comparatively rich. Farther south, in present-day Angola, the kings of Kongo used the slave trade to consolidate their power and voluntarily adopted Christianity. Kongo flourished until the late sixteenth century, when attackers from the interior destroyed it.

The slave-trading African kings and their communities used the trade as a way of disposing of "undesirables," including slaves whom they already owned, lawbreakers, and persons accused of witchcraft. But most slaves were simply victims of raids or wars. Moslem and European slave trading greatly stimulated conflicts among African communities.

Although European societies had used slaves since the time of ancient Greece and Rome, there were ominous differences in the European slavery that arose once the Portuguese began voyaging to West Africa. First, the new slave trade was a high-volume business that expanded steadily. Between

The Slave Trade: An African View

This iron casting from Benin shows a group of enslaved Africans, already dressed in western clothing.

1500 and 1600, perhaps 250,000 African slaves would land in the New World, and 50,000 would die en route. Another 200,000 would arrive between 1601 and 1621. Before the Atlantic slave trade finally ended in the nineteenth century, nearly 12 million Africans would be shipped in terrible conditions across the sea. Slavery on this scale had been unknown to Europeans since the collapse of the Roman Empire. Second, African slaves were treated exceptionally harshly. In medieval Europe slaves had primarily performed domestic service, but by 1450 the Portuguese and Spanish created large slave-labor plantations on their newly occupied islands along Africa's Atlantic coast, as well as in southern Portugal and on Spain's Mediterranean islands. These plantations produced sugar for European markets, using capital supplied by Italian investors to buy African slaves who toiled until death. In short, the African slaves owned by Europeans were destined for exhausting, mindless labor. By 1600 the "new slavery" had become a brutal link in an expanding commerce that ultimately would encompass all major Western nations.

Finally, race became the explicit basis of the "new slavery." Africans' blackness and their alien religion dehumanized them in European eyes. As their racial prejudice hardened, Europeans justified enslaving blacks with increasing ease. From the fifteenth century onward, European Christianity made few attempts to soften slavery's rigors, and race defined a slave. Because the victims of the "new slavery" were physically distinctive as well as culturally alien, slavery became a lifelong, hereditary, and despised status.

Columbus Reaches America

Europeans' varying motivations for expanding their horizons converged in the fascinating, contradictory figure of Christopher Columbus (1451–1509). The son of a ropemaker from the Italian port of Genoa, the young Columbus gained solid navigating experience as a sailor on voyages to West Africa and Iceland. His practical knowledge, self-taught geographical learning, and keen imagination drew him to speculations (circulating in late-fifteenth-century Europe) that Asia might be reached by sailing westward across the Atlantic. By the early 1480s this idea obsessed him. Religious fervor led Columbus to dream of carrying Christianity around the globe and liberating Jerusalem from Moslem rule, but he also burned with ambition to win wealth and glory. Although no portrait of Columbus painted from life exists, contemporaries agreed in describing him as a tall man of commanding presence, implacable in purpose.

Columbus would not be the first European to venture far out into the Atlantic. Besides the early Viking settlers at Vinland, fifteenth-century English fishermen may already have sailed as far west as the Grand Banks and even the North American coast. But Columbus was unique in the persistence with which he hawked his "enterprise of the Indies" around the royal courts of western Europe. John II of Portugal showed interest until Días's discovery of the Cape of Good Hope promised a surer way to India. Finally, in 1492, hoping to break a threatened Portuguese monopoly on direct trade with Asia, the rulers of newly united Spain—Queen Isabella of Castile and King Ferdinand of Aragon—accepted Columbus's offer. Picking up the westward-blowing trade winds at the Canary Islands, Columbus's three small ships reached San Salvador within a month.

Columbus's success derived from a gigantic miscalculation. North America lay about where he expected to find Japan, for he had combined Marco Polo's overestimate of Asia's eastward thrust with Ptolemy's underestimate of the earth's circumference. Another ancient Greek mathematician had calculated something close to the true circumference, and this figure was generally accepted by knowledgeable fifteenth-century Europeans; hence the skepticism that Columbus had aroused.

Word of Columbus's discovery caught Europeans' imaginations. It also induced Isabella and John II in 1494 to sign the Treaty of Tordesillas, which divided all future discoveries between Castile and Portugal. Meanwhile, Isabella had sent Columbus back to explore further, and he established a colony on Hispaniola, the Caribbean island today occupied by Haiti and the Dominican Republic. Columbus proved a poor administrator, and after his last voyages (1498–1502), he was shunted aside. He died an embittered man, convinced that he had reached the threshold of Asia, only to be cheated of his rightful rewards.

England's Henry VII (ruled 1485–1509) ignored Castile's and Portugal's claims of exclusive rights to new discoveries. In 1497 he sent the Italian navigator known in England as John Cabot westward into the Atlantic, tacking against the eastward winds of these latitudes. Cabot claimed for England either Nova Scotia or Newfoundland and the rich Grand Banks fisheries, but he disappeared at sea on a later voyage. Like Columbus, Cabot thought that he had reached Asia.

The more Columbus and others explored, the more apparent it became (to everyone except himself) that a vast landmass blocked the route to Asia. In 1500 the Portuguese claimed Brazil, and other voyages soon revealed a continuous coastline from the Caribbean to Brazil. In 1507 this landmass got its name when a publisher brought out a collection of voyagers' tales. One of the chroniclers was an Italian named Amerigo Vespucci. With a shrewd marketing touch, the publisher devised a catchy name for the new continent: America.

Getting past America and reaching Asia remained the early explorers' primary aim. In 1513 the Spaniard Vasco Núñez de Balboa chanced upon the Pacific Ocean when he crossed the narrow isthmus of Panama. Then in 1519 the Portuguese Ferdinand Magellan, sailing under the Castilian flag, began a voyage around the world by way of the stormy Magellan Straits at South America's southern tip. In an incredible feat of endurance, he crossed the Pacific to the Philippines, only to die fighting with local chiefs. One of his five ships and fifteen emaciated sailors finally returned to Spain in 1522, the first people to have sailed around the world.

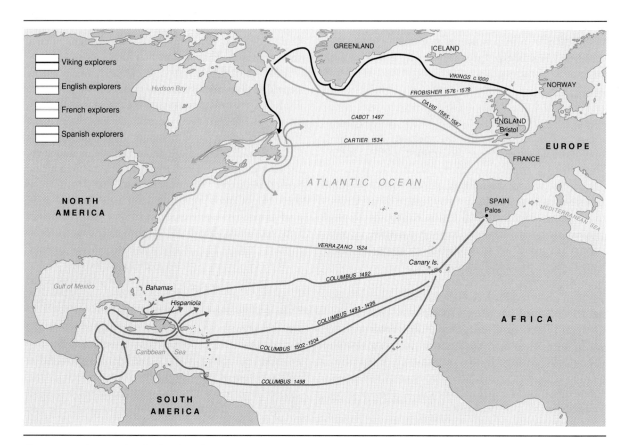

European Transatlantic Explorations, 1000–1587

Following Columbus's 1492 voyage, Spain's rivals soon began laying claim to parts of the New World based on the voyages of Cabot for England, Cabral for Portugal, and Verrazano for France. Later English and French exploration focused on finding a passage to Asia around or through Canada.

But Europeans hoped for easier access to East Asia's fabled wealth. The French king Francis I accepted the challenge of finding a "northwest passage" to Asia. In 1524 he dispatched the Italian navigator Verrazano to explore the North American coast from the Carolinas to Newfoundland. In two subsequent voyages, in 1534–1536, the French explorer Jacques Cartier carefully probed the coasts of Newfoundland, Quebec, and Nova Scotia and ascended the St. Lawrence as far as present-day Montreal. But Verrazano and Cartier found no gold and no northwest passage.

The Conquerors

Columbus was America's first slave trader and the first of the Spanish conquerors, or *conquistadores*. At his struggling colony on Hispaniola, he began exporting Indian slaves and created *encomiendas*—grants for the right to extract labor and other tribute from the Indians of a designated district. Other *conquistadores* would soon transplant this practice to the American mainland.

From the beginning *encomiendas* harshly exploited the native people, who died in droves from overwork, malnutrition, and disease. Portuguese slavers stepped in, supplying boatloads of Africans to replace the perishing Indians. But Spanish friars who came to Hispaniola to convert the Indians quickly sent back grim reports of Indian exploitation; and King Ferdinand (who had made money by selling *encomiendas*) felt sufficiently shocked to attempt to forbid the practice. No one, however, worried about the African slaves' fate.

Soon Spanish settlers were fanning out through the Caribbean in search of Indian slaves and gold.

In 1519 the restless nobleman Hernán Cortés (1485–1547) led a small band of followers to the Mexican coast. Destroying his boats and gathering Indian allies, he marched inland over towering mountain passes to conquer Mexico.

Spaniards had dreamed of a prize such as Mexico ever since they reached America. Mexico was rich: an impressive civilization had been evolving there for three thousand years, culminating in the mighty Aztec Empire. It was exotic: the priests and soldiers who dominated the empire raided neighboring peoples to seize victims for grisly human sacrifices. And Mexico was highly organized. The three hundred thousand inhabitants of the capital, Tenochtitlán, enjoyed fresh water supplied by means of elaborate engineering works; their urban society was highly stratified; and artisans produced a profusion of finely crafted pottery as well as stone, copper, silver, and gold implements. "We were amazed and said that it was like the enchantments they tell of [in stories], and some of our soldiers even asked whether the things that we saw were not a dream?" recalled one of Cortés's soldiers of his first glimpse of Tenochtitlán's pyramids, lakes, and causeways. Certainly the golden gifts that the Aztecs offered in the vain hope of buying off the invaders were no dream. "They picked up the gold and fingered it like monkeys," recalled an Indian. "Their bodies swelled with greed, and their hunger was ravenous. They hungered like pigs for that gold."

Cortés attacked and swiftly prevailed. He owed his astonishing victories partly to firearms and horses, which terrified the Aztecs, and partly to initial Aztec suppositions that the Spanish were the white, bearded gods whose return ancient legends had foretold. His success also resulted from his boldness and cunning, the Aztec emperor Moctezuma's fears, epidemics among the Indians, and the revolt of the Aztecs' subject peoples. By 1521 Cortés had overthrown the Aztecs and begun to build Mexico City on the ruins of Tenochtitlán. Soon the last Aztec emperor suffered defeat and execution, and within twenty years Central America lay at the Spaniards' feet. New Spain was born.

During the rest of the sixteenth century, other *conquistadores* and officials consolidated a great Hispanic empire stretching from New Spain (Mexico) to Argentina. Subduing America and enriching themselves never troubled the *conquistadores'* consciences. Before a battle a herald would reel off a proclamation in Spanish demanding the Indians'

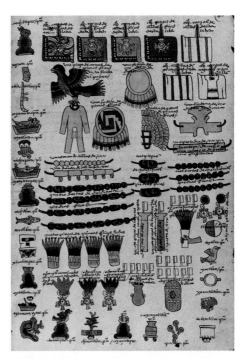

Aztec Wealth

The Aztec emperors' power and wealth derived from tribute paid by subject peoples. Here, in a report prepared by Aztecs for their Spanish conquerors, is a list of the blankets, jewelry, and other finery that various Mexican cities formerly owed Emperor Moctezuma. Symbols denoting each city appear down the left margin.

conversion to Christianity and shifting onto them the guilt for bloodshed if they resisted. From the beginning, however, the Spanish church and government worried that the *conquistadores* were becoming too powerful and abusive. The monarchs sent over hundreds of bureaucrats to govern in the hierarchical European manner and to defend Indian rights. Another army of Spanish friars established missions among the Indians and tried to lessen the native people's suffering. But the whole system was too cumbersome. "I obey, but I do not fulfill" became a standard bureaucratic dodge.

The human cost of the conquest was enormous. Mourned a vanquished Aztec:

Broken spears lie in the roads;
We have torn our hair in our grief.
The houses are roofless now . . .
And the walls are splattered with gore . . .
We have pounded our hands in despair
Against the adobe walls.

When Cortés landed in 1519, central Mexico's population had been about 25 million. By 1600 it had shrunk to between 1 million and 2 million. Peru and other regions experienced similar devastation. America had witnessed the greatest demographic disaster in history.

Warfare, forced labor, starvation, and mass slaughter accounted for some of the catastrophe, but the greatest killers were microbes. Native Americans lacked antibodies to Old World infections—above all, the deadly, highly communicable smallpox. From the first years of contact, frightful epidemics decimated Indian communities. In the West Indian islands, the entire native population perished within a half-century. In return, a virulent form of venereal syphilis spread from the New World to Europe shortly after Columbus's first voyage.

Yet the "Columbian exchange"—the biological encounter of the Old and New Worlds—was not limited to deadly germs. In addition to diseases, sixteenth-century Europeans also brought horses, cattle, sheep, swine, chickens, wheat and other grains, sugar cane, and numerous fruits and garden vegetables to America, besides iron metallurgy, firearms, the wheel, and weeds. In the next century, African slaves carried rice and yams with them across the Atlantic. The list of New World gifts to the Old World was equally impressive: corn, many varieties of beans, white and sweet potatoes, the tropical root crop manioc, tomatoes, squash, pumpkins, peanuts, vanilla, cacao, coffee, avocados, pineapples, chilis, tobacco, turkeys, canoes and kayaks, hammocks, snowshoes, and moccasins. Often several centuries passed before new plants became widely accepted across the ocean; for example, many Europeans suspected that potatoes and tomatoes were either poisons or aphrodisiacs until the nineteenth century, and Indians at first had to be forced to grow wheat. However, the worldwide exchange of food products enriched human diets and later made possible enormous population growth.

Another dimension of the meeting of Old and New Worlds was the mixing of peoples. Throughout the sixteenth century, between one hundred thousand and three hundred thousand Spaniards immigrated, 90 percent of them male. Particularly in towns, a racially blended population arose. Blacks who were imported as slaves occasionally mated with Indians, and white men fathered numerous

The Exotic Weed

Among the notable New World plants involved in the Columbian exchange was tobacco. Central to Indian ritual, smoking tobacco quickly became popular among Europeans as well.

children with Indian and black women. Although these population transfers and mixtures were paltry compared to the wholesale extermination of native Americans through disease and violence, they helped save some offspring of the native American population by transmitting Old World antibodies.

The New World supplied seemingly limitless wealth for Spain. Not only did some Spaniards grow rich from West Indian sugar plantations and Mexican sheep and cattle ranches, but immense quantities of silver crossed the Atlantic after rich mines in Mexico and Peru began producing in the 1540s. A robust trade between America and Spain grew up, which Castilian officials tried to regulate. Spain took in far more American silver than its economy could absorb, setting off inflation that eventually engulfed all Europe. Bent on dominating Europe, the Spanish kings needed ever more American silver to pay their armies. Several times they went bankrupt, and their efforts to squeeze more taxes from their subjects provoked in the 1560s the revolt of Spain's rich Netherlands provinces—modern Belgium, Holland, and Luxembourg. In the end, gaining access to American wealth cost Spain dearly.

The bloody history of Spain's American conquests and efforts to dominate Europe helped spin the "Black Legend"—northern Europeans' vision of a tyrannical, fanatically Catholic Spain intent on conquering everything in sight. Ironically, much of the Black Legend's lurid picture of American horrors derived from the writings of a devout Spanish friar, Bartolomé de Las Casas (1474–1566), who had repented his own participation (as a layman) in the subjugation of Hispaniola. By the end of the sixteenth century, Las Casas's noble hopes of justice for the Indians lay in ruins. The Spanish church became increasingly bureaucratic, intolerant, and restrictive. All this fueled the Black Legend. As Spain's struggle to reconquer the Netherlands and to dominate France spilled ominously near their homeland, Protestant Britons shuddered. But they also looked for opportunities across the Atlantic with which to strike back at Spain—and to enrich themselves.

Footholds in North America

As early as 1510, the flow of wealth from the New World to Spain attracted swarms of northern European pirates. Over the next century, northern Europeans grew familiar with the North American coast through exploratory voyages, fishing expeditions, a small-scale fur trade, and piracy and smuggling.

But all non-Spanish sixteenth-century attempts to plant colonies in North America failed. Although England and France had laid claim to parts of North America on the basis of early voyages by the Cabots, Verrazano, and Cartier, these claims remained hollow pretensions as long as Spain could exclude other Europeans by force. Only in the early seventeenth century did Spain lose this power. In 1607–1608 the English and the French finally began to exploit knowledge gained during the previous century and established centers for permanent colonies. The Dutch, now free of Spain, followed their example

by 1614. Within less than twenty years of the initial successful settlements, each colony developed an economic orientation, pattern of Indian relations, and a natural direction of geographic expansion that would endure throughout the colonial era. The first quarter of the seventeenth century marked the formative period of North America's modern history.

New Spain's Northern Borderlands

The Spanish had built their New World empire by subduing the Aztec and other Indian states, whose riches had attracted the invaders like a magnet. But in the borderlands north of Mexico, the absence of visible wealth and organized states discouraged conquest. Good agricultural land did not suffice. "As it was his object to find another treasure like that . . . of Peru," a witness wrote of southeastern North America's would-be *conquistador*, Hernán de Soto, he "would not be content with good lands nor pearls."

However, a succession of hopeful emulators of Cortés did invade large parts of what would become the United States, although most perished in the attempt. The earliest was Juan Ponce de León, the conqueror of Puerto Rico, who in 1512–1513 and again in 1521 trudged through Florida in search of gold and slaves. His quest ended in death in an Indian skirmish. Legends notwithstanding, Ponce de León had not sought a "fountain of youth," although sometimes Indians managed to get rid of troublesome Spaniards by telling them tall tales of wonders elsewhere.

Dreams of conquest would not die, despite the failure of Ponce and several later adventurers. Lured by hopes of finding a new Peru, de Soto and his party in 1537–1543 blundered from Tampa Bay to the Appalachians and back to southern Texas. Scouring the land for gold, de Soto harried the Indians mercilessly. "Think, then," an Indian chief appealed to him vainly,

> *what must be the effect on me and mine, of the sight of you and your people, whom we have at no time seen, astride the fierce brutes, your horses, entering with such speed and fury into my country, that we had no tidings of your coming—things so absolutely new, as to strike awe and terror into our hearts.*

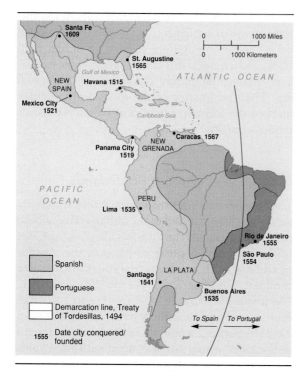

The Spanish and Portuguese Empires, 1610

By 1610 Spain dominated Latin America, including Portugal's possessions. Having devoted its energies to exploiting Mexico and the Caribbean, Spain had not yet expanded into what is now the United States, aside from establishing outposts in Florida and New Mexico.

De Soto also perished. Meanwhile, in 1540–1542 a second party under Coronado, drawn by rumors of a golden city called Cíbola, invaded the Southwest from Mexico. Coronado found the Grand Canyon, plundered the New Mexico pueblos, and roamed as far as Kansas before returning to Mexico, thinking himself a failure because he had found no gold. A third expedition, led by Juan Rodríguez Cabrillo, sailed along the California coast but likewise found nothing worth seizing.

For decades after these failed ventures, Spain's only interest in future U.S. lands lay in establishing a few strategic bases in Florida to keep out intruders. Later, in the 1580s, Spanish friars returned to the southwestern pueblo country, preaching Christianity and scouting the area's potential wealth. Encouraged by their reports, in 1598 Juan de Oñate led five hundred Spaniards into the upper Rio Grande Valley, where he proclaimed the royal col-ony of New Mexico, distributed *encomiendas,* and demanded tribute from the pueblo-dwelling Indians.

The new colony barely survived. The Spanish government had to replace Oñate in 1606 because of his excessive brutality. Finding no gold, many settlers went back. Those who stayed established Santa Fe in 1609, while others migrated to isolated ranches and fought off Navaho and Apache raiders. Eventually the missions' demands for labor service and their attempts to uproot pueblo religion produced an Indian backlash against Christianity (see Chapter 3). The Spanish would not be secure in New Mexico for a century.

Initial French Failures

In 1534 Jacques Cartier of France, searching for the northwest passage, identified the St. Lawrence River as one of North America's two primary avenues of entry. After 1600 this river would become the center of French colonization. (The other such avenue, also used by the French but in later years, was the Mississippi River.) Before finally planting permanent American colonies, however, France experienced more than a half-century of failure.

France made the first attempt at European colonization in North America in 1541, when ten ships carrying four hundred soldiers, three hundred sailors (including Cartier), and a few women sailed to the St. Lawrence Valley. Cartier returned to France in 1542 with what he thought were gold and diamonds but proved to be iron pyrite ("fool's gold") and quartz. The rest of the expedition ascended the St. Lawrence as far as the rapids, lost heart at the prospect of another Canadian winter, and went home.

The failed expedition of 1541–1542 seemed to verify the Spanish opinion, voiced by the cardinal of Seville, that "this whole coast as far [south] as Florida is utterly unproductive." The next French effort at colonization came in 1562, when French privateers (mariners licensed by their government to raid enemy shipping) briefly established a base in what is now South Carolina. In 1564 the French founded a settlement near modern-day Jacksonville, Florida, which the Spanish destroyed a year later, massacring all Frenchmen found to be Protestants. These failures, along with a civil war between French Catholics and Protestants, distracted the French from further colonization.

To lock France out of North America and to protect the Caribbean against seaborne northern European raiders, the Spanish in 1565 established the first permanent European settlement on future United States soil. This was the powerful fortress at St. Augustine, Florida. But because the Spanish considered Florida's interior worthless, St. Augustine never became more than a military stronghold and a base for religious missions.

Elizabethan England and the Wider World

In 1558, when Elizabeth I became queen, England was a minor power with a population of less than 5 million and stood on the sidelines as Spain and France grappled for supremacy in Europe. England's initial claims to North America had by now receded into the background, although hundreds of English fishing vessels voyaged annually to North American shores and to the Grand Banks. The English remained preoccupied with charting the direction of their religious Reformation and coping with domestic instability.

This instability, however, helped propel Elizabethan expansion. Shipping its unemployed poor overseas seemed a good solution to England's economic woes. "Surplus" English people transplanted to colonies across the ocean might not only provide raw markets for English cloth but also produce valuable export commodities. And the gentry of England's West Country (the southwestern peninsula jutting out into the Atlantic) itched for action. They were restless men, used to the sea, linked by family ties and Puritan sympathies, and frustrated by customs that limited the amount of family property inherited by younger sons. Sir Francis Drake, Sir John Hawkins, Sir Humphrey Gilbert, and Sir Walter Raleigh all fit this description and stood ready to lead England's overseas adventure.

But Spain blocked the way. When Elizabeth came to the throne, England and Spain were enjoying friendly relations. With the queen's support, Hawkins in the early 1560s made a tidy fortune raiding the Guinea coast for slaves and selling them legally to the Spanish; and Elizabeth stood by as the Spanish wiped out France's Florida colony in 1564. But the English worried about Spain's intervention in France's civil wars and its determined

Elizabethan Sea Dogs

Sir John Hawkins (1532–1595, right) and Sir Francis Drake (1540?–1596, center) led England's seaborne assault on Spain's New World empire. Thomas Cavendish (1555?–1592, left) followed Drake in sailing around the world in 1586–1588, capturing several Spanish galleons on the way. He later died at sea.

effort to crush the Netherlands revolt, as well as about the pope's call for Elizabeth's overthrow. Further, by now Englishmen had no incentive to trade legally with Spanish America: in 1568 the Spanish authorities in Mexico had chased Hawkins and Drake from the Caribbean. Secretly, Elizabeth stepped up her aid to French Protestants (the Huguenots), to the Calvinist rebels in the Netherlands, and to "sea dogs" like Hawkins and Drake—from whose voyages she took a share of the plunder. In the 1570s she encouraged merchants to invest in Atlantic-oriented ventures.

Meanwhile, the situation in Ireland, England's "back door," was deteriorating. As early as 1565, English troops fought to impose Tudor rule throughout the island. The conflict intensified when the pope and the Spanish began directly aiding Irish Catholics' resistance to the English. In the ensuing war that ground on through the 1580s, the English drove the Irish clans out of their strongholds (especially in northern Ireland, or Ulster) and established settlements ("plantations") of English and Scottish Protestant settlers—a profitable business for well-connected members of the gentry like Drake and Gilbert. Since Irish resistance did not depend on fortified cities or large armies, English commanders had to develop new tactics to subdue the mobile, armed Irish people, who could easily disappear into bogs and forests. The English practiced total war to break the rebellious population's spirit, inflicting starvation and mass slaughter by destroying villages in the winter. Commanders used terror to force local bands into submission. For example, Gilbert lined the path to his headquarters with Irish heads.

Elizabeth's generals justified these atrocities by claiming that the Irish were "savages." Ireland thus furnished precedents for strategies that the English later employed against North American Indians, whose customs, religion, and method of fighting likewise seemed to absolve Englishmen from guilt in waging exceptionally cruel warfare. Fighting in Ireland and settling fellow countrymen there, leading English colonizers such as Gilbert and Raleigh gained practical experience that they later applied in the New World.

England had two objectives in the Western Hemisphere in the 1570s. The first was to find the northwest passage to Asia and if possible to discover gold on the way; the second, in Drake's words, was to "singe the king of Spain's beard" by raiding Spanish fleets and ports from Spain to the West Indies. The search for the northwest passage only led to such embarrassments as explorer Martin Frobisher's return from the Canadian Arctic with a shipload of "fool's gold." However, privateering raids on the Spanish were both spectacularly successful and profitable for Drake's and Hawkins's financial backers, including merchants, gentry, government leaders, and Elizabeth herself. The most breathtaking enterprise was Drake's voyage around the world in 1577 in quest of sites for colonies. During this voyage he sailed up the California coast and entered San Francisco Bay.

Now deadly rivals, Spain and England sought to plant strategic bases against each other. In 1570–1571 the Spanish tried to establish a new outpost in Chesapeake Bay. They failed, largely because of Indian hostility. Then in 1578, Gilbert secured a royal patent (charter) to start an English colony in Newfoundland. Bad weather and unseaworthy ships at first prevented him from crossing the Atlantic, and after he at last took five ships to Newfoundland in 1583, he drowned on his return voyage.

But English colonial ventures did not cease. In 1584 Gilbert's half-brother Raleigh acquired the patent. Raleigh dispatched Arthur Barlowe to explore the coast farther south, closer to the Spanish—the region that the English had already named Virginia in honor of their virgin queen. Barlowe returned singing the praises of Roanoke Island (see "A Place in Time").

The Origins of Virginia

Claimed by the Spanish and English but occupied by neither, Virginia beckoned invaders. Although Barlowe and his fellow promoters exaggerated America's allure, here was a land of plenty.

The East Coast's native Americans spoke a variety of Algonkian languages and grouped themselves into numerous tribes. Early voyagers like Verrazano had commented on their large numbers, their health ("they live a long life and rarely fall sick"), their friendliness, and their eagerness to trade. Only the Maine Indians had been hostile—they had already learned to be wary of whites. Well they might be, for Europeans were unwittingly bringing them terrible tragedy. "The people began to die very fast, and many in a short space," an Englishman at Roanoke remarked, adding that the deaths invariably began after white men had visited an Indian village. From early in the sixteenth century, raging epidemics of smallpox and a dozen other Old World maladies scourged the defenseless Indians and exterminated entire tribes. Whole villages perished at once, with no one left to bury the dead. Ultimately up to 90 percent of the native population may have been lost. The Europeans came, one historian has written, not to a virgin land but to a widowed land.

But the English would find seizing Virginia no easy matter. Roanoke's sad fate illustrated several stubborn realities about early European experiences in North America. First, even a large-scale, well-financed colonizing effort could fail, given the settlers' unpreparedness for the American environment. Second, whites did not bring enough provisions for the first winter and consistently disdained growing their own food. Although some early English settlers were curious and open-minded about the Indians' way of life, all assumed that the Indians would feed them while they looked for gold—a sure recipe for trouble. Third, colonizing attempts would have to be self-financing: financially strapped monarchs like Elizabeth I would not throw good money after bad into America. Fourth, conflict with the Spanish hung menacingly over every European attempt to gain a foothold in North America.

In 1588 England won a spectacular naval victory over the Armada, a huge invasion fleet sent into the English Channel by Spain's Philip II. This famous victory preserved England's independence and demonstrated that the kingdom could repel attacks although it had little offensive military might. The war churned on as before. In 1595 Drake and Hawkins died fighting in the Caribbean. Raleigh wasted his political influence and physical health in fruitless quests for the legendary gilded king ("El Dorado") in South America. England, France, and the Netherlands formed an alliance to dismember the Spanish Empire, but the French backed out. Only the Netherlanders' naval assaults on Spanish and Portuguese* outposts around the world had devastating effects. England made no further moves to carve out American colonies until after 1600.

Yet overseas expansion still lured individual Englishmen. To sustain public interest in the New World, in 1589 and again in 1601 Richard Hakluyt published monumental collections of explorers' accounts, *The Principal Navigations, Voyages, and Discoveries of the English Nation*. But neither the English crown nor Parliament would agree to spend tax money on colonies, and Roanoke's failure had proved that private fortunes were inadequate to finance successful settlements. Only joint-stock companies—business corporations that would amass capital through sales of stock to the public—could raise funds for American settlement. Such stock offerings produced large sums, yet each investor could limit his risk to an amount that he could afford to lose. England's government henceforth would leave colonization to the private initiative of individuals or business groups and would spend no substantial sums on any colonies with the exception of (in the eighteenth century) Georgia and Nova Scotia.

---

*Between 1580 and 1640, Portugal and its colonies were annexed to Spain.

Elizabeth died in 1603, and her cousin, the king of Scotland, ascended the English throne as James I. The cautious and peace-loving king signed a truce with Spain in 1604. Seriously alarmed by Dutch naval victories, the Spanish considered England the lesser danger. The new Spanish king, Philip III, therefore conceded what his predecessors had always refused: a free hand to another power in part of the Americas. Spain renounced its claims to Virginia; England could colonize unmolested.

On April 10, 1606, James I granted a charter authorizing overlapping grants of land in Virginia to two separate joint-stock companies, one based in London and the other in Plymouth. The Virginia Company of Plymouth received a grant extending south from modern Maine to the Potomac River, while the Virginia Company of London's lands ran north from Cape Fear to the Hudson River. Whichever group established the first successful colony would have its boundaries extended one hundred miles at the other's expense. The colonists would be business employees, not citizens of a separate political jurisdiction, and the stockholders of each company would regulate their behavior.

The Virginia Company of Plymouth sent 120 men to Sagadahoc, at the mouth of the Kennebec River. Half left in 1608 after a hard Maine winter, and the rest went back to England a year later with Raleigh Gilbert (Humphrey's son) when he returned home to collect an inheritance. Soon thereafter the company disbanded.

The wealthy merchant Sir Thomas Smythe provided the leadership necessary for the Virginia Company of London to avoid a similar failure. Smythe's first expedition to Virginia comprised 144 men, of whom 39 died at sea. The initial immigrants included many members of the gentry, most of whom expected riches to fall into their laps. They chose a site on the James River, which they named Jamestown, in May 1607. Discipline quickly fell apart after the discovery of iron pyrite sparked a fool's gold rush. By September only 59 colonists were still alive, and they had neglected to plant crops. When relief ships arrived in January 1608 with 120 reinforcements, only 38 survivors remained at Jamestown.

Although short of workers who could farm, fish, hunt, and do carpentry, Jamestown most

Roanoke, 1584–1590

"We found the people most gentle, loving, and faithful, void of all guile and treason, and such as live after the manner of the golden age. The people only care how to defend themselves from the cold in their short winter, and to feed themselves with such meat as the soil affordeth. . . . The earth bringeth forth all things in abundance, as at the first creation, without toil or labor." Arthur Barlowe, who wrote these glowing words in 1584 after returning to England from Roanoke Island, on the coast of North Carolina, thought that he had found a paradise. To be sure, the native Americans seemed (to Barlowe) to fight cruel and bloody wars that had left them "marvelously wasted" and the country "desolate." But this was all the more reason why they should welcome English protection. To establish friendly reciprocity, the Indians' chief, Winginia, immediately offered to trade.

He beckoned us to come and sit by him, and being set he made all signs of joy and welcome, striking on his head and breast and afterwards on ours to show that we were all one, smiling and making show the best he could of all love and familiarity. After he had made a long speech unto us, we presented him with divers [various] things, which he received very joyfully and thankfully. . . . A day or two after this we fell to trading with them. . . . Of all things that he saw a bright tin dish most pleased him.

Sir Walter Raleigh (1552?–1618), *by an Unknown Artist*
Raleigh was the foremost advocate of colonization at the English court.

Shortly thereafter Barlowe returned home, taking two kidnapped Indians so that Englishmen could see actual "savages" and teach them English.

The voyagers had been sent by Sir Walter Raleigh, who dreamed of founding an American colony where English, Indians, and even blacks liberated from Spanish slavery could live together productively. Barlowe reported just what Raleigh wanted to hear. Raleigh persuaded Queen Elizabeth to dispatch ships and a company of soldiers to launch a colony at Roanoke, accompanied by painter John White and scientist Thomas Harriot.

At first all went well. Harriot carefully studied Indian culture, and White captured the Indians' life in paintings of extraordinary delicacy. In awe of the English, the Indians eagerly traded and shared their corn—which they grew with amazing ease: "Their country corn," Barlowe had already reported, "groweth three times in five months. . . . Only they cast the corn into the ground, breaking a little of the soft turf with a wooden matlock, or pickax. . . . They have also beans very fair of divers colors and wonderful plenty. Some growing naturally and some in their gardens. . . ." Why should the English ever work?

So the English refused to try growing their own food—and by the first winter, they had outlived their welcome. Fearing that the Indians were about to attack them, the English killed Winginia in June 1586. When Raleigh's friend Drake arrived soon after with a shipload of blacks whom he had rescued from the Spanish and planned to settle at Roanoke, most of the English were ready to quit. Casually abandoning the blacks, the English sailed back across the Atlantic.

Raleigh did not give up yet. He sent another expedition in the summer of 1586 commanded by Richard Grenville, who left 15 men at Roanoke before hurrying off to fight the Spanish. In 1587 Raleigh dispatched White back to Roanoke with 110 settlers and their last Indian friend, Manteo, whom the English baptized and proclaimed "lord" of the local Indians. White found no trace of the little English

(Left) **A Carolina Indian Mother and Child,** by *John White, 1585*

(Right) **A Carolina Indian Warrior in Body Paint,** by *John White, 1585*

(Below) **Carolina Indians Fishing,** by *John White, 1585*

Using canoes, weirs, nets, and spears, coastal Indians depended on fishing as an important source of their food.

garrison. Leaving the settlers (including his newborn granddaughter), he went home to bring more supplies.

But Spain's attack in the English Channel intervened. Drake and every other English seaman were needed to help repel the Armada of 1588. Not until 1590 could White return to Roanoke—and found only rusty armor, moldy books, and the word *CROATOAN* cut into a post. What had happened to the "lost colony"? Were the settlers killed by Indians? Did they starve or die in a hurricane or drown attempting to move to the nearby island of Croatoan? Or did they join the Indians? (A persistent theory is that they were absorbed into a North Carolina tribe whose modern descendants have such English traits as blue eyes.) The most recent authority to tackle the question believes that Roanoke survivors moved closer to Chesapeake Bay, only to be wiped out by the Powhatan Confederacy when the next English settlement was planted

at Jamestown, in 1607. But historians will probably never know with certainty.

By the time England first attempted to found a colony in America, almost a century had passed since Christopher Columbus's discoveries. In that century Spain had already carved out an American empire vaster than the empire of ancient Rome at an

appalling cost in human lives. By the 1580s the English thought that they could do better: to provide the benevolent rule that would foster multiracial harmony and prosperity. But Roanoke was a miserable failure, and not for seventeen years would the English try again. English leaders' initial hopes of bringing freedom to America were a poignant casualty.

needed effective leadership on the council that directed Virginia's affairs. The council's first president hoarded supplies, and its second was lazy and indecisive. In September 1608 the councilors turned to a brash soldier of fortune whose eagerness to settle arguments with his fists had landed him in irons for most of the 1607 voyage: the magnificent braggart Captain John Smith.

Although only twenty-eight years old and of yeoman origin, Smith had experience fighting Spaniards and Turks that prepared him well to assume control in Virginia. Immediately organizing all but the sick in well-supervised work gangs, he ensured sufficient food and housing for winter. Applying lessons learned in his soldiering days, he laid down rules for maintaining sanitation and hygiene to limit disease. Above all, he brought order through military discipline. During the winter of 1608–1609, Smith lost just a dozen men out of two hundred.

Smith also became the colony's best Indian negotiator. After local native Americans captured him in late 1607, Smith displayed such impressive courage that Powhatan, the leader of the nearby Powhatan Confederacy, arranged an elaborate reconciliation ceremony in which his daughter, Pocahontas, "saved" Smith's life during a mock execution. Smith maintained satisfactory relations with the Powhatan Confederacy, in part through his personality, but he also employed calculated demonstrations of English military strength to mask the settlers' actual weakness.

John Smith prevented Virginia from disintegrating as Sagadahoc had. The company's shareholders reorganized the colonial government in 1609, however, and replaced the council's president with Thomas De La Warr. The new governor sailed for Virginia with six hundred settlers, but he and a third of the expedition were shipwrecked off Bermuda. De La Warr's loss left the colony without effective leadership, for Smith could no longer claim any authority. Discipline soon crumbled, and crops were neglected as settlers scattered to hunt for gold. Smith returned to England in September after suffering a serious wound from a gunpowder explosion.

The five hundred men and women who remained at Jamestown had not laid away sufficient food for the winter, and with Smith gone, the

Indians turned hostile. A survivor of the winter left this account:

> So lamentable was our scarcity, that we were constrained to eat dogs, cats, rats, snakes, toadstools, horsehides, and what not; one man out of the misery endured, killing his wife powdered her up [with flour] to eat her, for which he was burned. Many besides fed on the corpses of dead men, . . . and indeed so miserable was our estate that the happiest day that some of them hoped to see was when the Indians had killed a mare, they wishing whilst she was boiling that Sir Thomas Smythe was upon her back in the kettle.

Of the five hundred residents at Jamestown in September 1609, about four hundred died by May 1610. The survivors stumbled down to a small ship and were sailing for home when they met Lord De La Warr and his shipwrecked contingent, just arriving in boats built on Bermuda. Their combined forces reoccupied Jamestown, but Virginia barely survived its "starving time."

De La Warr, a veteran of Irish campaigns, organized the settlers like a military garrison. The colony slowly grew, and by 1611 it had expanded forty miles beyond Jamestown, to modern-day Richmond. The English population remained small, just 380 in 1616, and it had yet to produce anything of value for the stockholders.

Tobacco emerged as Virginia's economic salvation. John Rolfe, an Englishman who married Pocahontas, spent several years perfecting a salable variety of tobacco and began planting it in Virginia. By 1618 the product commanded high prices, and that year Virginia exported large amounts of the crop. Thereafter Sir Thomas Smythe poured supplies and settlers into the colony.

To attract investment, the company started awarding large land grants to individuals who would pay the transportation of laborers to work their own property. Most of these laborers were indentured servants, who had to work for a fixed term of service (usually several years) in return for passage to America. The "plantations" that the new landowners established typically resembled the stockaded communities ("bawns") that English settlers built on confiscated lands in Ireland.

By 1622 Virginia still faced three serious problems. First, local officials systematically defrauded

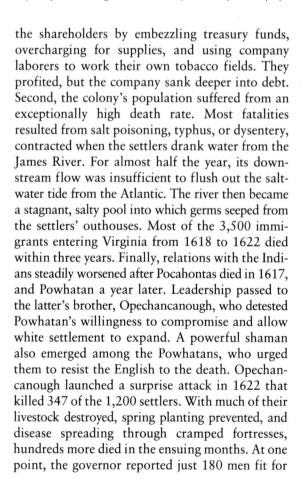

Artifacts from Early Virginia

This double-edged sword (shown with fragments of its guard and pommel) and elaborate pipe tamper (featuring a man wearing armor and and smoking a pipe) were unearthed at Flowerdew Hundred, an early English settlement near present-day Hopewell, Virginia, and date from the first half of the seventeenth century.

the shareholders by embezzling treasury funds, overcharging for supplies, and using company laborers to work their own tobacco fields. They profited, but the company sank deeper into debt. Second, the colony's population suffered from an exceptionally high death rate. Most fatalities resulted from salt poisoning, typhus, or dysentery, contracted when the settlers drank water from the James River. For almost half the year, its downstream flow was insufficient to flush out the saltwater tide from the Atlantic. The river then became a stagnant, salty pool into which germs seeped from the settlers' outhouses. Most of the 3,500 immigrants entering Virginia from 1618 to 1622 died within three years. Finally, relations with the Indians steadily worsened after Pocahontas died in 1617, and Powhatan a year later. Leadership passed to the latter's brother, Opechancanough, who detested Powhatan's willingness to compromise and allow white settlement to expand. A powerful shaman also emerged among the Powhatans, who urged them to resist the English to the death. Opechancanough launched a surprise attack in 1622 that killed 347 of the 1,200 settlers. With much of their livestock destroyed, spring planting prevented, and disease spreading through cramped fortresses, hundreds more died in the ensuing months. At one point, the governor reported just 180 men fit for

military duty against an enemy numbering in the thousands.

Nevertheless, Opechancanough could not hold his forces together for a long siege. Reorganizing the settlers, Governor Francis Wyatt then took the offensive after the company sent more men. Wyatt used tactics developed during the Irish war. He inflicted widespread starvation by destroying food supplies, conducted winter campaigns to drive Indians from their homes when they would suffer most, and fought (according to John Smith) as if he had "just cause to destroy them by all means possible." By 1625 the English had won the war, and the Indians had lost their best chance of driving out the intruders.

The clash left the Virginia Company bankrupt and James I concerned over complaints against its officers. After receiving a report critical of the company's management, James revoked its charter in 1624, and the next year Virginia became a royal colony. Only about five hundred Old World settlers now lived in Virginia, including a handful of Africans of uncertain status who had been brought in since 1619.* So the roots from which would

---

*Whether or not these first Africans were—or remained—slaves is unknown. The emergence of Virginia's African-American population will be traced in Chapter 2.

grow the Anglo-American and African-American peoples of Virginia were fragile indeed.

French, Dutch, and Swedish Fur Colonies

French, like English, fishermen worked the plenteous Grand Banks fisheries throughout the sixteenth century. The French sailors bartered with coastal Indians for skins of the beaver, a species almost extinct in Europe. By the late sixteenth century, as European demand for beaver hats skyrocketed, France came to see North America primarily as a source for this valuable commodity.

Between 1598 and 1604, a series of government-sponsored French fur-trading outposts appeared in Acadia (modern-day Nova Scotia). But only in 1608 did the first enduring French settlement on Canadian soil begin, founded by Samuel de Champlain at Quebec, far up the St. Lawrence River. Champlain wintered there with twenty-eight men, of whom twenty died.

Shrewdly understanding how to keep his settlement going, Champlain arranged for the Hurons and other nearby tribes to collect furs from farther inland and deliver them to Quebec. He also dispatched French agents to live for long periods with the native Americans. These *coureurs de bois* (runners of the woods) integrated themselves into Indian communities and became a personal link uniting French and Indian interests. In 1615, when four Catholic priests arrived at Quebec, the French also began energetic missionary work among the Indians. Results came slowly, but eventually many Indians converted to Catholicism, and the missionaries (mostly Jesuits) learned to perform valuable services as diplomats, explorers, and even military strategists.

Preservation of good relations with Indian allies was critical to Champlain's success. Nevertheless, New France remained tiny. By 1650 just 675 French

European Settlements in North America, 1565–1625

Except for St. Augustine, all European settlements founded before 1607 were abandoned by 1625. Despite the migration of ten thousand Europeans to North America's Atlantic coast by 1625, the total number of Spanish, English, French, and Dutch on the continent was then about eighteen hundred, of whom two-thirds lived in Virginia.

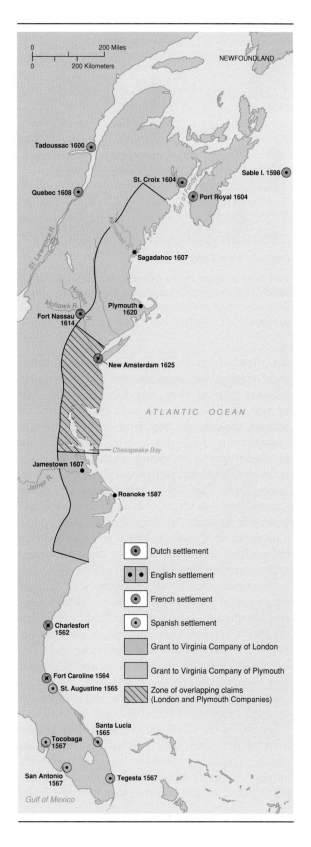

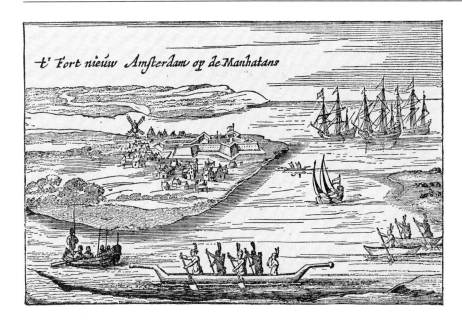

t' Fort nieuw Amsterdam op de Manhatans

New Amsterdam

After the Dutch "purchase" of Manhattan Island, the fortified settlement of New Amsterdam grew only slowly, as this view from 1651 (the earliest known depiction) clearly shows. Except for the tip, the island remained farmland or forest. Corn brought by canoe-paddling Indians also helped feed the settlement. Note the windmill, where grain was ground.

lived there. Meanwhile, a formidable rival challenged New France's fur trade: the Dutch.

The Dutch Republic* was one of the seventeenth century's great powers. Mighty at sea, the Hollanders built an empire stretching from Brazil to West Africa and what is now Indonesia. North America was for them a relatively minor sphere of activity. Even so, the Dutch played a key role in opening North America to Europeans.

As early as 1609, the Dutch East India Company had become interested in North America when its merchants learned of the broad, deep Hudson River flowing from the interior of present-day New York. By 1611 Dutch oceangoing ships were sailing far up the Hudson, and in 1614 the company built Fort Nassau near what would become Albany. Then in 1625 a second Dutch joint-stock company, the new West India Company, erected another fort on an island at the mouth of the Hudson. A year later, the company's representative, Peter Minuit, bought the island from local Indians and began a second settlement there. The island was named Manhattan; the settlement, New Amsterdam; and the entire colony, New Netherland. As in New

France, immigrants trickled in slowly; by 1643 the Dutch colony had only sixteen hundred residents.

New Netherland became North America's first multiethnic society. Barely half the settlers were Dutch; most of the rest were Germans, French, and Scandinavians. In 1643 the population included Protestants, Catholics, Jews, and Moslems, and eighteen European and African languages were spoken. But religion counted for little (in 1642 the colony had seventeen taverns but not one place of worship), and the settlers' get-rich-quick attitude sapped company profits as private individuals persisted in trading illegally in furs. Eventually the company bowed to the inevitable and legalized private fur trading. Lacking self-restraint to avoid friction with the Indians, the colonists meanwhile failed to maintain enough military strength to deter attack.

New Netherlanders lived by the fur trade. The Dutch tried to use the Iroquois Confederacy as their Indian intermediary, much as the French depended on the Hurons. To stimulate a flow of furs to New Netherland, in the 1620s Dutch traders obtained from the Indians of Long Island Sound large quantities of wampum (tiny seashells traditionally denoting spiritual power, which native Americans had long traded throughout the continent's interior) and used it to buy beaver pelts inland. Backed respectively by the French and the Dutch, Hurons and Iroquois became embroiled in an ever-deep-

---

*By 1588 the independence of the northern, Dutch-speaking part of Spain's rebellious Netherlands provinces was secure, but the southern Netherlands (modern Belgium and Luxembourg) remained under Spanish rule until 1713.

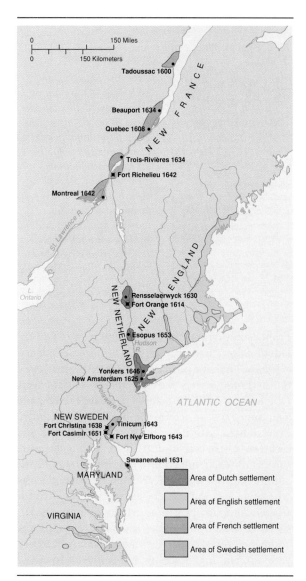

The Riverine Colonies of New France, New Netherland, and New Sweden, c. 1650

So that they could easily buy furs trapped by Indians farther inland, England's imperial rivals located their colonies along major river routes to the interior. The French settled along the St. Lawrence, the Dutch along the Hudson, and the Swedes along the Delaware.

ening contest to control the fur trade and maximize their profits in wampum, firearms, and alcohol. Overhunting soon drove up the price of beaver pelts, and intertribal wars grew correspondingly more violent. After 1642 the Dutch-armed Iroquois, in a series of bloody "beaver wars," destroyed

or scattered rival pro-French tribes like the Hurons. Then they attacked the French settlements along the St. Lawrence. "They come like foxes, they attack like lions, they disappear like birds," wrote a French Jesuit of the Iroquois.

Although the Dutch allied successfully with the Iroquois, their relations with their Indian neighbors, the Algonkians, were the worst of any Europeans. With its greedy settlers and military weakness, New Netherland had largely itself to blame. In 1643 all-out war erupted when Governor Willem Kiefft massacred previously friendly Algonkians, and by 1645 the Dutch could temporarily prevail only with English help and by inflicting terrible atrocities. But the fighting had cut New Netherland's population from sixteen hundred to seven hundred.

Another European challenger dangerously distracted the Dutch in their war with the Algonkians. In 1638 Sweden had planted a small fur-trading colony in the lower Delaware Valley. New Sweden diverted many furs from New Netherland. Annoyed, in 1655 the Dutch colony's stern, one-legged soldier-governor Peter Stuyvesant marched his militia against New Sweden. The four hundred residents of the rival colony peacefully accepted Dutch annexation. But New Netherland paid dearly for the victory. The Algonkians attacked during the militia's absence, this time destroying many scattered Dutch settlements and forcing Stuyvesant to ransom white captives.

Tiny though they were, the seventeenth-century French, Dutch, and Swedish colonies were not historically insignificant. New France became the nucleus of modern French Canada. New Netherland did not endure under Dutch rule (as we shall see in Chapter 3, in 1664 it fell to the English), yet the Dutch presence in what became New York lent a distinctive flavor to American life for centuries. Even short-lived New Sweden left a mark—the log cabin, that durable symbol of the American frontier, which Finnish settlers in the Swedish colony first introduced to the continent.

The Origins of New England: Plymouth Plantation

Still another rival entered the competition for the North American fur trade: the English who settled New England. In 1614 the ever-enterprising John

Smith, who explored its coast, gave New England its name. "Who," he asked, "can but approve this most excellent place, both for health and fertility?" An admirer of Cortés, Smith planned to conquer its "goodly, strong, and well-proportioned [Indian] people" and establish an English colony there. But his hope of settling an English colony in New England came to naught. As for the region's native peoples, microbes rather than soldiers did the grim business of destroying them as a terrible epidemic devastated the coastal tribes about 1616. In 1622 an Englishman found the ground littered with the "bones and skulls" of the unburied dead.

Against this tragic backdrop, in 1620 the Virginia Company of London gave a patent to some London merchants headed by Thomas Weston for a settlement near the Hudson River. Weston sent over 18 families (a total of 102 persons) in a small, leaky ship, the *Mayflower*. The colonists promised to send lumber, furs, and fish back to Weston in England for seven years, after which they would own the tract.

The expedition's leaders—but not all its members—belonged to a small religious community from the town of Scrooby in northern England. The group was made up of Puritans who had taken the radical step of withdrawing from the Church of England. Such "Separatists" risked the death penalty, and the Scrooby band had fled to the Netherlands to practice their religion freely. Unsatisfied there, they decided to immigrate to America under Weston's sponsorship.

The Pilgrims, as these people became known, missed their intended destination near the Hudson River. In November 1620 the *Mayflower* landed at Massachusetts Bay, outside the bounds of Virginia. Knowing that they had no legal right to be there, the Pilgrim leaders forced all the adult males in the group (including non-Separatists) to sign the Mayflower Compact before they landed. By this document they constituted themselves a "civil body politic"—that is, a civil government—under James I's sovereignty and established the colony of Plymouth Plantation.

Weakened by their journey and unprepared for winter, half the Pilgrims died within four months of landing. Those still alive in the spring of 1621 owed much to the aid of two Indians. One was Squanto, a local Indian who had been taken to Spain as a slave some years earlier, escaped to

Defending Plymouth Plantation

Nervous about their security despite the neighboring Indians' weakening through terrible epidemics, the Pilgrims at Plymouth used military force to overawe local tribes. This English helmet of steel and wrought iron was part of the equipment that a professional soldier like Miles Standish might have used to defend the settlement.

England, and made himself useful to potential New World colonists. Returning, he learned that he alone of his tribe of two thousand had survived an epidemic. The other friendly Indian, an Abenaki from Maine named Samoset, hoped to use the English as an ally against a rival tribe, the Narragansetts of modern-day Rhode Island. To stop the Pilgrims from stealing their food, the Indians taught the newcomers how to grow corn. The alliance that Squanto and Samoset arranged between Plymouth and local Wampanoag Indians headed by chief Massasoit united two weak parties, but with their firearms the Pilgrims became the dominant partner. By late 1621 Plymouth forced the local Indians to acknowledge English sovereignty. The Pilgrims' first Thanksgiving after the harvest of 1621 was a ceremony cementing the relationship, "at which time . . . we exercised our arms, many of the Indians coming amongst us, with some 90 men, whom for three days we entertained and feasted."

Plymouth's relations with the native Americans soon worsened, however. News of the Virginia massacre of 1622 hastened the Pilgrims' militarization of their colony (under the leadership of a professional soldier, Miles Standish) and threatening their Indian "allies" with their monopoly of firepower. By imposing stern discipline on themselves, the Pilgrims managed to become agriculturally self-sufficient. But they also offended the Indians by avoiding the close personal contact that the native peoples expected of an ally, and they made no attempt to convert the native Americans.

The Pilgrims were not so lucky—or shrewd—in dealing with their English patrons. Systematically cheated by their English sponsors, after seven years the Pilgrims had sunk so deeply into debt that they faced fifteen years' additional labor to free themselves. Fishing failed to be profitable, but they learned to trade their corn surpluses with the nonagricultural Indians of Maine for furs. By 1627 they had also agreed with the Dutch to divide the fur trade in the Connecticut River Valley. By the time Plymouth finally freed itself of obligations, the settlement had grown to several hundred persons on Cape Cod and in the southeastern corner of present-day Massachusetts.

At first an almost insignificant group, the Pilgrims were only one of several small English bands that immigrated to New England in the 1620s. Their importance was twofold. First, they helped inspire the American vision of sturdy, self-reliant, God-fearing folk crossing the Atlantic to govern themselves freely. Second, they foreshadowed the methods that later generations of white Americans would use to gain mastery over the Indians. In both respects, the Pilgrims were the vanguard of a mighty, voluntary migration of Puritans to New England in the 1630s.

Conclusion

The founding of the first Old World colonies on the North American mainland came late in the Age of Discovery—the era spanning the mid-fifteenth to the mid-seventeenth centuries, during which Europeans enormously expanded their geographical horizons. Among the previously unknown peoples whom Europeans encountered were the native Americans of the Western Hemisphere and the dark-skinned Africans living south of the Sahara Desert. Indians and Africans alike had adapted well to their environments, but Europeans found them in many respects strange, even sinister.

The displacement of Indians and the enslavement of Africans tarnished the early history of European settlement in the New World. Despite devastation by disease, however, native Americans yielded only slowly to foreign incursions. As for Africans, even the horrors of the Atlantic slave trade did not strip them entirely of their heritage, which they later nurtured into a distinctive African-American culture.

During the first third of the seventeenth century, the general outlines of European land claims in North America emerged, as did the basic elements of the various colonies' economic life. Establishing ranches in New Mexico and fortresses in Florida, Spain advanced as far north as seemed worth going. Virginia's victory over the Indians left the English in control in the Chesapeake, where tobacco had become the principal commercial crop. Here and in the fragile Plymouth colony, English settlers depended primarily on farming. The Dutch, Swedish, and French colonies existed mainly to trade in fish and furs, which soon became important to New Englanders as well. Of the non-English colonies, New France was geographically the best positioned to expand deep into the continent. By 1630 North America stood poised for two surges in colonial development: the great English migration across the Atlantic, and the involuntary migration of Africans to New World servitude.

Given the thousands of lives lost and the fortunes wasted, the first tiny European outposts in North America may seem a minor achievement. By the 1630s they were just beginning to take on an air of permanence, leading discontented Europeans to imagine that new societies could be created across the Atlantic free from the Old World's inherited problems or without painful labor. These dreamers seldom dared to cross the ocean, and those who did generally lost their illusions—or their lives—when faced with the rigors of a strange environment. The transplantation of Europeans into North America was hardly a story of inevitable triumph.

CHRONOLOGY

c. 600–1600 Rise of the great West African empires.

c. 1000 Vikings voyage to North America and establish a small settlement at Vinland.

c. 1400–1600 Renaissance era—first in Italy, then elsewhere in Europe.

1440 Portuguese slave trade in West Africa begins.

1488 Bartolomeu Días reaches the Cape of Good Hope.

1492 Christopher Columbus lands at San Salvador.

1497 John Cabot reaches Nova Scotia or Newfoundland.

1512–1521 Juan Ponce de León explores Florida.

1513 Vasco Núñez de Balboa views the Pacific Ocean.

1517 Protestant Reformation begins in Germany.

1519 Ferdinand Magellan embarks on round-the-world voyage.
Hernán Cortés begins conquest of Aztec empire.

1524 Giovanni da Verrazano explores the North American coast.

1534 Jacques Cartier explores Canada for France.

1540–1542 Francisco Vásquez de Coronado explores the southwestern United States.

1558 Elizabeth I becomes queen of England.

1565 St. Augustine founded.

1565–1580s English attempt to subdue Ireland.

1577 Francis Drake circumnavigates the globe.

1578 Humphrey Gilbert secures a patent to establish an English colony in Newfoundland.

1585–1587 Roanoke colony explored and founded.

1588 English defeat the Spanish Armada.

1598 New Mexico colony founded.

1603 James I becomes king of England.

1607 Jamestown colony founded.

1608 Samuel de Champlain founds Quebec.

1614 New Netherland colony founded.

1619 Large exports of tobacco from Virginia begin.
First Africans arrive in Virginia.

1620 Mayflower Compact signed; Plymouth Plantation founded.

1622 Powhatan Confederacy attacks Virginia colony.

1624 Revocation of Virginia Company's charter.

1625 Peter Minuit purchases Manhattan Island.

1638 New Sweden colony founded.

1643 War erupts between the Dutch and the Algonkian Indians.

1655 New Netherland colony peacefully takes over New Sweden.

For Further Reading

Paul Bohannan and Philip Curtin, *Africa and the Africans* (2d ed., 1971). A brief but comprehensive introduction to the African world—geography, society, culture, and history.

Fernand Braudel, *The Mediterranean and the Mediterranean World in the Age of Philip II* (2d ed., 1966; English trans., 1972). One of the greatest historical works of our time; examines the interactions of large "structures" of environment, economy, and events in sixteenth-century Europe and Africa.

Carl Bridenbaugh, *Vexed and Troubled Englishmen, 1590–1642* (1978). An excellent account of England during the age of expansion.

William Cronon, *Changes in the Land: Indians, Colonists, and the Ecology of New England* (1983). A pioneering study of the interactions of native Americans and European settlers with the New England ecosystem.

Francis Jennings, *The Invasion of America: Indians, Colonialism, and the Cant of Conquest* (1975). A brilliant, angry, and controversial corrective to traditional views of the settlement of North America.

Alvin Josephy, Jr., *The Indian Heritage of America* (1968). A comprehensive account of all Western Hemisphere native peoples, organized by cultural region and attentive to evolution over time.

D. W. Meinig, *The Shaping of America*, Vol. I: *Atlantic America, 1492–1800* (1986). A geographer's engrossing study of Europeans' encounter with North America and the rise of colonial society.

Roderick Nash, *Wilderness and the American Mind* (2d ed., 1973). An incisive essay on the changing ways in which untamed nature has captured the American imagination from colonial times to the rise of modern environmentalism.

J. H. Parry, *The Age of Reconnaissance* (1963). A comprehensive analysis of European exploration and the rise of European overseas empires from the fifteenth to the seventeenth centuries.

Additional Bibliography

Native Americans

James Axtell, *The European and the Indian: Essays on the Ethnohistory of Colonial North America* (1981) and *The Invasion Within: The Contest of Culture in Colonial North America* (1985); Harold Driver, *Indians of North America* (2d ed., 1969); Charles Hudson, *The Southeastern Indians* (1976); Jesse Jennings, ed., *Ancient North Americans* (1983); Karen Ordahl Kupperman, *Roanoke: The Abandoned Colony* (1984) and *Settling with the Indians: The Meeting of English and Indian Cultures in America, 1580–1640* (1980); Gary Nash, *Red, White, and Black: The Peoples of Colonial America* (2d ed., 1982); Neal Salisbury, *Manitou and Providence: Indians, Europeans, and the Making of New England, 1500–1643* (1982); Bernard Sheehan, *Savagism and Civility: Indians and Englishmen in Colonial Virginia* (1980); Anthony F. C. Wallace, *The Death and Rebirth of the Seneca* (1970); Wilcomb E. Washburn, *The Indian in America* (1975).

The Africans and Slavery

Philip Curtin, *The Atlantic Slave Trade: A Census* (1969) and *Economic Change in Precolonial Africa: Senegambia in the Era of the Slave Trade* (1975); Basil Davidson, *The African Genius* (1969); David Brion Davis, *The Problem of Slavery in Western Culture* (1966); J. S. Fage, *A History of Africa* (1978); Winthrop D. Jordan, *White Over Black: American Attitudes Toward the Negro 1550–1812* (1968); Robert July, *A History of the African People* (1970); Paul E. Lovejoy, *Transformations in Slavery: A History of Slavery in Africa* (1983); Richard Olaniyan, *African History and Culture* (1982); Jon Vogt, *Portuguese Rule on the Gold Coast, 1469–1682* (1979).

The Europeans

Fernand Braudel, *Civilization and Capitalism, 15th–18th Centuries* (3 vols., 1979; English trans., 1981); Peter Burke, *Popular Culture in Early Modern Europe* (1978); Carlo Cipolla, *Before the Industrial Revolution: Euro-*

pean Society and Economy, 1100–1700 (1976); L. A. Clarkson, *The Pre-Industrial Economy of England, 1500–1750* (1972); Patrick Collinson, *The Elizabethan Puritan Movement* (1967); Natalie Z. Davis, *Society and Culture in Early Modern France* (1975); A. G. Dickens, *The English Reformation* (1964); J. H. Elliott, *Imperial Spain, 1479–1716* (1963); G. R. Elton, *England Under the Tudors* (1974); J. R. Hale, *Renaissance Europe* (1971); Ralph Houlbrooke, *The English Family, 1450–1700* (1984); Peter Laslett, *The World We Have Lost: England Before the Industrial Age* (2d ed., 1971); Alan Macfarlane, *Witchcraft in Tudor and Stuart England* (1970); Stephen Ozment, *The Age of Reform, 1250–1550* (1980); Quentin Skinner, *The Origins of Modern Political Thought* (1978); Gerald Strauss, *Luther's House of Learning: Indoctrination of the Young in the German Reformation* (1978); Keith Thomas, *Religion and the Decline of Magic* (1971); Margo Todd, *Christian Humanism and the Puritan Social Order* (1988); Penry Williams, *The Tudor Regime* (1979); Keith Wrightson, *English Society, 1580–1680* (1982).

European Expansion and the Spanish Conquest

Fredi Chiappelli, ed., *First Images of America: The Impact of the New World on the Old* (2 vols., 1976); Alfred W. Crosby, Jr., *The Columbian Exchange: Biological and Cultural Consequences of 1492* (1972); Ralph Davis, *Rise of the Atlantic Economies* (1973); J. H. Elliott, *The Old World and the New, 1492–1650* (1970); Lewis Hanke, *The Spanish Struggle for Justice in the Conquest of America* (1965); Howard Mumford Jones, *O Strange New World* (1964); James Lockhart and Stuart B. Schwartz, *Early Latin America: A History of Colonial Spanish America and Brazil* (1983); S. E. Morison, *Admiral of the Ocean Sea: A Life of Christopher Columbus* (1942), *The European Discovery of America: The Northern Voyages*, A.D. *1500–1600* (1971), and *The Southern Voyages*, A.D. *1492–1616* (1974); J. H. Parry, *The Establishment of the European Hegemony: Trade and Expansion in the Age of the Renaissance* (1966); Carl O. Sauer, *Sixteenth Century North America* (1971).

Northern Europeans in North America

Nicholas P. Canny, *The Elizabethan Conquest of Ireland: A Pattern Established, 1565–1576* (1976); Thomas J. Condon, *New York Beginnings: Commercial Origins of the New Netherlands* (1968); Wesley Frank Craven, *Dissolution of the Virginia Company: The Failure of a Colonial Experiment* (1932); W. J. Eccles, *The Canadian Frontier, 1534–1760* (1969); George D. Langdon, Jr., *Pilgrim Colony: A History of New Plymouth, 1620–1691* (1966); Edmund S. Morgan, *American Slavery, American Freedom: The Ordeal of Colonial Virginia* (1975); David B. Quinn, *England and the Discovery of America, 1481–1620* (1974), *North America from Earliest Discovery to First Settlements: Norse Voyages–1612* (1977), and *Set Fair for Roanoke: Voyages and Colonies, 1584–1606* (1985); Oliver Rink, *Holland on the Hudson: An Economic and Social History of Dutch New York* (1986).

CHAPTER 2

Godly Order and Slavery: Seventeenth-Century New England, Caribbean, and Chesapeake Society

On the West Indian island of Barbados in 1692, a widowed Englishwoman named Sarah Horbin counted up her relatives to see who might deserve bequests of property in case her only son—a sailor whom Arab pirates were holding for ransom in an African prison—died. Through her kinsman John Seabury of Barbados, she had kept in contact with a dozen Seabury cousins in Massachusetts. She had also remained in touch with several Virginia relatives in the Empereur family and with a kinsman of her husband's, Andrew Rouse, who lived in the frontier zone between Virginia and Florida then simply called Carolina.

About one-third of those leaving England went to Ireland or the Netherlands, but the migration chiefly scattered these refugees across the Atlantic. By 1700 there were almost 250,000 persons of English birth or parentage in the New World, including 200,000 within the modern-day United States. The vast exodus provided British North America with its first large wave of immigrant settlers. Perhaps every fourth American alive today could be descended from someone who crossed the Atlantic with this surge of desperate humanity.

Sarah Horbin and her far-flung clan were part of a great migration of English women and men who built an empire almost absentmindedly for their mother country. From 1630 to 1660, at least 200,000 (and perhaps 250,000) English swarmed to foreign lands. By the mid-seventeenth century, England's population had reached 5.5 million, yet the kingdom was losing between 65,000 and 80,000 people every decade. Emigration from Spain, then a nation of 8 million, averaged about 20,000 per decade, while France, with a population of about 19 million, sent fewer than 10,000 persons overseas every ten years. About 1650 an English woman or man was five times more likely to emigrate than was a Spaniard, and twenty-five times more likely than an inhabitant of France.

Most of these refugees were the unwanted offspring of poverty and unemployment. Eighty percent of them were aged between fifteen and twenty-four. They generally had left their home communities looking for work, and, unsuccessful at finding it, signed on for America upon reaching a port city. The majority took ship only because they had no alternative.

The English government ignored this outpouring of youthful vigor. Its overseas possessions grew without any official plan for colonial expansion. The settlers who immigrated to—or found themselves stranded in—America received almost no financial help from the royal treasury and had to fend for themselves in a hostile world.

This freedom from centralized control allowed three very different societies to develop in seventeenth-century British North America: New England, the West Indies, and the Chesapeake. Each evolved distinctive systems of land use, labor, religious practice, and family and community experience. Barely one generation removed from England in 1690, Sarah Horbin on Barbados, her Seabury cousins in Massachusetts, and her Empereur kin in Virginia led lives that differed profoundly from one another.

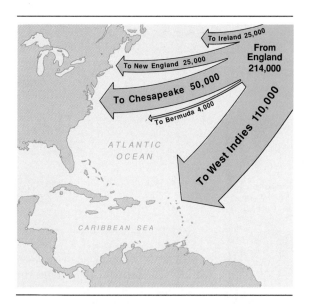

The Great English Migration, 1630–1660

During the great transatlantic English migration, the present-day United States received just one-third of English immigrants. The West Indies attracted twice as many colonists as went to the Chesapeake, and over four times as many as settled in New England.

The New England Way

Six years after returning to England from Jamestown, Captain John Smith led an expedition of whale hunters to that part of the North American coast then called Norumbega. He found no whales but came back with a profitable load of dried fish and a conviction that the land was destined for "men that have great spirits, but small means [or fortunes]." In 1616 Smith published *A Description of New England*, which gave the region its modern name.

Smith's pamphlet inspired persons discontented with the Church of England to view that area as a haven. The Pilgrims settled there by accident in 1620, and a few hundred others drifted in over the next decade, but not until 1630 did large-scale migration begin. Building communities based on religious ideals, these Puritans would found America's first utopian society.

The Puritan Impulse

Since the 1570s dissatisfied members of the Church of England had demanded that it be "purified" of traces of Roman Catholicism. These Puritans primarily wished to free the members of each congregation (laypersons) and their minister from outside interference by bishops. They also objected to ceremonies and practices inherited from Catholicism such as the Mass, elaborate church decoration, kneeling, and the use of priestly vestments or communion rails—the latter two implying that the clergy were separate from, and superior to, their congregations. Puritan ministers encouraged laypersons' participation in parish affairs and held simplified prayer meetings whose chief feature was a learned sermon.

Puritans differed among themselves about how to institute a reformed church. Non-Separatist Puritans upheld a state church, but one in which congregations were self-governing; they essentially attempted to reform the Church of England from within. Separatists, in contrast, rejected the concept of a state church and worshiped illegally outside the Church of England. Aside from the Separatists of Plymouth and Rhode Island, American Puritans were usually non-Separatists.

Insisting that it was not sufficient for a person to lead an outwardly moral life, Puritans argued that Christians must forge a commitment to serve God through a special act of spiritual rebirth (termed the *conversion experience, redemption,* or *sanctification*). At this moment of being "born again," a soul confronted the horrifying truth of its own unworthiness, sensed the majesty of God's righteousness, and felt the transcending power of divine love as God's saving grace made it worthy of entering heaven. Sanctification then cemented the individual to God as a "saint," or member of the "elect," who—though guaranteed eternal life in heaven—must still resist human sinfulness.

The conversion experience rarely came until an individual had deeply probed all personal weaknesses, learned to accept self-denial, and undergone repeated cycles of self-examination and repentance. For all but a few Puritans, this process, known as preparation for salvation, spanned several agonizing years spent in self-doubt and fear of losing one's soul, during which an individual struggled to gain self-mastery. Many saints who left accounts of their conversion experiences remembered a harrowing, exhausting sensation of relief and described themselves as having been "left smoaking" or "bruised" by the powerful rush of God's grace.

For many Puritans, the conversion process was understandably a torturous process. Poverty, loneliness, and fear so pervaded England that even the middle classes could not avoid feeling anxious over the future. Chronic unemployment and low wages constantly tempted the hard-pressed to become petty cheats. Even honest individuals had difficulty showing charity, since they also found life insecure. In a nation of rampant unemployment, many persons unable to make a decent living had to fight with despair, the impulse to desert their families, and the urge to drink. Because the faltering economy forced half of all men and women to delay marriage until after age twenty-five, young adults had to battle sexual temptation through much of their lives. In such desperate times, it was natural for many to doubt that they could set the example expected of saints.

In preparing for spiritual rebirth, Puritans fought to gain mastery over their own wills, to internalize a highly idealistic code of ethics, and to forge the inner strength to live by an uncompromising moral standard. By the time of his or her redemption, a Puritan had undergone a radical personality transformation that replaced doubt with certainty. It was this reorientation of character that produced the Puritans' strong sense of purpose, willingness to sacrifice, and ironclad discipline. The conversion experience molded individuals like the Puritan military and political leader Oliver Cromwell, who felt confident that he could conquer any enemy because he had already conquered himself.

By bending their wills to a higher purpose while preparing for salvation, a generation of English men and women unknowingly steeled themselves to tame a hostile frontier. Temporarily blocked from reforming England, they attempted to build a righteous society in a distant land with rocky soil, a short growing season, and few natural resources.

Ultimately they had just two advantages in conquering this wilderness: a holy violence burning within and a stubborn refusal to accept defeat.

Errand into the Wilderness

By 1600 Puritans held considerable influence in the Church of England and enjoyed significant support from both commoners and gentry. Thereafter, as the political environment grew threatening and the economy worsened in England, many Puritans took interest in colonizing New England.

James I (ruled 1603–1625), the founder of England's Stuart dynasty, bitterly opposed Puritan efforts to eliminate the office of bishop. The monarchy's right to name bishops greatly strengthened its power because bishops composed about a quarter of the House of Lords, the upper chamber of Parliament, which at the time had a strong voice in enacting laws. Bishops also controlled the clergy and thus could silence ministers whose sermons or writings criticized government policies. James made it clear that he saw Puritan attacks on bishops as a direct threat to himself when he snapped, "No bishop, no king."

After Charles I became king in 1625, Anglican authorities undertook a systematic campaign to eliminate Puritan influence within the church. With the king's backing, bishops insisted that services be conducted according to the Book of Common Prayer, which prescribed rituals similar to Catholic practices, and they dismissed Puritan ministers who refused to perform these "High Church" rites. Church courts, which judged cases involving religious law, harassed the Puritan laity with fines or excommunication.

Besides persecution, economic distress also drove Puritans into exile. Between 1550 and 1650, wages fell by half. Bad harvests and depressions plagued England. A 30 percent rise in population from 1590 to 1640 spawned massive unemployment. When economic crisis and the outbreak of the Thirty Years' War on the European continent prevented Germany from importing large amounts of English cloth after 1618, a deep recession gripped England's weaving industry, taking a severe toll on the heavily Puritan southeastern counties. In 1629 the Puritan John Winthrop surveyed his home county of Suffolk, recently a busy center of cloth

Decline in Real Wages in England, 1500–1700

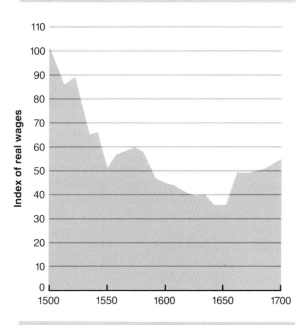

This index of real wages, which measures the drop in purchasing power due to inflation and declining wages, indicates that as the Great Migration began around 1630, living standards for English workers had suffered a steady reduction of about 60 percent since the base year, 1500.

SOURCE: E. H. Phelps Brown and S. V. Hopkins, "Builders' Wage-Rates, Prices and Population: Some Further Evidence," *Economica*, XXVI (1959), 18–38; adapted from D. C. North and R. P. Thomas, *The Rise of the Western World: A New Economic History* (Cambridge, England: Cambridge University Press, 1973), 111.

production, and cried out in anguish, "Why meet we so many wandering ghosts in the shape of men, so many spectacles of misery in our streets?"

In 1628 several Puritan merchants bought the claims of the Virginia Company of Plymouth, England, to land north of Plymouth colony between the Charles and Merrimack rivers. This group obtained a royal charter in 1629 to settle and govern the area.

A City upon a Hill

Four hundred Puritans arrived at Salem, Massachusetts, later in 1629 to prepare the way for others. Then in 1630 the company sent out its "great fleet" of eleven ships and seven hundred passengers under John Winthrop, who would serve as a governor of Massachusetts Bay almost continuously until 1649. In midvoyage the governor delivered a lay sermon titled "A Model of Christian Charity," describing the colony as a utopian alternative to old England.

Winthrop boldly announced that "we shall be as a city upon a hill, the eyes of all people are upon us." The settlers would build a godly community whose compelling example would shame England into repenting. The English government would then truly reform the church, and a revival of piety would create a nation of saints.

Winthrop denounced the self-destructive economic jealousy that bred class hatred. God intended that "in all times some must be rich and some poor," the governor explained, in order that the saints could display virtue appropriate to their station in life. The rich had an obligation to show charity and mercy; those less wealthy should live out their faith in God's will by demonstrating patience and

John Winthrop

During the passage to America, Winthrop urged his shipmates to build a society about which "men shall say of succeeding plantations: 'The Lord make it like that of New England.'"

fortitude. God expected the state's rulers to keep the greedy among the rich from exploiting the needy and to prevent the lazy among the poor from burdening their fellow citizens.

In outlining a divine plan in which all persons, rich and poor, depended on one another, Winthrop's sermon expressed a conservative European's understanding of traditional social reciprocity (see Chapter 1) and voiced the Puritans' deep dismay with the economic forces battering—and changing—English society. England had long since ceased to be a country of self-sufficient farm families living for generations in tight-knit communities. In most villages a handful of gentry landlords owned half the cultivated acreage; a small class of farmers known as yeomen—perhaps 20 percent of the rural population—held the rest; and about 30 percent of families achieved a decent standard of living by renting farms from the gentry or pursuing a craft. At the bottom of the social hierarchy, half or more of all English were landless laborers, servants, weavers, or spinners who had few possessions, raised little or none of their own food, and enjoyed no secure employment.

Winthrop's sermon implicitly criticized the breakdown of English society. Ever-growing numbers of desperate people tramped the road seeking work. Community ties frayed as villages experienced a turnover in population as high as 50 percent each decade. Family life deteriorated as household members scattered to find work. Perhaps a quarter of all children were hired out as servants to reside with strangers or were apprenticed to live with craftsmen willing to teach a trade that might save them from poverty.

The majority of England's people had no choice but to forsake their homes and compete fiercely for jobs. This floating population became increasingly individualistic, acquisitive, and materialistic. A new aggressiveness took root among vast numbers of brutalized people trapped in a market economy subject to frequent recessions.

Winthrop blamed this competitive spirit for fostering apathy toward human suffering. "What means then the bleating of so many oppressed with wrong," he had asked just before leaving England, "our shops full of rich wares, and under our stalls lye our own flesh in nakedness." Winthrop wanted charity to moderate the drive for profit, so that goods would be exchanged, wages set, and interest calculated in a manner that would allow a decent life for all. He expected the rich to serve God with their money, giving generously in time of need, and the less fortunate to sacrifice their time to serve in church, government, or the military.

Winthrop's shipboard sermon exemplified the main difference between New England's settlement and British colonization elsewhere. Other Englishmen in the New World would display the same acquisitive impulses transforming England, in particular by harshly exploiting labor. But the Puritans, while hoping for prosperity, believed that there were limits to legitimate commercial behavior. Puritans thought that moral self-restraint—or if need be, the government—should prevent merchants from taking advantage of shortages to squeeze out "excessive" profits. Above all, they hoped to turn religious idealism into a renewed sense of community. "It is a great thing," wrote an early New Englander, "to be a foundation stone in such a spiritual building." Massachusetts Bay would not be an extension of England but a reaction to it.

The Way of the Saints

Winthrop and the great fleet arrived in June 1630 at Boston harbor, and by fall six towns had sprung up in the city's modern limits. During the unusually severe first winter, 30 percent of Winthrop's party died, and an additional 10 percent went home in the spring. By mid-1631, however, thirteen hundred new settlers had landed, and more were on the way. The worst was over. The colony would never suffer another starving time. In contrast to early Virginia, Massachusetts Bay attracted disciplined, motivated men and women who established the colony on a firm basis within a year.

As non-Separatists, Massachusetts Puritans considered themselves spiritual members of the Church of England, but they created a system of church governance called congregationalism that completely ignored the authority of Anglican bishops. More than any other person, the Reverend John Cotton shaped American congregationalism. Called by some a walking library, this clergyman's prestige was so great that according to a fellow minister, Massachusetts settlers "could hardly believe that God would suffer Mr. Cotton to err."

Cotton's plan for governing the New England church placed control of each congregation squarely

Two Sketches of an Early Plymouth Meetinghouse *(left)*; **Interior of the "Old Ship Church," Hingham, Massachusetts** *(right)*

One early New Englander boasted that his community's meetinghouse had been erected "by our own vote, framed by our own hammers and saws, and by our own hands set in the convenientest place for us all." Hingham's First Parish Meeting House (1681, right) was built by ship carpenters. They simply constructed a ship's keel in reverse for the interior roof.

in the hands of the male saints. By majority vote these men chose their minister, elected a board of "elders" to handle finances, decided who else deserved recognition as saints, and otherwise ran the church. In contrast, in a typical English parish, a powerful gentry family would select a new pastor (subject to a bishop's formal approval), and all other important decisions would be made by the parish council, or vestry, which was virtually always composed of wealthy landlords rather than ordinary church members. New England thus allowed for much more democratic control of the church than did Anglicanism.

Congregationalism fused separating and non-separating Puritanism. Congregational churches followed the Separatist tradition by allowing only

saints to take communion and baptize their children, but as in non-Separatist practice, they obliged all adults (except a few scandalously wicked individuals) to attend services and pay set rates (or tithes) for their support. New England thus had a state-sponsored, or "established," church, whose relationship to civil government was symbolized by the fact that a single building—called a meetinghouse rather than a church—was used for both religious services and town business.

This "New England Way" also diverged from English practices by setting higher standards for identifying the elect. English Puritans usually accepted as saints those who could correctly profess the faith, had repented their sins, and lived free of scandal. Massachusetts Puritans, however, insisted that candidates for membership undergo a soul-baring examination before the congregation and describe their spiritual life and conversion experience—a procedure called the conversion relation.

English Puritans strongly criticized the conversion relation as an unnecessary barrier to membership that would intimidate humble saints who felt awkward about having neighbors vote on their state of grace. Many early Puritans shared the reluctance of Jonathan Fairbanks, who refused to give a public profession of grace before the church in Dedham, Massachusetts, for several years, until the faithful persuaded him with many "loving conferences." One Dublin, New Hampshire, woman who was denied membership after being overcome by nervousness started sobbing uncontrollably and cried out, "*Christ* hath called me, and bid me *come* . . . and shall I now be put by?" Ashamed and somewhat misty-eyed themselves, the congregation relented, but the episode perfectly showed the conversion relation's potential for causing embarrassment and pain. The conversion relation would emerge as the New England Way's most vulnerable point and a major cause of its eventual demise.

New Englanders, like most European Protestants, could scarcely imagine conversion without literacy. Fathers drilled their children in the catechism, a simple question-and-answer summary of religious beliefs. Young people read the Bible to feel the quickening of God's grace, and saints often recorded their lapses and spiritual insights in diaries. In 1642 Massachusetts Bay colony, concerned about parental laxness, ordered households to conduct regular catechism sessions. Evidently this did not suffice, because in 1647 the colony passed its famous Old Deluder Act. The law ordered every town of fifty or more households to appoint one father to whom all children could come for instruction, and every town of at least one hundred households to maintain a grammar school and a teacher capable of preparing students for university-level instruction. The law's name derived from its declaration that "one chief project of that old deluder, Satan, [is] to keep men from knowledge of the Scriptures" by encouraging ignorance. By 1671 most other Puritan colonies enacted similar legislation, which represented New England's first step toward public education even though none of these laws

required school attendance, and though boys were more likely to be taught reading and writing than were girls. In any case, the family remained New England's chief bastion against ignorance, as Boston's First Church recognized in 1669 when it ordered the congregation's elders to visit all households "and see how they are instructed in the grounds [elements] of religion."

But however diligent laypeople might be in reading the Bible and indoctrinating their children, clergymen had responsibility for leading saints to repentance and stimulating piety. The minister's role was to stir his parishioners' faith with direct, logical, and moving sermons understandable by average listeners, not just by a well-educated elite. The Puritans' preference for this "plain style" of preaching did not blind them to the need for a highly educated clergy. To produce learned ministers, Massachusetts chartered Harvard College in 1636.

Harvard not only trained ministers but also offered instruction in the arts and sciences. Freshmen entered Harvard as young teen-agers after demonstrating an ability to write and speak Latin and a knowledge of Greek grammar. Harvard

Harvard College

An eighteenth-century woman depicted the college—an institution that excluded her gender—in needlework.

offered a single curriculum emphasizing classical languages, logic, philosophy, and divinity. All students left their tiny four-by-six-foot rooms at 4:30 A.M. for a breakfast of bread and beer. After prayers at 5:00 A.M., students went to study hall prior to lectures, all given in Latin, from 8:00 to 11:00 A.M. Then came the main meal, washed down with more beer and eaten indoors with everyone wearing hats. After a recreation hour, tutors quizzed underclassmen in the morning lecture as upperclassmen gave Latin speeches before the president. At 4:00 P.M. all students broke for additional beer and bread before attending prayers at 5:00 P.M., after which came a study hour, a light supper, another recreation hour, and finally bed at 9:00 P.M.

Harvard's insistence on high standards led Oxford University in England to recognize Harvard degrees as equivalent to its own by 1648. From 1642 to 1671, the college produced 201 graduates, including 111 ministers. Harvard's alumni made New England the only part of England's overseas empire to possess a college-educated elite during the seventeenth century, and they ensured that the New England Way would not falter for lack of properly trained clergy.

Dissent and Expansion

Some Puritans dissented from Winthrop's vision of the city upon a hill. The first to challenge the New England Way was Roger Williams, who arrived in America in 1631. Williams was one of those rare individuals who stir controversy without making personal enemies. Radiating the joy of serving God, he quickly became one of the most respected and popular figures in Massachusetts. But Williams questioned the legal basis of congregationalism. Once he began to insist that church and state be entirely separate, the Massachusetts Bay government moved to silence him.

Puritans agreed that the church must be free of state control, and they opposed theocracy (government run by clergy). However, they believed that a holy commonwealth required cooperation between church and state. Williams took a different stance, arguing that civil government should remain absolutely uninvolved with religious matters, whether blasphemy (cursing God), failure to pay tithes, refusal to attend worship, or swearing oaths on the Bible in court. He derived this posi-

tion from the sixteenth-century Anabaptist tradition (see Chapter 1), which held that the elect must limit their association with society's sinners to protect God's church from contamination. Williams opposed any kind of compulsory church service or interference with private religious beliefs, not because he felt that all religions deserved equal respect (for he did not) but because he feared that the state would eventually corrupt the saints.

Believing that the very purpose of founding Massachusetts Bay was to protect true religion and prevent heresy, the political authorities declared Williams's opinions subversive and banished him in 1635. At his friend Winthrop's suggestion, he went south with four companions to a place that he called Providence, which he purchased from the Indians. At Williams's invitation, a steady stream of malcontents drifted to the group of settlements near Providence on Narragansett Bay, which eventually joined to form Rhode Island colony. (Orthodox Puritans scorned the place as "Rogues Island.") In 1644 Williams obtained permission from England to establish a legal government. True to Williams's ideals, Rhode Island was the only New England colony to practice religious toleration. Growing slowly, the colony's four towns had eight hundred settlers by 1650.

A second challenge to the New England Way came from Anne Hutchinson, whom Winthrop described as "a woman of haughty and fierce carriage, of a nimble wit and active spirit." The controversy surrounding Hutchinson was especially ironic since her ideas derived from the much-respected John Cotton's theology. Cotton insisted that true congregationalism required the saints to be entirely free of religious or political control by anyone who had not undergone a conversion experience. His refusal to give any authority or power over religion to the nonelect applied even to persons who led upright, blameless lives—at least until they had been reborn spiritually.

Anne Hutchinson extended Cotton's main point—that the saints must be free from interference by the nonelect—into a broad attack on clerical authority. Dissatisfied with the dull minister of her church, she began implying that he was not among the elect, and then asserted that the saints in his congregation might ignore his views if they believed that he lacked saving grace. She eventually alleged that all the colony's ministers except John

Cotton and her brother-in-law John Wheelwright had not been born again and so lacked authority over those, like herself, who were already saved.

By casting doubt on the clergy's spiritual state and denying the right of unsaved ministers to judge the saints, Hutchinson undermined the clergy's moral authority to interpret and teach Scripture. Critics charged that her beliefs would delude individuals into imagining that they were accountable to no one but themselves. Her followers consequently were called Antinomians, meaning those opposed to the rule of law. Hutchinson bore the additional liability of being a woman challenging traditional male roles in the church and state. The authorities would have prosecuted Hutchinson had she been a man, of course, but her gender made her seem an especially dangerous foe.

By 1636 Massachusetts Bay split into two camps. Hutchinson's supporters included merchants (like her husband) who disliked the government's economic restrictions on their business; young men chafing against the rigid control of church elders; and most women, protesting their exclusion from voting in church affairs. In 1636 the Antinomians were strong enough to have their

candidate elected governor, but they suffered defeat with Winthrop's return to office in 1637.

The victorious Winthrop brought Hutchinson to trial for heresy before the Massachusetts Bay legislature (the General Court). While John Cotton watched nervously, the legislators peppered her with questions. Hutchinson's knowledge of Scripture was so superior to that of her interrogators, however, that she would have been acquitted had she not claimed to have communicated directly with the Holy Spirit. Like virtually all Christians, orthodox Puritans believed that God had ceased to make known matters of faith by personal revelation since New Testament times. Thus Hutchinson's own words were sufficient to condemn her.

The General Court banished Hutchinson to Rhode Island. She later moved to New Netherland, where in 1643 she was killed by Indians. John Wheelwright led another exodus of Antinomians to Exeter, New Hampshire. Antinomianism's failure ended the last challenge capable of splitting congregationalism and ensured the New England Way's survival for two generations.

A less dramatic disagreement over the New England Way helped push yet a third wave of Puri-

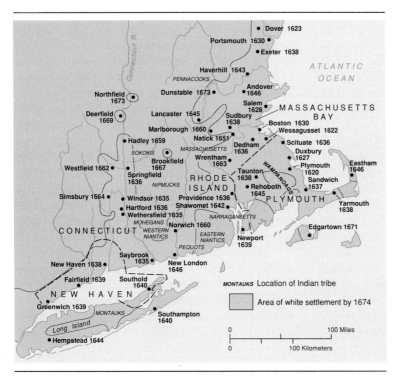

Colonizing New England, 1620–1674

Puritan expansion reached its maximum extent just before King Philip's War (see p. 59), which erupted largely as a result of the pressure of encroaching white settlement on the Wampanoags. New England's frontier did not expand beyond the area reached in 1674 until after 1715.

SOURCE: Frederick Merk, *History of the Westward Movement.* Copyright © 1979 by Lois Bannister Merk. Reprinted by permission of Alfred A. Knopf, Inc.

tans outside Massachusetts. Congregations at Dorchester and Newtown (present-day Cambridge) rejected the rigorous standards advocated by John Cotton for identifying the elect. Newtown's minister, Thomas Hooker, in particular took a more liberal attitude than Cotton toward admitting church members. Both groups asked the General Court's permission to relocate in the lower Connecticut River Valley, where unauthorized settlements had appeared at Windsor (1633) and Wethersfield (1634).

The General Court approved the settlers' plans, provided they would remain subject to Massachusetts authority for at least a year. In 1635 the Dorchester congregation went to Windsor. In 1636 Hooker and his congregation walked 120 miles to Hartford. Hooker's influence helped moderate Puritanism in Connecticut by establishing standards for church membership less strict than those in Massachusetts.

In 1639 Hartford, Windsor, and Wethersfield adopted a government, designed by Thomas Hooker, called the Fundamental Orders of Connecticut. Hooker modeled his government after that of Massachusetts Bay. Voting and officeholding were opened to all adult male landowners.

The southeastern third of modern-day Connecticut remained outside this agreement. Under John Davenport, a minister who felt that both Massachusetts Bay and Connecticut allowed too much moral laxness, this region set the strictest standards for verifying sainthood and based its laws most closely upon Old Testament examples. In 1643 the eight towns of this area united as the colony of New Haven.

The most fundamental threat to Winthrop's city upon a hill was that the people would abandon the ideal of a close-knit community to pursue self-interest. Although most Puritans welcomed the chance to found villages dedicated to stability, self-discipline, and a sense of mutual obligation, a large minority had come to America to find prosperity and social mobility. The most visibly ambitious colonists were merchants, whose activities fueled New England's economy but whose way of life challenged its ideals.

Merchants fit uneasily into a religious utopia that idealized social reciprocity and equated financial shrewdness with greed. They also clashed repeatedly with government leaders, who were trying to regulate prices so that consumers would not suffer from the chronic shortage of manufactured goods that afflicted New England.

In 1635, when the Massachusetts General Court forbade the sale of any item above 5 percent of its cost, Robert Keayne of Boston and other merchants objected. These men argued that they had to sell some goods at higher rates in order to offset losses from other sales, shipwrecked cargoes, and inflation. In 1639, after selling nails at 25 percent to 33 percent above cost—hardly profiteering—Keayne was fined heavily in court and forced to make a humiliating apology before his congregation.

Though a pious Puritan whose annual profits averaged just 5 percent, Keayne symbolized the dangerous possibility that a headlong rush for profits would lead New Englanders to forget that they were their brothers' keepers. "Worldly gain was not the end design of the people of *New-England*," warned the Reverend John Higginson, "but *Religion*." Controversies like the one involving Keayne were part of a struggle for New England's soul. At stake was the Puritans' ability to insulate their city upon a hill from a market economy that would strangle the spirit of community within a harsh new world of frantic competition.

Power to the Saints

To preserve the New England Way, the Puritans evolved political and religious institutions far more democratic than those in the mother country. Unlike the Virginia Company of London, the Massachusetts Bay Company established its headquarters in America and gave the right of electing the governor and his executive council to all male saints. In 1634, after public protest that the governor and council held too much power, each town gained the option of sending two delegates to the General Court. In 1644 the General Court became a bicameral (two-chamber) lawmaking body when the towns' deputies separated from the Governor's Council to form the House of Representatives.

Massachusetts did not require voters or officeholders to own property but bestowed full citizenship on every adult male accepted as a saint. By 1641 about 55 percent of the colony's twenty-three hundred men could vote. By contrast, English property requirements allowed fewer than 30 percent of adult males to vote.

Old England's basic unit of local government was the county court. Its members, the justices of the peace, not only decided legal cases as judges but also performed such administrative tasks as supervising road repairs, maintaining public buildings, and assessing taxes for official expenses. Gaining office by royal appointment rather than election, the justices were always members of the gentry selected because of their wealth and political connections. But an ocean away, New England's county courts primarily functioned as courts of law, and the vital unit of local administration was the town meeting. Town meetings decentralized authority over political and economic decisions to a degree unknown in either Great Britain or its other overseas colonies.

New England legislatures established a town by awarding a grant of land to several dozen heads of families. These individuals enjoyed almost unlimited freedom to lay out the settlement, organize its church, distribute land among themselves, set local tax rates, and make local laws. Each town determined its own qualifications for voting and holding office in the town meeting, although custom dictated that all male taxpayers (including non-saints) be allowed to participate. The meeting could exclude anyone from settling in town, or it could

grant the right of sharing in any future land distributions to newcomers, whose children would inherit this privilege.

Community Life

The local economy and environment left their stamp on New England towns. Of these communities the seaports often seemed least tight-knit because of their transient population, while towns in Plymouth colony tended to be little more than a few stores, a mill, and a meetinghouse serving farmers dwelling over a wide distance. Nevertheless, towns in Massachusetts, Connecticut, and what would become New Hampshire (part of Massachusetts until 1679) were broadly uniform, since most were farm communities resembling traditional English villages.

The founders usually granted each family a one-acre house lot (just enough for a vegetable garden) within a half-mile of the meetinghouse. The town meeting also gave each household strips of land or small fields farther out for its crops and livestock. Often an individual owned several parcels of land in different locations and had the

The Whipple House

This Ipswich, Massachusetts, home, part of which dates to c. 1640, is thought to be one of the oldest Anglo-American dwellings extant.

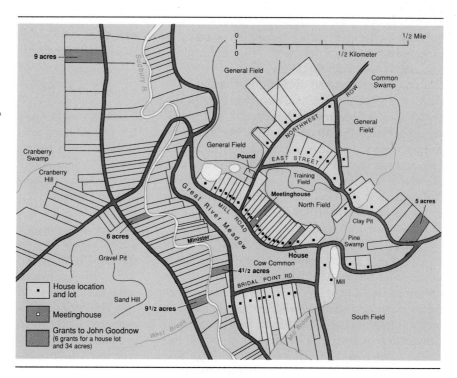

Land Divisions in Sudbury, Massachusetts, 1639–1656

Like other first-generation townsmen, John Goodnow lived on a small house lot near the meetinghouse. He pastured his livestock on "common" fields owned by the town and grew crops on thirty-four acres in five separate locations at a distance from his house.

SOURCE: Sumner Chilton Powell, *Puritan Village: The Formation of a New England Town* (Middletown, Conn.: Wesleyan University Press, 1963). Reprinted by permission.

right to graze a few extra animals on the town "commons."

Few aspects of early New England life are more revealing than the first generation's attempt in many, but not all, towns to keep settlement tightly clustered by granting families no more land than they needed to support themselves. Dedham's forty-six founders, for example, received 128,000 acres from Massachusetts Bay in 1636 yet gave themselves just 3,000 acres by 1656, or about 65 acres per family.

By separating a family's home from its farm acreage and forcing all residents to live within a mile of one another, town founders created a physical setting conducive to traditional reciprocity. In England, meanwhile, this mode of land division was coming to seem inefficient as farmers tried to produce a greater surplus for sale by consolidating their landholdings. By 1600 English agriculturalists preferred to live on scattered farms away from village centers, even though dispersion increased the difficulty of maintaining neighborly ties. New England's generally compact system of settlement forced people to interact with each other and also established an atmosphere of mutual watchfulness that promoted godly order.

Puritan Families

To the Puritans, society's foundation rested not upon the individual but upon the "little commonwealth"—the nuclear family. "*Well ordered families,*" declared minister Cotton Mather in 1699, "naturally produce a *Good Order* in other *Societies.*" In a proper Puritan family, the wife, children, and servants dutifully obeyed the husband. According to John Winthrop, a "true wife" thought of herself "in subjection to her husband's authority."

New Englanders defined matrimony as a contract subject to state regulation rather than a religious sacrament and so were married by justices of the peace instead of ministers. As a civil institution, a marriage could be dissolved by the courts in cases of desertion, bigamy, adultery, or physical cruelty. By permitting divorce, Puritans diverged radically from practices in England, where Anglican authorities rarely annulled marriages and civil divorces required a special act of Parliament. Still, New Englanders saw divorce as a remedy fit only for extremely wronged spouses, such as the Plymouth woman who discovered that her husband was simultaneously married to women in Boston, Barbados, and England. Massachusetts courts allowed just twenty-seven divorces from 1639 to 1692.

Because Puritans believed that healthy families were crucial to the community's welfare, they intervened whenever they discovered truly serious problems in a household. The courts disciplined unruly youngsters, disobedient servants, disrespectful wives, and violent or irresponsible husbands whose behavior seemed dangerous or unusually disruptive to a family. Churches also censured, and sometimes expelled, spouses who did not maintain domestic tranquillity. Negligent parents, one minister declared, "not only wrong each other, but they provoke God by breaking his law."

Although New England wives enjoyed significant legal protections against spousal violence and nonsupport and also had more freedom than their English counterparts to escape a failed marriage, they suffered the same legal disabilities borne by all Englishwomen. English common law allowed a wife no property rights independently of her husband unless he consented to a special prenuptial agreement giving her control over any property that she already owned. Only if a husband had no other heirs or wrote a will awarding his widow full control over their possessions could she claim rights over household property, although the law reserved lifetime use of a third of the estate for her support.

The structure and stability of New England families differed fundamentally from English households. In Great Britain infectious diseases combined with poor nutrition to produce steep levels of early death among adults, as well as high infant mortality. The typical male who reached age 18 could expect to die at about 53, while 18-year-old females on average faced an even shorter life span, to about 45, because so many pregnancies ended in death. English people married relatively late in the early seventeenth century, so that a typical family had just five children, of whom three would reach adulthood. Because perhaps one in six adults never married, this survival rate produced relatively modest population increases. So short was the span of life that, considering the late age of marriage, perhaps half of all English parents did not live long enough to see their first grandchild born. Most women who married in Manchester, England, in the 1650s, for example, were already orphans upon becoming brides.

In contrast, New England benefited from a remarkably benign disease environment. Although

Death in Seventeenth-Century New England

In the early years of settlement, the grave of the deceased was typically located on family land and marked by a plain stone. As the century unfolded, however, cemeteries increasingly sprang up near the meetinghouse, and intricately carved stones adorned the graves.

settlements were compact, minimal travel occurred between towns, especially in winter, when people were most susceptible to infection. Furthermore, easy access to land allowed families an adequate diet, which improved resistance to disease and lowered death rates associated with childbirth.

Consequently, New Englanders lived long and raised large families. Life expectancy for men reached 65, and women lived nearly that long. More than 80 percent of all infants survived long enough to get married. The 58 men and women who founded Andover, Massachusetts, for example, had 247 children; and by the fourth generation, the families of their descendants numbered 2,000 persons (including spouses who married in from other families). Despite the relatively small size and short duration of the Puritan exodus to New England (just 20,000 immigrants landed from 1630 to 1642, after which few newcomers arrived), the fact that about 70 percent of all settlers came as members of family groups soon resulted in a population evenly divided between males and females. This balance permitted rapid population growth without heavy immigration.

Its extraordinary rate of population growth enabled New England to become the only part of England's overseas empire that did not import large

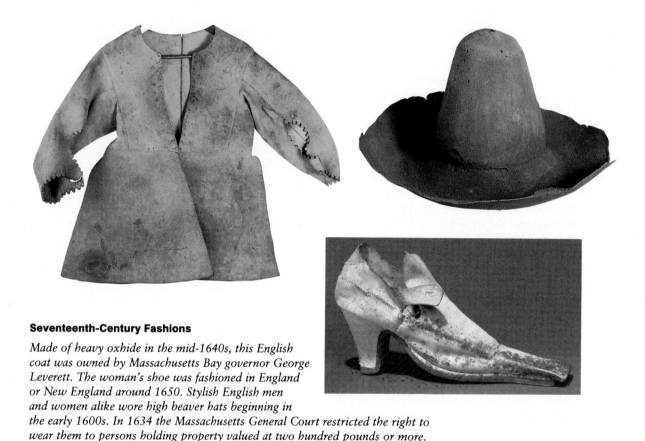

Seventeenth-Century Fashions

Made of heavy oxhide in the mid-1640s, this English coat was owned by Massachusetts Bay governor George Leverett. The woman's shoe was fashioned in England or New England around 1650. Stylish English men and women alike wore high beaver hats beginning in the early 1600s. In 1634 the Massachusetts General Court restricted the right to wear them to persons holding property valued at two hundred pounds or more.

numbers of indentured servants or slaves. Labor was in especially short supply in the first decades of settlement, when the colonists had to build towns and clear fields from dense forest. The first generation brought its labor with it, in the form of its own children.

Lacking any legal right to share in town land divisions until they became their fathers' heirs, the founding generation's children depended on their parents to provide them with acreage for a farm. Parents encouraged children, especially sons, to delay marriage and work for them in return for a bequest of land at a later date. Young males often stayed at home to till their fathers' fields until their late twenties, when they finally received their own land. Because the average family raised three or four boys to adulthood, parents could depend on thirty to forty years of work if their sons delayed marriage until about age twenty-six.

Families with more sons and daughters enjoyed a labor surplus that allowed them to send their children to work as apprentices or hired hands for others. However, this system of family labor was inefficient, for two reasons. First, the available supply of labor could not expand in times of great demand. Second, parents were reluctant to force their own children to work as hard as strangers. Nevertheless, family labor was the only system that New Englanders could afford.

Saddled with the triple burdens of a short growing season, rocky soil salted with gravel, and an inefficient system of land distribution that forced farmers to cultivate widely scattered strips, the colonists managed to feed large families and keep ahead of their debts, but few became wealthy from farming. Seeking greater fortunes than agriculture offered, seventeenth-century New Englanders soon turned lumbering, fishing, and rum distilling into major industries employing perhaps a fifth of all adults full-time and offering seasonal work to many farmers. As its economy became more diversified, New England prospered. But in the process, its inhabitants grew more worldly, only to discover that fewer and fewer of their children were emerging as saints.

The End of the Puritan Errand

As New Englanders struggled to make a living and curb dissent, old England fell into chaos. Charles I's efforts to impose taxes without Parliament's consent sparked a civil war in 1642. Alienated by years of religious harassment, Puritans gained control of the revolt, beheaded Charles in 1649, and eventually replaced the king with "Lord High Protector" Oliver Cromwell. Shortly after Cromwell's death, a provisional English government recalled the Stuarts and in 1660 crowned Charles II king.

The Stuart restoration doomed Puritanism in England. High Church Anglicans ruthlessly expelled Puritan ministers from their parishes and passed harsh laws forbidding Separatists from establishing churches and schools. One English saint summed up Puritan disillusionment: "God has spit in our face." The Restoration also left American Puritans without a mission. A generation of New England ministers had inspired their congregations to hope that their example would shame England into establishing a truly reformed church. However, having conquered a wilderness and built their city upon a hill, New Englanders discovered after 1660 that the eyes of the world were no longer fixed on them.

Simultaneously with the demise of English Puritanism, an internal crisis gripped the New England Way. The turmoil stemmed from the failure of the founding generation's children to declare themselves saints and accept full church membership. By 1650, for example, fewer than half the adults in John Winthrop's congregation were saints. The first generation believed that they had accepted a holy contract, or covenant, with God, which obliged them to establish a scripturally ordained church and charge their descendants with its preservation. In return for upholding this New England Way, God would make the city upon a hill prosper and shield it from corruption.

By 1650, however, relatively few second-generation Puritans had been willing to join the elect by making the required conversion relation before their congregation. One reason certainly was the

second generation's understandable reluctance to subject themselves to a grilling before relatives and friends. All children who matured in Puritan towns must have witnessed at least one person suffer an ordeal like that of Sarah Fiske. For more than a year, Fiske answered petty charges of speaking uncharitably about her relatives—especially her husband, Phineas—and then was admitted to the Wenham, Massachusetts, church only after publicly denouncing herself as worse "than any toad."

Through its passivity, the second generation expressed its preference for a more inclusive religious community, organized on traditional English practices for admitting saints to Puritan congregations. In England non-Separatist ministers had routinely certified adults as members worthy of taking communion upon hearing a private conversion relation, and they baptized *all* children. The second generation in America also rejected the public conversion-relation ritual as an unnecessary source of division and bitterness that undermined Christian fellowship. In this they differed from their parents, who used the conversion relation to affirm godly order by setting the highest standards for moral conduct.

Because Puritan churches baptized only babies born to saints, the second generation's unwillingness to submit to the conversion relation confronted their parents with the prospect that their own grandchildren would remain unbaptized unless standards for church membership were loosened. In 1662 a convention of clergy and laity devised a compromise known as the Half-Way Covenant, which permitted the children of all baptized members, including nonsaints, to receive baptism. This covenant allowed the founders' descendants to transmit church membership to their children, but it left these offspring "halfway" members who could not take communion or vote in church affairs. When forced to choose between a church system founded on a pure membership of the elect and one that embraced the entire community, New Englanders eventually sacrificed purity for community.

The Half-Way Covenant signaled the end of the New England Way. The elect had been unable to bring up a new generation of saints whose religious fervor equaled their own. Most adults chose to remain in "halfway" status for life, and the saints became a shrinking minority as the third and fourth generations matured. Sainthood tended to flow in certain families, and by the 1700s there were more women among the elect than men in most congregations. But since women could not vote in church affairs, religious authority stayed in male hands.

The Eclipse of the Indians

One reason why the Puritans spread so rapidly across New England was the utter devastation of the region's native population well before the English arrived. Microbes introduced by fishermen and other casual visitors killed perhaps 90 percent of New England's coastal Indians between 1616 and 1618, and the earliest Puritan immigrants had faced little opposition from the demoralized native survivors. After declining from 20,000 in 1600 to a mere 750 in 1631, the Massachusett tribe came under attack by Micmacs from eastern Canada and soon emerged as the first native Americans to become a colonized people in their own land. The Massachusett people sought military protection from Winthrop's settlers so eagerly that they sold most of their land by 1636, surrendered their independence in 1644, and agreed to try Christianity and "civilization" by moving to "praying towns" like Natick, a place given them by the General Court. In the praying towns, leaders chosen by the Puritans would teach the native Americans Christianity and English ways.

The expansion of English settlement nevertheless aroused Indian resistance. As Puritans moved into the Connecticut River Valley, friction developed with the Pequots, a populous tribe less affected than others by earlier epidemics and whose name meant "Destroyer" in Algonkian. After an attack on two ships and the killing of several sailors near Pequot territory, an expedition from Puritan Massachusetts marched into Connecticut in 1636 to take revenge on that tribe, although the Indians' guilt in the incident had never been firmly established. An alarmed English farmer at Saybrook, Connecticut, angrily protested to the invaders, "You come hither to raise these wasps about my ears, and then you will take wing and flee away."

After clumsily plundering an Indian village, the Massachusetts troops did return home, leaving Connecticut's 800 settlers to face 3,500 enraged enemies. Pequot raids took about thirty lives through April 1637, by which time the settlers had won allies among the Mohegan and Narragansett Indians. Heeding Thomas Hooker's stern advice "not to do this work of the Lord's revenge slackly," Captain John Mason then waged a ruthless campaign, using tactics similar to those devised by the English to break Irish resistance during the 1570s (see Chapter 1). Mason's troops made no distinction between warriors and civilians—and they took few prisoners. By late 1637 perhaps 800 Pequots were killed, and the Puritans' native American allies were daily carrying heads to Hartford for rewards.

This so-called Pequot War tipped the balance of military power to the English by smashing the Pequots, the region's most feared Indian nation. Opening the way for central New England's swift settlement, the war sped up the tendency for small Indian tribes to become dependent on whites as they found themselves surrounded by white settlement. The English victory in 1637 proved so decisive that New England remained at peace until 1676.

As white settlers moved onto the Indians' traditional lands, Puritan missionaries, believing that Christianity was incompatible with native American culture, widened efforts to convert them. Unlike missionaries from France and Spain, who appealed to the Indians' appreciation of ceremony and related Catholic doctrines to native American beliefs, the Puritans insisted that the converts master a complex theology of salvation completely foreign to Indian thinking. Only after suffering the shock of disease and depopulation, cultural disintegration, economic dependence, and submission to white government did any New England Indians accept Protestantism. From the founding of Natick in 1651 to 1675, John Eliot, New England's foremost missionary, coaxed Indians into a total of fourteen praying towns, which in this way became Anglo-America's first Indian reservations.

The "praying Indians," as the converts were known, worshiped in their own language and listened to Scripture read from Eliot's Algonkian-language *Up-Biblum God,* the first Bible printed in Anglo-America (1663). Cut off from their own culture and bombarded with alien concepts of sinfulness, converted Indians often acquired a highly negative self-image, experiencing confusion, depression, and excessive preoccupation with shame and guilt. Few red Puritans were ever baptized as saints, and only two praying towns established congregations free of outside white control.

By 1675 European diseases had steadily reduced New England's Indian population from 140,000 in 1600 to 10,000, of whom 2,000 lived in praying

John Eliot

Eliot's Algonkian translation of the Bible, Up-Biblum God *(1663), was the first Bible printed in America.*

towns. Meanwhile, the number of English had swollen to 50,000. White-Indian conflict became acute during the 1670s because of pressure imposed on several major tribes, surrounded by white settlers, to accept the legal authority of colonial courts. Tension ran especially high in the Plymouth colony, where the English had engulfed the large Wampanoag tribe and forced a number of humiliating concessions on their leader Metacomet, or "King Philip," the son of Massasoit, the Pilgrims' onetime ally.

In 1675 Plymouth hanged three Wampanoags for killing a Christian Indian and threatened to arrest Philip. A minor incident in which several Wampanoags were shot while burglarizing a farmhouse produced a steady escalation of violence; and Philip soon organized about two-thirds of the native Americans, including perhaps a third of all praying Indians, into a military alliance. "But little remains of my ancestor's domain, I am resolved not to see the day when I have no country," Philip declared as he and his followers ignited the conflict known as King Philip's War.

Philip's forces—unlike the Indian combatants in the Pequot War, few of whom had fought with guns—were as well armed as the whites. The Indians attacked 52 of New England's 90 towns (of which 12 were entirely destroyed), burned 1,200 houses, slaughtered 8,000 head of cattle, and killed 600 colonists.

The tide turned against Philip in 1676. English militiamen and praying Indians destroyed their enemies' food supplies and sold hundreds of captives into slavery, including Philip's wife and child. "It must have been as bitter as death to him," wrote Puritan clergyman Cotton Mather, "to lose his wife and only son, for the Indians are marvellously fond and affectionate toward their children." Perhaps three thousand Indians starved or fell in battle, including Philip himself.

King Philip's War reduced New England's Indian population by almost 40 percent and eliminated native American resistance to white expansion everywhere in the region except Maine and along the Canadian border. It also generated in whites an abiding hatred of all native Americans, even the Christian Indians who fought Philip. In 1677 ten praying towns were disbanded and all Indians restricted to the remaining four; all Indian courts were dismantled; and "guardians" were appointed to supervise the native Americans. Missionary activity largely ceased. "There is a cloud, a dark cloud upon the work of the Gospel among the poor Indians," mourned John Eliot. The surviving Indians became a steadily dwindling underclass of servants and tenants widely afflicted by poverty, debt, and alcoholism.

Economics, Salem, and Satan

In the three decades after the Half-Way Covenant's adoption in 1662, New Englanders endured an endless stream of sermons called jeremiads (after ancient Israel's prophet Jeremiah), in which the clergy berated them for failing to preserve the idealism of the region's founding generation. The ministers complained not about rising sinfulness—for the people remained law-abiding, industrious, and sober—but about their parishioners' increasing tendency to forget, as one minister emphasized in 1663, "that New-England is originally a plantation of Religion, not a plantation of trade." The jeremiads indicted New Englanders for becoming more worldly, more individualistic, and less patient with restrictions on their economic behavior.

By the late seventeenth century, growing opportunities for personal success, born of an expanding economy, were changing New England's character. Although the earliest Puritan settlers had hardly lacked economic ambitions, their overriding need for cooperation and unity while building a society from scratch led them to emphasize collective welfare above individual interest. By 1690, however, the problems facing towns or congregations—far less serious than in the early years—no longer required the same degree of communal effort. New Englanders now turned their energies into producing more goods for export and otherwise profiting from overseas trade or the local market economy.

As New Englanders pursued economic gain more openly, the fabric of community loosened and populations began dispersing away from town centers. Eager to expand their agricultural output, townsmen voted themselves much larger amounts of land after 1660 and insisted that it be located in one place. For example, Dedham, which distributed only three thousand acres from 1636 to 1656, parceled out five times as much in the next dozen years. Rather than continue living close together, farmers built homes on their outlying tracts and thereby sacrificed the close, neighborly ties that previously had arisen from frequent association. This process of "hiving out" often generated friction between townspeople settled near the meetinghouse (who usually dominated politics) and the "outlivers," whose distance from the town center generally limited their influence over local affairs.

Although early New England was hardly a simple society of subsistence farmers, a rough equality had prevailed among its residents, most of whom were small landowners with few luxuries. By the late seventeenth century, however, the region's occupational structure had become very complex, especially in its several port cities, and the distribution of wealth was growing more uneven. These developments undermined the spirit of community by sowing jealousy and creating the anxiety that a small minority might be profiting at the majority's expense. At the same time, New England's rising involvement in international trade led individuals—in both cities and the countryside—to act more competitively, aggressively, and impersonally toward one another. John Winthrop's vision of a religiously oriented community

sustained by a sense of reciprocity and charity was giving way to a world increasingly like the materialistic, acquisitive society that the original immigrants had fled in old England.

Nowhere in New England did these trends have more disturbing effects than in Salem, Massachusetts, which grew rapidly after 1660 to become the region's second-largest port. Trade made Salem prosperous but also destroyed the relatively equal society of humble fishermen and small farmers that had once existed. A sharp distinction emerged between the port's residents—especially its rich merchants—and outlying farmers. Prior to 1661 the richest 10 percent of Salem residents owned 21 percent of the town's property, but by 1681 the richest tenth possessed 62 percent of all wealth.

Salem's farmers lost not only social standing to the merchants but also political power. Before 1665 twice as many farmers as merchants had held the town meeting's highest offices, but thereafter, merchant officeholders outnumbered those who were farmers by six to one. Salem became highly vulnerable to internal conflict between its prosperous merchants and its agricultural folk.

About six miles west of Salem's meetinghouse lay the precinct of Salem Village (now Danvers), an economically stagnant district whose residents resented Salem Town's political domination. The village was divided between supporters of the Porter and Putnam families. Well connected with the merchant elite, the Porters enjoyed political prestige in Salem Town and lived in the village's eastern section, whose residents farmed richer soils and benefited somewhat from Salem Town's prosperity. In contrast, most Putnams lived in Salem Village's less fertile western half, had little chance to share in Salem Town's commercial expansion, and had lost the political influence that they once held in town. The rivalry between Porters and Putnams mirrored the tensions between Salem's urban and rural dwellers.

In late 1691 several Salem Village girls encouraged a West Indian slave woman, Tituba, to tell fortunes and talk about sorcery. When the girls later began behaving strangely, villagers assumed that they were victims of witchcraft. Pressed to identify their tormenters, the girls named an ill-tempered beggar, a bedridden old woman, and Tituba.

So far the incident was not unusual. Until the late seventeenth century, belief in witchcraft was

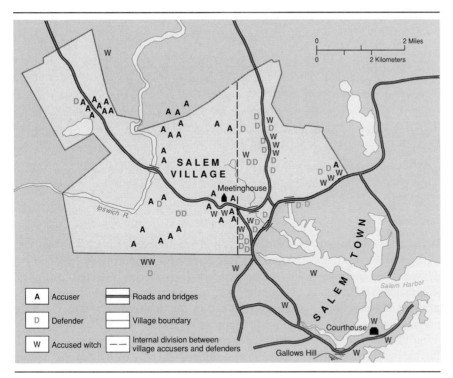

**The Geography
of Witchcraft:
Salem Village, 1692**

*Geographic patterns of
witchcraft testimony mir-
rored tensions within Salem
Village. Accused witches
and their defenders lived
mostly in the village's eastern division or in Salem
Town, while their accusers
overwhelmingly resided in
the village's western sector.*

SOURCE: Adapted from Paul
Boyer and Stephen Nissen-
baum, *Salem Possessed: The
Social Origins of Witchcraft*
(Cambridge, Mass.: Harvard
University Press, 1974).

very strong at all levels of European and American society. Between 1647 and 1691, New England courts tried eighty-one persons as witches, of whom sixteen were hanged. But unlike previous witchcraft episodes, in which officials questioned a few persons of low status in orderly hearings, events at Salem Village produced near panic and ensnared numerous prominent persons.

By April 1692 the girls had denounced two prosperous farm wives long considered saints in the local church, and they had identified the village's former minister as a wizard (male witch). In the judges' minds, fear of witchcraft overrode any doubts about the girls' credibility and led them to sweep aside normal procedural safeguards. Specifically the judges ignored the law's ban on "spectral evidence"—testimony that a spirit resembling the accused had been seen tormenting a victim. With the blessing of the village minister, himself a failed merchant, accusations multiplied until the jails overflowed with victims, including one suspect's four-year-old daughter, who would spend nine months in heavy chains.

The pattern of hysteria in Salem Village reflected that community's internal divisions. Most charges

came from the village's troubled western division, especially from Putnam family members, who lodged 46 of the 141 formal indictments. With two exceptions, those named as witches lived outside the village's western half; they primarily included persons connected economically or by marriage to the Porters—though no Porters were themselves named as witches—and several members of wealthy Salem Town families.

Anxieties concerning gender and age also influenced who became victims. Two-thirds of all accusers were girls aged between eleven and twenty, products of a society that had little sympathy for the emotional complexity of adolescence and that expected children to act like adults well before they possessed the self-control to do so. Those most frequently named as witches were middle-aged wives or widows, the very persons who most closely resembled an adolescent girl's mother. To a large extent, a group of immature girls were displacing resentment felt toward their mothers (who had the primary responsibility for bringing up daughters) onto other women whose families were viewed by the girls' parents or neighbors with jealousy or hostility.

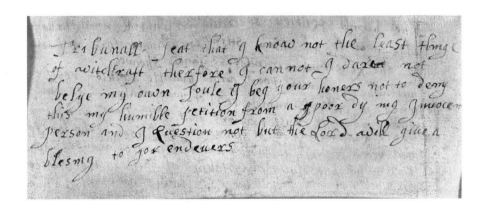

Petition of Mary Easty, 1690

In her petition Easty swore that "I know not the least thing of witchcraft."

The number of persons facing trial multiplied quickly. Those found guilty desperately tried to stave off death by implicating others. As the pandemonium spread beyond Salem, fear dissolved ties of friendship and family. A minister heard himself condemned by his own granddaughter. A seven-year-old girl helped send her mother to the gallows. A wife and daughter facing death testified against their own husband and father. Fifty persons saved themselves by confessing. Twenty others who would neither disgrace their name nor betray the guiltless went to their graves. Shortly before she was hanged, a victim of the witch hunters named Mary Easty begged the court to come to its senses: "I petition your honors not for my own life, for I know I must die . . . [but] if it be possible, that no more innocent blood be shed."

By late 1692 most Massachusetts ministers had expressed doubt that justice was being done. The clergy primarily objected that most convictions depended heavily upon spectral evidence. Increase Mather (Cotton's father, and a leading Puritan minister) in particular insisted that spectral evidence lacked legal credibility because the devil could manipulate it. Mather concluded that by accepting such evidence in court, New Englanders had fallen victim to a deadly game of "blind man's buffet" set up by Satan and were "hotly and madly, mauling one another in the dark." Backed by the clergy (and alarmed by an accusation against his wife), Governor William Phips forbade any further imprisonments for witchcraft in October—by which time more than a hundred individuals were in jail and twice that many stood accused—and shortly thereafter he suspended all trials. Phips ended the terror in early 1693 by pardoning all those convicted or suspected of witchcraft.

The witchcraft hysteria reflected profound anxieties over social change in New England. The underlying causes for this tension were evident in the antagonism of Salem Village's communally oriented farmers toward the competitive, individualistic, and impersonal way of life represented by Salem Town. In this clash of values, the rural villagers assumed the symbolic role of purging their city upon a hill of its commercial witches, only to leave the landscape desecrated by their gallows.

By the last years of the seventeenth century, the New England Way of John Winthrop had lost its relevance for the generation reaching maturity. Eighteenth-century New Englanders would be far less willing to accept society's right to restrict their personal behavior and economic freedom. The anxieties arising from this shift in values, which lay at the core of the witchcraft hysteria, faded after 1700 because of a general awareness that New England's stingy soil, harsh climate, and meager natural resources forced its inhabitants to become economically enterprising if they wished to avoid poverty.

By 1700 New Englanders had begun a transition from Puritans to "Yankees." True to their Puritan roots, the people would retain strong religious convictions and an extraordinary capacity for perseverance. Out of the striving to wring a living from an unsparing environment evolved the Yankee traits of ingenuity, shrewdness, and a sharp eye for opportunity, on which New Englanders would build a thriving international commerce—and later an industrial revolution.

The English Caribbean

Simultaneously with the appearance of New England's earliest settlements in the 1620s, a second wave of English colonization swept the West Indies. Between 1630 and 1642, more than twice as many British immigrants landed in the Caribbean as went to New England; indeed, almost 60 percent of the seventy thousand British who drifted overseas during these years embarked for either the Caribbean or the Western Atlantic provisioning base at Bermuda.

The English West Indies strongly influenced British North America. The Caribbean islands became the major market for New England's surplus foodstuffs, dried fish, and lumber. In the 1640s the British West Indians began adapting their economy to large-scale slave labor and devising a code of social conduct for nonwhites. In this way, the West Indies pioneered techniques of racial control that would later appear in the mainland colonies' plantation societies. After 1660 a large outmigration of English islanders added significantly to British North America's population.

No Peace Beyond the Line

In the sixteenth century, Spain claimed all the Caribbean, but the Spanish eventually concentrated on holding the four largest islands: Santo Domingo (or Hispaniola), Puerto Rico, Cuba, and Jamaica. By 1600 the West Indies had become a diplomatic no man's land, a region outside the legal limits of European treaties. Anyone sailing past the mid-Atlantic and south of the Tropic of Cancer's line forfeited the protection of international law. English, French, and Dutch felt free to settle uninhabited islands, and the Spanish felt equally free to exterminate trespassers on sight. Undeclared war was the normal state of affairs, and life was cheap, for no peace existed "beyond the line."

Successful English colonies appeared in the Caribbean only after Spain and the Dutch Republic went to war in 1621. Gambling that the Dutch would distract Spain from launching attacks against isolated outposts, English freebooters began seizing islands vacated by the Spanish. St. Kitts (St.

Christopher) was first in 1624, and by 1640 the English had established nearly twenty communities from the Bahamas to the waters off Nicaragua. Spanish troops soon destroyed most of these fledgling settlements but left the English entrenched on St. Kitts, Barbados, Montserrat, Nevis, and Antigua. Later, in 1655, Jamaica also fell to an English force.

Born of war, England's West Indian colonies matured in turmoil. Between 1640 and 1713, every major island but Barbados suffered at least one invasion by Carib Indians, Spaniards, French, or Dutch. After 1680 pirates from the Bahamas menaced British shipping until the Royal Navy exterminated them during the 1720s. Seven slave revolts rocked the English islands prior to 1713, and they left a bitter legacy of racial hatred on the crowded West Indies.

Sugar and Slaves

The English West Indies initially developed along lines similar to Virginia. Strong demand for tobacco led the first settlers to cultivate that plant almost exclusively. Even after the boom collapsed in 1629, the Caribbean colonists kept growing tobacco in hopes that prices would recover.

Since a single worker could tend only three acres per year, tobacco farming supported a large population on Barbados, St. Kitts, Antigua, Nevis, and Montserrat. By 1640 more colonists lived on these five islands (collectively half the size of Rhode Island) than in Virginia.

Tobacco was inexpensive to raise; it needed no equipment more costly than a curing shed. Thus tobacco growing gave individuals with small savings a chance to improve themselves. Although low prices inhibited upward mobility, and there emerged a distinct group of planters profitably working their estates with servant labor, through the 1630s the English West Indies remained a society with a large percentage of independent landowners, an overwhelmingly white population, and no extreme inequality of wealth.

An alternative to tobacco soon appeared, however, that rapidly revolutionized the islands' economy and society. During the early 1640s, Dutch merchants familiar with Brazilian methods of sugar production began encouraging the English to grow sugar cane. In return for selling their harvest to the

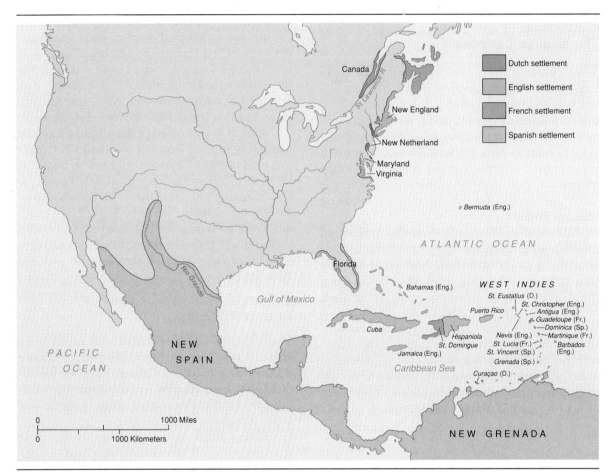

The Caribbean Colonies, 1660   *Aside from Jamaica, England's sugar colonies were clustered in the eastern Caribbean's Leeward Islands. Lying within easy reach of seaborne attack, every English island but Barbados was the scene of major fighting.*

Dutch, wealthy English planters learned how to raise and process this highly profitable crop.

Sugar could make a settler fabulously wealthy because it sold at unusually high prices, which escalated steadily for a century after its introduction on the islands. But sugar manufacture was also a complex process that required grinding, boiling, refining, and (for rum) distilling the cane immediately after cutting—before it lost its sweetness—and therefore was a very costly venture. Besides a large labor force, a sugar producer needed a mill, several caldrons, a still, and a number of outbuildings. Growing sugar required more capital than ordinary tobacco farmers possessed or could borrow as long as tobacco prices stayed low. Aggressively buying land, a few sugar planters on Bar-

bados closed off opportunity to small farmers by bidding up real-estate prices about 1,000 percent from 1643 to 1650. By 1680 a mere 7 percent of property owners held over half the agricultural acreage on Barbados, which grew 60 percent of the sugar exported to Britain. A typical sugar planter owned an estate of two hundred acres, while most Barbadians scratched a pitiful living from farms of ten acres or less.

Because the profit from sugar vastly exceeded that from any other crop, West Indian planters soon turned all available acreage into cane fields. They deforested every English island except mountainous Jamaica and greatly reduced the amount of land available for grain and livestock. The West Indies then quickly became dependent on outside sources for lumber and foodstuffs, and a flourishing market thus opened up for New England farmers, fishermen, and loggers.

Because planters needed three times as many workers per acre to raise cane as tobacco, rising sugar production greatly multiplied the demand for labor. Before 1640 West Indians had imported white servants who signed an indenture, or contract, to work without pay for four to six years in return for free passage to America. After 1640, however, sugar planters increasingly purchased slaves from the Dutch to do common field work and instead employed the indentured servants who came from Britain as overseers or skilled artisans.

Although slavery had died out in England after the eleventh century, English immigrants to the Caribbean quickly copied the example set there by Spanish slaveowners. On Barbados, for example, British newcomers imposed slavery on both blacks and Indians immediately after settling on that island in 1627. The Barbadian government in 1636 condemned every black brought there to lifelong bondage. All other English islanders likewise plunged into slaveowning with gusto.

Sugar planters preferred slaves to white servants because slaves could be driven harder and maintained less expensively. Unlike European servants, who wilted in the tropics, Africans could endure Caribbean conditions, because they had grown up in a hot, humid climate. White servants could use their contracts to demand decent food, clothes, and housing; but slaves, as mere property, had no rights, and masters could spend the bare minimum necessary to keep them alive. Most servants ended their indentures after four years, just as they were becoming efficient workers, but slaves toiled on until death. Although slaves initially cost two to four times more than servants, they proved a more economical long-term investment.

By 1670 the sugar revolution had transformed the British West Indies into a predominantly black and unfree society. In 1713 slaves outnumbered whites by a margin of four to one. Although the number of slaves shot up from approximately 40,000 in 1670 to 130,000 in 1713, the white population remained stable at about 33,000 because the planters' preference for slave labor greatly reduced the importation of indentured servants after 1670.

Declining demand for white labor in the West Indies diverted the flow of English immigration from the islands to mainland North America and so contributed to population growth there. Further, because the expansion of West Indian sugar plantations priced land beyond the reach of most whites, perhaps thirty thousand people left the islands from 1655 to 1700. Most whites who quit the West Indies also migrated to the mainland colonies—especially the Chesapeake, where they could continue growing tobacco.

West Indian Society

Within a generation of 1640, sugar transformed the West Indies into a starkly unequal world of haves and have-nots. At the pinnacle of society were a few fabulously rich families; composing just 7 percent of all whites, they owned more than half the land and held more than a hundred slaves apiece. The great majority of whites, however, survived on plots of ten acres or less and led a hardscrabble existence growing tobacco, cotton, or food crops.

At the bottom of Caribbean society were the slaves, who lived under a ruthless system of racial control imposed by the islands' European minority through laws known as slave codes. In 1661 Barbados passed the first comprehensive slave code, which served as a model for all colonies in the Caribbean and several on the North American mainland. The Barbados code professed to guarantee decent treatment for slaves (as did certain laws protecting indentured servants), but it failed to define an adequate diet or shelter, aside from requiring masters to furnish each woman with a dress and every man with a pair of pants and a hat. In effect, the code allowed owners to let their slaves run almost naked, house them in rickety shacks, and work them to exhaustion. Moreover, the Barbados code stripped slaves of all legal rights protected under English law. Unlike white servants, slaves could not be tried by juries. The law gave slaves no guarantee of a fair legal hearing and did not even forbid testimony obtained by torture.

In this way, West Indian governments allowed masters almost complete control over their human property. Their laws purposefully placed no limits on how or why a master could punish a slave. Consequently, slaves suffered vicious beatings and whippings. If a master killed a slave, he could not be punished unless a jury determined that he acted

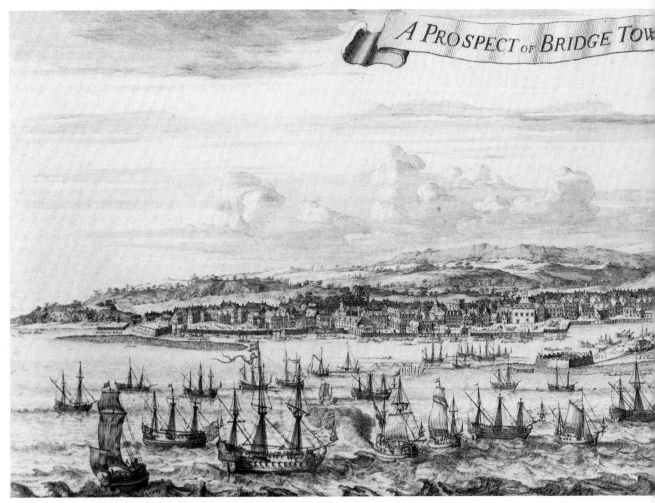

View of Bridge Town, Barbados, in 1695 *One historian has called this rare sketch, which was drawn on the deck of a ship, "the finest and most accurate seventeenth-century view of an English seaport in the New World."*

intentionally, and even then he could only be fined, not jailed or executed. The slave codes effectively legalized assault, battery, and involuntary manslaughter.

Slave codes, moreover, left those in bondage defenseless against *all* whites, not just their masters. Slaves could not testify in court against free persons. Barbados allowed any ordinary white who caught a slave at large without a pass to give him a "moderate whipping," which could include beatings of up to fifty lashes.

Finally, slave codes attempted to terrorize those in bondage into obedience through cruel and extreme punishments. Judges could order ears sliced off for theft of food, have slaves torn limb from limb for allegedly poisoning masters, and sentence rebels to be burned alive. Heads or other body parts of executed slaves often dangled gruesomely in public places to generate an atmosphere of dread.

Life in the Caribbean endured amid the constant violence inflicted on Catholic by Protestant, slave by master, and man by nature. Of the seventy-four settlers who founded Barbados in 1627, only six remained alive just eleven years later. A bubonic-plague epidemic killed an estimated one-third of the islanders from 1647 to 1649. Up to five thousand militiamen (every sixth Englishman in the Caribbean) perished while fighting to capture Jamaica from Spain in the 1650s. Hundreds regularly lost their lives in hurricanes. In 1692 an

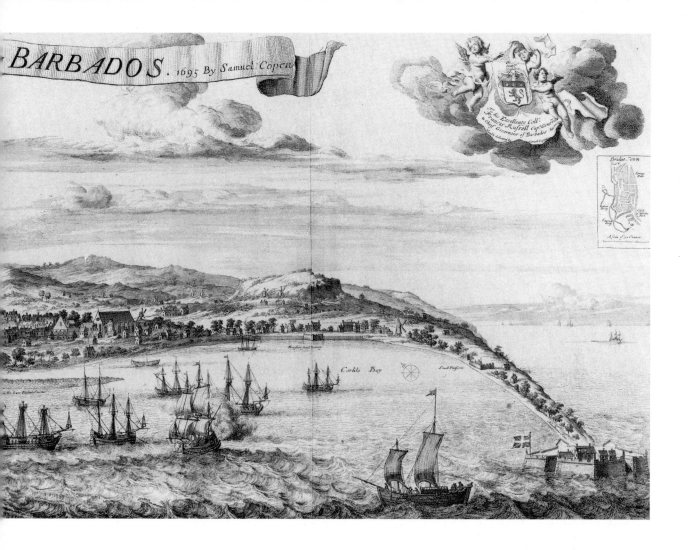

earthquake killed almost seven thousand Jamaicans out of a population of forty thousand. Malaria and yellow fever never ceased their slaughter. Immigrants usually died less than twenty years after arriving, at about thirty-eight years of age.

Mortality among blacks was especially frightful. Sugar production required arduous labor, but it was so profitable that planters had little incentive to keep their slaves healthy; they could well afford to replace those killed by overwork. Slaves usually arrived on the islands as men and women in their early twenties, and within ten years most were dead of exhaustion and abuse. So rapidly did the planters wear out field hands that, although they imported 264,000 Africans to the English West

Indies between 1640 and 1699, the slave population stood at just 100,000 in 1700.

Despite these appalling conditions, enslaved Africans did what they could to maintain a semblance of normal existence. They were more likely than island whites to start families, since the ratio of male to female slaves neared equality by 1670. (Still, a staggering mortality rate among slave spouses cut most marriages short, and half or more of all slave children died before age five.) In their daily lives, slaves retained much of their native heritage. African music survived in work songs and ceremonial dances and chants, including the mournful laments in which newly arrived Africans grieved over their fate. Very few converted to

Christianity; most clung to faith in ancestral spirits, and some committed suicide in the belief that their ghosts would return home. They also re-created African family structures, as well as marriage and funeral customs. In short, the islands' black culture displayed a far stronger African imprint than did the African-American way of life that would eventually emerge on the North American mainland.

Among white islanders, family cohesion was weak. Because about 80 percent of servants were male, most British settlers led wild lives as bachelors. Not until after 1700 did a sufficient number of white women inhabit the islands to give all white men the option of marriage. Even then high death rates robbed most children of at least one parent well before they reached maturity.

Organized religion withered in the English Caribbean. The number of clergymen never met the colonists' needs, so the majority of churches had no minister. Aside from the small Jewish minority, most whites rarely attended religious services. English islanders spent far more time in taverns drinking rum (popularly known as Old Kill-Devil) than in church. According to an old Caribbean joke, upon founding a new settlement, the Spanish first constructed a church, the Dutch first built a fort, and the English immediately set up a barroom. If drinking habits on Bermuda in the 1620s were typical, the average English islander consumed well over a gallon of distilled liquor each month.

Few white residents demonstrated any sense of community. The rich generally hired overseers to manage their estates and retired in luxury to England. The poor left in droves for other colonies. In sum, the English Caribbean was a society of materialistic fortune seekers trying to get rich quickly before death overtook them, and of slaves being worked to death.

The West Indian colonies were the first of England's overseas possessions to evolve into plantation societies. The most extreme examples of labor exploitation, racial subordination, and social stratification could indeed be found in these Caribbean colonies, but a similar pattern of development also characterized English settlements in Chesapeake Bay. By 1700 the Chesapeake resembled the Caribbean far more than it resembled New England, but only after enduring a tortured history of economic depression and violent unrest.

Chesapeake Society

Virginia's survival was no longer at stake when James I took control of the colony in 1624 from the bankrupt Virginia Company. The company had built a colony but destroyed itself in the process. Charles I ignored his new province. He and his successors refused to spend any significant amount of money on Virginia, even for the governors whom they appointed—whose salaries instead came from local taxes.

Royal indifference worked to the colonial elite's advantage by minimizing outside interference. Virginia's leaders experimented with various systems of local administration and succeeded in forcing reluctant governors to cooperate with their legislature. As in the West Indies, the environment and the dominant regional crop—tobacco in Virginia's case—determined the colonists' destiny. These same forces shaped life in Maryland and northeastern North Carolina, which, with Virginia, evolved a common Chesapeake culture.

State and Church

Virginia's first elected assembly did not meet until 1619 but thereafter convened regularly until the Virginia Company's charter was revoked. King James I, who then took over direct control of the colony, disliked representative government and planned to rule Virginia through a governor of his own choosing, who would appoint (and could dismiss) advisers to the newly created Royal Council. But Virginians petitioned repeatedly that their legislature be revived. In 1628 the new king, Charles I, grudgingly relented, but only to induce the assembly to lay a tax on tobacco exports that would transfer the cost of the colony's government from the crown to Virginia's taxpayers.

After 1630 the need for additional taxes led royal governors to call regular assemblies. The small number of elected representatives, or burgesses, initially met as a single body with the council to pass laws. During the 1650s the legislature split into two chambers—the House of Burgesses and the Governor's Council, whose members held lifetime appointments. Later royal colonies all established bicameral legislatures like Virginia's.

Local government varied widely during Virginia's first quarter-century. All individuals who commanded the militia, enforced the law, or held courts were appointed to office rather than elected. After experimenting with various institutions of local administration, in 1634 Virginia's settlers adopted England's county-court system. The courts' members, or justices of the peace, acted as judges; they also set local tax rates, paid county officials, and saw to the construction and maintenance of roads, bridges, and public buildings. As in England, this system was undemocratic, for the justices and the sheriffs, who administered the counties during the courts' recesses, gained office by the royal governor's appointment instead of by citizens' votes. Everywhere south of New England, unelected county courts would become the basic unit of local government by 1710.

First instituted in 1618, Anglican vestries governed each parish. The six vestrymen handled all church finances, determined who was deserving of poor relief, and investigated complaints against the minister. The taxpayers, who were legally obliged to pay fixed rates to the Anglican church, elected vestries until 1662, when the assembly made them self-recruiting and independent of the voters.

Because few counties supported more than one parish, many residents could not conveniently attend services. A chronic shortage of clergymen left many communities without functioning congregations. In 1662 just ten ministers served Virginia's forty-five parishes. Compared to New Englanders, Chesapeake dwellers felt religion's influence lightly, though not as lightly as English West Indians.

First Families

Virginia encountered great difficulty in developing a social elite able and willing to provide disinterested public service. The gentry sent by the Virginia Company to supervise its affairs were rarely suited for a frontier society. By 1630 all but a few of these gentlemen had either died or returned to England.

The next cycle of leaders were primarily middle class in origins, but over time they acquired great wealth. Most worked their way up into the company's highest positions and then built large estates by defrauding the stockholders. Others were rough-hewn gamblers who risked all on tobacco and won big. From 1630 to 1660, these individuals dominated Virginia's Royal Council and became even richer through land grants, tax exemptions, and public salaries. Because they had few or no children to assume their place in society, however, their influence died with them.

From 1660 to 1675, a third cycle of immigrants, who generally arrived after 1645, assumed political power. Principally members of English merchant families engaged in trade with Virginia, they had become planters. They usually emigrated with wealth, education, and burning ambition. By 1670 they controlled the Royal Council. Most of them profited from "public" service by obtaining huge land grants.

Unlike their predecessors, this group bequeathed their wealth and power to future generations, later known as the First Families of Virginia. Among them were the Burwell, Byrd, Carter, Harrison, Lee, Ludwell, Randolph, and Taylor families. Not only would the First Families dominate Virginia politics for two centuries, but a fifth of all American presidents would be descended from them.

Maryland

Until 1632 English colonization had resulted from the ventures of joint-stock companies, but afterward the crown repeatedly made presents of the Virginia Company's forfeited territory to reward English politicians. Overseas settlement thereafter resulted from grants of crown land to proprietors, who assumed the responsibility for peopling, governing, and defending their colonies.

In 1632 the first such grant went to Lord Baltimore (Cecilius Calvert) for a large tract of land north of the Potomac River and east of Chesapeake Bay, which he named Maryland in honor of England's Queen Henrietta Maria. Lord Baltimore also secured freedom from royal taxation, the power to appoint all sheriffs and judges, and the privilege of creating a local nobility. The only checks on the proprietor's power were the crown's control of war and trade and the requirement that an elected assembly approve all laws.

With Charles I's agreement, Lord Baltimore intended to create an overseas refuge for English Catholics, who constituted about 2 percent of England's population. Although English Catholics were rarely molested and many (like the Calverts) were very wealthy, they could not worship in public, had to pay tithes to the Anglican church, and could not hold political office.

In making Maryland a Catholic haven, Baltimore had to avoid antagonizing English Protestants. He sought to accomplish this by transplanting to the Chesapeake the old English institution of the manor—an estate on which a lord could maintain private law courts and employ as his chaplain a Catholic priest. Local Catholics could then come to the manor to hear Mass and receive the sacraments privately. Baltimore adapted Virginia's headright system by offering wealthy English Catholic aristocrats large land grants on condition that they bring settlers at their own cost. Anyone transporting five adults (a requirement raised to twenty by 1640) received a two-thousand-acre manor. Baltimore hoped that this arrangement would allow Catholics to survive and prosper in Maryland while making it unnecessary to pass any special laws alarming to Protestants.

Maryland's initial colonization proceeded quite smoothly. In 1634 the first two hundred settlers landed. Maryland was the first colony spared a starving time, thanks to the Calvert family's careful study of Virginia's early history. The new colony's success showed that English overseas expansion had come of age. Baltimore, however, stayed in England, governing as an absentee proprietor, and few Catholic settlers went to Maryland. From the outset, Protestants formed the majority of the population. Maryland became a society of independent landowners because land prices were low and few settlers consequently were willing to become tenants on the manors. These conditions doomed the Calverts' dream of creating on the Chesapeake a manorial system of mostly Catholic lords collecting rents. By 1675 all of Maryland's sixty nonproprietary manors had evolved into plantations.

There was little religious tension in Maryland in the colony's first years, although gradually the situation worsened. The Protestant majority dominated the colonial assembly's elective lower house, but many Catholics (including several Calvert relatives) became large landowners, held high public office in the colony, and dominated the appointive upper house. Serious religious problems first emerged in 1642, when Catholics and Protestants in the capital at St. Mary's argued over use of the city's chapel, which both groups had shared until that time. As antagonisms intensified, Baltimore

drafted the Act for Religious Toleration, which the assembly passed in 1649. Baltimore hoped that the statute would reinforce the Catholic minority's legal rights, but the law also reflected his consistent support for freedom of conscience. The toleration act was America's first law affirming liberty of worship. However, it did not protect non-Christians, nor did it separate church and state, since it empowered the government to punish religious offenses such as blasphemy.

The toleration act did not secure religious peace. In 1654 the Protestant majority barred Catholics from voting, ousted Governor William Stone (himself a Protestant), and repealed the toleration act. In 1655 Stone raised an army of both faiths to regain the government but was defeated at the Battle of the Severn River. The victors imprisoned Stone and hanged three Catholic leaders. Catholics in Maryland actually experienced more trouble than did their counterparts during the English Civil War, in which Catholics were seldom molested by the victorious Puritans.

Maryland remained in Protestant hands until 1658. Ironically, Lord Baltimore resumed control by order of the Puritan authorities then ruling England. Even so, the Calverts encountered enormous obstacles in governing Maryland during the next four decades because of Protestant resistance to any political influence by Catholics.

Life in the Chesapeake

Compared to colonists on England's tiny Caribbean sugar islands or in New England's compact towns (where five hundred people often lived within a square mile of the meetinghouse), Chesapeake residents had few neighbors. A typical community comprised about two dozen families in an area of twenty-five square miles, or about six persons per square mile. Friendship networks seldom extended beyond a three-mile walk from one's farm and rarely included more than twenty adults. Many, if not most, Chesapeake inhabitants lived in a constricted world much like that of Robert Boone, a Maryland farmer described by an Annapolis paper as having died at age seventy-nine "on the same Plantation where he was born in 1680, from which he never went 30 Miles in his Life."

The isolated folk in Virginia and Maryland and in the unorganized settlements of what would

"The Roaring Girl"

A picture of a smoker adorns the title page of this 1611 English play. Smoking tobacco had become a popular pastime in England, which by 1620 was a major market for American leaf.

become North Carolina shared a way of life shaped by one overriding fact: their future depended on the price of tobacco. Tobacco had dominated Chesapeake agriculture since 1618, when demand for the crop exploded and prices spiraled to dizzying levels. The boom ended in 1629 after prices sank a stunning 97 percent, from a high of 36 pence per pound to a penny. After stabilizing near 2.4 pence, tobacco rarely again fetched more than 10 percent of its former high.

Despite its plunge, tobacco stayed profitable as long as it sold for over two pence per pound *and* was cultivated on fertile soil near navigable water. The plant grew best on level ground with good internal drainage, so-called light soil, which was usually found beside rivers. Locating a farm along Chesapeake Bay or the region's web of rivers also

minimized transportation costs by permitting tobacco to be loaded on ships at wharves near one's home. Perhaps 80 percent of all Chesapeake homes lay within a half-mile of a riverbank, and most within six hundred feet of the shoreline.

From such waterfront bases, wealthy planters built wharves that served not only as depots for tobacco exports but also as distribution centers for imported goods. The planters' control of both export and import commerce stunted the growth of towns and the emergence of a powerful merchant class. Urbanization therefore proceeded slowly in the Chesapeake, even in a capital like Maryland's St.

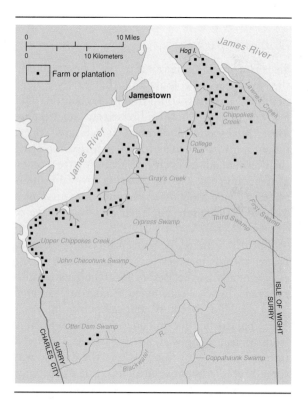

Pattern of Settlement in Surry County, Virginia, 1620–1660

Unlike the New England colonists, whose settlements were tightly nucleated around a town center (see the map of Sudbury, Massachusetts, on page 54), the Chesapeake population distributed itself thinly along the banks of rivers and creeks.

SOURCE: Thad W. Tate and David Ammerman, eds., *The Chesapeake in the Seventeenth Century* (Chapel Hill: University of North Carolina Press, 1979). Published for the Institute of Early American History and Culture. Reprinted by permission.

Mary's, which as late as 1678 was still a mere hamlet of thirty scattered houses.

Although the tobacco crash left small producers struggling to support themselves, cultivating the "weed" could generate a large income for anyone with a sizable work force. Tobacco thus sustained a sharp demand for labor that lured about 110,000 Britons to the Chesapeake from 1630 to 1700. Ninety percent of these immigrants were indentured servants. Virginia and Maryland encouraged masters to import workers by offering headrights (usually of fifty acres) for each person transported. Men were more valued as field hands than women, so 80 percent of servants were males aged about twenty.

Domestic Relations

So few women immigrated to the Chesapeake in the early years of colonization that barely a third of all male servants could find brides before 1650. Further, marriage occurred relatively late, because most inhabitants immigrated as servants whose indentures forbade them to wed before completing their term of labor. Their own scarcity gave women a great advantage in negotiating favorable marriages. Female indentured servants often managed to have their suitors buy their remaining time of service.

Death ravaged seventeenth-century Chesapeake society mercilessly and left domestic life exceptionally fragile. Before 1650 the greatest killers were diseases contracted from contaminated water: typhoid, dysentery, and salt poisoning. After 1650 malaria became epidemic as sailors returning from Africa, along with a few Africans, carried it into the marshy lowlands, where the disease was spread rapidly by mosquito bites. Life expectancy in the 1600s was about forty-eight for men and forty-four for women—slightly less than in England but nearly twenty years less than in New England. Servants died at horrifying rates, with perhaps 40 percent going to their graves within six years of arrival, and 70 percent by age forty-nine. Such high death rates severely crippled family life. Half of all persons married in Charles County, Maryland, during the late 1600s became widows or widowers within seven years. The typical Maryland family saw half of its four children die in childhood.

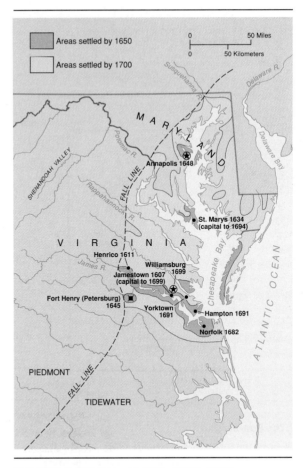

Colonizing the Chesapeake, 1607–1660

The Chesapeake frontier expanded slowly until after Indian defeat in the Second Powhatan War of 1644–1646. By 1700, when the European and African population had reached 110,000, newcomers had spread virtually throughout the tidewater.

Chesapeake women who lost their husbands tended to enjoy greater property rights than widows elsewhere. To ensure that their own children would inherit the family estate in the event that their widows remarried, Chesapeake men often wrote wills giving their wives perpetual and complete control of their estates. A widow in such circumstances gained economic independence yet still faced enormous pressure to marry a man who could produce income by farming her fields.

The combination of predominantly male immigration and devastating death rates notably retarded population growth. Although the Chesapeake had received perhaps 110,000 British immigrants between 1630 and 1700, its white population stood at just 69,000 in 1700. By contrast, a benign disease environment and a more balanced sex ratio among the 25,000 Puritans who immigrated to New England during the 1600s allowed that region's white population to climb to 91,000 by 1700.

The Chesapeake's dismal demographic history began improving in the late seventeenth century. By then resistance acquired from childhood immunities allowed native-born residents to survive into their fifties, or ten years longer than immigrants. As the number of families slowly rose, the ratio of men to women became more equal, since half of all children were girls. By 1690 an almost even division existed between the sexes. Thereafter, the white population grew primarily through an excess of births over deaths rather than through immigration, so that by 1720 the Chesapeake was primarily a native-born society.

Tobacco's Troubles

The massive importation of servants into the seventeenth-century Chesapeake made society increasingly unequal. Taking advantage of the headright system, a few planters built up large landholdings and then earned substantial incomes from their servants' labor. The servants' lot was harsh. Most were poorly fed, clothed, and housed. The exploitation of Chesapeake labor was hardly equaled anywhere in the English-speaking world outside the West Indies.

Servants faced a bleak future when their indentures ended. Having received no pay, they entered into freedom without savings. Virginia obliged masters to provide a new suit of clothes and a year's supply of corn to a freed servant. Maryland required these items plus a hoe and an ax and gave the right to claim fifty acres whenever an individual could pay to have the land surveyed and deeded.

Maryland's policy of reserving fifty acres for ex-servants permitted many of its so-called freedmen to become landowners. Two-thirds of all Chesapeake servants went to Virginia, however, where no such entitlement existed. After 1650 Virginia speculators monopolized most of the light

soil along riverbanks so essential for a profitable farm, and freedmen found land ever more unaffordable. Upward mobility was possible, but few achieved it.

After 1660 upward mobility almost vanished from the Chesapeake as the price of tobacco fell far below profitable levels, to a penny a pound. So began a depression lasting over fifty years. Despite their own tobacco losses, large planters earned other income from rents, interest on loans, some shopkeeping, and government fees.

Most landowners held on by offsetting tobacco losses with small sales of corn and cattle to the West Indies. A typical family nevertheless inhabited a shack barely twenty feet by sixteen feet and

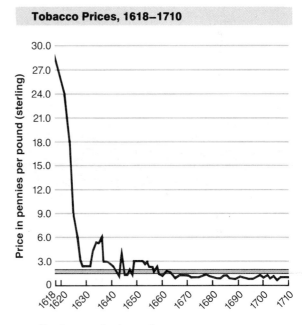

Tobacco Prices, 1618–1710

Price in pennies per pound (sterling)

⬛ Break-even price for producers

Even after its great plunge in the 1620s, tobacco remained profitable until about 1660, when its price fell below the "break-even" point—the income needed to support a family or pay off a farm mortgage.

SOURCE: Russell R. Menard, "The Chesapeake Economy, 1618–1720: An Interpretation" (unpublished paper presented at the Johns Hopkins University Seminar on the Atlantic Community, November 20, 1973), and "Farm Prices of Maryland Tobacco, 1659–1710," *Maryland Historical Magazine*, LVIII (Spring 1973), 85.

owned no more property than Adam Head of Maryland possessed when he died in 1698: three mattresses without bedsteads, a chest and barrel that served as table and chair, two pots, a kettle, "a parcell of old pewter," a gun, and some books. Most tobacco farmers lacked furniture, lived on mush or stew because they had just one pot, and slept on the ground—often on a pile of rags. Having fled poverty in England or the Caribbean for the promise of a better life, they found utter destitution in the Chesapeake.

Servants who completed their indentures after 1660 fared even worse, for the depression slashed wages well below the level needed to build savings and in this way placed landownership beyond their means. Lacking capital, those living as tenants could not afford to breed cattle for the West Indies, and they had little corn to sell after meeting their own needs. Ex-servants formed a frustrated and embittered underclass that seemed destined to remain landless and poor.

Bacon's Rebellion

By the 1670s these bleak conditions trapped most Virginia landowners in a losing battle against poverty and left the colony's freedmen verging on despair. Both groups were capable of striking out in blind rage if an opportunity presented itself to stave off economic disaster. In 1676 this human powder keg exploded in violence that left hundreds of Indians dead, dozens of plantations looted, and Virginia's capital, Jamestown, burned. The person who lit the match was Nathaniel Bacon, a wealthy, well-educated young Englishman who had immigrated to Virginia in 1674 and established a plantation. He was a bold man and an inspiring speaker, and Governor William Berkeley, a distant relative, had immediately appointed him to the Royal Council.

Virginia had been free of serious conflict with native Americans since the Second Powhatan War of 1644–1646. During that struggle, forces under Opechancanough, then nearly a century old but able to direct battles from a litter, killed five hundred of the colony's eight thousand whites before meeting defeat. By 1653 tribes encircled by English settlement began agreeing to remain within boundaries set by the government—in effect, on reservations. White settlement then expanded north

Virginia Indian, c. 1645

At the time that this contemporary sketch was made, Virginia's white settlers and Indians were embroiled in the Second Powhatan War.

to the Potomac River, and by 1675 Virginia's four thousand Indians were greatly outnumbered by forty thousand whites.

Provoked by white settlers, Indians in the Potomac Valley in 1676 made several attacks, in which thirty-six Virginians, including Bacon's overseer, died. Governor Berkeley proposed defending the panic-stricken frontier with an expensive chain of forts linked by patrols. Stung by low tobacco prices and taxes that took almost a quarter of their yearly incomes, small farmers preferred the less costly solution of waging a war of near extermination. Despite orders from Berkeley not to retaliate, three hundred settlers elected Bacon to lead them against nearby Indians in April 1676. Bacon's expedition found only peaceful Indians but massacred them anyway.

When he returned in June 1676, Bacon sought authority to wage war "against all Indians in generall." Bacon's new-found popularity forced the governor to grant his demand. The legislature voted a program designed to appeal to both hard-pressed taxpayers and ex-servants desperate for land. The assembly defined as enemies any Indians who left their villages without English permission (even if they did so out of fear of attack by Bacon), and declared their lands forfeited. Bacon's troops were free to plunder all "enemies" of their furs, guns, wampum, and corn harvests and also to keep Indian prisoners as slaves. The assembly's incentives for enlisting were directed at land-bound buccaneers eager to get rich quickly by seizing land and enslaving any Indians who fell into their clutches.

But Berkeley soon had second thoughts about letting Bacon's thirteen hundred men continue their frontier slaughter and called them back. The governor's order spared more Indians from attack, leading Bacon's men to rebel and march on Jamestown. Forcing Berkeley to flee across Chesapeake Bay, the rebels burned Jamestown, offered freedom to any servants or slaves owned by Berkeley's supporters who joined them, and then looted their enemies' plantations. At the very moment of triumph, however, Bacon died of dysentery in late 1676, and his followers dispersed.

The tortured course of Bacon's Rebellion revealed a society under deep internal stress. The revolt began as an effort to displace escalating tensions within white society onto local Indians. Because social success in Virginia depended on accumulating land and labor, small farmers and landless ex-servants alike responded enthusiastically to the prospect of taking Indian lands, stealing their furs, wampum, and harvests, and enslaving prisoners. So easily did the insurrection disintegrate into an excuse to plunder other whites, however, that it appears that the rebels were driven as much by economic opportunism as by racism. Bacon's Rebellion was an outburst of long-pent-up frustrations by marginal taxpayers and ex-servants, driven to desperation by the tobacco depression.

Slavery

Bacon's Rebellion exposed the crackling tensions underlying class relations among Chesapeake whites. This social instability derived in large part from the massive importation of indentured servants, who later became free agents in an economy that offered them little but poverty while their former masters seemingly prospered. But even before Bacon's Rebellion, the acute potential for class conflict was diminishing as Chesapeake planters gradually substituted black slaves for white servants (see "A Place in Time").

Early Virginians were still inching toward a system of racial bondage long after English West Indian planters had taken the plunge. A Dutch privateer sold the first Africans to Virginia in 1619, but it is unknown whether these individuals were treated as indentured servants or slaves. Very few blacks entered the Chesapeake before 1649 (the date of the earliest known contract for importing African slaves); of these, most became free, some bought farms and raised families, and a few later purchased other Africans.

Racial slavery developed in three stages in the Chesapeake. Blacks first began appearing from 1619 to 1640. Although Anglo-Virginians carefully dis-

Tobacco Label

Dating from about 1700, this English label for smoking tobacco features slaves on a Virginia tobacco plantation.

Middlesex County, Virginia, in the Seventeenth Century

On a sandy peninsula between tidewater Virginia's Rappahannock and Piankatank rivers lies Middlesex County, carved in 1668 out of sprawling Lancaster County. In the late 1640s, families had begun appropriating land here. Settlement was well under way by February 1651, when little Richard Perrott became "the first Man Child that was gott and borne in Rappahannock River of English parents." Richard's parents, like all the 83 families residing in Middlesex by 1668, lived on isolated "plantations" that raised corn and livestock for food and tobacco for sale.

These 83 families comprised 513 free people. They accounted for roughly half the county's residents and owned the other half of the population: 334 English indentured servants (mostly males aged 15–25) and 65 blacks brought from the West Indies. Servants and slaves were as much the head of household's responsibility as children. Blacks' conditions of servitude were still fluid, although a trend toward lifetime bondage had begun. Servants typically owed between four and twelve years' service, and half of those with four or more years to go would not live to enjoy freedom. Their lot was hard, but their labor essential. Each hoe-wielding laborer could cultivate two to three acres of tobacco plants, and owners could increase input only by adding to their labor force. Because planters such as Peter Montague faced "the whole loss of the . . . Cropp" when a servant ran away at the height of

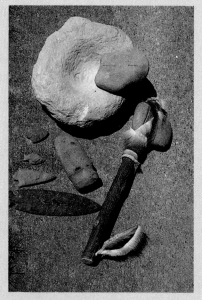

Indian Artifacts from Middlesex County

These early Indian relics include a grinding stone (top), several spear points (left), and a stone ax head (right). Native Americans continued to live in Middlesex County after the arrival of the first permanent English settlers around 1650 but gradually moved westward.

the season, unfree workers had some bargaining leverage.

Death lurked everywhere. On average, adult men and women died at ages 48 and 39 respectively—a life expectancy of fifteen years less than that of New Englanders. Thirty percent of all children under 18 lost both parents. The appearance of a highly lethal strain of malaria (which coincided with increasing imports of African-born slaves after 1680)

kept death rates high.

The prevalence of early death produced complex households in which stepparents might raise children with two or three different surnames. Mary, George Keeble's wife, bore seven children before being widowed at age 29, whereupon she immediately became Robert Beverley's wife. Mary died in 1678 at age 41 after having five children by Beverley, who then married Katherine Hone, a widow with one child. Upon Beverley's death in 1687, Katherine quickly wed Christopher Robinson, who had just lost his wife and needed a mother for his four children. Christopher and Katherine's household included children named Keeble, Beverley, Hone, and Robinson. This tangled chain of six marriages among seven people eventually produced twenty-five children who lived at least part of their lives with one or more stepparents.

For a sense of belonging, residents relied primarily on kin networks. Twice monthly, however, they could gather in the parish church for a short sermon, communion, and a chance to gossip, trade news, and sell livestock—always using tobacco as the medium of exchange. Monthly court sessions likewise brought people together to resolve disputes and see the county's prominent men installed in the petty local offices that helped define their status.

Property also counted in determining status. Toward the end of the century, a landowner's ability to work a holding depended pri-

Hewick Manor

Christopher Robinson arrived in Virginia from England about 1666 and built this stately brick home in 1678. Robinson, who served two terms in the Virginia House of Burgesses, was named England's secretary of foreign plantations in 1692, but he died the following year.

Christ Episcopal Church

This handsome brick structure was erected in 1714 on the site of an earlier wooden church. The churchyard contains the elaborately carved tabletop tombs of many seventeenth-century Middlesex County residents, among them members of the Beverley, Churchill, and Corbin families.

marily on owning slaves, for since the 1670s the supply of indentured English servants had been drying up. In 1698 the county's population stood at 1,771—30 percent unfree. But by a four-to-one margin, these unfree laborers were now black. Although slaves cost two or three times the going rate for servants, black teen-agers who survived could give twenty years' service before becoming "old"; further, immunities acquired from African ancestors gave slaves a greater likelihood of warding off malaria. In addition, many black women produced large new generations of slaves. Sharlott, for example, who came from Africa at age 12, bore thirteen children. By age 56 her master, Henry Thacker, owned twenty-two of her descendants, representing a 2,500 percent profit over her purchase price.

Facing narrowing opportuni-

ties in the 1690s, poorer whites began leaving Middlesex County at a rate of about two hundred per decade. In Virginia's interior they found abundant land and a more healthful climate. As whites who remained grew steadily more nervous about the rising number of enslaved blacks, local slave codes became more stringent. Masters, seldom gentle with white servants (who nevertheless lived with the family), used often brutal punish-

ments to keep slaves in line and generally housed their bondspeople in separate huts. In 1700 the county demanded "that Negroes not be kept att Quarters without overseers."

Between 1668 and 1740, Middlesex County's population was transformed from 93 percent white to 54 percent black. Half the population still owned the other half. But the race of the unfree laborers had changed, and they were now chattel slaves.

tinguished blacks from whites in official documents—in a manner that seems to show a tendency to discriminate according to race—they did not assume that every African was sold as a slave rather than as a servant who would eventually become free. During the second phase, spanning the years 1640–1660, unmistakable evidence survives that many blacks were treated as slaves and that their children inherited that status. Customary behavior apparently required that all blacks be treated as inferior to whites—even whites like indentured servants, who owed labor service to others. In the final phase, after 1660, whites officially recognized slavery and regulated it by law. Maryland first defined slavery as a lifelong, inheritable, racial status in 1661. Virginia followed suit in 1670. By 1705 strict legal codes defined the place of slaves in society and set standards of racial etiquette. Although this period saw slavery mature into a legal system, most of the specific practices enacted into law had evolved into custom before 1660.

Slavery was never considered a status appropriate for any white. Although the English could have enslaved enemies such as the Irish, Scots, and Spanish, they always reserved this complete denial of human rights for nonwhites. The English embarked on slavery as an "unthinking decision," one in which they unconsciously acted on the basis of a profoundly negative, emotional response to blackness and assumed that Africans were inferior to whites—and so uniquely suited for slavery.

As late as 1660, fewer than a thousand slaves lived in Virginia and Maryland. The number in bondage first became truly significant in the 1680s, when the Chesapeake's slave population almost tripled, rising from forty-five hundred to about twelve thousand. By 1700 nearly twenty thousand slaves resided in the region, and they made up 22 percent of the inhabitants. Even so, indentured servants still composed half of all unfree laborers in 1700.

Slavery replaced indentured servitude for economic reasons. First, it became more difficult to import indentured servants as the seventeenth century advanced, because a gradual decline in England's population between 1650 and 1700 reduced the number of persons willing to emigrate overseas. As England's population decreased, labor became more valuable at home, and wages rose by about 50 percent. Second, before 1690 the Royal African Company, which held a monopoly on selling slaves to the English colonies, shipped nearly all its cargoes to the West Indies, a situation that left few blacks available for sale to the Chesapeake. During the 1690s this monopoly was broken, and rival companies soon expanded the supply of slaves. Large shipments of Africans then began reaching the Chesapeake, though not in sufficient numbers to change the region's racial composition radically. Unlike the West Indies, the Chesapeake (including its backcountry) would remain predominantly white.

The emergence of slavery was critical in relaxing the economic strains within white society that had helped precipitate Bacon's Rebellion. Gradually after 1690, nonslaveowners came to see themselves as sharing a common interest with the upper class in maintaining social control over a race regarded as alien and threatening.

Conclusion   By 1690 England had planted three distinctive societies in the New World. At the northern and southern extremes were New England and the West Indies, which were appropriately polar opposites in regard to their racial composition, their organization of labor, their inhabitants' sense of community, the influence of religion, and the degree to which materialism governed social relations. Nevertheless, these two societies—like the rich and poor in John Winthrop's "A Model of Christian Charity"—had critical need of each other. The sugar islands could not feed themselves or supply their own lumber requirements, and New England relied on the Caribbean to purchase its surpluses of these goods.

The third English sphere in the New World, the Chesapeake, represented a middle ground, a place closely akin to the exploitative, uncertain, market-economy world of old England that most of its residents had left. As in the Old World, in the Chesapeake prosperity proved elusive during the seven decades after 1630, and economic hardship ultimately produced the chaos of Bacon's Rebellion. By 1700, however, a new mix of races and labor organization was emerging in the Chesapeake that would lay the basis for a remarkably vibrant society. At the core of this future dynamism would be a small, enterprising elite of "First Families" that would dominate the region's politics, economy, and culture very much in the manner of England's landed gentry.

In the course of the seventeenth century, New England evolved from a highly religious, community-oriented society to a region characterized by rising worldliness, individualism, and competitiveness. New Englanders ceased to be Puritans and became Yankees sometime in the early eighteenth century. Their collective character nevertheless continued to exhibit many traits rooted in the Puritan experience. In the Chesapeake, social development evolved in the opposite direction. As the number of blacks in their midst swelled and caused them to replace their former class antagonisms with a heightened sense of racial solidarity, the region's whites moved away from a fiercely competitive, openly materialistic, and frankly exploitative ethos toward a growing sense of community among themselves.

CHRONOLOGY

1603 James I becomes king of England.

1619 Virginia's first elected assembly meets.
Dutch privateer sells first African slaves to Virginia.

1625 Charles I becomes king of England.

1630 John Winthrop, "A Model of Christian Charity."
Massachusetts Bay colony founded.

1630– 1660 The great English migration to North America.

1633 First English settlements in Connecticut.

1634 Cecilius Calvert (Lord Baltimore) founds proprietary colony of Maryland.

1635 Roger Williams is banished from Massachusetts Bay; founds Providence, Rhode Island, in 1636.

1636 Harvard College established.

1637 Anne Hutchinson is tried by Massachusetts Bay colony and banished to Rhode Island.
Pequot War.

1639 Fundamental Orders of Connecticut.

1640s Large-scale slave-labor system takes hold in the West Indies.

1642 English Civil War begins.

1643 New Haven colony founded.

1644 Williams obtains permission to establish a legal government in Rhode Island.

1649 Earliest known contract for importing slaves to the Chesapeake.

1649 Lord Baltimore drafts Maryland's Act for
(cont.) Religious Toleration.

King Charles I beheaded.

1651– Natick, Massachusetts, and other New
1675 England "praying towns" established.

1653 First Indian reservation established in Virginia.

1660 Charles II becomes king of England in the Stuart restoration.

1661 Barbados government creates first comprehensive slave code.

Maryland defines slavery as a lifelong, inheritable racial status.

1662 Half-Way Covenant drafted.

1670 Virginia defines slavery as a lifelong, inheritable racial status.

1675– King Philip's (Metacomet's) War in New
1676 England.

1676 Bacon's Rebellion in Virginia.

1690s Collapse of the Royal African Company's monopoly on selling slaves to the English colonies; large shipments of Africans begin reaching the Chesapeake.

1692– Salem witchcraft trials.
1693

For Further Reading

Bernard Bailyn, *The New England Merchants in the Seventeenth Century* (1955). A masterful examination of the challenge posed to Puritan ideals by New England's merchants.

Jack P. Greene, *Pursuits of Happiness: The Social Development of Early Modern British Colonies and the Formation of American Culture* (1988). A brilliant synthesis of Chesapeake, Caribbean, and New England history.

Winthrop D. Jordan, *The White Man's Burden: Historical Origins of Racism in the United States* (1974). A brief yet definitive analysis of racism's origins.

Edmund S. Morgan, *American Slavery, American Freedom: The Ordeal of Colonial Virginia* (1975). The most penetrating analysis yet written on the origins of southern slavery.

Darrett B. Rutman, *Winthrop's Boston: A Portrait of a Puritan Town, 1630–1649* (1965). An illuminating description of the disintegration of Winthrop's "city upon a hill."

Darrett B. Rutman and Anita H. Rutman, *A Place in Time: Middlesex County, Virginia, 1650–1750* (1984). The best examination of community life in the early Chesapeake.

Alan Simpson, *Puritanism in Old and New England* (1955). The best short introduction to Puritanism ever written.

Additional Bibliography

Early New England

David Grayson Allen, *In English Ways: The Movement of Societies and the Transferral of English Local Law and Custom* (1981); James Axtell, *The School upon a Hill: Education and Society in Colonial New England* (1974); Emery Battis, *Saints and Sectaries: Anne Hutchinson and the Antinomian Controversy in the Massachusetts Bay Colony* (1962); Theodore Dwight Bozeman, *To Live Ancient Lives: The Primitivist Dimension in Puritanism* (1988); Charles L. Cohen, *God's Caress: The Psychology of Puritan Religious Experience* (1986); David Cressy, *Coming Over: Migration and Communication Between England and New England in the Seventeenth Century* (1987); Richard S. Dunn, *Puritans and Yankees: The Winthrop Dynasty of New England, 1630–1717* (1962); Stephen Foster, *Their Solitary Way: The Puritan Social Ethic in the First Century of Settlement in New England* (1971); Philip F. Gura, *A Glimpse of Sion's Glory: Puritan Radicalism in New England, 1620–1660* (1984); David D. Hall, *The Faithful Shepherd: A History of the New England Ministry in the Seventeenth Century* (1972); Charles E. Hambrick-Stowe, *The Practice of Piety: Puritan Devotional Disciplines in Seventeenth Century New England* (1982); Christine Leigh Heyrman, *Commerce and Culture: The Maritime Communities of Colonial Massachusetts* (1984); Kenneth A. Lockridge, *A New England Town: The First*

Hundred Years: Dedham, Massachusetts, 1636–1736 (1970); Robert Middlekauff, *The Mathers: Three Generations of Puritan Intellectuals, 1596–1728* (1971); Perry Miller, *The New England Mind*, 2 vols. (1939–1953); Edmund S. Morgan, *The Puritan Dilemma: The Story of John Winthrop* (1958) and *Visible Saints: The History of a Puritan Idea* (1963); Sumner Chilton Powell, *Puritan Village: The Formation of a New England Town* (1964); Darrett B. Rutman, *Husbandmen of Plymouth: Farms and Villages in the Old Colony, 1620–1649* (1967).

Witchcraft

Paul Boyer and Stephen Nissenbaum, *Salem Possessed: The Social Origins of Witchcraft* (1974); John P. Demos, *Entertaining Satan: Witchcraft and the Culture of Early New England* (1982); Carol F. Karlsen, *The Devil in the Shape of a Woman: Witchcraft in Colonial New England* (1987); Keith Thomas, *Religion and the Decline of Magic* (1971); Richard Weisman, *Magic, Science, and Religion in Seventeenth-Century Massachusetts* (1982).

The English West Indies

Carl Bridenbaugh and Roberta Bridenbaugh, *No Peace Beyond the Line: The English in the Caribbean, 1624–1690* (1972); Michael Craton and James Walvin, *A Jamaican Plantation: The History of Worthy Park, 1670–1970* (1970); Richard S. Dunn, *Sugar and Slaves: The Rise of the Planter Class in the English West Indies, 1624–1713* (1972); Richard B. Sheridan, *Sugar and Slavery: An Economic History of the British West Indies, 1623–1775* (1973).

Indian-White Relations

James Axtell, *The Invasion Within: The Contest of Cultures in Colonial North America* (1985); William Cronon, *Changes in the Land: Indians, Colonists, and the Ecology of New England* (1983); Francis Jennings, *The Invasion of America: Indians, Colonialism, and the Cant of Conquest* (1975); Yasuhide Kawashima, *Puritan Justice and the Indian: White Man's Law in Massachusetts, 1630–1763* (1986); Howard S. Russell, *Indian New England Before the Mayflower* (1980); Neal Salisbury, *Manitou and Providence: Indians, Europeans, and the Making of New England, 1500–1643* (1982); Alden T. Vaughan, *The New England Frontier: Puritans and Indians, 1620–1675* (1965).

Gender and Family

John P. Demos, *A Little Commonwealth: Family Life in Plymouth Colony* (1970); Philip Greven, *Four Generations: Population, Land, and Family in Colonial Andover, Massachusetts* (1970); Lyle Koehler, *A Search for Power: The "Weaker Sex" in Seventeenth-Century New England* (1980); Edmund S. Morgan, *The Puritan Family: Religion and Domestic Relations in Seventeenth-Century New England* (1966); Marylynn Salmon, *Women and the Law of Property in Early America* (1986); Roger Thompson, *Women in Stuart England and America: A Comparative Study* (1974); Laurel Thatcher Ulrich, *Good Wives: Image and Reality in the Lives of Women in Northern New England, 1650–1750* (1982); Nancy Woloch, *Women and the American Experience* (1984).

The Chesapeake

Warren M. Billings, ed., *The Old Dominion in the Seventeenth Century: A Documentary History of Virginia, 1606–1689* (1975); Timothy H. Breen and Stephen Innes, *"Myne Own Ground": Race and Freedom on Virginia's Eastern Shore, 1640–1676* (1980); Lois Green Carr et al., *Colonial Chesapeake Society* (1988); Wesley Frank Craven, *The Southern Colonies in the Seventeenth Century* (1949) and *White, Red, and Black: The Seventeenth-Century Virginian* (1971); Carville Earle, *The Evolution of a Tidewater Settlement Pattern: All Hallow's Parish, Maryland, 1650–1783* (1975); Ivor Noel Hume, *Martin's Hundred* (1982); Aubrey C. Land et al., eds., *Law, Society, and Politics in Early Maryland* (1977); Gloria L. Main, *Tobacco Colony: Life in Early Maryland, 1650–1720* (1982); William L. Shea, *The Virginia Militia in the Seventeenth Century* (1983); Thad Tate and David Ammerman, eds., *The Chesapeake in the Seventeenth Century: Essays on Anglo-American Society* (1979); Wilcomb E. Washburn, *The Governor and the Rebel: A History of Bacon's Rebellion in Virginia* (1957).

CHAPTER 3

Colonial Society Comes of Age, 1660–1750

Alexander Garden was furious with the young Anglican minister George Whitefield. Just over from England, Whitefield was stating publicly that the rest of Garden's ministers were unsaved and endangering their parishioners' souls. Garden, as the bishop of London's commissary (representative) in Charles Town, South Carolina, was responsible for the Church of England's well-being in the southern British colonies. He thought that he had plenty to contend with already—most pressingly, the numbing indifference of most of his flock—and did not appreciate one of his ministers' making waves. With Whitefield's descent on the colonies like a hurricane, Garden sensed that 1740 would not be a good year for established religion.

Calling Whitefield in for an interview, Garden demanded that the preacher explain his repeated attacks on South Carolina's Anglican ministry. He got more than he bargained for. Whitefield, it seemed, thought that Garden "was as ignorant as the rest" of the local clergy because he failed to teach the central Protestant doctrine of justification by faith alone (see Chapter 1). And Whitefield threatened to speak out against the commissary if Garden refused to condemn dancing and other public entertainments. Thunderstruck, Garden shot back that Whitefield would be suspended if he preached in any church in the province—to which Whitefield retorted that he would treat such an action as he would an order from the pope.

Garden got Whitefield out of his house but not out of his hair. The two men carried their dispute to the public. Garden accused Whitefield of jeopardizing the stability of colonial society. Whitefield accused the Anglican clergy of abandoning Calvinist doctrine in favor of the cold heresy of reason. An extraordinary orator, Whitehead stirred his listeners' passions, calling forth an "enthusiasm" for religion that undermined traditional order and deference. He inspired members of congregations to think themselves as good as, if not superior to, their ministers; wives, to question their husbands' piety; children, to claim divine grace that their parents did not feel; slaves, to believe that they too had souls; and common people, to insist that they were the equal of anyone else.

That was Whitefield's greatest crime—to be heard throughout America. He became the first national figure in North America, traveling thousands of miles to spread his doubts about the established religious order. Everywhere he went, the people poured out by the thousands to listen and feel, to sense individually the overwhelming power of a direct connection with God.

Sweeping through British North America in the 1740s, Whitefield encountered a vibrant society, a rapidly growing economy, and the beginnings of a richly diverse culture. By 1750 the colonies could claim the world's largest concentration of overseas Europeans; besides those of English stock, significant numbers descended from German, Irish, Scottish, Dutch, and French settlers. North America was also the enforced home of a burgeoning African population, by now slowly becoming English-speaking and Christian. Geographically, however, the people remained isolated from one another. Whitefield found it quicker to make the hazardous, disease-ravaged transatlantic voyage than to go overland from New England to Georgia.

A generation of imperial crisis and war with the French from 1685 to 1713 had forged among Anglo-America's whites a strong sense of shared allegiance to the English crown and of deeply felt Protestant heritage. Then, during the era of peace between 1713 and 1744, British Americans' provincialism faced the dual challenge of two vital yet conflicting European cultural currents. The first of these was the Enlightenment—the dissemination among the educated public of faith in reason rooted in an appreciation of natural science—which found its foremost American exponent in Benjamin Franklin. The second current was the religious revival pulsing across Protestant Europe in the 1730s

and 1740s, one of whose greatest prophets was George Whitefield. That Franklin and Whitefield became the first two Anglo-American public figures to win fame not only throughout the colonies but also in the entire Western world testifies to America's active participation in the culture of the age.

The peace and prosperity that characterized mid-eighteenth-century British North America would have astonished seventeenth-century colonists, clinging to their uncertain footholds on the edge of the transatlantic wilderness. But even though by 1740 life was becoming reasonably stable and secure, especially for upper-class Anglo-Americans, the Great Awakening let loose spiritual and social tremors that jolted colonial self-confidence. Alexander Garden's nervousness was hardly unreasonable.

The Restoration Colonies

In 1660 mainland Anglo-America remained a loose cluster of Chesapeake settlements with about thirty thousand struggling tobacco producers, and a New England enclave where some thirty-three thousand stubborn Puritans had built their city upon a hill. In between lay thinly populated New Netherland, an outpost of England's great commercial rival, the Dutch Republic.

With the end of the English Revolution and the Stuart restoration in 1660, English authorities almost immediately busied themselves with their North American colonies. Their least effective initiative was the revived Church of England's attempt to clean up organized religion in the Chesapeake— a "Sodom of uncleaness [*sic*] & a Pest house of iniquity," as one overwrought Anglican minister in Maryland described that colony about 1660. But because educated English clergymen resisted taking American parishes, reform of American Anglicanism never got very far.

Second, Parliament began passing laws collectively known as the Navigation Acts, designed to benefit England's commercial interests. Expanding upon a 1651 law, the Navigation Acts of 1660 and 1663 barred colonial merchants from exporting such commodities as sugar and tobacco anywhere except to England, and from importing goods in

non-English ships. The act of 1672 provided administrative machinery to enforce these rules.

Third, the Restoration set in motion a new wave of colony building that gave England control of the North American coast from Maine to South Carolina. A series of "Restoration colonies" appeared—Carolina, New York, New Jersey, and Pennsylvania. Before 1720 most settlers in the new colonies came from existing British North American provinces; but thereafter, these provinces attracted masses of Irish and German immigrants, in the process altering the colonies' purely English character.

English domestic politics figured prominently in the Restoration government's plans for America. Charles II (ruled 1660–1685) had clamoring supporters to reward. The Navigation Acts favored powerful commercial interests in England. The king entrusted the creation of the new colonies to important English politicians—the proprietors who organized settlement, oversaw governance (subject to loose control from London), and expected to profit handsomely.

In every Restoration colony, the proprietors created a system of land distribution that would bring them high income and ensure a stable social hierarchy. But, as earlier in Maryland, their plans

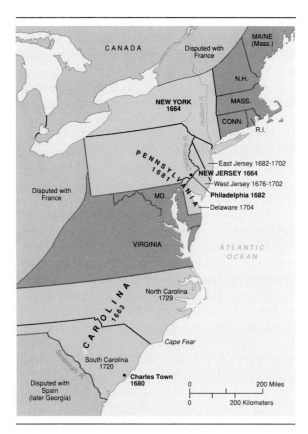

The Restoration Colonies

England's Restoration colonies were carved out of the claims or earlier colonial territory of rival European powers. Spain claimed the territory chartered as Carolina in 1663. Out of England's takeover of Dutch New Netherland in 1664 came the colonies of New York, East Jersey, West Jersey, Pennsylvania, and Delaware.

collided with the colonists' determination to better themselves. Dreams of stability soon waned, and by 1689 English attempts to impose a uniform system of rule across the Atlantic provoked a series of colonial rebellions, linked to an anti-Stuart revolution in England itself.

Carolina

During the 1650s several struggling, unauthorized little outposts were formed along the swampy coast from just south of Virginia to Spanish Florida by a few English settlers—"the dregs and gleanings of all other English Colonies," an early-eighteenth-century clergyman recalled. Some of these "dregs and gleanings" were New Englanders; others were

people who had failed to profit from the West Indian sugar boom. In 1663 Charles II bestowed this unpromising coast on several English supporters. The grateful proprietors named their colony Carolina in honor of Charles (*Carolus* in Latin).

Carolina grew haltingly at first. The proprietors organized the existing little settlements in the northern part of their domain as a separate district and established a bicameral legislative body for it. Then in 1669 one of the proprietors, Anthony Ashley Cooper, speeded up settlement by offering immigrants fifty-acre land grants for every family member, indentured servant, or slave they brought in. Cooper's action marked a turning point. In 1670 settlement of southern Carolina began when two hundred Barbadian and English settlers landed near modern-day Charleston, "in the very chops of the Spanish." Narrowly escaping destruction when a hurricane scattered Spanish warships sent to attack them, they wintered without enduring a "starving time." Soon they formed the colony's nucleus, with their own bicameral legislature distinct from that of the northern district.

Cooper and his secretary—John Locke, later acclaimed as one of the great philosophers of the age—devised an intricate plan for Carolina's settlement and government. Their Fundamental Constitutions of Carolina attempted to ensure the colony's stability by decreeing that political power and social rank should accurately reflect settlers' landed wealth. Thus they invented three orders of nobility, with "proprietors" on top, "landgraves" in the middle, and "caciques" at the bottom. Together this elite would hold two-fifths of all land, make laws through a Council of Nobles, and dispense justice through manorial law courts. Ordinary Carolinians with smaller landholdings were expected to defer to nobility, although they would enjoy religious toleration and the benefits of English common law.

The reality of Carolina's early settlement bore small resemblance to Locke's scheme. New arrivals who could get all the land they needed saw little reason to obey pseudofeudal lords and all but ignored most of the plans drawn up for them across the Atlantic.

Until 1680 about half the settlers of southern Carolina came directly from overcrowded Barbados, bringing with them a few slaves. Other settlers drifted in from mainland colonies to the north, as did a trickle of French Protestant refugees. The first colonists raised "Hoggs, & Cattle which they sell to the New-Comers, and with which they purchase Cloathes, and tools from them," and also sold beef to the West Indies. Cattle raising discouraged the widespread use of slaves, for herding required only a small labor force and afforded bondsmen too many tempting opportunities to run away. Because ranching yielded only modest profits, few striking disparities of wealth arose, and the slaves who accompanied the first Carolinians seem to have been spared the brutality widely meted out to blacks in the British Caribbean.

In northern Carolina life was much the same. Settled by Virginians and Marylanders, the region exported tobacco, lumber, and pitch, giving local people the name tarheels. As in southern Carolina, these activities did not at first produce enough profit to warrant maintaining many slaves, and so self-sufficient white families predominated. As late as 1720, the region was nine-tenths white.

But Carolina had not been created so that settlers could merely eke out a marginal existence.

Like the first Virginians, southern Carolinians sought a staple crop that could make them rich. By the early 1690s, they found it—rice. The grain was probably first brought by West Africans, for it constituted the basic foodstuff in Senegambia. Because rice, like sugar, enormously enriched a few men with capital to invest in costly dams, dikes, and slaves, it remade southern Carolina into a society resembling that of the West Indies. By earning annual profits of 25 percent, rice planters within a generation became the only colonial elite whose wealth rivaled that of the Caribbean sugar planters.

The Carolina rice planters' huge profits had to be reaped at someone's expense, however. No matter how inhumanly they might be driven, indentured English servants simply could not work in humid rice paddies swarming with mosquitoes. The planters' solution was to import an ever-growing force of African slaves. Unfortunately for these people, they had two major advantages to masters. First, perhaps 15 percent of the slaves imported into Carolina had cultivated rice in their home-

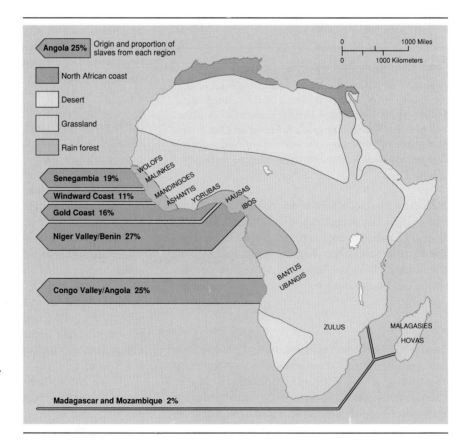

Old World Origins of North American Slaves, 1690–1807

Three-quarters of all Africans brought to British North America were sold to Europeans by African merchants operating between the Niger and Senegal rivers. Most slaves were captured or bought several hundred miles inland and marched to the coast for export.

land, and their expertise was vital in teaching whites how to raise the unfamiliar crop. Second, many Africans had partial immunity to malaria, the highly infectious and deadly disease transmitted by mosquito bites, which was endemic to coastal regions of West Africa and which African-born slaves (and infected slave ships' crews) carried to the New World. (Tragically, the antibody that helps ward off malaria also tends to produce the sickle-cell trait, a hereditary genetic condition often fatal to those children who inherit it.) The Africans' relatively low death rate from malaria made possible commercial rice production in Carolina. A tremendous demand for black slave labor resulted, for a typical rice planter farming 130 acres needed sixty-five slaves. The proportion of slaves in southern Carolina's population spurted from 17 percent in 1680 to 67 percent in 1720, when the region officially became the colony of South Carolina. South Carolina was Britain's sole eighteenth-century mainland colony with a black majority.

Rice thrived only within a forty-mile-wide coastal strip extending from Cape Fear (now in North Carolina) to present-day Georgia. The hot, humid, marshy lowlands quickly became infested with malaria. Carolinians grimly joked that the rice belt was a paradise in spring, an inferno in summer, and a hospital in the wet, chilly fall. In the worst months, planters' families usually escaped to the relatively cool and more healthful climate of Charles Town and let overseers supervise their harvests.

As long as Europeans outnumbered Africans, race relations could be somewhat relaxed. But as a black majority emerged and swelled, whites increasingly relied on force and fear to control their slaves. In 1696 Carolina adopted the galling restrictions and gruesome punishments of the Barbados slave code (see Chapter 2). Bondage in the mainland colony was becoming as cruel and harsh as in the West Indies.

In contrast to South Carolina, northern Carolina was long spared large-scale slavery; but tragedy also marred its early history as whites and native Americans there became locked in a bloody struggle. In 1711, provoked by white encroachments on their land and by several instances of whites' kidnapping Indians as slaves, the Tuscarora tribe destroyed New Bern, a frontier settlement of seven hundred Swiss immigrants. In retaliation, colonial

militia and the Tuscaroras' Indian enemies rampaged through the offending tribe's villages. By 1713, with a thousand of their people killed or enslaved (about one-fifth of the total population), the Tuscaroras surrendered. Nearly half the survivors migrated to New York, where they became the Sixth Nation of the Iroquois Confederacy.

Disunity was costly for Carolina Indians. After helping whites crush the Tuscaroras, the Yamasees of the southern Carolina lowlands found themselves beset by colonial fur traders who cheated, abused, and enslaved them. Finally, in 1715, the Yamasees led most nearby tribes in attacks that drove the settlements back to the coast. But the next year, the Carolina militia, which barely equaled the thousand warriors then harassing Charles Town, enrolled six hundred slaves and drove the Indians from the area suitable for rice production.

The Tuscarora and Yamasee wars cracked Indian opposition to Old World peoples' expansion in the Carolinas. The Tuscaroras largely abandoned the region. The Yamasees practically disappeared as a people, for those who were not killed in fighting, enslaved, or doomed by disease blended into the Creek nation farther inland.

The first two generations of Carolina settlers had cleared the unhealthy coastal regions, developed profitable exports, enslaved thousands of blacks, and crushed Indian resistance—all with little aid from the faraway proprietors, whose main activities had been vetoing many laws passed by the Carolina assemblies and appointing unpopular governors. Carolinians came to regard the proprietors as indifferent even to their defense. Exasperated, the southern Carolina assembly asked the British monarchy to take control, and in 1720 the king complied by making South Carolina a royal province. Proprietary rule finally ended in 1729, when North Carolina also became a royal colony.

Ten years later, in 1739, South Carolina was rocked by a powerful slave uprising, the Stono Rebellion. It began when twenty slaves robbed guns and ammunition from a store twenty miles from Charles Town, at the Stono River Bridge. Marching under a makeshift flag and crying "Liberty!" they collected eighty men and headed for Spanish Florida, a well-known refuge for runaways. Along the way they burned seven plantations and killed twenty whites, but they spared a Scottish innkeeper who "was a good Man and kind to his slaves."

Within a day mounted militia surrounded the slaves by a riverbank, cut them down mercilessly, and spiked a rebel head on every milepost between that spot and Charles Town. Disturbances elsewhere in the colony required more than a month to suppress, with insurgents generally "put to the most cruel Death." But white apprehension ran high, expressed in a new slave code that would remain essentially in force until the Civil War. The code kept South Carolina slaves under constant surveillance. Further, it threatened masters with fines for not disciplining slaves and required legislative approval for manumission (freeing of individual slaves). The Stono Rebellion thus speeded South Carolina's emergence as a rigid, racist, and fear-ridden society—and its failure showed slaves that armed uprisings were suicidal. Slaves still resisted after the revolt, but typically by feigning stupidity, running away, committing arson or sabotage, or poisoning masters. Not until 1831 would significant slave violence again break out on the mainland.

The Carolinas' rise had cost innumerable lives and untold suffering for enslaved blacks and displaced native Americans. Whites lived in an atmosphere of anxiety. Grim reality had triumphed over hazy English dreams of a stable society.

New York and the Jerseys

Like Carolina, the English colonies of New York and New Jersey had their origins in the speculative enterprise of Restoration courtiers close to Charles II. As in Carolina, here too upper-class proprietors hoped to create a hierarchical society in which they could profit from settlers' rents. These plans for the most part failed in New Jersey, as in Carolina. Only in New York did they come close to success.

In 1664, waging war against the Dutch Republic, Charles II dispatched a naval force to conquer New Netherland. Weakened by an earlier clash with local Indians, Dutch governor Peter Stuyvesant and four hundred poorly armed civilians surrendered peacefully. Nearly all the Dutch (including Stuyvesant himself) remained in the colony on generous terms.

Charles II made his brother James, Duke of York, proprietor of the new province and renamed it New York. When the duke became King James II in 1685, he proclaimed New York a royal colony. Immigration from New England, Britain, and France

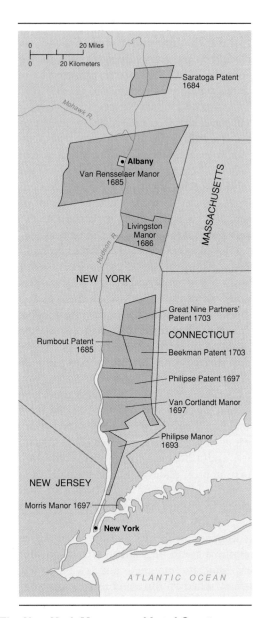

The New York Manors and Land Grants

Between 1684 and 1703, English governors awarded most of the best land east of the Hudson River as manors to prominent politicians—the majority of them Dutch—whose heirs became the wealthiest elite in the rural northern colonies.

boosted the population from five thousand in 1664 to twenty thousand in 1700, of whom just 44 percent were descended from the original New Netherlanders.

Abraham Wendell, *by an Unknown Artist, c. 1737*

Prosperous eighteenth-century Dutch residents of the Hudson River Valley commonly sat for their portraits. Among them was the well-to-do Albany patroon Abraham Wendell, shown here standing before his own land, stream, and mill.

New York's governors rewarded their most influential political supporters with large land grants. By 1703 five families held approximately 1.75 million acres (about half the area east of the Hudson River and south of Albany), which they withheld from sale in hope of creating manors with numerous rent-paying tenants. But the *patroons*—the Dutch name for manor lords—never became European-style lords oppressing peasant tenants, for unlike Europe, America had plenty of good land and too few farmers. The easy availability of other land along the Hudson kept the manors underpopulated and unprofitable until after 1700. *Patroons* could only attract tenants by offering favorable terms—building mills, lowering rents, and giving young families farm tools—and by dispensing evenhanded justice in their manor courts. Individual tenants thus did well, but their landlords did even better. Earning an enormous income from their rents, the New York *patroons* by 1750 formed a landed elite second only in wealth to the Carolina rice planters.

Ambitious plans likewise collided with American realities in New Jersey, which also was carved out of New Netherland. Immediately after the Dutch province's conquest in 1664, the Duke of York named two court favorites, Lord Berkeley and Sir Philip Carteret, as joint proprietors of New Jersey, an area then inhabited by less than six thousand native Americans and a few hundred Dutch and Swedes. From the beginning the New Jersey proprietors had difficulty controlling their province. By 1672 several thousand New Englanders had settled along the Atlantic shore. Quarreling with the absentee proprietors, they renounced allegiance to them at an extralegal meeting that the proprietary governor sneered at as the "disorderly assembled." Soon Berkeley and Carteret tired of wrangling with the unruly Puritans and sold the region to a group of even more contentious religious dissenters, called Quakers, who split the territory into the two colonies of West Jersey (1676) and East Jersey (1682).

East Jersey's new proprietors, a group of mostly Scottish Quakers, could no more successfully work with the local Puritans than had Berkeley and Carteret, while West Jersey's English Quakers squabbled constantly among themselves. The Jerseys' mix of Quakers, Anglicans, Puritans, Scottish Presbyterians, Dutch Calvinists, and Swedish Lutherans got along poorly with each other and even worse with the proprietors. The governments collapsed between 1698 and 1701 as mobs disrupted the courts. In 1702 the disillusioned proprietors finally surrendered their political powers to the crown, which proclaimed New Jersey a royal province.

Quaker Pennsylvania

The noblest attempt to carry out European-born concepts of justice and stability in founding a Restoration colony began in 1681. That year, Charles II paid off a huge debt to a supporter's heir by making this man, William Penn, the proprietor of the last unallocated tract of American territory at the king's disposal. Penn (1644–1718) had two aims in developing his colony. First, he was a Quaker and wanted to launch a "holy experiment" based on the teachings of the extremely radical English preacher George Fox. Second, "though I desire to extend religious freedom," he explained, "yet I want some recompense for my trouble." But Penn did not intend "Penn's Woods" to become merely a hunting ground for get-rich-quick speculators.

Quakers in late-seventeenth-century England stood well beyond the fringe of respectability. They appealed strongly to men and women at the bottom of the economic ladder, and they challenged the conventional foundation of the social order. George Fox, the movement's originator, had received his inspiration while wandering civil war–torn England's byways and searching for spiritual meaning among distressed common people. Tried on one occasion for blasphemy, he warned the judge to "tremble at the word of the Lord" and was ridiculed as a "quaker." Fox's followers called themselves the Society of Friends, but the name Quaker stuck. They were among the most radical of the many religious sects born in England during the 1640s and 1650s.

The core of Fox's theology was his belief that the Holy Spirit or "Inner Light" could inspire every soul. Mainstream Christians, by contrast, found any such claim of special communication with God highly suspicious, as Anne Hutchinson's banishment from Massachusetts Bay colony in 1636 had revealed. While trusting direct inspiration, Quakers also took great pains to ensure that individual opinions would not be mistaken for God's will. They felt confident that they understood Inner Light only after having reached near-unanimous agreement through intensive and searching discussion led by "Public Friends"—ordinary laypeople. In their simple religious services ("meetings"), Quakers sat silently until the Inner Light prompted one of them to speak.

Some of their beliefs led English Quakers to behave in ways that seemed disrespectful to government and the social elite and so aroused fierce hostility. For example, insisting that individuals deserved recognition for their spiritual state rather than their wealth or family status, Quakers refused to tip their hats to their social betters. For the same reason, they would not use the pronoun *you* (customarily employed when commoners spoke to members of the gentry), instead addressing everyone *thee* and *thou* as a token of equality. By wearing their hats in court, moreover, Quakers appeared to mock the state's authority; and by taking literally Scripture's ban on swearing oaths, they seemed to place themselves above the law. The Friends'

refusal to bear arms appeared unpatriotic and cowardly to many. Finally, Quakers accorded women unprecedented equality. The Inner Light, Fox insisted, could "speak in the female as well as the male." A number of fiery Quaker proselytizers were women, including Mary Dyer, a Rhode Island merchant's wife whom Fox converted when the couple returned to England. She went back to Rhode Island in 1658, helped organize Quaker groups there, and eventually was condemned for sedition and hanged in Massachusetts in 1660.

Not all Quakers came from the bottom of society. The movement's emphasis on quiet introspection and its refusal to adopt a formal creed also attracted well-educated and well-to-do individuals disillusioned by the quarreling of rival faiths. The possessor of a great fortune, William Penn was hardly a typical Friend, but there were significant numbers of merchants among the estimated sixty thousand Quakers in the British Isles in the early 1680s. Moreover, the industriousness that the Society of Friends encouraged in its members ensured that many humble Quakers were already accumulating money and property.

Quakers in England faced intense pressure to conform to the established church, but they throve on persecution. The courts severely fined those absent from Anglican services. Constables commonly collected fines by seizing Quakers' farm tools, equipment, or livestock and by destroying their looms or workbenches. Between 1660 and 1685, fifteen thousand Quakers were jailed, and many others suffered public whippings or facial disfigurements. Through all this adversity, they won a reputation for industriousness, even in prison. Jailed in 1669, William Penn found his fellow Quaker inmates busily engaged at crafts like weaving and spinning and absorbed in prayer during their work breaks. "The jail by that means became a meeting-house and a work-house," Penn proudly wrote, "for *they would not be idle anywhere.*"

Much care lay behind the Quaker migration to Pennsylvania that began in 1681, and it resulted in the most successful initial transplantation of Europeans in any North American colony. Penn sent an advance party to the Delaware Valley, where a thousand Swedes and Dutch already lived. After an agonizing voyage in which one-third of the passengers died, Penn arrived in 1682. Choosing a site for the capital, he named it Philadelphia—the "City

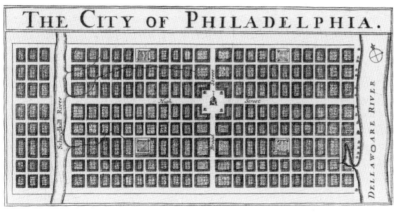

William Penn's Map of Philadelphia, c. 1681; Portrait of Penn,
by Francis Place

Central to William Penn's master plan for Philadelphia was the idea that each residence should stand in the middle of its plot, encircled by gardens and orchards. This pastel portrait is thought to be the most accurate likeness of Penn extant.

of Brotherly Love." By 1687 some eight thousand English Quaker refugees had joined Penn across the Atlantic. (Pennsylvania was the only Restoration colony besides West Jersey whose colonists before 1720 came primarily from Europe rather than other colonies.) Because most Quakers immigrated in family groups rather than as single males, a high birthrate resulted, and the population grew rapidly. In 1698 a Quaker reported that in Pennsylvania one seldom met "any young Married Woman but hath a Child in her belly, or one upon her lap."

As planned by its founder, Pennsylvania offered Friends the freedom not only to live diligently but also to make laws according to their ideals. Having experienced persecution, Penn hated intolerance and arbitrary government. Thus in drafting the colony's constitution, he proposed "to leave myself and my successors [as proprietor] no power of doing mischief, that the will of One man may not hinder the good of the whole company." But the Frame of Government (constitution) that Penn devised went through at least seven drafts before he was satisfied. After wavering between authoritarian and more democratic plans, Penn finally opted for a system with a strong executive branch (a governor and governor's council) and granted the lower legislative chamber (the assembly) only limited powers. Friends, forming the majority of the colony's pop-

ulation, dominated this elected assembly. Penn named Quakers (or persons sympathetic to them) as governor, judges, and sheriffs. Hardly a democrat, he feared "the ambitions of the populace which shakes the Constitution," and he intended to check "the rabble" as much as possible. Because he also insisted on the orderly disposition of property and hoped to avoid unseemly wrangling, he carefully oversaw land sales in the colony. To prevent haphazard growth and social turmoil in his "greene country towne," Philadelphia, Penn designed the city with a grid plan, laying out the streets at right angles and reserving small areas for parks.

Good planning ensured that Pennsylvania suffered no initial "starving time." The colony was also fortunate in experiencing no large-scale wars with native Americans for seventy years. Partly this resulted from the sparse Indian population in the Delaware Valley—probably no more than twenty thousand in the 1680s. To the Indians, Penn expressed a wish "to live together as Neighbours and Friends," and he tried to buy land fairly from them. However, Pennsylvania was not immune from localized Indian violence.

Pennsylvania seemed an ideal colony—intelligently organized, well financed, tolerant, open to all industrious settlers, and largely at peace with the Indians. Rich, level lands and a lengthy growing season produced bumper crops. Sharp West

Indian demand for its grain quickly generated widespread prosperity and by 1700 made Philadelphia a major port.

But like other attempts to base new American societies on preconceived plans or lofty ideals, Penn's "peaceable kingdom" soon bogged down in human bickering. In 1684 the founder returned to England to resolve boundary disputes with adjacent Maryland, and in his absence (until 1699) the settlers quarreled incessantly. Although Penn spent much money on his colony, an opposition party attacked his efforts to monopolize foreign trade and to make each landowner pay him a small annual fee. Bitter struggles between Penn's supporters in the governor's council and opponents in the assembly deadlocked the government. From 1686 to 1688, the legislature passed no laws and the council once ordered the lower house's speaker arrested. Penn's brief return to Pennsylvania from 1699 to 1701 helped little, but just before he sailed home, he made the legislature a unicameral (one-chamber) assembly and allowed it to initiate measures.

In addition, religious conflict shook Pennsylvania during the 1690s, when George Keith, a college-educated Public Friend, urged Quakers to adopt a formal creed. This would have changed the democratically functioning Quaker sect—in which the humblest member had equal authority in interpreting the Inner Light—into a more traditional church dominated by an educated clergy. The majority of Quakers rejected Keith's views in 1692, whereupon he joined the Church of England, taking some Quakers with him. Keith's heresy began a major decline in the Quaker share of Pennsylvania's population. The proportion fell further once Quakers ceased immigrating in large numbers after 1710. Finally, in 1748 Penn's heirs became Anglican. Pennsylvania's highest political offices thereafter went to Anglicans, although Friends remained predominant in the assembly.

William Penn met his strongest opposition in the counties on the lower Delaware River, where the best lands had been taken up by Swedes and Dutch. In 1704 these counties gained the right to elect their own legislature, but Penn continued to name their governor. Although the new colony of Delaware's separation temporarily strengthened the proprietor's party in what remained of Pennsylvania, by then the founder's dream of a harmonious society was dashed.

Sadness darkened Penn's last years. Having sunk a fortune into Pennsylvania, he later spent some months in a debtor's prison and died in debt. Long before, he had despaired at having to battle with the legislature's politicians, bent on economic and political advantage. As early as 1685, he begged them, "For the love of God, me, and the poor country, be not so governmentish; so noisy and open in your disaffection."

Penn's anguish summed up the dilemmas of the late-seventeenth-century Englishmen who had planned the Restoration colonies so carefully. Very little went according to expectation. Yet the Restoration colonies were a solid success. Before they were a quarter-century old, the middle colonies demonstrated that British America could benefit by encouraging pluralism. New York and New Jersey successfully integrated New Netherland's Swedish and Dutch population; and Pennsylvania, New Jersey, and Delaware refused to require residents to pay support for any official church. But meanwhile, the virtual completion of English claim staking along the Atlantic coast had set England on a collision course with France and Spain, the other European powers vying for North American territory.

Rivals for North America

France and Spain had established far-flung inland networks of fortified trading posts and missions that stood in marked contrast to England's compact settlements. To offset the English colonists' superiority in numbers, France and Spain enlisted native Americans as trading partners and military allies, and the two Catholic nations had far more success than English Protestants in converting Indians to Christianity. By 1720 a handful of missionaries, fur traders, and merchants—who rarely benefited from any military protection—had spread French and Spanish influence through two-thirds of the present-day United States.

England's rivals exercised varying degrees of control in developing their American colonies. Louis XIV's France, the supreme power in late-seventeenth-century Europe, poured in state resources, whereas Spain, then in deep decay, made little attempt to influence North American affairs from afar. In both cases, local officials and settlers assumed the primary burden for extending imperial control.

France Claims a Continent

By 1663 more than half a century's efforts had yielded little success for the struggling colony of New France. The Iroquois were choking its livelihood by intercepting convoys of beaver pelts from the interior. French settlement had advanced no farther up the St. Lawrence River than Jacques Cartier had penetrated 129 years before. The colony's white population of twenty-five hundred was less than half that of tiny New Netherland.

But 1663 marked the turning point for New France. That year, the trading company that had founded the colony relinquished control to Louis XIV. From 1663 to 1672, the French crown energetically built up the new royal colony's population by dispatching about six hundred settlers each year. About half were indentured servants who received land after three years' work and could marry among the hundreds of "kings' girls," female orphans shipped over with dowries. The royal government also sent fifteen hundred soldiers (most of whom eventually became settlers) to stop Iroquois interference with the French fur trade. In 1666 these troops marched into present-day New York, pan-

icking the local Mohawks into fleeing without a fight. Sobered by the burning of four villages, well stocked with winter food, the Iroquois Confederacy made a peace that lasted until 1680. Subsequently, New France enormously expanded its North American fur exports. The colony also began attracting hardy and ambitious upper-class adventurers such as the Sieur de La Salle, a former candidate for the priesthood who arrived in 1663 to seek his fortune but later had to evade creditors eager to clap him in a debtor's prison.

French activity quickly penetrated deep into the continent. Frenchmen swarmed westward seeking furs, and by 1670 one-fifth of them were *coureurs de bois*—independent traders unconstrained by government authority or dubious pasts. Living and intermarrying with the Indians, the *coureurs* built for France an empire resting solely on trade and goodwill among native peoples all over central North America. As early as 1672, fur trader Louis Jolliet and Jesuit missionary Jacques Marquette became the first white men known to have reached the upper Mississippi River (near modern Prairie du Chien, Wisconsin); they later paddled twelve hundred miles downstream, to the Mississippi's junction with the Arkansas River. Ten years later, the Sieur de La Salle descended the entire Mississippi to the Gulf of Mexico. When he reached the delta, La Salle formally claimed all the Mississippi basin—half the territory of the present-day

The Old World Encounters the New

Alexandre de Batz, a French visitor to New Orleans in 1735, drew these members of various native American tribes that French missionaries described. The six Indians at the center were Illinois people, a tribe among whom Father Marquette worked. Trade goods, including cured skins and kegs of fat, are lined up in the foreground.

continental United States—for Louis XIV, in whose honor he named the territory Louisiana. A small band of curious Indians watched the ceremony and then drifted away, serenely unaware that anything had changed for them.

Having asserted title to this vast empire, the French began settling the southern gateway into it. In 1698 the first French colonizers arrived near the mouth of the Mississippi. A year later, the French erected a fort near present-day Biloxi, Mississippi. In 1702 they occupied what is now Mobile, Alabama, as a fur-trading station. Founded in 1718, New Orleans became Louisiana's capital and port.

In no time Louisiana acquired a foul reputation, and few French immigrated there willingly. To boost its population, the government deported paupers and criminals, recruited German refugees, and encouraged large-scale slave imports. By 1732

two-thirds of lower Louisiana's fifty-eight hundred people were slaves. Life was dismal, even for whites. A thoroughly corrupt government ran the colony. The settlers could barely feed themselves, often escaping famine only by trading gunpowder for the Indians' corn. Even the priests reportedly could not get along with each other.

France's vast North American empire existed primarily to support trade with the Indians for furs. By 1744 *coureurs de bois* had explored as far west as North Dakota and Colorado and were buying beaver pelts and Indian slaves on the Great Plains. Only at widely scattered places did the French attempt other kinds of enterprise: for example, mining iron in modern-day Missouri and farming in what is now Illinois. Fewer than a thousand fur traders and soldiers held an immense domain for France. The all-important factor was maintaining

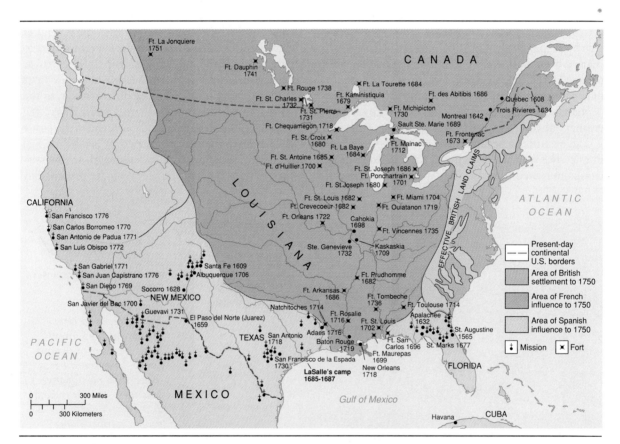

French and Spanish Occupation of North America, to 1776   *French fur traders became entrenched along the Great Lakes and upper Mississippi River between 1666 and 1700, after which they built many settlements in territory claimed by Spain along the Gulf of Mexico. Spanish colonization was concentrated in Florida, central Texas, the Rio Grande Valley, and southern California.*

good relations with the Indians, who after 1720 were the real bar to Spanish and English expansion.

Spain's Borderlands

In the 1680s the Spanish had meanwhile grown alarmed. La Salle had temporarily occupied an outpost near modern-day Houston from 1685 to 1687. To defend their borderland holdings, Spanish authorities in Mexico proclaimed the province of Texas (or Tejas) in 1691. But no permanent Spanish settlements appeared there until 1716, when Spaniards established four missions and a small garrison. The most flourishing of these was San Antonio de Valero, where friars constructed a fortified mission building later famous as the Alamo. The Spanish presence in Texas remained weak, however. By 1742 only eighteen hundred Spaniards and thirteen hundred Catholic Indians blocked the French intruders, and Spain displayed little urgency in building up the province.

Spanish preoccupation with unrest in New Mexico was a primary reason for this neglect of Texas. By 1680 about 2,800 Europeans—many of them scattered on isolated *ranchos* (ranches)—and 30,000 pueblo-dwelling Indians lived in New Mexico's Rio Grande Valley. That year, an Indian named Popé led a revolt, sparked by Spanish priests' efforts to outlaw the religious rituals central to the pueblo peoples' way of life. Popé's forces killed 400 whites (including most priests), captured Santa Fe, and drove the survivors south to El Paso (modern Juarez, Mexico). The pueblo peoples held Santa Fe until Popé died, in 1692, and their resistance seriously threatened Spanish rule down to the 1720s.

To repopulate New Mexico, Spain gave land grants of approximately twenty-six square miles wherever ten or more families founded a town. Strong fortifications arose to protect against future Indian attacks. As in the early New England towns, the settlers built homes on small lots around the church plaza, farmed separate fields nearby, grazed livestock at a distance, and shared a community woodlot and pasture.

By 1750 the Spanish in New Mexico numbered just 5,200, half of them in four towns. Meanwhile, the reduction of the pueblo population by an astonishing 55 percent since 1680, to a mere 13,500, finally eased the danger to Spanish settlements from this quarter, although nomadic Apaches and Navahos remained a menace to outlying *ranchos*. These livestock-raising centers, radiating out for many miles from little clusters of houses, monopolized vast tracts along the Rio Grande and blocked further town settlement. On the *ranchos* mounted cattle and sheep herders (*vaqueros*) created the way of life later associated with the American cowboy—featuring lariat and roping skills, cattle drives, roundups, and brandings. In this way, the horse reached the native Americans.

Recognizing the advantage that mounted men held over foot warriors, the Spanish tried to keep their horses away from the Indians, but horses escaped, were stolen, and were surreptitiously sold. Trade and natural increase spread the animals over the Southwest and the Great Plains. The introduc-

The Alamo

The eighteenth-century Franciscan mission stands today as a powerful symbol of the spirit of resistance felt by a small group fighting in 1836 for Texan Independence from Mexico (see Chapter 12).

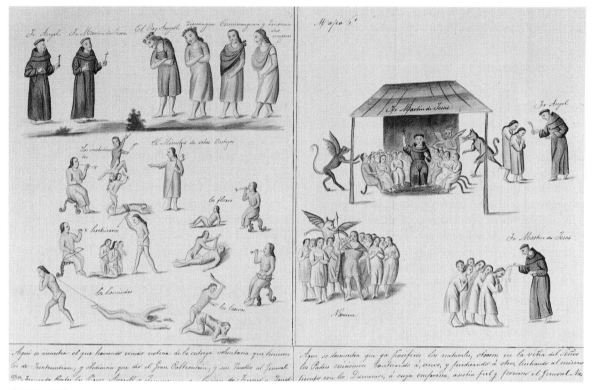

Mission Life

At top left, two priests greet an Indian chief and his three wives; below them, diso-bedient Indians are punished; right, demons dance as priests offer Mass and perform sacraments.

tion of the horse, which took place between the late sixteenth and the eighteenth centuries, was a pivotal event for the Plains Indians. Peaceful peoples who once had migrated slowly on foot, they became flamboyant mounted warriors.

It was missionaries, however, not farmers and herders, who shouldered the main burden of colonizing Spain's borderlands. Most often the first Spaniards to explore and map an area, the padres persuaded native American tribes to accept Spanish allegiance by gathering at a mission. Because soldiers seldom accompanied them, the missionaries organized their converts as defense forces against raiders. Thus new missions created a military shield for older Spanish settlements.

In this process, the native Americans often suffered unintentionally. Mission life slowly cut them off from their religion, traditional work habits, and language. Most devastating of all, the dense concentration of native peoples at places where they were exposed to Old World diseases spawned ter-

rible epidemics among them. The graveyards around the adobe mission churches were soon filled with hundreds of little crosses commemorating deceased Indian converts.

Spain's final burst of North American expansion began in 1700. That year, Austrian-born friar Eusebio Kino came north from Mexico to found Arizona's first mission (near present-day Tucson), and his explorations from this base disproved the longstanding myth that California was an island incapable of being settled. But not until 1769 did Franciscan friars led by Father Junípero Serra establish California's first mission, at San Diego. Over time, a string of missions inched up the coast, a day's march apart, to San Francisco. Government officials encouraged this mission-building effort mainly to plant a firm Spanish presence in California and thus forestall a coastal expansion of Russian outposts, which in the 1720s had sprung up in Alaska to tap the fur trade.

California's potential wealth in minerals and

agricultural land remained largely unexploited during the years of Spanish—and later Mexican—occupation. The Spanish crown awarded immense grants of California land to ex-soldiers and other pioneers for cattle ranches. With the best lands belonging to large estate owners or the church, all but a few California Indians lived rather humbly as farmers or artisans at the missions. Between 1785 and 1803, 40 percent of California's Indians became Catholic. But the white and mestizo (mixed Indian and European) population never rose above 4,000 during the eighteenth century, and exposure to European diseases reduced the mission Indians from an initial total of some 54,000 converts to 17,000 by 1832.

Spain also attempted an ambitious missionizing effort in Florida. By 1665, when scarcely 2,000 whites inhabited Florida, some 13,000 Indians were gathered in a chain of thirty-two missions near the border with southern Carolina. However, Spain's grip was uncertain, for after 1690 southeastern native peoples, among them the Creeks, fiercely retaliated against the English and their Indian allies, who had been plundering native villages for slaves. In light of the Spaniards' reluctance to give their Indian converts enough guns to protect themselves, mission building was less successful in Florida than elsewhere in Spanish North America.

By the mid-eighteenth century, the French and Spanish empires had reached their limits in North America. Spain controlled much of the southern Atlantic and Pacific coastlines. France exercised a subtle influence over the Mississippi, Ohio, and Missouri River valleys. Both empires, spread thin, depended heavily on Indian goodwill or acquiescence. In contrast, British North America was compact, aggressively expansionist, and usually antagonistic toward the native Americans.

Rebellion and War

As France and Spain widened their influence throughout North America, England's colonies seethed with unrest, triggered by the Stuart monarchs' attempt to tighten political control over the colonists. By the late 1680s, the monarchy had kindled sullen resistance as it assumed direct rule over New England and squelched representative government in eight provinces.

But royal centralization collapsed in 1689, after a revolution in England forced King James II into exile. In North America this rebellion sparked several uprisings and ushered in a long period of war with France. Most important, James's successors, William and Mary, reversed several objectionable royal policies and largely returned control of local affairs to the colonial elites.

Stuart Policies

As the sons of a king executed by Parliament, the last two Stuart monarchs disliked representative government. Charles II called Parliament into session rarely from 1674 to 1679, and not at all from 1681 until his death in 1685. James II (ruled 1685–1688) hoped to reign as an "absolute" monarch like France's Louis XIV, who never had to face a national parliament. Not surprisingly, neither English king had much sympathy for the American colonial assemblies.

Royal intentions of extending direct political control to North America first became evident in New York. The proprietor, Charles II's brother James, the Duke of York, considered elected assemblies "of dangerous consequence" and forbade legislatures to meet from 1664 to 1682. He relented from 1682 to 1686 but thereafter called none. Meanwhile, Charles showed a clear preference for naming high-ranking army men as colonial governors. Despite their new civilian status, these governors were the militia's commanders in chief, and their background made them well suited to crushing civilian dissent with armed force. From 1660 to 1685, Charles appointed former army officers to about 90 percent of all gubernatorial positions, thereby compromising the time-honored English tradition of holding the military strictly accountable to civilian authority. By 1680 such "governors general" ruled 60 percent of all American colonists. James II later continued this policy.

Ever resentful of outside meddling, New Englanders proved most stubborn in defending self-government and resisting Stuart policies. As early as 1661, the Massachusetts assembly politely but firmly declared its citizens exempt from all laws and royal decrees from England except for a declaration of war. The colony ignored the Navigation

Acts (see below) and continued welcoming Dutch traders. "The New England men break through and . . . trade to any place that their interest lead them," claimed Virginia's governor William Berkeley.

Soon Charles II targeted Massachusetts for special punishment. In 1679 he carved out of its territory a new royal colony, New Hampshire. Then in 1684 he declared Massachusetts itself a royal colony and revoked its charter, the very foundation of the Puritan city upon a hill. Puritan minister Increase Mather responded by openly calling on colonists to resist to the point of martyrdom.

Royal centralization in America culminated after James II ascended to the throne. In 1686 the new king consolidated Massachusetts, New Hampshire, Connecticut, Rhode Island, and Plymouth into a single administrative unit, the Dominion of New England. He added New York and the Jerseys in 1688. With this bold stroke, all legislatures in these colonies ceased to exist, and still another former army officer, Sir Edmund Andros, became the governor of the Dominion of New England, at Boston.

Massachusetts soon burned with hatred for the new governor. By "Exercise of an arbitrary Government," preached Salem's minister, "ye wicked walked on Every Side & ye Vilest of men ware [sic] exalted." Andros was indeed brutally arbitrary. He suppressed the legislature, limited towns to a single annual meeting, and jailed prominent citizens to crush protests. Further, Andros hit a raw nerve by forcing a Boston Puritan congregation to share its meetinghouse with an Anglican minister, and he even looked into the finances of Harvard College. Naturally, he also strictly enforced the Navigation Acts. "You have no more privileges left you," Andros reportedly told a group of outraged colonists, "than not to be sold for slaves." Other than his soldiers and a handful of recently arrived Anglican immigrants, however, Andros had no base of support in Massachusetts.

Tensions also ran high in New York, where Catholics held high political and military posts under the Duke of York's rule. By 1688 citizens feared that these Catholic officials would betray the colony to France. Many colonists had reason to believe that Andros's local deputy, Captain Francis Nicholson, was pro-Catholic. When Nicholson allowed the harbor's forts to deteriorate

and reacted skeptically to rumors of Indian hostility, New Yorkers suspected the worst.

The Glorious Revolution in England and America

New England Puritans' fury at Andros's forcing them to tolerate Anglicanism was matched by English Protestants' growing worries about the Stuarts' obvious predilection for Catholicism. The Duke of York became a Catholic in 1676, and Charles II converted on his deathbed. Both rulers violated Parliament's laws by issuing decrees that allowed Catholics to hold high office and worship openly. When seven Anglican bishops denounced one such edict in 1688, James II tried them as state enemies. English Protestants' fears that they would have to accept Catholicism intensified after both kings expressed their preference for allying with France just as Louis XIV was launching new persecutions of that country's Protestants in 1685.

The English tolerated James II's Catholicism only because his heirs, his daughters Mary and Anne, had remained Anglican. Then in 1688 James's wife bore a son, who would be raised—and might someday reign—as a Catholic. Aghast at the thought of a Catholic monarchy, some English politicians asked Mary and her husband, William of Orange (the Dutch Republic's leader) to intervene. When William and Mary led a small army to England in November 1688, most royal troops defected to them, and James II fled to France.

This bloodless revolution of 1688, also called the Glorious Revolution, created a "limited monarchy" as defined by England's Bill of Rights of 1689. The crown promised to summon Parliament annually, sign all its bills, and respect traditional civil liberties. The Glorious Revolution's vindication of limited representative government burned deeply into English political consciousness, and Anglo-Americans never forgot it. Anglo-Americans not only came to share English Protestants' pride in the Glorious Revolution but also struck their own blows for liberty. Soon Massachusetts, New York, and Maryland all rose up against local representatives of the Stuart regime.

By 1688–1689 New Yorkers and New Englanders felt increasingly threatened by French aggression. Rumors flew that a French fleet was planning to take New York and that Indians would

**King William and
Queen Mary**

raid Albany. By early 1689 pro-French Indians assaulted English settlements in Maine. Andros promptly led a force of English troops and Massachusetts militia to defend Maine. But when he refused to attack neutral Indians, the colonists suspected him of protecting treacherous French allies. Ordering his soldiers to guard the Maine frontier, Andros returned to Boston defenseless in the event of trouble there.

Meanwhile, news that England's Protestant leaders had risen up against James II had electrified New Englanders. On April 18, well before confirmation of the English revolt's success, Boston's militia arrested Andros and his councilors. (The governor tried to flee in women's clothing but was caught after an alert guard spotted a "lady" in army boots.) The "sensible Gentlemen" of Massachusetts—the old political leadership—acted in the name of William and Mary, risking their necks should James return to power in England. Massachusetts and every other New England colony swiftly resumed self-government.

William and Mary would have preferred continuing the Dominion, but in the face of single-minded colonial determination to break it up, they wisely desisted. They gave official consent to dismantling the Dominion and restored to the citizens of Connecticut and Rhode Island the right of electing their own governors. However, they kept Massachusetts a royal colony, and, though allow-

ing the province to absorb Plymouth, refused to let it regain New Hampshire.

In other respects, too, Massachusetts won only a partial victory. Despite Increase Mather's lobbying in London, the new royal charter of 1691 reserved to the crown the right of appointing the governor. Moreover, property ownership, not church membership, became the criterion for voting. Worst of all, the Puritan colony had to tolerate Anglicans, who were proliferating in the port towns. In a society trembling at divine displeasure over its ungodliness (see Chapter 2), this was indeed bitter medicine to swallow.

New York's counterpart of the anti-Stuart uprising was Leisler's Rebellion. Emboldened by news of Boston's April 18 coup and startled by rumors that Andros's deputy Nicholson had threatened to burn New York, the city's militia seized the harbor's main fort on May 31, 1689. With his authority strangled, Nicholson sailed for England. Captain Jacob Leisler of the militia took over command of the colony, repaired its run-down defenses, and called elections for an assembly. When English troops arrived at New York in 1691 and Leisler denied them entry to key forts for fear that their commander was loyal to James II, a skirmish resulted, and Leisler was arrested.

"Hott brain'd" Leisler unwittingly had set his own downfall in motion. He had jailed many New Yorkers for questioning his authority, only to find that his former enemies had gained the new governor's ear and persuaded him to charge Leisler with treason for firing on royal troops. A packed jury found Leisler and his son-in-law, Jacob Milborne, guilty. Both men went to the gallows insisting that they were dying "for the king and queen and the Protestant religion."

Quickly wresting control of the council and legal system, Leisler's enemies used the courts to plunder their opponents' estates. Their rampage ceased in 1695, when Parliament reversed Leisler's and Milborne's convictions and ordered them reburied with full honors. Following a triumphant, emotional procession in which half of New York's adults marched in a pouring rain to reinter the two martyrs, the Leislerians inflicted stinging reprisals on their enemies and would have executed Leisler's bitterest antagonist if a sympathetic governor had not pardoned him. Both parties fought ruthlessly to destroy the other; but not until most of their leaders had died, by about 1720, did Jacob Leisler's vengeful ghost cease stalking New York.

By 1689 Maryland too had suffered political turmoil revolving around the issues of arbitrary government and Catholic plots. The Protestant-dominated lower house and the Catholic officials in the upper chamber feuded endlessly. Lurking behind it all was the uncertainty of having a pro-Stuart Catholic as the colony's absentee proprietor. News of England's Glorious Revolution naturally heartened Maryland's Protestant majority, which had long chafed under Catholic rule. Hoping to prevent a repetition of minor religion-tinged uprisings that had flared in 1676 and 1681, Lord Baltimore sent a messenger from England in early 1689 to command Maryland's obedience to William and Mary. But the courier died en route. The colony's Protestants widely began to fear that their proprietor was a traitor who supported James II.

Soon John Coode, a leader of the 1681 revolt, and three others organized the Protestant Association to secure Maryland for William and Mary. These conspirators seem to have been motivated far more by their exclusion from high public office than by religion, for three of the four had Catholic wives. Coode's group seized the capital in July 1689, removed all Catholics from office, and requested that the crown take over the colony. They got their wish. Maryland became a royal province in 1691, and in 1692 it made the Church of England the established religion. Catholics, who composed less

than one-fourth of the population, lost the right to vote and thereafter could worship only in private.

Maryland stayed in royal hands until 1715. At that point, the fourth Lord Baltimore joined the Church of England and regained his proprietorship. (Ironically, the children of John Coode and of another Protestant Association mastermind then turned Catholic.) Maryland continued as a proprietary colony until 1776.

The revolutionary events of 1688–1689 decisively changed the colonies' political climate by reestablishing legislative government and ensuring religious freedom for Protestants. Dismantling the Dominion of New England and directing governors to call annual assemblies, William and Mary allowed the colonial elite to reassert control over local affairs and encouraged American political leaders to identify their interests with England. A foundation was thus laid for an empire based on voluntary allegiance rather than submission to raw power imposed from faraway London. The crowning of William and Mary opened a new era in which Americans drew rising confidence from their relationship to the English throne. "As long as they reign," wrote a Bostonian who helped topple Andros, "New England is secure."

A Generation of War

The Revolution of 1688 ushered in a quarter-century of warfare that convulsed Europe and the colonies alike. In 1689 England joined a general European coalition against France's Louis XIV, who supported James II's claim to the English crown. The resulting War of the League of Augsburg (which Anglo-Americans called King William's War) was the first struggle to embroil the colonies in European rivalries. For the next seventy-five years, North American soil would be an extension of Europe's battlefields.

In the American theater of King William's War, New Yorkers and Yankees launched a two-pronged invasion of Canada in 1690, with one prong aimed at Montreal and the second at Quebec. Lack of supplies caused the Anglo-American expedition marching on Montreal to disintegrate in the New York wilderness. Meanwhile, their strength sapped by smallpox, half-rations, and insufficient ammunition, two thousand Massachusetts militiamen eventually abandoned a lengthy siege of Quebec.

The war then degenerated into a series of cruel but inconclusive border raids against civilians on both sides.

Already weary from a new wave of Beaver Wars fought against Indians in the Ohio Valley since 1680 (see Chapter 1), the Iroquois of New York bore the bloodiest fighting in King William's War. Standing almost alone against their foes, the Five Nations faced overwhelming odds. Not only did their own English and Dutch allies meet with little success intercepting enemy war parties, but *coureurs de bois* had enlisted virtually all other Indians of the region as French combatants. In 1691 every Mohawk and Oneida war chief died in battle; by 1696 French armies had destroyed the villages of every Iroquois nation but the Cayugas and Oneidas. Hundreds of tribe members defected to the French and moved to Canada.

Although the war ended in 1697, the Iroquois staggered under Algonkian invasions until 1700. By then one-quarter of the Five Nations' 2,000 warriors had been killed or taken prisoner, or had deserted to Canada. The total Iroquois population declined 20 percent over twelve years, from 8,600 to 7,000. (By comparison, fewer than 900 English and Dutch, and perhaps no more than 400 French, died during the same period.)

In 1701, under French pressure, the Iroquois agreed not only to let Canada's governor settle their disputes with other Indians but also to stay neutral in future wars. Thereafter, the Iroquois perfected a delicate diplomacy that played off the English and French. Skillful negotiations brought the Iroquois far more success than had war by allowing them to keep control of their lands, rebuild their decimated population, and gain recognition as holding the balance of power along the Great Lakes.

In 1702 European war again erupted when England fought France and Spain in the War of the Spanish Succession, called Queen Anne's War by England's American colonists. This conflict taught Anglo-Americans painful lessons about their military weakness. Raiders from Canada destroyed several towns in Massachusetts and Maine. The Spanish invaded southern Carolina and nearly took Charles Town in 1706. Enemy warships captured many colonial vessels and landed looting parties along the Atlantic coast. Colonial sieges of Quebec and St. Augustine ended as expensive failures.

English forces had more success than their colonial counterparts and occupied the Hudson's

French Fort Builders

The French mania for establishing forts in America is the subject of this German engraving of c. 1700.

Bay region, as well as previously French Newfoundland and Acadia (later called Nova Scotia). When peace came in 1713 after nineteen years of vicious combat, however, the French and Indian hold on the continent's interior remained unbroken.

The most important consequence of the colonial wars was political in nature, not military. The wars instilled in Anglo-Americans a profound sense of dependence on Great Britain. The clashes with France vividly reminded Americans of the loyalty they owed William and Mary for ousting James II, who the colonists believed would have persecuted Protestants and ruled despotically. Anglo-Americans also came to recognize their own military weakness and the extent to which their shipping needed the Royal Navy's protection. Even as a new generation of English colonists matured, war was thus reinforcing their sense of British identity by buttressing their loyalty to the crown.

Peace and Expansion

The end of Queen Anne's War in 1713 introduced a generation of peace lasting until 1744. Britain's mainland colonies enjoyed exceptional growth in these years, with their population tripling from about 330,000 to 1 million. Settlement spread to the foothills of the Appalachians, and the new colony of Georgia was born. Rising prosperity dramatically improved living standards for most Americans and allowed the upper ranks of society to become graciously cultured and "enlightened."

A Burgeoning, Diversifying Population

In 1751 Pennsylvania businessman, publicist, and scientist Benjamin Franklin (1706–1790) wrote in an essay, *Observations Concerning the Increase of Mankind and the Peopling of the Colonies,* that "people increase in proportion to the number of marriages, and that is greater in proportion to the ease and convenience of supporting a family. When families can be easily supported, more persons marry, and earlier in life." Cities, he noted, retarded such growth: they were unhealthy and contained many people too poor to marry and rear families. But British America, with its small cities and great expanses of rural space, clearly seemed destined to grow and flourish. Estimating the colonies' population at 1 million, Franklin calculated that this number would double every twenty-five years. He exulted: "What an accession of power to the British empire!" Franklin knew whereof he spoke: he was the tenth child among seventeen siblings. He estimated colonial growth trends with amazing precision, and modern research has confirmed his reasoning about the factors driving population change in his era.

Every North American colony followed a similar demographic pattern. In the first years of settlement, numbers increased only through a continuous influx of immigrants, for settlers always died more quickly than children could be born to replace them. But at some point, males ceased to outnumber females, so that most adults could find mates. Moreover, because colonists married young and had large families, the population finally started inching up by natural increase (the excess of births over deaths). Rapid growth, however, began only when settlers also enjoyed good nutrition and a healthy environment—conditions that lowered infant mortality and extended adult life expectancy.

By 1645 the male-female ratio almost equalized in New England (see Chapter 2). Thereafter, favorable environmental conditions caused the population to shoot up. By 1690 the same spurt began in the Middle Atlantic colonies.

Demographic "takeoff" reached the South last. Only with the heavy importation of indentured servants did the southern population continue to expand in the seventeenth century. Even after 1690, when the southern colonies finally had roughly equal numbers of men and women, growth was slow because epidemic disease haunted the marshy tidewater. After Queen Anne's War, however, southern whites left the tidewater in droves, and by 1750 a majority of them resided in the piedmont, where the life expectancy equaled that in New England. Slaves came to form the greater part of the eighteenth-century tidewater population, but their death rate was lower than whites' because of their partial immunity to malaria.

After 1700, when life expectancy and family size in the South rose to levels typical of the North, British North America's growth rate far outpaced Great Britain's. Colonial women had an average of eight children and forty-two grandchildren; British women at the time typically bore five infants and had fifteen grandchildren. The ratio of Britain's population to that of the mainland colonies plummeted from 20 to 1 (1700) to 3 to 1 (1775).

Fully half of all colonial women bore more than eight children. This exceptionally high birthrate produced families like that of New Jersey resident Daniel Robbins, described in the *New England Weekly Journal* in 1733. By the time Robbins was 66, his wife had 13 children, of whom 11 had married and borne 62 offspring of their own. None of the Robbins's descendants had yet died, and more grandchildren were on the way. "Thus it appears," the *Weekly Journal* declared, "that said Daniel Robbins has successfully kept and fulfilled that great and necessary Commandment of *Multiply, be Fruitful,* and *Replenish the Earth.*" Such remarkable fertility was responsible for two-thirds of colonial population growth after 1700.

In the eighteenth century, immigration continued to contribute significantly to colonial population growth, though it became less important than natural increase. In the forty years after Queen Anne's War, the colonies absorbed 350,000 newcomers, 40 percent of them (140,000) slaves who had survived a sea crossing of sickening brutality. The approximately 210,000 whites who immi-

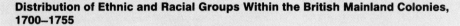

Distribution of Ethnic and Racial Groups Within the British Mainland Colonies, 1700–1755

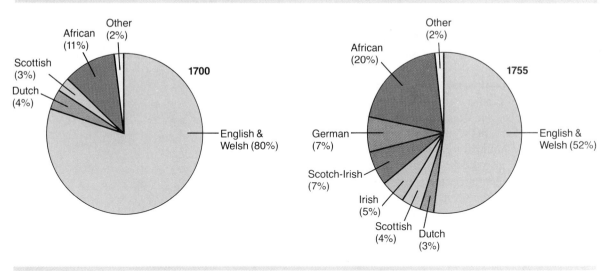

The impact of heavy immigration from 1720 to 1755 can be seen in the reduction of the English-Welsh stock from four-fifths of all colonists to a slight majority; in the doubling of the African-American population; and in the sudden influx of Germans and Irish, who together composed a fifth of all Anglo-Americans by 1755.

SOURCE: Thomas L. Purvis, "The European Ancestry of the United States Population," *William & Mary Quarterly,* LXI (1984), 85–101.

grated during these years included a sharply reduced share from England compared to the seventeenth century. Whereas between 1630 and 1700 an average of 2,000 English settlers landed annually (constituting 90 percent of all European immigrants), after 1713 the English contribution dropped to about 500 a year. Rising employment and higher wages in eighteenth-century England simply made voluntary immigration to America far less attractive than before. But economic hardship elsewhere in the British Isles and northern Europe supplied a steady stream of immigrants, and their coming ensured that white North Americans were growing more ethnically diverse.

Immigrants usually found the passage to America harrowing. A German in 1750 remembered "the ship . . . full of pitiful signs of distress . . . , all of them caused by the age and the highly salted state of the food . . . , as well as by the very bad and filthy water, which brings about the miserable destruction and death of many. . . . All this misery reaches its climax when . . . one

must suffer through two or three days and nights of storm, with everyone convinced that the ship with all aboard is bound to sink." This man's voyage lasted fifteen weeks.

The largest eighteenth-century white immigrant contingent comprised 100,000 newcomers from Ireland, two-thirds of them "Scots-Irish" descendants of sixteenth-century Scottish Presbyterians who had settled in northern Ireland. After 1718 Scots-Irish fled to America to escape rack renting (frequent increases in farm rents), and they commonly came as complete families. In contrast, 90 percent of all Catholic Irish immigrants arrived as unmarried male indentured servants. Rarely able to find Catholic wives, they generally abandoned their faith to marry Protestant women.

Meanwhile, from Germany came a wave of 65,000 settlers, most of them refugees from terrible economic conditions in the Rhine Valley. Wartime devastation had compounded the misery of Rhenish peasants, many of whom were squeezed onto plots of land too small to feed a family. One-third of these people financed their voyage as "redemptioners"—that is, they had sold themselves or their children as indentured servants. Most Germans were either Lutherans or Calvinists. But a significant minority belonged to small, pacifist religious sects that desired above all to be left alone.

Overwhelmingly, the eighteenth-century immigrants were poor. Those who became indentured servants had to give one to four years of work to an urban or rural master, who might well exploit them cruelly. Servants could be sold or rented out, beaten, granted minimal legal protection, kept from marrying, and sexually harassed; and attempted escape usually meant an extension of their service. But at the end of their term, most managed to collect "freedom dues," which could help them to marry and acquire land.

Whether or not they had been servants, few immigrants settled permanently in those parts of North America where land was relatively scarce and expensive—New England, New Jersey, lower New York, and the southern tidewater. (New Englanders in particular did not welcome people who might become public charges: "these confounded Irish will eat us all up," snorted one Bostonian.) Philadelphia became the immigrants' primary port of entry. So many foreigners passed through the "City of Brotherly Love" into underpopulated Pennsylvania that by 1755 the original English stock accounted for only one-third of the colony's population; the rest were mostly Germans, Irish, and Scots.

Rising numbers of immigrants traveled to the piedmont region, stretching along the eastern slope of the Appalachians. A significant German community developed in upper New York, and thousands of other Germans as well as Irish fanned southward from Pennsylvania into western Maryland. Many other Irish, Germans, and Scots arrived in the second-most popular gateway to eighteenth-century America, Charles Town, whence they would move on to settle the South Carolina piedmont. There they raised grain, livestock, and tobacco, generally without slaves. After 1750 both streams of immigration merged with an outpouring of Anglo-Americans from the Chesapeake in the rolling, fertile hills of western North Carolina. In 1713 few Anglo-Americans had lived more than fifty miles from the sea, but by 1750 one-third of all colonists resided in the piedmont.

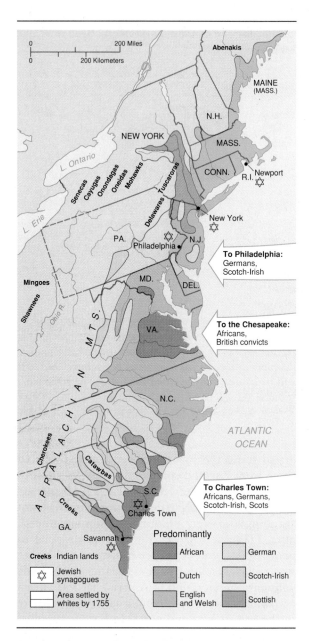

Immigration and Frontier Expansion, to 1755

A sharp rise in the importation of African slaves made much of the southern tidewater a predominantly black region. Immigrants from Germany, Ireland, and Scotland tended to settle in the piedmont. A significant Jewish population emerged in the seaports.

Immigrants found the piedmont rather easy to settle. Disease and war had already destroyed or scattered most of the native American population.

Only in upper New York did a continuing Indian presence block further white expansion (see "A Place in Time"). Elsewhere after 1713, few Indians remained within the triangular region bounded by Philadelphia, Albany, and southern Maine. The Chesapeake tribes had moved beyond Virginia's Shenandoah Valley, and in the Carolina piedmont, the remnants of the Tuscaroras and Yamasees drifted away. Then in the 1730s, smallpox killed perhaps half the fifty thousand Cherokees and Catawbas remaining in the Carolina piedmont. Native Americans explained their own depopulation in supernatural rather than scientific terms, but their conclusion was not far from the mark. "They have a superstition," wrote a Pennsylvania German in 1700, "that as many Indians die each year, as the number of Europeans that newly arrive."

English-stock colonists did not relish the influx of so many foreigners. Franklin spoke for many when he asked in his 1751 essay on population,

why should the Palatine boors [Germans] be suffered to swarm into our settlements, and, by herding together, establish their language and manners, to the exclusion of ours? Why should Pennsylvania, founded by the English, become a colony of aliens, who will shortly be so numerous as to Germanize us instead of us Anglicizing them, and will never adopt our language or customs any more than they can acquire our complexion?

In the same ungenerous spirit, Franklin objected to the slave trade largely because it would increase America's black population at the expense of industrious whites.

On another occasion, Franklin suggested that the colonists send rattlesnakes to Britain in return for the convict laborers dumped on American shores. Deportation of lawbreakers to America had been common enough in the seventeenth century, and between 1718 and 1783, some thirty thousand convicts arrived. A few were murderers; most were thieves; some were guilty of the most trivial offenses, like a young Londoner who "got intoxicated with liquor, and in that condition attempted to snatch a handkerchief from the body of a person in the street to him unknown. . . ." Convicts were sold as servants on arrival. Relatively few continued to commit crimes in America, and some managed eventually to establish themselves as back-country farmers. But like many contemporary Americans, colonial citizens seldom wished to absorb the victims of other nations' social problems.

Georgia

Yet for Parliament, solving England's social problems was a chief motive in chartering the new colony of Georgia in 1732. Parliament intended Georgia as a refuge where bankrupt debtors (who normally rotted in jail until their debt was repaid) could settle, their presence protecting South Carolina against attacks from Spanish Florida to the south. Meanwhile, the new colony's sponsors hoped that Georgia would flourish by exporting expensive commodities like wine and silk. Parliament even spent money to ensure the success of the colony, which became the only North American province (except Nova Scotia) in which the British government actually invested funds.

The moving spirit behind Georgia's foundation was tough-minded James Oglethorpe (1696–1785). He guided the colony's charter through Parliament (of which he was a member) and for the first ten years of Georgia's existence dominated the board of trustees that administered the province. A puritanical bachelor, he yearned to do good for the downtrodden. Although a soldier of fortune, he admired the pacifist Quaker William Penn, whom in several respects he resembled. Like Penn, he was doomed to disappointment.

Georgia took shape slowly during its first decade. Oglethorpe founded the port of entry, Savannah, in 1733, and by 1740 a small contingent— 2,800 colonists—had settled in the province. Almost half the immigrants came from Germany, Switzerland, and Scotland, and most had their overseas passage paid by the government. A small number of Jews were among the early settlers. Georgia thus began as the least English of all colonies. In 1742 Oglethorpe led 650 men in repelling 3,000 Spanish troops and refugee South Carolina slaves who had invaded Georgia aiming to destroy all English settlements as far as Charles Town. When peace returned in 1744, Georgia's survival was assured.

Idealistic concerns about human welfare, along with practical considerations of security, prompted Oglethorpe to try banning slavery and rum from Georgia, as well as to deal fairly with the Indians.

In 1750, about forty miles south of Lake Ontario lay the Seneca Indian village of Geneseo. Comprising about a hundred houses set amidst vast fruit orchards and beautiful vegetable fields, Geneseo was the largest community of the Senecas, the westernmost Iroquois people. The high seventeenth-century stockade had slowly crumbled during the long peace since 1713. As the village outgrew its former fortifications, the Senecas abandoned their decrepit homes and built replacements wherever they pleased, so that Geneseo sprawled without plan across a lovely meadow.

Decades of peace had brought the Senecas prosperity. In exchange for the furs that they sold at Albany, Seneca hunters kept Geneseo well supplied with British manufactures. Every Seneca household owned a gun, several metal pots, woven blankets, steel knives and hatchets, animal traps, iron needles, scissors, ready-made shirts, bells, mirrors, tweezers for extracting body hair, a mouth harp, copper armbands, rings, metallic earrings, and assorted charms. Dutch and English merchants did a lucrative business providing the Iroquois with these wares, as well as with enormous quantities of gunpowder, bullets, and whiskey. The Senecas dressed, slept, cooked, hunted, and entertained themselves using European goods, which they incorporated into their way of life without changing their underlying culture and values.

Iroquois life revolved around the longhouse. Measuring as much as seventy-five feet long and fifteen

Iroquois Silver Craft

Though lacking knowledge of silver and other metals until whites introduced them, the Iroquois thereafter became highly skilled metal crafters.

feet wide, the longhouse was a barracks that could hold up to sixty persons. Each family occupied a compartment twelve or fifteen feet long containing two sets of double-decker bunk beds about six feet wide. There was little privacy, for one hallway connected every compartment and people tramped through at all hours. An open fire smoldering all day in every family's quarters kept the atmosphere smoke-filled and stuffy.

Each longhouse sheltered the members of a particular clan, its symbol carved above the main entrance. Because ancestry was traced through the mother's line, women dominated the longhouse's social and economic activities. Elder women resolved problems between clan members and oversaw the distribution of property.

By raising the community's crops, women also bore the chief responsibility for preventing famine. An individual woman could claim exclusive rights to a field or an orchard, but few did so. The women cleared, planted, weeded, and harvested the fields of their clan in a leisurely but highly efficient fashion by organizing "working bees," during which they joked, sang, or gossiped their way through each day's labor. Aside from meat and fish that the men brought in, a mother furnished her family's entire diet: fruit, squash, pumpkins, herbs, bark teas, and especially succotash, a bean-corn mixture that provided all a healthy adult's protein needs. Iroquois women were such productive farmers that the Seneca nation, which numbered just thirty-five hundred people in 1750, raised perhaps a million bushels of corn each year.

The Iroquois also gave women considerable opportunity to influence the choice of leaders and other political decisions. The forty-nine Seneca clans sent representatives to the council of the League of the Iroquois, and whenever a delegate died, the senior women of the clan named his successor. Although men had formal responsibility for war and diplomacy, women's views carried substantial weight at village meetings. Women rarely spoke there, but they persuaded important individuals from their clans to voice females' views, and they lobbied undecided leaders to support their spokesmen. Because native Americans made decisions by persuasion

Hendrick, a Mohawk Chief, c. 1710

Hendrick, who posed for this formal portrait during a visit to London, sported European-style dress but personalized it with Iroquois touches such as the woven sash and wampum belt that he is holding. The Iroquois readily adopted European attire.

and consensus rather than by a simple majority vote, women were guaranteed a hearing—and they often prevailed.

As head of their clans, women could, moreover, insist that their kinsmen attack enemies for revenge or to seize a captive to replace a dead relative. Although such demands could not be legally enforced, they imposed a moral burden that men could not escape without seriously damaging their reputation. Consequently, Iroquois women instigated many small scale military actions by demanding vengeance or prisoners. Even during the relatively peaceful decades after Queen Anne's War ended in 1713, Seneca matrons sent several dozens of war parties against the Catawba Indians of South Carolina. The fate of Catawbas dragged back by these raiders depended on the women, who adopted most captives into their families but shared fully in slowly torturing to death those who seemed unfit to replace fallen relatives.

So the Senecas, like all Iroquois, depended heavily on women's contributions. The men roamed over a million square miles from South Carolina north to Hudson's Bay and west to the Mississippi River; frequently gone for several months at a stretch while trapping furs, they went off for shorter periods while hunting game, conducting diplomacy, or seeking captives. But during these absences, economically self-sufficient women could be counted on to feed the village. Additionally, in times of a conflict such as King William's War, when the Iroquois lost perhaps half their senior leaders in battle, elder women's political skills and wisdom guided untested younger men who were suddenly thrust into positions of high responsibility. And in more peaceful times, women preserved the memory of the past, passed traditions on to children, and kept peace within the cramped, smoke-filled longhouses. In short, women provided the economic self-sufficiency, political wisdom, and cultural memory that were essential to the Iroquois' continuation as a great people.

Family Life in a Seneca Longhouse

The baby hangs in a cradle-board; the man carves a wooden bowl.

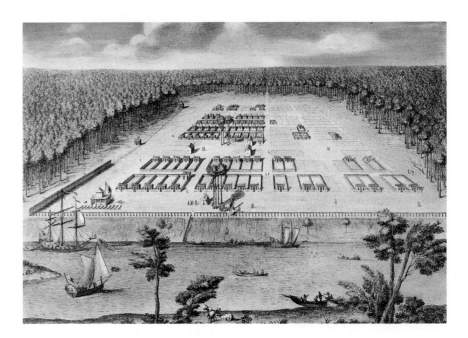

Earliest-Known View of Savannah, c. 1734

Oglethorpe hated slavery. "They live like cattle," he wrote to the trustees after viewing Charles Town's slave market. "If we allow slaves, we act against the very principles by which we associated together, which was to relieve the distressed." Slavery, he thought, degraded blacks, made whites lazy, and presented a terrible risk. South Carolina's Stono Rebellion of 1739 particularly alarmed him. Oglethorpe worried that wherever whites relied on a slave labor force, they courted slave revolts, which the Spanish could then exploit. As an abstainer from hard liquor (a trait that made him unusual in eighteenth-century America), he disapproved of the importation and distilling of spirits, and as the man responsible for the colony's security, he feared the effects of encouraging nearby Indians to drink. Oglethorpe was also atypical of his era in admiring the native Americans' seemingly simple, dignified way of life, and they responded by trusting him. As long as he remained the colony's leader, Georgia enjoyed good relations with the southeastern tribes.

At Oglethorpe's insistence, Parliament made Georgia the only colony where slavery was forbidden. He also pushed through a requirement that landholdings remain relatively small and that a male always occupy each farm. Thus fathers could pass on property only if they had male heirs. These measures were aimed at keeping rural Georgia populated by white farmer-soldiers, ready to leap to the colony's defense and uncorrupted by the urge to speculate in real estate or build up slave-labor plantations.

But Oglethorpe's well-intentioned plans failed completely. Few debtors arrived because Parliament set impossibly stringent conditions for their release from prison. Limitations on settlers' rights to sell or enlarge their holdings, as well as the ban on slavery, also kept settlement low. Raising exotic export crops proved impractical; as in South Carolina, only rice yielded a profit. Oglethorpe struggled against economic reality for a decade and then gave up. After the early 1740s, he took little part in Georgia's affairs. Then in 1750 the trustees finally legalized slavery, and other restrictions on the market for land also fell by the wayside. As a result, Georgia boomed. The population rose from four thousand residents in 1750 (including up to a thousand hitherto illegal slaves) to twenty-three thousand inhabitants in 1770, 45 percent of them blacks.

Georgia's settlement completed British colonization of the Atlantic seaboard. Having held Georgia against Spain and pushed the frontier west 150 miles, British expansion virtually halted after 1750. Anglo-Americans would not settle beyond the Appalachians until the 1770s. Nevertheless, the colonial population continued to grow rapidly,

James Oglethorpe and the Indians

In 1734 Oglethorpe visited London with Indians who had sold him land. Here the native Americans meet with Englishmen who have invested in the Georgia colony.

doubling every twenty-six years—almost exactly what Franklin had predicted in 1751. Had this rate continued, the U.S. population today would number around 850 million, second only to China's.

A Maturing Colonial Economy and Society

Britons who visited mid-eighteenth-century America were generally impressed at the sight of a sophisticated society and widespread economic prosperity. "The nobleness of the town," wrote an English naval officer after first viewing New York in 1756, "surprized me more than the fertile appearance of the country. I had no idea of finding a place in America, consisting of near 2,000 houses, elegantly built of brick, raised on an eminence and the streets paved and spacious, . . . but such is this city that very few in England can rival it in its show." Seven years later, when issuing orders for demobilizing royal troops stationed in the colonies, General Jeffery Amherst advised his regimen-

tal commanders to discourage their men from returning to the British Isles to be mustered out because "I would much rather they would take their Discharges in this country, where they can get their Livelyhood by working Easier than at Home."

The prosperity and social development that European visitors recorded, as well as the underlying rapid population growth and wide expansion of frontier settlement, were relatively new. By 1750 the colonies' brisk economic growth had been under way for only fifty to seventy-five years, depending on the region. Throughout the first half of the eighteenth century, colonial exports climbed steadily and allowed Anglo-Americans to enjoy a relatively high standard of living despite external controls imposed by Parliament.

British Economic Policy Toward America

Between 1651 and 1733, Parliament enacted a series of laws governing commerce between the British Isles and the overseas colonies. Historians label the rules of trade set forth in these laws the "navigation system," and they use the word *mercantilism* to describe the assumptions on which these laws rested. Both the navigation system and mercantilist thinking remained vigorously alive from the late seventeenth to the late eighteenth century, and they deeply affected North America's relationship with Great Britain.

Mercantilism was not a carefully elaborated economic theory. Rather, the word refers to European policymakers' aim of guaranteeing prosperity by making their own country as self-sufficient as possible—by eliminating dependence on foreign suppliers, damaging foreign competitors' commercial interests, and increasing their nation's net stock of gold and silver by selling more abroad than they bought. Mercantilist policies generally had the additional effect of favoring special interests such as chartered companies and merchants' guilds. Mercantilism was the antithesis of a competitive free-market system, which received its first great theoretical defense in Scottish economist Adam Smith's *The Wealth of Nations,* published in 1776. Until that revolutionary year, mercantilist thinking would dominate British policy almost unchallenged.

Parliament enacted England's first Navigation Act in 1651 to undercut the Dutch Republic's economic preponderance. Dutch shippers and merchants then controlled oceanic trade and probably owned three-quarters of northern Europe's commercial vessels; few Englishmen could compete with the well-financed and experienced Dutch traders. By the Navigation Acts, Parliament sought to exclude the Dutch from English trade and thereby to force England to build up its own merchant marine. Immediately after the Stuart restoration in 1660, Parliament reiterated these rules and also began protecting English manufactures from foreign competition. By 1750 a long series of Navigation Acts were in force, affecting the colonial economy in four major ways.

First, the laws limited all imperial trade to *British* ships, defined as those with British ownership and whose crews were three-quarters British. (Because Parliament wanted only to exclude the Dutch, not to discriminate against Americans, it classified all colonists, even blacks, as British.) When Parliament began strictly to enforce this requirement in the late seventeenth century, American colonists and some elements of the English business community alike objected, because the Dutch offered better prices, credit, and merchandise. After 1700, however, when Britain's merchant marine became equal to its Dutch competitors, this cause for complaint evaporated.

This new shipping restriction not only contributed to Great Britain's rise as Europe's foremost shipping nation but also laid the foundations for an American merchant marine. By the 1750s one-third of all imperial vessels were American-owned. The swift growth of this merchant marine diversified the colonial economy and made it more self-sufficient. The expansion of colonial shipping in turn hastened urbanization by creating a need for centralized docks, warehouses, and repair shops in America. By 1770 Philadelphia was the British Empire's second-largest port, after London, and New York City was not far behind. Shipbuilding emerged as a major colonial industry in these years, and by 1770 one-third of the "British" merchant marine was actually American-built.

The second major way in which the Navigation Acts affected the colonies lay in their barring the export of certain "enumerated goods" to foreign nations unless these items first passed through England or Scotland. The mainland's chief "controlled" items were tobacco, rice, furs, indigo (a Carolina plant that produced a blue dye), and naval stores (masts, hemp, tar, and turpentine). Parliament never restricted grain, livestock, fish, lumber, or rum, which altogether made up 60 percent of colonial exports. Further, American exporters of tobacco and rice—the chief commodities affected by enumeration—had their burdens reduced by two significant concessions. First, Parliament gave Americans a monopoly over the British market by excluding foreign tobacco, even though this hurt British consumers. (Rice planters enjoyed a natural monopoly because they had no competitors.) Second, Parliament tried to minimize the added cost of landing tobacco and rice in Britain (where customs officials collected duties on both) by refunding these duties on all tobacco and rice that the colonists later shipped to other countries. About 85 percent of all American tobacco and rice was eventually reexported and sold outside the British Empire.

The navigation system's third impact on the colonies was to encourage economic diversification in America. Parliament used British tax money to pay modest bounties to Americans producing

New York Harbor, c. 1760 *New York was a bustling colonial port in the mid-eighteenth century. In this colorful panorama, a group of militiamen drill, center; a French ship, possibly the catch of a privateer, is anchored to the left.*

such items as silk, iron, dyes, hemp, and lumber, which Britain would otherwise have had to import from other countries, and it raised the price of commercial rivals' imports by imposing protective tariffs on them.

On the surface, the trade laws' fourth consequence for the colonies was negative: they forbade Americans from competing with British manufacturers of clothing and steel. In practice, however, this prohibition had little effect, for it banned only *large-scale* manufacturing; colonial tailors, hatters, and housewives could continue to make any item of dress in their households or small shops. Manufactured by low-paid labor, British clothing imports to America generally undersold whatever the colonists could have produced at their higher labor costs. For this reason, Americans failed to establish a profitable clothing industry until after 1820. Steel manufacturing also depended on cheap labor, and not until the 1840s did either Great Britain or America develop a successful steel industry. The colonists were free to produce iron, however, and by 1770 they had built 250 ironworks employing thirty thousand men, a work force larger than the entire population of Georgia or of any provincial city. At the American Iron Company's

complex of eleven forges and furnaces near Ringwood, New Jersey, five hundred workers manned eleven furnaces that annually consumed eight square miles of timber as fuel. By 1770 British North America produced more iron than England and Wales, and only Sweden and Russia exceeded the colonies' output.

Colonial complaints against the navigation system raged in the late seventeenth century but rarely were heard after 1700. The trade regulation primarily burdened tobacco and rice exporters, whose income nevertheless was reduced by less than 3 percent. The commercial laws did raise the cost of non-British merchandise imported into the colonies, but seldom by enough to encourage smuggling (except in the case of tea from India and molasses from the French Caribbean). The great volume of colonial trade proceeded lawfully, and Americans probably smuggled much less than did Britons themselves. Anglo-American commerce provided mutual advantages for Britain and its colonies, and when Americans lost their trading rights in 1783, their commerce declined greatly. Although Parliament intended the laws only to benefit Britain, the navigation system had far from crippled the provincial economy. Rather, British North

Colonial Exports and Their Average Annual Value, 1768–1772

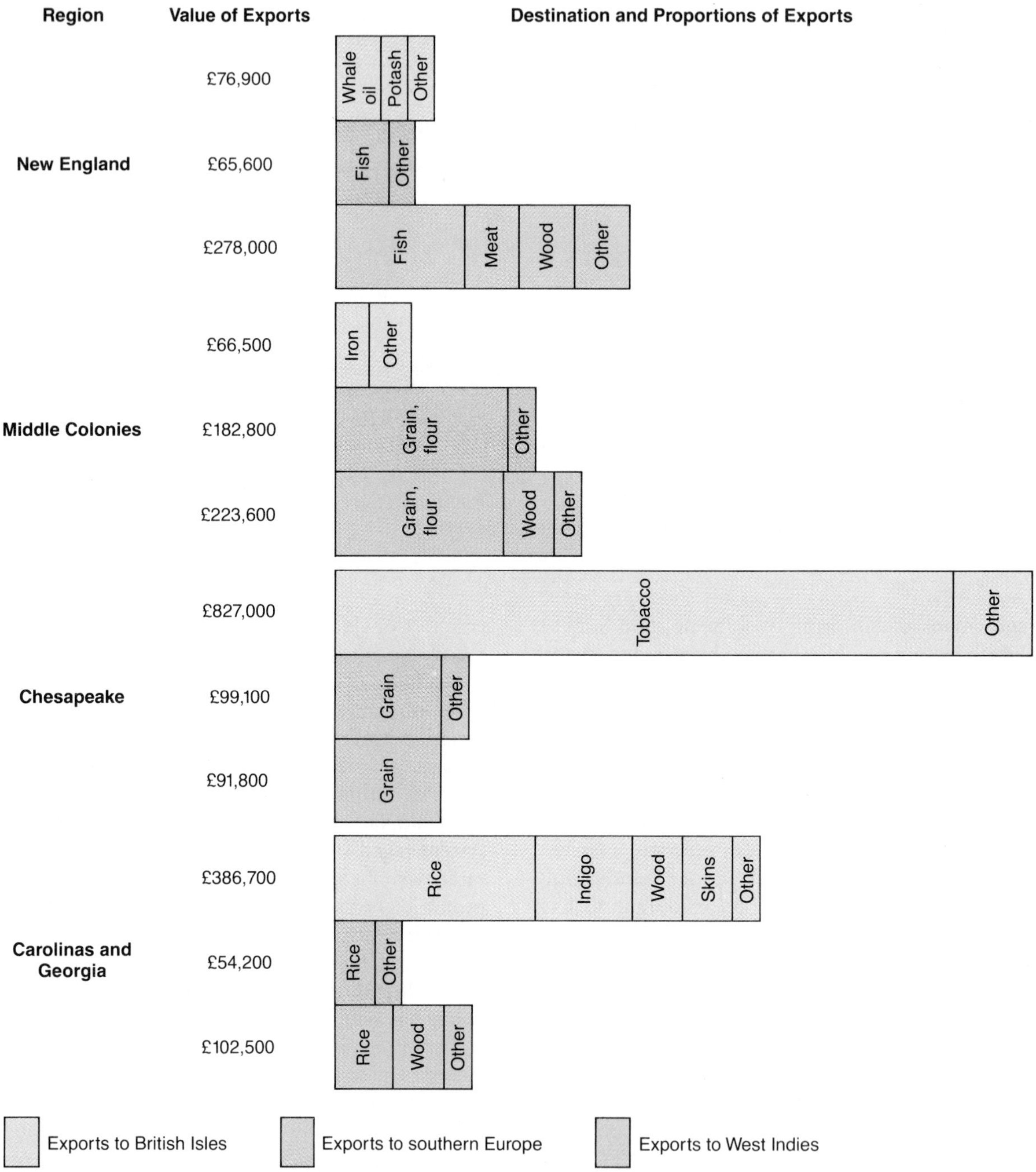

Region	Value of Exports	Destination and Proportions of Exports

New England

£76,900 — Whale oil | Potash | Other

£65,600 — Fish | Other

£278,000 — Fish | Meat | Wood | Other

Middle Colonies

£66,500 — Iron | Other

£182,800 — Grain, flour | Other

£223,600 — Grain, flour | Wood | Other

Chesapeake

£827,000 — Tobacco | Other

£99,100 — Grain | Other

£91,800 — Grain

Carolinas and Georgia

£386,700 — Rice | Indigo | Wood | Skins | Other

£54,200 — Rice | Other

£102,500 — Rice | Wood | Other

☐ Exports to British Isles   ☐ Exports to southern Europe   ☐ Exports to West Indies

Export patterns varied greatly among colonial regions. The South sent almost 80 percent of its exports to Great Britain, while more than half of northern exports went to the West Indies and another quarter was sold in southern Europe. The value of Chesapeake tobacco equaled that of almost all northern exports combined.

NOTE: Unlabeled segments represent miscellaneous exports.

SOURCE: James F. Shepherd and Gary M. Walton, *Shipping, Maritime Trade and the Economic Development of Colonial North America* (Cambridge, England: Cambridge University Press, 1972), 211–227.

America's economy grew at a per capita rate of 0.6 percent annually from 1650 to 1770, a pace twice that of Britain.

Eighteenth-Century Living Standards

Propelled by a tenfold increase in the volume of exports, colonial living standards rose dramatically from 1700 to 1770. Nowhere was Americans' newfound prosperity more evident than in the Chesapeake, which in the late seventeenth century had been a region of impoverished tenants battered by depressed tobacco prices. Not only did tobacco exports triple from 1713 to 1774, but prices slowly crept upward, in large part owing to a 75 percent reduction in marketing costs. The Chesapeake economy further benefited from sharply higher exports of wheat and corn, which by 1770 equaled 25 percent of tobacco sales. Thus within three generations of Bacon's Rebellion, the Chesapeake had ceased to be a region locked in pervasive poverty; instead, poverty was confined to a small underclass of whites attempting to farm marginal-quality soil. At the same time, a landholding small-planter element arose, so large that perhaps 30 percent of all white families owned slaves. Atop Chesapeake society, moreover, an elite of wealthy large landowners and slavemasters flourished after about 1700.

Living standards were highest in the mid-Atlantic, spanning the area from New York south to Delaware. In 1770 per capita wealth here exceeded the colonial average by 40 percent. These colonies' striking prosperity owed much to rich soils, a long-term climatic warming that lengthened the growing season after 1700, and brisk demand for livestock, wheat, and corn in the West Indies and (to a lesser extent) southern Europe.

Of all Anglo-Americans, New Englanders prospered least. Though hardly poor, Yankees were on average only half as wealthy as colonists elsewhere. Plagued by mediocre soil and a short growing season, New Englanders had to import grain to feed themselves. Yankees sent two-thirds of their livestock, lumber, and fish exports to the West Indies, and while their cattle raising remained profitable, a long-term decline in lumber prices stung the local economy. By the 1750s most New England towns had become overpopulated, bursting with more young men than could acquire enough land to support a family. In subsequent decades only migration to the frontier—to Vermont, Maine, Nova Scotia, and upper New York—would ease the pressure.

Many New Englanders survived economically by turning to the sea. By 1700 the Yankee merchant marine and fishing industry were the largest in the colonies, providing employment for every seventh man. This prosperity came at a heavy cost, however, for the sea was cruel and took perhaps every fifth sailor to a watery grave. (For this reason, the balcony on a ship captain's home from which his wife could watch for her husband's return to harbor became known as the widow's walk.)

Taken as a whole, the American colonies by the mid-eighteenth century enjoyed a standard of living that greatly exceeded that of Scotland or Ireland and approximated that of England and Wales. Steady overseas demand for colonial products spawned a prosperity that enabled Americans to consume a huge volume of British products. Consequently, the share of British exports sold to the colonies spurted from just 5 percent in 1700 to almost 40 percent by 1760. "You may depend upon it," remarked Pennsylvania judge William Allen in commenting on prospects for self-improvement, "this is one of the best poor man's countries in the world."

Rural Family Life

Although economic opportunity abounded for eighteenth-century immigrants and American-born colonists alike, personal success was hard won. A case in point is that of Aaron Leaming, the penniless orphan of a crippled English immigrant. By 1740 Leaming had risen through hard work to become one of New Jersey's richest residents. His rags-to-riches climb was certainly atypical, but his blunt advice to would-be emulators captured the essence of colonial opportunity: "Those who [do] not intend to die as poor as they were born must bestir themselves with great industry."

Because the vast majority of landowners had just enough acreage for a working farm, they could not provide their children with land of their own when they married. Moreover, since couples typically started having children in their mid-20s, had their last babies sometime after 40, and lived past 60, all but their youngest children would be approaching middle age before receiving any inheritance. Even children who obtained inheritances before turning 30 rarely got more than a sixth or seventh of their parents' estate, because most families wrote wills that divided property evenly—or almost so—among all daughters and sons. A young male had to build savings to buy farm equipment by working (from about age 16 to 23) as a field hand for his father or neighbors. Because mortgages usually required down payments of 33 percent, a young husband normally supported his growing family by renting a farm from the local gentry until his early or mid-30s.

Landownership came quickest to those farmers who could find seasonal or part-time work. Some learned a craft like carpentry that earned money year-round. Many more trapped furs, gathered honey and beeswax, or made cider, shingles, turpentine, or wampum. Whenever possible, farmers found wintertime jobs draining meadows, clearing fields, or fencing land for wealthier landowners who did not own slaves or indentured servants. Such nonagricultural work might gain an industrious farmer half again of his total income from selling crops and livestock.

Families worked off mortgages slowly because the long-term cash income from a farm (6 percent) about equaled the interest on borrowed money (5–8 percent). After making a down payment of one-third, a husband and wife generally satisfied the next third upon inheriting shares of their deceased parents' estates. They paid off the final third when their children reached their teens and the family could thus expand farm output with two or three full-time workers. Only by their late 50s, just as their youngest offspring got ready to leave home, could most colonial parents hope to free themselves of debt.

In general, the more isolated a community or the less productive its farmland, the more self-sufficiency and bartering its people practiced, although only the remotest settlements were completely self-sufficient. Almost all rural families depended heavily on wives' and daughters' production. Women contributed to their household's financial success by manufacturing items that the family would otherwise have to purchase. Besides cooking, cleaning, and washing, wives preserved food, boiled soap, made clothing, and tended the garden, dairy, orchard, poultry house, and pigsty. Women often sold dairy products to neighbors or export merchants, spun yarn into cloth for tailors, knitted

"The Queen of Sheba"

Mary Williams, a young girl of Massachusetts or New Hampshire, completed this brightly colored needle-point work in 1744. Though reflecting contemporary European design, the picture is distinctively American in composition and in the architectural and clothing styles that it depicts.

various garments for sale, and even vended their own hair for wigs. A farm family's ability to feed itself and its animals was worth about half of its cash income (a luxury that few European tenants had), and women did no less than men in meeting this end.

Legally, however, colonial American women found themselves constrained (see Chapter 2). A woman's single most autonomous decision was her choice of a husband. Once married, she lost control of her dowry (unless she was a New Yorker subject to old Dutch custom, which allowed her somewhat more authority). Still, widows controlled between 8 and 10 percent of all property in eighteenth-century Anglo-America, and some—among them Eliza Pinckney of South Carolina, the mother of several Revolutionary-era leaders—held large estates.

City women shared their country cousins' legal disability, and they worked equally hard to help support their households. Yet in one respect most city women differed. They and their families had to contend with narrowing, not expanding, economic prospects.

The Urban Paradox

The cities were colonial America's economic paradox. They shipped the livestock, grain, and lumber that enriched the countryside but were caught in a downward spiral of declining opportunity.

After 1740 economic success proved ever more elusive for the 4 percent of colonists who lived in cities. Poverty escalated rapidly in the three major seaports of Philadelphia, New York, and Boston. Debilitating ocean voyages left many immigrants too weak to work, and every incoming ship from Europe carried numerous widows and orphans. Moreover, the cities' poor rolls always bulged with the survivors of mariners lost at sea. High population density and poor sanitation in urban locales allowed contagious diseases to run rampant, so that half of all city children died before age twenty-one and urban adults lived ten years less on average than country folk.

Even the able-bodied found cities economically treacherous. Early-eighteenth-century urban artisans typically trained apprentices and employed them as journeymen for many years until the latter opened their own shops. After 1750, however, more and more employers kept their labor force only as long as business was brisk, and released workers when sales slowed; in 1751 a shrewd Benjamin Franklin recommended this practice as an intelligent way to use expensive labor. Recessions hit more frequently after 1720 and created longer spells of unemployment. As urban populations ballooned, wages correspondingly tended to shrink, while the cost of rents, food, and firewood shot up.

Urban poverty grew from insignificance before 1700 into a major problem in the mid-eighteenth century. By 1730 Boston could no longer shelter its destitute in the almshouse built in 1685, and by 1741 the town had declared every sixth citizen too poor to pay taxes. Not until 1736 did New York need a poorhouse (for just forty persons), but by 1772, 4 percent of its residents (over eight hundred people) required public assistance to survive. The number of Philadelphia families listed as poor on tax rolls jumped from 3 percent in 1720 to 11 percent by 1760.

Economic frustration disposed townspeople to turn to violence to defend their interests. Before 1710, for example, few serious disorders disrupted Boston, but between that year and 1750, the city experienced five major riots, aimed at suppressing prostitution, stopping the navy from drafting sailors, or protesting wartime profiteering. However, citizens used force only as a last resort to curb public nuisances. They usually achieved their goals through intimidation or property damage, after which they disbanded and let the law resume its course.

Most southern cities were tiny. Charles Town, however, became North America's fourth-largest

Lamplighter on Broad Street, *by William Chappel*

A lamplighter makes his rounds on New York City's Broad Street. Eighteenth-century American cities were crowded, disease-infested places where poverty was rampant.

city. South Carolina's capital offered gracious living to the wealthy planters who flocked to their townhouses during the months of worst heat and insect infestation on their plantations. But shanties on the city's outskirts sheltered a growing crowd of destitute whites. The colony encouraged whites to immigrate in hopes of reducing blacks' numerical preponderance, but some European newcomers could not reach frontier farms or find any work except as ill-paid roustabouts. Like their counterparts in northern port cities, Charles Town's poor whites competed for work with urban slaves whose masters rented out their labor, and racial tensions simmered.

Slavery's Wages

From 1713 to 1754, five times as many slaves poured onto mainland North America than in all the preceding years. The proportion of blacks in the colonies doubled, rising from 11 percent at the beginning of the century to 20 percent by midcentury. Slavery was primarily a southern institution, but 15 percent of its victims lived north of Maryland, mostly in New York and New Jersey. By 1750 every seventh New Yorker was a slave.

Because West Indian and Brazilian slave buyers outbid the mainland colonists, a mere 5 percent of transported Africans were ever sold within the present-day United States. Unable to buy as many male field hands as they needed, mainland masters had no choice but to accept numerous female workers, and they protected their investments by maintaining the slaves' health. These factors promoted family formation and increased life expectancy far beyond the levels in the Caribbean, where family life was unstable and high death rates resulted from overwork and disease (see Chapter 2). On the mainland by 1750, the rate of natural increase for African-Americans almost equaled that for whites.

For slaves, the economic progress achieved in colonial America by about 1750 meant primarily that masters could usually afford to keep them healthy. Rarely, however, did masters choose to make their human chattels comfortable. A visitor to a Virginia plantation from Poland (where most peasants lived in dire poverty) gave this impression of slaves' quality of life:

We entered some Negroes huts—for their habitations cannot be called houses. They are far

Blacks as a Percentage of the Total Population in Anglo-America 1650–1770

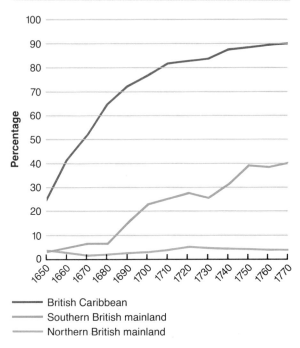

— British Caribbean
— Southern British mainland
— Northern British mainland

Wide differences developed in the racial composition of Britain's American colonies. By the mid-eighteenth century, the Caribbean sugar islands were almost 90 percent black, whereas the mainland colonies north of Maryland had become about 95 percent white. By 1750 slaves composed almost 40 percent of all mainland colonists south of Pennsylvania.

SOURCE: Robert W. Fogel and Stanley L. Engerman, *Time on the Cross* (Boston: Little, Brown, 1974), 21.

more miserable than the poorest of the cottages of our peasants. The husband and wife sleep on a miserable bed, the children on the floor . . . a little kitchen furniture amid this misery . . . a teakettle and cups . . . five or six hens, each with ten or fifteen chickens, walked there. That is the only pleasure allowed to the negroes.

To maintain slaves, masters normally spent just 40 percent of the amount paid for the upkeep of indentured servants. While white servants ate two hundred pounds of beef or pork yearly, most slaves consumed only fifty pounds of meat. The value of the beer and hard cider given to a typical servant alone equaled the expense of feeding and clothing the average slave. Masters usually provided adult slaves with eight quarts of corn and a pound of pork each week but expected them to grow their own vegetables, forage for wild fruits, and perhaps raise poultry.

Slaves worked for a far longer portion of their lives than whites. Slave children went to the fields as part-time helpers soon after reaching seven years and began working full-time between eleven and fourteen. Unlike white women, who did only light work in their dairies and gardens, female blacks routinely tended tobacco or rice crops, even when pregnant, and often worked outdoors in winter. Most slaves toiled until they died, although those in their sixties rarely performed hard labor.

The rigors of bondage did not, however, crush its victims' spirits. Slaves experienced love and formed families, and they constantly strove to win concessions from their owners. Despite the odds against them, slaves accumulated small amounts of property by establishing exclusive rights over their gardens and poultry, and they sometimes sold food to their masters. In 1769, for example, Thomas Jefferson made several purchases like the following:

gave negro for watermelon	7 pence
paid Fanny for 6 chickens	2 shillings
paid Cato for 1 doz eggs	3 pence

House slaves widely insisted on being tipped by guests for shining shoes and stabling horses. They sometimes sought presents aggressively on holidays, as a startled New Jersey tutor on a Virginia plantation discovered in 1774 when slaves demanding gifts of cash roused him from bed early Christmas morning.

In the South Carolina and Georgia rice country, slaves working under the highly favorable task system had control of about half their waking hours. Under tasking, each slave spent some hours caring for a quarter-acre—usually a half-day—after which his or her duties ended. By 1750 this system permitted certain slaves to keep hogs and sell surplus vegetables in Charles Town. A remarkable but atypical slave named Sampson earned enough money in his off-hours to hire another to work his own task, and became free in 1728.

By midcentury slaves made up 20 percent of New York City's population and formed a majority in Charles Town and Savannah. City life offered slaves advantages, most notably the chance for those with skills to hire themselves out and keep part of their wages. Many urban slaves could afford to dress well and to patronize taverns catering to black customers. By 1770 one-tenth of Savannah's slaves lived in rented rooms away from their owners. Though still in bondage, these blacks forced urban whites to allow them a substantial measure of personal freedom. But urban racial tensions could also

John Potter and His Family   *The Potters of Matunuck, Rhode Island, relax at tea. Note the presence of the black servant.*

run high, as in New York City in 1741, when nine slaves were burned at the stake for allegedly plotting arson.

Although slaves improved themselves and generally experienced robust health, most led lives of drudgery, lightened by few physical comforts. Prosperity also proved elusive for numerous white residents of the seaports, increasingly buffeted by poverty. These exceptions aside, middle-class eighteenth-century Anglo-Americans achieved a remarkably high standard of living, exceeded only by the Dutch and perhaps the English. The relatively few Americans at the top of the social pyramid lived more comfortably than the colonial middle class, but even the richest provincials enjoyed nothing like the opulence of Europe's titled aristocrats and the West Indian sugar kings.

The Consolidation of the Colonial Elites

"A man who has money here, no matter how he came by it, he is everything, and wanting [lacking] that he's a mere nothing, let his conduct be ever so irreproachable." Thus a Rhode Islander in 1748 described how colonial Americans defined high status. But once having achieved wealth, a man was expected by his contemporaries to behave with an appropriate degree of responsibility, to display dignity and generosity, and to be a community leader. In short, he was expected to act like a gentleman.*

Before 1700 the colonies' class structure was not readily apparent, because the rural elite's preference for buying land, servants, or slaves instead of luxuries perpetuated a homespun quality among the wealthy. In 1715 a traveler visiting one of Virginia's richest planters, Robert Beverley, noticed that his host owned "nothing in or about his house but just what is necessary, . . . [such as] good beds but no curtains and instead of cane chairs he hath stools made of wood." Unlike the British gentry, who did no manual labor, the colonial upper class included many individuals like West Jersey's Lieutenant Governor Thomas Olive, who commonly set aside his plowing to hold spontaneous court

sessions amid tree stumps as a favor to neighbors seeking his folksy "Jersey justice."

After 1720 well-to-do colonists began displaying their wealth more openly, particularly in their housing. The greater gentry—the richest 2 percent, who held about 15 percent of all property—constructed residences such as the Low House, New Jersey's most splendid home in 1741, and the Shirley mansion in Virginia. The lesser gentry, or second-wealthiest 2 to 10 percent, who held about 25 percent of all property, typically lived in a more modest fieldstone dwelling such as Pennsylvania's Lincoln homestead or a wood-frame house such as Whitehall in Rhode Island. In contrast, middle-class farmers commonly inhabited one-story wooden buildings with four small rooms and a loft.

The gentry also exhibited their wealth after 1720 by living in imitation of the European "grand style." They wore costly English fashions, drove carriages instead of wagons, and bought expensive chinaware, books, furniture, and musical instruments. They pursued a gracious life by studying foreign languages, learning formal dances, and cultivating polite manners. In sports their preference shifted to horse racing (on which they bet avidly) and away from cockfighting, a less elegant diversion. Their diets gained variety (as did those of most other eighteenth-century Americans), and gentry families indulged in rich, often unwholesome delicacies. A few young colonial males even got an English education.

For some rich colonials, affluence meant simply an opportunity to behave irresponsibly, but if they did so they generally incurred censure. For example, one young heir of the wealthy Livingstone family of New York was, his relatives complained, such a spendthrift that he was "scarce ever worth a groat in cash," the result of having "murdered his days with gamesters and Debauchers, and as he lived without a Fame, died without a memory."

For Chesapeake gentlemen, debt was a problem even if they lived virtuously. Tobacco planters were perpetually short of cash and in hock to British merchants who bought their crops and sold them imported goods on credit at high prices. Noted the Maryland assembly in 1697: "The trade of this province ebbs and flows according to the rise or fall of tobacco in the market of England." Planters could respond only in two ways. First, they could strive for as much self-sufficiency as possible on

---

*In the eighteenth century, the word *gentleman* meant an individual who not only conformed to socially accepted standards of behavior but also belonged to the upper class, or *gentry*.

The Shirley Plantation

The Shirley plantation on Virginia's James River was the nucleus of a self-contained world containing its own blacksmith, cooper, cobbler, and, of course, field slaves. Rare, gleaming silver graces the interior.

their estates—for example, by training their slaves to manufacture glass, bricks, tools, nails, and carriages. Second, they could diversify away from the region's tobacco monoculture (dependence on a single staple crop) by growing wheat or cutting timber. Self-sufficiency and diversification became more widely accepted objectives as the eighteenth century wore on, and after 1750 landowners like George Washington and Thomas Jefferson strongly advocated them.

In the eighteenth-century colonial cities, wealth remained highly concentrated. For example, New York's wealthiest 10 percent owned about 45 percent of the property throughout the eighteenth century. Similar patterns existed in Boston and Philadelphia. Set alongside the growth of a poor underclass in these cities, such statistics underscored the polarization of status and wealth in urban America on the eve of the Revolution. But as serious as this problem was becoming, no American cities experienced the vast gulf between elite wealth and mass poverty that was commonplace in eighteenth-century European towns.

The American colonial gentry and urban elite not only set the tone for society at large but also dominated politics. Governors invariably appointed members of the greater gentry to sit on their councils or as judges on the highest courts. Most representatives elected to the legislatures' lower houses (assemblies) also ranked among the wealthiest 2 percent, as did majors and colonels in the militia. In contrast, members of the lesser gentry sat less often in the legislature, but they commonly served as justices of the peace on the county courts and as militia officers up to captain.

Colonial America's only high-ranking elected officeholders were the members of the legislature's lower house. But outside New England (where any voter could hold office), legal requirements barred 80 percent of white men from running for the assembly, most often by specifying that a candidate must own a minimum of a thousand acres. (Farms then averaged 180 acres in the South and 120 acres in the mid-Atlantic colonies.) Even had there been no such property qualifications, however, few ordinary citizens could have afforded the high costs of elective office. Assemblymen received only living expenses, which might not fully cover the cost of staying at their province's capital, much less compensate a farmer or an artisan for his absence from farm or shop for six to ten weeks a year. Even members of the gentry grumbled about legislative duty, many of them viewing high office as "a sort of tax on them to serve the public at their own Expense besides the neglect of their business," according to Governor Lewis Morris of New Jersey.

For these reasons, political leadership fell to certain wealthy families with a tradition of public service. Nine families, for example, provided one-third of Virginia's royal councilors during the century after 1680. John Adams, a rising young Massachusetts politician, estimated that most towns in his colony chose their legislators from among just three or four families.

The colonies set liberal qualifications for male voters, but all provinces excluded women, blacks, and Indians from elections. In seven colonies voters had to own land (usually forty to fifty acres), and the rest demanded that an elector have enough property to furnish a house and work a farm with his own tools. About 40 percent of free men could not meet these requirements, but nearly all of these were indentured servants, single sons still living with parents, or young men just beginning family life. Nevertheless, most white males in America would vote by age forty, whereas two-thirds of all men in England and nine-tenths in Ireland could not and would never vote.

In rural areas voter participation was low unless a vital issue was at stake. The difficulties of voting limited the average rural turnout to about 45 percent. (This rate of participation was, however, better than in typical American elections today, apart from those for president.) Outside New England and Pennsylvania, which held regularly scheduled elections, governors changed legislatures according to no set pattern, so that elections might lapse for years and suddenly be held on very short notice. Colonists in isolated areas thus often had no knowledge of an upcoming contest. The fact that all polling took place at the county seat discouraged many electors from traveling long distances over poor roads to vote. Moreover, in New York, New Jersey, the Chesapeake colonies, and North Carolina, voters had to state their choice publicly, often face-to-face with the candidates. This procedure naturally inhibited participation on the part of those who might dissent. Finally, the absence of political parties also played a role in the turnout:

no institutional means existed to stimulate popular interest in politics and to mobilize voters in support of candidates. Office seekers nominated themselves and usually ran on their reputation rather than issues that might spur public interest.

In view of these various factors, indifference toward politics was not uncommon by the mid-eighteenth century. For example, to avoid paying legislators' expenses at the capital, numerous Massachusetts towns refused to choose assemblymen; in 1763, 64 of 168 towns held no elections. Thirty percent of men elected to South Carolina's assembly neglected to take their seats from 1731 to 1760, including a majority of those chosen in 1747 and 1749. Apathy would have been even greater had candidates not freely plied voters with alcohol. This "swilling the planters with bumbo" was most popular among Virginians: George Washington dispensed almost two quarts of liquor for each voter at the courthouse when first elected to the assembly in 1758. Such practices helped the elite in most eighteenth-century colonies build up a tradition of community leadership that would serve them well in the years of revolutionary crisis after 1763.

Only in the major seaports did a truly competitive political life flourish. Voter turnout was relatively high in the cities because of greater population density, better communications, and the use of secret ballots (except in New York). Further, the cities' acute economic difficulties stimulated political participation among urban voters, ever hopeful that the government might ease their problems. In politics as in economics, cities were an exception to the general pattern for Anglo-America.

The most significant political development after 1700 was the rise of the assembly as the preponderant force in American government. Except in Connecticut and Rhode Island (where voters elected their governor), the crown or the proprietors in England chose each colony's governor, who in turn named a council, or upper house of the legislature. Thus only through the assembly could members of the gentry defend their own interests. Until 1689 governors and councils took the initiative in drafting laws, and the assemblies rather passively followed their lead; but thereafter, the assemblies assumed a more central role in politics.

Colonial leaders argued that their legislatures should exercise the same rights as those won by Parliament in its seventeenth-century struggle with royal authority. Indeed, Americans saw their assemblies as miniature Houses of Commons, and they assumed that governors possessed only those powers exercised by the British crown. Since Parliament had won supremacy over the monarchy through the Bill of Rights in 1689, colonials felt that their governors had strictly limited powers and should defer to the assemblies in cases of disagreement.

The lower houses steadily asserted their prestige and authority by refusing to permit outside meddling in their proceedings, taking firm control over taxes and the budget, and especially by keeping a tight rein on executive salaries. Although governors had considerable powers (including the right to veto acts, call or dismiss assembly sessions at will, and schedule elections anytime), they were quite vulnerable to legislatures' financial pressure because they received no salary from British sources and relied on the assemblies for their income. Only through this "power of the purse" could assemblies force governors to sign laws opposed by the crown.

Moreover, because the British government had little interest in eighteenth-century colonial politics, the assemblies could seize considerable power at the governors' expense. The Board of Trade, which Parliament established in 1696, was charged with monitoring American developments and advising the crown on colonial affairs. But aside from its first decade and a vigorous period from 1748 to 1753, the board's small, inefficient staff lacked the vision and energy to provide the strong support needed by embattled governors wrestling to maintain royal authority. The board could have easily frustrated the assemblies' rise to power by persuading the crown to disallow objectionable colonial laws signed by the governors; but of 8,563 acts sent from the mainland between 1696 and 1776, the board had just 469 disapproved. The Board of Trade's ineffectiveness left a vacuum in royal policy that allowed the colonies to become self-governing in most respects except for trade regulation, restrictions on printing money, and declaring war.

Thus during the first half of the eighteenth century, most Americans prospered and some grew wealthy. Gradually, class distinctions became more sharply etched. But British North America had no centuries-old institutions to bolster aristocratic privilege: no hereditary nobility, powerful bureaucracy, standing army, or royal court. Even the Anglican church was weak, lacking American bishops. Without these traditions of rigid hierarchy, social expectations largely sufficed to ensure that the American upper class would receive appropriate deference and act with a sense of public responsibility.

Enlightenment and Awakening

Anglo-America was probably the world's most literate society in the eighteenth century. Perhaps 90 percent of New England's adult white male population and 40 percent of the women could write well enough to sign documents, thanks to the region's traditional support for primary education. Among white males elsewhere in the colonies, the literacy rate varied from about 35 percent to more than 50 percent. (In England, by contrast, no more than one-third of all males could read and write.) But how readily most of these people could (or would) read a book or write a letter was another matter. Ordinary Americans' reading fare at best encompassed only a few well-thumbed books: an almanac, a psalter, and the Bible. Colonial farmers and artisans inhabited the world of oral culture, in which ideas and information passed through the spoken word—a conversation with neighbors, an exchange of pleasantries with the local gentleman, a hot debate at the town meeting, a sermon by the minister. When uttered with feeling and sincerity, spoken words could move them with tremendous force.

However, members of the gentry, well-to-do merchants, educated ministers, and a few self-improving artisans lived in the world of print culture. Though costly, books and writing paper could open up eighteenth-century European civilization to men and women who could read. And a rich, exciting world it was. Great advances in natural science seemed to explain the laws of nature; human intelligence appeared poised to triumph over ignorance and prejudice; life itself looked as if it would at last become pleasant. Eminent men of letters such as France's Voltaire (1694–1778) corresponded with kings, awed the literate public, and dared to attack religious bigotry. For those who had the time to read and think, an age of optimism and progress had dawned: the Enlightenment. Upper-class Americans could not resist its charms and could be powerfully moved by the promise of its written words.

Enlightened Americans

American intellectuals like the self-taught scientist Benjamin Franklin drew their inspiration from Enlightenment ideals, which combined confidence in human reason with skepticism toward beliefs not founded on science or strict logic. One source of Enlightenment thought lay in the writings of English physicist Sir Isaac Newton (1642–1727), who in 1687 explained how universal gravitation ruled the universe. Newton's work captured Europe's imagination by demonstrating the harmony of natural laws and stimulated others to search for rational principles in medicine, law, psychology, and government.

> Nature and Nature's laws lay hid in night:
> God said: Let Newton be! and all was light

wrote English poet Alexander Pope, expressing the wonder that educated Europeans felt at Newton's revelations.

In the second quarter of the eighteenth century, no American more fully embodied the Enlightenment spirit than Franklin. Born in Boston in 1706, Franklin migrated to Philadelphia at age seventeen. He brought along skill as a printer, considerable ambition, and insatiable intellectual curiosity. In 1727 he gathered a small group of young men, mostly aspiring artisans like himself, into a club called the Junto, whose members pledged themselves to debate highbrow questions and collect useful information for their "mutual improvement."

In moving to Philadelphia, Franklin put himself in the right place at the right time, for the city was growing much more rapidly than Boston and was attracting English and Scottish merchants who shared Franklin's zest for learning. These men nudged Franklin's career along by lending him books and securing him printing contracts. In 1732 Franklin began to publish *Poor Richard's Almanack,* a collection of maxims and proverbs that made him famous. By age forty-two Franklin had earned enough money to retire from printing and devote himself to science and community service.

These dual goals—science and community benefit—were intimately related in Franklin's mind, for he believed that all true science would be useful in the sense of making everyone's life more comfortable. For example, experimenting with a kite, Franklin demonstrated in 1752 that lightning was electricity, a discovery that led to the useful lightning rod. Building on his Junto activities, Franklin organized the American Philosophical Society in 1743 to encourage "all philosophical experiments that let light into the nature of things, tend to increase the power of man over matter, and multiply the conveniences and pleasures of life." By 1769 this society had blossomed into an intercolonial network of amateur scientists.

Franklin left his mark on Philadelphia in other ways. He established its first volunteer fire company—complete with engine—in 1736, inspired the creation of a circulating library that held America's finest collection of scientific books, and in 1740 founded an academy that became the College of Philadelphia (now the University of Pennsylvania). From this institution sprang the colonies' first medical school in 1765.

Although several southern plantation owners, including Thomas Jefferson, ardently championed progress through science, the Enlightenment's primary centers in America were the seaboard cities, where the latest books and ideas from Europe circulated and gentlemen and self-improving artisans met in small societies to investigate nature. In the eyes of many of these individuals, the ideal was the Royal Society in London, the foremost learned society in the English-speaking world. Franklin and Cotton Mather became members of the Royal Society. In this respect, the Enlightenment, at least initially, strengthened the ties between colonial and British elites. While confident that science would benefit everyone, Enlightened Americans envisioned progress as gradual and proceeding from the top down. They trusted reason far more than they trusted the common people, whose judgment, especially on religious matters, seemed too easily deranged.

Just as Newton inspired the scientific bent of Enlightenment intellectuals, English philosopher John Locke's *Essay Concerning Human Understanding* (1690) led many to embrace "reasonable" or "rational" religion. Locke contended that ideas, including religion, are not inborn but are acquired by toilsome investigation of and reflection upon experience. To most Enlightened intellectuals, the best argument for the existence of God seemingly could be derived through study of the harmony and order of nature, which pointed to a rational Creator. Some individuals carried this argument a step further by insisting that where the Bible conflicted with reason, one should follow the dictates of reason rather than the Bible. Those who took the argument furthest were called Deists. Deists concluded that God, having created a perfect universe, did not miraculously intervene in its workings but rather left it alone to operate according to natural laws.

Americans influenced by the Enlightenment usually described themselves as Christians and attended church. But they feared Christianity's excesses, particularly as indulged in by fanatics who persecuted others in religion's name, and by "enthusiasts" who claimed miraculous visions and direct mandates from God. Mindful of Locke's caution that a human can never be *absolutely* certain of anything but his or her own existence, they distrusted zealots. Typically, Franklin contributed money to most of the churches in Philadelphia but thought that the religion's value lay mainly in its encouragement of virtue rather than in theological hair splitting.

Prior to 1740 Enlightened Americans usually associated fanaticism and bigotry with the bygone days of the early Puritans, and they looked on their own time as an era of progressive reasonableness. But a series of religious revivals known as the Great Awakening would soon shatter their complacency.

The Great Awakening

Viewing the world as orderly and predictable, rationalists were inclined to a sense of smug self-satisfaction. Franklin took the occasion of writing his will in 1750 to thank God for giving him "such a mind, with moderate passions" and "such a competency of this world's goods as might make a reasonable mind easy." But many Americans lacked a comfortable competency of worldly goods and lived neither orderly nor predictable lives. For example, in 1737 and 1738 an epidemic of diphtheria, a contagious throat disease, killed every tenth child under sixteen from New Hampshire to Pennsylvania. Such an event starkly reminded the colonists of the fragility of earthly life and turned their thoughts to religion.

A quickening of religious fervor began at scattered places in the colonies in the mid-1730s. Then in the 1740s, an outpouring of passionate Christian revivalism swept all of British North America. This "Great Awakening" cut across lines of class, status, and education. Even elites found themselves

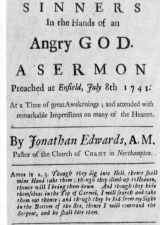

Jonathan Edwards; Title Page from "Sinners in the Hands of an Angry God"

Edwards's famous sermon warned the wicked of the terrible punishments awaiting them in the afterlife.

caught up in it, realizing the inadequacy of reason alone to move their hearts. Above all, the Great Awakening represented an unleashing of anxiety and longing among ordinary people living in a world of oral culture—anxiety about sin, and longing for salvation. And the answers that they received were conveyed through the spoken word. Some preachers of the Great Awakening were themselves intellectuals, comfortable amid the books and ideas of the print culture. But for all, religion was primarily a matter of emotional commitment.

In contrast to rationalists, who stressed the human potential for betterment, the ministers who roused their congregations into outbursts of religious fervor during the Great Awakening's revivals depicted the emptiness of material comfort, the utter corruption of human nature, the fury of divine wrath, and the need for immediate repentance. Although he was a brilliant intellect, well aware of contemporary science, the Congregationalist Jonathan Edwards, who led a revival at Northampton, Massachusetts, in 1735, drove home this message with breathtaking clarity. "The God that holds you over the pit of Hell, much as one holds a spider or other loathsome insect over the fire, abhors you," Edwards intoned in one of his famous sermons, "Sinners in the Hands of an Angry God." "His wrath toward you burns like fire; He looks upon you as worthy of nothing else but to be cast into the fire."

Even before Edwards's Northampton revival, two ministers in central New Jersey—the Presbyterian William Tennent and the Dutch Reformed Theodore Frelinghuysen—had stimulated conversions in prayer meetings called the Refreshings. But the event that brought these isolated threads of revival together was the arrival in 1739 of the charismatic George Whitefield, an English clergyman who had been stoking the fires of revival in the Anglican church. So overpowering was Whitefield's presence that some joked that he could make crowds swoon simply by saying "Mesopotamia," and English author Samuel Johnson thought Whitefield's magnetic appeal so potent that the priest would have been adored even if he preached from a tree wearing only a nightcap. Crowds exceeding twenty thousand could hear his booming voice clearly, and many wept at his eloquence.

Whitefield's American tour inspired thousands to seek salvation. Most converts were young

adults in their late twenties. In Connecticut alone, the number joining churches jumped from 630 in 1740 to 3,217 in 1741, and within four years of Whitefield's arrival, every fifth man and woman under forty-five had been "born again."

Whitefield's allure was so mighty that he even awed potential critics. Hearing him preach in Philadelphia, Benjamin Franklin first vowed to contribute nothing to the collection but gradually melted. So admirably did Whitefield conclude his sermon, Franklin recalled, "that I empty'd my Pocket wholly into the Collector's Dish, Gold and all." But divisions over the revivals quickly developed in Whitefield's wake and were widened by the tactics of some of his more extreme followers. For example, after leaving Boston in October 1740, Whitefield invited Gilbert Tennent (William's son) to follow "in order to blow up the divine flame lately kindled there." Denouncing Boston's established clergymen as "dead Drones" and lashing out at aristocratic fashion, Tennent built a following among the city's poor and downtrodden. So did another firebrand, the Congregationalist James Davenport, who once bellowed at his Southold, New York, congregation for twenty-four hours.

Exposing colonial society's social divisions, Tennent and Davenport corroded support for the revivals among established ministers and officials. Increasingly, the lines hardened between the revivalists, known as New Lights, and the rationalist clergy, or Old Lights, who dominated the Anglican, Presbyterian, and Congregational churches. In 1740 Gilbert Tennent published *The Danger of an Unconverted Ministry,* which hinted that most Presbyterian ministers lacked saving grace and hence were bound for hell, and urged their parishioners to abandon them for the New Lights. By thus sowing the seeds of doubt about individual ministers, Tennent was undermining one of the foundations of social order, for if the people could not trust their own ministers, whom could they trust?

Old Light rationalists fired back. In 1742 Charles Chauncy, a well-known Boston Congregationalist, condemned the revival as an epidemic of the "enthusiasm" that Enlightenment intellectuals so loathed. Chauncy particularly blasted those enthusiasts who mistook the ravings of their overheated imaginations for direct communications from God. He even provided a kind of checklist for spotting enthusiasts: look for "a certain wildness" in their eyes, the "quakings and tremblings" of their limbs, and foaming at the mouth, Chauncy suggested. Put simply, the revival had unleashed "a sort of madness."

The Great Awakening opened unprecedented splits in American Protestantism. In 1741 New and Old Light Presbyterians formed rival branches that did not reunite until 1758, when the revivalists emerged victorious. The Anglicans lost many members to New Light preachers, especially to Presbyterians and Baptists. Congregationalists splintered so badly that within twenty years of 1740, New Lights had seceded from one-third of all churches and formed separate parishes.

In Massachusetts and Connecticut, where the Congregational church was established by law, the secession of New Light parishes provoked bitter conflict. To force New Lights into paying tithes to their former church, Old Lights repeatedly denied new parishes legal status. Connecticut passed repressive laws forbidding revivalists to preach or perform marriages, and the colony expelled many New Lights from the legislature. In Connecticut's Windham County, an extra story had to be added to the jail to hold all the New Lights arrested for not paying tithes. Elisha Paine, a revivalist imprisoned at Windham for illegal preaching, continued giving sermons from his cell and drew such crowds that his followers built bleachers nearby to hear him. Paine and his fellow victims generated widespread sympathy for the New Lights, who finally won control of Connecticut's assembly in 1759.

Although New Lights made steady gains until the 1770s, the Great Awakening peaked in 1742. The revival then crested everywhere but in Virginia, where its high point came after 1755 with an upsurge of conversions by Baptists, who also suffered considerable legal harassment.

For all the commotion it raised at the time, the Great Awakening's long-term effects exceeded its immediate impact. First, the revival started the decline in the influence of Quakers (who were not significantly affected by the Great Awakening), Anglicans, and Congregationalists. As these churches' importance waned, the number of Presbyterians and Baptists increased after 1740, and that of Methodists (pro-revival offshoots of Anglicanism) rose after 1770. Ever since the late 1700s, these three churches have dominated American Protestantism. Second, the Great Awakening stimulated the founding of new colleges, for existing colleges were scarred in their opponents' eyes by their affiliations with either Old or New Lights. In 1746 New Light Presbyterians established the College of New Jersey (Princeton). Then followed King's College (Columbia) for Anglicans in 1754, the College of Rhode Island (Brown) for Baptists in 1764, Queen's College (Rutgers) for Dutch Reformed in 1766, and Dartmouth College for Congregationalists in 1769. Third, the revival

Nassau Hall *Officially chartered as the College of New Jersey, Princeton was popularly known in its early years as Nassau Hall, after the name of its principal building (center).*

marked the real emergence of black Protestantism, which was almost nonexistent before 1740. New Lights reached out to slaves, some of whom joined white churches and even preached at the revivals. Conversions came slowly, but by 1790 many blacks were Christians.

The Great Awakening also had the unintended effect of fostering religious toleration by blurring theological differences among New Lights. Though an Anglican who helped found Methodism, George Whitefield preached with Presbyterians such as Gilbert Tennent and Congregationalists like Jonathan Edwards. Revivalism emphasized inner experience over doctrine and implied that the true church was a fellowship of saints who shared saving grace. Revivalism thus prepared Americans to accept denominationalism, which today assumes that all Judeo-Christian churches are legitimate expressions of belief in God and deserve equal freedom and respect. Denominationalism would slowly emerge after the Revolution as the best means of accommodating religious diversity.

Historians have disagreed over whether the Great Awakening had political as well as religious effects. Although Tennent and Davenport called the poor "God's people" and flayed the wealthy, they never advocated a social revolution, and the Awakening did not produce any distinct political ideology. Yet by sensitizing the public to the corruption of those in authority, New Light ministers laid some of the groundwork for political revolutionaries a generation later, who would contend that royal government in America had grown corrupt and unworthy of obedience.

Conclusion

The aura of sanctified purpose lingered over Whitefield and his religious revival even after his death in Boston in 1770. In September 1775 a ragtag army of American rebels, marching through Massachusetts, paused on their way to attack the British stronghold at Quebec. Hoping to win a blessing for their risky venture, they broke open a tomb and prayed over a holy man's remains. The corpse was George Whitefield's.

By the 1750s the British mainland colonies had taken on the look of mature societies. For fifty years their population and wealth had been rising impressively. The mainland provinces were more populous than Scotland and almost one-third the size of England. White colonists' standard of living far exceeded those of Scotland and Ireland and equaled that of England. Literacy had spread widely in the northern colonies, and by 1766 Anglo-America had more institutions of higher learning than England, Scotland, and Ireland together. A self-confident Anglo-American upper class had garnered expertise in law, trade, finance, and politics.

While the mainland colonies had developed mature political systems that could even challenge royal authority, the Glorious Revolution of 1688–1689 and the imperial wars of 1689–1713 had bolstered the colonists' dependence on—and loyalty to—the British monarchy. Nonetheless, the colonists' British patriotism, which would be proven under enemy fire between 1744 and 1760, hinged on the assumption that they shared Britons' political rights. In particular, a crucial principle for them was the rough equality of power between the colonial legislatures and Great Britain's Parliament.

In 1763 Britain began challenging Americans' longstanding conceptions of their political rights and attempted to subordinate the colonies to Parliament's authority. In ignoring the colonies' tradition of self-government, however, Parliament would underestimate the vigor with which the colonial elite stood ready to defend local autonomy, even to the point of revolution. Nor did the British upper class have any inkling of the depth of righteous conviction that many ordinary Americans would feel in linking their defense of liberty with their obedience to God. Out of that potent mixture of self-reliant confidence and God-given mission, Americans would begin to forge a national consciousness.

CHRONOLOGY

1651–
1733 Parliament creates the navigation system to regulate British imperial commerce.

1660 Restoration of the Stuart dynasty to English throne.

1663 Sir John Colleton and others obtain title to Carolina.

1664 English conquer the Dutch colony of New Netherland, which becomes the English colony of New York.

Sir Philip Carteret and John, Lord Berkeley, become joint proprietors of the Jersey colony.

1670 Settlement of southern Carolina begins.

1672 Louis Jolliet and Jacques Marquette explore the Mississippi River.

1676 Quakers organize the colony of West Jersey.

1680–
1692 Pueblo revolt in New Mexico.

1681 William Penn founds the colony of Pennsylvania.

1682 Quakers organize the colony of East Jersey.

The Sieur de la Salle descends the Mississippi River to the Gulf of Mexico and claims the Mississippi basin for France.

1685 James II becomes king of England.

1686–
1689 Dominion of New England.

1688 Glorious Revolution in England; James II is deposed.

1689 William and Mary ascend to English throne.
Protestant Association organized in Maryland.
Leisler's Rebellion in New York.

1689–
1697 King William's War.

1690 John Locke, *Essay upon Human Understanding*.

1698 French begin settlements near the mouth of the Mississippi River.

1700 Father Eusebio Kino founds first Arizona mission.

1701 Iroquois adopt neutrality policy in future colonial wars.

1702–
1713 Queen Anne's War.

1711–
1713 Tuscarora War in North Carolina.

1715–
1716 Yamasee War in South Carolina.

1718 New Orleans founded.

1732 Georgia colony chartered.

1739 Great Awakening begins.
Stono Rebellion in South Carolina.

1743 Benjamin Franklin founds American Philosophical Society.

1769 Franciscan priests establish first California mission, at San Diego.

For Further Reading

Bernard Bailyn, *Voyagers to the West: A Passage in the Peopling of America on the Eve of the Revolution* (1986). Pulitzer Prize–winning study that, though dealing primarily with British immigration in the 1770s, throws important light on the motives of immigrants throughout the eighteenth century.

Richard L. Bushman, *From Puritan to Yankee: Character and the Social Order in Connecticut, 1690–1765* (1967). The best examination of social and cultural maturation in any colony.

Jack P. Greene and J. R. Pole, eds., *Colonial British America: Essays in the New History of the Early Modern Era* (1984). Essays by sixteen leading authorities summarizing the current status of scholarship on early America.

Rhys Isaac, *The Transformation of Virginia, 1740–1790* (1982). Pulitzer Prize–winning study of class relationships, race relations, and folkways at the time of the Great Awakening.

James H. Merrell, *The Indians' New World: Catawbas and Their Neighbors from European Contact Through the Era of Removal* (1989). A pathbreaking examination, with broad implications for understanding the native American past, of the interaction between South Carolina colonists and Catawba Indians.

Edwin J. Perkins, *The Economy of Colonial America* (2d ed., 1988). An authoritative, commonsensical, and highly readable overview of economic life in early America.

Phinizy Spalding, *Oglethorpe in America* (1977). An excellent introduction to Georgia's early struggle for survival.

Peter H. Wood, *Black Majority: Negroes in Colonial South Carolina from 1670 Through the Stono Rebellion* (1974). An engrossing study of slavery and racism as they evolved in the Lower South.

Additional Bibliography

The Restoration Colonies

Melvin B. Endy, Jr., *William Penn and Early Quakerism* (1973); Sung Bok Kim, *Landlord and Tenant in Colonial New York: Manorial Society, 1664–1775* (1978); Daniel C. Littlefield, *Rice and Slaves: Ethnicity and the Slave Trade in Colonial South Carolina* (1981); John A. Munroe, *Colonial Delaware: A History* (1973); Gary B. Nash, *Quakers and Politics: Pennsylvania, 1681–1726* (1968); John E. Pomfret, *The Province of East New Jersey, 1609–1702: The Rebellious Province* (1962), and *The Province of West New Jersey, 1609–1702: A History of the Origins of an American Colony* (1956); Robert C. Ritchie, *The Duke's Province: A Study of New York Politics and Society, 1664–1691* (1977); W. Stitt Robinson, *The Southern Colonial Frontier, 1607–1763* (1979); Robert M. Weir, *Colonial South Carolina: A History* (1983).

French and Spanish Expansion

John Francis Bannon, *The Spanish Borderlands Frontier, 1513–1821* (1970); W. J. Eccles, *The Canadian Frontier, 1534–1760* (1969), and *France in America* (1972); Charles Edwards O'Neill, *Church and State in French Colonial Louisiana: Policy and Politics to 1732* (1966); Edward H. Spicer, *Cycles of Conquest: The Impact of Spain, Mexico, and the United States on the Indians of the Southwest, 1533–1960* (1962); David J. Weber, ed., *New Spain's Far Western Frontier: Essays on Spain in the American West* (1979).

Rebellion and Imperial Warfare

Lois Green Carr and David W. Jordan, *Maryland's Revolution of Government, 1689–1692* (1974); Michael G. Hall, *Edward Randolph and the American Colonies, 1676–1703* (1960); Richard R. Johnson, *Adjustment to Empire: The New England Colonies, 1675–1715* (1981); David S. Lovejoy, *The Glorious Revolution in America, 1660–1692* (1972); Howard H. Peckham, *The Colonial Wars, 1689–1762* (1964); William Saunders Webb, *The Governors General: The English Army and the Definition of the Empire, 1569–1681* (1979).

Society, Economics, and Population Growth

Philip D. Curtin, *The Atlantic Slave Trade: A Census* (1969); Oliver M. Dickerson, *The Navigation Acts and the American Revolution* (1951); Thomas M. Doerflinger, *A Vigorous Spirit of Enterprise: Merchants and Economic Development in Revolutionary Philadelphia* (1986); A. Roger Ekirch, *Bound for America: The Transportation of British Convicts to the Colonies, 1718–1775* (1987); Richard Hofstader, *America at 1750: A Social Portrait* (1971); N. E. H. Hull, *Female Felons: Women and Serious Crime in Colonial Massachusetts* (1987); Allan Kulikoff, *Tobacco and Slaves: The Development of Southern Cultures in the Chesapeake, 1680–1800* (1986); Audrey Lockhart, *Some Aspects of Emigration from Ireland to the North American Colonies Between 1660 and 1775* (1976); John J. McCusker and Russell R. Menard, *The Economy of British America, 1607–1789* (1985); Edgar J. McManus, *Black Bondage in the North* 1973); Donald W. Meinig, *The Shaping of America: A Geographical Perspective on Five Hundred Years of History: Volume I, Atlantic America, 1492–1800* (1986); Gerald W. Mullin, *Flight and Rebellion: Slave Resistance in Eighteenth-Century Virginia* (1972); Gary B. Nash, *The Urban Crucible: The Northern Seaports and the Origins of the American Revolution* (abridged ed., 1986); Sharon V. Salinger, *"To Serve Well and Faithfully": Labor and Indentured Servants in Pennsylvania, 1682–1800* (1987); Daniel Blake Smith, *Inside the Great House: Family Life in Eighteenth-Century Chesapeake Society* (1980); Mechal Sobel, *The World They Made Together: Black and White Values in Eighteenth-Century Virginia* (1987); Gary M. Walton and James F. Shepherd, *The Economic Rise of Early America* (1979); Robert V. Wells, *The Population of the British Colonies in America Before 1776: A Survey of Census Data* (1975); Betty Wood, *Slavery in Colonial Georgia, 1730–1775* (1984).

The Enlightenment, Religion, and Politics

Patricia U. Bonomi, *Under the Cope of Heaven: Religion, Society, and Politics in Colonial America* (1986); Henry S. Commager, *The Empire of Reason: How Europe Imagined and America Realized the Enlightenment* (1977); Bruce C. Daniels, ed., *Power and Status: Essays on Officeholding in Colonial America* (1986); Robert J. Dinkin, *Voting in Provincial America: A Study of Elections in the Thirteen Colonies, 1680–1776* (1977); Edwin S. Gaustad, *The Great Awakening in New England* (1957); Jack P. Greene, *The Quest for Power: The Lower Houses of Assembly in the Southern Royal Colonies, 1689–1776* (1963); Thomas L. Purvis, *Proprietors, Patronage, and Paper Money: Legislative Politics in New Jersey; 1703–1776* (1986); Sally Schwartz, *A Mixed Multitude: The Struggle for Toleration in Colonial Pennsylvania* (1987); Charles S. Sydnor, *American Revolutionaries in the Making: Political Practices in Washington's Virginia* (1965); Patricia J. Tracy, *Jonathan Edwards, Pastor: Religion and Society in Eighteenth-Century Northampton* (1980); Carl J. Vipperman, *The Rise of Rawlins Lowndes, 1721–1800* (1978); Marilyn J. Westerkamp, *Triumph of the Laity: Scots-Irish Piety and the Great Awakening, 1625–1760* (1988); Esmond Wright, *Franklin of Philadelphia* (1986).

CHAPTER 4

The Road to Revolution, 1748–1776

In 1769 Benjamin Franklin was an agent for several American colonial assemblies and living in London, where he obtained an anonymous English pamphlet entitled *Good Humour*. Franklin bristled at the unknown author's charges that the colonists' recent opposition to parliamentary taxes represented "*a posture of hostility* against Great Britain." "There was no Posture of Hostility in America," Franklin angrily scribbled in the margin, "but Britain put herself in a Posture of Hostility against America."

As Franklin wrote those words, a constitutional crisis gripped the British Empire and was markedly affecting Britain's relationship with its overseas colonies. The conflict between the mother country and the American colonies arose suddenly after 1763, when Parliament attempted to tighten control over economic and political affairs in the colonies. Long accustomed to legislating for themselves, Americans resisted this unexpected effort to centralize decision making in London. American leaders like Franklin interpreted Britain's clampdown as calculated antagonism and were certain that Parliament's efforts to tax them would make a mockery of self-government in America.

Despite their apprehension over parliamentary taxes, colonial politicians usually expressed their opposition peacefully from 1763 to 1775, through such tactics as legislative resolutions and commercial boycotts. Few lost their lives during the twelve years prior to the battles at Lexington and Concord, the first military clashes of the Revolution, and all of those killed were American civilians rather than royal officials or soldiers. Even after fighting broke out, some colonists agonized for more than a year over whether to sever their political relationship with England—which even native-born Americans sometimes referred to affectionately as "home." Of all the world's colonial peoples, none became rebels more reluctantly than did Anglo-Americans in 1776.

Imperial Warfare

Between 1713, when Queen Anne's War ended, and the early 1740s, the American colonies enjoyed a generation of peace, punctuated only by a brief war with Spain fought in Georgia from 1739 to 1742. But then two major European wars spilled over into the New World. The first was known in Europe as the War of the Austrian Succession (1740–1748) and in America as King George's War (1744–1748). A second, far more decisive European struggle, the Seven Years' War (1756–1763), had as its American counterpart the French and Indian War, which engulfed the colonies from 1754 to 1760. These conflicts originated in rivalries among the great powers of Europe—Britain, France, Austria, Prussia, and Russia—but few colonists doubted that King George's War was also *their* war, or that their prosperity depended on a British victory in the Seven Years' War.

Yet these wars produced an ironically mixed effect. On one hand, they fused the bonds between the British and the Anglo-Americans. Fighting side by side, shedding their blood in the same cause, the British and the American colonists came to rely on each other as rarely before. At the same time, the conclusion of each war planted the seeds first of misunderstanding, then of suspicion, and finally of hostility between the former compatriots.

King George's War

King George's War largely followed the pattern of earlier conflicts under William and Mary and Queen Anne (see Chapter 3). Few battles involved more than six hundred men, most of the skirmishes consisted of raids and counterattacks along the Canadian border, and the French and their Indian allies attacked no English settlements south of New York.

King George's War produced just one major engagement, which would later embitter Anglo-American relations. In 1745 almost four thousand New Englanders under William Pepperell of Maine assaulted the French bastion of Louisbourg on the northern tip of Nova Scotia, which guarded the entrance to the St. Lawrence River. Upon learning that the expedition of raw recruits planned to take a fortress defended by 250 cannons mounted on stone walls thirty feet high, Benjamin Franklin (then a member of the Pennsylvania assembly) feared the worst. "Fortified towns are hard nuts to crack," he warned his brother in Boston, "and your teeth are not accustomed to it."

Unable to bring artillery with them, Franklin's Yankee countrymen obtained siege guns by storming the enemy's outer batteries and then captured ammunition from several unsuspecting French supply ships that sailed into their clutches. For almost seven weeks they shelled Louisbourg, lobbing in nine thousand cannonballs and six hundred bombs until every building was either crumbling or on fire. On June 17, 1745, Pepperell took the fortress and almost 1,500 prisoners, at a loss of only 167 of his troops.

The colonists did not enjoy the fruits of victory for long. After three more years of inconclusive warfare, Britain and France signed a treaty in 1748 that exchanged Louisbourg for a British outpost in India that the French had taken during the war.

The memory of how their stunning achievement at Louisbourg went for naught would rankle the colonists for a decade.

A Fragile Peace

King George's War had failed to establish either Britain or France as the dominant power in North America, and each side soon began preparations for another war. The French governor of Canada continued to maintain two forts on New York soil, at Niagara and Crown Point, as well as a pair of garrisons in territory claimed by Britain's King George II as part of Nova Scotia. It was the Ohio Valley, however, that became the tinderbox for Anglo-French conflict. Pennsylvania traders took advantage of the peace to surge into the valley, where they briefly established a flourishing fur trade with the local Indians. French soldiers responded by harassing and arresting the Pennsylvanians, and even killing some, until all were driven out by 1752. In 1753 the Canadians began building a chain of forts that would link the Ohio River with Louisiana and block British expansion westward. In the interwar years, the French also strengthened their military alliances with the western Indians and even gained some prestige among the Iroquois, who had taken no part in King George's War.

In response to French aggression, in mid-1754 delegates from seven colonies north of Virginia

"Join or Die," 1754

Benjamin Franklin published this well-known cartoon just before the Albany Congress convened. The snake symbolized the colonies' considerable divisions—a disunity that political leaders would have to struggle against in years to come.

gathered at Albany, New York, to lay plans for their mutual defense. By showering the wavering Iroquois with thirty wagonloads of presents, the colonists kept most of these Indians neutral. The delegates then endorsed a proposal for a colonial confederation, the so-called Albany Plan of Union, largely based on the ideas of Pennsylvania's Franklin and Massachusetts's Thomas Hutchinson. The plan called for a "Grand Council" representing all the colonial assemblies, with a crown-appointed "president general" as its executive officer. The Grand Council would devise policies regarding military defense and Indian affairs, and if necessary, it could demand funds from the colonies according to an agreed-upon formula. Although it provided a precedent for later American unity, the Albany Plan came to nothing, primarily because no colonial legislature would surrender the least control over its powers of taxation, even to fellow Americans and in the face of grave mutual danger.

Virginians meanwhile were on the verge of provoking an international incident in the Ohio Valley, which Virginia claimed. In 1753 the colony sent a twenty-one-year-old surveyor, George Washington, to demand that the French abandon their forts on the Allegheny River. The French refused, but Washington reported that Virginia might still block further Canadian expansion by occupying the strategic point where the Allegheny and Monongahela rivers joined to form the Ohio—the site of present-day Pittsburgh.

Returning in 1754 with three hundred colonial volunteers and one hundred British regulars, Washington found the French already occupying the juncture of the rivers and constructing Fort Duquesne there. He then built a crude defensive position about sixty miles southeast called Fort Necessity, near which his men killed several French soldiers in an ambush that brought swift retaliation. On July 4, 1754, after losing one-fourth of his men in a daylong battle, Washington surrendered Fort Necessity to an enemy force four times larger than his own and led the survivors home.

The Seven Years' War in America

Although France and Britain remained at peace in Europe until 1756, the action at Fort Necessity created a virtual state of war in North America. In response, nearly eight thousand Americans enlisted during 1755 to attack the Canadian strongholds menacing New York and Nova Scotia. That same year, British general Edward Braddock and a thousand Irish regulars arrived in North America to take Fort Duquesne.

Stiff-necked and scornful of colonial soldiers, Braddock expected his disciplined British regulars to make short work of the enemy and only dimly perceived the strength and resourcefulness of the forces gathering against him. Washington's failure in the Ohio Valley had driven the western Indians into an alliance with the French. On July 9, 1755, about nine hundred Canadians and Indians ambushed Braddock's force of British regulars and the Virginia volunteers under Washington nine miles east of Fort Duquesne. Riddled by three hours of steady fire from an unseen foe, Braddock's regulars finally broke and left Washington's Virginians to hold off the enemy while they retreated. Nine hundred regular and provincial soldiers died in Braddock's defeat, including Braddock himself, who succumbed on the retreat.

Following this engagement, Indian raids convulsed Pennsylvania, Maryland, Virginia, and even parts of New Jersey—all colonies that had escaped attack in previous wars. Meanwhile, neither of two Anglo-American armies that marched against the French fortresses at Niagara and Crown Point in New York reached its objective in 1755. The only successful British expedition that year was undertaken by two thousand New Englanders who seized two French forts that were putting Nova Scotia at risk. This campaign was memorable less for its military significance than for its tragic aftermath. Following the takeover of the French forts, the governor of Nova Scotia ordered the troops to drive thousands of local French-Canadian civilians, the Acadians, from their homes—often with nothing more than they could carry in their arms—and to burn their villages. This cruel expulsion stemmed from the Acadians' refusal to promise not to bear arms for France. Almost 5 percent of Canada's population was eventually deported in this way to the British colonies, from which many migrated to French Louisiana. There they became known as Cajuns.

Although Anglo-Americans outnumbered Canadians twenty to one, the French commander in chief, Louis Joseph Montcalm, maintained the offensive in 1756 and 1757. A daring and resourceful general, Montcalm benefited from large numbers of French regulars in Canada, over-

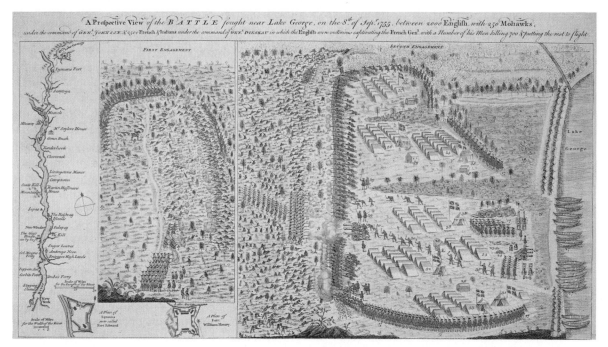

The Battle of Lake George *This contemporary drawing records the battle of September 8, 1755, in intricate detail. A force of 3,500 American provincials and 300 Indians under William Johnson defeated a mixed force of 2,000 French regulars, Canadians, and Indians, led by Baron Ludwig Dieskau, who were defending Crown Point.*

whelming Indian support, and the mobilization of nearly every able-bodied Canadian into a formidable militia that fought with the courage of desperate men. In contrast, the American colonies balked at providing many troops and frequently sent poorly trained men who had been enlisted for only a few months. "I would rather have no Troops," wrote a despairing British colonel in 1757, "than to be at the Trouble & expence to form them, & when they could begin to be able to perform their Duty, be oblig'd to disband them."

Confronted by the numerically superior but disorganized Anglo-Americans, the French seized Fort Oswego on Lake Ontario in 1756 and took Fort William Henry on Lake George in 1757. By now the French threatened central New York and western New England. In Europe, too, the war was going badly for Britain, which by 1757 seemed to be facing defeat on all fronts.

In this dark hour, one of the British ministers, William Pitt, took control of military affairs in the royal cabinet and reversed the downward course. Imaginative and single-minded in his conception

of Britain's imperial destiny, Pitt saw himself as the man of the hour. "I know," he declared, "that I can save this country and that no one else can." True to his word, Pitt reinvigorated British patriotism throughout the empire. By the war's end, he was the colonists' most popular hero, the symbol of what Americans and Englishmen could accomplish when united.

Hard pressed in Europe by France and its allies (which included Spain after 1761), Pitt preferred not to send large numbers of British regulars to America. Fewer than four thousand British troops arrived on the mainland from mid-1757 until Canada's conquest. Rather, Pitt believed that the key to crushing Canada lay in the mobilization of colonial soldiers. To encourage the Americans to assume the military burden, he promised that if the colonies raised the necessary men, Parliament would bear most of the cost of maintaining them.

Pitt's offer to free Americans from the war's financial burdens generated unprecedented support. The colonies organized twenty-one thousand troops in 1758, more soldiers than the crown sent

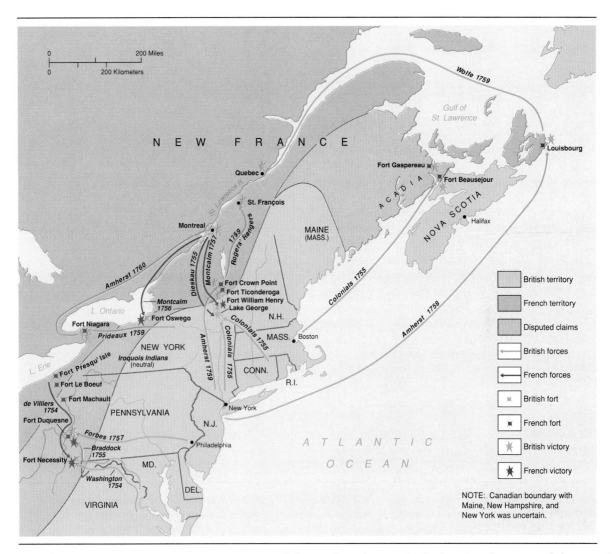

The Seven Years' War in America   *After experiencing major defeats early in the war, Anglo-American forces turned the tide against the French by taking Fort Duquesne in late 1757 and Louisbourg in 1758. After Canada fell in 1760, the fighting shifted to Spain's Caribbean colonies.* NOTE: The Canadian boundary with Maine, New Hampshire, and New York was uncertain.

to the mainland during the entire war, and raised an equal number in 1759. The resulting offensive under General Jeffery Amherst captured Fort Duquesne and Louisbourg by late 1758 and drove the French from northern New York the next year. In September 1759 Quebec fell after General James Wolfe defeated Montcalm on the Plains of Abraham outside that city, where both commanders died in battle. Canadian resistance ended in 1760, when Montreal surrendered.

France ceded all its territories on the North American mainland by the Treaty of Paris of 1763, which officially ended the Seven Years' War in both America and Europe. France gave Britain all of its lands east of the Mississippi and transferred title to its claims west of that river to Spain, which also gained New Orleans. In return for Cuba, which a British expedition had taken over in 1762, Spain ceded Florida to Britain. Spain's vast New World empire thus remained intact, but France's formerly

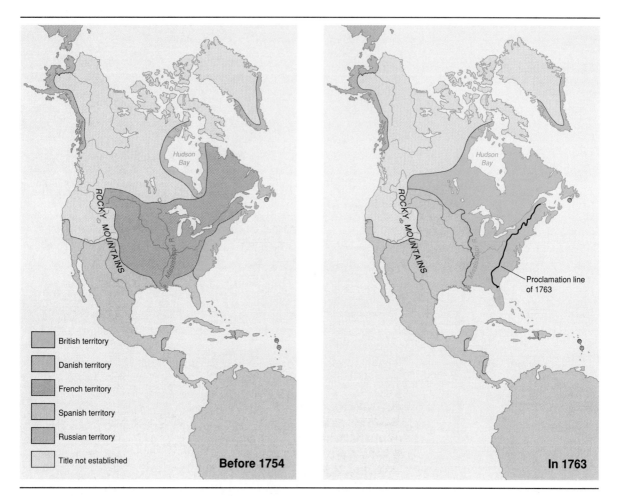

European Powers in the New World Before 1754 and in 1763

The Treaty of Paris (1763) divided France's North American empire between Britain and Spain. Hoping to prevent unnecessary violence between whites and Indians, Britain forbade any new white settlements west of the Appalachians' crest in the Proclamation of 1763.

extensive holdings were reduced to a few tiny fishing islands off Newfoundland and several thriving sugar islands in the West Indies. Britain seemed supreme in eastern North America.

Friction Between Allies

In England, public opinion assumed that credit for the North American victory belonged to the professional soldiers sent over from Britain. In fact, however, two of every five regulars who served had enlisted in America. Benjamin Franklin once complained that, although the force that captured two French forts on Nova Scotia's border in 1755 comprised two thousand Massachusetts troops and fewer than three hundred British regulars, "yet it could not be discovered by the Account ... published in the London Gazette, that there was a single New England man concern'd in the Affair."

The failure of the British people to understand Pitt's strategy had led them to underestimate the colonial soldiers' contribution to the war. Though realizing that the newly formed colonial units would not perform as well as veteran regiments, Pitt had nevertheless placed the American enlistees in charge of vital support roles: forming the reserve force in battle, performing essential supply functions, and holding frontier forts. This plan had the advantage of freeing the greatest number of British regulars for combat against the highly trained French, but it led the British public mistakenly to infer that the Americans had dodged their share of the fighting.

Pitt's promise to reimburse the colonial assemblies for their military expenses, moreover, angered Britons, who concluded that the colonists were escaping scot-free from the war's financial burden. Resentment amounting to rage against the colonists flared in Britain, especially among England's heavily taxed landlords. These members of the gentry had seen Britain's national debt nearly double during the war, from £72 million to over £123 million. At a time when the total debt of all the colonies collectively amounted to less than £1 million, the interest charges alone on the British debt came to more than £4 million a year. Staggering under the twin burdens of debt and taxes, the British thought it outrageous to repay Americans for defending themselves against an enemy on their own borders.

Worse, victory over the French did not end the British taxpayers' woes, for the settlement of the war indirectly spurred new Indian-white conflicts that drove the British debt even higher. With the French vanquished, the Indians feared that Anglo-American settlers would flock to areas of the Appalachian Mountains where the British military seemed determined permanently to occupy the western forts captured from France. To check British ambitions, an Ottawa chieftain named Pontiac forged an alliance among several western tribes and in May 1763 launched an offensive that sacked eight British forts near the Great Lakes and besieged two others at Pittsburgh and Detroit. After a relief column of Royal Americans and Scottish Highlanders routed a large Indian force at Bushy Run, Pennsylvania, an uneasy truce prevailed until a peace was negotiated in 1764.

Yet despite the native American defeat at Bushy Run, Pontiac's Alliance had not been decisively beaten. Hoping to conciliate the Indians and end the frontier fighting, the British government issued the Proclamation of 1763, which banned white settlement beyond the crest of the Appalachians. The proclamation angered colonies with western land claims, but it was intended only as a temporary measure to calm Indian fears about white expansion. The British, in fact, moved the line west just five years later to accommodate colonial land spec-

ulators. (One of those speculators was George Washington, who astutely kept buying western land because "any person who . . . neglects the present oppertunity [sic] of hunting out good Lands . . . will never regain it.") The real barrier to Anglo-American expansion into the Ohio Valley was not the Proclamation of 1763 but continuing Indian strength, which prevented whites from occupying lands west of Pittsburgh until 1775.

Pontiac's War also led the British government to conclude that ten thousand British soldiers should remain in North America to occupy the western territories that France had ceded and to intimidate the Indians. The British expected to spend £220,000 annually to maintain these troops, but the actual expense soared to nearly twice that figure. With the £20,000 needed to establish civil governments in Canada and Florida factored in, the burden of maintaining control over Britain's newly acquired territories would reach almost half a million pounds a year, fully 6 percent of Britain's peacetime budget. Britons considered it perfectly reasonable for the colonists to help offset this expense, which the colonists, however, saw as none of their responsibility. Added to British misunderstanding of the American role in the Seven Years' War, the question of who would pay this new debt further clouded relations between the peoples of Britain and the mainland colonies.

Imperial Reorganization

The Seven Years' War ended the era of "salutary neglect" that had characterized imperial oversight during most of the preceding half-century. Before 1763 Parliament had made few laws affecting the colonies, aside from the various Navigation Acts controlling trade (see Chapter 3). These laws, moreover, had not provoked dissatisfaction, for Americans widely accepted Britain's right to regulate their commerce but customs officers enforced the law loosely.

During the early 1760s, Parliament changed course, stirring up controversy in the process. The discontent centered first on new regulations that denied to Americans suspected of smuggling traditional rights essential for a fair trial. But the most striking departure from prior imperial practices came in Parliament's attempts to tax the colonies. Because Britain tightened its imperial grip gradually, however, Americans were slow to appreciate the extent of the changes under way. Following a minor dispute in 1761 over the use of legally dubious search warrants and growing friction raised by the Sugar Act of 1764, a major confrontation over parliamentary taxation flared in 1765 over the passage of the Stamp Act.

These measures coincided with the beginning of the reign of George III (ruled 1760–1820), who ascended to the throne at age twenty-two. In contrast to his immediate predecessors, George I and George II, who had been largely content to let veteran politicians in Parliament run the country, the new king distrusted the British political establishment. He was determined to have a strong influence on government policy, but he wished to reign as a constitutional monarch who cooperated with

Parliament and worked through prime ministers. However, neither his experience, his temperament, nor his philosophy suited George III to the formidable task of selecting satisfactory prime ministers to oversee the passage of imperial laws. Frequent clashes of personality and policy prompted the king to make abrupt changes in leadership at the very time when British government was trying to implement a massive reorganization of the empire. George's first prime minister, his friend and former tutor Lord Bute, lasted only from 1760 to 1763. Then in quick succession came the ministry of George Grenville from 1763 to 1765, that of the Marquis of Rockingham in 1766, the ministry of the ailing William Pitt in 1766, and a period of uncertain leadership that ended only in 1770, with the appointment of the ministry led by Frederick, Lord North.

The Writs of Assistance

British attempts to halt American merchants from trading with the enemy in the French West Indies during the Seven Years' War produced a crackdown on smuggling. In 1760 the royal governor of Massachusetts authorized revenue officers to employ a document called a writ of assistance to seize illegally imported goods. The writ was a general search warrant that permitted customs officials to enter any ships or buildings where smuggled goods might be hidden. Because the document required no evidence of probable cause for suspicion, most English legal authorities considered it unconstitutional. The writ of assistance also threatened the traditional respect accorded the privacy of a family's place of residence, since most merchants conducted business from their homes, where they might store inventory anywhere. The writ allowed a customs agent to ransack a merchant's house in search of illegal goods, even if there was no evidence of lawbreaking. (Today such warrants are illegal in Great Britain and the United States.)

Writs of assistance proved a powerful weapon against smuggling. In quick reaction to the writs, merchants in Boston, virtually the smuggling capital of the colonies, hired lawyer James Otis to challenge the constitutionality of these warrants. (Otis, a former prosecuting attorney for Boston's vice-admiralty court, had resigned his post in protest against the writs.) Arguing his case before the Mas-

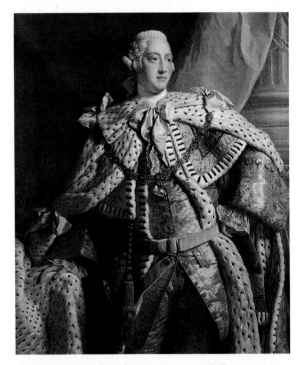

George III, *Studio of A. Ramsay, c. 1767*

Although unsure of himself and emotionally little more than a boy upon his accession to the English throne, George III possessed a deep moral sense and a fierce determination to rule as well as to reign.

sachusetts supreme court in 1761, Otis proclaimed that "an act against the Constitution is void"—even one passed by Parliament. But the court, heavily influenced by the opinion of Chief Justice Thomas Hutchinson, who noted the continuing use of identical writs in England, ruled against the merchants.

Despite having lost the case, Otis had expressed with absolute clarity the colonists' fundamental conception of Parliament's role under the British constitution. The British constitution was not a written document but a collection of customs and accepted principles that guaranteed certain rights to all citizens. Most British politicians assumed that Parliament's laws were themselves part of the constitution and hence that Parliament could alter the constitution at will. Like other Americans, Otis contended that Parliament possessed no authority to violate any of the traditional "rights of Englishmen," and he asserted that there were limits "beyond which if Parliaments go, their Acts bind not."

The Sugar Act

In 1764, just three years after Otis's court challenge, Parliament passed the Sugar Act with the goal of raising £100,000, a sum that would offset one-fifth of the military expenses in North America. Its enactment triggered a new round of tension between Britain and the colonies, for the Sugar Act ended Britain's longstanding policy of exempting colonial trade from revenue-raising measures. The Navigation Acts had not been designed to bring money into the British treasury but rather to benefit the imperial economy indirectly, by stimulating trade and protecting English manufacturers from foreign competition. The taxes that Parliament levied on colonial products entering Britain were paid by English importers who passed them on to consumers; they were not taxes paid by American producers. So little revenue did the Navigation Acts bring in (just £1,800 in 1763) that they did not even pay for the cost of their own enforcement, which came to about £8,000.

The Sugar Act amended the old Molasses Act of 1733, which had taxed all foreign molasses entering British America at 6 pence per gallon. Parliament had never intended this law to raise revenue but rather to serve as a protective tariff excluding French West Indian molasses from entering

British North America, where the colonists distilled it into rum. The Molasses Act increased the cost of rum by about half for all distillers using French molasses but allowed distillers to import molasses from the British West Indies duty-free. However, the British West Indies produced such large amounts of rum for local use that little surplus molasses remained for export. Mainland distillers needed about 3.5 million gallons of molasses annually, and they had no choice but to buy it from the French West Indies, which had huge surpluses to export. Because the Molasses Act's 6 pence duty was too high to pass on to consumers, American importers had commonly bribed customs officials into taking 1½ pence per gallon to look the other way when French molasses was unloaded. Aware of the widespread bribery, Parliament assumed, erroneously, that rum drinkers could stomach a 3 pence duty per gallon.

New taxes were not the only feature of the Sugar Act objectionable to Americans. The act's principal architect, British prime minister George Grenville, viewed it as a weapon against what he saw as an epidemic of colonial smuggling. Grenville exaggerated the extent of colonial smuggling, which was largely confined to tea and to French molasses, and he ignored the fact that illegal trade was rampant in Great Britain. In any event, the Sugar Act targeted a broad range of colonial commercial activities for control by establishing a host of new regulations. The law stipulated that colonists could export lumber, iron, skins, hides, whalebone, logwood, and many other commodities to foreign countries only if the shipments landed first in Britain. Previously, American ships had taken these products directly to the Netherlands or the German states, where captains purchased local goods and then sailed straight back to the colonies. By channeling this trade through Britain, Parliament hoped that colonial shippers would purchase more *imperial* wares for the American market and buy fewer goods from foreign competitors. Moreover, by slapping a heavy tax on the formerly thriving American business of carrying duty-free Portuguese wine from Madeira and the Azores to the colonists, the law also aimed to increase English merchants' sales of European wine.

These restrictions financially burdened several important sectors of American commerce that previously had been legal. The Sugar Act hit New

England especially hard, since its economy had depended heavily on exporting these items to continental Europe and also on quenching the colonists' thirst with Portuguese wine. By interfering with a profitable trade developed through American enterprise, the Sugar Act had the perverse effect of creating a new category of smuggling where none had existed before, because many colonial merchants ultimately ignored the law, which in their view senselessly sacrificed their interests.

The Sugar Act also vastly complicated the requirements for shipping colonial goods. A captain now had to fill out a confusing series of documents to certify his trade as legal, and the absence of any of them left his entire cargo liable to seizure. Moreover, the Sugar Act defined oceanic commerce so broadly that much of the trade between colonies, never before regulated, became subject to complex rules for compliance. The law's petty regulations made it virtually impossible for a great many colonial shippers to avoid committing technical violations of the Sugar Act, even if they traded in the only manner possible under local circumstances.

Finally, the Sugar Act disregarded many traditional English protections for a fair trial. First, the law allowed customs officials to transfer smuggling cases from the colonial courts (in which juries decided the outcome) to vice-admiralty courts, where a judge alone gave the verdict. Because the Sugar Act (until 1768) awarded vice-admiralty judges 5 percent of any confiscated cargo, judges had a financial incentive to find every defendant guilty. Second, until 1767 the law did not permit defendants to be tried where their offense allegedly had taken place (usually their home province) but required all cases to be heard in the vice-admiralty court at Halifax, Nova Scotia. Third, the law reversed normal courtroom procedures, which presumed innocence until guilt was proved, by requiring the defendant to disprove the prosecution's charge.

The Sugar Act was no idle threat. George Grenville ordered the navy to enforce the measure, and it did so vigorously. A Boston resident complained in 1764 that "no vessel hardly comes in or goes out but they find some pretense to seize and detain her." That same year, Pennsylvania's chief justice reported that customs officers were extorting fees from small boats carrying lumber across the Delaware River to Philadelphia from New Jersey and seemed likely "to destroy this little River-trade." "Men of war, cutters, marines with their bayonets fixed, judges of admiralty, collectors, comptrollers, searchers, . . . and a whole catalogue of pimps are sent hither," scowled a Massachusetts merchant in 1765, "not to protect our trade, but to distress it."

The Sugar Act alarmed colonists by sacrificing their economic interests and legal rights for the benefit of British merchants. Rather than pay the 3 pence tax, Americans continued smuggling molasses until 1766. Then, to discourage smuggling, Britain lowered the duty to 1 penny—less than the customary bribe American shippers paid to get their cargoes past inspectors. The law thereafter raised about £30,000 annually in revenue until 1775.

The Sugar Act confused Americans. They understood (correctly) that the Molasses Act of 1733 had never been meant as a revenue measure; in their eyes, it was a legitimate law intended to regulate trade. They therefore hesitated to denounce the Sugar Act as unconstitutional, for it seemingly only amended the Molasses Act. Notwithstanding, nine provincial legislatures protested that in passing the Sugar Act, Parliament had abused its authority to regulate trade. But seven of these objected on narrow grounds—either to its economic consequences for distillers or to its denial of traditional guarantees of a fair trial. Thus opposition to the Sugar Act failed to crystallize into a general defense of the no-taxation-without-representation principle. The law's burden fell overwhelmingly on Massachusetts, New York, and Pennsylvania, and other provinces had little interest in resisting a measure that did not affect them directly. In the end, the Sugar Act's immediate impact was minor. Soon a far more controversial issue would overshadow it—the Stamp Act.

The Stamp Act

The revenue raised by the Sugar Act did little to ease Britain's financial crisis. The national debt continued to rise, and the British public groaned under the weight of the second-highest tax rates in Europe. Particularly irritating to Britons was the fact that by 1765 their rates averaged 26 shillings per person, while the colonial tax burden varied

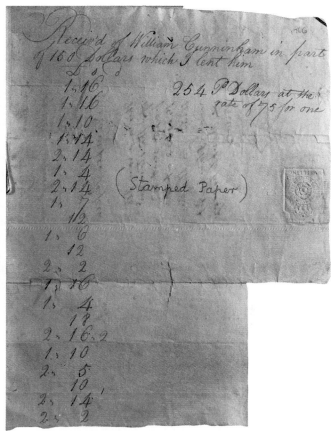

Tax Stamps

Under the Stamp Act, all legal and commercial documents had to bear tax stamps such as those shown here in closeup and on a business document.

from ½ to 1½ shillings per inhabitant, or barely 2 percent to 6 percent of the British rate. Well aware of how lightly the colonists were taxed, Grenville thought that fairness demanded a larger contribution to the empire's need.

To force the colonists to pay their share of imperial expenses, Parliament passed the Stamp Act in March 1765. The law obliged Americans to purchase and use special stamped (watermarked) paper for newspapers, customs documents, various licenses, college diplomas, and numerous legal forms necessary for recovering debts, buying land, and making wills. As with the Sugar Act, violators would face prosecution in vice-admiralty courts, without juries. The prime minister projected yearly revenues of £60,000 to £100,000, which would offset 12 percent to 20 percent of North American military expenses. Unlike the Sugar Act, which was an *external* tax on trade that fell mainly on merchants and ship captains, the Stamp Act levied an *internal* tax that few colonists could escape. Any-

one who made a will, transferred property, borrowed money, or bought playing cards or newspapers would pay the tax.

To Grenville and most of his supporters in Britain, the new tax seemed a small price for the benefits of the empire. Nevertheless, some Britons objected in principle to the tax, most notably William Pitt, who was Grenville's brother-in-law. In challenging the Stamp Act, Pitt emphasized that the colonists had never been subject to British revenue bills and taxed themselves through their own local assemblies.

Grenville agreed with Pitt that Parliament could not tax any British subjects unless they enjoyed representation in that body. But, Grenville and his followers contended, Americans *were* represented in Parliament, even if not one American actually elected any members. Americans, the prime minister claimed, shared the same status as the majority of British adult males, who either lacked sufficient property to vote or lived in large cities like

Sheffield, Manchester, and Birmingham—some more populous than the entire colony of Georgia in the mid-1760s—which had no seats in Parliament. Such persons were considered to be "virtually" represented in Parliament. The theory of virtual representation held that every member of Parliament stood above the narrow interests of his constituents and considered the welfare of *all* subjects when deciding issues. By definition, then, no Briton was represented by any particular individual in the House of Commons, but rather all imperial subjects, including Americans, could depend on each member of Parliament to protect their well-being.

Grenville and his supporters also denied that Americans were entitled to any exemption from British taxation because they elected their own assemblies. These legislative bodies were allegedly no different from English or Scottish town councils, whose local powers to pass laws and taxes did not nullify Parliament's authority over them. Accordingly, colonial assemblies were an adaptation to unique American circumstances and possessed no more power than Parliament allowed them to exercise.

The Colonial Perspective

The Stamp Act forced a choice on Americans. They would either have to confront the issue of parliamentary taxation head-on or surrender any claim to meaningful rights of self-government. However much they might admire and respect Parliament, few colonists imagined that it represented them. American spokesmen accepted the theory of virtual representation as valid for England and Scotland, but they denied that it could be extended to inhabitants of the colonies. In the American view, unless a lawmaker shared the interests of his constituents, he would have no personal stake in opposing bills contrary to their welfare. Americans recognized that members of Parliament would not impose oppressive taxes on their fellow residents of Great Britain, because the same taxes would also fall on their own estates and fortunes. The same members of Parliament, if left free to collect revenue in America, would have a clear incentive to shift the government's financial burden from themselves and their constituents onto the American colonists.

To Americans, Parliament's passage of the Stamp Act demonstrated both its indifference to their interests and the shallowness of the theory of virtual representation. Colonial agents in London had lobbied against passage of the law, and provincial legislatures had sent petitions—carefully worded statements of principle—warning against passage, but all to no avail. Parliament had dismissed the petitions without even a hearing. Parliament "must have thought us Americans all a parcel of Apes and very tame Apes too," concluded Christopher Gadsden of South Carolina, "or they would have never ventured on such a hateful, baneful experiment."

Although Americans rejected Parliament's claim to tax them, they did concede that it possessed *limited* powers of legislation. For example, the colonists believed that Parliament could standardize legal procedures throughout the realm to permit every British subject equal access to royal justice. The colonists also accepted the practical necessity for Parliament to regulate the empire's trade, even if their commerce was inconvenienced in the process.

Anglo-Americans considered the essential obligation of British allegiance to be loyalty to the crown, and their one unequivocal duty to be helping to defend the empire in wartime. The colonists insisted that they enjoyed a substantial measure of self-governance similar to that of Ireland, whose Parliament alone could tax its people but could not interfere with laws, like the Navigation Acts, passed by the British Parliament. In a speech before the Boston town meeting opposing the Sugar Act, James Otis expressed Americans' basic argument: "that by [the British] Constitution, every man in the dominions is a free man: that no parts of His Majesty's dominions can be taxed without consent: that every part has a right to be represented in the supreme or some subordinate legislature." In essence, Americans assumed that the empire was a loose federation in which their legislatures possessed considerable autonomy, rather than an extended nation governed directly from London.

Resisting the Stamp Act

Unlike the Sugar Act, the Stamp Act generated a political storm that rumbled through all the colonies in 1765. Every rank in society was caught up in the tempest—artisans, small farmers, planters, and merchants; women as well as men. Before the protest was over, upper-class community leaders had assumed direction of the colonial resistance movement.

In late May Patrick Henry, a twenty-nine-year-old Virginia lawyer with a talent for fiery oratory, dramatically conveyed the rising spirit of resistance. Henry persuaded the Virginia House of Burgesses to adopt several strongly worded resolutions denying Parliament's power to tax the colonies, and in the debate over the resolutions, the Speaker of the House cut him off just short of his uttering a treasonous wish that "some good American would stand up for his country"—presumably by assassinating the British tyrant responsible. Rather garbled accounts of Henry's resolutions electrified other Americans, and by the year's end, eight other colonial legislatures took a firm stand against British taxation.

Meanwhile, active resistance to the law was taking shape. In Boston by late summer, a group of mostly middle-class artisans, shopkeepers, and businessmen joined together as the Loyal Nine to fight the Stamp Act. They recognized that the stamp distributors, who alone could accept money for watermarked paper, were the law's weak link. If the public could pressure them into resigning before taxes became due on November 1, the Stamp Act would become inoperable. The Loyal Nine would propel Boston to the forefront of resistance.

It was no accident that Boston set the pace in opposing Parliament. Bostonians lived primarily by trade and distilling, and in 1765 they were not living well. No other port suffered so much from the Sugar Act's trade restrictions. The law burdened rum producers with a heavy tax on molasses, dried up a flourishing business of importing Portuguese wines, and prohibited the direct export of many New England products to profitable overseas markets. The city, moreover, was still struggling to recover from a great fire in 1760 that had burned 176 warehouses and left every tenth family homeless.

Widespread economic distress produced an explosive situation in Boston. A large segment of its population had good reason to blame British policies for the town's hard times. The situation was unusually dangerous because Bostonians were not only used to violence but seemed to enjoy mayhem for its own sake. The high point of each year

was November 5, Guy Fawkes Day, when thousands gathered to commemorate the failure of a Catholic plot in England in 1606 to blow up Parliament and kill King James I. On that day each year, mobs from the North End and the South End customarily burned gigantic figures of the pope. High spirits usually overflowed into violent confrontations in which unruly crowds battled each other with fists, stones, and barrel staves. After the brawlers in 1764 killed a small child who got in the way, the rival mobs made a truce that united them under a South End shoemaker named Ebenezer MacIntosh. MacIntosh commanded two thousand young toughs who could not imagine getting through 1765 without a major riot. The Loyal Nine soon enlisted these frustrated street fighters against Boston's stamp distributor, Andrew Oliver.

The morning of August 14 found a likeness of Oliver swinging from a tree guarded by a menacing crowd. Oliver apparently did not realize that the Loyal Nine were warning him to resign immediately, so at dusk MacIntosh and several hundred shouting followers demolished a new building of Oliver's at the dock. The mob then surged toward Oliver's house, where they ceremoniously beheaded his effigy and "stamped" it to pieces, an exercise designed in part to give him time to flee to safety. The crowd then shattered the windows of his home, smashed his furniture, and even tore out the paneling. When Lieutenant Governor Thomas Hutchinson and the sheriff tried to disperse the crowd, they were driven off under a barrage of rocks. Surveying his devastated home the next morning, Oliver announced his resignation.

Groups similar to the Loyal Nine but calling themselves the Sons of Liberty began forming throughout the colonies to follow Boston's example. A second house wrecking occurred at Newport, Rhode Island, on August 27, after the local stamp distributor ignored a fair warning to resign; he ruefully did so the next day. Upon seeing his store pulled down, Maryland's stamp master rode off in panic until his horse dropped dead of exhaustion in New Jersey. Most other distributors followed the example of James McIvers of New York, who fled the office as soon as he learned of Oliver's fate: "a storm was riseing," McIvers explained, "and I should soon feel it." Virginia's distributor abandoned his duties after learning that his own father was attacking him in the press. By November 1 every stamp man but two had resigned, and the holdouts did so shortly. Within a mere three months, a movement with no central direction had made Grenville's tax a dead letter.

Bitterness against the Stamp Act unleashed spontaneous, contagious violence. Twelve days after the first Boston riot, MacIntosh's mob demolished the elegant home of Thomas Hutchinson. The crowd indulged in a ten-hour orgy of drunken vandalism. This attack occurred in part because smugglers held grudges against Hutchinson for certain decisions he had given as chief justice and also because many financially pinched citizens saw him as a symbol of the royal policies crippling Boston's already troubled economy. Others lashed out in reaction to Hutchinson's efforts to stop the destruction of his brother-in-law Andrew Oliver's house. Ironically, Hutchinson privately opposed the Stamp Act.

Violence also got out of hand in Newport, Rhode Island. Unwilling to do their own dirty work, local merchants had arranged for John Webber, an English sailor just four days in town, to lead a gang of seamen against the provincial stamp distributor. Having accomplished that task, Webber turned on the merchants, publicly humiliated the sheriff, and seemed on the verge of plundering the town. The deposed stamp master—who was also the colony's attorney general—ended Newport's descent into anarchy by clapping Webber in jail.

The ten weeks from August 14 to November 1, 1765, were the most disorderly period of American opposition to British authority. The Sons of Liberty directed their violence against property, however, and invariably left avenues of escape for their victims. No one was killed or tarred and feathered, although some stamp distributors had their pride deeply wounded. Nevertheless, Webber's rampage and the frenzied assault on Hutchinson's mansion were instances of simple lawlessness. By September 1765 the leaders of the Sons of Liberty recognized that unless they prevented similar sprees in the future, they would discredit their cause. Thereafter, they directed public demonstrations with firm discipline and sometimes used military formations to maneuver hundreds of protesters like a small army. Especially fearful that a royal soldier or revenue officer might be shot or killed, the Sons of Liberty forbade their followers to carry weapons, even when facing armed adversaries. Realizing the value of martyrs, they resolved that the only lives lost over the issue of British taxation would come from their own ranks.

In October 1765 representatives of nine colonies met in New York City in the so-called Stamp Act Congress. The session was remarkable for the colonies' agreement on and bold articulation of the general principle that Parliament lacked authority to levy taxes outside Great Britain and to deny any person a jury trial. Only once before had a truly intercolonial meeting taken place—the Albany Congress, in 1754—and, as we have seen, its plea for unity had fallen on deaf ears. In 1765 the colonial response was entirely different. "The Ministry never imagined we could or would so generally unite in opposition to their measures," wrote a Connecticut delegate to the congress, "nor I confess till I saw the Experiment made did I."

Declarations of principle like these resolutions of the Stamp Act Congress helped to embolden and unify Americans, but words seemed futile in view of Parliament's earlier refusal to consider colonial objections to the stamp duties. "The most effectual way to procure a repeal," an anonymous writer in the *New York Gazette* suggested, "is to shew them [the British] that nothing will execute it but down right force. This will make them despair of ever executing it at all."

Indeed, the British were finding the Stamp Act unenforceable, and governmental business began grinding to a halt. By late 1765 most stamp distributors had resigned or fled under popular compulsion, and without the watermarked paper required by law, most royal customs officials and court officers were refusing to perform their duties. In response, legislators compelled the reluctant officials to resume operation by threatening to withhold their pay. At the same time, merchants obtained sailing clearances by insisting that they would sue if cargoes spoiled while delayed in port. By late December the courts and harbors of almost every colony were again functioning.

Thus the American upper class assumed control of the public outcry against the Stamp Act. Respectable gentlemen moved to keep an explosive situation from getting out of hand by taking over leadership of local Sons of Liberty groups, by coordinating protest through the Stamp Act Congress, and by having colonial legislatures restore normal business. Colonial leaders feared that chaos was

"The Fatal To-Morrow"

In his October 31, 1765, edition, the Pennsylvania Journal's *publisher explained to subscribers how the Stamp Act, which would take effect the following day, was forcing him to stop publishing awhile in order to "deliberate whether any methods can be found to elude the chains forged for us."*

about to break out, particularly if British troops landed to enforce the Stamp Act. A letter from an influential Pennsylvanian, John Dickinson, to William Pitt summed up how responsible colonials envisioned the dire consequences of revolutionary turmoil: "a multitude of Commonwealths, Crimes, and Calamities, Centuries of mutual jealousies, Hatreds, Wars of Devastation, till at last the exhausted provinces shall sink into savagery under the yoke of some fortunate Conqueror."

Such extreme consequences did not come to pass, though the Stamp Act still remained in effect. To force its repeal, New York's merchants agreed on October 31, 1765, to boycott all British goods, and businessmen in other cities soon followed their example. Because Americans purchased about 40 percent of England's manufactures, this non-importation strategy put the English economy in danger of recession. The colonial boycotts consequently triggered panic within England's business community, whose members descended on Parliament to warn that the Stamp Act's continuation would stimulate a wave of bankruptcies, massive unemployment, and political unrest.

For reasons unconnected with the Stamp Act, George Grenville had fallen from George III's favor in mid-1765 and had been succeeded by the Marquis of Rockingham. The new prime minister hesitated to advocate repeal because the overwhelming majority within the House of Commons was outraged at colonial defiance of the law. Then in January 1766 William Pitt, a steadfast opponent of the Stamp Act, boldly denounced all efforts to tax the colonies, declaring, "I rejoice that America has resisted." Parliamentary support for repeal thereafter grew, though only as a matter of practicality, not as a surrender of principle. In March 1766 Parliament revoked the Stamp Act, but only in conjunction with passage of the Declaratory Act, which affirmed parliamentary power to legislate for the colonies "in all cases whatsoever."

Because the Declaratory Act was written in general language, Americans interpreted its meaning to their advantage. Most colonial political leaders recognized that the law was modeled after an earlier statute of 1719 regarding Ireland, which was considered exempt from British taxation. The measure therefore seemed no more than a parliamentary exercise in saving face to compensate for the Stamp Act's repeal, and Americans ignored it. The House of Commons, however, intended that the colonists take the Declaratory Act literally to mean that they could not claim exemption from *any* parliamentary statute, including a tax law. The Stamp Act crisis thus ended in a fundamental disagreement between Britain and America over the colonists' political rights.

Although the Stamp Act crisis had not resolved the underlying philosophical differences between Britain and America, most Americans were eager to put the events of 1765 behind them, and they showered both king and Parliament with loyal statements of gratitude for the Stamp Act's repeal. The Sons of Liberty disbanded. Americans manifestly still possessed a deep emotional loyalty to "Old England" and concluded with relief that their active resistance to the law had slapped Britain's leaders back to their senses. Despite the unpleasant memories retained by each side after the Stamp Act's repeal, the empire remained in a position to mend its wounds with time.

Era of Crisis

From 1767 to 1773, Parliament pursued a confrontational policy that gradually corroded Americans' trust of Britain. British actions in these years created a climate of fear and alienation on the mainland that left most Americans convinced that the Stamp Act had not been an isolated mistake but part of a deliberate design to undermine colonial self-governance. Burdened by historically high levels of taxation, the British public strongly supported politicians who would compel Americans to contribute toward the cost of royal government in the colonies. Two untested leaders in the House of Commons responded to this public pressure: Charles Townshend and Lord North, neither of whom had much sympathy for the American position.

The Rise of Charles Townshend

In August 1766, in a move arising out of British politics, George III dismissed the Rockingham government and summoned William Pitt to form a cabinet. An opponent of taxing the colonies, Pitt had the potential to repair the Stamp Act's damage, for no man was more respected in America. However, Pitt's health collapsed in March 1767, and effective leadership passed to his chancellor of the exchequer (or treasurer) Charles Townshend. Townshend, who had earned a resolution of gratitude from the Massachusetts assembly for voting against the Stamp Act, seemed well suited to reassure the nervous colonists. What Americans did not know was that he was fickle, hungry for power, and believed that Parliament could tax them. As responsibility for the empire shifted to "Champagne Charley" (a name bestowed on Townshend after he delivered an extraordinarily rousing dinner speech while drunk), policy lurched in the same direction as George Grenville had taken.

Just as Townshend took office, a conflict arose with the New York legislature over the Quartering Act of 1765 (also known as the Mutiny Act). This law ordered colonial legislatures to pay for certain goods needed by soldiers stationed within their respective borders. The necessary items were relatively inexpensive barracks supplies such as candles, windowpanes, mattress straw, polish, and a small liquor ration. The Quartering Act applied only to troops in settled areas, not on the frontier. It did not force citizens to accept soldiers in private homes or require legislatures to build new barracks. Just five colonies fell under its provisions, and four of these generally complied.

Despite its seemingly petty stipulations, the law aroused resentment, for it constituted an *indirect* tax; that is, while it did not (like the Stamp Act) empower royal officials to collect money directly from the colonists, it obligated particular assemblies to raise a stated amount of revenue by whatever means they considered appropriate. The act fell lightly or not at all on most colonies; but New York, where more soldiers were stationed than any other province, found compliance very burdensome and refused to grant any supplies.

New York's resistance to indirect taxation produced a torrent of anti-American feeling in the House of Commons, whose members remained bitter at having had to withdraw the Stamp Act. Townshend responded by drafting the New York Suspending Act, which threatened to nullify all laws passed by the colony after October 1, 1767, if the assembly still refused to vote the supplies. By the time that George III signed the measure in June, however, New York had already appropriated the necessary funds.

Although New York's retreat averted further confrontation, the conflict over the Quartering Act revealed the full extent of anticolonial sentiment in the House of Commons. The incident demonstrated that British leaders would not hesitate to defend Parliament's sovereignty through the most drastic of all steps: by interfering with American claims to self-governance. What Townshend and others did not realize was that such a course of action would soon undermine a loyal people's political allegiance.

Townshend's Financial Policies

The new wave of British resentment toward the colonies coincided with an outpouring of British frustration over the government's failure to cut taxes from wartime levels. Discontent raged among the landed gentry, whose members took advantage of their domination of the House of Commons to slash their own taxes by 25 percent in 1767. This move cost the government £500,000 and prompted Townshend to propose laws that would increase colonial customs revenue and tax imports entering America.

Townshend reasoned that a closer surveillance of colonial trade would intercept more smuggled goods, pressure colonial merchants to rely more on legal imports, and thus enlarge customs duties. In 1767 he introduced legislation creating the American Board of Customs Commissioners, whose members would strictly enforce the Navigation Acts. This law raised the number of port officials, funded the construction of a colonial coast guard, and provided money for secret informers.

At the same time, Townshend sought to tax the colonists by exploiting an oversight in their arguments against the Stamp Act. In confronting the Stamp Act, Americans had emphasized their opposition to *internal* taxes—that is, to taxes levied directly on property, goods, or government services in the colonies—but had said little about Parliament's right to tax imports as they entered the colonies. Townshend and other British leaders chose to interpret this silence as evidence that the colonists accepted Britain's right to tax their trade—to impose "external" taxes. Yet not all British politicians were so mistaken. "They will laugh at you,"

predicted a now much wiser George Grenville, "for your distinctions about regulations of trade." Brushing aside Grenville's warnings, Parliament passed Townshend's Revenue Act of 1767 (popularly called the Townshend duties) in June and July 1767. The new law taxed glass, paint, lead, paper, and tea imported into the colonies.

On the surface, Townshend's contention that the Americans would submit to this external tax on imports was convincing, for the colonists had long accepted Parliament's right to regulate their overseas trade and had in principle acknowledged taxation as a legitimate form of regulation. Even the Sugar Act had not primarily aroused opposition in the colonies because it imposed taxes; rather, Americans had protested the law because it instituted impractical regulations for conducting trade and violated traditional guarantees of a fair trial.

Townshend's Revenue Act differed significantly from what Americans had long seen as a legitimate way of regulating trade through taxation. To the colonists, charging a duty was a lawful way for British authorities to control trade only if that duty excluded foreign goods by making them prohibitively expensive to consumers. The Revenue Act of 1767, however, set moderate rates that did not price goods out of the colonial market; clearly, its purpose was to collect money for the treasury. Thus from the colonial standpoint, Townshend's duties were taxes just like the Stamp Act duties.

Although Townshend had introduced the Revenue Act in response to the government's budgetary problems, he had an ulterior motive for establishing an American source of revenue. Traditionally, royal governors had depended on colonial legislatures to vote their salaries; for their part, the legislatures had often refused to allocate these salaries until governors had signed certain bills to which they were opposed. Through the Revenue Act, Townshend hoped to establish a fund that would pay the salaries of governors and other royal officials in America, thus freeing them from the assemblies' control. In effect, by stripping the assemblies of their most potent weapon, the power of the purse, the Revenue Act threatened to tip the balance of constitutional power away from elected colonial representatives and toward unelected royal officials.

In reality the Revenue Act would never yield anything like the income that Townshend anticipated. Of the various items taxed, only tea produced any significant revenue—£20,000 of the £37,000 that the law was expected to yield. And because the measure would serve its purpose only if British tea was affordable to colonial consumers (who could easily smuggle Dutch tea), Townshend eliminated £60,000 worth of import fees paid on East Indian tea entering Britain before transhipment to America. On balance, the Revenue Act *worsened* the British treasury's deficit by £23,000. By 1767 Britain's financial difficulties were more an excuse for, than the driving force behind, political demands to tax the colonies. From Parliament's standpoint, the conflict with America was becoming a test of national will over the *principle* of taxation.

The Colonists' Reaction

Parliament gave the colonists little time to plan resistance against the Townshend duties. Americans only learned of the Revenue Act shortly before it went into operation, and they hesitated over the appropriate response. The strong-arm tactics that sent stamp tax collectors into panicky flight would not work against the Townshend duties, which the navy could easily collect offshore, safe from any Sons of Liberty.

Resistance to the Revenue Act remained weak until December 1767, when John Dickinson published twelve essays entitled *Letters from a Farmer*. (Dickinson was in fact a lawyer, but he preferred to portray himself as a son of the soil because the legal profession was unpopular among the general population.) The essays, which appeared in nearly every colonial newspaper, emphasized that, although Parliament could regulate trade by voting duties capable of providing small amounts of "incidental revenue," it had no right to tax commerce for the single purpose of raising revenue. In other words, the legality of any external tax depended on its intent. No tax designed to produce revenue could be considered constitutional unless a people's elected representatives voted for it. Dickinson said nothing that the colonists had not stated or implied during the Stamp Act crisis. Rather, his contribution lay in persuading Americans that the many arguments that they had marshaled against the Stamp Act also applied to the Revenue Act.

For all their clarity and eloquence, the *Letters from a Farmer* did not suggest tactics for resisting the Townshend duties, which had already taken effect. Dickinson was a conservative, deeply opposed to turmoil: he averred that "the cause of liberty is a cause of too much dignity to be sullied by turbulence and tumult." Yet resistance quickly took shape, aided immeasurably by the leadership of Massachusetts and by the blundering of the British government.

Dickinson himself had grasped the critical importance of mobilizing the citizens of Massachusetts. In a letter to James Otis, the Boston lawyer famed for his arguments in the writs-of-assistance case, Dickinson acknowledged that "whenever the Cause of American Freedom is to be vindicated, I look towards the Province of Massachusetts Bay. She must, as she has hitherto done, first kindle the Sacred Flame that on such occasions must warm and illuminate the Continent." Soon after receiving the letter, Otis chaired a Boston town meeting that asked the Massachusetts legislature to oppose the Townshend duties. In response, the assembly in early 1768 called on one of its members, Samuel Adams, to draft a "circular letter" to every other legislature. Harvard-educated yet possessing a flair for the push-and-shove of local politics, Adams had helped bring the Sons of Liberty under respectable leadership in 1765. In time he would acquire a reputation in Britain as a fanatic for colonial rights, but he deliberately phrased the circular letter in moderate language in order to give it a wide appeal. Adams's circular letter forthrightly condemned both taxation without representation and the threat to self-governance posed by Parliament's making governors and other royal officials financially independent of the legislatures. Nonetheless, the document acknowledged Parliament as the "supreme legislative Power over the whole Empire," and it advocated no illegal activities.

Virginia's assembly warmly approved Adams's eloquent message and sent out a more strongly worded circular letter of its own, urging all colonies to oppose imperial policies that would "have an immediate tendency to enslave them." But most colonial legislatures reacted indifferently to these letters. In fact, resistance to the Revenue Act might have disintegrated had the British government not overreacted to the circular letters.

Indeed, parliamentary leaders regarded even the mild Massachusetts letter as "little better than an incentive to Rebellion." Disorganized by Townshend's sudden death in 1768, the king's Privy

Samuel Adams

A central player in the drive for American liberty, Adams wrote in 1774 that "I wish for a permanent union with the mother country, but only in terms of liberty and truth. No advantage that can accrue to America from such a union, can compensate for the loss of liberty."

Council directed Lord Hillsborough, first appointee to the new post of secretary of state for the colonies, to express the government's displeasure. Hillsborough flatly told the Massachusetts assembly to disown its letter, forbade all overseas assemblies to endorse it, and commanded royal governors to dissolve any colonial legislature that violated his instructions. George III later commented that he never met "a man of less judgment than Lord Hillsborough." A wiser man might have tried to divide the colonists by appealing to their sense of British patriotism, but Hillsborough had chosen a course guaranteed to unite them in anger.

To protest Hillsborough's crude bullying, many legislatures previously indifferent to the Massachusetts circular letter now adopted it enthusiastically. The Massachusetts House of Representatives voted 92–17 not to recall its letter. The number 92 immediately acquired symbolic significance for Americans; colonial politicians on more than one occasion drank 92 toasts in tipsy salutes to Massachusetts's action. In obedience to Hillsborough, royal governors responded by dismissing legislatures in Massachusetts and elsewhere. These moves played directly into the hands of Samuel Adams, James Otis, and John Dickinson, who wished to ignite widespread opposition to the Townshend duties.

While increasingly outraged over the Revenue Act, the colonists still needed some effective means of bringing pressure on Parliament for its repeal. One approach, non-importation, seemed especially promising because it offered an alternative to violence and would distress Britain's economy. In August 1768 Boston's merchants therefore adopted a non-importation agreement, and the tactic slowly spread southward. "Save your money, and you save your country!" became the watchword of the Sons of Liberty, who began reorganizing after two years of inactivity. Not all colonists supported non-importation, however. Its effectiveness ultimately depended on the compliance of merchants, whose livelihood relied, in turn, on buying and selling imports. In several major communities, including Philadelphia and Baltimore, merchants continued buying British goods until early 1769, and Charles Town (Charleston), South Carolina, did not cut off its purchases until July 1769. Far from complete, the boycott probably kept out no more than 40 percent of all imports from Britain.

Nevertheless, the exclusion of 40 percent of imports inflicted serious losses on British merchants and thereby heightened pressure within Britain for repeal of the Townshend duties. Yet the tactical value of non-importation was not restricted to damaging Britain's economy. It also hinged on convincing the British—and the colonists themselves—that all Americans were determined to sustain resistance, and on demonstrating that the American cause rested on the foundations of impeccable morality and sensible moderation. Colonial rhetoric therefore frequently included traditional religious appeals and harped on familiar lessons from ancient history. And it provided a unique opportunity for women to join in the protest against unconstitutional laws.

The Mobilization of Opinion

Samuel Adams once expressed hope that America would become a "Christian Sparta." By linking religion and ancient history, Adams was combining two of colonial leaders' most potent rhetorical appeals in rallying public protest. Almost every eighteenth-century American had been steeped in Protestantism since earliest childhood; and all whose education had gone beyond the basics had imbibed Greek and Latin learning, as well as seventeenth-century English literature. All these hallowed traditions, Americans believed, confirmed the legitimacy of their cause. "Having been initiated in youth, in the doctrines of civil liberty, as they were taught by such men as Plato . . . [and] Cicero . . . among the ancients; and such as . . . Milton [and] Locke . . . among the moderns," wrote the minister Jonathan Mayhew, "[and] having earlier still learnt from the holy scriptures, that wise, brave, and virtuous men were always friends of liberty . . . I would not, I cannot now, relinquish the fair object of my youthful affections, LIBERTY. . . ."

Recalling in later years the inspiring debate over the Stamp Act that he had witnessed in Virginia's House of Burgesses in 1765, Thomas Jefferson said of Patrick Henry that "he appeared to me to speak as Homer wrote." Jefferson was a typical educated man of his day in revering the ancient republics of Greece and Rome for their supposedly stern, virtuous devotion to liberty. The pamphlets, speeches, and public declarations that gentlemen like Jefferson and Dickinson wrote resounded with quotations from the ancient classics. These allusions served as constant reminders to upper-class Americans of the righteous dignity of their cause. But appeals to ordinary Americans had to draw upon deeper wellsprings of belief. Significantly, the power of Henry's oratory also reflected his ability (unique among Virginia political leaders) to evoke the colonists' religious fervor, which the Great Awakening had stirred.

Beginning with the Stamp Act protest, New England's clergymen mounted their pulpits and summoned their flocks to stand up for God and liberty. "A just regard to our liberties . . . is so far from being displeasing to God that it would be ingratitude to him who has given them to us to . . . tamely give them up," exhorted one minister. "We are bound in conscience to stand fast in the liberty with which Christ has made us free." Not quite so quickly, but in the end with equally heartfelt intensity, Baptist and other dissenting preachers took up the cause. Only Anglican ministers, who were accustomed to insist on the religious duty of obe-

dience to the crown, tried to stay neutral or opposed the protest; and many pacifist Quakers kept out of the fray. But to most American Protestant clergymen, memories of battling for the Lord in the old Calvinist tradition proved too powerful to resist.

Voicing such a message, "the black regiment" of clergymen in their dignified gowns exerted an enormous influence on public opinion. Far more Americans heard sermons (or read them in printed form) than had access to newspapers or pamphlets, and ministers always got a respectful hearing at town meetings. Community leaders' proclamations of days of "fasting and public humiliation"—in colonial America, a familiar means of focusing public attention on an issue and invoking divine aid—inspired sermons on the theme of God's sending the people woes only to strengthen and sustain them until victory. Even Virginia gentlemen not notable for their piety felt moved by such proclamations and ordered their families to comply. Moreover, protest leaders' calls for boycotting British luxuries meshed neatly with traditional pulpit warnings against frivolity and wastefulness. Few ordinary Americans escaped the unceasing public reminders that community solidarity against British tyranny and "corruption" meant rejecting sin and obeying God.

By associating their cause with Christian faith and ancient virtue, Americans were not using a particularly original strategy, for such allusions were commonplace eighteenth-century ways of appealing to public opinion. But another American means of mobilizing support was novel: the involvement of women in the protest movement. Women's enlistment in the cause unfolded slowly. Calling themselves the Daughters of Liberty, upper-class female patriots had played only a minor part in defeating the Stamp Act. Some had attended political rallies during the Stamp Act crisis, while others had reinforced colonial resolve by turning a cold shoulder to men unwilling to resist Grenville's tax.

In contrast, women assumed a highly visible role during the Townshend crisis. Clearly believing that colonial women could exert a persuasive moral influence on public opinion, American leaders encouraged them to protest the Revenue Act's tax on tea. Accordingly, in early 1770 more than three hundred "mistresses of families" in Boston denounced the consumption of the beverage. In some ways, such nonconsumption was a more

Mr. and Mrs. Thomas Mifflin, *by John Singleton Copley, 1773*

The Mifflins were prominent Philadelphians. Thomas, a merchant in his early years, sat in the Pennsylvania assembly, served as one of the youngest members of the First Continental Congress, and later joined the Continental Army, where he quickly rose to officer's rank. An ardent supporter of the American cause, Sarah Morris Mifflin here demonstrates her patriotism by spinning her own thread.

nized spinning bees. These events attracted intense publicity as evidence of American determination to fight parliamentary taxation. The colonial cause, noted a New York woman, had enlisted "a fighting army of amazons . . . armed with spinning wheels."

Spinning bees not only helped undermine the masculine prejudice that women had no place in public life but also endowed spinning and weaving, previously considered routine household tasks, with special political virtue. "[W]omen might recover to this country the full and free enjoyment of all our rights, properties and privileges," exclaimed the Reverend John Cleaveland of Ipswich, Massachusetts, in 1769; he then added with more than usual honesty that this "is more than the men have been able to do."

Spinning bees, combined with female support for boycotting tea, were dramatic demonstrations of American determination. Colonial leaders were waging a battle to convince public opinion in Britain that their society would stand firm in opposing unconstitutional taxes. Only if the British people believed that Americans—male and female—were truly united would they accept repeal of the Townshend duties. Female participation in symbolic protests forced the British public to appreciate the depth of colonial commitment to maintaining the non-importation agreements and so contributed significantly to Parliament's reluctant decision to rescind most of the Townshend duties.

Repeal of the Townshend Duties

In January 1770 Lord North became prime minister. Although described as a "great, heavy, booby-looking man" and noted for occasionally sleeping through debates in the House of Commons, North had ability and would retain his office until 1782. North favored eliminating most of the Townshend duties to prevent the American commercial boycott from widening, but to underscore British authority, he insisted on retaining the tax on tea. Parliament agreed, and in April 1770, giving in for the second time in three years to colonial pressure, it repealed most of the Townshend duties.

Parliament's partial repeal produced a dilemma for American politicians. They considered it intolerable that taxes remained on tea, the most profitable item for the royal treasury. Colonial leaders were unsure whether they should press on with the

effective tactic than non-importation, for while a minority of merchants might ignore non-importation on the basis of principle or financial interest, a refusal by colonists to consume imports would chill merchants' economic incentive to continue bringing in English products.

Nonconsumption agreements therefore quickly became popular and were extended to include English manufactures (mostly clothing) as well as tea. Again women played a vital role, because the boycott would fail unless the colonists replaced British imports with apparel of their own making. Responding to leaders' pleas that they expand domestic cloth production, women of all social ranks, even those who customarily did not weave their own fabric or sew their own clothing, organon-importation agreement until they achieved total victory, or whether it would suffice to maintain a selective boycott of tea. When the non-importation movement collapsed in July 1770, the Sons of Liberty resisted external taxation by voluntary agreements not to drink British tea. Through nonconsumption they succeeded in limiting revenue from tea to about one-sixth the level originally expected. This amount was far too little to pay the salaries of royal governors as Townshend had intended.

Yet American leaders took little satisfaction in having forced Parliament to compromise. The tea duty remained as a galling reminder that Parliament refused to retreat from the broadest possible interpretation of the Declaratory Act. Thus although the crisis passed in 1770, its legacy lingered long afterward. The tax on tea acted like a festering sore that slowly poisoned relations between Britain and its colonies. The Townshend crisis had begun the gradual process by which a loyal people lost all sense of allegiance to their mother country.

Customs Racketeering and Escalating Violence

Although few Americans had objected to the establishment in 1767 of the American Board of Customs Commissioners, that institution soon became a major source of controversy in the colonies. Townshend had wanted the board to bring honesty, efficiency, and more revenue to overseas customs operations, but it accomplished none of his goals. Instead, the new commissioners grew notorious for abusing the law rather than enforcing it, in order to enrich themselves through confiscated ships or cargoes.

The rapid expansion of the American customs service in 1767 coincided with new legal provisions that awarded a revenue officer one-third of the value of all goods and ships appropriated through a conviction of smuggling. The fact that fines could be tripled under certain circumstances provided an even greater incentive to seize illegal cargoes. Smuggling cases were heard in vice-admiralty courts, moreover, where the probability of conviction was extremely high. Had the new customs commissioners done their duty honestly and pursued smugglers vigorously, little dissension would have developed. But the prospect of accumulating a small fortune through seizures proved

too tempting. Soon revenue agents commonly perverted the law by filing charges for technical violations of the Sugar Act, even when no evidence existed of intent to conduct illegal trade.

Indeed, the Sugar Act afforded unscrupulous excise officials a virtual gold mine of opportunities to accuse honest shipowners and merchants of smuggling. Revenue agents most often exploited the provision that declared any cargo illegal unless it had been loaded or unloaded with a customs officer's written authorization. Many vessels transporting lumber or tobacco found it impossible to comply, because they typically picked up these items piecemeal at a succession of small wharves far from a customhouse. Previously, a ship captain received certification of such cargoes for overseas passage at the nearest harbor, but after 1764 such a procedure violated the Sugar Act, even if the captain had no intention of smuggling.

Under the new rules, even a captain who threw rotting provisions overboard while at sea could be found guilty of illegally unloading. One common device by which customs officials created opportunities for seizures was to accommodate local circumstances by bending the rules for a time (particularly by relaxing the strict loading requirements) and then suddenly to enforce the letter of the law. The American Board of Customs Commissioners thus embarked on a program of "customs racketeering" that constituted little more than a system of legalized piracy operating through the vice-admiralty courts to achieve its objectives.

Directly or indirectly, the Board of Customs Commissioners fed an upsurge in popular violence. Above all, customs commissioners' use of paid spies provoked retaliation. The *Pennsylvania Journal* in 1769 scorned these agents as "dogs of prey, thirsting after the fortunes of worthy and wealthy men." By the very fact that they betrayed the trust of employers, and sometimes of friends, informers aroused wild hatred in their victims and were roughly handled whenever found. Nearly all instances of tarring and feathering in these years were acts of private revenge against informers rather than acts of political reprisal.

Customs commissioners also fanned angry passions by invading the traditional rights of sailors. Longstanding maritime custom allowed a ship's crew to supplement their incomes by making small sales between ports. Anything stored in a sailor's chest was considered private property that did not have to be listed as cargo on the captain's manifest and so was exempt from the regulations of the Navigation Acts. After 1767, however, revenue agents began treating such belongings as cargo, thus establishing an excuse to seize the entire ship.

Under this new policy, crewmen saw their trunks ruthlessly broken open by arrogant inspectors and then lost trading stock worth several months' wages because it was not listed on the captain's loading papers. Sailors developed deep hatred for customs officers and eagerly awaited chances to get even. Not surprisingly, after 1767 inspectors fell increasingly victim to riots dominated by vengeful seafaring men. By enforcing the letter of the law while violating its spirit, the American Board of Customs Commissioners created a superheated climate that made such riots and assaults inevitable.

In British eyes, the violence perpetrated against customs officials not only tarnished the colonists' efforts to defend their rights but also seemed part of an American campaign to destroy royal authority. However, this perception was wrong. Although colonial leaders could not channel all resistance into peaceful petitions and boycotts (as they had done in protesting the Townshend duties) and could not always prevent periodic eruptions of outrage against royal officials' excesses, they vehemently opposed such tactics as counterproductive. "Let this be the language of all," wrote a Son of Liberty in the *Boston Gazette*: "no mobs, no confusion, no tumults."

Nowhere were customs agents and informers more detested than in Boston, where in June 1768 citizens finally retaliated against their tormentors. The occasion was the seizure of the colonial merchant John Hancock's sloop *Liberty*. A group of nearby sailors mercilessly beat the customs agents on the wharf and then decided to give every excise man in town the same lesson. The crowd swelled to several hundred as it surged through the streets hunting down its prey, and by day's end, the rioters had driven all revenue inspectors from Boston.

Hancock, reportedly North America's richest merchant and a leading opponent of British taxation, had become a chief target of the customs commissioners. Although a significant minority of Boston's merchants did smuggle, no firm evidence exists that Hancock was among them. Nevertheless, in

John and Dorothy Hancock, *by Edward Savage*

As president of the Second Continental Congress, Hancock, shown here with his wife, Dorothy, was the first to sign the Declaration of Independence.

1768 the customs commissioners used a perjured statement from a customs inspector to seize the *Liberty* for allegedly avoiding £700 in duties on Madeira wine worth £3,000. By then requesting the payment of triple charges on the wine, they made Hancock liable for a total fine of £9,000, an amount almost thirteen times greater than the taxes supposedly evaded.

Several flagrant violations of Hancock's right to a fair trial tainted his prosecution. For example, a customs inspector who refused to sign false statements against Hancock was fired but then promised the return of his job and a secret payment if he would cooperate. The Boston grand jury charged another customs inspector with lying under oath. The most damaging evidence against Hancock came from a customs informer, whose testimony would not have been allowed in any other English court because he stood to gain a third of the £9,000 fine that Hancock would pay if convicted. Furthermore, the presiding judge did not allow Hancock's lawyer to cross-examine prosecution witnesses; and because the judge questioned Hancock's witnesses privately, in his own chambers, Hancock's lawyer could not be sure whether their evidence had hurt or helped his case. Since the hearing took place in a vice-admiralty court, moreover, Hancock's fate depended not on a jury but on the same judge whose actions had prejudiced his defense.

Hancock's case forced Americans to reevaluate their former acceptance of the principle that Parliament had limited authority to pass laws for them. Prior to 1768 colonial leaders had single-mindedly denied Britain's power to tax them, without considering that freedoms of equal importance might also be jeopardized by other kinds of legislation. But by 1770 it was becoming clear that measures like the Sugar Act and the act creating the American Board of Customs Commissioners seriously endangered property rights and civil liberties. This realization led many Americans to expand their opposition from a rejection of taxation without representation to a more broadly based rejection of legislation without representation. By 1774 there would emerge a new consensus that Parliament possessed no lawmaking authority over the colonies except the right to regulate imperial commerce through statutes like the old Navigation Acts.

By 1770 the British government, aware of its customs officers' excesses, began reforming the service. The smuggling charges against Hancock were finally dropped because the prosecution feared that Hancock would appeal a conviction to England, where honest officials would take action against the persons responsible for violating his rights. But although the abuses largely ended by the early 1770s, the damage had been done. Townshend's American Board of Customs Commissioners contributed enormously to the colonists' growing suspicion of British motives and their progressive alienation from the mother country.

The Boston Massacre

As another consequence of the violence stirred up by the customs commissioners, a force of seventeen hundred British troops landed in Boston during the six weeks after October 1, 1768. By 1770 this military occupation, which directly resulted from the *Liberty* riots, provoked a fresh round of violence.

Boston rapidly took on the atmosphere of an occupied city and crackled with tension as armed sentries and resentful civilians traded insults. The mainly Protestant townspeople found it especially galling that many soldiers were Irish Catholics and a few, mostly drummers, were blacks. The majority of enlisted men, moreover, were free to seek employment following the morning muster. Often agreeing to work for less than local laborers, they generated fierce hostility in a community still plagued by unemployment.

The situation in Boston was tailor-made for a man like Samuel Adams, whose genius lay in shaping public opinion. Adams once said that his task

The Landing of British Troops in Boston, 1768

The patriot silversmith and engraver Paul Revere recorded the controversial event for posterity in this engraving. Revere also described the redcoats' "insolent Parade, [with] Drums beating, Fifes playing, and Colours flying up King Street."

was not to make events but to improve on them. By imposing nearly two thousand redcoats on a crowded, economically distressed, and violence-prone city of twenty thousand bullheaded Yankees, the British government gave Adams all the grist that he needed for his propaganda mill.

In October 1768 Adams began publishing the *Journal of the Times,* a magazine claiming to offer a factual account of abuses committed by the army and the customs service in Boston. Adams intended to make a bad situation worse by kindling outrage that would harden popular resistance against British authority. Although the troops behaved well by the period's standards (often better than the townspeople), the *Journal* rarely lacked for stories of civilians who were assaulted, insulted, or simply annoyed at hearing regimental musicians play mocking versions of "Yankee Doodle" on fifes and drums. Adams exaggerated every incident, published all rumors as if they were true, and invented stories whenever the times grew dull. Bostonians came to hate the redcoats more with every issue of Adams's *Journal,* and Americans elsewhere worried that their communities might be the next site of a military occupation.

Still, Bostonians endured their first winter as a garrison town without undue trouble and saw half the British troops sail home in mid-1769. Relations between the remaining soldiers and civilians then abruptly worsened. The deep-seated resentment against all who upheld British authority suddenly boiled over on February 22, 1770, when an unpopular customs informer fired bird shot at several children bombarding his house with rocks and killed an eleven-year-old German boy. The ever crafty Samuel Adams made sure that the tragedy served his cause well. He organized a burial procession to maximize the sense of horror at a child's death, relying on grief to unite the community in opposition to British policies. "My Eyes never beheld such a funeral," wrote his cousin John Adams. "A vast Number of Boys walked before the Coffin, a vast Number of Women and Men after it. . . . This Shews there are many more Lives to spend if wanted in the Service of their country."

Although the army had played no part in the shooting, it became a natural target for the townspeople's frustration and rage. A week after the boy's funeral, a disorderly crowd went looking for trouble and found it at the guardpost protecting the

The Boston Massacre, 1770, *Engraving by Paul Revere*

Shortly after the "massacre," one Bostonian observed that "unless there is some great alteration in the state of things, the era of the independence of the colonies is much nearer than I once thought it, or now wish it."

customs office. They pelted the sentry with insults, ice, rocks, and lumber until a captain and seven soldiers arrived. While the officer tried to disperse the mob, his men endured a steady barrage of flying objects and dares to shoot. One soldier finally did fire, after having been knocked down by a block of ice, and the others pulled their triggers without orders. Their uneven volley hit eleven persons, five of whom eventually died.

Burning hatreds produced by an intolerable situation underlay this so-called Boston Massacre. Once again Samuel Adams orchestrated a funeral fit for martyrs and used the occasion to solidify American opposition to British authority. Most colonists accepted the distorted account of the event published in Adams's *Journal* and reinforced by Paul Revere's famous engraving (see illustration above): that it was a ruthless attack on unarmed civilians who dared to stand up to military bullies. The "massacre" profoundly affected Americans, forcing many to confront the stark possibility that the British government might be bent on coercing them into paying unconstitutional taxes through naked force.

Drift and Division

The shock that followed the March 5 bloodshed marked the emotional high point of the Townshend crisis. Royal authorities in Massachusetts tried to defuse the situation in Boston by isolating all British soldiers on a fortified island in the harbor, and Governor Thomas Hutchinson promised that the soldiers who had fired would be tried. Patriot leader John Adams served as their attorney, with the intention not only to demonstrate Americans' commitment to impartial justice but also "to lay before [the people of Boston], the Law as it stood, that they might be apprized of the Dangers . . . which must arise from intemperate heats and irregular commotions." All but two of the soldiers were acquitted, and the ones found guilty suffered only a branding on their thumbs. Meanwhile, Parliament soon repealed all external taxes except the tea duty, leaving most colonists uncertain about whether their rights were still endangered. To the extent that Americans resisted at all, they did so passively by drinking smuggled tea.

From mid-1770 to 1772, Lord North's government virtually ignored the colonies. North's inaction undercut the influence of firebrands like Samuel Adams, who were left without an issue that could be used to stir discontent. The minister of John Hancock's congregation expressed the mood of the times well when he wrote in January 1771 that "there seems . . . to be a Pause in Politics."

During the lull Americans increasingly quarreled among themselves. New Hampshire and New York argued over title to modern-day Vermont, where settlers from both colonies fought a minor guerrilla war. Pennsylvania waged a frustrating legal battle with Virginia to defend its territory near Pittsburgh and had similar problems with Connecticut, which issued land grants around Wilkes-Barre and settled several hundred squatters there. But the most dramatic example of colonial divisiveness occurred in North Carolina, where widespread discontent over corrupt, inefficient government sparked a brief civil war between provincial officials and the so-called Regulators. The Regulators aimed to redress the grievances of North Carolinians living in the colony's western regions, who were underrepresented in the colonial assembly and who found themselves exploited by dishonest, self-serving officeholders appointed to their posts by eastern politicians. The Regulator movement climaxed on May 16, 1771, at the Battle of Alamance Creek. Leading an army of perhaps 1,300 eastern militia, North Carolina's royal governor defeated about 2,500 Regulators in a clash that left almost three hundred casualties. Although the Regulator uprising then disintegrated, it crippled the colony's subsequent ability to resist British authority.

The Committees of Correspondence

The truce in Anglo-American antagonisms lasted until 1772. In the fall of that year, Lord North's ministry began preparing to implement Townshend's goal of paying the royal governors' salaries out of customs revenue. The colonists had always viewed this intention to free the governors from legislative domination as a fundamental threat to representative government. In response, Samuel Adams persuaded Boston's town meeting to request that every Massachusetts community appoint persons responsible for exchanging information and coordinating measures to defend colonial rights. Of approximately 260 towns, about half immediately established "committees of correspondence," and most others did so within a year. From Massachusetts the idea spread throughout New England.

The committees of correspondence were the colonists' first attempt to maintain close and continuing political cooperation over a wide area. By linking almost every interior community to Boston through a network of dedicated activists, the system allowed Adams to conduct a campaign of political education for all of Massachusetts, and increasingly for all of New England. Adams sent out messages for each town's local committee to read at its town meeting, which would then debate the issues and adopt a formal resolution. Forcing tens of thousands of citizens to consider evidence that their rights were in danger, the system committed them to take a personal stand by voting.

Adams's most successful venture in whipping up public alarm came in June 1773, when he publicized certain letters of Massachusetts governor Thomas Hutchinson that Benjamin Franklin had obtained. Massachusetts town meetings discovered through the letters that their own chief executive had advocated "an abridgement of what are called English liberties" and "a great restraint of natural liberty." The publication of the Hutchinson correspondence confirmed American suspicions that a plot was afoot to destroy basic freedoms.

The shock produced by Hutchinson's letters led many colonists to take seriously the warnings of well-known English political writers like Lord Bolingbroke, John Trenchard, and Thomas Gordon. Beginning in the early eighteenth century, these and other "oppositionist" authors had argued that since 1720 prime ministers had exploited the treasury's vast resources to provide pensions, contracts, and profitable offices to politicians or had bought elections by bribing voters in small boroughs. According to these men, most members of Parliament no longer represented the true interests of their constituents but rather had sold their political souls for financial gain.

Often referring to themselves as the "country interest" (or "country party"), these writers expressed the frustrations of landowning taxpayers who were forced to support an expensive government dominated by a "court party" of non-elected officials close to the king. Eventually, this "country ideology" predicted, a power-hungry prime minister or a group of anonymous conspirators would use a corrupted Parliament to gain absolute power for themselves. By 1773 many Americans believed that this scenario was indeed unfolding and that the assault on their rights was part of a plot to establish a despotism.

Even before the committees of correspondence sprang up, an incident had occurred that reinvigorated American discontent. On June 9, 1772, the customs schooner *Gaspee* ran aground near Providence, Rhode Island. One of the last revenue cutters to engage in customs racketeering by plundering cargoes for technical violations of the Sugar Act, the *Gaspee* had acquired an odious reputation among Rhode Islanders. Its crew had frequently landed to steal fruit, unfenced livestock, and firewood, and the captain was said to be "more impe-

rious and haughty than the Grand Turk himself." Now helplessly stuck in the mud, the *Gaspee* presented too tempting a target for local inhabitants to resist. That night, more than one hundred disguised men burned it to the waterline, not for political reasons but for the simple pleasure of revenge.

The British government dispatched a commission to look into the attack, with instructions to send all suspects to England for trial. The investigators failed to identify any raiders and came back empty-handed. Nevertheless, Americans were alarmed that the ministry intended to dispense with another essential civil liberty, an accused citizen's right to be tried by a local jury.

In reaction to the *Gaspee* commission's instructions, Patrick Henry, Thomas Jefferson, and fellow Virginian Richard Henry Lee proposed in March 1773 that Virginia establish a permanent committee for corresponding with other colonies. Within a year every province but Pennsylvania had followed its example. By early 1774 colonial leaders were linked by a communications web for the first time since 1766.

In contrast to the brief, intense Stamp Act crisis, the dissatisfaction spawned by the Townshend duties and the American Board of Customs Commissioners persisted and gradually poisoned relations between Britain and America. In 1765 feelings of loyalty and affection toward Britain had remained strong in America and thus had helped disguise the depth of the division over the constitutional issue of taxation. By 1773, however, colonial allegiance was becoming conditional and could no longer be assumed.

Toward Independence

Although the British Empire remained superficially tranquil in early 1773, it had resolved none of its underlying constitutional problems. To a large degree, Americans ignored the continued taxation of tea because of a widespread expectation that Lord North would eventually have the duty repealed. Parliament suddenly blasted this unrealistic hope when it passed the Tea Act in 1773. This measure set off a chain reaction that started with the Boston

Tea Party in late 1773 and was followed by Parliament's attempt to retaliate through the Intolerable Acts in 1774, the First Continental Congress in September 1774, the outbreak of fighting in April 1775, and the colonists' declaration of their independence in July 1776.

The Tea Act

Colonial smuggling and nonconsumption had taken a heavy toll on Britain's East India Company, which enjoyed a legal monopoly on importing tea into the British Empire. By 1773, with tons of tea rotting in its warehouses, the East India Company was teetering on the brink of bankruptcy. But Lord North could not let the company fail. Not only did it pay substantial duties on the tea it imported into Britain, but it also provided huge indirect savings for the government by maintaining British authority in India at its own expense.

If the company could only control the colonial market, North reasoned, its chances for returning to profitability would greatly increase. Americans supposedly consumed more than a million pounds of tea each year, but by 1773 they were purchasing just one-quarter of it from the company. In May 1773, to save the beleaguered East India Company from financial ruin, Parliament passed the Tea Act, which eliminated all remaining import duties on tea entering England and thus lowered the selling price to consumers. (Ironically, the same saving could have been accomplished by repealing the Townshend tax, which would have ended colonial objections to the company's tea and produced enormous goodwill toward the British government.) To lower the price further, the Tea Act also permitted the company to sell its tea directly to consumers rather than through wholesalers.

These two concessions reduced the cost of East India Company tea in the colonies well below the price of all smuggled competition. Parliament expected simple economic self-interest to overcome American scruples about buying taxed tea. With the resulting revenue, the British government would finally be able to achieve Townshend's goal of making the royal governors independent of colonial assemblies by paying their salaries.

But the Tea Act alarmed many Americans, above all because they saw in it a menace to colonial representative government. By making taxed tea competitive in price with smuggled tea, the law in all likelihood would raise revenue, which the British government would use to pay royal governors. The law thus threatened to corrupt Americans into accepting the principle of parliamentary taxation by taking advantage of their weakness for a frivolous luxury. Quickly, therefore, the committees of correspondence decided to resist the importation of tea, though without violence and without the destruction of private property. Either by pressuring the company's agents to refuse acceptance or by intercepting the ships at sea and ordering them home, the committees would keep East India Company cargoes from being landed. In Philadelphia an anonymous "Committee for Tarring and Feathering" warned harbor pilots not to guide any ships carrying tea into port.

In Boston, however, this strategy failed. On November 28, 1773, the first ship came under the jurisdiction of the customhouse, to which duties would have to be paid on its cargo within twenty days. Otherwise, the cargo would be seized from the captain and the tea claimed by the company's agents (who included two of Governor Hutchinson's sons) and placed on sale. When Samuel Adams, John Hancock, and other leading citizens repeatedly asked the customs officers to issue a special clearance for the ship's departure, they found themselves blocked by the governor's refusal to compromise.

On the evening of December 16, Samuel Adams convened a meeting in Old South Church. He informed the five thousand citizens of Hutchinson's insistence upon landing the tea, told them that the grace period would expire in a few hours, and announced that "this meeting can do no more to save the country." About fifty young men disguised as Indians thereupon yelled a few war whoops and headed for the wharf, followed by most of the crowd.

Adams's disciplined band of youths assaulted no one and damaged nothing but the hated cargo. Thousands lined the waterfront to see them heave forty-five tons of tea overboard. For almost an hour, the onlookers stood silently transfixed, as if at a religious service, while they peered through the crisp, cold air of a moonlit night. The only sounds were the steady chop of hatchets breaking open wooden

The Boston Tea Party, 1773

This 1793 engraving is the earliest-known American depiction of the event.

chests and the soft splash of tea on the water. When their work was finished, the participants left quietly, and the town lapsed into a profound hush—"never more still and calm," according to one observer.

The Intolerable Acts

Boston's "Tea Party" inflamed the British. Lord North fumed that only "New England fanatics" could imagine themselves oppressed by inexpensive tea. A Welsh member of Parliament drew wild applause by declaring that "the town of Boston ought to be knocked about by the ears, and destroy'd." In vain did the great parliamentary orator Edmund Burke plead for the one action that could end the crisis. "Leave America . . . to tax herself. . . . Leave the Americans as they anciently stood. . . ." The British government, however, swiftly asserted its authority by enacting four Coercive Acts that, together with the unrelated Quebec Act, became known to Americans as the Intolerable Acts.

The first of the Coercive Acts, the Boston Port Bill, became law on April 1, 1774. It ordered the navy to close Boston harbor unless the Privy Council certified by June 1 that the town had arranged to pay for the ruined tea. Lord North's cabinet deliberately imposed this impossibly short deadline in order to ensure the harbor's closing, which would lead to serious economic distress. The gov-

ernment therefore refused to let a group of London merchants post bond for the necessary £9,000.

The second Coercive Act, the Massachusetts Government Act, had actually been under consideration before the Boston Tea Party. This law revoked the Massachusetts charter and restructured the government to make it less democratic. The colony's upper house would no longer be elected annually by the assembly but appointed for life by the crown. The governor gained absolute control over the naming of all judges and sheriffs. Jurymen, previously elected, were now appointed by sheriffs. Finally, the new charter forbade communities to hold more than one town meeting a year without the governor's permission. These changes brought Massachusetts's government into line with that of other royal colonies, but the colonists interpreted them as evidence of hostility toward representative government.

The final two Coercive Acts—the Administration of Justice Act and the Quartering Act—rubbed salt into the wounds. The first of these permitted any person charged with murder while enforcing royal authority in Massachusetts (such as the British soldiers indicted for the Boston Massacre) to be tried in England or in other colonies. The second allowed the governor to requisition *empty* private buildings for housing troops. These measures, along with the appointment of General Thomas Gage, Britain's military commander in North America, as the new governor of Massachusetts,

Thomas Gage

The commander in chief of Britain's forces in America from 1763 to 1775, Gage in April 1775 would issue the fateful order for British troops to march to Concord and seize the rebel arms stored there (p. 158).

struck New Englanders as proof of a plan to place them under a military despotism.

Americans learned of the Quebec Act along with the previous four statutes and associated it with them. Intended to cement loyalty to Britain among conquered French-Canadian Catholics, the law established Roman Catholicism as Quebec's official religion. This provision alarmed Protestant Anglo-Americans, who widely associated Catholicism with arbitrary government. Furthermore, the Quebec Act gave Canada's governors sweeping powers but established no legislature. It also permitted property disputes (but not criminal cases) to be decided by French law, which did not use juries. Additionally, the law extended Quebec's territorial claims south to the Ohio River and west to the Mississippi, a vast area in which several colonies had land claims.

The Intolerable Acts convinced New Englanders that the crown was plotting to corrode traditional English liberties throughout North America. Many believed that after starving Boston into submission, the governor of Massachusetts would appoint corrupt sheriffs and judges to crush political dissent through rigged trials. The Quartering Act would repress any resistance by forcing troops on an unwilling population. The Administration of Justice Act, which the colonists cynically called the Murder Act, would encourage massacres by preventing local juries from convicting soldiers who killed civilians. Once resistance in Massachusetts had been smashed, the Quebec Act would serve as a blueprint for extinguishing representative government throughout the colonies. Parliament would revoke every colony's charter and introduce a government like Quebec's. Elected assemblies, freedom of religion for Protestants, and jury trials would all disappear.

Intended by Parliament simply to punish Massachusetts—and particularly that rotten apple in the barrel, Boston—the Intolerable Acts instead pushed most colonies to the brink of revolution. Repeal of these laws became, in effect, the colonists' nonnegotiable demand. Of the twenty-seven reasons justifying the break with Britain that the Americans cited in their 1776 Declaration of Independence, six concerned these statutes.

Virginia's response to the Intolerable Acts was particularly important because that colony could provide more military manpower than any other. Sentiment for active resistance first solidified in the Virginia assembly, whose members returned to their counties and enlisted the local gentry in the cause of firmly opposing the offensive laws. As the upper class quickly pulled together, the leading planters undertook a program of political education for the colony's ordinary citizens, who up to that point had been apathetic about the Anglo-American confrontation. On public occasions such as court days and militia musters, the gentry spoke repeatedly of the need to support Massachusetts, persuading voters to commit themselves to resistance by signing petitions against the Intolerable Acts. Within two years the gentry had mobilized Virginia's free population overwhelmingly against Parliament, and it was clear that if war broke out, the British Army would face united resistance not only in New England but also in Virginia.

The First Continental Congress

In response to the Intolerable Acts, the extralegal committees of correspondence of every colony but Georgia sent delegates to a Continental Congress in Philadelphia. Among those in attendance when the Congress assembled on September 5, 1774, were the colonies' most prominent politicians: Samuel and John Adams of Massachusetts; John Jay of New York; Joseph Galloway and John Dickinson of Pennsylvania; and Patrick Henry, Richard Henry Lee, and George Washington of Virginia. The fifty-six delegates had come together to find a way of defending American rights short of war, and in interminable dinner parties and cloakroom chatter, they took one another's measure.

The First Continental Congress opened by endorsing a set of extreme statements of principle called the Suffolk Resolves that recently had placed Massachusetts in a state of passive rebellion. Adopted by delegates at a convention of Massachusetts towns just as the Continental Congress was getting under way, the resolves declared that the colonies owed no obedience to any of the Intolerable Acts, that a provisional government should collect all taxes until the former Massachusetts charter was restored, and that defensive measures should be taken in the event of an attack by royal troops. The Continental Congress also voted to boycott all British goods after December 1 and to cease exporting almost all goods to Britain and its West Indian possessions after September 1775 unless a reconciliation had been accomplished. This agreement, the Continental Association, would be enforced by locally elected committees of "observation" or "safety," whose members in effect were usurping control of American trade from the royal customs service.

Such bold defiances were not to the liking of all delegates. Jay, Dickinson, Galloway, and other moderates who dominated the middle-colony contingent most feared the internal turmoil that would surely accompany a head-on confrontation with Britain. These "trimmers" (John Adams's scornful phrase) vainly opposed non-importation and tried unsuccessfully to win endorsement of Galloway's plan for a "Grand Council," an American legislature that would share with Parliament the authority to tax and govern the colonies.

Finally, however, the delegates summarized their principles and demands in their Declaration of Rights. This document conceded to Parliament the power to regulate colonial commerce, but it argued that all previous parliamentary efforts to impose taxes, enforce laws through admiralty courts,

suspend assemblies, and unilaterally revoke charters were unconstitutional. By addressing the Declaration of Rights to the king rather than Parliament, Congress was imploring George III to end the crisis by dismissing those ministers responsible for passing the Intolerable Acts.

The Fighting Begins

Most Americans hoped that their resistance would jolt Parliament into renouncing all authority over the colonies except trade regulation. But a minority of the colonial elite took alarm, and bonds between men formerly united in outlook sometimes snapped. John Adams's onetime friend Jonathan Sewall, for example, charged that the Congress had made the "breach with the parent state a thousand times more irreparable than it was before." Fearing that Congress was enthroning "their *High Mightinesses,* the MOB," he and like-minded Americans fell back on their loyalty to the king. In England meanwhile, George III sniffed rebellion in the Congress's actions. His instincts, and those of American loyalists, were correct. A revolution was indeed brewing.

To solidify their defiance, the American resistance leaders coerced waverers and loyalists (or "Tories," as they were often called). Thus the elected committees that Congress had created to enforce the Continental Association often turned themselves into vigilantes, compelling merchants who still traded with Britain to burn their imports and make public apologies, browbeating clergymen who preached pro-British sermons, and pressuring Americans to adopt simpler diets and dress in order to relieve their dependence on British imports. Additionally, in colony after colony, the committees took on governmental functions by organizing volunteer military companies and extralegal legislatures. By the spring of 1775, colonial patriots had established provincial "congresses" that paralleled and rivaled the existing colonial assemblies headed by royal governors.

The uneasy calm was first broken in April 1775, in Massachusetts. There as elsewhere, citizens had prepared for the worst by collecting arms and organizing extralegal militia units (locally known as minutemen) whose members could respond instantly to an emergency. The British government ordered Massachusetts governor Gage to quell the "rude rabble" by arresting the principal patriot leaders. Aware that most of these had already fled Boston, Gage instead sent 700 British soldiers on April 19, 1775, to seize military supplies that the colonists had stored at Concord. Two couriers, William Dawes and Paul Revere, quickly alerted nearby towns of the British troops' movements and target. At Lexington about 70 minutemen hastily drawn up on the town green attempted to oppose the soldiers. After a confused skirmish in which 8 minutemen died and a single redcoat was wounded, the British pushed on to Concord. There they found few munitions but encountered a growing swarm of armed Yankees (see "A Place in Time"). When some minutemen mistakenly became convinced that the town was being burned, they exchanged fire with the British regulars and touched off a running battle that continued most of the sixteen miles back to Boston. By day's end the redcoats had lost 273 men, but they had gained some respect for Yankee courage.

These engagements awakened the countryside, and by the evening of April 20, some twenty thousand New Englanders were besieging the British garrison in Boston. Acting on their own authority, on May 10 Vermonter Ethan Allen and a motley collection of New Englanders overran Fort Ticonderoga on Lake Champlain, partly with the intent of using its captured cannon in the siege of Boston. That same day, the Second Continental Congress convened in Philadelphia. Most delegates still opposed independence and at Dickinson's urging agreed to send a "loyal message" to George III. Dickinson composed what became known as the Olive Branch Petition; excessively polite, it nonetheless presented three demands: a cease-fire at Boston, repeal of the Intolerable Acts, and negotiations to establish guarantees of American rights. Events quickly overtook this effort at reconciliation. The Olive Branch Petition reached London at the same time as news of a battle fought just outside Boston on June 17. In this engagement British troops attacked colonists entrenched on Breed's Hill and Bunker Hill. Although successfully dislodging the Americans, the British suffered 1,154 casualties out of 2,200 men, compared to a loss of 311 Yankees. After Bunker Hill the British public wanted retaliation, not reconciliation, and on August 23 the king proclaimed New England in a state of rebellion. In December Parliament declared all the colonists rebellious and made their ships subject to seizure.

The Failure of Reconciliation

Despite the turn of events, most Americans clung to hopes of reconciliation. Even John Adams, who believed in the inevitability of separation, described himself as "fond of reconciliation, if we could reasonably entertain Hopes of it on a constitutional basis." Yet the same Americans who pleaded for peace passed measures that Britain could only construe as rebellious. Before the delegates to the Continental Congress even heard about the Battle of Bunker Hill, they voted to establish an "American continental army" and appointed George Washington its commander.

Still, most Americans resisted independence, partly because they clung to the notion that evil ministers rather than the king were forcing unconstitutional measures on them and partly because they expected that saner heads would rise to power in Britain. On both counts they were wrong. The Americans exaggerated the influence of Pitt, Burke, and their other friends in Britain. For example, when Burke proposed in March 1775 that Parliament acknowledge the colonists' right to raise and dispose of taxes, he was voted down by a thumping majority in Parliament. Lord North's sole counterproposal was to allow the colonists to tax themselves, but on condition that they collect whatever sum of money Parliament ordered. This concession amounted to no more than involuntary self-taxation, and it had the full endorsement of George III, who consistently supported the North ministry.

The Americans' sentimental attachment to the king, the last emotional barrier to their accepting independence, finally crumbled in January 1776 with the publication of Thomas Paine's *Common Sense*. A former corsetmaker and schoolmaster, Paine immigrated to the colonies from England late in 1774 with a letter of introduction from Benjamin Franklin, a penchant for radical politics, and a gift for writing plain and pungent prose that anyone could understand. Paine told Americans what they had been unable to bring themselves to say: kingship was an institution dangerous to liberty, undemocratic, and inappropriate to Americans. The king was "the royal brute" and a "hardened, sullen-tempered Pharaoh." By repudiating monarchy and creating a republic, "we have it in our power to begin the world over again."

By Paine's estimate *Common Sense,* printed in both English and German, sold more than one hundred thousand copies within three months, equal to one for every fourth or fifth adult male. The *Connecticut Gazette* described it as "a landflood that sweeps all before it." By the spring of 1776, Paine's pamphlet had dissolved lingering allegiance to George III and removed the last psychological barrier to independence.

Independence at Last

John Adams described the movement toward independence as a coach drawn by thirteen horses, which could not reach its destination any faster than the slowest ones were willing to run. New England was already in rebellion, and Rhode Island declared itself independent in May 1776. The middle colonies hesitated to support revolution because they feared, correctly, that the war would largely be fought over control of Philadelphia and New York. Following the news in April that North Carolina's congressional delegates were authorized to vote for

independence, the South began pressing for separation. Virginia's extralegal legislature soon instructed its delegates at the Second Continental Congress to propose independence, which Richard Henry Lee did on June 7. Formally adopting Lee's resolution on July 2, Congress created the United States of America.

The task of drafting a statement to justify the colonies' separation from England fell to Virginia delegate Thomas Jefferson. Congress reviewed his manuscript on July 3 and approved it the next day. The Declaration of Independence never mentioned Parliament by name—even though the central point of dispute since 1765 had been Parliament's legislative powers—because Congress was unwilling to imply, even indirectly, that it held any authority over America. Jefferson instead indicted the king for "repeated injuries and usurpations, all having in direct object the establishment of an absolute tyranny over these states." The declaration recited these "injuries" but above all emphasized the crown's apparent intention to establish a "despotism."

Jefferson elevated the colonists' grievances from a dispute over English freedoms to a struggle for

History Preserved

The Pennsylvania State House was the site of the Declaration of Independence's signing (at which this inkstand was used) and of the constitutional convention. During the latter, Washington sat in this handsome mahogany half-sun chair.

Concord, Massachusetts, in 1775

About 2 A.M. on April 19, 1775, the alarm bell in Concord, Massachusetts, started to ring furiously. Normally, it summoned men to turn out with fire buckets, but on this night drowsy citizens (including the town's minister, Reverend William Emerson) ambled toward the town square clutching muskets. Concord's minutemen were gathering to oppose 750 British troops marching to seize arms and ammunition stored in their town. Concord's mobilization on that chilly spring night was sure evidence that the colonies were teetering on the brink of revolution.

Until recently, the citizens had been loyal British subjects. Like other rural New Englanders, they had been indifferent to the British Empire's political crisis until they had debated Boston's circular letter of November 20, 1772. Thereafter, Concord's town meeting endorsed a steady flow of correspondence from Boston denouncing unconstitutional parliamentary laws. In June 1774, 80 percent of Concord men signed a strongly worded pledge to boycott British goods until the Intolerable Acts were repealed. By March 6, 1775, all but three men in town had sworn to uphold the Continental Congress against Massachusetts's royal governor, General Thomas Gage. Within the brief span of thirty months, Concord had shed its apathy and become united in resisting the Intolerable Acts.

As dawn approached, the townspeople hid bullets and gunflints throughout their houses, concealed gunpowder in the woods, and buried cannon and muskets. Fifteen-year-old Milicent Barrett, the granddaughter of the minutemen's colonel, supervised teen-age girls in the manufacture of cartridges. Reinforcements for Concord's 150 minutemen arrived from nearby towns. Word came that the British had opened fire on Lexington's minutemen, but no one knew if blood had been shed.

At daybreak Captain David Brown marched his company toward Lexington and promptly ran into the British. Sizing up the situation, Brown swung back to Concord with drums beating and fifes squealing. "We had grand music," Corporal Amos Barrett later recalled. Badly outnumbered, Colonel James Barrett evacuated the town center and took up position on high ground overlooking the Concord River bridge to await reinforcements.

After posting a guard at the bridge, just out of the minutemen's range, the British scoured the town for military equipment. Much of what little remained behind was saved by the town's women, who outwitted redcoats sent to search their homes. Mrs. Amos Wood tricked an officer who correctly suspected the presence of hidden ammunition into believing that a locked room sheltered panic-stricken women. "I forbid anyone entering this room," commanded the chivalrous Englishman. Hannah Barnes bluffed a search party out of entering a room that contained a chest filled with money needed to buy additional military supplies.

The British regulars dumped five hundred pounds of bullets into a pond, destroyed sixty barrels of flour, and found two cannon. They also accidentally set fire to the courthouse and a blacksmith shop,

"The White Cockade" *Fifer Luther Blanchard and drummer Francis Barker played this martial tune shortly before the skirmish near the bridge.*

Concord, April 19, 1775 *In a contemporary illustration, engraver Amos Doolittle recorded the British troops' arrival in town.*

which they saved before serious damage resulted. But the minutemen on the ridge became enraged by the rising smoke.

"Will you let them burn the town down?" screamed hotheaded Lieutenant Joseph Hosmer at Colonel Barrett. Now commanding four hundred men, Barrett decided to reenter the town and led his men toward the hundred redcoats guarding the bridge. The British withdrew across the river and fired several warning shots. One round wounded Luther Blanchard, a fifer who had been merrily playing a marching tune. Suddenly, smoke billowed from the British ranks and musketballs whistled across the water. Captain Isaac Davis and Private Abner Hosmer, volunteers from nearby Acton, fell dead. "For God's sake, fire," shouted Captain Jonathan Buttrick to his Concord company, which shot a volley at the British that killed three soldiers and wounded nine others.

The skirmish lasted only two or three minutes. The British withdrew to the town center. The min-

British Looters

A colonial cartoonist caught the redcoats in a looting spree during their retreat from Concord.

utemen crossed the river but then broke ranks and milled about in confusion. Both sides kept their distance until noon, when the British started to march back to Boston.

The British delay in leaving Concord allowed hundreds of minutemen to arrive from neighboring towns. At Meriam's Corner, these reinforcements began harassing the redcoats in a running battle that continued for sixteen miles. "Every man," recalled Private Thaddeus Blood, "was his own commander." By day's end almost three hundred royal troops were killed, wounded, or missing, and eighty colonists lay dead or injured.

Concord citizens escaped the day with slight losses: four men wounded, none dead. The war, however, had barely begun, and before it was over, Concord sent off every able-bodied man between the ages of eighteen and forty to serve in the army. After the war the fight at the bridge assumed mythic dimensions for Americans, who celebrated the patriots who dared death at "the rude bridge that arched the flood" and "fired the shot heard 'round the world." But Concord citizens were too familiar with the events to romanticize them. In 1792 they unemotionally tore up the historic bridge and built a more convenient crossing several hundred yards down river.

universal human rights. His eloquent emphasis on the equality of all individuals and their natural entitlement to justice, liberty, and self-fulfillment expressed the Enlightenment's deepest longing for a government that would rest on neither legal privilege nor the exploitation of the majority by the few.

Jefferson addressed the Declaration of Independence as much to Americans uncertain about the wisdom of independence as to world opinion, for he wanted to convince his fellow citizens that social and political progress could no longer be accomplished within the British Empire. The declaration never claimed that perfect justice and equal opportunity existed in the United States; rather, it challenged the Revolutionary generation and all who later inherited the nation to bring this ideal closer to reality.

Conclusion

The most moving section of the Declaration of Independence's original draft was directed to the people of England, whom Jefferson regretfully reminded that "we might have been a free and great people together." Congress eliminated these words, which expressed the feelings of most Americans all too well, for in a civil war it is never wise to dwell on the matter of shedding common blood. Throughout the long imperial crisis, Americans had repeatedly pursued the goal of reestablishing the empire as it had functioned before 1763, when colonial trade was protected and encouraged—not taxed and plundered—by the Navigation Acts, and when colonial assemblies had exercised exclusive power over taxation and internal legislation. These reluctant revolutionaries now had to face the might of Europe's greatest imperial power and win their independence on the battlefield. They also had to decide to what degree they would implement the idealistic vision evoked in Jefferson's declaration. Neither task would prove simple or easy.

CHRONOLOGY

1733 Molasses Act.

1744–1748 King George's War.

1754–1760 French and Indian War (in Europe, the Seven Years' War, 1756–1763).

1760 George III becomes king of Great Britain.

1763 Pontiac's War.

1764 Sugar Act.

1765 Stamp Act.
Quartering Act.
Loyal Nine formed in Boston to oppose the Stamp Act.
Sons of Liberty band together thoughout the colonies.
Stamp Act Congress.
Colonists begin boycott of British goods.

1766 Stamp Act repealed.
Declaratory Act.

1767 New York Suspending Act.

American Board of Customs Commissioners created.

Revenue Act (Townshend duties).

John Dickinson, *Letters from a Farmer*.

1768 Massachusetts "circular letter."

Boston merchants adopt the colonies' first non-importation agreement.

John Hancock's ship *Liberty* seized by Boston customs commissioner.

British troops arrive in Boston.

1770 Townshend duties, except tea tax, repealed.

Boston Massacre.

1771 Battle of Alamance Creek in North Carolina.

1772 Gaspee incident in Rhode Island.

Committees of correspondence begin in Masschusetts and rapidly spread.

1773 Tea Act.

Boston Tea Party.

1774 Coercive (Intolerable) Acts.

Quebec Act.

First Continental Congress meets and adopts Suffolk Resolves.

Continental Association.

Colonists' Declaration of Rights and Grievances.

1775 Battles of Lexington and Concord.

Second Continental Congress meets.

Olive Branch Petition.

Battles at Breed's Hill and Bunker Hill.

1776 Thomas Paine, *Common Sense*.

Declaration of Independence.

For Further Reading

Bernard Bailyn, *The Ideological Origins of the American Revolution* (1967). Pulitzer Prize–winning examination of the political heritage that shaped colonial resistance to British authority.

Jack P. Greene, *Peripheries and Center: Constitutional Development in the Extended Politics of the British Empire and the United States 1607–1788* (1987). A thorough study of how inherited English legal traditions and colonial political experience not only influenced Americans from 1763 to 1776 but also shaped the later course of American constitutional thought.

Robert A. Gross, *The Minutemen and Their World* (1976). An eloquent and evocative examination of Concord, Massachusetts, in the Revolutionary era.

Pauline Maier, *From Resistance to Revolution: Colonial Radicals and the Development of American Opposition to Britain, 1765–1776* (1972). An insightful, definitive examination of how colonial leaders strove to force the repeal of unconstitutional laws with a minimum use of violence.

Robert Middlekauff, *The Glorious Cause: The American Revolution, 1763–1789* (1982). A judicious, learned, and highly readable narrative of the events leading to Independence.

Edmund S. Morgan and Helen M. Morgan, *The Stamp Act Crisis: Prologue to Revolution* (rev. ed., 1963). The most penetrating, and now classic, analysis of colonial constitutional principles regarding the limits on Parliament's taxing power.

Robert R. Palmer, *The Age of the Democratic Revolution: Vol. I, The Challenge* (1959). Bancroft Prize–winning examination of the American Revolution in comparison to events in England, Ireland, and France.

Additional Bibliography

The Military Background

Fred Anderson, *A People's Army: Massachusetts Soldiers and Society in the Seven Years' War* (1984); Sylvia R. Frey, *The British Soldier in America: A Social History of Military Life in the Colonial Period* (1981); Douglas E. Leach, *Arms for Empire: A Military History of the British Colonies in North America, 1607–1763* (1973); Richard Middleton, *The Bells of Victory: The Pitt-Newcastle Ministry and the Conduct of the Seven Years' War, 1757–1762* (1985); John Shy, *Toward Lexington: The Role of the British Army in the Coming of the American Revolution* (1965).

Taxing and Regulating Trade

Thomas C. Barrow, *Trade and Empire: The British Customs Service in Colonial America* (1967); Oliver M. Dickerson, *The Navigation Acts and the American Revolution* (1951); Michael Kammen, *Empire and Interest: The American Colonies and the Politics of Mercantilism* (1970); John P. Reid, *In a Rebellious Spirit: The Argument of Facts, the Liberty Riot, and the Coming of the American Revolution* (1979); John W. Tyler, *Smugglers and Patriots: Boston Merchants and the Advent of the American Revolution* (1986); Carl Ubbelohde, *The Vice-Admiralty Courts and the American Revolution* (1960).

Constitutional Issues

Richard L. Bushman, *King and People in Provincial Massachusetts* (1985); David L. Jacobson, ed., *The English Libertarian Heritage: From the Writings of John Trenchard and Thomas Gordon in "The Independent Whig" and "Cato's Letters"* (1965); Richard Koebner, *Empire* (1961); John G. A. Pocock, *Three British Revolutions: 1641, 1688, 1776* (1980); Jack R. Pole, *Political Representation in England and the Origins of the American Republic* (1966); John P. Reid, *Constitutional History of the American Revolution: The Authority of Rights* (1986), *Constitutional History of the American Revolution: The Power to Tax* (1987), and *In a Defiant Stance: The Conditions of Law in Massachusetts Bay, the Irish Comparison, and the Coming of the American Revolution* (1977).

Religious Influences

Ruth H. Bloch, *Visionary Republic: Millennial Themes in American Thought, 1756–1800* (1985); Patricia U. Bonomi, *Under the Cope of Heaven: Religion, Society, and Politics in Colonial America* (1986); Carl R. Bridenbaugh, *Mitre and Sceptre: Transatlantic Faiths, Ideas, Personalities, and Politics, 1689–1775* (1962); Jack P. Greene and William G. McLaughlin, *Preachers and Politicians: Two Essays on the Origin of the American Revolution* (1977); Nathan O. Hatch, *The Sacred Cause of Liberty: Republican Thought and the Millennium in Revolutionary New England* (1977).

Resistance

David Ammerman, *In the Common Cause: American Response to the Coercive Acts of 1774* (1974); Richard D. Brown, *Revolutionary Politics in Massachusetts: The Boston Committees of Correspondence and the Towns, 1772–1774* (1970); Ian R. Christie and Benjamin W. Labaree, *Empire or Independence, 1760–1776: A British-American Dialogue on the Coming of the American Revolution* (1976); Peter C. Hoffer, *Revolution and Regeneration: Life Cycle and the Historical Vision of the Generation of 1776* (1983); Michael G. Kammen, *A Rope of Sand: The Colonial Agents, British Politics, and the American Revolution* (1968); Benjamin W. Labaree, *The Boston Tea Party* (1964); Mary Beth Norton, *Liberty's Daughters: The Revolutionary Experience of American Women, 1750–1800* (1980); Richard A. Ryerson, *The Revolution Is Now Begun: The Radical Committees of Philadelphia, 1765–1776* (1978); John Sainsbury, *Disaffected Patriots: London Supporters of Revolutionary America, 1769–1782* (1987); Peter Shaw, *American Patriots and the Rituals of Revolution* (1981); Neil R. Stout, *The Perfect Crisis: The Beginnings of the Revolutionary War* (1976); Peter D. G. Thomas, *The Townshend Duties Crisis: The Second Phase of the American Revolution, 1767–1773* (1987); Robert W. Tucker and David C. Hendrickson, *The Fall of the First British Empire: Origins of the War of American Independence* (1982); Hiller B. Zobel, *The Boston Massacre* (1970).

Biographies

Bernard Bailyn, *The Ordeal of Thomas Hutchinson* (1974); Richard R. Beeman, *Patrick Henry: A Biography* (1974); John Brooke, *King George III* (1972); Milton E. Flower, *John Dickinson: Conservative Revolutionary* (1983); Eric Foner, *Tom Paine and Revolutionary America* (1976); William M. Fowler, Jr., *The Baron of Beacon Hill: A Biography of John Hancock* (1979); Pauline Maier, *The Old Revolutionaries: Political Lives in the Age of Samuel Adams* (1980); Dumas Malone, *Jefferson the Virginian* (1948); John C. Miller, *Sam Adams: Pioneer in Propaganda* (1936); Peter D. G. Thomas, *Lord North* (1974).

CHAPTER 5

The Forge of Nationhood, 1776–1788

In November 1775 General George Washington ordered Colonel Henry Knox to bring the British artillery recently captured at Fort Ticonderoga to the siege of Boston. Washington knew firsthand of the difficulties of wilderness travel, especially in the winter, and he must have wondered if this city-bred officer was up to the task. Only twenty-five years old and a Boston bookseller with little experience in the woods, Knox was nevertheless the army's senior artillerist, largely because he had read several books on the subject while business in his store was dull.

Knox and his men built crude sleds to haul their fifty-nine cannons through dense forest covered by two feet of snow. On good days they moved these sixty tons of artillery about seven miles. On two very bad ones, they shivered for hours in freezing water while retrieving guns that had fallen through the ice at river crossings. As their oxen grew weak from overexertion and poor feed, the men had to throw their own backs into pulling the cannons across New York's frozen landscape. On reaching the Berkshire Mountains in western Massachusetts, their pace slowed to a crawl as they trudged uphill through snow-clogged passes. Forty days and three hundred miles after leaving Ticonderoga, Knox and his exhausted New Yorkers reported to Washington in late January 1776. The Boston bookseller had more than proved himself: he had accomplished one of the Revolution's great feats of endurance.

The guns from Ticonderoga placed the outnumbered British in a hopeless position and forced them to evacuate Boston on March 17, 1776. A lifelong friendship formed between Washington and Knox. Knox served on the Virginian's staff throughout the war and accepted his request to be the nation's first secretary of war in 1789.

Friendships like the one between Washington and Knox were almost as revolutionary as the war that produced them. Because inhabitants of different colonies had little opportunity to become acquainted before 1775, their outlooks had remained narrowly confined within the borders of their provinces. This localism was well entrenched at the start of the war. George Washington at first described New Englanders as "an exceeding dirty and nasty people." Yankee soldiers irritated troops from distant colonies such as Virginia with smug assumption of superiority expressed in their popular marching song "Chester," whose rousing lyrics rang out:

> Let tyrants shake their iron rod,
> and slavery clank her galling chains.
> We fear them not, we trust in God.
> New England's God forever reigns.

The Revolution gave northerners and southerners their first real chance to learn what they had in common, and they soon developed mutual admiration. George Washington, who in the war's early days dismissed New England officers as "the most indifferent kind of people I ever saw," changed his mind after meeting men like Henry Knox.

In July 1776 the thirteen colonies had out of desperation declared independence and established a new nation. But it took the War for Independence to create American citizens. Only as a result of the collective hardships experienced during eight years of terrible fighting did the inhabitants of the thirteen states cease to see themselves simply as military allies and come to accept each other as fellow citizens.

The return of peace in 1783 left Americans with a false sense of security. Major problems remained unsolved and ignored. The national government's authority withered as the states increasingly failed to provide the financial support necessary to finance federal operations. During the 1780s far-sighted leaders perceived two great challenges. Could they preserve the national spirit born during the war before it evaporated? If so, could they find a means of providing the central government with the ability to uphold its financial obligations and command respect from foreign countries, and yet not threaten interference with each state's right to legislate for itself or endanger individual liberties? They would not even begin to overcome these challenges until 1789.

America's First Civil War

The Revolution was both a collective struggle that marched a sizable portion of the American people against Britain and a civil war between inhabitants of North America. Eventually, it would degenerate into a brothers' war of the worst kind, conducted without the restraint, mutual respect, and compassion that would characterize the next prolonged encounter between Americans, the bloody Civil War of the 1860s. From a military standpoint, the Revolution's outcome depended not only on the ability of the supporters of independence, called the Whigs, to wear down the British army but also on the Whigs' success in suppressing fellow North Americans' opposition to independence. The magnitude of these tasks frequently disheartened the Whigs, but it also united them. Without the disappointments and sacrifices suffered from 1775 to 1783, Americans might never have developed the commitment to nationhood essential to prevent their new country from splintering into several smaller republics.

The Loyalists

As late as January 1776, most colonists still hoped that declaring independence from Britain would not be necessary. Not surprisingly, when separation came six months later, many Americans remained unconvinced that it was justified. About 20 percent of all whites either opposed the rebellion actively or refused to support the Continental Congress unless threatened with fines or imprisonment. While these internal enemies of the Revolution called themselves loyalists, they were "Tories" to their Whig foes. Whigs remarked, but only half in jest, that "a tory was a thing with a head in England, a body in America, and a neck that needed stretching."

Loyalists avowed many of the same political values as did the Whigs. Like the Whigs, they usually opposed Parliament's claim to tax the colonies. Many loyalists thus found themselves fighting for a cause with which they did not entirely agree, and as a result large numbers of them would find it relatively easy to change sides during the war. Most doubtless shared the apprehension expressed in 1775 by the Reverend Jonathan Boucher, a well-known Maryland loyalist, who preached with two loaded pistols lying on his pulpit cushion: "For my part I equally dread a Victory by either side."

Loyalists disagreed, however, with the Whigs' insistence that only independence could preserve the colonists' constitutional rights. The loyalists denounced separation as an illegal act certain to ignite an unnecessary war. Above all, they retained a profound reverence for the crown and deeply believed that if they failed to defend their king, they would sacrifice their personal honor.

The most important factor in determining loyalist strength in any area was the degree to which prominent local Whigs had successfully convinced the mass of voters that representative government was endangered by the king and Parliament. Town leaders in New England, the Virginia gentry, and the rice planters of South Carolina's seacoast all vigorously pursued a program of political education and popular mobilization from 1772 to 1776. Repeatedly explaining the issues at public meetings, these elites shook the mass of citizens from their apathy and persuaded the overwhelming majority in favor of resistance. As a result, probably no more than 5 percent of whites in these areas were committed loyalists in 1776. Where the leading families acted indecisively, however, their communities remained divided when the fighting began. Because the gentry of New York and New Jersey were especially reluctant to declare their allegiance to either side, the proportion of loyalists was highest there. Those two states eventually furnished about half of the twenty-one thousand Americans who fought in loyalist military units.

The next most significant factor influencing loyalist military strength was the geographical distribution of recent British immigrants, who closely identified with their homeland, not America, and overwhelmingly opposed independence. Among these newcomers were thousands of British soldiers who had served in the French and Indian War and then remained in the colonies, usually in New York, where they could obtain two-hundred-acre land grants. Further, more than 125,000 English, Scots, and Irish landed from 1763 to 1775—the greatest number of Britons to arrive during any dozen years of the colonial era. Major centers of loyalist sympathy existed wherever large concentrations of such British-born people lived. In New York, Georgia, and the backcountry of North and South Carolina, where the native-born Britons were heavily concentrated, the proportion of loyalists among whites probably ranged from 25 percent to 40 percent in 1776. In wartime the British army organized many Tory units comprising immigrants from the British Isles, including the Loyal Highland Emigrants, the North Carolina Highlanders, and the Volunteers of Ireland. After the war foreign-born loyalists composed a majority of those persons compensated by the British for property losses during the Revolution—including three-quarters of all such claimants from the Carolinas and Georgia.

Loyalism also fed on the presence of ethnic and religious minorities outside of the main currents of colonial society. For example, a small number of German, Dutch, and French religious congregations that resisted use of the English language felt indebted to the British government for their religious freedom and doubted that their rights would be as safe in an independent nation dominated by Anglo-Americans. Yet on balance, these ethnic and religious minorities provided few loyalists. The great majority of Germans in Pennsylvania, Maryland, and Virginia, for example, had started to assimilate into the English-speaking mainstream by 1776 and would overwhelmingly support the Whig cause.

One group with distinctive ethnic and religious characteristics—Canada's French Catholics—composed the most significant North American minority to hold loyalist sympathies. Although they had fought against the British in the French and Indian War, French-Canadian Catholics feared domination by the Anglo-Americans. The Quebec Act of 1774 had guaranteed their religious freedom and their continued use of French civil law. Remembering that the American colonists had denounced this measure and demanded its repeal, French Catholics worried that their privileges would disappear if they were absorbed into an independent Protestant America.

Canadian anxieties intensified in mid-1775, when the Continental Congress ordered Continental forces to "free" Canada from British tyranny unless this action was "disagreeable" to the French population. In reality, Congress cared little what the French-Canadians thought, for Congress believed that a conquest of Canada was essential to block a British invasion from the north. In 1775 Continental armies (one of them led by Benedict Arnold, a fervent patriot who later turned traitor) marched into Canada and attacked Quebec but suffered defeat on December 31, 1775. French Catholics emerged from the shock of invasion more loyal to the crown than ever before. The Whigs never even attempted to win over the other recently founded mainland colonies—Nova Scotia and East and West Florida—whose small populations of mainly recent immigrants were firmly dominated by British military authorities.

American loyalists would also draw wartime support from both slaves and native Americans. As a deeply alienated group within society, slaves quickly realized that the Revolution was not intended to benefit them. In 1766, when a group of slaves, inspired by the protests against the Stamp Act, had marched through Charleston, South Carolina, shouting "Liberty!" they had faced arrest for inciting a rebellion. By 1775 it was the British who most often offered liberty to enslaved Americans. For example, in 1775 Lord Dunmore, governor of Virginia, promised freedom to any slave who enlisted in the cause of restoring royal authority. About eight hundred blacks joined him before he fled the colony. During the war at least twenty thousand American slaves ran away to sign on as laborers or soldiers in the Royal Army. Among the Whig slaveholders who saw many of his slaves escape to British protection was Thomas Jefferson.

Native Americans had long resented the presence of white colonists on their lands, and during the war only the Oneidas and Tuscaroras (two member tribes of the Iroquois Confederacy) in New York and the Catawbas in South Carolina supported the Whig cause. Elsewhere in the original thirteen colonies and throughout the region west of the Appalachian Mountains, the British could count on Indian support or neutrality.

Toward loyalists collectively, Whigs reserved an intense hatred, far greater than their antipathy toward the British army, and loyalists responded with equal venom. Each side saw its cause as so sacred that opposition by a fellow American was an unforgivable act of betrayal. The worst atrocities committed during the war were inflicted by Americans upon each other.

The Opposing Sides

Britain entered the war with two major advantages. First, in 1776 the 11 million inhabitants of the British Isles greatly outnumbered the 2.5 million Americans, one-third of whom were either slaves or loyalists. Second, Britain possessed the world's largest navy and one of its best professional armies. Nevertheless, the royal military establishment grew during the war years to a degree that strained Britain's resources. The army more than doubled from 48,000 to 111,000 men, not only in North America but also in the British Isles and the West Indies. To meet its manpower needs, the British government had to raise the recruiting bonuses paid to get men to enlist, lower physical requirements, widen age limits, and sometimes enroll soldiers forcibly. But even these measures failed to provide the required numbers. Without hiring 30,000 German mercenaries known as Hessians

Woodcut from "A New Touch on the Times . . . . By a Daughter of Liberty, Living in Marblehead," 1779

Americans on the home front as well as in the front lines experienced stunning wartime hardships. This illustration of a female partisan holding a musket accompanied a poem by Molly Gutridge, whose theme was women's sacrifice and suffering in a seaport economy upset by war.

and later enlisting 21,000 loyalists, Britain could not have met its manpower needs.

Despite its smaller population, the United States mobilized its people more effectively than did Britain. By the end of the war, the Americans had enlisted or drafted into the Continental Army or the state militias perhaps half of all free males from age sixteen to forty-five—about 220,000 troops—compared to the 162,000 Britons, loyalists, and Hessians who served in the British army.

Britain's ability to crush the rebellion was further weakened by the decline in its seapower that had resulted from peacetime budget cuts after 1763. Midway through the war, half of the Royal Navy's ships sat in dry dock awaiting major repairs.

Although the navy expanded rapidly from 18,000 to 111,000 sailors, it lost 42,000 men to desertion and 20,000 to disease or wounds. In addition, Britain's merchant marine suffered mightily from raids by the numerous American privateers newly outfitted from the colonies' thriving merchant marine. During the war rebel privateers and the fledgling U.S. Navy would capture over 2,000 British merchant vessels and 16,000 crewmen.

Britain could ill afford these losses, for it faced a colossal task in trying to supply its troops in America. While at one time or another the British army controlled all the major American cities, British soldiers ventured into the agricultural hinterland only at their peril and hence could not easily round up supplies. In fact, almost all the food consumed by the army, a third of a ton per soldier per year, had to be imported from Britain. Seriously overextended, the navy barely kept the army supplied and never effectively blockaded American ports.

Mindful of the enormous strain that the war imposed, British leaders faced serious problems maintaining their people's support for the conflict. The war more than doubled the national debt. Bur-

An American Soldier of 1778,
by Friedrich von Germann

dened by record taxes, the politically influential landed gentry could not be expected to vote against their pocketbooks forever.

The United States faced different but no less severe wartime problems. First, one-fifth of its free population was openly disloyal. Second, although the state militias sometimes performed well in hit-and-run guerrilla skirmishes and were also effective in intimidating loyalists and wavering Whigs and in requisitioning war supplies, they lacked the training to fight pitched battles. Congress recognized that independence would never be secured if the United States relied on guerrilla tactics, avoided major battles, and allowed the British to occupy all major population centers. Moreover, because European powers would interpret U.S dependence on guerrilla warfare as evidence that Americans could not drive out the British army, that strategy would doom efforts by the Continental Congress to gain foreign loans and diplomatic recognition.

The Continental Army thus had to fight in the standard European fashion of the times. Professional eighteenth-century armies relied on expert movements of mass formations. Victory often depended on rapid maneuvers to crush an enemy's undefended flank or rear. Attackers needed exceptional skill in close-order drill in order to fall on an enemy before he could reform and return fire. Because muskets had a range of under one hundred yards, armies in battle were never far apart. Battles usually occurred in open country with space for maneuver. The troops advanced within musket range of each other, stood upright without cover, and fired volleys at one another until one line weakened from its casualties. Discipline, training, and nerve were essential if soldiers were to stay in ranks while comrades fell beside them. The stronger side then attacked at a quick walk with bayonets drawn and drove off its opponents.

In 1775 Britain possessed a well-trained army with a strong tradition of bravery under fire. In contrast, the Continental Army had neither an inspirational heritage nor many experienced officers or sergeants who might turn raw recruits into crack units. Consequently, the Americans experienced a succession of heartbreaking defeats in the war's early years. Yet to win the war, the Continentals did not have to destroy the British army but only prolong the rebellion until Britain's taxpayers lost patience with the struggle. Until then,

American victory would hinge heavily on the ability of one man to keep his army fighting despite defeat. He was George Washington.

George Washington

Few generals ever looked and acted the role as much as Washington. He spoke with authority and comported himself with dignity. At six feet two inches, he stood a half-foot taller than the average man of his day. Powerfully built, athletic, and hardened by a rugged outdoor life, he was one of the war's few generals whose presence on the battlefield could inspire troops to heroism.

Washington's military experience began at age twenty-two, when he had taken command of a Virginia regiment raised to resist French claims in the Ohio Valley (see Chapter 4). He had lost his first battle to a force vastly outnumbering his own. A year later, at Braddock's defeat, he had placed himself at the point of greatest danger and had two horses killed under him, besides having his hat shot off and his coat ripped by five bullets. His reputation for courage reached England, where he had briefly become a minor hero. Above all, Washington's early military experience—his mistakes and lost battles—taught him lessons that he might not have learned from easy, glorious victories. He discovered the dangers of overconfidence and the need for determination in the face of defeat. He also learned much about American soldiers, especially that they performed best when led by example and treated with respect.

With Virginia's borders safe from attack in 1758, Washington had resigned his commission and become a tobacco planter. He had sat in the Virginia House of Burgesses, where his influence had grown, not because he thrust himself into every issue but because others respected him and sought his opinion. Having emerged as an early, though not outspoken, opponent of parliamentary taxation, he had also sat in the Continental Congress. In the eyes of the many who valued his advice and remembered his military experience, Washington was the logical choice to head the Continental Army.

War in Earnest

Henry Knox's successful transport of artillery from Ticonderoga to Boston prompted the British to evacuate Boston in March 1776 and to move on to New York, which they wished to seize and use as a base for conquering New England. Under two brothers—General William Howe and Admiral Richard, Lord Howe—130 warships carrying 32,000 royal troops landed near New York harbor in the summer of 1776. Defending New York, America's second-largest city, were 18,000 poorly trained soldiers under George Washington.

On August 27, 15,000 of William Howe's men nearly overwhelmed the 10,500 troops whom Washington had stationed on Long Island, just across a river from New York City. Inflicting over 1,000 casualties while losing fewer than 400 men, the British were on the verge of annihilating the Americans. But Washington executed a masterful night evacuation to New York City, saving 9,500 soldiers and most of his artillery from certain capture. He himself was the last American to board a boat.

By the third week of September 1776, the Continental Army around New York included more than 16,000 men fit to bear arms. Over the next three months, the British killed or took prisoner one-quarter of these troops and drove the survivors into headlong retreat across New Jersey. By early December, when Washington crossed the Delaware River from New Jersey into Pennsylvania, he had fewer than 7,000 troops fit for duty. Thomas Paine accurately described these demoralizing days as "the times that try men's souls."

With the British in striking distance of Philadelphia, Washington decided to seize the offensive before the morale of his army and country collapsed completely. On Christmas night, 1776, he led his troops back into New Jersey and attacked a Hessian garrison at Trenton, where he captured 918 Germans and lost only 4 Continentals. Washington then attacked 1,200 British at Princeton on January 3, 1777, and killed or took captive one-third of them while sustaining only 40 casualties.

These American victories at Trenton and Princeton had several important consequences. At a moment when defeat seemed inevitable, they boosted civilian and military morale. In addition, by checking the British offensive, they frustrated Howe's plans to pacify New Jersey by persuading inhabitants opposed to or skeptical of independence to rally to the British cause. Although nearly 5,000 New Jerseyans with loyalist sympathies swore allegiance to the crown late in 1776, Washington's victories forced the British early in 1777 to remove

The Battle of Princeton (1777), *by William Mercer, c. 1790*

In the battle's first phase, fought south of the town, the American advance guard clashed with redcoats who were en route to Trenton, where they planned to link up with Lord Cornwallis. The British had the upper hand until George Washington and the main Continental force arrived, attacked, and drove them off.

virtually all their New Jersey garrisons to New York, while Washington established winter quarters at Morristown, New Jersey, only twenty-five miles from New York City.

As long as they had enjoyed the support of the redcoats, New Jersey's loyalists had plundered local Whigs. Now stripped of British protection, the loyalists fell prey to the rebel militia, who drove thousands of loyalists into British-held New York, where many joined the Royal Army. Other loyalists formed guerrilla bands to raid their former neighbors; still others fled into South Jersey's forbidding Pine Barrens, from which they pillaged their ex-tormentors. Until 1782, when the state militia destroyed the last band of Pine Barren Tories, New Jersey's Whigs fell victim to a barrage of ambushes and assassinations. The state suffered civil war at its worst.

While lingering until 1782, New Jersey loyalism never recovered from the blow it received when the British evacuated the state early in 1777. The state militia became a relentless police force dedicated to rooting out political dissent. The mili-

tia disarmed known loyalists, jailed their leaders, and kept a constant watch on suspected Tories. Ironically, the British themselves contributed to the undermining of New Jersey loyalism, for prior to the Battle of Trenton, British commanders had failed to prevent an orgy of looting by their troops that damaged loyalists and Whigs equally. Surrounded by armed enemies and facing constant danger of arrest, most loyalists who remained in the state bowed to the inevitable and swore allegiance to the Continental Congress; more than a few ex-loyalists themselves joined the rebel militia. The same process was eventually repeated following British invasions of New York in 1777, Georgia in 1778, and the Carolinas in 1779. Upon regaining the upper hand, Whig militias ruthlessly pursued loyalists aiding the redcoats, forced many to flee, and coerced most into renouncing the crown.

Not all loyalists shifted sides, however. The war drove perhaps one of every six loyalists into exile in Canada, Britain, or the West Indies. Twenty percent of all New Yorkers may have left the United States by 1784. When the British evacuated Savannah in 1782, 15 percent of all whites in Georgia accompanied them. Most of those who departed were evidently British immigrants, whose mobility and lack of local roots made exile easier. Whether loyalists changed sides or became political refugees, loyalism declined as a force during the war. By 1782 few active loyalists remained outside British lines.

The Turning Point

Shortly after the battles of Trenton and Princeton, the Marquis de Lafayette, a young French aristocrat, joined Washington's staff. Lafayette was twenty years old, highly idealistic, very brave, and infectiously optimistic. Given Lafayette's close connections with the French court, his presence in America indicated that the French king, Louis XVI, might recognize U.S. independence and perhaps declare war on Britain. Before recognizing the United States, however, Louis wanted proof that the Americans could win a major battle, a feat they had not yet accomplished.

Louis did not have to wait long. In the summer of 1777, the British launched a two-pronged assault intended to crush American resistance in New York State and thereby isolate New England. Pushing off from Montreal, a force of regulars and their Iroquois allies, marching under Lieutenant Colonel Barry St. Leger, would proceed south along Lake Ontario and invade central New York from Fort Oswego in the west, while General John Burgoyne would lead the main British force south from Quebec through eastern New York and link up with St. Leger near Albany.

The British would have faced a formidable task under any circumstances; but to complicate matters, General William Howe, the British commander in chief in North America, chose to launch a *second* major campaign in the summer of 1777, which was aimed at the American capital, Philadelphia. Howe intended to draw the Continentals south to the defense of their capital, defeat them in battle, and then use Philadelphia as a base for building loyalist support in the mid-Atlantic region. Howe's fateful decision to move against Philadelphia meant that neither he nor the modest force that he had left behind in New York City under General Henry Clinton could decisively aid St. Leger or Burgoyne if their invasion of New York misfired.

Unfortunately for Howe, nothing went according to plan in New York. St. Leger's force of 1,900 advanced a hundred miles and halted to besiege 750 New York Continentals at Fort Stanwix. Unable to take the post after three weeks, and finding himself deserted by the Iroquois, who suffered heavy losses in a battle with the local militia near Oriskany, St. Leger retreated in late August 1777.

Meanwhile, on July 6 Burgoyne's 8,300 British and Hessians had taken Fort Ticonderoga, about a hundred miles north of Albany. But by now Burgoyne's supply lines were overstretched, and a force that he dispatched to seize supplies at Bennington, Vermont, was repulsed with heavy losses. Along with the 900 troops that Burgoyne had detached to garrison Fort Ticonderoga, his losses in Vermont depleted his army and gave General Horatio Gates time to collect nearly 17,000 American troops for an attack. Gates fought two indecisive battles near Saratoga in the fall, inflicting another 1,200 casualties on Burgoyne. Surrounded and hopelessly outnumbered, Burgoyne's 5,800 troops honorably laid down their arms on October 17, 1777.

The diplomatic impact of the Battle of Saratoga rivaled its military significance and made it the war's turning point. Early in December 1777, news of the battle reached France, where Benjamin Franklin had recently arrived as the U.S. ambassador. Although one of America's wealthiest, wisest, and most sophisticated men, Franklin shrewdly captured the French imagination by appearing in a fur cap and playing the part of an innocent backwoods philosopher. Turning himself into the court's latest fad, Franklin won widespread French sympathy for the United States. Then with the victory at Saratoga, France became convinced that the Americans could win the war and thus deserved diplomatic recognition.

In February 1778 France therefore formally recognized the United States. Four months later, it went to war with Britain. Spain declared war on Britain in 1779, but as an ally of France, not the United States, and the Dutch Republic joined them in the last days of 1780. Now facing a coalition of enemies, Britain had no allies of its own.

Of all the American allies, only France sent troops to the United States, and they did nothing of significance until 1781. Nonetheless, the coalition forced Britain to send thousands of soldiers to Ireland and the West Indies to guard against

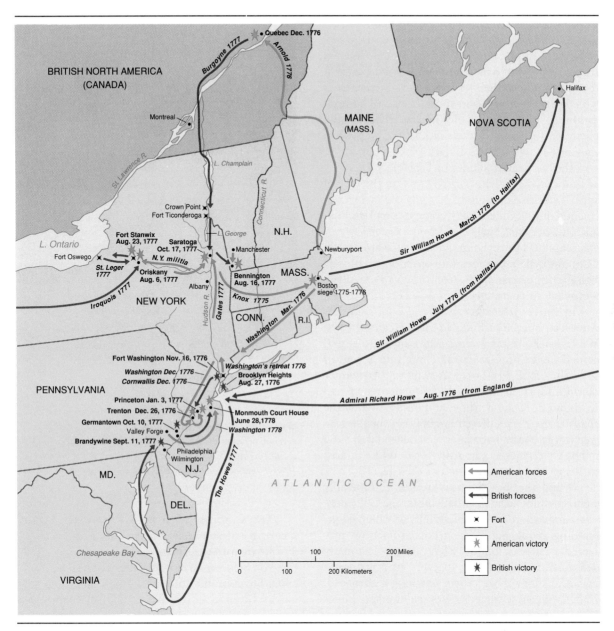

The War in the North, 1776–1779

Following the British evacuation of Boston, the war shifted to New York City, which the British held from 1776 to 1783. In 1777 Britain's success in taking the U.S. capital, Philadelphia, was offset by defeat in upstate New York. The hard-fought battle of Monmouth Court House, New Jersey, ended the northern campaigns in 1778.

French invasion, thus reducing the manpower available to fight in the United States. The French and Spanish navies, which together approximately equaled the British fleet, won several large battles, denied Britain control of the sea, and punctured the Royal Navy's blockade.

The Continentals Mature

While Gates and Burgoyne maneuvered in upstate New York, Howe landed 18,000 troops near Philadelphia in late August. With Washington at their head and Lafayette at his side, 16,000 Continentals paraded through the imperiled city on August 24,

1777. "They marched twelve deep," John Adams wrote to his wife Abigail, "and yet took up above two hours in passing by." Adams noted that the troops were well armed and uniformed but that they did not keep their heads straight or wear their hats cocked properly—in short, they still had not acquired "quite the air of soldiers." They would pay a fearful price for their lack of training when they met Howe's professionals.

The two armies collided on September 11, 1777, at Brandywine Creek, Pennsylvania. In the face of superior British discipline, not only did most Continental units crumble but Congress soon fled Philadelphia in panic, enabling Howe to occupy America's capital. Howe again defeated Washington at Germantown on October 4. In one month's bloody fighting, 20 percent of the Continentals were killed, wounded, or captured.

In early December 1777, 11,000 tentless American survivors huddled round campfires at Whitemarsh, Pennsylvania. Short on rations and chilled to the bone from marching into a wall of sleet, they took a full week to walk to their winter quarters fourteen miles away. A fourth of them had worn out at least one shoe, and on days when the roads froze, they suffered horribly on the ice-covered ridges. Washington later remembered that "you might have tracked the army from White Marsh to Valley Forge by the blood of their feet."

While the British army rested comfortably eighteen miles away in Philadelphia, the Continentals stumbled around the bleak hills of Valley Forge, building crude huts. The troops somehow preserved a sense of humor, which they occasionally demonstrated by joining together in a thousand voices to squawk like crows watching a cornfield. Underlying these squawks was real hunger: James Varnum reported on December 20 that his Connecticut and Rhode Island troops had gone the two previous days without meat and three days without bread.

The army slowly regained its strength but still lacked training. The Continentals had forced Burgoyne to surrender more by their overwhelming numbers than by their skill. Indeed, when Washington's men had met Howe's forces on equal terms, they lost badly. The Americans mainly lacked the ability to march as compact units and maneuver quickly. Regiments often straggled single-file into battle and then wasted precious time forming to attack, and few troops were expert in bayonet drill.

Friedrich von Steuben

The Prussian-born Steuben arrived in the United States in December 1777. Although the government and the army alike felt deep disillusionment over the value of foreign officers at that time, the talented Steuben overcame this disability and was appointed the Continental Army's major-general in 1778.

The Continental Army's ill-trained recruits received a desperately needed boost in February 1778, when the German soldier of fortune Friedrich von Steuben arrived at Valley Forge. The short, squat Steuben did not look like a soldier, but this earthy German instinctively liked Americans and became immensely popular. He had a talent for motivating men (sometimes by staging humorous tantrums featuring a barrage of German, English, and French swearing); but more important, he possessed administrative genius. In a mere four months, General Steuben almost single-handedly turned the army into a formidable fighting force.

General Henry Clinton, now British commander in chief, evacuated Philadelphia in mid-1778 and marched to New York. The Continental Army got its first opportunity to demonstrate Steuben's training when it caught up with Clinton's rear guard at Monmouth Court House, New Jersey, on June 28, 1778. Although the Americans initially faltered, Washington re-formed them along a strong defensive position. Clinton ordered his best units against Washington's line, only to see them thrown back at bayonet point. The battle raged for six hours in one-hundred-degree heat until Clinton broke off contact. Expecting to renew the fight at daybreak, the Americans slept on their arms, but Clinton's army slipped away before then. The British would never again win easy victories, except when they faced more militiamen than Continentals.

The Battle of Monmouth ended the contest for the North. Clinton occupied New York, which the Royal Navy made safe from attack. Washington kept his army nearby to watch Clinton. Meanwhile, the Whig militia hunted down the last few Tory guerrillas and extinguished loyalism.

Frontier Campaigns

A different kind of war developed west of the Appalachians and along the western borders of New York and Pennsylvania. The numbers engaged in these frontier skirmishes were relatively small, but the fighting was fierce and the stakes were high. In 1776 few Anglo-Americans had a clear notion of the western boundaries of the new nation; by 1783, when the Peace of Paris concluded the war, whites had established enough settlements west of the Appalachians to justify their claim to the Mississippi River as their western border. So while the frontier campaigns did not determine the outcome of the war, they had a significant impact on the future shape of the United States.

In the 1760s Daniel Boone and other "long knives" had begun exploring west of the Cumberland Gap, the main pass through the southern Appalachians. They were astonished to find no permanent Indian settlements within the sixty thousand square miles of what are now Kentucky and central Tennessee. This vast area could be opened to settlement if the native Americans would sell their claims to it. The Iroquois sold their title in 1768, as did the Cherokees in 1775. The Shawnees, who dwelled in what is now Ohio, also accepted whites' occupation of Kentucky, but only after their defeat in 1774 by the Virginia militia in Lord Dunmore's War. Having surrendered their claims at gunpoint, the Shawnees felt no obligation to honor Dunmore's treaty, and for the next forty years, this embittered Indian nation would stand at the forefront of resistance to white expansion in the Ohio Valley.

The permanent settlement of Kentucky began in 1775, and of central Tennessee the year after. White expansion into the Ohio Valley made the western Indians firm British allies. Native Americans elsewhere overwhelmingly supported the British.

As Daniel Boone's career in Kentucky illustrates, Anglo-Americans paid a heavy price holding the West for the Continental Congress. Boone survived numerous ambushes, at least seven skirmishes, and three pitched battles. In 1778 he and thirty men, assisted by their wives and children, stood off more than four hundred Indians at Boonesborough. Boone himself was twice shot and twice captured. Indians also killed two of his sons, a brother, and two brothers-in-law, besides wounding another brother four times and capturing a daughter, who was herself later wounded as well.

However, the Indian attacks failed to drive white settlers from Kentucky (see "A Place in Time"). In June 1778, 175 militiamen left what is now Louisville to put an end to British authority north of the Ohio River. Their leader was George Rogers Clark, a twenty-six-year-old colonel who had spent the previous four years fighting native Americans in Kentucky. Clark used news of the recent French-American alliance to persuade the militia at the distant French settlements in present-day Illinois and at Vincennes, Indiana, to become U.S. citizens. He then established his headquarters at Kaskaskia, Illinois.

But Britain's commander at Detroit, Colonel Henry Hamilton, leading five hundred regulars and Indians who outnumbered Clark's riflemen more than four to one, retook Vincennes in December. A realistic officer might have retreated, and a brave officer might have prepared to defend Kaskaskia, but Clark decided to attack Vincennes. In the dead of winter, he led his Kentuckians through 180 miles of barren plains flooded by heavy rains. They waded across three icy rivers, all shoulder-deep. The men survived on half-rations because the downpours had driven most wildlife to higher ground.

Clark had gambled that Hamilton's Indians would have gone home, but he learned with dismay that two hundred remained at Vincennes. Undaunted, the resourceful Clark now resorted to espionage. He employed a French spy to deceive

Bryan's Station, Kentucky, in 1782

The War for American Independence was more than a military clash between British redcoats and American continentals disciplined to fight in rigid formations. The conflict also pitted American against American, as loyalist and patriot bands met in hundreds of small, bloody backcountry encounters. And for thousands of native Americans, the war meant a chance to defend their homeland against the settlers spilling westward across the Appalachians.

In 1782 the war came to Bryan's Station, five miles east of Lexington, Kentucky. Founded three years earlier by five of Daniel Boone's brothers-in-law, the fort was surrounded by a twelve-foot-high stockade and sheltered thirty-nine houses. The settlers risked attack by Indians every time they ventured out—even the women, who left the fort regularly, under armed escort, to milk cows, weed gardens, and draw water from a nearby spring. In August Bryan's Station got word to send its men to join a local militia rally, for a pro-British force of three hundred Wyandot Indians and sixty white Canadians, led by the Pennsylvania loyalist Captain William Caldwell, was raiding Kentucky. At neighboring Hoy's Station, the attackers had abducted two children and ambushed a rescue party.

Caldwell's men headed straight for Bryan's Station, silently surrounding it on the night of August 15 as the settlement's men and women were casting bullets and readying their muskets. At daybreak, as the fort's captain, John Craig, prepared to lead forty-three men to Hoy's Station, an African-born slave noticed that the usual chorus of singing birds had given way to an eerie silence. In broken English he warned of an unseen enemy. Soon the defenders shot a poorly concealed Indian, whose companions, however, did not betray their presence by firing back—not even to stop two Bryan's Station men who trotted off to summon help. Craig realized that the attackers were waiting to ambush

the main body of men just outside the fort.

The defenders of Bryan's Station practiced their own deception. They desperately needed water in order to avoid dehydration while fighting under the broiling sun; but men trying to reach the spring would be cut down in a crossfire. If the Indians' intent, however, was to lull the settlers' suspicions, the native Americans might let women through. So, pretending total ignorance of danger, the women went to fetch the water. They walked barefoot as usual (although shoes would have helped them run faster if pursued), and they took a dozen girls, one of them shielding her mother by walking in front. Even when one woman saw a hand

Bryan's Station

175a

A Kentucky Rifle *It is believed that a resident of Bryan's Station used this rifle in the defense of the fort in 1782.*

clutching a hatchet under a bush, they maintained their composure at the spring and resisted the urge to rush to safety. After fifteen agonizing minutes, they returned with the water.

Caldwell's men attacked at midmorning. A few Indian decoys had tried to lure the defenders away from one side of the fort, but Craig's men kept their discipline and drove back the main force when it swarmed toward them. A steady pounding of musket fire and a rain of flaming arrows followed. While their men held the enemy at bay, the women reloaded guns and molded bullets while their children pulled flaming arrows out of roofs and doused fires. Little Betsy Johnson calmly plucked a blazing arrow from her infant brother Richard's cradle.

Help arrived by late afternoon, when the defenders' ammunition was running so low that their wives had begun melting pewter plates into bullets. Fourteen mounted militiamen galloped through a hail of enemy fire to reach the fort safely. Meanwhile, thirty other unmounted men in the relief party engaged the foe in a confused hand-to-hand fight. Outnumbered ten to one, the reinforcements lost six men before breaking off the battle.

Certain that more militiamen were on the way, Caldwell ended the siege. But that night, the settlers listened helplessly as the jeering loyalists trampled their crops and killed their livestock. The next morning's light unveiled a scene of desolation. A hundred acres of corn lay wasted, most of the potatoes and vegetables had been uprooted, and the carcasses of five hundred cattle, hogs, and sheep littered the ground.

The defenders had lost two men but had killed or wounded thirty attackers. Bryan's Station never again came under siege, and within two years its residents abandoned it for isolated farms; but war with the Indians went on for a decade. Richard Mentor Johnson, whose cradle had been hit by a fiery arrow, later received a gold sword from Congress for bravery in the War of 1812, and in 1837 he became vice president of the United States.

Fetching Water *In a twentieth-century reenactment, Bryan's Station women leave the safety of the fort to draw water from the nearby spring.*

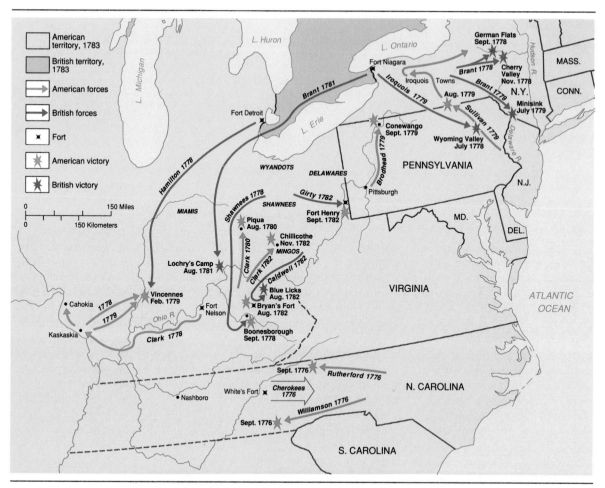

The War in the West, 1776–1779

George Rogers Clark's victory at Vincennes in 1779 gave the United States effective control of the Ohio Valley. Carolina militiamen drove attacking Cherokees far back into the Appalachians in 1776. In retaliation for their raids on New York and Pennsylvania, John Sullivan inflicted widespread starvation on the Iroquois by burning their villages and winter food supplies in 1779.

the native Americans into believing that he commanded a thousand men, prompting the Indians to flee. Carefully hiding his true strength, he then besieged the fort. The British commander surrendered Vincennes and twelve cannons on February 24, 1779, because he too concluded that he was badly outnumbered. Clark's victory not only eliminated British forts south of Detroit but also gave the United States a strong claim to retain the region north of the Ohio River.

In the East meanwhile, the Iroquois in New York remained neutral until 1777. Then the Six Nations of the Iroquois Confederacy split, with all

but the Tuscaroras and most Oneidas providing warriors for St. Leger's invasion of New York. Led by the exceptionally gifted Mohawk Joseph Brant, the Iroquois devastated the Pennsylvania and New York frontiers in 1778; they killed 340 Pennsylvania militia at Wyoming, Pennsylvania, alone and probably slew an equal number in their other raids. In 1779 the U.S. general John Sullivan retaliated by invading the Iroquois country with 3,700 Continentals and several hundred Tuscaroras and Oneidas. Sullivan fought just one battle, near present-day Elmira, New York, in which his artillery routed Brant's warriors. After he subsequently

Detroit in 1794

Detroit was a French outpost from 1701 to 1760. The British occupied it for the next thirty-six years, using it after 1775 as a staging area for their frontier forays on white settlers.

burned two dozen Indian villages and destroyed a million bushels of corn, most Iroquois fled without food into Canada. Untold hundreds starved during the next winter, when more than sixty inches of snow fell.

In 1780 Brant's thousand warriors fell upon the Tuscaroras and Oneidas and then laid waste to Pennsylvania and New York for two years. But this final whirlwind of Iroquois fury masked reality: Sullivan's campaign had destroyed the Iroquois peoples' heartland, and by 1783 their population had declined by perhaps one-third in eight years. The Six Nations would never truly recover.

Victory in the South

After 1778, as Britain formulated a new strategy that reflected changed circumstances, the war's focus shifted to the South. With the entry of France and Spain into the war, the conflict had acquired international dimensions; Britain was suddenly locked in a struggle that raged from India to Gibraltar to the West Indies and the American mainland. By

securing ports in the South, the British would acquire the flexibility to move their forces back and forth between the West Indies and the United States as necessity dictated. In addition, the South looked like a relatively easy target. General Henry Clinton recalled that in 1778 a British force of 3,500 troops had taken Savannah, Georgia, without great difficulty, and he expected that a renewed invasion of the South would tap a huge reservoir of loyalist support. In sum, the British plan was to seize key southern ports and, with the aid of loyalist militiamen, move back toward the North, pacifying one region after another.

The plan unfolded smoothly at first. Sailing from New York with 9,000 troops, Clinton forced the surrender of Charleston, South Carolina, and its 3,400-man garrison on May 12, 1780. Clinton then returned to New York with a third of his army, leaving mopping-up operations in the South to Lord Charles Cornwallis, now in command of British forces in that region. However, the British quickly found that there were fewer loyalists than they had expected. The Carolinas and Georgia did contain a sizable loyalist population, whose members enlisted by the thousands in royal militia units. Most were British immigrants, and Scots were especially prominent. But southern loyalism had suffered a serious blow in 1776, when Britain's Cherokee allies, settling scores of their own, had attacked the Carolina frontier and killed residents indiscriminately. Numerous Tories had switched sides, joining the Whig militia to defend their homes.

After the British capture of Charleston, the loyalist militia, embittered by countless instances of harsh treatment under Whig rule, lost little time in taking revenge. Whigs struck back whenever possible. So began an escalating cycle of revenge, retribution, and retaliation that engulfed the Lower South through 1782.

This southern war became intensely **personal.** Individuals often chose sides not for political rea-

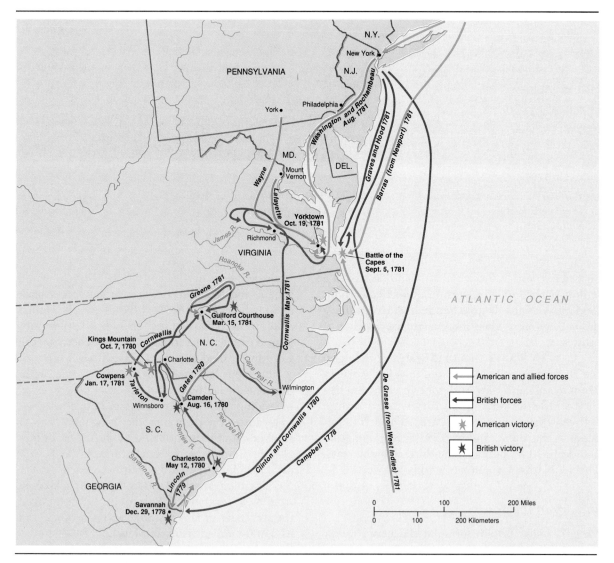

The War in the South, 1778–1781

By 1780 Britain held the South's major cities, Charleston and Savannah, but could not establish control over the backcountry because of resistance from Nathaniel Greene's Continentals. By invading Virginia, Lord Cornwallis placed himself within striking distance of Washington's U.S. and French forces, a decision that rapidly led to the British surrender at Yorktown in October 1781.

sons but to avenge an outrage perpetrated by the other. For example, Thomas Sumter and Andrew Pickens, South Carolina's two foremost Whig guerrillas, both took up arms after Tories plundered their plantations in 1780. And when another South Carolinian, the Tory William Cunningham, learned that his brother had been whipped to death by Whig militiamen from Ninety-Six, South Carolina, he grimly walked sixty miles to Ninety-Six to find and kill the officer responsible. Afterward, while leading loyalist guerrillas, Cunningham earned the nickname Bloody Bill.

An obscure rebel whose involvement in these confused vendettas seems typical was the Whig sympathizer Andrew Meaden of North Carolina. For Meaden, the Revolution was a true civil war: he never once saw a British regular during his two years' service but did all his fighting against loyalists or Cherokees. Meaden later recalled how in July 1780, he "volunteered under Captain George Wailes from Rowan Co. . . . to march in his company against some Tories, who had shot Capt. Yorke while a prisoner. . . . We made great exertions to take Capt. Fannan, a Tory, who had shot Capt. Yorke. . . . But he eluded our pursuit. . . . We took some Tories prisoner, whipped some, and compelled them to take the oath of allegiance." Like many of his generation, Meaden, fighting more for vengeance than politics, slowly became brutalized.

But the southern conflict was not all guerrilla warfare. Washington, forced by Clinton's continued occupation of New York City to stay in the North with most of the Continental Army, sent General Horatio Gates to take command in the South. With only a small force of Continentals at his disposal, however, Gates had to rely on poorly trained militiamen. In August 1780 Cornwallis inflicted a crushing defeat on Gates at Camden, South Carolina. Fleeing after firing a single volley, Gates's militia left his badly outnumbered Continentals to be overrun. Camden was the worst American defeat of the war.

Washington responded by relieving Gates of command and sending General Nathaniel Greene to confront Cornwallis. Greene subsequently fought three major battles between March and September 1781, and he lost all of them. "We fight, get beat, rise, and fight again," he wrote back to Washington. Still, Greene won the campaign, for he gave the Whig militia the protection they needed to hunt

down loyalists, stretched British supply lines until they began to snap, and sapped Cornwallis's strength by inflicting much heavier casualties than the British general could afford. Greene's dogged resistance forced Cornwallis to leave the Carolina backcountry in American hands and to lead his battered troops into Virginia.

Secure in New York City, Clinton wanted Cornwallis to return to Charleston and renew his Carolina campaign, but Cornwallis had a mind of his own and established a new base at Yorktown, Virginia, near the coast. From Yorktown Cornwallis hoped to fan out into Virginia and Pennsylvania, but he never got the chance. Cornwallis's undoing began on August 30, 1781, when a French fleet from the West Indies, commanded by Admiral De Grasse, dropped anchor off the Virginia coast and landed troops near Yorktown. Soon Lafayette joined them, leading a small force of Continentals. Meanwhile, Washington made enough feints at New York City to prevent Clinton from coming to Cornwallis's aid and then moved his army south to tighten the noose around the British. Trapped in Yorktown, Cornwallis's 6,000 British stood off 8,800 Americans and 7,800 French for three weeks. They finally surrendered with military honors on October 19, 1781.

The Peace of Paris

"Oh God!" Lord North exclaimed upon hearing of Yorktown, "It's all over." Indeed, Cornwallis's surrender drained the will of England's overtaxed gentry to fight and forced the government to commence peace negotiations. John Adams, Benjamin Franklin, and John Jay were America's principal diplomats at the peace talks in Paris, which began in June 1782.

Military realities largely influenced the terms of the peace. Britain recognized American independence and stipulated the evacuation of all royal troops from U.S. soil. Although the vast majority of Americans lived in the thirteen states clustered near the eastern seaboard, the British had little choice but to award the United States all lands east of the Mississippi, for by 1783 twenty thousand Anglo-Americans lived west of the Appalachians, and Clark's victories had given Americans control of the Northwest. The treaty also gave the United

States important fishing rights off the Grand Banks of Canada.

On the whole, the settlement was highly favorable to the United States, but it did not resolve all disputes. In a separate treaty, Britain transferred East and West Florida back to Spain, but the boundaries designated by this treaty were ambiguous. Spain interpreted the treaty to mean that it regained the same Florida territory that it had ceded to Britain in 1763. But Britain's treaty with the United States named the thirty-first parallel as the Floridas' northern border, well south of the area claimed by Spain. Spain and the United States would dispute the northern boundary of Florida until 1795.

The Peace of Paris also planted the seeds of several future disputes between Britain and the United States. Although the United States promised to urge the state legislatures to compensate loyalists for their property losses and agreed that no legal bars would prevent British creditors from collecting prewar debts, several state governments later refused to pay back loyalists and erected barriers against British creditors. In response, the British failed to honor their treaty pledge to return slaves confiscated by their troops.

The Peace of Paris ratified American independence, but winning independence had exacted a heavy price. At least 5 percent of all free white males aged sixteen to forty-five died in the war. If the present-day U.S. population fought a war with comparable casualties, 2.5 million people would be killed. Only the Civil War produced a higher ratio of casualties to the nation's population. Further, while the war secured American independence, it did not settle two important issues: what kind of society America was to become and what sort of government the new nation would possess. Yet the war had a profound impact on both questions.

Revolutionary Society

Two forces shaped the social effects of the Revolution: first, the principles articulated in the Declaration of Independence; and second, the dislocations caused by the war itself. These factors combined to change relationships between members of different classes, races, and sexes momentously.

Egalitarianism

Between 1700 and 1760, social relations between elites and the common people had grown more formal, distant, and restrained. Members of the gentry had attempted to emphasize their social position by living far beyond the means of ordinary families. As the 1760s unfolded, however, the need to mobilize widespread support for the rising Whig movement had led the upper class to minimize their displays of wealth. Members of the gentry instinctively realized that by dressing in a fashion closer to the average citizen, they could build a sense of common cause. Thus the upper classes began wearing homespun rather than imported English clothes as early as 1768 and subsequently watched their popularity soar. When the First Families of Virginia organized minutemen companies in 1775, they threw away their expensive militia uniforms and dressed in homespun hunting shirts; then even the poorest farmer would not be too embarrassed to enlist because of his humble appearance. By 1776 the visible distinctions of wealth had been noticeably reduced.

Then came war, which accelerated the erosion of class differences by forcing the gentry, who held officers' rank, to show respect to the ordinary folk serving as privates. Indeed, the soldiers demanded to be treated with consideration, especially in light of the ringing words of the Declaration of Independence, "All men are created equal." The soldiers would follow commands, but not if they were addressed as inferiors. General Steuben reported to a European army officer: "You say to your soldier, 'Do this,' and he doeth it, but I am obliged to say 'This is the reason why you ought to do that,' and he does it."

The best officers realized this fact immediately. Some, among them General Israel Putnam of Connecticut, went out of their way to show that they felt no superiority to their troops. While inspecting a regiment digging fortifications around Boston in 1776, Putnam saw a large stone nearby and told a noncommissioned officer to throw it onto the outer wall. The individual protested, "Sir, I am a corporal." "Oh," replied Putnam, "I ask your pardon, sir." The general then dismounted his horse and hurled the rock himself, to the immense delight of the troops working there.

A majority of men of military age were exposed to treatment of this sort in the course of the war. Soldiers came to expect that their worth as individuals would be recognized by their officers, at least within the limits allowed by the army. After these common soldiers returned to civilian life, they retained a sense of self-esteem and insisted on respectful treatment. As these feelings of personal pride gradually translated into political behavior and beliefs, it became highly unlikely that the majority of voters would again accept candidates who scorned the common people. The war thus subtly but fundamentally democratized Americans' political assumptions.

The gentry's sense of social rank also diminished as they met men who rose through ability rather than through advantages of wealth or family. The war produced numerous examples like James Purvis, the illiterate son of a nonslaveowning Virginia farmer, who joined the First Virginia Regiment as a private in 1775, soon rose to sergeant, and then taught himself to read and write so that he could perform an officer's duties. Captain Purvis fought through the entire war and impressed his well-born officers as "an uneducated man, but of sterling worth." As elites saw more and more middle-class farmers and even artisans performing responsibilities previously thought to be above their station in life, they developed a new appreciation that a person's merit was unrelated to his wealth.

This new emphasis on equality did not extend to blacks, women, or native Americans, but it undermined the tendency to believe that wealth or distinguished family background conferred a special claim to public office. "[O]ne should consider himself as good a man as another," declared the *New Jersey Gazette* in 1780, "and not be brow beaten or intimidated by riches or supposed superiority." After the war even a fraternal organization of veteran Continental Army officers, the Society of the Cincinnati, evoked widespread alarm because its charter gave membership to sons and their descendants who, it was feared, might evolve into a hereditary aristocracy.

In short, Revolutionary-generation Americans came to insist that virtue and sacrifice defined a citizen's worth independently of his wealth. Citizens widely began to view members of the "natural aristocracy"—those who had demonstrated fitness for government service by personal accomplishments—as the ideal candidates for political office. This natural aristocracy had room for a few self-made men such as Benjamin Franklin, as well as for those, like Jefferson and John Hancock, born into wealth. Voters still elected the wealthy to office, but not if they flaunted their money. And members of the gentry increasingly acted like the "harmless aristocrats" of Virginia described by Judge St. George Tucker, who "never failed to pull off their hats to a poor man whom they met, and generally appeared to me to shake hands with every man in a Court-yard or a Church-yard."

A Revolution for Blacks

The wartime situation of African-Americans contradicted the ideals of equality and justice for which Americans were fighting. About five hundred thousand blacks—20 percent of the total population—inhabited the United States in 1776, of whom all but about twenty-five thousand lived in bondage. Even those who were free could not vote, lived under curfews and other galling restrictions, and lacked the guarantees of equal justice held by the poorest white criminal. Free blacks could expect no more than grudging toleration, and few slaves ever gained their freedom.

Although the United States was a "white man's country" in 1776, the war opened some opportunities to blacks. Amid the confusion of war, some slaves, among them Jehu Grant of Rhode Island, ran off and posed as freemen. Grant later recalled his excitement "when I saw liberty poles and the people all engaged for the support of freedom, and I could not but like and be pleased with such a thing." Blacks also made their way into the Continental Army. Even though the army late in 1775 forbade the enlistment of any African-Americans, some blacks were already fighting in units during the siege of Boston, and the ban on black enlistments started to collapse in 1777. All states but Georgia and South Carolina eventually recruited blacks.

Approximately five thousand blacks served in the Continental forces, most from the North. The majority of blacks who enlisted were slaves serving with their masters' consent, usually in integrated units. In 1781 a German mercenary described Rhode Island's black regiment as "the most neatly dressed, the best under arms, and the most precise in its maneuvers."

For the most part, these wartime opportunities for blacks grew out of the army's need for manpower rather than a white commitment to equal justice for African-Americans. In fact, until the mid-eighteenth century, few in the Western world had criticized slavery at all. Like disease and sin, slavery was considered part of the natural order. But in the decade before the Revolution, American opposition to slavery had swelled. The first American prohibition against slaveowning came from the annual leadership conference (known as the yearly meeting) of the New England Quakers in 1770. The yearly meetings of New York and Philadelphia Quakers followed suit in 1776, and by 1779 the Quakers had compelled their members to free 80 percent of their slaves.

While the Quakers aimed mainly to abolish slaveholding within their own ranks, the Declaration of Independence's broad assertion of natural rights and human equality spurred a more general attack on the institution of slavery. Between 1777 and 1784, Vermont, Pennsylvania, Massachusetts, Rhode Island, and Connecticut ended slavery. New York did so in 1799, and New Jersey in 1804. New Hampshire, unmoved by petitions like that written in 1779 by Portsmouth slaves demanding liberty "to dispose of our lives, freedom, and property," never freed its slaves; but by 1810 there were none in the state.

The movement against slavery reflected the Enlightenment's emphasis on gradual change, initiated by leaders who carefully primed public opinion. The Revolutionary generation, rather than advocating slavery's immediate abolition, favored steps that would weaken the institution and in this way bring about its eventual demise. Most state abolition laws provided for gradual emancipation, typically declaring all children born of a slave woman after a certain date—often July 4—free. (Such individuals still had to work, without pay, for their mother's master for up to twenty-eight years.) Furthermore, the Revolution's leaders did not press for decisive action against slavery in the South, out of fear that widespread southern emancipation would either bankrupt or end the Union. Instead, a southern slave's claim to freedom had to be balanced by an owner's demand for compen-

Alexander Spotswood Payne with His Brother, John Robert Dandridge Payne, and Their Nurse, c. 1790–1800

The Payne children, members of a wealthy eighteenth-century family, posed with their black nurse. The Revolution vastly modified the social and intellectual climate in which slavery had flourished in America for more than a century without substantial challenge.

sation for lost labor. But the United States, already deeply in debt as a result of the war, could not have financed immediate abolition in the South, and any attempt to have done so without compensation would have driven that region into secession. "Great as the evil is," observed Virginia's James Madison in 1787, "a dismemberment of the union would be worse."

Yet even in the South, slavery worried the consciences of prominent Whigs. When one of his slaves ran off to join the British and later was recaptured, Madison concluded that it would be hypocritical to punish the runaway "merely for coveting that liberty for which we have paid the price of so much blood." Still, Madison did not free the slave, and no state south of Pennsylvania abolished slavery. Nevertheless, every state but North Carolina passed laws making it possible for masters to manumit (set free) slaves without posting large sums of money as bond for their good behavior. By 1790 the number of free blacks in Virginia and Maryland had risen from about four thousand in 1775 to nearly twenty-one thousand, or about 5 percent of all African-Americans there.

These "free persons of color" faced the future destitute of money. Most had purchased their freedom by spending their small cash savings earned in off-hours and were past their physical prime. Once free, they found whites reluctant to hire them or to pay equal wages. Black ship carpenters in Charleston, South Carolina, for example, earned one-third less than their white coworkers in 1783. Under such circumstances, most free blacks remained poor laborers or tenant farmers. However, even under such extreme disadvantages, some free blacks became landowners or skilled craftsmen. One who achieved considerable fame was Benjamin Banneker of Maryland, a self-taught mathematician and astronomer. Later, in 1789, he served on the commission that designed Washington, D.C., and after 1791 he published a series of almanacs.

Free blacks relied on one another for help. Self-help among African-Americans largely flowed through religious channels. Because racially separate churches provided mutual support, self-pride, and a sense of accomplishment, free blacks began founding their own Baptist and Methodist congregations after the Revolution. In 1787 black Methodists in Philadelphia started the congregation that by 1816 would become the African Methodist Episcopal church. Black churches, the greatest source of inner strength for most African-Americans ever since, had their origins in the Revolutionary period.

Most states granted important civil rights to free blacks during and after the Revolution. Free blacks had not participated in colonial elections in the North, but they gained this privilege everywhere there by 1780. Most northern states repealed or stopped enforcing curfews or other colonial laws restricting their freedom of movement. Free blacks in the South could cast ballots in North Carolina, Maryland, and Delaware by 1783 and soon gained this right in Kentucky and Tennessee. These same states generally changed their laws to guarantee free blacks equal treatment in court hearings.

The Revolution neither ended slavery nor brought equality to free blacks, who continued to be treated as second-class citizens. But it did begin a process by which slavery could be extinguished. In half the nation, public opinion no longer condoned human bondage, and southerners increasingly viewed slavery as a necessary evil—an attitude that implicitly recognized its immorality.

Slavery had begun to crack, and even the hold of racism seemed to be weakening.

Women in the New Republic

"To be adept in the art of Government is a prerogative to which your sex lay almost exclusive claim," wrote Abigail Adams to her husband John in 1776. She was one of the era's shrewdest and tartest political commentators and her husband's political confidante and best friend, but she had no public role. Indeed, for most women and almost all men in the 1780s, a woman's duty was to maintain her household and raise her children.

Apart from the fact that some states eased women's difficulties in obtaining divorces, the Revolution did not significantly affect the legal position of women. Women did not gain any new political rights, although New Jersey's 1776 constitution did not exclude them from voting and a law in force in that state from 1790 to 1807 referred to voters as "he and she." On the whole, the Revolution did far more for African-Americans than for white women. The assumption that women were naturally dependent—either as children subordinate to their parents or as wives to their husbands—continued to dominate discussions of the female role.

Nonetheless, the Revolutionary era witnessed the beginnings of a challenge to this attitude. Throughout the 1760s Whig orators had pointed to women's sacrifices to keep their families clothed during the colonial boycotts as evidence of Americans' patriotic solidarity. While these effusive declarations of women's importance to the patriot cause were meant mainly for British ears, American women heard them and took them seriously. For example, Massachusetts's Mercy Otis Warren, known before the imperial crisis for her polished, nonpolitical poetry, turned her pen to political satire in the early 1770s. In her play *The Group* (1775), she lampooned leading Massachusetts Tories under such names as Judge Meagre, Sir Spendall, and Hum Humbug.

Gradually, the subordination of women, which once was taken for granted, became the subject of debate. The Massachusetts essayist and poet Judith Sargent Murray contended in 1779 that the sexes had equal intellectual ability and deserved equal education. Murray hoped that "sensible and informed" women would improve their minds, not

Women in Revolutionary Society

As republican ideals and the female wartime experience joined forces to alter both women's self-images and prevailing social attitudes, postwar America witnessed notable changes in the lives of white women. (Left) Mrs. William Moseley, a republican mother idealized in portraiture with her son; (center) Judith Sargent Murray, a proponent of equal education for women; and (right) the Westtown Boarding School, established by the Society of Friends in 1794 to expand women's educational opportunities in the mid-Atlantic states.

rush into marriage (as she had at eighteen), and instill republican ideals in their children. After 1780 the urban upper class founded numerous private schools, or academies, for girls, and these provided to American women their first widespread opportunity for advanced education. Massachusetts also established an important precedent in 1789, when it forbade any town to exclude girls from its elementary schools. Further, American women who chafed at the restrictions of their domestic role took heart from the publication in 1792 of the English radical Mary Wollstonecraft's *Vindication of the Rights of Women.* While feeling obliged to condemn Wollstonecraft's intemperate language and sexually liberated lifestyle, many American women approved her passionate defense of female moral equality.

Although the great struggle for female political equality would not begin until the nineteenth century, the frequent Revolutionary-era assertions that women were intellectually and morally men's peers provoked scattered calls late in the eighteenth century for political equality. In 1793 Priscilla Mason, a spunky schoolgirl graduating from one of the

female academies, blamed "*Man,* despotic man" for shutting women out of the church, the courts, and government. In her salutatory oration, she urged that a women's senate be established by Congress to evoke "all that is human—all that is *divine* in the soul of woman."

Priscilla Mason had pointed out a fundamental problem in republican egalitarianism: what, besides being a virtuous wife and mother, should a woman *do* with her education? Men and women would grapple to resolve this question for generations to come.

The Revolution and Social Change

The American Revolution left the overall distribution of wealth in the nation unchanged. Because the 3 percent of Americans who fled abroad as loyalists represented a cross-section of society, their departure left the new nation's class structure unaltered. Loyalists' confiscated estates tended to be bought up by equally well-to-do Whig gentlemen. Overall, the American upper class seems to have owned about as much of the national wealth in 1783 as it did in 1776.

In short, the Revolution did not obliterate social distinctions nor even challenge all of them. Class distinctions, racial injustice, and the subordination of women persisted into the nineteenth century. In particular, the institution of slavery survived intact in the South, where the vast majority of slaves lived. Yet the Revolutionary era set in motion significant social changes. Increasingly, the members of the gentry had to earn respect by demonstrating their competence and by treating the common people with dignity. The Revolution dealt slavery a decisive blow in the North, greatly enlarged the free-black population, and awarded free people of color important political rights. While the momentous era did not bring women political equality, it placed new issues pertaining to the relations between the sexes on the agenda of national debate. And inevitably, the social changes wrought by the Revolution also deeply affected American political values.

Forging a Government

Americans had drawn many political conclusions from the imperial crisis of the 1760s, including the conviction that without vigilance by the people, governments would become despotic. But before the Declaration of Independence, few Americans had given much thought to forming governments of their own. While guiding and inspiring the Whigs, the Continental Congress lacked the sovereign powers usually associated with governments, including the authority to impose taxes.

During the war years, Whigs quickly recognized the need to establish governmental institutions to sustain the war effort and to buttress the United States' claim to independent nationhood. But the task of forging a government would prove arduous, in part because of the inevitable upheavals of war. In addition, the state governments that Americans formed after the Declaration of Independence reflected two different and often conflicting impulses: on one hand, the traditional ideas and practices that had guided Anglo-Americans for much of the eighteenth century; on the other, the republican ideals that found a receptive audience in America in the 1760s and early 1770s.

"Can America be happy under a government of her own?" asked Thomas Paine in 1776. He answered his own question: "as happy as she pleases: she hath a blank sheet to write upon."

Tradition and Change

In establishing the Revolutionary state governments, Whigs relied heavily on ideas about government inherited from the colonial experience. For example, most Whigs took for granted the value of bicameral legislatures. As we have seen, the colonial legislatures in the royal provinces had consisted of two houses: an elected lower chamber (or assembly) and an upper chamber (or council) appointed by the governor or chosen by the assembly. These two-part legislatures resembled Parliament's division into the House of Commons and House of Lords and symbolized the assumption that a government should give separate representation to aristocrats and common people.

Revolutionary Americans also accepted the longstanding practice of setting property requirements for voters and elected officials. In the prevailing view, only the ownership of property, especially land, made it possible for voters to think and act independently. Whereas tenant farmers and hired laborers might sell their votes or vote against their best judgment to avoid displeasing their landlords or employers, property holders could express their opinions freely. This association between property and citizenship was so deeply ingrained that even radical firebrands such as Samuel Adams opposed allowing all males—much less women—to vote and hold office.

The notion that elected representatives should exercise independent judgment in leading the people rather than simply carry out the popular will also survived from the colonial period and restricted the democratization of politics. Although Americans today take political parties for granted, the idea of parties as necessary instruments for identifying and mobilizing public opinion was alien to the eighteenth-century political temper, which equated parties with "factions"—selfish groups that advanced their own interests at the expense of the public good. In general, candidates for office did not present voters with a clear choice between pol-

Revolutionary Americans

The Revolutionary generation witnessed the emergence of a new brand of politics as ideals of liberty and equality accelerated longstanding tendencies among the people.

icies calculated to benefit rival interest groups; instead, they campaigned on the basis of their personal reputations and fitness for office. As a result, voters did not know where office seekers stood on specific issues and hence found it hard to influence governmental actions.

Another colonial practice that persisted into the 1770s and 1780s was the equal (or nearly equal) division of legislative seats among all counties or towns, regardless of differences in population. Inasmuch as representation had never before been apportioned according to population, a minority of voters normally elected a majority of assemblymen. Additionally, many offices that later would become elective—such as sheriffs and justices of county courts—were appointive in the eighteenth century.

In sum, the colonial experience provided no precedent for a democratization of the United States during the Revolutionary era. Whigs showed little inclination to extend the vote to all free males. Nor did they favor the election of county officials, representation in assemblies based on population, or the development of a party system that would encourage candidates to state their political beliefs forthrightly.

Yet without intending to extend political participation, Whigs found themselves pulled in a democratic direction by the logic of the imperial crisis of the 1760s and 1770s. The colonial assemblies, the most democratic parts of colonial government, had led the fight against British policy during Americans' ideological clash with the mother country, while the executive branch of colonial governments, filled by royal governors and their appointees, had repeatedly locked horns with the assemblies. Whigs entered the Revolution dreading executive officeholders and convinced that even elected governors could no more be trusted with power than could monarchs. Recent history seemed to confirm the message hammered home by British country ideology (see Chapter 4) that those in power tended to become either corrupt or dictatorial. Consequently, Revolutionary statesmen proclaimed the need to strengthen legislatures at the governors' expense.

Despite their preference for vesting power in popularly elected legislatures, Whigs described themselves as republicans rather than democrats. Although used interchangeably today, these words had different connotations in the eighteenth century. At worst, democracy suggested mob rule; at best, it implied the concentration of power in the hands of an uneducated multitude. In contrast, republicanism presumed that government would be entrusted to capable leaders, elected for their superior talents and wisdom. For most republicans, the ideal government would delicately balance the interests of different classes to prevent any one group from gaining absolute power. Some Whigs, including John Adams, thought that a republic could include a hereditary aristocracy or even a monarchy as part of this balance, but most thought otherwise. Having blasted one king in the Declaration of Independence, Whigs had no desire to enthrone another. Still, their rejection of hereditary aristocracy and monarchy posed a problem for Whigs as they set about drafting state constitutions: how to maintain balance in government amid pervasive distrust of executive power.

Reconstituting the States

The state governments that Americans constructed during the Revolution reflected both the traditional and radical features of their thought. In keeping with colonial traditions, eleven of the thirteen states established bicameral legislatures. In all but a few states, the great majority of officeholders, at both the state and the county level, were still appointed rather than elected. Only one state, Pennsylvania, attempted to ensure that election districts would be roughly equal in population, so that a minority of voters could not elect a majority of legislators. Nine of the thirteen states reduced property requirements for voting, but none abolished such qualifications entirely, and most of the reductions were quite modest.

Yet the persistence of these conservative features should not obscure the pathbreaking components of the state constitutions. Above all, they were *written* documents whose adoption usually required popular ratification and which could be changed only if the people voted to amend them. In short, having rejected Parliament's right to tax them, Americans also jettisoned the British conception of a constitution as a body of customary arrangements and practices, insisting instead that constitutions were written compacts that defined and limited the powers of rulers. Moreover, as a final check on governmental power, the revolutionary constitutions spelled out citizens' fundamental rights. By 1784 all state constitutions included explicit bills of rights that outlined certain freedoms beyond governmental control. In sum, governments were no longer to serve as the final judge of the constitutionality of their activities.

The state constitutions reflected Whig thought in other ways, too. In most states the governor became an elected official, and elections themselves occurred far more frequently. Prior to 1776 colonial elections, typically called at the governor's pleasure, most often took place every three or four years. In contrast, after 1776 each state scheduled annual elections except South Carolina, which held them every two years. While most state and county offices remained appointive, the power

of appointments was transferred from the governor to the legislature. Legislatures usually appointed judges and could reduce their salaries or impeach them (try them for wrongdoing). But the new constitutions took their largest bite out of the governors' powers. Pennsylvania actually eliminated the office of governor, while other states stripped the executive branch of nearly all authority. By relieving governors of most appointive powers, denying them the right to veto laws, and making them subject to impeachment, the constitutions turned governors into figureheads who simply chaired an executive council that made militia appointments and supervised financial business.

As the new state constitutions weakened the executive branch and vested more power in the legislatures, they also made the legislatures, especially the upper chambers, more responsive to the will of the people. Nowhere could the governor appoint the upper chamber. Eight constitutions written before 1780 allowed voters to select both houses of the legislature, one (Maryland) used a popularly chosen "electoral college" for its upper house, and the remaining "senates" were filled by vote of their assemblies. Pennsylvania and Georgia abolished the upper house and substituted a single-chamber unicameral legislature. The Whigs' assault on the executive branch and their enhancement of legislative authority reflected their bitter memories of royal governors who had acted arbitrarily to prorogue (dismiss) assemblies and control government through their power of appointment, and it underscored the influence of "country-party" ideologues, who had warned that republics' undoing began with executive usurpation of authority.

In their first flush of revolutionary enthusiasm, few Whigs imagined that the legislatures themselves could become tyrannical. Yet most were familiar with the argument of the French Baron de Montesquieu (1689–1755) in *The Spirit of the Laws* that a proper division of political power would balance the executive, legislative, and judicial branches. By concentrating power in legislatures, the state constitutions provided no such balance. Gradually, however, Whigs paid more attention to the principle of balanced government. For example, Massachusetts revised its constitution in 1780 to strengthen the office of governor, while Georgia and Pennsylvania substituted bicameral for unicameral legislatures by 1790. Other states raised property qualifications for members of the upper chamber in a bid to encourage the "senatorial element" and to make room for men of "Wisdom, remarkable integrity, or that Weight which arises from property."

In general, the state constitutions written in the 1780s balanced power more evenly among branches of the government than had those composed in 1776–1777. Nonetheless, in comparison to the colonial-era royal governors, state executives continued to be relatively weak. Further, despite Whigs' efforts to bolster the upper chamber, or senate, as a balance against excesses of the lower house, the individuals elected to state senates did not seem notably wealthier or wiser than the members of the lower house. Even after Whigs raised the property requirements for senators, voters sent virtually indistinguishable groups to both houses. This failure of the "senatorial element" to emerge led republicans to reevaluate the purpose of bicameral legislatures. While social distinctions existed in the United States, none were so extreme as to merit institutionalization in a separate branch of the legislature. Whigs gradually altered their defense of bicameral legislatures by emphasizing that these bodies could act as useful checks on each other rather than as institutional embodiments of different social classes. If either house passed unwise measures, the other could block their enactment. Thus bicameralism itself became a functional safeguard against legislative abuses.

The Whigs' deference to the principle of balanced government revealed a central feature of their thought. Gradations among social classes and restrictions on the expression of popular will troubled them far less than the prospect of tyranny by those in power. But Whigs also believed that social divisions, if deep-seated and permanent, could jeopardize republican liberty. While more committed to liberty than to equality, some Whig leaders attempted to implement major social changes through legislation by the new state governments. In Virginia, for example, between 1776 and 1780 (when he became governor), Thomas Jefferson drafted a series of bills to promote greater equality. In October 1776 he persuaded the Virginia legislature to abolish entails, legal requirements that prevented an heir and all his descendants from selling or dividing an estate. Although entails were easy to break through special laws—Jefferson himself had escaped from the restrictions of one—he hoped that their elimination would strip wealthy families of the opportunity to amass land continuously and become an overbearing aristocracy. Through Jefferson's efforts, Virginia also ended primogeniture, the legal requirement that the eldest son inherit all a family's property in the absence of a will. Thereby, Jefferson hoped to ensure a continuous division of wealth. By 1791 no state provided for primogeniture, and just two allowed entails.

These years also witnessed the end of state-established churches in most of the country. New England, whose political climate was the nation's most conservative, resisted this reform, and the Congregational church continued to collect tithes (church taxes) until 1817 in New Hampshire, 1818 in Connecticut, and 1833 in Massachusetts. But in every state where colonial taxpayers had supported the Anglican church, such support was abolished by 1786. Thomas Jefferson best expressed the ideal behind disestablishment in his Statute for Religious Freedom (1786), whose preamble resounded with a defense of religious freedom at all times and places. "Truth is great," proclaimed Jefferson, "and will prevail if left to itself."

The American Revolution, wrote Thomas Paine in 1782, was intended to ring in "a new era and give a new turn to human affairs." This was an ambitious declaration and seemed to conflict with the Whigs' tendency to borrow from the past institutions such as state senates and property requirements for voting. Paine's point was not that the unique features of some constitutions, such as the termination of primogeniture and the disestablishment of the Anglican church, outweighed the traditional elements of the constitutions. Instead, he was expressing the Whigs' view—which lay at the heart of their republican ideal—that *all* political institutions now were being judged by the standard of whether they served the public good rather than the interests of the powerful few. More than any single innovation of the era, it was this new way of thinking that made the Whigs revolutionary.

The Articles of Confederation

While Whigs poured most of their political energies into the state governments, in 1776 John Dickinson, who had stayed in Congress despite having refused to sign the Declaration of Independence, drafted a proposal for a national government, which he called the Articles of Confederation. Congress adopted a weakened version of the Articles and sent it to the states for ratification in 1777. The Articles established a single-chamber national Congress, elected by the state legislatures, in which each state had only one vote. Congress could request funds from the states but could enact no tax of its own without every state's approval, nor could it regulate interstate or overseas commerce.

The proposed government's omissions were notable. The Articles did not provide for an executive branch. Rather, congressional committees oversaw financial, diplomatic, and military affairs. Nor was there a judicial system by which the national government could compel allegiance to its laws. Finally, the Articles would not become operational until approved by all thirteen state legislatures. Twelve states agreed to the new government by 1779, but Maryland delayed, refusing to sign until all states claiming lands north of the Ohio River turned these territories over to the United States. Maryland lawmakers wanted to keep Virginia and New York from expanding to such a degree that they would dominate the new nation. Beginning in 1781, northwestern claims by individual states were abandoned, and the Articles finally became law in March.

The Articles explicitly reserved to each state "its sovereignty, freedom and independence" and established a form of government in which Americans were citizens of their own states first and of

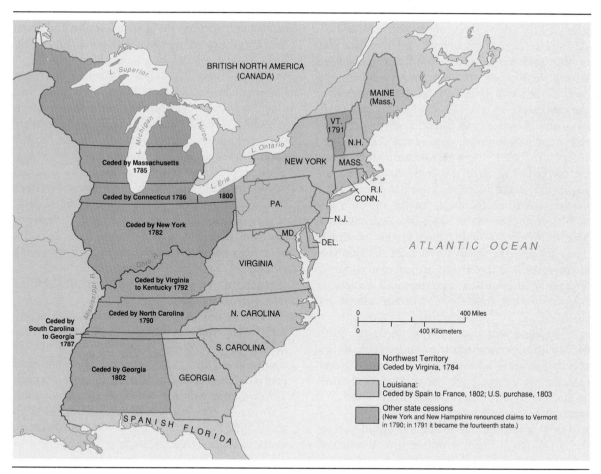

State Claims to Western Lands, and State Cessions to the Federal Government, 1782–1802

Eastern states' surrender of land claims paved the way for new state governments in the West. Georgia was the last state to cede its western lands, in 1802.

the United States second. As John Adams later explained, the Whigs of 1776 never thought of "consolidating this vast Continent under one national Government" but instead erected "a Confederacy of States, each of which must have a separate government." Much as they distrusted the concentration of power in the hands of executives on the state level, Whigs had deep misgivings about a strong national government.

The Articles worked satisfactorily during the war, as the fear of military defeat ensured cooperation from the states. The advent of peace, however, made most politicians complacent and exposed the Confederation's impracticalities. The United States ended the Revolution burdened with difficult problems that could not be solved by a government with so little power.

Yet in its brief history, the Confederation not only achieved American independence but also provided for administration of western lands. The states surrendered responsibility for more than 160 million acres north of the Ohio River to Congress during the Revolution. To establish uniform procedures for surveying this land, Congress enacted the Ordinance of 1785. The law established as the basic unit of settlement a township six miles square. Every township would be subdivided into thirty-six sections of 640 acres each, one of which would be reserved as a source of income for schools. Subsequently, in the Northwest Ordinance of 1787, Congress defined the steps for the creation and admission of new states. This law designated the area north of the Ohio River as the Northwest Territory and provided for its later division into states. It forbade slavery while the region remained a territory, although the citizens could legalize the institution after statehood (as Illinois almost did in 1824).

The Northwest Ordinance outlined three stages for admitting states into the Union. First, during the initial years of settlement, Congress would appoint a territorial governor and judges. Second, as soon as five thousand adult males lived in a territory, the people would write a temporary constitution and elect a legislature that would pass the territory's laws. Third, when the total population reached sixty thousand, the settlers would write a state constitution, which Congress would have to approve before granting statehood.

The Ordinance of 1785 and the Northwest Ordinance became the Confederation's major contributions to American life. These laws set the basic principles for surveying the frontier, allowed territorial government at an early stage of settlement, and provided reasonable standards for statehood. Both measures served as models for organizing territories later acquired west of the Mississippi River. The Northwest Ordinance also established a significant precedent for banning slavery from certain territories. But because Indians, determined to keep out white settlers, controlled virtually the entire region north of the Ohio River, the Confederation's ordinances respecting the Northwest had no immediate effect.

The Northwest Territory seemed to offer enough rich land to guarantee future citizens landownership for centuries. This fact satisfied American republican sentiment, which placed great importance upon opening the West for settlement out of fears that the rapidly growing U.S. population would quickly exhaust the land east of the Appalachians and so create a large class of tenants and poor laborers who would lack the property needed to vote. By poisoning politics through class conflict, such a development would undermine the equality that republicans thought essential for a healthy nation. In the anticipated westward push by whites, Thomas Jefferson and other republican thinkers hoped to avoid conflict with the northwestern Indians by assimilating them into white society. However, since native Americans had no desire to abandon their own culture, republican anxieties over preserving economic opportunity by giving white settlers access to western lands made war inevitable and sowed the seeds of eventual Indian removal farther west.

At postwar treaty negotiations, native Americans repeatedly heard U.S. commissioners scornfully declare: "You are a subdued people . . . we claim the country by conquest." Under threats of continued warfare, the Indians initially gave in. The Iroquois, who lost about 10 percent of their warriors by fighting on the British side, gave up about half their land in New York and Pennsylvania in several treaties made at Fort Stanwix in 1784. Then at the Treaty of Fort McIntosh in 1785, the major northwestern tribes signed away most of present-day Ohio. These settlements outraged most

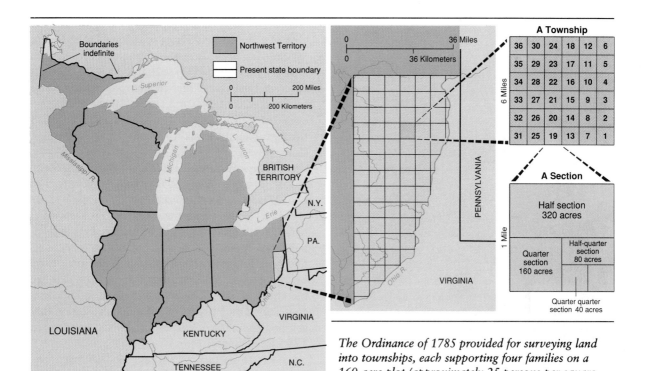

The Northwest, 1785–1787

The Ordinance of 1785 provided for surveying land into townships, each supporting four families on a 160-acre plot (approximately 25 persons per square mile). In 1787 the Northwest Ordinance stipulated that states would ultimately be created in the region.

native Americans, who denied that their negotiators had authority to give up tribal lands. By 1786 the Indians had repudiated both treaties.

The Indians' resistance stemmed in large part from their confidence that the British—still a presence in the West—would provide the arms and ammunition they needed to defy the United States. Britain had refused to abandon seven forts on the nation's northwestern frontier, officially because several state legislatures had blocked the collection of prewar debts owed British merchants and had also refused to compensate loyalists for wartime property losses. In April 1784, however, well before Britain knew about the violation of these provisions of the peace treaty, its colonial office had secretly ordered the governor of Canada to hold those forts. With Indian support, Britain hoped eventually to reestablish its claim to the Northwest Territory.

The Mohawk Joseph Brant emerged as the inspiration behind Indian resistance to white encroachments. Courageous in battle, skillful in diplomacy, and highly educated (he had translated the Bible into Iroquois), Brant became a minor celebrity when he visited King George at London in 1785. At British-held Fort Detroit in 1786, he helped organize the northwestern Indians into a military alliance to exclude white settlers north of the Ohio River. But Brant and his Mohawks, who had relocated beyond American reach in Canada, could not win support from the Iroquois still living in New York. John Sullivan's campaign of 1779 (see above) had left the Six Nations unwilling to risk another such invasion.

The Confederation confronted similar problems in the Southeast, where Spanish officials were goading Indians to harass Anglo-American settlers in Tennessee and Georgia. The Spanish found a brilliant ally in the Creek Alexander McGillivray, a sickly but shrewd diplomat who was three-quarters white. In the Treaty of Augusta (1783), the Creeks had surrendered extensive territory in Georgia that McGillivray intended to regain. Patiently holding back his warriors for three years, McGillivray negotiated a secret treaty with Spain that promised the Creeks weapons so that they

Joseph Brant, *by Wilhelm von Moll Berczy, c. 1800*

In the 1780s several Indian leaders—among them Brant (a Mohawk), Blue Jacket (a Shawnee), and Little Turtle (a Miami)—worked to create a northwestern Indian confederation that would strengthen native American resolve not to bargain with land-hungry whites.

could protect themselves "from the Bears and other fierce Animals." When McGillivray finally unleashed his forces in 1786, he assaulted only occupants on the disputed lands and wisely offered a cease-fire after winning his objective. Eager to avoid voting taxes for a costly war, state politicians let him keep the land.

Besides intriguing with the southeastern Indians, Spain attempted to deny western settlers permission to ship their crops down the Mississippi River to New Orleans, the only port from which they could profitably export their goods. Having negotiated a separate treaty with Britain (see above), Spain had not signed the Peace of Paris, by which Britain promised the United States export rights down the Mississippi, and in 1784 the Spanish closed New Orleans to Anglo-American com-

merce. To negotiate trading privileges at New Orleans, the United States sent John Jay to Spain. Jay failed to win concessions, but he returned with a treaty that opened up valuable Spanish markets to eastern merchants and renounced Spanish claims to disputed southwestern lands—at the cost, however, of relinquishing American export rights through New Orleans for twenty years. Although Congress rejected this Jay-Gardoqui Treaty in 1786, the treaty infuriated westerners and southerners, whose interests seemed to have been sacrificed to benefit northern commerce.

The Confederation was no more successful at prying trade concessions from Britain. Before Independence almost 60 percent of northern exports had gone to the British West Indies, but after 1783 Britain closed West Indian ports to the Yankee merchant marine. The loss of these island markets contributed mightily to an economic depression that gripped the nation, and especially its seaports, in 1784 (see Chapter 6).

Next to its lack of success in diplomacy, the Confederation's greatest failure lay in its inability to prevent national bankruptcy. Winning the war had cost the nation's six hundred thousand taxpayers a staggering $160 million, a sum that exceeded by 2,400 percent the taxes raised to pay for the Seven Years' War. To finance the War for Independence, which cost far more than the nation could immediately collect through taxation, the government had borrowed funds from abroad and printed its own paper money, called Continentals. Lack of public faith in the government destroyed 98 percent of the value of the Continentals from 1776 to 1781, an inflationary disaster that gave rise to the expression "not worth a Continental."

Faced with a desperate financial situation, Congress turned to a wealthy, self-made Philadelphia merchant, Robert Morris, who in 1781 became the nation's superintendent of finance. Morris proposed that the states authorize the collection of a national import duty of 5 percent to finance the congressional budget and to guarantee interest payments on the war debt. Because the Articles stipulated that every state had to approve the levying of national taxes, the import duty failed to pass in 1782 when Rhode Island alone rejected it.

Hoping to panic the country into creating a regular source of national revenue, Morris and New York congressman Alexander Hamilton then engi-

Robert Morris

Morris assumed almost dictatorial powers over the nation's finances in his role as superintendent of finance. As a delegate to the Philadelphia Convention in 1787, he would support a strong federal government.

neered a dangerous gamble known later as the Newburgh Conspiracy. In 1783 the two men secretly persuaded the army's officers (then encamped at Newburgh, New York) into bluffing that they would mutiny unless the treasury obtained the taxation authority needed to raise their pay, which was months in arrears. But George Washington, learning of the conspiracy before it was carried out, ended the plot by delivering a speech that appealed to his officers' honor and left them unwilling to proceed. Although Morris never intended that a mutiny actually occur, his willingness to take such a risk demonstrated the country's perilous financial straits.

When peace came in 1783, Morris found it impossible to secure adequate funding for the United States. That year, Congress sent another tax measure to the states, but once again a single legislature, this time New York's, blocked it. From then on, the states steadily decreased their contributions to Congress. By the late 1780s, the states had fallen behind nearly 80 percent in providing the

funds that Congress requested to operate the government and honor the national debt.

In sum, the Articles of Confederation had achieved nothing significant except the ordinances of 1785 and 1787. The government's disunity and financial embarrassments invited both foreign aggression and attacks by western Indians on frontier settlers. "I see one head gradually turning into thirteen," George Washington soberly commented in 1780; "I see the powers of Congress declining too fast." By 1787 his apprehensions had become a reality.

Shays's Rebellion

But for an outbreak of violence in Massachusetts late in 1786, the Confederation might have tottered on indefinitely. Since 1784 a recession had gripped Massachusetts after the state had lost its best market, the British West Indies. To worsen matters, the state legislature voted early in 1786 to pay off its Revolutionary debt in three years. This ill-considered policy necessitated a huge tax hike that exceeded the ability of many marginal farmers to pay. The plight of Massachusetts farmers was especially severe in the western counties, where agriculture was least profitable. Late in 1786 farmer and former Revolutionary War officer Daniel Shays led some two thousand angry men in an attempt to shut down the courts in three of these western counties, and thereby stop sheriffs' auctions for unpaid taxes and prevent foreclosures on farm mortgages. Although routed by the state militia after several skirmishes, Shays's followers won control of the Massachusetts legislature in 1787, cut taxes, and secured a pardon for their leader.

Shays's supporters had limited objectives, were dispersed with relatively little bloodshed, and never seriously posed the danger of anarchy. But his uprising symbolized for critics of the weak national government the Republic's fragility under the Confederation. By threatening to seize weapons from a federal arsenal at Springfield, Massachusetts, the Shaysites had unintentionally reminded nationalists how pitifully defenseless the United States had become. At the same time, rumors were flying that the Spanish had offered export rights at New Orleans to westerners if they would secede from the Union. Nationalists wondered whether Shays's Rebellion might trigger secessionist movements elsewhere. Washington had earlier worried that one head was turning into thirteen, but now it seemed possible that one might turn into thirty or forty separate heads.

Not everyone shared these apprehensions. In contrast to New England, the mid-Atlantic and southern states were emerging from a depression, thanks to rising tobacco and food exports to Europe. Taxpayers in these sections, moreover, were paying off war debts easily. Further, the regions' numerous small farming families, living in relatively isolated communities and trading largely with neighbors, were in quiet times widely indifferent to national politics. But the minority of people intensely dissatisfied with the Confederation was growing. Urban artisans, for example, hoped for a stronger national government that would impose a uniformly high tariff and thereby protect them from foreign competition. Merchants and shippers wanted a government powerful enough to secure trading privileges for them, while land speculators and western settlers preferred a government capable of pursuing a more activist policy against the Indians. To these groups were now added those political leaders who saw in Shays's Rebellion a sign of worse things to come.

Shortly before the outbreak of the rebellion, delegates from five states had assembled at Annapolis, Maryland. They had intended to discuss means of promoting interstate commerce but instead called for a general convention to propose amendments to the Articles of Confederation. Accepting their suggestion, Congress asked the states to appoint delegations to meet in Philadelphia.

The Philadelphia Convention

In May 1787 fifty-five delegates from every state but Rhode Island began gathering at the Pennsylvania State House in Philadelphia, later known as Independence Hall. Among them were figures of established reputation like George Washington, Benjamin Franklin, John Dickinson, and Robert Morris, as well as talented newcomers such as Alexander Hamilton and James Madison. Most were wealthy and in their thirties or forties, and nineteen owned slaves. More than half had legal training.

The convention immediately closed its sessions to the press and the public, kept no *official* journal, and even appointed chaperones to accompany the

aged and talkative Franklin to dinner parties lest he disclose details of what was happening. Although these measures opened the members of the convention to the charge of acting undemocratically and conspiratorially, the delegates thought secrecy essential to ensure themselves freedom of debate without fear of criticism from home.

The delegates shared a "continental" or "nationalist" perspective, instilled through their extended involvement with the national government. Thirty-nine had sat in Congress, where they had seen the Articles' defects firsthand. These delegates had outgrown the localism that was typical of state politicians and had come to appreciate how much Americans were alike. In the postwar years, they had become convinced that unless the national government were freed from the state legislatures' control, the country would fall victim to foreign aggression or simply disintegrate.

The convention faced two basic issues. The first was whether to tinker with the Articles (as the state legislatures had formally instructed the delegates to do) or to scrap the Articles and draw up an entirely new frame of government. The second fundamental question was how to balance the conflicting interests of large and small states. James Madison of Virginia, who had entered Congress in 1780 at twenty-nine, proposed an answer to each issue. Despite his youth and almost frail build, Madison commanded enormous respect for his profound knowledge of history and the passionate intensity that he brought to debates.

Madison's Virginia Plan, introduced by his fellow Virginian Edmund Randolph in late May, boldly called for the establishment of a national government rather than a federation of states. Madison's blueprint gave Congress virtually unrestricted rights of legislation and taxation, the power to veto any state law, and authority to use military force against the states. As delegate Charles Pinckney of South Carolina immediately saw, the Virginia Plan was designed "to abolish the State Govern[men]ts altogether." The Virginia Plan specified a bicameral legislature and fixed representation in both houses of Congress proportionally to each state's population. The voters would elect the lower house, which would then choose delegates to the upper chamber from nominations submitted by the legislatures. Both houses would jointly name the country's president and judges.

The Assembly Room in Independence Hall

Much history was made in this room. The Declaration of Independence was signed here in 1776, and the constitutional-convention delegates met in this chamber in 1787.

Madison's scheme aroused immediate opposition, however, especially his call for the states to be represented according to their population—a provision highly favorable to his own Virginia. On June 15 William Paterson of New Jersey offered a counterproposal, the so-called New Jersey Plan, which recommended a single-chamber congress in which each state had an equal vote, just as under the Articles.

Despite their differences over representation, Paterson's and Madison's proposals alike would have strengthened the national government at the states' expense. No less than Madison, Paterson wished to empower Congress to raise taxes, regulate interstate commerce, and use military force against the states. The New Jersey Plan, in fact, was the first to define congressional laws and treaties as the "supreme law of the land"; it would also have established courts to force reluctant states and their citizens to accept these measures.

The New Jersey Plan was highly significant because it exposed the convention's great stumbling block: the question of representation. The Virginia Plan would have given the four largest states a majority in both houses. The New Jersey Plan would have allowed the seven smallest states, which included just 25 percent of all Americans, to control Congress. By July 2 the convention had arrived "at a full stop," as Roger Sherman of Connecticut noted. To end the impasse, the delegates

assigned a member from each state to a "grand committee" dedicated to compromise. The panel adopted a proposal offered earlier by the Connecticut delegation: an equal vote for each state in the upper house and proportional voting in the lower house. Madison and the Virginians doggedly fought this so-called Connecticut Compromise, but they were voted down on July 17. The convention overcame the remaining hurdles rather easily in the next two months.

As finally approved on September 17, 1787, the Constitution of the United States was an extraordinary document, and not merely because it successfully reconciled the conflicting interests of the large and small states. Out of hard bargaining among different states' representatives emerged the Constitution's delicate balance between the desire of nearly all delegates for a stronger national government and their fear that governments tended to grow despotic. The Constitution augmented national authority in several ways. Although it did not incorporate Madison's proposal to give Congress a veto over state laws, it vested in Congress the authority to lay and collect taxes, to regulate commerce among the states (interstate commerce), and to conduct diplomacy. States could no longer coin money, interfere with contracts and debts, or tax interstate commerce. All acts and treaties of the United States became "the supreme law of the land." All state officials had to swear to uphold the

James Madison

Although one of the Philadelphia Convention's young-est delegates, Madison of Virginia was among its most politically astute. He played a central role in the Constitution's adoption.

Constitution, even against acts of their own states. The national government could use military force against any state.

These provisions added up to a complete abandonment of the principle on which the Articles of Confederation had rested: that the United States was a federation of independent republics known as states, with all authority concentrated in their legislatures. Yet still concerned about too strong a federal system, the Constitution's framers devised two ways to restrain the power of the new national government. First, they established three distinct branches—executive, legislative, and judicial—within the national government; and second, they designed a system of checks and balances to prevent any one branch from dominating the other two. The framers systematically applied to the national government the principle of a *functional* separation of powers, an idea that had been evolving in the states since about 1780. In the bicameral Congress, states' equal representation in the Senate was offset by the proportional representation, by population, in the House; and each chamber could

block hasty measures demanded by the other. Further, where the state constitutions had deliberately weakened the executive, the Constitution gave the president the power to veto acts of Congress; but to prevent capricious use of the veto, Congress could override the president by a two-thirds majority in each house. The president could conduct diplomacy, but only the Senate could ratify treaties. The president named his cabinet, but only with Senate approval. The president and all his appointees could be removed from office by a joint vote of Congress, but only for "high crimes," not for political disagreements.

To further ensure the independence of each branch, the Constitution provided that the members of one branch would not choose those of another, except for judges, whose independence was protected by lifetime appointment. For example, the president was to be selected by an electoral college, whose members the states would select as their legislatures saw fit. The state legislatures also elected the members of the Senate, while the election of delegates to the House of Representatives was achieved by popular vote.

In addition to checks and balances, the founders improvised a novel form of federalism—a system of shared power and dual lawmaking by the national and state governments—in order to place limits on central authority. Not only did the state legislatures have a key role in electing the president and senators, but the Constitution could be amended by the votes of three-fourths of the state legislatures. Thus the convention devised a form of government that differed significantly from Madison's plan to establish a "consolidated" national government entirely independent of, and superior to, the states.

A key assumption behind federalism was that the national government would limit its activities to foreign affairs, national defense, regulating commerce, and coining money. The states otherwise had full freedom to act autonomously on purely internal matters. Regarding slavery in particular, each state retained full authority.

The Philadelphia Convention treated slavery as a political, not a moral issue; it allowed three-fifths of all slaves to be counted for congressional representation (a formula used since 1783 to assess state contributions to Congress). The Constitution forbade any state's people to prevent the return of runaway slaves to another state. The only cases in which the Constitution interfered with slavery were such national matters as overseas commerce and (presumably) administration of the territories (since the Constitution did not repudiate the Northwest Ordinance's law on slavery). The Constitution explicitly permitted Congress to ban the importation of slaves after 1808.

While leaving much authority to the states, the Constitution established a national government clearly superior to the states in several spheres, and it utterly abandoned the notion of a federation of virtually independent states. Having thus strengthened national authority, the convention had to face the issue of ratification. For two reasons, it seemed unwise to submit the Constitution to state legislatures for ratification. First, the framers realized that the state legislatures would reject the Constitution, which shrank their power relative to the national government. Second, most of the framers repudiated the idea—implicit in ratification by existing state legislatures—that the states composed the foundation of the new government. The opening words of the Constitution—"We the People of the United States"—underlined the delegates' growing conviction that the government had to be based on the consent of the American people themselves, "the fountain of all power" in Madison's words.

In the end, the Philadelphia Convention provided for the Constitution's ratification by special state conventions composed of delegates elected by the people. Approval by only nine such conventions would put the new government in operation. Because any state refusing to ratify would remain under the Articles, the possibility existed that the country might divide into two nations.

Under the Constitution the framers expected the nation's "natural aristocracy" to continue exercising political leadership; but did they also intend to rein in the democratic currents set in motion by the Revolution? In one respect they did, by curtailing what most nationalists considered the excessive power of popularly elected legislatures. But the Constitution made no attempt to control faction and disorder by suppressing liberty—a "remedy," wrote Madison, that would be "worse than the disease." The framers did provide for one crucial democratic element in the new government, the House of Representatives. Equally important,

the Constitution recognized the American people as the ultimate source of political legitimacy. Moreover, by making the Constitution flexible and amendable (though not easily amendable) and by dividing political power among competing branches of government, the framers made it possible for the national government to be slowly democratized in ways unforeseen in 1787, without turning into a tyranny of ideologues or temporary majorities. Madison eloquently expressed the founders' intention of controlling the dangers inherent in any society:

> *If men were angels, no government would be necessary. If angels were to govern men, neither external nor internal controls on government would be necessary. In framing a government which is to be administered by men over men, the great difficulty lies in this: You must first enable the government to control the governed; and in the next place, oblige it to control itself. A dependence on the people is no doubt the primary control on the government; but experience has taught mankind the necessity of external precautions.*

Ratification

The Constitution's supporters began the campaign for ratification without significant national support. Most Americans had expected that the Philadelphia Convention would offer only limited amendments to the Articles. A majority therefore hesitated to adopt the radical restructuring of government that had been proposed. Undaunted, the Constitution's friends moved decisively to marshal political support. In a clever stroke, they called themselves Federalists, a term that implied that the Constitution balanced the relationship between the national and state governments and thereby lessened the opposition of those hostile to a centralization of national authority.

The Constitution's opponents commonly became known as Antifederalists. This negative-sounding title probably hurt them, for it did not convey the crux of their argument against the Constitution—that it was not "federalist" at all since it failed to balance the power of the national and state governments. Indeed, many Antifederalists doubted whether any such balance was possible. In their view, either the national or the state gov-

George Mason

Mason fought the Constitution's ratification, insisting on the inclusion of a bill of rights. He deeply opposed the delegates' compromise on the slave trade, a practice that he deemed "disgraceful to mankind."

devised a system of checks and balances to guard against tyranny, but no one could be certain that the untried scheme would work. For all its checks and balances, in addition, the Constitution nowhere contained ironclad guarantees that the new government would protect the liberties of individuals or the states. The absence of a bill of rights made an Antifederalist of Madison's nationalist ally and fellow Virginian, George Mason, the author of the first such state bill in 1776.

Although the Antifederalists advanced some formidable arguments, they rarely matched their opponents in vigor. The intellectual horizons of the Antifederalists usually were bounded by the state politics with which they were familiar; few of them had acquired the national outlook that service in the Continental Army or Congress had imparted to their opponents. The Antifederalists could count among their number the Virginia firebrand Patrick Henry but no one with Madison's learning, Hamilton's genius, or the national prestige of Washington and Franklin. While their antagonists carefully planned how to elect sympathetic delegates to the ratifying conventions, the Antifederalists failed to create a sense of urgency among their supporters, assuming incorrectly that a large majority would rally to them. Only one-quarter of the voters turned out to elect delegates to the state ratifying conventions, however, and most had been mobilized by Federalists.

Federalist delegates prevailed in eight conventions between December 1787 and May 1788, in all cases except one by margins of at least two-thirds. Such lopsided votes seldom reflected the Federalists' greater organizational skills compared to their opponents, rather than the degree of popular support for the Constitution. Advocates of the new plan of government did indeed ram through approval in some states "before it can be digested or deliberately considered" (in the words of a Pennsylvania Antifederalist). Only Rhode Island and North Carolina rejected the Constitution and thus refused to join the new United States.

But unless Virginia and New York ratified, the new government would not be workable. Antifederalist sentiment in both states (and elsewhere) ran high among small farmers, who saw the Constitution as a scheme favoring city dwellers and monied interests. Prominent political leaders in these two states called for refusing ratification, includ-

ernments would dominate the Republic; no even division of power could be achieved. By augmenting national authority, Antifederalists maintained, the Constitution would ultimately doom the states.

The Antifederalist arguments expressed a deep-seated Anglo-American suspicion of concentrated power. Unquestionably, the Constitution gave the national government unprecedented authority in an age when almost all writers on politics taught that the sole means of preventing despotism was to restrain the power of government officials. Compared to a national government, which inevitably would be distant from the people in an era when news traveled slowly, the state governments struck Antifederalists as far more responsive to the popular will. "The vast Continent of America cannot be long subjected to a Democracy if consolidated into one Government. You might as well attempt to rule Hell by Prayer," wrote a New England Antifederalist. True, the framers had

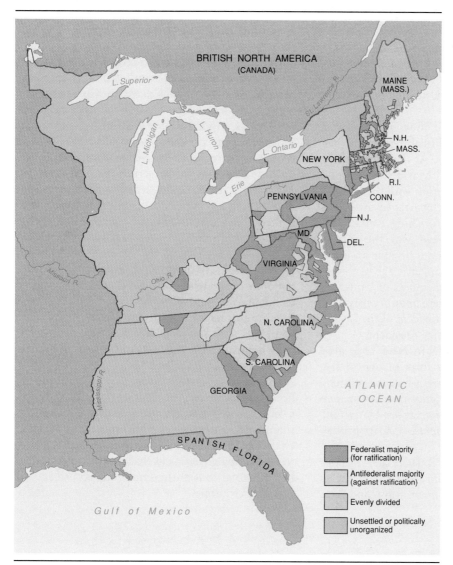

Federalist and Anti-federalist Strongholds, 1787–1790

Antifederalist support came from interior regions where geographic isolation bred a narrow, localistic perspective. Federalists drew their primary backing from densely populated areas along major transportation routes, where trade, mobility, and frequent contact with persons in other states encouraged a nationalistic identity.

ing New York governor George Clinton and Virginia's Richard Henry Lee, George Mason, Patrick Henry, and future president James Monroe.

The Constitution became the law of the land on June 21, 1788, when the ninth state, New Hampshire, ratified by the close vote of 57–47. At that moment debate was still under way in the Virginia convention. The Federalists won crucial support from the representatives of the Alleghany counties—modern West Virginia—who wanted a strong national government capable of ending Indian raids across the Ohio River. Western Vir-

ginians' votes, combined with James Madison's logic and the growing support for the Constitution among tidewater planters, proved too much for Henry's spellbinding oratory. On June 25 the Virginia delegates ratified by a narrow 53 percent majority.

The struggle was even closer and more hotly contested in New York. Antifederalists had solid control of the state convention and would probably have voted down the Constitution, but then news arrived of New Hampshire's and Virginia's ratification. The Federalist forces, led by Alexander Hamilton and John Jay, began hinting strongly that if the convention voted to reject, pro-Federalist New York City would secede from the state and join the Union alone, leaving upstate New York a landlocked enclave. When a number of Antifederalist delegates took alarm at this threat and switched sides, New York ratified on July 26, by a 30–27 vote.

So the Antifederalists went down in defeat, and they did not survive as a political movement. Yet they left an important legacy. At their insistence, the Virginia, New York, and Massachusetts conventions ratified the Constitution with the accompanying request that the new charter be amended to include a bill of rights protecting Americans' basic freedoms. So widespread was the public demand for a bill of rights that it became an inevitable item on the new government's agenda, even as the states were choosing members of Congress and as presidential electors were unanimously designating George Washington president of the United States, with John Adams as vice president.

Antifederalists' objections in New York also stimulated a response in the form of one of the greatest works of political analysis ever written: *The Federalist,* a series of eighty-five newspaper essays penned by John Jay, Alexander Hamilton, and James Madison. *The Federalist* papers probably had little or no influence on the voting in the New York State convention. Rather, their importance lay in providing a glimpse of the framers' intentions in designing the Constitution, and thus powerfully shaping the American philosophy of government. The Constitution, insisted *The Federalist*'s authors, had a twofold purpose: first, to defend the minority's rights against majority tyranny; and second, to prevent a stubborn minority from blocking well-considered measures that the majority believed necessary for the national interest. Critics, argued *The Federalist,* had no reason to fear that the Constitution would allow a single economic or regional interest to dominate. In the profoundest essay in the series, *Federalist* No. 10, Madison rejected the Antifederalist argument that establishing a republic for a nation as large as the United States would unleash a chaotic contest for power and ultimately leave the majority exploited by a minority. "Extend the sphere," Madison insisted, "and . . . you make it less probable that a majority of the whole will have a common motive to invade the rights of other citizens, . . . [or will be able to] act in unison with each other." The country's very size and diversity would theoretically neutralize the attempts of factions to manipulate unwise laws through Congress.

Madison's analysis was far too optimistic, however. As the Antifederalists predicted, the Constitution afforded enormous scope for special interests to influence the government. The great challenge for Madison's generation would be how to maintain a government that would provide equal benefits to all but at the same time accord special privileges to none.

Conclusion

The entry of North Carolina into the Union in late 1789 and of Rhode Island in May 1790 marked the final triumph of the nationalism born of the War for Independence. The devastating eight-year conflict swept up half of all men of military age and made casualties of one-fifth of these. Never before had such a large part of the population been called on to make sacrifices in a common cause of this magnitude.

The collective experience of fighting together as countrymen made many veterans self-consciously American. After several years in the army, General Nathaniel Greene of Rhode Island condemned the "prejudices" of those with "local attachments." "I feel the cause and not the place," Greene said; "I would as soon go to Virginia [to fight] as stay here [New England]." The distractions of peace almost allowed this sentiment to evaporate, but the Constitution offered the firmest proof that a growing number of Americans now felt comfortable viewing themselves as a common people rather than citizens of allied states.

CHRONOLOGY

1770 Yearly Meeting of New England Quakers prohibits slaveowning—first American ban on slaveholding.

1775 Virginia governor Lord Dunmore promises freedom to any slave assisting in the restoration of royal authority.

First white settlement in Kentucky.

Mercy Otis Warren, *The Group.*

1776 British troops evacuate Boston.

British defeat American forces under George Washington in fighting around New York City.

American victory in Battle of Trenton.

1777 American victory in Battle of Princeton.

British general John Burgoyne surrenders at Saratoga.

Battle of Brandywine Creek; British occupy Philadelphia.

British general William Howe defeats Washington at Battle of Germantown.

1778 France formally recognizes the United States.

France declares war on Britain.

Philadelphia evacuated by British general Henry Clinton; Battle of Monmouth Court House (New Jersey).

George Rogers Clark captures Kaskakia (Ill.), Cahokia (Ill.), and Vincennes (Ind.).

British occupy Savannah.

1779 Spain declares war on Britain.

George Rogers Clark's recapture of Fort Vincennes.

1780 British seize Charleston.

Dutch Republic declares war on Britain.

1781 Articles of Confederation become law.

Battle of Yorktown; British general Charles Cornwallis surrenders.

1782 British evacuate Savannah.

Paris peace negotiations begin.

1783 Peace of Paris.

1784 Spain closes New Orleans to American trade.

1785 Ordinance of 1785.

Treaty of Fort McIntosh.

1786 Congress rejects Jay-Gardoqui Treaty.

Fort Detroit Indian conference leads to resumption of Indian warfare.

Virginia adopts Thomas Jefferson's Statute of Religious Freedom.

1786–1787 Shays's Rebellion in Massachusetts.

1787 Northwest Ordinance.

Philadelphia Convention; federal Constitution signed.

1788 James Madison, Alexander Hamilton, and John Jay, *The Federalist.*

Federal Constitution becomes law.

1792 Mary Wollstonecraft, *Vindication of the Rights of Women.*

For Further Reading

Jack P. Greene, ed., *The American Revolution: Its Character and Limits* (1987). Leading scholars' analysis of how Americans dealt with the problem of applying their political ideals to an imperfect society without endangering the nation's survival.

Don Higginbotham, *The War of American Independence: Military Attitudes, Policies, and Practice, 1763–1789* (1971). An excellent examination of how military policies and events affected society and reflected contemporary attitudes toward war.

Linda K. Kerber, *Women of the Republic: Intellect and Ideology in Revolutionary America* (1980). A pathbreaking study of how the Revolution affected women's legal and social status.

Robert Middlekauff, *The Glorious Cause: The American Revolution, 1763–1789* (1982). The best compre-

hensive account of military and political developments through the Philadelphia Convention.

Benjamin Quarles, *The Negro in the American Revolution* (1961). An authoritative study of blacks' role in the War for Independence and the struggle's consequences for them.

Charles Royster, *A Revolutionary People at War: The Continental Army and American Character* (1980). An illuminating analysis of how Revolutionary Americans created and fought in an army and what this reveals about their emotions, attitudes, and ideals.

Gordon Wood, *The Creation of the American Republic, 1776–1787* (1969). The most comprehensive treatment of the evolution of American political thought from the creation of the first state governments to the Philadelphia Convention.

Additional Bibliography

The Military Struggle

Wallace Brown, *The King's Friends: The Composition and Motives of the American Loyalist Claimants* (1965); Richard Buel, Jr., *Dear Liberty: Connecticut's Mobilization for the Revolutionary War* (1980); Robert M. Calhoon, *The Loyalists in Revolutionary America, 1760–1781* (1973); E. Wayne Carp, *To Starve the Army at Pleasure: Continental Army Administration and American Political Culture, 1775–1783* (1984); Lawrence D. Cress, *Citizens in Arms: The Army and the Militia in American Society to the War of 1812* (1982); Jonathan R. Dull, *A Diplomatic History of the American Revolution* (1985); William M. Fowler, *Rebels Under Sail: The American Navy During the Revolution* (1976); Barbara Graymont, *The Iroquois in the American Revolution* (1972); Ira D. Gruber, *The Howe Brothers and the American Revolution* (1972); Ronald Hoffman and Peter J. Albert, eds., *Arms and Independence: The Military Character of the American Revolution* (1984); Ronald Hoffman and Thad W. Tate, eds., *An Uncivil War: The Southern Backcountry During the American Revolution* (1985); James K. Martin and Mark E. Lender, *A Respectable Army: The Military Origins of the Republic, 1763–1789* (1982); William H. Nelson, *The American Tory* (1961); James O'Donnell, *Southern Indians in the American Revolution* (1973); Howard H. Peckham, *The Toll of Independence: Engagements and Battle Casualties of the American Revolution* (1974); John Shy, *A People Numerous and Armed: Reflections on the Military Struggle for American Independence* (1976); Paul H. Smith, *Loyalists and Redcoats: A Study in British Revolutionary Policy* (1964); Jack M. Sosin, *The Revolutionary Frontier, 1763–1783* (1967).

Revolutionary Society

Robert A. Becker, *Revolution, Reform, and the Politics of American Taxation, 1763–1783* (1980); Ira Berlin and Ronald Hoffman, eds., *Slavery and Freedom in the Age of the American Revolution* (1983); Joy Day Buel and Richard Buel, Jr., *The Way of Duty: A Woman and Her Family in Revolutionary America* (1984); Jeffrey J. Crow and Larry E. Tise, *The Southern Experience in the American Revolution* (1978); Linda Grant DePauw, *Founding Mothers: Women in America in the Revolutionary Era* (1975); Peter C. Hoffer, *Revolution and Regeneration: Life Cycle and the Historical Vision of the Generation of 1776* (1983); Rhys Isaac, *The Transformation of Virginia, 1740–1790* (1982); Michael Kammen, *A Season of Youth: The American Revolution and the Historical Imagination* (1978); Duncan J. MacLeod, *Slavery, Race, and the American Revolution* (1974); Jackson Turner Main, *The Social Structure of Revolutionary America* (1965); John E. Selby, *The Revolution in Virginia, 1775–1783* (1988); Kenneth Silverman, *A Cultural History of the American Revolution: Painting, Music, Literature, and the Theatre in the Colonies and the United States from the Treaty of Paris to the Inauguration of George Washington, 1763–1789* (1976).

Politics and Constitutionalism

Willi Paul Adams, *The First American Constitutions: Republican Ideology and the Making of the State Constitutions in the Revolutionary Era* (1980); Richard Beeman et al., eds., *Beyond Confederation: Origins of the Constitution and American National Identity* (1987); Van Beck Hall, *Politics Without Parties: Massachusetts,*

1780–1791 (1972); Donald S. Lutz, *Popular Consent and Popular Control: Whig Political Theory in the Early State Constitutions* (1980); Forrest McDonald, *E Pluribus Unum: The Formation of the American Republic, 1776–1790* (1965), and *Novus Ordo Seclorum: The Intellectual Origins of the Constitution* (1985); Jackson Turner Main, *The Antifederalists: Critics of the Constitution, 1781–1788* (1961), and *Political Parties Before the Constitution* (1973); Anne M. Ousterhout, *A State Divided: Opposition in Pennsylvania to the American Revolution* (1987); John G. A. Pocock, *The Machiavellian Moment: Florentine Political Thought and the Atlantic Republican Tradition* (1975); Norman K. Risjord, *Chesapeake Politics, 1781–1800* (1978); David P. Szatmary, *Shays' Rebellion: The Making of an Agrarian Insurrection* (1980).

Biographies

James T. Flexner, *Washington: The Indispensable Man* (1974); Don Higginbotham, *Daniel Morgan: Revolutionary Rifleman* (1961); Isabel Thompson Kelsay, *Joseph Brant, 1743–1807: Man of Two Worlds* (1984); Ralph Ketcham, *Benjamin Franklin* (1966), and *James Madison: A Biography* (1971); Dumas Malone, *Jefferson and the Rights of Man* (1951); David Nelson, *Anthony Wayne, Soldier of the Early Republic* (1985), and *William Alexander, Lord Stirling* (1987); Charles Royster, *Light-Horse Harry Lee and the Legacy of the American Revolution* (1981); George T. Thayer, *Nathaniel Greene: Strategist of the American Revolution* (1960); Carl J. Vipperman, *The Rise of Rawlins Lowndes, 1721–1800* (1978); William B. Willcox, *Portrait of a General: Sir Henry Clinton in the War of Independence* (1964).

CHAPTER 6

Launching the New Republic, 1789–1800

Early in 1789 a mysterious stranger from New Orleans named André Fagot appeared in Nashville, Tennessee. Fagot was officially there to talk business with local merchants, but in reality he was a Spanish agent sent to stir up discontent. For years, westerners had agonized over the American government's failure to win Spanish permission for them to export crops through New Orleans, without which their settlements would never flourish. Fagot made westerners a tempting offer—unrestricted export privileges at New Orleans, which promised to ensure them prosperity. But in return, they would have to request that Spain annex Tennessee to its Louisiana colony.

Fagot found many local residents willing to discuss becoming Spanish subjects. One of his more enthusiastic contacts was a young lawyer recently arrived from the Carolinas. Aware that poor communities could support only poor lawyers, the Carolinian was drawn irresistibly to the plot. Learning that Spain would give valuable land grants in the lower Mississippi Valley to anyone who renounced United States citizenship, the lawyer began visiting Spanish Louisiana regularly to investigate settling there. Fagot probably placed little reliance on this brash conspirator, who had a wild temper and a reputation for gambling and drinking. In 1789 he seemed just another frontier opportunist. But in little more than a quarter-century, the Nashville lawyer would become the country's most popular hero and the symbol of American nationalism. He was Andrew Jackson.

The fact that even Jackson could talk secession to Spanish agents underscores the fragility of the United States in 1789, one year after the Constitution's ratification. North Carolina (which controlled Tennessee territory) and Rhode Island had not yet joined the Union. Westerners appeared to be abandoning the new government. The United States faced the prospect that foreign powers would slice off western territory. The nation could conceivably have disintegrated into several smaller republics, much as Latin America would splinter into numerous nations after rebelling against Spain in the early nineteenth century.

Few incoming American presidents have confronted as many grave problems as did George Washington in 1789. The West might well have separated from the Union. Indians and frontier whites fought endlessly. Foreign restrictions on U.S. exports threatened the nation's economy. The treasury was bankrupt, and the government's credit in a shambles.

The most serious obstacles facing the United States in 1789 were overcome by the time Washington's second administration ended in 1797, but only at the price of unleashing fiercely emotional party divisions among citizens. By 1798 a sense of crisis gripped the nation. The party in power resorted to political repression. Fearing that a fair election might be impossible and that the national government was slipping into despotism, the opposing party desperately tried to justify the right of state legislatures to veto federal laws. In the election of 1800, each side damned the other in increasingly irresponsible rhetoric. Only when the election had been settled—by the narrowest of margins—could it be said that the United States had managed to avoid dissolution and preserve civil liberties for its citizens.

The Fragile New Nation

By 1789 six years had elapsed since Britain had recognized U.S. independence, but for many Americans peace had brought problems rather than prosperity. Restrictions on export markets endangered the livelihoods of innumerable farmers, sailors, and merchants. Foreign efforts to prevent Americans from settling the frontier frustrated influential land speculators and toiling pioneers. The Confederation's default on the national debt had injured tens of thousands of Revolutionary creditors from all levels of society by delaying their compensation, and even after 1788 there was no guarantee that the new government would honor their claims fully. All these conditions had helped convince prominent Americans that a new constitution and a new government were desperately needed. But Antifederalists had not disappeared from public life, and supporters of the new government faced enormous pressure to succeed.

In the first two decades under the Constitution, it proved impossible for the government to devise policies that would provide equal benefits throughout the land. The different regions' interests varied greatly and often conflicted. Other fissures also became apparent in American society: among blacks, Indians, and whites; between emerging capitalists and wage-earning workers; above all, among citizens who interpreted the republican ideology of the Revolutionary years in different ways.

Regional and ideological conflicts would split the new nation's Congress, first into factions and then into hostile parties—just what the Constitution's framers had hoped to avoid. And political polarization would also bring into focus something else that few members of the Philadelphia Convention had favored: a rising demand for a *democratic* republic.

The West

Most U.S. territory from the Appalachians to the Mississippi River belonged to those peoples whom the Declaration of Independence had condemned as "merciless Indian savages." Divided into more than eighty tribes and numbering perhaps 150,000

persons in 1789, these native Americans were struggling to preserve their way of life. During the Revolutionary War, Anglo-Americans had dealt the Iroquois and Cherokees a punishing series of blows. But most Indians, although bloodied, continued to resist threats to their land. Tribes in the Ohio Valley formed a defensive confederacy in 1786 (see Chapter 5). The powerful southeastern tribes refused to acknowledge American rule. Great Britain openly backed Indian resistance in the Northwest, and Spain armed the southeastern native Americans. As the Constitution took effect, the federal government faced the prospect of having to force Britain and Spain to abandon the Indians and then of negotiating land purchases from them.

Confronting the inland Indians were approximately two hundred thousand whites and blacks who had hacked homesteads out of the raw wilderness. Although their ranks included some well-to-do planters and merchants, most families found life exceedingly harsh. Above all, frontier settlers were isolated and vulnerable. By 1786 a succession of Indian war parties spread death, destruction, and anxiety from Pennsylvania to Georgia. In Kentucky alone, where just 74,000 settlers lived in 1790, more than 1,500 pioneers were killed or captured in Indian raids from 1784 to 1790—a casualty rate twice as high as that of the Revolutionary War. Frontier people retaliated ruthlessly. "The people of Kentucky," wrote an army officer trying to end the fighting, "will carry on private expeditions against the Indians and kill them whenever they meet them, and I do not believe there is a jury in all Kentucky will punish a man for it."

Whites could conquer the Indians only by mustering overwhelming military force and threatening entire tribes with starvation by ravaging their villages and stocks of winter food. Such large-scale operations lay beyond the capability of poorly equipped, ill-trained frontier militia. This fact became obvious in 1786, when a lack of supplies forced 1,200 Kentuckians marching under George Rogers Clark against the Indians of the Great Lakes region to abandon their campaign. If Clark, who had prevailed against enormous odds during the

Revolution, found himself thus overwhelmed, clearly only federal forces could defeat the Indians. But in 1789 the U.S. Army's total strength was 672 soldiers, less than half the number of warriors that the northwestern Indian confederation could raise. Little wonder that the weakness of the U.S. government caused many frontier folk to despair—and to decide that the United States had forfeited their loyalty. Clark spoke for untold Kentuckians in 1788 when he declared that "no property or person is safe under a government so weak as that of the United States."

Nevertheless, militia raids across the Ohio River did force the Miamis, Shawnees, and Delawares gradually to evacuate southern Indiana and Ohio. These Indians' withdrawal northward, toward the Great Lakes, tempted whites to make their first settlements in what is now Ohio. In the spring of 1788, about fifty New Englanders sailed down the Ohio River in a bullet-proof barge named the *Mayflower* and founded the town of Marietta. That same year, some Pennsylvanians and New Jerseyites established a second community north of the Ohio, on the site of modern-day Cincinnati. By then the contest for the Ohio Valley was nearing a decisive stage.

Westerners felt a special bitterness toward the British. The recent enemy's continued occupation of seven forts on American soil seemed the mainspring of the unceasing border fighting. Royal diplomats justified this violation of the Peace of Paris by citing certain states' failure to compensate loyalists for confiscated property and to honor prewar debts owed by U.S. citizens. But these complaints served only as pretexts for retarding American expansion westward until Britain could sponsor an Indian buffer state south of the Great Lakes and possibly annex the region to Canada. Meanwhile, the lingering British presence in the Northwest allowed Canadian fur traders to maintain a brisk business there.

Spaniards' intentions of acquiring U.S. territory were equally transparent, particularly when they hinted that Indian raids on the frontier would stop if the settlers asked for Spanish citizenship. Spain exerted even more formidable leverage on westerners by closing New Orleans to American commerce in 1784. This action lured some leading westerners into a web of secret negotiations known

Spanish Claims to American Territory, 1783–1796

Spain refused to recognize Britain's 1783 cession to the United States of all territory north of the 31st parallel. The Spanish occupied Florida as it had been ceded to Britain in the Treaty of Paris (1763) and claimed all or part of five future states south of the Tennessee River and west of the Flint River.

as the Spanish Conspiracy. Noting that Congress under the Articles of Confederation seemed ready to accept the permanent closing of New Orleans in return for Spanish concessions elsewhere (see Chapter 5), many westerners began talking openly of secession. "I am decidedly of the opinion," anxiously wrote Kentucky's attorney general in 1787, "that this western country will in a few years Revolt from the Union and endeavor to erect an Independent Government." In 1788 Tennessee conspirators boldly advertised their flirtation with Spain by naming a large district along the Cumberland River after Spain's governor in New Orleans. Most westerners who accepted Spanish favors and gold meant only to pocket badly needed cash in return for vague promises of goodwill. The episode showed, however, that leading citizens were susceptible to foreign manipulation and subversion. As young Andrew Jackson concluded in 1789, making some arrangements with the Spanish seemed "the only immediate way to obtain peace with the Savage [Indians]."

The South

Meanwhile, southerners watched the deterioration of Anglo-American fortunes in the West with particular concern. Many southern citizens had acquired a personal stake in trans-Appalachian affairs because Virginia and North Carolina had rewarded Revolutionary soldiers with western land. Whether these veterans intended to move west themselves or to profit by selling their rights to others, all wanted to see the western territories prosper. Hoping to make a quick fortune in land speculation, southern planters (including George Washington) had borrowed heavily to buy frontier real estate; but uncertainty about the West's future made them worry that land prices would crash. By 1789 a potent combination of small farmers and landed gentry in the South had become enraged at foreign barriers to frontier expansion and eagerly supported politicians, among them Thomas Jefferson and James Madison, who advocated strong measures against the British and Spanish.

Aside from the frustrated ambitions of southern land speculators, however, the region's economy had largely recovered from the Revolution. The South was exporting as much tobacco by 1786 as before the Revolution and was earning prices that equaled or exceeded prewar levels. Furthermore, the southern economy had become increasingly diversified as grain harvests rose sharply in the Chesapeake, hemp production expanded noticeably in Virginia, and indigo culture temporarily revived in South Carolina and Georgia. Agricultural income seemingly was growing less dependent on the fate of one or two staple crops than during the colonial era. The South's recovery lagged only in the coastal districts of South Carolina, where the war had taken an especially destructive course. By 1789 agriculture and commerce had recuperated to such an extent that every southern state except South Carolina had made substantial progress in retiring its war debt.

The North

In the North, in such states as Pennsylvania and New York, agricultural production benefited from a steady demand for foodstuffs and by 1788 had largely recovered from the Revolution's ravages. As famine stalked Europe, American farmers in the Delaware and Hudson River valleys prospered from climbing export prices.

New Englanders were not so fortunate. A short growing season and poor soil kept yields so low, even in the best of times, that farmers barely produced enough grain for local consumption. New Englanders also faced both high taxes to repay the money borrowed to finance the Revolution and a tightening of credit that spawned countless lawsuits against debtors. These problems had sparked Shays's Rebellion in 1786 and still defied solution. Whereas most southern states had largely eliminated their war debts and the Middle Atlantic states had made great progress in managing theirs, New England taxpayers remained under a crushing obligation. Economic depression only aggravated the region's chronic overpopulation. Young New England men continued migrating to the frontier

Regional Diversity, c. 1790–1800

(Right) Rockett's Landing on the James River, in the heart of fertile land near the head of the tidewater; (center) the New England countryside near Worcester, Massachusetts; (far right) a Pennsylvania barn. The interests and commercial activities of the sections varied markedly in the Republic's early years.

or to the cities, and their discontent and restless mobility loosened the bonds of parental authority and left many women without marriage prospects.

New England's fishing fleet and merchant marine also discovered the high price of independence. Prior to 1775, when every colonial vessel enjoyed the protection of the Navigation Acts, the region's maritime community had employed approximately 15 percent of all adult males. After Independence, however, Britain quickly slapped strict limitations on U.S. commerce. The new republic's ships lost all rights to carry cargoes to the West Indies and faced high customs fees for landing products in Great Britain. For the most part, American foodstuffs, lumber, and tobacco were welcome in Britain only if they arrived in British ships. Because half of all U.S. exports went to Great Britain or its West Indian colonies, these restrictions allowed British shippers to increase their share of the Atlantic trade at American expense.

Only with difficulty did the U.S. merchant marine survive in these years. Resourceful captains took cargoes to the French West Indies, Scandinavia, and even China. Wily Yankee skippers were also surprisingly successful in smuggling foodstuffs to the British West Indies under the very nose of the Royal Navy. Nevertheless, British policies imposed real hardship on New England, whose economy depended heavily on fishing and ocean commerce. By 1791 discriminatory British treatment had reduced the number of seamen in the Massachusetts cod and whale fisheries by 42 percent compared to the 1770s. Recognizing that Great Britain could not be forced to grant trade concessions, New England's leaders preferred to solve the problem through peaceful accommodation, an approach entirely opposite to western and southern preferences for direct confrontation with Britain—even at the risk of war.

Entrepreneurs, Artisans, and Wage Earners

After 1783, through the enterprise of an ambitious, aggressive class of businessmen, the northern economy became less dependent on farming. Most of these individuals had begun as merchants, and they now used their profits to invest in factories, ships, government bonds, and banks (see "A Place in Time"). These men believed that the United States would gain strength if Americans balanced agriculture with banking, manufacturing, and commerce, and they wanted to limit American dependence on imported British manufactures. They also insisted that the nation needed a healthy merchant marine standing ready to augment U.S. naval forces in wartime.

Philadelphia in the 1790s

*F*rom 1790 to 1800, Philadelphia was the United States' capital, largest city, main financial market, and intellectual and scientific center. Home to forty-four thousand people in 1790, by 1800 Philadelphia almost doubled its population. This growth occurred despite a frightful yellow-fever epidemic in 1793, which cost several thousand lives and sent everyone (including President Washington and the entire federal government) fleeing until cooler weather killed the infection-bearing mosquitoes. A constant stream of country people and foreign immigrants poured in, and large numbers of Germans, French, Irish, and Scots kept Philadelphia's population diverse.

Most Philadelphians belonged to artisan families practicing such trades as carpentry, bricklaying, tailoring, and leatherworking. These crafts supplied the city's elite with elegant imitations of the latest European fashions in dress, furniture, and housing. Modestly endowed artisans, small merchants, and professional men lived comfortably, if not opulently. Such was not the case for many of the newcomers, who generally found themselves trapped amid the expanding ranks of propertyless, ill-paid wage workers.

Among poor Philadelphians were 1,640 blacks counted by the 1790 census, all but 210 of them free. (Pennsylvania had enacted gradual emancipation in 1780.) Whereas some slaves had been trained in skilled trades like blacksmithing, young free men of color

Delaware River Front, Philadelphia, *by Thomas Birch*

The port of Philadelphia hummed with activity in the 1790s. Its wharves welcomed goods from all over the world, and Pennsylvania manufactures and farm products lined the riverfront, waiting for export.

found themselves excluded from such crafts and relegated to menial work. Still, free blacks strove to improve their lot: they maintained seven schools and a Methodist congregation led by a former slave. All these were segregated.

The richest 10 percent of Philadelphians owned about half the city's wealth. This upper crust included old Quaker merchant families, recent wartime profiteers, and hustling new entrepreneurs. Philadelphia was still a preindus-

trial city entirely dependent on foreign trade for its existence, and most of its wealthiest men made their fortunes in commerce.

Philadelphia's economic environment was treacherous, however. Given rapidly changing market conditions, merchants had to be ever ready to act decisively. They repeatedly gambled everything in hopes of developing new overseas markets for Delaware Valley foodstuffs or of expanding the sphere within which they could retail European-made

The Bank of Pennsylvania, *by Benjamin Latrobe, 1798*

Philadelphia, William Penn's "greene country towne," was a major financial center from 1790 to 1800. The city's banks and merchant exchange were among the United States' finest buildings in these years. The writer James Fenimore Cooper remarked that Philadelphia's splendid architecture was "a tribute to [the] gold . . . to be expected here."

imports. Overseas trade was the most nerve-wracking of all Philadelphia businesses. From 1785 to 1791, bankruptcies reduced the number of trading firms from 514 to 440. Of the sixty-five wealthiest traders operating in 1779, only nine were still in business seventeen years later. The survivors were calculating, daring, and grasping.

In 1776, into this competitive commercial world came the half-blind French immigrant Stephen Girard. Relying on a quick mind and a scrappy, abrasive personality, Girard struggled for years just to avoid bankruptcy. But he exemplified the traits necessary for commercial success in Philadelphia—a determination to conduct his business personally (even when laid up with a painful head wound) and a willingness to take chances. "Since I have not as much as I desire, it seems necessary for me to take some risks or remain always poor." By

1795 he ranked high among the city's wealthiest individuals.

Girard's phenomenal success stemmed from his refusal to imitate conservative businessmen, who demonstrated a "prudence that will risk nothing." He and his fellow entrepreneurs helped propel Philadelphia into the industrial age. They provided two essential elements that would transform the city's economy—capital amassed from foreign trade, and a readiness to take chances by investing in business ventures unrelated to commerce. Merchants had founded the city's banking system in 1781; later merchants would pool funds to establish competing banks. Among these was one started by Girard in 1812 that remained in operation until the 1970s. These banks were critical in providing venture capital for the building of factories. Many merchants also lent directly to entrepreneurs who were unable to obtain

loans from commercial banks, thus expanding opportunity for new areas of economic activity. Some merchants even invested in factories directly and lent important managerial skills that contributed to the success of these infant industries.

Amid the shifting sands of precarious commerce and embryonic industrial capitalism, Girard and his competitors in the 1790s helped a flourishing, cultured city continue to prosper. The well-to-do could even afford to send their daughters to the Young Ladies' Academy, founded in 1787 by Dr. Benjamin Rush. "The patriot—the hero—the legislator," Dr. Rush grandly proclaimed, "would find the sweetest reward for their toils, in the approbation of their wives"—and how better could young women bestow this approval than by being educated themselves? Among the subjects that they studied was bookkeeping.

Philadelphia's bustling commerce and entrepreneurial enterprise produced social strain. Journeymen printers and leatherworkers, for example, organized and struck in a vain attempt to avoid becoming permanent wage earners. Yet the city's most notable political pressure group of the 1790s did not promote class conflict. In this organization, Philadelphia's Democratic Society, artisan masters rubbed shoulders with members of the professional elite like Dr. Rush and famed scientist David Rittenhouse—and with entrepreneur Stephen Girard. What united these republican enthusiasts were a conviction that individuals of talent and ambition ought not be held back by special interests, an admiration for revolutionary France, and a determination to preserve the liberty so hard won in the American Revolution.

Such entrepreneurs stimulated a flurry of innovative business ventures that pointed toward the future. The country's first private banks were founded in the 1780s in Philadelphia, Boston, and New York. Philadelphia merchants created the Pennsylvania Society for the Encouragement of Manufactures and the Useful Arts in 1787. This organization promoted the immigration of English artisans familiar with the latest industrial technology, including Samuel Slater (see Chapter 8), who established the nation's first modern water-powered textile factory at Pawtucket, Rhode Island, in 1793. In 1791 investors from New York and Philadelphia started the Society for the Encouragement of Useful Manufactures, which attempted to demonstrate the potential of large-scale industrial enterprises by building a factory town at Paterson, New Jersey. That same year, New York merchants and insurance underwriters organized America's first formal association for trading government bonds, out of which the New York Stock Exchange evolved.

Many of these early enterprises ended in financial ruin, however, because they proved premature or unrealistic. Not a few of their promoters shared the fate of Philadelphia businessman Robert Morris, who had signed both the Declaration of Independence and Constitution yet would spend three years in a debtor's prison after 1798. But the vision of these men was ultimately vindicated, for as often happens, failure preceded success: in the nineteenth century, the United States gradually became an industrial society.

Yet in 1789 the northeastern cities remained overwhelmingly preindustrial, without large factories. Half the urban work force consisted of "mechanics," whose ranks included both master artisans and journeymen. Mechanics manufactured goods by hand, typically in workshops where the master and his family employed a few journeymen or apprentices. Journeymen changed jobs frequently; those hired in Samuel Ashton's Philadelphia cabinet shop, for example, stayed an average of just six months between 1795 and 1803. Moreover, well-to-do artisan households, as well as professional and upper-class families, employed numerous servants. And masters and other employers could draw upon the growing ranks of low-paid day workers, who included most free blacks and many orphans, widows, and drifters.

Certificate of the "New York Mechanick Society," c. 1785

In the face of changing times and narrowing opportunity, many urban artisans organized societies to set wages and working hours.

Mechanics tended to follow in their fathers' occupational footsteps. They lived in close-knit neighborhoods with others who practiced their trade and with whom they enjoyed such traditional pastimes as drinking, marching, and "mobbing." Their wives and daughters often helped in the shop but rarely sought outside employment unless widowed or orphaned. Despite their industriousness and thrift, mechanics faced stiff competition from British manufacturers, who increasingly used labor-saving machinery and unskilled, low-paid labor. Consequently, American mechanics were disposed to support political leaders willing to raise the price of imported British goods through a national tariff. Most mechanics had supported the Constitution, hoping that it would create a strong and assertive national government.

A few artisans succeeded in adapting techniques of large-scale production to their crafts. The textile-finishing, printing, furniture-making, and construction trades most successfully exploited new technology or unskilled wage labor; they offered many opportunities for master artisans to establish flourishing family businesses. But most mechanics were either reluctant to abandon traditional household-oriented shops for an impersonal factory system or else could not modernize for lack of credit, which was scarce and expensive. Many artisans thus found opportunity shrinking, and they responded by organizing societies to set wages and working hours. Over the long run, the artisan community would contract as mechanics themselves became wage earners working for entrepreneurial industrialists; but in the 1790s these trends were only beginning to emerge.

In 1789 virtually all politically conscious Americans—entrepreneurs and merchants, urban mechanics and frontier settlers, nationalists and Antifederalists, northerners and southerners—expressed their hopes for the nation's future in terms of republican ideals. These lofty goals of selfless service to the general good had helped community leaders rally the public behind them in resisting British encroachments since the 1760s. Republican ideology had guided the men who hammered out state constitutions and the new federal Constitution, and it had also helped Antifederalists state their case against the Constitution. Now in the 1790s, how to interpret republican ideals, with their abiding distrust of government power, became a nagging question in the cut-and-thrust of everyday politics. Most Americans thought that they knew what republican virtue meant, and most tended to condemn rivals' views as the road to corruption. Noting in *The Federalist* the numerous divergent meanings of the word *republican,* James Madison had concluded that "no satisfactory one would ever be found."

Constitutional Government Takes Shape

Traveling slowly over the nation's miserable roads, the men entrusted with launching the federal experiment began assembling in New York, the new national capital, in March 1789. Because so few members were on hand, Congress opened its session a month late. George Washington did not arrive until April 23 and only took his oath of office a week later.

The slowness of these first halting steps, however, disguised the seriousness of the tasks at hand. The country's elected leaders had to make far-reaching decisions on several critical questions left

unresolved by the Constitution's framers. For example, the Constitution gave the president no formal responsibility for preparing a legislative agenda, although it allowed him wide discretion by directing him to make periodic reports on the state of the Union and by permitting him to recommend matters for Congress's consideration. The Philadelphia Convention likewise had not specified whether cabinet officers would be accountable to Congress or to the president. Nor did the Constitution say how the federal court system should be structured. Finally, widespread distrust of any government unrestrained by a bill of rights required that Congress prepare amendments for the states' consideration, but the exact scope and character of these amendments remained to be determined. "We are in a wilderness," wrote James Madison, "without a footstep to guide us."

Consequently, even though the Constitution had been ratified as the supreme law of the land, its framers' intentions might still have been reversed. The First Congress could easily have weakened presidential authority, limited access to federal courts, or passed amendments resurrecting features of the Articles of Confederation. Antifederalists conceivably could have convoked another constitutional convention, ostensibly to prepare a bill of rights but actually to rewrite the entire Constitution. In 1789 the nation's future remained unsettled in these, as in many other, regards.

Defining the Presidency

No office in the new government aroused more suspicion than the presidency. Many feared that the president's powers could make him a virtual king. Public apprehension remained in check only because of George Washington's reputation for honesty. Washington tried to calm fears of unlimited executive power. His careful behavior established important precedents that until the 1820s restrained his successors from becoming actively involved in the preparation of legislation.

The Constitution mentioned the executive departments only in passing, required the president to obtain the Senate's approval for his nominees to head these bureaus, and made all executive personnel liable to impeachment. Otherwise, Congress was free to determine the organization and accountability of what became known as the cabinet. The first cabinet, established by Congress, consisted of four departments, headed by the secretaries of state, treasury, and war and by the attorney general. Vice President John Adams's tie-breaking vote defeated a proposal that would have forbidden the president from dismissing cabinet officers without Senate approval. This outcome reinforced the president's authority to make and carry out policy; it also separated the powers of the executive and legislative branches beyond what the Constitution required, and so made the president a more equal partner with Congress.

President Washington suggested few laws to Congress. Rarely did he speak out against opponents of government policy, and generally he limited his public statements to matters of foreign relations and military affairs. He deferred to congressional decisions concerning domestic policy whenever possible and cast only two vetoes during his eight-year tenure (1789–1797).

Washington tried to reassure the public that he was above favoritism and conflicts of interest. Believing himself duty-bound to seek advice from a wide range of opinions, he balanced his cabinet with southerners and northeasterners. When Secretary of State Thomas Jefferson opposed certain policies of Secretary of the Treasury Alexander Hamilton, Washington implored Jefferson not to leave his post, even though the president supported Hamilton.

"He is polite with dignity, affable without familiarity, distant without haughtiness, grave without austerity, modest, wise, and good." So Abigail Adams, the wife of the vice president, described Washington. Once the government had settled into Philadelphia (the nation's capital from 1790 to 1800), the president enjoyed the private company of wealthy citizens, but he felt truly comfortable only at his Virginia estate, Mount Vernon, or on the Pennsylvania farm he rented. More than any other national leader, Washington sincerely strove to understand the aspirations of the two groups that dominated American society—northeastern merchants and entrepreneurs, and southern planters. Like most republican leaders, he believed that the proper role for ordinary citizens was not to set policy through elections but rather to choose well-educated, politically sophisticated men who would make laws in the people's best

interest, though independently of direct popular influence.

The president endured rather than enjoyed the pomp of office. Suffering from a variety of ailments that grew as the years passed, Washington longed to escape the presidency. Only with difficulty was he persuaded to accept reelection in 1792. He feared dying while in office and thus setting the precedent for a lifetime presidency. With great anxiety he realized that "the preservation of the sacred fire of liberty and the destiny of the republican model of government are . . . *deeply*, perhaps *finally*, staked on the experiment entrusted to the hands of the American people." Should he contribute to that experiment's failure, he feared, his name would live only as an "awful monument."

National Justice and the Bill of Rights

The Constitution merely authorized Congress to establish federal courts below the level of the Supreme Court; it had offered no guidance as to how the judicial system should be structured. And although the Constitution specifically barred the federal government from committing such abuses as passing ex post facto laws* and bills of attainder,[†] the absence of a comprehensive bill of rights had led several delegates at Philadelphia to refuse to sign the Constitution and had been a major point of attack by Antifederalists. The task of filling in these gaps fell to the First Congress.

In 1789 many citizens feared that the new federal courts would ride roughshod over local customs. Every state had gradually devised a unique, time-honored blend of judicial procedures appropriate to local circumstances. Any attempt to force states to abandon their legal heritage would have produced strong counterdemands that federal justice be narrowly restricted. Bowing to such sentiments, Congress might have drastically curtailed the scope and power of the federal judiciary or

---

*Ex post facto law: a law criminalizing previously legal actions and punishing those who have been engaging in such actions.

[†]Bill of attainder: a legislative act proclaiming a person's guilt and stipulating punishment without a judicial trial.

limited the federal judicial system to the Supreme Court. Congress might also have forbidden federal judges to accept cases from the states on a range of subjects (as permitted by Article III, Section 2). Such actions by Congress would have tipped the balance of power in the new nation to the states.

But when it passed the Judiciary Act of 1789, which created the federal-court system, Congress did not seek to hobble the national judiciary. Yet the act managed to quiet popular apprehensions by establishing in each state a federal district court that operated according to local procedures. A district-court ruling could be appealed to a federal circuit court. Each circuit court consisted of one district-court judge and two Supreme Court justices (who would travel among certain states between Supreme Court sessions), and the three would decide cases according to state laws. But as the Constitution stipulated, the Supreme Court exercised final jurisdiction. Congress had struck a reasonable compromise that respected state traditions while offering wide access to federal justice.

In fulfilling its mandate to guarantee personal liberties, the First Congress sifted through 210 proposals for constitutional amendments. There was no consensus, however, as to what a bill of rights should provide, and a strong possibility existed that Antifederalists would manipulate the widespread public desire for protection of individual rights into a campaign to return power to the states. James Madison, who had been elected to the House of Representatives, battled fiercely to keep the Constitution's opponents from undermining the powers essential for a firm national government. It was Madison who played the leading role in drafting the ten amendments that became known as the Bill of Rights when ratified by the states in December 1791.

Madison insisted that the first eight amendments guarantee personal liberties, not strip the national government of any necessary authority. All but one of these eight affirmed the rights of individuals rather than of state governments. Their most important provisions protected public debate, religious beliefs, and procedures for fair trials. The Ninth and Tenth amendments reserved to the people or to the states powers not allocated to the federal government under the Constitution, but Madison headed off proposals to limit federal power

more explicitly. In general, the Bill of Rights imposed no serious check on the framers' nationalist objectives.

The Bill of Rights made only one concession toward what would soon be termed states' rights. That sole exception was the Second Amendment, ensuring the *collective* right of each state's populace to maintain a militia free of federal interference. The implications of this "right to keep and bear arms" were profoundly disturbing. Its prominence as the second of the ten amendments, moreover, emphasized lingering fears that a powerful central government might degenerate into tyranny. In adopting the Second Amendment, the nation's politicians were playing with fire, for it represented nothing less than an invitation to civil war.

Once the Bill of Rights was in place, the federal judiciary moved decisively to establish its authority. In 1793, in *Chisholm* v. *Georgia,* the Supreme Court ruled that a state could be sued in federal courts by nonresidents. The next year, the Court declared its right to determine the constitutionality of congressional statutes in *Hylton* v. *United States* and to strike down state laws in *Ware* v. *Hylton.* But Congress decided that the Court had encroached too far on states' authority in *Chisholm,* and in 1794 it voted to overturn this decision through a constitutional amendment. Ratified in 1798, the Eleventh Amendment revised Article III, Section 2, so that private citizens could no longer undermine states' financial autonomy by using federal courts to sue another state's government in civil cases and claim money from that state's treasury. The defeat of *Chisholm* stands as one of the handful of instances in American history whereby the Supreme Court was subsequently overruled by a constitutional amendment.

By endorsing the Eleventh Amendment, Congress expressed its recognition that federal power could threaten vital local interests. Such awareness had been growing since the early 1790s, rupturing the nationalist coalition that had written the Constitution, secured its ratification, and dominated the First Congress. A dramatic sign of this split was James Madison's shift from nationalist to critic of excessive federal power in 1790–1791. Up to this time, Madison and most of his fellow nationalists had not thought very deeply about how federal power should be used. The chief exception was

Alexander Hamilton, whose bold program alienated many like-minded nationalists by demonstrating that federal policies could be shaped to reward special interests.

National Economic Policy and Its Consequences

Realizing that war would jeopardize national survival, Washington concentrated his attention on diplomacy and military affairs. His reluctance to become involved with pending legislation enabled his energetic secretary of the treasury, Alexander Hamilton, to set the administration's domestic priorities. Hamilton quickly emerged as the country's most imaginative and dynamic statesman by formulating a sweeping program for national economic development. But Hamilton's agenda proved deeply divisive.

Hamilton and His Objectives

Born in the West Indies in 1755, Hamilton had sailed to New York in 1772 to enroll at King's College (now Columbia University), where he had emerged as a passionate defender of American rights. He had entered the Continental Army in 1775, distinguished himself in battle several times, and won the nickname the Little Lion.

During his four years on Washington's staff, Hamilton developed an exceptionally close relationship with his commander in chief. Hamilton's mother had been the mistress of a Scottish merchant who had abandoned her and their children when Alexander was about ten. For Hamilton, Washington helped fill the emotional void created by his own father's desertion. At the same time, for the childless Washington, Hamilton became almost a son. Hamilton thus gained extraordinary influence over Washington, who despite misgivings frequently supported the younger man's policies.

Hamilton formulated his financial proposals to strengthen the nation against foreign enemies and also to lessen the threat of disunion. The most immediate danger concerned national security: the possibility of war with Great Britain, Spain, or both.

The Republic could finance a full-scale war only by borrowing heavily, but because Congress under the Articles of Confederation had failed to redeem or pay interest on the Revolutionary debt, the nation's credit had been ruined abroad and at home. The country's economy also seemed unequal to fighting a major European power. War with Britain would mean a blockade, which would strangle commerce and stop the importation of necessary manufactured goods. French assistance had overcome this danger during the Revolution; but France's navy had declined greatly since 1783 (while the British had vastly improved theirs). Moreover, growing political instability in France was transforming America's wartime ally into an uncertain friend. Unless the United States achieved self-sufficiency in the manufacture of vital industrial products and maintained a strong merchant marine ready for combat, its chances of surviving a second war with Britain appeared slim.

Hamilton also feared that the Union might disintegrate because of Americans' tendency to think first of their local loyalties and interests. He himself felt little personal identification with his adopted state, New York. His six years in the Continental Army produced a burning nationalistic faith. For him, the Constitution's adoption had been a close victory of national over state authority. Now he worried that the states might reassert power over the new government. If this happened, he doubted whether the nation could prevent ruinous trade discrimination between states, deter foreign aggression, and avoid civil war.

Both his wartime experiences and his view of human nature forged Hamilton's political beliefs. An enthusiastic young patriot who had fought bravely during the Revolution's darkest hours, Hamilton had grown profoundly disillusioned by civilian profiteering. Like many disappointed idealists, he became a cynic who believed that few could live up to his own standards. Thus he came to share the conviction of many other nationalists that the Republic's population (like the rest of humanity) would never show limitless self-sacrifice and virtue. Hamilton concluded that the federal government's survival depended on building support among politically influential citizens through a straightforward appeal to their financial interests. Private ambitions would then serve the national welfare.

Charming and brilliant, vain and handsome, a notorious womanizer, and thirsting for fame and power, Hamilton himself exemplified the worldly citizen whose fortunes he hoped to link to the republic's future. But to the growing ranks of his opponents, Hamilton would embody the dark forces luring the Republic to its doom—a man who, Jefferson wrote, believed in "the necessity of either force or corruption to govern men."

Report on the Public Credit

Seeking guidance on how to restore the nation's credit worthiness, in 1789 Congress directed the Treasury Department to evaluate the status of the Revolutionary debt. Hamilton seized the opportunity to devise policies that would not only rebuild the country's credit but also entice a key sector of the upper class to place their prestige and capital at its service. Congress received his Report on the Public Credit in January 1790. The report listed $54 million in United States debt: $42 million owed to Americans, and the rest to foreigners. Hamilton estimated that on top of the national debt, the states had debts of $25 million, an amount that included several million dollars that the United States had promised to reimburse, such as Virginia's expenses in defending settlements in the Ohio Valley.

Hamilton's first major recommendation was that the federal government compensate anyone possessing debt certificates issued by the Continental Congress at their full value. The government would obtain the necessary money by "funding" the debt—that is, raising the $54 million needed to honor the national debt by selling an equal sum in new bonds. Holders of the original debt could then be repaid in full unless they preferred to receive the reissued bonds. Retainers of the new bonds would earn 4 percent interest, and to pay that interest, Congress would levy duties on imports.

Second, the report proposed that the federal government pay off the state debts remaining from the Revolution. Such obligations would be funded along with the national debt in the manner described above. Once again, current holders would receive full value with interest.

Hamilton argued that the continued failure of certain states to honor their obligations would undermine U.S. credit in overseas markets. While this reasoning contained a kernel of truth, it masked his most important motive. He saw the federal assumption of state debts as a chance for the national government to win the gratitude and loyalty of state creditors by honoring their claims before the remaining states could manage to pay them. Since legislatures awash in debt wanted to avoid piling more taxes on the voters, they would accept any relief, regardless of Hamilton's actual intentions.

Hamilton exhorted the government to use the money earned by selling federal lands in the West to pay off the $12 million owed to Europeans as quickly as possible. The Treasury could easily accumulate the interest owed on the remaining $42 million by collecting customs duties on imports and excise taxes on whiskey distillers. An essential feature of Hamilton's plan was the creation of a "sinking fund"—a sum of money reserved solely for guaranteeing future interest payments, into which revenues would be "sunk." This precaution would establish public confidence by assuring bond holders that their investments would be safe because the government would always have funds to pay them their interest promptly. Furthermore, Hamilton proposed that money owed to American citizens should be made a permanent debt. That is, he urged that the government *not* attempt to repay the $42 million principal but instead keep paying interest to persons wishing to hold bonds as an investment. If Hamilton's recommendation were adopted, the only burden on the taxpayers would be the small annual cost of 4 percent interest. It

Continental Currency

Alexander Hamilton, *by John Trumbull, 1792*

Hamilton's self-confident pride clearly shows through in this portrait, painted at the height of his influence in the Washington administration.

would then be possible to uphold the national credit at minimal expense, without ever having to pay off the debt itself.

Hamilton advocated a perpetual debt above all as a lasting means of uniting the economic fortunes of the nation's creditors to the United States. In an age when financial investments were notoriously risky, the federal government would protect the savings of wealthy bond holders through conservative policies but still offer an interest rate competitive with the Bank of England's. The guarantee of future interest payments would act as the explicit link uniting the interests of the moneyed class with those of the government. Few other investments would entail so little risk.

The Report on the Public Credit provoked immediate controversy. While no one in Congress doubted that its provisions would fully restore the country's fiscal reputation, many objected that those

least deserving of reward would gain the most. The original owners of more than three-fifths of the debt certificates issued by the Continental Congress (ranging from George Washington to Revolutionary patriots of modest means) had long before sold theirs at a loss, many out of dire financial necessity. Foreseeing Hamilton's intentions, wealthy speculators, on the other hand, had by then accumulated large holdings at the expense of unsuspecting original owners. Now these astute speculators stood to reap huge gains, even collecting interest that had fallen due before they had purchased the certificates. "That the case of those who parted with their securities from necessity is a hard one, cannot be denied," Hamilton admitted. But making exceptions would be even worse.

To Hamilton's surprise, Madison—once an advocate of national assumption of state debts—emerged as one of the chief opponents of reimbursing current holders at face value. Madison tried but failed to obtain compensation for original owners who had sold their certificates. Congress rejected his suggestions partly because some congressmen were themselves speculators but primarily because preventing fraudulent claims would have been impossible.

Had Congress allowed popular pressure to influence how it repaid public creditors, however, the nation would have found it very hard to borrow money during future emergencies. Hamilton's policy was defensible and virtually inevitable; but it generated widespread resentment because it rewarded rich profiteers while ignoring the wartime sacrifices of ordinary citizens.

Opposition to assuming the state debts also ran high. Only the New England states, New Jersey, and South Carolina had failed to make effective provisions for paying their creditors. Understandably, the issue stirred the fiercest indignation in the South, which except for South Carolina had extinguished 83 percent of its debt. To allow residents of the laggard states to escape heavy taxes while others had liquidated theirs at great expense seemed to reward irresponsibility. Many Virginians, among them Madison, opposed Hamilton not only for reasons of high principle but also because of their state's self-interest. South Carolina became the sole southern state that supported Hamilton's policies.

Southern hostility almost defeated assumption. In the end, however, Hamilton managed to save his proposal by exploiting the strong desire among Virginians to relocate the national capital in their region. Virginians expected that moving the capital would make their state the crossroads of the country and thus help preserve its position as the nation's largest, most influential state. In return for the northern votes necessary to transfer the capital to the Potomac River, Hamilton secured enough Virginians' support to win the battle for assumption. Yet the debate over state debts alienated most southerners by confirming their suspicions that other regions monopolized the benefits of a stronger union.

Congressional enactment of the Report on the Public Credit dramatically reversed the nation's fiscal standing. Formerly scorned as a beggar country, the United States saw its financial reputation soar in 1790. Europeans grew so enthusiastic for U.S. bonds that by 1792 some securities were selling at 10 percent above face value.

Reports on the Bank and Manufactures

In December 1790 the secretary of the treasury presented Congress with a second message, the Report on a National Bank. Having managed to restore full faith in greatly undervalued certificates, Hamilton in effect had significantly expanded the stock of capital available for investment. He intended to direct that money toward projects that would diversify the national economy through a federally chartered bank.

The proposed bank would raise $10 million through a public stock offering. The Treasury would hold one-fifth of the stock and name one-fifth of the directors, but four-fifths of the control would fall to private hands. Private investors could purchase shares by paying for three-quarters of their value in government bonds. In this way, the bank would capture a significant portion of the recently funded debt and make it available for loans; it would also receive a substantial and steady flow of interest payments from the Treasury. Anyone buying shares under these circumstances had little chance of losing money and was positioned to profit handsomely.

Hamilton argued that the Bank of the United States would cost the taxpayers nothing and greatly benefit the nation. It would provide a safe place for the federal government to deposit tax revenues, make inexpensive loans to the government when taxes fell short, and help relieve the scarcity of hard cash by issuing paper notes that would circulate as money. Furthermore, it would possess authority to regulate the business practices of state banks. Above all, the bank would provide much needed credit to expand the economy.

Finally, Hamilton called for American economic self-sufficiency. He admired the "prodigious effect" on Great Britain's national wealth that the recent expansion of factories had stimulated in that nation, and he wanted to encourage similar industrialization in the United States. His Report on Manufactures of December 1791 advocated protective tariffs on foreign imports to foster domestic manufacturing, which in turn would both attract immigrants and create national wealth. Elsewhere the secretary called for assisting the merchant marine against British trade restrictions by reducing duties on goods imported into the United States on American ships and by offering subsidies (called bounties) for fishermen and whalers. These measures would also indirectly protect the national bank's loans to industrialists and shippers.

Hamilton's Challenge to Limited Government

In the eyes of many of the new government's supporters, Hamilton's plan to establish a permanent national debt violated the principle of equality among citizens; it seemed to favor the interests of public creditors over those of other Americans. Hamilton's critics also denounced his proposal for a national bank, interpreting it as a dangerous scheme that would give a small, elite group special power to influence the government.

The bank issue drew Thomas Jefferson into the ranks of Hamilton's opponents. It was almost an article of faith among Revolutionary-generation Americans like Madison and Jefferson that the Bank of England had undermined the integrity of government in Britain. Shareholders of the new Bank of the United States could just as easily become the tools of unscrupulous politicians. If significant numbers in Congress also owned bank stock, they would likely vote in support of the bank even at the cost of the national good. To Jefferson, the bank was "a machine for the corruption of the legislature [Congress]." Representative John Taylor of Virginia predicted that its vast wealth would enable the bank to take over the country, which would thereafter, he quipped, be known as the United States of the Bank.

Opponents' strongest argument against the bank was their claim of its unconstitutionality. The Constitution had given Congress no specific authorization to issue charters of incorporation. Unless Congress adhered to a "strict interpretation" of the Constitution, critics argued, the central government might oppress the states and trample individual liberties, just as Parliament had done to the colonies. Strictly limiting the powers of the government seemed the surest way of preventing the United States from degenerating into a corrupt despotism, as Britain had.

Congress approved the bank by only a thin margin. Doubtful of the bank's constitutionality, Washington turned for advice to both Jefferson and Hamilton. Jefferson scarcely understood banking, but he deeply feared political corruption and did not want to extend government power beyond the letter of the Constitution. "To take a single step beyond the boundaries thus specifically drawn around the powers of Congress is to take possession of a boundless field of power no longer susceptible of any definition," warned Jefferson. Hamilton fought back, urging Washington to sign the bill. Because Congress could enact all measures "necessary and proper" (Article I, Section 8), Hamilton contended that the only unconstitutional activities were those actually *forbidden* to the national government. In the end, the president accepted Hamilton's cogent argument for a "loose interpretation" of the Constitution. In February 1791 the Bank of the United States obtained a charter guaranteeing its existence for twenty years. Washington's acceptance of the principle of loose interpretation was the first victory for those advocating an active, assertive national government.

Madison and Jefferson also strongly opposed Hamilton's proposal to encourage industry through protective tariffs on foreign manufactures. They viewed such protectionism as an unfair subsidy promoting uncompetitive industries that would founder without government support. Moreover, tariffs doubly injured the majority of citizens, first by imposing heavy import taxes that were passed on to consumers and then by reducing the incentive for American manufacturers to produce goods

at a lower cost than imports. Together these results unjustifiably raised prices. The only beneficiaries would be individuals shielded from overseas competition and institutions, like the bank, that lent them money. Fearing that American cities might develop a dangerous class of dependent and politically volatile poor people, Jefferson and Madison saw industrialization as a potential menace to the Republic's stability.

Congress ultimately refused to approve a high protective tariff. Nevertheless, Hamilton succeeded in setting higher duties on goods imported into the United States by British vessels than on items carried by American ships. As a result, the tonnage of such goods carried by the American merchant marine more than tripled from 1789 to 1793. Congress also approved subsidies for New England's beleaguered whale and cod fisheries in 1792.

Hamilton's Legacy

Hamilton's attempt to erect a base of political support by appealing to economic self-interest proved highly successful. His arrangements for rescuing the nation's credit provided enormous gains for the speculators, merchants, and other "monied men" of the port cities who by 1790 held most of the Revolutionary debt. As holders of bank stock, these same groups had yet another reason to use their prestige on behalf of national authority. Assumption of the state debts liberated taxpayers from a crushing burden in New England, New Jersey, and South Carolina. Hamilton's efforts to promote industry, commerce, and shipping struck a responsive chord among the Northeast's budding entrepreneurs and hard-pressed artisans,

Those attracted to Hamilton's policies called themselves Federalists, in large part to imply (incorrectly) that their opponents had formerly been Antifederalists. Despite the Federalists' effort to associate themselves with the Constitution, they actually favored a "consolidated" (centralized) national government instead of a truly federal system with substantial powers left to the states. Federalists dominated public opinion in New England, New Jersey, and South Carolina besides enjoying considerable support in Pennsylvania and New York.

However, Hamilton's program sowed dissension in sections of the country where Federalist economic policies provided few benefits. Resentment ran high among those who felt that the government appeared to be rewarding special interests. This situation appeared a perversion of the common understanding that the Constitution had been ratified to bring equal advantages to all Americans. Southern reaction to Hamilton's program, for example, was overwhelmingly negative. Few southerners (aside from some wealthy Charleston merchants) had retained Revolutionary certificates until 1789. By that date only South Carolina of all the southern states had any significant remaining Revolutionary debt. The Bank of the United States had few southern stockholders, and it allocated very little capital for loans there.

Hamilton's plans for commercial expansion and industrial development likewise seemed irrelevant to the interests of the West, where agriculture promised to be exceptionally profitable if only the right to export through New Orleans would be guaranteed. In Pennsylvania and New York, too, the uneven impact of Hamiltonian policies generated dissatisfaction. Resentment against a national economic program whose main beneficiaries seemed to be eastern "monied men" and Yankees who refused to pay their debts gradually united westerners, southerners, and many individuals in the mid-Atlantic region into a political coalition that challenged the Federalists for control of the government and called for a return to the "true principles" of republicanism.

The Whiskey Rebellion

Hamilton's financial program not only sparked an angry political debate in Congress but also helped ignite a civil insurrection called the Whiskey Rebellion. Severely testing the federal government's authority, this insurrection was the young republic's first serious crisis.

Because the national government's assumption of state debts required more revenue than import duties alone could provide, Hamilton had recommended on excise tax on domestically produced whiskey. He insisted that his proposal would distribute the expense of financing the national debt evenly across the United States. He even alleged that the country's morals would improve if higher prices induced Americans to drink less liquor, a contention enthusiastically endorsed by Philadel-

phia's College of Physicians. Though Congress complied with Hamilton's request in March 1791, many members doubted that Americans (who on average annually imbibed six gallons of hard liquor per adult) would submit tamely to sobriety. James Jackson of Georgia, for example, warned the administration that his constituents "have long been in the habit of getting drunk and that they will get drunk in defiance of a dozen colleges or all the excise duties which Congress might be weak or wicked enough to pass."

The accuracy of Jackson's prophecy became apparent in September 1791, when a crowd tarred and feathered an excise agent near Pittsburgh. Western Pennsylvanians found the new tax especially burdensome. Unable to ship their crops to world markets through Spanish New Orleans, most farmers had grown accustomed to distilling their rye or corn into alcohol, which could be carried across the Appalachians at a fraction of the price charged for bulky grain. Hamilton's excise equaled 25 percent of whiskey's retail value, enough to wipe out a frontier farmer's profit.

The law furthermore specified that all trials concerning tax evasion be conducted in federal courts. Any western Pennsylvanian indicted for noncompliance thus had to travel three hundred miles to Philadelphia. Not only would the accused then face a jury of unsympathetic easterners, but he would have to bear the cost of a long journey and lost earnings while at court, in addition to fines and other court penalties if found guilty. Consequently, western Pennsylvanians had justifiable reasons for complaining that local circumstances made the whiskey tax excessively burdensome.

Moreover, Treasury officials rarely enforced the law rigorously outside western Pennsylvania. An especially diligent excise inspector lived near Pittsburgh, whose efforts to collect the tax increasingly enraged local residents and in time touched off massive resistance.

Initially, most residents preferred to protest the tax peacefully, through mass meetings and petitions to Congress. Only a frustrated, reckless minority resorted to violence. However, these hotheads not only attacked federal revenue officers without giving Congress a chance to respond to their grievances but even turned on their own neighbors, destroying property and occasionally pinning down farmers with rifle fire for hours. In several instances the rebels terrorized or tarred and feathered others simply for criticizing their actions. Opposition to the whiskey tax degenerated into random violence that overshadowed the legitimate complaints of western Pennsylvanians.

Large-scale resistance erupted in July 1794. One hundred men attacked a U.S. marshal serving sixty delinquent taxpayers with summonses to appear in court at Philadelphia. A crowd of five hundred burned the chief revenue officer's house after a shootout with federal soldiers assigned to protect him. Roving bands torched buildings, assaulted tax collectors, chased government supporters from the region, and flew a flag symbolizing an independent country that they hoped to create from six western counties.

The frontier turmoil played directly into the Washington administration's hands. Hamilton blasted the rebellion as simple lawlessness, in particular because Congress had reduced the tax rate per gallon in 1792 and just recently had voted to allow state judges in western Pennsylvania to hear trials. Washington concluded that failure to respond strongly to the uprising would encourage similar outbreaks in other frontier areas where lax enforcement had allowed distillers to escape paying taxes.

Washington accordingly summoned 12,900 militiamen from Pennsylvania, Maryland, Virginia, and New Jersey to march west under his command. Opposition evaporated once the troops reached the Appalachians, and the president left Hamilton in charge of making arrests. Of about 150 suspects seized, Hamilton sent twenty in irons to Philadelphia. Two men received death sentences, but Washington eventually pardoned them both, noting that one was a "simpleton" and the other "insane."

The Whiskey Rebellion was a milestone in determining limits on public opposition to federal policies. In the early 1790s, many Americans still assumed that it was legitimate to protest unpopular laws using the same tactics with which they had blocked parliamentary measures like the Stamp Act. Indeed, western Pennsylvanians had justified their resistance with exactly such reasoning. Before 1794 the question of how far the people might go in resisting federal laws remained unresolved because, as Washington declared, "We had given no testi-

mony to the world of being able or willing to support our government and laws." But by firmly suppressing the first major challenge to national authority, Washington served notice that if citizens wished to change the law, they could do so only through constitutional procedures—by making their dissatisfaction known to their elected representatives and if necessary electing new representatives.

The United States in a Hostile World

By 1793 disagreements over foreign affairs had emerged as the primary source of friction in American public life. The political divisions created by Hamilton's financial program hardened into ideologically oriented factions that argued vehemently over whether the country's foreign policy should be pro-French or pro-British.

The United States faced a particularly hostile international environment in the 1790s. European powers restricted American trade, stirred up Indian raids on the frontier, claimed large areas of western territory, and maintained military garrisons on U.S. soil. Because the United States was a weak nation whose economic well-being depended heavily on exports, foreign-policy issues loomed large in national politics. Disputes over foreign relations would poison public life from 1793 to 1815.

Defending the West

The most serious perils to the nation's future rose from British and Spanish attempts to detach the West from the United States. In the early years of Washington's administration, Spanish officials commonly bribed numerous well-known political figures in Tennessee and Kentucky, among them a former general on Washington's staff, James Wilkinson, whose unscrupulous intrigues would continue well past 1800. Thomas Scott, a congressman from western Pennsylvania, meanwhile schemed with the British. Between 1791 and 1796, the federal government anxiously admitted Vermont, Kentucky, and Tennessee to the Union, partly in the hope of strengthening their sometimes flickering loyalty to the United States.

Like all subsequent strong presidents, Washington jealously guarded his prerogative to conduct foreign affairs. Consulting with the Senate as the Constitution required, he nevertheless tried to keep tight control of foreign policy. Realizing that he could not quickly resolve the complex western problem, Washington pursued a course of patient diplomacy that was intended "to preserve the country in peace if I can, and to be prepared for war if I cannot." The prospect of peace improved in 1789 when Spain unexpectedly opened New Orleans to American commerce, although exports remained subject to a 15 percent duty that westerners bitterly resented. Still, secessionist sentiment gradually subsided.

Washington now moved to weaken Spanish influence in the West by neutralizing Spain's most important ally, the Creek Indians. The Creeks numbered more than twenty thousand, including perhaps five thousand warriors, and they bore a fierce hostility toward Georgian settlers, whom they called *Ecunnaunuxulgee*, or "the greedy people who want our lands." In 1790 the Creek leader Alexander McGillivray signed a peace treaty with the United States (a secret provision of which promised him a large annual bribe) that permitted whites to occupy lands in the Georgia piedmont fought over since 1786, but which in other respects preserved Creek territory against white expansion. Washington insisted that Georgia restore to the Creeks' allies, the Chickasaws and Choctaws, the vast area along the Mississippi River known as the Yazoo Tract, which Georgia claimed and had begun selling off to white land speculators.

Hoping to conclude a similar agreement with Great Britain's Indian allies, the United States sent an envoy to the Great Lakes tribes in 1790. The Miamis responded by burning a captured American to death. Late that same year, the president's first effort to force peace through military action failed when General Josiah Harmar abandoned his march against the Miamis after the loss of nearly two hundred of his soldiers. A second campaign ended in disaster on November 4, 1791, when Indians killed nine hundred men out of a force of fourteen hundred led by General Arthur St. Clair.

Washington's efforts to pacify the frontier lay in a shambles. Not only had two military expeditions suffered defeat in the Northwest Territory, but in 1792 the Spanish had persuaded the Creeks to renounce their treaty with the federal government and to resume hostilities. Ultimately, the damage done to U.S. prestige by these setbacks convinced many Americans that the combined strength of Britain and Spain could be counterbalanced only by an alliance with France.

France and Factional Politics

One of the most momentous events in history, the French Revolution began in 1789 with the meeting (for the first time in almost two centuries) of France's legislative assembly, the Estates General. Americans remained fundamentally sympathetic to the revolutionary cause as the French abolished nobles' privileges, wrote a constitution, and bravely repelled invading armies from Austria and Prussia. France became a republic early in 1793; it then pro-

"The Contrast"

In a contemporary cartoonist's view, the winning of American liberty seemed an orderly and peaceful process as compared to the bloody struggle for French liberty.

claimed a war of all peoples against all kings, in which it assumed that the United States would eagerly enlist.

Enthusiasm for a pro-French foreign policy raged in the South and on the frontier, in particular after France went to war against Spain and Great Britain in 1793. Increasingly, western settlers and southern speculators in frontier lands hoped for a decisive French victory in Europe that, they reasoned, would leave Britain and Spain militarily too exhausted to continue meddling in the West. The United States could then insist on free navigation of the Mississippi, force the evacuation of British garrisons, and end both nations' support of Indian resistance.

Moreover, a slave uprising in France's Caribbean colony of Saint Domingue (modern-day Haiti), in which the British became involved, soon generated passionate anti-British sentiment in the South. White southerners grew alarmed for the future of slavery and their own lives as thousands of terrified French planters fled to the United States from Saint Domingue with accounts of how British invaders in 1793 had supported the rebellious slaves. The blacks had fought with determination and inflicted heavy casualties on the French. Southern whites concluded that the British had intentionally sparked a bloodbath on the island and worried that a British-inspired race war would engulf the South as well. Anti-British hysteria even began to undermine South Carolina's loyalty to Federalist policies.

After 1790 American reactions to the French Revolution diverged sharply in the North and the South, in large measure for economic reasons. In the North merchants' growing antagonism toward France reflected not only their conservatism but also their strong awareness that good relations with Britain were essential for their region's prosperity. Virtually all the nation's merchant marine operated from northern ports, and by far the largest share of U.S. foreign trade was with Great Britain. Merchants, shippers, and ordinary sailors in New England, Philadelphia, and New York feared that an alliance with France would provoke British retaliation against this valuable commerce, and they argued that the United States could win valuable concessions by demonstrating friendly intentions toward Great Britain. Indeed, important members of Parliament, including Prime Minister William Pitt the Younger, seemed to favor liberalizing trade with the United States.

Southerners had no such reasons to favor Britain. Southern spokesmen like Jefferson and Madison viewed Americans' reliance on British commerce as a menace to national self-determination and wished to divert most U.S. trade to France. Jefferson and Madison repeatedly demanded that British imports be reduced through the imposition of discriminatory duties on cargoes shipped from England and Scotland in British vessels. Their recommendations gravely threatened the economic well-being of Britain, which sold more manufactured goods to the United States than to any other country. In the heat of the debate, Federalist opponents of a discriminatory tariff warned that the English would not stand by while a weak French ally pushed them into depression. If Congress adopted this program of trade retaliation, Hamilton predicted in 1792, "there would be, in less than six months, an open war between the United States and Great Britain."

After declaring war on Britain and Spain in 1793, France actively tried to embroil the United States in the conflict. (The treaty of alliance of 1778 still bound the United States to come to France's aid.) The French dispatched Edmond Genêt as minister to the United States with orders to enlist American mercenaries to conquer Spanish territories and attack British shipping. Much to the French government's disgust, however, President Washington issued a proclamation of American neutrality on April 22.

Meanwhile, Citizen Genêt (as he was known in French Revolutionary style) had arrived on April 8. He found no shortage of southern volunteers for his American Foreign Legion despite America's official neutrality. Making generals of George Rogers Clark of Kentucky and Elisha Clarke of Georgia, Genêt directed them to seize the Spanish garrisons at New Orleans and St. Augustine. Clark openly defied Washington's Neutrality Proclamation by advertising for recruits for his mission in Kentucky newspapers; Clarke began drilling three hundred troops on the Florida border. But the French failed to provide adequate funds for either campaign. And as for the American recruits, while all were willing to fight for France, few were

The Frigate L'Embuscade ("Ambush")

During Washington's presidency, French-outfitted raiders such as L'Embuscade *snatched merchant vessels from American coasts. The seizures defied U.S. authority and hindered the Republic's quest for neutrality in the war between France and Britain.*

willing to fight for free, and so both expeditions eventually disintegrated in 1794 for lack of French money to supply them.

However, Genêt did not need funds to outfit privateers, whose crews were paid from captured plunder. By the summer of 1793, almost a thousand Americans were at sea in a dozen ships flying the French flag. These privateers seized more than eighty British vessels and towed them to United States ports, where French consuls sold the ships and cargoes at auction.

The British Crisis

Even though the Washington administration swiftly closed the nation's harbors to Genêt's buccaneers and requested the French ambassador's recall, his exploits provoked an Anglo-American crisis. George III's ministers decided that only a massive show of force would deter further American aggression. Accordingly, on November 6, 1793, the Privy Council issued secret orders confiscating any foreign ships trading with French islands in the Caribbean. The council purposely delayed publishing these instructions until after most American ships

carrying winter provisions to the Caribbean left port, so that their captains would not know that they were sailing into a war zone. The Royal Navy then seized more than 250 American vessels, a high price for Genêt's troublemaking.

Meanwhile, the U.S. merchant marine was suffering a second galling indignity—the drafting of its crewmen into the understrength Royal Navy. Thousands of British sailors, including numerous naval deserters, had previously fled to U.S. ships, where they hoped to find an easier life than under the tough, poorly paying British system. In late 1793 British naval officers began routinely inspecting American crews for British subjects, whom they then impressed (forcibly enlisted) as the king's sailors. Overzealous commanders sometimes broke royal orders by taking U.S. citizens, and in any case the British did not recognize former subjects' right to adopt American citizenship. Impressment scratched a raw nerve in most Americans, who recognized that the federal government's willingness to defend its citizens from such contemptuous abuse was a critical test of national character.

Next the British boldly challenged the United States for control of the West. In February 1794

Canada's royal governor delivered an inflammatory speech at an Indian council, denying U.S. claims north of the Ohio River and urging his listeners to destroy every white settlement in the Northwest. Soon British troops were building an eighth garrison on U.S. soil, Fort Miami, near present-day Toledo, Ohio. Meanwhile, the Spanish encroached further upon territory owned by the United States by building Fort San Fernando in 1794 at what is now Memphis, Tennessee.

Hoping to halt the drift toward war, Washington launched a desperate diplomatic initiative in 1794. He sent Chief Justice John Jay to Great Britain, dispatched Thomas Pinckney to Spain, and authorized General Anthony Wayne to negotiate a treaty with the Indians of the Ohio Valley.

Having twice defeated federal armies, the Indians scoffed at Washington's peace offer. But the tide turned as Wayne led three thousand regulars and Kentucky militiamen deep into the Indian homeland and ruthlessly razed every village within his reach. On August 20, 1794, his troops routed a thousand Indians at the Battle of Fallen Timbers just two miles from British Fort Miami. Wayne's army marched past the post in a provocative victory parade and then built an imposing stronghold to challenge British authority in the Northwest, appropriately named Fort Defiance. Indian morale plummeted. In August 1795 Wayne compelled twelve northeastern tribes to sign the Treaty of Greenville, which opened most of modern-day Ohio to white settlement and ended Indian hostilities for sixteen years.

Wayne's success allowed John Jay to win a major diplomatic victory in London: a British promise to withdraw troops from American soil. He also managed to gain access to West Indian markets for small American ships, but only by bargaining away U.S. rights to load cargoes of sugar, molasses, and coffee from the Caribbean. On other points, Jay found the British unyielding. Aside from fellow Federalists, few Americans could interpret Jay's Treaty as preserving peace with honor.

Jay's Treaty left Britain free not only to violate American neutrality but also to ruin a profitable commerce by restricting U.S. trade with French ports during wartime. Many opponents, moreover, passionately decried Jay's failure to end

Negotiating the Treaty of Greenville

In this detail of a contemporary painting believed to have been done by a member of General Wayne's staff, Chief Little Turtle speaks to Wayne, who stands with one hand behind his back.

impressment and predicted that Great Britain would thereafter force even more Americans into the Royal Navy. And southerners resented that Jay had not achieved their long-sought goal of compensation for slaves taken away by the British army during the Revolution. As the Federalist-dominated Senate ratified the treaty by a one-vote margin in 1795, Jay nervously joked that he could find his way across the country by the fires of rallies burning him in effigy.

Despite its unpopularity, Jay's Treaty probably represented the utmost that a weak, politically divided United States could have extracted from mighty Britain. Although enormously unpopular, the treaty was one of the Washington administration's major accomplishments. First, it defused an explosive crisis with Great Britain before war became inevitable. Second, it ended a twelve-year British occupation of U.S. territory. Third, the treaty provided for the settlement, by arbitration, of the claims of British merchants who were owed American debts from before 1776, and it also arranged for U.S. citizens' compensation for property seized by the Royal Navy in 1793 and 1794. Americans benefited disproportionately when these accounts were finally settled by 1804: they received $10,345,000, compared to just $2,750,000 awarded to the British creditors.

Although the Senate rejected the provision granting limited trading rights with the West Indies in return for a British monopoly over certain commodities, Jay's Treaty played a critical role in stimulating an enormous expansion of American trade. British governors in the West Indies used the treaty's ratification as an excuse to proclaim their harbors open to U.S. ships. Other British officials permitted Americans to develop a thriving commerce with India, even though this trade infringed on the East India Company's monopoly. Within a few years after 1795, American exports to the British Empire shot up 300 percent because the United States had unofficially gained "most-favored-nation" status as a means of restoring good relations.

On the heels of Jay's Treaty came an unqualified diplomatic triumph engineered by Thomas Pinckney. Ratified in 1796, the Treaty of San Lorenzo with Spain (also called Pinckney's Treaty) won westerners the right of unrestricted, duty-free access to world markets via the Mississippi River. Spain also promised to recognize the 31st parallel as the United States' southern boundary, to dismantle all fortifications on American soil, and to discourage Indian attacks against western settlers.

By 1796 the Washington administration thus had successfully defended the country's territorial integrity, restored peace to the frontier, opened the Mississippi for western exports, made it possible for northeastern shippers to regain British markets, and kept the nation out of a dangerous European war. As the popular outcry over Jay's Treaty demonstrated, however, the nation's foreign policy had left Americans much more deeply divided in 1796 than they had been in 1789.

Battling for the Nation's Soul

Neither the Constitution nor *The Federalist* had envisioned organized political parties, and none existed in 1789 when Washington became president. By the end of his second term, however, politically conscious Americans had split into two hostile parties, Federalists and Republicans.

The unfolding struggle transcended the economic and sectional differences so evident in earlier disputes about Hamiltonian finance and the possibility of war with Britain. After 1796 a battle raged over the very future of representative government, culminating in the election of 1800, whose outcome would determine whether the nation's political elite could accommodate demands from ordinary citizens for a more active and influential role in determining government policy. No issue was more important or hotly argued than the matter of officeholders' accountability to their constituents.

Ideological Confrontation

By the mid-1790s the French Revolution had forced Americans to reassess their political values. American attitudes toward events in France divided sharply after that nation's revolutionary regime turned radical in 1793–1794, sending thousands of "counterrevolutionaries" to the guillotine. The polarization of American opinion assumed a strongly, though not completely, regional dimension.

The Republican Court, *by Daniel Huntington*

Federalists emphasized the dignity of the national government by staging sumptuous balls and formal receptions. Administration critics saw these affairs as an effort to emulate European court life. Washington, although mindful of upholding presidential dignity, found public functions tedious, and his stiff formality often masked his personal discomfort.

For northern Federalists, revolutionary France became an abomination—"an open hell," thundered Massachusetts Federalist Fisher Ames, "still ringing with agonies and blasphemies, still smoking with sufferings and crimes." New England was the nation's most conservative, religiously oriented region, and most of its people came to detest the French government's disregard for civil rights and its attempt to substitute the adoration of Reason for the worship of God. Middle Atlantic businessmen, who were perhaps less religious than New Englanders but hardly less conservative, condemned French leaders as evil radicals who incited the poor against the rich. A minority of well-off northern merchants and professional men, however, continued to look favorably upon the French Revolution, primarily out of loyalty to deeply felt republican principles.

Federalists trembled at the thought of guillotines and "mob rule" looming in the United States' future. Memories of Shays's Rebellion and the Whiskey Rebellion made their fears reasonable. So did the tendency of artisans in Philadelphia and New York to bandy the French revolutionary slogan "Liberty, Equality, Fraternity" and to admire pro-French political leaders such as Jefferson. Moreover, Citizen Genêt had openly encouraged

vocal opposition to the Washington administration until the faction in the French government that he represented fell from power—and even more troubling, he had found hundreds of Americans willing to fight for France. Federalists worried that all of this was just the tip of an iceberg.

By the mid-1790s Federalist leaders had concluded that it was unwise and perhaps dangerous to involve the public too deeply in politics. The people, they believed, were not evil-minded but simply undependable and could easily fall prey to such a rabble rouser as Genêt. As Senator George Cabot of Massachusetts put it, "The many do not think at all." For Federalists, democracy meant "government by the passions of the multitude," though they also felt that the people, if properly led, could stand as a powerful (but passive) bulwark against anarchy. Indeed, they *did* trust ordinary property owners to judge a candidate's personal fitness for high office. Federalists consequently argued that citizens need not be presented with choices over policy during elections; instead, voters ought to choose candidates according to their personal merits. Thus they favored a representative government, in which elected officials would rule in the people's name but would be independent of direct popular influence.

"Where Liberty Dwells, There Is My Country"

Motifs of republican virtue and liberty were widely reproduced in the nation's early years. In this coverlet of toile manufactured in England for American sale, the shield-bearing Columbia, symbolizing the United States, leads a fur-capped Benjamin Franklin in his elevation to divine status.

Preserving order, the Federalists maintained, required demonstrating the dignity of the government and forging a close, visible relationship between the government and the upper class. Such a spectacle would not only reassure citizens that their future was in competent hands but also set high standards that few radicals could meet. As early as 1789, Vice President John Adams had tried to give the president and other high officials royal-sounding titles like "His High Mightiness." (Adams had failed amid much ridicule, including being lampooned as "His Rotundity.") During the 1790s government officials continued to dramatize their social distance from average citizens. Members of Congress and the cabinet dressed in high fashion, traveled in expensive coaches, appeared with retinues of servants, and attended endless formal dinners and balls, which served as grand opportunities for the upper class to flaunt its wealth. Federalists insisted that they ruled *of* and *for* the people, but they took pains to symbolize that their government was not *by* the people.

The Federalists aimed to limit public office to wise and virtuous men who would vigilantly protect liberty. This objective was consistent with eighteenth-century fears that corruption and unchecked passion would undermine society, for in republican theory a "virtuous" government need not be directly responsible to public opinion. If (as many assumed) democracy meant "mob rule," then political virtue and direct democracy were incompatible. The Federalists' profound suspicion of the common people therefore was deeply rooted not only in old-fashioned social reciprocity (see Chapter 1) and in conservative colonial political traditions but also in republican ideology itself.

A very different understanding of republican ideology influenced Jefferson, Madison, and others alienated by Federalist measures. Although some critics of the administration surfaced in New England and the Middle Atlantic states, Antifederalist sentiment ran particularly high in the South. Indeed, the southern interpretation of republicanism stressed the corruption inherent in a powerful government dominated by a highly visible few, and southerners widely insisted that liberty would be safe only if power was diffused among virtuous, independent citizens. Thus Antifederalist southerners feared popular participation in politics far less than northern Federalists. Further, few southern planters were strongly religious, and many had absorbed the Enlightenment's faith that the free flow of ideas would inevitably ensure progress. They also felt confident of their ability to lead (and be elected by) the smaller farmers. Consequently, southerners felt exhilarated by the events unfolding in France; they saw the French as fellow republicans, carrying on a work of universal revolution that would replace hereditary privilege with liberty, equality, and brotherhood. Unlike northern Federalists, nervous about urban mobs, southern planters faced the future with optimism and viewed attempts to inhibit widespread political participation as unworthy of educated gentlemen.

Self-interest, too, drove men like Jefferson and Madison to rouse ordinary citizens' concerns about civic affairs. Political apathy was widespread in the early 1790s, a situation that favored the Federalists by making it unlikely that they would be criticized for passing unwise laws. If, however, the Federalists could be held accountable to the public, they would think twice before enacting measures opposed by the majority; or if they persisted in advocating misguided policies, they would ultimately be removed from office. Such reasoning led Jefferson, a wealthy landowner and large slaveholder, to say, "I am not among those who fear the people; they and not the rich, are our dependence for continued freedom."

Efforts to turn public opinion against the Federalists had begun in October 1791 with the publication of the nation's first opposition newspaper, the *National Gazette*. Then in 1793–1794, popular dissatisfaction with the government's policies led to the formation of several dozen Democratic (or Republican) societies, primarily in seaboard cities but also in the rural South and in frontier towns. Their memberships ranged from planters and merchants to artisans and sailors. Conspicuously absent were clergymen, the poor, and blacks.

Sharply critical of the Federalists, the societies spread dissatisfaction with the Washington administration's policies. Because many of the clubs arose during Genêt's ministry, and because all of them also acclaimed revolutionary France, Federalists assumed (wrongly) that their members were acting as foreign agents. Federalists interpreted their emotional appeals to ordinary people as demagoguery and denounced the societies' followers as "democrats, mobocrats, & all other kinds of rats."

The Federalists feared that the societies would grow into revolutionary organizations. Washington privately warned that "if [the clubs] were not counteracted (not by prosecutions, the ready way to make them grow stronger) or did not fall into disesteem . . . they would shake the government to its foundation." During the Whiskey Rebellion, the president publicly denounced "certain self-created societies." So great was his prestige that the societies temporarily broke up. But by attacking them, Washington had at last ended his nonpartisan stance and identified himself unmistakably with the Federalists. The censure would cost him dearly.

The Republican Party and the Election of 1796

Neither Jefferson nor Madison belonged to a Democratic society. However, these private clubs helped publicize administration critics' views, and they initiated into political activity numerous voters who would later support Jefferson's and Madison's Republican party. Ironically, Madison had earlier been one of the most outspoken opponents of political parties.

In the early 1790s, politically active Americans believed that deliberately organizing a political faction or party was a corrupt, subversive action. The Constitution's framers had neither wanted nor planned for political parties, and in *The Federalist* No. 10, Madison had claimed that the Constitution would prevent the rise of national political factions. Republican ideology commonly assumed that factions or parties would fill Congress with politicians of little ability and less integrity, pursuing selfish goals at the expense of national welfare. Good citizens, it was assumed, would shun partisan scheming. These ideals, however, began to waver as controversy mounted over Hamilton's program and foreign policy. President Washington still tried to set an example of impartial leadership by seeking advice from both camps. (He did not know that in their partisan zeal both Hamilton and Jefferson maintained indiscreet contacts with British and French diplomats, respectively.) But Jefferson finally resigned from the cabinet in 1793, and thereafter even the president could not halt the widening political split. Each side saw itself as the guardian of republican virtue and attacked the other as an illegitimate "cabal" (faction).

In 1794 party development reached a decisive stage. Shortly after Washington had openly identified himself with Federalist policies, followers of Jefferson who called themselves Republicans* successfully attacked the Federalists' "pro-British" leanings in many local elections and won a slight majority in the House of Representatives. The election signaled the Republicans' transformation from a faction of officeholders to a broad-based party capable of coordinating local political campaigns throughout the nation.

Federalists and Republicans alike used the press to mold public opinion in the 1790s. In this decade American journalism came of age as the number of newspapers multiplied from 92 to 242, mostly in New England and the Middle Atlantic states. By 1800 newspapers had perhaps 140,000 paid subscribers (about one-fifth of the eligible voters), and their secondhand readership probably exceeded 300,000. Newspapers of both camps were libelous and irresponsible. They cheapened the quality of public discussion through incessant fear mongering and character assassination. Republicans stood accused of plotting a reign of terror and of wishing to turn the nation over to France. Federalists faced repeated charges of favoring a hereditary aristocracy and even of planning to establish an American dynasty by marrying off John Adams's daughter to George III. Such tactics whipped up mutual distrust and made political debate emotional and subjective. Nevertheless, the newspaper warfare stimulated many citizens to become politically active, even if for the wrong reasons.

Behind the inflammatory rhetoric, the Republicans' central charge was that the Federalists had evolved into a faction bent on enriching wealthy citizens at the taxpayers' expense. In 1794 a Republican writer claimed that Federalist policies would create "a privileged order of men . . . who shall enjoy the honors, the emoluments, and the patronage of government, without contributing a farthing to its support." Although almost every Republican leader, too, was well born, Republicans asserted that the Federalists planned to re-create the atmosphere of a European court through highly publicized state dinners, formal balls, and other dazzling entertainments. The Republicans

*Jefferson and Madison preferred the party name *Republican* rather than the radical-sounding *Democratic*.

George Washington, *by Jean Antoine Houdon, 1788–1792*

The French sculptor Houdon created this magnificent life-size statue of Washington from a life mask and exact measurements. It depicts Washington in a role with which he was comfortable: that of an ordinary citizen-farmer.

erred in claiming that their opponents were scheming to introduce legal privilege, aristocracy, and monarchy. But they correctly identified the Federalists' fundamental assumption: that citizens' worth could be measured in terms of their money.

Republican charges that the president secretly supported alleged Federalist plots to establish a monarchy enraged Washington. "By God," Jefferson reported him swearing, "he [the president] would rather be in his grave than in his present situation . . . he had rather be on his farm than to be made *emperor of the world*." Further, the president took alarm at the stormy debate over Jay's Treaty, and he dreaded the nation's polarization into hostile factions. Republicans' abuse sharply stung him. "As for you, sir," sneered Thomas Paine in a pamphlet, "treacherous in private friendship . . . and a hypocrite in public life, the world will be puzzled to decide whether you are an apostate or an impostor, whether you have abandoned good principles or ever had any." Lonely and surrounded by mediocre advisers after Hamilton's return to private life, Washington decided in the spring of 1796 to retire after two terms. Four years earlier, Madison had drafted the president's parting message to the nation; but now Washington called on Hamilton to give a sharp political twist to his Farewell Address.

The heart of Washington's message was a vigorous condemnation of political parties. Partisan alignments, he insisted, endangered the republic's survival, especially if they became entangled in disputes over foreign policy. Washington warned that the country's safety depended on citizens' avoiding "excessive partiality for one nation and excessive dislike of another." Otherwise, independent-minded "real patriots" would be overwhelmed by demagogues championing foreign causes and paid by foreign governments. Aside from scrupulously fulfilling its existing treaty obligations and maintaining its foreign commerce, the United States must avoid "political connection" with Europe and its wars. If the United States gathered its strength under "an efficient government," it could defy any foreign challenge; but if it became sucked into Europe's quarrels, violence, and corruption, then the republican experiment was doomed. Washington and Hamilton had skillfully turned the central argument of republicanism against their Republican critics. They had also evoked a vision of America virtuously isolated from foreign intrigue and power politics, which would remain a potent inspiration until the twentieth century.

Washington left public life in 1797 and died in 1799. Like many later presidents, he went out amid a barrage of criticism. During his brief retirement, the nation's political division into Republicans and Federalists hardened. Each party consolidated its hold over particular states and groups of voters, leaving the electorate almost equally divided.

As the election of 1796 approached, the Republicans cultivated a large, loyal body of voters. Their efforts to marshal support marked the first time since the Revolution that the political elite had effectively mobilized ordinary Americans to take an interest in public affairs. The Republicans' constituency included the Democratic societies, workingmen's clubs, and immigrant-aid associations.

Immigrants became a prime target for Republican recruiters. During the 1790s the United States absorbed perhaps twenty thousand French refugees from Saint Domingue and more than sixty thousand Irish, including some conspirators exiled for plotting against British rule. Although potential immigrant voters were few—composing less than 2 percent of the electorate—the Irish in particular could exert crucial influence in Pennsylvania and New York, where public opinion was closely divided and a few hundred immigrant voters could tip the balance away from the Federalists. In short, Irish immigrants could provide the Republicans with a winning margin in the two states, and the Republicans' pro-French and anti-British rhetoric ensured enthusiastic Irish support.

In 1796 the presidential candidates were Vice President John Adams, supported by the Federalists, and the Republicans' Jefferson. Republicans expected to win as many southern electoral votes and congressional seats as the Federalists counted on in New England, New Jersey, and South Carolina. The crucial "swing" states were Pennsylvania and New York, where the Republicans tried mightily to tip the balance by wooing the large immigrant (particularly Irish) vote. In the end, however, the Republicans took Pennsylvania but not New York, and so Jefferson lost the presidency by just three electoral votes. The Federalists narrowly regained control of the House and maintained their firm grip on the Senate. But by a political fluke possible under the Constitution at the time, Jefferson became vice president.*

The new president exemplified both the strengths and the weaknesses of an intellectual. His brilliance, insight, and idealism have rarely been equaled among American presidents. Like most intellectuals, however, Adams was more comfortable with ideas than with people, more theoretical than practical, and rather inflexible. He inspired trust and often admiration but could not command

---

*The Constitution then stipulated that the presidential candidate with the second-highest electoral vote would become vice president. This was one example of the Constitution's failure to provide for political partisanship.

Adams Family Farm
John Adams, *by Gilbert Stuart, 1826 (Detail)*

The Adamses hailed from Quincy, Massachusetts. John Adams was born in the house at the right; his son, John Quincy Adams, in the saltbox at the left. Soon after the elder Adams's death, John Quincy Adams, himself now president, commissioned a final portrait; this gentle and distinguished canvas was the result.

personal loyalty. His wisdom and historical vision were drowned out in highly emotional political debate. Adams's rational, reserved personality was likewise ill suited to inspiring the electorate, and he ultimately proved unable to unify the country.

The French Crisis

Adams was initially fortunate, however, that French provocations produced a sharp backlash against the Republicans. The French interpreted Jay's Treaty as an American attempt to assist the British in their war against France. On learning of Jefferson's defeat, the French ordered the seizure of American ships carrying goods to British ports; and within a year the French had plundered more than three hundred vessels. The French government rubbed in its contempt for the United States by directing that every American captured on a British naval ship (even those involuntarily impressed) should be hanged.

Hoping to avoid war, Adams sent a peace commission to Paris. But the French foreign minister, Charles de Talleyrand, refused to meet the dele-

gation, instead promising through three unnamed agents ("X, Y, and Z") that talks could begin after he received $250,000 and France obtained a loan of $12 million. This barefaced demand for a bribe became known as the XYZ Affair. Americans reacted to it with outrage. "Millions for defense, not one cent for tribute" became the nation's battle cry as the 1798 congressional elections began.

The XYZ Affair discredited the Republicans' foreign policy views, but the party's leaders compounded the damage by refusing to condemn French aggression and opposing Adams's call for defensive measures. The Republicans tried to excuse French behavior, while the Federalists rode a wave of militant patriotism. In the 1798 elections, Jefferson's supporters were routed almost everywhere, even in the South.

Congress responded to the XYZ Affair by arming fifty-four ships to protect American commerce. The new warships were at once put to use in what has become known as the Quasi-War—an undeclared Franco-American naval conflict in the Caribbean from 1798 to 1800, during which U.S.

forces seized ninety-three French privateers at the loss of just one vessel. The British navy meanwhile extended the protection of its convoys to America's merchant marine. By early 1799 the French were a nuisance but no longer a serious threat at sea.

Despite the president's misgivings, the Federalists in Congress tripled the regular army to ten thousand men in 1798, with an automatic expansion of land forces to fifty thousand in case of war. But the risk of a land war with the French was minimal. In reality, the Federalists primarily wanted a military force ready in the event of a civil war, for the crisis had produced near-hysteria about conspiracies that were being hatched by French and Irish malcontents flooding into the United States.

Federalists were well aware that the French legation was not only engaged in espionage but also making treasonous suggestions to prominent persons. The government knew, for example, that in 1796 General Victor Collot had traveled from Pittsburgh to New Orleans under orders to investigate the prospects for establishing a pro-French, independent nation west of the mountains, and also that he had examined strategic locations to which rebellious frontier dwellers might rally. The State Department heard in 1798 that France had created in the West "a party of mad Americans ready to join with them at a given Signal."

The Alien and Sedition Acts

The Federalists, moreover, insisted that the likelihood of open war with France required stringent legislation to protect national security. In 1798 the Federalist-dominated Congress accordingly passed four measures known collectively as the Alien and Sedition Acts. Adams neither requested nor particularly wanted these laws, but he deferred to congressional judgment and signed them.

Both parties cooperated in writing the first of the four laws, the Alien Enemies Act, which was designed to prevent wartime spying or sabotage. This measure outlined procedures for determining whether the citizens of a hostile country posed a threat to the United States; if so, they were to be deported or jailed. The law established fundamental principles for protecting national security and respecting the rights of enemy citizens. It was to

operate only if Congress declared war and so was not used until the War of 1812 (see Chapter 7).

Second, the Alien Friends Act was a peacetime statute enforceable until June 25, 1800. It authorized the president to expel any foreign residents whose activities he considered dangerous. The law did not require proof of guilt, on the assumption that spies would hide or destroy evidence of their crime. Republicans maintained that the law's real purpose was to deport prominent immigrants critical of Federalist policies.

Republicans also denounced the third law, the Naturalization Act. This measure increased the residency requirement for U.S. citizenship from five to fourteen years (the last five continuously in one state), with the purpose of reducing Irish voting.

Finally came the Sedition Act, the only one of these measures enforceable against U.S. citizens. Although its alleged purpose was to distinguish between free speech and attempts at encouraging others to violate federal laws or to overthrow the government, the act nevertheless defined criminal activity so broadly that it blurred any real distinction between sedition and legitimate political discussion. Thus it forbade an individual or group "to oppose any measure or measures of the United States"—wording that could be interpreted to ban any criticism of the party in power. Another clause made it illegal to speak, write, or print any statement about the president that would bring him "into contempt or disrepute." Under such restrictions, for example, a newspaper editor might face imprisonment for disapproving of an action by Adams or his cabinet members. The Federalist *Gazette of the United States* expressed the twisted logic of the Sedition Act perfectly: "It is patriotism to write in favor of our government—it is sedition to write against it."

Sedition cases were heard by juries, which could decide if the defendant had really intended to stir up rebellion or was merely expressing political dissent. But whatever way one looked at it, the Sedition Act interfered with free speech. Ingeniously, the Federalists wrote the law to expire in 1801 (so that it could not be turned against them if they lost the next election) and to leave them free meanwhile to heap abuse on the *vice* president, Jefferson.

Federalist enforcement of the first of the repressive new laws, the Alien Friends Act, produced mixed results. The president signed a deportation order for French agent Collot, who escaped capture. No expulsions were actually carried out under the law, although two of Collot's assistants and several dozen other French sailed home before they could be forcibly removed.

The real target of Federalist repression was the U.S. opposition press. Four of the five largest Republican newspapers were charged with sedition just as the election of 1800 was getting under way. The attorney general used the Alien Friends Act to threaten an Irish journalist, John Daly Burk, with expulsion (Burk went underground instead). Scottish editor Thomas Callender was on the verge of being deported when he suddenly qualified for citizenship. Now unable to expel Callender, the government tried him for sedition before an all-Federalist jury, which sent him to prison for criticizing the president.

Federalist leaders never intended to fill the jails with Republican martyrs. Rather, they wanted to use a small number of highly visible prosecutions to intimidate most journalists and candidates into keeping quiet during the election of 1800. The attorney general charged seventeen persons with sedition and won ten convictions. Among the victims was the Republican congressman Matthew Lyon of Vermont ("Ragged Matt, the democrat," to the Federalists), who spent four months in prison for publishing a blast against Adams.

Vocal criticism of Federalist repression erupted only in Virginia and Kentucky. During the summer of 1798, militia commanders in these states mustered their regiments, not to drill but to hear speeches demanding that the federal government respect the Bill of Rights. Entire units then signed petitions denouncing the Alien and Sedition Acts. The symbolic implications of these protests were sobering. Young men stepped forward to sign petitions on drumheads with a pen in one hand and a gun in the other, as older officers who had fought in the Continental Army looked on approvingly. It was not hard to imagine Kentucky rifles being substituted for quill pens as the men who had led one revolution took up arms again.

Ten years earlier, opponents of the Constitution had warned that giving the national government extensive powers would eventually endanger freedom. By 1798 their prediction had come true.

Shocked Republicans realized that because the Federalists controlled all three branches of the government, neither the Bill of Rights nor the system of checks and balances protected individual liberties. In this context, the doctrine of states' rights was first advanced as a means of preventing the national government from violating basic freedoms.

Madison and Jefferson anonymously wrote two manifestoes on states' rights that the assemblies of Virginia and Kentucky officially endorsed in 1798. Madison's Virginia Resolutions and Jefferson's Kentucky Resolutions declared that the state legislatures had never surrendered their right to judge the constitutionality of federal actions and that they retained an authority called interposition, which enabled them to protect the liberties of their citizens. A set of Kentucky Resolutions adopted in November 1799 added that objectionable federal laws might be "nullified" by the states. The terms *interposition* and *nullification* were not defined, but their intention was obviously to prevent residents from being tried for breaking an unconstitutional law. The Virginia and Kentucky legislatures must have understood that interposition would ultimately challenge the jurisdiction of federal courts and perhaps require that state militia march into a federal courtroom to halt proceedings at bayonet point.

Although no other states endorsed these resolutions (most in fact expressed disapproval), their passage demonstrated the great potential for violence in the late 1790s. So did a minor insurrection called the Fries Rebellion, which broke out in 1799 when crowds of Pennsylvania German farmers released prisoners jailed for refusing to pay taxes needed to fund the national army's expansion. Fortunately, the disturbance collapsed just as federal cavalry arrived, and the only casualties were several head of rebellious cattle shot by trigger-happy soldiers.

The nation's leaders increasingly acted as if a crisis were imminent. Vice President Jefferson hinted that events might push the southern states into secession from the Union. The normally sensible President Adams hid guns in his home. After passing through Richmond and learning that state officials were purchasing thousands of muskets for the militia, an alarmed Supreme Court justice wrote in January 1799 that "the General Assembly of

Virginia are pursuing steps which will lead directly to civil war." A tense atmosphere hung over the Republic as the election of 1800 neared.

The Election of 1800

In the election the Republicans rallied around Jefferson for president and the wily New York politician Aaron Burr for vice president. The Federalists meanwhile became mired in wrangling between Adams and the extreme "High Federalists" who looked to Alexander Hamilton for guidance. That the nation survived the election of 1800 without a civil war or the disregard of voters' wishes owed chiefly to the good sense of the more moderate leaders of both parties. Thus Jefferson and Madison discouraged radicalism that might provoke intervention by the national army. Even more credit belonged to Adams for rejecting High Federalist demands that he ensure victory by deliberately sparking an insurrection or asking Congress to declare war on France.

"Nothing but an open war can save us" argued Adams's High Federalist secretary of the treasury. But when the president suddenly discovered the French willing to seek peace in 1799, he proposed a special diplomatic mission. "Surprise, indignation, grief & disgust followed each other in quick succession," said a Federalist senator on hearing the news. Adams obtained Senate approval for his envoys only by threatening to resign and so make Jefferson president, an action that he later described with justifiable pride as "the most disinterested . . . in my whole life." The High Federalists were so outraged that they tried unsuccessfully to dump Adams. Hamilton denounced him as a fool, but this ill-considered maneuver rallied most New Englanders around their stubborn, upright president.

Adams's negotiations with France did not achieve a settlement until 1801, but the expectation that normal—and perhaps friendly—relations with the French would resume prevented the Federalists from exploiting charges of Republican sympathy for the enemy. Without the immediate threat of war, moreover, voters grew resentful that in merely two years, taxes had soared 33 percent to support an army that had done nothing except chase terrified Pennsylvania farmers. As the danger of war receded, voters gave the Federalists less credit

for standing up to France and more blame for ballooning the national debt by $10 million.

Two years after their triumph in the 1798 elections, support for the Federalists had eroded sharply. High Federalists who had hoped for war spitefully withheld the backing that Adams needed to win. The Republicans meanwhile redoubled their efforts to elect Jefferson. They were especially successful in mobilizing voters in Philadelphia and New York, where artisans, farmers, and some entrepreneurs were ready to forsake the Federalists, whom they saw as defenders of entrenched privilege and upstart wealth. Amid the excitement, political apathy waned. Voter turnouts in 1800 leaped to more than double those of 1788, rising from about 15 percent to almost 40 percent, and in hotly contested Pennsylvania and New York more than half the eligible voters participated.

Playing on their opponent's reputation as a religious free thinker, the Federalists forged a case against Jefferson that came down to urging citizens to vote for "GOD—AND A RELIGIOUS PRESIDENT; or impiously declare for JEFFERSON—AND NO GOD!!!" But this ploy did not prevent thousands of deeply religious Baptists, Methodists, and other dissenters from voting Republican. Nor did voters know that Adams was scarcely more conventional in his religious views than Jefferson.

Adams lost the presidency by just 8 electoral votes out of 138. He would have won if his party had not lost control of New York's state senate, which chose the electors, after a narrow defeat in New York City. Unexpectedly, Jefferson and his running mate Burr also carried South Carolina because his backers made lavish promises of political favors to that state's legislators.

Although Adams lost, Jefferson's election was not assured. The Republicans had failed to select in advance one elector who would not vote for Burr, so the electoral college deadlocked in a Jefferson-Burr tie.* The choice of president devolved upon the House of Representatives, where thirty-five ballots over six days produced no result. Finally, Delaware's only representative, a Federalist, aban-

---

*The Twelfth Amendment (ratified in 1804) eliminated the possibility of such problems. It stipulated that electors vote for presidential and vice-presidential candidates as a pair; no longer would the runner-up in the presidential contest become vice president.

doned Burr and gave Jefferson the presidency by history's narrowest margin.

Deferring Equality

The election of 1800 did not make the United States more democratic. Rather, it prevented rigidly anti-democratic prejudices from blocking future political liberalization. The Republican victory also repudiated the Federalist willingness, so evident in Hamilton's plans, to create a base of support for the government through special-interest legislation. Such self-serving goals led critics like Madison to condemn the Federalists for "substituting the motive of private interest for public duty." After 1800 government policies would be judged by Jefferson's standard of "equal rights for all, special privileges for none."

But not all Americans won equal rights. Women took no part in politics, and few people felt that they should. As for the native Americans, the nation's diplomatic gains came largely at their expense; and foreign-policy issues rarely concerned the aspirations of African-Americans. Moreover, in the Republic's early years, white Americans lost much of the idealism that Revolutionary ideology had inspired, and they began to assume that racial minorities could never be more than second-class citizens at best.

Indian Decline

By 1795 most eastern Indian tribes had suffered severe reductions in population and territory. Innumerable deaths had resulted from battle, famine, exposure to the elements during flight from enemies, and disease. From 1775 to 1795, the Cherokees declined from 16,000 to 10,000 and the Iroquois fell from about 9,000 to 4,000. Meanwhile, in the quarter-century before 1800, Indians may have forfeited more land than the area inhabited by whites in 1775.

Frontier warfare had sapped the strength of many Indian cultures. Young adults grew indifferent toward traditional ways. Unable to strike back at whites, Indians inflicted violence on one another and often consumed enormous quantities of whis-

Osage Warrior, *by Charles de Saint-Mémin, c. 1804*

As the nineteenth century opened, most native Americans clung tightly to their traditional lifestyles and values.

key. The situation among the Iroquois was all too typical. "The Indians of the Six Nations," wrote a federal official in 1796, "have become given to indolence, drunkenness, and thefts, and have taken to killing each other."

The Indians' predicament spawned a profound social and moral crisis within the tribes, most notably among the Iroquois. Handsome Lake, an Iroquois tribal leader, tried to halt his people's decline by borrowing from the white man's world. Despite his own problems with liquor, he sought to end alcoholism among Indians by appealing to their religious traditions. Even more radically, he welcomed Quaker missionaries and federal aid earmarked for teaching whites' agricultural methods to Iroquois men, who had to look for a new livelihood after the loss of their hunting grounds. Some, to be sure, sneered at advice that they should work like white farmers; said one, only "squaws and hedgehogs are made to scratch the ground." But

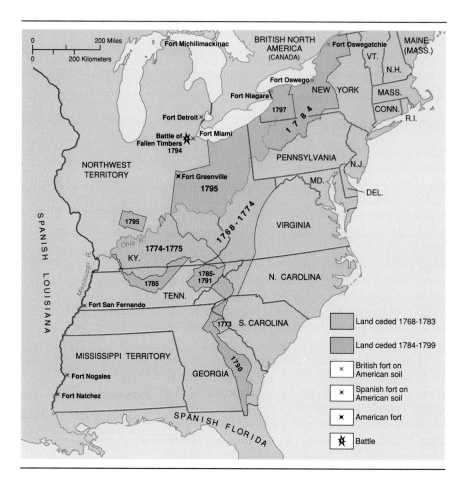

Indian Land Cessions, 1768–1799

Between 1768 and 1775, western Indians sold off vast territories, though only in undesirable mountainous regions or unoccupied Kentucky hunting grounds. Pressure by U.S. military forces from 1784 to 1799 led to the native Americans' first involuntary cessions since the early eighteenth century of large, inhabited Indian lands.

many Iroquois men welcomed the change. It was the women who resisted most, because they stood to lose their collective ownership of farmland, their control of the food supply, and their place in tribal councils. Women who did not accept Handsome Lake's and the Quakers' urging to exchange farming for housewifery found themselves accused of witchcraft, and some were killed. Even so, cultural conversion proceeded very slowly.

White attitudes toward native Americans would change significantly after the 1790s. Eighteenth-century Anglo-Americans attributed the Indians' distinctive way of life to their upbringing and expected that the native peoples would eventually match whites' cultural achievements. Indians—unlike blacks—did not seem to eighteenth-century whites a separate race. But the Iroquois' partial willingness to adopt white ways proved quite exceptional: in contrast, most native Americans

clung tightly to traditional values, much to whites' frustration and annoyance. By 1800 whites were growingly perceiving native Americans as incapable of change—as "redskins," a distinct and inferior race that white American society could never absorb. Native Americans, in short, were becoming aliens in their own land, regarded by more and more whites as a deadweight on the nation's progress.

Redefining the Color Line

The Republic's first years marked the high tide of black Americans' Revolutionary era success in bettering their lot. Although racism had not disappeared, Jefferson's eloquent words "all men are created equal" had awakened many whites' consciences. By 1790, 8 percent of all African-Americans enjoyed freedom—many having purchased

Number and Percentage of Free Blacks, by State, 1800

State	Total Number of Free Blacks	Free Blacks as a Percentage of Total Black Population
Massachusetts	7,378	100%
Vermont	557	100%
New Hampshire	855	99%
Rhode Island	3,304	90%
Pennsylvania	14,564	89%
Connecticut	5,300	85%
Delaware	8,268	57%
New York	10,374	33%
New Jersey	4,402	26%
Maryland	19,587	16%
Virginia	20,124	6%
North Carolina	7,043	5%
South Carolina	3,185	2%
Georgia	1,019	2%
Kentucky	741	2%
Tennessee	309	2%
UNITED STATES	108,395*	11%

* Total includes figures from the District of Columbia, Mississippi Territory, and Northwest Territory. These areas are not shown on the chart.

Within a generation of the Declaration of Independence, a large free black population emerged that included every ninth African-American. In the North, only in New Jersey and New York did most blacks remain slaves. Almost half of all free blacks lived in the South. Every sixth black in Maryland was free by 1800.

SOURCE: U.S. Bureau of the Census.

liberty or earned it through wartime service. Ten years later, 11 percent controlled their own fate. Various state reforms meanwhile attempted to improve slaves' conditions. In 1791, for example, the North Carolina legislature declared that the former "distinction of criminality between the murder of a white person and one who is equally an human creature, but merely of a different complexion, is disgraceful to humanity" and authorized the execution of whites who murdered slaves. By 1794 most states had outlawed the Atlantic slave trade.

Hesitant measures to ensure free blacks' legal equality also appeared in the 1780s and early 1790s. Most states dropped restrictions on their freedom of movement, protected their property, and allowed them to enroll in the militia. Of the sixteen states in the Union by 1796, all but three either permitted free blacks to vote or made no specific attempt to exclude them. Further, the federal Constitution

required no racial test for citizenship and counted everyone except slaves equally for congressional representation. But before the 1790s ended, the trend toward lessening social and legal distances between the races ended. Abolitionist sentiment ebbed, slavery became more entrenched, and whites demonstrated unmistakable reluctance to accept even free blacks as fellow citizens.

Federal law led the way in restricting blacks' rights. When Congress established procedures for naturalizing aliens in 1790, it limited eligibility to foreign whites. The federal militia law of 1792 required whites to enroll in local units but allowed states to exclude free blacks, an option that state governments increasingly chose. The navy and the marine corps forbade nonwhite enlistments in 1798. Delaware stripped free blacks of the vote in 1792, and by 1807 Maryland, Kentucky, and New Jersey had followed suit. Free blacks continued to vote and serve in integrated militia organizations in many localities after 1800 (including the slave states of North Carolina and Tennessee), but the number of places that treated them as the political equals of whites dropped sharply in the early 1800s.

An especially revealing indication of changing racial attitudes occurred in 1793, when Congress enacted the Fugitive Slave Law. This law required judges to award possession of a runaway slave upon any formal request by a master or his representative. Accused runaways not only were denied a jury trial but also were sometimes refused permission to present evidence of their freedom. Slaves' legal status as property disqualified them from claiming these constitutional privileges, of course, but the Fugitive Slave Law denied *free* blacks the legal protections that the Bill of Rights guaranteed them as citizens. Congress nevertheless passed this measure without serious opposition. The law marked a striking departure from the atmosphere of the 1780s, when state governments had invariably given whites and free blacks the same legal privileges. By 1793 white Americans clearly found it easy to forget that the Constitution had not limited citizenship to their race, and fewer of them felt honorbound to protect black rights.

The bloody slave revolt on Saint Domingue notably undermined the trend toward abolition and reinforced the kind of fears that spawned racism. Reports of the slaughter of French slaveowners made Americans hesitate to criticize slavery in the United States and helped transform the image of blacks from that of victims of injustice to one of a potential menace. In August 1800 smoldering southern white fears were kindled when a slave insurrection broke out near Virginia's capital, Richmond. Having secretly assembled weapons, more than a thousand slaves planned to march on Richmond. State militiamen, called out by Governor James Monroe, swiftly put down the conspiracy and executed some thirty-five slaves, including the leader, Gabriel Prosser. "I have nothing more to offer than what General Washington would have had to offer, had he been taken by the British officers and put to trial by them," said one rebel before his execution. "I have ventured my life in endeavoring to obtain the liberty of my countrymen, and I am a willing sacrifice to their cause."

Gabriel's Rebellion confirmed whites' anxieties that Saint Domingue's terrifying experience could be replayed on American soil. For years thereafter, isolated uprisings occurred, and rumors persisted that a massive revolt was brewing. Antislavery sentiment diminished quickly. By 1810 abolitionists ceased to exert political influence, and not until the 1830s would the antislavery movement recover from the damage inflicted by the Saint Domingue revolt.

By the time Thomas Jefferson assumed the presidency in 1801, free blacks had suffered a subtle erosion of their substantial political gains since 1776, and slaves were no closer to freedom. Two vignettes poignantly communicate blacks' plight. In 1799, near death, George Washington freed all of his relatively few slaves and gave them small sums of money to start a new life. But Martha Washington refused to emancipate the much larger group of Mount Vernon slaves who were her personal property. Meanwhile, across the Potomac, work was proceeding on the new national capital that would bear the first president's name. Enslaved blacks performed most of the labor. African-Americans were manifestly losing ground.

Conclusion

The United States had survived the perils of birth. By 1801 the dangers of civil war and national disintegration had abated, though they had not vanished. A peaceful transition of power, unprecedented in history, occurred when the Federalists allowed Thomas Jefferson to become president. But ideological hatreds remained strong, and the West's allegiance to the Union was by no means assured. Racial tensions were growing, not diminishing. It remained to be seen whether Jefferson's liberal version of republicanism could serve as a better philosophy of government than the Federalists' conservative republicanism.

CHRONOLOGY

1787 Pennsylvania Society for the Encouragement of Manufactures and the Useful Arts established.

1789 George Washington sworn in as first president.
Judiciary Act of 1789.
French Revolution begins.

1790 Alexander Hamilton submits his Report on the Public Credit and Report on a National Bank to Congress.

1791 Bank of the United States is granted a twenty-year charter.
Vermont admitted to the Union.
Bill of Rights ratified.
Slave uprising begins in French colony of Saint Domingue.
Society for the Encouragement of Useful Manufactures founded.
Hamilton submits his Report on Manufactures to Congress.

1792 Kentucky admitted to the Union.

1793 Fugitive Slave Law.
Chisholm v. *Georgia.*
Large-scale exodus of French planters from Saint Domingue to the United States.
France declares war on Britain, Spain, and Holland.

1793 Washington's Neutrality Proclamation.
(cont.) Democratic societies established.

1794 *Hylton* v. *United States.*
Ware v. *Hylton.*
Whiskey Rebellion in western Pennsylvania.
General Anthony Wayne's forces rout Indians in the Battle of Fallen Timbers.

1795 Jay's Treaty with Britain ratified.
Treaty of Greenville.

1796 Tennessee admitted to the Union.
Treaty of San Lorenzo (Pinckney's Treaty) ratified.
Washington's Farewell Address.
John Adams elected president.

1798 XYZ Affair.
Alien and Sedition Acts.
Eleventh Amendment to the Constitution ratified.

1798– Virginia and Kentucky Resolutions.
1799

1798– United States fights Quasi-War with France.
1800

1799 Fries Rebellion in Pennsylvania.

1800 Gabriel's Rebellion in Virginia.
Thomas Jefferson elected president.

For Further Reading

Lance Banning, *The Jeffersonian Persuasion: Evolution of a Party Ideology* (1978). A fresh interpretation of the intellectual assumptions that underlay Jeffersonian political principles.

Richard Buel, Jr., *Securing the Revolution: Ideology in American Politics, 1789–1815* (1972). A detailed examination of the party battles of the 1790s and the factors that contributed to the Jeffersonians' eventual victory.

Ralph Ketcham, *Presidents Above Party: The First American Presidency, 1789–1829* (1984). A comprehensive study of the ideals of nonpartisan leadership that guided the behavior of the first six presidents.

Drew R. McCoy, *The Elusive Republic: Political Economy in Jeffersonian America* (1980). An insightful portrayal of the influence of economic considerations on early national political thought.

Charles R. Ritcheson, *Aftermath of Revolution: British Policy Toward the United States, 1783–1795* (1969). A judicious, thoroughly researched account of Anglo-American diplomacy to Jay's Treaty.

James M. Smith, *Freedom's Fetters: The Alien and Sedition Laws and American Civil Liberties* (rev. ed., 1966). The most comprehensive study of the country's first great crisis in civil rights.

Gerald Stourzh, *Alexander Hamilton and the Idea of Republican Government* (1970). A bold, sweeping description of Hamilton's personal values, understanding of republicanism, and political policies.

Additional Bibliography

Early National Society

Ira Berlin, *Slaves Without Masters: The Free Negro in the Antebellum South* (1974); James Essig, *Bonds of Wickedness: American Evangelicals Against Slavery, 1770–1808* (1982); Alfred N. Hunt, *Haiti's Influence on Antebellum America* (1989); Robert McColley, *Slavery and Jeffersonian Virginia* (1964); Curtis P. Nettles, *The Emergence of a National Economy, 1775–1815* (1962); Douglass C. North, *The Economic Growth of the United States, 1790–1860* (1961); Howard B. Rock, *Artisans of the New Republic: The Tradesmen of New York City in the Age of Jefferson* (1979); George C. Rogers, Jr., *Charleston in the Age of the Pinckneys* (1969); Bernard W. Sheehan, *Seeds of Extinction: Jeffersonian Philanthropy and the American Indian* (1973); Charles G. Steffen, *The Mechanics of Baltimore: Workers and Politics in the Age of Revolution, 1763–1812* (1984); Barbara M. Tucker, *Samuel Slater and the Origins of the American Textile Industry, 1790–1860* (1984); Anthony F. C. Wallace, *The Death and Rebirth of the Seneca* (1970).

Diplomatic, Military, and Western Affairs

Harry Ammon, *The Genêt Mission* (1973); Steven R. Boyd, ed., *The Whiskey Rebellion: Past and Present Perspectives* (1985); Colin G. Calloway, *Crown and Calumet: British-Indian Relations, 1783–1815* (1987); Jerald A. Combs, *The Jay Treaty: Political Battleground of the Founding Fathers* (1970); Alexander DeConde, *Entangling Alliance: Politics and Diplomacy under George Washington* (1958), and *The Quasi-War: The Politics and Diplomacy of the Undeclared War with France, 1797–1801* (1966); Felix Gilbert, *To the Farewell Address: Ideas of Early American Foreign Policy* (1961); Reginald Horsman, *The Frontier in the Formative Years, 1783–1815* (1970); Richard H. Kohn, *Eagle and Sword: The Federalists and the Creation of the Military Establishment in America, 1783–1802* (1975); Daniel G. Lang, *Foreign Policy in the Early Republic: The Law of Nations and the Balance of Power* (1985); Bradford Perkins, *The First Rapprochement: England and the United States, 1795–1805* (1955); Thomas P. Slaughter, *The Whiskey Rebellion: Frontier Epilogue to the American Revolution* (1986); William Stinchcombe, *The XYZ Affair* (1980); Wiley Sword, *President Washington's Indian War: The Struggle for the Old Northwest, 1790–1795* (1985); Mary K. B. Tachau, *Federal Courts in the Early Republic: Kentucky, 1789–1816* (1978); J. Leitch Wright, *Britain and the American Frontier, 1783–1815* (1975).

Politics

Joyce Appleby, *Capitalism and a New Social Order: The Republican Vision of the 1790s* (1984); Richard Beeman, *The Old Dominion and the New Nation, 1788–1801* (1972); Rudolph M. Bell, *Party and Faction in American Politics: The House of Representatives, 1789–1801* (1974); William N. Chambers, *Political Parties in a New Nation: The American Experience, 1776–1809* (1963); Noble E. Cunningham, Jr., *The Jeffersonian Republicans: The Formation of Party Organization, 1789–1801* (1957); Paul Goodman, *The Democratic Republicans of Massachusetts* (1964); John F. Hoadley, *Origins of American Political Parties, 1789–1803* (1986); Stephen G. Kurtz, *The Presidency of John Adams: The Collapse of Federalism, 1795–1800* (1957); John C. Miller, *The Federalist Era, 1789–1801* (1960); Carl E. Prince, *New*

Jersey's Jeffersonian Republicans: The Genesis of an Early Party Machine, 1789–1817 (1967); Lisle A. Rose, *Prologue to Democracy: The Federalists in the South, 1789–1800* (1968); Robert A. Rutland, *The Birth of the Bill of Rights, 1776–1791* (1955); Bernard Schwartz, *The Great Rights of Mankind* (1977); Donald H. Stewart, *The Opposition Press of the Federalist Period* (1969); Alfred F. Young, *The Democratic Republicans of New York: The Origins, 1763–1797* (1967); John Zvesper, *Political Philosophy and Rhetoric: A Study of the Origins of American Party Politics* (1977).

Biographies

John R. Alden, *George Washington: A Biography* (1984); Ralph A. Brown, *The Presidency of John Adams* (1975); Gerard H. Clarfield, *Timothy Pickering and American Diplomacy, 1795–1800* (1969); Jacob E. Cooke, *Alexander Hamilton* (1982); Marcus Cunliffe, *George Washington: Man and Monument* (1958); Ralph Ketcham, *James Madison: A Biography* (1971); Adrienne Koch, *Jefferson and Madison: The Great Collaboration* (1950); Milton Lomask, *Aaron Burr: The Years from Princeton to Vice President, 1756–1805* (1979); Forrest McDonald, *Alexander Hamilton: A Biography* (1979); Dumas Malone, *Jefferson and the Ordeal of Liberty* (1962); Richard B. Morris, *John Jay: The Nation and the Court* (1967); Paul D. Nelson, *Anthony Wayne: Soldier of the Early Republic* (1985); Merrill Peterson, *Thomas Jefferson and the New Nation: A Biography* (1970); Peter Shaw, *The Character of John Adams* (1976); Page Smith, *John Adams* (1962).

CHAPTER 7

Jeffersonianism and the Era of Good Feelings

Arriving at a diplomatic reception in 1803, the British minister to the United States, Anthony Merry, was aghast to find the American president, Thomas Jefferson, "ACTUALLY STANDING IN SLIPPERS DOWN AT THE HEELS." Such "utter slovenliness and indifference to appearances," Merry concluded, could only be "intended as an insult, not to me personally, but to the sovereign I represented." In fact, Jefferson intended no insult. He never paid much attention to his dress and believed that pomp and fanfare had gotten out of hand in the administrations of George Washington and John Adams. Jefferson's casual dress, including his penchant for wearing slippers on public occasions, reflected both his personal preference and his desire to restore "republican simplicity" to the American government. That same desire led Jefferson to walk to his inaugural and then back to his boarding house, and later to substitute written messages for personal appearances before Congress.

The appearance of the new capital, Washington, reinforced Merry's impression of Americans' shabbiness. Designed for the traffic of London and the elegance of Versailles, Washington possessed neither in 1800. It could boast of two public buildings of note, the president's mansion and the Capitol, both unfinished and separated by a mile and a half of swampy terrain. The best that could be said for the place, a British visitor observed, was that the partridges nesting around the Capitol's wall provided excellent shooting.

Washington's spare arrangements mirrored conditions in the young nation. In 1800 the two most populous states, Virginia and Pennsylvania, contained fewer than fourteen inhabitants per square mile. At a time when London reported more than a million inhabitants and Paris more than half a million, no American city held even seventy thousand people. The poor quality or utter lack of roads forced Americans to live very isolated from each other. Stagecoaches running between Baltimore and Washington, for example, had to pass through a virtually trackless forest. To get to Washington from Monticello, his home in Virginia, President Jefferson had to cross five rivers that lacked bridges.

This isolation ensured that the political horizons of most Americans were limited by the physical boundaries of their own towns or villages. Republicans and Federalists clashed venomously in Washington, but in many rural areas, neither party aroused intense support. The outgoing president, John Adams, had not seen himself as the leader of a political party. The incoming president, Thomas Jefferson, did play the role of party leader and in this respect was a more modern figure than Adams. But neither Jefferson's Republicans nor the rival Federalists had any effective grassroots organization. However sharp the clashes between Republicans and Federalists in Washington, national issues only occasionally concerned ordinary Americans. Women, slaves, and the propertyless were legally barred from voting, and even those citizens who were eligible to vote often found national issues remote and uninteresting. Few voters ever laid eyes on a president. Jefferson, for example, had not been in New England since 1784, and he never did ven-

243

ture west of the Appalachian Mountains or south of Virginia.

Despite its deeply ingrained localism, America was to experience the most extraordinary national events between 1800 and 1820. In swift succession, the United States would double its land area; survive a bizarre scheme by a former vice president to divide the Union; stop all its trade with Europe in an effort to avoid war, and then go to war anyway and nearly lose; conclude a peace more favorable than it had a right to expect; and almost disintegrate in a battle over statehood for Missouri while simultaneously profiting from European power concessions that would extend its territorial claims from the Atlantic to the Pacific.

The intrusion of so dizzying a sequence of events upon a society known for its sleepy provinciality was not altogether accidental. Because communications were poor, the age proved congenial to adventures like Jefferson's vice president, Aaron Burr, who hatched wild conspiracies with the hope of succeeding before his plans became common knowledge. Furthermore, the strength of local attachments among the common people somewhat insulated leaders like Jefferson and his successor, James Madison, from their constituents. This insulation, in turn, enabled Jefferson and Madison to view politics on a grand scale. In their eyes, politics was more a process for transforming philosophical ideas into realities than for accommodating the special needs of diverse groups.

America's newness also contributed to the philosophical or ideological cast of its politics. Because there had never before been a transfer of political power from a defeated party to a victorious party, no one was sure how the Republicans would behave in office or what would become of the Federalists. The absence of precedents that might have quietly settled certain issues meant that seemingly minor questions such as replacement of Federalist officeholders became occasions for major philosophical clashes between the Republicans and the Federalists. In sum, one of the tasks that faced Jefferson and Madison was to devise and gain popular acceptance of ground rules to guide the operations of republican government.

The Age of Jefferson

Although basically a dispassionate man, Thomas Jefferson aroused deep emotions in others. His admirers saw him as a vigilant defender of popular liberty, an aristocrat who trusted the people. His detractors, pointing to his doubts about some Christian doctrines and to his early defense of the French Revolution, portrayed him as an infidel and a frenzied radical. Jefferson had so many facets that it was hard not to misunderstand him. Trained in law, he spent much of his prepresidential life in public office—as governor of Virginia, secretary of state under Washington, and vice president under John Adams. His interests included the violin, architecture, languages, and science. He designed his own mansion, Monticello, in Virginia; studied Latin, Greek, French, Italian, Anglo-Saxon, and several Indian languages; and served for nearly twenty years as president of the American Philosophical Society, the nation's first and foremost scientific organization. He viewed himself as a stronger friend of equality than either Washington or Adams; yet he owned more than two hundred slaves.

History convinced Jefferson that republics collapsed from within, not from without. Hostile neighbors notwithstanding, the real threat to freedom was posed by governments that progressively undermined popular liberty. Taxes, standing armies, and corrupt officials had made governments the masters, rather than the servants, of the people. Anyone who doubted this lesson of history needed only to look at the French Revolution; Jefferson had greeted it with hope and then watched in dismay as Napoleon Bonaparte assumed despotic power in 1799.

To prevent the United States from sinking into tyranny, Jefferson advocated that state governments retain considerable authority. He reasoned that in a vast republic marked by strong local

Jefferson's Monticello

Located in Virginia's piedmont region, Jefferson's mansion Monticello revealed his taste, scientific curiosity, and penchant for gadgetry. The device on his desk, known as a polygraph, enabled him to duplicate his letters in a pre-photocopier age.

attachments, state governments were more immediately responsive to the popular will than was the government in Washington. He also believed that popular liberty required popular virtue. For republican theorists like Jefferson, virtue consisted of a disposition to place the public good ahead of one's private interests and to exercise vigilance to keep governments from growing out of control. To Jefferson, the most vigilant and virtuous people were educated farmers, who were accustomed to act and think with sturdy independence. The least vigilant were the inhabitants of cities. Jefferson regarded cities as breeding grounds for mobs and as menaces to liberty. When the people "get piled upon one another in large cities, as in Europe," he wrote, "they will become corrupt as in Europe."

Despite his deep philosophical beliefs, Jefferson was not impractical. Of all the charges leveled at him by contemporaries, the most inaccurate was that he was a dreamy philosopher incapable of governing. "What is practicable," he wrote, "must often control pure theory." He studied science not because he liked to ponder abstract puzzles but because he believed that every scientific advance would increase human happiness. All true knowledge was useful knowledge. This practical cast of mind revealed itself both in his inventions—he designed an improved plow and a gadget for duplicating letters—and in his presidential agenda.

Jefferson's "Revolution"

Jefferson described his election as a revolution, but the revolution he sought was to restore the country to the liberty and tranquillity it had known before Alexander Hamilton's economic program and John Adams's Alien and Sedition Acts: to reverse the drift into despotism that he had detected during the 1790s. One alarming sign of this drift was the growth of the national debt by $10 million under

Explosion of the Intrepid

In September 1804 the American fireship Intrepid, *loaded with powder and intending to penetrate Tripoli harbor and explode enemy ships, blew up before reaching its target, killing Captain Richard Somers and his crew. Seven months earlier, commanded by Lieutenant Stephen Decatur, the* Intrepid *had destroyed the American frigate* Philadelphia, *which had fallen into Tripolitan hands. Britain's Lord Nelson reportedly described Decatur's exploit as "the most bold and daring act of the age."*

the Federalists. Jefferson and his secretary of the treasury, the Swiss-born Albert Gallatin, objected to the debt on both political and economic grounds. Hamilton had argued that by giving creditors a financial stake in the health of the federal government, a national debt would strengthen that government. Jefferson and Gallatin disagreed. Merely to pay the interest on the debt, there would have to be taxes, which Jefferson and Gallatin opposed for many of the same reasons that they opposed the debt. Taxes would suck money from industrious farmers, the backbone of the Republic, and put it in the hands of wealthy creditors, parasites who lived off interest payments. Further, Jefferson and Gallatin feared that revenue from taxes would tempt the government to build such a menace to liberty as a standing army.

Jefferson and Gallatin succeeded in getting Congress to repeal most internal taxes, but this repeal left the government dependent on revenue from the tariff, which was inadequate to pay off the debt. The only alternative was to slash expenditures. Jefferson closed American embassies in Madrid, Lisbon, and The Hague to save money and to signal his intention of pulling the United States out of European entanglements, and he cut the army from 4,000 to 2,500 men. The navy, however, was a different matter. In 1801 he ordered a naval squadron into action in the Mediterranean against the so-called Tripolitan (or Barbary) pirates of North Africa. For centuries, the Moslem rulers of Tripoli, Morocco, Tunis, and Algiers had solved their own budgetary problems by engaging in piracy and extorting tribute in exchange for protection; seamen whom they captured were held for ransom or sold into slavery. Most European powers handed over the fees demanded, but Jefferson calculated that going to war would be cheaper than paying high tribute to maintain peace. While suffering its share of reverses during the ensuing fighting, the United States did not come away empty-handed. In 1805 it was able to conclude a peace treaty with Tripoli for roughly half the price that it had been paying annually for protection.

Jefferson was not a pacifist and would continue to use the navy to gain respect for the American flag, but he and Gallatin placed economy ahead of military preparedness. Gallatin calculated that the nation could be freed of debt in sixteen years if administrations held the line on expenditures. In Europe, the Peace of Amiens (1802) brought a temporary halt to the hostilities between Britain and France that had threatened American shipping in the 1790s, and buoyed Jefferson's confidence that minimal military preparedness was a sound policy. The Peace of Amiens, he wrote, "removes the only danger we have to fear. We can now proceed without risks in demolishing useless structures of expense, lightening the burdens of our constituents, and fortifying the principles of free government." This may have been wishful thinking, but it rested on a sound economic calculation, for the vast territory of the United States could never be secured from attack without astronomical expense.

Jefferson and the Judiciary

In his inaugural address, Jefferson reminded Americans that their agreements were more basic than their disagreements. "We have called by different name brothers of the same principle," he proclaimed. "We are all republicans; we are all federalists." He was enough of a realist to know that the political conflict would not evaporate, but he sincerely hoped to allay fear of the Republican party and to draw moderate Federalists over to his side. There was a chance of success. He and John Adams had once been friends. The two shared many views, and each was suspicious of Hamilton. But the eventual reconciliation between Adams and Jefferson (they renewed their friendship after Jefferson's presidency), and more generally between Federalists and Republicans, would not occur during Jefferson's administration, largely because of bitter feelings over the composition and control of the judiciary.

In theory, Jefferson believed that talent and virtue rather than political affiliation were the primary qualifications for judgeships. In theory, the Federalists believed the same, but they had rarely detected either talent or virtue among the Republicans, and in 1800 not a single Republican sat on the federal judiciary. For Republicans, the crowning blow was the Federalist-sponsored Judiciary Act, passed on February 27, 1801. On the surface, this law had a nonpartisan purpose. By creating sixteen new federal judgeships, the act promised to relieve Supreme Court justices of the burden of riding far from Washington to hear cases. But the act contained several features that struck Jefferson as objectionable, including a provision to reduce the number of justices on the Supreme Court from six to five. This provision threatened both to strip Jefferson of his first opportunity to appoint a justice and to perpetuate Federalist domination of the judiciary.

Recalling the federal courts' zealousness in enforcing the Alien and Sedition Acts, and dismayed by the absence of Republicans on the federal judiciary, Jefferson saw in the Judiciary Act of 1801 a confirmation of his fears that the Federalists were retreating into the judiciary as a stronghold, "and from that battery all the works of Republicanism are to be beaten down and erased." Any lingering doubts Jefferson might have had about Federalist intentions were swept away by the actions of outgoing president John Adams during his last days in office. Between December 12, 1800, the day on which Adams's defeat in the election became clear, and March 4, 1801, the date of Jefferson's inauguration, Adams appointed several last-minute, or "midnight," judges. All federal judges appointed by Adams under provisions of the Judiciary Act were prominent Federalists. Some had been defeated for office during the election of 1800. One had captained a loyalist regiment during the Revolution, and three were brothers or brothers-in-law of John Marshall, the Federalist chief justice who was also the reputed author of the Judiciary Act of 1801.

Some radical Jeffersonians believed that judges should be elected, but Jefferson himself had no quarrel with the practice of appointing judges to serve during "good behavior" (normally for life); indeed, he thought that an independent judiciary was vital to the success of republican government. But the Federalists seemed to be turning the judiciary into an arm of their party, and in defiance of the popular will. Ironically, it was not the midnight appointments that Adams actually made but one that he left unfinished that stiffened Jefferson's resolve to seek repeal of the Judiciary Act. On his last day in office, Adams appointed an obscure Federalist, William Marbury, as justice of the peace in the District of Columbia but then failed to deliver Marbury's commission before midnight. With Jefferson in office, the new secretary of state, James Madison, refused to release the commission. Marbury petitioned the Supreme Court for a writ of mandamus,* ordering Madison to make the delivery. Chief Justice Marshall then called on Madison to show cause why he should not be compelled to hand over the commission. Although the Supreme Court did not decide the case of *Marbury* v. *Madison* until 1803, Jefferson detected in Marshall's

---

*Mandamus: an order from a higher court commanding that a specified action be taken.

John Marshall, *by Chester Harding*

Marshall served as U.S. chief justice under six presidents, several of whom were infuriated by his opinions. During Marshall's tenure, the Supreme Court asserted its authority to declare laws passed by Congress unconstitutional and affirmed the supremacy of the national government over state governments.

maneuvers the early signs of still another Federalist scheme to use the judiciary to advance partisan interests, and in 1802 he won congressional repeal of the Judiciary Act. The Federalists were in despair. The Constitution, moaned Federalist senator Gouverneur Morris, "is dead. It is dead."

As John Marshall would soon demonstrate, however, the Federalist judiciary was alive and brimming with energy. Like Jefferson, Marshall was a Virginian, but he was the son of an ordinary farmer, not an aristocrat. Marshall's service in the Continental Army during the Revolution had instilled in him (as in Alexander Hamilton) a burning attachment to the Union rather than to any state, and in the 1790s he had embraced the Federalist party. In 1803 Marshall's long-awaited

decision in *Marbury* v. *Madison* came down. Marshall tossed the Republicans a few crumbs by ruling that the Supreme Court could not compel Madison to deliver William Marbury's commission. With twisting logic, Marshall then argued that the Court could not issue a writ of mandamus (the writ Marbury sought) in its original jurisdiction because its power to do so, although explicitly granted by Congress in the Judiciary Act of 1789, was not explicitly granted by the Constitution. Hence that part of the Judiciary Act of 1789 that gave the Court power to issue writs of mandamus was unconstitutional. Next Marshall proceeded to trample on the crumbs by lecturing Madison about his moral duty (as opposed to his legal obligation) to have delivered the commission.

From the perspective of constitutional history, the key part of Marshall's decision is not that he left a minor official like Marbury without legal recourse nor that he delivered an uncalled-for lecture to Madison, but that he declared part of the Judiciary Act of 1789 unconstitutional. This was the first time that the Court had declared an act of Congress unconstitutional. It would not do so again until 1857, but an important precedent had been set.

Marshall's decision, however, had a different significance for Jefferson. Along with most mainstream Republicans, Jefferson thought that the courts did have a right to engage in judicial review (that is, to declare legislative acts unconstitutional). As far as judicial review went, Jefferson merely held that courts had no *exclusive* right of review; other branches of the government should also have the right to review the constitutionality of measures before them. Since Marshall's decision in *Marbury* did not assert that courts alone could declare laws unconstitutional, Jefferson had no quarrel with the principle of judicial review as Marshall advanced it. What infuriated Jefferson was Marshall's gratuitous lecture to Madison, which was really a lecture to Jefferson as Madison's superior. The lecture struck Jefferson as another example of Federalist partisanship with respect to the judiciary.

While the *Marbury* decision was brewing, the Republicans had already taken the offensive against the judiciary by moving to impeach (charge with wrongdoing) two Federalist judges, John Pickering of the New Hampshire District Court and Samuel

Chase of the United States Supreme Court. The particulars of the two cases differed. Pickering was an insane alcoholic who behaved in a bizarre manner in court. In one case, he decided against the prosecution before hearing any of its witnesses and then taunted the district attorney that even if he could present forty thousand witnesses, "they will not alter the decree." Chase, a notoriously partisan Federalist, had rigorously enforced the Sedition Act of 1798 and had jailed several Republican editors, including one whom Jefferson had befriended. To Republicans, Chase was the devil incarnate; all of them knew that Chase's name formed the correct ending of a popular ditty:

> *Cursed of thy father, scum of all that's base,*
> *Thy sight is odious, and thy name is . . .*

Despite these differing details, the two cases raised the same issue. The Constitution provided that federal judges could be removed solely by impeachment, which could be considered only in cases of "Treason, Bribery and other high Crimes and Misdemeanors." Was impeachment an appropriate way to get rid of judges who were insane or excessively partisan? Despite misgivings among Federalists and some Republicans about charging an obviously insane man with crimes and misdemeanors, the Senate voted to convict Pickering on March 12, 1804. That same day, the House of Representatives voted to indict Chase. John Randolph, one of Jefferson's supporters in Congress, so completely botched the prosecution of Chase that he failed to obtain the necessary two-thirds majority for conviction on any of the charges. But even if Randolph had done a competent job, Chase might still have gained acquittal, because moderate Republicans were coming to doubt whether impeachment was a solution to the issue of judicial partisanship.

Chase's acquittal ended Jefferson's skirmishes with the judiciary. Although his radical followers continued to attack the principles of judicial review and an appointed judiciary as undemocratic, Jefferson objected to neither. He merely challenged Federalist use of judicial power for political goals. Yet there was always a gray area between law and politics. Federalists did not necessarily see a conflict between protecting the Constitution and advancing their party's cause. Nor did they use their control of the federal judiciary to undo Jef-

ferson's "revolution" of 1800. The Marshall court, for example, upheld the constitutionality of the repeal of the Judiciary Act of 1801. For his part, Jefferson never proposed to impeach Marshall. In supporting the impeachments of Pickering and Chase, Jefferson was trying to make the judiciary more responsive to the popular will by challenging a pair of judges whose behavior had been outrageous. No other federal judge would be impeached for more than fifty years.

The Louisiana Purchase

Jefferson's goal of avoiding foreign entanglements would remain beyond reach as long as European powers had large landholdings in North America. In 1800 Spain, a weak and declining power, controlled East and West Florida as well as the vast Louisiana Territory. The latter alone was equal in size to the United States at that time. In the Treaty of San Ildefonso (October 1, 1800), Spain ceded the Louisiana Territory to France, which was fast emerging under Napoleon Bonaparte as the world's foremost military power. It took six months for news of the treaty to reach Jefferson and Madison but only a few minutes for them to grasp its significance.

Jefferson had long dreamed of an "empire of liberty" extending across North America and even into South America, an empire to be gained not by military conquest but by the inevitable expansion of the free and virtuous American people. An enfeebled Spain constituted no real obstacle to this expansion. As long as Louisiana had belonged to Spain, time was on the side of the United States. But Bonaparte's capacity for mischief was boundless. What if Bonaparte and the British reached an agreement that gave England a free hand in the Mediterranean and France a license to expand into North America? Then the United States would be sandwiched between the British in Canada and the French in Louisiana. What if Britain refused to cooperate with France? In that case, Britain might use its naval power to seize Louisiana before the French took control, thereby trapping the United States between British forces in the South and West as well as in the North and West.

Although Americans feared these two possibilities, Bonaparte actually had a different goal. During the 1790s he had dreamed of a French empire in the Middle East, but his defeat by the British fleet at the Battle of the Nile in 1798 had blasted this dream. Now Bonaparte devised a plan for a new French empire, this one bordering the Caribbean and the Gulf of Mexico. The fulcrum of the empire was to be the Caribbean island of Santo Domingo (today comprising Haiti and the Dominican Republic). He wanted to use Louisiana not as a base from which to threaten the United States but as a breadbasket for an essentially Caribbean empire. His immediate task was to subdue Santo Domingo, where a bloody slave revolution in the 1790s had resulted by 1800 in the takeover of the government by the black statesman Toussaint L'Ouverture (see Chapter 6). Bonaparte dispatched an army to reassert French control and to reestablish slavery, but yellow fever and fierce resistance on the part of former slaves combined to destroy the army.

As a slaveholder himself, Jefferson tacitly approved Bonaparte's attempted reconquest of Santo Domingo; as a nationalist, he continued to fear a French presence in Louisiana. This fear intensified in October 1802, when the Spanish colonial administrator in New Orleans issued an order prohibiting the deposit of American produce in New Orleans for transshipment to foreign lands. Because American farmers west of the Appalachians depended on New Orleans as a port for the cash crops that they shipped down the Mississippi River, the order was a major provocation to Americans. The order had in fact originated in Spain, but most Americans assumed that it had come from Bonaparte, who, while he now owned Louisiana, had not yet taken possession of it. An alarmed Jefferson wrote to a friend that "the day that France takes possession of N. Orleans . . . we must marry ourselves to the British fleet and nation."

The combination of France's failure to subdue Santo Domingo and the termination of American rights to deposit produce in New Orleans stimulated two crucial decisions, one by Jefferson and the other by Bonaparte, that ultimately resulted in the United States' purchase of Louisiana. First, Jefferson nominated James Monroe and Robert R. Livingston to negotiate with France for the purchase of New Orleans and as much of the Floridas as possible. (Because West Florida had repeatedly changed hands between France, Britain, and Spain,

no one was sure who owned it.) Meanwhile, Bonaparte, mindful of his military failure in Santo Domingo and of American opposition to French control of Louisiana, had concluded that his projected Caribbean empire was not worth the cost. In addition, he planned to recommence the war in Europe and needed cash. Accordingly, he decided to sell *all* of Louisiana. After some haggling between the American commissioners and Bonaparte's minister, Talleyrand, a price of $15 million was settled upon. (One-fourth of the total represented an agreement by the United States to pay French debts owed to American citizens.) For this sum the United States gained an immense, uncharted territory west of the Mississippi River. No one knew its exact size; Talleyrand merely observed that the bargain was noble. But the purchase virtually doubled the area of the United States at a cost, omitting interest, of 13½¢ an acre. It is small wonder that at the signing of the treaty, Livingston claimed that "this is the noblest work of our whole lives. . . . From this day the United States take their place among the powers of the first rank."

Because Jefferson's commissioners had exceeded their instructions, however, the president had doubts about the constitutionality of the purchase. No provision of the Constitution explicitly gave the government authority to acquire new territory or to incorporate it into the Union. Jefferson therefore drafted a constitutional amendment that authorized the acquisition of territory and prohibited the American settlement of Louisiana for an indefinite period. Fearing that an immediate and headlong rush to settle the area would lead to the destruction of the Indians and to an orgy of land speculation, Jefferson wanted to control development so that Americans could advance "compactly as we multiply." Few Republicans, however, shared Jefferson's constitutional reservations, and the president himself soon began to worry that ratification of an amendment would take too long and that Bonaparte might in the meantime change his mind about selling Louisiana. Consequently, he quietly dropped the amendment and submitted the treaty to the Senate, where it was quickly ratified.

It is easy to make too much of Jefferson's dilemma over Louisiana. He was wedded to strict construction of the Constitution, believing that the Constitution should be interpreted according to its letter. But he was also committed to the principle of establishing an "empire of liberty." Doubling the size of the Republic would guarantee land for American farmers, the backbone of the Republic and the true guardians of liberty. Like the principle of states' rights to which Jefferson also subscribed, strict construction was not an end in itself but a means to promote republican liberty. If that end could be achieved by some way other than strict construction, so be it. In addition, Jefferson was alert to practical considerations. Most Federalists opposed the Louisiana Purchase on the grounds that it would decrease the relative importance of their strongholds on the eastern seaboard. As the leader of the Republican party, Jefferson saw no reason to hand the Federalists an issue by dallying over ratification of the treaty.

The Lewis and Clark Expedition

Louisiana dazzled Jefferson's imagination. Here was an immense territory about which Americans knew virtually nothing. No one was sure of its western boundary. A case could be made for the Pacific Ocean, but Jefferson was content to claim that Louisiana extended at least to the mountains west of the Mississippi. No one, however, was certain of the exact location of these mountains, because

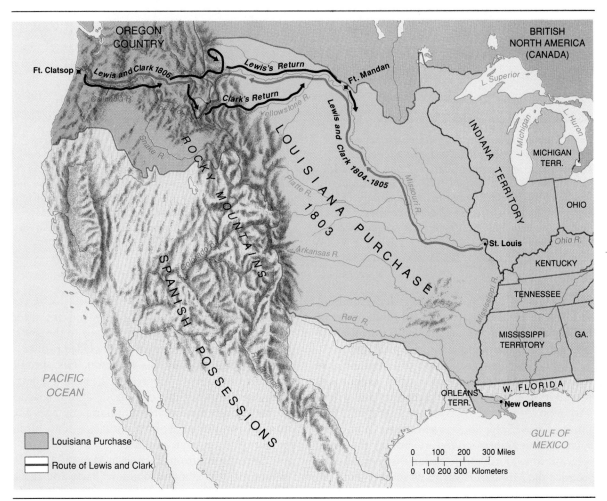

The Louisiana Purchase and the Exploration of the West   *The explorations of Lewis and Clark demonstrated the vast extent of the area purchased from France.*

Meriwether Lewis, *by Charles Wilson Peale*

Lewis grew up near Jefferson's Virginia home and, under Jefferson's guidance, developed a thirst for knowledge as well as for adventure. Lewis became Jefferson's personal secretary in 1801 and in that capacity read Jefferson's first State of the Union message to Congress. In 1803 Jefferson secured a congressional appropriation of $2500 to finance the expedition that Lewis would lead.

William Clark, *by Charles Wilson Peale*

Brother of the famed Indian fighter George Rogers Clark, William Clark served at the Battle of Fallen Timbers. William Clark's daring and resourcefulness aided the Louisiana expedition in times of crisis, as did his skill at map making. He later became governor of the Missouri Territory and an outspoken advocate of the interests of the Indians whom he had fought in his youth.

few Americans had ever seen them. Jefferson himself had never been more than fifty miles west of his home in Virginia. Thus the Louisiana Purchase was both a bargain and a surprise package.

Even before the acquisition of Louisiana, Jefferson had planned an exploratory expedition; picked its leader, his personal secretary and fellow Virginian Lieutenant Meriwether Lewis; and sent him to Philadelphia for a crash course in sciences such as zoology, astronomy, and botany that were relevant to exploration. Jefferson instructed Lewis to trace the Missouri River to its source, cross the western highlands, and follow the best water route to the Pacific. In requesting congressional funding for the expedition, Jefferson stressed the commer-

cial possibilities that it might uncover; along the line of the Missouri and beyond, the Indians' trade in pelts might be diverted from Canada to the south. But the advance of scientific knowledge probably had a higher priority for Jefferson. His specific instructions to Lewis focused on the need to obtain accurate measurements of latitude and longitude; to gather information about Indian languages and customs; and to learn about climate, plants, birds, reptiles, insects, and volcanoes.

Setting forth from St. Louis in May 1804, Lewis, his second-in-command William Clark, and about fifty others followed the Missouri River and then the Snake and Columbia rivers. In the Dakota country, Lewis and Clark hired a French-Canadian

Calumet

This calumet, a pipe used by the North American Indians for such ceremonies as the ratification of treaties (and hence called a peace pipe), was typical of the items that Lewis and Clark brought back from their exploration of the Louisiana Territory.

fur trader, Toussaint Charbonneau, as a guide and interpreter. Slow-witted and inclined to panic in crises, Charbonneau proved a mixed blessing, but his wife, Sacajawea, who accompanied him on the trip, made up for his failings. A Shoshone and probably no more than sixteen years old in 1804, Sacajawea had been stolen by a rival tribe and then claimed by Charbonneau, perhaps in settlement for a gambling debt. When first encountered by Lewis and Clark, she had just given birth to a son; indeed, her infant's presence helped to reassure Indian tribes of the expedition's peaceful intent. Additionally, Sacajawea showed Lewis and Clark how to forage for wild artichokes and other plants, often their only food, by digging into the dens where rodents stored them. Clutching her baby, she rescued most of the expedition's scientific instruments after a storm capsized one of its boats on the Missouri River.

The group finally reached the Pacific in November 1805 and then returned to St. Louis, but not before collecting a mass of scientific information, including the disturbing fact that more than three hundred miles of mountains separated the Missouri from the Columbia. It also produced a sprinkling of tall tales, many of which Jefferson believed, about gigantic Indians, soil too rich to grow trees, and a mountain composed of salt. Jefferson's political opponents railed that he would soon be reporting the discovery of a molasses-filled lake. For all the ridicule, the expedition stimulated rather than dampened interest in the West.

The Election of 1804

Jefferson's acquisition of Louisiana left the Federalists dispirited and without a popular national issue. As the election of 1804 approached, the main threat to Jefferson was not the Federalist party but his own vice president, Aaron Burr. In 1800 Burr had tried to take advantage of a tie in the electoral college to gain the presidency, a betrayal in the eyes of most Republicans, who assumed that he had been nominated for the vice presidency. While the adoption in 1804 of the Twelfth Amendment, which required separate and distinct ballots in the electoral college for the presidency and vice presidency, put an end to the possibility of an electoral tie for the presidency, it did not put an end to Burr. Between 1801 and 1804, Burr entered into enough intrigues with the Federalists to convince the Republicans that it would be unsafe to renominate him for the vice presidency. The Republicans in Congress rudely dumped Burr in favor of George Clinton. Without a hope of success, the Federalists nominated Charles C. Pinckney and Rufus King and then watched their candidates go down to crushing defeat in the election. The Federalists carried only two states, failing to hold even Massachusetts. Jefferson's overwhelming victory brought his first term to a fitting close; between 1801 and 1804, the United States had doubled its territory, taken steps to pay off its debt, and remained at peace. In short, Jefferson basked in the sun of success.

The Election of 1804		
Candidates	Parties	Electoral Vote
THOMAS JEFFERSON	Democratic-Republican	162
Charles C. Pinckney	Federalist	14

The Gathering Storm

The sky was not cloudless for long. In gaining control of Louisiana, the United States had benefited from the preoccupation of European powers with their own struggles. The nation would again benefit from this preoccupation between 1814 and 1823. But between 1803 and 1814, the renewal of the Napoleonic wars in Europe turned the United States into a pawn in a chess game played by others and helped to make Jefferson's second term far less successful than his first. In fact, the very success of his first administration contained the germs of problems that would plague his second term. As long as the two parties could compete on a more or less even basis, as in the election of 1800, leaders within each party could demand unity as a prerequisite for victory. But as the Federalist opposition weakened, unity among Republicans became less important, and they increasingly fell victim to internal squabbles.

Jefferson's Coalition Fragments

For the moment, the election of 1804 eliminated the Federalists as a force in national politics. More troubling to Republicans than Federalist opposition was factionalism within their own party, much of it the product of the inventive and perverse mind of Aaron Burr. Burr suffered a string of reverses in 1804. After being denied renomination as vice president, he entered into a series of intrigues with a faction of despairing and extreme (or "High") Federalists in New England. Led by Senator Timothy Pickering of Massachusetts, these High Federalists plotted to sever the Union by forming a pro-British "Northern Confederacy," composed of Nova Scotia (part of British-owned Canada), New England, New York, and even Pennsylvania. Although most Federalists disdained the plot, Pickering and others settled on Burr as their leader and helped him gain the Federalist nomination for the governorship of New York. Alexander Hamilton, who had thwarted Burr's plans for the presidency in 1800 by throwing his weight behind Jefferson, now foiled Burr a second time by allowing the publication of his "despicable opinion" of Burr. Defeated by a Republican in the election for New York's governor, Burr challenged Hamilton to a duel and

mortally wounded him at Weehawken, New Jersey, on July 11, 1804.

Under indictment in two states for his murder of Hamilton, Burr, still vice president, now hatched a scheme so bold that it gained momentum initially because his political opponents seriously doubted that even Burr was capable of such machinations. He allied himself with the unsavory general James Wilkinson, formerly the highest military officer in the U.S. Army and now military governor of the Louisiana Territory. Wilkinson had been on Spain's payroll intermittently as a secret agent since the 1780s. Together Burr and Wilkinson conspired to separate the western states into an independent confederacy south of the Ohio River. In addition, Wilkinson had long entertained the idea of an American conquest of Mexico, and Burr now added West Florida as a possible target. They presented these ideas to westerners as having the covert support of the administration, to the British as a way to attack Spanish-owned Mexico and West Florida, and to the Spanish (removing Mexico and West Florida as targets) as a way to divide up the United States.

Jefferson, who described Burr as a crooked gun that never shot straight, let the plot germinate for more than a year before taking action. In October 1806 he finally denounced the conspiracy publicly. By that time Burr and about sixty followers had left their staging ground, an island in the upper Ohio River, and were making their way down the Ohio and Mississippi rivers to join Wilkinson at Natchez. But Wilkinson was not there to greet Burr and his several boatloads of conspirators with their many conspiracies. Recognizing that Jefferson was now moving against Burr and that the British were uninterested in supporting the plot, Wilkinson wrote to Jefferson to report the conspiracy and then took refuge in New Orleans, where he proclaimed himself the most loyal of the president's followers.

A few weeks later, Jefferson officially denounced the conspiracy. Now Burr panicked. He tried to escape to West Florida but was intercepted; brought back to Richmond, he was put on trial for treason. Chief Justice Marshall presided at the trial and charged the jury that the prosecution had to prove not merely that Burr had treasonable intentions but also that he had committed treasonable acts, a virtually impossible task inasmuch as the conspiracy had fallen apart before Burr accomplished what he had planned. Jefferson was furious, but Marshall was merely following the clear wording of the Constitution, which deliberately made treason difficult to prove. The jury returned a verdict of "not proved," which Marshall entered as "not guilty." Still under indictment for his murder of Hamilton, Burr fled to Europe, where he tried to interest Napoleon in making peace with Britain as a prelude to a proposed Anglo-French invasion of the United States and Mexico. He returned to the United States in 1812 and, in keeping with his reputation as a womanizer, fathered two illegitimate children in his seventies and was divorced for adultery at eighty. Perhaps the most puzzling man in American history, he died in 1836.

Jefferson and the Quids

In addition to the Burr conspiracy, Jefferson faced a challenge from a group of Republicans known as the Quids*, who were led by fellow Virginian John Randolph. Randolph was a man of abounding eccentricities. An early illness had left him beardless, with a soprano voice, and probably sexually impotent. Like a dart, his wit was sharp and piercing. For all his peculiarities and biting witticisms, however, Randolph was a man of principle. Although much younger than Jefferson, he stood squarely in the tradition of the "country" ideology of the 1770s, that set of beliefs that had celebrated the honest wisdom of the plain farmer against the corruption of rulers and "court" hangers-on and that had warned incessantly against the natural tendency of all governments to encroach upon liberty. Jefferson had started out with the same beliefs but had gradually recognized their limitations. By definition, country ideology was a stance for those out of power, an ideology of opposition rather than of governance. In gaining political power, Jefferson had learned the need for compromise. Randolph, in contrast, remained frozen in an earlier time and denounced every change as a decline from the purity of 1776. He once said that he would throw all politicians to the dogs if he had less respect for dogs.

After serving in the House of Representatives between 1801 and 1805, Randolph began to turn on Jefferson. First, he blasted Jefferson for backing

a compromise in the Yazoo land scandal. In 1795 the Georgia legislature had sold the huge "Yazoo" tract (35 million acres of land comprising most of present-day Alabama and Mississippi) for a fraction of its value to four land companies that had bribed virtually the entire legislature. Following public outrage, the next legislature canceled the sale, but not before many investors had purchased land in the expectation of reselling it at a higher price. The cancellation of the sale threatened to bankrupt these investors, who had bought land to which they now no longer held legal title. For Jefferson, the scandal posed a moral challenge, since some of the purchasers, knowing nothing of the bribery, had bought the land in good faith. It also confronted him with a political challenge, since some of the buyers were northerners whom Jefferson hoped to woo into the Republican party. In 1803 a commission that included Secretary of State Madison and Treasury Secretary Gallatin awarded 5 million acres to Yazoo purchasers as a compromise. For Randolph, the compromise was itself a scandal, further evidence of the decay of republican virtue.

Randolph next collided with Jefferson over the president's request for a congressional appropriation of $2 million to purchase East and West Florida from Spain. Characteristically, Randolph raged less at the idea of obtaining the Floridas than at Jefferson's apparent act of deception in requesting money for extraordinary diplomatic expenses without officially informing Congress of the real object of the expenditures. Jefferson had sound reasons for preferring to keep negotiations over the Floridas out of the limelight, and he privately informed members of Congress, including Randolph, of his plans for the purchase; but to Randolph, it all seemed like another betrayal of virtue. He proclaimed, "I don't understand this double set of opinions and principles—the one ostensible, the other real; I hold true wisdom and cunning to be utterly incompatible."

The Suppression of American Trade

Burr's acquittal and Randolph's taunts shattered the aura of invincibility that had surrounded Jefferson after the Louisiana Purchase and the election of 1804. Now foreign affairs began to pose an even sharper challenge to his administration. In 1803 the Peace of Amiens collapsed. Britain and

---

*Quid: a name taken from the Latin *tertium quid* or "third thing." Roughly, a dissenter.

France resumed their war. While the United States remained neutral, many European nations joined the fray. Britain reacted to American neutrality with contempt. Much of Britain's information about the United States came from Federalists, who viewed the American republic as feeble and Jefferson as a pro-French romantic, and from British visitors to the United States, usually aristocrats, who sent back unflattering portraits of a rudderless democracy without effective leadership.

Britain concluded that there was little to fear from America, but the British attitude contained a dose of envy as well as contempt for the United States. While Britain was locked in a struggle against Napoleon, whom the British viewed as the enemy of all humanity, the United States was prospering at Britain's expense. Between 1790 and 1810, American ship tonnage nearly tripled. American vessels carried sugar and coffee from French and Spanish colonies in the Caribbean to Europe. This trade not only provided Napoleon with supplies but also drove down the price of sugar and coffee from the British West Indies by adding to the glut of these commodities on world markets. It was easy for the British to conclude that American prosperity was the cause of Britain's economic difficulties.

The basis of the American prosperity was the reexport trade—an American adaptation to the British Rule of 1756, which stated that trade closed in time of peace could not be opened in time of war. For example, in peacetime, France usually restricted to French ships the transportation of products such as sugar from the French West Indies. According to the Rule of 1756, the ships of a neutral country such as the United States could not replace French ships as carriers now that the war between France and Britain made French vessels fair game for the British navy. The American response to the Rule of 1756 was the "broken voyage." American vessels would carry produce from the Spanish and French West Indies to an American port, unload it and pass it through customs, then reload it and reexport it to Europe as *American* produce. Between 1795 and 1805, the British tolerated broken voyages but thereafter charted a new course. Seeking now to strangle French commerce as well as to defeat Napolean's armies, Britain pursued total war against France. A sign of the new policy was a British court's decision in the 1805 *Essex* case declaring broken voyages illegal.

The British followed the *Essex* decision in May 1806 with the first of several trade regulations known as Orders in Council, which established a blockade of part of the continent of Europe. In theory, this Order in Council softened the *Essex* decision by allowing American vessels to trade with French possessions as long as they carried their cargoes to Britain rather than to a continental port controlled by France. But Napoleon responded in November 1806 with his Berlin Decree, which proclaimed a blockade of the British Isles; any ship attempting to enter or leave a British port was now subject to seizure by France. The British answered the Berlin Decree with another Order in Council, this one requiring all neutral ships trading in the blockaded zones of Europe to stop at British ports to secure licenses. Napoleon replied in December 1807 by tightening his so-called Continental System with the Milan Decree, which proclaimed that any vessel that submitted to British regulations or allowed itself to be searched by the Royal Navy was subject to seizure by France.

This dizzying sequence of proclamations and counterproclamations effectively outlawed virtually all American trade. If an American ship submitted to search by a British ship or secured a British license to trade, it became a French target; if it avoided the British and reached a French-controlled port, it became a British target. Both Britain and France seized American ships, but British seizures were far more humiliating to Americans. France was a weaker naval power than Britain; much of the French fleet had been destroyed by the British at the Battle of Trafalgar in October 1805. Accordingly, most of France's seizures of American ships occurred in European ports where American ships had been lured by Napoleon's often inconsistent enforcement of his Continental System. In contrast, British warships hovered just beyond the American coast. Off New York, for example, the Royal Navy stopped and searched virtually every American vessel. At times, U.S. ships had to line up a few miles from the American coast to be searched by the Royal Navy.

Impressment

On top of these provocations, the British added that of impressment. At issue was the seizure from American merchant ships, and the subsequent pressing into service, of purported British sailors who had deserted from the Royal Navy.

British sailors had good reason to be discontented with the navy. Aside from the fact that discipline on the Royal Navy's "floating hells" was often brutal, wages were much lower than on American ships. The pay of an able-bodied seaman on a British ship was only around seven dollars a month, compared to twenty-five to thirty-five dollars a month on American ships. As a result, at a time when war intensified Britain's need for sailors, the Royal Navy suffered a high rate of desertion to U.S. ships; for example, in 1807 the American frigate *Constitution* carried a crew of 419 men, of whom 149 were British subjects.

Impressed sailors led harrowing lives that included frequent escapes and recaptures. One seaman suffered impressment on eleven separate occasions; another, on the verge of his third recapture, drowned himself rather than spend another day in the Royal Navy. The British practice of impressment was not only cruel to individuals but galling to American pride, because many deserters from the Royal Navy had acquired American naturalization papers and become American citizens. The British impressed these men anyway on the principle that once a Briton, always a Briton. At times, the British also impressed American-born citizens, even when the latter produced documentation proving their American birth. Americans with Irish-sounding names were especially suspect. One New Englander related how a British captain barked at him that "I was a damned Irish Yankee and I have as good a right [duty] to serve his majesty as he had." Between 1803 and 1812, the British impressed over six thousand American citizens. Although impressment did less damage to the American economy than the seizure of ships, it was even more humiliating.

Any doubts that Americans had about British arrogance evaporated in June 1807 when a British warship, HMS *Leopard,* patrolling off Hampton Roads, Virginia, attacked an unsuspecting American frigate, USS *Chesapeake,* and forced it to surrender. The British then boarded the vessel and seized four supposed deserters. One, a genuine deserter, was later hanged; the other three were former Britons, now American citizens, who had "deserted" only from impressment. Even the British had never before asserted their right to seize

deserters off government ships. The so-called *Chesapeake* Affair enraged the country. Jefferson remarked that he had not seen so belligerent a spirit in America since 1775. Yet while making some preparations for war, the president sought peace —first by conducting fruitless negotiations with Britain to gain redress for the *Chesapeake* outrage, and second by steering the Embargo Act through Congress in December 1807.

The Embargo

By far the most controversial legislation of either of Jefferson's administrations, the Embargo Act prohibited vessels from leaving American ports for foreign ports. Technically, it prohibited only exports, but its practical effect was to stop imports as well, for few foreign ships would venture into American ports if they had to leave without cargo. Amazed by the boldness of the act, a British newspaper described the embargo as "little short of an absolute secession from the rest of the civilized world."

Jefferson advocated the embargo as a means of "peaceable coercion." By restricting French and British (especially British) trade with the United States, he hoped to pressure both nations into respecting American neutrality. But the embargo did not have the effect that Jefferson intended. Although British sales to the United States dropped 50 percent between 1807 and 1808, the British quickly found new markets in South America, where rebellions against Spanish rule had flared up, and in Spain itself, where a revolt against Napoleon had opened trade to British shipping. Further, the Embargo Act itself contained some loopholes. For example, it allowed American ships blown off course to put in at European ports if necessary; suddenly many captains were reporting that adverse winds had forced them across the Atlantic. Treating the embargo as a joke, Napoleon seized whatever American ships he could lay hands on and then informed the United States that he was only helping to enforce the embargo. The British were less amused, but the embargo confirmed their view that Jefferson was an ineffectual philosopher, an impotent challenger compared with Napoleon.

The harshest effects of the embargo were felt not in Europe but in the United States. Some thirty thousand American seamen found themselves out of work. Merchants stumbled into bankruptcy by

Joseph Peabody, *by Charles Osgood*

The Revolutionary soldier Joseph Peabody (1757–1844) built a large fleet of seafaring vessels after the war and became the leading merchant in Salem, Massachusetts. The embargo severely disrupted Peabody's thriving importation of pepper, tea, indigo, and other products from China, the Mediterranean, and the West Indies.

twice the ship tonnage per capita of any other state and more than a third of the entire nation's ship tonnage in foreign trade. (The earnings of the Massachusetts merchant fleet that year were equal to the entire revenue of the U.S. government in 1806.) For a state so dependent on foreign trade, the embargo was a calamity. Wits reversed the letters of *embargo* to form the phrase "O grab me."

The picture was not entirely bleak. The embargo forced a diversion of merchants' capital into manufacturing. In short, unable to export produce, Americans began to make products. Before 1808 the United States had only fifteen mills for fashioning cotton into textiles; by the end of 1809, an additional eighty-seven mills had been constructed. But none of this comforted merchants already ruined or mariners driven to soup kitchens. Nor could New Englanders forget that the source of their misery was a policy initiated by one of the "Virginia lordlings," "Mad Tom" Jefferson, who knew little about New England and who had a dogmatic loathing of cities, the very foundations of New England's prosperity. A Massachusetts poet wrote:

> *Our ships all in motion once whitened the*
> *   ocean,*
> *They sailed and returned with a cargo;*
> *Now doomed to decay they have fallen a prey*
> *To Jefferson, worms, and embargo.*

The Election of 1808

Even before the Embargo Act, Jefferson had announced that he would not be a candidate for reelection. With his blessing, the Republican congressional caucus nominated James Madison and George Clinton for the presidency and vice presidency, while the Federalists countered with Charles C. Pinckney and Rufus King, the same ticket that had made a negligible showing in 1804. In 1808 the Federalists staged a modest comeback, gaining twenty-four congressional seats. Still, Madison won 122 of 175 electoral votes for president, and the Republicans retained comfortable majorities in both houses of Congress.

Several factors contributed to the Federalists' revival in 1808. First, the embargo gave them the national issue that they had long lacked. Also, younger Federalists, represented by men like Har-

the hundreds, and jails swelled with debtors. A New York City newspaper ruefully noted that the only activity still flourishing in the city was prosecution for debt. Farmers, too, were devastated. Unable to export their produce or sell it at a decent price to hard-pressed urban dwellers, many farmers could not earn enough cash to pay their debts. In desperation, one farmer in Schoharie County, New York, sold his cattle, horses, and farm implements, worth eight hundred dollars before the embargo, for fifty-five dollars. Speculators who had purchased land expecting to sell it later at a higher price also took a beating, because cash-starved farmers stopped buying land. "I live and that is all," wrote one New York speculator. "I am doing no business, cannot sell anybody property, nor collect any money."

The embargo fell hardest on New England and particularly on Massachusetts, which in 1807 had

The Election of 1808		
Candidates	Parties	Electoral Vote
JAMES MADISON	Democratic-Republican	122
Charles C. Pinckney	Federalist	47
George Clinton	Democratic-Republican	6

rison Gray Otis of Massachusetts and Robert G. Harper of South Carolina, were making their influence felt. Old-time Federalists, expecting the voters to defer naturally to gentlemen, had refused to campaign actively for votes, and they judged it disgraceful that their Republican opponents treated voters to barbecues and staged mass meetings. The younger Federalists, on the other hand, deliberately imitated the vote-winning techniques that had proved successful for the Republicans.

The Failure of Peaceable Coercion

To some contemporaries, the diminutive "Little Jemmy" Madison (he was only five feet, four inches tall) seemed a weak and shadowy figure alongside the commanding presence of Jefferson. But in fact, Madison, who faced a situation that would have confused anyone, brought to the presidency an intelligence and a capacity for systematic thought that matched Jefferson's. Like Jefferson, Madison believed that American liberty had to rest on the virtue of the people and that that virtue was critically tied to the growth and prosperity of agriculture. More clearly than Jefferson, Madison also recognized that agricultural prosperity depended on the vitality of American trade, for Americans would continue to enter farming only if they could get their crops to market. In particular, the British West Indies, dependent on the United States for much of their lumber and grain, struck Madison as a natural trading partner for the United States. Britain alone could not fully supply the West Indies. Therefore, if the United States embargoed its own trade with the West Indies, Madison reasoned, the British would be forced to their knees before Americans could suffer severe losses from the embargo. Britain, he wrote, was "more vulnerable in her commerce than in her armies."

The problem was that the American embargo was coercing no one. Increased trade between Canada and the West Indies after 1808 made a shambles of Madison's plan to pressure Britain by blocking American trade to the West Indies. On March 1, 1809, Congress repealed the Embargo Act and substituted the weaker, although face-saving, Non-Intercourse Act. This act opened American trade to all nations except Britain and France and authorized the president to restore trade with either nation if it ceased to violate neutral rights. But the act failed to persuade the British or the French to respect American shipping. Grasping at straws, Madison then negotiated an agreement with David Erskine, the British minister in Washington, to reopen American trade in return for a British promise to revoke its Orders in Council. That same day, June 10, 1809, some six hundred American ships sailed for Britain. But Erskine had acted without orders. British Foreign Secretary George Canning disavowed the Erskine agreement as soon as he got wind of it, and Madison was forced to reembargo trade with Britain.

Madison called Canning's policy a "mixture of fraud and folly," but Canning thought that he was pursuing a level-headed course of action and had trouble understanding American belligerence. Canning and most British statesmen saw the world as containing a few great powers like Britain and France and innumerable small and weak powers. When great powers waged war against each other, there were no neutrals. Weak nations such as the United States should logically seek the protection of a great power. Since Britain was a natural trading partner for the United States, Americans should recognize, the reasoning went, that their best interests would be served by peacefully submitting to dependency on Britain. The problem was that Jefferson and Madison refused to accept this British conception of power relationships. In their view, the United States, however weak its military, was a nation founded on majestic principles that made it morally superior to Europe. The stepchildren of vanity and ambition, Europe's wars were of no concern to Americans. Jefferson wrote of France and England: "The one is a den of robbers and the other of pirates."

As an economic boom swept across Britain in 1809, the failure of the American policy of peaceable coercion was becoming obvious. Nor was that policy having a noticeable impact on France. Holding the same view of international power relations as the British, Napoleon tried to manipulate the United States into a collision course with Britain. Confronted by implacable hostility from Britain and France, Congress continued to drift. In May 1810 it substituted Macon's Bill No. 2 for the Non-Intercourse Act. The Macon legislation reopened trade with Britain and France and then offered a clumsy bribe to each: if either Britain or France repealed its restrictions on neutral shipping, the United States would halt all commerce with the other. Jumping at the opportunity presented by Macon's Bill No. 2, Napoleon promised to repeal his edicts against American trade. Madison snapped at the bait and proclaimed non-intercourse against Britain. But Napoleon had no intention of respecting American neutrality. His plan all along had been to trick the Americans into a posture of hostility toward Britain, and he continued to seize American ships spotted in French-controlled ports. Peaceable coercion had become a fiasco.

The Push into War

Madison soon found himself faced not only by a hostile Britain and France but by militants within his own party who demanded more aggressive policies. Most of these men were southerners and westerners. Coming from regions where honor was a sacred word, they were infuriated by insults to the American flag. In addition, when an economic recession struck the South and West between 1808 and 1810, South Carolina's John C. Calhoun and others realized that British policies were wrecking the economies of their regions. Consequently, a war spirit began to pulsate in the veins of several young congressmen elected in 1810. Drawn mainly from the South and West, these hotbloods formed a cohesive group, dubbed the "war hawks," in the House of Representatives. Their leader was a thirty-four-year-old Kentuckian, Henry Clay, who preferred war to the "putrescent pool of ignominious peace." With the support of the other war hawks, such as Calhoun, Richard M. Johnson of Kentucky, and William R. King of North Carolina—all of them future vice presidents—Clay was elected to the speakership of the House over the aging Nathaniel Macon, the author of Macon's Bill No. 2.

Tecumseh and the Prophet

Voicing a more emotional and pugnacious nationalism than Jefferson and Madison, the war hawks called for the expulsion of the British from Canada and the Spanish from the Floridas. Their demands merged with western settlers' fears that the British in Canada were actively recruiting the Indians to halt the march of American settlement. These fears, groundless but plausible, became intense when the Shawnee chief Tecumseh and his half-brother the Prophet sought to unite several tribes in Ohio and the Indiana territory against American settlers. Demoralized by the continuing loss of Indian lands to the whites and by the ravages of Indian society

Tenskwatawa, the Prophet

In periods of crisis, the native American cultures often gave rise to prophets—religious revivalists of sorts—such as Tecumseh's brother Tenskwatawa. Known to non-Indians as the Prophet, Tenskwatawa tried to revive traditional Indian values and customs such as the common ownership of land and the wearing of animal skins and furs. His religious program blended with Tecumseh's political program to unite the western tribes.

by alcoholism, Tecumseh and the Prophet (himself a reformed alcoholic) tried to unify their people and revive traditional Indian virtues. Both men believed that the Indians had to purge themselves of liquor and other corrupting messengers of white civilization as part of this revival. For example, to express his rejection of the whites' ways, Tecumseh long refused to learn English.

The aspirations of these Shawnee leaders set them on a collision course with Governor William Henry Harrison of the Indiana Territory. A wily bargainer, Harrison had purchased much of central and western Indiana from the Miami and the Delaware Indians in the Treaty of Fort Wayne (1809) for the paltry sum of ten thousand dollars. When Tecumseh's Shawnee people had refused to sign the treaty, however, Harrison began to regard the brilliant and charismatic Indian leader as an enemy.

With white settlers in Indiana convinced that Tecumseh's effort to unite the Indians was a British-inspired scheme, Harrison gathered an army in September 1811 and marched against a Shawnee encampment, the Prophet's Town, at the junction of the Wabash and Tippecanoe rivers. Then in November the Shawnees, led by the Prophet (Tecumseh was off recruiting Creek Indians), attacked Harrison. In the ensuing Battle of Tippecanoe, the Shawnees were beaten, the Prophet's Town was destroyed, and the Prophet was discredited in Tecumseh's eyes for his premature attack. Ironically, the Battle of Tippecanoe, which made Harrison a national hero, accomplished precisely what it had been designed to prevent. Never before a British agent, Tecumseh now joined with the British.

Congress Votes War

By the spring of 1812, President Madison had reached the decision that war with Britain was inevitable. On June 1 he sent his war message to Congress. Meanwhile, an economic depression struck Britain, partly because the American policy of restricting trade with that country had finally started to work. Under pressure from its merchants, Britain repealed the Orders in Council on June 23, but by then Congress, unaware that the British were contemplating repeal of the orders, had passed the declaration of war. It was still possible, of course, for Madison to revoke the declaration now that the maritime issue had been partly

settled. The British cabinet believed that he would do so. What the British failed to comprehend, however, was how much more belligerent American political leaders, particularly Republicans, had become between 1810 and 1812.

While both war hawks and westerners had contributed to this hostile mood, neither held the key to the vote in favor of war. The war hawks composed a minority within the Republican party; the West was still too sparsely settled to have many representatives in Congress. Rather, the votes of Republicans in populous states like Pennsylvania, Maryland, and Virginia were the main force propelling the war declaration through Congress. Most opposition to war came from Federalist strongholds in Massachusetts, Connecticut, and New York. Because Federalists were so much stronger in the Northeast than elsewhere, congressional opposition to war revealed a sectional as well as a party split. In general, however, southern Federalists opposed the war declaration, while northern Republicans supported it. In other words, the vote for war followed party lines more closely than sectional lines. Much like James Madison himself, the typical Republican advocate of war had not wanted war in 1810 nor even in 1811 but had been led by the accumulation of grievances to demand it in 1812.

The Causes of the War

In his war message, Madison listed impressment, the continued presence of British ships in American waters, and British violations of neutral rights as grievances that justified war. But none of these complaints was new. Taken together, they do not fully explain why Americans went to war in 1812 rather than earlier—for example, in 1807 after the *Chesapeake* affair. Madison also listed British incitement of the Indians as a stimulus for war. This grievance of recent origin contributed to war feeling in the West. "The War on the Wabash," a Kentucky newspaper proclaimed, "is purely British. The British scalping knife has filled many habitations both in this state as well as in the Indiana Territory with widows and orphans." But the West had too few American inhabitants to account for the nation's being propelled into war. A more important underlying cause was the economic recession that affected the South and West after

1808—and the conviction, held by John C. Calhoun and others, that British policy was damaging America's economy. Finally, the fact that Madison rather than Jefferson was president in 1812 was of major importance. Jefferson had believed that the only motive behind British seizures of American ships was Britain's desire to block American trade with Napoleon. Hence Jefferson had concluded that time was on America's side; the seizures would stop as soon as the war in Europe ceased. In contrast, Madison had become persuaded that Britain's real motive was to strangle American trade once and for all and thereby eliminate the United States as a trading rival. War or no war in Europe, Madison saw Britain as a menace to America. In his war message, he stated flatly that Britain was meddling with American trade not because that trade interfered with Britain's "belligerent rights" but because it "frustrated the monopoly which she covets for her own commerce and navigation."

The War of 1812

The popular American war slogan in June 1812 was "Free Trade and Sailors' Rights," and maritime issues had indeed been the centerpiece of Madison's war message. Yet Americans marched rather than sailed to war; they aimed at Canada, not at the British fleet. There were several reasons for this strategy. First, the growth of Canadian exports to the West Indies after 1808 had convinced Madison that Canada was not a snowbound wasteland but a key prop of the British Empire, an indispensable component of Britain's designs to strangle American trade. Moreover, an attack on Canada seemed a practical tactic. Between 1800 and 1812, the Republicans had consistently preferred economy to preparedness. They had shrunk the national debt from $83 million to $27.5 million, and as a result the American navy contained only six frigates, three sloops of war, and a number of smaller vessels, including gunboats. A brainchild of Jefferson, the gunboats were little more than floating gun docks designed for harbor defense. They often sank when they ventured forth to sea and at times could not even hold anchor in harbors. When a hurricane blew one gunboat eight

miles inland onto a cornfield, the Federalists mordantly toasted it as the finest ship "upon earth."

Thus unable to challenge Britain at sea, Americans looked north to Canada as a practical objective. Few Americans expected a prolonged or difficult struggle. The United States outstripped Canada in everything: 25 to 1 in population, 9 to 1 in militia, 7 to 5 in regular army soldiers. Further, not only were the best British troops in Europe fighting Napoleon but three out of every five settlers in Canada were Americans from New York, Pennsylvania, and Connecticut. These settlers, now technically Canadians, had been lured north by cheap land but feared the British more than they feared their kin on the American side. To Jefferson, the conquest of Canada seemed "a mere matter of marching."

Expectations of an easy victory, however, rested on a much shakier foundation than many Americans realized. First, the British had an invaluable ally in the native Americans, who proved to be terrifying as well as tough warriors. Although not the only ones to commit atrocities, the Indians struck fear in beholders by dangling scalps from their belts. The British quickly learned to play on this fear, in some cases forcing Americans to surrender by hinting that the Indians might be uncontrollable in battle. Second, most American generals were aged and incompetent, and one of the only good ones, Andrew Jackson, was long denied a federal commission, on political grounds. And the American state militias, the darlings of republican theorists because they seemed a safe alternative to a standing army, were filled with Sunday soldiers who "hollered for water half the time, and whiskey the other. . . ." Their lack of training aside, few militiamen really understood the goals of the war. In fact, outside Congress, there simply was not much blood lust in 1812. In New England, where opposition to the war was widespread, the people had little stomach for an invasion of Canada. (The loyal minority in New England, however, did provide the army with more regiments than either the middle states or the South.) President Madison was able to raise only 10,000 one-year volunteers out of the 50,000 authorized by Congress. In Kentucky, the home of the prominent war hawk Henry Clay (who boasted that his constituents were spoiling for a fight), only 400 answered the first call for volunteers. This lukewarm response in all sections indicates not only that most people viewed Canada as remote but also that national political issues did not necessarily penetrate deeply into American society in 1812. Local attachments remained stronger than national ones.

The military campaigns of the war developed in two broad phases. From the summer of 1812 to the spring of 1814, the Americans assumed the offensive position, launching a succession of poorly coordinated and generally unsuccessful attacks on Canada. From the spring of 1814 into early 1815, the British took the offensive and achieved some spectacular victories while losing key battles.

On to Canada

Whereas some Americans wanted to commence the war with an attack on Montreal, the ardor of western politicians dictated that the opening offensive occur in the West. In July 1812 sixty-year-old General William Hull led an American army from Detroit into Canada, but the ingenious Tecumseh cut his supply line. Hull then retreated to Detroit. Unnerved by the sight of Tecumseh and by the hint of the British commander, General Isaac Brock, that "the numerous body of Indians who have attached themselves to my troops will be beyond my control the moment the contest commences," Hull surrendered two thousand men to thirteen hundred British and native American troops.

Now the British concentrated their strength against a mixed force of regulars and New York militia menacing Canada north of Niagara Falls. While the American regulars marched into Canada, the New York militiamen, contending that they had volunteered only to protect their homes, not to invade Canada, refused to cross their state line. As the militia looked on from the American side, a detachment of American regulars was crushed by the British at the Battle of Queenston (October 12, 1813). Again the daunting Indian presence proved decisive. Winfield Scott, later to become a candidate for the presidency of the United States, negotiated the American surrender as Mohawk Indians were attacking his men. The third American offensive of 1812 never got off the ground. The sixty-two-year-old general Henry Dearborn was to have moved on Montreal via Lake Champlain. He had advanced twenty miles north of Plattsburgh by November 19, when the militia refused to go any further. Thus Dearborn returned to Plattsburgh.

Under General William Henry Harrison, the Americans renewed their offensive in 1813 and tried to retake Detroit. A succession of reverses convinced Harrison that offensive operations were futile as long as the British controlled Lake Erie. During the winter of 1812–1813, Captain Oliver H. Perry constructed a little fleet of vessels out of green wood, cannon captured in a raid on York (Toronto), and supplies dragged across the snow from Pittsburgh to his headquarters at Presqu'ile (Erie). Perry encountered and destroyed a British squadron at Put-in-Bay on the western end of Lake Erie on September 10, 1813, reporting "We have met the enemy, and they are ours." Losing control of Lake Erie, the British pulled back from Detroit, but Harrison overtook and defeated a combined British and Indian force at the Battle of the Thames on October 5. Tecumseh, now a legend among the whites, died in the battle; Colonel Richard Johnson's claim, never proved, to have killed Tecumseh later contributed to Johnson's election as vice president of the United States.

The Naval War

Even before their victory at Put-in-Bay, Americans had achieved sensational successes on the high seas. Republican tightfistedness had not altogether succeeded in starving the United States Navy. However small, the navy had entered the war with three of the largest and fastest frigates afloat — the *Constitution,* the *United States,* and the *President.* On August 19, 1812, the *Constitution* destroyed HMS *Guerrière* in the mid-Atlantic and on December 29 wrecked HMS *Java* off Brazil. In October the *United States,* under Captain Stephen Decatur, captured HMS *Macedonian* off the African coast and brought the ship back to New London, Connecticut, as a prize. But these victories had more psychological than strategic value. While they gave Americans something to cheer, the British clamped a blockade on the American coast, starting with Delaware Bay and Chesapeake Bay in the fall of 1812 and extending to New York in the spring of 1813 and to New England in the spring of 1814. The *United States* was now corked in the bottle of New York harbor, the *President* in New Haven, and the *Constitution* in Boston. Nor did Perry's victory on Lake

The Constitution Ranging Alongside the Guerrière, *by Michael Felice Corne, 1812 (Detail)*

The Constitution *won more battles than any other early American frigate. Its most famous victory was over H.M.S.* Guerrière *in August 1812. Known affectionately as Old Ironsides, it was saved from demolition in 1830 by the poet Oliver Wendell Holmes, became a schoolship for the U.S. Naval Academy, was nearly confiscated by the fledgling Confederate navy in 1861, and today survives as a naval relic in Boston harbor.*

Erie and Harrison's at the Battle of the Thames hasten the conquest of Canada. Efforts to invade Canada in the Niagara area, and to gain control of Lake Ontario, failed.

The British Offensive

Britain's military fortunes crested in the spring of 1814. After his disastrous invasion of Russia in 1812 and a series of defeats in 1813, France's Napoleon abdicated as emperor in April 1814, and Britain began to move regulars from Europe to North America. The British quickly found, however, that earlier defeats had toughened the Americans, who were now fighting to defend their homes rather than to invade Canada. The first sign of trouble for the British came on the Niagara front in July 1814, when attacking redcoats were stopped by fierce American resistance at the battles of Chippewa (July 5) and Lundy's Lane (July 25).

The main British thrust came not on the Niagara front but down Lake Champlain. At the head of ten thousand British veterans, the largest and best-equipped British army ever sent to North America, General Sir George Prevost advanced south via the lake at the end of August and reached Plattsburgh on September 6. Prevost's plan was to split the New England states from the rest of the country. At Plattsburgh, however, he encountered a well-entrenched American army. Resolving that he had to control the lake before attacking Plattsburgh, Prevost called up his fleet, but an American naval squadron under Captain Thomas Macdonough defeated the British squadron on September 11. Dispirited, Prevost abandoned the campaign.

Ironically, the British achieved a far more spectacular success in an operation originally designed merely as a diversion from their main thrust down Lake Champlain. In 1814 a British army sailed from Bermuda for Chesapeake Bay, landed near Washington, and on August 24 met a larger American force, composed mainly of militia, at Bladensburg, Maryland. The Battle of Bladensburg quickly became the "Bladensburg races" as the American militia fled, almost without firing a shot. The British then descended on Washington. Madison, who had witnessed the Bladensburg fiasco, escaped into the Virginia hills. His wife, Dolley, pausing only long enough to load her silver, a bed, and a portrait of George Washington onto her carriage, hastened to join her husband, while British troops ate the supper prepared for the Madisons at the presidential mansion. Then they burned the mansion along with other public buildings in Washington. A few weeks later, the British attacked

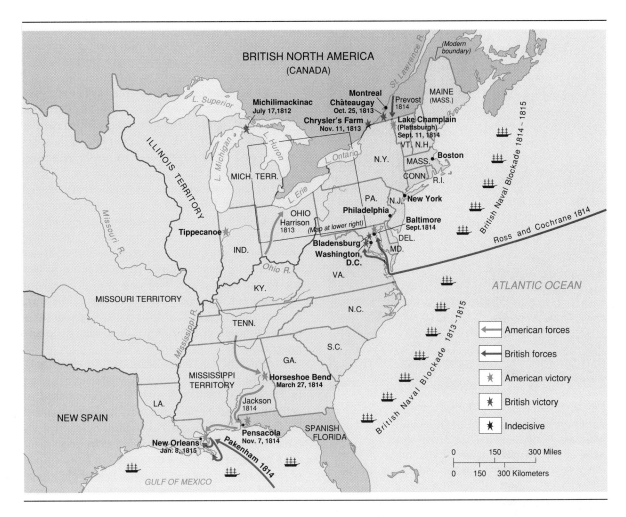

Major Battles of the War of 1812

Most of the war's major engagements occurred on or near the United States' northern frontier; but the Royal Navy blockaded the entire Atlantic coast, and the British army penetrated as far south as Washington and New Orleans.

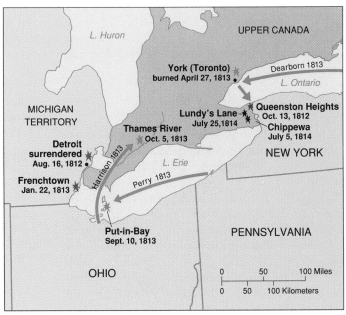

Dolley Madison, *by Gilbert Stuart, 1804*

As the attractive young wife of Secretary of State James Madison, Dolley Madison acted virtually as the nation's First Lady during the administration of Jefferson, a widower. Friendly, tactful, and blessed with an unfailing memory for names and events, she added to her reputation as an elegant hostess after her husband became president.

Baltimore, but after failing to crack its defenses, they broke off the operation.

The Treaty of Ghent

In August 1814 negotiations to end the war commenced between British and American commissioners at Ghent, Belgium. The British appeared to command a strong position. Having frustrated American designs on Canada, they stood poised for their Lake Champlain initiative. In reality, however, their position was not as strong as it appeared and would grow weaker as negotiations progressed.

With Napoleon's abdication as emperor, Britain's primary goal had become a favorable and lasting peace in Europe; the British had little to gain from prolonging a minor war in America. Mindful of their superior military position, they demanded territorial concessions from the United States. The American naval victory at Plattsburgh, however, brought home to Britain the fact that after two years of fighting, the British controlled neither the Great Lakes nor Lake Champlain. The spectacular raid on Washington had no strategic significance, and so the British gave way on the issue of territorial concessions. The final treaty, signed on Christmas Eve 1814, restored the status quo ante bellum*: the United States neither gained nor lost territory. Several additional issues, including the fixing of a boundary between the United States and Canada, were referred to joint commissions for future settlement. Nothing was done about impressment, but with Napoleon out of the way, neutral rights became a dead issue. Because there was no longer a war in Europe, there were no longer neutrals.

Ironically, the most dramatic American victory of the war came after the conclusion of peace. In December 1814 a British army, composed of veterans of the Napoleonic wars and commanded by General Sir Edward Pakenham, descended on New Orleans. On January 8, 1815, two weeks after the signing of the Treaty of Ghent but before word of the treaty had reached America, Pakenham's force attacked an American army under General Andrew ("Old Hickory") Jackson. Already a legend for his ferocity as an Indian fighter, Jackson inspired little fear among the British, who advanced into battle far too confidently, but he did strike enough terror in his own men to prevent another American rout. In an hour of gruesome carnage, Jackson's troops shredded the line of advancing redcoats, killing Pakenham and inflicting more than two thousand casualties while losing only thirteen Americans.

The Hartford Convention

Because the Treaty of Ghent had already concluded the war, the Battle of New Orleans had little significance for diplomats. Indirectly, however, it had an impact on domestic politics by eroding Federalist strength.

---

*Status quo ante bellum: Latin for the state of affairs before the war.

The comeback that the Federalists had made in the election of 1808 had continued into the 1812 campaign. Buoyed by hostility to the war in the Northeast, the Federalists had thrown their support behind DeWitt Clinton, an antiwar Republican. Although Madison won the electoral vote 128–89, Clinton carried all of New England except Vermont, as well as New York and New Jersey. American military setbacks in the war intensified Federalist disdain for the new Madison administration. Indeed, from their bastions in New England (see "A Place in Time"), Federalists saw a nation misruled for over a decade by Republican bunglers. Jefferson's attack on the judiciary had seemed to threaten the rule of law. His purchase of Louisiana, a measure of doubtful constitutionality, had enhanced Republican strength and reduced the relative importance of Federalist New England in the Union. The Embargo Act had severely damaged New England's commerce. Now "Mr. Madison's War" was bringing fresh misery to New England in the form of the British blockade. A few Federalists began to talk of New England's secession from the Union. Most, however, rejected the idea, believing that they would soon benefit from popular disfavor with the war and spring back into power.

In late 1814 a Federalist convention met in Hartford, Connecticut. While some advocates of secession were present, moderates took control and passed a series of resolutions summarizing New England's grievances. At the root of these grievances lay the belief that New England was becoming a permanent minority in a nation dominated by southern Republicans who failed to understand New England's commercial interests. Accordingly, the convention proposed to amend the Constitution to abolish the three-fifths clause (which gave the South a disproportionate share of votes in Congress by allowing it to count slaves as a basis of representation), to require a two-thirds vote of Congress to declare war and to admit new states into the Union, to limit the president to a single term, to prohibit the election of two successive presidents from the same state, and to bar embargoes lasting more than sixty days. As bold as these proposals were, their timing was disastrous for the Federalists. News of the Treaty of Ghent and of Jackson's victory at New Orleans dashed the Federalists' hopes of gaining broad popular support. The goal of the Hartford Convention had been to assert states' rights rather than disunion, but to many the proceedings smelled of a traitorous plot. The restoration of peace, moreover, stripped the Federalists of the primary grievance that had fueled the convention. In the election of 1816, Republican James Monroe, Madison's hand-picked successor, swept the nation over negligible Federalist opposition. He would win reelection in 1820 with only a single dissenting electoral vote. As a force in national politics, the Federalists were finished.

The Election of 1816

Candidates	Parties	Electoral Vote
JAMES MONROE	Democratic-Republican	183
Rufus King	Federalist	34

The Election of 1820

Candidates	Parties	Electoral Vote
JAMES MONROE	Democratic-Republican	231
John Quincy Adams	Independent Republican	1

The Election of 1812

Candidates	Parties	Electoral Vote
JAMES MADISON	Democratic-Republican	128
DeWitt Clinton	Federalist	89

The Awakening of American Nationalism

The United States emerged from the War of 1812 bruised but intact. In its first major war since the Revolution, the American republic had demonstrated not only that it could fight on even terms

Bulfinch's Boston

During the first quarter of the nineteenth century, Boston shed its quaint colonial-era character and was transformed into a bustling commercial hub and one of the most important towns in the independent nation. Formerly a community dotted with frame houses and boxy brick residences—most with small farms, gardens, and orchards—Boston became a prosperous seaport in the early years of the republic, a charming place dominated by tree-fringed streets and stately brick homes inhabited by the town's elites.

Bostonians' success in maritime industry underlay this metamorphosis. Shipping, cod fishing, and whaling thrived in the port town. Boston's waterfront was ever alive with graceful, gently bobbing sailing ships—a riot of masts. Bostonians going about their business on the harborfront clomped along in their wagons, their horses' progress sometimes impeded by the ships' bowsprits jutting out into the streets. Along the way they passed wharf after wharf lined with the brick warehouses and countinghouses that had sprung up to manage Bostonians' widening sea trade. In 1794 eighty humming quays gave a distinctive commercial flavor to the waterfront.

A highly profitable commerce with Europe, the East Indies, and China fueled the furious seaside activity, along with shipping to ports in the East Indies and elsewhere in the United States. Boston merchants and sea captains built fortunes from their shipping and fish-

ing ventures; some voyages realized profits of more than $100,000, a huge take for the times. New England cotton manufacturers benefited handsomely too as savvy Yankees began to turn a former home industry into a large-scale business operation that supplied the duck and canvas for the harbor's panorama of sails. The fledgling American navy also needed sails; those for the *Constitution* had to be made in an old grain storehouse because no other town structure was long enough.

Even before the imposition of the embargo that stifled this lucrative trade, Boston, the home of many of President Thomas Jefferson's most bitter Federalist critics, among them George Cabot and Harrison Gray Otis, was a thorn in Jefferson's side. A Federalist elite ran the city, dominating its politics and culture as well as its maritime economy. Composing the elite were not only the merchants upon whom the town's commercial prosperity rested but also the lawyers who controlled its judicial offices, as well as men who had made a fortune in real estate. These upper-crust Bostonians supported the town's cultural institutions, such as the Boston Athenaeum, the nation's largest private library; the American Academy of Arts and Sciences; and Harvard College in nearby Cambridge. Austere and even frigid in their manners, Boston's Federalist leaders were a study in contrast to friendly, backslapping Virginia squires.

Following a grand tour of Europe, the architect Charles Bul-

Charles Bulfinch, *by Mather Brown, 1786*

Bulfinch learned about architecture as a boy by browsing in the well-stocked architectural library of his maternal grandfather, the wealthy Charles Apthorp. In the 1780s Bulfinch's interest was further stimulated by his visits to Rome, Florence, and London and by the encouragement of Thomas Jefferson.

finch, in love with the classical style that he had seen in ancient Roman ruins, designed the majestic Massachusetts State House (completed in 1798) and the gracious mansions on Beacon Hill from which Boston's Federalists looked down upon "their" prosperous city. Bulfinch did more than cater to the elite; the scion of colonial aristocrats, he was part of the elite and served as Boston's police chief. The vast majority of Bostonians, of course, shared none of the privileges and splendor enjoyed by Bulfinch and others of the elite; artisans, mariners, and laborers looked up to Beacon Hill, not down from it. Yet even when Jefferson's Republicans began to score victories in Massachusetts, Boston stayed solidly Federalist.

How could the Federalists retain their political control for so long? Part of the answer is that Boston artisans and laborers remembered how the elite families had supported the Revolution and the Constitution. In addition, the Federalist elite profited from the attitude still prevailing among the common people that social superiors deserved respect and even obedience. Historians call this attitude deference, and there was a lot of it in Boston. To secure deference, the elite paid careful attention to dress. Powdered wigs, lace ruffles, silk stockings, and gold canes were all part of a carefully fashioned image that members of the elite projected when they walked the streets. This attention to image was important, especially among elite families like

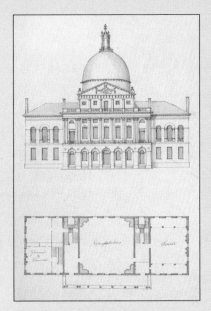

Massachusetts State House

Like Jefferson, Bulfinch admired the classical style of ancient Greece and Rome. But Bulfinch was less inclined than Jefferson to copy ancient buildings literally. Bulfinch's design for the Massachusetts State House reflects the symmetry of neoclassicism; unlike Jefferson's plan for the Virginia Capitol, it is not based on any particular Roman structure.

the Cabots and the Lowells, recent arrivals to Boston who had made their fortunes during and after the Revolution. If deference showed any sign of weakening, the Boston elite could and did fall back on its control of elections. Until 1822, for example, Boston Brahmins beat back efforts to establish decentralized polling places. All Bostonians voted in Faneuil Hall under the eyes of the elite, and only after presenting evidence of property owning.

Bulfinch advised young men against becoming architects, for he believed that few new buildings would be constructed in Boston. His attitude reflected the fact that Boston's population had grown by only 10 percent between 1743 and 1790. Immigrants avoided stuffy Federalist Boston. Adventurers and radicals found New York and Philadelphia more congenial. Yet even as Bulfinch designed his stately mansions, the city was changing. Its population rose from 18,000 in 1790 to nearly 34,000 in 1810, and to 58,000 in 1826. By the 1820s the city had become too large and diverse to follow the leadership of a single elite. By the late 1820s, new political alignments had shattered Federalist domination of Boston's politics.

The Tea Party, *by Henry Sargent, c. 1821 (Detail)*

Bulfinch's Federalist patrons craved elegant interiors and could afford wall-to-wall carpeting. Tea parties like this unified as well as entertained Boston's elite.

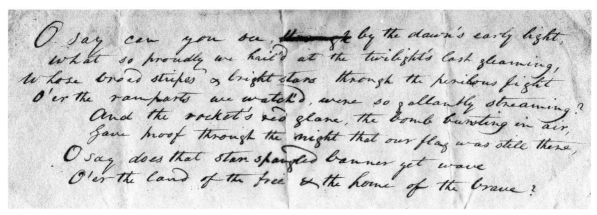

Manuscript for "The Star-Spangled Banner" *(Detail)*

against a major power but also that republics could fight wars without turning themselves into despotisms. The war produced more than its share of symbols of American nationalism. Whitewash cleared the smoke damage to the presidential mansion; thereafter, it became known as the White House. The British attack on Fort McHenry, guarding Baltimore, prompted a young observer, Francis Scott Key, to compose "The Star-Spangled Banner." The Battle of New Orleans boosted Andrew Jackson onto the stage of national politics and became a source of legends about why the Americans had won the battle. It appears to most scholars today that the British lost because Pakenham's men, advancing within range of Jackson's riflemen and cannon, unaccountably paused and became sitting ducks. But in the wake of the battle, Americans spun a different tale. The legend arose that Jackson owed his victory not to Pakenham's blundering tactics but to hawk-eyed Kentucky frontiersmen whose rifles picked off the British with unerring accuracy. In fact, many frontiersmen in Jackson's army had not carried rifles; even if they had, gunpowder smoke would have obscured the enemy. But none of this mattered at the time. Just as Americans preferred militia to professional soldiers, they chose to believe that their greatest victory of the war was the handiwork of amateurs.

Madison's Nationalism and the Era of Good Feelings

The War of 1812 had three major political consequences. First, it eliminated the Federalists as a national political force. Second, it went a long way toward convincing the Republicans that the nation was strong and resilient, capable of fighting a war while maintaining the liberty of its people. The third consequence was an outgrowth of the first two. With the Federalists tainted by disloyalty and with fears about the fragility of republics fading, Republicans increasingly embraced some doctrines long associated with the Federalists. In a message to Congress in December 1815, Madison called for federal support for internal improvements, tariff protection for the new industries that had sprung up during the embargo, and the creation of a new national bank. (The charter of the first Bank of the United States had expired in 1811.) In Congress another Republican, Henry Clay of Kentucky, proposed similar measures, which he called the American System, with the aim of making the nation economically self-sufficient and free from dependency on Europe. In 1816 Congress chartered the Second Bank of the United States and enacted a moderate tariff. Federal support for internal improvements proved to be a thornier problem. Madison favored federal aid in principle but believed that a constitutional amendment was necessary to authorize it. Accordingly, he vetoed an internal-improvements bill passed in 1817.

As Republicans adopted positions that they had once disdained, an "Era of Good Feelings" dawned on American politics. A Boston newspaper, impressed by the warm reception accorded President Monroe while touring New England, coined the phrase in 1817. It has stuck as a description of Monroe's two administrations, from 1816 to 1824.

Compared with Jefferson and Madison, Monroe was neither brilliant, polished, nor wealthy, but he keenly desired to heal the political divisions that a stronger intellect and personality might have inflamed. The phrase "Era of Good Feelings" reflects not only the war's elimination of some divisive issues but also Monroe's conscious effort to avoid political controversies. But the good feelings were paper-thin. Madison's 1817 veto of the internal-improvements bill revealed the persistence of disagreements about the role of the federal government under the Constitution. Furthermore, the embargo, the War of 1812, and the continuation of slavery had aroused sectional animosities that a journalist's phrase about good feelings could not dispel. Not surprisingly, the postwar consensus began to unravel almost as soon as Americans recognized its existence.

John Marshall and the Supreme Court

Jefferson's old antagonist John Marshall continued to preside over the Supreme Court during the Monroe administrations and in 1819 issued two opinions that stunned Republicans. The first case, *Dartmouth College* v. *Woodward,* centered on the question of whether New Hampshire could transform a private corporation, Dartmouth College, into a state university. Marshall concluded that the college's original charter, granted to its trustees by George III in 1769, was a contract. Since the Constitution specifically forbade states to interfere with contracts, New Hampshire's effort to turn Dartmouth into a state university was unconstitutional. The implications of Marshall's ruling were far-reaching. Charters or acts of incorporation provided their beneficiaries with various legal privileges and were sought by businesses as well as by colleges. In effect, Marshall said that once a state had chartered a college or business, it surrendered both its power to alter the charter and, in large measure, its authority to regulate the beneficiary.

A few weeks later, the chief justice handed down an even more momentous decision in the case of *McCulloch* v. *Maryland.* The issue here was whether the state of Maryland had the power to tax a national corporation, specifically the Baltimore branch of the Second Bank of the United States. The bank was a national corporation, chartered by Congress, but most of the stockholders were private citizens who reaped whatever profits the bank made. Speaking for a unanimous Court, Marshall ignored these private features of the bank and concentrated instead on two issues. First, did Congress have the power to charter a national bank? Nothing in the Constitution, Marshall conceded, explicitly granted this power. But the Constitution did authorize Congress to lay and collect taxes, to regulate interstate commerce, and to declare war. Surely these enumerated powers, he reasoned, implied a power to charter a bank. Marshall was clearly engaging in a broad, or "loose," rather than strict, construction (interpretation) of the Constitution. The second issue was whether a state could tax an agency of the federal government that lay within its borders. Marshall argued that any power of the national government, express or implied, was supreme within its sphere. States could not interfere with the exercise of federal powers. A tax by Maryland on the Baltimore branch was such an interference and hence was plainly unconstitutional.

Marshall's decision in the *McCulloch* case dismayed many Republicans. Although Madison and Monroe had supported the establishment of the Second Bank of the United States, the bank had made itself unpopular by tightening its loan policies during the summer of 1818. This contraction of credit triggered a severe depression, the Panic of 1819, that gave rise to considerable distress throughout the country, especially among western farmers. At a time when the bank was widely blamed for the panic, Marshall's ruling stirred controversy by placing the bank beyond the regulatory power of any state government. His decision, indeed, was as much an attack on state sovereignty as it was a defense of the bank. The Constitution, Marshall argued, was the creation not of state governments but of the people of *all* the states and thus was more fundamental than state laws. His reasoning assailed the Republican theory, best expressed in the Virginia and Kentucky resolutions of 1798–1799, that the Union was essentially a compact among states. Republicans had continued to view state governments as more immediately responsive to the people's will than was the federal government and to regard the compact theory of the Union as a guarantor of popular liberty. As Republicans saw it, Marshall's *McCulloch* decision, along with his decision in the *Dartmouth College* case, stripped state governments of the power to impose the will of their people upon corporations.

The Missouri Compromise

The fragility of the Era of Good Feelings again became apparent in the prolonged controversy between 1819 and 1821 over the territory of Missouri. In February 1819 the House of Representatives was considering a bill to admit Missouri as a slave state. James Tallmadge, Jr., a New York Republican, offered an amendment that prohibited the further introduction of slaves into Missouri and provided for the emancipation, at age twenty-five, of all slave offspring born after Missouri's admission as a state. Following bitter debate, the House approved the bill with Tallmadge's amendment. The Senate, after an equally rancorous debate, struck the amendment from the Missouri bill. In each chamber the vote on the Tallmadge amendment followed sectional lines, with the South virtually unanimously opposed to the provisions regarding slavery and the North predominantly in

support. "This momentous question," Jefferson worried, "like a fire bell in the night, awakened and filled me with terror."

American politics had long been torn by sectional conflict, and slavery had at times figured in this discord, notably in the debate at the Constitutional Convention over the three-fifths clause. Yet prior to 1819 slavery had not been the primary factor in sectional division. Issues like Alexander Hamilton's economic program and the Jay Treaty had done more than slavery to polarize the country along sectional lines. During the 1790s Jefferson's main fear had been that Federalist economic policies were favoring northern commercial development at the expense of southern agriculture. After 1800 Federalist opposition to the Louisiana Purchase and to the War of 1812 grew mainly out of concern that the now dominant Republicans were

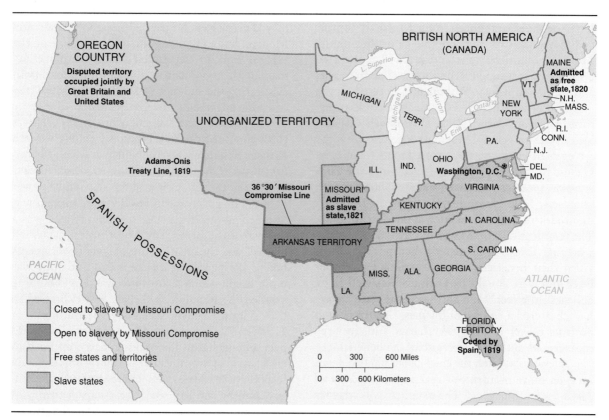

The Missouri Compromise, 1820–1821

The Missouri Compromise temporarily quelled controversy over slavery by admitting Maine as a free state and Missouri as a slave state, and by prohibiting slavery in the remainder of the Louisiana Purchase south of 36° 30′.

sacrificing New England's political and commercial interests to those of the South and West. The Hartford Convention of 1814 had been a reaction not so much to the spread of slavery as to the decline of New England's political influence.

For various reasons, the Missouri question thrust slavery into the center of this long-standing sectional conflict. In 1819 the Union had eleven free and eleven slave states. The admission of Missouri as a slave state would upset this balance to the advantage of the South. Noting that every president since John Adams had been a Virginian, Federalists portrayed the admission of Missouri as part of a conspiracy to perpetuate the rule of Virginia slaveholders. Republicans countered by pointing to the relatively sudden emergence in the House of Representatives of a vocal antislavery block, which included many northern Federalists, and to the growing number of Federalist-dominated societies in the North that promoted the manumission (freeing) of slaves. In response to these developments, some Republicans began to view all efforts to restrict slavery as part of a plot by the Federalists to divide northern and southern Republicans and thus regain political power. In sum, by 1819 the slavery issue had become intertwined with the prevailing distrust between the parties and between the sections.

Virtually every issue that was to wrack the Union during the next forty years was present in the controversy over Missouri: southern charges that the North was conspiring to destroy the Union and to end slavery; accusations by northerners that southerners were conspiring to extend the institution. For a while, leaders doubted that the Union would survive the crisis. House Speaker Henry Clay wrote that the words *civil war* and *disunion* were commonly uttered, almost without emotion. But a series of congressional agreements in 1820 and 1821, known collectively as the Missouri Compromise, resolved the crisis.

The first of these agreements involved the balance between slave states and free states. At the same time that Congress was considering statehood for Missouri, Maine was seeking admission as a free state. In 1820 Congress agreed to admit Maine as a free state, to pave the way for Missouri's admission as a slave state, and to prohibit slavery in the remainder of the Louisiana Purchase

territory north of 36°30′ (the southern boundary of Missouri). But compromise did not come easily. The components of the eventual compromise passed by close and ominously sectional votes. Additionally, no sooner had the compromise been forged than it nearly fell apart. As a prelude to statehood, Missourians drafted a constitution that prohibited free blacks from entering their territory. This provision raised a thorny question, for some eastern states recognized free people of color as citizens, who, as such, were protected from discrimination by the federal Constitution, which clearly stated that "Citizens of each State shall be entitled to all Privileges and Immunities of Citizens in the several States." Balking at Missourians' exclusion of free blacks, antislavery northerners barred Missouri's admission into the Union until 1821, when Henry Clay engineered a new agreement. This second Missouri Compromise prohibited Missouri from discriminating against citizens of other states but left open the issue of whether free blacks were citizens.

The Missouri Compromise was widely viewed as a southern victory. The South had gained admission of Missouri, whose acceptance of slavery was controversial, while conceding to the North the admission of Maine, whose rejection of slavery inspired no controversy at all. Yet the South had conceded to freedom a vast block of territory north of 36°30′. While much of this territory was unorganized Indian country that some viewed as unfit for white habitation, it would not remain a wilderness for long. Also, the Missouri Compromise reinforced the principle, originally set down by the Northwest Ordinance of 1787, that Congress had the right to prohibit slavery in some territories. Southerners had implicitly accepted the argument that slaves were not like other forms of property that could be moved from place to place at will.

Foreign Policy Under Monroe

American foreign policy between 1816 and 1824 reflected more consensus than conflict. The end of the Napoleonic Wars and the signing of the Treaty of Ghent had removed most of the foreign-policy disagreements between Federalists and Republicans. Moreover, Monroe was fortunate to have as his secretary of state an extraordinary diplomat,

John Quincy Adams. An austere and scholarly man whose library equaled his house in monetary value, Adams was a tough negotiator and a fervent nationalist. Although he was the son of the last Federalist president, he had been the only Federalist in the Senate to support the Louisiana Purchase. He later backed the embargo, joined the Republican party, served as minister to Russia, and was one of the negotiators of the Treaty of Ghent.

As secretary of state, Adams moved quickly to strengthen the peace with Great Britain. During his term the United States and Britain signed the Rush-Bagot Treaty of 1817, which effectively demilitarized the Great Lakes by severely restricting the number of ships that the two powers could maintain there. Next the British-American Convention of 1818 fixed the boundary between the United States and Canada from the Lake of the Woods west to the Rockies and restored to Americans the same fishing rights off Newfoundland that they had enjoyed before the War of 1812. As a result of these two agreements, for the first time since Independence, the United States had a secure border with British-controlled Canada and could turn its attention southward and westward.

Adams's dealings with the Spanish, who still owned East Florida and claimed West Florida, were also successful. It had never been clear whether the Louisiana Purchase included West Florida. Acting as if it did, the United States in 1812 had simply added a slice of West Florida to the state of Louisiana and another slice to the Mississippi Territory. In 1818 Andrew Jackson, the American military commander in the South, seizing upon the pretext that Florida was both a base for Seminole Indian raids into American soil and a refuge for fugitive slaves, invaded East Florida, hanged two British subjects, and captured Spanish forts. Jackson had acted without explicit orders, but Adams supported the raid, guessing correctly that it would panic the Spanish into further concessions. In 1819 Spain agreed to the Adams-Onís (or Transcontinental) Treaty. By its terms, Spain ceded East Florida to the United States, renounced its claims to all of West Florida, and agreed to a southern border of the United States that ran from the Mississippi River along the Sabine River (separating Texas from Louisiana) and then westward along the Red and Arkansas rivers to the Rocky Mountains, finally following the forty-second parallel to the Pacific. For the first time, the United States had a legitimate claim to the Pacific coast.

The Monroe Doctrine

John Quincy Adams had long believed that God and nature had ordained that the United States would eventually span the entire continent of North America. Throughout his negotiations leading up to the Adams-Onís Treaty, he made it clear to Spain that should the Spanish not concede some of their territory in North America, the United States might seize all of it, including Texas and even Mexico. Americans were fast acquiring a reputation as an aggressive people. Yet Spain was concerned with larger issues than the encroachment of Americans. Its primary objective was to suppress the revolutions against Spanish rule that had broken out in South America. To accomplish this, Spain sought support from the European monarchs who had organized the Holy Alliance in 1815. The brainchild of the czar of Russia, the Holy Alliance proclaimed lofty Christian principles as a justification for quashing revolutions everywhere. Although most of the crowned heads of Europe joined the alliance, the British, distracted by trouble at home, stayed aloof. Britain's main goal was to prevent a new eruption of revolutionary France. To this end, Britain had joined the Quadruple Alliance (Austria, Britain, Prussia, and Russia) and, since there was some overlap in the members of the two leagues, hoped to control the Holy Alliance without actually joining it. But the Holy Alliance had a mind of its own, and by 1822 its members were talking of helping Spain suppress the South American revolutions. In response, British foreign minister George Canning proposed that the United States and Britain issue a joint statement opposing any European interference in South America while pledging that neither would annex any part of Spain's old empire in the New World.

This was the background of the Monroe Doctrine, as President Monroe's message to Congress on December 2, 1823, later came to be called. The message announced three key principles: that unless American interests were involved, the United States' policy was to abstain from European wars; that the "American continents" were not "subjects for future colonization by any European power"; and that any attempt at European colonization in the New World would be construed by the United States as an unfriendly act. Monroe's message was in harmony with some aspects of Canning's proposals. But Monroe accepted the position of Secretary of State Adams that it was better for the United States to make a declaration of policy on its own than to "come in as cock-boat in the wake of the British man-of-war." Specifically, Monroe and Adams rejected Canning's insistence that both Britain and the United States pledge never to annex any part of Spain's former territories. Adams had long believed that Texas and Cuba would one day fall under American control as a consequence of the law of "political gravitation." "We have no intention of seizing either Texas or Cuba," Adams wrote. "But the inhabitants of either or both of them may exercise their primitive rights, and solicit a union with us. . . . Without entering now into the enquiry

of the expediency of our annexing Texas or Cuba to our Union, we should at least keep ourselves free to act as emergencies arise and not tie ourselves down to any principle which might immediately afterward be brought to bear against ourselves."

As Adams wished, the Monroe Doctrine kept open the American option to extend control over Texas and Cuba while simultaneously sanctioning American recognition of the new Latin American governments. It is easy to ridicule the doctrine as merely a unilateral pronouncement by the United States. It was in fact widely derided in Europe. Fear of the British navy, not the Monroe Doctrine, prevented the Holy Alliance from intervening in South America. Yet by keeping open its options to annex territory, the United States was using the Monroe Doctrine to claim a preeminent position in the New World.

Conclusion

Although the diplomatic achievements of John Quincy Adams and James Monroe were formidable, the greatest accomplishment of the early Republic's leaders was to fashion a workable body of political institutions and customs to govern the young nation. The framers of the Constitution had not anticipated the rise of political parties, and when Jefferson took office in 1801, it was unclear how a victorious party would behave. The range of possibilities was great. Some feared that the Republicans would amend the Constitution to ensure their political ascendancy. One reason why Jefferson's early actions against the judiciary had terrified Federalists was that they viewed his maneuverings as part of a larger plan to destroy them.

As it turned out, Jefferson did not destroy the Federalists; they destroyed themselves. Until the embargo, they failed to come up with a popular national issue, and then they rode opposition to the embargo and to the War of 1812 for too long. When the war ended, a surge of national pride swept the Federalists aside. The election of 1800 had generated anxiety bordering on hysteria; that of 1820 produced yawns. Indeed, the nation was almost too peaceful. Federalist collapse and the embrace by the Republicans of former Federalist policies like the tariff and national banking blurred divisions once sharp.

James Monroe's reelection in 1820 marked the high point of the Republican surge. Even as Republicans congratulated themselves on the emergence of an era of apparent good feelings, the signs of future divisions were growing. The furor over the Missouri Compromise shattered sectional harmony. Subtle changes were starting to occur in American society—changes that would create new political issues and divisions by 1830.

CHRONOLOGY

1800– John Adams's midnight
1801 appointments.

1801 Thomas Jefferson's inauguration.

1802 Repeal of the Judiciary Act of 1801.
Yazoo land compromise.
American right of deposit at New Orleans revoked.

1803 *Marbury* v. *Madison*.
Conclusion of the Louisiana Purchase.

1804 Judge John Pickering convicted by the Senate.
Impeachment of Justice Samuel Chase.
Aaron Burr kills Alexander Hamilton in a duel.
Jefferson elected to a second term.

1804– Lewis and Clark expedition.
1806

1805 Start of the Burr conspiracy.
Chase acquitted by the Senate.
Essex case.

1806 British government issues the first Order in Council.
Napoleon's Berlin Decree.

1807 Burr acquitted of treason.
Chesapeake Affair.
Napoleon's Milan Decree.
Embargo Act passed.

1808 James Madison elected president.

1809 Non-Intercourse Act passed; Embargo Act repealed.

1810 Macon's Bill No. 2.

1811 Battle of Tippecanoe.

1812 Orders in Council revoked.
United States declares war on Britain.
Madison reelected to a second term.
General William Hull surrenders at Detroit.
USS *Constitution* defeats HMS *Guerrière*.
Battle of Queenston.

1813 Battle of Lake Erie (Put-in-Bay).
Battle of the Thames.

1814 Battles of Chippewa and Lundy's Lane.
Battle of Bladensburg.

British burn Washington, D.C.
Captain Thomas Macdonough's naval victory at the Battle of Plattsburgh.
Hartford Convention.
Treaty of Ghent signed.

1815 Battle of New Orleans.

1816 James Monroe elected president.
Second Bank of the United States chartered.

1817 Rush-Bagot Treaty.

1818 British-American Convention of 1818.
Andrew Jackson invades East Florida.

1819 Adams-Onís (Transcontinental) Treaty.
Dartmouth College v. *Woodward*.
McCulloch v. *Maryland*.

1820 Monroe reelected to a second term.

1820– Missouri Compromise.
1821

1823 Monroe Doctrine.

For Further Reading

Henry Adams, *History of the United States During the Administrations of Jefferson and Madison,* 9 vols. (1889–1891). A classic study by the great-grandson of John Adams.

Irving Brant, *James Madison,* vols. 4–6 (1953–1961). The standard biography of Madison.

Forrest McDonald, *The Presidency of Thomas Jefferson* (1976). A lively overview.

Dumas Malone, *Jefferson and His Time,* vols. 4 and 5 (1970, 1974). An extremely comprehensive biography.

Merrill Peterson, *Thomas Jefferson and the New Nation: A Biography* (1970). The best one-volume biography of Jefferson.

Marshall Smelser, *The Democratic Republic, 1801–1815* (1968). A thorough general work.

J. C. A. Stagg, *Mr. Madison's War: Politics, Diplomacy and Warfare in the Early Republic* (1983). An important reinterpretation of the causes of the War of 1812.

Additional Bibliography

Political Ideologies

Joyce Appleby, *Capitalism and a New Social Order: The Republican Vision of the 1790s* (1984); Lance Banning, *The Jeffersonian Persuasion: Evolution of a Party Ideology* (1978); Drew McCoy, *The Elusive Republic: Political Economy in Jeffersonian America* (1980).

Political Parties

James Banner, *To the Hartford Convention: The Federalists and the Origins of Party Politics in the Early Republic, 1789–1815* (1967); Noble E. Cunningham, *The Jeffersonian Republicans and Power: Party Operations, 1801–1809* (1963); David Hackett Fischer, *The Revolution of American Conservatism: The Federalist Party in the Era of Jeffersonian Democracy* (1965); Ronald P. Formisano, *The Transformation of Political Culture: Massachusetts Parties, 1790s–1840s* (1983); Robert M. Johnstone, Jr., *Jefferson and the Presidency: Leadership in the Young Republic* (1978); David P. Jordan, *Political Leadership in Jefferson's Virginia* (1983); Linda K. Kerber, *Federalists in Dissent: Imagery and Ideology in Jeffersonian America* (1970); Shaw Livermore, *The Twilight of Federalism: The Disintegration of the Federalist Party, 1815–1830* (1962); James S. Young, *The Washington Community: 1800–1828* (1966).

Political Leaders

Thomas P. Abernethy, *The Burr Conspiracy* (1954); Robert Dawidoff, *The Education of John Randolph* (1979); Milton Lomask, *Aaron Burr,* 2 vols. (1979, 1982); Samuel Eliot Morison, *Harrison Gray Otis, 1765–1848: The Urbane Federalist* (1962); Robert Shalhope, *John Taylor of Caroline: Pastoral Republican* (1978).

Law and the Judiciary

Leonard Baker, *John Marshall: A Life in Law* (1974); Albert J. Beveridge, *John Marshall,* 4 vols. (1916–1919); Richard E. Ellis, *The Jeffersonian Crisis: Courts and Politics in the Young Republic* (1971); Charles G. Haines, *The Role of the Supreme Court in American Government and Politics, 1789–1835* (1944); Peter C. Hoffer and N. E. H. Hull, *Impeachment in America, 1635–1805* (1984); Morton J. Horwitz, *The Transformation of American Law, 1780–1860* (1977).

The War of 1812 and Its Prologue

Pierre Berton, *The Invasion of Canada* (1980); Roger H. Brown, *The Republic in Peril* (1964); A. L. Burtt, *The United States, Great Britain, and British North America* (1940); Harry L. Coles, *The War of 1812* (1965); Reginald Horsman, *The Causes of the War of 1812* (1962); Bradford Perkins, *Prologue to War: England and the United States, 1805–1812* (1961); Julius W. Pratt, *Expansionists of 1812* (1925); Louis M. Sears, *Jefferson and the Embargo* (1927); Burton Spivak, *Jefferson's English Crisis: Commerce, Embargo, and the Republican Revolution* (1979).

Nationalism and Sectionalism

Harry Ammon, Jr., *James Monroe: The Quest for National Identity* (1971); George Dangerfield, *The Awakening of American Nationalism, 1815–1828* (1965) and *The Era of Good Feelings* (1952); Don E. Fehrenbacher, *The South and Three Sectional Crises* (1980); Glover Moore, *The Missouri Compromise, 1819–1821* (1953); Donald L. Robinson, *Slavery in the Structure of American Politics, 1765–1820* (1971).

John Quincy Adams and the Monroe Doctrine

Samuel F. Bemis, *John Quincy Adams and the Foundations of American Foreign Policy* (1949); Walter LaFeber, ed., *John Quincy Adams and the American Continental Empire* (1965); Ernest R. May, *The Making of the Monroe Doctrine* (1975); Dexter Perkins, *Hands Off: A History of the Monroe Doctrine* (1951) and *The Monroe Doctrine, 1823–1826* (1927).

CHAPTER 8

The Transformation of American Society, 1815–1840

In 1835 William Kirkland and his wife, Caroline, left the private school that they had run in Geneva, New York, and moved to Detroit, in the Michigan Territory. William's plan was simple. He and Caroline would teach in Detroit long enough to earn money to invest in land. Detroit was being flooded by immigrants from the East who, as Caroline wrote, "came to buy land,—not to clear and plough, but as men buy a lottery ticket or dig for gold—in the hope of unreasonable and unearned profits." Although William intended to found a settlement in the wilderness rather than merely to buy and sell land, he, too, hoped to get rich in the West.

Reared in cultivated refinement in New York City and educated at excellent Quaker schools, Caroline had her own notions about the West. The novels and travelers' accounts that she had read projected conflicting but invariably rosy images of the frontier: the West was a land of boundless treasure, a vast garden eager to yield the fruits of its soil, and a romantic wilderness through which one could easily drive a carriage on a moonlit night.

After serving for a year as the principal of a school for young ladies in Detroit, William acquired thirteen hundred acres of land in Livingston County, sixty miles northwest of Detroit, and laid out his settlement around the village of Pinckney. But life in Pinckney failed to live up to the Kirklands' expectations. Instead of a quaintly romantic cottage, Caroline found herself forced to live in a tiny log cabin, far too small for her fancy eastern furniture. Equally disconcerting to the Kirklands was westerners' attitude toward others' possessions.

Frontier people thought that they had a right to borrow anything that Caroline owned, with no more than a blunt declaration that "you've got plenty." "For my own part," Caroline related, "I have lent my broom, my thread, my tape, my spoons, my cat, my thimble, my scissors, my shawl, my shoes; and have been asked for my combs and brushes: and my husband, for his shaving apparatus and his pantaloons."

Other surprises were in store for the Kirklands. Accustomed to servants, Caroline found that even poor western girls refused to hire themselves out permanently as household help. As William noted, occasionally a poor girl would enter service long enough to earn money for a new dress, "but never as a regular calling, or with an acknowledgement of inferior station." Yet the Kirklands gradually realized that the peculiarities of westerners sprang not from selfishness or laziness but from an underlying belief in equality. For example, westerners' penchant for borrowing arose from their attitude that frontier men and women had to share and share alike, or go under.

Caroline turned her experiences in Michigan to good advantage by writing a fictionalized account of them, *A New Home—Who'll Follow?* (1839). Justly hailed as the first realistic account of western life, *A New Home* established Caroline's literary reputation, which she continued to build after she and William returned to New York in 1843.

Between 1815 and 1840, many Americans like the Kirklands ventured into the West and had their visions of easy living punctured by the harsh realities of the frontier. Even those who remained in the East had to adjust—to the successive waves of economic and social change that swept the nation after the conclusion of the War of 1812. For westerners and easterners alike, improvements in transportation (the so-called transportation revolution) were spearheaded by the completion in 1825 of the Erie Canal. This "revolution" both stimulated interregional trade and migration and encouraged an unprecedented development of towns and cities. The new urban dwellers, in turn, formed a market not only for agricultural produce but also for the products of the industries springing up in New England and the major northeastern cities.

Viewed superficially, these changes did not greatly affect the way most Americans lived. Whether in 1815 or 1840, the majority of Americans dwelled outside of cities, practiced agriculture for a living, and traveled on foot or by horse. Yet this surface impression of continuity is misleading, because by 1840 many farmers had moved to the West. The nature of farming had also changed, as farmers increasingly raised crops for sale in distant markets rather than merely for their families' consumption. While most Americans still depended on agriculture, by 1840 alternatives to farming abounded. The rise of such alternatives, in turn, had an impact on some of the most basic social relationships: between parents and children, and between wives and husbands.

Westward Expansion and the Growth of the Market Economy

The spark that ignited these changes was the spread of Americans across the Appalachian Mountains. In 1790 the vast majority of the people resided east of the mountains and within a few hundred miles of the Atlantic Ocean. But by 1840 one-third lived between the Appalachians and the Mississippi River. In this area, known at the time as the West, settlers were buffeted by a succession of unexpected social and economic forces.

The Sweep West

This outward thrust of the population occurred in a series of bursts. The first began even before the 1790s and was reflected in the admission of four new states into the Union between 1791 and 1803: Vermont, Kentucky, Tennessee, and Ohio. Then, after an interlude of over ten years that saw the admission of only one new state, Louisiana, six states entered the Union between 1816 and 1821: Indiana, Mississippi, Illinois, Alabama, Maine, and Missouri. Even as Indiana and Illinois were gaining statehood, settlers were pouring farther west into Michigan. Ohio's population jumped from 45,000 in 1800 to 581,000 by 1820 and 1,519,000 by 1840; Michigan's, from 5,000 in 1810 to 212,000 by 1840.

An adventuring spirit carried some Americans far beyond the Mississippi. The Lewis and Clark expedition whetted interest in the Far West, and in 1811 a New York merchant, John Jacob Astor, founded the fur-trading post of Astoria at the mouth of the Columbia River in the Oregon Country. In the 1820s and 1830s, fur traders also operated along the Missouri River from St. Louis to the Rocky Mountains and beyond. At first, whites relied on the native Americans to bring them furs, but during the 1820s white trappers or "mountain men"— among them, Kit Carson, Jedidiah Smith, and the mulatto Jim Beckwourth—gathered furs on their own while performing astounding feats of survival in harsh surroundings.

Jedidiah Smith was representative of these men. Born in the Susquehanna Valley of New York in 1799, Smith moved west with his family to Pennsylvania and Illinois and in 1822 signed on with an expedition bound for the upper Missouri River. In the course of this and subsequent explorations, he was almost killed by a grizzly bear in the Black Hills of South Dakota, learned from the Indians to trap beaver and shoot buffalo, crossed the Mojave Desert into California, explored California's San Joaquin Valley, and hiked back across the Sierras and the primeval Great Basin to the Great Salt Lake, a trip so forbidding that even the Indians avoided it.

Their exploits popularized in biographies, the mountain men became legends in their own day.

The Mountain Men

Rocky Mountain trappers or "mountain men" were among the most colorful and individualistic of nineteenth-century Americans. Entrepreneurs who trapped beavers for their pelts (which were used until the 1830s to make hats), the mountain men were also hunters, explorers, and adventurers who lived "a wild Robin Hood kind of life" with "little fear of God and none at all of the Devil."

They were, however, atypical migrants. For most pioneer settlers, the West meant the area between the Appalachians and the Mississippi River, the region today known as the Midwest, and before 1840 very few ventured into the Far West. In contrast to Jedidiah Smith, whose unquenchable thirst for adventure led to his death at the hands of Comanches in 1831, most pioneers sought stability and security. The newspaper reports, pamphlets, and letters home that told easterners what to expect in the West usually stressed that western living was bountiful rather than harsh or even risky. A legislator in the Missouri Territory wrote in 1816 that in the states west of the Appalachians, "there neither is, nor, in the nature of things, can there ever be, any thing like poverty there. All is ease, tranquility and comfort."

Western Society and Customs

In their desire for stability, pioneers usually migrated as families rather than as individuals. Because they needed to get their crops to market, most settlers between 1790 and 1820 clustered near the navigable rivers of the West, especially the magnificent water system created by the Ohio and Mississippi rivers. Only with the spread of canals in the 1820s and 1830s, and later of railroads, did westerners feel free to venture far from rivers. In addition, westerners often clustered with people who hailed from the same region back east. For instance, in 1836 a group of farmers from nearby towns met at Castleton, Vermont, listened to a minister intone from the Bible, "And Moses sent them to spy out the land of Canaan," and soon established the town of Vermontville in Michigan. Other migrants to the West were less organized than these latter-day descendants of the Puritans, but most hoped to settle among familiar faces in the West. Finding southerners already well entrenched in Indiana, for example, New Englanders tended to prefer Michigan.

Far from seeking isolation, most westerners craved sociability. Even before there were towns and cities in the West, farm families joined with their neighbors in group sports and festivities. Men met for games that, with a few exceptions like marbles (popular among all ages), were tests of strength or agility. These included wrestling, lifting weights, pole jumping (for distance rather than height), and a variant of the modern hammer toss. Some of these games were brutal. In gander pulling, horseback riders competed to pull the head off a gander whose neck had been stripped of feathers and greased. Women usually combined work and play in quilting and sewing parties, carpet tackings, and even chicken and goose pluckings. Social activities brought the sexes together. Group corn huskings usually ended with dances; and in a variety of "hoedowns" and "frolics," even westerners who in theory might disapprove of dancing promenaded to singing and a fiddler's tune.

Within western families, there was usually a clear division of labor between men and women. Men performed most of the heaviest labor such as cutting down trees and plowing fields, but women had many chores. Women usually rose first in the morning, because their work included milking the cows as well as preparing breakfast. Women also fashioned the coverlets that warmed beds in unheated rooms, and prior to the spread of factory-made clothing in the 1830s, they made shirts, coats, pants, and dresses on home spinning wheels for family use. They often helped butcher hogs. They knew that the best way to bleed a hog was to slit its throat while it was still alive, and after the bleeding, they were adept at scooping out the innards, washing the heart and liver, and hanging

them to dry. There was nothing dainty about the work of pioneer women.

Most western sports and customs had been transplanted from the East. Gander pulling, for example, had been a popular pastime in Virginia before it made its way to the frontier. Yet the West had a character of its own. Before 1830 few westerners could afford elegant living. Cowpaths did double duty as sidewalks in country towns. The West contained no more than a sprinkling of elegant mansions. Even in the wealthy cotton-growing regions of Alabama and Mississippi, most planters lived in rough conditions prior to 1830. Their relative lack of refinement made westerners easy targets for easterners' contemptuous jibes. Criticisms of the West as a land of half-savage yokels tended, in turn, to give rise to counterassertions by westerners that they lived in a land of honest democracy and that the East was soft and decadent. The exchange of insults fostered a regional identity among westerners that further shaped their behavior. Priding themselves on their simple manners, westerners were often not only hostile to the East but also intolerant of those westerners who had pretensions to gentility. On one occasion, a traveler who hung up a blanket in a tavern to cover

Merrymaking at a Wayside Inn, *by Pavel Svinin*

Country inns served as social centers for rural neighborhoods as well as stopping places for travelers.

his bed from public gaze had it promptly ripped down. On another, a woman who improvised a screen behind which to retire in a crowded room was dismissed as "stuck up." And a politician who rode to a public meeting in a buggy instead of on horseback lost votes.

The Federal Government and the West

Of the various causes of expansion to the Mississippi from 1790 to 1840, the one that operated most generally and uniformly throughout the period was the growing strength of the federal government. Even before the Constitution's ratification, several states had ceded their western land claims to the national government, thereby creating the bountiful public domain. The Land Ordinance of 1785 had set forth plans for surveying and selling parcels of this public treasure to settlers. The Northwest Ordinance of 1787 provided for the orderly transformation of western territories into states. The Louisiana Purchase of 1803 brought the entire Mississippi River under American control, and the Transcontinental Treaty of 1819 wiped out the last vestiges of Spanish power east of the Mississippi. The federal government directly stimulated settlement of its expanding landholdings by inducing soldiers to enlist during the War of 1812 in return for promises of land after the war. With 6 million acres allotted to these so-called military bounties, many former soldiers pulled up roots and tried farming in the West. To facilitate westward migration, Congress authorized funds in 1816 for continued construction of the National Road, a highway begun in 1811 that reached Wheeling, Virginia, on the Ohio River, in 1818 and Vandalia, Illinois, by 1838. Soon the road was thronged with settlers. "Old America seems to be breaking up," a traveler on the National Road wrote in 1817. "We are seldom out of sight, as we travel on this grand track towards the Ohio, of family groups before and behind us."

While whites gained innumerable advantages from having a more powerful national government behind them, the rising strength of that government brought misery to the Indians. Virtually all the foreign-policy successes during the Jefferson, Madison, and Monroe administrations worked to the native Americans' disadvantage. Both the Louisiana Purchase and the Transcontinental Treaty

stripped them of Spanish protection. In the wake of the Louisiana Purchase, Lewis and Clark bluntly told the Indians that they must "shut their ears to the counsels of bad birds" and listen henceforth only to the Great Father in Washington. The outcome of the War of 1812 also worked against the native Americans; indeed, the Indians were the only real losers of the war. Early in the negotiations leading to the Treaty of Ghent, the British had insisted on the creation of an Indian buffer state in the Old Northwest, between the United States and Canada. But after the American victory at the Battle of Plattsburgh, the British dropped the demand and essentially abandoned the Indians to the Americans.

The Removal of the Indians

As white settlers poured into the West, they found in their path sizable pockets of Indians, particularly in the South. The Cherokees, Creeks, Choctaws, Chickasaws, and Seminoles—whom non-Indians collectively called the Five Civilized Tribes—occupied large parts of Tennessee, Georgia, Alabama, Mississippi, and Florida. Years of commercial dealings and intermarriage with non-Indians had created in all these tribes an influential minority of mixed-bloods, who had heeded the call of white missionaries to embrace Christianity and agriculture. Among the Cherokees, for example, not only was agriculture practiced, but some Indians built looms and gristmills and even owned slaves. One of their chiefs, Sequoyah, devised a written form of the Cherokee language, while other Cherokees published their own newspaper, the *Cherokee Phoenix*.

In whites' eyes, these were extraordinary accomplishments, and the federal government welcomed them as signs of advancing "civilization" among the Indians. But "civilizing" the native Americans did not always work to the government's advantage. While some assimilated mixed-bloods willingly sold tribal lands to the government and moved west, others, recognizing that their prosperity depended on commercial dealings with whites, resisted removal. In addition, within the "civilized" tribes, the majority of Indians were full-bloods. Although some full-bloods willingly moved west, most were keen to retain their ancestral lands in the East and were contemptuous both of whites

Tahlequah, Indian Territory

The sufferings of the southeastern Indian tribes along the Trail of Tears did not end when the Cherokees, Choctaws, Chickasaws, Creeks, and other nations arrived in the Indian Territory that is now Oklahoma. Most of the tribes found that the federal government failed to deliver fully on promises of supplies and that white merchants, who had contracted to feed the native Americans until they could raise their own crops, often cheated them. At times, white contractors bought up Indian claims for corn rations for cash, which the Indians then spent on whiskey. One white agent reported seeing two thousand drunken Creeks, more than 10 percent of the entire tribe, on a single day in 1837.

Yet left to their own devices, the southeastern Indians were thriving in their new western home by the 1840s. In addition to establishing farms and small factories, the native Americans developed a passion for education. With the aid of white missionaries, they built elementary schools and academies. They operated printing presses that turned out schoolbooks, hymnals, and catechisms in the Creek, Choctaw, and Cherokee languages as well as in English. Some historians have concluded that the native Americans' school system was the best west of the Mississippi in the 1840s. As white Americans trekked to Texas and California during that decade, moreover, they came to depend on

the food and other supplies that they purchased from the transplanted southeastern Indians.

With prosperity, the tribes gradually overcame their internal political divisions. Rival Cherokee factions, for example, united in 1839 and established a seat of government at Tahlequah, a village in present-day eastern Oklahoma, near the Illinois River. But the "civilized" tribes continued to suffer from raids by the nomadic prairie Indians such as the Osages and Comanches. In June 1843 Tahlequah became the scene of a most extraordinary council of tribes. Some four thousand delegates from seventeen Indian nations, including the seven-foot-tall Osage leader Black Dog and the son of Tecumseh, crowded into Tahlequah to hear the presiding Cherokee chief, John Ross, proclaim: "By peace our condition has been improved in the pursuits of civilized life. We should, therefore, extend the hand of peace from tribe to tribe, till peace is established between every nation of red men within the reach of our voice." In addition to destroying a thousand gallons of whiskey, the council agreed on a compact that provided for punishment of offenders from one tribe who raided another tribe.

No Indian council, however, could remove the source of intertribal raiding: the steady shrinkage of the nomadic Indians' hunting grounds caused by the relentless advance of white settlement and by

the very prosperity of the civilized Indians. Reduced to near starvation, the Osages and Comanches continued to raid the civilized tribes' livestock until these nomads themselves were forced onto reservations.

Cherokee Hunter,
by Baroness Hyde de Neuville, 1820
On the eve of their removal to the West, the Cherokees and the other southeastern tribes had increasingly abandoned their traditional hunting, fishing, and gathering for agriculture and trade.

Chief John Ross, *by John Rubens Smith, 1841*

After becoming the principal chief of the eastern Cherokees in 1828, Ross, who was only one-eighth Cherokee himself, emerged as a leading opponent of Jackson's Indian-removal policy.

Choctaw Girls

These young Choctaws, members of one of the Five Civilized Tribes, were photographed in the Oklahoma Indiana Territory.

Tahlequah Council, 1843, *by John Mix Stanley*

The seventeen-tribe council of the summer of 1843 was intended to establish friendly ties between the Cherokee exiles and the Indian Territory's Plains peoples.

and of mixed-bloods who bartered away tribal land to whites. When the Creek mixed-blood chief William McIntosh sold to the government all Creek lands in Georgia and two-thirds of Creek lands in Alabama in the Treaty of Indian Springs (1825), other Creeks executed him.

As whites' demands for Indian lands reached the boiling point during the 1820s, the traditional policy of negotiating treaties piecemeal with the Indians came under fire. Andrew Jackson embodied the whites' new militancy. Jackson was one of the first prominent government officials to recognize that the balance of power between native Americans and whites had shifted drastically since the American Revolution. His victory over the Creeks at the Battle of Horseshoe Bend in 1814 had convinced him that the Indians were much weaker than whites often realized. And because they were weakening, Jackson could see no justification for continuing "the farce of treating with the Indian tribes." The Indians were not independent nations, Jackson argued, but were subject to the laws of whatever state they resided in.

When Jackson became president in 1829, he promptly instituted a more coercive removal policy. His policy reflected not only his disdain for the Indians but also his conviction that, as long as the Indians stayed in the East, the "real" Indians who still retained their "savage" ways would be exploited by mercenary whites and self-serving mixed-bloods. In 1830 he secured from a divided Congress passage of the Indian Removal Act, which granted the president funds and authority to remove native Americans by force if necessary. By then, Georgia and other states were putting overwhelming pressure on the Indians. Resolutions pushed through the Georgia legislature provided that after 1830 Indians could not be parties to or witnesses in legal cases involving whites. By the late 1820s, the Creeks in Georgia and Alabama started to move west. In 1836 the Georgia militia attacked Creeks still in the state, and when starving Creeks raided white settlements for food, federal troops finished the job begun by the militia. In 1836 fifteen thousand Creek Indians, most of the Creek nation, were removed, many in chains and handcuffs, and resettled west of the Mississippi.

A similar fate befell the other "civilized" tribes of the South. Treaties signed in 1830 and 1832 achieved the removal of the Choctaws from Mississippi and the Chickasaws from northern Missis-

sippi and northwestern Alabama. The visiting Frenchman Alexis de Tocqueville witnessed the arrival of the Choctaws, including "the wounded, the sick, newborn babies, and the old men on the point of death," at Memphis on the Mississippi. "I saw them embark to cross the great river, and the sight will never fade from my memory. Neither sob nor complaint rose from that silent assembly. Their afflictions were of long standing, and they felt them to be irremediable." Most Seminoles were removed from Florida, but only after a bitter war between 1835 and 1842 that cost the federal government $20 million.

The Cherokees, the most assimilated of all southern tribes, staged the most ingenious defense by petitioning the U.S. Supreme Court for an injunction against enforcement of the Indian Removal Act of 1830. Although the Cherokees had drafted a constitution in 1827 for a Cherokee republic within Georgia, Chief Justice John Marshall, in the case of *Cherokee Nation* v. *Georgia* (1831), ruled that the Cherokees were neither a state nor a foreign nation and hence lacked standing to bring suit. But Marshall acknowledged that prolonged occupancy gave the Cherokees a right to their land, and a year later, he clarified the Cherokees' legal position in *Worcester* v. *Georgia*, by holding that they were a "domestic dependent nation" entitled to federal protection from molestation by Georgia.

But Marshall's decision had little impact. Jackson ignored it, reportedly sneering, "John Marshall has made his decision; now let him enforce it." The Cherokees themselves were divided into a majority anti-removal faction and a minority pro-removal faction. Federal agents persuaded a pro-removal chief to sign the Treaty of New Echota (1835), which ceded all Cherokee land to the United States for $5.6 million and free transportation west. Most Cherokees denounced the treaty, and on June 22, 1839, a party of Cherokees took revenge by murdering its three principal signers, including a former *Cherokee Phoenix* editor. But the Cherokees' fate had already been sealed. Between 1835 and 1838, bands of Cherokees straggled west to the Mississippi along the so-called Trail of Tears. Unlike the Creeks, the Cherokees policed their own removal, but this fact did not lessen their physical and spiritual sufferings. Between 2,000 and 4,000 of the 16,000 migrating Cherokees died.

Indians in the Northwest Territory fared no

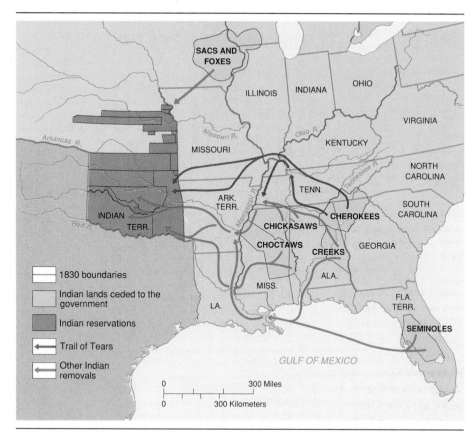

The Removal of the Native Americans to the West, 1820–1840

The so-called Trail of Tears, followed by the Cherokees, was one of several routes along which various tribes migrated on their forced removal to reservations west of the Mississippi.

better. A series of treaties extinguished their land titles, and most moved west of the Mississippi. The removal of the northwestern Indians was notable for two uprisings. The first, led by Red Bird, a Winnebago chief, began in 1827 but was quickly crushed. The second was led by a Sac and Fox chief, Black Hawk, who resisted removal until 1831 and then moved his people west of the Mississippi, only to return the following year. In June 1832 federal troops and Illinois militia furiously attacked his band and virtually annihilated Black Hawk's followers as they tried to recross the Mississippi into Iowa. Black Hawk's downfall induced the other Old Northwest tribes to cede their lands. Between 1832 and 1837, the United States acquired nearly 190 million acres of Indian land in the Northwest for $70 million in gifts and annuities.

The Agricultural Boom

In pushing Indians from the path of white settlers, the federal government was responding to whites' demands for land and more land. Depleted soil and overcrowding had long driven eastern farmers west, but after the War of 1812, a new incentive—the bounding prices of agricultural commodities such as wheat, corn, and cotton—pulled settlers westward in search of better farmland. Several factors accounted for the skyrocketing farm prices. First, Britain and France, exhausted by the Napoleonic Wars, were importing wheat and corn from America, and the United States had swiftly captured former British markets in the West Indies and former Spanish markets in South America. In addition, the beginnings of industrialization in New England even before the war combined with the westward migration of New England farmers to create a demand in the eastern United States for western foodstuffs. So as domestic and foreign demand intensified, commodity prices rose between 1815 and 1819. The West's splendid river systems made it possible for farmers in Ohio to ship wheat and corn down the Ohio River to the Mississippi and then down the Mississippi to New Orleans. There wheat and corn were either sold or transshipped to the East, the West Indies, South America, or

Europe. Just as government policies were making farming in the West possible, high prices for foodstuffs were making it attractive.

Eli Whitney and the Cotton Gin

While the prospect of raising wheat and corn was pulling farmers toward the Old Northwest, the irresistible lure of cotton was creating a frenzied rush to settle the Old Southwest, particularly the states of Alabama and Mississippi on the Gulf of Mexico.

As early as the 1790s, demand in the British textile industry for raw cotton was stimulating the cultivation of the crop along the coastal strip of South Carolina and Georgia. The soil and climate there were ideal for growing long-staple "sea-island" cotton, a variety whose fibers could easily be separated from its shiny black seed by squeezing it through rollers. But in the South's upland and interior regions, the only cotton that would thrive was the short-staple variety, whose green seed stuck so tenaciously to the fibers that rollers merely crushed the seeds and ruined the fibers. It was as if southerners had discovered gold only to find that they could not mine it. But in 1793 a Connecticut Yankee, Eli Whitney, rescued the South by inventing the cotton gin during a brief stopover at the Georgia plantation of a Yale classmate. Whitney's gin was simplicity itself. He impaled short-staple cotton fibers onto iron pins that he inserted into a cylinder, then rotated the cylinder to push the fibers through iron guards. As the seeds dropped conveniently into a box below, the fibers were gathered by rotating brushes positioned on the far side of the guards.

Whitney and his classmate quickly patented the gin, but neither made much money off it. The device was so simple that it was easy to copy, and within a few years, other inventors marked improved gins that used saw-toothed cylinders rather than iron pins. But Whitney's invention removed at a stroke one of the main obstacles to the spread of cotton planting. Short-staple cotton quickly proved itself a wonderful crop. The British could not get enough of it. The explosive thrust of small farmers and planters from the seaboard South into the Old Southwest resembled a gold rush. By 1817 "Alabama fever" gripped the South. At the United States land office in Huntsville, sales of public land in 1818 reached $7 million; good land sold for $30

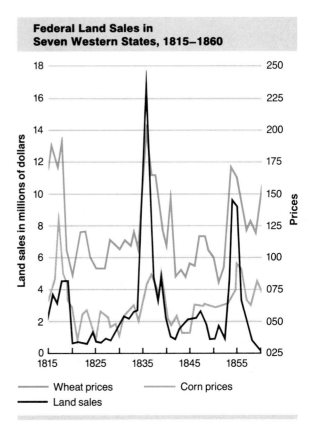

Federal Land Sales in Seven Western States, 1815–1860

Land sales from the public domain tended to rise and fall with the prices of wheat and corn. The higher the price that farmers could obtain for these commodities, the more land they purchased.

SOURCE: Douglass North, *The Economic Growth of the United States 1790–1860* (New York: Norton, 1966), 137.

to $50 an acre. By 1820 half of the nation's cotton was produced west of the Appalachians in the gulf states of Alabama and Mississippi. Cotton production tripled between 1816 and 1826, and the story was only beginning. Between 1831 and 1836, the value of cotton exports rose 300 percent. Accounting for less than a quarter of all American exports between 1802 and 1807, cotton composed just over half by 1830 and nearly two-thirds by 1836.

The Rise of the Market Economy

To farmers, the high prices of agricultural commodities between 1815 and 1819 appeared an unmixed blessing. Most planned to grow enough food to feed their families (called subsistence agriculture) *and* a cash crop like wheat or cotton to sell in local or distant markets (called commercial agriculture, or the "market economy"). Farming for markets was not new; many farmers had done so during the colonial era. What was new after the War of 1812 was the extent to which farmers entered the market economy. High crop prices tempted many former subsistence farmers into the commercial economy. Often these individuals had little experience with commercial dealings and little idea of what they were getting into. Commercial agriculture exposed farmers to innumerable new risks. First, cash crops like wheat and cotton were sold to persons whom the farmers themselves frequently never met, in places that they never saw. Second, farmers had no control over the fluctuations of distant markets. Further, there was inevitably an interval, often a long one, between harvesting a cash crop and selling it. To sustain themselves during the interval, farmers had to borrow money. Thus commercial agriculture forced farmers into short-term debt in the hope of long-term profit.

The debt was frequently worse than most had expected. In the first place, many western farmers had to borrow money to buy their land. The roots of this indebtedness for land lay, in turn, in the federal government's inability to devise an effective policy for transferring the public domain directly into the hands of small farmers.

Federal Land Policy

Partisan and sectional pressures buffeted federal land policy like a kite in a March wind. The result was a succession of land laws between 1796 and 1820, each of which sought to undo the damage caused by its predecessor.

Because their political bases lay in the East, the Federalists had been reluctant during the 1790s to encourage headlong settlement of the West. Nevertheless, they were eager to raise revenue for the federal government from land sales. They reconciled these goals—retarding actual settlement while gaining revenue—by encouraging the sale of huge tracts of land to wealthy speculators, individuals who did not intend to farm the land but planned instead to hold it until its value rose and then sell off parcels to farmers. Even during the 1790s, land speculators were swarming through the area east of the Appalachians. The Holland Land Company, for example, composed mainly of Dutch investors,

bought up much of western New York and western Pennsylvania. A federal land law passed in 1796 reflected Federalist aims by establishing a minimum purchase of 640 acres at a minimum price of two dollars an acre and by allowing only a year for full payment. Few small-scale farmers could afford land from the public domain on these terms.

Believing that the small farmer was the backbone of the Republic, and fully aware of Republican political strength in the West, Thomas Jefferson and the Republicans took a different tack. Starting in 1800, federal land laws increasingly reflected the Republicans' desire to ease the transfer of the public domain to farmers. Even so, few proposed giving land to farmers outright. The Republicans needed revenue from land sales if they were to extinguish the national debt. Accordingly, the land law of 1800 dropped the minimum purchase to 320 acres and allowed up to four years for full payment but kept the minimum price at $2.00 an acre. In 1804 the minimum purchase came down to 160 acres; and in 1820, to 80 acres. The minimum price also declined from $2.00 an acre in 1800 to $1.64 in 1804 and to $1.25 in 1820.

Although land policy was steadily liberalized, small farmers did not necessarily benefit immediately. Federal land laws between 1800 and 1820 were nervous responses to the fact that much of the public domain was still being bought up by speculators, no matter what Congress did. All land in the public domain was first sold at auction, usually for much more than the two-dollar minimum. With agricultural prices soaring, speculators assumed that land would continue to rise in value and accordingly were willing to bid high on new land. In ignorance of their real value, veterans of the War of 1812 often sold their land warrants to speculators. Josiah Meigs, the commissioner of the government's General Land Office, reported cases of veterans who had sold warrants for 160 acres for as little as two hundred dollars.

The growing availability of credit after the War of 1812 fed speculation. The chartering of the Second Bank of the United States in 1816 had the dual effect of increasing the amount of money in circulation and stimulating the chartering of private banks within states (state banks). The circulation of all banks grew from $45 million in bank notes in 1812 to $100 million in 1817. The stockholders and directors of these banks viewed them less as a sound investment for their capital (many directors

Independence, Squire Jack Porter, *by Francis Blackwell Mayer, 1858*

This painting of Captain John Porter, a War of 1812 veteran who later owned a farm in western Maryland, captures the independence and self-sufficiency that antebellum Americans associated with agriculture. With no boss to command him, Squire Porter relaxed and smoked his pipe whenever he chose.

actually had very little capital when they started state banks) than as agencies that could lend them money for land speculation. Secretary of the Treasury William H. Crawford observed in 1820 that banks had been incorporated "not because there was capital seeking investment, not because the places where they were established had commerce and manufacturers which required their fostering aid; but because men without active capital wanted the means of obtaining loans, which their standing in the community would not command from banks or individuals having real capital and established credit." In short, banks were founded so that they could lend their directors money for personal investment in land speculation. The result was an orgy of land speculation between 1815 and 1819. In 1819 sales of public land were over 1,000 percent greater than the average of the 1800–1814 period.

The Speculator and the Squatter

Nevertheless, most of the public domain eventually found its way into the hands of small farmers. Because speculators gained nothing by holding land for prolonged periods, they were only too happy to sell it when the price was right. In addition, a familiar frontier type, the squatter, exerted a restraining influence on the speculator.

Even before the creation of the public domain, squatters had helped themselves to western land; George Washington himself had been unable to drive squatters off lands that he owned in the West. Squatters were an independent and proud lot, scornful of their fellow citizens, who were "softened by Ease, enervated by Affluence and Luxurious Plenty, & unaccustomed to Fatigues, Hardships, Difficulties or dangers." Disdaining land speculators above all, squatters formed claims associations to police land auctions and prevented speculators from bidding up the price of land. Squatters also pressured Congress to allow them "preemption" rights—that is, the right to purchase at the minimum price land that they had already settled on and improved. Seeking to undo the pernicious effects of its own laws, Congress responded by passing special preemption laws for squatters in specific areas and finally, in 1841, acknowledged a general right of preemption.

But preemption laws were of no use to farmers

who arrived after speculators had already bought up land. Having spent their small savings on livestock, seed, and tools, these settlers then had to buy land from speculators on credit at vicious interest rates that ranged as high as 40 percent. Saddled by steep indebtedness, many western farmers had no choice but to skimp on subsistence crops while expanding cash crops in the hope of paying off their creditors. Farmers in these years were not merely entering the market economy; they were lunging into it.

Countless farmers who had carried basically conservative expectations to the West and who had hoped to establish self-sufficient farms in a land of abundance quickly became economic adventurers. Wanting land that they could call their own, but forced to raise cash crops in a hurry, many farmers worked their acreage to exhaustion and thus had to keep moving in search of new land. The phrase "the moving frontier" refers not only to the obvious fact that with each passing decade, the line of settlement shifted farther west but also to the fact that the same people kept moving. The experience of Abraham Lincoln's parents, who migrated from the East through several farms in Kentucky and then to Indiana, was representative of the westward trek.

The Panic of 1819

In 1819 the land boom collapsed like a house of cards, the victim of a financial panic. The Panic of 1819 had several long-term causes, all of which illustrated how deeply the American economy— and "independent" American farmers—had become dependent on foreign trade and loose credit. The textile factories that had sprung up during the embargo had not shared in the postwar economic boom. With the conclusion of the Napoleonic Wars in 1815, British exporters unloaded their overflowing textile inventories on the American market at bargain prices that undercut American-made textiles. Because bank credit was readily available, Americans had enough cash to purchase these British manufactures. In the case of agriculture, despite the postwar boom in agricultural exports to Europe, the United States actually *imported* more than it exported between 1815 and 1819. In addition, after 1817 the combination of a bumper crop in Europe and a business recession in Britain trimmed the

foreign demand for American wheat, flour, and cotton at the very time when American farmers were becoming more dependent on agricultural exports to pay their debts.

Closer to home, the loose practices of state banks contributed mightily to the panic. Like the Bank of the United States, the state banks issued their own bank notes. In the absence of any national system of paper money, these notes served as a circulating medium. A bank note was just a piece of paper with a printed promise from the bank's directors to pay the bearer on demand a certain amount of specie (gold or silver coinage). State banks had long emitted far more bank notes than they could redeem. Further, because the Bank of the United States had more branches than any state bank, notes of state banks were often presented by their holders to branches of the Bank of the United States for redemption. Whenever the Bank of the United States redeemed a state bank note in specie, it became a creditor of the state bank.

In reaction to the overemission of state bank notes, the Bank of the United States began in the summer of 1818 to insist that state banks redeem in specie their notes that were held by the Bank of the United States. To pay their debts to the Bank of the United States, state banks had to demand that borrowers repay loans. The result was a general curtailment of credit throughout the nation, but particularly in the West.

The biggest losers were the land speculators, who had bought huge tracts with the expectation that prices would rise but now found prices tumbling. Land that had once sold for as much as $69 an acre dropped to $2 an acre. Land prices fell, in turn, because the credit squeeze drove down the market prices of staples like wheat, corn, cotton, and tobacco. Cotton, which sold for 32¢ a pound in 1818, sank as low as 17¢ a pound in 1820. Since farmers could not get much cash for their crops, they could not pay the debts that they had incurred to buy land. Since speculators could not collect money owed them by farmers, the value of land that they still held for sale collapsed.

The significance of the panic lay not only in the economic damage it did but also in the conclusions that many Americans drew from it. First, the panic left a bitter taste about banks, particularly the Bank of the United States, which was widely blamed for the hard times. In addition, the panic dramatized the vulnerability of American factories to cheap foreign competition (a vulnerability evident even before the economic downturn) and thereby stimulated demands for the protection of domestic industries. These demands would lead to the passage of higher tariffs in 1824 and 1828. Finally, plummeting prices for cash crops demonstrated how much farmers were coming to depend on distant markets. In effect, it took a severe business reverse to show farmers the extent to which they had become businessmen. The fall in the prices of cash crops intensified the search for better forms of transportation to reach those faraway markets. If the cost of transporting crops could be cut, farmers could keep a larger share of the value of their crops and thereby adjust to falling prices.

The Transportation Revolution: Steamboats, Canals, and Railroads

Most forms of transportation available to Americans in 1820 had severe drawbacks. The great rivers west of the Appalachians ran primarily from north to south and hence could not by themselves connect western farmers with eastern markets. The National Road, with its crushed-stone surface, was a well-built highway that advanced farther west each year. In addition, between 1815 and 1825, several northern states chartered private companies to build toll roads (turnpikes). But roads could not solve the nation's transportation problems. Aside from the fact that horse-drawn wagons could carry limited produce, roads were expensive to maintain. Turnpike companies generally found the income from tolls inadequate to cover the outlays for repairs. After 1825 the pace of investment in turnpikes slackened, and the interest of both public and private investors shifted toward the development of waterways.

In 1807 Robert R. Livingston and Robert Fulton successfully introduced a steamboat popularly known as the *Clermont* on the Hudson River. Livingston and Fulton soon gained a monopoly from the New York legislature to run a ferry service on the Hudson between New York and New Jersey. So spectacular were their profits that rival entrepreneurs secured a license from Congress to operate a competing ferry service and thereby challenged the Livingston-Fulton monopoly. A long court battle followed. Finally, in 1824 the U.S. Supreme Court decided against the monopoly in the famous case of *Gibbons* v. *Ogden*. Speaking for a unanimous Court, Chief Justice John Marshall ruled that commerce included not merely the exchange of products but navigation as well. This was an important finding, because the Constitution clearly empowered Congress to regulate commerce "among the several States." In the event of a conflict between state and congressional regulation of commerce, Marshall continued, the congressional power must prevail. Thus Marshall upheld the competitors (who had a license from Congress) and effectively broke the Livingston-Fulton monopoly. In the wake of Marshall's decision, state efforts to establish monopolies over river trade quickly collapsed. The number of steamboats operating on western rivers jumped from 17 in 1817 to 69 in 1820 and to 727 by 1855.

Prior to the introduction of steamboats on the Mississippi, flatboats (simply floating rafts) carried produce downriver. Since they were unable to navigate upstream, the flatboats were broken up and sold for firewood in New Orleans. The return voyage was made either by foot or horse through Indian country, or by sailing vessels from New Orleans to Philadelphia or New York and then by foot or horse across the Appalachians to the West.

Interior of a Flatboat, *by Charles-Alexandre Lesueur, 1826*

Not all flatboats that carried produce and pioneers on American rivers were floating rafts. Many had roomy interiors that accommodated whole families, provisions, and even barn animals.

Keelboats—similar to flatboats but moved by a rudder—could make the upstream voyage, though at a snail's pace. It took a keelboat three or four months to complete the 1,350-mile journey from New Orleans to Louisville. In contrast, steamboats could travel upstream at a relatively fast speed. As early as 1817, a steamboat made the trip in twenty-five days. Moreover, although the English had developed steam-propulsion technology in the eighteenth century, between 1820 and 1840, Americans discovered many practical techniques for increasing the effectiveness of steamboats. The gradual introduction of long, shallow hulls made steamboats suitable for use in shallow water (particularly the stretch of the Mississippi-Ohio river system from Louisville to Pittsburgh). The result was an extension of the navigation season; hot, dry summer weather that lowered water levels no longer forced steamboats out of service.

Steamboats became more ornate as well as more practical. To compete for passengers, they began to offer luxurious cabins and lounges (called saloons). The saloon of the *Eclipse,* a Mississippi steamboat, was the length of a football field and featured skylights, chandeliers, a ceiling criss-crossed by Gothic arches, and mahogany furniture covered with velvet. Such "elegance bordering on magnificence" helped to reassure westerners that whatever easterners might say, they were not savage backwoods people but polished and urbane citizens. Yet most steamboat passengers only glimpsed this elegance. Saloons were reserved for the small minority who booked "cabin" passage. The majority of travelers purchased "deck" passage, which entitled them to sleep on a cotton bale if they were lucky enough to find one, on the floor if they were not.

Whether cabin or deck passengers, all steamboat travelers confronted the hazards of this mode of navigation. Fires were common—not surprisingly, in view of the fact that steamboats needed huge furnaces and often carried combustible cargoes like oil and hay. Collisions claimed many lives. The worst, occurring in 1837 on the Mississippi, killed several hundred Creek Indians who were being transported by steamer to reservations in the West. Submerged snags often cracked the fragile hulls of fast-moving steamers: British novelist Charles Dickens described the Mississippi above Cairo, Illinois, as "an enormous ditch . . . choked and obstructed everywhere by huge logs and whole forest trees." Moreover, because little was known about the reaction of metals under stress, boiler explosions destroyed many steamboats, not to mention their passengers. So common were such explosions that one company introduced a line of steamboats on the Hudson River that, for safety's sake, carried the passengers in tow on a barge. Yet nothing could stifle Americans' love of steamboats; for all their perils, they could navigate swiftly upriver.

Once steamboats had demonstrated the feasibility of upriver navigation, popular enthusiasm for internal improvements shifted away from turnpikes and toward canals. As late as 1816, the United States had only a hundred miles of canals. Not only did Americans know little about building canals in these early years, but the capital required to construct them was mind-boggling. Even Thomas Jefferson dismissed the idea of canals as "little short of madness." However, the invention of the steamboat, the abundance of western settlers desperate for access to markets, and the natural endowment of the Great Lakes combined to make the lure of canals irresistible. Canals offered the prospect of connecting the superb Mississippi-Ohio river system with the Great Lakes, and the Great Lakes with eastern markets.

The construction of the Erie Canal was the first major canal project. Started by New York State in 1817, the canal at its completion stretched for 363 miles between Albany and Buffalo. The Erie Canal was ten times longer than any previous American canal and by far the longest in the Western world. More than a waterway, it was a capstone of the sometimes fragile Era of Good Feelings, a symbol of American ingenuity and peaceful progress. As part of the celebration of its completion in 1825, a procession of American steamboats formed a perfect circle of salute around two British warships anchored in New York Harbor. The British responded by striking up "Yankee Doodle," to which the Americans replied with "God Save the King." Through the Erie Canal, New York City was linked by inland waterways (the Hudson River, the canal itself, and Lake Erie) all the way to Ohio.

In New England the Blackstone Canal (1824–1828) created a water highway between Worcester, Massachusetts, and the Narragansett Bay in Rhode Island. By 1834 the Main Line (or Pennsylvania) Canal connected eastern Pennsylvania with Pitts-

Erie Canal, *by John William Hill, 1831*

Construction of the Erie Canal was a remarkable feat—all the more so because the United States did not possess a single school of engineering at the time. The project's heroes were lawyers and merchants who taught themselves engineering, and brawny workmen, often Irish immigrants, who hacked a waterway through the forests and valleys of New York.

burgh. The Main Line Canal was an even more remarkable feat of engineering than the Erie because it crossed the Allegheny Mountains with the aid of a railroad. Canal boats on this system had to be built in collapsible sections; they were disassembled upon reaching the mountains and then carried up one side and down the other on cable cars. As these canals spread like fingers from east to west, a similar system of canals was under construction from west to east. By 1836 the Ohio and Erie Canal stretched from Portsmouth on the Ohio River to Cleveland on Lake Erie. The Miami and Erie Canal ran from Cincinnati to Dayton, where plans called for it to join a railroad line to Sandusky on Lake Erie. From Lake Erie, packets and steamboats could carry produce to the Erie Canal and on to Albany and New York City. In 1836, 365,000 bushels of western wheat entered the milling city of Rochester on the Erie Canal and left as 369,000 barrels of flour bound for eastern New York.

The canal boom drastically cut shipping costs. In 1817, just before construction began on the Erie Canal, the cost of transporting wheat from Buffalo to New York City was three times the market value of wheat in New York City, while the transportation costs for corn and oats over the same route were, respectively, six and twelve times their market value in New York City. Average freight charges between Buffalo and New York City dropped from 19¢ a ton per mile in 1817 to less than 2¢ a ton per mile in 1830. Throughout the nation, canals reduced shipping costs from 20¢ to 30¢ a ton per mile before 1815 to 2¢ to 3¢ a ton per mile by the 1830s.

When another economic depression hit in the late 1830s, various states found themselves overcommitted to costly canal projects and ultimately scrapped many. Yet even as the canal boom was ending, railroads were spreading. In 1825 the world's first railroad devoted to general transportation began operation in England, and by 1840 some three thousand miles of track had been laid in America, about the same as the total canal mileage in 1840. During the 1830s investment in American railroads actually exceeded that in canals. Cities like Baltimore and Boston, which lacked major inland waterway connections, turned to railroads to enlarge their share of the western market. The Baltimore and Ohio Railroad, chartered in 1828, took business away from the Chesapeake and Ohio Canal farther south. Blocked by its Berkshire Mountains from building a canal to the Erie, Massachusetts chartered the Boston and Worcester Railroad in 1831 and the Western Railroad (from Worcester to Albany) in 1833.

Faster, cheaper to build, and able to reach more places, railroads had obvious advantages over canals and contributed to the growth of communities that were remote from waterways. But railroads' potential was only slowly realized. Most early railroads ran between cities in the East rather than from east to west and carried more passengers than freight. Not until 1849 did freight revenues exceed passenger revenues, and not until 1850 was the East Coast connected by rail to the Great Lakes.

Several factors explain the relatively slow spread of interregional railroads. Unlike canals, which were built directly by state governments, most railroads

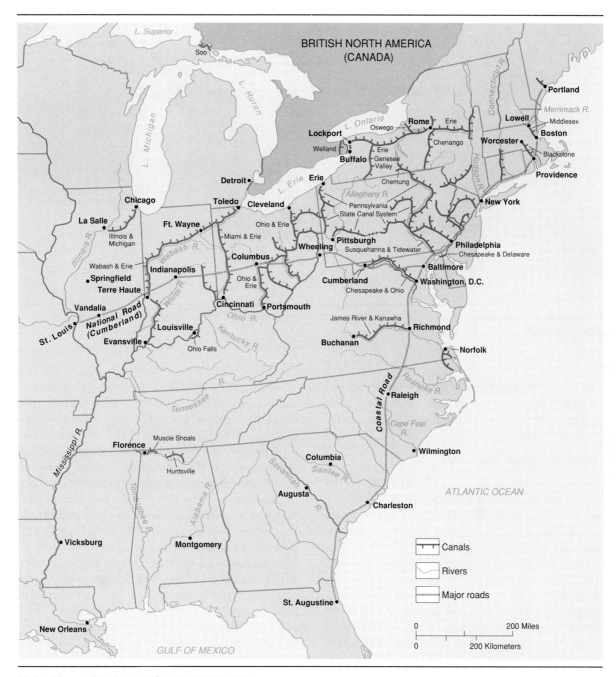

Major Rivers, Roads, and Canals, 1825–1860

Railroads and canals increasingly tied the economy of the Midwest to that of the Northeast.

were constructed by private corporations seeking quick profits. To minimize their original investment, railroad companies commonly resorted to cost-cutting measures such as covering wooden rails with iron bars. As a result, while relatively cheap to build, American railroads needed constant repairs and were even more vulnerable than canals to economic fluctuations. In contrast, while expensive to construct, canals needed relatively little maintenance and were kept in operation for decades after

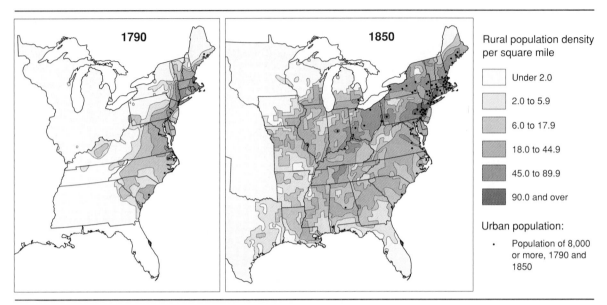

Population Distribution, 1790 and 1850

By 1850 high population density characterized parts of the Midwest as well as the Northeast.

SOURCE: *1900 Census of Population, Statistical Atlas*, plates 2 and 8.

railroads appeared. Moreover, it remained cheaper to ship bulky commodities such as iron ore, coal, and nonperishable agricultural produce by canal.

The Growth of the Cities

The transportation revolution contributed to the rapid growth of towns and cities. In 1820 only 6.1 percent of the population lived in places of 2,500 or more inhabitants, and only 2 cities, New York and Philadelphia, had more than 100,000 people. Four of the 10 largest cities in the United States in 1820 had fewer than 15,000 inhabitants. The next forty years witnessed, in relative terms, the most rapid urbanization in American history. By 1860 nearly 20 percent of the population lived in places of 2,500 or more. New York City's population rose from 124,000 in 1820 to 800,000 in 1860. By 1860 there were 8 American cities larger than the largest city in 1820. An even more revealing change was the transformation of sleepy villages of a few hundred into thriving towns of several thousand. In 1820 only 56 incorporated towns could boast between 2,500 and 10,000 inhabitants; by 1850 there were over 350 such towns. The Erie Canal transformed Rochester, New York, for example, from a village of a few hundred people in 1817 to a thriving town of 9,000 by 1830.

City and town growth occurred with dramatic suddenness, especially in the West. Pittsburgh, Cincinnati, and St. Louis were little more than villages in 1800. The War of 1812 stimulated the growth of Pittsburgh, whose iron forges provided shot and weapons for American soldiers, and Cincinnati, which became a staging ground for attacks on the British in the Old Northwest. Meanwhile, St. Louis acquired some importance as a fur-trading center. Then between 1815 and 1819, the agricultural boom and the introduction of the steamboat transformed all three places from outposts with transient populations of hunters, traders, and soldiers into bustling cities. Cincinnati's population, for example, nearly quadrupled between 1810 and 1820 and doubled in the 1820s.

With the exception of Lexington, Kentucky, whose lack of access to water forced it into relative stagnation after 1820, all the prominent western cities were river ports: Pittsburgh, Cincinnati, and Louisville on the Ohio; St. Louis and New Orleans on the Mississippi. Except for Pittsburgh, all were essentially commercial hubs rather than manufacturing centers and were flooded by individuals extremely eager to make money. In 1819 land speculators in St. Louis were bidding as much as a thousand dollars an acre for lots that had sold for thirty dollars an acre in 1815. Waterfronts endowed

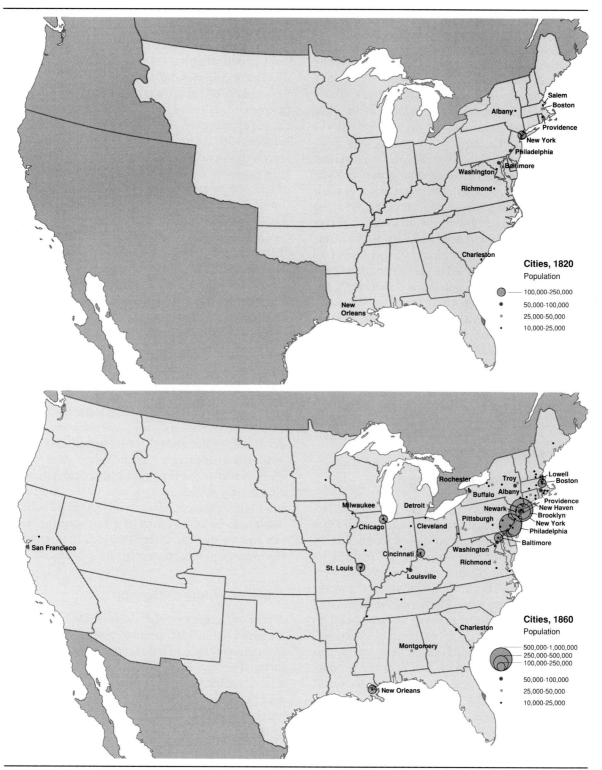

American Cities, 1820 and 1860   *In 1820 most cities were seaports. By 1860, however, cities dotted the nation's interior, in large measure because of the transportation revolution.*
SOURCE: *Statistical Abstract of the United States.*

with natural beauty were swiftly overrun by stores and docks. "Louis Ville, by nature is beautiful," a visitor wrote, "but the handy Work of *Man* has instead of improving destroy'd the works of Nature and made it a detestable place."

The transportation revolution acted like a fickle god, selecting some cities for growth while sentencing others to relative decline. Just as the steamboat had elevated the river cities over land-locked Lexington, the completion of the Erie Canal shifted the center of western economic activity toward the Great Lakes. The result was a gradual decline in the importance of river cities and a rise between 1830 and 1860 in the importance of lake cities such as Buffalo, Cleveland, Detroit, Chicago, and Milwaukee. In 1830 nearly 75 percent of all western city dwellers lived in the river ports of New Orleans, Louisville, Cincinnati, and Pittsburgh, but by 1840 the proportion had dropped to 20 percent.

The growth of cities and towns was spurred initially by the transportation revolution and the development of interregional trade. Urban expansion received an added boost from the rise of manufacturing between 1815 and 1840.

The Rise of Manufacturing

Today we customarily equate the word *manufacturing* with industrialization—that is, with large factories, machinery, and mass production. But the literal meaning of *manufacturing* is "making by hand." During the colonial era, most products were made by hand, either in households or in the work-shops of skilled artisans. The period between 1815 and 1860 marked a transition from colonial to modern manufacturing. Household, or "cottage," industries declined, while large factories and power-driven machinery came to dominate the production of cotton textiles. But small shops were still responsible for a great deal of manufacturing. As late as 1860, the average manufacturing establishment contained only eight workers.

Few Americans believed in 1860 that they lived in an industrial society; most continued to think of the United States as a nation of farmers and small producers. This self-image, however, was misleading. By 1850 the 20 percent of the labor force engaged in manufacturing produced about 30 percent of the national output. Furthermore, industrialization was starting to affect many crafts besides textile making.

Industrialization was not a single occurrence, a kind of tidal wave that washed away traditional forms of manufacturing. Rather, it was a gradual process with several distinct stages. First, the tasks involved in making a product were subdivided, so that instead of making a whole product, each worker made only a part. Next, workers were gathered into factories with rooms devoted to specialized operations performed by hand or by simple machines. Finally, power-driven machinery replaced fabrication by hand. These three stages arrived quickly and almost simultaneously in New England's cotton textile industry, but many crafts—includ-ing the making of shoes, hats, guns, trunks, and saddles—experienced at least the first two stages before 1860. Many variations of this pattern appeared between 1815 and 1860. In some crafts, task subdivision and simple machinery were intro-duced without the creation of large factories. In others, like shoe manufacturing, the subdivision of tasks and the emergence of large factories occurred before the introduction of power-driven machin-ery. Because the growth of industrialization was gradual and uneven, it was not always clear to men and women at the time that traditional hand fab-rication by skilled artisans was in the process of becoming obsolete. They still imagined skilled artisans to be at the center of manufacturing with-out recognizing the extent to which industrializa-tion was tumbling them from their pedestals.

Causes of Industrialization

A host of factors stimulated industrialization. The Embargo Act of 1807 persuaded merchants barred from foreign trade to redirect their capital into fac-tories. The War of 1812 sparked support for pro-tective tariffs to end American economic depen-dence on Europe; particularly in the 1820s, tariffs reduced imports of English cloth and contributed to the 15.4 percent average annual rise in Ameri-can cloth products between 1815 and 1833. Improvements in transportation made it possible for manufacturers to sell finished products in dis-tant markets and provided an incentive to increase production. In addition, a popular preference for factory-made rather than homemade products developed wherever the transportation revolution reached. Household production declined not only in cities but in rural areas along canals and railroads and never gained a secure footing in the West. The more farmers went into the business of selling as well as raising crops, the more they were inclined to buy articles like shoes and clothes rather than make them.

Industrialization also depended on immigration. Five million people migrated from Europe to the United States between 1790 and 1860. Some came to escape political oppression (the United States was the only nation in which a large segment of the working class could vote), but more immigrated in search of economic opportunity. The bulk of these newcomers were either German or Irish, and over 80 percent arrived after 1840 (see Chapter 12). All contributed to industrialization as laborers and as consumers. But the immigrants who played the greatest role in launching industrialization were not the Germans or the Irish but the much smaller numbers of British immigrants. Industrialization had started in Britain during the mid-eighteenth century, and by 1790 Britain had a class of artisans who understood the workings of machines. Men like Samuel Slater learned the "mystery" of textile production as apprentices to factory masters in England and then evaded British laws against emigration (Slater did so by leaving in disguise), carrying their knowledge of machines to America in their heads.

Although Britain had a head start in developing the technology relevant to industrialization, Americans made contributions of their own. Unlike Britain, America had no craft organizations (called guilds) that tied artisans to a single trade. As a result, American artisans freely experimented with machines outside their craft. In the 1790s wagon maker Oliver Evans of Delaware, for example, built an automated flour mill that required only a single supervisor to look on as the grain poured in from one side and was discharged from the other as flour. In addition, the relatively high wages paid to American workers gave manufacturers an incentive to find substitutes for expensive hand labor in order to make products as quickly and cheaply as possible. After inventing the cotton gin, Eli Whitney in 1798 filled a government contract for ten thousand muskets by using unskilled workers to make identical parts that could be interchanged from musket to musket. The idea of interchangeable parts actually originated in Europe, but the United States led all nations in applying the idea in factories—so much so that it came to be called the American system of manufacturing.

New England Industrializes

New England became America's first industrial region. The gradual strangulation of American trade by Britain's Orders in Council, Napoleon's Continental System, and Jefferson's embargo hit New England more severely than regions less dependent on European trade. Incentives were thus provided for New England's merchants to invest in manufacturing. In addition, New England's rivers were numerous, swift-flowing, and ideally suited to provide water power for mills. At the same time, the region's soil, thin and rocky in many places, forced young men off the land and into the westward flow of migration, while leaving villages and towns with a surplus of young women. The textile mills that multiplied in New England after 1815 depended on the labor of the sisters who had stayed at home while their brothers headed west or moved to the cities.

Within New England the main innovation came in the manufacture of cotton textiles. In 1790 Samuel Slater arrived in Pawtucket, Rhode Island, and established there the first permanent American mill for spinning cotton into yarn through the use of the spinning frame invented by the Englishman Richard Arkwright. Starting with nine workers, Slater had a hundred by 1800 and constructed other mills around Rhode Island and Massachusetts. Slater's mills performed only two of the many operations needed to turn raw cotton into clothing: carding, or fashioning broad laps of cotton into fine strands or slivers, and spinning these strands into yarn. The actual weaving of yarn Slater contracted out to women working in their homes. This "putting-out" system reinforced rather than challenged the traditional position of household, or "cottage," industry.

The incorporation in 1813 of the Boston Manufacturing Company by a group of merchant capitalists called the Boston Associates began a new chapter in the relationship between factories and

Samuel Slater's Mill

Slater's mill in Pawtucket, Rhode Island, was the birthplace of the U.S. textile industry.

cottage industries. Starting with a capital stock of $400,000 (more than ten times the stock of a typical Rhode Island mill), the Boston Manufacturing Company in quick succession established cotton textile factories in the Massachusetts towns of Waltham on the Charles River and Lowell on the Merrimack. By 1836 the Boston Associates had a total investment of $6.2 million in eight companies employing more than six thousand workers.

Size was not the only factor that distinguished these new mills from Slater's. In contrast to Slater's mills, the Waltham and Lowell factories produced finished products and thus challenged the cottage industries that Slater's system had sustained. Additionally, the Waltham and Lowell mills upset the traditional ordering of New England society to a degree that Slater never contemplated. Slater had sought to preserve tradition by hiring entire families to work in his mill complexes, just as entire families had traditionally worked on farms. He hired men to raise crops on nearby land owned by the factory while their wives and children tended the machines inside. Under this arrangement, children were never out of parental sight for long. In contrast, 80 percent of the workers in the mills operated by the Boston Manufacturing Company were unmarried women between the ages of fifteen and thirty, who had been lured from New England's farms by the promise of factory work. Mary Paul,

a Vermont teen-ager, settled her doubts about leaving home for work in Lowell by concluding that "I . . . must work where I can get more pay." While these young women often wrote home, they rarely saw their parents. In place of traditional family discipline, the Waltham and Lowell operatives, as the mill workers were called, experienced new kinds of restraints. The Boston capitalists who financed the mills did not personally oversee them; rather, they delegated oversight to managers, who imposed their own forms of discipline on the work force. Operatives had to live either in boarding houses built by the factory owners or in licensed private dwellings. Company regulations required operatives to attend church on the Sabbath, to observe a 10:00 P.M. curfew, and to accept what one minister called the "moral police of the corporations." At least initially, most young female operatives submitted without complaint to the "moral police."

A major reason why the corporations enforced high moral standards was to give the mills a good reputation so that New England farm girls would continue to be attracted into factory work. Yet mill conditions were far from attractive. To prevent the threads from snapping, the factories had to be kept humid. To create this condition, overseers nailed the windows shut and sprayed the air with water. Operatives also had to contend with flying dust and the deafening roar of the machines. Then keener

Mill Girls

New England's humming textile mills were a magnet for untold numbers of independence-seeking young women in antebellum America.

competition and a worsening economy in the late 1830s led the mill owners to reduce wages and speed up work schedules. Such conditions were common in nineteenth-century factories, but in Lowell and Waltham, they were intensified by the basic impersonality of the system. Each of the major groups that contributed to the system lived in a self-contained world. The Boston Associates raised capital but rarely visited the factories. Their agents, all men, gave orders to the operatives, mainly women. Some 800 Lowell mill women quit work in 1834 to protest a reduction in wages. Two years later, there was another "turnout," this time involving 1,500 to 2,000 women. These were the largest strikes in American history to that date. They are noteworthy as strikes not only of employees against employers but also of women against men.

Manufacturing in New York City and Philadelphia

With their large size, reliance on female labor, and dependence on machinery, the Lowell and Waltham textile mills were the most conspicuous examples of industrialization before 1840. In contrast to such planned factory towns, cities like New York and Philadelphia during the 1820s and 1830s witnessed an industrialization that lacked even the appearance of orderliness, depended far less on machinery and on female workers, occurred in small firms as well as in large ones, and encompassed a greater range of products, including shoes, saddles, tools, rope, hats, and gloves.

While diverging from the Lowell-Waltham model, the factories of New York and Philadelphia exposed workers to some of the same forces encountered by New England mill girls. By expanding the market for manufactures, the transportation revolution had turned some urban craftsmen, auctioneers, and merchants into aggressive merchandisers who scoured the country for orders. As a result, by 1835 New York City's ready-made clothing industry, for example, was supplying cheap dungarees and shirts to western farmers and even southern slaves; in the 1840s it was providing expensive suits for well-to-do customers. In turn, the possibility of reaching distant markets intensified competition and spurred businessmen to slash the cost of their products by increasing output, cutting wages, or both. In New England the Boston Associates had responded by introducing machines, but New York City lacked an easily harnessable source of water power, and before 1840 few machines existed that could speed up the fabrication of products like shoes. Thus factory owners in cities like New York and Philadelphia had to use different tactics to increase their share of the marketplace: they hired large numbers of unskilled or semiskilled workers, many of them women, and paid them low wages to perform simple, specialized hand operations like stitching cloth and soling shoes. In place of the colonial artisan who had fabricated the whole shoe on demand for a customer, such unskilled or semiskilled laborers no longer made whole shoes and rarely even saw a customer.

This subdivision of tasks (without the use of machines) characterized a great deal of industrialization before 1840 and occurred in a variety of work settings. In the boot and shoe industry that developed after 1820 in eastern Massachusetts, especially at Lynn, workers were gradually gathered into large factories to perform specialized operations in different rooms. In metropolises like New York and Philadelphia, the pattern was a little different. Here, while some large factories appeared in nearly all crafts, much of the subdivision of tasks took place in small shops, garrets, or homes. Because of the population density in these cities, it was unnecessary to gather workers into large factories. Middlemen could simply subcontract tasks out to widows, immigrants, and others who would fashion parts of shoes or saddles or dresses anywhere that light would enter. "We have been in some fifty cellars in different parts of the city," a New York *Tribune* reporter wrote in 1845, "each inhabited by a shoe-maker and his family. The floor is made of rough plank laid loosely down, and the ceiling is not quite so high as a tall man. The walls are dark and damp and . . . the miserable room is lighted only by a shallow sash partly projecting above the surface of the grounds and by the little light that struggles from the steep and rotting stairs. In this apartment often lives the man and his work bench, the wife, and five or six children of all ages; and perhaps a palsied grandfather and grandmother and often both. . . . Here they work, here they cook, they eat, they sleep, they pray. . . ."

In further contrast to places like Lowell and Waltham, which had not even existed in the eighteenth century, New York and Philadelphia were home to artisans with proud craft traditions and independence. Those with a skill like cutting leather or clothing, which was still in demand and took years to master, continued to earn good wages. Others grew rich by turning themselves into businessmen who spent less time making products than taking trips to obtain orders and who then hired workers to fill the orders. Thus industrialization did not reduce all artisans to misery. But many artisans, even though skilled, found themselves on the downslope. Increasingly faced with factory competition, they could either eke out a living as independent artisans by working longer hours and by skimping on food or other necessaries, or enter factories at low wages as semiskilled or unskilled workers. In 1835 Philadelphia shoemakers complained that factory owners had reaped "large fortunes, by reducing wages, making huge quantities of work, and selling at reduced prices, while those

of us who have served time to the trade and have been anxious to foster its interests, have had to abandon the business and enter the system of manufacturing."

In the late 1820s, skilled artisans in New York, Philadelphia, and other cities began to form trade unions and "workingmen's" political parties to protect their interests. Disdaining association with unskilled workers, most of these groups initially sought to restore privileges and working conditions that artisans had once enjoyed rather than to act as leaders of unskilled workers. But the steady deterioration of working conditions in the early 1830s tended to throw skilled and unskilled workers into the same boat. When coal heavers in Philadelphia struck for a ten-hour day in 1835, they were quickly joined by carpenters, cigar makers, shoemakers, leather workers, and other craftsmen in the United States' first general strike.

The emergence of organized worker protest underscored the mixed blessings of economic development. While some benefited from the new commercial and industrial economy, others found their economic position deteriorating. By the 1830s many Americans wondered whether their nation was truly a land of equality.

Equality and Inequality

Observers of antebellum (pre–Civil War) America sensed that changes were sweeping the country but had trouble describing them or agreeing on their direction. Alexis de Tocqueville, a French nobleman who spent nine months in America in 1831–1832, and whose two-volume *Democracy in America* (1835, 1840) contained both extraordinary insights and oversights, pinpointed the "general equality of condition among the people" as the fundamental fact from which all other characteristics of American society flowed. Yet Tocqueville's oft-cited observation about equality represented only part of his thinking about the extent of social democracy in America. He filled his private journal with references to inequalities. Tocqueville believed that these inequalities were less visible, but not necessarily less authentic, than those in France. He was struck by how American servants insisted on being called the "help" and on being viewed as neighbors invited to assist in running a household rather than as a class of permanent menials. But he certainly recognized that there were rich and poor in America.

While Tocqueville argued with himself, Americans disagreed with each other. Some insisted that wealth was "universally diffused." Others, like New York merchant Philip Hone, described an unhappy society in which "the two extremes of costly luxury in living, expensive establishments, and improvident waste are presented in daily and hourly contrast with squalid misery and hopeless destitution."

What assumptions and considerations explain these conflicting evaluations? Tocqueville viewed everything in comparative terms. America had more social equality than France. It was not just that American *servants* took on airs; in America, *merchants,* who in France were disdained by the titled nobility, were among other groups who considered themselves equal to anyone. Other observers generalized about the whole society after examining only part of it. Almost all contemporaries struggled to find the right words to describe the changes. They applied traditional terms like *artisan* and *farmer* to people whose activities no longer conformed to the conventional image of what artisans and farmers did. Similarly, they tossed around words like *democracy* and *equality* without always recognizing that equality before the law was one thing, equality of opportunity another, and social equality a third.

For all these reasons, it is difficult to get what mariners call a fix on American society before the Civil War. Using refined techniques of measurement, however, historians have drawn a more detailed and complete portrait of antebellum society than the profile sketched by contemporaries. The following discussion applies mainly to northern society. The South, whose "peculiar institution" of slavery created a distinctive social structure and set of social relationships, is examined separately in Chapter 10.

Growing Inequality: The Rich and the Poor

The gap between the rich and the poor, which had increased during the late eighteenth century, widened further during the first half of the nineteenth century. Although Americans portrayed them as oases of equality, farm areas contained a good deal of inequality. In 1850 the poorest 40 percent of native-born farmers owned less than one hundred dollars worth of property, while the richest 30 percent to 40 percent of farmers owned three-fourths or more of the total farm property. But the truly striking inequalities developed in the cities, where a small fraction of the people owned a huge share of urban wealth. In Boston, for example, the richest 10 percent of the population owned a little over half of the city's real estate and personal property in 1771. By 1833 the richest 4 percent owned 59 percent of the wealth, and by 1848 nearly two-thirds of the wealth. By 1848, 81 percent of Boston's population owned only 4 percent of its wealth. In New York City, the richest 4 percent owned nearly half the wealth in 1828 and more than two-thirds by 1845. These statistics are representative of trends that affected all major cities. By 1860 the wealthiest 10 percent in Baltimore, St. Louis, and New Orleans held more than 80 percent of the wealth. A similar if less extreme trend toward the concentration of wealth affected towns like Jacksonville, Illinois, and Poughkeepsie, New York.

Although commentators celebrated the self-made American who rose "from rags to riches," few individuals actually accumulated their wealth in this way. The vast majority of those who became extremely rich started out with considerable wealth. Fewer than five of every hundred wealthy men started poor, and close to ninety of every hundred started rich. The old-fashioned way to make money was to inherit it, marry into more, and then invest wisely. There were just enough instances of fabulously successful poor boys like John Jacob Astor, who built a fur-trading empire, to sustain popular belief in the rags-to-riches myth, but not enough to turn that myth into a reality.

Their splendid residences as well as their wealth set the rich apart. The urban rich built imposing mansions clustered in neighborhoods. In 1828 over half of the 500 wealthiest families in New York City lived on only 8 of the city's more than 250 streets, while during the early 1830s, half of Boston's wealthy families lived on but 8 of its 325 streets. Social clubs also separated the rich from others. The Philadelphia Club, founded in 1834, was a stronghold for proper Philadelphians. By the late 1820s, New York City had a club so exclusive that it was called just The Club. Tocqueville noted

View of St. Louis, *by Leon Pomarede, 1832*

When the trans-Mississippi fur trade declined in the 1830s, the steamboats that plied the Mississippi and Missouri rivers became the key to St. Louis's expansion. The economic gap between the city's rich and poor widened as St. Louis grew.

that in America "the wealthiest and most enlightened live among themselves." Yet Tocqueville was also struck by how the rich feigned respect for equality when they moved about in public. They rode in ordinary rather than sumptuous carriages, brushed elbows easily with the less privileged, and avoided the conspicuous display of wealth that marked their private lives.

At the opposite end of the social ladder were the poor. By today's standards, most antebellum Americans were poor: they lived "close to the margin" of poverty, depended heavily on their children's labor to meet expenses, had little money to spend on medical care or recreation, and were subject to unemployment, not just during general economic downturns but from month to month, even in times of prosperity. Freezing weather, for instance, could temporarily throw day laborers, factory workers, and boatmen out of work. In 1850 an estimated three out of eight males over the age of twenty owned little more than their clothing and the cash in their pockets.

In evaluating economic status, it is important to recognize that statistics on the distribution of wealth to some extent mask the fact that the accumulation of property takes place over an entire lifetime and increases with age. With its extraordinary high birthrate, antebellum America was overwhelmingly a nation of young people with little property; not all of them would remain propertyless as they grew older.

We must also keep in mind that when antebellum Americans themselves spoke of poverty, they were not thinking of the condition of hardship that affected most people. Instead, they were referring to a state of dependency, a total inability to fend for oneself, that affected *some* people. They often called this dependency pauperism. The absence of health insurance and old-age pensions condemned many infirm and aged people to pauperism. Widows whose children had left home might also have a hard time avoiding pauperism. Contemporaries usually classified all such people as the "deserving" poor and contrasted them with the "undeserving" poor—such as indolent loafers and drunkards whose poverty was self-willed. Most moralists claimed that America was happily free of a permanent class of paupers. They assumed that since pauperism resulted either from circumstances beyond anyone's control, such as old age and disease, or from voluntary decisions to squander money on liquor, it could not afflict entire groups generation after generation.

This assumption was comforting but also misleading, because a class of people who could not escape poverty was emerging in the major cities during the first half of the nineteenth century. One source of this class was immigration. As early as 1801, a New York newspaper called attention to boatloads of immigrants with large families, without money or health, and *"expiring from the want of sustenance."* The arrival of huge numbers of Irish immigrants during the 1840s and 1850s made a bad situation worse. The Irish were among the poorest immigrants ever to arrive in America. Fleeing famine in Ireland, they found even worse conditions in noxious slums like New York's infamous Five Points district. Starting with the conversion of a brewery into housing for hundreds of people in 1837, the Five Points became probably the worst slum in America.

The Irish were not only poor but, as Catholics, also belonged to a church despised by the Protestant majority. In short, they were different and had little claim on the kindly impulses of most Protestants. But even the Protestant poor came in for rough treatment in the years between 1815 and 1840. The more Americans convinced themselves that success was within everyone's grasp, the less they accepted the traditional doctrine that poverty was ordained by God, and the more they were inclined to hold the poor responsible for their own poverty. Ironically, even as many Americans blamed the poor for being poor, they practiced discrimination that kept some groups mired in enduring poverty. Nowhere was this more true than in the case of northern free blacks.

Free Blacks in the North

Prejudice against blacks was deeply ingrained in white society throughout the nation. Although slavery had largely disappeared in the North by 1820, laws penalized blacks in many ways. One form of discrimination was to restrict the blacks' right to vote. In New York State, for example, a constitutional revision of 1821 eliminated property requirements for white voters but kept them for blacks. Rhode Island banned blacks from voting in 1822; Pennsylvania did so in 1837. Throughout the half-century after 1800, blacks could vote on equal terms with whites in only one of the nation's major cities, Boston. Efforts were also made to bar free blacks from migrating to other states and cities. Missouri's original constitution authorized the state legislature to prevent blacks from entering the state "under any pretext whatsoever." Free blacks were often barred from public conveyances and facilities and were either excluded from public schools in major cities or forced into segregated schools. Segregation was the rule in northern jails, almshouses, and hospitals. But of all restrictions on free blacks, the most damaging was the social pressure that forced them into the least skilled and lowest-paying occupations throughout the northern cities. Recollecting his youthful days in Providence, Rhode Island, in the early 1830s, the free black William J. Brown wrote: "To drive carriages, carry a market basket after the boss, and brush his boots, or saw wood and run errands was as high as a colored man could rise." Although a few free blacks became successful entrepreneurs and grew moderately wealthy, urban free blacks were only half as likely as city dwellers in general to own real estate.

The "Middling Classes"

The majority of antebellum Americans lived neither in splendid wealth nor in grinding poverty. Most belonged to what men and women of the time called the middling classes. Even though the wealthy owned an increasing proportion of all wealth, most people's standard of living rose between 1800 and 1860, particularly between 1840 and 1860, when per capita income grew at an annual rate of around 1.5 percent.

Americans applied the term *middling classes* to farmers and artisans, whose ideal was self-employment. These were the nation's sturdy "producers." Commentators criticized the rich for luxury and the poor for depravity, but they rarely had anything bad to say about the middling classes, whom they regarded as steady and dependable, the

The Blacksmith's Shop, *by Eastman Johnson, 1863*

Blacksmiths were indispensable artisans in antebellum America. At their forges, which served as both social and industrial centers, they made or repaired horseshoes, nails, rifles, saws, wagon axles, chains, bear traps, and farm implements of every sort.

real America. Yet life in the middle was unpredictable, filled with jagged ups and downs. Words like *farmer* and *artisan* were often misleading, for they gave a greater impression of steadiness and stability than was really the case. For example, Asa G. Sheldon, born in Massachusetts in 1788, described himself in his autobiography as a farmer, offered advice on growing corn and cranberries, and gave speeches about the glories of farming. While Sheldon undoubtedly knew a great deal about farming, he actually spent very little time tilling the soil. In 1812 he began to transport hops from New England to brewers in New York City, and he soon extended this business to Philadelphia and Baltimore. He invested his profits in land, but rather than farm the land, he made money selling its timber. When a business setback forced him to sell his property, he was soon back in operation "through the disinterested kindness of friends" who lent him money, with which he purchased carts and oxen. These he used to get contracts for filling in swamps in Boston and for clearing and grading land for railroads. From all this and from the backbreaking labor of the Irish immigrants he hired to do the

shoveling, Sheldon the "farmer" grew prosperous. But his prosperity in fact owed little to farming.

The increasingly commercial and industrial economy of antebellum America created opportunities for success and forced individuals like Sheldon to make adaptations. Not everyone, though, had an opportunity for success. Had it not been for the intervention of wealthy friends, Sheldon would have ended up in a poorhouse. Many lacked kindly friends with money to lend. Some, like Sheldon, rose. Others, like Allan Melville, father of novelist Herman Melville, slipped down the slope. An enterprising import merchant, Allan Melville had an abounding faith in his nation, in "our national Eagle, 'with an eye that never winks and a wing that never tires,'" and in the inevitable triumph of honesty and prudence. The Melvilles lived comfortably in Albany and New York City, but in the late 1820s, Allan's business, never robust, sagged. By 1830 he was begging his father for a loan of $500, proclaiming that "I am destitute of resources and without a shilling—without immediate assistance I know not what will become of me." He got the $500 plus an additional $3,000, but the downward spiral continued. In 1832 he died, broken in spirit and nearly insane.

The case of artisans also illustrates the perils of life in the middling classes. During the colonial period, artisans had formed a proud and cohesive group whose members often attained the goal of self-employment. They owned their own tools, made their own products on order from customers, boarded their apprentices and journeymen in their homes, and passed their skills on to their sons. By 1850, in contrast, artisans had entered a new world of economic relationships. This was true even of a craft like carpentry that did not experience any industrial or technological change. Town and city growth in the wake of the transportation revolution created a demand for housing. Some carpenters, usually those with access to capital, became contractors who took orders for more houses than they could build themselves and who then hired large numbers of journeymen to do the construction work. Likewise, as we have seen, in the early industrialization of shoe manufacturing during the 1820s, some shoemakers spent less time crafting shoes than making trips to obtain orders for their products, then hired workers to fashion parts of shoes. In effect, the old class of artisans was breaking apart into two new groupings. On one side were artisans who had become businessmen or entrepreneurs; on the other, journeymen with little prospect of self-employment.

An additional characteristic of the middling classes (one that they shared with the poor) was a high degree of transiency, or "spatial mobility." Farmers who cultivated land intensively in order to raise a cash crop and so get out of debt exhausted their land quickly and had to move on. Artisans displaced from skilled jobs by machines found that much unskilled work was seasonal and that they had to move from job to job to survive. Canal workers and boatmen had to secure new work when waterways froze. Even for city dwellers, to shift jobs often meant changing residences, for the cities were spreading out at a much faster rate than was public transportation. Some idea of the degree of transiency can be gained from a survey made by the Boston police on Saturday, September 6, 1851. At a time when Boston's population was 145,000, the survey showed that from 6:30 A.M. to 7:30 P.M., 41,729 people entered the city and 42,313 left.

Alcohol in the Early Republic

Antebellum economic change improved many lives but also imposed new pressures. In a society in which some individuals outstripped others in the race for riches, most felt compelled to succeed. But when they failed, more and more Americans came to believe that their failure was not the product of fate or divine will, as had traditionally been thought, but of individual lack of enterprise. By stripping away the older idea that personal failure reflected God's will, the commercialization and industrialization of American society made the individual bear the whole burden of failure. In this context, Americans increasingly turned to alcoholic binges in these years, as a way not to explain their inadequacies but to soften them, by retreating into the mellow stupor of intoxication.

A tradition of drinking had been inherited from the eighteenth century, and the spread of the population across the Appalachians further stimulated the production and consumption of liquor. Before 1830 western farmers commonly distilled grain into spirits. Annual per capita consumption of rum, whiskey, gin, and brandy rose until it exceeded seven gallons by 1830, nearly triple today's rate.

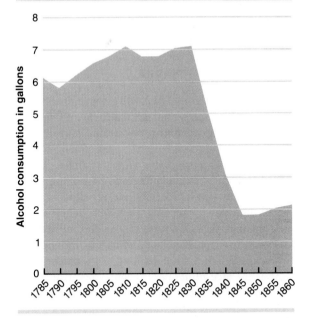

Absolute Alcohol Consumption, per Capita, of Drinking-Age (15+) Population

The temperance movement, which arose in the late 1820s and was dedicated to encouraging abstinence from alcoholic beverages, had a decisive impact on American drinking patterns.
SOURCE: From *The Alcoholic Republic: An American Tradition* by W. J. Rorabaugh. Copyright 1979 by Oxford University Press, Inc. Reprinted by permission.

By the late 1820s, the average adult male was drinking a half-pint of liquor a day. So much a part of the cultural scene did drinking become that one enterprising Irish immigrant, Sam Patch, even charged spectators to watch him jump, inebriated, into rivers. In 1829 he finally miscalculated and drunkenly plunged to his death in Genesee Falls near Rochester, New York. Far more typical than Patch's spectacular leaps were brawls among drunken lumbermen and canal workers. But it was not just manual workers who fell victim to the "demon" of liquor, for many physicians, lawyers, and bankers sought in intoxication a temporary feeling of achievement, power, and success.

The multiplying risks and opportunities that confronted Americans both widened the gap between social classes and increased the psychological burdens on individuals. Commercial and industrial growth also placed pressure on such basic social relationships as those between lawyers and their clients, ministers and their parishioners, and children and their parents.

The Revolution in Social Relationships

Following the War of 1812, the growth of interregional trade, commercial agriculture, and manufacturing disrupted many traditional social relationships and forged new ones. Two broad generalizations encompass these changes. First, Americans questioned authority to an unprecedented degree. In 1775 they had rebelled against their king. Now, it seemed, they were rebelling as well against their lawyers, physicians, ministers, and even their parents. An attitude of individualism sprouted and took firm root in antebellum America. Once *individualism* had meant nothing more than selfishness, but now Americans used the word to signify positive qualities: self-reliance and the conviction that each person was the best judge of his or her own true interests. Ordinary Americans might still agree with the opinions of their leaders, but only after they had thought matters through on their own. Those with superior wealth, education, or social position could no longer expect the automatic deference of the common people.

Second, even as Americans widely proclaimed themselves a nation of self-reliant individualists and questioned the traditional basis of authority, they sought to construct new foundations for authority. For example, among middle-class women, the idea developed that they possessed a "separate sphere" of authority in the home. In addition, individuals increasingly joined with others in these years to form voluntary associations through which they might influence the direction that their society would take.

The Attack on the Professions

The first phase in this alteration of social relationships was the erosion of traditional forms of authority. In the swiftly changing antebellum society, claims to social superiority were questioned as never before. The statesman Harrison Gray Otis put it in a nutshell in 1836: "Everywhere the disposition is found among those who live in the val-

leys to ask those who live on the hills, 'How came we here and you there?' "

Intense criticism of lawyers, physicians, and ministers exemplified this assault on authority. As far back as the 1780s, Benjamin Austin, a radical Boston artisan, had complained that lawyers needlessly prolonged and confused court cases so that they could charge high fees. Between 1800 and 1840, a wave of religious revivals known as the Second Great Awakening (see Chapter 9) sparked new attacks on the professions. Some revivalists blasted the clergy for creating complicated theologies that ordinary men and women could not comprehend, for drinking expensive wines, and for fleecing the people. One religious revivalist, Elias Smith, extended the criticism to physicians, whom he accused of inventing Latin and Greek names for diseases in order to disguise their own ignorance of how to cure them.

Attacks on the learned professions peaked between 1820 and 1850. In medicine a movement arose under the leadership of Samuel Thomson, a farmer's son with little formal education, to eliminate all barriers to entry into the medical profession. Thomson believed that anyone could understand the principles of medicine and become a physician. His crusade was remarkably successful. By 1845 every state had repealed laws that required licenses and education to practice medicine. Meanwhile, attacks on lawyers sharpened, and relations between ministers and their parishioners grew tense and acrimonious. In colonial New England, ministers had usually served a single parish for life, but by the 1830s a rapid turnover of ministers was becoming the norm as finicky parishioners commonly dismissed clergymen whose theology displeased them. Ministers themselves were becoming more ambitious—more inclined to leave small, poor congregations for large, wealthy ones.

The increasing commercialization of the economy contributed both to the growing number of professionals and to the attacks on them. The rise of the market economy intensified the demand for lawyers and physicians; the number of medical schools, for example, grew from one in 1765 to twenty in 1830 and sixty-five in 1860. Like so many other antebellum Americans, these freshly minted lawyers and doctors often were transients without deep roots in the towns that they served and without convincing claims to social superiority.

Describing lawyers and physicians, a contemporary observer wrote: "Men dropped down into their places as from clouds. Nobody knew who or what they were, except as they claimed, or as a surface view of their character indicated." A horse doctor one day would the next day hang up his sign as "Physician and Surgeon" and "fire at random a box of his pills into your bowels, with a vague chance of hitting some disease unknown to him, but with a better prospect of killing the patient, whom or whose administrator he charged some ten dollars a trial for his marksmanship."

The questioning of authority was particularly sharp on the frontier. Here, to eastern and foreign visitors, it seemed that every man they met was a "judge," "general," "colonel," or "squire." In a society in which everyone was new, such titles were easily adopted but just as easily challenged. Where neither law nor custom sanctioned claims of superiority, would-be gentlemen substituted an exaggerated sense of personal honor. Obsessed with their fragile status, many of these "gentlemen" reacted testily to the slightest insult. Dueling became a widespread frontier practice. At a Kentucky militia parade in 1819, a colonel's dog jogged onto the field and sat at his master's knee. Enraged by this breach of military decorum, the regiment's general ran the dog through with his dress sword. A week later, general and colonel met with pistols at ten paces. The colonel was killed; the general, crippled for life.

The Challenge to Family Authority

In contrast to the public, philosophical attacks on the learned professions, children engaged in a quiet questioning of parental authority. Economic change created new opportunities that forced young people to choose between staying at home to help their parents and venturing out on their own. Writing to her parents in Vermont shortly before taking a job in a Lowell textile mill, eighteen-year-old Sally Rice quickly got to the point: "I must of course have something of my own before many more years have passed over my head and where is that something coming from if I go home and earn nothing. You may think me unkind but how can you blame me if I want to stay here. I have but one life to live and I want to enjoy myself as I can while I live."

A similar desire for independence propelled young men to leave home at earlier ages than in the past and to strike out on their own. Although the great migration to the West was primarily a movement of entire families, movement from farms to towns and cities within regions was frequently spearheaded by restless and single young people. Two young men in Virginia put it succinctly: "All the promise of life seemed to us to be at the other end of the rainbow—somewhere else—anywhere else but on the farm. . . . And so all our youthful plans had as their chief object the getting away from the farm."

Antebellum Americans also widely wished to be free of close parental supervision, and their changing attitudes influenced courtship and marriage. Many young people who no longer depended on their parents for land insisted on privacy in courting and wanted to decide for themselves when to marry. Increasingly, too, romantic love between the partners rather than parental preferences determined decisions to marry. Where seventeenth-century Puritans had advised young people to choose marriage partners whom they *could* love, by the early 1800s, young men and women viewed romantic love as the indispensable basis for a successful marriage. "In affairs of love," a young lawyer in Maine wrote, "young peoples hearts are generally much wiser than old peoples heads."

One sign of young people's growing control over courtship and marriage was the declining likelihood that the young women of a family would marry in their exact birth order. Traditionally, fathers had wanted their daughters to marry in the order of their birth, to avoid planting the suspicion that there was something wrong with one or more of them. Toward the end of the eighteenth century, however, the practice ceased to be customary, as daughters were making their own marital decisions. Another mark of the times was the growing number of long engagements. Having made the decision to marry, some young women were reluctant to tie the knot, fearing that marriage would snuff out their independence. For example, Caroline and William Kirkland were engaged for seven years before their marriage in 1828. Equally striking was the increasing number of young women who chose not to marry. Catharine Beecher, the daughter of the prominent minister Lyman Beecher, broke off her engagement to a young man during the 1820s, despite her father's pressure to marry him. She later renewed the engagement, but after her fiancé's death in a shipwreck, she remained single for the rest of her life.

Thus young people lived more and more in a world of their own. Not surprisingly, moralists reacted with alarm and flooded the country with books of advice to youth such as William Alcott's *The Young Man's Guide,* which went through thirty-one editions between 1833 and 1858. The number of such advice books sold in antebellum America was truly vast, but to an amazing extent, they all said the same thing. They did not advise young men and women to return to farms, and they assumed that parents had little control over them. Rather, their authors exhorted youths to develop habitual rectitude, self-control, and "character." It was an age not just of the self-made man but also of the self-made youth.

Wives, Husbands

Another class of advice books pouring from the antebellum presses counseled wives and husbands on their rights and duties. These were a sign that relations between spouses, too, were changing. Young men and women who, as teen-agers, had grown accustomed to making decisions on their own were more likely than their ancestors to approach wedlock as a compact between equals. Of course, wives remained unequal to their husbands in many tangible ways, the most obvious being the continuation into the 1830s of the traditional legal rule that married women could not own property. But relations between wives and husbands were changing during the 1820s and 1830s toward a form of equality.

One source of the change was the rise of a potent ideology known as the doctrine of separate spheres. Traditionally, women had been viewed as subordinate to men in all spheres of life. Now middle-class men and women developed a kind of separate-but-equal doctrine that portrayed men as superior in making money and governing the world and women as superior for their moral influence on family members. One of the most important duties assigned to the sphere of women was the raising of children. During the eighteenth century, ministers had addressed sermons to fathers to remind them of their duty to govern the family, but by the 1830s child-rearing manuals increasingly appealed to mothers rather than fathers. "How entire and

perfect in this dominion over the unformed character of your infant," the popular writer Lydia Sigourney proclaimed in her *Letters to Mothers* (1838). Advice books instructed mothers to discipline their children by loving them and withdrawing affection when they misbehaved rather than by using corporal punishment. A whipped child might become more obedient but would remain sullen and bitter. In contrast, the gentler methods advised in manuals promised to penetrate to the child's heart, to make the child want to do the right thing.

The idea of a separate women's sphere blended with a related image of the family and the home as secluded refuges from a society marked by commotion and disorder. The popular culture of the 1830s and 1840s painted an alluring portrait of the pleasures of home life through songs like "Home, Sweet Home" and poems such as Henry Wadsworth Longfellow's "The Children's Hour" and Clement Moore's "A Visit from St. Nicholas." The publication of Moore's poem coincided with the growing popularity of Christmas as a holiday season in which family members gathered to exchange warm affection. Even the physical appearance of houses changed as architects offered new designs for the ideal home. The prominent architect Andrew Jackson Downing published plans for peaceful single-family homes that he hoped would offset the "spirit of unrest" and the feverish pace of American life. In Downing's view, houses should contain welcoming porches, comfortable piazzas, overhanging roofs with high gables, and deep eaves to evoke sentiment. He wrote of the ideal home: "There should be something to love. There must be nooks about it, where one would love to linger; windows, where one can enjoy the quiet landscape at his leisure; cozy rooms, where all fireside joys are invited to dwell."

As a prophet, Downing deserves high marks, because one of the motives that has impelled many Americans to flee cities for suburbs in the twentieth century has been the desire to achieve ownership of a single-family residence. However, in the 1820s and 1830s, this ideal was beyond the reach of most people—not just blacks, immigrants, and sweatshop workers, but much of the middle class as well. In the countryside, while middle-class farmers still managed productive households, these were anything but tranquil: wives milked cows and bled hogs, and children fetched wood, drove cows to pasture, and chased blackbirds from cornfields.

The Ephraim Hubbard Foster Family, *by Ralph E. W. Earl, c. 1824*

This painting literally captures the child-centeredness of middle-class families in antebellum America by placing a child in the middle of the family group.

In the cities, middle-class families often had to sacrifice their privacy by taking in boarders to supplement family income.

Still, the doctrine of separate spheres for men and women, and the image of the home as a calming refuge from a harsh world, were powerful ideals, and virtually the only ones projected in antebellum magazines. Although they were ideals rather than descriptions of reality, they did intersect with the real world at *some* points. For example, the decline of cottage industries and the rising number of urban families headed by merchants, lawyers, or brokers (all of whom worked away from their homes) gave married women more time to spend on child rearing. Above all, even if they could not afford to live in a Downing-designed house, married women found that they could use the doctrine of separate spheres and the image of the home as a refuge to gain new power within their families. A subtle implication of the doctrine of separate spheres was that women should have control not only over the discipline of children but also over the more fundamental issue of the number of children that they would bear.

In 1800 the United States had had one of the highest birthrates ever recorded for a civilized nation. The average woman bore 7.04 children. It is safe to say that married women had become pregnant as often as possible. In the prevailing farm economy, children were valuable for carrying out essential tasks and, as time passed, for relieving aging parents of the burden of heavy farm labor. Most parents had assumed that the more children, the better. However, the spread of a commercial economy raised troublesome questions about children's economic value. Unlike a farmer, a merchant or lawyer could not send his children to work at the age of seven or eight. The average woman, who had borne 7.04 children in 1800, was bearing only 5.02 by 1850, and 3.98 by 1900. The birthrate remained high among blacks and among many immigrant groups, but it slumped drastically among native-born whites, particularly in towns and cities. The birthrate also declined in rural areas, but more sharply in rural villages than on farms, and more sharply in the East, where land was scarce, than in the West, where abundant land created continued incentives for parents to have many children.

For the most part, the decline in the birthrate was accomplished by abstinence from sexual intercourse or by *coitus interruptus* (withdrawal of the male organ before ejaculation) or by abortion. By the 1840s such abortionists as New York City's notorious Madame Restell advertised remedies for "female irregularities," a common euphemism for unwanted pregnancies. There were no foolproof birth-control devices, and as much misinformation as information circulated about the techniques of birth control. Nonetheless, interest in birth-control devices was intensifying. In 1832 Charles Knowlton, a Massachusetts physician, described the procedure for vaginal douching in his book *Fruits of Philosophy*. Although Knowlton was frequently prosecuted and once jailed for obscenity, efforts to suppress his ideas only resulted in their being publicized even more. By 1865 popular tracts had familiarized Americans with a wide range of birth-control methods, including the rubber condom and the vaginal diaphragm. Whatever the method, the decision to limit family size was usually reached jointly by wives and husbands. Economic and ideological considerations blended together. Husbands could note that the economic value of children was declining; wives, that having fewer children would give them more time to nurture each one and thereby carry out the duties of the woman's sphere.

Supporters of the ideal of separate spheres did not advocate full legal equality for women. Indeed, the idea of separate spheres was an explicit *alternative* to legal equality. But the concept did enhance women's power within marriage by justifying their demands for influence over such vital issues as child rearing and the frequency of pregnancies. In addition, it allowed some women a measure of independence from the home. For example, it sanctioned Catharine Beecher's travels to lecture women on better ways to raise children and manage their households.

Horizontal Allegiances and the Rise of Voluntary Associations

As some forms of authority, such as that of parents over their children and of husbands over their wives, were weakening, Americans devised new ways through which individuals could extend their influence over others. The pre–Civil War period witnessed the widespread substitution of *horizontal* allegiances for *vertical* allegiances. An example of vertical allegiance is found in the traditional patriarchal family, wherein a wife and children looked up to the father for leadership. Another example occurs in the small eighteenth-century workshop, where apprentices and journeymen took direction from the master craftsman and even lived in the craftsman's house, subject to his authority. Common to these examples is the idea of authority

flowing from the top down. In a vertical allegiance, people in a subordinate position identify their best interests with the interests of their superiors rather than with those of other individuals in the same subordinate position.

When social relationships began to assume a horizontal form, several new patterns emerged. While the older kind of vertical relationships did not disappear, they became less important in people's lives. Relationships now arose that linked those in a similar position. For example, in large textile mills during the 1830s, many operatives discovered that they had more in common with each other than with their managers and overseers. Similarly, wives were increasingly inclined to form associations that bound them with other married women. Young men formed associations with other young men. None of these associations was intended to overthrow traditional authority. Many of them in fact professed to strengthen the family or community. But all represented the substitution of new allegiances for old ones.

A sign of the change can be seen in the large number of voluntary associations formed in the 1820s and 1830s. These were associations that arose apart from government and sought to accomplish some goal of value to their members. Tocqueville observed that in France the government stood at the head of every enterprise but that in America "you will be sure to find an association."

At the most basic level, the voluntary associations encouraged sociability. As transients and newcomers flocked into towns and cities, they tended to join with others who shared similar characteristics, experiences, or interests. Gender was the basis of many voluntary societies. Of twenty-six religious and charitable associations in Utica, New York, in 1832, for instance, one-third were exclusively for women. Race was still another basis for voluntary associations. Although their names did not indicate it, Boston's Thompson Literary and Debating Society, its Philomathean Adelphic Union for the Promotion of Literature and Science, and New York City's Phoenix Society were all organizations for free blacks.

Promoting sociability, however, was not the only benefit of voluntary associations. These associations also allowed their members to assert their influence at a time when traditional forms of authority were weakening. For example, voluntary associations proved compatible with the idea that women had a separate sphere. As long as a woman could argue that her activities were in the best interests of the home, she could escape the kitchen long enough to join maternal associations (where mothers exchanged ideas about child rearing), temperance associations (where they promoted abstinence from alcoholic beverages), and moral-reform societies. These latter societies, which multiplied in the 1830s and 1840s, combated prostitution.

Temperance and moral-reform societies had a dual purpose. They sought to suppress well-known vices *and* to enhance women's power over men. Temperance advocates assumed that intemperance was a male vice. Moral reformers attributed the prevalence of prostitution to the lustfulness of men who, unable to control their passions, exploited poor and vulnerable girls. While exhorting prostitutes to give up their line of work, moral reformers also tried to shame brothel patrons into chastity by publishing their names in newspapers. Just as strikes in Lowell in the 1830s were a form of collective action by working women, temperance and moral-reform societies represented collective action by middle-class women to increase their influence in society. Here as elsewhere, the tendency of the times was to forge new forms of horizontal allegiance between like-minded Americans.

Conclusion

Alexis de Tocqueville described the United States of the 1830s as remarkable not for "the marvellous grandeur of some undertakings" but for the "innumerable multitude of small ones." In fact, a number of grand enterprises *were* undertaken between 1815 and 1840, among them the construction of the Erie Canal and the establishment of the Lowell mills. But Tocqueville was basically correct. The distinguishing feature of the period was the amount of small to medium-size enterprises that Americans embarked upon: commercial farms of modest proportions, railroads that ran for a few hundred miles, manufacturing companies that employed five to ten workers.

The changes of the period were modest in comparison to those that would come in the late nineteenth century, when industrial firms routinely employed hundreds of workers and railroads spanned the continent. Nevertheless, to antebellum Americans, it seemed as if the world of their ancestors was breaking apart. In 1800 no human or machine had been able to sustain motion at more than ten miles an hour. The railroads changed that. In 1800 it had been natural to assume that the limits of trade were set by the limits of rivers. Canals changed that. Everywhere traditional assumptions about what was "natural" were challenged.

As traditional assumptions eroded, new ones took their place. Ties to village leaders and even to parents weakened, but new bonds with the like-minded and with age peers emerged. Individualism became a major force in the sense that a widening circle of Americans insisted on the right to shape their own economic destinies. "No man in America is contented to be poor," a magazine proclaimed, "or expects to continue so." Yet Americans did not desire isolation from each other. Voluntary associations based on the personal preferences of their members, rather than on custom, proliferated. A host of advice books aimed at young people, wives, and husbands tried to teach Americans how to play the new roles thrust upon them by economic and social change. The marriage manual was as much a part of antebellum America as the Erie Canal or the Boston Manufacturing Company.

The social transformations of 1815 to 1840 not only changed the private lives of Americans but also brought a host of new political issues to the fore, as we shall see in Chapter 9.

CHRONOLOGY

1790 Samuel Slater opens his first Rhode Island mill for the production of cotton yarn.

1793 Eli Whitney invents the cotton gin.

1807 Robert R. Livingston and Robert Fulton introduce the steamboat *Clermont* on the Hudson River.

1811 Construction of the National Road begins at Cumberland, Maryland.

1813 Incorporation of the Boston Manufacturing Company.

1816 Second Bank of the United States chartered.

1817 Erie Canal started.

1819 Economic panic, ushering in four-year depression.

1820– Growth of female moral-reform societies.
1850

1820s Expansion of New England textile mills.

1824 *Gibbons* v. *Ogden*.

1825 Completion of the Erie Canal.

1828 Baltimore and Ohio Railroad chartered.

1830 Indian Removal Act passed by Congress.

1831 *Cherokee Nation* v. *Georgia*.
Alexis de Tocqueville begins visit to the United States to study American penitentiaries.

1832 *Worcester* v. *Georgia*.

1834 First strike at the Lowell mills.

1837 Economic panic begins a depression that lasts until 1843.

1840 System of production by interchangeable parts perfected.

For Further Reading

Rowland Berthoff, *An Unsettled People: Social Order and Disorder in American History* (1971). A stimulating interpretation of American social history.

Ray A. Billington, *Westward Expansion: A History of the American Frontier* (1949). The standard study of westward movement and settlement.

Daniel Boorstin, *The Americans: The National Experience* (1965). A provocative interpretation of American society in the first half of the nineteenth century.

Carl Degler, *At Odds: Women and the Family in America from the Revolution to the Present* (1980). A fine overview of the economic and social experiences of American women.

George R. Taylor, *The Transportation Revolution, 1815–1860* (1951). The standard general study of the development of canals, steamboats, highways, and railroads.

Sean Wilentz, *Chants Democratic: New York City and the Rise of the American Working Class, 1788–1850* (1983). A stimulating synthesis of economic, social, and political history.

Additional Bibliography

Agriculture and the Westward Movement

Thomas D. Clark, *The Rampaging Frontier* (1939); Charles Danhof, *Change in Agriculture: The Northern United States, 1820–1870* (1969); Paul W. Gates, *The Farmer's Age: Agriculture, 1815–1860* (1960); William H. Goetzmann, *Explorations and Empire: The Explorer and the Scientist in the Winning of the American West* (1966); Malcolm Rohrbough, *The Land Office Business: The Settlement and Administration of American Public Lands, 1789–1837* (1968).

Indians

Robert F. Berkhofer, Jr., *The White Man's Indian: Images of the American Indian from Columbus to the Present*

(1979); John R. Finger, *The Eastern Band of Cherokees, 1819–1900* (1984); Michael D. Green, *The Politics of Indian Removal: Creek Government and Society in Crisis* (1982); William G. McLoughlin, *Cherokees and Missionaries, 1789–1839* (1984); Roy H. Pearce, *The Savages of America* (1965); Richard Slotkin, *Regeneration Through Violence: The Mythology of the American Frontier, 1600–1860* (1973); Wilcomb E. Washburn, *The Indian in America* (1975).

The Transportation Revolution

Albert Fishlow, *American Railroads and the Transformation of the Ante-Bellum Economy* (1965); Robert W. Fogel, *Railroads and American Economic Growth: Essays in Econometric History* (1964); Carter Goodrich, *Government Promotion of American Canals and Railroads, 1800–1890* (1960); Erik F. Haites, James Mak, and Gary M. Walton, *Western River Transportation: The Era of Early Internal Development, 1800–1860* (1975); Harry N. Scheiber, *The Ohio Canal Era: A Case Study of Government and the Economy, 1820–1861* (1969); R. E. Shaw, *Erie Water West* (1966).

Communities

Stuart Blumin, *The Urban Threshold: Growth and Change in a Nineteenth-Century American Community* (1976); Don H. Doyle, *The Social Order of a Frontier Community: Jacksonville, Illinois, 1825–1870* (1978); Clyde Griffen and Sally Griffen, *Natives and Newcomers: The Ordering of Opportunity in Mid-Nineteenth-Century Poughkeepsie* (1978); Paul Johnson, *A Shopkeeper's Millennium: Society and Revivals in Rochester, New York, 1815–1837* (1978); Richard C. Wade, *The Urban Frontier* (1964); Anthony F. C. Wallace, *Rockdale: The Growth of an American Village in the Early Industrial Revolution* (1977).

Immigrants

Rowland Berthoff, *British Immigrants in Industrial America* (1953); Kathleen N. Conzen, *Immigrant Milwaukee, 1836–1860* (1976); Jay P. Dolan, *The Immigrant Church: New York's Irish and German Catholics, 1815–1860* (1975); Oscar Handlin, *Boston's Immigrants: A Study in Acculturation* (rev. ed., 1959); Marcus L. Hansen, *The Atlantic Migration, 1607–1860* (1940); Philip Taylor, *The Distant Magnet: European Emigration to the United States of America* (1971); Carl Wittke, *The Irish in America* (1956).

Technology

Siegfried Giedion, *Mechanization Takes Command* (1948); H. J. Habakkuk, *American and British Technology in the Nineteenth Century* (1962); Otto Mayr and Robert C. Post, eds., *Yankee Enterprise: The Rise of the American System of Manufactures* (1981); Merritt R. Smith, *Harpers Ferry Armory and the New Technology* (1977).

Manufacturing and Economic Growth

W. Elliot Brownlee, *Dynamics of Ascent* (1974); Stuart Bruchey, *The Roots of American Economic Growth, 1607–1861* (1965); Thomas C. Cochran, *Frontiers of Change: Early Industrialism in America* (1981); Alan Dawley, *Class and Community: The Industrial Revolution in Lynn* (1976); Thomas Dublin, *Women at Work: The Transformation of Work and Community in Lowell, Massachusetts, 1826–1860* (1979); Bruce Laurie, *Working People of Philadelphia, 1800–1850* (1980); Douglass North, *The Economic Growth of the United States, 1790–1860* (1961); Peter Temin, *The Jacksonian Economy* (1969); Barbara Tucker, *Samuel Slater and the Origins of the American Textile Industry, 1790–1860* (1984).

Rich and Poor

Leonard P. Curry, *The Free Black in Urban America, 1800–1850* (1981); Peter Knights, *The Plain People of Boston, 1830–1860* (1971); Raymond A. Mohl, *Poverty in New York, 1785–1825* (1971); Edward Pessen, *Riches, Class, and Power Before the Civil War* (1973); William J. Rorabaugh, *The Alcoholic Republic: An American Tradition* (1979); Stephan Thernstrom, *Poverty and Progress* (1964).

Professions

Daniel H. Calhoun, *Professional Lives in America: Structure and Aspiration, 1750–1850* (1965); Donald M. Scott, *From Office to Profession: The New England Ministry, 1750–1850* (1978); Richard Shryock, *Medical Licensing in America, 1650–1965* (1967).

Women and the Family

Nancy F. Cott, *The Bonds of Womanhood: 'Woman's Sphere' in New England, 1780–1835* (1977); Suzanne Lebsock, *The Free Women of Petersburg: Status and Culture in a Southern Town, 1784–1860* (1984); James C. Mohr, *Abortion in America: The Origins and Evolution of National Policy, 1800–1900* (1978); Glenda Riley, *Women and Indians on the Frontier, 1825–1915* (1984); Ellen K. Rothman, *Hands and Hearts: A History of Courtship in America* (1987); Mary Ryan, *Cradle of the Middle Class: The Family in Oneida County, New York, 1790–1865* (1981); Kathryn K. Sklar, *Catharine Beecher: A Study in American Domesticity* (1973); Gwendolyn Wright, *Building the Dream: A Social History of Housing in America* (1981).

CHAPTER 9

Politics, Religion, and Reform
in Antebellum America

In 1824 the Marquis de Lafayette, former major general in the Continental Army and a Revolutionary War hero, accepted the invitation of President James Monroe and Congress and revisited the United States. For thirteen months as "the Nation's Guest," Lafayette traveled to every state and received a welcome that fluctuated between warm and tumultuous. There seemed no limits to what Americans would do to show their admiration for this "greatest man in the world." "There were," a contemporary wrote, "*La Fayette* boots—*La Fayette* hats—*La Fayette* wine—and *La Fayette* everything." In New York City, some fervid patriots tried to unhitch the horses from Lafayette's carriage and pull it up Broadway themselves.

Lafayette had contributed mightily to the Revolution's success. Americans venerated him as a living embodiment of the entire Revolutionary generation fast passing from the scene. The majority of Americans alive in 1824 had been born since George Washington's death in 1799. John Adams and Thomas Jefferson survived, but they were along in years. Both would die on July 4, 1826, fifty years to the day since the signing of the Declaration of Independence. Seizing on Washington's remark that he loved Lafayette "as my own son," Americans toasted the Frenchman as a cherished member of the family of Revolutionary heroes. In Charleston the toast ran: "WASHINGTON, our Common Father—*you* his favorite *son*"; in New Jersey, "LA FAYETTE, a living monument of greatness, virtue, and faithfulness still exists—a second Washington is now among us."

The festive rituals surrounding Lafayette's visit symbolized Americans' conviction that they had remained true to their heritage of republican liberty. The embers of conflict between Federalists and Republicans that once had seemed to threaten the Republic's stability had cooled; the Era of Good Feelings still reigned over American politics in 1824. Yet even as Americans were turning Lafayette's visit into an affirmation of their ties to the Founders, those ties were fraying in the face of new challenges. Westward migration and growing economic individualism, the forces underlying these challenges, shaped politics mightily between 1824 and 1840. The impact of economic and social change shattered old assumptions and contributed to a vigorous new brand of politics.

This transformation led to the birth of a second American party system, in which two new parties, the Democrats and the Whigs, replaced the Republicans and the Federalists. More was at work here than a change of names. The new parties took advantage of the transportation revolution to spread their messages to the farthest corners of the nation and to arouse voters in all sections. The new parties' leaders were more effective than their predecessors at organizing grassroots support, more eager to make government responsive to the popular will, and more likely to enjoy politics and welcome conflict as a way to sustain interest in political issues.

Not all Americans looked to politics as the pathway to their goals. Some, in fact, viewed politics as suited only to scoundrels and could identify with the sentiments of the Detroit workingman who wrote in 1832 that he "did not vote. I'll [have] none of sin." Despairing of politics, many men and women became active in reform movements pursuing various goals, among them the abolition of slavery, the suppression of the liquor trade, improved public education, and equality for women. Strongly held religious beliefs impelled reformers into these causes, while simultaneously increasing their distrust of politics. Yet even reformers hostile to politics gradually found that the success of their reforms depended on their ability to influence the political process.

During the 1820s and 1830s, the political and reform agendas of Americans diverged increasingly from those of the Founders. The Founders had feared popular participation in politics, enjoyed their wine and rum, left an ambiguous legacy on slavery, and displayed only occasional interest in women's rights. Yet even as Americans shifted their political and social priorities, they continued to venerate the Founders, who in death meant even more than in life. Histories of the United States, biographies of Revolutionary patriots, and torchlight parades that bore portraits of Washington and Jefferson alongside those of Andrew Jackson all helped to reassure the men and women of the young nation that they were remaining loyal to their republican heritage.

The Transformation of American Politics, 1824–1832

In 1824 Andrew Jackson and Martin Van Buren, who would lead the Democratic party in the 1830s, and John Quincy Adams and Henry Clay, who would help to guide the rival National Republican (or Whig) party in the 1830s, all belonged to the same political party—the Republican party of Thomas Jefferson. Yet by 1824 the Republican party was coming apart at the seams under pressures generated by industrialization in New England, the spread of cotton cultivation in the South, and westward expansion. These forces sparked issues that would become the basis for the new political division between Democrats and Whigs. In general, those Republicans (augmented by a few former Federalists) who retained Jefferson's suspicion of a strong federal government and preference for states' rights became Democrats; those Republicans (along with many former Federalists) who believed that the national government should actively encourage economic development became Whigs.

Regardless of which path a politician chose, all leaders in the 1820s and 1830s had to adapt to the rising democratic idea of politics as a forum for the expression of the will of the common people rather than as an activity that gentlemen conducted for the people. Gentlemen could still gain election to office, but their success now depended less on their education or wealth than on their ability to identify and follow the will of the majority. Americans still looked up to their political leaders, but the leaders could no longer look down on the people.

Democratic Ferment

The process by which politics gradually became more democratic took several forms. In one state after another, the requirement, common in the eighteenth century, that voters own property was scaled down to a stipulation that voters merely pay poll taxes. Maryland, South Carolina, Massachusetts, Connecticut, and New York all liberalized their suffrage laws for white voters between the 1790s and 1821, and none of the eight new states admitted between 1796 and 1821 required voters to own property. Moreover, written ballots replaced the old custom of voting aloud (called *viva voce* or "stand up" voting), which had enabled social superiors to influence their inferiors at the polls. Many appointive offices became elective. In 1821, for example, New York abolished its five-member Council on Appointments, which had controlled the appointment of some fifteen thousand public officials, including every mayor in the state. While the electoral college remained in place, the practice of allowing state legislatures to choose presidential electors gave way to the selection of electors by popular vote. In 1800, rather than voting for Thomas Jefferson or John Adams, most Americans could do no more than vote for the men who would vote for the men who would vote for Jefferson or Adams. By 1824, however, legislatures chose electors in only six states, and by 1832 in only one (South Carolina).

Nothing did more to undermine the old barriers to the people's expression of their will than a fierce tug of war between the Republicans and the Federalists in the 1790s and early 1800s. Since party survival depended on the ability to win elections, political parties had to court voters. First the Republicans and then the Federalists learned to woo voters by staging grand barbecues at which men from Massachusetts to Maryland washed down free clams and oysters with free beer and whiskey. Wherever one party was in the minority, it sought to increase the number of eligible voters in order to turn itself into the majority party. In the South, where the Republicans were strong, they showed little interest in increasing the size of the electorate, but in the North they built a following by advocating expanded suffrage. Federalists played the same game when it suited their needs; the initiator of suffrage reform in Maryland, for example, was an aristocratic Federalist.

The democratization of politics developed at an uneven pace, however. As late as 1820, the Republican and Federalist parties continued to be organized from the top down. To nominate candidates, for example, both parties relied on the caucus, a meeting of party members in the legislature, rather than on popularly elected nominating conventions. Moreover, few party leaders rushed to embrace the *principle* of universal white manhood suffrage. Even the newly admitted western states tried at first to imitate the suffrage restrictions of the East and abandoned them only when

it became clear that in a region where nearly everyone's land title was in dispute, to require property ownership for voting merely invited fraud. Nor did the democratization of politics necessarily draw more voters to the polls. Waning competition between the Republicans and the Federalists between 1816 and 1824—the years spanning the Era of Good Feelings—deprived voters of clear choices and turned national politics into a boring spectacle.

Yet no one could mistake the tendency of the times: to oppose the people or democracy had become a formula for political suicide. The people, a Federalist moaned, "have become too saucy and are really beginning to fancy themselves equal to their betters." Whatever their convictions, politicians learned to adjust.

The Election of 1824

Partially submerged political tensions surfaced in the election of 1824 and inflicted sudden death on the Era of Good Feelings. Even before the election, President Monroe's Republican coalition was cracking under pressure from its rival sectional components. In 1824 five candidates, all Republicans, ended up vying for the presidency. John Quincy Adams emerged as New England's favorite. South Carolina's brilliant John C. Calhoun contended with Georgia's William Crawford, an old-school Jeffersonian, for southern support. Out of the West marched Henry Clay of Kentucky, ambitious, crafty, and confident that his American System of protective tariffs and federally supported internal improvements would endear him to the manufacturing regions of the East as well as to the New West.

Clay's belief that he was holding a solid block of western states was punctured by the rise of a fifth candidate, Andrew Jackson of Tennessee. At

The Election of 1824

Candidates	Parties	Electoral Vote	Popular Vote	Percentage of Popular Vote
JOHN QUINCY ADAMS	Democratic-Republican	84	108,740	30.5
Andrew Jackson	Democratic-Republican	99	153,544	43.1
William H. Crawford	Democratic-Republican	41	46,618	13.1
Henry Clay	Democratic-Republican	37	47,136	13.2

first, none of the other candidates took Jackson seriously. But he was popular on the frontier and in the South and stunned his rivals by gaining the support of opponents of the American System from Pennsylvania and other northern states.

Although the Republican congressional caucus chose Crawford as the party's official candidate early in 1824, the caucus could no longer unify the party. Three-fourths of the Republicans in Congress had refused to attend the caucus. Crawford's already diminished prospects evaporated when he suffered a paralyzing stroke. Impressed by Jackson's support, Calhoun withdrew from the race and ran unopposed for the vice presidency. In the election, Jackson won more popular and electoral votes than any other candidate (Adams, Crawford, Clay) but failed to gain a majority, as required by the Constitution. Thus the election was thrown into the House of Representatives, whose members had to choose from the three top candidates—Jackson, Adams, and Crawford. Hoping to forge an alliance between the West and Northeast in a future bid for the presidency, Clay gave his support to Adams. Clay's action secured the presidency for Adams, but when Adams promptly appointed Clay his secretary of state, Jackson's supporters raged that a "corrupt bargain" had cheated Jackson of the presidency. Although there is no evidence that Adams had traded Clay's support for an explicit agreement to appoint Clay his secretary of state (an office from which Jefferson, Madison, Monroe, and Adams himself had risen to the presidency), the allegation of a corrupt bargain was widely believed. It formed a cloud that hung over Adams's presidency.

John Quincy Adams as President

Adams's appointment of Clay as his secretary of state was the first of several clumsy miscalculations that cloaked his presidency in controversy. Basically, Adams failed to understand the changing political climate. In his first annual message to Congress in December 1825, the president made a series of proposals that might have won acclaim in 1815 but that only antagonized interests that had grown more powerful and alert in the ensuing decade. He proposed, for example, a program of federal support for internal improvements, an idea that

John Quincy Adams

John Quincy Adams was the first president to pose for the camera. His expression here reveals his austere and determined personality.

had gained support from Republicans like Henry Clay, the architect of the American System, after the War of 1812. Between 1819 and 1825, however, opponents of the American System had multiplied. Strict Jeffersonians (often called Old Republicans), among them the Virginian John Randolph, had consistently attacked federal aid for internal improvements as unconstitutional, but they were no longer the mainstays of the opposition. Adams's call for federal support for improvements came within a few months of New York's completion of the Erie Canal. Because New York had built the canal with its own money, its senator, Martin Van Buren, opposed federal aid for internal improvements; such support would only enable other states to construct rival canals.

In addition, Adams infuriated southerners by proposing to send American delegates to a conference of newly independent Latin American nations in Panama. Southerners feared that U.S. attendance would imply recognition of Haiti, a black republic that had gained its independence from France through a slave revolution. Both the sharp debate over the Missouri Compromise in 1819–1820 and the discovery of a planned slave revolt in South Carolina in 1822 (organized by a free black, Denmark Vesey) had shaken southern slaveholders and generated hostility to Adams's proposal. If Adams had simply recognized that he was antagonizing important groups and responded by seeking new bases of support, he might have saved himself. But he clung to an increasingly obsolete notion of the president as a custodian of the public good who stayed aloof from factions and parties. Far from purging his political opponents, he appointed several to high office and thereby alienated even his friends. As late as 1829, he wrote blithely: "I have no wish to fortify myself by the support of any party whatever."

The Rise of Andrew Jackson

As Adams's popularity ebbed, Andrew Jackson's star rose. Jackson's victory over the British in the Battle of New Orleans in 1815 had given him a national reputation. The fact that he was a Tennessee slaveholder, a renowned Indian fighter, and a militant advocate of Indian removal endeared Jackson to the South. Where Adams tried to uphold treaties between the federal government and the Indians that gave the native Americans the option of staying in the East, Jackson urged that southerners be allowed a free hand in pushing the Indians westward. Southerners praised Jackson's stance as a noble application of the Jeffersonian principle of states' rights and recognized that it would satisfy their hunger for land. Furthermore, as the only presidential candidate in the election of 1824 with no connection to the Monroe administration, Jackson was in an ideal position to capitalize on what John C. Calhoun called "a vague but widespread discontent" in the wake of the Panic of 1819 that left people with "a general mass of disaffection to the Government" and "looking out anywhere for a leader."

While Adams moved sluggishly, Jackson's supporters swiftly established committees throughout the country. Two years before the election of 1828, towns and villages across the United States buzzed with furious but unfocused political activity. With the exception of the few remaining Federalists, almost everyone called himself a Republican. There were Republicans who were "Adams men," others who were "Jackson men," and still others who styled themselves "friends of Clay." Amid all the political confusion, few realized that a new political system was being born. The man most alert to the signs of the times was Martin Van Buren, who was to become vice president during Jackson's second term and president upon Jackson's retirement.

Van Buren exemplified a new breed of politician debuting on the national scene in the 1820s. A tavernkeeper's son, he had started his political career at the bottom, in county politics, and worked his way up to New York's governorship. In Albany he built a powerful political machine, the Albany Regency, composed mainly of men like himself from the lower and middling ranks. His archrival in New York politics, DeWitt Clinton, was all that Van Buren was not—tall, handsome, aristocratic, and brilliant. But Van Buren had a geniality that made ordinary people feel comfortable and an uncanny ability to sense in which direction the political winds were about to blow. Van Buren loved politics, which he viewed as a wonderful game; he was one of the first prominent American politicians to make personal friends from among his political enemies.

The election of 1824 convinced Van Buren of the need for renewed two-party competition. Without the discipline imposed by a strong opposition party, the Republicans in 1824 had splintered into sectional pieces. No candidate had secured an electoral majority, and the House of Representatives had decided the outcome amid charges of intrigue and corruption. It would be better, Van Buren concluded, to let all the shades of opinion in the nation be reduced to two. Then the parties would clash, and a clear popular winner would emerge. Jackson's strong showing in the election persuaded Van Buren that "Old Hickory" could lead a new political party. In the election of 1828, this party, which gradually became known as the Democratic party, put up Jackson for president and Calhoun for vice president. Its opponents, increasingly calling themselves the National Republicans, rallied behind Adams and his running mate, treasury secretary Richard Rush. Slowly but surely, the second American party system was taking shape.

The Election of 1828

The 1828 campaign was a vicious, mudslinging affair. The National Republicans attacked Jackson as a murderer (between duels and military executions, he was directly responsible for the deaths of several men), a drunken gambler, and an adulterer. The adultery charge caused Jackson the greatest pain. His wife, the beloved, ailing, and soon-to-die Rachel, had sought a divorce from her first husband, Lewis Robards. She had married Jackson believing that her divorce was complete, only to find that it was not. "Ought a convicted adulteress and her paramour husband," the Adams men taunted, "be placed in the highest office of this free and Christian land?" Jackson's supporters replied in kind. They accused Adams of wearing silk underwear, being rich, being in debt, and having gained favor with the czar of Russia by trying to provide him with a beautiful American prostitute.

Although both sides engaged in mudslinging, Jackson's men had better aim. Charges by Adams's supporters that Jackson was an illiterate backwoodsman only added to Jackson's popular appeal by making him seem just like an ordinary citizen. Jackson's supporters portrayed the clash as one between "the *democracy* of the *country,* on the one hand, and a *lordly purse-proud aristocracy* on the other." Jackson, they said, was the common man incarnate—his mind unclouded by learning, his morals simple and true, his will fierce and resolute. In contrast, Jackson's men represented Adams as an aristocrat, a dry scholar whose learning obscured the truth, a man who could write but not fight. Much of this, of course, was wild exaggeration. Jackson was a wealthy planter, not a simple backwoodsman. But it was the kind of exaggeration that people wanted to hear. Uncorrupt, natural, plain, Jackson was presented as the common man's image of his better self.

The election swept Jackson into office with more than twice the electoral vote of Adams. Yet the popular vote, much closer, made it clear that the people were not simply responding to the personalities or images of the candidates (though these dominated the campaign). The vote also reflected

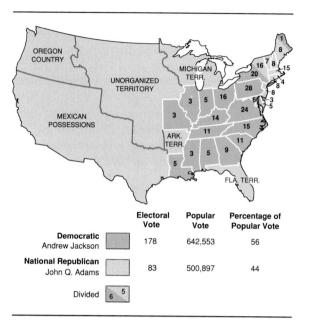

		Electoral Vote	Popular Vote	Percentage of Popular Vote
Democratic Andrew Jackson		178	642,553	56
National Republican John Q. Adams		83	500,897	44
Divided		6		

The Election of 1828

the strongly sectional bases of the new parties. The popular vote was close only in the middle states and the Northwest. Adams gained double Jackson's vote in New England; Jackson received double Adams's vote in the South, and nearly triple Adams's vote in the Southwest.

Jackson in Office

For all its fanfare, the campaign had revealed little about Jackson's stands on major issues. On such key questions as federal aid for internal improvements and the tariff, Jackson had sent out conflicting signals. In Tennessee he had aggressively pursued wealth and opposed legislation for the relief of debtors. Yet he understood the popular feelings that had carried him to the presidency and, once in office, played the role of defender of the people against the forces of privilege.

His first policy on coming to office was to openly support the principle of "rotation in office"—the removal of officeholders of the rival party—which critics called the spoils system. Jackson did not invent this policy: many of his predecessors had employed it. Nor did he pursue it with unusual thoroughness, for he removed only about one-fifth of the federal officeholders whom he inherited from Adams. But Jackson defended removal on new and democratic grounds. The duties of officeholders were so plain and simple, he argued, that any intelligent man could perform them. By moving civil servants into and out of office at will, Jackson hoped not only to give as many individuals as possible a chance to work for the government but also to prevent the emergence of an elite bureaucracy that operated beyond the will of the people.

Although Jackson's policy toward the civil service ruffled feathers, it did not produce deep sectional or ideological division. But the issues of federal support for internal improvements and protective tariffs ignited sectional controversy. The South had fewer canals and roads than other sections and, in 1830, fewer plans to build them. Its main cash crop, cotton, was nonperishable and could be transported by rivers and the ocean. Accordingly, southerners were cool toward spending federal money for internal improvements. Jackson, whose firmest political base was in the South, became convinced that federal support for internal improvements was a lavish giveaway program prone to corruption. He also believed that such funding violated the principle that Congress could appropriate money only for objectives shared by *all* Americans, such as national defense, not for the objectives of particular sections or interests. Accordingly, in 1830 Jackson vetoed a bill to provide federal support for a road in Kentucky between Maysville and Lexington.

Coupled with the almost simultaneous passage of the Indian Removal Act (see Chapter 8), the Maysville Road veto enhanced Jackson's popularity in the South. The tariff issue, however, sternly tested the South's allegiance to Jackson. In 1828, while John Quincy Adams was still in office, Jackson's supporters in Congress had contributed to the final passage of a bill that favored western agricultural interests by raising tariffs (import taxes) on imported hemp, wool, fur, flax, and liquor as well as New England manufacturing interests by raising the tariff on imported textiles. The South, which had few industries to protect from foreign competition, was left high and dry, for tariffs effectively raised the cost of manufactured goods for southerners. Jackson's followers had assumed that the support of the South could be taken for granted in the upcoming election and that embittered southerners would blame the Adams administration for this "Tariff of Abominations." In reality,

Jackson rather than Adams would bear the brunt of the South's ire over the tariff.

Nullification

The tariff of 1828 laid the basis for a rift between Jackson and his vice president, John C. Calhoun, that was to shake the foundations of the Republic. Early in his career, Calhoun had been an ardent nationalist. He had entered Congress in 1811 as a "war hawk," supported the protectionist tariff of 1816, and dismissed strict construction of the Constitution as refined philosophical nonsense. During the late 1820s, however, Calhoun changed course. Calhoun the nationalist gradually became Calhoun the states' rights sectionalist. The reasons for his shift were complex. He had supported the tariff of 1816 essentially as a measure conducive to national defense in the wake of the War of 1812. By encouraging infant industries, he had reasoned, the tariff would free the United States from dependence upon Britain and provide revenue for military preparedness. By 1826, however, few Americans perceived national defense as a priority. Further, the infant industries of 1816 had grown into troublesome adolescents that demanded higher and higher tariffs.

There was also the matter of Calhoun's fierce ambition. He longed to be president. Jackson had stated that he would serve only one term, and as vice president, Calhoun assumed that he would succeed Jackson. To do so, however, he had to maintain the support of his native South Carolina and of the South in general. As the center of cotton production shifted to the Southwest—Alabama and Mississippi—South Carolina's economy declined during the 1820s, and South Carolinians largely blamed protective tariffs. Tariffs not only drove up the price of manufactured goods but also threatened to reduce the sale of British textile products in the United States. Such a reduction might eventually lower the British demand for southern cotton and cut cotton prices. The more New England industrialized, the clearer it became that tariff laws were pieces of sectional legislation. New Englanders like Massachusetts's eloquent Daniel Webster swung toward protectionism; southerners responded with militant hostility.

Calhoun followed the Virginia and Kentucky resolutions of 1798–1799 in viewing the Union as a compact by which the states had conferred lim-

Andrew Jackson, *by Thomas Sully, 1845*

John C. Calhoun, *by Charles Bird King, c. 1825*

Jackson, defeated in the presidential election of 1824, won handily four years later. The magnetic Calhoun, Jackson's vice president, broke with Jackson over nullification and the Peggy Eaton affair and resigned the vice presidency in 1832.

ited and specified powers on the federal government. While the Constitution did empower Congress to levy tariffs, Calhoun insisted that only tariffs that raised revenue for such common purposes as defense were constitutional. Set so high that it deterred foreign exporters from shipping their products to the United States, the tariff of 1828 could raise little revenue, and hence it failed to meet Calhoun's criterion of constitutionality: that federal laws benefit everyone *equally*. In 1828 Calhoun anonymously wrote the widely circulated *South Carolina Exposition and Protest,* in which he spelled out his argument that the tariff of 1828 was unconstitutional and that aggrieved states therefore had the right to nullify, or override, the law within their borders.

Vehement opposition to tariffs in the South, and especially in South Carolina, rested on more than economic considerations, however. Southerners feared that a federal government that passed tariff laws favoring one section over another might also pass laws meddling with slavery. Because Jackson himself was a slaveholder, the fear of federal interference with slavery was perhaps farfetched. But South Carolinians, long apprehensive of assaults

on their crucial institution of slavery, had many reasons for concern. South Carolina was one of only two states in which blacks composed a majority of the population in 1830. Moreover, in 1831 a bloody slave revolt led by Nat Turner boiled up in Virginia. That same year, William Lloyd Garrison established *The Liberator,* an abolitionist newspaper. These developments did not add up to a real challenge to slavery. However, they were enough to convince many troubled South Carolinians that a line had to be drawn against tariffs and the possibility of future interference with slavery.

Jackson Versus Calhoun

Like Calhoun, Jackson was strong-willed and proud. Unlike Calhoun, he was already president and the leader of a national party that included supporters in pro-tariff states like Pennsylvania (which had gone for Jackson in the election of 1828). Thus to retain key northern support while soothing the South, Jackson devised two policies.

The first was the distribution of surplus federal revenue to the states. Tariff schedules kept some goods out of the United States but let many others in for a price. The price, in the form of duties on imports, became federal revenue. In these years before federal income taxes, tariffs were a major source of federal revenue. Jackson hoped that this revenue, fairly distributed among the states, would remove the taint of sectional injustice from the tariff and force the federal government to restrict its own expenditures. All of this was good Jeffersonianism. Second, Jackson hoped to ease tariffs down from the sky-high tariff of 1828.

Calhoun disliked the idea of distributing federal revenue to the states because he believed that such a policy could become an excuse to maintain tariffs forever. But he was loath to break openly with Jackson. Between 1828 and 1831, Calhoun muffled his protest, hoping that Jackson would lower the tariff and that he, Calhoun, would retain both Jackson's favor and his chances for the presidency. Congress did pass new, slightly reduced tariff rates in 1832, but these did not come close to satisfying South Carolinians.

Even before passage of the tariff of 1832, two issues that had nothing to do with tariffs ruptured personal relations between Calhoun and Jackson. In 1829 Jackson's secretary of war, John H. Eaton, married the daughter of a Washington tavern-keeper. By her own account, Peggy O'Neale Eaton was "frivolous, wayward, [and] passionate." Before the marriage Peggy had acquired the reputation of being too forward with the boarders in her father's tavern, one of whom had been Eaton. After the marriage she and Eaton were snubbed socially by Calhoun's wife and by his friends in the cabinet. Peggy's only supporters were Martin Van Buren, the secretary of state, and President Jackson himself, who never forgot how his own wife had been wounded by slander during the campaign of 1828. Jackson concluded that the entire Eaton affair was a plot inspired by Calhoun to discredit him and advance Calhoun's own presidential aspirations.

To make matters worse, in 1830 Jackson received convincing documentation of his suspicion that back in 1818, Calhoun, as secretary of war under President Monroe, had urged that Jackson be punished for his unauthorized raid into Spanish Florida. The revelation that Calhoun had tried to stab him in the back in 1818, combined with the snubbing of Peggy Eaton, convinced Jackson that he had to "destroy [Calhoun] regardless of what injury it might do me or my administration." A symbolic confrontation occurred between Jackson and Calhoun at a Jefferson Day dinner in April 1830. Jackson proposed the toast: "Our Union: It must be preserved." Calhoun responded: "The Union next to Liberty the most dear. May we always remember that it can only be preserved by distributing equally the benefits and burdens of the Union."

The stage was now set for a direct clash between the president and his vice president over nullification. In 1831 Calhoun acknowledged his authorship of the *South Carolina Exposition and Protest*. In November 1832 a South Carolina convention nullified the tariffs of 1828 and 1832 and forbade the collection of customs duties within the state. Jackson reacted quickly. He despised nullification, calling it an "abominable doctrine" that would reduce the government to anarchy, and he loathed the South Carolina nullifiers as "unprincipled men who would rather rule in hell, than be subordinate in heaven." Jackson even began to send arms to loyal Unionists in South Carolina, and in December 1832 he issued a proclamation that while promising South Carolinians further tariff reductions, lambasted nullification as itself unconstitutional. The Constitution, he emphasized, had established "a single nation," not a league of states.

The crisis eased in March 1833 when Jackson signed into law two measures—"the olive branch and the sword," in the words of one historian. The olive branch was the tariff of 1833 (also called the Compromise Tariff), which provided for a gradual but significant lowering of duties between 1833 and 1842. The sword was the Force Bill, authorizing the president to use arms to collect customs duties in South Carolina.

Like most of the accommodations by which the Union lurched from one sectional crisis to the next before the Civil War, the Compromise of 1833 grew out of a mixture of partisanship and statesmanship. The moving spirit behind the Compromise Tariff was Kentucky's senator Henry Clay, who had long favored high tariffs. A combination of motives brought Clay and the nullifiers together in favor of tariff reduction. Clay feared that without concessions to South Carolina on tariffs, the Force Bill would produce civil war. Further, he was apprehensive that without compromise, the principle of protective tariffs would disappear under the wave of Jackson's immense popularity. In short, Clay would rather take responsibility for lowering tariffs than allow the initiative on tariff questions to pass to the Jacksonians. For their part, the nullifiers hated Jackson and defiantly toasted "Andrew Jackson: On the soil of South Carolina he received an humble birthplace. May he not find it in a traitor's grave!" While recognizing that South Carolina had failed to gain support for nullification from other southern states and that they would have to bow to pressure, the nullifiers preferred that Clay, not Jackson, be the hero of the hour. Accordingly, they supported Clay's Compromise Tariff and formally rescinded the nullification proclamation. Everywhere Americans now hailed Clay, once known as hotheaded and impetuous, as the Great Compromiser. Even Martin Van Buren frankly stated that Clay had "saved the country."

The Bank Veto

One reason why Jackson signed Clay's compromise tariff into law was that he did not have strong convictions about an alternative. Inclined to react passionately to most issues, Jackson was relatively flexible and open-minded on the subject of tariffs. In sharp contrast, as a result of some disastrous financial speculations early in his career, Jackson had come to office with a deep suspicion of all banks, all paper money, and all exclusive monopolies. On each count, the Bank of the United States was a likely target.

In 1816 the Second Bank of the United States had received a twenty-year charter from Congress. As a creditor of state banks, the Bank of the United States could contract the lending capacity of the state banks whenever it chose by demanding that they redeem in specie (gold or silver coinage) their bank notes that were held by the Bank of the United States. Because most banks emitted more notes than they could redeem in specie, the Bank of the United States exerted an often healthy restraint on excessive lending by state banks.

Many aspects of the Bank of the United States, however, made it controversial. As we have seen, its decision to contract credit had precipitated the Panic of 1819, for which it was widely blamed. Furthermore, at a time when privilege was coming under fire, the bank was undeniably a privileged institution. First, it was the official depository for federal revenue, a fact that greatly increased its capacity to lend money and that gave it a commanding position over all state banks. Second, while the federal government accorded it privileges not

available to any other bank, the Bank of the United States was only remotely under the federal government's control. The bank's stockholders were private citizens—a "few Monied Capitalists," in Jackson's words. Although chartered by Congress, the bank was located not in Washington but in Philadelphia. The federal government appointed a majority of the bank's directors but allowed them considerable independence.

No one better typified the bank's distance from the push and shove of politics than its president, Nicholas Biddle. A polished aristocrat, Biddle had once edited a literary magazine (after his marriage to an heiress freed him of the need to make money), and he continued to write poetry in his spare time. As bank president, he viewed himself as a public servant whose duty was to keep the bank above politics. Knowing nothing of Jackson's loathing of banks, Biddle had voted for Jackson in 1824 and 1828. Jackson would give Biddle many opportunities to repent these votes.

In his first annual message to Congress in 1829, Jackson questioned "both the constitutionality and expediency" of the Bank of the United States. Strongly influenced by Henry Clay, Biddle resolved to seek recharter of the bank in 1832, four years before its existing charter expired. With his eyes on the presidential election of 1832, Clay sensed that a pro-bank stand would boost his own chances in the election. Although Biddle and Clay secured congressional approval to recharter, Jackson promptly vetoed the recharter bill. He denounced the bank as a private and privileged monopoly that drained the West of specie, was immune to taxation by states (as Chief Justice Marshall had established in his 1819 *McCulloch* v. *Maryland* decision), gathered inordinate power into the hands of a few men, and made "the rich richer and the potent more powerful." Failing to persuade Congress to override Jackson's veto, Clay now pinned his hopes on gaining the presidency himself.

The Election of 1832

By 1832 Jackson's views on major issues were considerably clearer than in 1828. The Indian Removal Act, his vetoes of the Maysville Road Bill and the recharter of the Bank of the United States, his policy of distributing federal revenues, and his lowering of tariffs all marked him as a strong defender of states' rights. But at the same time, his vigorous

The Election of 1832				
Candidates	Parties	Electoral Vote	Popular Vote	Percentage of Popular Vote
ANDREW JACKSON	Democratic	219	687,502	55.0
Henry Clay	National Republican	49	530,189	42.4
William Wirt	Anti-Masonic	7 ⎱	33,108	2.6
John Floyd	National Republican	11 ⎰		

response to nullification had established him as a staunch Unionist. States' rights and Unionism were compatible doctrines. While cherishing the Union, Jackson believed that the states were far too diverse to accept strong, purposeful direction from the federal government. The safest course was to allow the states considerable freedom, so that they would remain contentedly within the Union and reject dangerous doctrines like nullification.

Despite earlier statements to the contrary, Jackson ran again, selecting Martin Van Buren, now clearly the heir apparent, as his running mate to replace Calhoun, who had resigned. Against Jackson the National Republicans put up Henry Clay. Clay's platform was his American System of protective tariffs, national banking, and federal support for internal improvements. The election of 1832, the first in which national nominating conventions chose the candidates, was more issue-oriented than the vicious campaign of 1828. But Jackson continued to benefit from his great personal popularity. He carried 219 electoral votes to Clay's 49 and even took pro-bank and pro-tariff Pennsylvania. Clay's economic nationalism made him popular in pro-tariff New England. But Clay could not topple Jackson's stronghold in the South, while Jackson chalked up support in the North and West as well as the South. Secure in office for another four years, Jackson was ready to finish the job of dismantling the Bank of the United States.

The Bank Controversy and the Second Party System

Coming late in Andrew Jackson's first term, the veto of the bank's recharter had relatively little impact on the election of 1832. However, between 1833 and 1840, banking became an issue that ignited extraordinary popular passion. In no period of American history have issues relating to banking generated keener public interest than during these seven years. Jackson's veto of recharter unleashed a tiger that threatened to devour all banks.

Why did banking so raise people's temperature? Part of the answer lay in the fact that the U.S. government did not issue paper currency of its own; there were no "official" dollar bills as we know them today. Paper money took the form of notes (promises to redeem in specie) emitted by private banks. As a consequence, private bankers had enormous influence over economic transactions and could easily be viewed by ordinary people as sinister. In addition, a basic issue lurked behind most of the banking debates of the 1830s. What sort of society would the United States become? If paper money circulated in abundance, businessmen and farmers could readily obtain loans to open factories or buy more land. Such an economy would be speculative in the sense that it would raise expectations for profit while posing risks. A sudden slump in the prices of industrial or agricultural products would leave businessmen and farmers mired in debt. Furthermore, a speculative economy would not benefit everyone equally. Factory owners would reap profits, but their employees would have to perform poorly paid and often unhealthy work. Would the United States be a nation that embraced swift economic development, even at the price of allowing some to get rich quickly off investments while others languished? Or would it be a nation characterized by more modest growth in traditional molds, but one anchored by "honest" manual work and frugality?

Before the answer to any of these questions was clear, the banking issue dramatically transformed American politics. It contributed mightily to the emergence of opposition to the Democrats and to the steady expansion of popular interest in politics.

The War on the Bank

Once reelected, Jackson could have allowed the bank to die a natural death when its charter ran out in 1836. But viewing the bank not only as a monopoly but as a symbol of all the exclusive privileges that were robbing the nation of its republican ideals, Jackson and several of his rabid followers feared the bank as a kind of dragon that would grow new limbs even as old ones were cut off. As Frederick Robinson, a radical New York Jacksonian, put it: "Kill the great monster and the whole brood which are hatched and nourished over the land will fall an easy prey. But if we suffer it to escape with life, however wounded, maimed, and mutilated, it will soon recover its wonted strength, its whole power to injure us, and all hope of its destruction must be forever renounced." When Biddle, in anticipation of further moves against the bank by Jackson, began to call in the bank's loans and contract credit during the winter of 1832–1833, Jacksonians saw their darkest fears confirmed. The bank, Jackson assured Van Buren, "is trying to kill me, but I will kill it."

Rather than allow the bank to die naturally, Jackson embarked on a policy of removing federal deposits from the Bank of the United States and placing them in state banks. The policy was controversial even within the administration; Jackson dismissed two secretaries of the treasury before he finally found one, Maryland's Roger B. Taney, who would implement the policy.

Once in place, the policy of removing deposits only raised a new and even thornier issue. Those state banks that became the depositories for federal revenue could use that revenue as the basis for issuing more paper money and for extending more loans. In short, the removal policy enabled state banks to increase their lending capacity. But Jackson hated both paper money and a speculative economy in which capitalists routinely took out large loans. The policy of removal seemed a formula for producing exactly the kind of economy that Jackson wanted to abolish. Jackson recognized the danger and hoped to sharply limit the number of state banks that would become depos-

itories for federal revenue. But as state banks increasingly clamored for the revenue, the number of state-bank depositories soon multiplied beyond Jackson's expectations. There were twenty-three by the end of 1833. Critics dubbed them "pet banks" because they were usually selected for their loyalty to the Democratic party. During the next few years, fueled by paper money from the pet banks and by an influx of foreign specie to purchase cotton and for investment in canal projects, the economy entered a heady expansion. Jackson could not stem the tide. In 1836, pressured by Congress, he reluctantly signed into law the Deposit Act, which both increased the number of deposit banks and loosened federal control over them.

Jackson's policy of removing deposits deepened a split within his own Democratic party between advocates of soft money (paper) and those of hard money (gold or silver coinage, or specie). Both sides agreed that the Bank of the United States was evil, but for different reasons. Soft-money Democrats resented the bank's role in periodically contracting credit and restricting the lending activities of state banks; their hard-money counterparts disliked the bank because it sanctioned an economy based on paper money. Prior to the Panic of 1837, the soft-money position was more popular among Democrats outside of Jackson's inner circle of advisers than within that circle. For example, western Democrats had long viewed the Bank of the United States' branch in Cincinnati as inadequate to supply their need for credit and favored an expansion of banking activity.

Aside from Jackson and a few other figures within the administration, the most articulate support for hard money came from a faction of the Democratic party in New York called the Locofocos. The Locofocos grew out of various "workingmen's" parties that had sprouted during the late 1820s in northern cities and that called for free public education, the abolition of imprisonment for debt, and a ten-hour workday. Most of these parties had collapsed within a few years, but in New York the "workies" had gradually been absorbed by the Democratic party. Once in the party, the workingmen were hard to keep in line. Composed of a mixture of intellectuals and small artisans and journeymen threatened by economic change, they worried about inflation, preferred to be paid in specie, and distrusted banks and paper

Jackson Versus the Bank

Andrew Jackson, aided by Martin Van Buren (center), attacks the Bank of the United States, which, like the many-headed serpent Hydra of Greek mythology, keeps sprouting new heads. The largest head belongs to Nicholas Biddle, the Bank's president.

money. In 1835 a faction of workingmen had broken away from Tammany Hall, the main Democratic party organization in New York City, and held a dissident meeting in a hall whose candles were illuminated by a newfangled invention, the "loco foco," or match. Thereafter, these radical workingmen were known as Locofocos.

The Rise of Whig Opposition

During Jackson's second term, the opposition National Republican party changed its name to the Whig party. More important, the opposition began to broaden its base in both the South and the North. Jackson's magnetic personality had swept him to victory in 1828 and 1832. But as the profile of Jackson's administration became more sharply delineated—as Jackson's vague Jeffersonianism of 1829 gave way to hard-and-fast positions against the Bank of the United States, federal aid for internal improvements, protective tariffs, and nullification—the opposition drew into its fold increasing numbers alienated by Jackson's policies.

Jackson's crushing of nullification, for example, led some of its southern supporters into the Whig party, not because the Whigs favored nullification but because they opposed Jackson. Jack-

son's war on the Bank of the United States produced the same result. His policy of removing deposits from the bank pleased some southerners but dismayed others who had been satisfied with the bank and who did not share westerners' mania for even cheaper and easier credit. Jackson's opposition to federal aid for internal improvements also alienated some southerners who feared that the South would languish behind the North unless it began to push ahead with improvements. Because so much southern capital was tied up in slavery, pro-improvement southerners looked to the federal government for aid, and when they met with a cold shoulder, they drifted into the Whig party. None of this added up to an overturning of the Democratic party in the South; the South was still the Democrats' firmest base. But the Whigs were making significant inroads, particularly in southern market towns and among planters who had close ties to southern bankers and merchants.

Meanwhile, in the North, social reformers were infusing new vitality into the opposition to Jackson. These reformers wanted to improve American society by attacking the sale of liquor, opposing slavery, bettering public education, and elevating public morality. Most opponents of liquor (temperance reformers) and most public-school reformers gravitated to the Whigs. Whig philosophy was more compatible with the reformers' goals than Democratic ideals. Where Democrats maintained that the government should not impose a uniform standard of conduct on a diverse society, the Whigs' commitment to Clay's American System implied an acceptance of active intervention by the government to change society. Reformers wanted the government to play a positive role specifically by suppressing the liquor trade and by establishing centralized systems of public education. Thus a shared sympathy for active government programs tended to unite Whigs and reformers.

Reformers also indirectly stimulated new support for the Whigs from native-born Protestant workers. The reformers, themselves almost all Protestants, widely distrusted immigrants, especially the Irish, who viewed drinking as a normal recreation and who, as Catholics, suspected (correctly) that the public schools favored by reformers would teach Protestant doctrines. The rise of reform agitation and its frequent association with the Whigs drove the Irish into the arms of the Democrats but, by the same token, gained support for the Whigs from many native-born Protestant workers who were contemptuous of the Irish.

Of all the sources of Whig strength, none, however, was more remarkable than Anti-Masonry, a protest movement against the secrecy and exclusiveness of the Masonic lodges, which had long provided prominent men with fraternal fellowship and exotic ritual. The spark that set off the Anti-Masonic crusade was the abduction and disappearance in 1826 of William Morgan, a stonemason in Genesee County, New York, who had threatened to expose the secrets of the Masonic order. Every effort to solve the mystery of Morgan's disappearance ran into a stone wall because local sheriffs, judges, and jurors were themselves Masons seemingly bent on obstructing the investigation. Throughout the Northeast the public became increasingly aroused against the Masonic order, and rumors spread that Masonry was a powerful conspiracy of the rich to suppress popular liberty, a secret order of men who loathed Christianity, and an exclusive retreat for drunkards.

Beginning as a movement of moral protest in New York, Anti-Masons soon organized the Anti-Masonic party and scored remarkable successes, gaining temporary control of Vermont and Penn-sylvania and holding the balance of power in New York and Massachusetts. As the political power of Anti-Masonry became evident, both parties courted it, the Whigs more successfully than the Democrats. The Whigs' ability to capitalize on Anti-Masonry partly reflected the fact that Anti-Masons displayed the same hatred for vice as the Whig reformers. Anti-Masons usually advocated temperance, and some attacked slavery. They insisted that membership in Masonic lodges, like the consumption of liquor, was sinful. A number of leading Whigs, among them Henry Clay, were themselves Masons, but they knew a good thing when they saw it; by 1834 the Whigs were rapidly absorbing Anti-Masonry. Anti-Masonry brought into the Whig party in the North a broadly based constituency that protested "aristocracy" with the same zeal as the Jacksonians did. In this way, Anti-Masonry helped to free the Whig party of the charge that it was merely a tool of the rich.

By 1836 the Whigs had become a national party with widespread appeal. In both the North and South, they attracted those with close ties to the market economy—commercial farmers, planters, merchants, and bankers. In the North they also gained support from reformers, evangelical clergymen (especially Presbyterians and Congregationalists), Anti-Masons, and manufacturers. In the South they appealed to some former nullificationists; Calhoun himself briefly became a Whig. Everywhere the Whigs assailed Jackson as an imperious dictator, "King Andrew I"; indeed, they had taken the name "Whigs" to associate their cause with that of the American patriots who had opposed King George III in 1776.

The Election of 1836

As the election of 1836 approached, the Whigs lacked only a national leader. Henry Clay came close, but he was scarred by many political battles and additionally could not shake his reputation as a man who spent his days at the gaming table and his nights in brothels. Unable to agree on a single candidate, the Whigs ran four sectional candidates: William Henry Harrison of Ohio in the Old Northwest, Hugh Lawson White of Tennessee and W. P. Mangum of North Carolina in the South, and Daniel Webster of Massachusetts in the East. The Whig strategy was to prevent Vice President

The Election of 1836

Candidates	Parties	Electoral Vote	Popular Vote	Percentage of Popular Vote
MARTIN VAN BUREN	Democratic	170	765,483	50.9
William H. Harrison	Whig	73		
Hugh L. White	Whig	26	739,795	49.1
Daniel Webster	Whig	14		
W. P. Mangum	Whig	11		

Martin Van Buren, the Democratic candidate, from gaining the required majority of electoral votes. That would force the election into the House of Representatives, where the Whigs thought that they had a chance to win.

Van Buren, whose star in the Democratic party had risen as Calhoun's had fallen, captured 170 electoral votes to 124 for the four Whigs combined. The Whig strategy obviously had backfired, but there were signs of trouble ahead for the Democrats. In the South the Whigs ran virtually even in the popular vote and captured Georgia and Tennessee. Even in the southern states held by Van Buren, the Democratic proportion of the popular vote was much smaller than in 1832; in North Carolina, for example, it dropped from 70 percent to 53 percent.

The Panic of 1837

Jackson left office in March 1837 in a sunburst of glory. Hailed as "the greatest man of his age" and presented with innumerable children named after him, his return to his Nashville home became a triumphal procession. But the public's mood quickly became less festive, for no sooner was Van Buren in office than a severe depression began.

The years 1835 and 1836 had witnessed a speculative boom fed by Jackson's policy of removing federal deposits from the Bank of the United States and placing them in state banks. In 1830 there were 329 banks in the nation with a total capital of $110 million. By 1835 the number of banks had increased to 704, with a total capital of $231 million. The value of bank notes in circulation grew from $61 million in 1830 to $149 million in 1837. Commodity prices rose an average of 13 percent a year in 1835 and 1836. Land sales

skyrocketed. States made new commitments to build canals. In 1836, for example, Illinois began construction of the Illinois and Michigan Canal in order to link Lake Michigan with the Illinois and Mississippi rivers. Then in May 1837 prices began to tumble, and bank after bank suspended specie payments. After a short rally, the economy crashed again in 1839. The Bank of the United States, which had continued to operate as a state bank with a Pennsylvania charter, failed. Nicholas Biddle himself was charged with fraud and theft. Banks throughout the nation again suspended specie payments.

The ensuing depression was far more severe and prolonged than the economic downturn of 1819. Those lucky enough to find work saw their wage rates drop by roughly one-third between 1836 and 1842. In despair, many workers turned to the teachings of William Miller, a New England religious enthusiast whose reading of the Bible convinced him that the end of the world was imminent. Dressed in black coats and stovepipe hats, Miller's followers roamed urban sidewalks and rural villages in search of converts. Many Millerites sold their possessions and purchased white robes to ascend into heaven on October 22, 1843, the date on which Millerite leaders calculated the world would end. Ironically, by then the worst of the depression was over, but at its depths in the late 1830s and early 1840s, the economic slump fed the gloom that made poor people receptive to Miller's predictions. A New Yorker rich enough to afford a private joke confided to his diary that people everywhere were "out of kash, out of kredit, out of karacter and out of klothes."

The origins of the depression were both national and international. In July 1836 Jackson had issued a proclamation called the Specie Circular, which

Note of the "Humbug Glory Bank"

In the Panic of 1837, many notes from real banks were not worth much more than this funny money, adorned by an ass and a shady character.

provided that after August 15 only specie was to be accepted in payment for public lands. The Specie Circular was one of Jackson's final affirmations of his belief that paper money encouraged people to embark on speculative, get-rich-quick schemes, sapped "public virtue," and robbed "honest labour of its earnings to make knaves rich, powerful and dangerous." He hoped that the Specie Circular would reverse the damaging effects of the Deposit Act of 1836, which he had signed reluctantly. The Specie Circular took the wind out of the speculative boom by making banks hesitant to issue more of the paper money that was fueling the boom, because western farmers eager to buy public lands would now demand that banks immediately redeem their paper in specie. Although the Specie Circular chilled bankers' confidence, it was not the sole or even the major reason for the depression. There were international causes as well, most notably the fact that in 1836, Britain, in an effort to restrain the outflow of British investment, checked the flow of specie from its shores to the United States.

The Search for Solutions

Van Buren came to office with a well-deserved reputation as a crafty politician; contemporaries called him the "sly fox" and the "little magician." Now he had to act decisively, for the depression was causing misery not only for ordinary citizens but for the Democratic party as well. Railing against "Martin Van Ruin," the Whigs in 1838 swept the governorship and most of the legislative seats in Van Buren's own New York.

To regain the political initiative, the president called for the creation of an Independent Treasury. Instead of depositing its revenue in state banks, the federal government would keep the revenue itself and thereby withhold public money from the grasp of business corporations. Introduced in Congress in 1837, the Independent Treasury Bill finally passed in 1840. With a flourish, Van Buren signed it into law on July 4, 1840; his supporters hailed it as America's second Declaration of Independence.

The establishment of the Independent Treasury reflected the basic Jacksonian suspicion of an alliance between the federal government and banking. From the moment that it was introduced, the Independent Treasury Bill promised not only to give the Democrats a clear national issue around which to rally but to get the federal government out of the banking business. But the Independent Treasury proposal failed to address the banking issue on the state level. Jackson's dismemberment of the Bank of the United States had not slowed the establishment of state banks, whose number by 1840 had grown to over nine hundred. While holding charters from state governments, these banks were privately controlled institutions whose loans to businessmen and farmers fueled the kind of speculative economy that Jacksonians feared.

Whigs and Democrats differed sharply in their approach to the multiplication of state banks. Eager to encourage economic development, Whigs in New York and elsewhere introduced the idea of "free banking." Free banking allowed any group to start a bank as long as its members met general state requirements. In the eyes of Whigs, Jackson's Specie Circular, not banks themselves, had caused the depression. In contrast, Democrats took a different view of both the causes of the depression and the value of state banks. Disillusioned by the collapse of the speculative boom of 1835–1836, a growing number of Democrats blamed the depression on banks and paper money and adopted the hard-money stance long favored by Jackson and his advisers. In Louisiana and Arkansas, Democrats successfully prohibited banks altogether. Elsewhere, Democrats imposed severe legislative restrictions on banks—for example, by banning the emission of paper money in small denominations. In sum, after 1837 the Democrats became an anti-bank, hard-money party.

The Election of 1840

Despite the depression, Van Buren gained his party's renomination. Avoiding their mistake of 1836, the Whigs settled on a single candidate, Ohio's William Henry Harrison, and ran former Virginia senator John Tyler as vice president. A relatively minor force in the Whig party, Harrison was sixty-seven years old and barely eking out a living on a farm. The Whigs picked him because he had few enemies. Early in the campaign, the Democrats made a fatal mistake by ridiculing Harrison as "Old Granny," a man who desired only to spend his declining years in a log cabin sipping cider. Without knowing it, the Democrats had handed the

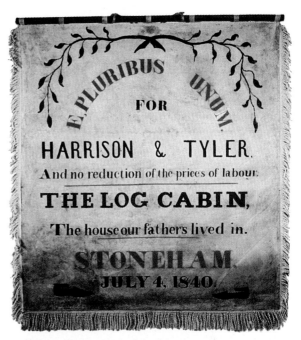

Harrison and Tyler Log Cabin Banner

By July 1840 few Americans needed to be reminded that "the house our fathers lived in" was a log cabin, the Whig campaign symbol.

Whigs the most famous campaign symbol in American history. The Whigs immediately reminded the public that Harrison had been a rugged frontiersman, the hero of the Battle of Tippecanoe, and a defender of all frontier people who lived in log cabins.

Refusing to publish a platform, the Whigs ran a "hurrah" campaign. They used log cabins for headquarters, sang log-cabin songs, gave out log-cabin cider, and called their newspaper the *Log Cabin*. For a slogan, they trumpeted "Tippecanoe and Tyler too." When not celebrating log cabins, they attacked Van Buren as a soft aristocrat who lived in "regal splendor." While Harrison was content to drink hard cider from a plain mug, the Whigs observed, Van Buren had turned the White House into a palace fit for an oriental despot and drank fine wines from silver goblets while he watched people go hungry in the streets.

The election results gave Harrison a clear victory. Van Buren carried only seven states and failed even to hold his own New York. The depression would have made it difficult, if not impossible, for any Democrat to have triumphed in 1840, but Van

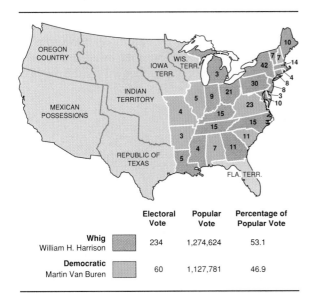

	Electoral Vote	Popular Vote	Percentage of Popular Vote
Whig William H. Harrison	234	1,274,624	53.1
Democratic Martin Van Buren	60	1,127,781	46.9

The Election of 1840

Buren had other disabilities besides the economic collapse. Unlike Harrison and Jackson, he had no halo of military glory. Moreover, Van Buren ran a surprisingly sluggish campaign. Prior to 1840 the Whigs had been slower than the Democrats to mobilize voters by new techniques. But in 1840 it was Van Buren who directed his campaign the old-fashioned way by writing encouraging letters to key supporters, while Harrison broke with tradition and went about the country (often on railroads) campaigning. Ironically, Van Buren, the master politician, was beaten at his own game.

The Second Party System Matures

In losing the presidency in 1840, Van Buren actually received 400,000 more popular votes than any previous presidential candidate. The total number of votes cast in presidential elections had risen from 1.2 million in 1828 to 1.5 million in 1836 to 2.4 million in 1840. The leap in the size of the popular vote between 1836 and 1840, 60 percent, is the greatest proportionate jump between consecutive elections in American history. Neither lower suffrage requirements nor population growth was the main cause of this change. Rather, the spurt in the popular vote resulted from a jump in the percentage of eligible voters who *chose* to vote. In the three elections before 1840, the proportion of white males who voted had fluctuated between 55 percent and 58 percent; in 1840 it rose to 80 percent.

Both the depression and the frenzy of the log-cabin campaign had jolted previously indifferent voters to go to the polls. Yet voter turnouts stayed up even after prosperity returned in the 1840s. The second party system, which had been developing slowly since 1828, reached a high plateau in 1840 and remained there for more than a decade. What gave politicians their appeal in the eyes of ordinary people were not only their rousing campaign techniques but also the strong contrasts and simple choices that they could present. The gradual hardening of the line between the two parties stimulated enduring popular interest in politics.

No less than the tariff and banking, reform also aroused partisan passions by 1840. Yet many of the seeds of the reform movements that burst upon the national scene in the 1830s were initially sown in the field of religion rather than politics.

The Rise of Popular Religion

In *Democracy in America,* Alexis de Tocqueville pointed out an important difference between France and the United States. "In France I had almost always seen the spirit of religion and the spirit of freedom pursuing courses diametrically opposed to each other; but in America I found that they were intimately united, and that they reigned in common over the same country." From this assertion Tocqueville drew a startling conclusion: religion was "the foremost of the political institutions" of the United States.

In calling religion a political institution, Tocqueville did not mean that Americans gave special political privileges to any particular denomination. Rather, he was referring to the way in which religious impulses reinforced American democracy and liberty. Just as Americans demanded that politics be made accessible to the average person, they insisted that ministers preach doctrines that appealed to ordinary people. The most successful ministers were those who used plain words to move the heart, not those who tried to dazzle their listeners with theological complexities. Increasingly, too, Americans demanded theological doctrines that put individuals in charge of their own religious destiny. They thrust aside the Calvinist doctrine that God had arbitrarily selected some people for salvation and others for damnation and substituted the belief that anyone could attain heaven.

Thus heaven as well as politics became democratized in these years. This harmony between religious and democratic impulses owed much to a series of religious revivals known as the Second Great Awakening.

The Second Great Awakening

The Second Great Awakening had begun in Connecticut during the 1790s and set ablaze one section of the nation after another during the following half-century. At first, educated Congregationalists and Presbyterians such as Yale University's president Timothy Dwight had dominated the revivals. But as they moved from Connecticut to frontier states like Tennessee and Kentucky, the

Methodist Camp Meeting *Frontier revivals occurred outdoors, lasted for days, and attracted an abundance of women and children as well as men.*

revivals had undergone striking changes that were typified by the rise of camp meetings. Camp meetings were gigantic revivals in which members of several denominations gathered together in sprawling open-air camps for up to a week to hear revivalists proclaim that the Second Coming of Jesus was near and that the time for repentance was now. The most famous camp meeting had occurred at Cane Ridge, Kentucky, in August 1801, when a huge crowd had come together on a hillside to listen to thunderous sermons and to sing hymns and experience the influx of divine grace. One eyewitness vividly described the meeting:

> At night, the whole scene was awfully sublime. The ranges of tents, the fires, reflecting light amidst the branches of the towering trees; the candles and lamps illuminating the encampment; hundreds moving to and fro, with lights or torches, like Gideon's army; the preaching, praying, singing, and shouting, all heard at once, rushing from different parts of the ground, like the sound of many waters, was enough to swallow up all the powers of contemplation.

The Cane Ridge revival had been an episode of the larger Great Kentucky Revival of 1800–1801.

Among the distinguishing features of these frontier revivals was the appearance of "exercises" in which men and women rolled around like logs, jerked their heads furiously (a phenomenon known simply as the jerks), and grunted like animals (the "barking exercise"). Observing the apparent pandemonium that had broken loose, critics had blasted the frontier frenzy for encouraging fleshly lust more than spirituality and complained that in revivals, "more souls were begot than saved." In fact, the early frontier revivals had challenged traditional religious customs. The most successful frontier revivalist preachers were not educated men but ordinary farmers and artisans who had experienced powerful religious conversions and who had contempt for learned ministers with their dry expositions of doctrine.

No religious denomination had been more successful on the frontier than the Methodists. With fewer than seventy thousand members in 1800, the Methodists had by 1844 become America's largest Protestant denomination, claiming a little over a million members. In contrast to New England Congregationalists and Presbyterians, Methodists emphasized that religion was primarily a matter of the heart rather than the head. Too, the frontier

Methodists disdained a "settled" ministry—that is, ministers tied to fixed parishes. Instead, they preferred itinerant circuit riders—young, unmarried men—who moved on horseback from place to place and preached in houses, open fields, or wherever else listeners gathered.

Although the frontier revivals disrupted religious custom, they also worked to promote law, order, and a sense of morality on the frontier. For all the jerks, rolls, and barks that they produced, they ultimately advanced values such as sobriety, hostility to dueling, and an abhorrence of the violence so common in frontier living. Drunken rowdies who tried to invade camp meetings met their match in brawny itinerants like the Methodist Peter Cartwright. It was not only in camp meetings that Cartwright and his peers sought to raise the moral standard of the frontier. The basic unit of Methodist discipline on the frontier was the "class." When revivals broke up, the converted formed these tiny groups of twelve or so members who met weekly to provide mutual encouragement of both religion and morality. In these class meetings, Methodists chastised each other for drunkenness, fighting, fornication, gossiping, and even sharp business practices.

Eastern Revivals

By the 1820s the center of the Second Great Awakening was shifting from the frontier back to the East. The revival fires glowed with peculiar intensity in an area of western New York that became known as the Burned-Over District. Although not a frontier area in the 1820s, western New York was filled with transplanted New Englanders whose ancestors had experienced the Great Awakening in the eighteenth century and who hungered for their own religious experiences. After the completion of the Erie Canal, the region was also a magnet for winners and losers in the restless pursuit of wealth. In sum, it was a fertile field of high expectations and bitter discontent.

The man who harnessed these anxieties to religion was Charles G. Finney. Finney began his career as a lawyer, but after a religious conversion in 1821, which he described as a "retainer from the Lord Jesus Christ to plead his cause," he became a Presbyterian minister and conducted revivals in towns along the canal like Rome and Utica. While he also found time for trips to New York and Boston, his greatest "harvest" came in the thriving canal city of Rochester in 1830–1831.

The Rochester revival had several features that justify Finney's reputation as the "father of modern revivalism." First, it was a citywide revival in which all denominations participated. Finney was a pioneer of cooperation among Protestant denominations. In addition, in Rochester and elsewhere, Finney introduced devices for speeding conversions. Among these were the "anxious seat," a bench to which those ready for conversion were led so that they could be made objects of special prayer, and the "protracted meeting," which went on nightly for up to a week. Finney's emphasis on revival techniques sharply distinguished him from eighteenth-century revivalists, including Jonathan Edwards. Where Edwards had portrayed revivals as the miraculous work of God, Finney made them out to be human creations. The divine spirit flowed in revivals, but humans made them happen. Finally, although a Presbyterian, Finney flatly rejected the Calvinist belief that humans had a natural and nearly irresistible inclination to sin (the doctrine of "human depravity"). Rather, he affirmed, sin was purely a voluntary act; no one *had* to sin. Men and women could will themselves out of sin just as readily as they had willed themselves into it. Indeed, he declared, it was theoretically possible for men and women to will themselves free of all sin — to live perfectly. Those who heard Finney and similar revivalists came away convinced that they had experienced the washing away of all past guilt and the beginning of a new life. "I have been born again," a young convert wrote. "I am three days old when I write this letter."

The assertions that people could live without sin ("perfectionism") and that revivals were human contrivances made Finney a controversial figure. Yet his ideas came to dominate "evangelical" Protestantism, forms of Protestantism that focused on the need for an emotional religious conversion. He was successful because he told people what they wanted to hear: that their destinies were in their own hands. A society that celebrated the "self-made" individual found plausible Finney's assertion that even in religion, people could make of themselves what they chose. Moreover, compared to most frontier revivalists, Finney had an unusually dignified style. Taken together, these factors gave him a potent appeal to merchants, lawyers, and small manufacturers in the towns and cities of the North. Finally, more than most revivalists, Finney recognized that without the mass participation of women, few revivals would have gotten off the ground. During the Second Great Awakening, female converts outnumbered male converts by about two to one. Finney encouraged women to give public testimonials of their religious experiences in church, and he often converted husbands by first converting their wives and daughters. After a visit by Finney, Melania Smith, the wife of a Rochester physician who had little time for religion, greeted her husband with a reminder of "the woe which is denounced against the families which call not on the Name of the Lord." Soon Dr. Smith heeded his wife's pleading and joined one of Rochester's Presbyterian churches.

Critics of Revivals: The Unitarians

Whereas some praised revivals for saving souls, others doubted that they produced permanent changes in behavior and condemned them for encouraging "such extravagant and incoherent expressions, and such enthusiastic fervor, as puts common sense and modesty to the blush."

One small but influential group of revival critics was the Unitarians. The basic doctrine of Unitarianism—that Jesus was not divine but merely an exemplary human being—had gained quiet acceptance among religious liberals during the eighteenth century. However, it was not until the early nineteenth century that Unitarianism emerged as a formal denomination with its own churches, ministry, and national organization. In New England in these years, hundreds of Congregational churches were torn apart by the withdrawal of socially prominent families who had embraced Unitarianism and by legal battles over which group—Congregationalists or Unitarians—could occupy church property. Although Unitarians won relatively few converts outside New England, their tendency to attract the wealthy and educated gave them influence beyond their numbers.

Unitarians criticized revivals as uncouth emotional exhibitions and argued that moral goodness should be cultivated by a gradual process of "character building," in which the individual learned to model his or her behavior on that of Jesus rather than by a sudden emotional conversion as in a revival. Yet Unitarians and revivalists shared the belief that human behavior could be changed for the better. Both rejected the Calvinist emphasis on innate human wickedness. William Ellery Channing, a Unitarian leader, claimed that Christianity had but one purpose: "the perfection of human nature, the elevation of men into nobler beings."

The Rise of Mormonism

The Unitarians' assertion that Jesus Christ was human rather than divine challenged a basic doctrine of orthodox Christianity. Yet Unitarianism proved far less controversial than another of the new denominations of the 1820s and 1830s, the Church of Jesus Christ of Latter-day Saints, or Mormons. Its founder, Joseph Smith, grew to manhood in one of those families that seemed in constant motion to and fro but never up. After moving his family nearly twenty times in ten years, Smith's ne'er-do-well father settled in Palmyra, New York, in the heart of the Burned-Over District. As a boy, Smith's imagination teemed with plans to find buried treasure, while his religious views were convulsed by the conflicting claims of the denominations that thrived in the region. "Some were contending for the Methodist faith, some for the Presbyterian, and some for the Baptists," Smith later wrote. He wondered who was right and who wrong, or whether they were "all wrong together."

The sort of perplexity that Smith experienced was widespread in the Burned-Over District, but his resolution of the confusion was unique. Smith claimed that an angel led him to a buried book of revelation and to magic stones for use in translating it. He completed his translation of this Book of Mormon in 1827. The Book of Mormon tells the story of an ancient Hebrew prophet, Lehi, whose descendants came to America and created a prosperous civilization that looked forward to the appearance of Jesus as its savior. Jesus had actually appeared and performed miracles in the New World, the book claimed, but the American descendants of Lehi had departed from the Lord's ways and quarreled among themselves. God had cursed some with dark skin; these were the American Indians, who, when later discovered by Columbus, had forgotten their history.

Despite his astonishing claims, Smith quickly

gathered followers. The appeal of Mormonism lay partly in its positioning of America at the center of Christian history and partly in Smith's assertion that he had discovered a new revelation. The idea of an additional revelation beyond the Bible appeared to some to resolve the turmoil created by the Protestant denominations' inability to agree on what the Bible said or meant.

Smith and his followers steadily moved west from New York to Ohio and Missouri and then to Illinois, where they built a model city, Nauvoo, and a magnificent temple supported by thirty huge pillars. By moving west, the Mormons hoped to draw closer to the Indians, whose conversion was one of their goals, and to escape persecution. Smith's claim to have received a new revelation virtually guaranteed a hostile reception for the Mormons wherever they went, because Smith had undermined the authority of the Bible, one of the two documents (the other being the Constitution) upon which the ideals of the American republic rested.

Smith added fuel to the fire when he reported in 1843 that he had received still another revelation, this one sanctioning the Mormon practice of having multiple wives, or polygyny. Although Smith did not publicly proclaim polygyny as a doctrine, its practice among Mormons was a poorly kept secret. Smith's self-image also intensified the controversy that boiled around Mormonism. Refusing to view himself as merely the founder of another denomination, he saw himself as a prophet, the "Second Mohammed," and believed that Mormonism would be to Christianity what Christianity had been to Judaism: a grand, all-encompassing, and higher form of religion. He himself was the "King of the Kingdom of God." In 1844 he announced his candidacy for the presidency of the United States. But the state of Illinois was already moving against him. Charged with treason, he was jailed in Carthage, Illinois, and along with his brother, murdered there by a mob in June 1844.

Despite persecution, the Mormons won converts, not only in the United States but in the teeming slums of English factory cities from which Mormon agents brought thousands to America. In the thirty years after 1840, the number of Mormons grew from six thousand to two hundred thousand. After Smith's death a new leader, Brigham Young, led the main body of Mormons from Nauvoo to the Great Salt Lake Valley in Utah, which

Handcart Pioneers

The painter of these pioneer Mormons trekking to Utah, Carl Christian Anton Christensen, was attracted to Mormonism by missionaries in his native Denmark. Christensen immigrated to America in 1857 and with his bride walked thirteen hundred miles from Iowa City to Utah, pulling his possessions in a crude, two-wheeled handcart.

then was still under the control of Mexico. There Mormons established an independent republic, the state of Deseret. A thousand miles from Illinois, they prospered. Their isolation, combined with the firm control of Young, the "Old Boss," kept the rank and file in line. Polygyny, which Young officially proclaimed as a church doctrine, did not produce the hoped-for increase in Mormon numbers, but it did guarantee that Mormons would remain a people apart from the mainstream of American society. Above all, the Mormons were industrious and deeply committed to the welfare of other Mormons. Cooperation among Mormons took several forms, not the least of which was the practice of devoting each Mormon's "surplus" production to public projects like irrigation. Mormons transformed the valley into a rich oasis. When Utah came under American control after the Mexican War, they dominated its government.

Although Mormonism is one of the few religions to have originated in the United States, the antebellum Mormons pushed against the currents of American religion and society. They rejected the Bible as the sole source of revelation, substituted polygyny for monogamy, and elevated economic cooperation above competitiveness. Mormonism appealed to the downtrodden and insecure rather than to the prosperous and secure. It offered the downcast an explicit alternative to dominant religious and social practices. In this respect, Mormonism mirrored the efforts of several religious communal societies whose members resolutely set themselves apart from society. In general, these religious communitarians were less numerous, controversial, and long-lasting than the Mormons, but one group among them, the Shakers, has continued to fascinate Americans.

The Shakers

The leader of the Shakers (who derived their name from a convulsive religious dance that was part of their ceremony) was Mother Ann Lee, the illiterate daughter of an English blacksmith. Lee had set sail for America in 1774, and her followers soon organized a tightly knit community in New Lebanon, New York. In this and in other communities, the Shakers proved themselves able craftsmen. Shaker furniture became a byword for its beauty and strength. But for all their achievements as craftsmen, the Shakers were fundamentally otherworldly and hostile to materialism. Lee insisted that her followers abstain from sexual intercourse, believed that the end of the world was imminent, and derived many of her doctrines from trances and heavenly visions that she claimed to have. Among these doctrines was her conviction that at the Second Coming, Jesus would take the form of a woman, herself.

Her teachings about the evils of sexual relations would quickly have doomed the Shakers to extinction had it not been for the spread of religious revivalism in 1790. Turning up at Cane Ridge and other revival sites, Shaker missionaries made off with converts whom the revivals had loosened

Shakers, New Lebanon, New York   *Opposed to marriage, Shakers could increase their numbers only by gaining converts. After the Civil War, they failed in this mission. When this photograph was taken, about 1872, there were just over two thousand Shakers in the United States.*

from their traditional religious moorings. At their peak during the second quarter of the nineteenth century, the Shakers numbered about six thousand in eight states.

Shakers and Mormons chose to live apart from society. But the message of most evangelical Protestants, including Charles G. Finney, was that religion and economic individualism—a person's pursuit of wealth—were compatible. Most revivalists told people that getting ahead in the world was acceptable as long as they were honest, temperate, and bound by the dictates of their consciences. By encouraging assimilation into rather than retreat from society, evangelicalism provided a powerful stimulus to the manifold reform movements of the 1820s and 1830s.

The Age of Reform

Despite rising popular interest in politics between 1824 and 1840, large numbers of people were excluded from politics. Women were not allowed to vote, and blacks generally suffered rather than benefited from the gradual liberalization of voting requirements. By 1860 most northern states denied free people of color the right to vote. Too, the political parties did not welcome the intrusion of controversial issues like slavery, nor did they show much interest in women's rights.

During the 1820s and 1830s, unprecedented numbers of men and women overcame the limits of political parties by joining organizations that aimed to improve society. Some sought to abolish slavery; others, to elevate the position of women, to suppress liquor, or to improve the treatment of criminals and the insane. Many worked for the betterment of public education, and a resourceful minority attempted to establish utopian communities in which individuals could live harmoniously apart from society in idyllic settings. At times, the reformers cooperated with politicians, and when they did, it was usually with Whigs rather than Democrats. But the reformers' primary allegiance was to their own causes rather than to political parties. Indeed, politics struck most reformers as a sorry spectacle that allowed a man like Andrew Jackson, a duelist who married a divorcée, to become

president and that routinely rewarded persons who would sacrifice any principle for victory at the polls.

Reformers were energized by the moral exhilaration that came from believing that they were on God's side of any issue. Religious revivalism contributed to their intense moralism. Virtually all prominent temperance reformers of the 1820s and 1830s, for example, had been inspired initially by revivals. Religious conversions also propelled some men and women into abolition. However, revivalism and reform were not always so intimately linked. Prominent school reformers were frequently religious liberals either hostile or indifferent to revivals, and similarly a disproportionate number of early women's rights advocates were either Unitarians or Quakers. And while some abolitionists owed their first flush of idealism to revivals, others did not, and almost all came to criticize the Protestant churches for condoning slavery. Yet even those reformers opposed to revivalism borrowed the evangelical preachers' language and psychology by looking upon drunkenness, ignorance, and inequality as sins that called for immediate repentance and change.

Historians have advanced conflicting interpretations of antebellum reformers. Some see reformers as noble and tireless crusaders for a better society; others portray them as unbalanced fanatics who would hammer all people into a single, arbitrary standard of righteousness. Both sides have a point. Reformers were usually high-minded men and women who gained neither wealth nor security from their commitment to causes. Yet reform did have a dark side. Reformers did not hesitate to coerce people into righteousness. They pushed for legal prohibition of liquor and for compulsory education. For criminals they designed penitentiaries on highly repressive principles. In retrospect, their priorities were often misplaced. Assailing intemperance with fury, they paid less attention to the slums and working conditions that stimulated drinking. Reform enlisted far more advocates of temperance than of women's rights, and more supporters of public-school reform than of the abolition of slavery.

Although the reform movements appealed to those excluded from or repelled by politics, most lacked the political parties' national organizations. The primary center of reform was New England and those areas of New York and the

Midwest settled by New Englanders. Southerners actively suppressed abolition, displayed only mild interest in temperance and education reform, ignored women's rights, and looked upon utopian communities as signs of the mental instability of northern reformers.

The War on Liquor

Agitation for temperance (either total abstinence from alcoholic beverages or moderation in their use) intensified during the second quarter of the nineteenth century. Temperance reformers addressed a growing problem: per capita consumption of alcohol had risen steadily between 1800 and 1830. With some justification, reformers saw alcoholic excess as a male indulgence whose bitter consequences (spending wages on liquor instead of food) were suffered by women and children. Not surprisingly, temperance was a banner behind which millions of women were to march during the nineteenth century.

There had been agitation against intemperance before 1825, but that year the Connecticut revivalist Lyman Beecher ushered in a new phase when, in six widely acclaimed lectures, he thundered against all use of alcohol. A year later, evan-

gelical Protestants created the American Temperance Society, the first national temperance organization. By 1834 some five thousand state and local temperance societies were loosely affiliated with the American Temperance Society. Where previous temperance supporters had advised moderation in the use of spirits, the American Temperance Society followed Beecher in demanding total abstinence. The society flooded the country with tracts denouncing the "amazing evil" of strong drink and urged churches to expel any members who condoned alcohol.

Among the main targets of the evangelical temperance reformers were moderate drinkers among the laboring classes. In the small shops where a handful of journeymen and apprentices worked informally, passing the jug every few hours was a time-honored way to relieve fatigue and monotony. But with the rise of large factories, new demands arose for a disciplined work force. Factory owners with precise production schedules to meet needed orderly and steady workers. Thus evangelical temperance reformers quickly gained manufacturers' support. In East Dudley, Massachusetts, for example, three factory owners refused to sell liquor in factory stores, calculating that any profits from the sale would be more than offset by

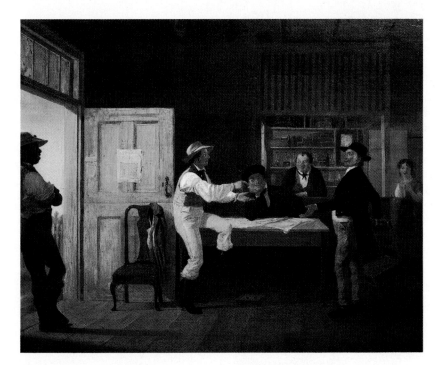

Politicians in a Country Bar,
by James Clooney, 1844

The temperance movement did not deter politicians from soliciting voters in a likely place.

Rochester, New York, in the 1820s and 1830s

When Captain Oliver H. Perry defeated the British at the Battle of Lake Erie (1813), he did an unsought favor for a tiny settlement started by Colonel Nathaniel Rochester in western New York. Perry's victory, while giving the Americans control of Lake Erie, reminded them of their inability to control Lake Ontario. The original plans for a waterway across New York had projected a route from Albany on the Hudson River to Oswego on Lake Ontario. But since the Lake Ontario border with Canada remained insecure, canal planners shifted to a southerly and much longer route, from Albany to Lake Erie, that passed through Rochester. Situated at the falls of the Genesee River, with abundant water power for flour mills, Rochester was already producing 26,000 barrels of flour a year in 1818. The completion of the Erie Canal in 1825 transformed Rochester from a small milling center into America's first inland boom town (see Chapter 8). In 1828 Rochester exported 200,000 barrels of flour. Its population leaped from 1,500 in 1820 to more than 12,000 by 1834.

During the 1820s Rochester experienced growing social fragmentation. Increasingly, a spirit of acquisitiveness took root in the town. In past days master artisans had boarded and supervised a few

journeymen in their own homes and exclusively served local customers. Now the master craftsmen traveled through the countryside in search of more business. To fill the additional orders from distant buyers, they subdivided the tasks of making shoes and other commodities and gradually replaced the semiskilled journeymen whom they had once boarded with unskilled laborers who lived apart, in working-class neighborhoods. Increasing rowdiness accompanied this growing division of the social classes. Taverns multiplied; in 1827 alone almost a hundred persons procured licenses to sell liquor. Town fathers blamed liquor for a horrifying spectacle in 1829, when hundreds paid to see the none-too-sober Sam Patch plunge to his death in a widely publicized leap over the main falls of the Genesee.

With social upheavals came political divisions. By the mid-1820s

Genesee Scenery, by *Thomas Cole*

Cole captured the beautiful countryside around Rochester in this colorful view featuring the falls of the Genesee.

Early View of Rochester

This 1835 view looks eastward across the Erie Canal. Buffalo Street (now Main Street) is at the center.

the handful of elite families like that of Nathaniel Rochester could no longer govern the town's diverse interests. The Anti-Masonic movement, which began near Rochester, acted as a magnet for those discontented with the leading families, virtually all of whose male members were Masons. "Reason seems to have lost her empire," a member of the Rochester clan complained, "and Charity to have resigned her seat."

For merchant Josiah Bissell, Sam Patch's fatal leap was the last straw. Long dismayed by rampant drunkenness and Sabbath breaking

Nathaniel Rochester,
by Colby Kimble, 1822

in Rochester, Bissell and like-minded citizens had tried in 1828 to suppress stagecoach and boat travel on Sunday, to force observance of the Sabbath on *"that large mass of the community who neither fear God nor obey man."* On the Sunday after Sam Patch's death, Bissell invited the leading evangelist, Charles G. Finney, to conduct a revival in Rochester.

Finney's revivals in Rochester during 1830 and 1831 drew hundreds into the churches. Now demure women were shouting "Blessed be the Name of Jesus" in church. "We are either marching toward heaven or towards hell," a convert wrote to his sister. "How is it with you?"

Nevertheless, the revivals failed to unify the town. The rise of Anti-Masonry in the 1820s had fragmented Rochester's politics to the point where no leader, religious or political, could mend the pieces. Rather than restoring unity, Finney contributed a new and ideological basis to the town's divisions by tying religious conversion to temperance. During the 1830s most town supporters of the revivals became Whigs: evangelical Presbyterians, including numerous manufacturers and merchants converted by Finney, soon formed the core of Roch-

ester's Whig party. A respectable number of anti-liquor workers followed their lead. In contrast, the Jacksonian Democrats drew their support from Catholics, unchurched Protestant workers, and grocers and retailers who served working-class neighborhoods. Opposing restrictions on the sale of liquor, Rochester's Jacksonians took the view that the individual's conscience rather than legislation should guide morality, and they opposed efforts to force the substitution of cold water for liquor. Asked how her husband would vote, a woman in a working-class neighborhood replied: "Why he has always been [for] Jackson, and I don't think he has joined the Cold Water."

The temperance issue acted as a filter through which national issues like the Bank of the United States made their way into Rochester during the 1830s. The same people who opposed Jackson's removal of deposits from the bank supported temperance. Yet temperance was more than just another issue at election time. It served as the *premier* issue in Rochester. Their response to temperance shaped the basic political orientation of Rochester's voters and guided their allegiances when a controversial issue like banking appeared on the horizon.

lost working time and "the scenes of riot and wickedness thus produced."

Workers showed little interest in temperance before the late 1830s. But after the Panic of 1837, a new stage of temperance agitation sprang up in the form of the Washington Temperance Societies. Starting in Baltimore in 1840, the Washingtonians were more likely to be mechanics (workingmen) and laborers than ministers and manufacturers. Many were reformed drunkards, and most had concluded that their survival in the harsh climate of depression depended on their commitment to sobriety and frugality. For example, Charles T. Woodman, a baker, had been forced by the collapse of his business to flee Boston for Philadelphia to escape his creditors. Like most Washingtonians, Woodman blamed his ruin on the revival of his "old habit" of drink. The forces dislocating workers in the late 1830s were often far beyond their control. Part of the appeal of temperance was that it lay *within* their control. Take care of temperance, a Washingtonian assured a Baltimore audience, and the Lord would take care of the economy.

For all their differences from earlier temperance associations, the Washingtonians reflected the impact of revivals even more than did the American Temperance Society. Viewing drinking as sinful, they held "experience meetings," in which members described their "salvation" from liquor and their "regeneration" through abstinence (or "teetotalism"*). Their wives joined "Martha Washington" societies, in which they pledged to smell their husbands' breath each night and paraded with banners that read "Teetotal or No Husband." The Washingtonians spread farther and faster than any other antebellum temperance organization.

As temperance won new supporters, anti-alcohol crusaders gradually shifted their tactics from calls that individuals abstain to demands that cities and towns, and even states, ban all traffic in liquor (see "A Place in Time"). This shift from moral suasion to legal prohibition was controversial even within the movement. But by the late 1830s, prohibition was scoring victories. In 1838 Massachusetts prohibited the sale of distilled spirits in amounts less than fifteen gallons; in 1851 Maine banned the manufacture and sale of all intoxicating beverages. Controversial though these laws were, the temperance movement earned a measure of success. After rising steadily between 1800 and 1830, per capita consumption of distilled spirits began to fall during the 1830s. The rate of consumption during the 1840s was less than half that in the 1820s.

Public-School Reform

No less than temperance reformers, school reformers worked to encourage orderliness and thrift in the common people. Rural America's so-called district schools provided reformers with one of their main targets. One-room log or clapboard cabins containing pupils aged anywhere from three to twenty or more, the district schools taught farmers' children to read and count but little more. Those who attended the district schools never forgot their primitive conditions or harsh discipline: "the woodpile in the yard, the open fire-place, the backless benches," and the floggings until "the youngster vomited or wet his breeches."

For all their drawbacks, the district schools enjoyed support from rural parents, who financed them by a mixture of tuition payments, property taxes, and fuel contributions and by boarding the teachers in their homes. But reformers saw these schools in a different light. Centered in industrializing states like Massachusetts and Connecticut, the reformers insisted that schools had to equip children for the emerging competitive and industrial economy. The most articulate and influential of the reformers, former Massachusetts lawyer and state senator Horace Mann, in 1837 became the first secretary of the newly created Massachusetts Board of Education, and for the next decade, he promoted a sweeping transformation of public education. Mann's goals included shifting the burden of financial support for schools from parents to the state, grading the schools (that is, classifying pupils by age and attainment), extending the school term from two or three months to as many as ten months, introducing standardized textbooks, and compelling attendance. In place of loosely structured schools that were mere appendages of the family, Mann and other reformers advocated highly structured institutions that would occupy most of the child's time and energy.

School reformers hoped not only to combat ignorance but to spread uniform cultural values by

---

*Teetotal: coined by an English laborer at a temperance meeting in 1834, *teetotal* was merely an emphatic form of *total*.

exposing all children to identical experiences. Children would arrive at school at the same time and thereby learn punctuality. Graded schools that matched children against their age peers would stimulate the competitiveness needed in a rapidly industrializing society. Children would all read the same books and absorb such common sayings as "Idleness is the nest in which mischief lays its eggs." The McGuffey readers, which sold 50 million copies between 1836 and 1870, created a common curriculum and preached industry, honesty, sobriety, and patriotism.

But antebellum educational reformers faced challenges at every turn. Mindful that the short terms and informal arrangements of district schools harmonized with the farming seasons, rural people resisted standardization and centralization. In Massachusetts, representatives of farm areas nearly succeeded in abolishing Mann's board of education in 1840. From a different direction, urban Catholics sniped at the reformers' rigid Protestantism. In New York City, Bishop John Hughes led demands during the early 1840s for public support of parochial schools. Hughes pointed out that the textbooks used in public schools contained anti-Catholic and anti-Irish barbs; one textbook warned, for example, that Catholic immigrants threatened to turn America into the "common sewer of Ireland." And in both rural and urban areas, the laboring poor opposed compulsory education as a menace to parents dependent on their children's wages.

Yet the reformers enjoyed remarkable success in overcoming opposition. Although reform did not make significant gains in the South (see Chapter 10), much of the North remodeled its schools along the lines advocated by Mann. Most northern states continued to finance schools by a mixture of public tax support and tuition payments, but the balance gradually shifted toward tax support. School terms lengthened, and schools increasingly were graded. In 1852 Massachusetts passed the nation's first compulsory-attendance law.

The school reformers prevailed, in part, because their opposition was fragmented. Neither Protestant farmers nor urban Catholics thought much of school reform, but these groups thought even less of each other. In part, too, reformers succeeded because they gained influential allies. The so-called workingmen's parties that arose in the late 1820s shared the school reformers' enthusiasm for free

public education. Manufacturers, who needed a disciplined work force, could not help but notice how much emphasis reformers placed on punctuality. Many merchants, lawyers, and progressive farmers sensed that the district schools were unsuited to an age of rapid economic change and accordingly supported reform. And reform-minded women not only preferred the gentle methods of discipline that Mann advocated but recognized, too, that the grading of schools would facilitate women's entry into teaching. It was widely believed that a woman could never control the assortment of three- to twenty-year-olds found in a one-room schoolhouse, but managing a class of eight- or nine-year-olds was a different matter. Catharine Beecher stated bluntly: "A profession is to be created for women. . . . This is the way in which thousands of intellectual and respectable women, who toil for a pittance scarcely sufficient to sustain life, are to be relieved and educated." Whereas in 1800 most teachers had been male, women gradually took the place of men in the classroom wherever school reform left its mark. By 1900 about 70 percent of the nation's schoolteachers were women.

School reform also appealed to native-born Americans alarmed by the swelling tide of immigration. The public school emerged as the favorite device by which reformers forged a common American culture out of an increasingly diverse society. "We must decompose and cleanse the impurities which rush into our midst" through the "one infallible filter—the SCHOOL."

School reformers were assimilationists in the sense that they hoped to use public education to give children common values through shared experiences. In one respect, however, these reformers wore blinders on the issue of assimilation, for few stressed the integration of black and white children. When black children were fortunate enough to get any schooling, it was usually in segregated schools. Black children who entered integrated public schools met with such virulent prejudice that black leaders in northern cities frequently preferred segregated schools.

Abolition

Antislavery sentiment among whites flourished in the Revolutionary era but declined in the early nineteenth century. The main antislavery organization founded between 1800 and 1830 was the

**Game of Chance:
Auctioneers and Slaves**

Games and toys were meant to educate as well as to amuse children. This game, manufactured in Maine in the mid-nineteenth century, encouraged children to abhor slavery.

American Colonization Society (1817), which displayed little moral outrage against slavery. The society proposed a plan for gradual emancipation, with compensation to the slaveowner, and the shipment of freed blacks to Africa. This proposal attracted support from some slaveholders in the Upper South who would never have dreamed of a general emancipation.

At its core, colonization was hard-hearted and softheaded. Colonizationists assumed that blacks were a degraded race that did not belong in American society, and they underestimated the growing dependence of the South's economy on slavery. Confronted by a soaring demand for cotton and other commodities, few southerners were willing to free their slaves, even if compensated. In any event, the American Colonization Society never had enough funds to buy freedom for more than a fraction of slaves. Between 1820 and 1830, only 1,400 blacks migrated to Liberia, and most were already free. In striking contrast, the American slave population, fed by natural increase (the excess of births over deaths), rose from 1,191,000 in 1810 to more than 2,000,000 in 1830.

During the 1820s the main source of radical opposition to slavery was blacks themselves. Blacks had little enthusiasm for colonization. Most American blacks were native- rather than African-born. How, they asked, could they be sent back to a continent that they had never left? "We are *natives* of this country," a black pastor in New York proclaimed. "We only ask that we be treated as well as *foreigners.*" In opposition to colonization, blacks formed scores of abolition societies. In 1829 the Boston free black David Walker published an *Appeal* for a black rebellion to crush slavery.

Not all whites acquiesced to the continuance of slavery. In 1821 the Quaker Benjamin Lundy began a newspaper, the *Genius of Universal Emancipation,* and put forth proposals that no new slave states be admitted, that the internal slave trade be outlawed, that the three-fifths clause of the Constitution be repealed, and that Congress abolish slavery wherever it had the authority to do so. In 1828 Lundy hired a young New Englander, William Lloyd Garrison, as an assistant editor. Prematurely bald and with steel-rimmed glasses, and typically donning a black suit and black cravat, Garrison looked more like a schoolmaster than a rebel. But in 1831, when he launched his own newspaper, *The Liberator,* he quickly established himself as the most famous and controversial white abolitionist. "I am in earnest," Garrison wrote. "I will not equivocate—I will not excuse—I will not retreat a single inch—AND I WILL BE HEARD."

Garrison's battle cry was "immediate emancipation." In place of exiling blacks to Africa, he substituted the truly radical notion that blacks should enjoy civil (or legal) equality with whites. He greeted slaves as "a Man and a Brother," "a Woman and a Sister." Even Garrison, however, did not think that all slaves could be freed overnight. "Immediate emancipation" meant that all people had to realize that slavery was sinful and its continued existence intolerable.

Garrison quickly gained support from the growing number of black abolitionists. A black barber in Pittsburgh sent Garrison sixty dollars to help with *The Liberator.* Black agents sold subscriptions. Three-fourths of *The Liberator*'s subscribers in the early years were black. The escaped slave Frederick Douglass and a remarkable freed slave who named herself Sojourner Truth proved eloquent lecturers against slavery. Douglass could rivet an audience with an opening line. "I appear before the immense assembly this evening as a thief and a robber," he gibed. "I stole this head, these limbs, this body from my master, and ran off with them."

Relations between black and white abolitionists were not always harmonious. White abolitionists called for legal equality for blacks but not necessarily for social equality. Not without racial prejudice, they preferred light- to dark-skinned Negroes and, Garrison excepted, were hesitant to admit blacks to antislavery societies. Yet the prejudices of white abolitionists were mild compared to those of most whites. A white man or woman could do few things less popular in the 1830s than become an abolitionist. Mobs, often including colonizationists, repeatedly attacked abolitionists. For example, a Boston mob, searching for a British abolitionist in 1835, found Garrison instead and dragged him through town on the end of a rope. An abolitionist editor, Elijah Lovejoy, was murdered by a mob in Alton, Illinois, in 1837.

Abolitionists drew on the language of revivals and described slavery as sin, but the Protestant churches did not rally behind abolition as strongly as behind temperance. Lyman Beecher roared against the evils of strong drink but whimpered about those of slavery and in 1834 tried to suppress abolitionists at Cincinnati's Lane Theological Seminary. In response, Theodore Dwight Weld, an idealistic follower of Charles G. Finney, led a mass withdrawal of students. These "Lane rebels" formed the nucleus of abolitionist activity at the antislavery Oberlin College.

As if external hostility were not enough, abolitionists argued continually with each other. The American Anti-Slavery Society, founded in 1833, was the scene of several battles between Garrison and prominent New York and midwestern abolitionists such as the brothers Lewis and Arthur Tappan, Theodore Dwight Weld, and James G. Birney. One of the issues between the two sides was whether abolitionists should enter politics as a distinct party. In 1840 Garrison's opponents ran Birney for president on the ticket of the newly formed Liberty party. As for Garrison himself, he was increasingly rejecting *all* laws and governments, as well as political parties, as part of his doctrine of "nonresistance." In 1838 he and his followers had founded the New England Non-Resistance Society. The

starting point of the doctrine was the fact that slavery depended on force. Garrison then added that all governments ultimately rested on force; even laws passed by elected legislatures needed police enforcement. Because Garrison viewed force as the opposite of Christian love, he concluded that Christians should refuse to vote, hold office, or have anything to do with government. It is a small wonder that many abolitionists thought of Garrison as extreme, or "ultra."

The second issue that divided the American Anti-Slavery Society concerned the role of women in the abolitionist movement. In 1837 Angelina and Sarah Grimké, daughters of a South Carolina slaveholder, embarked on an antislavery lecture tour of New England. Women had become deeply involved in antislavery societies during the 1830s, but always in female auxiliaries affiliated with those run by men. What made the Grimké sisters so controversial was that they drew mixed audiences of men and women to their lectures at a time when it was thought indelicate for women to speak before male audiences. Clergymen chastised the Grimké sisters for lecturing men rather than obeying them.

Such criticism backfired, however, because the Grimkés increasingly took up the cause of women's rights. In 1838 each wrote a classic of American feminism. Sarah produced her *Letters on the Condition of Women and the Equality of the Sexes,* while Angelina contributed her *Letters to Catharine E. Beecher* (Lyman Beecher's daughter and a militant opponent of female equality). Some abolitionists tried to dampen the feminist flames. The abolitionist poet John Greenleaf Whittier dismissed women's grievances as "paltry" compared to the "great and dreadful wrongs of the slave." Even Theodore Dwight Weld, who had married Angelina Grimké, wanted to subordinate women's rights to antislavery. But the fiery passions would not be extinguished. Garrison, welcoming the controversy, promptly espoused women's rights and urged that women be given positions equal to men in the American Anti-Slavery Society. In 1840 the election of a woman, Abby Kelley, to a previously all-male committee split the American Anti-Slavery Society wide open. A substantial minority of pro-feminist delegates left—some to join the Liberty party, others to follow Lewis Tappan into the new American and Foreign Anti-Slavery Society.

The disruption of the American Anti-Slavery

Society did not greatly damage abolitionism. The national society had never had much control over the local societies that had grown swiftly during the mid-1830s. By 1840 there were more than fifteen hundred local societies, principally in Massachusetts, New York, and Ohio. By circulating abolitionist tracts, newspapers, and even chocolates with antislavery messages on their wrappers, these local societies kept the country ablaze with agitation.

One of the most disruptive abolitionist techniques was to flood Congress with petitions calling for an end to slavery in the District of Columbia. Congress had no time to consider all the petitions, but to refuse to address them meant depriving citizens of their right to have petitions heard. In 1836 southerners secured congressional adoption of the "gag rule," which automatically tabled abolitionist petitions and thus prevented discussion of them in Congress. Ex-president John Quincy Adams, then a representative from Massachusetts, led the struggle against the gag rule and finally secured its repeal in 1845. The debate over the gag rule subtly shifted the issue from the abolition of slavery to the constitutional rights of free expression and petitioning Congress. Members of Congress with little sympathy for abolitionists found themselves attacking the South for suppressing the right of petition. In a way, the gag-rule episode vindicated Garrison's tactic of stirring up emotions on the slavery issue. By holding passions over slavery at the boiling point, Garrison kept the South on the defensive. The less secure southerners felt, the more they were tempted into clumsy overreactions like the gag rule.

Women's Rights

The position of American women in the 1830s contained many contradictions. Women could not vote. If married, they had no right to own property (even inherited property) or to retain their own earnings. Yet the spread of reform movements provided women with unprecedented opportunities for public activity without challenging the prevailing belief that their proper sphere was the home. By suppressing liquor, for example, women could claim that they were transforming wretched homes into nurseries of happiness.

The argument that women were natural guardians of the family was double-edged. It justified reform activities on behalf of the family, but it undercut women's demands for legal equality. Let women attend to their sphere, the counterargument ran, and leave politics and finance to men. So deeply ingrained was sexual inequality, indeed, that most feminists did not start out intending to attack it. Instead, their experiences in other reform movements, notably abolition, led them to the issue of women's rights.

Among the early women's rights advocates who started their reform careers as abolitionists were the Grimké sisters, the Philadelphia Quaker Lucretia Mott, Lucy Stone, and Abby Kelley. Like abolition, the cause of women's rights revolved around the conviction that differences of race and gender were unimportant and incidental. "Men and women," Sarah Grimké wrote, "are CREATED EQUAL! They are both moral and accountable beings, and whatever is *right* for man to do, is *right* for woman." The most articulate and aggressive advocates of woman's rights, moreover, tended to gravitate to William Lloyd Garrison rather than to more moderate abolitionists. Garrison, himself a vigorous feminist, repeatedly stressed the peculiar degradation of women under slavery. The early issues of *The Liberator* contained a "Ladies' Department" headed by a picture of a kneeling slave woman imploring, "Am I Not a Woman and a Sister?" It was common knowledge that slave women were vulnerable to the sexual demands of white masters. Garrison denounced the South as a vast brothel and described slave women as "treated with more indelicacy and cruelty than cattle."

While their involvement in abolition aroused advocates of women's rights, the discrimination that they encountered within the abolition movement infuriated them and impelled them to make women's rights a separate cause. In the 1840s Lucy Stone became the first abolitionist to lecture solely on women's rights. When Lucretia Mott and other American women tried to be seated at the World's Anti-Slavery Convention in London in 1840, they were relegated to a screened-off section. The incident made a sharp impression not only on Mott but on Elizabeth Cady Stanton, who had elected to accompany her abolitionist husband to the meeting as a honeymoon trip. In 1848 Mott and Stanton organized a women's rights convention at Seneca Falls, New York, that proclaimed a Declaration of Sentiments. Modeled on the Declaration of Independence, the Seneca Falls Declaration began

Elizabeth Cady Stanton
(far left) **and Lucretia Mott**

Most newspapers ridiculed the Seneca Falls convention that Stanton and Mott organized to advance women's rights. Over three hundred people attended.

with the assertion that "all men and women are created equal." The convention passed twelve resolutions, and only one, a call for the right of women to vote, failed to pass unanimously; but it did pass. Ironically, after the Civil War, the call for woman suffrage became the main demand of women's rights advocates for the rest of the century.

Although its crusaders were resourceful and energetic, women's rights had less impact than most other reforms. Temperance and school reform were far more popular, and abolitionism created more commotion. Women would not secure the right to vote throughout the nation until 1920, fifty-five years after the Thirteenth Amendment would abolish slavery. One reason for the relatively slow advance of women's rights was that piecemeal gains —such as married women's securing the right to own property in several southern states by the late 1830s—satisfied many women. The cause of women's rights also suffered from a close association with abolitionism, which was unpopular. In addition, the advance of feminism was slowed by the competition that it faced from the alternative ideal of domesticity. By sanctioning activities in reforms such as temperance and education, the cult of domesticity provided many women with worthwhile pursuits beyond the family. In this way, it blunted the edge of female demands for full equality.

Penitentiaries and Asylums

Reform efforts took shape during the 1820s to combat poverty, crime, and insanity by establish-ing highly regimented institutions, themselves products of striking new assumptions about the causes of deviancy.

In the colonial era, Americans had viewed poverty as neither the fault of its victims nor a sign of a defective social order. Rather, poverty was seen as a permanent condition of society, ordained by God to test Christians' humility and charity. Men and women thought of crime, too, as an enduring feature of society. Faced with punishment, individual criminals might mend their ways, but new lawbreakers would take their place. So ingrained were the defects of human nature that some would always choose the way of crime.

Several developments undermined these assumptions during the first half of the nineteenth century. Not only were poverty and crime rising, but in the swiftly growing cities, each was more visible than in the past. Alarmed legislators launched investigations into the causes of both indigence and crime, from which they concluded that deviant behavior often resulted from exposure to drunken fathers and broken homes. The failure of parental discipline, not the will of God or the wickedness of human nature, lay at the root of evil.

Few Americans would have reached these conclusions (or even undertaken the investigations that led to them) had it not been for their growing belief that the moral qualities of the individual were changeable rather than fixed. Both religious revivalists and reformers increasingly came to think that human nature could be altered by the right combination of moral influences. Most grasped the optimistic implications. "The study of the *causes* of crime," William Ellery Channing concluded, "may lead us to its *cure*."

To cure crime, reformers created substitutes for parental discipline, most notably the penitentiary. Penitentiaries were prisons marked by an unprecedented degree of order and discipline. Of course, colonial Americans had incarcerated criminal offenders, but jails had been used mainly to hold prisoners awaiting trial or to lock up debtors. For much of the eighteenth century, the threat of the gallows rather than of imprisonment had deterred wrongdoers. In contrast, nineteenth-century reformers believed that rightly managed, penitentiaries would bring about the sincere reformation of offenders.

To purge offenders' violent habits, reformers usually insisted on solitary confinement. Between 1819 and 1825, New York built penitentiaries at Auburn and Ossining (Sing Sing), in which prisoners were confined by night in small, windowless cells. By day they could work together but never speak and rarely even look at each other. Some reformers criticized this "Auburn system" for allowing too much contact and preferred the rival "Pennsylvania system," in which each prisoner spent all of his or her time in a single cell (each with a walled courtyard for exercise) and received no news or visits from the outside.

Antebellum America also witnessed a remarkable transformation in the treatment of poor people. The prevailing colonial practice of offering relief to the poor by supporting them in a household ("outdoor relief") gradually gave way to the construction of almshouses for the infirm poor and workhouses for the able-bodied poor ("indoor relief"). The argument for indoor relief was much the same as the argument for penitentiaries: plucking the poor from their demoralizing surroundings and exposing them to a highly regimented institution could change them into virtuous, productive citizens. However lofty the motives behind workhouses and almshouses, the results were often abysmal. In 1833 a legislative committee found that the inmates of the Boston House of Industry were packed seven to a room and included unwed mothers, the sick, and the insane as well as the poor.

As for insane people, those living in a work-

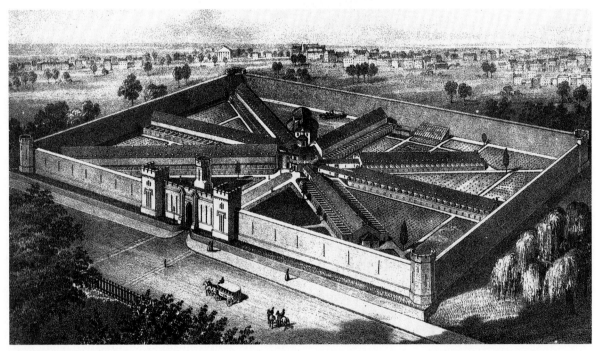

The Eastern Penitentiary *Built in Pennsylvania in 1820, this prison, in its geometrically precise layout, reflected prison reformers' concern with total control.*

house such as the Boston House of Industry were relatively well off, for many experienced even worse treatment by confinement in prisons. In 1841 an idealistic Unitarian schoolteacher, Dorothea Dix, was teaching a Sunday school class in a jail in East Cambridge, Massachusetts, and discovered there insane people kept in an unheated room. Dix pursued her investigation and visited jails and almshouses throughout the state. In 1843 she presented a memorial to the state legislature, which described the insane confined "in *cages, closets, cellars, stalls, pens! Chained, naked, beaten with rods, and lashed into obedience.*" With the support of Horace Mann and the Boston reformer Samuel G. Howe, she encouraged legislatures to build insane asylums, and by the time of the Civil War, twenty-eight states, four cities, and the federal government had constructed public mental institutions.

Penitentiaries, workhouses, and insane asylums all reflected the same optimistic belief that deviancy could be erased by resettling deviants in the right environment. But what was the "right" environment? In some aspects, the answer was clearcut. Heated rooms were better than frigid ones, and sober parents preferable to drunkards. But reformers demanded much more than warm rooms and responsible parents. Reformers were convinced that the unfettered freedom and individualism of American society were themselves defects in the environment and that the poor, criminal, and insane needed extraordinary regimentation if they were to change. Prison inmates were to march around in lock step; in workhouses the poor, treated much like prisoners, were often forbidden to leave or receive visitors without permission. The idealism behind such institutions was genuine, but later generations would question reformers' underlying assumptions.

Utopian Communities

The belief that individuals could live perfectly, which tinged most antebellum reform movements, took its most extreme form in the experimental societies or "utopian" communities that flourished in these years. Although varying widely in their philosophies and arrangements, utopian communities had some common features. Their founders were intellectuals who designed their communities as alternatives to the prevailing competitive economy and as models whose success would inspire imitation. Unlike the Shakers and the Mormons, the utopians did not claim to have visions of God or visits from angels. Nor did they burn their bridges to society.

American interest in utopian communities first spurted during the 1820s. In 1825 British industrialist and philanthropist Robert Owen founded the New Harmony community in Indiana. Owen had already acquired a formidable reputation (and a fortune) from his management of cotton mills at New Lanark, Scotland. His innovations at New Lanark had substantially improved his workers' educational opportunities and living conditions and left him convinced that similar changes could transform the lives of working people everywhere. He saw the problem of the early industrial age as social rather than political. The form of government (whether republican, aristocratic, or monarchical) mattered less than the arrangement of work and living conditions. If social arrangements could be perfected, all vice and misery would disappear; human character was formed, "without exception," by people's surroundings or environment. The key to perfecting social arrangements lay, in turn, in the creation of small, planned communities—"Villages of Unity and Mutual Cooperation," each to contain a perfect balance of occupational, religious, and political groups.

Lured to the United States by cheap land and by Americans' receptivity to experiments, Owen confidently predicted that by 1827 the northern states would embrace the principles embodied in New Harmony. Unfortunately, by 1827 there was little left to embrace, for the community had quickly fallen apart. New Harmony had attracted more than its share of idlers and fanatics, and Owen had not always helped matters. He had spent too much time on the road publicizing the community and not enough time managing it. He had clashed with clergymen, who still believed that Original Sin, not environment, shaped human character. Yet Owenism survived the wreckage of New Harmony. The ideas that the human character was formed by environment and that cooperation was superior to competition had a potent impact on urban workers for the next half-century. Owen's ideas, for example, impelled workingmen's leaders to support educational reform during the late 1820s.

In the early 1830s, the utopian impulse weakened, only to revive amid the economic chaos of the late 1830s and 1840s. Appalled by the misery that came with economic depression, small bands of idealists gathered anew in experimental communities whose names—Hopedale, Fruitlands, Brook Farm—suggested idyllic retreats. Their founders' visions were fired by intense but unconventional forms of Christianity. Adin Ballou, a Universalist minister who founded Hopedale, near Milford, Massachusetts, described it as a "miniature Christian republic." Brook Farm, near Boston, was mainly the creation of a group of religious philosophers called transcendentalists. Most transcendentalists, including Ralph Waldo Emerson and George Ripley, had started as Unitarians but sought to revitalize Unitarianism—and indeed, all denominations—by proclaiming the infinite spiritual capacities of ordinary men and women.

Like other utopias, Brook Farm was both a retreat and a model. Convinced that the competitive commercial life of the cities was unnatural, philosophers welcomed the opportunity to engage in elevated discussions after a day perspiring in the cabbage patch. Although Brook Farm never had more than a hundred residents, it attracted several renowned writers. Emerson visited it, and novelist Nathaniel Hawthorne lived there for a period; Brook Farm's literary magazine, *The Dial,* became a forum for transcendentalist ideas about philosophy, art, and literature (also see Chapter 11). The utopians at Brook Farm also tried out the scheme of social organization devised by the French utopian Charles Fourier. Fourier's ideas, which resembled Owen's, called for dividing society into small cooperative units called phalanxes. In the words of one historian, Fourierism "offered a rigid, almost regimented plan designed to free people to be what nature meant them to be." Fourierism caught on as far west as Wisconsin and Iowa; at least twenty-eight Fourierist communities sprang up between 1841 and 1858.

Few utopias enjoyed success to match their ambition. Brook Farm disbanded in 1849; Hopedale, in 1853. In general, utopian communities were less durable and attracted fewer people than religious communities such as those of the Shakers and Mormons. In contrast to the religious communitarians, the utopians kept open their avenues to society and moved back and forth between their communities and antislavery or women's rights conventions. Utopians neither sought nor attained the kind of grip on the allegiance of their members held by a Mother Ann Lee or a Joseph Smith.

Oneida

A notable exception to this generalization—a reform community that was both durable and exclusive—was the Oneida community in New York State. Started by Yale graduate John Humphrey Noyes in 1847, Oneida lasted until 1881. A friend of many reformers, Noyes in 1834 took Charles G. Finney's idea of perfectionism to a logical extreme by announcing that he had achieved perfection and was henceforth incapable of sinning. By 1837 Noyes had decided that those who could not sin had no need for exclusive institutions like marriage. Within a few years, he put "communism in love" to practical effect by exchanging wives with one of his followers.

To ordinary minds, Noyes was simply an adulterer; indeed, one reason why he fled to Oneida was to avoid prosecution for adultery. But Noyes preferred to call his doctrine "complex marriage"; a man or woman who had achieved perfection could have sexual intercourse with any number of perfected partners. Despite appearances, Noyes did not view complex marriage as a way to loosen sexual standards. Rather, he created elaborate rules to restrict the occasions of intercourse. The general idea was for the most spiritually advanced members of the community to father the most children. Appropriately, "Father" Noyes fathered more than anyone else.

Noyes's ideas about sex reflected his belief that any exclusive attachment between husband and wife worked against the interests of women by burdening them with excessive numbers of children and with "kitchen slavery." By establishing rules to govern intercourse, he hoped to reduce the number of children. Other arrangements at Oneida also evidenced Noyes's commitment to greater equality for women. Not only were women given a voice in decisions that affected the community, but they were relieved of much household drudgery by Noyes's decree that Oneidans eat only one formal meal a day (breakfast). Even child rearing became a communal, rather than exclusively maternal, responsibility at Oneida. As soon as children were able to walk, they were placed in a communal nursery.

Oneida's significance went beyond complex marriage. Noyes was an abolitionist. By the 1850s, when southerners thought about abolitionists, they thought of Noyes as well as Garrison. To defenders of slavery, the North seemed in the grip of licentious crackpots whose calls for the abolition of slavery were only the first step in a barbaric restructuring of all social relationships.

Conclusion

During the 1820s and 1830s, American society burst beyond its traditional physical and intellectual boundaries. Everywhere the old leadership provided by the Revolutionary generation gave way to new leaders born after 1775. Surrounded by weak foreign neighbors and at peace with the great powers of Europe, Americans, without much restraint from traditional or external threats, grappled with the implications of a changing society.

Political parties, religious revivals, and reform movements responded to social change in ways that were novel and inventive but never uniform. By reducing the innumerable interests and opinions that composed American society to two alternatives—the Democrats and the Whigs—the second party system gave direction to the conflicts that were created by economic and social change. Those excluded from politics or dismayed by the compromises into which politicians routinely entered turned to the churches and to reform movements as vehicles for change. Yet religion and reform were not simply alternatives to politics, for each intersected politics at scores of points. The closer one drew to 1840, the greater were the number of intersections. Temperance advocates began to demand legal prohibition of liquor; some abolitionists turned to the Liberty party; some feminists demanded the vote; utopians became political targets. Politics became a medium that even those antagonistic to politics had to understand.

CHRONOLOGY

1800– 1801 Great Kentucky Revival.

1817 American Colonization Society founded.

1824 John Quincy Adams elected president by the House of Representatives.

1826 American Temperance Society organized.

1828 Andrew Jackson elected president.
Congress passes the "Tariff of Abominations."
John Calhoun anonymously writes *South Carolina Exposition and Protest.*

1830 Jackson's Maysville Road Bill veto.
Indian Removal Act.

1830– 1831 Charles G. Finney's Rochester revival.

1831 William Lloyd Garrison starts *The Liberator.*

1832 Jackson vetoes recharter of the Bank of the United States.

Jackson reelected president.

South Carolina Nullification Proclamation.

1833 Force Bill.

Compromise Tariff.

American Anti-Slavery Society founded.

South Carolina nullifies the Force Bill.

1834 Whig party organized.

1836 Congress imposes the gag rule.

Deposition Act.

Specie Circular.

Martin Van Buren elected president.

1837 Horace Mann becomes secretary of the Massachusetts Board of Education.

Economic depression sets in.

Murder of Elijah Lovejoy by proslavery mob.

Grimké sisters set out on lecture tour of New England.

1838 Garrison's New England Non-Resistance Society founded.

Publication of Sarah Grimké's *Letters on the Condition of Women* and Angelina Grimké's *Letters to Catharine E. Beecher.*

1839 Depression deepens as the Bank of the United States fails.

1840 Independent Treasury Act passed.

William Henry Harrison elected president.

First Washington Temperance Society started.

1841 Dorothea Dix begins exposé of prison conditions.

Brook Farm Community founded.

1848 Seneca Falls Convention.

For Further Reading

Lee Benson, *The Concept of Jacksonian Democracy: New York as a Test Case* (1961). A major revisionist interpretation of the period.

William W. Freehling, *Prelude to Civil War* (1966). A major study of the nullification crisis.

Richard P. McCormick, *The Second American Party System: Party Formation in the Jacksonian Era* (1966). An influential work stressing the role of political leaders in shaping the second party system.

Edward Pessen, *Jacksonian America: Society, Personality, and Politics* (rev. ed., 1979). A comprehensive interpretation of the period that emphasizes the lack of real democracy in American society and politics.

Arthur M. Schlesinger, Jr., *The Age of Jackson* (1945). A classic study, now dated in some of its interpretations but still highly readable.

Fred Somkin, *Unquiet Eagle: Memory and Desire in the Idea of American Freedom, 1815–1860* (1967). A penetrating study of American political values.

Alice F. Tyler, *Freedom's Ferment* (1944). A comprehensive survey of reform movements.

Ronald G. Walters, *American Reformers, 1815–1860* (1978). An insightful study of nineteenth-century reform, incorporating recent scholarship.

Chilton Williamson, *American Suffrage: From Property to Democracy, 1760–1860* (1960). The standard study of changing requirements for voting.

Additional Bibliography

Political Leaders

Donald B. Cole, *Martin Van Buren and the American Political System* (1984); James C. Curtis, *The Fox at Bay: Martin Van Buren and the Presidency, 1837–1841* (1970); Richard B. Latner, *The Presidency of Andrew Jackson: White House Politics, 1829–1837* (1979); John Niven, *Martin Van Buren and the Romantic Age* (1983); Major L. Wilson, *The Presidency of Martin Van Buren* (1984); C. M. Wiltse, *John C. Calhoun: Nullifier, 1829–1839* (1949).

Political Parties

Jean H. Baker, *Affairs of Party: The Political Culture of Northern Democrats in the Mid-Nineteenth Century* (1983); Ronald P. Formisano, *The Birth of Mass Political Parties, 1827–1861* (1971) and *The Transformation of American Political Culture: Massachusetts Parties, 1790s–1840s* (1983); Daniel W. Howe, *The Political Culture of the American Whigs* (1980); Robert V. Remini,

The Election of Andrew Jackson (1963) and *Andrew Jackson and the Course of American Empire* (1977); Harry L. Watson, *Jacksonian Politics and Community Conflict: The Emergence of the Second American Party System in Cumberland County, North Carolina* (1981); Sean Wilentz, *Chants Democratic: New York City and the Rise of the American Working Class, 1788–1850* (1983).

Banking and the Economy

Bray Hammond, *Banks and Politics in America from the Revolution to the Civil War* (1957); John M. McFaul, *The Politics of Jacksonian Finance* (1972); William G. Shade, *Banks or No Banks: The Money Question in Western Politics* (1972); James Roger Sharp, *The Jacksonians Versus the Banks: Politics in the United States After the Panic of 1837* (1970); Peter Temin, *The Jacksonian Economy* (1965).

Religious Revivals

Sydney E. Ahlstrom, *A Religious History of the American People*, 2 vols. (1975); Leonard J. Arrington, *The Mormon Experience* (1979) and *Brigham Young: American Moses* (1985); John Boles, *The Great Revival, 1787–1805* (1972); Whitney Cross, *The Burned-Over District* (1950); Klaus J. Hansen, *Mormonism and the American Experience* (1981); William G. McLoughlin, *Modern Revivalism* (1959); Donald G. Mathews, *Religion in the Old South* (1977).

Relationships Between Religion and Reform

Gilbert Barnes, *The Anti-Slavery Impulse* (1933); Clifford S. Griffin, *Their Brothers' Keepers: Moral Stewardship in the United States* (1960); Mary Ryan, *Cradle of the Middle Class: The Family in Oneida County, New York, 1790–1865* (1981); Timothy L. Smith, *Revivalism and Social Reform* (1957).

Temperance

Jed Dannenbaum, *Drink and Disorder: Temperance Reform in Cincinnati from the Washingtonian Revival to the WCTU* (1984); Ian Tyrrell, *Sobering Up: From Temperance to Prohibition in Antebellum America* (1979).

Educational Reform

Carl F. Kaestle, *Pillars of the Republic: Common Schools and American Society, 1780–1860* (1983); Carl F. Kaestle and Maris A. Vinovskis, *Education and Social Change in Nineteenth-Century Massachusetts* (1980); Michael B. Katz, *The Irony of Early School Reform* (1968); Stanley K. Schultz, *The Culture Factory: Boston Public Schools 1789–1860* (1973).

Abolitionists

Robert H. Abzug, *Passionate Liberator: Theodore Dwight Weld and the Dilemma of Reform* (1980); David B. Davis, *The Problem of Slavery in the Age of Revolution, 1770–1823* (1975); Lawrence J. Friedman, *Gregarious Saints: Self and Community in American Abolitionism, 1830–1870* (1982); Blanche Glassman Hersh, *The Slavery of Sex: Feminist Abolitionists in America* (1978); Jane A. Pease and William H. Pease, *They Who Would Be Free: Blacks' Search for Freedom, 1830–1861* (1974); Lewis Perry, *Radical Abolitionism: Anarchy and the Government of God in Antislavery Thought* (1973); Benjamin Quarles, *Black Abolitionists* (1969); Leonard L. Richards, *"Gentlemen of Property and Standing": Anti-Abolition Mobs in Jacksonian America* (1970); Ronald G. Walters, *The Antislavery Appeal: American Abolitionists After 1830* (1976); Bertram Wyatt-Brown, *Lewis Tappan and the Evangelical War Against Slavery* (1969).

Women's Rights

Lois Banner, *Elizabeth Cady Stanton* (1980); Barbara J. Berg, *The Remembered Gate — The Woman and the City, 1800–1860* (1978); Carl N. Degler, *At Odds: Women and the Family in America from the Revolution to the Present* (1980); Ellen C. DuBois, *Feminism and Suffrage: The Emergence of an Independent Women's Movement in America, 1848–1869* (1978); Elisabeth Griffith, *In Her Own Right: The Life of Elizabeth Cady Stanton* (1984); Gerda Lerner, *The Grimké Sisters from South Carolina: Rebels Against Slavery* (1967); Keith Melder, *Beginnings of Sisterhood: The American Woman's Rights Movement, 1800–1850* (1977).

Institutional Reformers

Gerald W. Grob, *Mental Institutions in America: Social Policy to 1875* (1973); W. David Lewis, *From Newgate to Dannemora: The Rise of the Penitentiary* (1965); Robert Mennel, *Thorns and Thistles* (1973); David Rothman, *The Discovery of the Asylum* (1971).

Utopian Communities

Arthur E. Bestor, *Backwoods Utopias: The Sectarian and Owenite Phases of Communitarian Utopianism in America, 1663–1829* (1950); Maren Lockwood Carden, *Oneida: Utopian Community to Modern Corporation* (1969); Michael Fellman, *The Unbounded Frame: Freedom and Community in Nineteenth-Century American Utopianism* (1973); J. F. C. Harrison, *Quest for the New Moral World: Robert Owen and the Owenites in Britain and America* (1969).

CHAPTER 10

The Old South and Slavery, 1800–1860

During the winter of 1831–1832, an intense debate over the future of slavery galvanized Virginians. A slave insurrection led by Nat Turner in August 1831 aroused new anxieties, particularly among the nonslaveholding whites in the western part of the state. "What is to be done?" an editorial writer in the *Richmond Enquirer* queried. "Oh my God, I don't know, but something must be done." Plans for a gradual emancipation of slaves, one of them advanced by Thomas Jefferson's grandson, leaped onto the state's political agenda. For a period, opponents of slavery held the initiative and protested against the institution with a fury that would have cheered antislavery northerners. Slavery, according to one Virginian, was "a mildew which has blighted in its course every region it has touched from the creation of the world." In the words of another, slavery "is ruinous to whites; retards improvements; roots out our industrious population; banishes the yeomanry from the country; and deprives the spinner, the weaver, the smith, the shoemaker, and the carpenter of employment and support." In the end, the advocates of emancipation went down to defeat, but only narrowly, and mainly because the state legislature was grossly malapportioned in favor of eastern slaveholders and against western nonslaveholders.

However narrow, the defeat of Virginia's emancipationists at the start of the 1830s marked a point of no return for the region known to history as the Old South. The Old South gradually took shape between the 1790s and 1860. As late as the American Revolution, *south* referred more to a direction than to a place. But by the 1850s, southerners were publishing books with titles like *Sociology for the South* and *Social Relations in Our Southern States* that took for granted the South's separate regional identity. The distinctive feature of the Old South was that it condoned slavery at a time when the institution had come under attack everywhere else in the civilized world. In 1775 slavery had known no sectional boundaries in America. However, by 1800 nearly every northern state had either abolished slavery or adopted a plan for the gradual emancipation of slaves within its borders, and Congress banned the importation of slaves in 1808. Thereafter, opposition to slavery intensified, not only in the United States, but in Europe and South America. Without too much exaggeration, Senator James Buchanan of Pennsylvania proclaimed in 1842: "All Christendom is leagued against the South upon the question of domestic slavery."

Virginians' debate over slavery in 1831–1832 underscored the internal divisions within Virginia and the South as a whole. In every southern state, nonslaveholding farmers, or yeomen, composed a majority of the white population throughout the antebellum period. Further, among the states that would secede and in 1861 form the Confederate States of America, there was a basic distinction between the Upper South (Virginia, North Carolina, Tennessee, and Arkansas) and the Lower, or Deep, South (South Carolina, Georgia, Florida, Alabama, Mississippi, Louisiana, and Texas). Socially and economically, the Upper South relied far less than the Lower South on slavery and on cotton. With varied agricultural economies based on the raising of wheat, tobacco, hemp, vegetables, and livestock, the states of the Upper South bore many resemblances to the free states of the North. Politically, the Upper South approached secession far more reluctantly than the Lower South.

For all of its internal variety, however, the Old South possessed strong bonds of unity that derived from slavery. The defense of slavery gradually united white opinion in the South. After reaching a climax in Virginia in 1831–1832, southern white opposition to slavery steadily weakened, and most whites came to dread the thought of a general emancipation of slaves. Although the Upper South

hesitated about secession in 1861, it withdrew from the Union not because of doubts about slavery but because of doubts as to whether secession would defend slavery. In the final analysis, the Upper and Lower Souths were merely parts of a single Old South, because slavery gave southern society such a distinctive cast. Although reminded by daily contact with whites of the contempt in which their race was held, blacks could do little to escape bondage. Slavery scarred all social relationships in the Old South: between blacks and whites, among whites, and even among blacks. Without slavery there never would have been an Old South.

King Cotton

The traditional cash crops of the South declined in the late eighteenth century. That old standby tobacco, a crop notorious for depleting soil nutrients, depended on foreign markets that were essentially undependable, especially after Independence stripped American trade of British protection. Tidewater Virginia, once the center of tobacco production, had dwindled economically to a shadow of its former self. North Carolina, whose soil had been depleted by tobacco, so languished that contemporaries called it the Rip Van Winkle of the Union. Rice provided the coastal region of South Carolina with a major cash crop, but rice could not be grown inland. Cotton growing was also

confined to seaboard areas. Indeed, in 1790 the South's population was concentrated in states bordering on the Atlantic. Three out of every four southerners lived in Maryland, Virginia, North Carolina, and South Carolina, and one out of every three in Virginia alone.

The contrast between the South of 1790 and that of 1850 was stunning. By 1850 only one out of every seven white southerners lived in Virginia. One out of every three white southerners lived in seven flourishing states (Alabama, Arkansas, Florida, Louisiana, Mississippi, Missouri, and Texas) admitted to the Union after 1800. What had transformed the stagnant South of 1800 into the dynamic

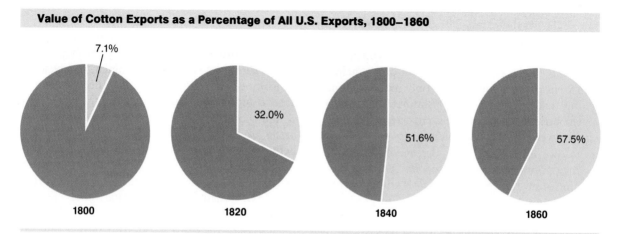

Value of Cotton Exports as a Percentage of All U.S. Exports, 1800–1860

7.1%

32.0%

51.6%

57.5%

1800   1820   1840   1860

By 1840 cotton accounted for more than half of all U.S. exports.

and bustling South of 1850? The answer, in a word, is cotton. The growth of the British textile industry in the late eighteenth century had created a huge demand for cotton and provided a stimulus to the development of the cotton gin. The removal of the Indians (see Chapter 8) opened the way to the expansion of cotton production in new territories. Armed with cotton gins, settlers swept into Alabama and Mississippi after 1815. By 1860 Mississippi had become the leading cotton producer in the nation, and settlers had already pushed farther west, into east Texas. At its peak the cotton belt (or "Cotton Kingdom") stretched from South Carolina, Georgia, and northern Florida in the east through Alabama, Mississippi, central and western Tennessee, and Louisiana, and from there on to Arkansas and Texas.

The Lure of Cotton

To British traveler Basil Hall, it seemed that all southerners could talk about was cotton. "Every flow of wind from the shore wafted off the smell of that useful plant; at every dock or wharf we encountered it in huge piles or pyramids of bales,

and our decks were soon choked with it. All day, and almost all night long, the captain, pilot, crew, and passengers were talking of nothing else." With its warm climate, wet springs and summers, and relatively dry autumns, the Lower South was especially suited to the cultivation of cotton. In contrast to the sugar industry, which thrived in southeastern Louisiana, cotton required neither expensive irrigation canals nor costly machinery. Sugar was a rich man's crop that demanded a considerable capital investment to grow and process. But cotton could be grown profitably on any scale. A cotton farmer did not even need to own a gin; commercial gins would serve him. Nor did a cotton farmer have to own slaves; in 1860, 35 percent to 50 percent of all farmers in the cotton belt owned no slaves. Cotton was profitable for anyone, even nonslaveholders, to grow; it promised to make poor men prosperous and rich men kings.

Although modest cotton cultivation did not require slaves, large-scale cotton growing and slavery grew together. As the southern slave population nearly doubled between 1810 and 1830, cotton employed three-fourths of all southern slaves. Owning slaves made it possible to harvest vast tracts

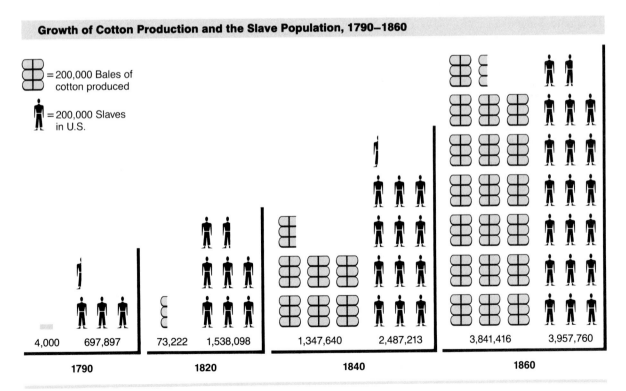

Growth of Cotton Production and the Slave Population, 1790–1860

= 200,000 Bales of cotton produced

= 200,000 Slaves in U.S.

4,000	697,897	73,222	1,538,098	1,347,640	2,487,213	3,841,416	3,957,760

1790	1820	1840	1860

Cotton and slavery rose together in the Old South.

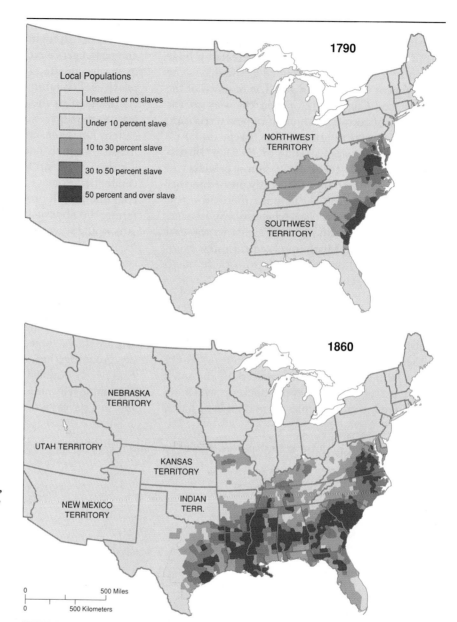

Distribution of Slaves, 1790 and 1860

In 1790 the majority of slaves resided along the southeastern seaboard. By 1860, however, slavery had spread throughout the South, and slaves were most heavily concentrated in the Deep South states.

SOURCE: Reprinted with permission of Alfred A. Knopf, Inc. from *Ordeal by Fire: The Civil War and Reconstruction* by James M. McPherson. Copyright 1982 by Alfred A. Knopf, Inc.

of cotton speedily, a crucial advantage because a sudden rainstorm at harvest time could pelt cotton to the ground and soil it. Slaveholding also enabled planters to increase their cotton acreage and hence their profits.

An added advantage of cotton lay in its compatibility with the production of corn. Corn could be planted earlier or later than cotton and harvested before or after. Since the cost of owning a slave was the same whether or not he or she was working, corn production enabled slaveholders to utilize slave labor when slaves were not employed on cotton. Nonslaveholding cotton growers also found it convenient to raise corn, and by 1860 the acreage devoted to corn in the Old South actually *exceeded* that devoted to cotton. Corn fed both families and the livestock that flourished in the South (in 1860 the region had two-thirds of the nation's hogs). From an economic standpoint, corn and cotton gave the South the best of both worlds. Fed by intense demands in Britain and New England, the price of cotton remained high, with the result that money flowed into the South. Because of southern self-sufficiency in growing corn and in raising hogs that thrived on the corn, money was not drained out of the region to pay for food produced in the North. In 1860 the twelve wealthiest counties in the United States were all in the South.

Ties Between the Lower and Upper South

Sugar and cotton were the main cash crops in the Lower South. The agriculture of the Upper South, founded on tobacco, hemp, wheat, and vegetables, depended far less than that of the Lower South on a few great cash crops. Yet the Upper South identified with the Lower South rather than with the agricultural regions of the free states. The reasons were social, political, and even psychological. Many settlers in states like Alabama and Mississippi had

come from Upper South states like Virginia and North Carolina. All white southerners benefited from the three-fifths clause of the Constitution, which enabled them to count slaves as a basis for congressional representation. All southerners were stung by abolitionists' criticisms of slavery, drawing no distinction between the Upper and Lower South. Importantly, too, economic ties linked the Upper and Lower South. The profitability of cotton and sugar in the Lower South increased the value of slaves throughout the South. Between 1790 and 1860, perhaps a million or more slaves were herded across state lines in the Old South. Roughly three-fourths of these slaves moved with their masters, while the remainder were sold as individuals. The sale of slaves from states with declining or stagnant plantation economies (Maryland, Virginia, and South Carolina) to those with booming economies (Alabama, Mississippi, Louisiana, Arkansas, and Texas) became a huge business. Arguing against a proposal for the gradual emancipation of slaves, Professor Thomas R. Dew of Virginia's College of William and Mary stated in

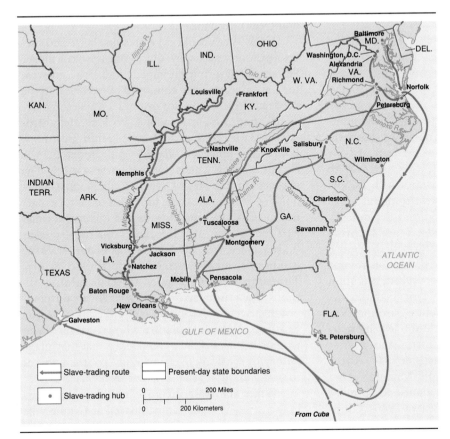

The Internal Slave Trade, 1810–1860

An internal slave trade developed after the slave trade with Africa ended in 1808. With the growth of cotton production, farmers in the Upper South found it profitable to sell their slaves to planters in the Lower South.

1832, "Virginia is, in fact, a *negro* raising State for other States; she produces enough for her own supply, and six thousand a year for sale." Without the sale of its slaves, Dew concluded, "Virginia will be a desert."

The North and South Diverge: Economic Patterns

The South had emerged from a slump in the last quarter of the eighteenth century to become a region of dynamic change between 1800 and 1860. But it had changed in ways that only widened the distance between it and the North. At a time when the North was experiencing rapid urbanization, the South remained predominantly rural. In 1820 the proportion of the southern population living in urban areas was about half that of New England and the mid-Atlantic states; by 1860 the proportion had dropped to a third.

One reason for the rural character of the South was that it contained very little industry. Although a third of the population of the United States in 1850 lived there, the South accounted for only 10 percent of the nation's manufacturing. The industrial output of the entire South in 1850 was less than that of New Hampshire and only one-third that of Massachusetts. Between 1840 and 1860, the South's share of the capital invested in American manufacturing actually *declined*, from 20 percent to 16 percent.

Yet the South had advocates of both industrialization and factories. A minority of southerners, among them editor J. D. B. De Bow of New Orleans, applauded industrialization as a way to revive the economies of older states such as Virginia and South Carolina, to retard migration to the Southwest, to reduce the South's dependency on northern manufactured products, and by proving that slavery had not transformed the South into a backwater, to quiet "the slanderous tongue of northern fanatics." Pleas for industrialization met with some success as a few large manufacturing companies took root. In South Carolina William Gregg, a prosperous Charleston jewelry merchant, zealously advocated industrialization after touring New England's textile mills in 1844. A year later, he started the Graniteville Manufacturing Company, which owned nine thousand spindles and three hundred looms by the late 1840s. Graniteville became a company town, with lumber mills,

gristmills, and a machine shop as well as textile mills. In Richmond Joseph Reid Anderson guided the Tredegar Iron Works to success. By 1860 the Tredegar Works ranked fourth among the nation's largest producers of iron products, and during the Civil War, it contributed greatly to the Confederate cause. Farther southwest, Daniel Pratt constructed an industrial village near Montgomery, Alabama, in which he produced cotton textiles and ginned raw cotton.

These striking examples of industrial success in the Old South, however, do not change the general picture. Industrial output in the South ran somewhat behind that of the West and far behind that of New England and the Middle Atlantic states. Compared to factories in New England, New York, and Pennsylvania, those of the South were small; they produced mainly for nearby markets; and they were much more closely tied to agriculture. The leading northern industries turned hides into tanned leather and leather into shoes, or cotton into threads and threads into suits. In contrast, while the South had some textile and shoe factories, its leading industries were only a step removed from agriculture. They turned grain into flour, corn into meal, and trees into lumber.

If the South could develop some large and successful industries, why did it not develop more? Slavery did not in itself impede industrial growth, for slaves were widely employed in factories. In the Tredegar Iron Works, for example, Anderson overcame opposition from white workers and introduced slaves into skilled rolling-mill positions. Indirectly, however, slavery did undercut the enthusiasm of whites for industrialization. The prospect of industrial slavery troubled most slaveholders. Slaves who were hired out to factory masters in cities like New Orleans and Richmond could pass themselves off as free, and often they acted as if they were free by negotiating better working conditions and by shifting from factory to factory. The same objection applied to small rural workshops. Even rural factories drew slaves off the plantations, where discipline could be more easily enforced. A Virginia planter who rented his slaves to an iron manufacturer complained that they made money by working overtime and "got the habit of roaming about and *taking care of themselves.*"

White laborers, of course, could be employed in factories. William Gregg proved at Graniteville that supposedly unruly southern whites could be

Port and City of New Orleans, *The South's largest city, New Orleans was also the main port of exit for cotton*
by Marie Adrien Persac, 1858 *and Mississippi Valley produce.*

forged into a disciplined labor force. But any effort to introduce extensive industrialization faced a major problem: to raise capital for industrialization, planters would have had to sell their slaves. They had little incentive to do so. Cash crops like cotton and sugar were proven winners, while the benefits of industrialization remained remote and doubtful. Moreover, industrialization threatened to disrupt social relations, a southerner contended, by introducing "filthy, overcrowded, licentious factories" and by attracting antislavery white immigrants to the South. As long as southerners believed that an economy founded on cash crops would remain profitable, they had little reason to leap into the uncertainties of industrialization.

The North and South Diverge: Education in a Cotton Economy

Compared to the antebellum North, the Old South made only meager provisions for public elementary schools. Flurries of enthusiasm for public education periodically swept the South, but without much effect. Southerners flatly rejected the idea of com-

pulsory education, which was gaining ground in the North by the 1850s, and they were reluctant to tax property to support education. The idea of educating slaves in any kind of school became increasingly abhorrent to southern legislatures; indeed, lawmakers made it a crime even to teach slaves to read. Some public aid flowed to state universities and to schools for white paupers, but for most whites, the only available schools were private. As a result, white illiteracy, which had been more extensive in the South than in the North during the eighteenth century, remained high in the South even as it declined in the North during the antebellum period. For example, nearly 60 percent of the North Carolinians who enlisted in the United States Army before the Civil War were illiterate. The comparable proportion for northern enlistees was less than 30 percent.

Various factors help to explain why the South lagged behind the North in the field of public education. Because the Lower South's economy relied so heavily on cotton, state revenues rose and fell with the price of cotton, and so did legislative enthusiasm for education. In addition, the South's low population density made it difficult to provide public schools for all children. The idea of having a public school within walking distance of each child was appealing until one realized just how far each child would have to walk. But a low population density did not stop midwestern states from energetically promoting public education. The most probable reason for the South's failure to develop effective public schools was widespread indifference to the idea.

As was true of southern arguments in favor of industrialization, pro-education proclamations abounded, but these issued from a small segment of the leadership and often fell on deaf ears. Agricultural, self-sufficient, and independent, the middling and poor whites of the South remained unconvinced of the need for public education. They had little dependency on the printed word, few complex commercial transactions, and infrequent dealings with urban people. Even the large planters, some of whom did support public education, had a less intense commitment to it than did northern manufacturers. Where many northern businessmen accepted Horace Mann's argument that public schools would create a more orderly and alert work force, planters had no need for an educated white work force, for they already had a black one that they were determined to keep illiterate lest it acquire through books ideas about freedom.

Cotton and Southern Progress

Because the South diverged so sharply from the North, it is tempting to view the South as backward and lethargic, doomed to be bypassed by its more energetic northern sisters. Increasingly, northerners associated the spread of cities and factories with progress. Finding few cities and factories in the South, they concluded that the region was a stranger to progress as well. A northern journalist wrote of white southerners in the 1850s: "They work little, and that little, badly; they earn little, they sell little; they buy little, and they have little—very little—of the common comforts and consolations of civilized life."

Yet the white South did not lack progressive features. In 1840 per capita income in the white South was only slightly below the national average, and by 1860 it exceeded the national average. While it is true that southerners made few contri-

butions to technology to rival those of northerners, many southerners had a progressive zeal for agricultural improvement. The Virginian Edmund Ruffin, who allegedly touched off the Civil War by firing the first cannon on Fort Sumter in 1861 and committed suicide in despair at the South's defeat in 1865, was an enthusiastic supporter of crop rotation and of the use of fertilizer and an important figure in the history of scientific agriculture.

Rather than viewing the Old South as economically backward, it is better to see it merely as different. Cotton was a wonderful crop, and southerners could hardly be blamed for making it their ruler. "No! You dare not make war upon cotton; no power on earth dares to make war upon it," a senator from South Carolina proclaimed in 1858. "Cotton is king."

Social Relations in the White South

Antislavery northerners often charged that slavery twisted the entire social structure of the South out of shape. By creating a permanent black underclass of bondsmen, they alleged, slavery robbed lower-class whites of the incentive to work, reduced them to shiftless misery, and rendered the South a premodern throwback in an otherwise progressive age.

Stung by northern allegations that slavery turned the white South into a region of rich planters and wretchedly poor common folk, Alabama lawyer Daniel R. Hundley retorted that "the middle classes of the South constitute the greater proportion of her citizens, and are likewise the most useful members of her society" and that even the planters "wear homespun every day and work side by side with their slaves." Turning the tables on his northern antagonists, Hundley contended that the real center of white inequality was the North, where merchants and financiers paraded in fine silks and never soiled their hands with manual labor.

In reality, what makes the white South both difficult and interesting to study is that it was a curious amalgam of aristocratic and democratic, premodern and modern features. Although it contained considerable class inequality, property ownership was widespread. Rich planters occupied seats in state legislatures out of proportion to their numbers in the population, but they did not necessarily get their way, nor did their political agenda always differ from that of other whites. Practices like slaveholding and dueling not only survived but intensified in the Old South at a time when they were dying out elsewhere in the civilized world. Visitors to the South sometimes thought that they were traveling backward in time. "It seems as if everything had stopped growing, and was growing backwards," novelist Harriet Beecher Stowe wrote of the South. Yet like northerners, white southerners were restless, acquisitive, eager to make money, skillful at managing complex commercial enterprises, and when they chose, even capable of becoming successful industrialists.

The Social Groups of the White South

While all agricultural regions of the South contained slaveholders and nonslaveholders, there was considerable diversity within each group. There were slaveholders in every southern state who owned vast estates, magnificent homes, and hundreds of slaves, but most lived more modestly. In 1860 one-quarter of all white families in the South owned slaves. Of these, nearly half owned fewer than five slaves, and nearly three-quarters had fewer than ten slaves. Only 12 percent owned twenty or more slaves, and only 1 percent had a hundred or more. Large slaveholders clearly were a minority within a minority. Nonslaveholders also formed a diverse group. Most were landowners whose farms drew on the labor of family members, but the South also contained nonslaveholding whites who squatted on land in the so-called pine barrens or piney woods and who scratched out a livelihood by raising livestock, hunting and fishing, and planting a few acres of corn, oats, or sweet potatoes.

Despite all the diversity, one might reasonably divide the South's social structure into four main groups—the planters, the small slaveholders, the yeomen (or family farmers), and the people of the pine barrens—although even this classification is a little arbitrary. Historians usually classify as planters those who owned twenty or more slaves, the minimum number considered necessary for specialized plantation agriculture. Yet in any group of twenty slaves, some were likely to be too old and others too young to work. Arguably, a planter needed more than twenty slaves to run a plantation. Similarly, those with fewer than twenty slaves

are usually described as small slaveholders, but an obvious difference separated an individual who owned ten to nineteen slaves and one who owned fewer than five. The former was close to becoming a planter; the latter was only a step removed from the yeomen. A great deal depended on where one lived. In the low country and delta regions of the South, the planters dominated; most small slaveholders in these areas had dealings with the planters and looked to them for leadership. In the hilly upland regions, the yeoman were dominant, and small slaveholders tended to acquire their outlook.

Of course, many lawyers, physicians, merchants, and artisans, who did not fall into any of these four main groups, also made the Old South their home. But because the South was fundamentally rural and agricultural, those outside of agriculture usually identified their interests with one or another of the four agricultural groups. Rural artisans and merchants had innumerable dealings with the yeoman. Urban merchants and lawyers depended on the planters and absorbed their outlook on most issues. (Some of the most articulate defenders of plantation slavery, including Daniel R. Hundley, were trained as lawyers.) Similarly, slave traders relied on the plantation economy for their livelihood. Nathan Bedford Forrest, the uneducated son of a humble Tennessee blacksmith, made a fortune as a slave trader in Natchez, Mississippi. When the Civil War broke out, Forrest enlisted in the Confederate army as a private and rose swiftly to become the South's greatest cavalry general. "That devil Forrest," the Yankees called him. Plantation slavery directed Forrest's allegiances as surely as it did those of planters like Jefferson Davis, the Confederacy's president.

Planters and Plantation Mistresses

With porticoed mansion and fields teeming with slaves, the plantation still stands at the center of the popular image of the Old South. This romanticized view, reinforced by novels and motion pictures like *Gone with the Wind*, is not entirely misleading, for the South contained plantations that travelers found "superb beyond description." Whether devoted to cotton, tobacco, rice, or sugar, the plantations were characterized by a high degree of division of labor. In the 1850s Bellmead, a tobacco plantation on Virginia's James River, was virtually an agricultural equivalent of a factory village. Its more than one hundred slaves were classified into the domestic staff (butlers, waiters, seamstresses, laundresses, maids, and gardeners), the pasture staff (shepherds, cowherds, and hog drivers), outdoor craftsmen (stonemasons and carpenters), indoor craftsmen (blacksmiths, carpenters, shoemakers, spinners, and weavers), and the field hands. Such a division of labor was inconceivable without an abundance of slaves and land. Wade Hampton's cotton plantation near Columbia, South Carolina, encompassed twenty-four hundred acres of land. With such resources, it is not surprising that large plantations could generate incomes that contemporaries viewed as immense ($20,000—$30,000 a year). Immense is an even better description of the worth (rather than income) of some planters. At his death in 1851, South Carolina's Nathaniel Heyward owned fourteen rice plantations; a cotton plantation; a sawmill and pine land; horses, mules, and cattle worth $20,000; nine residences in Charleston; and furniture valued at $180,000, silver plate at $15,000, old wine at $3,000, and securities and cash amounting to $200,000. This represented the *small* part of his estate. The large portion was his more than two thousand slaves valued at over a million dollars.

During the first flush of settlement in the piedmont and trans-Appalachian South, in the eighteenth century, most well-off planters had been content to live in simple log cabins. In contrast, between 1810 and 1860, elite planters often vied with each other to build stately mansions. Some, like Lyman Hardy of Mississippi, hired architects. Hardy's "Auburn," built in 1812 near Natchez, featured Ionic columns and a portico thirty-one feet long and twelve feet deep. Others copied designs from books like Andrew Jackson Downing's *The Architecture of Country Houses* (1850), which sold sixteen thousand copies between 1850 and 1865. Nor did the popular Greek Revival and Georgian styles exhaust planters' options. In 1859 Joseph A. S. Acklen, who owned several plantations near the junction of the Red and Mississippi rivers, began a country house in the style of a Gothic castle, with a great hall and more than fifty rooms.

However impressive, these were not typical planters. The wealth of most planters, especially in states like Alabama and Mississippi, consisted primarily in the value of their slaves rather than

Lyman Hardy's Auburn, Natchez, Mississippi

Designed by one transplanted Yankee and owned by another, Auburn, with its tall columns topped by lavish Ionic capitals, showed the influence of neoclassical architecture in the Old South.

in such finery as expensive furniture or silver plate. In monetary terms, slaves were worth a great deal, as much as seventeen hundred dollars for a field hand in the 1850s. Planters could convert their wealth into cash for purchasing luxuries only by selling slaves. A planter who sold his slaves ceased to be a planter and relinquished the South's most prestigious social status. Not surprisingly, most planters clung to large-scale slaveholding, even if it meant scrimping on their lifestyles. A northern journalist observed that in the Southwest, men worth millions lived as if they were not worth hundreds.

Planters had to worry constantly about profitability, for the fixed costs of operating plantations—including hiring overseers, housing and feeding slaves, and maintaining cotton gins and other equipment—were considerable. Their drive for profits led planters to search constantly for more and better land, to organize their slaves into specialized work gangs for maximum efficiency, and to make their plantations self-sufficient in food. Their quest for profits also impelled planters to cultivate far-flung commercial connections. Like any commodity, cotton went up and down in price. Sometimes the fluctuations were long-term; more often, the price fluctuated seasonally. In response to these rises and falls, planters assigned their cotton to commercial agents in cities. These agents held the cotton until the price was right and extended credit to enable the planters to pay their bills before the cotton was sold. Thus indebtedness became part of the plantation economy. Persistent debt intensified the planters' quest for more profits to escape from the burden of debt. Planters enjoyed neither repose nor security.

Plantation agriculture placed psychological strains as well as economic burdens on planters and their wives. Frequent moves disrupted circles of friends and relatives, all the more so because migration to the Southwest carried families into progressively less settled, more desolate areas. In 1850 those regions of the South with thriving plantation economies—notably Alabama, Mississippi, and southeastern Louisiana—had only recently emerged from the frontier stage; as late as 1860, the Mississippi Delta contained vast tracts of unsettled land. In the 1850s New York journalist Frederick Law Olmsted was surprised to find planters in the Southwest living in fairly crude homes whose only distinguishing features were whitewashed exteriors and, at times, expensive rugs over roughly planked floors. "Their early frontier life," Olmsted wrote, "seems to have destroyed their capacity to enjoy many of the usual luxuries of civilized life."

For plantation women, migration to the Southwest often amounted to a fall from grace, for many of them had grown up in seaboard elegance, only to find themselves in isolated regions, surrounded by slaves, and bereft of the companion-

Sugar Mill on Bayou Teche, Olivier Plantation, *by Marie Adrien Persac, 1861*

Elite southerners, chickens, and a peacock enjoy a sunny day in this placid scene of a gracious Louisiana sugar plantation.

ship of white social peers. "I am sad tonight, sickness preys on my frame," wrote a bride who moved to Mississippi in 1833. "I am alone and more than 150 miles from any near relative in the wild woods of an Indian nation." At times wives lacked even their husbands' companionship. Plantation agriculture kept men on the road, scouting new land for purchase, supervising outlying plantations, and transacting business in New Orleans or Memphis. "Almost four weeks, and am I to be depriv'd of the pleasure of seeing you for weeks to come, it makes the tears fall fast from my poor Eyes," a lonely wife wrote her distant husband.

Planters and their wives found various ways to cope with their isolation from civilized society. Many spent long periods of time in cities and left the management of plantations to overseers. In 1850 fully one-half the planters in the Mississippi Delta were absentees living in or near Natchez or New Orleans rather than on their plantations. Yet in 1850 only 30 percent of planters with a hundred or more slaves employed white overseers; the majority did not escape from the task of managing their estates. In response, many made plantation life more sociable by engaging in lavish hospitality. But hospitality imposed enormous burdens on plantation wives, who might have to entertain as many as fifteen people for breakfast and attend to the needs of visitors who stayed for days. Indeed, in the plantation economy, wives had even less leisure than their husbands. Aside from raising their own children and caring for guests, plantation mistresses supervised house slaves, made carpets and clothes, looked after outlying buildings like smokehouses and dairies, and planted garden fruits and vegetables. Plantation women were anything but the delicate idlers of legend. In the absence of their husbands or fathers, they frequently kept the plantation accounts. An Alabama politician expected his daughter to report the exact amounts of corn and cotton planted at each of his plantations.

Among the greatest sorrows of some plantation mistresses was the presence of the mulatto children, who stood as daily reminders of their husbands' infidelity. Mary Boykin Chesnut, an astute Charleston woman and famous diarist, commented: "Any lady is ready to tell you who is the father of all the mulatto children in everybody's household but her own. These, she seems

to think, drop from clouds." Insisting on sexual purity for white women, southern gentlemen followed a looser standard for themselves. After the death of his wife, the brother of the famous abolitionist sisters Sarah and Angelina Grimké fathered three mulatto children. The gentlemanly code usually tolerated such transgressions as long as they were not paraded in public—but at times, even if they were. Richard M. Johnson of Kentucky, the man who allegedly killed Tecumseh during the War of 1812, was elected vice president of the United States in 1836 despite having lived openly for years with his black mistress.

The isolation, drudgery, and humiliation that planters' wives experienced turned very few against the system. When the Civil War came, they supported the Confederacy as enthusiastically as any group. However much they might hate living as white islands in a sea of slaves, they recognized no less than their husbands that their wealth and position depended on slavery.

The Small Slaveholders

In 1860, 88 percent of all slaveholders owned fewer than twenty slaves, and most of these possessed fewer than ten slaves. Some slaveowners were not even farmers: one out of every five was employed outside of agriculture, usually as a lawyer, physician, merchant, or artisan.

As a large and extremely diverse group, small slaveholders experienced conflicting loyalties and ambitions. In the upland regions, they absorbed the outlook of yeomen (nonslaveowning farmers), the numerically dominant group. Typically, small upland slaveholders owned only a few slaves and rarely aspired to become large planters. In contrast, in the low country and delta regions, where planters formed the dominant group, small slaveholders often aspired to planter status. In these planter-dominated areas, someone with ten slaves could realistically look forward to the day when he would own thirty. The deltas were thus filled with ambitious and acquisitive individuals who linked success to owning more slaves. Whether one owned ten slaves or fifty, the logic of slaveholding was much the same. The investment in slaves could be justified only by setting them to work on profitable crops. Profitable crops demanded, in turn, more and better land. Much like the planters, the small slaveholder of the low country and delta areas were restless and footloose.

The social structure of the deltas was fluid but not infinitely so. Small slaveholders were usually younger than large slaveholders, and many hoped to become planters in their own right. But as the antebellum period wore on, a clear tendency developed toward the geographical segregation of the small slaveholders from the planters in the cotton belt. Small slaveholders led the initial push into the cotton belt in the 1810s and 1820s, while the large planters, reluctant to risk transporting their hundreds of slaves into the still turbulent new territory, remained in the seaboard South. Gradually, however, the large planters ventured into Alabama and Mississippi. Colonel Thomas Dabney, a planter originally from tidewater Virginia, made several scouting tours of the Southwest before moving his family and slaves to the region of Vicksburg, Mississippi, where he started a four-thousand-acre plantation. The small slaveholders already on the scene at first resented Dabney's genteel manners and misguided efforts to win friends. He showed up at house raisings to lend a hand, but the hands he lent were not his own, which remained gloved, but those of his slaves. The small slaveholders muttered about transplanted Virginia snobs. Dabney responded to complaints simply by buying up much of the best land in the region. In itself, this was no loss to the small slaveholders. They had been first on the scene, and it was their land that the Dabneys of the South purchased. Dabney and men like him quickly turned the whole region from Vicksburg to Natchez into one of large plantations. The small farmers took the proceeds from the sale of their land, bought more slaves, and moved elsewhere to grow cotton. Small slaveholders gradually transformed the region from Vicksburg to Tuscaloosa, Alabama, into a belt of medium-size farms with a dozen or so slaves on each.

The Yeomen

Nonslaveholding family farmers, or yeomen, composed the largest single group of southern whites. Most were landowners. Landholding yeomen, because they owned no slaves of their own, frequently hired slaves at harvest time to help in the fields. In an area where the land was poor, like eastern Tennessee, the landowning yeomen were typically subsistence farmers, but most grew some crops for the market. Whether they engaged in subsistence or commercial agriculture, they controlled landholdings far more modest than those of the planters—more likely in the range of fifty to two hundred acres than five hundred or more acres. Yeomen could be found anywhere in the South, but they tended to congregate in the upland regions. In the seaboard South, they populated the piedmont region of Georgia, South Carolina, North Carolina, and Virginia; in the Southwest they usually lived in the hilly upcountry, far from the rich alluvial soil of the deltas. A minority of yeomen did not own land. Typically young, these men resided with and worked for landowners to whom they were related.

The leading characteristic of the yeomen was the value that they attached to self-sufficiency. As nonslaveholders, they were not carried along by the same logic that impelled slaveholders to acquire more land and plant more cash crops. Although most yeomen raised cash crops, relative to planters, they devoted a higher proportion of their acreage to subsistence crops like corn, sweet potatoes, and oats than to cash crops. The ideal of the planters was profit with modest self-sufficiency; that of the yeomen, self-sufficiency with modest profit.

Yeomen dwelling in the low country and delta regions dominated by planters were often dismissed as "poor white trash." But in the upland areas, where they constituted the dominant group, the yeomen were highly respectable. There they coexisted peacefully with the slaveholders, who typically owned only a few slaves (large planters were rare in the upland areas). Both the small slaveholders and the yeomen were essentially family farmers. With or without the aid of a few slaves, fathers and sons cleared the land and plowed, planted, and hoed the fields. Wives and daughters planted and tended vegetable gardens, helped at harvest, occasionally cared for livestock, cooked, and made clothes for the family.

In contrast to the far-flung commercial transactions of the planters, who depended on distant commercial agents to market their crops, the economic transactions of yeomen usually occurred within the neighborhood of their farms. Yeomen

Corn Husking, *by Eastman Johnson, 1860*

Grown by the South's nonslaveholding yeomen, corn rather than cotton was the region's principal crop. Yeomen ate corn in various forms, including bread and grits, and fed corn to their livestock, which provided them with meat and milk.

often exchanged their cotton, wheat, or tobacco for goods and services from local artisans and merchants. In some areas they sold their surplus corn to the herdsmen and drovers who made a living in the South's upland regions by specializing in the raising of hogs. Along the French Broad River in eastern Tennessee, some twenty thousand to thirty thousand hogs were fattened for market each year; at peak season, a traveler would see a thousand hogs a mile. When driven to market, the hogs were quartered at night in huge stock stands, veritable hog "hotels," and fed with corn supplied by the local yeomen.

The People of the Pine Barrens

One of the most controversial groups in the Old South comprised independent whites of the wooded "pine barrens." In a region marked by slaveholding, widespread landownership, and agriculture, these people stood out as deviants. Composing about 10 percent of southern whites, they were neither slaveholders nor (as a rule) landowners nor primarily farmers. Rather, they typically put up crude cabins, cleared a few acres of surrounding land (on which they usually squatted), planted some corn

between tree stumps, and grazed hogs and cattle in the woods. Their simple diet—cornmeal and pork supplemented by fish and game—did not differ much from that of the yeomen or slaves. But their way of life was different. They did not raise cash crops, nor did they engage in the daily routine of orderly work that marked family farmers. With their ramshackle houses and handful of stump-strewn acres, they appeared to be lazy and shiftless.

Antislavery northerners cited the people of the pine barrens as proof that slavery degraded nonslaveholding whites. A southern defender of slavery, Daniel R. Hundley, summarized the antislavery argument: "Look at the Poor Whites of the South, . . . and behold the fruits of slavery." Then he attacked the argument. The pine barrens folk were poor, he conceded, but unlike the paupers of the northern cities, they could fend for themselves. Hundley's contention was well founded. The people of the pine barrens acquired a degree of self-sufficiency to which the South's climate and customs contributed. Mild winters made it possible to graze livestock in the woods for much of the year. Furthermore, the South retained the legal tradition (rapidly being dismantled in the antebellum North) of treating unfenced and unimproved land as available for public use. Despite complaints, the people of the pine barrens (along with many yeomen) hunted on land belonging to others as long as it was neither enclosed nor improved.

The economic independence of the pine barrens dwellers shaped their attitudes toward work. The men were reluctant to hire themselves out as farm laborers, and even when they did, they refused to perform "slave" tasks like caring for cattle and fetching wood and water. The women had similar attitudes. They might sew or quilt on hire, but they refused to become servants.

It is misleading to think of these people as victimized or oppressed. Many lived in the pine barrens out of choice. The grandson of a farmer who had migrated from Emanuel County, Georgia, to the Mississippi pine barrens explained his grandfather's motives in these words: "The truth is it looks like Emanuel County. The turpentine smell, the moan of the winds through the pine trees, and nobody within fifty miles of him, [were] too captivating . . . to be resisted, and he rested there."

Conflict and Consensus in the White South

Planters tangled with yeomen on several issues in the Old South. With their extensive economic dealings and need for credit, planters and their urban commercial allies inclined toward the Whig party, which was generally more sympathetic to banking and economic development. Cherishing their self-sufficiency, and economically independent, the yeomen tended to be Democrats.

The occasions for conflict between these groups were minimal, however, and an underlying political unity reigned in the South. Especially in the Lower South, each of the four main social groups—planters, small slaveholders, yeomen, and pine barrens people—tended to cluster in different regions. The delta areas that planters dominated contained relatively small numbers of yeomen. In other regions small slaveowners, families with ten to fifteen slaves, predominated. In the upland areas far from the deltas, the yeomen congregated. And the people of the pine barrens lived in a world of their own. There was more geographical intermingling of groups in the Upper South than in the Lower, but throughout the South each group attained a degree of independence from the others. With widespread

landownership and relatively few factories, the Old South basically was not a place where whites worked for other whites, and this tended to minimize friction among whites.

In addition, the white South's political structure was sufficiently democratic to prevent any one social group from gaining exclusive control over politics. It is true that in both the Upper and the Lower South, the majority of state legislators were planters. Large planters, those with fifty or more slaves, were represented in legislatures far out of proportion to their numbers in the population. Yet these same planters owed their election to the popular vote. The white South was affected by the same democratic currents that swept northern politics between 1815 and 1860, and the newer states of the South had usually entered the Union with democratic constitutions that included universal white manhood suffrage—the right of all adult white males to vote.

While yeomen often voted for planters, the nonslaveowners did not issue their elected representatives a blank check to govern as they pleased. During the 1830s and 1840s, Whig planters who favored banks faced intense and often successful opposition from Democratic yeomen. These yeomen blamed banks for the Panic of 1837 and pressured southern legislatures to restrict bank operations. On banking issues, nonslaveholders got their way often enough to nurture their belief that they ultimately controlled politics and that slaveholders could not block their goals.

Conflict over Slavery

Nevertheless, there was considerable potential for conflict between the slaveholders and nonslaveholders. The white carpenter who complained in 1849 that "unjust, oppressive, and degrading" competition from slave labor depressed his wages surely had a point. Between 1830 and 1860, slaveholders gained an increasing proportion of the South's wealth while declining as a proportion of its white population. The size of the slaveholding class shrank from 36 percent of the white population in 1831 to 31 percent in 1850 to 25 percent in 1860. A Louisiana editor warned in 1858 that "the present tendency of supply and demand is to concentrate all the slaves in the hands of the few, and thus excite the envy rather than cultivate the sympathy of the people." That same year, the governor of Florida proposed a law guaranteeing to each white person the ownership of at least one slave. Some southerners began to support the idea of Congress's reopening the African slave trade to increase the supply of slaves, bring down their price, and give more whites a stake in the institution.

As the debate over slavery in Virginia during 1831–1832 (see this chapter's introduction) attests, slaveholders had good reasons for uncertainty over the allegiance of nonslaveholders to the "peculiar institution" of slavery. The publication in 1857 of Hinton R. Helper's *The Impending Crisis of the South,* which called upon nonslaveholders to abolish slavery in their own interest, revealed the persistence of white opposition to slavery. On balance, however, slavery did not create profound and lasting divisions between the South's slaveholders and nonslaveholders. Although antagonism to slavery flourished in parts of Virginia up to 1860, proposals for emancipation dropped from the state's political agenda after 1832. In Kentucky, a state with a history of antislavery activity that dated back to the 1790s, calls for emancipation were revived in 1849 in a popular referendum. But the pro-emancipation forces went down to crushing defeat. Thereafter, the continuation of slavery ceased to be a political issue in Kentucky and elsewhere in the South.

The rise and fall of pro-emancipation sentiment in the South raises a key question. Since the majority of white southerners were nonslaveholders, why did they not attack the institution more consistently? To look ahead, why were so many of them to fight ferociously and die bravely during the Civil War in defense of an institution in which they appeared not to have had any real stake? There are various answers to these questions. First, some nonslaveholders hoped to become slaveholders. Second, most simply accepted the racist assumptions upon which slavery rested. Whether slaveholders or nonslaveholders, white southerners dreaded the likelihood that emancipation might encourage "impudent" blacks to entertain ideas of social equality with whites. Blacks might demand the right to sit next to whites in railroad cars and even make advances to white women. "Now suppose they [the slaves] was free," a white southerner told a northern journalist in the 1850s, "you see they'd all think themselves just as good as we; of course they would if they was free. Now just suppose you had a family of children, how would you like to hev a niggar steppin' up to your darter?" Slavery, in short, appealed to whites as a legal, time-honored, and foolproof way to enforce the social subordination of blacks. Finally, no one knew where the slaves, if freed, would go or what they would do. After 1830 a dwindling minority of northerners and southerners still dallied with the idea of colonizing freed blacks in Africa, but that alternative increasingly seemed unrealistic in a society where slaves numbered in the millions. Without colonization, southerners concluded, emancipation would produce a race war. In 1860 Georgia's governor sent a blunt message to his constituents, many of them nonslaveholders: "So soon as the slaves were at liberty thousands of them would leave the cotton and rice fields . . . and make their way to the healthier climate of the mountain region [where] we should have them plundering and stealing, robbing and killing." There was no mistaking the conclusion. Emancipation would not merely deprive slaveholders of their property, it would jeopardize the lives of nonslaveholders.

The Proslavery Argument

As slaveholders and nonslaveholders closed ranks behind slavery, southerners increasingly defended the institution as a positive good rather than as a necessary evil. Between 1830 and 1860, southern intellectuals such as James Henry Hammond, Edmund Ruffin, and William Gilmore Simms of South Carolina and Nathaniel Beverley Tucker, George F. Holmes, and George Fitzhugh of Virginia constructed a theoretical defense of slavery. They contended that slavery was a venerable institution that had flourished in the most refined civilizations. A slave society in ancient Athens, Holmes noted, had produced Plato and Aristotle, and Roman slaveholders had "conquered the world, legislated for all succeeding ages, and laid the broad foundations of modern civilization and modern institutions." In the eyes of these apologists for slavery, the antiquity and universality of the institution proved that inequality was a natural human condition.

Furthermore, they noted, inequality existed in the North as well as the South, with the difference that northern inequality resulted in the exploita-

Old Kentucky Home, *by Eastman Johnson, 1859*

This portrait of banjo-plucking, carefree slaves projected the white South's view of slavery as a benign institution.

tion of the weak, while southern inequality led to the protection of the weak by the strong. Northern mill owners used their "wage slaves" and then discarded them; in contrast, southern masters and slaves were bound together by a "*community* of interests." Southerners portrayed slavery as a costly and inefficient labor system, but one that allowed and even compelled masters to treat slaves well by attending to their health, clothing, and discipline. "You have been chosen," Tucker told students at the College of William and Mary, "as the instrument, in the hand of God for accomplishing the great purpose of his benevolence."

The rise of the proslavery argument coincided with a shift in the position of the southern churches on slavery. During the 1790s and early 1800s, some Protestant ministers had assailed slavery as immoral. By the 1830s, however, most members of the clergy had convinced themselves that slavery was not only compatible with Christianity but also necessary for the proper exercise of the Christian religion. Like the proslavery intellectuals, clergymen contended that slavery provided the opportunity to display Christian responsibility toward one's inferiors, while it helped blacks develop Christian virtues like humility and self-control. With this conclusion solidified, southerners increasingly attacked antislavery evangelicals in the North for disrupting the allegedly superior social arrangement of the South. In 1844 the Methodist Episcopal church split into northern and southern wings. In 1845 Baptists formed a separate Southern Convention. Even earlier, southerners and conservative northerners had combined in 1837 to drive the antislavery New School Presbyterians out of that denomination's main body. All this added up to a profound irony. In 1800 southern evangelicals had been more critical of slavery than southerners as a whole. Yet the evangelicals effectively seceded from national church organizations long before the South seceded from the Union.

Honor and Violence in the Old South

Almost everything about the Old South struck northern visitors as extreme. Although inequality certainly flourished in the North, no group in northern society was as deprived as the slaves. The Irish immigrants who arrived in the North in great waves in the 1840s often owned no property, but unlike the slaves, they were not in themselves a form of property. Not only did northerners find the gap between the races in the South extreme, but individual southerners seemed to run to extremes. One minute they were hospitable and gracious; the next, savagely violent. Abolitionists were not the only ones to view the Old South as a land of extremes. "The Americans of the South," Alexis de Tocqueville asserted, "are brave, comparatively ignorant, hospitable, generous, easy to irritate, violent in their resentments, without industry or the spirit of enterprise."

Violence in the White South

No one who lived in a southern community, a northern journalist noted in the 1850s, could fail to be impressed with "the frequency of fighting with deadly weapons." Throughout the colonial and antebellum periods, violence deeply colored the daily lives of white southerners. In the 1760s a minister described backcountry Virginians "biting one anothers Lips and Noses off, and gowging one another—that is, thrusting out anothers Eyes, and kicking one another on the Cods [genitals], to the Great damage of many a Poor Woman." In the 1840s a New York newspaper described a fight between two raftsmen on the Mississippi that started when one accidentally bumped the other into shallow water. When it was over, one raftsmen was dead; the other boasted, "I can lick a steamboat. My fingernails is related to a sawmill on my mother's side, . . . and the brass buttons on my coat have all been boiled in poison." Gouging out eyes became a specialty of sorts among poor whites. On one occasion, a South Carolina judge entered his court to find a plaintiff, a juror, and two witnesses all missing one eye. Stories of eye gougings and ear bitings lost nothing in the telling and became part of the folklore of the Old South. Mike Fink, a legendary southern fighter and hunter, boasted that he was so mean that in infancy, he refused his mother's milk and cried out for a bottle of whiskey. Yet beneath the folklore lay the reality of violence that gave the Old South a murder rate as much as ten times higher than that of the North.

The Code of Honor and Dueling

At the root of most violence in the white South lay intensified feelings of personal pride that themselves reflected the inescapable presence of slaves. Every day of their lives, white southerners saw slaves who were degraded, insulted, and powerless to resist. This experience had a searing impact on whites, for it encouraged them to react violently to even trivial insults in order to demonstrate that they had nothing in common with slaves. Among gentlemen this exaggerated pride took the form of a code of honor. In this context, honor can best be defined as an extraordinary sensitivity to one's reputation, a belief that one's self-esteem depends on the judgment of others. In the antebellum North, moralists celebrated a rival ideal, character—the quality that enabled an individual to behave in a steady fashion regardless of how others acted toward him or her. A person possessed of character acted out of the promptings of conscience. In contrast, in the honor culture of the Old South, the slightest insult, as long as it was perceived as intentional, could become the basis for a duel (see "A Place in Time").

Formalized by British and French officers during the Revolutionary War, dueling gained a secure niche in the Old South as a means by which gentlemen dealt with affronts to their honor. To outsiders, the incidents that sparked duels seemed so trivial as to be scarcely credible: a casual remark accidentally overheard, a harmless brushing against the side of someone at a public event, even a hostile glance. Yet dueling did not necessarily terminate in violence. Dueling constituted part of a complex code of etiquette that governed relations among gentlemen in the Old South and, like all forms of etiquette, called for a curious sort of self-restraint. Gentlemen viewed dueling as a refined alternative to the random violence of lower-class life. The code of dueling did not dictate that the insulted party leap at his antagonist's throat or draw his pistol at the perceived moment of insult. Rather, he was to remain cool, bide his time, settle on a choice of weapons, and agree to a meeting place. In the interval, negotiations between friends of the parties sought to clear up the "misunderstanding" that had evoked the challenge. In this way, most confrontations ended peaceably rather than on the field of honor at dawn.

Although dueling was as much a way of settling disputes peaceably as of ending them violently, the ritual could easily terminate in a death or maiming. Dueling did not allow the resolution of grievances by the courts, a form of redress that would have guaranteed a peaceful outcome. As a way of settling personal disputes that involved honor, recourse to the law struck many southerners as cowardly and shameless. Andrew Jackson's mother told the future president: "The law affords no remedy that can satisfy the feelings of a true man."

In addition, dueling rested on the assumption that a gentlemen could recognize another gentleman and hence would know when to respond to a challenge. Nothing in the code of dueling compelled a gentleman to duel someone beneath his status, because such a person's opinion of a gentleman hardly mattered. An insolent porter who insulted a gentleman might get a whipping but did not merit a challenge to a duel. Yet it was often difficult to determine who was a gentleman. The Old South teemed with pretentious, would-be gentlemen. A clerk in a country store in Arkansas in the 1850s found it remarkable that ordinary farmers who hung around the store talked of their honor and that the store's proprietor, a German Jew, carried a dueling pistol.

The Southern Evangelicals and White Values

With its emphasis on the personal redress of grievances and its inclination toward violence, the ideal of honor had a potential for conflict with the values preached by the southern evangelical churches, notably the Baptists, Methodists, and Presbyterians. These evangelical denominations were on the rise even before the Great Kentucky Revival of 1800–1801 and continued to grow in the wake of the revival. With forty-eight thousand southern members in 1801, for example, the Methodists reported eighty thousand by 1807. All of the evangelical denominations stressed humility and self-restraint, virtues that stood in contrast to the entire culture of show and display that buttressed the extravagance and violence of the Old South.

Prior to 1830 most southern gentlemen looked down on the evangelicals as uncouth fanatics, and even after 1830 evangelical values scarcely dominated the South's white leadership. But evangelicals gradually shed their image as illiterate backwoods people by founding colleges like Randolph Macon (Methodist, 1830) and Wake Forest (Baptist, 1838) and by exhorting pious women, who composed two-thirds of the membership of evangelical churches, to make every home "a sanctuary, a resting place, a shadow from the heats, turmoils, and conflicts of life, and an effectual barrier against ambition, envy, jealousy, and selfishness." During the 1830s evangelical values and practices like revivalism began to penetrate even the Episcopal church, the denomination long preferred by the gentry.

Southern evangelicals rarely attacked honor as such, but they railed against dueling, brawling, intemperance, and gambling and, in the words of a Georgia woman, the "*Revenge, Ambition, Pride*" that undergirded these practices. By the 1860s the South contained many Christian gentlemen like the bible-quoting Presbyterian general Thomas J. "Stonewall" Jackson, fierce in a righteous war but a sworn opponent of strong drink, the gaming table, and the duel.

Life Under Slavery

Slavery, the institution that lay at the root of the code of honor and other distinctive features of the Old South, has long inspired controversy among historians. Some have portrayed slavery as a benevolent institution in which blacks lived contentedly under kind masters; others, as a cruel and inhuman system that drove slaves into constant rebellion. Neither view is accurate, but both contain a germ of truth. There were kind masters who accepted the view expressed by a Baptist minister in 1854: "Give your servants that which is just and equal, knowing that you also have a Master in heaven." Moreover, some slaves developed genuine affection for their masters. Yet slavery was an inherently oppressive institution that forcefully appropriated the life and labor of one race for the material benefit of another. Despite professions to the contrary by apologists for slavery, the vast majority of slaveholders exploited the labor of blacks to earn a profit. Kind masters might complain about cruel overseers, but the masters hired and paid the overseers to get as much work as possible out of blacks. When the master of one plantation chastised his overseer for "barbarity," the latter replied: "Do you not remember what you told me the time you employed me that [if] I failed to make you good crops I would have to leave?" Indeed, kindness was a double-edged sword, for the benevolent master came to expect grateful affection from his slaves and then interpreted that affection as loyalty to the institution of slavery. In fact, blacks felt little, if any, loyalty to slavery. When northern troops descended upon plantations during the Civil War, masters were dismayed to find many of their most trusted slaves deserting to Union lines.

While the kindness or cruelty of masters made some difference to slaves, the most important

Edgefield District, South Carolina, in the Antebellum Era

*L*ocated on the western edge of South Carolina near the Georgia border, Edgefield District combined features of the aristocratic lowcountry, to which it was linked by the Savannah River, and the yeoman-dominated upland regions of the Old South. Most Edgefield whites were small farmers or agricultural workers. In 1860 a majority did not own any slaves, and a sizable minority had no land. Yet the invention of the cotton gin had attracted wealthy lowcountry planters to Edgefield, and by 1860 the district had become the state's leading cotton producer. These planters formed the nucleus of the district's elite. By 1860 the wealthiest 10 percent of white heads of household in Edgefield controlled 57 percent of the district's real and personal property. Intermarriage strengthened ties within the elite. By the time of the Civil War, the leading families, among them the Butlers, Bonhams, Brookses, Simkinses, and Pickenses, had intermarried.

Black slaves were the basis of upper-crust Edgefield's wealth. By 1860 slaves outnumbered whites by 50 percent in the district. The vast majority of Edgefield's black bondsmen were field slaves. Almost all of those dwelling on the great plantations worked under the "gang" system, by which they were divided into a number of groups, each performing a specified amount of work. (The gang system stood in contrast to the "task" system, in which individual slaves carried out designated chores.) The plantations' "plow gangs" comprised

Pierce Mason Butler

A leading Edgefield politician, Butler was befriended early in his career by John Calhoun, who secured an army commission for him. Joining Calhoun in the early 1830s in support of nullification, Butler was elected governor of South Carolina in 1836. He led the Palmetto regiment in the Mexican War and was killed in action in 1847.

strong young men and occasionally some women, whereas "hoe gangs" generally included elderly slaves and women. A small number of Edgefield's slaves were skilled artisans who did blacksmithing and carpentry on the district's omnipresent farms. Whether field hands or skilled craftsmen, most slaves lived with their families in simple, rude one-room cabins in close proximity to the dwellings of other slaves. An Edgefield black born into slavery in

Francis Wilkinson Pickens

Pickens came to Edgefield to study and practice law. A relative of Calhoun, he favored nullification. Elected governor of South Carolina just before its secession from the Union in 1860, Pickens once said that "before a free people can be dragged into a war, it must be in defense of great national right as well as national honor."

1852 recalled that the slaves "had houses of weatherboards, big enough for [a] chicken coop—man, wife, and chillun [live] dere."

Only one-quarter of Edgefield's whites owned twenty or more of such slaves in 1860. This elite minority accounted for possession of nearly two-thirds of the district's slaves. Using their slaves not only as agrarian workers but as collateral for loans, the great planters agreed with John C. Calhoun's

369a

northern-bred son-in-law Thomas Green Clemson—the owner of the Edgefield plantation called Canebreak—that "slaves are the most valuable property in the South, being the basis of the whole southern fabric." Yet despite the yawning gap between the wealth of the planters and the income of most other whites, class conflict did not convulse antebellum Edgefield's white society, which as a whole was tightly unified. Verbal assaults on "aristocrats" did sweep through the district from time to time, but lawyers (whom the people treated with suspicion because they did not work with their hands) rather than planters bore the brunt of these attacks.

Religion contributed mightily to this harmony reigning within Edgefield's white society. Indeed, religion was at the core of both family life and community life in the district and significantly molded the world view of the people. Although many churches dotted the countryside, so dispersed was Edgefield's population—the district contained only two incorporated towns—that ministers were limited. Thus devout Episcopalian planters and zealous Baptist yeomen farmers often found themselves sitting side by side listening to whatever traveling preacher had happened through their neighborhood. As a further boon to white solidarity, Edgefield's small farmers depended on the plantation lords to gin and market their cotton, and during the harvest they often rented slaves from the great planters. Nonslaveholding yeomen were likelier than small slaveowners to be dissatisfied with their lot in life, and many moved west into the states of Georgia, Alabama, Mississippi, and Louisiana rather than stay and complain about the rich. Nearly 60 percent of Edgefield's white heads of household in 1850 no longer

Trinity Episcopal Church

Well-known local families, among them the Butlers, Brookses, Pickenses, and Wigfalls, were members of this elite Edgefield church.

resided in the district in 1860.

The code of honor further unified the whites. Like southern gentlemen elsewhere, Edgefield's male elite saw affronts to honor behind every bush. Two military officers once fought a duel because one questioned the other's chess moves. Louis Wigfall, an Edgefield planter who later served as a Confederate senator from Texas and who was rumored to be "half drunk all the time," posted signs denouncing as cowards those who refused to accept his innumerable challenges to duels. Yet however much the code of honor set individual against individual, it could unify a region. For example, in 1856 Preston Brooks, a United States congressman from Edgefield, brutally caned Massachusetts senator Charles Sumner on the Senate floor after Sumner had delivered an antislavery oration that

dealt roughly with one of Brooks's relatives. As Representative Brooks later wrote to his constituents, it was not just the honor of a relative that he sought to defend. Rather, he had set himself up as a "sentinel" guarding the honor of every white South Carolinian against the slanderous tongues of northerners. By the mid-1850s growing attitudes like this were demonstrating that the battle lines clearly had been drawn between southerners and northerners. The time seemed to be fast approaching when, as Edgefield newspaper editor Arthur Simkins observed, southern planters' "rich blessings . . . inherited from a virtuous ancestry" would lead them to band together to strongly oppose "mobocratic tendencies in American society" flourishing in the Northeast's "larger cities and more populous manufacturing towns."

determinants of their experiences under slavery depended on such impersonal factors as the kind of agriculture in which they were engaged, whether they resided in rural or urban areas, and whether they lived in the eighteenth or nineteenth century. The experiences of slaves working on cotton plantations in the 1830s differed drastically from those of slaves in 1700, for reasons unrelated to the kindness or brutality of masters.

The Maturing of the Plantation System

Slavery changed significantly between 1700 and 1830. In 1700 the typical slave was a young man in his twenties who had recently arrived aboard a slave ship from Africa or the Caribbean and worked in company with other recent arrivals on isolated small farms. Drawn from different African regions and cultures, few such slaves spoke the same language. Because commercial slave ships contained twice as many men as women, and because slaves were widely scattered, blacks had difficulty finding sexual partners and creating a semblance of family life. Further, as a result of severe malnutrition, black women who had been brought to North America on slave ships bore relatively few children. Thus the slave trade had a devastating effect on natural increase among blacks. Without importations, the number of slaves in North America would have declined between 1710 and 1730.

In contrast, by 1830 the typical North American slave was as likely to be female as male, had been born in America, spoke a form of English that made possible communication with other slaves, and worked in the company of numerous other slaves on a plantation. The key to the change lay in the rise of plantation agriculture in the Chesapeake and South Carolina during the eighteenth century. Plantation slaves had an easier time finding mates than those on the remote farms of the early 1700s. As the ratio between slave men and women fell into balance, marriages occurred with increasing frequency between slaves on the same or nearby plantations. The native-born slave population began to rise after 1730 and soared after 1750. Importations of African slaves gradually declined after 1760, and Congress banned them in 1808.

Work and Discipline of Plantation Slaves

In 1850 the typical slave experience was to work on a large farm or plantation with at least ten fellow bondsmen. That year, almost three-quarters of all slaves were owned by masters with ten or more slaves, and just over one-half lived on units of twenty or more slaves. To understand the daily existence of the typical antebellum slave, then, requires an examination of the work and discipline routines common on large-scale farming operations.

The day of antebellum plantation slaves usually began an hour before sunrise with the sounding of a horn or bell. After a sparse breakfast, slaves marched to the fields. A traveler in Mississippi described a procession of slaves on their way to work. "First came, led by an old driver carrying a whip, forty of the largest and strongest women I ever saw together; they were all in a simple uniform dress of bluish check stuff, the skirts reaching little below the knee; their legs and feet were bare; they carried themselves loftily, each having a hoe over the shoulder, and walking with a free, powerful swing, like *chasseurs* on the march." Then came the plow hands, "thirty strong, mostly men, but few of them women. . . . A lean and vigilant white overseer, on a brisk pony, brought up the rear."

As this account indicates, slave men and women worked side by side in the fields. Female slaves who did not labor in the fields scarcely idled their hours away. A former slave, John Curry, described how his mother milked cows, cared for the children whose mothers worked in the fields, cooked for field hands, did the ironing and washing for her master's household, and took care of her own seven children. Plantations never lacked tasks for slaves of either sex. As former slave Solomon Northup noted, "ploughing, planting, picking cotton, gathering the corn, and pulling and burning stalks, occupies the whole of the four seasons of the year. Drawing and cutting wood, pressing cotton, fattening and killing hogs, are but incidental labors." Regardless of the season, the slave's day stretched from dawn to dusk. Touring the South in the 1850s, Frederick Law Olmsted prided himself on rising early and riding late but added: "I always found the negroes in the field when I first looked out, and generally had to wait for the negroes to come from the field to have my horse fed when I stopped

Black Women and Men on a Trek Home, South Carolina

Much like northern factories, large plantations made it possible to impose discipline and order on their work force. Here black women loaded down with cotton join their men on the march home after a day in the fields.

for the night." When darkness made field work impossible, slaves toted cotton bales to the gin-house, gathered wood for supper fires, and fed the mules. Weary from their labors, they slept in log cabins on wooden planks. "The softest couches in the world," a former bondsmen wryly observed, "are not to be found in the log mansions of a slave."

Although virtually all antebellum Americans worked long hours, no laboring group experienced the same combination of long hours and harsh discipline as slave field hands. Northern factory workers did not have to put up with drivers who, like one described by Olmsted, walked among the slaves with a whip, "which he often cracked at them, sometimes allowing the lash to fall lightly upon their shoulders." The lash did not always fall lightly. The annals of American slavery contain stories of repulsive brutality. Pregnant slave women were sometimes forced to lie in depressions in the ground and endure whipping on their backs, a practice that supposedly protected the fetus while abusing the mother. The disciplining and punishment of slaves was often left to white overseers and

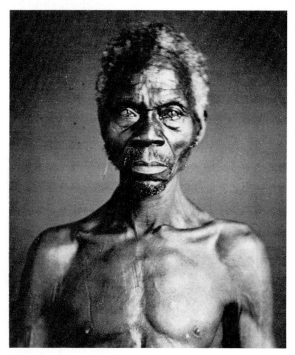

Renty

Renty, a native of the Congo, served on a South Carolina plantation in 1850, the year this daguerreotype was taken.

black drivers rather than to masters. "Dat was de meanest devil dat ever lived on the Lord's green earth," a former Mississippi slave said of his driver. The barbaric discipline meted out by others twinged the conscience of many a master. But even masters who professed Christianity viewed the disciplining of slaves as a priority—indeed, as a Christian duty to ensure the slaves' proper "submissiveness." The black abolitionist Frederick Douglass, once a slave, recalled that his worst master had been converted at a Methodist camp meeting. "If religion had any effect on his character at all," Douglass related, "it made him more cruel and hateful in all his ways."

Despite its relentless, often brutal discipline, plantation agriculture gave a minority of slaves opportunities for advancement, not from slavery to freedom but from unskilled and exhausting field work to semiskilled or skilled indoor work. Some slaves developed skills like blacksmithing and carpentry and learned to operate cotton gins. Others were trained as cooks, butlers, and dining-room attendants. These house slaves became legendary for their arrogant disdain of field hands of poor whites. The legend often distorted the reality, for house slaves were as subject to discipline as field slaves. "I liked the field work better than I did the house work," a female slave recalled. "We could talk and do anything we wanted to, just so we picked the cotton." Yet slave craftsmen and indoor servants occupied higher rungs than field hands on the social ladder of slavery.

The Slave Family

Masters thought of slaves as naturally promiscuous and flattered themselves into thinking that they alone held slave marriages together. Masters did have an incentive to encourage slave marriages in order to bring new slaves into the world and to discourage slaves from running away. Some masters baked wedding cakes for slaves and later arbitrated marital disputes. James Henry Hammond, the governor of South Carolina and a large slaveholder, noted in his diary how he "flogged Joe Goodwyn and ordered him to go back to his wife. Ditto Gabriel and Molly and ordered them to come together. Separated Moses and Anny finally."

Yet this picture of benevolent masters holding together naturally promiscuous slaves is misleading. The keenest challenge to the slave family came not from the slaves themselves but from slavery. The law provided neither recognition of nor protection for the slave family. While some slaveholders were reluctant to break slave marriages by sale, such masters could neither bequeath this reluctance to their heirs nor avoid economic hardships that might force them to sell off slaves. The reality, one historian has calculated, was that on average,

Slave Market in Richmond, Virginia, *by Eyre Crowe, 1852*

The sale of enslaved blacks in antebellum markets such as this made stable family life an impossibility for innumerable southern slaves.

The Hermitage   *These slave quarters were part of the Hermitage plantation in Savannah, Georgia.*

a slave would witness in a lifetime the sale of eleven family members.

Naturally, the commonplace buying and selling of slaves severely disrupted the slaves' attempts to create a stable family life. Poignant testimony to the effects of sale on slave families, and to the desire of slaves to remain near their families, was provided by an advertisement for a runaway slave in North Carolina in 1851. The advertisement described the fugitive as presumed to be "lurking in the neighborhood of E. D. Walker's, at Moore's Creek, who owns most of his relatives, or Nathan Bonham's who owns his mother; or, perhaps, near Fletcher Bell's, at Long Creek, who owns his father." Small wonder that a slave preacher pronounced a slave couple married "until death or *distance* do you part."

Aside from their disruption by sale, slave families experienced separations and degradations from other sources. The marriage of a slave woman gave her no protection against the sexual demands of a master nor, indeed, of any white. The slave children of white masters at times became targets of the wrath of white mistresses. Sarah Wilson, the daughter of a slave and her white master, remembered that as a child, she was "picked on" by her

mistress until the master ordered his wife to let Sarah alone because she "got big, big blood in her." Slave women who worked in the fields usually were separated from their children by day; young sons and daughters often were cared for by the aged or by the mothers of other children. When slave women took husbands from nearby (rather than their own) plantations, the children usually stayed with the mother. Hannah Chapman remembered that her father tried to visit his family under cover of darkness "because he missed us and us longed for him." But if his master found him, "us would track him the nex' day by de blood stains."

Despite enormous obstacles, the relationships within slave families were often intimate and, where possible, long-lasting. In the absence of legal protection, slaves developed their own standards of family morality. A southern white woman observed that slaves "did not consider it wrong for a girl to have a child before she married, but afterwards were extremely severe upon anything like infidelity on her part." When given the opportunity, slaves sought to solemnize their marriages before clergymen. White clergymen who accompanied the Union army into Mississippi and Louisiana in the closing years of the Civil War conducted thousands of marriage rites for slaves who had long viewed themselves as married and who now desired a formal ceremony and registration.

Although slaves tried to solemnize their marriage vows in the same fashion as whites, the slave family did not merely copy the customs of white families. In white families, for example, the parent-child bond overrode all others; slaves, in contrast, emphasized ties between children and their grandparents, uncles, and aunts as well as parents. Such broad kinship ties marked the West African cultures from which many slaves had originally been brought to America, and they were reinforced by the separations between children and one or both parents that routinely occurred under slavery. Frederick Douglass never knew his father and saw his mother infrequently, but he vividly remembered his grandmother, "a good nurse, and a capital hand at making nets for catching shad and herring." In addition, slaves often created "fictive" kin networks; in the absence of uncles and aunts, they simply named friends their uncles, aunts, brothers, or sisters. In effect, slaves invested non-kin relations with symbolic kin functions. In this way, they helped protect themselves against the involuntary disruption of family ties by forced sale and established a broader community of obligation. When plantation slaves greeted each other as "brudder," they were not making a statement about actual kinship but about obligations that they felt for each other. Apologists for slavery liked to argue that a "community of interests" bound masters and slaves together. In truth, the real community of interests was the one that slaves developed among themselves in order to survive.

The Longevity, Diet, and Health of Slaves

In general, slaves in the United States reproduced faster and lived longer than slaves elsewhere in the Western Hemisphere. The evidence comes from a compelling statistic. In 1825, 36 percent of all slaves in the Western Hemisphere lived in the United States, while Brazil accounted for 31 percent. Yet of the 10 million to 12 million African slaves who had been imported to the New World between the fifteenth and nineteenth centuries, only some 550,000 (about 5 percent) had come to North America, while 3.5 million (nearly 33 percent) had been brought to Brazil. Mortality had depleted the slave populations of Brazil and the Caribbean to a far greater extent than in North America.

Several factors account for the different rates between the United States on one hand and Brazil and the Caribbean on the other. First, the sex ratio among slaves equalized more rapidly in North America, encouraging earlier and longer marriages and more children. Second, because growing corn and raising livestock were compatible with cotton cultivation, the Old South produced plenty of food. The normal ration for a slave was a peck of cornmeal and three to four pounds of fatty pork a week. Slaves often supplemented this nutritionally unbalanced diet with vegetables grown in small plots that masters allowed them to farm and with catfish and game. In the barren winter months, slaves ate less than in the summer; in this respect, however, they did not differ much from most whites.

As for disease, slaves had greater immunities to both malaria and yellow fever than did whites, but they suffered more from cholera, dysentery, and diarrhea. In the absence of privies, slaves usually relieved themselves behind bushes; urine and feces washed into the sources of drinking water and caused many diseases. Yet slaves developed some remedies that while commonly ridiculed by whites, were effective against stomach ailments. For example, the slaves' belief that eating white clay would cure dysentery and diarrhea rested on a firm basis, for we know now that kaolin, an ingredient of white clay, is a remedy for these ailments.

Although slave remedies were often more effective than those of white physicians, slaves experienced higher mortality rates than whites. At any age, a slave looked forward to a shorter life than a white, but most strikingly in infancy. Rates of infant mortality for slaves were at least twice those of whites. Between 1850 and 1860, fewer than two out of three black children survived to the age of ten. Whereas the worst mortality occurred on plantations in disease-ridden, low-lying areas, pregnant, overworked field hands often miscarried or gave birth to weakened infants even in healthier regions. Masters allowed pregnant women to rest, but rarely enough. "Labor is conducive to health," a Mississippi planter told a northern journalist; "a healthy woman will rear most children."

Slaves off Plantations

Although plantation agriculture gave some slaves, especially males, opportunities to acquire specialized skills, it imposed a good deal of supervision on them. The greatest opportunities for slaves were reserved for those who worked off plantations and farms, either as laborers in extractive industries like mining and lumbering or as artisans in towns and cities. Because the lucrative cotton growing attracted so many whites onto small farms, a perennial shortage of white labor plagued almost all the nonagricultural sectors of the southern economy. As a consequence, there was a steady demand for slaves to drive wagons, to work as stevedores (ship-cargo handlers) in port cities, to man river barges, and to perform various tasks in mining and lumbering. In 1860 lumbering employed sixteen thousand workers, most of them slaves who cut trees, hauled them to sawmills, and fashioned them into useful lumber. In sawmills black engineers fired and fixed the steam engines that provided power. In iron-ore ranges and ironworks, slaves not only served as laborers but occasionally supervised less skilled white workers. In Richmond and Petersburg in Virginia, some six thousand slaves processed chewing tobacco. In addition, just as mill girls composed the labor force of the booming textile industry in New England, slave women and children worked in the South's infant textile mills.

Behind all of this were some basic, long-standing features of southern society. Even before the rise of cotton, the profitability of southern cash crops like rice and indigo had pulled white labor out of towns and cities and indirectly provided considerable scope for slaves to work as skilled artisans. In the eighteenth century, cities like Charleston and Savannah had a large class of highly skilled slave blacksmiths and carpenters. This tradition continued into the next century and affected both enslaved and free blacks. Whether slave or free, blacks generally found it easier to work in skilled occupations in southern cities than in northern cities during the antebellum period. Not only did tradition open up skilled crafts to blacks, but the South did not attract the same flow of immigrant labor to compete with blacks as did the North.

As a result, despite slavery's stranglehold on black society, some southern blacks enjoyed opportunities in cities that were denied to blacks in northern cities. For the most part, enslaved blacks who worked in factories or in extractive industries like lumbering and mining were not owned by their employers. Rather, they were hired out by their rural masters to urban employers. If conditions in factories or mines deteriorated to the point where slaves grew ill or died, rural masters would refuse

to provide urban employers with more slaves. So it was in the interest of white supervisors to keep conditions of work for slaves off the plantations at a tolerable level. Watching the loading of a steamboat with cotton bales, Frederick Law Olmsted was amazed to see slaves sent to the top of the bank to roll the bales down to Irishmen who stowed them on the ship. Asking the reason for this arrangement, Olmsted was told: "The niggers are worth too much to be risked here; if the Paddies [Irish] are knocked overboard, or get their backs broke, nobody loses anything."

Life on the Margin: Free Blacks in the Old South

When the British were marching on New Orleans late in 1814, Andrew Jackson called upon the free blacks of the city to rally to the American flag. Many did, and they played a significant role in Jackson's victory early in 1815 at the Battle of New Orleans. Indeed, free blacks were more likely than

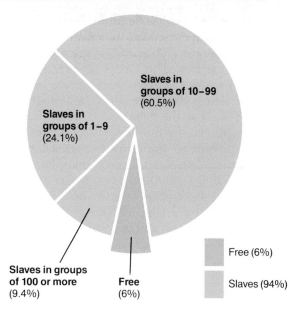

Black Society in the Old South, c. 1860

Slaves in groups of 10–99 (60.5%)

Slaves in groups of 1–9 (24.1%)

Slaves in groups of 100 or more (9.4%)

Free (6%)

Free (6%)

Slaves (94%)

*All states in which slavery was legal in 1860

Slaves greatly outnumbered free blacks in the Old South. Most slaves were owned by masters with ten or more slaves.

SOURCES: *Eighth Census of the United States, 1860: Population by Age, Sex, Race,* and Lewis C. Gray, *History of Agriculture in the Southern United States* (New York: Kelley, 1933).

southern blacks in general to live in cities. In 1860 one-third of the free blacks in the Upper South and more than half in the Lower South were urban.

The relatively specialized economies of the cities provided free people of color with opportunities to become carpenters, coopers (barrel makers), barbers, and even small traders. A visitor to an antebellum southern market would find that most of the meat, fish, vegetables, and fruit had been prepared for sale by free blacks. Urban free blacks formed their own fraternal orders and churches; a church run by free blacks was often the largest house of worship in a southern city. In New Orleans free blacks had their own literary journals and opera. In Natchez a free black barber, William Tiler Johnson, invested the profits of his shop in real estate, acquired stores that he rented out, purchased slaves and a plantation, and even hired a white overseer.

As Johnson's career suggests, some free blacks were highly successful. But free blacks were always vulnerable in southern society and became more so as the antebellum period wore on. While free blacks continued to increase in absolute numbers (a little more than a quarter-million free people of color dwelled in the South in 1860), the rate of growth of the free black population slowed after 1810. Between 1790 and 1810, this population had more than tripled, to 108,265. The reason for the slowdown after 1810 was that fewer southern whites were setting slaves free. Until 1820 masters with doubts about the rightness of slavery frequently manumitted (freed) their black mistresses and mulatto children, and some set free their entire work forces (as Jefferson had done upon his death in 1826). In the wake of the Nat Turner rebellion in 1831 (see below), laws restricting the liberties of free blacks were tightened. During the mid-1830s, for example, most southern states made it a felony to teach blacks to read and write. Every southern state forbade free blacks to enter that state, and in 1859 Arkansas ordered all free blacks to leave.

So while a free black culture flowered in cities like New Orleans and Natchez, that culture did not reflect the conditions under which most free blacks lived. Free blacks were tolerated in New Orleans, in part because there were not too many of them. A much higher percentage of blacks were free in the Upper South than in the Lower South. Further, although a disproportionate number of free blacks lived in cities, the majority lived in rural areas, where whites lumped them together with slaves. Even a successful free black like William Tiler Johnson could never dine or drink with whites. When Johnson attended the theater, he sat in the colored gallery.

The position of free blacks in the Old South contained many contradictions. So did their minds. As the offspring, or the descendants of offspring, of mixed liaisons, a disproportionate number of free blacks had light brown skin. Some of them were as color-conscious as whites and looked down on "darky" field hands and coal-black laborers. Yet as whites' discrimination against free people of color intensified during the late antebellum period, many free blacks realized that such a future as they had was as blacks, not as whites. Feelings of racial solidarity grew stronger among free blacks in the 1850s, and after the Civil War, the leaders of the freedmen were usually blacks who had been free before the war.

Slave Resistance

The Old South contained the seeds of organized slave insurrections. In the delta areas of the Lower South, where blacks outnumbered whites, enslaved blacks experienced continuous forced labor on plantations and communicated their bitterness to each other in the slave quarters. Free blacks in the cities could have provided leadership for rebellions. Rumors of slave conspiracies flew around the southern white community, and all whites knew of the massive black insurrection that had destroyed French rule in Santo Domingo.

Yet only three organized rebellions occurred in the Old South, and taken together, they illustrate more the futility than the possibility of a slave insurrection. In 1800 Virginia slave Gabriel Prosser's planned slave uprising was betrayed by other slaves, and Prosser and his followers were executed. That same year, a South Carolina slave, Denmark Vesey, won fifteen hundred dollars in a lottery and bought his freedom. Purchasing a carpentry shop in Charleston and becoming a preacher at that city's African Methodist Episcopal church, Vesey built a cadre of dedicated black followers, including a slave of the governor of South Carolina and a black conjurer named Gullah Jack. In 1822 they devised a plan to attack Charleston and seize all the city's arms and ammunition, but they were betrayed by other slaves and executed.

The Nat Turner rebellion, which occurred in 1831 in Southampton County, Virginia, was the only one of the three slave insurrections to result in the death of whites. Gloomy and introspective by nature, Nat Turner taught himself to read and write in childhood and became a prodigious reader of the Bible. He gained recognition from slaves as a preacher of electrifying sermons delivered in woodland clearings or in the shacks where slaves gathered to hear "real preachin'." Soon he added a reputation for visions and prophecy; he told, for example, of seeing white and black angels warring in the sky. Yet for all his gifts—a white later said that Turner had "a mind capable of attaining any-thing"—Turner's life was one of onerous field work, punctuated by a sale that separated him from his wife and that reminded him that whites measured his value only in cash.

In 1831 Turner's conviction of the injustice of slavery, intensified by his reading of the Bible and by his own experiences, boiled over. Slaves who had long venerated him as a prophet now took him as their "general." In August he set out with a handful of slaves armed with axes and clubs. Gathering recruits as they moved from plantation to plantation, Turner and his followers killed all white men, women, and children they encountered. Before the rebellion was suppressed and Turner hanged, fifty-five whites had been slain, a number roughly equal to Turner's force at its peak strength.

Turner's rebellion stunned the South. In the widely circulated *Confessions of Nat Turner,* which Turner dictated to a white lawyer while awaiting execution, Turner's steadfast belief in the justice of his cause flashed again. When asked, "Do you not find yourself mistaken now?," Turner replied, "Was not Christ crucified?" In company with the earlier slave uprising in Santo Domingo, Turner's rebellion convinced white southerners of the ever-present threat of a slave insurrection. Yet neither the Turner rebellion nor the Prosser and Vesey plots ever had a chance of success. The latter two were conspiracies that never got off the ground. During the Turner rebellion, several slaves alerted their masters to the threat, less out of loyalty to slavery than from a correct assessment of Turner's chances. Despite constant fears of slave rebellion, the Old South experienced far less in the way of organized

Slave with Bells

Like cats, some slaves were belled to make escape difficult.

rebellion than did the Caribbean region and South America.

Why is this so? First, although slaves formed a majority in South Carolina and a few other states, they did not constitute a *large* majority in any state. Second, in contrast to the Caribbean, an area of absentee landlords and sparse white population, the white presence in the Old South was formidable, and the whites had all the guns and soldiers. Reviewing Gabriel's Rebellion, Governor James Monroe of Virginia commented: "The superiority in point of numbers, in the knowledge and use of arms, and indeed every other species of knowledge which the whites have over the blacks in this Commonwealth, is so decisive that the latter could only sustain themselves for a moment in a rebellion against the former." The rumors of slave conspiracies that periodically swept the white South demonstrated to blacks the promptness with which whites could muster forces and mount slave patrols. Third, the development of family ties among slaves made them reluctant to risk death and leave their children parentless. Finally, blacks who ran away or plotted rebellions had no allies. Southern Indians routinely captured runaway slaves and exchanged them for rewards; some Indians even owned slaves.

Short of rebellion, slaves could try to escape to freedom in the North. Perhaps the most ingenious, Henry Brown, induced a friend to ship him from Richmond to Philadelphia in a box and won immediate fame as "Box" Brown. Some light mulattoes passed as whites. More often, fugitive slaves borrowed, stole, or forged passes from plantations or obtained papers describing them as free. Frederick Douglass borrowed a sailor's papers in making his escape from Baltimore to New York City in 1838. Some former slaves, among them Harriet Tubman and Josiah Henson, made repeated trips back to the South to help other slaves escape. These sundry methods of escape fed the legend of the "Underground Railroad," supposedly an organized network of safe houses owned by white abolitionists who spirited blacks to freedom. In reality, fugitive slaves owed very little to abolitionists. Some white sympathizers in border states did provide safe houses for blacks, but these houses were better known to watchful slave catchers than to most blacks.

Escape to freedom was a dream rather than an alternative for most blacks; out of millions of slaves, probably fewer than a thousand escaped to the North. Yet slaves often ran away from masters, not to escape to freedom but to visit spouses or avoid punishment. Most runaways remained in the South; indeed, some returned to former, kinder masters. During the eighteenth century, African slaves had often run away in groups to the interior and sought to create self-sufficient colonies or villages of the sort that they had known in Africa. But once the United States had acquired Florida, long a haven for runaways, few uninhabited places remained in the South to which slaves could escape.

Despite poor prospects for permanent escape, slaves could disappear for prolonged periods into the free black communities of southern cities. Because whites in the Old South depended so heavily on black labor, slaves enjoyed a fair degree of practical freedom to drive wagons to market and to come and go when they were off plantations. Slaves hired out or sent to a city might overstay their leave and even pass themselves off as free.

The experience of slavery has sometimes been compared to the experience of prisoners in penitentiaries or on chain gangs, but the analogy is misleading. The supervision that slaves experienced was sometimes intense (for example, when working at harvest time under a driver), but often lax; it was irregular rather than consistent.

The fact that antebellum slaves frequently enjoyed some degree of practical freedom did not change the underlying oppressiveness of slavery. But it did give slaves a sense that they had certain rights on a day-to-day basis, and it helped to deflect slave resistance into forms that were essentially furtive rather than open and violent. Theft was so common that planters learned to keep their tools, smokehouses, closets, and trunks under lock and key. Overworked field hands might leave valuable tools out to rust, or feign illness, or simply refuse to work. As an institution, slavery was vulnerable to such tactics; unlike free laborers, slaves could not be fired for negligence or malingering. Frederick Law Olmsted found slaveholders in the 1850s afraid to inflict punishment on slaves "lest the slave should abscond, or take a sulky fit and not work, or poison some of the family, or set fire to the dwelling, or have recourse to any other mode of avenging himself."

Olmsted's reference to arson and poisoning reminds us that not all furtive resistance was peaceful. Arson and poisoning, both common in African culture as forms of vengeance, were widespread in the Old South, and the fear of each even more so. Dysentery and similar ailments afflicted whites as well as blacks. Masters could never be sure about why they were sick; to put it differently, they could never be sure that they had not been poisoned.

Arson, poisoning, work stoppages, and negligence were alternatives to violent rebellion. Yet these furtive forms of resistance differed from rebellion. The goal of rebellion was freedom from slavery. The goal of furtive resistance was to make slavery bearable. The kind of resistance that slaves usually practiced sought to establish customs and rules that would govern the conduct of masters as well as that of slaves without challenging the institution of slavery as such. Most slaves would have preferred freedom but settled for less. "White folks do as they please," an ex-slave said, "and the darkies do as they can."

The Emergence
of African-American Culture

A distinctive culture emerged among blacks in the slave quarters of antebellum plantations. This culture drew on both African and American sources, but it was more than a mixture of the two. Enslaved blacks gave a distinctive twist to the American as well as African components of their culture.

The Language of Slaves

Before slaves could develop a common culture, they had to be able to communicate with each other. During the colonial period, verbal communication among slaves had often been difficult, for most slaves had been born in Africa, which contained an abundance of cultures and languages. The captain of a slave ship noted in 1744:

> As for the languages of Gambia [in West Africa], they are so many and so different that the Natives on either Side of the River cannot understand each other; which, if rightly consider'd, is no small happiness to the Europeans who go thither to trade for slaves.

In the pens into which they were herded before shipment and on the slave ships themselves, however, Africans developed a "pidgin"—that is, a language that has no native speakers but in which people with different native languages can communicate. Pidgin is not unique to black people. When Tarzan announced, "Me Tarzan, you Jane," he was speaking English pidgin. Nor is English pidgin the only form of pidgin; slaves sent to South America developed Spanish and Portuguese pidgins.

Many of the early African-born slaves learned English pidgin poorly or not at all, but as American-born slaves came to compose an increasingly large proportion of all slaves, English pidgin took root. Indeed, it became the only language most slaves knew. Like all pidgins, this was a simplified language. Slaves usually dropped the verb *to be* (which had no equivalent in African tongues) and either ignored or confused genders. Instead of saying "Mary is in the cabin," they said, "Mary, he in cabin." To negate, they substituted *no* for *not*, saying, "He no wicked." English pidgin contained several African words. Some, like *banjo,* became part of standard English; others, like *goober* (peanut), became part of southern white slang. Although they picked up pidgin terms, whites ridiculed field hands' speech. Some slaves, particularly house servants and skilled artisans, learned to speak standard English but had no trouble understanding the pidgin of field hands. However strange pidgin sounded to some, it was indispensable for communication among slaves.

African-American Religion

The development of a common language marked the first step in the forging of African-American culture. No less important was the religion of the slaves.

Africa contained rich and diverse religious customs and beliefs. Some of the early slaves were Moslems; a few had acquired Christian beliefs either in Africa or in the New World. But the majority of the slaves transported from Africa were neither Moslems nor Christians but rather worshipers in one of many native African religions. Most of these religions, which whites lumped together as heathen, drew little distinction between the spiritual and material worlds. Any event or development, from a storm to an earthquake or an illness, was assumed to stem from supernatural forces. These forces were represented by God, by spirits that inhabited the woods and waters, and by the spirits of ancestors. In addition, the religions of West Africa, the region from which most American slaves originally came, attached special significance to water, which suggested life and hope.

The majority of the slaves brought to America in the seventeenth and eighteenth centuries were young men who may not have absorbed much of this religious heritage before their enslavement. In any case, Africans differed from each other in their specific beliefs and practices. For these reasons, African religions could never have unified blacks in America. Yet some Africans probably clung to their beliefs during the seventeenth and eighteenth centuries, a tendency made easier by the fact that whites undertook few efforts before the 1790s to convert slaves to Christianity. Further, dimly remembered African beliefs such as the reverence for water may have predisposed slaves to accept Christianity when they were finally urged to do so, because water had a symbolic significance for Christians, too, in the sacrament of baptism. The Christianity preached to slaves by Methodist and Baptist revivalists during the late eighteenth and nineteenth centuries, moreover, resembled African religions in that Christianity also drew few distinctions between the sacred and the secular. Just as Africans believed that a crop-destroying drought or a plague resulted from supernatural forces, the early revivalists knew in their hearts that every drunkard who fell off his horse and every Sabbath-breaker struck by lightning had experienced a deliberate and direct punishment from God.

By the 1790s blacks formed about a quarter of the membership of the Methodist and Baptist denominations. Yet masters continued to fear that a Christianized slave would be a rebellious slave. Converted slaves in fact played a significant role in each of the three major slave rebellions in the Old South. The leaders of Gabriel Prosser's rebellion in 1800 used the Bible to prove that slaves, like the ancient Israelites, could prevail against overwhelming numbers. Denmark Vesey read the Bible, and most of the slaves executed for joining his conspiracy belonged to Charleston's African Methodist church. Nat Turner was both a preacher and a prophet.

Despite the subversive impact of Christianity on some slaves, however, these uprisings, particularly the Nat Turner rebellion, actually stimulated Protestant missionaries to intensify their efforts to convert slaves. Missionaries pointed to the self-taught Turner to prove that slaves would hear about Christianity in any event and that organized efforts to convert blacks were the only way to ensure that slaves learned correct versions of Christianity, which emphasized obedience rather than rebellion. Georgia missionary and slaveholder Charles Colcock Jones reassuringly told white planters of the venerable black preacher who, upon receiving some abolitionist tracts in the mails, promptly turned them over to the white authorities for destruction. A Christian slave, the argument ran, would be a better slave rather than a bitter slave. For whites, the clincher was the split of the Methodists, Baptists, and Presbyterians into northern and southern wings by the mid-1840s. Now, they argued, it had finally become safe to convert slaves, for the churches had rid themselves of their antislavery wings. Between 1845 and 1860, the number of black Baptists doubled.

Bibby Mosby

Bibby Mosby was a "mammy" enslaved to the family of a Charlottesville, Virginia, judge from about 1830 to 1863.

The experiences of Christianized blacks in the Old South illustrate many of the contradictions of life under slavery. Urban blacks often had their own churches, but in the rural South, where the great majority of blacks lived, slaves worshiped in the same churches as whites. Although the slaves sat in segregated sections, they heard the same sermons and sang the same hymns as whites. Some black preachers actually developed followings among whites, and Christian masters were sometimes disciplined by biracial churches for abusing Christian slaves in the same congregation. The churches were, in fact, the most interracial institutions in the Old South. Yet none of this meant that Christianity was an acceptable route to black liberation. Ministers went out of their way to remind slaves that spiritual equality was not the same as civil equality. The effort to convert slaves gained momentum only to the extent that it was becoming certain that Christianity would not change the basic inequality of southern society.

Although they listened to the same sermons as whites, slaves did not necessarily draw the same conclusions. It was impossible to Christianize the slaves without telling them about the Chosen People, the ancient Jews whom Moses led from captivity in Pharaoh's Egypt into the Promised Land of Israel. Inevitably, slaves drew parallels between their own condition and the Jews' captivity. Like the Jews, blacks concluded, they themselves were "de people of de Lord." If they kept the faith, then, like the Jews, they too would reach the Promised Land. The themes of the Chosen People and the Promised Land ran through the sacred songs, or "spirituals," that blacks sang, to the point where Moses and Jesus almost merged:

> *Gwine to write to Massa Jesus,*
> *To send some Valiant Soldier*
> *To turn back Pharaoh's army, Hallelu!*

A listener could interpret a phrase like "the Promised Land" in several ways; it could refer to Israel, to heaven, or to freedom. From the perspective of whites, the only permissible interpretations were Israel and heaven, but some blacks, like Denmark Vesey, thought of freedom as well. The ease with which slaves constructed alternative interpretations of the Bible also reflected the fact that many plantations contained black preachers, slaves trained by white ministers to spread Christianity among blacks. When in the presence of masters or white ministers, these black preachers usually just repeated the familiar biblical command: "Obey your master." Often, however, slaves met for services apart from whites, usually on Sunday evenings but at times during the week as well. Then the message changed. A black preacher in Texas related how his master would say "tell them niggers iffen they obeys the master they goes to Heaven." The minister quickly added, "I knowed there's something better for them, but I daren't tell them 'cept on the sly. That I done lots. I tells 'em iffen they keep praying, the Lord will set 'em free."

Some slaves privately interpreted Christianity as a religion of liberation from the oppression of slavery, but most recognized that their prospects for freedom were slight. On the whole, Christianity did not turn them into revolutionaries. Neither did it necessarily turn them into model slaves. What it did accomplish was to provide slaves with a view of slavery different from their masters' outlook. Where the masters argued that slavery was a benign and divinely ordained institution in blacks' best interests, Christianity told them that slavery was really an affliction, a terrible and unjust institution, but one that God had allowed in order to test their faith. For having endured slavery, he would reward blacks. For having created it, he would punish masters.

Black Music and Dance

Compared to the prevailing cultural patterns among elite whites, the culture of blacks in the Old South was extremely expressive. In religious services, blacks shouted "Amen" and let their bodily movements reflect their feelings long after white religious observances, some of which had once been similarly expressive, had grown sober and sedate. Northern journalist Frederick Law Olmsted recorded how, during a slave service in New Orleans during the 1850s, parishioners "in indescribable expression of ecstasy" exclaimed every few moments: "Glory! oh yes! yes!—sweet Lord! sweet Lord!"

Slaves also expressed their feelings in music and dance. Drawing on their African musical heritage, which used hand clapping to mark rhythm, American slaves made rhythmical hand clapping—called patting juba—an indispensable accompaniment to dancing, because southern law forbade them to own "drums, horns, or other loud instruments, which may call together or give sign or notice to one another of their wicked designs and intentions." Slaves also played an African instrument, the banjo, and beat tin buckets as a substitute for drums. Whatever instrument they played, their music was tied to bodily movement. Sometimes slaves imitated white dances like the minuet, but in a way that ridiculed the high manners of their masters. More often, they expressed themselves in a dance African in origin, emphasizing shuffling steps and bodily contortions rather than the erect precision of whites' dances.

Whether at work or at prayer, slaves liked to sing. Work songs describing slave experiences usually consisted of a leader's chant and a choral response:

> *I love old Virginny*
>   *So ho! boys! so ho!*
> *I love to shuck corn*
>   *So ho! boys! so ho!*
> *Now's picking cotton time*
>   *So ho! boys! so ho!*

The Banjo Lesson, *by Henry O. Tanner, c. 1893*

Tanner, a black artist, captured African-Americans' rich musical traditions and close family bonds in this evocative painting.

Masters encouraged such songs, believing that singing induced the slaves to work harder and that the innocent content of most work songs proved that the slaves were happy. Recalling his own past, Frederick Douglass came closer to the truth when he observed that "slaves sing most when they are most unhappy. The songs of the slave represent the sorrows of his heart; and he is relieved by them, only as an aching heart is relieved by its tears."

Blacks also sang religious songs, later known as spirituals. The origin of spirituals is shrouded in obscurity, but it is clear that by 1820 blacks at camp meetings had improvised what one white described as "short scraps of disjointed affirmations, pledges, or prayers lengthened out with long repetition choruses." As this description suggests, whites usually took a dim view of spirituals and tried to make slaves sing "good psalms and hymns" instead of "the extravagant and nonsensical chants, and catches, and hallelujah songs of their own composing." Indeed, when around whites, blacks often sang hymns like those of Isaac Watts and other great white evangelicals, but nothing could dampen slaves' enthusiasm for songs of their own making.

Spirituals reflected the potent emphasis that the slaves' religion put on deliverance from earthly travails. To a degree, the same was true of white hymns, but spirituals were more direct and concrete. Slaves sang, for example,

> *In that morning, true believers,*
> *In that morning,*
> *We will sit aside of Jesus*
> *In that morning,*
> *If you should go fore I go,*
> *In that morning,*
> *You will sit aside of Jesus*
> *In that morning,*
> *True believers, where your tickets*
> *In that morning,*
> *Master Jesus got your tickets*
> *In that morning.*

Another spiritual proclaimed: "We will soon be free, when the Lord will call us home."

Conclusion   The emergence of an African-American culture was one among many features that made the Old South distinctive. With its huge black population, lack of industries, and dispersed white population, the South seemed a world apart. Even while finding individual southerners agreeable, northerners increasingly recognized the differences between their region and the South in the antebellum years. Whether or not they believed that the federal government should tamper with slavery, northerners grew convinced that slavery had cut the South off from progress and had turned it into a region of "sterile land, and bankrupt estates."

Conversely, to most white southerners, the North, and especially the industrial Northeast, appeared to be the region that deviated from the march of progress. Southerners noted that most Americans—indeed, most people throughout the world—practiced agriculture and that agriculture made the South a more comfortable place for millions than factories rendered the North. In reaction to northern assaults on slavery, southerners portrayed the institution as a time-honored and benevolent response to the natural inequality of the black and white races. Southerners pointed to the slaves' adequate nutrition, their embrace of evangelical Protestantism, the affection of some slaves for their masters, and even their work songs as evidence of the slaves' contentment.

In reality, few if any slaves accepted slavery. Although slaves rebelled infrequently and had little chance for permanent escape, they often engaged in covert resistance to their bondage. The slaves embraced Christianity, but they understood it differently than whites. Where Christianity taught whites the need to make slaves submissive, it taught slaves the gross injustice of human bondage.

CHRONOLOGY

1790s Methodists and Baptists start to make major strides in converting slaves to Christianity.

1793 Eli Whitney invents the cotton gin.

1800 Gabriel Prosser leads a slave rebellion in Virginia.

1808 Congress prohibits external slave trade.

1812 Louisiana, the first state formed out of the Louisiana Purchase, is admitted to the Union.

1816–1819 Boom in cotton prices stimulates settlement of the Southwest.

1817 Mississippi enters the Union.

1819 Alabama enters the Union.

1819–1820 Missouri Compromise.

1822 Denmark Vesey's conspiracy is uncovered in South Carolina.

1831 William Lloyd Garrison starts *The Liberator*. Nat Turner leads a slave rebellion in Virginia.

1832 Virginia legislature narrowly defeats a proposal for gradual emancipation.

Virginia's Thomas R. Dew writes an influential defense of slavery.

1835 Arkansas admitted to the Union.

1837 Economic panic begins, lowering cotton prices.

1844– Methodist Episcopal and Baptist churches
1845 split into northern and southern wings over slavery.

1845 Florida and Texas admitted to the Union.

1849 Sugar production in Louisiana reaches its peak.

1849– Period of high cotton prices.
1860

1857 Hinton R. Helper, *The Impending Crisis of the South.*

1859 John Brown's raid on Harpers Ferry.

1860 South Carolina secedes from the Union.

For Further Reading

John B. Boles, *Black Southerners, 1619–1869* (1983). An excellent synthesis of recent scholarship on slavery.

Orville Vernon Burton, *In My Father's House Are Many Mansions: Family and Community in Edgefield, South Carolina* (1985). An extremely valuable study of the South Carolina upcountry.

Wilbur J. Cash, *The Mind of the South* (1941). A brilliant interpretation of southern history.

Bruce Collins, *White Society in the Antebellum South* (1985). A very good, brief synthesis of southern white society and culture.

William J. Cooper, *Liberty and Slavery: Southern Politics to 1860* (1983). A valuable synthesis and interpretation of recent scholarship on the antebellum South in national politics.

Clement Eaton, *The Growth of Southern Civilization, 1790–1860* (1961). A fine survey of social, economic, and political change.

Robert W. Fogel and Stanley L. Engerman, *Time on the Cross: The Economics of American Negro Slavery* (1974). A controversial book that uses mathematical models to analyze the profitability of slavery.

Eugene D. Genovese, *Roll, Jordan, Roll: The World the Slaves Made* (1974). The most influential work on slavery in the Old South written during the last twenty years; a penetrating analysis of the paternalistic relationship between masters and slaves.

James Oakes, *The Ruling Race: A History of American Slaveholders* (1982). An important attack on the ideas of Eugene D. Genovese.

U. B. Phillips, *American Negro Slavery* (1918). A work marred by racial prejudice but containing a wealth of information about the workings of slavery and the plantation system. The same description fits another major book by Phillips, *Life and Labor in the Old South* (1929).

Kenneth M. Stampp, *The Peculiar Institution: Slavery in the Ante-Bellum South* (1956). A standard account of the black experience under slavery.

Charles S. Sydnor, *The Development of Southern Sectionalism, 1819–1848* (1948). A description of the growing split between North and South over slavery and related issues.

William R. Taylor, *Cavalier and Yankee: The Old South and American National Character* (1961). An imaginative study of the northern and southern mind through the eye of literature.

Additional Bibliography

The Economic and Social Structure of the White South

William L. Barney, *The Road to Secession* (1972); Fred Bateman and Thomas Weiss, *A Deplorable Scarcity: The Failure of Industrialism in the Slave Economy* (1981); Orville V. Burton and Robert McMath, eds., *Class, Conflict, and Consensus* (1982); Mary B. Chesnut, *A Diary from Dixie* (edited by Ben Ames Williams, 1949); Blanche Henry Clark, *The Tennessee Yeoman, 1840–1860* (1942); Catherine G. Clinton, *The Plantation Mistress: Women's World in the Old South* (1982); Barbara J. Fields, *Slavery and Freedom on the Middle Ground: Maryland During the Nineteenth Century* (1985); Elizabeth Fox-Genovese, *Within the Plantation Household: Black and White Women of the Old South* (1988); Eugene Genovese, *The Political Economy of Slavery* (1965); Steven Hahn, *The Roots of Southern Populism: Yeomen Farmers and the Transformation of the Georgia Upcountry, 1850–1890* (1983); Daniel R. Hundley, *Social Relations in Our Southern States* (1860); Suzanne Lebsock, *The Free Women of Petersburg: Status Culture in a Southern Town, 1784–1860* (1984); Forrest McDonald and Grady McWhiney, "The Antebellum Southern Herdsman: A Reinterpretation," *Journal of Southern History* 41 (May 1975): 147–66; Frank L. Owsley, *Plain Folk of the Old South* (1949); Whitman H. Ridgway, *Community Leadership in Maryland, 1790–1840* (1979); Anne F. Scott, *The Southern Lady: From Pedestal to Politics, 1830–1930* (1970); Julia F. Smith, *Slavery and Plantation Growth in Antebellum Florida* (1973); Herbert Weaver, *Mississippi Farmers, 1850–1860* (1945); Ralph A. Wooster, *Politicians, Planters, and Plain Folk* (1975); Gavin Wright, *The Political Economy of the Cotton South* (1978).

The Values of the White South

Edward L. Ayers, *Vengeance and Justice: Crime and Punishment in the Nineteenth-Century American South* (1984); David T. Bailey, *Shadow on the Church: Southwestern Evangelical Religion and the Issue of Slavery, 1783–1860* (1985); Dickson D. Bruce, *Violence and Culture in the Antebellum South* (1979); William J. Cooper, *The South and the Politics of Slavery, 1829–1856* (1978); Clement Eaton, *The Mind of the Old South* (1964); James D. Essig, *The Bonds of Wickedness: American Evangelicals Against Slavery, 1770–1808* (1982); Drew G. Faust, *A Sacred Circle: The Dilemma of the Intellectual in the Old South, 1840–1860* (1977) and *James Henry Hammond and the Old South: A Design for Mastery* (1982); John Hope Franklin, *The Militant South* (1966); George M. Fredrickson, *The Black Image in the White Mind: The Debate on Afro-American Character and Destiny, 1817–1914* (1971) and *White Supremacy: A Comparative Study in American and South African History* (1981); Alison G. Freehling, *Drift Toward Dissolution: The Virginia Slavery Debate of 1831–1832* (1982); Elliott J. Gorn, " 'Gouge and Bite, Pull Hair and Scratch': The Social Significance of Fighting in the Southern Backcountry," *American Historical Review* XC (February 1985): 18–43; Michael Hindus, *Prison and Plantation: Crime, Jusice, and Authority in Massachusetts and South Carolina, 1767–1878* (1980); John McCardell, *The Idea of a Southern Nation: Southern Nationalists and Southern Nationalism* (1979); Donald G. Mathews, *Religion in the Old South* (1977); Ronald Takaki, *A Pro-Slavery Crusade: The Agitation to Reopen the African Slave Trade* (1980); J. Mills Thornton, *Politics and Power in a Slave Society: Alabama, 1800–1860* (1978); Bertram Wyatt-Brown, *Southern Honor: Ethics and Behavior in the Old South* (1982).

Black Experience and Culture in the Old South

Ira Berlin, *Slaves Without Masters: The Free Negro in the Antebellum South* (1974); John Blassingame, *The Slave Community* (1972); Judith Wragg Chase, *Afro-American Art and Craft* (1971); Leonard P. Curry, *The Free Black in Urban America, 1800–1850: The Shadow of the Dream* (1981); Carl N. Degler, *Neither Black Nor White: Slavery and Race Relations in Brazil and the United States* (1971); Dena J. Epstein, *Sinful Tunes and Spirituals: Black Folk Music to the Civil War* (1977); Claudia D. Goldin, *Urban Slavery in the American South, 1820–1860* (1976); Herbert G. Gutman, *The Black Family in Slavery and Freedom, 1759–1925* (1976); Vincent Harding, *There Is a River: The Black Struggle for Freedom in America* (1981); Jacqueline Jones, *Labor of Love, Labor of Sorrow: Black Women, Work, and the Family from Slavery to the Present* (1985); Lawrence W. Levine, *Black Culture and Black Consciousness: Afro-American Folk Thought from Slavery to Freedom* (1977); Stephen B. Oates, *The Fires of Jubilee* (1975); Leslie H. Owens, *This Species of Property: Slave Life and Slave Culture in the Old South* (1976); Albert J. Raboteau, *Slave Religion* (1978); George P. Rawick, *From Sundown to Sunup: The Making of a Black Community* (1972); Robert S. Starobin, *Industrial Slavery in the Old South* (1970); Thomas L. Webber, *Deep Like Rivers: Education in the Slave Quarters, 1831–1865* (1978).

CHAPTER 11

Life, Leisure, and Culture, 1840–1860

Americans, wrote Alexis de Tocqueville, "care but little for what has been, but they are haunted by visions of what will be." British novelist Charles Dickens remarked that while the watchword of the English was "All right," that of Americans was "Go ahead." Indeed, a belief in irreversible progress captivated Americans in the 1840s and 1850s. Each passing year seemed to offer new evidence for Thomas Jefferson's prediction that Europe "will have to lean on our shoulders and hobble along by our side."

Inventiveness and material betterment loomed large in American conceptions of progress. Agricultural innovations helped farmers produce a surplus of food despite a swiftly rising population. Americans could confidently brush aside the gloomy forecast of Britain's Thomas Malthus, who at the end of the eighteenth century had argued that a growing population would exhaust its food supply and suffer famine. During the two decades before the Civil War, material progress also affected transportation and industry. Railroads ribboned their way throughout the eastern United States. The widening use of steam power and the perfection of manufacturing on the principle of interchangeable parts contributed to lower commodity prices and a gradual rise in real wages. The evidence of prosperity lay not only in higher wages but also in the multiplication of conveniences that transformed such everyday activities as cooking, eating, and drinking.

American achievements in agriculture, industry, and transportation led to growing demands in these years that the United States throw off any lingering cultural dependence on Europe. Some contemporaries began to insist that Americans read books written by their countrymen, while others called for the development of a distinctive American literary and artistic style. No less than economic innovation, literary and artistic inventiveness did make a mark on antebellum America. The period between 1820 and 1860 produced Washington Irving, the first American man of letters to gain fame throughout Europe; James Fenimore Cooper, the first American novelist to make a living continuously and exclusively by his writing; Henry Wadsworth Longfellow, the first nationally famous American poet; Edgar Allan Poe, the first and only American to invent a new literary genre, the detective story; and the Hudson River school of painting, the first native school of American painting. In 1820 a British critic had asked rhetorically: "In the four quarters of the Globe, who reads an American book?" By 1860 the answer was clear, for Europeans and Americans alike had learned to cherish Irving, Cooper, Ralph Waldo Emerson, Nathaniel Hawthorne, and other luminaries of what is often called the American Renaissance.

For the most part, antebellum Americans equated material, cultural, and moral progress. Samuel F. B. Morse, for example, expected that his invention of the telegraph in 1844 would not only speed communication but end war as well. Similar high expectations greeted other innovations. Advances in the technology of printing, a clergyman enthused in 1851, "multiply the word of God literally with every minute."

Yet progress had its darker side. Spread unevenly throughout the society, technological advances neither prevented nor ameliorated the depression of the late 1830s and early 1840s and had little positive impact on the poor. Periodic cholera epidemics reminded Americans that technology, in the shape of railroads and steamboats, could transport disease as well as food. Leading writers of the period, among them the philosopher and essayist Henry David Thoreau, questioned the easy assumption that material progress would stimulate moral progress. For the first time, widespread anxieties arose about the despoliation of the American landscape, and conscious efforts were launched to preserve enclaves of nature as parks and retreats safe from the advance of civilization.

Technology and Economic Growth

As evidence that they were a progressive people, Americans increasingly pointed to the march of "technology." The word *technology* was popularized after 1829 to describe how an understanding of scientific principles could be used to transform the practical conveniences of life. "We have invented more useful machines within twenty years," a Bostonian wrote in the 1830s, "than have been invented in all Europe." To those familiar with the progress of invention, *DeBow's Review* observed in 1846, "scarcely anything now will appear impossible."

Belief in the progressive effects of technology sprang from widely varying quarters. In 1836 the conservative Whig Daniel Webster contended that machines would advance civilization because they could perform the work of ten people without consuming food or clothing. At the other end of the political spectrum, a Lowell mill girl and labor organizer, Sarah Bagley, wrote in 1847: "It is emphatically the age of improvement. The arts and sciences have been more fully developed and the great mass of society are feeling its improvement." Practical science promised to make everyone's life more comfortable. The benefits of technology seemed to be democratic.

The technical innovations that transformed the quality of life in antebellum America included the steam engine, the cotton gin, the reaper, the use of interchangeable parts in manufacturing, the sewing machine, and most dazzling of all, the telegraph. Several of these innovations, including the steam engine and the principle of interchangeable parts, had originated in Europe. But Americans had a flair for investing in others' inventions and for perfecting their own, to the point where the inventions became profitable. Improvements in Eli Whitney's cotton gin between 1793 and 1860, for example, led to an eightfold increase in the amount of cotton that could be ginned in a day. Of course, technology did not benefit everyone. Improve-

Woman at Singer Sewing Machine

Asked to repair a sewing machine that did not do continuous stitching, Isaac M. Singer invented one that did. Patented in 1851, the Singer machine quickly dominated the market. Although most early sewing machines were used in factories, some had made their way into households by 1860.

ments in the cotton gin served to rivet slavery firmly in place by making the South more dependent on cotton. Technology also rendered many traditional skills obsolete and thereby undercut the position of artisans. But technology contributed to improvements in transportation and increases in productivity, which in turn lowered commodity prices and raised the living standards of a sizable body of free Americans between 1840 and 1860.

Agricultural Advancement

Confronted by the superior fertility of western soil, many easterners abandoned wheat production and migrated to the West or took jobs in America's expanding factories. Others developed new agricultural techniques and specialties. In Orange County, New York, for example, farmers fed their cows on the best clover and bluegrass and emphasized cleanliness in the processing of dairy products. Through these practices, they produced a superior butter that commanded more than double the price of ordinary butter and even gained a reputation in Europe. Still other eastern farmers continued to produce wheat, but to stay competitive with westerners, they turned to the use of fertilizers. By fertilizing their fields with plaster left over from the construction of the James River Canal, Virginia wheat growers raised their average yield per acre to fifteen bushels by the 1850s, up from an average of only six bushels in 1800. Similarly, during the 1840s American cotton planters began to import guano, left by the droppings of sea birds on islands off Peru, for use as a fertilizer. Fertilizers helped eastern cotton farmers close the gap created by the greater fertility of southwestern soil for cotton.

Like cotton, wheat presented a harvesting problem. Use of the traditional hand sickle consumed prodigious amounts of time and labor, all the more so because cut wheat had to be picked up and bound. Ever since the eighteenth century, inventors in Europe had experimented with horse-drawn machines to replace sickles. But until Cyrus McCormick came on the scene, the absence of the right combination of technical skill and business enterprise had relegated mechanical reapers to the realm of tinkerers' dreams. In 1834 McCormick, a Virginian, patented a mechanical reaper that both drew on and improved previous designs. Opening

a factory in Chicago in 1847, McCormick began to manufacture reapers by mass production and introduced aggressive marketing techniques such as deferred payments and money-back guarantees.

The North rather than the South provided the main market for McCormick's reaper and for those of his many competitors. With its reliance on slave labor, the South had far less incentive to mechanize agriculture. Even without the reaper, wheat was fast becoming to the midwestern farmer what cotton was to his southern counterpart. "The wheat crop is the great crop of the North-west, for exchange purposes," an agricultural journal noted in 1850. "It pays debts, buys groceries, clothing and lands, and answers more emphatically the purposes of trade among the farmers than any other crop." By harvesting grain seven times more rapidly than traditional methods, and with half the labor force, the reaper guaranteed the preeminence of wheat on the midwestern prairies of Illinois, Indiana, Iowa, and Missouri. McCormick sold 80,000 reapers by 1860, and this was only the beginning. During the Civil War, he made immense profits by selling more than 250,000 reapers. Ironically, just as a Connecticut Yankee, Eli Whitney, had stimulated the foundation of the Old South's economy by his invention of the cotton gin, Cyrus McCormick, a proslavery southern Democrat, would help the North win the Civil War. The reaper would keep northern agricultural production high at a time when labor shortages caused by the mobilization of troops might otherwise have slashed production.

Technology and Industrial Progress

Although Americans had made several important technical innovations before 1820, the early growth of American manufacturing depended mainly on *imported* technology. Gradually, however, American industries gained a reputation abroad for their own innovations. As early as 1835, a British observer reported that a woolen mill in Lowell, Massachusetts, contained a remarkable number of labor-saving contrivances. In 1853 a small-arms factory in England reequipped itself with machine tools (machines that shaped metal products) manufactured by two firms in the backwoods of Vermont. Americans had relatively few reservations about investing in technology. After finishing a tour of American factories in 1854, a noted British engineer concluded that "wherever [machinery] can be introduced as a substitute for manual labor, it is universally and willingly resorted to."

During the 1840s and 1850s, American industries advanced toward perfecting manufacturing by the use of interchangeable parts. Eli Whitney had introduced this idea (often called the American system of manufacturing) to the United States in 1798, but in Whitney's day the manufacture of guns or other items by the use of interchangeable parts required a great deal of time-consuming hand filing before the parts could be fitted together. In the 1840s American factories immeasurably improved the quality of their machine tools and thereby eliminated much of the need for hand filing. As a result, it became possible to substitute parts that were made in one year for those fabricated in another. In 1853 a British commission investigating American technology looked on in amazement as the superintendent of the Springfield, Massachusetts, armory ordered rifles produced in ten consecutive years to be stripped and their parts reassembled at random.

The American system of manufacturing contained several distinctive advantages. Traditionally, damage to any part of a mechanical contrivance had rendered the whole useless, for no new part would fit. With the perfection of manufacturing by interchangeable parts, however, replacements could be ordered for damaged parts. In addition, the improved machine tools upon which the American system depended enabled entrepreneurs to push inventions swiftly into mass production. The likelihood that inventions would quickly enter production in turn attracted investors. By the 1850s Connecticut firms like Smith and Wesson were mass-producing the revolving pistol, which Samuel Colt had invented in 1836. Sophisticated machine tools made it possible, a manufacturer wrote, to increase production "by confining a worker to one particular limb of a pistol until he had made two thousand." The sewing machine, invented in 1846 by Elias Howe, entered mass production only two years later.

Americans also displayed an eagerness to eliminate the constraints of time and space. An impatient people inhabiting a huge area, they seized enthusiastically on Samuel F. B. Morse's invention of the telegraph in 1844. "The advantages to be

Samuel F. B. Morse

Morse had various interests besides the telegraph. In the 1820s he became a well-known portrait painter and in the 1830s a leading anti-Catholic. He later grew interested in women's higher education and co-founded Vassar College in 1865.

derived from the adoption of the Electric Telegraph," a British engineer noted in 1854, "have in no country been more promptly appreciated than in the United States. A system of communication that annihilates distance was felt to be of vital importance, both politically and commercially, in a country so vast, and having a population so widely scattered." The speed with which Americans formed telegraph companies and erected lines stunned the British. "No private interests can oppose the passage of a line through any property," the same British engineer wrote. "There are no committees, no counsel, no long array of witnesses and expensive hearings; compensation is made simply for damage done, the amount being assessed by a jury, and generally on a most moderate estimate. With a celerity that is surprising a company is formed, a line is built, and operations are commenced." Although telegraph lines usually transmitted political and commercial messages, some cities adapted them for reporting fires. By the early 1850s, Boston had an elaborate system of telegraph stations from which news of a blaze could be swiftly transmitted to fire companies throughout the city. Whatever their use, telegraph lines spread rapidly. By 1852 more than fifteen thousand miles of lines connected cities as distant as Quebec, New Orleans, and St. Louis.

The Railroad Boom

The same penchant for overcoming the natural limits imposed by time and space drove antebellum Americans to make an extraordinary investment in railroads. To an even greater degree than the telegraph, the railroad embodied progress through technology.

In 1790 even European royalty could travel no faster than fourteen miles an hour, and that only with frequent changes of horses. Yet by 1850 an ordinary American could travel on a train at three times that speed. The swift, comfortable transport that American railroads provided for the common man and woman dramatized the democratic promise of technology more vividly than any other technological innovation of the time.

In Europe railroads usually had several classes of travel. The common people were traditionally herded into crowded cars and seated on wooden benches or chairs. Only those who paid to travel first-class enjoyed a modicum of luxury. In contrast, in America there was only *one* class of railroad travel (except for blacks, who were often forced to sit separately). Furthermore, American inventors introduced a level of comfort that astonished Europeans. They experimented with adjustable upholstered seats that could be turned in whatever direction the train was traveling and that could be converted into couches at night. In effect, everyone could travel first-class. Americans, a Frenchman observed, had "a perfect passion for railroads" and loved them "as a lover loves his mistress."

Yet in the 1830s little about the railroads appeared lovable. The first trains were drawn by horses rather than by locomotives; a few actually used sails for power. Those with locomotives showered their passengers' clothing with sparks, for the riding cars were often open to the air. In the absence of brakes, passengers at times had to get out and pull trains to stops. Without means of

illumination, trains rarely ran at night. Scheduling posed problems because the United States did not adopt standard time until 1883 (see Chapter 17); at noon in Boston, it was twelve minutes before noon in New York. Moreover, trains en route faced innumerable delays. Because most railroads owned only a single track, trains had to wait on sidings for other trains to pass. Since a train's whereabouts remained a mystery once it had left a station, such waits could seem interminable.

Between 1840 and 1860, a stunning transformation occurred in the size of the rail network and in the power and convenience of trains. Railroad track increased from three thousand to thirty thousand miles. Passengers now traveled in flat-roofed coaches. Illumination by kerosene lamps made night travel possible. Locomotives gained in power to the point where they no longer had to be pulled uphill by horses or by stationary engines. Fifty thousand miles of telegraph wires enabled dispatchers to communicate with trains on route and to reduce delays.

Passengers nevertheless still confronted inconveniences. Sleeping accommodations remained crude and schedules erratic. Since individual railroads continued to use track of different gauges, frequent changes of train (eight between Charleston and Philadelphia in the 1850s) remained a necessity. Yet nothing could slow the advance of railroads or cure Americans' mania for them. By 1860 the United States had more track than the rest of the nations of the world combined.

Just as canals had spearheaded the first phase of the transportation revolution, railroads led the second phase during the 1840s and 1850s. Canals were not abandoned; the Erie Canal, for example, did not reach its peak volume until 1880. But railroads, providing much faster transport and being less vulnerable to winter frosts, gradually overtook canals, first in passenger and then in freight traffic. By 1860 the value of goods transported by railroad greatly exceeded that carried by canals.

As late as 1860, few rail lines extended west of the Mississippi, but railroads had spread like spiderwebs east of the great river. The 1840s saw vigorous railroad construction in New England; by 1850 Massachusetts had half of the track that it would possess in 1950. Elsewhere to the east of the Mississippi, the railroad boom developed mainly in the 1850s, when twenty-two thousand miles of

The Express Train

Snaking through the wilderness, trains promised to conquer distance without upsetting nature's harmony.

BRITISH NORTH AMERICA (CANADA)

Railroads, 1850

Railroads built 1850 -1860

0 · · · · 500 Miles
0 · · · · 500 Kilometers

Railroad Growth, 1850–1860

Rail ties between East and Midwest greatly increased during the railroad "boom" of the 1850s.

track were added to the nation's rail network. In the South railroads transformed places like Chattanooga and Atlanta into thriving commercial hubs. The most important development of the 1850s, however, lay in the forging of rail lines between the East and the Midwest (or "Old Northwest"). The New York Central and the Erie railroads joined eastern New York to Buffalo; the Pennsylvania Railroad connected Philadelphia and Pittsburgh; and the Baltimore and Ohio linked Baltimore to Wheeling, Virginia (now West Virginia). Simultaneously, intense construction in Ohio, Indiana, and Illinois created trunk lines that joined each of these routes. By 1860 rail lines ran from Buffalo to Cleveland, Toledo, and Chicago; from Pittsburgh to Fort Wayne; and from Wheeling to Cincinnati and on to St. Louis.

The completion of rail links between the East and Midwest rerouted much of the commerce of the nation's interior. Before the 1850s most of the agricultural surplus of the Upper Mississippi Val-

ley had made its way down the river to New Orleans for transshipment to the East. Although a railroad between New Orleans and Cincinnati was finally completed in 1859, the earlier completion of the east-west trunk lines had already deflected the flow of grain, livestock, and dairy products directly to the East, bypassing the Mississippi Valley. Gradually, Chicago supplanted New Orleans as the nation's main interior commercial hub. In 1849 Chicago had virtually no rail service, but by 1860 eleven railroads radiated from it.

Too, the forging of east-west rail trunks dramatically stimulated the settlement and agricultural development of the Midwest. By 1860 Illinois, Indiana, and Wisconsin had replaced Pennsylvania, Ohio, and New York as the leading wheat-growing states. Although settlers usually arrived in advance of the railroads, the trains gave hot pursuit. Further, by enabling midwestern farmers to speed their produce to the East, railroads greatly increased the value of their farms and thereby promoted additional settlement. By encouraging settlement, moreover, railroads indirectly stimulated the industrial development of the Midwest, because new settlers needed lumber for fences and houses, and mills to grind wheat into flour. Cities like Chicago, Davenport, Iowa, and Minneapolis grew not only as railroad hubs but as centers of lumber and flour trade.

Railroads also propelled the growth of small towns along their routes. The Illinois Central Railroad, which had more track than any other road in 1855, made money not only from its traffic but also from real-estate speculation. Purchasing land for stations along its route, the Illinois Central then laid out towns around the stations. The selection of Manteno, Illinois, as a stop of the Illinois Central, for example, transformed the site from a crossroads without a single house in 1854 into a bustling town of nearly a thousand in 1860, replete with hotels, lumberyards, grain elevators, and gristmills. (The Illinois Central even dictated the naming of streets. In the towns along its route, streets running east and west were always named after trees, and those running north and south were numbered. Soon one town looked much like the next.) By the Civil War, few thought of the railroad-linked Midwest as a frontier region or viewed its inhabitants as pioneers.

As the nation's first big business, the railroads transformed the conduct of business. During the early 1830s, railroads, like canals, depended on financial aid from state governments. With the onset of depression in the late 1830s, however, state governments scrapped overly ambitious railroad projects. Convinced that railroads burdened them with high taxes and blasted hopes, voters turned against state aid, and in the early 1840s, several states amended their constitutions to bar state funding for railroads and canals. The federal government took up some of the slack, but federal aid did not provide a major stimulus to railroads before 1860. Rather, part of the burden of finance passed to city and county governments in agricultural areas that wanted to attract railroads. Municipal governments, for example, often gave railroads rights-of-way, grants of land for stations, and public funds.

The dramatic expansion of the railroad network in the 1850s, however, strained the financing capacity of local governments and required a turn toward private investment, which had never been absent from the picture. Well aware of the economic benefits of railroads, individuals living near the roads had long purchased railroad securities issued by governments and had directly bought stock in railroads, often paying by contributing their labor to building the roads. But the large roads of the 1850s needed more capital than such small investors could generate. Gradually, the center of railroad financing shifted to New York City, and in fact, it was the railroad boom of the 1850s that helped to make Wall Street the nation's greatest capital market. The securities of all the leading railroads were traded on the floor of the New York Stock Exchange during the 1850s. In addition, the growth of railroads turned New York City into the center of modern investment firms. The investment firms evaluated the securities of railroads in Toledo or Davenport or Chattanooga and then found purchasers for these securities in New York, Philadelphia, Paris, London, Amsterdam, and Hamburg. Controlling the flow of funds to railroads, the investment bankers began to exert influence over the railroads' internal affairs by supervising administrative reorganizations in time of trouble. A Wall Street analyst noted in 1851 that railroad men seeking financing "must remember that money is power, and that the [financier] can dictate to a great extent his own terms."

Rising Prosperity

Technological advances also improved the lives of consumers by bringing down the price of many commodities. For example, clocks that cost $50 to fabricate by hand in 1800 could be produced by machine for 50¢ by 1850. In addition, the widening use of steam power contributed to a 25 percent rise in the average worker's real income (actual purchasing power) between 1840 and 1860. Early-nineteenth-century factories, which had depended on water wheels to propel their machines, of necessity had to shut down when the rivers or streams that powered the wheels froze. With the spread of steam engines, however, factories could stay open longer and workers could increase their annual wages by working more hours. Cotton textile workers were among those who benefited: although their hourly wages showed little gain, their average annual wages rose from $163 in 1830 to $176 in 1849 to $201 by 1859.

Standard Workingman's Budget, New York City, 1853

Item of Expenditure	Amount
Groceries	$273.00
Rent	100.00
Clothing, bedding, etc.	132.00
Furnishings	20.00
Fuel	18.00
Lights	10.00
Taxes, water, commutation	5.00
Physicians' and druggists' charges	10.00
Traveling	12.00
Newspapers, postage, library fees	10.00
	$590.00
Church, charity, etc.	10.00
Total annual expenditures	$600.00

SOURCE: *New York Times*, November 8, 1853. The expenditures are supposed to be those of a family of four, "living moderately."

Workingman's Budget, Philadelphia, 1851

Item of Expenditure	Amount
Butcher's meat (2 lb. a day)	$ 72.80
Flour (6½ barrels a year)	32.50
Butter (2 lb. a week)	32.50
Potatoes (2 pecks a week)	26.00
Sugar (4 lb. a week)	16.64
Coffee and tea	13.00
Milk	7.28
Salt, pepper, vinegar, starch, soap, soda, yeast, cheese, eggs	20.80
Total expenditures for food	$221.52
Rent	$156.00
Coal (3 tons a year)	15.00
Charcoal, chips, matches	5.00
Candles and oil	7.28
Household articles (wear, tear, and breakage)	13.00
Bedclothes and bedding	10.40
Wearing apparel	104.00
Newspapers	6.24
Total annual expenditures	$538.44

SOURCE: *New York Daily Tribune*, May 27, 1851. These amounts are supposed to be the minimum upon which a family of five could live. Items have been rearranged and converted to an annual basis for this table.

The growth of towns and cities also contributed to an increase in average annual wages. Farmers experienced the same seasonal fluctuations as laborers in the early factories. In sparsely settled rural areas, the onset of winter traditionally brought hard times; as demand for agricultural labor slumped, few alternatives existed to take up the slack. "A year in some farming states such as Pennsylvania," a traveler commented in 1823, "is only of eight months duration, four months being lost to the laborer, who is turned away as a useless animal." In contrast, densely populated towns and cities offered more opportunities for annual work. The urban dockworker thrown out of his job as a result of frozen waterways might find work as a hotel porter or an unskilled indoor laborer.

Towns and cities also provided women and children with new opportunities for paid work. (Women and children had long performed many vital tasks on farms, but rarely for pay.) The wages of children between the ages of ten and eighteen came to play an integral role in the nineteenth-century family economy. Family heads who earned more than $600 a year might have been able to afford the luxury of keeping their children in school, but most breadwinners were fortunate if they made $300 a year. Although the cost of many basic commodities fell between 1815 and 1860 (another consequence of the transportation revolution), most

families lived close to the margin. Budgets of workingmen's families in New York City and Philadelphia during the early 1850s reveal annual expenditures of $500–$600, with more than 40 percent spent on food, 25–30 percent on rent, and most of the remainder on clothing and fuel. Such a family obviously could not survive on the annual wages of the average male head of household. It needed the wages of its children and, at times, those of the wife as well.

Life in urban wage-earning families was not necessarily superior to life in farming communities. A farmer who owned land, livestock, and a house did not have to worry about paying rent or buying fuel for cooking and heating, and rarely ran short of food. Many Americans continued to aspire to farming as the best of all occupations. But to purchase, clear, and stock a farm involved a considerable capital outlay that could easily amount to five hundred dollars, and the effort promised no rewards for a few years. The majority of workers in agricultural areas did not own farms and were exposed to the seasonal fluctuations in demand for agricultural labor. In many respects, they were worse off than urban wage earners.

The economic advantages that attended living in cities help to explain why so many Americans moved to urban areas during the first half of the nineteenth century. As a further attraction, during the 1840s and 1850s, cities also provided their residents with an unprecedented range of comforts and conveniences.

The Quality of Life

In addition to large-scale transformations in production, transportation, and income, the two decades before the Civil War witnessed subtle alterations in the quality of everyday life in the United States. Less visible and dramatic than those wrought by the railroad, these changes in everyday experiences occurred for the most part within the privacy of homes and affected such routine activities as eating, drinking, and washing. Technological improvements in these years made the daily home-life experiences of Americans far more comfortable. "Think of the numberless contrivances and inventions for our comfort and luxury which the last half dozen years have brought forth," the poet Walt Whitman exclaimed to his readers, and you will "bless your star that fate has cast your lot in the year of Our Lord 1857." Indeed, the patent office in Washington was flooded with sketches of reclining seats, sliding tables, beds convertible into chairs, lounges convertible into cradles, street-sweeping machines, and fly traps. Machine-made furniture began to transform the interiors of houses. Stoves revolutionized heating and cooking. By bringing fresh vegetables to city dwellers, railroads stimulated important changes in diet.

Despite all of the talk of comfort and progress, many Americans, however, experienced little improvement in the quality of their lives. Technological advances made it possible for the middle class to enjoy luxuries formerly reserved for the rich but often widened the distance between the middle class and the poor. At a time when the interiors of urban, middle-class homes were becoming increasingly lavish, the urban poor congregated in cramped and unsightly tenements. In addition, some aspects of life remained relatively unaffected by scientific and technical advances. Medical science, for example, made a few advances before 1860, but none that rivaled the astonishing changes wrought by the railroad and the telegraph.

The benefits rather than the limitations of progress, however, gripped the popular imagination. Few Americans accepted the possibility that progress could neglect such an important aspect of everyday life as health. Confronted by the failure of the medical profession to rival the achievements of Cyrus McCormick and Samuel F. B. Morse, Americans embraced popular health movements that sprang up outside of the medical profession and promised to conquer disease by the precepts of diet and regimen.

Housing

During the early 1800s, urban dwellings had grown far more standardized than previously. Builders had responded to the swift growth of cities by erecting quickly constructed row houses—uniform attached dwellings increasingly made of brick. Where city dwellers in the eighteenth century usually had lived in unattached frame houses of one or two stories, all of which looked different and faced in different directions, their nineteenth-century counterparts were more likely to inhabit row houses. Some praised the uniformity of row houses as democratic, but others condemned the structures as monotonous. "The great defect in the houses," an English visitor observed, "is their extreme uniformity—when you have seen one, you have seen all."

The average row house was narrow and long, fifteen to twenty feet across, thirty to forty feet from front to back. Most had open spaces in the rear for gardens, pigs, privies, and cisterns. Row houses were not all alike. In the nineteenth century, middle-class row houses were larger (3 to 3½ stories) than working-class row houses (2 to 2½ stories). Between 1830 and 1860, moreover, the interiors of middle-class row houses became more elaborate than those of common laborers. Such features as cast-iron balconies (especially popular in the South), elegant doors, curved staircases, carved columns between rooms, and rooms with fanciful, asymmetrical shapes distinguished the row houses of the middle class from those of the less fortunate.

As land values rose in the early nineteenth century (as much as 750 percent in Manhattan between 1785 and 1815), renting rather than owning homes became more common. By 1815 more than half of the homes in the large cities were rented, usually by artisans, journeymen, and day laborers. Soaring land values also led to the subdividing of many row houses for occupancy by several families or boarders. The worst of these subdivided houses were called tenements and became the usual habitats of Irish immigrants and free blacks.

In rural areas, the quality of housing depended on the date of settlement as much as on social class. In recently settled areas, the standard dwelling was a rude, one-room log cabin with floors made of split logs that allowed drafts to seep in, roofs that let in snow, crude chimneys made of sticks and clay, and windows covered by oiled paper or cloth. As rural communities matured, however, log cabins gave way to frame houses of two or more rooms with glass windows and better insulation. Most of these houses were built on a principle known as the balloon frame. Originally, *balloon frame* was a term used by traditional artisans to express their contempt for houses that appeared so flimsily constructed as to risk blowing away. In place of foot-thick heavy timbers that were laboriously fitted together, the balloon-frame house had a skeleton of thin sawed timbers nailed together in such a way that every strain ran against the grain of the wood. The strength of balloon-frame houses soon confounded their critics, while their simplicity and cheapness endeared them to western builders with neither the time nor the skill to cut heavy beams and fit them into each other.

Home Furniture

Furniture trends between 1840 and 1860 revealed the widening gap between the lifestyles of the prosperous and those of the poor. Families in the middle and upper classes increasingly decorated their parlors with a style of furniture known as French antique or rococo. Rococo furniture reflected both the affluence and the formality of middle- and upper-class families. In such households, the ideal

Family Group

In this daguerreotype taken about 1852, a family relaxes in their parlor, which is furnished in the ornate style popular during this period.

parlor required a seven-piece matched set: an armchair for the husband, a smaller and less expensive lady's chair for his wife, a sofa, and four parlor chairs for guests and children. Rococo furniture was by definition ornate. Upholstered chairs, for example, displayed intricate scrolls depicting vines, leaves, or flowers and had curved legs with ornamental feet (called cabriole legs). The heavily upholstered backs of sofas often contained designs of rose blossoms topped by carved medallions. Artisans framed hanging mirrors with intricately fashioned and gilded moldings that depicted birds, flowers, and even young women. The finished products frequently weighed so much that they threatened to tumble from the wall.

The highly ornamented rococo furniture marked its possessors as people of substantial wealth. At the same time, the rise of mass production in such furniture centers as Grand Rapids, Michigan, and Cincinnati brought the rococo style within the financial reach of the middle class and thereby helped to close the gap between the truly wealthy (who often imported their furniture from France) and those who were merely well off. Unable to afford even mass-produced rococo pieces, however, the great majority of Americans had to be content with simpler furniture. Technological advances in the fabrication of furniture tended to level taste between the middle and upper classes while simultaneously marking those classes off from everyone else.

Heating, Cooking, and Diet

In the 1840s the transportation and industrial revolutions affected such basic household features as heating, cooking, and diet. As soon as the transportation revolution had opened distant markets, some iron foundries began to specialize in the production of cast-iron stoves. By the late 1840s, stoves were rapidly displacing open hearths for both heating and cooking.

The blaze of the open hearth had a romantic attraction for poets, but the hearth was an inefficient source of warmth: most of the heat was lost up the chimney. Because of their superior ability to retain heat, stoves allowed families to reduce expenditures on wood and coal. Stoves were also superior to hearths for cooking. Housewives could leave meals unattended on stoves, and they no longer

ran the danger of scorching their dresses while bending to reach into open flames. In addition, several dishes could be cooked at once on a stove. In this way, stoves contributed to the growing variety of the American diet.

By the 1840s most stoves burned coal rather than wood. Before 1830 English and Welsh immigrants had taught Americans how to hew coal (that is, mine it with heavy instruments), and the discovery in eastern Pennsylvania of a superior variety of coal called anthracite guaranteed a steady supply. Coal was not without drawbacks, however. A faulty coal-burning stove could fill a room with poisonous carbon monoxide. But coal burned far longer than wood and reduced the time and expense that families had traditionally devoted to acquiring fuel.

As more and more people congregated in towns and cities, and as transportation improved, urban markets for the sale of country produce multiplied. Railroads brought fresh vegetables, which in the eighteenth century had been absent even from lavish banquet tables, into towns and cities. Railcars also carried in fresh fish, poultry, and fruit. By 1860 Boston and St. Louis each had ten large public markets. Even small towns in the Midwest were likely to have public markets by the 1840s.

Despite the improvements wrought by the transportation revolution, personal diets were still subject to seasonal fluctuations. Only the rich could afford fruits out of season, for they alone could afford to buy sugar in sufficient quantities to preserve fruit. (The Florida and California citrus fruit industries still lay in the future.) Indeed, preserving almost any kind of food presented problems. Although Americans pioneered technical advances in the harvesting and storing of ice before 1840, home iceboxes were rare before 1860. One contemporary writer recommended that housewives bury meat in the snow to keep it from spoiling, but salt remained the most widely used preservative. One reason why antebellum Americans ate more pork than beef was that salt affected the taste of pork less objectionably than the flavor of beef.

Water and Sanitation

Rural homes rarely had running water. Water was brought in from wells, springs, or cisterns; used; carried outside again; and dumped. During the early

1800s, the same had been true in cities, but with increasing population density, alarm rose about the threat to well water posed by leakage from outdoor privies. In response, some cities had constructed public waterworks. In 1823 Philadelphia had completed a system that brought water along aqueducts and through pipes from the Schuylkill and Delaware rivers to street hydrants. Visiting Philadelphia in 1842, Charles Dickens marveled that the city "is most bountifully provided with fresh water, which is showered and jerked about, and turned on, and poured off every where." During the 1840s and 1850s, several other major cities constructed similar waterworks. New York City completed the Croton aqueduct (which brought water into the city from reservoirs to the north) in the 1840s, and Cleveland, Detroit, Hartford, Louisville, and Cincinnati built waterworks during the 1850s. By 1860 sixty-eight public water systems operated in the United States.

Although these municipal water systems stood among the most impressive engineering triumphs of the age, their impact is easily exaggerated. Many small cities like Rochester and Poughkeepsie, New York, had no waterworks in 1860. As late as 1862, Louisville had only 239 houses connected to its system. The 53,000 customers of New York City's system in 1856 composed less than a tenth of the city's population. Even with the establishment of waterworks, few houses had running water; the incoming water usually ended its journey at a street hydrant. As in rural areas, families had to carry water into and out of houses. Moreover, houses blessed with running water rarely possessed hot water. Before one could take a bath, water had to be heated on the stove or over the fireplace. Not surprisingly, people rarely bathed. A New England physician claimed in 1832 that not one in five of his patients took one bath a year. Fewer than fourteen hundred baths served New York City in 1855.

Because Americans bathed infrequently, their bodily odors undoubtedly were pungent, but so were smells of every sort. Even fashionable residential streets often contained stables backed by mounds of manure. Municipal sanitation departments were virtually nonexistent. Street cleaning was mainly the responsibility of private contractors, who gained a reputation for slackness in discharging their duties. To supplement the work of such undependable contractors, Americans relied on hogs, which they let roam freely and scavenge.

Thomas Dusenberry, Plumber

Advertisements pointed out the marvelous possibilities of fresh water from New York City's Croton reservoir.

(Scavenging hogs that turned down the wrong street often made tasty dinners for the poor.) The abundance of outdoor privies added to the stench. Flush toilets were rare outside of cities, and within cities provisions for sewerage lagged behind those for waterworks. With a population of 178,000 in 1860, Boston had only about five thousand flush toilets, a far higher ratio of toilets to people than most cities could report. Americans normally answered calls of nature by trips to outdoor privies, whose unpleasant smells they suppressed mainly by the application of shovelsful of dirt.

Comforts and conveniences later taken for granted were still rare in 1860. Conveniences like stoves and folding beds that made their way into the home, far from liberating women from housework, merely elevated the standards of housekeeping. In her widely popular *Treatise on Domestic*

Economy (1841), Catharine Beecher used technological advances to justify her contention that women had a duty to make every house a "glorious temple" by utilizing space and other resources more efficiently. None of this, however, changes the fact that middle-class antebellum Americans increasingly boasted of how comfortable their lives were becoming and pointed to the steady improvement in wages, diet, and water supplies as tangible marks of betterment.

Disease and Health

Despite a slowly rising standard of living, Americans remained vulnerable to disease. Between 1793, when an outbreak of yellow fever had devastated Philadelphia, and 1918–1919, when an influenza epidemic killed more than half a million Americans (and at least 20 million people worldwide), epidemics posed a constant but unpredictable threat. In 1832–1833 the combined effects of cholera and yellow fever had killed perhaps a fifth of New Orleans's population. Cholera returned to the United States in 1849 and carried off 10 percent of St. Louis's population while dealing staggering blows to most other cities.

Although not the only threats to health, epidemic diseases were the most visible and feared dangers. With grim irony, the transportation revolution increased the peril from epidemics. The cholera epidemic of 1832 had the dubious distinction of being America's first national epidemic. Its course followed that of the transportation revolution. One route of the epidemic ran from New York City up the Hudson River, across the Erie Canal to Ohio, and down the Ohio River to the Mississippi and New Orleans; the other route followed shipping up and down the East Coast from New York City.

Each major antebellum epidemic of cholera or yellow fever intensified public calls for the establishment of municipal health boards, and by the 1850s most major cities had formed such agencies. However, so few powers did city governments give them that the boards could not even enforce the reporting of diseases. In fact, public health generally remained a low-priority issue, because many doubted that any project supported by the widely distrusted medical profession could be of much value. Distrust of physicians in part grew out of the long-standing popular belief that an elite med-

CHOLERA.

THE
DUDLEY BOARD OF HEALTH,
HEREBY GIVE NOTICE, THAT IN CONSEQUENCE OF THE
Church-yards at Dudley
Being so full, no one who has died of the CHOLERA will be permitted to be buried after *SUNDAY* next, (To-morrow) in either of the Burial Grounds of *St. Thomas's*, or *St. Edmund's*, in this Town.
All Persons who die from CHOLERA, must for the future be buried in the Church-yard at Netherton.
BOARD of HEALTH, DUDLEY.
September 1st, 1832.
W. MAURICE, PRINTER, HIGH STREET, DUDL.

Cholera

So full did some cemeteries become during the 1832 cholera epidemic that the residents of certain communities were directed to bury their dead elsewhere.

ical profession had no place in a democracy (see Chapter 8). But the inability of physicians to find a satisfactory explanation for epidemic diseases also contributed to hostility toward the profession.

Prior to 1860 no one understood that tiny organisms called bacteria caused both cholera and yellow fever. Rather, rival camps of physicians battled furiously and publicly over the merits of the "contagion" theory versus those of the "miasm" theory. Insisting that cholera and yellow fever were transmitted by touch, contagionists called for vigorous measures to quarantine affected areas. In contrast, supporters of the miasm theory argued that poisonous gases (miasms) emitted by rotting vegetation or dead animals carried disease through the air. The miasm theory led logically to the conclusion that swamps should be drained and streets cleaned. Neither theory, however, was consistent with the evidence. Quarantines failed to check cholera and yellow fever (an argument against the contagionist theory), while many residents of filthy slums and stinking, low-lying areas contracted neither of the two diseases (a refutation of the miasm theory). Confronted by this inconclusive debate between medical experts, municipal leaders refused to delegate more than advisory powers to health boards dominated by physicians. After the worst epidemic in the city's history, a New Orleans editor stated in 1853 that it was "much safer to follow the common sense and unbiased opinion of the intelligent mass of the people than the opinions of medical men . . . based upon hypothetical theories."

Although most epidemic diseases baffled antebellum physicians, a basis for forward strides in surgery was laid during the 1840s by the discovery of anesthetics. Prior to 1840 young people often entertained themselves at parties by inhaling nitrous oxide, or "laughing gas," which produced sensations of giddiness and painlessness; and semicomical demonstrations of laughing gas became a form of popular entertainment. (Samuel Colt, the inventor of the revolver, had begun his career as a traveling exhibitor of laughing gas.) But nitrous oxide had to be carried around in bladders, which were difficult to handle, and in any case, few recognized its surgical possibilities. Then in 1842 Crawford Long, a Georgia physician who had attended laughing-gas frolics in his youth, employed sulfuric ether (an easily transportable liquid with the same properties as nitrous oxide) during a surgical operation. Long failed to follow up on his discovery, but four years later William T. G. Morton, a dentist, successfully employed sulfuric ether during an operation at Massachusetts General Hospital in Boston. Within a few years, ether came into wide use in American surgery.

The discovery of anesthesia improved the public image of surgeons, long viewed as brutes who hacked away at agonized patients. Furthermore, by making longer operations possible, anesthesia encouraged surgeons to take greater care than previously during surgery. Nevertheless, the failure of most surgeons to recognize the importance of clean hands and sterilized instruments partially offset the benefits of anesthesia before 1860. In 1843 Boston physician and poet Oliver Wendell Holmes, Sr., published an influential paper on how the failure of obstetricians to disinfect their hands often spread a disease called puerperal fever among mothers giving birth in hospitals. Still, the medical profession only gradually accepted the importance of disinfection. Operations remained as dangerous as the diseases or wounds that they tried to heal. The mortality rate for amputations hovered around 40 percent, and during the Civil War, 87 percent of soldiers who suffered abdominal wounds died from them.

Popular Health Movements

Doubtful of medicine and skeptical of the benefits of public health, antebellum Americans turned to a variety of therapies and regimens that promised to give them healthier and longer lives. One popular response to disease was hydropathy, or the "water cure," which filtered into the United States from Europe during the 1840s. By the mid-1850s the United States had twenty-seven hydropathic sanatoriums, which claimed to offer by cold baths and wet packs "an abundance of water of dewy softness and crystal transparency, to cleanse, renovate, and rejuvenate the disease-worn and dilapidated system." The water cure held a special attraction for well-off women, partly because hydropathics professed to relieve the pain associated with childbirth and menstruation and partly because hydropathic sanatoriums were congenial gathering places in which middle-class women could relax and exercise in private.

In contrast to the water cure, which necessitated the time and expense of a trip to a sanatorium, a health system that anyone could adopt was propounded by Sylvester Graham, a temperance reformer turned popular health advocate. Alarmed by the 1832 cholera epidemic, Graham counseled changes in diet and regimen as well as total abstinence from alcohol. Contending that Americans ate too much, he urged them to substitute vegetables, fruits, and coarse, whole-grain bread (called Graham bread) for meat and to abstain from spices, coffee, and tea as well as from alcohol. Soon Graham added sexual "excess" (by which he meant most sex) to his list of forbidden indulgences. Vegetables were preferable to meat, according to Graham, because they provoked less hunger. The food cravings of the "flesh-eater" were "greater and more imperious" than those of the vegetarian.

Many of Graham's most enthusiastic disciples were reformers. Grahamites had a special table at the Brook Farm community. Until forced out by outraged parents and hungry students, one of Graham's followers ran the student dining room at reformist Oberlin College. Much like Graham, reformers traced the evils of American society to the unnatural cravings of its people. Abolitionists, for example, contended that slavery intensified white men's lust and contributed to the violent behavior of white southerners. Similarly, Graham believed that eating meat stimulated lust and other aggressive impulses.

Yet Graham's doctrines attracted a broad audience that extended beyond the perimeters of the reform movements. Many towns and cities had boarding houses whose tables were set according to his principles. His books sold well, and his public lectures were thronged. Like hydropathy, Grahamism addressed the popular desire for better health at a time when orthodox medicine seemed to do more damage than good. Graham used religious phrases that were familiar to churchgoers and then channeled those concepts toward nonreligious goals. Luxury was "sinful," disease resembled hell, and health was a kind of heaven on earth. In this way, he provided simple and familiar assurances to an audience as ignorant as he was of the true causes of disease.

Phrenology

The belief that each person was ultimately the master of his or her own destiny marked the popular antebellum health movements. A similar impulse underlay phrenology, the most popular of the scientific fads that swept antebellum America.

Originating with the Viennese physician Franz J. Gall, phrenology centered on the idea that the human mind was composed of thirty-seven distinct faculties, or "organs," each localized in a different part of the brain. Phrenologists thought that the degree of each organ's development determined the shape of the skull, so that they could accurately analyze an individual's character by examining the bumps and depressions of the skull. During the 1830s Johann Spurzheim, a student of Gall, and George Combe, a Scot, transported phrenology to the United States, where it commanded serious attention from educated dabblers in science, including Horace Mann and Henry Ward Beecher, Lyman Beecher's son and, after midcentury, the most prominent American clergyman.

In the 1840s phrenology entered a new phase in the hands of the brothers Orson and Lorenzo Fowler. A graduate of Amherst College, where he had been a classmate of Henry Ward Beecher, Orson Fowler originally intended to become a Protestant missionary. Instead, he became a missionary for phrenology and opened a publishing house in New York City (Fowlers and Wells) that marketed books on phrenology everywhere. When some critics argued that phrenology was godless because it eliminated the idea of the human soul, the Fowlers pointed to a huge organ called Veneration to establish that people were naturally religious. When others said that phrenology was pessimistic because a person presumably could not change the shape

of his or her skull, the Fowlers retorted that every desirable organ could be improved by exercise. Lorenzo Fowler reported that several of his skull bumps had actually grown. Orson Fowler wrapped it all into a tidy slogan: "Self-Made, or Never-Made."

Drawing phrenological charts of oneself or one's friends became a parlor game of sorts during the 1840s and 1850s, but phrenology appealed to Americans less as a pastime than as a "practical" science. In a mobile and individualistic society where people routinely transacted business with strangers, phrenology promised to provide at a glance a quick assessment of others. Merchants used phrenological charts to pick suitable clerks, and young maidens induced their fiancés to undergo phrenological analyses before tying the knot. Before phrenology, a supporter declared, "the wisest of men had no means of deciding, with anything like certainty, the talents or character of a stranger."

Phrenology did not cure disease, but phrenologists had close ties to the popular health movement. Fowlers and Wells issued the *Water-Cure Journal* after 1848 and brought out Sylvester Graham's *Lectures on the Science of Human Life*. Orson Fowler filled his popular phrenological books with tips on the evils of coffee, tea, meat, spices, and sex that could have been plucked from Graham's writings. As a "science," phrenology sprang from the same impulse as the health movements—the belief that anyone could understand and obey the "laws" of life.

Unlike hydropathy, phrenology did not require any investment of money. Unlike Grahamism, it did not call for painful abstinence. Easily understood and practiced by the average person, and filled with the promise of universal betterment, phrenology was the ideal science for antebellum America. Just as Americans invented machines to better their lives, they were not above inventing "sciences" that promised human betterment.

Democratic Pastimes

Between 1830 and 1860, technology increasingly transformed leisure as well as work. At times, the impact of technology on leisure was indirect. For example, as factory-made clothing displaced homespun, many middle-class women had more free time and occupied it by reading. By 1860 women composed the bulk of the novel-reading public, and fiction by and about women so flooded the country that Nathaniel Hawthorne complained of competition from a "damned pack of female scribblers." But technology's main effect on leisure was direct. In the years before the Civil War, Americans became dependent on types of recreation that were manufactured and sold. Recreation became a commodity that people purchased in the form of cheap newspapers and novels as well as affordable tickets to plays, museums, and lectures.

Just as the Boston Associates had daringly capitalized on new technology to produce textiles at Lowell and Waltham, imaginative entrepreneurs utilized technology to make and sell entertainment. Men like James Gordon Bennett, one of the founders of the penny press in America, and P. T. Barnum, the greatest showman of the nineteenth century, amassed fortunes by sensing what people wanted and then employing available technology to satisfy their desire. To a degree, indeed, these men induced the public to want what they had to sell. Barnum, for example, had a genius for using newspaper publicity to pique popular interest in curiosities that he was about to exhibit.

Bennett and Barnum thought of themselves as purveyors of democratic entertainment. They would sell their wares cheaply to anyone. Barnum's famous American museum in New York City catered to a wide variety of social classes that paid to view paintings, dwarfs, mammoth bones, and other attractions. By marketing the American Museum as family entertainment, Barnum helped to break down barriers that had long divided the pastimes of husbands from those of their wives. Similarly, the racy news stories in Bennett's *New York Herald* provided its vast audience with a common stock of information and topics for conversation. In these ways, the impact of technology on amusement was democratic.

Technology also ignited the process by which individuals became spectators rather than the creators of their own amusements. Americans had long found ways to enjoy themselves. Even the gloomiest Puritans had indulged in games and sports. After 1830, however, the burden of providing entertainment began to shift from individuals to

entrepreneurs who supplied ways to amuse the public.

Newspapers

In 1830 the typical American newspaper was a mere four pages long, with the front and back pages devoted almost wholly to advertisements. The second and third pages contained editorials, details of ship arrivals and of their cargoes, reprints of political speeches, and notices of political events. Few papers depended on their circulation for profit; even the most prominent papers had a daily circulation of only one thousand to two thousand. Rather, papers often relied on subsidies from political parties or factions. When a party gained power, it inserted paid political notices only in papers loyal to it. "Journalists," a contemporary wrote, "were usually little more than secretaries dependent upon cliques of politicians, merchants, brokers, and office seekers for their prosperity and bread."

Newspaper Boy, *by Edward Bannister, 1869*

Newsboys such as this one poignantly painted by the black artist Edward Bannister were a familiar sight on nineteenth-century street corners.

As a result, newspapers could be profitable without being particularly popular. Because of their potential for profit, new papers were constantly being established. But most had limited appeal. The typical paper sold for six cents an issue at a time when the average daily wage was less than a dollar. Papers often seemed little more than published bulletin boards. Merely records of events, they typically lacked the exciting news stories and eye-catching illustrations that later generations would take for granted.

The 1830s witnessed the beginnings of a stunning transformation. Technological changes, most of which originated in Europe, vastly increased both the supply of paper (still made from rags) and the speed of printing presses. The substitution of steam-driven cylindrical presses for flatbed hand presses led to a tenfold increase in the number of printed pages that could be produced in an hour. Enterprising journalists, among them the Scottish-born James Gordon Bennett, grasped the implications of the new technology. Newspapers could now rely on vast circulation rather than on political subsidies to turn a profit. To gain circulation, journalists like Bennett slashed the price of newspapers. In 1833 the *New York Sun* became America's first penny newspaper, and Bennet's *New York Herald* followed in 1835. By June 1835 the combined daily circulation of New York's three penny papers reached 44,000; in contrast, before the dawn of the penny press in 1833, the city's eleven dailies had a combined daily circulation of only 26,500. Spearheaded by the penny papers, the combined daily circulation of newspapers throughout the nation rose from roughly 78,000 in 1830 to 300,000 by 1840. The number of weekly newspapers spurted from 65 in 1830 to 138 in 1840.

Cheapness was not the only feature of the penny papers. Dependent on circulation and advertising rather than on subsidies, the penny press revolutionized the marketing and format of papers. Where single copies of the six-cent papers were usually available only at the printer's office, newsboys hawked the penny papers on busy street corners. Moreover, the penny papers subordinated the recording of political and commercial events to human-interest stories of robberies, murders, rapes, and abandoned children. They dispatched reporters to police courts and printed transcripts of trials. As sociologist Michael Schudson observes, "The penny press invented the modern concept of 'news.'" Rather than merely recording events, the penny papers wove events into gripping stories. They invented not only news but also news reporting. Relying on party stalwarts to dispatch copies of speeches and platforms, and reprinting news items from other papers, the older six-cent papers did little, if any, reporting. In contrast, the penny papers employed their own correspondents and were the first papers to use the telegraph to speed news to readers.

Some penny papers were little more than scandal sheets, but the best, like Bennett's *New York Herald* and Horace Greeley's *New York Tribune* (1841), pioneered modern financial and political reporting. From its inception, the *Herald* contained a daily "money article" that substituted the analysis and interpretation of financial events for the dull recording of commercial facts. "The spirit, pith, and philosophy of commercial affairs is what men of business want," Bennett wrote. The relentless snooping of the *Tribune*'s Washington reporters outraged politicians. In 1848 *Tribune* correspondents were temporarily barred from the House floor for reporting that Representative Sawyer of Ohio ate his lunch (sausage and bread) each day in the House chamber, picked his teeth with a jackknife, and wiped his greasy hands on his pants and coat.

The Popular Novel

Like newspapers, novels became enormously popular between 1830 and 1860. Of course, novels had been read long before 1830, and some authors, among them the Scot Sir Walter Scott, had gained a wide following. But the cost of novels before 1830 had restricted their sales. Each of Scott's novels, for example, was issued in a three-volume set that retailed for as much as thirty dollars. During the 1830s and 1840s, the impact of the transportation revolution and technical advances in printing brought down the price of novels. As canals and railroads opened crossroads stores to the latest fiction, publishers in New York and Philadelphia vied to deliver inexpensive novels to the shelves. By the 1840s cheap paperbacks that sold for as little as seven cents began to flood the market.

Those who did not purchase such fictional books could read serializations in newspapers that were devoted mainly to printing novels. The most successful of these story papers was the *New York Ledger*, which a young Scotch-Irish immigrant, Robert Bonner, started in the mid-1840s. Like James Gordon Bennett, the lord of the penny press, Bonner had a genius for identifying what the public wanted and for launching publicity extravaganzas. To herald the serialization of one novel, Bonner spent twenty thousand dollars and arranged the firing of a one-hundred-gun salute in City Hall Park. By 1860 the *Ledger* had an astonishing weekly circulation of four hundred thousand.

The most popular fiction on the market in the 1840s and 1850s was the sentimental novel, which sought to evoke feelings or emotions. The tribulations of orphans and the deaths of children filled the pages of these tearjerkers. In Susan Warner's *The Wide, Wide World* (first serialized in 1850), the heroine burst into tears on an average of every other page for two volumes. Sentimentalism was not confined to novels. The popular writer Lydia Sigourney wrote a poem on the death of a canary that had accidentally been starved to death.

Women contributed the main audience for sentimental novels. This genre was a kind of women's fiction, written by women about women and mainly for women. The most lucrative occupation open to women before the Civil War, writing often attracted those in desperate need of cash. Hard times had lured many renowned female novelists into the field. Susan Warner, for example, had been brought up in luxury and then tossed into poverty by the financial ruin of her father in the Panic of 1837. Mrs. E. D. E. N. Southworth, who gained fame and fortune from *The Hidden Hand* (first serialized in 1859) and other novels, turned to writing after a broken marriage left her supporting two children on a teacher's salary of $250 a year.

Women's fiction dealt with more than the flow of tears. A major theme in the novels of Susan Warner and Mrs. Southworth was that women could conquer any obstacle. Women's novels challenged the stereotype of the male as the trusty provider and of the female as the delicate dependent by portraying men as liars, drunken lechers, or vicious misers and depicting women as resourceful and strong-willed. In the typical plot, a female orphan or a spoiled rich girl thrown on hard times, or a dutiful daughter plagued by a drunken father, learned grittily to master every situation. The moral was clear. Women could overcome trials and make the world a better place. Few of the novelists were active feminists, but their writings provided a glimpse into the private feelings of their female readers.

The Theater

During the 1850s novelists like the Englishman Charles Dickens and the American Harriet Beecher Stowe, the author of *Uncle Tom's Cabin*, were as well known through dramatizations of their work as by sales of their books. Antebellum theaters were large (twenty-five hundred to four thousand seats in some cities) and crowded by all classes. With seats as cheap as twelve cents and rarely more than fifty cents, the typical theater audience included lawyers and merchants and their wives, artisans and clerks, sailors and noisy boys, and a sizable body of prostitutes. Prostitutes usually sat in the top gallery, called the third tier, "that dark, horrible, guilty" place. The presence of prostitutes in theaters was taken for granted; the only annoyance came when they left the third tier to solicit customers in the more expensive seats.

The prostitutes in attendance were not the only factor that made the antebellum theater vaguely disreputable. Theatrical audiences were notoriously rowdy. They showed their feelings by stamping their feet, whistling, hooting at villains, and throwing potatoes or garbage at the stage when they did not like the characters or the acting. Individual actors developed huge followings, and the public displayed at least as much interest in the actors as in the plays. In 1849 a long-running feud between the leading American actor, Edwin Forrest, and the popular British actor William Macready ended with a riot at New York City's Astor Place that left twenty people dead.

The Astor Place riot demonstrated the broad popularity of the theater. Forrest's supporters included a following of Irish workers who loathed the British and appealed to the "working men" to rally against the "aristocrat" Macready. Macready, who projected a more polished and intellectual image than Forrest, attracted the better-educated classes. Had not all classes patronized the theater, the riot probably would never have occurred.

The plays themselves were as diverse as the audiences. Most often performed were melodramas, whose plots resembled those of sentimental novels. Vice was punished, virtue rewarded, and the heroine finally married the hero. Yet the single most popular dramatist was William Shakespeare. In 1835 audiences in Philadelphia witnessed sixty-five performances of Shakespeare's plays. Americans who may never have read a line of Shakespeare grew familiar with Othello, King Lear, Desdemona, and Shylock. Theatrical managers adapted Shakespeare to a popular audience. They highlighted the swordfights and assassinations, cut some speeches, omitted minor characters, and pruned words or references that might have offended the audience's sense of propriety. For example, they substituted *pottels* for *urinals* and quietly advanced Juliet's age at the time that she falls in love with Romeo from fourteen to eighteen. They occasionally changed sad endings to happy ones. The producers even arranged for short performances or demonstrations between acts of Shakespeare—and indeed, of every play. During such an interlude, the audience might have observed a brief impersonation of Tecumseh or Aaron Burr, jugglers and acrobats, a drummer beating twelve drums at once, or a three-year-old who weighed a hundred pounds.

Minstrel Shows

The Yankee or "Brother Jonathan" figure who served as a stock character in many antebellum plays helped audiences to form an image of the ideal American as rustic, clever, patriotic, and more than a match for city slickers and decadent European aristocrats. In a different way, the minstrel shows that Americans thronged to see in the 1840s and 1850s forged enduring stereotypes that buttressed white Americans' sense of superiority by diminishing black people.

Minstrel shows arose in northern cities in the 1840s, as blackfaced white men took to the stage to present an evening of songs, dances, and humorous sketches. Minstrelsy borrowed some authentic elements of African-American culture, especially dances characterized by the sliding, shuffling step of southern blacks, but most of the songs had origins in white culture. Such familiar American songs as Stephen Foster's "Camptown Races" and "Massa's in the Cold Ground," which first aired in min-

Dan Bryant, the Minstrel

Bryant was one of many antebellum popularizers of black minstrelsy. One of the earliest known minstrelsy performances occurred in Boston in 1799, when the white man Gottlieb Graupner, reportedly made up as a black, sang and accompanied himself on the banjo.

strel shows, reflected white Americans' notions of how blacks sang more than it represented authentic black music. In addition, the images of blacks projected by minstrelsy both catered to and reinforced the prejudices of the working-class whites who dominated the audience of minstrel shows. Minstrel troupes usually depicted blacks as stupid, clumsy, and obsessively musical and emphasized the Africanness of blacks by giving their characters names like the Ethiopian Serenaders and their acts titles like the Nubian Jungle Dance and the African Fling. At a time of intensifying political conflict over race, minstrel shows planted images and expectations about blacks' behavior through stock characters. These included Uncle Ned, the tattered, humble, and docile slave, and Zip Coon, the arrogant urban free black who paraded around in a high hat, long-tailed coat, and green vest and who lived off his girlfriends' money. Minstrels lampooned blacks who assumed public roles by portraying them as incompetent stump speakers who called Patrick Henry "Henry Patrick," referred to John Hancock as "Boobcock," and confused the word *statute* with *statue*.

By the 1850s major cities from New York to San Francisco had several minstrel theaters. Touring professional troupes and local amateur talent even brought minstrelsy to small towns and villages. Mark Twain later recalled how minstrelsy had burst upon Hannibal, Missouri, in the early 1840s as "a glad and stunning surprise." So popular was the craze that minstrels even visited the White House and entertained Presidents John Tyler, James K. Polk, Millard Fillmore, and Franklin Pierce.

P. T. Barnum

The remarkable career of P. T. Barnum exemplified the intersection of virtually all of the forces that made entertainment a profitable business in antebellum America. As a young man in his native Bethel, Connecticut, Barnum savored popular journalism by starting a newspaper, the *Herald of Freedom,* that assailed wrongdoing in high places. Throughout his life, he thought of himself as a public benefactor and pointed to his profits as proof that he gave people what they wanted. Yet honesty was never his strong suit. As a small-town grocer in Connecticut, he regularly cheated his customers on the principle that they were trying to cheat him. Barnum, in short, was a hustler raised in the land of the Puritans, a cynic and an idealist rolled into one.

After moving to New York City in 1834, Barnum started a new career as an entrepreneur of popular entertainment. His first venture exhibited a black woman, Joice Heth, whom Barnum billed as the 169-year-old former slave nurse of George Washington. Barnum neither knew nor cared how old Joice was (in fact, she was probably around 80); it was enough that people would pay to see her. Strictly speaking, he cheated the public, but he knew that many of his customers shared his doubts about Joice's age. Determined to expose Barnum's gimmick, some poked her to see whether she was really a machine rather than a person. He was playing a game with the public, and the public with him.

In 1841 Barnum purchased a run-down museum in New York City, rechristened it the American

P. T. Barnum and Tom Thumb

Charles Stratton, whom Barnum renamed General Tom Thumb, was a midget. When discovered by Barnum in Bridgeport, Connecticut, in 1842, Tom was nearly five years old, stood only two feet tall, and had gained a mere six pounds since birth. Characteristically, Barnum immediately advertised Tom as an eleven-year-old and took him on tour.

Museum, and opened a new chapter in the history of popular entertainment. The founders of most earlier museums had intended an educational purpose. They exhibited stuffed birds and animals, specimens of rock, and portraits. Most of these museums, however, had languished for want of public interest. Barnum, in contrast, made piquing public curiosity the main goal. To attract people, he added collections of curiosities and faked exhibits. Visitors to the American Museum could see ventriloquists, magicians, albinos, a five-year-old midget whom Barnum named General Tom Thumb and later took on a tour of Europe, and the "Feejee Mermaid," a shrunken oddity that Barnum billed as "positively asserted by its owner to have been taken alive in the Feejee Islands." By 1850 the American Museum had become the best-known museum in the nation and a model for popular museums in other cities.

Blessed with a genius for publicity, Barnum recognized that newspapers could invent as well as report news. One of his favorite tactics was to puff his exhibits by writing letters (under various names) to newspapers, in which he would hint that the scientific world was agog over some astonishing curiosity of nature that the public could soon see for itself at the American Museum. But Barnum's success rested on more than publicity. A staunch temperance advocate, he provided regular lectures at the American Museum on the evils of alcohol and soon gave the place a reputation as a center for safe family amusement. Finally, Barnum tapped the public's insatiable curiosity about natural wonders. In 1835 the editor of the *New York Sun* had boosted his circulation by claiming that a famous astronomer had discovered pelicans and winged men on the moon. At a time when each passing year brought new technological wonders, the public was ready to believe in anything, even the Feejee Mermaid.

The Quest for Nationality in Literature and Art

Sentimental novels, melodramas, minstrel shows, and the American Museum belonged to the world of popular culture. All these genres lacked the dignity and originality that would endear them to those seeking cultural expressions that would reflect the American national spirit and command respect abroad. The limits of the popular genres—with their frequent crudity and their interchangeable plots, characters, and themes—did not escape the notice of reflective observers. During the 1830s Ralph Waldo Emerson emerged as the most influential spokesman for those who sought a national literature and art.

"Our day of dependence, our long apprenticeship to the learning of other lands, draws to a close," Emerson announced in his address "The American Scholar" (1837). For too long, Emerson affirmed, Americans had deferred to European precedents in literature and learning. Now the time had come

for the American people to trust themselves. Let "the single man plant himself indomitably on his instincts and there abide," and "the huge world will come round to him."

Contemporaries proclaimed "The American Scholar" an intellectual Declaration of Independence and praised Emerson for having "cut the cable" that still moored the United States to European thought. Yet Emerson's plea for cultural autonomy was hardly new; ever since the Revolution, Americans had been calling for cultural as well as political independence from Britain. In the 1780s Noah Webster, the famous compiler of textbooks and dictionaries that substituted phonetic American spellings for British spellings, had warned that basing American literature on European taste and manners was as foolish as constructing "a durable and stately edifice . . . upon the mouldering pillars of antiquity."

"The American Scholar" had an electrifying effect for several reasons. First, as Emerson recognized, the democratic spirit of the age had made Americans more self-reliant. Successful in their political and material lives, they no longer felt the need to defer to European standards. In addition, the dramatic impact of Emerson's address reflected his ability to adapt an international literary movement known as romanticism to American conditions. Originating in Europe in the second half of the eighteenth century, romanticism challenged the rival impulse known as classicism (or neoclassicism). Classicists described standards of beauty and taste as universal and decreed that the most desirable literary productions display elegance and polish. In contrast, romantics argued that each nation had to discover its own unique literary genius. They further insisted that great literature reflect not only national character but also the most profound emotions of the writer. Where classicists expected that all fine literature and art would conform to an identical standard of elegance, romantics sought individuality in literary and artistic expression.

As we have seen, during the 1830s the transcendentalist movement emerged as a challenge to Unitarianism, and in their literary work, Emerson and other transcendentalists evolved a uniquely American form of romanticism. Dismissing the prevailing idea that all knowledge came through the senses, transcendentalists argued instead that such basic conceptions as those of God and freedom were inborn. Knowledge resembled sight—

an instantaneous, direct perception of truth. Emerson concluded that learned people enjoyed no special advantages in the pursuit of truth. All persons could see the truth if only they would trust the promptings of their hearts. Applied to the United States, transcendentalist doctrine led to the exhilarating conclusion that a young, democratic society could produce as noble a literature and art as the more traditional societies of Europe. While such a fledgling, democratic society might lack elegance and polish, it could draw upon the inexhaustible resources of the common people.

Literary Geography

Emerson's "The American Scholar" coincided with a flowering of distinctively American literature and art, often called the American Renaissance, that had been gaining momentum since the 1820s. By 1837 the American public had grown as familiar with native-born authors such as Washington Irving and James Fenimore Cooper as with such lions of the British literary world as Sir Walter Scott and Charles Dickens. Emerson did not initiate this outpouring of native talent, but he expressed its ideals and helped to shape its direction.

Of all the regions of the United States, New England had the most fertile soil for literature. Its poets ranged from the urbane Henry Wadsworth Longfellow and polished Boston aristocrats like Oliver Wendell Holmes, Sr., and James Russell Lowell to the farm-born, self-taught Quaker John Greenleaf Whittier. Boston also became the home of George Bancroft, William Hickling Prescott, Francis Parkman, and John Lothrop Motley, the four most distinguished historians of the antebellum period. Twenty miles from Boston lay Concord, the home of Emerson, Nathaniel Hawthorne, the eccentric Henry David Thoreau, and the brilliant philosopher and critic Margaret Fuller. Not far from Concord lay Fruitlands, a utopian community where Louisa May Alcott, the author of *Little Women* (1868), passed part of her childhood under the sometimes dizzying influence of her unworldly father, Bronson Alcott. Farther to the west was Amherst, the residence of Emily Dickinson. Shy and reclusive, she lived out her entire fifty-six years on the same street ("I do not go from home," she stated with characteristic pithiness), where she wrote exquisite poems that examined, in her own words, every splinter in the groove of

the brain. Dreading the corruption of her art by commercialism, she staunchly refused to publish her verse.

Most New Englanders did not share Emily Dickinson's horror of publicity. Nineteenth-century New England writers and publishers widely exported their region's culture. By the end of the century, schoolchildren throughout the nation were turning pages of Longfellow's *Evangeline* (1847) and *The Song of Hiawatha* (1855), Whittier's *Snow-Bound* (1866), and Lowell's antislavery *The Biglow Papers* (1848). What had begun as a regional culture became enshrined as a national culture, and for this reason alone, New England's literary renaissance deserves special recognition.

New England, however, always faced a challenge from New York, the home of Irving, Cooper, and later of Walt Whitman and Herman Melville. Even before the flowering of American literature, New York had abounded with literary clubs, composed for the most part of wealthy young lawyers and merchants. It was in New York that the wealthy and gifted Irving had made his reputation with the publication of the comedic *Diedrich Knickerbocker's A History of New York* (1809). After serving in the War of 1812, Irving had left the United States for Europe and had not returned until 1832. Yet his *Sketch Book* (1820), which contained "Rip Van Winkle" and "The Legend of Sleepy Hollow," continued to endear him to Americans, who displayed a boastful pride in the literary accomplishments of their best-known writer.

The literary flowering affected all regions. Southerners such as William Gilmore Simms, the author of *The Yemassee* (1835), acquired reputations that spread beyond their native section. Although he did most of his writing in New York and Philadelphia, Edgar Allan Poe was a Virginian by upbringing and emotional identification. In the lower and westerly regions of the Old South, Augustus B. Longstreet and Johnson J. Hooper crafted humorous sketches that captured a kind of backcountry roguishness and rowdiness so extravagant that it became hilarious. Longstreet's *Georgia Scenes* (1835) described gander pulling, eye gouging, and other frontier pastimes. Hooper's *Some Adventures of Captain Simon Suggs* (1846) related how Suggs cheated his own father at cards to obtain a horse and how he went to a camp meeting to get religion and came away with the contents of the collection box instead.

**Washington Irving;
Rip Van Winkle**

Visiting Britain in 1817, Irving met Sir Walter Scott, who urged him to study German legends for fictional material. Irving took this advice and borrowed heavily from the German legend of "Peter Klaus" for "Rip Van Winkle," his most famous tale.

Not all antebellum writers, however, have passed the test of time. Irving's writings now strike critics as examples of a comfortable second-ratedness. Although polished poets, neither Longfellow nor Whittier was notably innovative. Dickinson was a genius, but born in 1830, she did most of her writing after 1860. In retrospect, regional humorists like Longstreet and Hooper are significant mainly because they foreshadowed a far greater humorist, Mark Twain.

Yet within the large circle of antebellum writers, the genius of seven individuals continues to shine: Cooper, Emerson, Thoreau, Whitman, Hawthorne, Melville, and Poe. Cooper and Emerson basked in public esteem in their day, but neither Hawthorne nor Poe gained the popular audience that each believed he deserved. The antebellum public largely ignored the remaining three—Thoreau, Whitman, and Melville. Creativity rather than popularity became the unifying characteristic of these seven writers. Each challenged existing literary conventions and created new ones. Cooper demonstrated the possibility of writing a novel using distinctively American literary themes. Emerson gave a new direction to an old literary form, the essay. Thoreau wrote about nature in a way that captured not only its beauty but its constant activity. By breaking with the conventions of rhyme and meter, Whitman breathed new vitality into poetry. As a writer of both short fiction and poetry, Poe went far to free literature from the insistence that it preach a moral and to establish the principle that fiction and poetry be judged by the pleasure that they imparted. Hawthorne and Melville turned the novel into a vehicle for exploring the depths of human psychology.

James Fenimore Cooper and the Quest for Literary Independence

Until well after 1800, British literature had dominated American literary taste. With the publication of *Waverley* (1814), a historical novel set in Britain in the 1740s, the star of Sir Walter Scott had begun its spectacular ascent on the American horizon. Americans had named more than a dozen towns Waverley; advertisements for subsequent novels by Scott had borne the simple caption, "By the author of *Waverley*."

Because he wrote historical novels under Scott's influence, James Fenimore Cooper, born in 1789, has often been called the American Scott. But this designation is misleading, for the enormously popular Cooper achieved a remarkable creativity in his own right. His most important innovation was to introduce to fiction such an American type as the frontiersman Natty Bumppo ("Leatherstocking") and such a distinctly American theme as the conflict between the customs of primitive life on the frontier and the irresistible advance of civilization. Starting with the publication of *The Pioneers* (1823), both the career of Leatherstocking and the conflict between nature and civilization unfolded in Cooper's novels, notably *The Last of the Mohicans* (1826), *The Pathfinder* (1840), and *The Deerslayer* (1841). Cooper's popularity was enhanced by his remarkable productivity. He averaged a novel a year for thirty-one years and once said that he found it harder to read his novels than to write them. The reading public knew what to expect of Cooper and rewarded him with its patronage.

Cooper's success marked the first step in a process that saw Americans develop an imaginative literature of their own. They still read British novels, but they increasingly enjoyed American writers. In 1800 American authors accounted for a negligible proportion of the output of American publishers. By 1830, 40 percent of the books published in the United States were written by Americans; and by 1850, 75 percent.

Emerson, Thoreau, and Whitman

Emerson's advocacy of a national literature extended beyond his urgings in "The American Scholar." In writings of his own, he tried (not always successfully) to capture the brisk language of the common people of the United States. Furthermore, he encouraged younger American writers like Thoreau and Whitman. Whitman, extravagantly patriotic, contrasted sharply with Emerson and Thoreau, who often criticized the materialism and aggressiveness of their countrymen. The ideal of nationality in literature clearly did not always mean the uncritical celebration of Americans and American policies. But the uniquely American prose or poetry that flowed from the pens of these three writers did share a strong common feature: it emphasized the spontaneous and vivid expression of personal feelings over learned analysis, which the writers associated with European traditions.

Born in 1803, Emerson served briefly as a Unitarian minister. During the 1830s he carved out a new career for himself as a public lecturer. The topics of his addresses, most of which he published as essays, appeared to be broad and general: "Beauty," "Nature," "Power," "Representative

Men," and "New England Reformers." But a unique pungency and vividness characterized his language. For example, in "The American Scholar," in which Emerson emphasized the importance of independent thought on the part of the true scholar, his language was striking: "Let him [the scholar] not quit his belief that a popgun is a popgun, though the ancient and honorable of the earth affirm it to be the crack of doom." Equally remarkable was Emerson's way of developing his subjects. A contemporary compared listening to Emerson to trying to see the sun in a fog; one could see light but never the sun itself. As a transcendentalist who believed that knowledge reflected the voice of God within every person and that truth was inborn and universal, Emerson never amassed evidence or presented systematic arguments to prove his contentions. Rather, he relied on a sequence of vivid and arresting though often unconnected assertions. The argument was hard to follow (one listener thought she might have better understood Emerson if she had stood on her head), but the overall effect dazzled the audience.

Emerson had a magnetic attraction for intellectually inclined young men and women who did not fit easily into American society. Henry David Thoreau, born in 1809 in Concord, Massachusetts, where Emerson took up residence during the 1830s, was representative of the younger Emersonians. Yet a crucial difference separated the two men. Adventurous in thought, Emerson was basically unadventurous in action. As contemplative as Emerson, Thoreau was more of a doer. At one point, Thoreau went to jail rather than pay his poll tax. This revenue, he knew, would support the war against Mexico, which he viewed as part of a southern conspiracy to extend slavery. The experience led Thoreau to write *Civil Disobedience* (1849), in which he defended the right to disobey unjust laws.

In the spring of 1845, Thoreau moved a few miles from Concord into the woods near Walden Pond. There he constructed a simple cabin on land owned by Emerson and spent the next two years providing for his wants away from civilization. Thoreau's stated purpose in retreating to Walden was to write a description (later published) of a canoe trip that he and his brother had taken down the Concord and Merrimack rivers in 1839. During his stay in the woods, however, he conceived and wrote a much more important book, *Walden*

(1854). A contemporary described *Walden* as "the log-book of his woodland cruise," and indeed, Thoreau filled its pages with descriptions of hawks and wild pigeons, his invention of raisin bread, his trapping of the woodchucks that despoiled his vegetable garden, and his construction of a cabin for exactly $28.50. Few writers have matched Thoreau's ability to capture both the details and the cycles of nature and to give the reader the sensation of being present at the scene. But true to transcendentalism, Thoreau had a larger message. His woodland retreat taught him that he (and by implication, others) could satisfy material wants with only a few weeks' work each year and thereby leave more time for reexamining life's purpose. The problem with Americans, he said, was that they turned themselves into "mere machines" to acquire wealth without asking why. Thoreau bore the uncomfortable truth that material and moral progress were not as intimately related as Americans liked to think.

One of Ralph Waldo Emerson's qualities was an ability to sympathize with such dissimilar personalities as Thoreau and Walt Whitman—the former eccentric, reclusive, and critical; the latter self-taught, outgoing, exuberant, and in love with virtually everything about America except slavery. Born in 1819, Whitman left school at eleven and became a printer's apprentice and later a journalist and editor for various newspapers in Brooklyn, Manhattan, and New Orleans. A familiar figure at Democratic party functions, he marched in the vanguard of party parades and put his pen to the service of the party's free-soil wing.

Journalism gave Whitman an intimate knowledge of ordinary Americans; the more he knew them, the more he liked them. His reading of Emerson nurtured his belief that America was to be the cradle of a new citizen in whom natural virtue would flourish unimpeded by European corruption, a man like Andrew Jackson, that "massive, yet most sweet and plain character." The threads of Whitman's early career came together in his major work, *Leaves of Grass*, a book of poems first published in 1855 and reissued with additions in subsequent years.

Leaves of Grass shattered most existing poetic conventions. Not only did Whitman write in free verse (that is, most of his poems had neither rhyme nor meter), but the poems were also lusty and blunt at a time when delicacy reigned in the literary world.

Walt Whitman

Whitman is today considered one of the major nineteenth-century poets, but in his day many derided his verse as indecent. In 1865 Whitman lost his job with the U.S. government when his superiors found out that he was the author of Leaves of Grass.

Whitman wrote of "the scent of these arm-pits finer than prayer" and "winds whose soft-tickling genitals rub against me." No less remarkably, Whitman intruded himself into his poems, one of which he titled "Song of Walt Whitman" (and later retitled "Song of Myself"). Although Whitman thought well of himself, it was not egotism that propelled him to sing of himself. Rather, he viewed himself—crude, plain, self-taught, and passionately democratic—as the personification of the American people. He was

> Comrade of raftsmen and coalmen, comrade
> of all who shake hands and welcome to
> drink and meat,
> A learner with the simplest, a teacher of the
> thoughtfullest.

By 1860 Whitman had acquired a considerable reputation as a poet. Nevertheless, the original edition of *Leaves* (a run of only about eight hundred copies) was ignored or derided as a "heterogeneous mass of bombast, egotism, vulgarity, and nonsense." One reviewer suggested that it was the work of an escaped lunatic. Only Emerson and a few

411

others reacted enthusiastically. Within two weeks of publication, Emerson, never having met Whitman, wrote: "I find it the most extraordinary piece of wit and wisdom that America has yet contributed." Emerson had long called for the appearance of "the poet of America" and knew in a flash that in Whitman, that poet had arrived.

Hawthorne, Melville, and Poe

In "The American Scholar," Emerson called upon American writers to create a democratic literature by comprehending "the near, the low, the common"—the everyday experiences of ordinary Americans. However exhilarating a message, Emerson's plea had a negligible impact on the major writers of fiction during the 1840s and 1850s—Nathaniel Hawthorne, Herman Melville, and Edgar Allan Poe. Hawthorne, for example, set *The Scarlet Letter* (1850) in New England's Puritan past, *The House of the Seven Gables* (1851) in a mansion haunted not by ghosts but by memories of the past, and *The Marble Faun* (1859) in Rome. Poe set several of his short stories such as "The Murders in the Rue Morgue" (1841), "The Masque of the Red Death" (1842), and "The Cask of Amontillado" (1846) in Europe; as one critic has noted, "His art could have been produced as easily had he been born in Europe." Melville did draw materials and themes from his own experiences as a sailor and from the lore of the New England whaling industry, but for his novels *Typee* (1846), *Omoo* (1847), and *Mardi* (1849), he picked the exotic setting of islands in the South Seas; and for his masterpiece *Moby-Dick* (1851), the ill-fated whaler *Pequod*. If the only surviving documents from the 1840s and 1850s were its major novels, historians would face an impossible task in describing the appearance of antebellum American society.

The unusual settings favored by these three writers partly reflected their view that American life lacked the materials for great fiction. Hawthorne, for example, bemoaned the difficulty of writing about a country "where there is no shadow, no antiquity, no mystery, no picturesque and gloomy wrong, nor anything but a commonplace prosperity in broad and simple daylight, as is happily the case with my dear native land." In addition, psychology rather than society riveted the attention of these three writers; each probed the depths of the human mind rather than the intricacies of social

relationships. Their preoccupation with analyzing the mental states of their characters grew out of their underlying pessimism about the human condition. Emerson, Whitman, and (to a degree) Thoreau optimistically believed that human conflicts could be resolved if only individuals followed the promptings of their better selves. In contrast, Hawthorne, Melville, and Poe viewed individuals as bundles of conflicting forces that, even with the best intentions, might never be reconciled.

Their pessimism led them to create characters obsessed by pride, guilt, a desire for revenge, or a quest for perfection and then to set their stories along the byways of society, where they would be free to explore the complexities of human motivation without the jarring intrusion of everyday life. For example, in *The Scarlet Letter* Hawthorne turned to the Puritan past in order to examine the psychological and moral consequences of the adultery committed by Hester Prynne and the minister Arthur Dimmesdale. So completely did Hawthorne focus on the moral dilemmas of his central characters that he conveyed little sense of the social life of the Puritan village in which the novel is set. Melville, who dedicated *Moby-Dick* to Hawthorne, shared the latter's pessimism. In the novel's Captain Ahab, Melville created a frightening character whose relentless and futile pursuit of the white whale fails to fill the chasm in his soul and brings death to all of his mates save the narrator, Ishmael. Poe also channeled his pessimism into creative achievements of the first rank. In perhaps his finest short story, "The Fall of the House of Usher" (1839), he demonstrated an uncanny ability to weave the symbol of a crumbling mansion with the mental agony of a crumbling family.

Hawthorne, Melville, and Poe did not heed Emerson's call to write about the everyday experiences of their fellow countrymen. Nor did they follow Cooper's lead by creating distinctively American heroes. Yet each contributed to an indisputably American literature. Ironically, their conviction that the lives of ordinary Americans provided inadequate materials for fiction led them to create a uniquely American fiction, one marked less by the description of the complex social relationships of ordinary life than by the analysis of moral dilemmas and psychological states. In this way, they unintentionally fulfilled a prediction made by Alexis de Tocqueville that writers in democratic nations, while rejecting many of the traditional sources of fiction, would explore the abstract and universal questions of human nature.

American Landscape Painting

American painters also sought to develop nationality in art between 1820 and 1860. Lacking a mythic past of the sort represented by the gods and goddesses of the ancient world, Americans subordinated history and figure painting to landscape painting. Yet just as Hawthorne had complained about the flat, commonplace character of American society, the painters of the Hudson River school recognized that the American landscape lacked the European landscape's "poetry of decay" in the form of ruined castles and crumbling temples. Like everything else in the United States, the landscape was fresh, relatively unencumbered by the human imprint. This fact posed a challenge to the Hudson River school painters.

The Hudson River school flourished from the 1820s to the 1870s. Numbering more than fifty painters, it is best represented by Thomas Cole, Asher Durand, and Frederic Church. All three men painted scenes of the region around the Hudson River, a waterway that Americans compared in majesty to the Rhine. But none was exclusively a landscapist. Some of Cole's most popular paintings were allegories, including *The Course of Empire*, a sequence of five canvases depicting the rise and fall of an ancient city and clearly implying that luxury doomed republican virtue. Nor did these artists paint only the Hudson. Church, a student of Cole and internationally the best known of the three, painted the Andes Mountains during an extended trip to South America in 1853. After the Civil War, the German-born Albert Bierstedt applied many Hudson River school techniques in his monumental canvases of the Rocky Mountains.

The writings of Washington Irving and the

Twilight in the Wilderness, by Frederick E. Church, 1860   *Like many Hudson River school paintings, Church's* Twilight in the Wilderness, *often considered his masterpiece, creates a mood of almost religious majesty.*

Central Park, New York City, in 1858

In 1858 Frederick Law Olmsted and Calvert Vaux entered the competition for the design of New York City's proposed Central Park. Already famous for his newspaper accounts of his tours through the slave states, Olmsted was keenly interested in landscapes. The British-born Vaux had been a partner of Andrew Jackson Downing, who, before his untimely death in 1852, had gained renown as America's foremost landscape architect. Both Olmsted and Vaux shared the widening fear that urban and industrial growth was destroying the American landscape and robbing the nation of its natural treasures. By the 1830s factory villages like Lowell and Waltham had turned into bustling cities, and by 1850 New York City had become a metropolis of more than half a million people. Pavement and houses threatened eventually to obliterate every parcel of open land. The "march of improvement," an observer warned in 1835, "is as destructive in its course, of everything verdant in nature, as the passage of an army of locusts over a field of grain."

So Olmsted and Vaux called for the creation of parks—enclaves of unspoiled nature in or near cities. They drew inspiration from a movement that developed in the 1830s to construct artistically landscaped "rural" cemeteries on the outskirts of cities. This movement for rural cemeteries addressed the practical problems spawned as urban developers churned up graves and as entrepreneurs plastered tombstones with handbills announcing

Frederick Law Olmsted

Olmsted's design for Central Park brought him fame and many commissions. Over his long career, he designed almost eighty parks, including Brooklyn's Prospect Park, Chicago's Jackson Park, and Boston's Back Bay Park. He also designed thirteen college campuses, among them those of Stanford University and the University of California at Berkeley.

new business ventures. But the rural-cemetery movement also reflected the ideal expressed by Emerson and Thoreau that nature was a source of spiritual refreshment. The opening of the Mount Auburn Cemetery just outside Boston in 1831 prompted an orator to proclaim that cemeteries "are not for the dead. They are for the living." Cemeteries modeled on Mount Auburn bore names that evoked images of pastoral beauty—"Laurel Hill," "Harmony Grove," "Wood Lands,"

"Green Mount," and "Greenwood." Like Mount Auburn, which some thirty thousand people a year were visiting by midcentury, they became tourist attractions.

From the cemetery movement and other sources, Olmsted and Vaux derived the principle that nature could always be improved upon by moving earth to form little hills and valleys. The result would be "picturesque"; that is, it would remind viewers of the landscapes that they had seen in pictures. Some advocates of the picturesque, among them the painter Frederic Church, preferred a wild and sublime naturalism, signified by jutting mountains and raging rivers, but Olmsted and Vaux favored gentle, pastoral scenery marked by rolling hills and placid lakes. With the blessing of the venerable Washington Irving, whose early writings had popularized the scenery along the Hudson River, Olmsted and Vaux wove their ideas into a plan called "Greensward." Not only did Greensward win the competition, but Olmsted secured the coveted appointment as the park's architect in chief.

Greensward prevailed over competing plans based on profoundly different visions of the ideal public park. Its main opposition came from advocates of bisecting the park with a grand boulevard, like the Champs Elysées in Paris, that would run from Fifty-ninth Street to the south wall of an existing reservoir with the aid of a suspension bridge across water and "a flight of marble steps" up to the reservoir. Olmsted and Vaux, in contrast, wanted the park to look as rural as possible, showing nothing of the city. A bordering line of trees screened out buildings. Within the park, brooks were filled in ("mere rivulets are uninteresting," Olmsted and Vaux proclaimed), and ninety-five miles of drainage pipes were dug to create lakes from the reservoir's water. Made as unobtrusive as possible, four sunken thoroughfares were cut through the park to carry coaches from east to west. The effect was to make Central Park an idealized version of nature. As Olmsted recognized, "The Park throughout is a single work of art."

Viewing Central Park as a secluded retreat in the heart of the city, Olmsted hoped that the park would encourage harmony between the rich and the poor by providing all classes with a meeting place free of the tensions generated by acquisitiveness. In cities, he wrote, our minds are "brought into close dealings with other minds without any friendly flowing toward them, but

Underpass and Traffic on Transverse Road

Olmsted used depressed roadways so that those who came to Central Park for enjoyment would not be upset by urban traffic.

rather a drawing from them." Most of the city's laboring poor, however, equated the value of the park with the employment opportunities, rather than the recreational prospects, that it offered. The city's Democratic administration used the construction jobs created by the park to reward its largely immigrant following. Olmsted complained that "the pretense of work was merely a form of distributing public money to the poor, and my office was for several days regularly surrounded by an organized mob carrying a banner inscribed 'Bread and Blood.' This

mob sent in to me a list of 10,000 names of men alleged to have starving families, demanding that they should immediately be put to work."

Olmsted kept his workers in line by "rigidly discharging any man who failed to work industriously and behave in a quiet and orderly manner." "Quiet and orderly" is a fair description of Olmsted's expectations of the appropriate behavior not only of his laborers but of all city dwellers. Noise so jangled his nerves that he worked late into the night, and he assumed that others shared his longing for quiet. But in fact, the laboring poor usually preferred more boisterous amusements than Central Park could provide. Frequenting the saloon, cheering at the prizefight, and running with the city's fire companies were more typical working-class entertainments than strolling in the park. And those laborers who did prefer the park often lived too far away and worked too long a day for a visit. An observer noted in 1873 that "the greater part of the laboring population" did not have the free time to enjoy the park. Even before it became clear that the park's clientele would be drawn mainly from the middle and upper classes, the bloody draft riots of 1863 (see Chapter 14), in which Irish mobs took over much of the city and lynched blacks, underscored the fact that Central Park had only limited potential to blunt social strife.

Skating in Central Park

Olmsted designed Central Park for all forms of outdoor amusements, including the highly popular ice skating.

opening of the Erie Canal had sparked artistic interest in the Hudson during the 1820s. Interest was kept alive in subsequent decades by popular fears that, as one contemporary expressed it in 1847, "the axe of civilization is busy with our old forests." As the "wild and picturesque haunts of the Red Man" became "the abodes of commerce and the seats of civilization," he concluded, "it behooves our artists to rescue from its grasp the little that is left before it is too late."

The Hudson River painters wanted to do more than preserve a passing wilderness. Their special contribution to American art was to emphasize emotional effect over accuracy. Cole's use of rich coloring, billowing clouds, massive gnarled trees, towering peaks, and deep chasms so heightened the dramatic impact of his paintings that the poet and editor William Cullen Bryant compared them to "acts of religion." Similar motifs marked Church's paintings of the Andes Mountains, which used erupting volcanoes and thunderstorms to evoke dread and a sense of majesty (see "A Place in Time"). Lacking the ruined castles and crumbling temples that dotted European landscapes, the Americans strove to capture the natural grandeur of their own landscape.

The "Diffusion" of Literature and Art

Just as Emerson contended that the democratizing spirit of his age would encourage Americans to discover their cultural identity, many of his contemporaries argued that in a democratic society, the educated had a duty to "diffuse" or spread enlightenment among the common people. Some hoped that inexpensive books and magazines would automatically bring fine literature to the masses. Reflecting on the declining cost of printed material, a clergyman concluded in 1841 that "genius sends its light into cottages." Many others, however, feared that the public would prefer the sensational penny-press fiction and the predictable sentimental novels to more elevating intellectual fare, and they pointed to the need for organized efforts to instruct and uplift American minds.

Advocates of systematic popular instruction turned not only to the public schools but also to lyceum lectures to popularize knowledge. The brainchild during the 1820s of Josiah Holbrook, an eccentric Connecticut inventor and educator, lyceums were essentially local organizations that

sponsored public lectures. The topics and audiences of these lectures were diverse. In the winter of 1851–1852, for example, the lyceum in Belfast, Maine, sponsored lectures on astronomy, biology, physiology, geology, conversation, reading, the cultivation of memory, popular illusions concerning the Middle Ages, Iceland, the equality of the human condition, the true mission of women, and the domestic life of the Turks. Audiences usually included professional men, merchants, farmers, artisans, and a large number of middle-class women.

The lecturers were also a diverse lot. Prior to 1840 most were well-known locals who wished to show off their learning before admiring neighbors. But between 1840 and 1860, the spread of railroads contributed to the creation of a group of nationally known lecturers, a virtual road show of the American Renaissance. Emerson, for example, delivered some sixty lectures in Ohio alone between 1850 and 1867. Known in the 1830s as a radical and eccentric Yankee philosopher, he acquired a reputation throughout the North as a venerable sage by 1860. Another popular lecturer, the poet and world traveler Bayard Taylor, enthralled audiences everywhere with his descriptions of Arabia, Greece, Russia, and Japan. Taylor's frequent appearances in the garb of a cossack or an Arab (complete with scimitar) only heightened the effect. Tickets to lectures sold for as little as twelve cents, but so large were the crowds (up to two thousand) that some literary figures could command the then astounding fee of $125 per lecture. Most lecturers were content with more modest rewards; one stalwart of the lyceum circuit claimed that he did it for "F.A.M.E.—Fifty and My Expenses." Herman Melville, no more popular as a lecturer than as a novelist, pledged, "If they will pay expenses and give a reasonable fee, I am ready to lecture in Labrador or on the Isle of Desolation off Patagonia."

Railroads, the spread of public education, and lower costs for newspapers and books helped bring audiences and lecturers together. Newspapers, for example, announced the comings and goings of lecturers. Bayard Taylor began to receive invitations to lecture only after the public had read his published accounts of his travels. Originating in New England, lyceums expanded quickly across the northern states and made inroads into the South.

The spread of lyceums revealed a broad popular hunger for knowledge and refinement. By 1840 thirty-five hundred towns had lyceums. Yet 1840 was also the year of the log-cabin campaign, which blasted Martin Van Buren for displays of refinement as fully as Andrew Jackson's supporters had earlier gouged John Quincy Adams for being a man of learning. Americans clearly were of two minds on the subject of learning.

This ambivalence toward refined knowledge was nowhere sharper than in the West. Westerners often prided themselves on their rough ways. Western almanacs sprinkled stories of Davy Crockett and other unlettered western heroes among their weather predictions and planting advice, and some western writers fiercely resisted cultural penetration from the East. Yet the West was filled with eastern missionaries who were eager to dispel the notion that westerners were crude backwoods folk and who cultivated learning as well as Protestantism by building scores of colleges, academies, and lyceum halls. In 1800 there was only one college in what is now the Midwest; by 1850 there were nearly seventy, more than in any other region. "They drive schools along with them, as shepherds drive their flocks," clergyman Henry Ward Beecher observed of westerners. "They have herds of churches, academies, lyceums, and their religious and educational institutions go lowing along the western plains, as Jacob's herd lowed along the Syrian hills." Western newspapers sometimes railed at transplanted easterners for "namby-pamby, uptownish" lyceum lectures, but audiences flocked to listen to emissaries of eastern refinement.

Antebellum America contained missionaries for art as well as for knowledge. During the 1840s the American Art Union tried to cultivate popular interest in art by catering to the people's penchant for gambling. For five dollars a year, subscribers to the union received both an engraving of an American painting and a lottery ticket for an original American painting. With agents in towns from Maine to Missouri, the American Art Union had sixteen thousand subscribers by 1849 and half a million visitors to its gallery in New York City. At a time when few American homes had wallpaper, which was imported and expensive, picture collecting became a fad.

The movements to popularize knowledge and art bridged the cultural gap between classes but never closed it. Further, the popularization of culture carried a hidden price tag. In bringing learning and art to the masses, creative thinkers had to soften their ideas. Lyceum lecturers, for example, usually avoided controversy. Even Emerson, whose early pronouncements on religion were extremely controversial, learned to pull his punches on the lyceum circuit. While his epigrammatic style of presenting his ideas made him eminently quotable, his vagueness made it possible to quote him on both sides of most issues. Similarly, while the American Art Union distributed some paintings by Thomas Cole, it also disseminated a lot of mediocre paintings that the public liked. Charged with encouraging mediocrity, the Art Union responded bluntly that, since "no one affects to fear mediocrity in religion or learning, why should we fear it in art?"

Conclusion

Hailed as progressive and democratic, technological advances transformed the lives of millions of Americans between 1840 and 1860. The introduction of the mechanical reaper increased wheat production and substantiated a federal official's contention in 1860 that "the ratio of increase of the principal agricultural products of the United States had more than kept pace with the increase of population." The gradual introduction of steam power reduced the vulnerability of factories to the vagaries of the weather, stretched out the employment season, and increased both productivity and annual income. The widespread introduction of coal-burning stoves not only warmed houses but, in conjunction with the spread of railroads, brought greater variety to the American diet. Technology also left an enduring mark on leisure pursuits. By bringing down the cost of printing, technical advances stimulated the rise of the penny press and the inexpensive novel, vastly increased the size of the reading public, and encouraged efforts to popularize knowledge.

Even dissenters usually directed their fire at technology's effects rather than at technology itself. Sylvester Graham wanted Americans to return to simpler lives, but he understood that vegetarianism depended on railroads to bring fresh produce into cities. The bright possibilities rather than the dark potential of technology impressed most antebellum Americans. Yet technology scarcely obliterated class and ethnic differences, nor did it quiet sectional strife. Even as the penny press and the telegraph spread throughout the nation, Americans were finding that speedier communication could not bridge their differences over slavery.

CHRONOLOGY

1820 Washington Irving, *The Sketch Book.*

1823 Philadelphia completes the first urban water-supply system.
James Fenimore Cooper, *The Pioneers.*

1826 Josiah Holbrook introduces the idea for lyceums.
Cooper, *The Last of the Mohicans.*

1831 Mount Auburn Cemetery opens.

1832 A cholera epidemic strikes the United States.

1833 The *New York Sun*, the first penny newspaper, is established.

1834 Cyrus McCormick patents the mechanical reaper.

1835 James Gordon Bennett establishes the *New York Herald.*

1837 Ralph Waldo Emerson, "The American Scholar."

1841 P. T. Barnum opens the American Museum.

1842 Edgar Allan Poe, "The Murders in the Rue Morgue."

1844 Samuel F. B. Morse patents the telegraph.
The American Art Union is established.
Poe, "The Raven."

1846 W. T. G. Morton successfully uses anesthesia.

1849 Second major cholera epidemic.
Astor Place theater riot leaves twenty dead.

1850 Nathaniel Hawthorne, *The Scarlet Letter.*

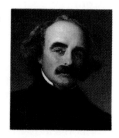

1851 Hawthorne, *The House of the Seven Gables.*
Herman Melville, *Moby-Dick.*
Erie Railroad completes its line to the West.

1852 Pennsylvania Railroad completes its line between Philadelphia and Pittsburgh.

1853 Ten small railroads are consolidated into the New York Central Railroad.

1854 Henry David Thoreau, *Walden.*

1855 Walt Whitman, *Leaves of Grass.*

1856 Pennsylvania Railroad completes Chicago link.
Illinois Central completed between Chicago and Cairo, Illinois.

1857 Baltimore–St. Louis rail service completed.

1858 Frederick Law Olmsted is appointed architect in chief for Central Park.

For Further Reading

Carl Bode, *The Anatomy of American Popular Culture, 1840–1861* (1959). A useful general survey.

E. Douglas Branch, *The Sentimental Years, 1836–1860* (1934). A gracefully written, breezy, and informative narrative.

Ann Douglas, *The Feminization of American Culture* (1977). An analysis of the role of the middle-class women and liberal ministers in the cultural sphere during the nineteenth century.

Siegfried Giedion, *Mechanization Takes Command*

(1948). An interpretive overview of the impact of technology on Europe and America.

Barbara Novak, *Nature and Culture: American Landscape Painting, 1825–1875* (1982). An insightful study of the relationships between landscape painting and contemporary religious and philosophical currents.

Gwendolyn Wright, *Building the Dream: A Social History of Housing in America* (1981). An exploration of the ideologies and policies that have shaped American housing since Puritan times.

Additional Bibliography

Technology, Progress, and the Standard of Living

Ruth Schwartz Cowan, *More Work for Mother: The Ironies of Household Technology from the Open Hearth to the Microwave* (1983); Durand Echeverria, *Mirage in the West: A History of the French Image of American Society to 1815* (1957); H. J. Habakkuk, *American and British Technology in the Nineteenth Century* (1962); Dolores Hayden, *The Grand Domestic Revolution: A History of Feminist Designs for American Homes, Neighborhoods, and Cities* (1981); David A. Hounshell, *From the American System to Mass Production, 1800–1932* (1984); John F. Kasson, *Civilizing the Machine: Technology and Republican Values in America, 1776–1900* (1976); Stanley Lebergott, *The Americans: An Economic Record* (1984); Edgar W. Martin, *The Standard of Living in 1860* (1942); Susan Strasser, *Never Done: A History of American Housework* (1983).

Railroads

Eugene Alvarez, *Travel on Southern Antebellum Railroads, 1828–1860* (1974); Alfred D. Chandler, *The Visible Hand: The Managerial Revolution in American Business* (1977); Thomas C. Cochran, *Railroad Leaders, 1845–1890* (1953); Stewart H. Holbrook, *The Story of American Railroads* (1947); Edward C. Kirkland, *Men, Cities and Transportation: A Study in New England History, 1820–1900* (1948); Robert J. Parks, *Democracy's Railroads: Public Enterprise in Michigan* (1972); John F. Stover, *American Railroads* (1961).

Disease and Health

John D. Davies, *Phrenology: Fad and Science* (1955); John S. Haller, Jr., *American Medicine in Transition, 1840–1910* (1981); Stephen Nissenbaum, *Sex, Diet, and Debility in Jacksonian America: Sylvester Graham and Health Reform* (1980); Martin S. Pernick, *A Calculus of Suffering: Pain, Professionalism, and Anesthesia in Nineteenth-Century America* (1985); Charles Rosen-

berg, *The Cholera Years: The United States in 1832, 1849, and 1866* (1962); Paul Starr, *The Social Transformation of American Medicine* (1982).

Popular Culture

Jean H. Baker, *Affairs of Party: The Political Culture of Northern Democrats in the Mid-Nineteenth Century* (1983); Carl Bode, *The American Lyceum: Town Meeting of the Mind* (1968); David Grimsted, *Melodrama Unveiled: American Theater and Culture, 1800–1850* (1968); Karen Halttunen, *Confidence Men and Painted Women: A Study in Middle-Class Culture in America, 1830–1870* (1982); Neil Harris, *Humbug: The Art of P. T. Barnum* (1973); Russell Lynes, *The Tastemakers* (1949); Dan Schiller, *Objectivity and the News: The Public and the Rise of Commercial Journalism* (1981); Michael Schudson, *Discovering the News: A Social History of American Newspapers* (1978); Donald Scott, "The Popular Lecture," *Journal of American History* 66 (March 1980):791–809; Robert C. Toll, *Blacking Up: The Minstrel Show in Nineteenth-Century America* (1974).

Literature

Nina Baym, *Woman's Fiction: A Guide to Novels by and About Women in America, 1820–1870* (1978); Vincent Buranelli, *Edgar Allan Poe* (1977); William Charvat, *The Profession of Authorship in America, 1800–1870* (edited by Matthew J. Bruccoli, 1968); David Levin, *History as Romantic Art: Bancroft, Prescott, Motley, and Parkman* (1963); Kenneth S. Lynn, *Mark Twain and Southwestern Humor* (1972); James Mellow, *Nathaniel Hawthorne in His Time* (1980); Henry Nash Smith, *Democracy and the Novel: Popular Resistance to Classic American Writers* (1978); Benjamin T. Spencer, *The Quest for Nationality: An American Literary Campaign* (1957); Tony Tanner, *The Reign of Wonder: Naiveté and Reality in American Literature* (1965); Larzer Ziff, *Literary Democracy: The Declaration of Cultural Independence in America* (1981).

Visual Arts

Elizabeth Barlow, *Frederick Law Olmsted's New York* (1972); Thomas Bender, *Toward an Urban Vision: Ideas and Institutions in Nineteenth-Century America* (1975); Albert Fein, *Frederick Law Olmsted and the Environmental Tradition* (1972); Neil Harris, *The Artist in American Society: The Formative Years, 1790–1860* (1966); Louis L. Noble, *The Life and Times of Thomas Cole* (1964); Raymond J. O'Brien, *Landscape and Scenery of the Lower Hudson Valley* (1981); Laura Wood Roper, *FLO: A Biography of Frederick Law Olmsted* (1973); Bryan J. Wolf, *Romantic Re-Vision: Culture and Consciousness in Nineteenth-Century American Painting and Literature* (1982).

CHAPTER 12

Immigration, Expansion, and Sectional Conflict, 1840–1848

Considering themselves uniquely civilized and progressive, many antebellum Americans found the idea that God had ordained the spread of their civilization over all of North America irresistible. "Americans regard this continent as their birthright," proclaimed Sam Houston, the first president of the independent republic of Texas, in 1847. Those whom Americans saw as less civilized, notably the Indians and the Mexicans, could rightfully be dispossessed of their land in order to make way for "our mighty march."

This was not idle talk. In less than a thousand days of feverish activity during the administration of President James K. Polk, the United States increased its land area by 50 percent. The nation not only annexed Texas and successfully negotiated with Britain to acquire that part of Oregon south of the forty-ninth parallel but also fought a war with Mexico that led to the acquisition of California and New Mexico. Americans justified these takeovers on some of the same grounds that they had used earlier to dispossess the Indians of their lands. South Carolina's John C. Calhoun boasted that nothing could prevent Americans, "an industrious and civilized race," from "passing into an uninhabited country where the power of the owners is not sufficient to keep them out." Some commentators even contended that expansion was a blessing in disguise for peoples whom Americans deemed less progressive than themselves. Calling in 1848 for the annexation of all of Mexico, a New York journalist argued that the acquisition of that territory would give "an entirely new character and new development to her population."

Beyond expanding its physical boundaries, the United States swelled dramatically in population during the 1840s and 1850s, in part because of a spectacular rise in European immigration. The number of immigrants who entered the United States in these two decades alone exceeded the nation's entire population in 1790. European immigration soared during the mid-1840s, at the same time that the nation plunged into expansion.

Although antebellum immigration and territorial expansion had different sources, the two developments became closely linked. For example, as the penny press whipped up fervor for expansion among the urban immigrant masses, they increasingly championed efforts to push the national boundary to the Pacific. Most immigrants, moreover, supported the Democratic party, which embraced expansion far more enthusiastically than the rival Whig party. The immigrant vote helped to tip the election of 1844 to the Democrats and brought an ardent expansionist, James K. Polk, to the White House.

Beyond these direct connections between immigration and expansion, immigration indirectly stimulated expansion. New immigrants, particularly the Irish, crowded into cities and factory towns in search of work at a time when the post-1837 depression kept the wages of native-born workers low. Ugly outbursts of anti-immigrant feeling reflected the mounting tensions between the immigrant and native-born populations. A number of influential Democrats concluded that the best solution to the intensifying class and ethnic conflict lay in expanding the national boundaries, bringing more land under cultivation, and attracting immigrants to that land, in the process recapturing the ideal of America as a nation of self-sufficient farmers.

Moreover, Democrats advocated expansion as a means of reducing strife between the sections. Expansion into Oregon would gratify the North; expansion into Texas would please the South. Some influential Democrats even argued that Texas would become a kind of highway along which slaves and free blacks alike would wend their way over the horizon and into Mexico. In this way, the argument ran, expansion would gradually drive the sectionally divisive issue of race out of politics.

In reality, expansion brought sectional antagonism to the boiling point, split the Democratic party in the late 1840s, and set the nation on the path to the Civil War.

Newcomers and Natives

Between 1815 and 1860, 5 million European immigrants landed in the United States. Of these, 4.2 million arrived between 1840 and 1860; 3 million of them came in the single decade from 1845 to 1854. This ten-year period witnessed the largest immigration proportionate to the total population (then around 20 million) in American history. The Irish led the way as a source of immigration between 1840 and 1860, with the Germans running a close second. Smaller contingents continued to immigrate to the United States from England, Scotland, and Wales, and a growing number came from Norway, Sweden, Switzerland, and Holland. But by 1860 fully three-fourths of the 4.1 million foreign-born Americans were either Irish or German.

Expectations and Realities

A desire for religious freedom drew some immigrants to the United States. For example, when Mormon missionaries actively recruited converts in the slums of English factory towns, a number of English migrated to America. Many emigrants from Norway were Quakers fleeing persecution by the official Lutheran clergy. But a far larger number of Europeans sailed for America to better their economic condition. Their hope was fed by a continuous stream of travelers' accounts and letters from relatives describing America as a utopia for poor people. German peasants learned that they could purchase a large farm in America for the price of renting a small one in Germany. English men and women were told that enough good peaches and apples were left rotting in the orchards of Ohio to sink the British fleet.

Hoping for the best, emigrants often encountered the worst. Their problems began at ports of embarkation, where hucksters frequently sold them worthless tickets and where ships scheduled to leave in June might not sail until August. Countless emigrants spent precious savings in waterfront slums while awaiting departure. The ocean voyage itself proved terrifying; many emigrants had never set foot on a ship. Most sailed on cargo ships as steerage passengers, where, for six weeks or more, they endured quarters almost as crowded as on slave ships.

For many emigrants, the greatest shock came when they landed. "The folks aboard ship formed great plans for their future, all of which vanished quickly after landing," wrote a young German from Frankfurt in 1840. Immigrants quickly discovered that farming in America was a perilous prospect at best. Aside from lacking the capital to start a farm, most immigrants had to confront the fact that farming in the United States bore little resemblance to farming in Europe. European farmers valued the associations of their communities. Their social and cultural lives revolved around villages that were fringed by the fields that they worked. In contrast, as many immigrants quickly learned, American farmers lived in relative isolation. They might belong to rural neighborhoods in which farmers on widely scattered plots of land met occasionally at revivals or militia musters. But they lacked the compact village life of European farmers, and

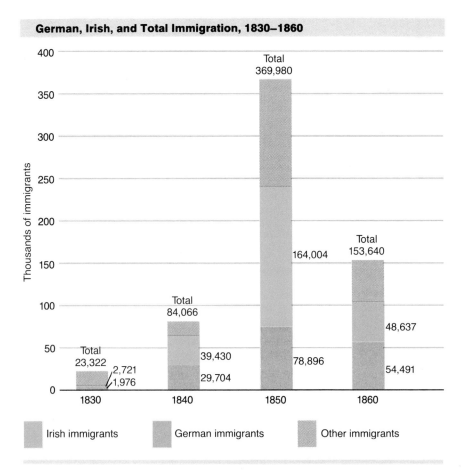

German, Irish, and Total Immigration, 1830–1860

Thousands of immigrants

- 1830: Total 23,322 — 2,721 — 1,976
- 1840: Total 84,066 — 39,430 — 29,704
- 1850: Total 369,980 — 164,004 — 78,896
- 1860: Total 153,640 — 48,637 — 54,491

Irish immigrants   German immigrants   Other immigrants

Irish and German immigrants led the more than tenfold growth of immigration between 1830 and 1860.

SOURCE: U.S. Bureau of the Census, *Historical Statistics of the United States, Colonial Times to 1970*, Bicentennial Edition (Washington, D.C., 1975).

they possessed an individualistic psychology that led them to speculate in land and to move frequently. One Irish immigrant farmer, writing home to complain of the distance between farms, noted bitterly, "I can hardly yet forgive the persons that advised me to come here."

Despite the shocks and dislocations caused by migration, certain patterns emerged in the distribution of immigrants within the United States. Initially shaped by trade routes, these patterns were then perpetuated by custom. Most of the Irish settlers before 1840 departed from Liverpool on sailing ships that carried English manufactures to eastern Canada and New England in return for timber. On arrival in America, few of these Irish had the capital to become farmers, and hence they crowded into the urban areas of New England, New York, Pennsylvania, and New Jersey, where they could more easily find jobs. In contrast, German emigrants usually left from continental ports on ships

engaged in the cotton trade with New Orleans. However, deterred from settling in the South by the presence of slavery, the oppressive climate, and the lack of economic opportunity, the Germans congregated in the upper Mississippi and Ohio valleys, especially in Illinois, Ohio, Wisconsin, and Missouri. Geographical concentration also characterized most of the smaller groups of immigrants. More than half of the Norwegian immigrants, for example, settled in Wisconsin, where they typically became farmers.

On balance, immigrants were less likely to pursue agriculture in the New World than in Europe. Both the Germans and, to an even greater degree, the Irish tended to concentrate in cities. By 1860 these two groups formed more than 60 percent of the population of St. Louis; nearly half the population of New York City, Chicago, Cincinnati, Milwaukee, Detroit, and San Francisco; and well over a third that of New Orleans, Baltimore, and Boston. These fast-growing cities created an intense demand for the labor of people with strong backs and a willingness to work for low wages. Irish construction gangs built the houses, new streets, and aqueducts that were changing the face of urban America and dug the canals and railroads that threaded together the rapidly developing cities. A popular song recounted the fate of the thousands of Irishmen who died of cholera contracted during the building of a canal in New Orleans:

> *Ten thousand Micks, they swung their picks,*
>   *To build the New Canal*
> *But the choleray was stronger 'n they.*
>   *An' twice it killed them awl.*

The cities provided immigrants with the sort of community life that seemed lacking in farming settlements. Immigrant societies like the Friendly Sons of St. Patrick took root in cities and combined with associations like the Hibernian Society for the Relief of Emigrants from Ireland to welcome the throngs of newcomers.

The Germans

In the mid-nineteenth century, the Germans were an extremely diverse group. In 1860 Germany was not a nation-state like France or Britain, but a collection of principalities and small kingdoms. German immigrants thought of themselves as Bavarians, Westphalians, or Saxons rather than as Germans. Moreover, the German immigrants included Catholics, Protestants (usually Lutherans), and Jews as well as a sprinkling of freethinkers who denounced the ritual, clergy, and doctrines of all religions. Although few in number, these critics were vehement in their attacks on the established churches. A pious Milwaukee Lutheran complained in 1860 that he could not drink a glass of beer in a saloon "without being angered by anti-Christian remarks or raillery against preachers."

German immigrants came from a wide range of social classes and occupations. The majority had engaged in farming, but a sizable minority were professionals, artisans, and tradespeople. Heinrich Steinweg, an obscure piano maker from Lower Saxony, arrived in New York City in 1851, anglicized his name to Henry Steinway, and in 1853 opened the firm of Steinway and Sons, which quickly

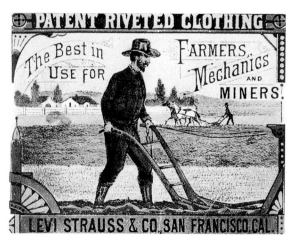

Levi Strauss's Jeans

A far cry from today's designer jeans, Levi Strauss's sturdy work pants quickly caught on with laborers.

achieved international acclaim for the quality of its pianos. Levi Strauss, a Jewish tailor from Bavaria, migrated to the United States in 1847. Upon hearing of the discovery of gold in California in 1848, Strauss gathered rolls of cloth and sailed for San Francisco. When a miner told him of the need for durable work trousers, Strauss fashioned a pair of overalls from canvas. To meet a quickly skyrocketing demand, he opened a factory in San Francisco; his cheap overalls, later known as blue jeans or Levi's, made him famous as well as rich.

For all their differences, the Germans were bound together by their common language, which strongly induced recent immigrants to the United States to congregate in German neighborhoods. Even prosperous Germans bent on climbing the social ladder usually did so within German neighborhoods. Germans formed their own militia and fire companies, sponsored parochial schools in which German was the language of instruction, started German-language newspapers, and organized their own balls and singing groups. The range of voluntary associations among Germans was almost as broad as among native-born Americans.

Other factors beyond their common language brought unity to the German immigrants. Ironically, the Germans' diversity also promoted their solidarity. For example, because they were able to supply their own doctors, lawyers, teachers, journalists, merchants, artisans, and clergy, the Germans had little need to go outside their own neighborhoods. Moreover, economic self-sufficiency conspired with the strong bonds of their language to encourage a clannish psychology among the German immigrants. While admiring the Germans' industriousness, native-born Americans resented their economic success and disdained their clannishness. German refugee Moritz Busch complained that "the great mass of Anglo-Americans" held his countrymen in contempt. The Germans responded by becoming even more clannish. In turn, their psychological separateness made it difficult for the Germans to be as politically influential as the Irish immigrants.

The Irish

Between 1815 and 1860, Irish immigration to the United States passed through several stages. Irish soldiers who fought against the United States in the War of 1812 had returned to their homeland with reports that America was a paradise filled with fertile land and abundant game, a place where "all a man wanted was a gun and sufficient ammunition to be able to live like a prince." Among the Irish who subsequently emigrated between 1815 and the mid-1820s, Protestant small landowners and tradespeople in search of better economic opportunity predominated.

From the mid-1820s to the mid-1840s, the character of Irish immigration to the United States gradually changed. Increasingly, the immigrants were Catholics drawn from the poorer classes, many of them tenant farmers whom Protestant landowners had evicted as "superfluous." Protestant or Catholic, rich or poor, 800,000 to a million Irish immigrants entered the United States between 1815 and 1844. Then, between 1845 and the early 1850s, a blight destroyed every harvest of Ireland's potatoes, virtually the only food of the peasantry, and spawned one of the most gruesome famines in history. The Great Famine inflicted indescribable suffering on the Irish peasantry and killed perhaps a million people. One landlord characterized the surviving tenants on his estate as no more than "famished and ghastly skeletons." To escape the ravages of famine, 1.8 million Irish migrated to the United States in the decade after 1845. Whereas earlier Irish immigrants had been predominantly poor and Catholic, the famine Irish were overwhelmingly so. Indeed, a quarter to a third of the Irish who arrived during the years 1845–1855 could speak only Irish.

Irish Catholics usually entered the work force at or near the bottom. The popular image of Paddy with his pickax and Bridget the maid contained a good deal of truth. Irish men in the cities dug cellars and often lived in them; outside the cities, they dug canals and railroad beds. Irish women often became domestic servants. Compared to other immigrant women, a high proportion of Irish women entered the work force, if not as maids then often as textile workers. By the 1840s Irish women were displacing native-born women in the textile mills of Lowell and Waltham. Poverty drove Irish women to work at early ages, and the outdoor, all-season work performed by their husbands turned many of them into working widows. Winifred Rooney became a nursemaid at the age of seven and an errand girl at eleven. She then learned needlework, a skill that helped her support her family after her husband's early death. The high proportion of employed Irish women reflected more than their poverty. Compared to the predominantly male German immigrants, more than half of the Irish immigrants were women, most of whom were single adults. In both Ireland and America, the Irish usually married late, and many never married. For Irish women to become self-supporting was only natural.

The lot of most Irish people was harsh. One immigrant described the life of the average Irish laborer in America as "despicable, humiliating, [and] slavish"; there was "no love for him—no protection of life—[he] can be shot down, run through, kicked, cuffed, spat upon—and no redress, but a response of 'served the damn son of an Irish b____ right, damn him.' " Yet some Irish struggled up the social ladder. In Philadelphia, which had a more varied industrial base than Boston, Irish men made their way into iron foundries, where some became foremen and supervisors. Other Irish rose into the middle class by opening grocery and liquor stores.

The varied occupations pursued by Irish immigrants brought them into conflict with two quite different groups. The poorer Irish who dug canals and cellars, hauled cargo on the docks, washed

Irish Emigrants

Eager Irish emigrants crowd to board a County Kerry mail coach that will carry them to a port town and eventually to a new life in America.

laundry for others, and served white families competed directly with equally poor free blacks. This competition stirred up Irish animosity toward blacks and a hatred of abolitionists. At the same time, enough Irish men eventually secured skilled or semiskilled jobs that clashes with native-born white workingmen became unavoidable.

Anti-Catholicism, Nativism, and Labor Protest

The hostility of native-born whites toward the Irish often took the form of anti-Catholicism. Anti-Catholicism had been a strong, if latent, impulse among American Protestants since the early Puritan days. The surge of Irish immigration during the second quarter of the nineteenth century revived anti-Catholic fever. For example, in 1834 rumors circulated among Boston Protestants that a Catholic convent in nearby Charlestown contained dungeons and torture chambers. The mother superior turned away a delegation of officials demanding to inspect the convent. Soon the building lay in ashes, the victim of a Protestant mob. In 1835 Samuel F. B. Morse, the future inventor of the telegraph, warned that the despotic governments of Europe were systematically flooding the United States with Catholic immigrants as part of a conspiracy to destroy republican institutions. "We must first stop this leak in the ship," he wrote, "through which the muddy waters from without threaten to sink us." That same year, the combative evangelical Protestant Lyman Beecher issued *A Plea for the West,* a tract in which he warned faithful Protestants of an alleged Catholic conspiracy to send immigrants to the West in sufficient numbers to dominate the region. A year later, the publication of Maria Monk's best-selling *Awful Disclosures of the Hotel Dieu Nunnery in Montreal* rekindled anti-Catholic hysteria. Although Maria Monk was actually a prostitute who had never lived in a convent, she professed to be a former nun. In *Awful Disclosures,* she described how the mother superior forced nuns to submit to the lustful advances of priests who entered the convent by a subterranean passage.

At the root of a great deal of the anti-Catholicism of the 1830s and 1840s lay native-born Americans' escalating fears of cheap competition from Irish workers. Increasingly tense rivalry for jobs was a strong impulse, for example, behind the burning of the Charlestown convent in 1834. Compared to fantastic notions of Catholic conspiracies to take over the country, anxieties over cheap Irish competition for jobs were fairly realistic. The Irish were crowding into the United States at a time when the wages of Protestant, native-born artisans and journeymen were already being depressed by the subdivision of tasks that accompanied early industrialization and by the aftermath of the Panic of 1837 (see Chapter 9). In response, young Protestant workingmen in their

424

twenties, threatened by Irish competition, formed the backbone of the many nativist (anti-immigrant) societies that multiplied during the 1840s. Most of these societies eventually developed political offshoots. The Order of the Star-Spangled Banner, for example, by 1854 evolved into the Know-Nothing or American party, which became a major political force in the 1850s.

Nativist outbursts were not labor's only response to the wage cuts that accompanied the depression. Some agitators began to advocate land reform as a solution to workingmen's economic woes. Americans had long cherished the notion that a nation so blessed by abundant land as the United States need never give rise to a permanent class of factory "wage slaves." In 1844 the English-born radical George Henry Evans organized the National Reform Association and rallied supporters with the slogan "Vote Yourself a Farm." Evans advanced neo-Jeffersonian plans for the establishment of "rural republican townships," composed of 160-acre plots for workers. He quickly gained the backing of artisans who preferred such "agrarian" notions to a further advance of the industrial order that was undermining their position. Evans was also supported by a number of middle-class intellectuals, among them Horace Greeley, the editor of the *New York Tribune.*

Land reformers argued that workers' true interests could never be reconciled with an industrial order in which factory operatives sold their labor for wages. By engaging in wage labor, they said, workers abandoned any hope of achieving economic independence. These reformers most appealed to articulate and self-consciously radical workers, particularly artisans and small masters whose independence was being threatened by factories and who feared that American labor was "fast verging on the servile dependence" common in Europe. But land reform offered little to factory operatives and wage-earning journeymen who completely lacked economic independence. In an age when a horse cost the average worker three months' pay and most factory workers dreaded "the horrors of wilderness life," the idea of solving industrial problems by resettling workers on farms seemed a pipe dream.

The land reformers believed that only a fundamental restructuring of economic relations would improve the condition of workers. They therefore opposed strikes for short-term wage increases. In contrast, labor unions, less idealistic in their goals, were more sympathetic to strikes. Unions had flourished in a number of cities during the mid-1830s and then experienced a resurgence in the mid-1840s as the effects of the depression wore off. They appealed to several groups indifferent to land reform. For example, as refugees from an agricultural society, desperately poor Irish immigrants could more realistically hope to improve their status through unions and strikes rather than through farming. The most celebrated strike in the New York City area in the 1840s was organized by Irish dockworkers in Brooklyn. Women workers also formed unions in the 1840s. In 1845 tailoresses and seamstresses organized the Ladies Industrial Association in New York City; their leader, Elizabeth Gray, proclaimed, "Too long have we been bound down by tyrant employers."

Agitation by labor unionists generated considerable commotion in the 1840s and resulted in a few victories for workers. In the landmark case of *Commonwealth* v. *Hunt* (1842), the Massachusetts Supreme Court ruled that labor unions, or "combinations," were not illegal monopolies that restrained trade. But because less than 1 percent of the work force belonged to a labor union during the 1840s, there were sharp limits to the impact of unions.

Although immigrant and native-born workers at times united to support land reform or unions, profound divisions along ethnic and religious lines split the antebellum working class. Even after labor had gained a modest victory in the *Commonwealth* v. *Hunt* decision, employers freely fired union agitators and replaced them with cheap immigrant labor. "Hundreds of honest laborers," a labor paper reported in 1848, "have been dismissed from employment in the manufactories of New England because they have been suspected of knowing their rights and daring to assert them." This kind of repression effectively blunted agitation for the ten-hour day (at a time when workers typically toiled for twelve to fourteen hours). The drive for a shorter workday had gained support in the 1840s from a number of organizations, among them the Lowell Female Reform Association.

During the 1830s and 1840s, tensions between

native-born and immigrant workers inevitably became intertwined with the political divisions of the second party system.

Labor Protest and Immigrant Politics

Very few immigrants had ever cast a vote in an election prior to their arrival in America, and only a small fraction were refugees from political persecution. Political upheavals had erupted in Austria and several of the German states in the turbulent year of 1848 (the so-called Revolutions of 1848), but among the million German immigrants to the United States, only about ten thousand were political refugees, or "Forty-Eighters."

Once they had settled in the United States, however, many immigrants became politically active. They quickly found that urban political organizations, some of them dominated by earlier immigrants, would help them to find lodging and employment—in return for votes. Both the Irish and the Germans identified overwhelmingly with the Democratic party. An obituary of 1837 that described a New Yorker as a "warm-hearted Irishman and an unflinching Democrat" could have been written of millions of other Irish. By 1820 the Irish had taken over Tammany Hall, the New York City Democratic organization. Similarly, the Germans became stalwart supporters of the Democrats in cities like Milwaukee and St. Louis.

The immigrants' worries about staying financially afloat partly explain their widespread Democratic support. Andrew Jackson had given the Democratic party an antiprivilege and anti-aristocratic coloration, and most immigrants, especially the Irish, saw the Democrats as more sympathetic than the Whigs to the common people. Moreover, many Irish immigrants turned to the Democrats because antislavery was more closely identified in the North with the Whig party than with the Democratic party. The Irish loathed abolitionism out of fear that emancipated slaves would migrate north and compete with them for unskilled jobs.

Beyond these economic considerations, most Irish and German immigrants saw the Whigs as more of a threat than the Democrats to their moral and religious values. The identification of the Whigs with temperance reform, for example, pushed the Irish and Germans toward the Democrats, for both immigrant groups had hearty traditions of drinking. The fact that some prominent temperance reformers, including Lyman Beecher, were also leading anti-Catholics further strengthened the allegiance of Catholic immigrants to the anti-temperance Democrats. Public-school reform, a major Whig goal, also drew fire from immigrants. The Irish looked upon school reform as a menace to the Catholicism of their children; the Germans saw it as a threat to the integrity of their language and culture.

These economic, moral, and religious views composed a volatile mixture in the immigrants' minds and turned them against the Whig party. The emotional cleavage between the two parties at times provoked violence. For example, in Philadelphia, contention between Irish Democrats and native-born Whigs over temperance became intertwined in the early 1840s with a conflict over the use of the Protestant King James rather than the Catholic Douay version of the Bible for the scriptural readings that began each school day in the public schools. Fiery Protestant politicians hostile to Catholics and Democrats mounted soapboxes to denounce "popery" and the alleged efforts of Catholics to "kick " the Bible out of the schools. Soon Protestant mobs descended on Catholic neighborhoods, and before the militia quelled these "Bible Riots," thirty buildings lay in charred ruins and at least sixteen people had been killed.

The Bible Riots spotlighted not only the interplay of nativism, religion, and politics but also the way in which local issues shaped the immigrants' political allegiances. Liquor regulations and school laws, for example, were city or state concerns rather than federal responsibilities. Yet the Democratic party that the immigrants so widely supported in their battles over local matters served them as a kind of school of broad, national principles. It taught them to venerate George Washington, to revere Thomas Jefferson and Andrew Jackson, and to view "monied capitalists" as parasites who would tremble when the people spoke. It introduced immigrants to Democratic newspapers, Democratic picnics, and Democratic parades. The Democrats, by identifying their party with all that they thought best about the United States, helped give immigrants a sense of themselves as Americans. By the same token, the Democratic party introduced immigrants to national issues. It redirected politi-

The Bible Riots *Religious differences and job competition between native-born Americans and immigrants triggered Philadelphia's bloody Bible Riots in June 1844.*

cal loyalties that often had been forged on local issues into the arena of national politics. During the 1830s the party had persuaded immigrants that national measures like the Bank of the United States and the tariff, seemingly remote from their daily lives, were vitally important to them. Now during the 1840s, the Democrats would try to convince immigrants that national expansion advanced their interests.

The West and Beyond

As late as 1840, Americans who referred to the West still meant the area between the Appalachian Mountains and the Mississippi River or just beyond, a region that included much of the present-day Midwest. Beyond the states bordering the Mississippi lay an inhospitable region unlike any that the earlier settlers had ever known. Those who ventured west of Missouri encountered the Great Plains, a semiarid plateau with few trees. Winds blowing east from the Rocky Mountains sucked the moisture from the soil. Bands of nomadic Indians—including the Pawnees, Kiowas, and Sioux—roamed

this territory and gained sustenance mainly from the buffalo. They ate its meat, wore its fur, and covered their dwellings with its hide. Aside from some well-watered sections of northern Missouri and eastern Kansas and Nebraska, the Great Plains presented would-be farmers with massive obstacles.

The formidable barrier of the Great Plains did not stop settlement of the West in the long run. Temporarily, however, it shifted public interest toward the verdant region lying beyond the Rockies, the Far West.

The Far West

With the Transcontinental (or Adams-Onís) Treaty of 1819, the United States had given up to Spain its claims to Texas west of the Sabine River. This had left Spain in undisputed possession not only of Texas but also of California and the vast territory of New Mexico. Combined, California and New Mexico included all of present-day California and New Mexico as well as modern Nevada, Utah, and Arizona, and parts of Wyoming and Colorado. Two years later, a series of revolts against Spanish rule had culminated in the independence of Mexico and in Mexico's takeover of all North

American territory previously claimed by Spain. The Transcontinental Treaty also had provided for Spain's cessation to the United States of its claims to the country of Oregon north of the forty-second parallel (the northern boundary of California). Then in 1824 and 1825, Russia abandoned its claims to Oregon south of 54°40' (the southern boundary of Alaska). In 1827 the United States and Britain, each of which had claims to Oregon based on discovery and exploration, revived an agreement (originally signed in 1818) for joint occupation of the territory between 42° and 54°40', a colossal area that contemporaries could describe no more precisely than the "North West Coast of America, Westward of the Stony [Rocky] Mountains" and that included all of modern Oregon, Washington, and Idaho as well as parts of present-day Wyoming, Montana, and Canada.

Collectively, Texas, New Mexico, California, and Oregon composed an area larger than Britain, France, and Germany combined. Such a vast region should have tempted any nation, but during the 1820s Mexico, Britain, and the United States viewed the Far West as a remote and shadowy frontier. By 1820 the American line of settlement had only reached Missouri, well over 2,000 miles (counting detours for mountains) from the West Coast. El Paso on the Rio Grande and Taos in New Mexico lay, respectively, 1,200 and 1,500 miles north of Mexico City. Britain, of course, was many thousands of miles from Oregon.

Far Western Trade

The earliest American and British outposts on the West Coast were trading centers established by merchants who had reached California and Oregon by sailing around South America and up the Pacific. Between the late 1790s and the 1820s, for example, Boston merchants had built a thriving exchange of coffee, tea, spices, cutlery, clothes, and hardware—indeed, anything that could be bought or manufactured in the eastern United States—for furs (especially those of sea otters), cattle, hides, and tallow (rendered from cattle fat and used for making soap and candles). Between 1826 and 1828 alone, Boston traders took more than 6 million cattle hides out of California; in the otherwise undeveloped California economy, these hides, called "California banknotes," served as the main medium

of exchange. During the 1820s the British Hudson's Bay Company developed a similar trade in Oregon and northern California.

The California trade occasioned little friction with Mexico. Producing virtually no manufactured goods, Hispanic people born in California (called *californios*) were as eager to buy as the traders were to sell—so eager that they sometimes rowed out to the vessels laden with goods, thus sparing the traders the trip ashore. Those traders who did settle in California, like the American Thomas O. Larkin and the Swiss-born John Sutter, quickly learned to speak Spanish and became assimilated into Mexican culture.

Farther south, trading links developed during the 1820s between St. Louis and Santa Fe along the famed Santa Fe Trail. The Panic of 1819 left the American Midwest short of cash and its merchants burdened by unsold goods. Pulling themselves up from adversity, however, plucky midwesterners loaded wagon trains with tools, utensils, clothing, windowpanes, and household sundries each spring and rumbled westward to Santa Fe, where they traded their merchandise for mules and New Mexican silver. To a far greater extent than had Spain, Mexico welcomed this trade. Indeed, by the 1830s more than half the goods entering New Mexico by the Santa Fe Trail trickled into the mineral-rich interior provinces of Mexico such as Chihuahua and Sonora, with the result that the Mexican silver peso, which midwestern traders brought back with them, quickly became the principal medium of exchange in Missouri.

Some Americans ventured north from Santa Fe to trap beaver in what is today western Colorado and eastern Utah. The profitability of the beaver trade also encouraged merchants and trappers like the "mountain man" Jedediah Smith (see Chapter 8) to venture directly from St. Louis into the Rockies in competition with both the Santa Fe traders and agents of the Hudson's Bay Company. On the Green River in Mexican territory, the St. Louis–based trader William Ashley in 1825 inaugurated an annual rendezvous or encampment where traders exchanged beaver pelts for supplies, thereby saving themselves the trip to St. Louis. With the aid of Ashley's encampments, the St. Louis traders gradually wrested the beaver trade from their Santa Fe competitors.

For the most part, American traders and trap-

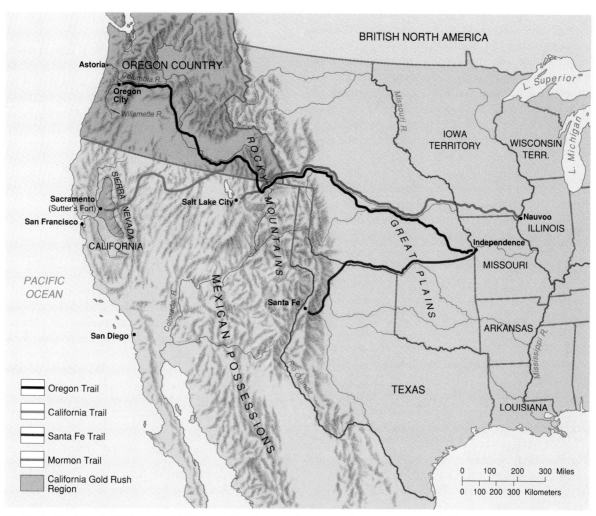

Trails to the West, 1840   *By 1840 several trails carried pioneers from Missouri and Illinois to the West.*

pers operating on the northern Mexican frontier in the 1820s and 1830s posed more of a threat to the beaver than to Mexico's provinces. (If silk hats had not become fashionable in Europe in the mid-1830s, the beaver might have been hunted to extinction.) Not only did the Mexican people of California and New Mexico depend on the American trade for manufactured goods, but Mexican officials in both provinces relied on customs duties to support their governments. In New Mexico the government often had to await the arrival of the annual caravan of traders from St. Louis before it could pay its officials and soldiers.

Although the relations between Mexicans and Americans were mutually beneficial during the 1820s, the potential for conflict was never absent. Spanish-speaking, Roman Catholic, and accustomed to a more hierarchical society, the Mexicans formed a striking contrast to the largely Protestant, individualistic Americans. And while few American traders themselves became permanent residents of Mexico, many returned with glowing reports of the climate and fertility of Mexico's northern provinces. By the 1820s American settlers were already moving into eastern Texas. At the same time, the ties that bound the central government of Mexico to its northern frontier provinces were starting to fray.

Mexican Government in the Far West

Spain, and later Mexico, recognized that the key to controlling the frontier provinces lay in promoting their settlement by civilized Hispanic people—that is, by Spaniards, Mexicans, and Indians who had embraced Catholicism and agriculture. The mission had long been the key instrument of Spanish expansion on the frontier. By the early nineteenth century, missions stretched up the California coast from San Diego to San Francisco and into the interior of New Mexico and Texas.

The Spanish mission combined political, economic, and religious goals—an arrangement alien to the American separation of church and state. The Franciscan priests who staffed the missions were paid government agents who endeavored to convert the Indians and to settle them on mission lands. By 1823 more than twenty thousand Indians lived on the lands of the twenty-one California missions. To protect the missions, the Spanish often constructed forts, or presidios, near them. San Francisco was the site of a mission and a presidio founded in 1776 and did not develop as a town until the 1830s.

Dealt a blow by the successful struggle for Mexican independence, Spain's system of missions and presidios declined in the late 1820s and 1830s. The Mexican government gradually "secularized" the missions by distributing their lands to ambitious government officials and private ranchers. Freed from the supervision of Franciscan priests, some former mission-dwelling Indians became forced laborers in white communities, but many returned to their nomadic ways and joined with Indians who had always resisted the missions. During the 1820s and 1830s, these "barbaric Indians"—notably, the Comanches, Apaches, Navahos, and Utes—terrorized the Mexican frontier by stealing livestock and carrying off Hispanic women and children. Apaches and Comanches attacked New Mexico and Texas, and the Comanches swept into northern Mexico, striking within 150 miles of Mexico City. The legislature of the Mexican state of Chihuahua complained in 1846 that "we travel the roads at their [the Indians'] whim; we cultivate the land where they wish and in the amount that they wish."

Mexican policy was partly responsible for this upsurge in terrorism. With the secularization of the missions, Hispanic ranchers had turned some native Americans into virtual slaves on ranches now bloated by the addition of former mission lands. In addition, Mexican frontier dwellers thought little of raiding Indian tribes for domestic servants. "To get Indian girls to work for you," a descendant of Hispanic settlers recalled, "all you had to do was organize a company against the Navahos or Utes or Apaches and kill all the men you could and bring captive the children." In short, the "barbaric Indians" had many scores to settle with the Mexicans.

Because the overofficered and corrupt Mexican army had little taste for frontier fighting, Mexican settlers on the frontier could not rely on the military for protection against the Indians. Consequently, few Mexicans ventured into the undeveloped, lawless territories. Few areas in the Western Hemisphere potentially so rich were so underpopulated. In 1836 New Mexico contained about 30,000 people of Hispanic culture; California, about 3,200; and Texas, 4,000. Separated by vast distances from their government in Mexico City, which often seemed indifferent to their welfare, and dependent on American traders for the necessities of civilization, the Mexicans of the frontier provinces formed only a frail barrier against the advance of American settlement.

The American Settlement of Texas

Unlike the provinces of New Mexico and California, the Mexican state known as Coahuila-Texas lacked the natural protection of mountains and deserts. During the post-1815 cotton boom, small bands of southern farmers began to push across the Sabine River into eastern Texas in search of more land for cotton cultivation. In addition, after the Panic of 1819, many debt-ridden Americans in the Midwest and South found flight into Texas a convenient escape from creditors. By 1823 some three thousand Americans lived in eastern Texas. In 1824 the Mexican government began actively to encourage American colonization of Texas as a way to bring in manufactured goods (of which the Mexicans produced virtually none) and to gain protection against the Indians. Expecting that American settlers would live peacefully under Mexican rule, the Mexican government bestowed generous land grants on agents (known as *empresarios*) who contracted to bring Americans into Texas. The most successful of these *empresarios*, Stephen F. Austin, had attracted some three hundred

Stephen F. Austin

By founding Anglo-American settlements in Texas in the 1820s, Austin and other empresarios *helped the Mexican government fill the sparsely populated region.*

American families to Texas by 1825. Other *empresarios* followed suit, and by 1830 some seven thousand Americans lived in Texas, more than double the Mexican population dwelling there.

Although Mexico gained some advantages from the American immigration into Texas, the Americans proved a mixed blessing to the Mexican people. Some unscrupulous American traders, like the notorious Harlan Coffee, provoked the Indians to raid Mexican settlements and seize livestock to trade for American liquor and guns. Other American immigrants were roustabouts who moved to Texas to escape debts and sheriffs. But even law-abiding Americans posed a problem. Unlike the relatively assimilated American traders in California, the settlers of Texas were farming families who dwelled in eastern Texas, apart from the Mexicans who had congregated in the western part of the state. Although naturalized as Mexican citizens, the American settlers distrusted the Mexicans and complained constantly about the creaking, erratic Mexican judicial system. Above all, Mexico had not bargained for the size and speed of the American immigration. The first news of the Americans, Mexican general Manuel Mier y Terán wrote in 1828, "comes from discovering them on land

already under cultivation." Four years later, Mier y Terán committed suicide in despair over Mexico's inability to stem and control the American advance.

As early as 1826, an American *empresario*, Haden Edwards, led a revolt against Mexican rule, but Mexican forces, aided by Stephen F. Austin, quickly crushed the uprising. Although, like Austin, most Americans were still willing to live in Texas as naturalized Mexican citizens, during the early 1830s, the allegiance of the Americans to the Mexican government was severely eroded. In 1830 Mexico closed Texas to further immigration from the United States and, having emancipated its own slaves in 1829, forbade the introduction of more slaves to Texas. The latter measure struck directly at the Americans, many of whom were slaveholders. However, Mexico lacked the military might to enforce its decrees. Between 1830 and 1834, the number of Americans in Texas doubled. In 1834 Austin secured repeal of the 1830 prohibition on American immigration, and by 1835 an estimated one thousand Americans a month were crossing into Texas. In 1836 Texas contained some 30,000 white Americans, 5,000 black slaves, and 4,000 Mexicans.

As American immigration swelled, Mexican politics grew increasingly unstable. "The political character of this country," Austin wrote, "seems to partake of its geological features—all is volcanic." From its inception, the government of the Mexican republic had rested on a precarious balance between liberals (or federalists), who favored popular liberty and decentralized government, and conservative centralists, who sought to concentrate power in the hands of military and church officials in Mexico City. In 1834 Mexican president Antonio López de Santa Anna ousted leading liberals from his government and began to restrict the powers of the regimes in Coahuila-Texas and other Mexican states. His actions ignited a series of rebellions in the Mexican states, the most important of which became known as the Texas Revolution.

The Texas Revolution

Santa Anna's brutality in crushing most of the rebellions alarmed Austin and others. Austin initially had taken a moderate position. He hoped to cooperate with Mexican liberals to restore the Mexican Constitution of 1824 and to secure greater autonomy for Texas within Mexico. At the outset, he did not favor Texas's independence from Mexico. When Santa Anna invaded Texas in the fall of 1835, however, Austin cast his lot with the more radical Americans who wanted outright independence.

At first, Santa Anna's army met with success. In late February 1836, his force of 4,000 men laid seige to San Antonio, whose 200 Texan defenders retreated into an abandoned mission, the Alamo. After repelling repeated attacks and inflicting more than 1,500 casualties on Santa Anna's army, the remaining 187 Texans, including such famed frontiersmen as Davy Crockett and Jim Bowie, were wiped out to the last man on March 6. A few weeks later, Mexican troops massacred some 350 Texas prisoners at Goliad.

Even before these events, Texas delegates had met in a windswept shed in the village of Washington, Texas, and declared Texas independent of Mexico. The rebels by then had settled on a military leader, Sam Houston, for their president. A

Sam Houston

This photo, taken in his sixties, shows Houston as a prosperous and successful statesman. But in his youth Houston had a reputation for wildness. In 1829 he resigned Tennessee's governorship and lived dissolutely for three years among the Cherokees.

giant man who wore leopard-skin vests, Houston retreated east to pick up recruits (mostly Americans who crossed the border to fight Santa Anna). Houston turned and surprised Santa Anna on a prairie near the San Jacinto River in April. Shouting "Remember the Alamo," Houston's army of eight hundred tore through the Mexican lines, killing nearly half of Santa Anna's men in fifteen minutes and taking Santa Anna himself prisoner. Houston then forced Santa Anna to sign a treaty (which the Mexican government never ratified) recognizing the independence of Texas.

American Settlements in California, New Mexico, and Oregon

California and New Mexico, both less accessible than Texas, exerted no more than a mild attraction for American settlers during the 1820s and 1830s. Only a few hundred Americans resided in New Mexico in 1840; that same year, California con-

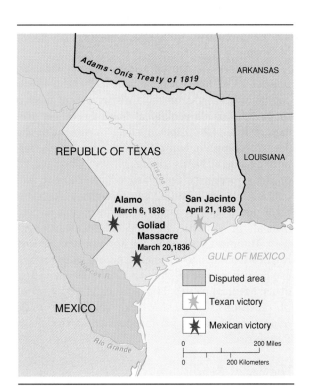

Major Battles in the Texas Revolution, 1835–1836

Sam Houston's victory at San Jacinto was the decisive action of the war and avenged the massacres at the Alamo and Goliad.

tained perhaps four hundred Americans. A contemporary observed that the Americans living in California and New Mexico during these years "are scattered throughout the whole Mexican population, and most of them have Spanish wives. . . . They live in every respect like the Spanish."

Yet the beginnings of change were already evident. California's Hispanic population generally welcomed American immigration as a way to encourage economic development. In addition, some Americans who settled in California before 1840 sent back highly favorable reports of the region to induce immigration. California was said to be a land of "perpetual spring," inhabited only by lazy Mexicans. One story, tongue-in-cheek, told of a 250-year-old man who had to leave the region when he finally wanted to die. Such reports produced their intended effect. During the 1840s an ever-widening stream of Americans migrated to the interior Sacramento Valley, where they lived geographically and culturally apart from the Mexicans. For these land-hungry settlers, no sacrifice seemed too great if it led to California. In 1848 John and Cornelia Sharp abandoned their hardscrabble farm in Ohio and built a flatboat that carried them and their seven children on the Ohio and Missouri rivers to Independence, Missouri. Arriving nearly destitute, they worked for almost four years to earn enough to continue their journey to California.

Oregon, with its abundant farmland, beckoned settlers from the Mississippi Valley. During the 1830s missionaries like the Methodist Jason Lee moved into Oregon's Willamette Valley, and by 1840 the area contained some five hundred Americans. Enthusiastic reports sent back by Lee piqued interest in Oregon. An orator in Missouri described Oregon as a "pioneer's paradise" where "the pigs are running around under the great acorn trees, round and fat and already cooked, with knives and forks sticking in them so that you can cut off a slice whenever you are hungry." Indeed, to some Oregon seemed even more attractive than California. Oregon was already jointly occupied by Britain and the United States, and its prospects for eventual U.S. annexation appeared better than California's.

The Overland Trail

Whatever their destination, Americans who journeyed west in the 1840s faced extraordinary obstacles. Little was known about the terrain between Missouri and the West Coast. In fact, little was known about the coast itself; as late as 1846, no detailed map of California existed. The few available guidebooks contained as much myth as truth. Lansford Hastings's *Emigrant's Guide to Oregon and California* (1845) deliberately tried to steer settlers away from Oregon and toward California.

Westport Landing, *by W. H. Jackson*

Now part of Kansas City, Westport Landing was typical of the Missouri River towns from which wagon trains began the long journey to the West.

LAND HO!

"WESTWARD THE STAR OF EMPIRE TAKES ITS WAY."

WANTED,

Ten good, substantial, intelligent, and independent-minded FARMERS, who either own farms in this region worth $3000 each, or who can command $1500 each on or before the first day of June next, and $1500 more in one year from that date, to form a Company and go to Illinois for the purpose of settling *together* on 3500 acres of land, (being 350 acres a-piece) each having 250 acres of first rate prairie, and 100 acres of excellent timber contiguous. Also, to become interested in 640 acres more adjoining, commanding a water power as great as that of Rochester, and a beautiful Town site, late the residence of a celebrated Indian Chief, who owned the whole tract; hence these lands have remained unsettled, whilst the surrounding country is settled with industrious and prosperous farmers. The title of the purchaser from the Indian has lately been confirmed by an act of Congress and sanctioned by the President, and is therefore perfect. These lands are situated on the banks of a beautiful river, near the Illinois & Michigan Canal,—now nearly completed,—and in the bosom of a country, which, for scenic beauty and fertility, is not surpassed on this side of the Rocky Mountains.

The subscriber has the above tract of land at his disposal, and no better lands or pleasanter location can be found in the whole range of the vast regions of the West. Come on, then, gentlemen, to the number of seven more (three are already waiting for you) and make out the number, and then depute some two, three, or four, of the wisest ones amongst you, to go and examine for you all. There is no romance about this, of which you can be convinced by calling on the subscriber, at B. Newton's Tavern, Palmyra, where maps of the lands may be seen, and where he will explain to you more fully the objects in view, and the advantages of obtaining a portion of these lands, water power and village property. Those who wish to make inquiry will please call soon, as the subscriber is about to depart for the west in a few weeks.

N. B.—The undersigned has two or three farms for sale in this county, which will be sold cheap for prompt pay. Also a house and lot in this village.

A. H. HOWLAND.

Palmyra, Oct. 29, 1841.

Land Ho!

Dwelling on the quality of farmland and the availability of timber and water power, advertisements lured pioneers westward with promises of prosperity and comfort rather than romance and adventure.

Unfortunately, Hastings devised shortcuts to California that drastically understated the distance across such formidable barriers as the Great Salt Desert. One victim of Hastings's misguidance, the Donner party, which set out from Illinois in 1846, lost so much time following his advice that its members became snowbound in the High Sierra and reached California only after the survivors had turned to cannibalism.

Emigrants responded to the extraordinary challenges of the overland trail by cooperating closely with each other. Most set out in huge wagon trains rather than as individuals; so large did the trains become that the voyagers found it necessary to draw up codes of law and elect officers for the trip. But even the most dedicated officers were hard pressed to coordinate the schedules of hundreds of wagons, and in practice the caravans often splintered into smaller parties composed of friends and relatives.

The family represented the most important single form of cooperation on the overland trail. Even before their departure from midwestern farms, women often spent months preserving food and making clothes for the trip. Once under way, women packed and unpacked the wagon each day, milked the cows brought along to stock the new farm in the West, cooked meals on open fires (even if it meant standing for hours with an umbrella to protect the flame from rain), and assisted with the childbirths that occurred on the trail at about the same frequency as in the nation as a whole. Men yoked and unyoked the oxen, drove the wagons and stock, and went off with other men on hunting parties. Men occasionally tried their hand at cooking, but as one noted briskly, "It is more slavish work than I had anticipated." On balance, the division of men's and women's work on the trail reflected firmly entrenched traditions.

One additional task of men was to stand guard against Indian raids, but most emigrants found the Indians whom they encountered cooperative. Indeed, emigrants came to depend on the native Americans as guides for crossing dangerous rivers like the Columbia and as couriers to carry messages back to eastern settlements. Soon the emigrants complained less about the violence of the Indians than about their shrewdness at driving bargains. "The Indian is a financier of no mean ability," a female emigrant wrote, "and invariably comes out A–1 in a bargain." The Indians profited not only by selling fish and vegetables to emigrants but also by exacting tribute for the right to pass through their territory and by collecting tolls for passage over crude bridges. Emigrants who refused to pay usually found that their livestock disappeared. The Indians' pilfering from the wagon trains was far more common than violent assaults on emigrants. The popular image of the isolated wagons surrounded by war-whooping Indians is misleading, because the wagons rarely traveled alone and the native Americans rarely attacked.

Yet tales of Indian massacres increasingly blazed in the eastern press during the 1840s and 1850s. In 1855 several newspapers reported the annihilation of 300 travelers in a wagon train by 2,000 bloodthirsty Sioux and Cheyenne Indians and then described how the sole survivor walked all the way to Oregon. This story and others like it were as fictional as they were juicy. But fraudulent reports of Indian attacks predisposed emigrants to distrust all native Americans. Nervous, trigger-happy emigrants at times provoked Indian assaults. Yet the number of emigrants killed by native Americans on the overland trail remained modest. Between 1840 and 1860, fewer than 400 emigrants lost their lives in Indian attacks, whereas slightly more than 400 Indians were killed by emigrants.

Between 1840 and 1848, an estimated 11,500 emigrants followed an overland trail to Oregon, while some 2,700 reached California. These numbers were modest and concentrated in the years from 1844 to 1848. Yet even small numbers could make a huge difference in the Far West, for the British could not effectively settle Oregon at all, and the Mexican population in California was small and scattered. By 1845 California clung to Mexico by the thinnest of threads. The territory's Hispanic population, the *californios*, felt little allegiance to Mexico, which they contemptuously referred to as the "other shore." Nor did they feel any allegiance to the United States. Some *californios* wanted independence from Mexico; others looked to the day when California might become a protectorate of Britain or perhaps even France. But these *californios*, with their shaky allegiances, now faced a growing number of American settlers whose political sympathies were not at all divided.

The Politics of Expansion

The major issue that arose as a by-product of westward expansion was whether the United States should annex the independent Texas republic. In the mid-1840s the Texas-annexation issue generated the kind of political passions that banking questions had ignited in the 1830s, and became

entangled with equally unsettling issues relating to California, New Mexico, and Oregon. Between 1846 and 1848, a war with Mexico and a dramatic confrontation with Britain settled all these questions on terms favorable to the United States.

Yet at the start of the 1840s, western issues occupied no more than a tenuous position on the national political agenda. From 1840 to 1842, questions relating to economic recovery—notably, banking, the tariff, and internal improvements—dominated the attention of political leaders. Only after politicians failed to address the economic issues coherently did opportunistic leaders thrust issues relating to expansion to the top of the political agenda.

The Whig Ascendancy

The election of 1840 brought the Whig candidate William Henry Harrison to the presidency and installed Whig majorities in both houses of Congress. The Whigs had raced to power with a program, based on Henry Clay's American System, to stimulate economic recovery, and they had excellent prospects of success. They quickly repealed Van Buren's darling, the Independent Treasury. They then planned to substitute some kind of national "fiscal agent," which, like the defunct Bank of the United States, would be a private corporation chartered by Congress and charged with regulating the currency. The Whigs also favored a tariff, but with a twist. In the past, Whigs had supported a "protective" tariff, one set so high as to discourage the importation of goods that would compete with the products of American industries. Now the Whigs proposed a modification in the form of a "revenue" tariff, one high enough to provide "incidental" protection for American industries but low enough to allow most foreign products to enter the United States. The duties collected on these imports would accrue to the federal government as revenue. The Whigs then planned to distribute this revenue to the states for internal improvements, a measure as popular among southern and western Whigs as the tariff was among northeastern Whigs.

The Whig agenda might have breezed into law had it not been for the untimely death of Harrison after only one month in office. With Harrison's demise, Vice President John Tyler, an upper-crust Virginian who had been put on the ticket in 1840 to strengthen the Whigs' appeal in the South, assumed the presidency. From virtually every angle, the new president proved a disaster for the Whigs.

Tyler, a former Democrat who had become a Whig mainly out of dismay at Andrew Jackson's tendency to veto acts of Congress, favored the Democratic policy of states' rights. Ironically, as president, Tyler himself used the veto to shred his new party's program. In August 1841 a Whig bill to create a new national bank became the first casualty of Tyler's veto. Stunned, the Whig majority in Congress quickly passed a modified banking bill, only to see Tyler veto it as well.

Congressional Whigs fared little better on the issues of the tariff and the distribution of tariff revenues to the states. The Compromise Tariff of 1833 had provided for a gradual scaling down of tariff duties, until none was to exceed 20 percent by 1842. Amid the depression of the early 1840s, however, the provision for a 20 percent maximum tariff appeared too low to generate revenue. Without revenue, the Whigs would have no money to distribute among the states for internal improvements and no program with national appeal. In response, the Whig congressional majority passed two bills in the summer of 1842 that simultaneously postponed the final reduction of tariffs to 20 percent and ordered distribution to the states to proceed. Tyler promptly vetoed both bills. Tyler's mounting vetoes infuriated the Whig leadership. "Again has the imbecile, into whose hands accident has placed the power, vetoed a bill passed by a majority of those legally authorized to pass it," screamed the *Daily Richmond Whig*. Some Whigs talked of impeaching Tyler. Finally, in August, Tyler, needing revenue to run the government, signed a new bill that maintained some tariffs above 20 percent but abandoned distribution to the states.

Tyler's erratic course confounded and disrupted his party. By maintaining some tariffs above 20 percent, the tariff of 1842 satisfied northern manufacturers, but by abandoning distribution, it infuriated many southerners and westerners. Northern Whigs succeeded in passing the bill with the aid of many northern Democrats, particularly pro-tariff Pennsylvanians, while large numbers of Whigs in the Upper South and West opposed the tariff of 1842.

In the congressional elections of 1842, the Whigs paid a heavy price for failing to enact their program. While retaining a slim majority in the Senate, they lost control of the House to the Democrats. Now the nation witnessed one party in control of the Senate, its rival in control of the House, and a president who appeared to belong to neither party.

Tyler and the Annexation of Texas

Although a political maverick disowned by his party, Tyler ardently desired a second term as president. Domestic issues offered him little hope of building a popular following, but foreign policy was another matter. In 1842 Tyler's secretary of state, Daniel Webster, concluded a treaty with Great Britain, represented by Lord Ashburton, that settled a long-festering dispute over the boundary between Maine and the Canadian province of New Brunswick. Awarding more than half the disputed territory to the United States, the Webster-Ashburton Treaty was popular in the North. Tyler reasoned that if he could now arrange for the annexation of Texas, he would build a national following.

The issue of slavery, however, had long clouded every discussion of Texas. By the late 1830s, antislavery northerners, among them John Quincy Adams, had concluded that both the Texas Revolution and subsequent proposals to annex Texas formed the core of an elaborate southern conspiracy to extend slavery into the Southwest. Several pieces of evidence seemed to point to this conclusion. Settled by slaveholders, Texas would certainly become a slave state. In fact, some southerners had talked openly of creating as many as four or five slave states out of the vast region encompassed by Texas. Further, as Adams pointed out in 1838, the slaveholding president Andrew Jackson had raised no objection when southerners had violated American neutrality by crossing into Texas in time to fight in the Battle of San Jacinto. All of this occurred, Adams added, at a time when southerners had started to defend slavery as a positive good rather than as a necessary evil.

Nevertheless, Tyler was not deterred from throwing the full weight of his administration behind the annexation of Texas. In the summer of 1843, the president launched a propaganda campaign for annexation. He justified his crusade by reporting that he had learned of certain British designs on Texas, which Americans, he argued, would be prudent to forestall. Tyler's campaign was fed by reports from his unofficial agent in London, Duff Green, a protégé of John C. Calhoun and a man whom John Quincy Adams contemptuously dismissed as an "ambassador of slavery." Green assured Tyler that as a prelude to undermining slavery in the United States, the British would pressure Mexico to recognize the independence of Texas in return for the abolition of slavery there. Calhoun, who became Tyler's secretary of state early in 1844, embroidered these reports with fanciful theories of British plans to use abolition as a way to destroy rice, sugar, and cotton production in the United States and gain for itself a monopoly on all three staples.

In the spring of 1844, Calhoun and Tyler submitted to the Senate for ratification a treaty, secretly drawn up, annexing Texas to the United States. Among the supporting documents accompanying the treaty was a letter from Calhoun to Richard Pakenham, the British foreign minister in Washington, that defended slavery as beneficial to blacks, the only way to protect them from "vice and pauperism." Antislavery northerners no longer had to look under the carpet for evidence that the impulse behind annexation lay in a desire to protect and extend slavery; now they needed only to read Calhoun's words. Both Martin Van Buren, the leading northern Democrat, and Henry Clay, the most powerful Whig, came out against immediate annexation, on grounds that annexation would provoke the kind of sectional conflict that each had sought to bury. By a vote of 35–16, the treaty went down to crushing defeat in the Senate. Decisive as it appeared, however, this vote only postponed the final decision on annexation to the upcoming election of 1844.

The Election of 1844

Tyler's ineptitude turned the presidential campaign into a free-for-all. The president hoped to succeed himself in the White House, but he lacked a base in either party. Testing the waters as an independent, he could not garner adequate support and was forced to drop out of the race.

Henry Clay had a secure grip on the Whig nomination. Martin Van Buren appeared to have an equally firm grasp on the Democratic nomination, but the issue of annexation split his party.

1844 Campaign Banner

Clay hoped to convince the public that the Whig programs of high tariffs and the distribution of tariff revenues would restore prosperity, here represented by a well-dressed farmer and his well-fed horse.

Trying to appease all shades of opinion within his party, Van Buren stated that he would abide by whatever Congress might decide on the annexation issue. Van Buren's attempt to evade the issue succeeded only in alienating the modest number of northern annexationists, led by Michigan's former governor Lewis Cass, and the much larger group of southern annexationists. At the Democratic convention, Van Buren and Cass effectively blocked each other's nomination. The resulting deadlock was broken by the nomination of James K. Polk of Tennessee, the first "dark-horse" nominee in American history.

Although little known outside the South, the slaveholding Polk was the favorite of southern Democrats, who accurately described him as the "bosom friend of [Andrew] Jackson, and a pure whole-hogged Democrat, the known enemy of banks and distribution." On the Texas issue, Polk supported immediate "reannexation," a curious turn of phrase that reflected Andrew Jackson's belief that Texas had been part of the Louisiana Purchase until unwisely ceded to Spain by the Transcontinental Treaty of 1819. Indeed, Polk followed Old Hickory's lead so often that he became known as Young Hickory.

Gibing "Who is James K. Polk?" the Whigs derided Polk's nomination. Polk himself marveled at his turn of fortune, for he had lost successive elections for the governorship of Tennessee. Yet he proved a wily campaign strategist. To satisfy pro-tariff Pennsylvania Democrats, Polk adjusted his position on the tariff to hold out some hope for protection. In addition, Polk and supporters like Senator Robert J. Walker of Mississippi managed to convince many northerners that the annexation of Texas would advance their interests. By foiling alleged British plans to abolitionize Texas, Walker contended, annexation would make Texas a safe haven for slavery and draw both slaves and free blacks away from states bordering the North. Failure to annex, on the other hand, would prevent the westward dispersal of the South's slave population, intensify racial tensions in the existing slave states, and increase the chances of a race war that would spill over into the North. However far-fetched, Walker's arguments played effectively on the racial phobias of many northerners and helped Polk detach annexation from Calhoun's narrow, pro-southern defense of it.

In contrast to the Democrats, who established a clear direction in their arguments, Clay kept muddying the waters. In the spring of 1844, he had opposed the annexation treaty. Then he sent conflicting messages to his followers throughout the summer of 1844, saying that he had nothing against annexation as long as it would not disrupt sectional harmony. Finally, in September 1844 he again came out against annexation. Clay's shifts on annexation alienated his southern supporters and prompted a small but influential body of northern antislavery Whigs to desert to the Liberty party, which had been organized in 1840. Devoted to the abolition of slavery by political action, the Liberty party nominated Ohio's James G. Birney for the presidency.

Annexation was not the sole issue of the campaign. The Whigs' failure to enact their tariff and banking policies under Tyler alienated some traditional Whig support. In addition, as the Philadelphia Bible Riots demonstrated, long-simmering tensions between native-born Americans and immigrants were boiling over in key northern states in 1844. The Whigs infuriated immigrant voters by nominating Theodore Frelinghuysen as Clay's running mate. A leading Presbyterian layman, Frelinghuysen gave "his head, his hand, and his heart" to temperance and an assortment of other Protestant causes. His presence on their ticket fixed the image of the Whigs as the orthodox Protestant party and roused the largely Catholic foreign-born voters to turn out in large numbers for the Democrats.

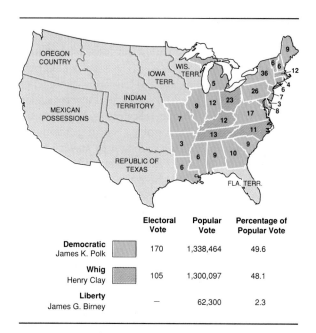

		Electoral Vote	Popular Vote	Percentage of Popular Vote
Democratic James K. Polk		170	1,338,464	49.6
Whig Henry Clay		105	1,300,097	48.1
Liberty James G. Birney		—	62,300	2.3

The Election of 1844

On the eve of the election in New York City, so many Irish marched to the courthouse to be qualified for voting that the windows had to be left open for people to get in and out. "Ireland has re-conquered the country which England lost," an embittered Whig moaned. Polk won the electoral vote 170–105, but his margin in the popular vote was only 38,000 out of 2.6 million votes cast, and he lost his own state of Tennessee by 113 votes. In most states the two main parties contended with each other on close terms, a sign of the maturity of the second party system. A shift of 6,000 votes in New York, where the immigrant vote and Whig defections to the Liberty party hurt Clay, would have given Clay both the state and the presidency.

Manifest Destiny

The election of 1844 demonstrated one incontestable fact: the annexation of Texas had more national support than Clay had realized. The surging popular sentiment for expansion that made the underdog Polk rather than Clay the man of the hour reflected a growing conviction among the people that America's natural destiny was to expand into Texas and all the way to the Pacific.

Expansionists emphasized extending the "area of freedom" and talked of "repelling the contaminating proximity of monarchies upon the soil that we have consecrated to the rights of man." For contemporary young Americans like Walt Whitman, such restless expansionism knew few limits. "The more we reflect upon annexation as involving a part of Mexico, the more do doubts and obstacles resolve themselves away," Whitman wrote. "Then there is California, on the way to which lovely tract lies Santa Fe; how long a time will elapse before they shine as two new stars in our mighty firmament?"

Americans awaited only a phrase to capture this ebullient spirit of continentalism. In 1845 John L. O'Sullivan, a New York Democratic journalist, wrote of "our manifest destiny to overspread and to possess the whole of the continent which Providence has given us for the development of the great experiment of liberty and federated self-government entrusted to us."

Advocates of Manifest Destiny used lofty language and routinely invoked God and Nature to sanction expansion. Inasmuch as most spokesmen for Manifest Destiny were Democrats, many of whom supported the annexation of Texas, northern Whigs frequently dismissed Manifest Destiny as a smoke screen aimed at concealing the evil intent of expanding slavery. In reality, many advocates of Manifest Destiny were neither supporters of slavery nor zealous annexationists. Oregon and California loomed more prominently in their minds than Texas. For despite their flowery phrases, these expansionists rested their case on hard material calculations. Most blamed the post-1837 depression on the failure of the United States to acquire markets for its agricultural surplus and saw the acquisition of Oregon and California as solutions. A Missouri Democrat observed that "the ports of Asia are as convenient to Oregon as the ports of Europe are to the eastern slope of our confederacy, with an infinitely better ocean for navigation." An Alabama Democrat praised California's "safe and capacious harbors," which, he assured, "invite to their bosoms the rich commerce of the East."

Expansionists desired more than profitable trade routes, however. At the heart of their thinking lay an impulse to preserve the predominantly agricultural character of the American people and thereby to safeguard democracy. Most expansionists associated the industrialization that was transforming America with social stratification and class strife, and many saw the concentration of impoverished Irish immigrants in cities and factory towns as evidence of the common people's shrinking opportunities for economic advancement. After a tour of New England mill towns in 1842, John L. O'Sullivan warned Americans that should they fail to encourage alternatives to factories, the United States would sink to the level of Britain, a nation that the ardent Democratic expansionist James Gordon Bennett described as a land of "bloated wealth" and "terrible misery."

Most Democratic expansionists came to see the acquisition of new territory as a logical complement to their party's policies of low tariffs and opposition to centralized banking. Where tariffs and banks tended to "favor and foster the factory system," expansion would provide farmers with land and with access to foreign markets for their produce. As a consequence, Americans would continue to become farmers, and the foundations of the Republic would remain secure. The acquisition of California and Oregon would provide enough land and harbors to sustain not only the 20 million Americans of 1845 but the 100 million that some expansionists projected for 1900 and the 250 million that O'Sullivan predicted for 1945.

The expansionists' message, especially as delivered by the penny press in such newspapers as Bennett's *New York Herald*, made sense to the laboring poor of America's antebellum cities. The *Herald*, the nation's largest-selling newspaper in the 1840s, played upon the anxieties of its working-class readers by arguing relentlessly for the expulsion of the British from Oregon and for thwarting alleged British plans to abolitionize the United States. These readers, many of them fiercely antiblack, anti-British Irish immigrants, welcomed any efforts to open up economic opportunities for the common people. Most also favored the perpetuation of slavery, for the freeing of slaves would throw masses of blacks into the already intense competition for jobs.

The expansionists with whom these laboring-class readers sided drew ideas from Thomas Jefferson, John Quincy Adams, and other leaders of the early Republic who had proclaimed the American people's right to displace uncivilized or European people from the path of their westward movement. Early expansionists, however, had feared that overexpansion might create an ungovernable empire. Jefferson, for example, had proposed an indefinite restriction on the settlement of Louisiana. In contrast, the expansionists of the 1840s, citing the virtues of the telegraph and the railroad, believed that the problem of distance had been "literally annihilated." James Gordon Bennett claimed that the telegraph would render the whole nation as compact and homogeneous as New York City. Ironically, while many expansionists pointed with alarm to the negative effects of industrialization on American society, their confidence in technology convinced them that the nation could expand with minimal risk to the people.

Polk and Oregon

The most immediate impact of the growing spirit of Manifest Destiny was to escalate the issue of Oregon. To soften northern criticism of the still-pending annexation of Texas, the Democrats had included in their platform for the election of 1844 the assertion that American title "to the whole of the Territory of Oregon is clear and unquestionable." Taken literally, the platform committed the party to acquire the entire area between California and 54°40′, the southern boundary of Alaska. Since Polk had not yet been elected, the British could safely ignore this extraordinary claim for the moment, and in fact, the Oregon issue had aroused far less interest during the campaign than had the annexation of Texas. But in his inaugural address, Polk reasserted the "clear and unquestionable" claim to the "country of Oregon." If by this Polk meant all of Oregon, then the United States, which had never before claimed any part of Oregon north of the forty-ninth parallel, had executed an astounding and belligerent reversal of policy.

Polk's objectives in Oregon, however, were more subtle than his language. He knew that the United States could never obtain all of Oregon without a war with Britain, and he wanted to avoid that. He proposed to use the threat of hostilities to persuade the British to accept what they had repeatedly rejected in the past: a division of Oregon at the forty-ninth parallel. Such a division would give the United States both the excellent deep-water harbors of Puget Sound and the southern tip of British-controlled Vancouver Island. For their part, the British had long held out for a division along the Columbia River, which entered the Pacific far south of the forty-ninth parallel.

Polk's comments in his inaugural speech roused among westerners a furious interest in acquiring

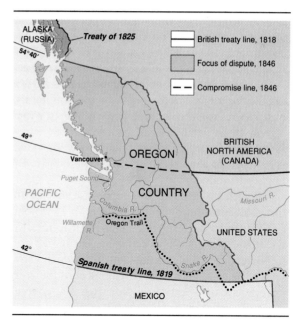

Oregon Boundary Dispute

Although demanding that Britain cede the entire Oregon Territory south of 54°40′, the United States settled for a compromise at the forty-ninth parallel.

the whole territory. Mass meetings adopted such resolutions as "We are all for Oregon, and *all* Oregon in the West" and "The Whole or None!" Further, each passing year brought new American settlers into Oregon. Even John Quincy Adams, who advocated neither the annexation of Texas nor the 54°40′ boundary for Oregon, believed that the American settlements in Oregon gave the United States a far more reasonable claim to the territory than mere exploration and discovery gave the British. The United States, not Britain, Adams contended, was the nation bound "to make the wilderness blossom as the rose, to establish laws, to increase, multiply, and subdue the earth," all "at the first behest of God Almighty."

In April 1846 Polk secured from Congress the termination of joint British-American occupation of Oregon and promptly gave Britain the required one year's notice. With joint occupation abrogated, the British could either go to war over American claims to 54°40′ or negotiate. They chose to negotiate. Although the British raged against "that ill-regulated, overbearing, and aggressive spirit of American democracy," they had too many domestic and foreign problems to welcome a war over what Lord Aberdeen, the British foreign secretary, dismissed as "a few miles of pine swamp." The ensuing treaty provided for a division at the forty-ninth parallel, with some modifications. Britain retained all of Vancouver Island as well as navigation rights on the Columbia River. The Senate ratified the treaty (with the proviso that Britain's navigation rights on the Columbia were merely temporary) on June 15, 1846.

The Origins of the Mexican War

Even as Polk was challenging Britain over Oregon, the United States and Mexico moved steadily toward war. The impending conflict had both remote and immediate causes. One long-standing grievance lay in the failure of the Mexican government to pay some $2 million in debts owed to American citizens. In addition, bitter memories of the Alamo and of the Goliad massacre continued to arouse in Americans a loathing of Mexicans. Above all, the issue of Texas embroiled relations between the two nations. Mexico still hoped to regain Texas or at least to keep it independent of the United States, a nation whose policies toward blacks seemed to most Mexicans evidence of an inherent national cruelty. Once in control of Texas, the Mexicans feared, the United States might seize other Mexican provinces, perhaps even Mexico itself, and treat the citizens of Mexico much as it had treated its slaves.

Unfortunately for Mexico, Polk's election boosted the strength of pro-annexation forces in the United States. The arguments that Polk and Senator Robert J. Walker had put forth during the election campaign of 1844 had persuaded many northerners of the national, rather than purely sectional, benefits of annexing Texas. Recognizing the growing popularity of annexation, both houses of Congress passed a resolution in February 1845 to annex Texas. Soon after taking office, Polk dispatched agents to the Texas republic to gain acceptance of annexation. Some Texans feared that annexation would provoke an invasion of Texas by Mexico, which had never formally recognized Texas's independence and which now served notice that it "would consider equivalent to a declaration of war against the Mexican Republic the passage of an act for an incorporation of Texas with the territory of the United States."

Confronted by Texan timidity and Mexican belligerence, Polk moved on two fronts. To sweeten the pot for the Texans, he supported their claim to the Rio Grande as the southern boundary of Texas. This claim ran counter to Mexico's view that the Nueces River, a hundred miles northeast of the Rio Grande, bounded Texas. The area between the Nueces and the Rio Grande was largely uninhabited, but the stakes were high. Although only a hundred miles southwest of the Nueces at its mouth on the Gulf of Mexico, the Rio Grande meandered west and then north for nearly two thousand miles and encircled a huge slice of territory, including part of New Mexico. The Texas that Polk proposed to annex thus encompassed far more land than the Texas that had gained independence from Mexico in 1836. Reassured by Polk's support, a Texas convention voted overwhelmingly on July 4, 1845, to accept annexation. In response to Mexican war preparations, Polk then made a second move, ordering American troops under General Zachary Taylor to the edge of the disputed territory. Taylor took up a position at Corpus Christi, a tiny Texas outpost situated just south of the Nueces and hence in territory still claimed by Mexico.

Never far from Polk's thoughts in his insistence on the Rio Grande boundary lay his desire for California and for its fine harbors of San Diego and San Francisco. In fact, Polk had entered the White House with the firm intention of extending American control over California. By the summer of 1845, his followers were openly proclaiming that if Mexico went to war with the United States over Texas, "the road to California will be open to us." Then in October 1845, Polk received a dispatch from Thomas O. Larkin, the American consul at Monterey, California, that warned darkly of British designs on California but ended with the optimistic assurance that the Mexicans in California would prefer American to British rule. Larkin's message gave Polk the idea that California might be acquired by the same methods as Texas: revolution followed by annexation.

Visions of new territorial acquisitions were dancing merrily in Polk's mind when Texas accepted annexation in July 1845. With Taylor's troops at Corpus Christi, the next move belonged to Mexico. Unfortunately, Mexico had difficulty making any firm moves, for its politics had slipped again into turmoil with the ouster of Santa Anna by General José Herrera in December 1844. Herrera's own position in Mexican politics was shaky, and prodded by the British, he agreed to receive a delegation from the United States to reach an amicable settlement. Simultaneously, Polk, locked in a war of words with the British over Oregon, decided to give negotiations with Mexico a try. In November 1845 he sent an emissary, the Spanish-speaking John Slidell, to Mexico City. Slidell's final instructions were to gain Mexican recognition of the annexation of Texas, including the Rio Grande boundary, in return for the United States' assumption of all financial claims on the part of American citizens against the Mexican government. Polk also authorized Slidell to offer up to $25 million for New Mexico and California or, failing this, to offer $5 million for New Mexico alone.

By the time Slidell reached Mexico City on December 6, 1845, the threat of a military revolt led by General Mariano Paredes had pushed the Herrera government to the brink of collapse. Too weak to negotiate any concessions to the United States, Herrera refused to receive Slidell. In response to Mexico's refusal to negotiate, Polk now ordered Taylor to march from Corpus Christi southward to the north bank of the Rio Grande. Still viewing the Rio Grande as the key to the Far West, Polk hoped that Taylor's presence on the river would spur the Mexicans to attack. Mexican aggression, the president anticipated, would unify Americans and would quiet northerners who were suspiciously contrasting Polk's willingness to compromise on Oregon with his continuing belligerence toward Mexico. "Why," a Chicago newspaper asked, "should we not compromise our difficulties with Mexico as well as with Great Britain?" Polk had no intention of compromising on the Texas boundary, but if it came to war, he wanted a united country behind him.

On May 9, 1846, Polk notified his cabinet that he could no longer await a Mexican attack and that he must send a war message to Congress. A few hours after the cabinet adjourned, news arrived that a Mexican force had crossed the Rio Grande and ambushed two companies of Taylor's troops. Now the prowar press had its martyrs. "*American blood has been shed on American soil!*" one of Polk's followers proclaimed. On May 11 Polk informed Congress that war "exists by the act of Mexico herself" and called for a $10 million appropriation to fight the war.

Polk's disarming assertion that the United States was already at war provoked furious opposition in

Congress, where John C. Calhoun briefly united with antislavery Whigs to protest the president's high-handedness. Polk's opponents pointed out that the Mexican attack on Taylor's troops had occurred in territory that no previous administration had claimed as part of the United States. By announcing that war already existed, moreover, Polk seemed to be undercutting Congress's power to declare war and using a mere border incident as a pretext for plunging the nation into a general war to acquire more slave territory. The pro-Whig *New York Tribune* warned its readers that Polk was "precipitating you into a fathomless abyss of crime and calamity." Antislavery poet James Russell Lowell of Massachusetts wrote of the Polk Democrats:

> They just want this Californy
>   So's to lug new slave-states in
> To abuse ye, an' to scorn ye,
>   An' to plunder ye like sin.

But Polk had maneuvered the Whigs into a corner. Few Whigs could forget that the opposition of the Federalists to the War of 1812 had wrecked the Federalist party, and few wanted to appear unpatriotic by refusing to support Taylor's beleaguered troops. Swallowing their outrage, most Whigs backed appropriations for war against Mexico.

Throughout the negotiations with Britain over Oregon and with Mexico over Texas, Polk had demonstrated his ability to pursue his goals unflinchingly. A humorless, austere man who banned dancing and liquor at White House receptions, Polk inspired little personal warmth, even among his supporters. But he possessed clear objectives and a single-mindedness in their pursuit. At every point, he had encountered opposition on the home front: from Whigs who saw him as a reckless adventurer; from northerners of both parties opposed to any expansion of slavery; and from John C. Calhoun, who loathed Polk for his high-handedness and feared that a war with Britain would strip the South of its market for cotton. Yet Polk triumphed over all opposition, in part because of his opponents' fragmentation, in part because of expansion's popular appeal, and in part because of the weakness of his foreign antagonists. Reluctant to fight over Oregon, Britain chose to negotiate. Too weak to negotiate, Mexico chose to fight over territory that it had already lost (Texas) and for territories over which its hold was feeble (California and New Mexico).

The Mexican War

Most European observers expected Mexico to win the war. With a regular army four times the size of the American forces, Mexico had the added advantage of fighting on home ground. The United States, which had botched its one previous attempt to invade a foreign nation, Canada in 1812, now had to sustain offensive operations in an area remote from American settlements.

In contrast to the Europeans, expansionists in the United States hardly expected the Mexicans to fight at all. A leading Democrat confidently predicted that Mexico would offer only "a slight resistance to the North American race" because its mixed Spanish and Indian population had been degraded by "amalgamation." Newspaper publisher James Gordon Bennett proclaimed that the "imbecile" Mexicans were "as sure to melt away at the approach of [American] energy and enterprise as snow before a southern sun."

In fact, the Mexicans did not prove to be superior in battle, but neither were they cowardly. They fought bravely and stubbornly, though with little success. In May 1846 Taylor, a sixty-two-year-old veteran of the War of 1812, defeated the Mexicans in two battles north of the Rio Grande and then crossed the river to defeat them again at Matamoros and to capture the major northern Mexican city of Monterrey in September. Taylor's victories touched off a wave of enthusiasm in the United States. Recruiting posters blared: "Here's to Old Zach! Glorious Times! Roast Beef, Ice Cream, and Three Months' Advance!" Already the Whigs were touting Taylor, "Old Rough and Ready," for the presidency in 1848.

After taking the supposedly impregnable Monterrey, however, Taylor, starved for supplies, granted the Mexicans an armistice by which he pledged not to pursue them for eight weeks. Eager to undercut Taylor's popularity, and judging him "wholly unqualified for the command he holds," Polk now stripped Taylor of half his men and assigned them to General Winfield Scott. Polk ordered Scott to prepare an amphibious assault on Vera Cruz, a city on the Gulf of Mexico far to the south, and to proceed overland to Mexico City. Before Scott could attack Vera Cruz, however, Taylor gained even greater fame. Seeking to win an easy victory over Taylor's depleted army, Santa Anna, who had made another of his many comebacks in Mexican politics, led an army of twenty thousand men north to dislodge Taylor. The two armies met at the Battle of Buena Vista, February 22–23, 1847. After a series of futile charges, Santa Anna's men, demoralized by the superior American artillery, retreated.

The Siege of Vera Cruz *(above)*
War News from Mexico *(left), by Richard Caton Woodville, 1848; The Mexican conflict was the first war that sent newspaper reporters to the front. Americans hungrily read their accounts of such engagements as the siege of Vera Cruz.*

Battle of Buena Vista, *by Carl Nebel, 1847*

Zachary Taylor's victory over the Mexicans at Buena Vista made him a national hero.

While Taylor was winning fame in northern Mexico, and before Scott had launched his attack on Vera Cruz, American forces farther north were dealing decisive blows to the remnants of Mexican rule in New Mexico and California. In the spring of 1846, Colonel Stephen Kearny marched an army from Fort Leavenworth, Kansas, toward Santa Fe. Like the pioneers on the Oregon Trail, Kearny's men faced immense natural obstacles as they marched over barren ground. "No grass for 4 days," one of Kearny's officers wrote his wife. "The regulars have spirit, and volunteers would not make it without them." Finally reaching New Mexico, Kearny took the territory by a combination of bluff, bluster, and perhaps bribery, without firing a shot. The Mexican governor, following his own advice that "it is better to be thought brave than to be so," fled at Kearny's approach. After suppressing a brief rebellion by Mexicans and Indians, Kearny sent a detachment of his army south into Mexico. There, having marched six thousand miles from Fort Leavenworth, these troops joined Taylor in time for the Battle of Buena Vista.

Like New Mexico, California fell easily into American hands. In 1845 Polk had ordered Commodore John D. Sloat and his Pacific Squadron to occupy California's ports in the event of war with Mexico. To ensure victory, Polk also dispatched a courier overland with secret orders for one of the most colorful and important actors in the conquest of California, John C. Frémont. A Georgia-born adventurer, Frémont had married Jessie Benton, the daughter of the powerful senator Thomas Hart

Benton of Missouri. Benton used his influence to have accounts of Frémont's explorations in the Northwest (mainly written by Jessie Benton Frémont) published as government documents. All of this earned glory for Frémont as "the Great Pathfinder." Finally overtaken by Polk's courier in Oregon, Frémont was instructed to proceed to California and to "watch over the interests of the United States." Interpreting his orders liberally, Frémont rounded up some American insurgents, seized the town of Sonoma, and proclaimed the independent "Bear Flag Republic" in June 1846. The combined efforts of Frémont, Sloat, his successor David Stockton, and Stephen Kearny (who arrived in California after capturing New Mexico) quickly established American control over California.

The final and most important campaign of the war saw the conquest of Mexico City itself. In March 1847 Winfield Scott landed near Vera Cruz at the head of twelve thousand men and quickly pounded the city into submission. Moving inland, Scott encountered Santa Anna at the seemingly impregnable pass of Cerro Gordo, but a young captain in Scott's command, Robert E. Lee, helped to find a trail that led around the Mexican flank to a small peak overlooking the pass. There Scott planted howitzers and, on April 18, stormed the pass and routed the Mexicans. Scott now moved directly on Mexico City. Taking the key fortresses of Churubusco and Chapultepec (where another young captain, Ulysses S. Grant, was cited for bravery), Scott took the city on September 13, 1847.

In virtually all these encounters on Mexican

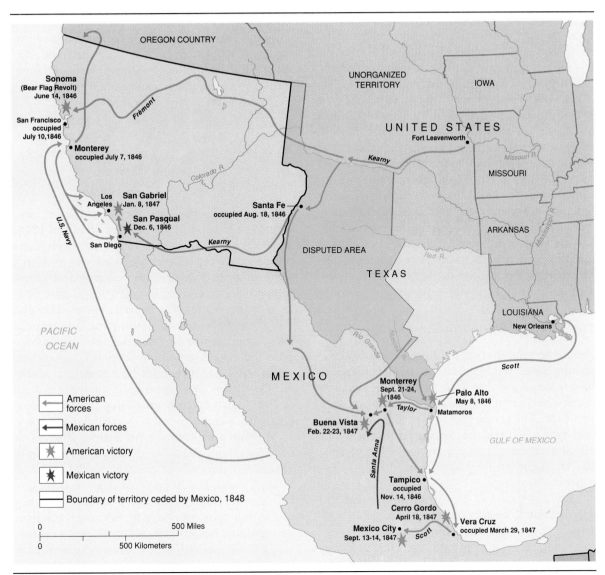

Major Battles of the Mexican War   *The Mexican War's decisive campaign began with General Winfield Scott's capture of Vera Cruz and ended with his conquest of Mexico City.*

soil, the Mexicans enjoyed numerical superiority. In the final assault on Mexico City, Scott commanded eleven thousand troops against Santa Anna's twenty-five thousand. But doom stalked the Mexican army. Hampered by Santa Anna's nearly unbroken string of military miscalculations, the Mexicans fell victim to the vastly superior American artillery and to the ability of the Americans to organize massive military movements. The "barbarians of the North" (as the Mexicans called the American soldiers) died like flies from yellow fever, and they carried into battle the agonies of

venereal disease, which they picked up (and left) in every Mexican town that they took. But the Americans benefited from the unprecedented quality of their weapons, supplies, and organization.

By the Treaty of Guadalupe Hidalgo (February 2, 1848), Mexico ceded Texas with the Rio Grande boundary, New Mexico, and California to the United States. In return, the United States assumed the claims of American citizens against the Mexican government and paid Mexico $15 million. Although the United States gained the present states of California, Nevada, New Mexico, Utah, most of Arizona, and parts of Colorado and Wyoming, some rabid expansionists in the Senate denounced the treaty because it failed to include all of Mexico. But the acquisition of California, with its excellent Pacific ports of San Diego and San Francisco, satisfied Polk. Few senators, moreover, wanted to annex the mixed Spanish and Indian population of Mexico. A writer in the *Democratic Review* expressed the prevailing view that "the annexation of the country [Mexico] to the United States would be a calamity," for it would incorporate into the United States "ignorant and indolent half-civilized Indians," not to mention "free negroes and mulattoes" left over from the British slave trade. In this way, the virulent racism of American leaders allowed the Mexicans to retain part of their nation. On March 10, 1848, the Senate ratified the treaty by a vote of 38 to 10.

The Mexican War in the Popular Mind

Occurring amid the rise of the penny press and the popular novel, the Mexican War became the most fully reported war that America had yet fought and the first conflict in which war correspondents were employed. The extensive coverage given to battlefield victories fueled the soaring nationalism and helped to submerge political divisions. "We are now all Whigs and all Democrats," an Indiana newspaper declared.

Romance as well as patriotism gripped the popular mind. Writers portrayed the war as evidence that the noble, chivalric streak in the American character could prevail over the grasping materialism of American society. To a generation fed on the historical novels of Sir Walter Scott, it seemed that the age of chivalry had returned. Innumerable popular war novels, with titles like *The Texan Ranger; or, The Maid of Matamoros*, mingled patriotism and romance by relating how American soldiers routed Mexican men only to fall in love with Mexican women.

The main beneficiary of the publicity swirling out of the war was Zachary Taylor. Taylor had the right combination of qualities to enchant a people in search of heroes. To those who danced to the hastily composed "Rough and Ready Polka" and the "General Taylor Quick Step," Taylor's military genius seemed equaled only by his democratic bearing and conspicuously ordinary manner. In

contrast to the more soldierly Winfield Scott ("Old Fuss and Feathers"), Taylor went into battle wearing a straw hat and plain brown coat. To an idolizing public, even Taylor's short stature and inclination to corpulence became an advantage; some said that he resembled Napoleon.

The war made Taylor a military hero. The conflicts that spun out of the war would now boost his political career.

Intensifying Sectional Divisions

Despite the wartime patriotic enthusiasm, sectional conflict sharpened between 1846 and 1848. To a degree, this conflict intensified over issues unrelated to expansion. Many of the problems stemmed from Polk's uncompromising and literal-minded Jacksonianism.

Once in office, Polk not only had restored the Independent Treasury, a measure that dismayed the Whigs, but also had eroded the unity of his own party by pursuing Jacksonian policies on tariffs and internal improvements. The numerous northern Democrats who supported a modestly protective tariff had taken heart during the 1844 campaign from Polk's promise to combine a revenue tariff with a measure of protection. But Polk's administration, glutted with southerners, quickly abandoned any talk of protection. The tariff of 1846, fashioned by Robert J. Walker, who became Polk's secretary of the treasury, slashed all duties to the minimum necessary for revenue. Polk then disappointed western Democrats, thirsting for federal aid for internal improvements, by vetoing a law that they supported, the Rivers and Harbors Bill of 1846. To these western Democrats, this veto appeared to be another sign of the pro-southern tilt of Polk's presidency and did more to weaken western support for Polk than his abandonment of the fight for the 54°40′ boundary of Oregon.

Ultimately, however, sectional conflict over tariffs and internal improvements proved of far less importance than the battles generated by territorial expansion. Polk held true to his belief that expansion had provided an "additional guaranty for the preservation of the Union itself." Like most Jacksonian Democrats, he saw the bursting of the nation's boundaries as a way to disperse the population, weaken dangerous tendencies toward centralized government, and retain the agricultural and democratic character of the United States. In Polk's judgment, expansion would accomplish these objectives whether the new territory acquired were slave or free. Focusing attention on slavery in the territories struck him as "not only unwise but wicked." The Missouri Compromise, prohibiting slavery north of 36°30′, impressed him as a simple and permanent solution to the problem of territorial slavery.

Yet many northerners were coming to see slavery in the territories as a profoundly disruptive issue that could not be resolved merely by extending the 36°30′ line to the Pacific. Some antislavery Whigs, especially those from abolitionist strongholds in New England and Ohio, opposed *any* extension of slavery, on moral grounds. But these Whigs, still a minority in their party, posed no immediate threat to Polk. A more damaging challenge emerged within Polk's own party: from a group of northern Democrats who, while not viewing slavery as morally evil, feared that an extension of slavery into California and New Mexico (parts of each lay north of 36°30′) would deter free laborers from settling those territories. These Democrats argued that competition with slave labor clearly degraded free labor, that the westward extension of slavery would create a barrier to the westward migration of free labor, and that such a barrier would intensify the social problems already evident in the East: excessive concentration of population, labor protest, class strife, and social stratification.

The Wilmot Proviso

A young Democratic congressman from Pennsylvania, David Wilmot, became the spokesman for these disaffected northern Democrats. On a sizzling night in August 1846, he introduced an amendment to an appropriations bill for the upcoming negotiations with Mexico over Texas, New Mexico, and California. This amendment, known as the Wilmot Proviso, stipulated that slavery be prohibited in any territory acquired by the negotiations. Neither an abolitionist nor a critic of Polk on tariff policy, Wilmot spoke for those loyal Democrats who had supported the annexation of Texas on the assumption that Texas would be the last slave state. Wilmot's intention was not to split his party along sectional lines but to hold Polk to

what Wilmot and other northern Democrats took as an implicit understanding: Texas for the slaveholders, California and New Mexico for free labor. With strong northern support, the proviso passed in the House but stalled in the Senate. Polk refused to endorse it, and most southern Democrats opposed any barrier to the expansion of slavery south of the Missouri Compromise line. Accepting the view that the westward extension of slavery would reduce the concentration of slaves in the older regions of the South and thus lessen the chances of a slave revolt, southern Democrats tried to put as much distance as possible between themselves and Wilmot.

The proviso raised unsettling constitutional issues. Calhoun and fellow southerners contended that since slaves were property, slaveholders enjoyed the Constitution's protection of property and could carry their slaves wherever they chose. This position led to the conclusion (drawn explicitly by Calhoun) that the Missouri Compromise of 1820, prohibiting slavery in the territories north of 36°30′, was unconstitutional. On the other side were many northerners who cited the Northwest Ordinance of 1787, the Missouri Compromise, and the Constitution itself, which gave Congress the power to "make all needful rules and regulations respecting the territory or other property belonging to the United States," as justification for congressional legislation over slavery in the territories. With the election of 1848 approaching, politicians of both sides, eager to hold their parties together and avert civil war, searched frantically for a middle ground.

The Election of 1848

The Whigs now confronted a major problem and a splendid opportunity. The problem derived from the fact that the nation had returned to prosperity after 1843 without any apparent help from the Whig economic program of national banking, high tariffs, and federal aid for internal improvements. After having asserted that their policies alone could pull the nation out of the depression, the Whigs had watched in dismay as the nation returned to prosperity under the Democrat Polk's program of an independent treasury, low tariffs, and no federal aid for internal improvements. Never before had Clay's American System seemed so irrelevant. The Whigs' opportunity grew out of the fact that the Wilmot Proviso had gravely embarrassed southern

San Francisco in the Gold Rush

San Francisco became a favorite destination for newcomers in the gold rush. Its population spurted from 1,000 in 1849 to 50,000 in 1856. Few American towns had presented less likely prospects for growth. The Spanish had constructed a presidio and a mission on the site in 1776, and a small town Yerba Buena, had sprung up around the mission. But when the United States took possession of Yerba Buena in July 1846, the town stretched for only a few streets in each direction and contained a mere 150 people who huddled amid its low mountains and fog-enshrouded sand hills. Arriving in the summer of 1846, a boatload of 200 Mormons more than doubled the population of Yerba Buena, which became San Francisco in 1847.

The gold rush transformed the town into "a pandemonium of city" in the words of John Woodhouse Audubon, who became stranded there by Christmas 1849, on his way to the gold fields. San Francisco quickly emerged as the main supply depot for miners and prospectors in the interior. At first, virtually all commodities that passed through the city originated outside of California. Lumber came from Maine and Oregon, flour from Chile and Virginia, sugar from Hawaii, and manufactured goods from the eastern states and Britain. This reliance on imports shaped the town's occupational structure between 1849 and 1853. San Francisco's economy was so top-heavy with merchants and storekeepers that those willing to drive carts (draymen) or unload ships or build houses could command wages that elsewhere would have seemed unbelievable. A New

Montgomery Street, San Francisco, 1850, *Daguerreotype by Frederick Coombs*

In the view of historian William H. Goetzmann and art historian William N. Goetzmann, San Francisco was "the final living embodiment of Manifest Destiny, a golden dream city of great instant wealth."

England–born lawyer seriously considered giving up his practice to become a drayman, for "they pay a man to drive a cart fifteen to twenty dollars a day," a generous wage at the time. By the mid-1850s the establishment of iron foundries and flour mills relieved the growing city's dependence on imports, but the supply of commodities remained uncertain, and commodity prices continued to gyrate crazily. Flour that cost $10 a barrel one month might jump to $19 the next. Real-estate prices also soared during the early rush, particularly near the waterfront. The city's economy was vulnerable to crashes as precipitous as its booms. A commercial panic in 1855 produced nearly two

hundred bankruptcies and left close to $7 million in uncollectable debts.

The variety of San Francisco's population rivaled the volatility of its economy. Emigrants came from the four corners of the globe. By the 1850s the Irish outnumbered every other group of foreign-born immigrants. Many Irish were convicts who arrived by way of Australia, to which they had been exiled as punishment for their crimes. China, France, and Italy, nations that did not contribute many immigrants to other parts of the United States before 1860, all sent sizable contingents to San Francisco. Part of the city's tiny black population was also foreign-born. Richard Dalton, for example, came from the West Indies as a steward on a steamer and then labored on the ships that plied the Sacramento and San Joaquin rivers to Sacramento and Stockton. Indeed, no other U.S. city contained people from more parts of the world, and only two, St. Louis and Milwaukee, had a higher proportion of foreign-born residents in 1860. In addition, by the early 1850s, San Francisco contained six to ten times as many men as women.

In a city bursting with rival ethnic and racial groups and lacking the constraints imposed by family responsibilities, violence became a principal noncommercial activity. Audubon reported how the place teemed with men "more blasphemous, and with less regard for God and his commands than all I have ever seen on the Mississippi." A young clergyman wrote in 1851 that "most of our citizens if not all go armed" and confessed that he carried a harmless-looking cane, which "will be found to contain a sword two-and-a-half feet long." The city's small fledgling police force posed little challenge to criminals. For protection, some businessmen organized disbanded soldiers into an extralegal force called the Hounds. Unfortunately, the Hounds soon terrorized the people whom they were supposed to protect. In response, in 1851 San Francisco's merchants organized the first of several Committees of Vigilance, which patrolled the streets, deported undesirables, and tried and hanged thieves and murderers.

The vigilantes turned out during subsequent outbursts of lawlessness. In 1855 a gambler named Charles Cora insulted the wife of William Richardson, a U.S. marshal. Richardson then insulted Cora's mistress, a prostitute. A crusading editor, William King, joined the fight on Richardson's side, and a political hack and longtime antagonist of King, James Casey, added his barbs to the fray. The outcome revealed much about law and order in early San Francisco. Richardson armed himself and sought out Cora in a saloon, only to be shot to death by Cora; Casey shot and killed King on a street. Vigilantes then seized Cora and Casey, tried them in secret, and hanged them.

These incidents underscore the city's religious and ethnic tensions as well as its atmosphere of easy violence. Richardson was a southerner and a Protestant, and his supporter King crusaded against the Catholic church. While less than models of virtue, their opponents Cora and Casey had been raised Catholics and resented attacks on the religion of their parents. Americans thought of the Far West as a land of opportunity where past antagonisms and traditions would be eradicated, but all the divisions of the larger society were reproduced in San Francisco. The major racial, regional, religious, and ethnic groups kept their distance from each other. Blacks were forced to sit in segregated parts of theaters and to attend segregated schools. Southern and New England Protestants worshiped at different churches. Immigrants from Europe also divided on the basis of language and nationality. German, Polish, Russian, and Anglo-American Jews each maintained separate religious congregations.

Regional and ethnic antagonisms even threatened at times to disrupt the harmony within the city's political parties. Transplanted southerners and Irish immigrants, for example, vied with each other for control of the Democratic party. But at election time, these groups laid aside their antagonisms and united against the rival parties. The Germans usually joined the Irish to ally with the Democrats, whereas the Whigs (and later the Know-Nothings and the Republicans) drew support from former New Englanders, from temperance advocates, and from some immigrants who resented the brash and brawling Irish. In this way, party politics gave coherence to the city's divisions and provided a generally peaceful outlet for the populace's overheated tempers.

San Francisco Saloon, *by Frank Marryat*

Mexicans, Chinese, Yankees, and southerners drink together in an ornate San Francisco saloon in the booming gold-rush days.

The Election of 1848

Candidates	Parties	Electoral Vote	Popular Vote	Percentage of Popular Vote
ZACHARY TAYLOR	Whig	163	1,360,967	47.4
Lewis Cass	Democratic	127	1,222,342	42.5
Martin Van Buren	Free-Soil		291,263	10.1

Democrats. Although many antislavery northern Whigs had supported Wilmot's amendment, the proviso's origin in the Democratic party provided southern Whigs with a windfall, for they could now portray themselves as the only dependable guardians of the South's interests.

These considerations inclined the majority of Whigs toward Zachary Taylor. As a Louisianian and large slaveholder, Taylor had an obvious appeal to the South. As a political newcomer who had never voted in a presidential election, he had no loyalty to Clay's American System. As a war hero, he might have a broad national appeal. Nominating Taylor, the Whigs presented him as an ideal man "without regard to creeds or principles" and ran him without any platform.

Because Wilmot was one of their own, the Democrats faced a greater challenge. They could not ignore the issue of slavery in the territories, but if they embraced the positions of either Wilmot or Calhoun, they would suffer an unmendable sectional fracture. With Polk declining to stand for reelection, the Democrats nominated Lewis Cass of Michigan, who solved their problem by evolving a doctrine of "squatter sovereignty," or popular sovereignty as it was later called. Cass argued that the issue of slavery in the territories should be kept out of Congress "and left to the people of the confederacy in their respective local governments." In other words, let the actual settlers in each territory decide the issue for themselves. Cass's position benefited from both its arresting simplicity and its vagueness. Was he saying that Congress had the power to prohibit slavery in the territories but, in the interests of sectional harmony, should leave the issue to each territory? Or did he mean that Congress lacked any power to legislate on slavery in the territories? As a further complication, the doctrine of squatter sovereignty did not establish a clear time frame for territorial action. Did the doctrine mean that the first territorial legislature could

abolish slavery, or did it intend that the final decision on slavery had to await the moment of admission to the Union? In actuality, few Democrats wanted definitive answers to these questions. The very vagueness of squatter sovereignty added to its appeal, for Democrats north and south were free to interpret it to their own advantage to their constituents.

Although both parties tried to steer around the issue of slavery in the territories, neither one fully succeeded. A pro–Wilmot Proviso faction of the Democratic party in New York, called the Barnburners, broke away from the party. Proclaiming their dedication to "Free Trade, Free Labor, Free Speech, and Free Men," the Barnburners courted Liberty party abolitionists and antislavery "Conscience" Whigs, who were dismayed by their party's nomination of the slaveholding Taylor. In August 1844 Barnburners, Conscience Whigs, and former Liberty party adherents met in Buffalo, created the Free-Soil party, and nominated Martin Van Buren on a platform opposing any extension of slavery. Van Buren's motives in accepting this third-party nomination reflected both lingering bitterness at his rejection by the Democrats in 1844 (a defeat engineered largely by Lewis Cass) and alarm at the increasingly southern domination of the party under Polk.

The Whig candidate, Taylor, benefited from the opposition's alienation of key northern states over the tariff issue, from Democratic disunity over the Wilmot Proviso, and from his glowing military record. He captured a majority of the electoral votes in both the North and the South. While failing to carry any state, the Free-Soil party ran well enough in the North to demonstrate the grassroots popularity of opposition to the extension of slavery. Defections to the Free-Soilers, for example, probably cost the Whigs the state of Ohio. Van Buren wrote that the new party had gained "more than we had any right to expect." Indeed, by showing that opposition to the spread of slavery had far greater popular appeal than the abolitionism of the old Liberty party, the Free-Soilers sent the Whig and Democratic parties a message that these parties would be unable to ignore in future elections.

The California Gold Rush

When Wilmot had first made public his proviso, the issue of slavery in the Far West was more abstract than practical, because Mexico had not yet ceded any territory and relatively few Americans resided in either California or New Mexico. Nine days before the signing of the Treaty of Guadalupe Hidalgo, however, an American carpenter discovered gold while constructing a sawmill in the foothills of California's Sierra Nevada range. A frantic gold rush was on within a few months. A San Francisco paper complained that "the whole country from San Francisco to Los Angeles, and from the shore to the base of the Sierra Nevada, resounds with the sordid cry to gold, GOLD, GOLD! while the field is left half-planted, the house half-built, and everything neglected but the manufacture of shovels and pickaxes." (Deprived of its staff, advertisers, and subscribers, the newspaper then suspended publication.) By December 1848 pamphlets with titles like *The Emigrant's Guide to the Gold Mines* had hit the streets of New York City.

To speed the gold-rushers to their destination, builders constructed sleek clipper ships like Donald McKay's *Flying Cloud*, which made the eighteen-thousand-mile trip from New York to San Francisco around Cape Horn in a record eighty-nine days on its maiden voyage in 1851. But most gold-rushers traveled overland. Overland emigrants to California rose from 400 in 1848 to 25,000 in 1849 and to 44,000 in 1850 (see "A Place in Time").

With the gold rush, the issue of slavery in the Far West became practical as well as abstract, and immediate rather than remote. In 1849 gold attracted a hundred thousand newcomers to California, including Mexicans, free blacks, and slaves brought by planters from the South. White prospectors loathed the thought of competing with any of these groups and wanted to drive all of them out of the gold fields. Spawned by disputed claims and prejudice, violence mounted, and demands grew for a strong civilian government in California to replace the ineffective military government left over from the war. Polk began to fear that without a satisfactory congressional solution to the slavery issue, Californians might organize a government independent of the United States. The gold rush thus guaranteed that the question of slavery in the Mexican cession would be the first item on the agenda for Polk's successor and, indeed, for the nation.

Conclusion

By calling their destiny manifest, Americans of the 1840s implied that they had no other course than to annex Texas, seize California and New Mexico, and secure the lion's share of Oregon. Obstacles might arise, but most believed that barriers to expansion would melt away in the face of a dynamic and resolute people.

This image of expansion as inevitable had deep roots in the experiences and values of the American people. Fed by immigration, the population continued to leap forward; by 1850 the United States had nearly five times its population in 1800. The fate of Mexican rule in Texas was sealed as much by the overwhelming numerical superiority of the American settlers as by Sam Houston's brilliant victory at the Battle of San Jacinto. In addition, expansion rested on a sequence of propositions that seemed self-evident to many antebellum Americans: that a nation of farmers would never experience sustained misery; that given the chance, most Americans would rather work on farms than in factories; and that expansion would provide more land for farming, reduce the dangerous concentration of people in cities, and restore opportunity for all.

Beyond all the talk of inevitable expansion, however, Americans saw their society's divisions deepen in the 1840s, not only between native-born and immigrant people but also between northerners and southerners. Expansion proved so controversial that it split the Democratic party over the Wilmot Proviso, widened the gap between northern and southern Whigs, and spurred the emergence of the Free-Soil party. Victorious over Mexico and enriched by the discovery of gold in California, Americans counted the blessings of expansion in these years but began to fear its costs.

CHRONOLOGY

1818 The United States and Britain agree on joint occupation of Oregon for a ten-year period.

1819 Transcontinental (Adams-Onís) Treaty.

1821 Mexico gains independence from Spain.

1822 Stephen F. Austin founds the first American community in Texas.

1824–1825 Russia abandons its claims to Oregon south of 54°40′.

1826 Haden Edwards leads an abortive rebellion against Mexican rule in Texas.

1827 The United States and Britain renew their agreement on joint occupation of Oregon for an indefinite period.

1830 Mexico closes Texas to further American immigration.

1834 Antonio López de Santa Anna comes to power in Mexico.

Austin secures repeal of the ban on American immigration into Texas.

1835 Santa Anna invades Texas.

1836 Texas declares its independence from Mexico.

Fall of the Alamo.

Goliad massacre.

Battle of San Jacinto.

1840 William Henry Harrison elected president.

1841 Harrison dies; John Tyler becomes president.

Tyler vetoes Whig National Banking Bill.

1842 Whigs abandon distribution.

Webster-Ashburton Treaty.

1843 Tyler launches campaign for Texas annexation.

1844 Philadelphia Bible Riots.

Senate rejects treaty annexing Texas.

James K. Polk elected president.

1845 Congress votes joint resolution to annex Texas.

Texas accepts annexation by the United States.

Mexico rejects Slidell mission.

1846 Congress ends the joint occupation of Oregon.

Zachary Taylor defeats the Mexicans in two battles north of the Rio Grande.

The United States declares war on Mexico.

John C. Frémont proclaims the Bear Flag Republic in California.

Congress votes to accept a settlement of the Oregon boundary issue with Britain.

Walker Tariff (tariff of 1846).

Colonel Stephen Kearny occupies Santa Fe.

Wilmot Proviso introduced.

Taylor takes Monterrey.

1847 Taylor defeats Santa Anna at the Battle of Buena Vista.

Vera Cruz falls to Winfield Scott.

Mormons establish the state of Deseret.

Mexico City falls to Scott.

Lewis Cass's principle of "squatter sovereignty."

1848 Gold discovered in California.

Treaty of Guadalupe Hidalgo signed.

Taylor elected president.

For Further Reading

Ray A. Billington, *The Far Western Frontier, 1830–1860* (1956). A comprehensive narrative of the settlement of the Far West.

William R. Brock, *Parties and Political Conscience: American Dilemmas, 1840–1850* (1979). An excellent interpretive study of the politics of the 1840s.

William H. Goetzmann, *When the Eagle Screamed: The Romantic Horizon in American Diplomacy, 1800–1860* (1966). A lively overview of antebellum expansionism.

Thomas R. Hietala, *Manifest Design: Anxious Aggrandizement in Late Jacksonian America* (1985). A fine revisionist study that stresses the economic impulse behind expansion.

Maldwyn A. Jones, *American Immigration* (1960). An excellent brief introduction to immigration.

Charles G. Sellers, *James K. Polk: Continentalist, 1843–1846* (1966). An outstanding political biography.

Henry Nash Smith, *Virgin Land: The American West as Symbol and Myth* (1950). A classic study of westward expansion in the American mind.

Additional Bibliography

Immigration, Nativism, and Labor Protest

Lee Benson, *The Concept of Jacksonian Democracy: New York as a Test Case* (1961); Ray A. Billington, *The Protestant Crusade, 1800–1860: A Study of the Origins of Nativism* (1938); R. A. Burchell, *The San Francisco Irish, 1848–1880* (1980); Kathleen Conzen, *Immigrant Milwaukee, 1836–1860* (1976); Alan Dawley, *Class and Community: The Industrial Revolution in Lynn* (1976); Hasia R. Diner, *Erin's Daughter in America* (1983); Oscar Handlin, *Boston's Immigrants* (rev. ed., 1969); Bruce Laurie, *Working People of Philadelphia, 1800–1850* (1980); Lawrence J. McCaffrey, *The Irish Diaspora in America* (1984); Kerby A. Miller, *Emigrants and Exiles: Ireland and the Irish Exodus to North America* (1985); Earle F. Niehaus, *The Irish in New Orleans, 1800–1860* (1965); LaVern J. Rippley, *The German-Americans* (1976); Dennis P. Ryan, *Beyond the Ballot Box: A Sound History of the Boston Irish, 1845–1917* (1983); Norman Ware, *The Industrial Worker, 1840–1860* (1964); Sean Wilentz, *Chants Democratic: New York City and the Rise of the American Working Class, 1788–1850* (1984); Carl Wittke, *The Irish in America* (1956).

The Far West

John W. Caughey, *The California Gold Rush* (1975); Malcolm Clark, Jr., *Eden Seekers: The Settlement of Oregon, 1818–1862* (1981); Douglas H. Daniels, *Pioneer Urbanites: A Social and Cultural History of Black San Francisco* (1980); Arnoldo De Leon, *They Called Them Greasers: Anglo Attitudes Toward Mexicans in Texas, 1821–1900* (1983); John Mack Faragher, *Women and Men on the Overland Trail* (1979); William H. Goetzmann, *Exploration and Empire: The Explorer and the Scientist in the Winning of the American West* (1966); Neal Harlow, *California Conquered: War and Peace on the Pacific, 1846–1850* (1982); Theodore J. Karaminski, *Fur Trade and Exploration: Opening of the Far Northwest, 1821–1852* (1983); Robert J. Loewenberg, *Equality on the Oregon Frontier* (1976); Roger W. Lotchin, *San Francisco, 1846–1856: From Hamlet to City* (1974); Frederick Merk, *History of the Westward Movement* (1978); R. W. Paul, *California Gold* (1947); Leonard Pitt, *The Decline of the Californios: A Social History of the Spanish-Speaking Californians, 1846–1890* (1966); Alfred Robinson, *Life in California* (1891); John I. Unruh, Jr., *The Plains Across: Overland Emigrants and the Trans-Mississippi West, 1840–1860* (1979); David J. Weber, *The Mexican Frontier, 1821–1846: The American Southwest Under Mexico* (1982).

The Politics and Diplomacy of Expansion

K. Jack Bauer, *The Mexican War, 1846–1848* (1974); William C. Binkley, *The Texas Revolution* (1952); Gene M. Brack, *Mexico Views Manifest Destiny* (1976); Seymour Connor and Odie Faulk, *North America Divided: The Mexican War, 1846–1848* (1971); William J. Cooper, *Liberty and Slavery: Southern Politics to 1860* (1983); Bernard DeVoto, *The Year of Decision, 1846* (1943); Norman A. Graebner, *Empire on the Pacific: A Study in American Continental Expansion* (1955); Reginald Horsman, *Race and Manifest Destiny: The Origins of American Racial Anglo-Saxonism* (1981); Marquis James, *The Raven: The Story of Sam Houston* (1929); Robert W. Johannsen, *To the Halls of the Montezumas: The Mexican War in the American Imagination* (1985); Ernest McPherson Lander, Jr., *Reluctant Imperialist: Calhoun, the South Carolinian, and the Mexican War* (1980); Frederick Merk, *Slavery and the Annexation of Texas* (1972); David M. Pletcher, *The Diplomacy of Annexation: Texas, Oregon, and the Mexican War* (1973); Joseph G. Raybeck, *Free Soil: The Election of 1848* (1970); John H. Schroeder, *Mr. Polk's War: American Opposition and Dissent, 1846–1848* (1971); Charles G. Sellers, *James K. Polk: Jacksonian, 1795–1843* (1957); Joel H. Silbey, *The Shrine of Party: Congressional Voting Behavior, 1841–1852* (1967); Otis A. Singletary, *The Mexican War* (1960).

CHAPTER 13

From Compromise to Secession, 1850–1861

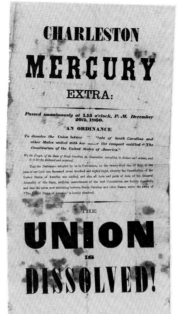

Between December 1859 and February 1860, Washington's political community witnessed one of the most remarkable deadlocks in the history of the House of Representatives. After forty-four ballots the House had still failed to elect a Speaker, the individual responsible for appointing the committees that the House needed to function. Too weak to elect one of their own, southerners repeatedly blocked the election of the early front-runner, Ohio Republican John Sherman.

Elections for the speakership had produced prolonged deadlocks in the past, but never before had tempers so flared. Now many congressmen armed themselves before entering the House chamber. During one debate a pistol fell from the pocket of a New York representative; other congressmen, thinking that he had drawn his pistol, leaped at him. A South Carolinian observed that "the only persons who do not have a revolver and a knife are those who have two revolvers." Although the election of the obscure and inoffensive William Pennington of New Jersey finally broke the deadlock, the tense atmosphere in Congress mirrored the division between the North and the South that would soon lead to the secession of the slave states from the Union.

Secession, a southern newspaper editor conceded in 1861, was a desperate measure. But, he quickly added, "We must recollect that we live in desperate times." A series of confrontations with the North over the status of slavery in the territories fed this growing sense of desperation in the South. Viewing the West as a boundless field of economic opportunity for themselves, northerners abhorred the idea of competing with slaves there for jobs and thus zealously resisted the westward advance of slavery. During the 1850s a growing number of northerners embraced the doctrine known as free soil, the belief that Congress had to prohibit slavery in all the territories. Free-soilers like New York's Republican senator William H. Seward and Illinois's senatorial candidate Abraham Lincoln did not call for the abolition of slavery in the southern states, but they did define the conflict between slavery and freedom as national in scope. In 1858 Seward spoke of an "irrepressible conflict" between slavery and freedom and predicted that either the wheat fields of the North would become slave or the cotton fields of the South free. Invoking the biblical warning that "a house divided against itself cannot stand," Lincoln made the same point in 1858: "I believe that this nation cannot exist permanently half slave and half free." In the eyes of these men, the only solution lay in a congressional prohibition of slavery in the territories.

The doctrine of free soil ultimately rested on an image of the good society as one in which free individuals worked to achieve economic self-sufficiency as landowning farmers, self-employed artisans, and small shopkeepers. Like free-soil northerners, white southerners valued economic independence, but they insisted that without slaves to do society's menial jobs, common white people could never attain economic self-sufficiency. By 1850 most southern whites had persuaded themselves that slavery was an institution that treated blacks humanely while enabling whites to enjoy comfortable lives.

These differing images of the good society made conflict over slavery in the territories virtually unavoidable. White southerners interpreted free-soil attacks on territorial slavery as slaps in their faces. Nothing infuriated them more than the idea that they could not take their property, slaves, anywhere that they chose. Increasingly, too, southerners viewed free-soilers' hostility as a thinly disguised attempt to corrode the foundations of slavery in both the territories and the South itself. When the abolitionist John Brown recklessly attempted to spark a southern slave insurrection in 1859, innumerable southerners concluded that only the extreme step of secession could safeguard the South against northern onslaughts. "Not only our property," a southern newspaper editor proclaimed in 1861, "but our honor, our lives and our all are involved."

The Compromise of 1850

Ralph Waldo Emerson had predicted that an American victory in the Mexican War would be akin to swallowing arsenic, and his forecast proved disturbingly accurate. When the Treaty of Guadalupe Hidalgo was signed in 1848 to end the war, the United States contained an equal number (fifteen) of free and slave states. The vast territory ceded by Mexico (the Mexican cession) threatened to upset this balance in ways that few could have foreseen. Further, all of the proposed solutions to the problem of slavery in the Mexican cession—a free-soil policy, extension of the Missouri Compromise line, and popular sovereignty—ensured controversy. The prospect of "Free Soilism, Wilmot Provisoism, and all such tomfoolery" horrified southerners. The idea of extending the Missouri Compromise line, 36°30′, to the Pacific, which would allow slavery in New Mexico and southern California, antagonized northerners committed to free soil. (This second proposal simultaneously angered southern extremists, notably John C. Calhoun and his followers, by conceding to Congress the right to bar slavery in any of the territories.) The third solution, popular (or "squatter") sovereignty, which promised to ease the issue of slavery extension out of national politics by allowing each territory to decide the question for itself, offered the greatest hope for compromise. Yet popular sovereignty would appease neither those opposed in principle to the expansion of slavery nor those opposed to prohibitions on its expansion.

As statesmen fashioned their positions on slavery extension, the flow of events plunged the nation into a crisis. In the spring of 1849, the nonslaveholding Mormons in Deseret drew up a constitution and sought admission to the Union. (The state of Deseret had been established by Brigham Young's followers on soil that had become part of the United States with the Treaty of Guadalupe Hidalgo.) Then in the fall of 1849, Californians, their numbers swollen by thousands of gold-rushers, framed a constitution that banned slavery, and in 1850 they petitioned for statehood. (From the standpoint of popular sovereignty, California had jumped the gun, for Congress had not yet recognized it as a territory.) To complicate matters, Texas, admitted as a slave state in 1845, laid claim to the eastern half of New Mexico, a region where the future of slaves remained in doubt.

By 1850 these territorial issues had become intertwined with two other concerns. Northern orators had long denounced slavery and the sale of slaves in the District of Columbia, within the shadow of the federal government. For their part, southerners had often complained that northerners were flouting the Fugitive Slave Act, which Congress had passed in 1793, and were actively frustrating slaveholders' efforts to catch runaways on northern soil and return them to the South. Any broad compromise between the sections would have to take into account northern demands for a restriction on slavery in the District of Columbia and southern insistence on a more effective fugitive-slave law.

Zachary Taylor at the Helm

Although elected president in 1848 without a platform, Zachary Taylor came to office with a clear position on the issue of slavery in the Mexican cession. A slaveholder himself, he took for granted the South's need to defend slavery. Taylor insisted that southerners would best protect slavery if they refrained from rekindling the issue of slavery in the territories. He rejected Calhoun's idea that the protection of slavery in the southern states ultimately depended on the expansion of slavery into the western territories. In Taylor's eyes, neither California nor New Mexico was suited to slavery; in 1849 he told a Pennsylvania audience that "the people of the North need have no apprehension of the further extension of slavery."

Although Taylor looked to the exclusion of slavery from California and New Mexico, his position differed from that embodied in the Wilmot Proviso, the free-soil measure proposed in 1846 by a northern Democrat. The proviso had insisted that *Congress* bar slavery in the territories ceded by Mexico. Taylor's plan, in contrast, left the decision to the states. Recognizing the preponderance of free-staters in California, Taylor had prompted Californians to bypass the territorial stage that normally preceded statehood, to draw up their constitution in 1849, and to apply directly for admission as a free state. The president strongly hinted that he expected New Mexico, where slavery had been abolished under Mexican rule, to do the same.

Taylor's strategy appeared to promise a quick, practical solution to the problem of slavery extension. It would give the North two new free states. At the same time, it would acknowledge a position upon which all southerners agreed: a *state* could bar or permit slavery as it chose. This conviction in fact served as the very foundation of the South's defense of slavery, its armor against all the onslaughts of the abolitionists. Nothing in the Constitution forbade a state to act one way or the other on slavery.

Despite its practical features, Taylor's plan dismayed southerners of both parties. Having gored the Democrats in 1848 as the party of the Wilmot Proviso, southern Whigs expected more from the president than a proposal that in effect yielded the proviso's goal—the banning of slavery in the Mexican cession. Many southerners, in addition, questioned Taylor's assumption that slavery could never take root in California or New Mexico. To one observer, who declared that the whole controversy over slavery in the Mexican cession "related to an imaginary negro in an impossible place," south-

erners pointed out that both areas already contained slaves and that slaves could be employed profitably in the mining of gold and silver. "California is by nature," a southerner proclaimed, "peculiarly a slaveholding State." Calhoun trembled at the thought of adding more free states. "If this scheme excluding slavery from California and New Mexico should be carried out—if we are to be reduced to a mere handful . . . wo, wo, I say to this Union." Disillusioned with Taylor, nine southern states agreed to send delegations to a southern convention that was scheduled to meet in Nashville in June 1850.

Henry Clay Proposes a Compromise

Taylor might have been able to contain mounting southern opposition if he had held a secure position in the Whig party. But the leading Whigs, among them Daniel Webster of Massachusetts and Kentucky's Henry Clay, each of whom had presi-

Henry Clay

Although unsuccessful in five presidential bids, Clay was a towering figure in the Senate, to which he was first elected during Jefferson's presidency. Ultimately, his long congressional service worked against his presidential aspirations, for he made many enemies over the years. But his knowledge of the Senate gave him the tools to forge compromises.

dential aspirations, never reconciled themselves to Taylor, a political novice. Early in 1850 Clay boldly challenged Taylor's leadership by forging a set of compromise proposals to resolve the range of contentious issues. Clay proposed (1) the admission of California as a free state; (2) the division of the remainder of the Mexican cession into two territories, New Mexico and Utah (formerly Deseret), without federal restrictions on slavery; (3) the settlement of the Texas–New Mexico boundary dispute on terms favorable to New Mexico; (4) as a pot-sweetener for Texas, an agreement that the federal government would assume the considerable public debt of Texas; (5) in the District of Columbia, the continuance of slavery but the abolition of the slave trade; and (6) a more effective fugitive-slave law.

Clay rolled all of these proposals into a single "omnibus" bill, which he hoped to steer through Congress. The debates over the omnibus during the late winter and early spring of 1850 witnessed the last major appearances on the public stage of Clay, Webster, and Calhoun, the trio of distinguished senators whose lives had mirrored every public event of note since the War of 1812. Clay played the role of the conciliator, as he had during the controversy over Missouri in 1820 and again during the nullification crisis in the early 1830s. He warned the South against the evils of secession and assured the North that nature would check the spread of slavery more effectively than a thousand Wilmot Provisos. Gaunt and gloomy, a dying Calhoun listened as another senator read his address, in which Calhoun summarized what he had been saying for years: the North's growing power, enhanced by protective tariffs and by the Missouri Compromise's exclusion of slaveholders from the northern part of the Louisiana Purchase, had created an imbalance between the sections. Only a decision by the North to treat the South as an equal could now save the Union. Three days later, Daniel Webster, who believed that slavery, "like the cotton-plant, is confined to certain parallels of climate," delivered his memorable "Seventh of March" speech. Speaking not "as a Massachusetts man, nor as a Northern man, but as an American," Webster chided the North for trying to "reenact the will of God" by legally excluding slavery from the Mexican cession and declared himself a forthright proponent of compromise.

However eloquent, the conciliatory voices of Clay and Webster made few converts. With every call for compromise, some northern or southern speaker would rise and inflame passions. The antislavery New York Whig William Seward, for example, enraged southerners by talking of a "higher law than the Constitution"—namely, the will of God against the extension of slavery. Clay's compromise became tied up in a congressional committee. To worsen matters, Clay, who at first had pretended that his proposals were in the spirit of Taylor's plan, broke openly with the president in May, while Taylor attacked Clay as a glory-hunter.

As the Union faced its worst crisis since 1789, a series of events in the summer of 1850 eased the way toward a resolution. When the Nashville convention assembled in June, extreme advocates of "southern rights," called the fire-eaters because of their recklessness, boldly made their presence felt. But talk of southern rights smelled suspiciously like a plot to disrupt the Union. "I would rather sit in council with the six thousand dead who have died of cholera in St. Louis," Senator Thomas Hart Benton of Missouri declared, "than go into convention with such a gang of scamps." Only nine of the fifteen slave states, most in the Lower South, sent delegates to the convention, and moderates took control and isolated the extremists. Then Zachary Taylor, after eating and drinking too much at an Independence Day celebration, fell ill with gastroenteritis and died on July 9. His successor, Vice President Millard Fillmore of New York, quickly proved himself more favorable than Taylor to the Senate's compromise measure by appointing Daniel Webster as his secretary of state. Next, after the compromise suffered a devastating series of amendments in late July, Stephen A. Douglas of Illinois took over the floor leadership from the exhausted Clay. Recognizing that the compromise lacked majority support in Congress, Douglas jettisoned Clay's strategy by chopping the omnibus into a series of separate measures and seeking to secure passage of each bill individually. This ingenious tactic worked beautifully. By summer's end, in the Compromise of 1850, Congress had passed each component of Clay's plan: statehood for California; territorial status for Utah and New Mexico, allowing popular sovereignty; resolution of the Texas–New Mexico boundary disagreement; federal assumption of the Texas debt; abolition of the

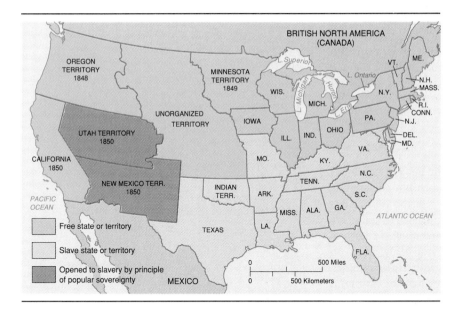

OREGON TERRITORY 1848

MINNESOTA TERRITORY 1849

BRITISH NORTH AMERICA (CANADA)

UNORGANIZED TERRITORY

UTAH TERRITORY 1850

CALIFORNIA 1850

NEW MEXICO TERR. 1850

PACIFIC OCEAN

INDIAN TERR.

TEXAS

MEXICO

WIS.

IOWA

MO.

ARK.

MISS.

LA.

ILL.

MICH.

IND.

OHIO

KY.

TENN.

ALA.

GA.

VA.

N.C.

S.C.

ATLANTIC OCEAN

FLA.

L. Superior

L. Michigan

Huron

L. Ontario

Erie

PA.

N.Y.

VT.

ME.

N.H.

MASS.

R.I.

CONN.

N.J.

DEL.

MD.

Free state or territory

Slave state or territory

Opened to slavery by principle of popular sovereignty

0   500 Miles

0   500 Kilometers

The Compromise of 1850

The Compromise of 1850 admitted California as a free state. Utah and New Mexico were left open to slavery or freedom on the principle of popular sovereignty.

slave trade in the District of Columbia; and a new fugitive-slave law.

Assessing the Compromise

President Fillmore hailed the compromise as a "final settlement" of sectional divisions, and Clay's reputation for conciliation reached new heights. Yet the compromise did not bridge the underlying differences between the two sections. Far from leaping forward to save the Union, Congress had backed into the Compromise of 1850; the majority of congressmen in one or another section opposed virtually all of the specific bills that made up the compromise. Most southerners, for example, voted against the admission of California and the abolition of the slave trade in the District of Columbia; the majority of northerners opposed the Fugitive Slave Act and the organization of New Mexico and Utah without a forthright congressional prohibition of slavery. These measures passed only because the minority of congressmen who genuinely desired compromise combined with the majority in either the North or the South who favored each specific bill.

Each section both gained and lost from the Compromise of 1850. The North won California as a free state, New Mexico and Utah as likely future free states, a favorable settlement of the Texas–New Mexico boundary (most of the disputed area was awarded to New Mexico, a probable free state), and the abolition of the slave trade in the District of Columbia. The South's benefits were cloudier. By stipulating popular sovereignty for New Mexico and Utah, the compromise, to most southerners' relief, had buried the Wilmot Proviso's insistence that Congress formally prohibit slavery in these territories. But to southerners' dismay, the position of the free-soilers remained viable, for the compromise left open the question of whether Congress could prohibit slavery in territories outside of the Mexican cession.

Not surprisingly, southerners reacted ambivalently to the Compromise of 1850. In southern state elections during the fall of 1850 and in 1851, pro-compromise, or Unionist, candidates thrashed anti-compromise candidates who talked of southern rights and secession. But even southern Unionists did not dismiss the possibility of secession. Unionists in Georgia, for example, forged the celebrated Georgia platform, which threatened secession if Congress either prohibited slavery in New Mexico or Utah or repealed the fugitive-slave law.

The one clear advantage gained by the South, a more stringent fugitive-slave law, quickly proved a mixed blessing. Because few slaves had been taken into the Mexican cession, the question of slavery there had a hypothetical quality. However, the issues raised by the new fugitive-slave law were far from hypothetical, because the law authorized real southerners to pursue real fugitives on northern soil. Here was a concrete issue to which the average northerner, who may never have seen a slave and who cared little about slavery a thousand miles away, would respond with fury.

Enforcement of the Fugitive Slave Act

Northern moderates accepted the Fugitive Slave Act as the price that the North had to pay to save the Union. But the law contained a string of features distasteful to moderates and outrageous to staunchly antislavery northerners. It denied alleged fugitives the right of trial by jury, did not allow them to testify in their own behalf, permitted their return to slavery merely on the testimony of the claimant, and enabled court-appointed commissioners to collect ten dollars if they ruled for the slaveholder but only five dollars if they ruled for the fugitive. In authorizing federal marshals to raise posses to pursue fugitives on northern soil, the law threatened to turn the North into "one vast hunting ground." In addition, the law targeted not only recent runaways but also those who had fled the South *decades* earlier. For example, it allowed slave-catchers in 1851 to wrench a former slave from his family in Indiana and return him to the master from whom he had fled in 1832. Above all, the law brought home to northerners the uncomfortable truth that the continuation of slavery depended on their complicity. By legalizing the activities of slave-catchers on northern soil, the law reminded northerners that slavery was a national problem, not merely a peculiar southern institution.

Antislavery northerners assailed the law as the "vilest monument of infamy of the nineteenth century." "Let the President . . . drench our land of freedom in blood," proclaimed Ohio's Whig congressman Joshua Giddings, "but he will never make us obey that law." His support for the law turned Senator Daniel Webster of Massachusetts into a villain in the eyes of the very people who for years had revered him as the "godlike Daniel." The abolitionist poet John Greenleaf Whittier wrote of his fallen idol:

> *All else is gone; from those giant eyes*
> *The soul has fled:*
> *When faith is lost, when honor dies,*
> *The man is dead.*

Advertisement for an Antislavery Play

This banner, promoting a spectacle of realistic scenes of slavery, illustrates the zeal and indignation of the antislavery movement.

Efforts to catch and return fugitive slaves inflamed feelings in both the North and the South. In 1854 a Boston mob, aroused by antislavery speeches, broke into a courthouse and killed a guard in an abortive effort to rescue the fugitive slave Anthony Burns. Determined to prove that the law could be enforced "even in Boston," President Franklin Pierce sent a detachment of federal troops to escort Burns to the harbor, where a ship carried him back to slavery. No witness would ever forget the scene. As five platoons of troops marched with Burns to the ship, some fifty thousand people lined the streets. As the procession passed, one Bostonian hung from his window a black coffin bearing the words "THE FUNERAL OF LIBERTY." Another draped an American flag upside down as a symbol that "my country is eternally disgraced by this day's proceedings." The Burns incident shattered the complacency of conservative supporters of the Compromise of 1850. "We went to bed one night old fashioned conservative Compromise Union Whigs," the textile manufacturer Amos A. Lawrence wrote, "and waked up stark mad Abolitionists." A Boston committee later successfully purchased Burns's freedom, but the fate of many fugitives was far less happy. One such unfortunate was Margaret Gaines, who, about to be captured and sent back to Kentucky as a slave, slit her daughter's throat and tried to kill her other children rather than witness their return to slavery.

In response to the Fugitive Slave Act, vigilance committees sprang up in many northern communities to spirit endangered blacks to safety in Canada. As another ploy, lawyers used obstructive tactics to drag out legal proceedings and thus raise the slave-catchers' expenses. Then during the 1850s, nine northern states passed "personal-liberty laws." By such techniques as forbidding the use of state jails to incarcerate alleged fugitives, these laws aimed to bar state officials from enforcing the law.

Northern resistance to the Fugitive Slave Act affected not only slaves who ran away from the South but also those who fled from masters visiting the North. In 1852 Juliet Lemmon of Virginia took eight of her slaves to New York City, where a judge set free all eight, on grounds that New York law prohibited slavery. In conjunction with the frequent cold stares, obstructive legal tactics, and occasional violence encountered by slaveholders who ventured north to capture runaways, incidents like this one helped demonstrate to southerners that opposition to slavery boiled only shallowly beneath the surface of northern opinion. In the eyes of most southerners, the South had gained little more from the Compromise of 1850 than the Fugitive Slave Act, and now doubts surrounded even that northern concession. After witnessing riots against the Fugitive Slave Act in Boston in 1854, a young Georgian studying law at Harvard wrote to his mother: "Do not be surprised if when I return home you find me a *confirmed disunionist.*"

Uncle Tom's Cabin

The publication in 1852 of Harriet Beecher Stowe's novel *Uncle Tom's Cabin* aroused wide northern sympathy for fugitive slaves. Stowe, the daughter of the famed evangelical Lyman Beecher and the younger sister of Catharine Beecher, the stalwart advocate of domesticity for women, greeted the Fugitive Slave Act with horror and outrage. In a memorable scene from the novel, she depicted the slave Eliza escaping to freedom, clutching her infant son while bounding across ice floes on the Ohio River. Yet Stowe targeted slavery itself more than

merely the slave-catchers who served the institution. Much of her novel's power derives from its intimation that even good intentions cannot prevail against so evil an institution. Torn from his wife and children by sale and shipped on a steamer for the Lower South, the black slave Uncle Tom rescues little Eva, the daughter of kindly Augustine St. Clare, from drowning. In gratitude, St. Clare purchases Tom from a slave-trader and takes him into his home in New Orleans. But after St. Clare's death, his cruel widow sells Tom to the vicious (and northern-born) Simon Legree, who whips Tom to death. Stowe played effectively on the emotions of her audience by demonstrating to an age that revered family life how slavery tore the family apart.

Three hundred thousand copies of *Uncle Tom's Cabin* were sold in 1852, and 1.2 million by the summer of 1853. Dramatized versions, which added dogs to chase Eliza across the ice, eventually reached perhaps fifty times the number of people as the novel itself. As a play, *Uncle Tom's Cabin* enthralled working-class audiences normally indifferent, if not hostile, to abolitionism. During one stage performance, a reviewer for a New York newspaper

Uncle Tom and Little Eva *(detail)*

The American public became familiar with Uncle Tom and Little Eva not only through Harriet Beecher Stowe's novel but also through paintings like this 1853 scene by the black artist Robert Stuart Duncanson.

observed that the gallery was filled with men "in red woollen shirts, with countenances as hardy and rugged as the implements of industry employed by them in the pursuit of their vocations." Astonished by the silence that fell over these men at the point when Eliza escapes across the river, the reviewer turned to discover that many of them were in tears.

The impact of *Uncle Tom's Cabin* cannot be precisely measured. Although the novel stirred deep feelings, it reflected the prevailing stereotypes of blacks far more than it overturned commonly held views. Stowe portrayed only light-skinned blacks as aggressive and intelligent; she depicted dark-skinned blacks such as Uncle Tom as docile and submissive. In addition, some of the stage dramatizations softened the novel's antislavery message. In one version, which P. T. Barnum produced, Tom was rescued from Legree and returned happily as a slave to his original plantation.

Surgery on the plot, however, could not fully excise the antislavery message of *Uncle Tom's Cabin*. Although the novel hardly lived up to the prediction of proslavery lawyer Rufus Choate that it would convert 2 million people to abolitionism, it did push many waverers toward a more aggressively anti-southern and antislavery stance. Indeed, fear of its impact inspired a host of southerners to pen anti–Uncle Tom novels. As historian David Potter has concluded, the northern attitude toward slavery "was never quite the same after *Uncle Tom's Cabin*."

The Election of 1852

The issue of the enforcement of the Fugitive Slave Act fragmented the Whig party. The majority of northern Whigs, strongly supportive of free soil, had opposed the passage of the Fugitive Slave Act and now were leading defiance of the law. This increasingly vocal and potent northern free-soil wing put southern Whigs on the spot, for these southerners had long come before the southern electorate as the party best able to defend slavery within the Union.

The Whigs' nomination in 1852 of General Winfield Scott, the Mexican War hero, in place of the pro-compromise Millard Fillmore, widened the sectional split in their party. Although a Virginian, Scott had fallen under the influence of Senator William H. Seward of New York, a leader of the party's free-soil wing, and owed his nomination to northern votes. During the campaign Scott issued only a single, feeble endorsement of the Compromise of 1850, far less than southern Whigs needed if they were to brand the Democrats as the party of disunion and portray themselves as the party of both slavery and the Union.

The Democrats suffered from divisions of their own. In 1848 defectors from the Democratic party, led by Martin Van Buren, had formed the core of the Free-Soil party, which had gained over 10 percent of the popular vote. By 1852, however, most of the Free-Soilers of 1848, hungry for the spoils of office, returned to the Democratic party. As an idea rather than as a third party, free soil continued to win adherents between 1848 and 1852, but most converts to the idea of free soil gravitated to the Whig rather than the Democratic party.

The Democratic convention began as a three-sided struggle among Lewis Cass of Michigan, James Buchanan of Pennsylvania, and Stephen A. Douglas of Illinois but ended with the nomination of a dark horse, Franklin Pierce of New Hampshire. Handsome, charming, and friendly, Pierce had served in Congress and in the Mexican War. But his appeal to the Democrats rested less on his political experience or his undistinguished war record (during a battle near Mexico City, he had passed out after having been thrown from his horse) than on his acceptability to all factions of the party. The

The Election of 1852				
Candidates	Parties	Electoral Vote	Popular Vote	Percentage of Popular Vote
FRANKLIN PIERCE	Democratic	254	1,601,117	50.9
Winfield Scott	Whig	42	1,385,453	44.1
John P. Hale	Free-Soil		155,825	5.0

"ultra men of the South," a friend of Pierce noted, "say they can cheerfully go for him and none, none say they cannot." In both the North and the South, the Democrats rallied not only behind the Compromise of 1850 but behind the idea of applying popular sovereignty to *all* the territories. In the most one-sided election since 1820, Pierce swept twenty-seven of the thirty-one states and won the electoral vote 254–42. The outcome was particularly galling for southern Whigs, who had soared to new heights four years previously. Compared to the 49.8 percent of the popular vote in the South won by Zachary Taylor in 1848, in 1852, Scott could claim only 35 percent of the southern vote. In state elections during 1852 and 1853, moreover, the Whigs were devastated in the South; one Whig stalwart lamented "the decisive breaking-up of our party."

The Collapse of the Second Party System

Franklin Pierce had the dubious distinction of being the last presidential candidate for eighty years to win the popular and electoral vote in both the North and the South. Not until 1932 did another president, Franklin D. Roosevelt, repeat this accomplishment. Pierce was also the last president to hold office under the second party system—Whigs against Democrats. For two decades the Whigs and the Democrats had battled, often on even terms, in both national sections. Then, within the four years of Pierce's administration, the Whig party disintegrated. In its place two new parties, first the American ("Know-Nothing") party, and then the Republican party, arose.

Unlike the Whig party, the Republican party was a purely sectional, northern party. Its support came from former northern Whigs and from discontented northern Democrats. The Democrats survived as a national party, but with a base so shrunken in the North that in 1856, the Republican party, although scarcely a year old, swept two-thirds of the free states.

For decades the second party system had kept the conflict over slavery in check by giving Americans other issues—banking, internal improvements, tariffs, nativism, and temperance—to argue over. Support for banks, paper money, tariffs, and temperance had helped to unify northern and southern Whigs, while opposition to the Whigs on these issues bound northern and southern Democrats together. By the early 1850s, however, some of the issues that Whigs had long used to court voters in both sections had lost their clarity and urgency. This development exposed the Whigs' internal division over free soil as a raw wound. When Stephen A. Douglas in 1854 put forth a proposal to organize the vast Nebraska territory without restrictions on slavery, he ignited a firestorm that consumed the Whig party.

The Waning of the Whigs

Even before the conflagration created by Douglas's Nebraska bill, the Whig party's grip on its constituents was weakening. An economic boom from the late 1840s to the mid-1850s made the Whigs' policy of a high protective tariff seem unnecessary, because the boom occurred at a time when the *low* Walker Tariff of 1846 was in force. The Whigs also suffered from a severe miscalculation on immigration. The spectacular rise in immigration between 1845 and 1854 impaled the Whigs on the horns of a dilemma. Most immigrants settled in the North and voted Democratic. The Whigs could have responded to this fact either by continuing to align themselves with prohibition and nativism or by bidding for the immigrant (largely Catholic) vote. In 1844 and again in 1848, they had chosen the former strategy, but every year brought more immigrants and greater risks to Whigs who ignored the power of the immigrant vote. In the presidential campaign of 1852, New York Whig senator William H. Seward had tried to reverse his party's direction by touting the Whig Winfield Scott as sympathetic to Catholicism. Scott had allowed his daughters to attend a Catholic convent school, and during the Mexican War, he had been careful to respect property belonging to the Catholic church in Mexico. Seward's strategy backfired, however: Catholic immigrants continued to vote Democratic, and native-born Protestant Whigs were outraged by this softening of their party's anti-immigrant stand.

As the Whigs' traditional stands on the tariff and nativism lost their potency, the party was increasingly unable to disguise its internal split over slavery. Of the two parties—Whig and Democratic—the Whigs had the larger, more aggressive free-soil wing. By the early 1850s, the Fugitive Slave Act had widened the chasm between antislavery "Conscience" Whigs, such as senators Charles Sumner of Massachusetts and Benjamin Wade of Ohio, and the so-called Cotton Whigs, northern manufacturers and southern planters with a shared financial stake in cotton. Sumner's contemptuous description of the Cotton Whigs as an alliance of "the lords of the loom" and "the lords of the lash" underscored the Whig party split. Only the thinnest of threads held the Whig party together by 1852, and these would soon snap under the pressure of mounting conflict over the future of slavery in the Nebraska Territory.

The Kansas-Nebraska Act

Signed by President Pierce at the end of May 1854, the Kansas-Nebraska Act dealt a shattering blow to the already weakened second party system. Moreover, the law triggered a renewal of the sectional strife that many Americans believed that the Compromise of 1850 had buried. The origins of the act lay in the seemingly uncontroversial advance of midwestern settlement. Farm families in Iowa and Missouri had long dreamed of establishing homesteads in the vast prairies to their west, and their congressional representatives had repeatedly introduced bills to organize the territory west of these states, so that Indian land titles could be extinguished and a basis for government provided. Too, since the mid-1840s, advocates of national expansion had looked to the day when a railroad would link the Midwest to the Pacific; and St. Louis, Milwaukee, and Chicago had vied to become the eastern end of the projected Pacific railroad.

In January 1854 Senator Stephen A. Douglas of Illinois proposed a bill to organize Nebraska as a territory. An ardent expansionist, Douglas had formed his political ideology in the heady atmosphere of Manifest Destiny during the 1840s. As early as the mid-1840s, he had embraced the ideas of a Pacific railroad and the organization of Nebraska as ways in which to guarantee a continuous line of settlement between the Midwest and the Pacific. While he preferred a railroad from his home town of Chicago to San Francisco, Douglas dwelled on the national benefits that would attend

construction of a railroad from *anywhere* in the Midwest to the Pacific. Such a railroad would enhance the importance of the Midwest, which could then hold the balance of power between the older sections of the North and South and guide the nation toward unity rather than disruption. In addition, westward expansion through Nebraska with the aid of a railroad struck Douglas as an issue, comparable to Manifest Destiny, around which the contending factions of the Democratic party would unite.

Douglas recognized two sources of potential conflict over his Nebraska bill. First, some southerners advocated a rival route for the Pacific railroad that would start at either New Orleans or Memphis. Second, Nebraska lay within the Louisiana Purchase and north of the Missouri Compromise line of 36°30′, a region closed to slavery. Unless Douglas made some concessions, southerners would have little incentive to vote for his bill, because the organization of Nebraska would simultaneously create a potential free state and increase the chances for a northern, rather than a southern, railroad to the Pacific. As the floor manager of the Compromise of 1850 in the Senate, Douglas thought that he had an ideal concession to offer to the South. The Compromise of 1850 had applied the principle of popular sovereignty to New Mexico and Utah, territories outside of the Louisiana Purchase and hence unaffected by the Missouri Compromise. Why not assume, Douglas reasoned, that the Compromise of 1850 had taken the place of the Missouri Compromise *everywhere*? Believing that expansion rather than slavery was uppermost in the public's mind, Douglas hoped to avoid controversy over slavery by ignoring the Missouri Compromise. But he quickly came under pressure from southern congressmen, who wanted an explicit repudiation of the Missouri Compromise. Soon southerners forced Douglas to state publicly that the Nebraska bill "superseded" the Missouri Compromise and rendered it "void." Still under pressure, Douglas next agreed to a division of Nebraska into two territories: Nebraska to the west of Iowa, and Kansas to the west of Missouri. Because Missouri was a slave state, most congressmen assumed that the division aimed to secure Kansas for slavery and Nebraska for free soil.

The modifications of Douglas's original bill set off a storm of protest. Congressmen quickly

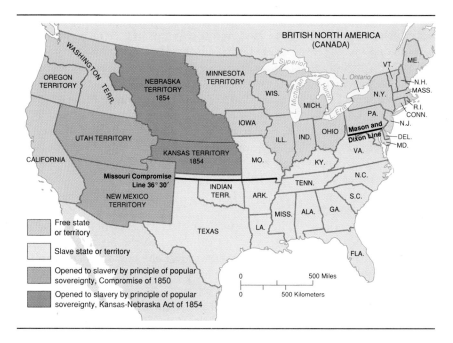

The Kansas-Nebraska Act, 1854

Kansas and Nebraska lay within the Louisiana Purchase, north of 36°30', and hence were closed to slavery until Stephen A. Douglas introduced his bills in 1854.

Map legend:
- Free state or territory
- Slave state or territory
- Opened to slavery by principle of popular sovereignty, Compromise of 1850
- Opened to slavery by principle of popular sovereignty, Kansas-Nebraska Act of 1854

tabled the Pacific railroad (which, in the turn of events, would not be built until after the Civil War) and focused on the issue of slavery extension. A group of "Independent Democratic" northern congressmen, composed of Conscience Whigs and free-soil Democrats, assailed the bill as "part and parcel of an atrocious plot" to violate the "sacred pledge" of the Missouri Compromise and to turn Kansas into a "dreary region of despotism, inhabited by masters and slaves." Their rage electrified southerners, many of whom initially had reacted indifferently to the Nebraska bill. Some southerners had opposed an explicit repeal of the Missouri Compromise from fear of stimulating sectional discord; others doubted that Kansas would attract many slaveholders. But the furious assault of antislavery northerners united the South behind the Kansas-Nebraska bill by turning the issue into one of sectional pride as much as slavery extension.

Despite the uproar, Douglas successfully guided the Kansas-Nebraska bill through the Senate, where it passed by a vote of 37 to 14. In the House of Representatives, where the bill passed by little more than a whisker, 113 to 100, the true dimensions of the conflict became apparent. Not a single northern Whig representative in the House voted for the bill, while the northern Democrats divided evenly, 44 to 44.

The Surge of Free Soil

Douglas obviously had miscalculated the reaction to his Kansas-Nebraska bill. Amid the clamor over the bill, he conceded that he could now travel to Chicago by the light of his own burning effigies. Yet Douglas was neither a fool nor a political novice. Rather, he was the victim of a political force, the surge of feeling for free soil, that exploded under his feet.

Support for free soil united northerners who could agree on little else. Many northern free-soilers were racists who opposed letting any blacks, free or slave, into the West. In 1851 and 1853, racist free-soil advocates in Iowa and Illinois secured the passage of laws prohibiting settlement by black people; and in Iowa, Michigan, and Wisconsin, free-soilers refused by overwhelming majorities to allow blacks to vote. In Oregon, after rejecting slavery by a three-to-one majority in 1857, voters excluded all blacks from the state by an eight-to-one majority. But laws excluding blacks from western settlement were not always enforced, and not all free-soilers were racist. Some rejected slavery on moral grounds and opposed blatantly racist legislation. However, as the abolitionist George W. Julian accurately observed, the antislavery convictions of many westerners were grounded on a "perfect, if not supreme" hatred of blacks.

Although split over the morality of slavery, free-soilers agreed that slavery impeded whites' progress. Most free-soilers accepted Abraham Lincoln's portrayal of the North as a society of upwardly mobile farmers, artisans, and small businessmen and subscribed to the doctrine of "free labor"—the idea that in America, any enterprising individual could escape the class of wage labor and attain self-employment. "The man who labored for another last year," Lincoln insisted, "this year labors for himself, and next year he will hire others to labor for him." Because a slave worked for nothing, the free-soil argument ran, no free laborer could compete with a slave. A territory might contain only a handful of slaves or none at all, but as long as Congress refused to prohibit slavery in the territories, the institution could gain a foothold. Then slavery would grow, and free labor would wither; competition with slave labor would either drive out free labor or deter free labor from entering. Wherever slavery appeared, a free-soiler proclaimed, "labor loses its dignity; industry sickens; education finds no schools; religion finds no churches, and the whole land of slavery is impoverished."

Furthermore, free-soilers flatly rejected the idea that slavery had natural limits. As long as slaves could enter a territory, they believed, slaveholders would find tasks for them. In 1851 a free-soiler warned that "slavery is as certain to invade New Mexico and Utah, as the sun is to rise." By 1854 free-soilers were predicting that once secure in Kansas, slavery would invade the Minnesota Territory.

One free-soiler articulated the growing suspicions of many when he branded the Kansas-Nebraska Act "a part of a continuous movement of slaveholders to advance slavery over the entire North." At every turn, the free-soilers contended, the spread of slavery depended on the complicity of politicians. At the heart of the free-soil argument lay the belief that southern planters, southern politicians, and their northern dupes like Stephen A. Douglas were conspiring to spread slavery. And rather than any single event, there emerged a *pattern* of events—the Fugitive Slave Act, the repeal of the Missouri Compromise, and the Kansas-Nebraska division—that convinced free-soilers that a diabolical Slave Power was spreading its tentacles like an octopus. "I voted for the compromise measures of 1850, with the exception of the fugitive slave law," wrote a Whig congressman from Massachusetts, "and had little sympathy with abolitionists, but the repeal of the Missouri Compromise, that most wanton and wicked act, so obviously designed to promote the extension of slavery, was too much to bear. I now advocate the freedom of Kansas under all circumstances and at all hazards, and the prohibition of slavery in all territories now free."

The Ebbing of Manifest Destiny

The Kansas-Nebraska Act strained Democratic harmony and embarrassed the Pierce administration. The hubbub over the law doomed Manifest Destiny, the issue that had unified the Democrats in the 1840s.

Pierce had come to office as a champion of Manifest Destiny. In 1853 his emissary James Gadsden concluded a treaty with Mexico for the purchase of a strip of land south of the Gila River (now southern Arizona and part of southern New Mexico), an acquisition favored by advocates of a southern railroad route to the Pacific. The fiercely negative reaction to the so-called Gadsden Purchase, however, pointed up the mounting suspicions of expansionist aims. Encountering stiff northern opposition, Gadsden's treaty gained Senate approval in 1854 only after an amendment slashed nine thousand square miles from the purchase. Clearly, the same sectional rivalries that were brewing conflict over the existing territory of Nebraska were threatening to engulf proposals to gain *new* territory.

Pierce encountered even more severe buffeting when he tried to acquire the island of Cuba. Even as Congress was wrestling with the Kansas-Nebraska bill, Mississippi's former senator John A. Quitman was planning a massive filibustering (unofficial) military expedition—to seize Cuba from Spain. Pierce himself wanted to purchase Cuba and may have encouraged Quitman as a way to scare Spain into selling the island. However, northerners, aroused by the Kansas-Nebraska bill, increasingly viewed filibustering as another manifestation of the Slave Power's conspiracy to grab more territory for the "peculiar institution." Pierce, alarmed by northern reaction to the Kansas-Nebraska bill and by signs that Spain planned to defend the island militarily, forced Quitman to scuttle the planned expedition.

Pierce still hoped to purchase Cuba, but events quickly slipped out of his control. In October 1854 the American ambassadors to Great Britain, France, and Spain, two of them from the South, met in Belgium and issued the unofficial Ostend Manifesto, which called upon the United States to acquire Cuba by any necessary means, including force, and then to welcome the island "into that great family of states of which the Union is the Providential Nursery." Already beset by the storm over the Kansas-Nebraska Act, and faced by northern outrage at the threat of aggression against Spain, Pierce quickly repudiated the manifesto.

Despite the Pierce administration's opposition to the Ostend Manifesto, the idea of expansion into the Caribbean continued to attract southerners, including the Tennessee-born adventurer William Walker. Slightly built and so shy and unassuming that he usually spoke with his hands in his pockets, Walker seemed an unlikely soldier of fortune. Yet between 1854 and 1860, the year when he was executed by a firing squad in Honduras, Walker led a succession of filibustering expeditions into Central America. Taking advantage of civil chaos in Nicaragua, he made himself the chief political force in that nation, reinstituted slavery there, and talked openly of making Nicaragua a United States colony. Southern expansionists also kept the acquisition of both Cuba and parts of Mexico at the top of their agenda and received some support from northern Democrats. As late as 1859, President James Buchanan, Pierce's successor, tried to persuade Congress to appropriate funds for the purchase of Cuba.

For all of the proclamations and intrigues that surrounded the movement for southern expansion in the 1850s, the expansionists' actual strength and goals remained open to question. Many planned filibustering expeditions never got off the ground. With few exceptions the adventurers were shady characters whom southern politicians might admire but upon whom they could never depend. Moreover, a sizable body of southerners did not support the idea of southward expansion. The largely Whig sugar planters in Louisiana, for example, opposed acquiring Cuba, on grounds that once Cuba was annexed, its sugar would enter the United States duty-free and compete with American sugar.

Still, southern expansionists created enough commotion to worry antislavery northerners that the South aspired to establish a Caribbean slave empire. Like a card in a poker game, the threat of expansion southward was all the more menacing for not being played. As long as the debate over the extension of slavery focused on territories in the continental United States, slavery's prospects for expansion were limited and, Kansas aside, seemed fairly dim. If parts of the Caribbean were added to the United States, however, all these calculations would have to change.

The Rise and Fall of the Know-Nothings

While fracturing the harmony of the Democrats, the Kansas-Nebraska Act also wrecked the Whig party. In the immediate aftermath of the law, most northern Whigs hoped to blame the Democrats for the act, revive their fortunes in the North, and entice defectors from the free-soil Democrats to their side. In the state and congressional elections of 1854, the Democrats were drubbed, losing sixty-six congressional seats in the north. But the Whig party failed to benefit from the backlash against the Democrats. However disillusioned they were by the Kansas-Nebraska Act, few northern Democrats would align with their traditional Whig opponents, while many northern Whigs, mindful of southern Whig support for the Kansas-Nebraska Act, decided to quit the party. In the Midwest defecting Whigs and free-soil Democrats turned to a bewildering variety of new parties that bore such names as the Peoples', Independent, and Republican parties. "The Whig party, *as a party*, are completely disbanded," an Indiana Democrat wrote. "They have not *as a party*, brought out a single candidate."

In the traditional Whig strongholds of the Northeast, the new American, or Know-Nothing, party emerged as the principal alternative to the Whigs and Democrats. The Know-Nothings evolved out of a secret nativist organization, the Order of the Star-Spangled Banner, founded in 1849. (The party's popular name, Know-Nothing, derived from the standard response that members gave to inquiries about its activities: "I know nothing.") One of many such societies that mushroomed in response to the unprecedented immigration of the 1840s, the Order of the Star Spangled Banner had sought to rid the

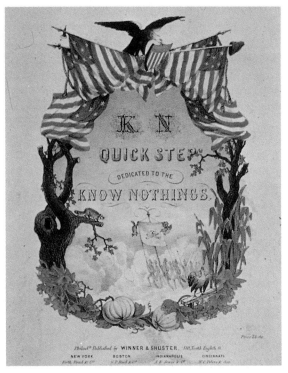

Know-Nothing Quickstep

By 1856, when the American (or Know-Nothing) party ran Millard Fillmore for president, the Know-Nothings had shed their secrecy to the point of commissioning party songs.

United States of immigrant and Catholic political influence by pressuring the existing parties to nominate only native-born Protestants to office and by advocating an extension of the naturalization period before immigrants could vote. Late in 1853 the order made inroads in politics as the American party. The Know-Nothings often astonished political observers by electing candidates whom the regular parties did not even know were running. The party received an additional boost when northern voters, disillusioned with the traditional parties over passage of the Kansas-Nebraska Act, turned to the Know-Nothings. In 1854 Know-Nothings captured the governorship, all the congressional seats, and almost all the seats in the state legislature in Massachusetts. By 1855 they controlled all of the New England states except Vermont and Maine and even made gains in Kentucky, Maryland, Missouri, and Texas.

Explaining the success of the Know-Nothings, one politician observed that the people "want a Paddy [Irish] hunt and on a Paddy hunt they will go." Indeed, hostility to immigrants and Catholics lay at the core of Know-Nothingism. Yet the Know-Nothings added some new dimensions to the long-standing nativist antagonism against Catholics and immigrants. Remembering the abortive attempt of some Whigs to court the Catholic vote in the election of 1852, the Know-Nothings trusted neither of the traditional parties. As Senator Charles Sumner of Massachusetts put it, "The people are tired of the old parties and they have made a new channel." Most Know-Nothing leaders were young, few were wealthy, and all dismissed the old parties as run by cliques of corrupt politicians. In addition, Know-Nothings stressed their opposition to the Slave Power and to slavery extension and presented themselves not only as anti-Catholic but also as antislavery. Indeed, an obsessive fear of conspiracies unified the Know-Nothings' stands on both Catholicism and slavery. Just as they declaimed against the pope for allegedly conspiring to subvert the American republic, they saw everywhere the evil influence of the Slave Power.

After rising spectacularly between 1853 and 1855, the star of Know-Nothingism nevertheless plummeted and gradually disappeared from the horizon after 1856. Various factors account for the Know-Nothings' failure to sustain their early success. First, the Know-Nothings proved as vulnerable as the Whigs and the Democrats to sectional splits over slavery. Although stronger in the North than in the South, the Know-Nothings developed a southern wing composed mainly of former Whigs, and in 1856 the northern and southern wings of the American party nominated different presidential candidates. Second, the former northern Whigs in search of an antislavery alternative to the Democrats found it impossible to reconcile the antislavery position of northern Know-Nothings with the latter's anti-Catholicism and nativism. One such Whig refugee, Illinois congressman Abraham Lincoln, asked pointedly: "How can anyone who abhors the oppression of negroes be in favor of degrading classes of white people?" We began by declaring, Lincoln continued, "that 'all men are created equal.' We now practically read it 'all men are created equal except negroes.' When the Know-

Nothings get control, it will read 'All men are created equal, except Negroes and foreigners and Catholics.'" Third, the secrecy of the Know-Nothings, which seemed as darkly conspiratorial as the very evils that Know-Nothings claimed to attack, also contributed to the party's demise. Finally, even success worked against the Know-Nothings, for once in office they proved unable to stop immigration or to suppress Catholicism, and soon they began to look like just another bunch of bumbling politicians.

The Republican Party

Even before the luster started to wear off Know-Nothingism, the Republican party, which sprang up in several states in 1854 and 1855, emerged as a refuge for antislavery voters. The new party was basically a coalition of "formers": former northern Whigs enraged at the southern Whigs' support for the Kansas-Nebraska Act; former northern Democrats dismayed by southerners' domination of their party; and in time, former Know-Nothings.

The need to harmonize these diverse constituencies forced Republican leaders into a juggling act. Because the Republican party contained a sizable group of former Democrats and former Whigs, issues like the tariff, banking, and internal improvements, which traditionally had divided Whigs and Democrats, had the potential to sever Republican unity. To maintain internal harmony during their early years, the Republicans thus usually ignored national economic issues. Similarly, anti-immigrant feeling and anti-Catholicism were potentially divisive issues for the new party. Many ex-Whig converts to the Republican party persisted in their anti-immigrant, anti-Catholic stance. But because the new party included former Democrats, the Republicans usually avoided public blasts at immigrants, who had traditionally voted Democratic. Even on the slavery issue, the Republican party held various shades of opinion in uneasy balance: at one extreme, conservatives who merely wanted to restore the Missouri Compromise; at the other, a small faction of former Liberty party abolitionists; and in the middle, a sizable body of free-soilers.

No single issue did more to unify the Republicans around their free-soil center and to build the new party's fortunes than the outbreak of violence in Kansas, which quickly gained for the territory the name Bleeding Kansas.

Bleeding Kansas

In the wake of the Kansas-Nebraska Act, Boston-based abolitionists had organized the New England Emigrant Aid Company to send antislavery settlers into Kansas. The abolitionists' aim was to stifle escalating efforts to turn Kansas into a slave state. But antislavery New Englanders arrived slowly in Kansas; the bulk of the territory's early settlers came from Missouri or elsewhere in the Midwest. Very few of these early settlers opposed slavery on moral grounds. Some, in fact, favored slavery; others wanted to keep all blacks, whether slave or free, out of Kansas. "I kem to Kansas to live in a free state," exclaimed a clergyman, "and I don't want niggers a-trampin' over my grave."

Despite most settlers' racist leanings and utter hatred of abolitionists, Kansas became a battleground between proslavery and antislavery forces. In March 1855 thousands of proslavery Missourian "border ruffians," led by Senator David R. Atchison, crossed into Kansas to vote illegally in the first election for a territorial legislature. Drawing and cocking their revolvers, they quickly silenced any judges who questioned their right to vote in Kansas. These proslavery advocates probably would have won an honest election, because they would have been supported by the votes both of slaveholders and of nonslaveholders horrified at rumors that abolitionists planned to use Kansas as a colony for fugitive slaves. But by stealing the election, the proslavery forces committed a grave tactical blunder. A cloud of fraudulence thereafter hung over the proslavery legislature subsequently established at Lecompton, Kansas. "There is not a proslavery man of my acquaintance in Kansas," wrote the wife of an antislavery farmer, "who does not acknowledge that the Bogus Legislature was the result of a gigantic and well planned fraud, that the elections were carried by an invading mob from Missouri." This legislature then further darkened its image by expelling several antislavery legislators and passing a succession of outrageous acts. These laws limited officeholding to individuals who would swear allegiance to slavery, punished the

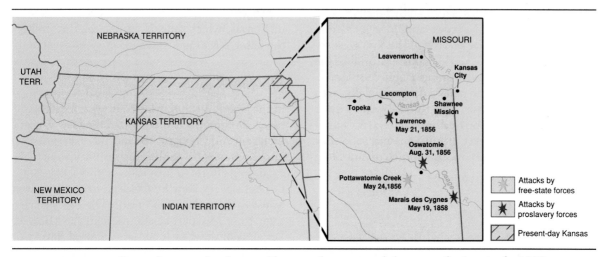

Bleeding Kansas   *Kansas became a battleground between free-state and slave-state factions in the 1850s.*

harboring of fugitive slaves by ten years' imprisonment, and made the circulation of abolitionist literature a capital offense.

The legislature's actions set off a chain reaction. Free-staters, including a small number of abolitionists and a much larger number of settlers enraged by the proceedings at Lecompton, organized a rival government at Topeka, Kansas, in the summer and fall of 1855. In response, the Lecompton government in May 1856 dispatched a posse to Lawrence, where free-staters, heeding the advice of antislavery minister Henry Ward Beecher that rifles would do more than Bibles to enforce morality in Kansas, had taken up arms and dubbed their guns "Beecher's Bibles." Riding under flags emblazoned "SOUTHERN RIGHTS" and "LET YANKEES TREMBLE AND ABOLITIONISTS FALL," the proslavery posse tore through the town like a hell-bent mob. Although the intruders did not kill anyone, they burned several buildings and destroyed two free-state printing presses—enough to earn their actions in the Republican press as "THE SACK OF LAWRENCE."

The next move belonged to John Brown. The son of a Connecticut abolitionist, Brown had drifted through business failures, bankruptcy, and even a charge of embezzlement, sustained only by his belief that God had ordained his misfortunes to test him. The sack of Lawrence convinced Brown that God now beckoned him, in the words of a neighbor, "to break the jaws of the wicked." In late May Brown led seven men, including his four sons and his son-in-law, toward the Pottawatomie Creek near

Lawrence. Setting upon five men associated with the Lecompton government, they shot one to death and hacked the others to pieces with broadswords. Brown's "Pottawatomie massacre" struck terror into the hearts of southerners and completed the transformation of "bleeding Kansas" into a battleground between the South and the North. A month after the massacre, a South Carolinian living in Kansas wrote to his sister:

> I never lie down without taking the precaution to fasten my door and fix it in such a way that if it is forced open, it can be opened only wide enough for one person to come in at a time. I have my rifle, revolver, and old home-stocked pistol where I can lay my hand on them in an instant, besides a hatchet and an axe. I take this precaution to guard against the midnight attacks of the Abolitionists, who never make an attack in open daylight, and no Proslavery man knows when he is safe in this Ter[ritory.]

In Kansas popular sovereignty flunked its major test. Instead of quickly resolving the issue of slavery extension, popular sovereignty merely institutionalized the division over slavery by creating two rival governments, in Lecompton and Topeka. The Pierce administration then shot itself in the foot by denouncing the Topeka government and recognizing only its Lecompton rival. Pierce had forced northern Democrats into the awkward position of appearing to ally with the South in support of the fraudulently elected legislature at Lecompton. Nor did popular sovereignty keep the slavery issue out of national politics. On the day before the sack of Lawrence, Republican senator Charles Sumner of Massachusetts delivered a bombastic and wrathful speech, "The Crime Against Kansas," in which he verbally whipped most of the United States Senate for complicity in slavery and singled out Senator Andrew Butler of South Carolina for his choice of "the harlot, slavery" as his mistress and for the "loose expectoration" of his speech (a nasty reference to the aging Butler's tendency to drool). Sumner's oration stunned most senators. Douglas wondered aloud whether Sumner's real aim was "to provoke some of us to kick him as we would a dog in the street." Two days later a relative of Butler, Democratic representative Preston Brooks of South Carolina, strode into the Senate chamber, found Sumner at his desk, and struck him repeatedly with a cane. The hollow cane broke after five or six blows, but Sumner required stitches, experienced shock, and did not return to the Senate for three years. Brooks became an instant hero in the South, and the fragments of his cane were "begged as sacred relics." A new cane, presented to Brooks by the city of Charleston, bore the inscription "Hit him again."

Now "Bleeding Kansas" and "Bleeding Sumner" united the North. The sack of Lawrence, Pierce's recognition of the proslavery Lecompton government, and Brooks's actions seemed to clinch the Republican argument that an aggressive slaveocracy held white northerners in contempt. Abolitionists remained unpopular in northern opinion, but southerners were becoming even less popular than abolitionists. Northern migrants to Kansas coined a name reflecting their feelings toward southerners: "the pukes." Other northerners attacked the slaveholding migrants to Kansas as the "Missouri savages." By denouncing the Slave Power more than slavery itself, Republican propagandists sidestepped the issue of slavery's morality, which divided their followers, and focused on portraying southern planters as arrogant aristocrats and the natural enemies of the laboring people of the North.

The Election of 1856

The election of 1856 revealed the scope of the political realignments of the preceding few years. In this, its first presidential contest, the Republican party nominated John C. Frémont, the famed

"pathfinder" who had played a key role in the conquest of California during the Mexican War. The Republicans then maneuvered the northern Know-Nothings into endorsing Frémont. The southern Know-Nothings picked the last Whig president, Millard Fillmore, as their candidate, while the Democrats dumped Pierce for the seasoned James Buchanan of Pennsylvania. A four-term congressman and long an aspirant to the presidency, Buchanan finally secured his party's nomination because he had the good luck to be out of the country (as minister to Great Britain) during the furor over the Kansas-Nebraska Act. As a signer of the Ostend Manifesto, he was popular in the South: virtually all of his close friends in Washington were southerners.

The campaign quickly turned into two separate races—Frémont versus Buchanan in the free states and Fillmore versus Buchanan in the slave states. In the North the candidates divided clearly over slavery extension; Frémont's platform called for a congressional prohibition of slavery in the territories, while Buchanan pledged congressional "non-interference." In the South Fillmore appealed to traditionally Whig voters and called for moderation in the face of secessionist threats. But by nominating a well-known moderate in Buchanan, the Democrats undercut some of Fillmore's appeal. Although Fillmore garnered more than 40 percent of the popular vote in ten of the slave states, he carried only Maryland. In the North Frémont outpolled Buchanan in the popular vote and won eleven of the sixteen free states; if Frémont had carried Pennsylvania and either Illinois or Indiana, he would have won the election. As it turned out, Buchanan, the only truly national candidate in the race, secured the presidency.

The election yielded three clear conclusions. First, the American party was finished as a major national force. The Know-Nothings had made fools out of themselves by endorsing Frémont, widely (although incorrectly) rumored to be a Roman Catholic, and by nominating Fillmore, who had never even attended a meeting of a Know-Nothing lodge. In the wake of the election, most northern Know-Nothings went over to the Republicans, while the southerners who had voted for Fillmore were left without any real party home. Second, although in existence scarcely more than a year, lacking any base in the South, and running a political novice, the Republican party did very well. A purely sec-

The Election of 1856				
Candidates	Parties	Electoral Vote	Popular Vote	Percentage of Popular Vote
JAMES BUCHANAN	Democratic	174	1,832,955	45.3
John C. Frémont	Republican	114	1,339,932	33.1
Millard Fillmore	American	8	871,731	21.6

tional party had come within reach of capturing the presidency. Finally, as long as the Democrats could unite behind a single national candidate, they would be hard to defeat. To achieve such unity, however, the Democrats would have to find more James Buchanans—"doughface" moderates who would be acceptable to southerners and who would not drive even more northerners into Republican arms.

The Crisis of the Union

No one ever accused James Buchanan of impulsiveness or fanaticism. Although he disapproved of slavery, he believed that his administration could neither restrict nor end the institution. In 1860 he would pronounce secession a grave wrong, but he would again affirm that his administration could not stop it. Understandably, contemporaries hailed his election as a victory for moderation. Yet his administration encountered a succession of controversies, first over the famed *Dred Scott* decision of the Supreme Court, then over the proslavery Lecompton constitution in Kansas, next following a raid by John Brown on Harpers Ferry, Virginia, and finally concerning secession itself. Ironically, a man who sought to avoid controversy presided over one of the most controversy-ridden administrations in American history. Buchanan's problems arose less from his own actions than from the fact that the forces driving the nation apart were already spinning out of control by 1856. By the time of Buchanan's inauguration, southerners who looked north saw creeping abolitionism in the guise of free soil, while northerners who looked south saw an insatiable Slave Power. Once these images had taken hold in the minds of the American people, politicians like Buchanan had little room for maneuver.

The Dred Scott *Case*

Pledged to congressional "non-interference" with slavery in the territories, Buchanan had long looked to the courts for a judicious and nonpartisan resolution of the vexatious issue of slavery extension. A case that appeared to promise such a solution had been winding its way through the courts for years; on March 6, 1857, two days after Buchanan's inauguration, the Supreme Court handed down its decision in *Dred Scott* v. *Sandford*.

Dred Scott, a slave, had been taken by his master during the 1830s from the slave state Missouri into Illinois and the Wisconsin Territory, areas respectively closed to slavery by the Northwest Ordinance of 1787 and by the Missouri Compromise. After his master's death, Scott sued for his freedom on the grounds of his residence in free territory. A jury sided with Scott and set him free. On appeal, however, the Missouri supreme court overturned the jury's decision in 1852 and returned Scott to slavery. Subsequently, Scott's new owner moved to New York while leaving Scott in Missouri, a turn of events that encouraged Scott to sue in the federal courts (which had jurisdiction over suits brought by citizens of one state against those of another). In 1856 the case finally reached the Supreme Court.

The Court faced two key issues. Did Scott's residence in free territory during the 1830s make him free? Next, regardless of the answer to this question, did Scott, again enslaved in Missouri, have a right to sue in the federal courts? The Court could have resolved the case on narrow grounds by answering the second question in the negative, but Buchanan wanted a far-reaching decision that would deal with the broad issue of slavery in the territories.

In the end, Buchanan got the broad ruling that he sought, but one so controversial that it settled little. In the most important of six separate majority opinions, Chief Justice Roger B. Taney, a

James Buchanan

Polished, affable, and cosmopolitan, Buchanan loathed extremists and instinctively searched for the middle ground on every issue. It was his misfortune to be president at a time when the middle ground was disappearing.

seventy-nine-year-old Marylander whom Andrew Jackson had appointed to succeed John Marshall in 1835, began with the narrow conclusion that Scott, a slave, could not sue for his freedom. Then the thunder started. No black, whether a slave or a free person decended from a slave, could become a citizen of the United States, Taney continued. Next Taney whipped the thunderheads into a tornado. Even if Scott had been a legal plaintiff, Taney ruled, his residence in free territory years earlier did not make him free, because the Missouri Compromise, whose provisions prohibited slavery in the Wisconsin Territory, was *itself* unconstitutional. The compromise, declared Taney, violated the Fifth Amendment's protection of property (including slaves) from deprivation without due process of law.

Contrary to Buchanan's hopes, the decision touched off a new blast of controversy over slavery in the territories. The antislavery press flayed it as a "willful perversion" filled with "gross historical falsehoods." Taney's ruling gave Republicans more evidence that a fiendish Slave Power conspiracy gripped the nation. Although the Kansas-Nebraska Act had effectively repealed the Missouri Compromise, the Court's majority now rejected even the *principle* behind the compromise, the idea that Congress could prohibit slavery in the territories. Five of the six justices who rejected this principle were from slave states. The Slave Power, a northern paper bellowed, "has marched over and annihilated the boundaries of the states. We are now one great homogenous slaveholding community."

Like Stephen Douglas after the Kansas-Nebraska Act, President Buchanan now appeared as another northern dupe of the slaveocracy. Republicans restrained themselves from open defiance of the decision only by insisting that it did not bind the nation; Taney's comments on the constitutionality of the Missouri Compromise, they contended, amounted merely to *obiter dicta*, opinions unnecessary to settling the case.

Reactions to the decision underscored the fact that by 1857 no "judicious" or nonpartisan solution to slavery extension was possible. Anyone who still doubted this needed only to read the fast-breaking news from Kansas.

The Lecompton Constitution

While the Supreme Court wrestled with the abstract issues raised by the expansion of slavery, Buchanan sought a concrete solution to the gnawing problem of Kansas, where the free-state government at Topeka and the officially recognized proslavery government at Lecompton viewed each other with profound distrust. Buchanan's plan for Kansas looked simple: an elected territorial convention would draw up a constitution that would either permit or prohibit slavery; Buchanan would submit the constitution to Congress; Congress would then admit Kansas as a state.

Unfortunately, no sooner had Buchanan devised his plan than it began to explode in his face. Popular sovereignty, the essence of Buchanan's plan, demanded fair play, a scarce quality in Kansas. The territory's history of fraudulent elections left both sides reluctant to commit their fortunes to the polls. An election for a constitutional convention took place in June 1857, but free-staters, by now a majority in Kansas, boycotted the election on grounds that the proslavery side would rig it. Dominated by proslavery delegates, a constitutional convention then met and drew up a frame of government, the Lecompton constitution, that protected the rights of those slaveholders already living in Kansas to their slave property and provided for a referendum in which voters could decide whether to allow in more slaves.

The Lecompton constitution created a dilemma for Buchanan. A supporter of popular sovereignty, he had gone on record in favor of letting the voters in Kansas decide the slavery issue. Now he was confronted by a constitution drawn up by a convention that had been elected by less than 10 percent of the eligible voters, by plans for a referendum that would not allow voters to remove slaves already in Kansas, and by the prospect that the proslavery side would conduct the referendum no more honestly than it had others. Yet Buchanan had compelling reasons to accept the Lecompton constitution as the basis for Kansas's admission as a state. The South, which had provided him with 112 of his 174 electoral votes in 1856, supported the constitution. Buchanan knew, moreover, that only about two hundred slaves resided in Kansas, and he believed that the prospects for slavery in the remaining territories were slight. The contention over slavery in Kansas struck him as another example of how extremists could turn minor issues into major ones. To accept the constitution and speed the admission of Kansas as either a free state or a slave state seemed the best way to pull the rug from beneath the extremists and quiet the commotion in Kansas. Accordingly, in December 1857 Buchanan formally endorsed the Lecompton constitution.

Buchanan's decision provoked a bitter attack from Senator Stephen A. Douglas. What rankled Douglas and many others was that the Lecompton convention, having drawn up a constitution, then allowed voters to decide only whether more slaves could be brought into the territory. "I care not whether [slavery] is voted down or voted up," Douglas declared. But to refuse to allow a vote on the constitution itself, with its protection of existing slave property, smacked of a "system of trickery and jugglery to defeat the fair expression of the will of the people."

Even as Douglas broke with Buchanan, events in Kansas took a new turn. A few months after electing delegates to the convention that drew up the Lecompton constitution, Kansans had gone to the polls to elect a territorial legislature. So flagrant was the fraud in this election—one village with thirty eligible voters returned more than sixteen hundred proslavery votes—that the governor disallowed enough proslavery returns to give free-staters a majority in the legislature. After the drafting of the Lecompton constitution, this territorial legislature called for a referendum on the entire document. Where the Kansas constitutional convention's goal had been to restrict the choice of voters to the narrow issue of the future introduction of slaves, the territorial legislature sought a referendum that would allow Kansans to vote against the protection of existing slave property as well as the introduction of more slaves.

In December 1857 the referendum called earlier by the constitutional convention was held. Boycotted by free-staters, the constitution with slavery passed overwhelmingly. Two weeks later, in the election called by the territorial legislature, the proslavery side abstained, and the constitution went down to crushing defeat. Having already cast his lot with the Lecompton convention's election, Buchanan simply ignored this second election. But he could not ignore the obstacles that the division in Kansas created for his plan to bring Kansas into the Union under the Lecompton constitution. When he submitted the plan to Congress, a deadlock in the House forced him to accept a proposal for still another referendum. This time, Kansans were given the choice between accepting or rejecting the entire constitution, with the proviso that rejection would delay statehood. Despite the proviso, Kansans overwhelmingly voted down the constitution.

Not only had Buchanan failed to tranquilize Kansas, but he had alienated northerners in his own party. His support for the Lecompton constitution confirmed the suspicion of northern Democrats that the southern Slave Power pulled all the important strings in their party. Douglas became the hero of the hour for northern Democrats and even for some Republicans. "The bone and sinew of the Northern Democracy are with you," a New Yorker wrote to Douglas. Yet Douglas himself could take little comfort from the Lecompton fiasco, as his cherished formula of popular sovereignty increasingly looked like a prescription for civil strife rather than harmony.

The Lincoln-Douglas Debates

Despite the acclaim that he gained in the North for his stand against the Lecompton constitution, Douglas faced a stiff challenge in Illinois for re-election to the United States Senate. Of his Republican opponent, Abraham Lincoln, Douglas said: "I shall have my hands full. He is the strong man of his party—full of wit, facts, dates—and the best stump speaker with his droll ways and dry jokes, in the West."

Physically as well as ideologically, the two men formed a striking contrast. Tall (6′4″) and gangling, Lincoln once described himself as "a piece of floating driftwood." Energy, ambition, and a passion for self-education had carried him from the Kentucky log cabin where he was born in 1809 through a youth filled with odd occupations (farm laborer, surveyor, rail-splitter, flatboatman, and storekeeper) into law and politics in his adopted Illinois. There he had capitalized on westerners' support for internal improvements to gain election to Congress in 1846 as a Whig. Having opposed the Mexican War and the Kansas-Nebraska Act, he joined the Republican party in 1856.

Douglas was fully a foot shorter than the towering Lincoln. But his compact frame contained astonishing energy. Born in New England, Douglas appealed primarily to the small farmers of southern origin who populated the Illinois flatlands. To these and others, he was the "little giant," the personification of the Democratic party in the West. The campaign quickly became more than just another Senate race, for it pitted the Republican party's rising star against the Senate's leading Democrat and, thanks to the railroad and the telegraph, received unprecedented national attention.

Although some Republicans extolled Douglas's stand against the Lecompton constitution, to Lincoln nothing had changed. Douglas was still Douglas, the author of the infamous Kansas-Nebraska Act and a man who cared not whether slavery was voted up or down as long as the vote was honest. Opening his campaign with the "House Divided" speech ("this nation cannot exist permanently half slave and half free"), Lincoln reminded his Republican followers of the gulf that still separated his doctrine of free soil from Douglas's popular sovereignty. Douglas dismissed the house-divided doctrine as an invitation to secession. What mattered to him was not slavery, which he viewed as merely an extreme way to subordinate an allegedly inferior race, but the continued expansion of white settlement. Like Lincoln, he wanted to keep slavery out of the path of white settlement. But unlike his rival, Douglas believed that popular sovereignty was the surest way to attain this goal without disrupting the Union.

The high point of the campaign came in a series of seven debates held from August 21 to October 15, 1858. The idea for the debates was floated by Lincoln, who hoped to gain by them public recognition, and accepted by Douglas, who viewed the encounters as a way of putting an end to Lincoln's practice of speaking in each Illinois town as soon as Douglas had left. The Lincoln-Douglas debates mixed political drama with the atmosphere of a festival. For the debate at Galesburg, for example, dozens of horse-drawn floats descended on the town from nearby farming communities. One bore thirty-two pretty girls dressed in white, one for each state, and a thirty-third, who dressed in black with the label "Kansas" and carried a banner proclaiming "THEY WON'T LET ME IN."

Douglas used the debates to portray Lincoln as a virtual abolitionist and advocate of racial equality. Both charges were calculated to doom Lincoln in the eyes of the intensely racist Illinois voters. In response, Lincoln affirmed that Congress had no constitutional authority to abolish slavery in the South, and in one debate he asserted bluntly that "I am not, nor ever have been in favor of bringing about the social and political equality of the white, and black man." However, fending off charges of extremism was getting Lincoln nowhere; so in order to seize the initiative, he tried to maneuver Douglas into a corner.

In view of the *Dred Scott* decision, Lincoln asked in the debate at Freeport, could the people of a territory lawfully exclude slavery? In essence, Lincoln was asking Douglas to reconcile popular sovereignty with the *Dred Scott* decision. Lincoln had long contended that the Court's decision rendered popular sovereignty as thin as soup boiled from the shadow of a pigeon that had starved to death. If, as the Supreme Court's ruling affirmed, Congress had no authority to exclude slavery from

Abraham Lincoln

Clean-shaven at the time of his famous debates with Douglas, Lincoln would soon grow a beard to give himself a more distinguished appearance.

Stephen A. Douglas

Douglas's politics were founded on his unflinching conviction that most Americans favored national expansion and would support popular sovereignty as the fastest and least controversial way to achieve it. Douglas's self-assurance blinded him to rising northern sentiment for free soil.

a territory, it seemingly followed that a territorial legislature created by Congress also lacked power to do so. To no one's surprise, Douglas replied that notwithstanding the *Dred Scott* decision, the voters of a territory *could* effectively exclude slavery simply by refusing to enact laws that gave legal protection to slave property.

Douglas's "Freeport doctrine" salvaged popular sovereignty but did nothing for his reputation among southerners, who preferred the guarantees of the *Dred Scott* decision to the uncertainties of popular sovereignty. While Douglas's stand against the Lecompton constitution had already tattered his reputation in the South ("he is already dead there," Lincoln affirmed), his Freeport doctrine stiffened southern opposition to his presidential ambitions.

Lincoln faced the problem throughout the debates that free soil and popular sovereignty, although distinguishable in theory, had much the same practical impact. Neither Lincoln nor Douglas doubted that popular sovereignty, if fairly applied, would keep slavery out of the territories. In order to keep the initiative and sharpen their differences, Lincoln shifted in the closing debates toward attacks on slavery as "a moral, social, and political evil." He argued that Douglas's view of slavery as merely an eccentric and rather unsavory southern custom would dull the nation's conscience and facilitate the legalization of slavery everywhere. But Lincoln compromised his own position by rejecting both abolition and equality for blacks.

Neither man scored a clear victory in argument, and the senatorial election itself settled no major issues. Douglas's supporters captured a majority of the seats in the state legislature, which at the time was responsible for electing United States senators. But despite the racist leanings of most Illinois voters, Republican candidates for the state legislature won a slightly larger share of the popular vote than did their Democratic rivals. Moreover, in its larger significance, the contest solidified the sectional split in the national Democratic party and made Lincoln famous in the North and infamous in the South.

John Brown's Raid

Although Lincoln explicitly rejected abolitionism, he often spoke of free soil as a step toward the "ultimate extinction" of slavery in the South. Predictably, many southerners ignored the distinction between free soil and abolition and concluded that Republicans and abolitionists were inseparable components of an unholy alliance against slavery. Indeed, to many southerners, the entire North seemed locked in the grip of demented leaders bent on civil war. One of the South's more articulate defenders of slavery, for example, equated the doctrine of the abolitionists with those of "Socialists, of Free Love and Free Lands, Free Churches, Free Women and Free Negroes—of No-Marriage, No-Religion, No-Private Property, No-Law and No-Government."

No single event did more to rivet this image of the North in southerners' minds than the raid in 1859 on the federal arsenal at Harpers Ferry, Virginia, by John Brown, the brooding religious zealot responsible for the Pottawatomie massacre in Kansas three years earlier. At the head of twenty-one

men, Brown seized the arsenal on October 16, 1859, in the hope of igniting a massive slave uprising, first in Virginia and then throughout the South. But Brown neglected to inform the slaves of his plans and even failed to provision his men with enough food to last a day. A detachment of federal troops, commanded by Lieutenant Colonel Robert E. Lee, quickly overpowered the raiders. Convicted of treason, Brown was hanged on December 2, 1859.

If this had been the whole story, southerners might have dismissed the raid as the act of an isolated lunatic. Captured correspondence, however, revealed that Brown, far from acting alone, had extensive ties to prominent northern abolitionists. These northerners had provided both moral and financial support for Brown's plan to invade Virginia, free the slaves, and "purge this land with blood." Any lingering southern doubts about the scope of the conspiracy vanished when parts of the North responded to Brown's execution with memorial services and tolling bells. Ralph Waldo Emerson exulted that Brown would "make the gallows as glorious as the cross," and William Lloyd Garrison proclaimed his support for "every slave insurrection at the South and in any slave country." Republicans, including Lincoln and Senator William Seward of New York, denounced Brown's raid, but southerners suspected that Brown's failure, rather than the deed itself, provoked the repudiation.

Although Brown had failed to start a slave insurrection, his abortive raid rekindled southern fears of slave uprisings. Every village church bell in the North that tolled in honor of Brown, a South Carolinian declared, "proclaims to the South the approbation of that village of insurrection and servile war." In the wake of Brown's raid and throughout 1860, rumors flew around the South of assorted slave plots to devastate the region. Vigilantes turned out to battle conspiracies that existed only in their own minds. For example, a horde of southern defenders mobilized to rout the thousands of abolitionists who were rumored to be conspiring to pillage northeastern Texas. In North Carolina white mobs raided an encampment of Irish canal workers said to be in league with the slaves. In various other incidents, vigilantes rounded up thousands of slaves, whipped some into confessing to nonexistent plots, and then lynched them. The hysteria played into the hands of the southern-rights extremists known as the fire-eaters. Indeed, this faction actively encouraged the witch hunt by

The Last Moments of John Brown
by Thomas Hovenden

By the day of his hanging, Brown had become a martyr in northern eyes. Although the artist showed Brown kissing a black child, in fact no blacks were present. On his way to the gallows, Brown handed a note to a guard predicting that "the crimes of this guilty land will never be purged away but with Blood."

spreading tales of slave conspiracies in the press so that southern voters would turn to them as alone able to "stem the current of Abolition."

Although southern fears of slave insurrections proved unfounded, nothing calmed those apprehensions. Nor did it make any difference to southerners that Seward and Lincoln denounced Brown's raid. Most southerners interpreted the evidence linking Brown to abolitionists as just the tip of an iceberg and concluded that the abolitionists themselves were mere agents of the Republican party. Had not the Republicans repeatedly assailed slavery and sought unconstitutionally to bar its expansion? Had not Seward spoken of an "irrepressible conflict" between freedom and slavery? The incident at Harpers Ferry, declared resolutions passed by the Tennessee legislature, was "the natural fruit of this treasonable 'irrepressible conflict' doctrine put forth by the great head of the Black Republi-

can party and echoed by his subordinates." In the final analysis, southerners contended, John Brown, abolitionists, and Republicans all rested their case on the same premise: that slaves were somehow an illegitimate form of property and that the South deserved only scorn for its "peculiar institution."

The South Contemplates Secession

Convinced that they were menaced not only by the eccentric William Lloyd Garrisons of the North but also by the Republican party that had swept two-thirds of the northern states in the election of 1856, southerners increasingly spoke of secession from the United States as their only recourse. "The South must dissever itself," a South Carolinian insisted, "from the rotten Northern element."

Southerners reached this conclusion gradually,

and often reluctantly. In 1850 few southerners could have conceived of transferring their political and emotional allegiances from the United States to some new nation. Relatively insulated from the main tide of immigration, southerners thought of themselves as the most American of Americans. The fire-eaters, many of whom ardently desired secession, by no means represented southern thought. But the events of the 1850s brought a growing number of southerners to the conclusion that the North had deserted the true principles of the Union. Southerners interpreted northern resistance to the Fugitive Slave Act and to slavery in Kansas as either illegal or unconstitutional, and they viewed headline-grabbing phrases like "irrepressible conflict" and "a higher law" as virtual declarations of war on the South. In southerners' eyes, it was the North, not the South, that had grown peculiar.

This sense of the North's deviance tinged reports sent home by southern visitors to the North during the 1850s. Southerners complained bitterly of the "impudence and want of politeness" of northern free blacks. A Mississippi planter could scarcely believe his eyes, for example, when he witnessed a group of northern free blacks refusing to surrender their seats to a party of white women. Abolitionist hecklers rankled southern lecturers in the North. When assured by their northern friends that such hostility to the South's institutions did not reflect the whole of northern opinion, southerners could only wonder why northerners kept electing Republicans to office. Southerners even began to question whether it was wise to allow southern youth to attend northern colleges, where their minds might be poisoned by descriptions of their slaveholding parents as "graceless barbarians." Southern visitors increasingly described their northern trips as ventures into "enemy territory" and "a totally different country."

In this context of fraying sectional ties, John Brown's raid had an electrifying effect on southern opinion. Thousands of southerners, a Richmond newspaper editor observed after the raid, "who, a month ago, scoffed at the idea of a dissolution of the Union as a madman's dream . . . now hold the opinion that its days are numbered, its glory perished." Another southerner proclaimed that the Brown incident had revealed "the width and depth of the abyss which renders asunder two nations, apparently one." A pamphlet published in 1860

embodied in its title the growing conviction of southerners that *The South Alone Should Govern the South*.

Viewed as a practical tactic to secure concrete goals, secession did not make a great deal of sense. Some southerners contended that secession would make it easier for the South to acquire more territory for slavery in the Caribbean; yet the South was scarcely united in desiring additional slave territory in Mexico, Cuba, or Central America. States like Alabama, Mississippi, and Texas contained vast tracts of unsettled land that could be converted to cotton cultivation far more easily than the Caribbean. Other southerners continued to complain that the North blocked the access of slaveholders to territories in the continental United States. But it is unclear how secession would solve this problem. If the South were to secede, the remaining continental territories would belong exclusively to the North, which could then legislate for them as it chose. Nor would secession stop future John Browns from infiltrating the South to provoke slave insurrections.

Yet to dwell on the impracticality of secession as a choice for the South is to miss the point. Talk of secession was less a tactic with clear goals than an expression of the South's outrage at the irresponsible and unconstitutional course that southerners viewed the Republicans as taking in the North. It was not merely that Republican attacks on slavery sowed the seeds of slave uprisings. More fundamentally, southerners believed that the North was treating the South as its inferior—indeed, as no more than a slave. "Talk of Negro slavery," exclaimed southern proslavery philosopher George Fitzhugh, "is not half so humiliating and disgraceful as the slavery of the South to the North." Having persuaded themselves that slavery made it possible for them to enjoy unprecedented freedom and equality, white southerners took great pride in their homeland. They bitterly dismissed Republican portrayals of the South as a region of arrogant planters and degraded white common folk. Submission to the Republicans, declared the Democratic senator Jefferson Davis of Mississippi, "would be intolerable to a proud people."

Nevertheless, as long as the pliant James Buchanan occupied the White House, southerners did no more than *talk* about secession. Once aware that Buchanan had declined to seek reelection, however, they anxiously awaited the election of 1860.

The Election of 1860

As a single-issue, free-soil party, the Republicans had done well in the election of 1856. To win in 1860, however, they would have to broaden their appeal in the North, particularly in states like Pennsylvania and Illinois that they had lost in 1856. To do so, Republican leaders had concluded, they needed to forge an economic program to complement their advocacy of free soil.

A severe economic slump following the so-called Panic of 1857 furnished the Republicans a fitting opening. The depression shattered more than a decade of American prosperity and thrust economic concerns to the fore. In response, in the late 1850s, the Republicans developed an economic program based on support for a protective tariff (popular in Pennsylvania) and on two issues favored in the Midwest, federal aid for internal improvements and the granting of free 160-acre homesteads to settlers out of publicly owned land. By proposing to make these homesteads available to immigrants who were not yet citizens, the Republicans went far to shed their nativist image that lingered from their early association with the Know-Nothings. Carl Schurz, an 1848 German political refugee who had campaigned for Lincoln against Douglas in 1858, now labored mightily to bring his antislavery countrymen over to the Republican party.

The Republicans' desire to broaden their appeal also influenced their choice of a candidate. At their convention in Chicago, they nominated Abraham Lincoln over the early front-runner, William H. Seward of New York. Although better known than Lincoln, Seward failed to convince his party that he could carry the key states of Pennsylvania, Illinois, Indiana, and New Jersey. (Rueful Republicans remembered that their presidential candidate John C. Frémont would have won in 1856 if he had carried Pennsylvania and one of the remaining three states.) Lincoln held the advantage not only of hailing from Illinois but also of projecting a more moderate image than Seward on the slavery issue. Seward's penchant for controversial phrases like "irrepressible conflict" and "higher law" had given him a radical image. Lincoln, in contrast, had repeatedly affirmed that Congress had no constitutional right to interfere with slavery in the South and had explicitly rejected the "higher law" doctrine. The Republicans now needed only to widen their northern appeal.

The Democrats, however, who still claimed to be a national party, had to bridge their sectional divisions. The *Dred Scott* decision and the conflict over the Lecompton constitution had weakened the northern Democrats and emboldened the southern Democrats. While Douglas desperately defended popular sovereignty against the free-soil doctrine, southern Democrats increasingly abandoned popular sovereignty for the crisp assurances of the *Dred Scott* decision. Heartened by Chief Justice Taney's ruling that Congress lacked the power to exclude slavery from the territories, many southerners now concluded that Congress had an obligation to safeguard slavery in any territory. In February 1860 Senator Jefferson Davis of Mississippi introduced a set of resolutions calling for the federal government to enforce the *Dred Scott* decision by actively protecting territorial slavery.

The Davis resolutions never stood a chance of adoption by Congress. Nevertheless, they embarrassed the Douglas Democrats. No northern Democrat could win an election on a platform calling for the congressional protection of slavery in the territories. As a Georgia Democrat opposed to the Davis resolutions commented: "Hostility to Douglas is the sole motive of the movers of this mischief. I wish Douglas defeated . . . , but I do not want him and his friends crippled or driven off. Where are we to get as many or as good men in the North to supply their places?"

The Democratic party's internal turmoil boiled over at its Charleston convention in the spring of 1860. Failing to force acceptance of a platform guaranteeing federal protection of slavery in the territories, the delegates from the Lower South stalked out. The convention adjourned to Baltimore, where a new fight broke out over the question of seating hastily elected, pro-Douglas slates of delegates from the Lower South states that had seceded from the Charleston convention. The decision to seat these pro-Douglas slates led to another walkout, this time by delegates from Virginia and other states in the Upper South. The remaining delegates nominated Douglas, while the seceders marched off to another hall in Baltimore and nominated Buchanan's vice president, John C. Breckenridge of Kentucky, on a platform calling for the

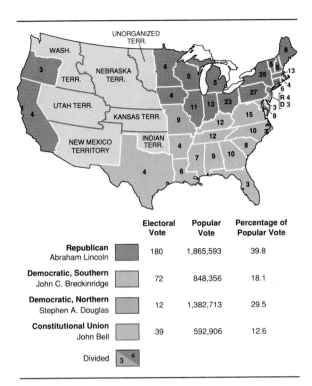

	Electoral Vote	Popular Vote	Percentage of Popular Vote
Republican Abraham Lincoln	180	1,865,593	39.8
Democratic, Southern John C. Breckinridge	72	848,356	18.1
Democratic, Northern Stephen A. Douglas	12	1,382,713	29.5
Constitutional Union John Bell	39	592,906	12.6
Divided	3 4		

The Election of 1860

congressional protection of slavery in the territories. Unable to rally behind a single nominee, the divided Democrats thus ran two candidates, Douglas and Breckenridge. The disruption of the Democratic party was now complete.

The South still contained an appreciable number of moderates, often former Whigs who had joined with the Know-Nothings behind Fillmore in 1856. In 1860 these moderates, aided by former northern Whigs who opposed both Lincoln and Douglas, forged the new Constitutional Union party and nominated John Bell, a Kentucky slaveholder who had opposed both the Kansas-Nebraska Act and the Lecompton constitution. Calling for the preservation of the Union, the new party took no stand on the divisive issue of slavery extension.

With four candidates in the field, voters faced a relatively clear choice. Lincoln conceded that the South had a constitutional right to preserve slavery but demanded that Congress prohibit its extension. At the other extreme, Breckenridge insisted that Congress had to protect slavery in any territory that contained slaves. This left the middle ground to Bell and Douglas, the latter still committed to popular sovereignty but in search of a verbal for-

mula that might reconcile it with the *Dred Scott* decision. Despite this four-way race, Lincoln won a clear majority of the electoral vote, 180 to 123 for his three opponents combined. Although Lincoln gained only 39 percent of the popular vote, his popular votes were concentrated in the North, the majority section, and were sufficient to carry every free state. Douglas ran a respectable second to Lincoln in the popular vote but a dismal last in the electoral vote. As the only candidate to campaign in both sections, Douglas suffered from the scattered quality of his votes and carried only Missouri. Bell won Virginia, Kentucky, and Tennessee, while Breckenridge captured Maryland and the Lower South.

The Movement for Secession

As the dust from the election settled, southerners faced a disconcerting fact: a man so unpopular among southerners that his name had not even appeared on the ballot in much of their section was now president. Lincoln's election struck most of the white South as a calculated northern insult. The North, a South Carolina planter told a visitor from England, "has got so far toward being abolitionized as to elect a man avowedly hostile to our institutions." Few southerners believed that Lincoln would fulfill his promise to protect slavery in the South, and most feared that he would act as a mere front man for more John Browns. "Now that the black radical Republicans have the power I suppose they will Brown us all," a South Carolinian lamented. An uneducated Mississippian residing in Illinois expressed his reaction to the election more bluntly:

> It seems the north wants the south to raise cotton and sugar rice tobacco for the northern states, also to pay taxes and fight her battles and get territory for the purpose of the north to send her greasy Dutch and free niggers into the territory to get rid of them. At any rate that was what elected old Abe President. Some professed conservative Republicans Think and say that Lincoln will be conservative also but sir my opinion is that Lincoln will deceive them. [He] will undoubtedly please the abolitionists for at his election they nearly all went into fits with Joy.

Some southerners had threatened secession at the prospect of Lincoln's election; now the moment

Charleston in the Secession Crisis, 1860–1861

After securing the nomination of Pennsylvania's James Buchanan for the presidency in 1856, northern Democrats made a conciliatory gesture to the South. They agreed to hold their party's 1860 convention in Charleston, South Carolina. Time would give northerners many opportunities to regret that gesture. Long in decline, with only a few overpriced hotels, Charleston offered little as a convention city. The supporters of Stephen A. Douglas had to convert the second floor of a meeting hall into a giant dormitory, where they slept in rows of beds and baked in one-hundred-degree heat. Far more troubling to the delegates who descended on the city in April 1860 was the hysteria that consumed Charleston in reaction to John Brown's raid on Harpers Ferry six months earlier. Mounted police, armed with swords and muskets, patrolled the streets, and vigilantes combed the byways in search of abolitionists. Panicked Charlestonians viewed every northerner in the city—whether a politician, a traveling salesman, or a schoolteacher—as "necessarily imbued with doctrines hostile to our institutions."

Suspicion and harassment greeted northern sojourners, but Charleston's blacks endured a virtual reign of terror after "the late outrage at Harpers Ferry." A little under half the city's population in 1860 was black, and 81 percent of the blacks were slaves. White southerners distrusted urban slaves, most of whom lived apart from their rural

Slave Badges

The badges that they were forced to wear constantly reminded Charleston's slaves of their bondage.

masters and were hired out to city employers. Indeed, some slaves took advantage of their distance from their masters to hire themselves out for wages, a practice that whites feared would infect slaves with the notion that they were free. In addition, white workingmen resented competition from urban slaves in the skilled trades, and they used the furor over John Brown's raid to pressure the city's mayor into enforcing an old and long-neglected ordinance that slaves working away from their masters wear badges. Those without badges were rounded up and jailed, and their masters fined.

Charleston's enslaved blacks were not the sole targets of the city's increasingly repressive mood. Few southern cities had more visible or well-organized communities of free blacks than Charleston. Composed mainly of mulattos who

took pride in their light skin and assembled in the Brown Fellowship Society, Charleston's free people of color formed a brown aristocracy of skilled tailors, carpenters, and small tradesmen. Free blacks like John Marsh Johnson worshiped in the same Episcopal church as such elite whites as Christopher G. Memminger, a prominent lawyer and politician who would soon become the Confederacy's secretary of the treasury. The financial prosperity of these free blacks depended on the white aristocrats who frequented their stores, admired their thrift and sobriety, and took comfort in their apparent loyalty. When a bill calling for the enslavement or expulsion of South Carolina's free blacks came before the state legislature in 1859, Memminger reminded the legislators that a free black had helped to expose Denmark Vesey's planned uprising of slaves back in 1822. Heartened by the support of Memminger and others, John Marsh Johnson congratulated himself for predicting "from the onset that nothing would be done affecting our position."

Johnson little realized the extent to which the world of Charleston's free blacks was in danger of falling apart. The city had been a center of southern-rights radicalism since the days of the nullification crisis. Charleston was the home of the fire-eater, Robert Barnwell Rhett; and it always rolled out the welcome carpet for Edmund Ruffin, a Virginia drumbeater for slavery. Further, after John Brown's raid, even moderate citizens, including former

Unionists, were embracing secession. The cause of secession demanded, in turn, that elite whites unite with working-class whites in a common front against the North. During the 1850s Charleston's working-class whites had grown increasingly powerful and aggressive; the increase in their numbers gave the city a white majority in 1860, for the first time in its history. Working-class whites feared competition from any blacks but had a special loathing for free blacks, who on Sundays dared "to draw up in fine clothes" and "wear a silk hat and gloves" and who celebrated weddings by drinking champagne and riding to the church in elegant carriages.

Soon free blacks became the victims of the growing cooperation between elite and working-class whites. Indeed, by August 1860 Charleston was in the grip of an "enslavement crisis." The same police dragnets that had snared urban slaves without badges now trapped innumerable free blacks as well. Unenslaved blacks suddenly had to prove that they were free, a tall order inasmuch as South Carolina had long prohibited the freeing of slaves. For decades white masters who wanted to free favored slaves had resorted to complicated legal ruses, with the result that many blacks who had lived for years as free people could not prove that they were free and were forced back into slavery. Abandoning his initial optimism, John Marsh Johnson wrote nervously to his brother-in-law to report "cases of persons who for 30 yrs. have been paying capitation Tax [as free persons of color] & one of 35 yrs. that have to go back to bondage & take out their Badges." Many other free African-Americans fled to the North.

A religious man, Johnson believed that God helped those who

First Shots of the Civil War

Stunned Charleston residents crowded the city's rooftops to view the firing on Fort Sumter—a siege that lasted thirty-four hours.

helped themselves. Rather than "supinely wait for the working of a miracle by having a Chariot let down to convey us away," he resolved in late August 1860 to stay and endure the "present calamity." By then, however, the Democratic party had snapped apart under the pressure of southern demands for the congressional recognition of slavery in all the territories. "The last party pretending to be a national party, is broken up," the secessionist Charleston *Mercury* exulted, "and the antagonism of the sections of the Union has nothing to arrest its fierce collision." In December 1860 another convention meeting in Charleston would proclaim South Carolina's secession from the United States. In April 1861, only a year after the Democratic delegates had assembled in Charleston for their party's convention, shore batteries along Charleston's harbor would open fire on Fort Sumter. This action set in motion a train of events leading to the extinction of slavery itself. Ironically, after the Civil War, the free blacks who had weathered the enslavement crisis of 1860 would emerge as the leaders of the city's black people, all of them now free.

View of Charleston, 1846, *by Henry Jackson*

Picturesque Charleston was home to many of South Carolina's most rabid secessionists.

of choice had arrived. On December 20, 1860, a South Carolina convention voted unanimously for secession; and by February 1, 1861, Alabama, Mississippi, Florida, Georgia, Louisiana, and Texas had followed South Carolina's lead (see "A Place in Time"). On February 4 delegates from these seven states met in Montgomery, Alabama, and established the Confederate States of America.

Despite the abruptness of southern withdrawal from the Union, the movement for secession had been, and continued to be, laced with uncertainty. Many southerners had resisted calls for immediate secession. Even after Lincoln's election, fire-eating secessionists had met fierce opposition in the Lower South from so-called cooperationists, who called upon the South to act in unison or not at all. Many cooperationists had hoped to delay secession in order to wring concessions from the North that might remove the need for secession. Jefferson Davis, who was inaugurated in February 1861 as the first president of the Confederacy, was a most reluctant secessionist, and he remained in the United States Senate for two weeks after his own state of Mississippi had seceded. Even zealous advocates of secession had a hard time reconciling themselves to secession and believing that they were no longer citizens of the United States. "How do you feel now, dear Mother," a Georgian wrote, "that *we* are in a foreign land?"

In the month after the establishment of the Confederate States of America, moreover, secessionists suffered stinging disappointments in the Upper South. Virginia, North Carolina, Tennessee, Arkansas, and the border slave states of Maryland, Kentucky, Delaware, and Missouri all rejected calls for secession. Various factors account for the Upper South's reluctance to embrace the movement. In contrast to the Lower South, which had a guaranteed export market for its cotton, the Upper South depended heavily on economic ties to the North, bonds that would be severed by secession. Further, with proportionately far fewer slaves than the Lower South, the states of the Upper South and the border states doubted the loyalty of their sizable nonslaveholding populations to the idea of secession. Virginia, for example, had every reason to question the allegiance to secession of its nonslaveholding western counties, which would soon break away to form Unionist West Virginia. Few in the Upper South could forget the raw nerve touched by the

Jefferson Davis

Davis brought an abundance of public experience to the Confederate presidency. Wounded in the Mexican War, he had served in the U.S. Senate, became secretary of war under President Franklin Pierce, and negotiated the Gadsden Purchase.

publication in 1857 of Hinton R. Helper's *The Impending Crisis of the South*. A nonslaveholding North Carolinian, Helper had described slavery as a curse upon poor white southerners and thereby questioned one of the most sacred southern doctrines, the idea that slavery rendered all whites equal. If secession were to spark a war between the states, moreover, the Upper South appeared to be the likeliest battleground. Whatever the exact weight assignable to each of these factors, one point is clear: the secession movement that South Carolina so boldly started in December 1860 seemed to be falling apart by March 1861.

The Search for Compromise

The lack of southern unity confirmed the long-standing belief of Lincoln and most Republicans that the secessionists' talk, and even their actions, contained more bluster than substance. Seward

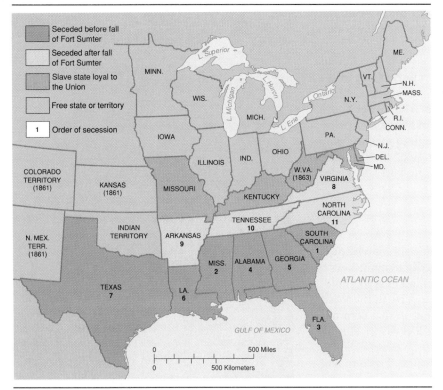

Secession

Four key states—Virginia, Arkansas, Tennessee, and North Carolina—did not secede until after the fall of Fort Sumter. The border slave states of Maryland, Delaware, Kentucky, and Missouri stayed in the Union.

described secession as the work of "a relatively few hotheads," and Lincoln expected that the loyal majority of southerners would soon wrest the initiative from the fire-eating minority.

This perception among the Republicans stiffened their resolve to resist the compromises that some moderates were trying to forge. In the immediate wake of South Carolina's secession, Senator John J. Crittenden of Kentucky brought forth the most important of the compromises. Crittenden's plan included calls for the compensation of owners of runaway slaves, the repeal of the North's personal-liberty laws, a constitutional amendment to prohibit the federal government from ever interfering with slavery in the southern states, and another constitutional amendment that would restore the Missouri Compromise line for the remaining territories and guarantee federal protection of slavery below the line. This last amendment proved to be the sticking point. Lincoln stood firm against any abandonment of free soil. "On the territorial issue," he wrote to a southerner, "I am inflexible." In the face of steadfast Republican opposition, the Crittenden plan collapsed.

Lincoln's opposition to compromise rested partly on his belief that a loyal majority of southerners would soon overturn secession. The president-elect, however, almost certainly exaggerated the strength and dedication of southern Unionists. In reality, many of the southern opponents of the fire-eating secessionists were sitting on the fence and hoping for major concessions from the North; their allegiance to the Union was conditional, not unconditional. Lincoln can be faulted for his misreading of southern opinion. But even if his assessment had been accurate, it is unlikely that he would have accepted the Crittenden plan. Republicans viewed the plan as a surrender rather than a compromise, because it hinged on the abandonment of free soil, the principle on which the Republican party had been founded. In addition, as Lincoln well knew, some southerners still talked of seizing more territory for slavery in the Caribbean. In proposing to extend the 36°30′ line, the Crittenden plan specifically referred to territories "hereafter acquired," a veiled reference to future Caribbean expansion. If he were to accept the Crittenden compromise, Lincoln feared that it would be only a matter of time "till we shall have to take Cuba as a condition upon which they [the seceding states] will stay in the Union."

Beyond these considerations, the precipitous secession of the Lower South subtly changed the question that Lincoln faced. The issue was no longer slavery extension but secession. The Lower South had left the Union in the face of losing a fair election. For Lincoln to have caved in to such pressure would have violated majority rule, the principle upon which the nation, not just his party, had been founded.

The Coming of War

By the time that Lincoln took office in March 1861, little more than a spark was needed to ignite a war. Lincoln pledged in his inaugural address to "hold, occupy, and possess" federal property in the seven states that had seceded, an assertion that committed him to the defense of Fort Pickens in Florida and Fort Sumter in the harbor of Charleston, South Carolina. William Seward, whom Lincoln had appointed secretary of state, now became obsessed with the idea of conciliating the Lower South in order to hold the Upper South in the Union. In addition to advising the evacuation of federal forces from Fort Sumter, Seward hatched a bizarre scheme to reunify the nation by provoking a war with France and Spain. But Lincoln brushed aside Seward's advice. Instead, the president informed the governor of South Carolina of his intention to supply Fort Sumter with much-needed provisions, but not with men and ammunition. To gain the dubious military advantage of attacking Fort Sumter before the arrival of relief ships, Confederate batteries began to bombard the fort shortly before dawn on April 12. The next day, the fort's garrison surrendered.

Proclaiming an insurrection in the Lower South, Lincoln now appealed for seventy-five thousand militiamen from the loyal states to suppress the rebellion. His proclamation pushed citizens of the Upper South off the fence upon which they had perched for three months. "I am a Union man," one southerner wrote, "but when they [the Lincoln administration] send men south it will change my notions. I can do nothing against my own people." In quick succession, Virginia, North Carolina, Arkansas, and Tennessee leagued with the Confed-

Lincoln's First Inauguration

In his inaugural, Lincoln, in the shadow of the still unfinished Capitol dome, assured the South that he would not interfere with slavery in states where it existed, but he warned that "the central idea of secession is the essence of anarchy."

eracy. After acknowledging that "I am one of those dull creatures that cannot see the good of secession," Robert E. Lee resigned from the United States Army rather than lead federal troops against his native Virginia.

The North, too, was ready for a fight, less to abolish slavery than to punish secession. Worn out from his efforts to find a peaceable solution to the issue of slavery extension, and with only a short time to live, Stephen Douglas assaulted "the new system of resistance by the sword and bayonet to the results of the ballot-box" and affirmed: "I deprecate war, but if it must come I am with my country, under all circumstances, and in every contingency."

Conclusion

Thus during the 1850s the gap widened between northerners and southerners on the vexing issue of slavery extension. Popular sovereignty, which in 1850 struck many Americans as a practical solution to slavery in the territories, foundered in Kansas amid civil strife and turmoil over the Lecompton constitution. As support for popular sovereignty withered, sentiment for free soil gained ground in the North. In the South the *Dred Scott* decision provided judicial support for the position that Congress had to protect slavery in whatever territories it appeared.

Although the differences between northern and southern opinion on the slavery-extension issue sharpened and widened during the tempestuous decade, the two sections stood far apart by 1850. The Compromise of 1850 merely papered over an already considerable gulf. Decades of industrial expansion had convinced northerners of the value of free labor, a view that excluded competition with slaves. Yet decades of agricultural prosperity had persuaded southerners of the economic and moral value of slavery. The success of their system made southerners antagonistic to any suggestion that slave property was inferior to other property.

Despite this clear division by 1850, secession germinated for ten years before flowering. More than a broad disagreement over slavery in the territories was needed to push the South into secession. Before the South took that drastic step, it had to convince itself that the North aimed not merely to bar the spread of slavery but also to corrode the moral and political foundations of southern society. Several events persuaded the South that such was indeed the North's intention: northern fury over the Kansas-Nebraska bill, the emergence of the purely sectional Republican party, northern opposition to the *Dred Scott* decision, and John Brown's raid on Harpers Ferry. Once southerners came to believe that northern attacks on slavery's expansion were tactics in a wider campaign to reduce the South to subjection and "slavery," secession became a natural recourse.

As an expression of principled outrage, secession fittingly capped a decade in which each side had clothed itself in principles. The conflicts over principle that marked the 1850s were deeply embedded in the nation's political heritage. Both sides, North and South, laid claim to the ideals of the Constitution, but each understood those ideals differently. For northerners wedded to free soil, liberty meant an individual's freedom to pursue self-interest without competition from slaves. For white southerners, liberty meant their freedom to dispose of their legally acquired property as they saw fit. Similarly, both sides subscribed to the rule of law, which each accused the other of deserting. Northerners found evidence of southern treachery in the voting fraud that culminated in the Lecompton constitution. Southerners pointed to northern defiance of the Fugitive Slave Act and, later, of the *Dred Scott* decision, and to northern complicity in John Brown's raid. In the end, war broke out between siblings who, although they claimed the same inheritance, had become virtual strangers to each other.

CHRONOLOGY

1846 Wilmot Proviso.

1848 Treaty of Guadalupe Hidalgo ends Mexican War.
Free-Soil party formed.
Zachary Taylor elected president.

1849 California seeks admission to the Union as a free state.

1850 Nashville convention assembles to discuss the South's grievances.
Compromise of 1850.

1852   Harriet Beecher Stowe, *Uncle Tom's Cabin.*
Franklin Pierce elected president.

1853   Gadsden Purchase.

1854   Ostend Manifesto.
Kansas-Nebraska Act.
William Walker leads a filibustering expedition into Nicaragua.

1854–   Know-Nothing and Republican parties
1855   emerge.

1855   Proslavery forces steal the election for a territorial legislature in Kansas.
Proslavery Kansans establish a government in Lecompton.
Free-soil government established in Topeka, Kansas.

1856   The "Sack of Lawrence."
John Brown's Pottawatomie massacre.
James Buchanan elected president.

1857   *Dred Scott* decision.
President Buchanan endorses the Lecompton constitution in Kansas.
Panic of 1857.

1858   Congress refuses to admit Kansas to the Union under the Lecompton constitution.
Lincoln-Douglas debates.

1859   John Brown's raid on Harpers Ferry.

1860   Abraham Lincoln elected president.
South Carolina secedes from the Union.

1861   The remaining Lower South states secede.
Confederate States of America established.
Crittenden compromise plan collapses.
Lincoln takes office.
Firing on Fort Sumter; Civil War begins.
Upper South secedes.

For Further Reading

Eric Foner, *Free Soil, Free Labor, Free Men: The Ideology of the Republican Party Before the Civil War* (1970). An outstanding analysis of the thought, values, and components of the Republican party.

Michael F. Holt, *The Political Crisis of the 1850s* (1978). A lively reinterpretation of the politics of the 1850s.

Allan Nevins, *The Ordeal of the Union* (vols. 1–2, 1947). A very detailed, highly regarded account of the coming of the Civil War.

David Potter, *The Impending Crisis, 1848–1861* (1976). The best one-volume overview of the events leading to the Civil War.

Additional Bibliography

The Compromise of 1850 and Its Aftermath

Stephen W. Campbell, *The Slave Catchers* (1968); Thomas F. Gossett, *Uncle Tom's Cabin and American Culture* (1985); Holman Hamilton, *Prologue to Conflict: The Crisis and Compromise of 1850* (1964); Thelma Jennings, *The Nashville Convention* (1980); Thomas D. Morris, *Free Men All: The Personal Liberty Laws of the North, 1780–1861* (1974); Chaplain W. Morrison, *Democratic Politics and Sectionalism: The Wilmot Proviso Controversy* (1967).

Political Realignment, 1852–1856

Carleton Beales, *Brass Knuckles Crusade: The Great Know-Nothing Conspiracy* (1961); Eugene Berwanger, *The Frontier Against Slavery: Western Anti-Negro Prejudice in the Slavery Extension Controversy* (1967); Ronald P. Formisano, *The Birth of Mass Political Parties: Michigan, 1827–1861* (1971); Michael F. Holt, *Forging a Majority: The Formation of the Republican Party in Pittsburgh* (1969); James A. Rawley, *Race and Politics: "Bleeding Kansas" and the Coming of the Civil War*

(1969); Geoffrey W. Wolff, *The Kansas-Nebraska Bill* (1977).

The South and the Sectional Crisis

Charles H. Brown, *Agents of Manifest Destiny: The Lives and Times of the Filibusterers* (1978); Avery Craven, *The Growth of Southern Nationalism, 1848–1861* (1953); Clement Eaton, *The Mind of the Old South* (1967); John Hope Franklin, *The Militant South, 1800–1861* (1970) and *A Southern Odyssey: Travelers in the Antebellum North* (1976); Michael P. Johnson and James L. Roark, eds., *No Chariot Let Down: Charleston's Free People of Color on the Eve of the Civil War* (1984); John McCardell, *The Idea of a Southern Nation: Southern Nationalists and Southern Nationalism, 1830–1861* (1979); Robert E. May, *The Southern Dream of a Caribbean Empire, 1854–1861* (1973); Rollin G. Osterweiss, *Romanticism and Nationalism in the Old South* (1949); Ronald L. Takaki, *A Proslavery Crusade: The Agitation to Reopen the African Slave Trade* (1971); J. Mills Thornton, *Politics and Power in a Slave Society* (1978).

The Disruption of the Union

William L. Barney, *The Road to Secession* (1972) and *The Secessionist Impulse* (1974); Steven A. Channing, *Crisis of Fear: Secession in South Carolina* (1970); Ollin-ger Crenshaw, *The Slave States in the Presidential Election of 1860* (1969); David Donald, *Charles Sumner and the Coming of the Civil War* (1960); Don E. Fehrenbacher, *The Dred Scott Case* (1978) and *Prelude to Greatness: Lincoln in the 1850s* (1962); George B. Forgie, *Patricide in the House Divided: A Psychological Interpretation of Lincoln and His Age* (1979); Henry V. Jaffa, *Crisis of the House Divided: An Interpretation of the Lincoln-Douglas Debates* (1959); Robert W. Johannsen, *Stephen A. Douglas* (1973); Michael Johnson, *Secession and Conservatism in the Lower South: The Social and Ideological Bases of Secession in Georgia, 1860–1861* (1983); Albert J. Kirwan, *John J. Crittenden: The Struggle for the Union* (1962); Milton Klein, *President James Buchanan: A Biography* (1962); Paul C. Nagel, *One Nation Indivisible: The Union in American Thought* (1964); Allan Nevins, *The Emergence of Lincoln* (2 vols., 1950); Roy F. Nichols, *The Disruption of American Democracy* (1948); Stephen B. Oates, *To Purge This Land with Blood: A Biography of John Brown* (1970); David Potter, *Lincoln and His Party in the Secession Crisis* (1942); Elbert B. Smith, *The Presidency of James Buchanan* (1975); Kenneth Stampp, *And the War Came: The North and the Secession Crisis, 1860–1861* (1970); R. A. Wooster, *The Secession Conventions of the South* (1962).

CHAPTER 14

Reforging the Union: Civil War, 1861–1865

With the fall of Fort Sumter in April 1861, northerners and southerners rushed to arms. "They sing and whoop, they laugh: they holler to de people on de ground and sing out 'Good-bye,'" remarked a slave watching rebel troops depart. "All going down to die." Longing for the excitement of battle, the first volunteers enlisted with hopes of adventure and glory. Garish uniforms reflected their expectation of martial romance. Gaudiest of all were the northern Zouave regiments, whose members patterned their dress on that of French troops in North Africa, who, in turn, modeled their uniforms on a notion of what the Turks wore into battle: baggy red pantaloons, spotless white gaiters, and fezzes. Marching to war in dashing attire provided more than an outlet for romantic yearnings: it also gave boys a chance to act like men. A contemplative New Yorker, who sent two teen-aged sons to enlist, marveled how the war provided "so much manhood suddenly achieved." In their early letters home, victorious soldiers exulted over their transformation in battle. "With your first shot you become a new man," an Alabama volunteer wrote to his father. Neither volunteers nor politicians expected a long or bloody war. Most northern estimates ranged from one month to a year. Southerners also looked forward to a speedy war. One rebel could lick ten Yankees, southerners liked to think, because "the Yankee army is filled with the scum of creation."

These expectations of military glory and quick fame proved the first of many miscalculations. Actual battlefield experiences scarcely conformed to the early volunteers' rosy visions. For most soldiers, achieving manhood meant surviving in fetid army camps and inuring themselves to the stench of death. "We don't mind the sight of dead men no more than if they were dead hogs," a Union soldier claimed after one engagement. Soldiers rapidly learned the value of caution in battle. When "solid shot is cracking skulls like eggshells," a northern volunteer wrote, "the consuming passion is to get out of the way." You learn, a southerner wrote, to become "cool and deliberate."

These were the reactions of the lucky ones. One out of every five soldiers who fought in the Civil War died in it. The 620,000 American soldiers who lost their lives between 1861 and 1865 nearly equaled the number of American soldiers killed in all the nation's earlier and later wars combined. The war's gruesome destructiveness shattered politicians' expectations as well as soldiers' romantic visions. Once it became clear that the war could not be ended by a few battles, leaders on both sides contemplated strategies once unpalatable and even unthinkable. The South, where the hand of government had always fallen lightly on the citizenry, found that it had to draft men into its army and virtually extort supplies from its civilian population. By the end of the war, the Confederacy was even prepared to arm its slaves in an ironically desperate effort to save a society founded on slavery. The North, which began the war with the restricted objective of overcoming secession, and which explicitly disclaimed any intention of interfering with slavery, found that in order to win, it had to shred the fabric of southern society by destroying slavery. For politicians as well as soldiers, the war turned into a series of surprises.

Mobilizing for War

North and South alike were unprepared for war. In April 1861 the Union had only a small army of sixteen thousand men, scattered all over the country, mostly in the West. One-third of the officers of the Union army had resigned to join the Confederacy. The Union seemed to hang by a thread politically. The nation had not had a strong president since James K. Polk in the 1840s. Its new president, Abraham Lincoln, struck many observers as a yokel. That such a government could marshal its people for war seemed at best a doubtful proposition. The federal government had levied no direct taxes on its citizens for decades, and it had never drafted anyone into its army. Fortunately for the Union, the Confederacy was even less prepared, for it had no tax structure, no navy, only two tiny gunpowder factories, and poorly equipped, unconnected railroad lines.

During the first two years of the war, both sides would have to overcome these deficiencies, raise and supply large armies, and finance the heavy costs of war. In each region mobilization for war expanded the powers of the central government to an extent that few had anticipated.

Recruitment and Conscription

The Civil War armies were the largest organizations ever created in America; by the end of the war, over 2 million men would have served in the Union army and 800,000 in the Confederate army. In the first flush of enthusiasm for war, volunteers rushed to the colors. "I go for wiping them out," a Virginian wrote to his governor. A similar zest for enlistment engulfed the North. "Without seriously repressing the ardor of the people, I can hardly stop short of twenty regiments," the governor of Ohio informed Lincoln. "War! and volunteers are the only topics of conversation or thought," an Oberlin College student wrote to his brother in April 1861. "I cannot study. I cannot sleep. I cannot work, and I don't know as I can write."

At first, the raising of armies depended on local efforts rather than on national or even state direction. Citizens opened recruiting offices in their hometowns, held rallies, and signed up volunteers. "The walls are covered with placards from military companies offering inducements to recruits," a war

"A Great Rush"

This recruiting poster lured volunteers by promises of bounties and threats of the draft.

correspondent wrote from New York, where shops were "devoted to . . . rifles, pistols, swords, plumes, long boots, saddles, bridles, camp beds, canteens." As a consequence of this recruitment system, regiments were usually composed of soldiers from the same locale. Localism and voluntarism did not stop with the recruitment of troops. In the South cavalrymen were expected to provide their own horses, and uniforms everywhere were left mainly to local option. In both armies officers up to the rank of colonel were elected by other officers and enlisted men.

This informal and democratic way of raising and organizing soldiers conformed to the nation's political traditions. Americans had argued for generations that the freely given consent of the people, not the dictates of the government, could alone create an army in a republic. Because of its length and gruesome destructiveness, the Civil War would place insupportable stress on this tradition, however. As early as July 1861, the Union instituted examinations for officers, and its practice of electing officers gradually died out. In addition, as casualties mounted, military demand soon exceeded the supply of volunteers. Because nearly half of its 1861 volunteers had enlisted for only a year, the Confederacy felt the pinch first and in April 1862 enacted the first conscription law in American history. All able-bodied white males aged eighteen to thirty-five would be required to serve in the military for three years. Subsequent amendments raised the age limit to forty-five and then to fifty, and lowered it to seventeen.

The Confederacy's Conscription Act aroused little enthusiasm among southerners. Opponents charged that the draft was an assault on state sovereignty by a despotic regime and that the law would "do away with all the patriotism we have." Exemptions applied to many occupations, from religious ministry to shoemaking, and these angered the nonexempt. So did a loophole, closed in 1863, that allowed the well-off to purchase substitutes. Hostility also mounted over an amendment, the so-called 20-Negro law, that exempted an owner or overseer of twenty or more slaves from service. Although southerners widely feared that the slave population could not be controlled if all able-bodied white males were away in the army, the 20-Negro law evoked complaints about "a rich man's war but a poor man's fight."

Despite opposition, the Confederate draft became increasingly hard to evade, and this fact stimulated volunteering. Only one soldier in five was a draftee, but four out of every five eligible white southerners served in the Confederate army. In addition, a new conscription law, passed in 1864, required all soldiers then in the army to stay in for the duration of the war. This requirement ensured that a high proportion of Confederate soldiers would be battle-hardened veterans.

Once the army was raised, the Confederacy faced the challenge of supplying it. At first, the South lacked facilities to produce arms and ammunition and relied on imports from Europe, weapons confiscated from federal arsenals situated in the South, and guns captured on the battlefield. These stopgap measures bought time until an

industrial base was established. By 1862 the Confederacy had a competent head of ordnance (weaponry), Josiah Gorgas. Working through Gorgas and other officials, the Confederacy assigned ordnance contracts to privately owned factories like the Tredegar Iron Works in Richmond, provided loans to establish new factories, and created government-owned industries like the giant Augusta Powder Works in Georgia, the largest in North America at the time. The South lost few, if any, battles for want of munitions.

The Confederacy was less successful in supplying its troops with clothing and food. Southern soldiers frequently went without shoes; during the South's invasion of Maryland in 1862, thousands of Confederate soldiers had to be left behind because they could not march barefoot on Maryland's macadamized roads. Late in the war, Robert E. Lee's Army of Northern Virginia ran out of food but never out of ammunition. The South's supply problems had several sources: railroads that fell into disrepair or were captured, an economy that relied more heavily on producing tobacco and cotton than growing food, and Union invasions early in the war that overran the livestock and grain-raising districts of central Tennessee and Virginia. Close to desperation, the Confederate Congress passed the Impressment Act in 1863, which authorized army officers to take food from reluctant farmers at prescribed rates. This law was even more unpopular than the Conscription Act, and farmers regarded impressment agents as legalized thieves. The same law empowered agents to impress slaves into labor for the army, a provision that provoked even more resentment. Slaveowners were willing to give up their relatives to military service, a Georgia congressman noted, "but let one of their negroes be taken and what a howl you will hear."

The industrial North could more easily supply its troops with arms, clothes, and food than could the South. However, keeping a full army was another matter. When the initial tide of enthusiasm for enlistment passed and the terms of the early recruits ended, Congress followed the Confederacy's example and turned to conscription. The Enrollment Act of March 1863 made every able-bodied white male citizen aged twenty to forty-five eligible for draft into the Union army.

Like the Confederate conscription law of 1862, the Enrollment Act granted exemptions, although only to high government officials, ministers, and

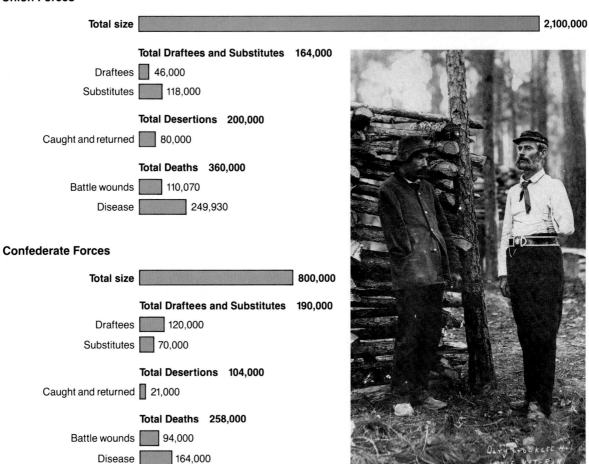

Union Forces

Total size — 2,100,000

Total Draftees and Substitutes 164,000
Draftees — 46,000
Substitutes — 118,000

Total Desertions 200,000
Caught and returned — 80,000

Total Deaths 360,000
Battle wounds — 110,070
Disease — 249,930

Confederate Forces

Total size — 800,000

Total Draftees and Substitutes 190,000
Draftees — 120,000
Substitutes — 70,000

Total Desertions 104,000
Caught and returned — 21,000

Total Deaths 258,000
Battle wounds — 94,000
Disease — 164,000

Total Civil War Deaths Compared to U.S. Deaths in Other Wars

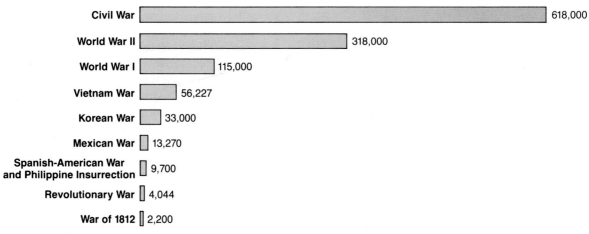

Civil War	618,000
World War II	318,000
World War I	115,000
Vietnam War	56,227
Korean War	33,000
Mexican War	13,270
Spanish-American War and Philippine Insurrection	9,700
Revolutionary War	4,044
War of 1812	2,200

The Civil War had profound human costs. North and South, there was hardly a family that did not grieve for a loved one or friend killed during the war. Armless or legless veterans were a common sight in American cities, towns, and rural districts well into our present century.

men who were the sole support of widows, orphans, or indigent parents. It also offered two means of escaping the draft: substitution, or paying another man who would serve instead; and commutation, paying a $300 fee to the government. To provide draft machinery, the law divided each state into enrollment districts and gave them quotas to meet, first through volunteers and then through the draft. The new system was difficult to administer and chaotic in practice. Enrollment districts often competed for volunteers by offering cash payments (bounties); dishonest "bounty jumpers" repeatedly registered and deserted after collecting their payment. And as in the South, conscription aroused opposition. Democrats denounced it as a violation of individual liberties and states' rights, while ordinary citizens of little means resented the commutation and substitution provision and leveled their own "poor man's fight" charges. Still, as the Confederates had learned, the law stimulated volunteering. Only 8 percent of Union soldiers were draftees or substitutes.

Financing the War

The recruitment and supply of huge armies lay far beyond the capacity of American public finance at the start of the war. During the 1840s and 1850s, annual federal spending had averaged only 2 percent of the gross national product.* With such meager expenditures, the federal government could meet its revenue needs from tariff duties and from income brought in by the sale of public lands. In fact, the government had not imposed any direct taxes on its citizens for thirty years. During the war, however, annual federal expenditures gradually rose to 15 percent of the gross national product, and the need for new sources of revenue became urgent. Yet even in the face of massive wartime expenditures, neither the Union nor the Confederacy initially showed much enthusiasm for imposing taxes. Aside from the fact that Americans were unaccustomed to paying taxes to their national government, both sides expected the war to be short, and neither wanted the knock of the tax collector

---

*Gross national product (GNP): the sum, measured in dollars, of all goods and services produced in a given year. By contrast, in the 1980s the federal budgets averaged about 25 percent of GNP.

to dampen patriotic spirit. In August 1861 the Confederacy enacted a small property tax and the Union an income tax, but both measures were halfhearted, and neither raised much revenue. The Union's first income-tax law actually postponed collection until 1863.

Still needing revenue, both sides turned to war bonds; that is, to loans from citizens, to be repaid by future generations. The patriotic fervor of the early war years helped to sell these bonds. Southerners quickly bought up the Confederacy's first bond issue ($15 million) in 1861. That same year, a financial wizard, Philadelphia banker Jay Cooke, led a successful campaign to induce the northern public to subscribe to a much larger bond issue ($150 million). But in themselves bonds did not answer the requirements of wartime finance, because they had to be paid for in gold or silver coin (specie), which was in short supply. Soaking up most of its available specie, the South's first bond issue threatened to be its last, while in the North many hoarded their gold rather than spend it on bonds.

Recognizing the limitations of taxation and of bond issues, the Union and the Confederacy began to print paper money. Early in 1862 Lincoln signed into law the Legal Tender Act, which authorized the issue of $150 million of the so-called greenbacks. Christopher Memminger, the Confederacy's treasury secretary, and Salmon P. Chase, his Union counterpart, shared a distrust of paper money, but each came around to the idea because, as Chase bluntly put it, *"The Treasury is nearly empty."* The availability of paper money would make it easier to pay soldiers, to levy and raise taxes, and to sell war bonds. The Legal Tender Act not only authorized the issuance of the greenbacks but also provided for the emission of $500 million of war bonds purchasable with greenbacks.

Yet doubts about paper money lingered. Unlike gold and silver, which had established market values, the value of paper money depended mainly on the public's confidence in the government that issued it. To bolster that confidence, Union officials made the greenbacks legal tender (that is, acceptable in payment of most public and private debts) and then overcame their early reservations about taxes by imposing increasingly stiff taxes on everything from income to liquor, yachts, and billiard tables. The steady flow of tax revenue into the federal treasury strengthened public confidence in the government's ability to meet its obligations and helped to check the inflationary tendency inherent in paper money.

In contrast, the Confederacy never made its paper money legal tender, an omission that inevitably raised the suspicion that the southern government had little confidence in its own paper issues. To compound the problem, the Confederacy raised less than 5 percent of its wartime revenue from taxes. (The comparable figure for the North was 21 percent.) The Confederacy did enact a comprehensive tax measure in 1863, but Union invasions disrupted its ability to collect taxes. In addition, the South's relatively undeveloped system of internal transportation made tax collection a hit-or-miss proposition. For example, the Confederacy's tax measures of 1863 included a tax-in-kind, a sort of tithe. After feeding their families, farmers had to pledge one-tenth of their crops to the government. Because thousands of agents were sent to collect it, the tax-in-kind brought results, but it fell disproportionately on farmers who lived near the railroads traveled by tax collectors. Some of the food collected, moreover, rotted in government warehouses for want of transportation. To many farmers, it seemed that the Confederacy's tax policies were both unfair and incompetently administered.

In the face of the Confederacy's sorry performance in collecting taxes, confidence in the South's paper money quickly evaporated, and the value of Confederate paper in relation to gold plunged disastrously. The Confederacy responded by printing more paper money, a billion dollars of it by 1865, but this action merely accelerated southern inflation. While prices in the North rose about 80 percent during the war, the Confederacy suffered an inflation rate in excess of 9,000 percent. What cost a southerner one dollar in 1861 cost forty-six dollars by 1864.

By raising taxes, floating bonds, and printing paper money, both the Union and the Confederacy broke with the hard-money, minimal-government traditions of American public finance. For the most part, these changes occurred as unanticipated and often reluctant adaptations to wartime conditions. But in the North the Republicans took advantage of the departure of the southern Democrats from Congress to push through one measure that they and their Whig predecessors had long advocated, a system of national banking. In February 1863 Congress passed the National Bank Act over the

concerted opposition of the northern Democrats. This law established criteria by which a bank could obtain a federal charter and issue national bank notes (notes backed by the federal government). One intended effect of the law was to give private bankers an incentive to purchase war bonds, because once a private bank had obtained a federal charter, it could issue national bank notes up to 90 percent of the value of the war bonds that it held.

The North's ability to revolutionize its system of public finance during the war reflected not only its longer experience with the complex financial transactions required by its industrial and commercial economy but also its greater political cohesion during the war.

Political Leadership in Wartime

The Civil War pitted rival political systems as well as armies and economies against each other. The South entered the war with several apparent political advantages. Lincoln's call for militiamen to suppress the rebellion had transformed hesitators in the South into tenacious secessionists. "Never was a people more united or more determined," a New Orleans resident wrote in the spring of 1861 to her brother-in-law, who was serving in Lincoln's cabinet. "There is but one mind, one heart, one action." Moreover, since the founding of the United States, the South had produced a disproportionate share of the nation's strong presidents: Washington, Jefferson, Madison, Monroe, Jackson, and Polk. Now President Jefferson Davis of the Confederacy, as a former war secretary and United States senator, possessed experience, honesty, courage, and what one officer described as "a jaw sawed in *steel*."

In contrast, the Union's list of political liabilities appeared lengthy. Loyal but contentious, northern Democrats wanted to prosecute the war without conscription, without the financial centralization represented by the National Bank Act, and without the abolition of slavery. Within the rival Republican party, Lincoln had trouble commanding respect. Unlike Davis, he had served in neither the cabinet nor the Senate, and his informal western manners inspired little confidence among eastern Republicans. Northern setbacks early in the war convinced most Republicans in Congress that Lincoln was an ineffectual leader. Vocal criticism of Lincoln sprang from a group of Republi-

President Abraham Lincoln

In this photo taken four days before Lincoln's assassination, the strains of the long wartime crisis show clearly on the president's face.

cans who became known as the Radicals and who included Secretary of the Treasury Salmon P. Chase, Senator Charles Sumner of Massachusetts, and Representative Thaddeus Stevens of Pennsylvania. The Radicals never formed a tightly knit cadre; on some issues they cooperated with Lincoln. But they did criticize him early in the war for failing to make the emancipation of the slaves a war goal and later for being too eager to readmit the conquered rebel states into the Union.

Lincoln's distinctive style of leadership encouraged and simultaneously disarmed opposition within the Republican party. Keeping his counsel to himself until ready to act, he met criticism with homespun anecdotes that caught his opponents off guard. The Radicals frequently concluded that Lincoln was a prisoner of the conservative wing of the party, while conservatives complained that Lincoln was too close to the Radicals. But Lincoln's cautious reserve had the dual benefit of leaving open his lines of communication with both wings of the party and fragmenting his opposition. Lincoln shrewdly brought several of his critics into

his cabinet, including Chase. Not only did Chase, once secure in the cabinet, moderate his criticism of the president, but he proved an excellent administrator.

In contrast, Jefferson Davis had a knack for making enemies. A West Pointer, he would rather have led the army than the government, and he used his sharp tongue to win arguments rather than to win over his foes. Davis's cabinet suffered from frequent resignations; the Confederacy had five secretaries of war in four years, for example. In particular, Davis's relations with his vice president, Alexander Stephens of Georgia, bordered on disastrous. A wisp of a man, Stephens weighed less than a hundred pounds and looked like a boy with a withered face. But he compensated for his slight physique with a tongue as acidic as Davis's. Leaving Richmond, the Confederate capital, in 1862, Stephens spent most of the war in Georgia, where he sniped at Davis as "weak and vacillating, timid, petulant, peevish, obstinate."

The conflict between Davis and Stephens involved not only a clash of personalities but also an ideological division, a rift, in fact, like that at the heart of the Confederacy. Although the Confederate Constitution, drafted in February 1861, resembled the United States Constitution in several ways, the southern charter explicitly guaranteed the sovereignty of the Confederate states and prohibited the Confederate Congress from enacting protective tariffs and from supporting internal improvements (measures long opposed by southern voters). For Stephens and other influential Confederate leaders—among them, governors Joseph Brown of Georgia and Zebulon Vance of North Carolina—the Confederacy existed not only to protect slavery but, equally important, to enshrine the doctrine of states' rights. (Brown condemned the Confederate Conscription Act as the most severe blow at constitutional liberty in American history.) In contrast, Davis's main objective was to secure the independence of the entire South from the North, a goal that frequently led him to override the wishes of state governors for the good of the Confederacy as a whole.

This difference between Davis and Stephens bore some resemblance to the discord between Lincoln and the northern Democrats. Like Davis, Lincoln believed that winning the war demanded an enhancement of the central government's power; like Stephens, northern Democrats resisted governmental centralization. But Lincoln could control his opponents more effectively than Davis, not only because, by temperament, he was more suited than Davis to conciliation but also because of the different nature of party politics in the two sections.

In the South the Democrats and the remaining Whigs agreed to suspend party rivalries for the duration of the war. However, this decision, made to promote southern unity, actually encouraged disunity. Without the institutionalization of conflict that party rivalry provided, southern politics tended to disintegrate along personal and factional lines. Lacking a party organization to back him, Davis could not mobilize votes to pass measures that he favored through the Confederate Congress, nor could he depend on the support of party loyalists throughout the slave states. In contrast, in the Union, northern Democrats' organized opposition to Lincoln tended to unify the Republicans. In the 1862 elections, which occurred at a low ebb of Union military fortunes, the Democrats won control of five large states, including Lincoln's own Illinois. Republican leaders drew the right conclusion from these Democratic gains: no matter how much they disdained Lincoln, they had to rally behind him or risk being driven from office by the Democrats. Ultimately, the Union would develop more political cohesion than the Confederacy, not because it had fewer divisions but because it managed its divisions more effectively.

Securing the Union's Borders

Even before large-scale fighting began, Lincoln moved swiftly to safeguard Washington, which was bordered by two slave states (Virginia and Maryland) and filled with Confederate sympathizers. A week after the firing on Fort Sumter, a Baltimore mob attacked a Massachusetts regiment bound for Washington, but enough troops slipped through to protect the capital. Lincoln then dispatched federal troops to Maryland, where he suspended the writ of habeas corpus*; in effect, federal troops could now arrest pro-secession Marylanders without formally charging them with specific offenses. Mind-

ful that strong Unionist sentiment flourished in the western part of the state, and cowed by Lincoln's bold moves, the Maryland legislature rejected secession. Delaware, another border slave state, quickly followed suit.

Next Lincoln authorized the arming of Union sympathizers in Kentucky, a slave state with a Unionist legislature, a secessionist governor, and a thin chance of staying neutral. Lincoln also stationed troops under General Ulysses S. Grant just across the Ohio River from Kentucky, in Illinois. When a Confederate army invaded Kentucky early in 1862, the state's legislature turned to Grant to drive it out. Officially, at least, Kentucky became the third slave state to declare for the Union. The fourth, Missouri, was ravaged by four years of fighting between Union and Confederate troops and between sundry bands of guerrillas and bushwackers, including William Quantrill, a Confederate desperado, and his murderous apprentices, Frank and Jesse James. Despite savage fighting and the divided loyalties of its people, Missouri never left the Union.[†]

By holding these four border slave states—Maryland, Delaware, Kentucky, and Missouri—in the Union, Lincoln kept open his lines to the free states and gained access to the river systems in Kentucky and Missouri that led into the heart of the Confederacy. (In 1862 invasions of the South by river would provide the North with most of its early military successes.) Lincoln's firmness, particularly in the case of Maryland, scotched charges that he was weak-willed, and it demonstrated how the crisis forced the president to exercise long-dormant powers. Although in the case *Ex parte* Merryman (1861), Chief Justice Roger B. Taney ruled that Lincoln had exceeded his authority in suspending the writ of habeas corpus in Maryland, the president, citing the Constitution's authorization of the writ's suspension in "Cases of Rebellion" (Article I, Section 9), insisted that he, rather than Congress, would determine whether a rebellion existed; and he ignored Taney's ruling.

---

*Habeas corpus: a court order requiring that the detainer of a prisoner bring the person in custody to court and show cause for his or her detention.

[†]Admitted to the Union in 1863, West Virginia became the fifth border state. This state originated in the refusal of thirty-five counties in the predominantly nonslaveholding region of Virginia west of the Shenandoah Valley to follow the state's leaders into secession in 1861.

In Battle, 1861–1862

The Civil War was the first war to rely extensively on railroads, the telegraph, mass-produced weapons, joint army-navy tactics, iron-plated warships, rifled guns and artillery, and trench warfare. All of this lends some justification to its description as the first modern war. But to the participants, slogging through muddy swamps and weighed down with equipment, the war hardly seemed modern. In many ways, the soldiers had the more accurate perspective, for the new weapons did not always work, and both sides employed tactics that were more traditional than modern.

Armies, Weapons, and Strategies

Compared to the Confederacy's 9 million people, of whom over one-third were slaves, the Union had 22 million people in 1861. The North also had 3.5 times as many white men of military age, 90 percent of all U. S. industrial capacity, and two-thirds of its railroad track. Yet the Union faced a daunting challenge. Its goal was to force the South back into the Union, whereas the South was fighting merely for its independence. To subdue the Confederacy, the North would have to sustain offensive operations over an area comparable in size to the part of Russia that the French emperor Napoleon had invaded in 1812 with unforgettably disastrous results.

Measured against this challenge, the Union's advantages in population and technology shrank. The North had more men, but needing to defend long supply lines and occupy captured areas, it could commit a smaller proportion of them to frontline duty. The South, on the other hand, with black slaves as the basis of its labor force, could assign a higher proportion of its white male population to combat. As for technology, the North required, and possessed, superior railroads. Fighting defensively

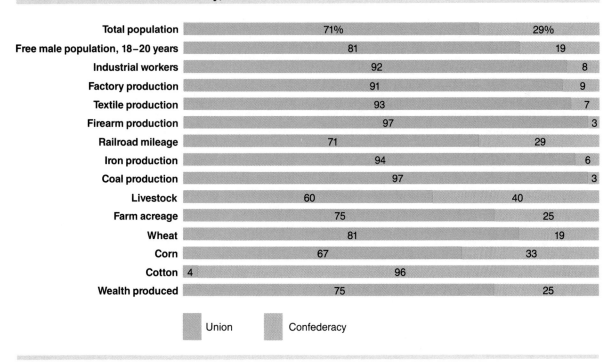

Comparative Population and Economic Resources of the Union and the Confederacy, 1861

	Union	Confederacy
Total population	71%	29%
Free male population, 18–20 years	81	19
Industrial workers	92	8
Factory production	91	9
Textile production	93	7
Firearm production	97	3
Railroad mileage	71	29
Iron production	94	6
Coal production	97	3
Livestock	60	40
Farm acreage	75	25
Wheat	81	19
Corn	67	33
Cotton	4	96
Wealth produced	75	25

At the start of the war, the Union enjoyed huge advantages in population, industry, railroad mileage, and wealth produced.

SOURCE: *The Times Atlas of World History* (New Jersey: Hammond, Inc., 1978).

Blacksmiths in Washington

These blacksmiths could shoe five hundred horses a day. Once finished with the horses, they would start on mules, of which the Union army had over one hundred thousand.

on so-called interior lines, the South could shift its troops relatively short distances within its defensive arc without relying on railroads, whereas the North had to move its troops and supplies huge distances around the exterior of the arc. To the North's disadvantage, not only could railroads easily be sabotaged by guerrillas, but once Union troops moved away from their railroad bases, their supply wagons often bogged down on wretched southern roads, which frequently became watery ditches in bad weather. Even on good roads, horses and mules, which themselves consumed supplies, were needed to pull wagons; an invading army of 100,000 men required 35,000 horses or mules. Finally, also to the Confederacy's benefit, southerners had an edge in soldiers' morale, for Confederate troops battled on home ground. "No people ever warred for independence," a Confederate general acknowledged, "with more relative advantages than the Confederates."

The Civil War witnessed experiments with a variety of newly developed weapons, including the submarine, the repeating rifle, and the multibarreled Gatling gun, the forerunner of the machine gun. Yet these futuristic innovations had less impact on the war than did the perfection in the 1850s of a bullet whose powder would not clog a rifle's spiraled internal grooves after a few shots. Like the smoothbore muskets that both armies had employed at the start of the war, most improved rifles had to be reloaded after each shot. But where the smoothbore musket had an effective range of only

eighty yards, the Springfield or Enfield rifles widely employed by 1863 could hit targets accurately at four hundred yards.

The development of the rifle posed a challenge to long-accepted military tactics. The tactical manuals used at West Point in the 1840s and 1850s had identified the mass infantry charge against an opponent's weakest point as the key to victory. These manuals assumed that defenders armed with muskets would be able to fire only a round or two before being overwhelmed. The same assumption led tacticians to disdain trenches; against assaulting infantry, trenches would become mere traps for defenders. Armed with rifles, however, a defending force could fire several rounds before closing with the enemy. Attacking forces would now have far greater difficulty getting close enough to thrust bayonets; in fact, less than 1 percent of the casualties in the Civil War resulted from bayonet wounds.

Thus the rifle produced some changes in tactics during the war. Both sides gradually came to understand the value of trenches, which provided defenders with some protection against the withering fire of attacking forces. By 1865 trenches pockmarked the landscape in Virginia and Georgia. In addition, widening employment of the rifle forced generals to rely less on cavalry. Traditionally, the cavalry had ranked among the most prestigious components of an army, in part because cavalry charges were often devastatingly effective and in part because the cavalry helped to maintain

Life in the Field

The implements in this Union army–owned field surgical kit could remove bullets but not stop infection. The British-made five-shot revolver reached the South despite the Union blockade. A Confederate officer owned the brass-and-leather-adorned field glass.

The bullet-rent trousers belonged to a Union officer wounded at Peachtree Creek. Although he survived the war, he endured repeated operations in the remaining forty-five years of his life to remove tissue infected by the bullet.

class distinctions within the army. Indeed, at the start of the war, one of the clearest Confederate advantages lay in the quality of its cavalry. But rifles reduced the effectiveness of cavalry by increasing the firepower of foot soldiers. Bullets that might miss the rider would at least hit the horse. Thus as cavalry charges against infantry became more difficult, both sides adapted by relegating cavalry to reconnaissance missions and to raids on supply trains.

Although the rifle exposed traditional tactics to new hazards, by no means did it invalidate those tactics. The attacking army still stood an excellent chance of success if it achieved surprise. The South's lush forests provided abundant opportunities for an army to sneak up on its opponent. For example, at the Battle of Shiloh in 1862, Confederate attackers surprised and almost defeated a larger Union army despite the rumpus created by green rebel troops en route to the battle, many of whom fired their rifles into the air to see if they would work.

Achieving such complete surprise normally lay beyond the skill or luck of generals. In the absence of any element of surprise, disaster became a likely result for the attacking army. At the Battle of Fredericksburg in December 1862, Confederate troops inflicted appalling casualties on Union forces attacking uphill over open terrain, while at Gettysburg in July 1863, Union riflemen and artillery shredded charging southerners. But generals might still achieve partial surprise by hitting an enemy before it had concentrated its troops; in fact, this is what the North tried to do at Fredericksburg. Because surprise often proved effective, most generals continued to believe that their best chance of success lay in striking an unwary or weakened enemy with all the troops they could muster rather than in relying on guerrilla or trench warfare.

Much like previous wars, the Civil War was fought basically in a succession of battles during which exposed infantry traded volleys, charged, and countercharged. Whichever side withdrew from the field usually was thought to have lost the battle, but the losing side frequently sustained lighter casualties than the supposed victors. Both sides had trouble exploiting their victories, for neither had airplanes to hammer or tanks to envelop retreating columns. As a rule, the beaten army moved back a few miles from the field to lick its wounds; the winners stayed in place to lick theirs. Politicians on both sides denounced their generals as timorous fools for not pursuing a beaten foe, but these politicians rarely understood how difficult it was for a mangled victor to gather horses, mules, supply trains, and exhausted soldiers for a new attack. Until the end of the war, the only cases of entire armies actually surrendering arose from captured garrisons. Not surprisingly, for much of the war, generals on both sides concluded that the best defense was a good offense.

To the extent that the North had a long-range strategy in 1861, it lay in the so-called Anaconda plan. Devised by the Mexican War hero General Winfield Scott, the plan called for the Union to blockade the southern coastline and to thrust, like a huge snake, down the Mississippi River. Scott expected that this sealing off and severing of the Confederacy would make the South recognize the futility of secession and restore southern Unionists to power. The Anaconda plan promised a relatively bloodless end to the war, but Scott, himself a southern Unionist, exaggerated the strength of Unionist spirit in the South. Furthermore, although Lincoln ordered a blockade of the southern coast a week after the fall of Fort Sumter, the North hardly had the troops and naval flotillas to seize the Mississippi in 1861. Thus while the Mississippi remained an obvious objective, northern strategy did not unfold according to any blueprint like the Anaconda plan.

Early in the war, the pressing need to secure the border slave states, particularly Kentucky and Missouri, dictated Union strategy west of the Appalachian Mountains. Once in control of Kentucky, northern troops plunged southward into Tennessee. The Appalachians tended to seal this western theater off from the eastern theater, where the Confederacy's decision to move its capital from Montgomery, Alabama, to Richmond, Virginia, shaped the Union strategy. "Forward to Richmond" became the Union's first war cry.

Stalemate in the East

Before they could reach Richmond, one hundred miles southwest of Washington, Union troops would have to dislodge a Confederate army brazenly encamped at Manassas Junction, only twenty-five miles from the Union capital. Lincoln ordered General Irvin McDowell to attack his former West Point classmate, Confederate general P. G. T. Beauregard. "You are green, it is true," Lincoln told McDowell, "but they are green also; you are all green alike." In the resulting First Battle of Bull Run (or First Manassas),* amateur armies clashed in bloody chaos under a blistering July sun. The engagement was a spectacle that contrasted vividly with the picnicking of the well-dressed Washington dignitaries who had gathered to view the action. Aided by last-minute reinforcements and by the disorganization of the attacking federals, Beauregard routed the larger Union army.

After Bull Run, Lincoln replaced McDowell with General George B. McClellan as commander of the Union's Army of the Potomac. Another West Pointer, McClellan had served with distinction in the Mexican War and mastered the art of administration by managing various midwestern railroads in the 1850s. Few generals could match his ability to turn a ragtag mob into a disciplined fighting force. His soldiers adored him, but Lincoln quickly became disenchanted with his new commander. Lincoln believed that the key to a Union victory lay in simultaneous, coordinated attacks on several fronts. In this way, the North could exploit its advantage in manpower and resources and negate the South's advantage of interior lines. McClellan, a proslavery Democrat, hoped to maneuver the South into a relatively bloodless defeat and then negotiate a peace that would readmit the Confederate states with slavery intact.

McClellan soon got an opportunity to demonstrate the value of his strategy. After Bull Run,

---

*Because the North usually named battles after the nearest body of water and the South after the nearest town, many Civil War battles are known by two names.

the Confederates had pulled back behind the Rappahannock River and awaited the Union onslaught against Richmond. Rather than directly attack the Confederate army, McClellan formulated a plan in the spring of 1862 to move the Army of the Potomac by water to the tip of the peninsula formed by the York and James rivers and then move northwestward up the peninsula to Richmond. McClellan's plan had several advantages. Depending on water transport rather than on railroads (which Confederate cavalry could cut), the McClellan strategy reduced the vulnerability of northern supply lines. By dictating an approach to Richmond from the southeast, it threatened the South's supply lines. By aiming for the capital of the Confederacy rather than for the Confederate army stationed northeast of Richmond, finally,

McClellan hoped to maneuver the southern troops into a futile attack on his army in order to avert a destructive siege of Richmond.

By far the most massive military campaign in American history to that date, the Peninsula Campaign at first unfolded smoothly. Three hundred ships transported seventy thousand men and immense stores of supplies to the tip of the peninsula. Reinforcements soon swelled McClellan's army to one hundred thousand. Although Confederate reinforcements also poured into the peninsula, by late May McClellan was within five miles of Richmond.

If the war had been a chess game, McClellan would have become a grand master. But after luring the Confederacy to the brink of defeat, McClellan hesitated. Overestimating the Confed-

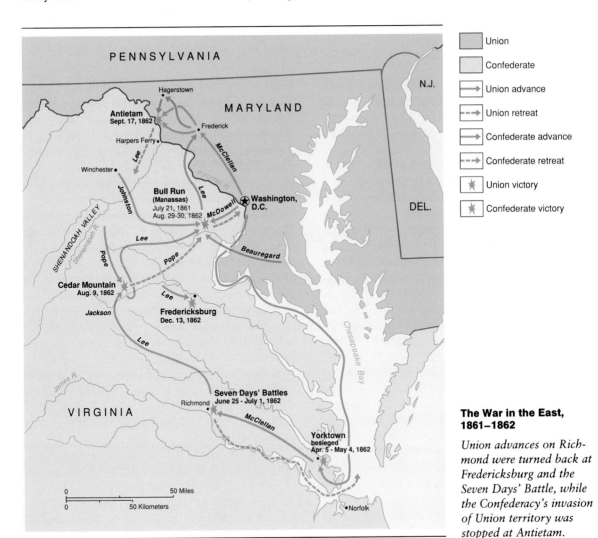

The War in the East, 1861–1862

Union advances on Richmond were turned back at Fredericksburg and the Seven Days' Battle, while the Confederacy's invasion of Union territory was stopped at Antietam.

Dead Soldiers at Antietam *These dead rebel gunners lie next to the wreckage of their battery at Antietam. The building, a Dunker church, was the site of furious fighting.*

erates' strength, he refused to launch a final attack on Richmond without the reinforcements that he expected, which were turned back by Confederate general Thomas "Stonewall" Jackson in the Shenandoah Valley. While McClellan delayed, General Robert E. Lee took command of the Confederacy's Army of Northern Virginia. An opponent of secession and so courteous that at times he seemed too gentle, Lee nevertheless possessed the qualities that McClellan most lacked, boldness and a willingness to accept casualties. Seizing the initiative, Lee attacked McClellan in late June. The ensuing Seven Days' Battles, fought in the forests east of Richmond, cost the South nearly twice as many men as the North and ended in a virtual slaughter of Confederates at Malvern Hill. But it was his own northern casualties that unnerved McClellan, and he began to send increasingly panicky reports to Washington. Lincoln, who cared little for McClellan's peninsula strategy, ordered McClellan to call off the campaign and return to Washington.

With McClellan out of the picture, Lee and his lieutenant, Stonewall Jackson, now boldly struck north and, at the Second Battle of Bull Run (Second Manassas), routed a Union army under General John Pope that had been held back from the peninsula to guard Washington. Lee's next stroke was even bolder. Crossing the Potomac River in early September 1862, he invaded western Mary-

land, where the forthcoming fall harvest could provide him with desperately needed supplies. By seizing western Maryland, moreover, Lee could threaten Washington, indirectly relieve pressure on Richmond, improve the prospects of peace candidates in the North's upcoming fall elections, and possibly induce Britain and France to recognize the Confederacy as an independent nation. But McClellan met Lee at the Battle of Antietam (or Sharpsburg) on September 17. Although a tactical draw, Antietam proved a strategic victory for the North, for Lee subsequently called off his invasion and retreated south of the Potomac. Heartened by the apparent success of northern arms, Lincoln then issued the Emancipation Proclamation, a war measure that freed all slaves under rebel control (see below). Talk of success, however, ignored the carnage of the twenty-four thousand casualties at Antietam that made it the bloodiest day of the entire war. A Union veteran recollected that one part of the battlefield contained so many bodies that a man could have walked through it without stepping on the ground.

Complaining that McClellan had "the slows," Lincoln faulted his commander for not pursuing Lee after the battle and replaced him with General Ambrose Burnside, who thought himself, and soon proved himself, unfit for high command. In December 1862 Burnside led 122,000 federal troops against 78,500 Confederates at the Battle of Fredericksburg. Burnside captured the town of Fredericksburg, northeast of Richmond, but then sacrificed his army in futile charges up the heights west of the town. Even Lee was shaken by the northern casualties. "It is well that war is so terrible—we should grow fond of it," he murmured to an aide during the battle. Richmond remained, in the words of a popular southern song, "a hard road to travel." The war in the East had become a stalemate.

The War in the West

The Union fared better in the West. Unlike the geographically limited eastern theater, the war in the West shifted over a vast and crucially important terrain that provided access to rivers leading directly into the South. The West also spawned new leadership. During the first year of war, an obscure Union general, Ulysses S. Grant, proved his competence. A West Point graduate, Grant had fought in the Mexican War and retired from the army in 1854 with a reputation for heavy drinking. He then had embarked on ventures in farming and in business, all of them dismal failures. When the Civil War began, he had gained an army commission through political pressure.

In 1861–1862 Grant retained control of two border states, Missouri and Kentucky. Moving into Tennessee, he captured two strategic forts, Fort Henry on the Tennessee River and Fort Donelson on the Cumberland. Grant then headed south to attack Corinth, Mississippi.

Corinth was a major railroad junction through which troops and supplies could be transported from the east to Memphis on the Mississippi River. In early April 1862, Confederate forces under generals Albert Sidney Johnston and P. G. T. Beauregard tried to relieve the Union pressure on Corinth by a surprise attack on Grant's army, encamped twenty miles north of the town, in southern Tennessee near a church named Shiloh. Hoping to whip Grant before the imminent arrival of twenty-five thousand Union reinforcements under General Don Carlos Buell, the Confederates exploded from the woods near Shiloh before breakfast and almost drove the federals into the Tennessee River. Beauregard cabled Richmond with news of a splendid Confederate victory. But Grant and his lieutenant, William T. Sherman, steadied the Union line. Buell's

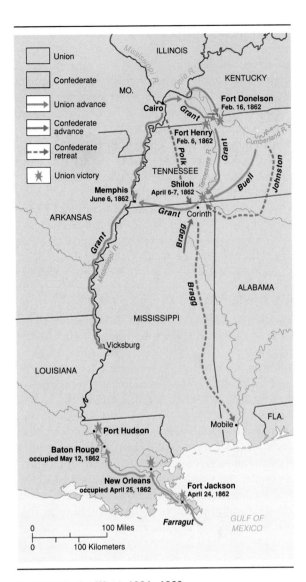

The War in the West, 1861–1862

By the end of 1862, the North held New Orleans and the entire Mississippi River except for the stretch between Vicksburg and Port Hudson.

reinforcements arrived in the night, and a Union counterattack drove the Confederates from the field the next day. Although Antietam would soon erase the distinction, the Battle of Shiloh was the bloodiest in American history to that date. Of the seventy-seven thousand men engaged, twenty-three thousand were killed or wounded, including Confederate general Albert Sidney Johnston, who bled to death from a leg wound. Defeated at Shiloh, the Confederates soon evacuated Corinth.

To attack Grant at Shiloh, the Confederacy had stripped the defenses of New Orleans, leaving only three thousand militia to guard its largest city. A combined Union land-sea force under General Benjamin Butler, a Massachusetts politician, and Admiral David G. Farragut, a Tennessean loyal to the Union, quickly capitalized on the opportunity. Blasting his way past two river forts south of New Orleans, Farragut took the city in late April and soon added Baton Rouge and Natchez to his list of conquests. Meanwhile, another Union flotilla moved down the Mississippi and captured Memphis in June. Now the North controlled the entire river, save for a two-hundred-mile stretch between Port Hudson, Louisiana, and Vicksburg, Mississippi.

Ironclads and Cruisers: The Naval War

By plunging its navy into the Confederacy like a dagger, the Union was exploiting one of its clearest advantages. The North began the war with over forty active warships against none for the South, and with the technology and industrial capacity to produce many more. Indeed, by 1865 the United States had the largest navy in the world. Steam-driven ships could penetrate the South's excellent river system from any direction and thereby turn a peacetime advantage into a wartime liability. For example, the Confederacy had stripped New Orleans's defenses in the belief that the real threat to the city would come from the north, only to find Farragut slipping in from the south.

Despite its size, the Union navy faced an extraordinary challenge in its efforts to blockade the South's thirty-five hundred miles of coast. Early in the war, small, sleek Confederate blockade-runners darted in and out of southern harbors and inlets with little chance of capture. The North gradually tightened the blockade by outfitting tugs, whalers, excursion steamers, and ferries as well as frigates to patrol southern coasts. The proportion of Confederate blockade-runners that made it through dropped from 90 percent early in the war to 50 percent by 1865. Even more than tightening the blockade, however, northern seizure of rebel ports and coastal areas shrank the South's foreign trade. In daring amphibious assaults during 1861 and 1862, the Union captured the excellent harbor of Port Royal, South Carolina, the coastal islands off South Carolina, and most of North Carolina's

river outlets. Naval patrols and amphibious operations contributed to a decline in the South's ocean trade to one-third its prewar level.

Although its resources were meager, the South made impressive efforts to offset the North's naval advantage. Early in the war, the Confederacy raised the scuttled Union frigate *Merrimac,* sheathed its sides with an armor of iron plate, rechristened it *Virginia,* and dispatched it to attack wooden Union ships in Hampton Roads, Virginia. The *Merrimac* quickly destroyed two northern warships but met its match in the hastily built Union ironclad the *Monitor.* In the first engagement of ironclads in history, the two ships fought an indecisive battle on March 9, 1862. The South constructed other ironclads and even the first submarine, which dragged a mine through the water to sink a Union ship off Charleston in 1864. Unfortunately, the "fish" failed to resurface and went down with its victim. But short of mechanics and iron-fabricating shops, the South could never build enough ironclads to overcome the North's supremacy in home waters. The Confederacy had more success

Deck of the *Monitor*

Although much smaller than its famous rival the Merrimac *(C.S.S.* Virginia)*, the Union ironclad* Monitor *benefited from its shallow draft, speed, and maneuverability. Its flat, raftlike shape made it hard to hit.*

on the high seas, where wooden, steam-driven commerce raiders like the *Alabama* and the *Florida* (both built in England) wreaked havoc on the Union's merchant marine. Commerce raiding, however, would not tip the balance of the war in the South's favor, because the North, unlike its opponent, did not depend on imports for war materials. The South would ultimately lose the naval war.

The Diplomatic War

While armies and navies clashed in 1861–1862, conflict developed on a third front, diplomacy. At the outbreak of the war, the Confederacy began a campaign to gain European recognition of its status as an independent nation. Southern confidence in a swift diplomatic victory ran high. Planning to establish a colonial empire in Mexico, Napoleon III of France had grounds to welcome the permanent division of the United States. Moreover, the upper classes in France, and also in Britain, were widely viewed as sympathetic to the aristocratic South and eager for the downfall of the brash Yankee republic. Furthermore, for years such influential southerners as South Carolina's senator and governor James Henry Hammond had contended that an embargo of cotton exports would bring Britain to its knees. These southerners reasoned that Britain, dependent on the South for four-fifths of its cotton, would break the Union blockade and provoke a war with the North rather than watch its textile workers sink into revolutionary discontent under the weight of an embargo.

Leaving nothing to chance, the Confederacy in 1861 dispatched emissaries James Mason to Britain and John Slidell to France to lobby for recognition of the South as an independent nation. When a Union ship captain, acting without orders, boarded the British vessel the *Trent,* which was carrying Mason and Slidell, and brought the two men to Boston as prisoners, British tempers exploded. "You may stand for this," Britain's prime minister, Lord Palmerston, roared to his cabinet, "but damned if I will." But cooler heads soon prevailed. Recognizing that one war at a time was enough, President Lincoln released Mason and Slidell.

Settlement of the *Trent* affair did not eliminate friction between the United States and Britain. The construction in British shipyards of two Confederate commerce raiders, the *Florida* and the *Alabama,* evoked protests from Union diplomats. In 1863 the United States minister to London, Charles Francis Adams (the son of former president John Quincy Adams), threatened war if two British-built ironclads commissioned by the Confederacy, the so-called Laird rams, were turned over to the South. Armed with long spikes below the water, the powerful rams posed a genuine threat to the Union blockade of the South. Britain, however, capitulated to Adams's protests and purchased the rams for its own navy.

On balance, the South fell far short of its diplomatic objectives. While recognizing the Confederacy as a belligerent, neither Britain nor France ever recognized it as a nation. Basically, the Confederacy overestimated its hand. For several reasons, the South's vaunted "cotton diplomacy" failed dismally. The Confederate government talked of embargoing cotton exports in order to bring the British to their knees, but in reality, the government never controlled more than 15 percent of the South's cotton. Planters conducted business as usual by raising cotton and trying to slip it through the blockade. The South ultimately lost its share of the British market anyway; with 77 percent of that market in 1860, it held only 10 percent by 1865. But the South's declining share of the British cotton market resulted from forces beyond its control and yielded no political advantages. Bumper cotton crops in the late 1850s had glutted the British market by the start of the war and weakened British demand for cotton. In addition, Britain had responded to the threat of a cotton embargo by developing new suppliers in Egypt and India, thereby buffering itself from southern pressure. Gradually, too, the North's tightened blockade restricted southern exports.

The South also exaggerated Britain's stake in helping the Confederacy. As a naval power that had frequently blockaded its own enemies, Britain's diplomatic interest lay in supporting the Union blockade in principle; from Britain's standpoint, to help the South break the blockade would set a precedent that easily could boomerang. Finally, although France and Britain often talked of recognizing the Confederacy, the timing never seemed quite right. The Union's success at Antietam in 1862 and Lincoln's subsequent issuance of the Emancipation Proclamation dampened Europe's enthusiasm for recognition at a crucial juncture. By transforming the war into a struggle to end slavery, the Emancipation Proclamation produced an upsurge of pro-Union feeling in antislavery Britain, particularly among liberals and the working class. Workingmen in Manchester, England, wrote Lincoln to praise his resolve to free the slaves and to reassure him of "our warm and earnest sympathy." The proclamation, wrote Henry Adams (diplomat Charles Francis Adams's son) from London, "has done more for us here than all of our former victories and all our diplomacy."

Emancipation Transforms the War

"I hear old John Brown knocking on the lid of his coffin and shouting 'Let me out! Let me out!'" abolitionist Henry Stanton wrote to his wife after the fall of Fort Sumter. "The Doom of Slavery is at hand." In 1861 this prediction seemed wildly premature. In his inaugural address that year, Lincoln had stated bluntly, "I have no purpose, directly or indirectly, to interfere with the institution of slavery in the states where it exists." Yet in the space of two years, the North's priorities underwent a decisive transformation. A mixture of practical necessity and ideological conviction thrust the emancipation of the slaves to the forefront of northern war goals.

The rise of emancipation as a Union war goal reflected the changing character of the war itself. As late as July 1862, General George McClellan had written to Lincoln to restate his conviction that "neither confiscation of property . . . or forcible abolition of slavery should be contemplated for a moment." As the struggle dragged on, however, demands for the prosecution of "total war" intensified in the North. Even northerners who saw no moral value in abolishing slavery were starting to recognize the military value of emancipation as a technique to cripple the South's resources.

From Confiscation to Emancipation

Union policy on emancipation developed in stages. As soon as northern troops began to invade the South, questions arose about the disposition of captured rebel property, including slaves. Slaves who fled behind the Union lines were sometimes considered "contraband"—enemy property liable to seizure—and were put to work for the Union army. Whereas some northern commanders viewed this practice a useful tool of war, others did not, and the Lincoln administration was evasive. To establish an official policy, Congress in August 1861 passed the first Confiscation Act, which authorized the seizure of all property used in military aid of the rebellion, including slaves. By the terms of this act, slaves who had been employed directly by the Confederate armed services and who later fled to freedom became "captives of war." But nothing in the act actually freed these contrabands, nor did the law apply to contrabands who had not worked for the Confederate military.

Several factors underlay the Union's cautious approach to the confiscation of rebel property. Officially maintaining that the South's rebellion lacked any legal basis, Lincoln argued that southerners were thus still entitled to the Constitution's protection of property. The president also had practical reasons to walk softly. The Union not only contained four slave states but also held a sizable body of proslavery Democrats who flatly opposed turning the war into a crusade against the South's social institutions. If the North in any way tampered with slavery, these Democrats feared, "two or three million semi-savages" might come north and compete with white workers. Mindful of the considerable northern opposition to turning a limited policy of confiscation into a general program of emancipation, Lincoln assured Congress in December 1861 that the war would not become a "remorseless revolutionary struggle."

From the start of the war, however, Lincoln faced pressure from the loosely knit but determined Radical Republicans to adopt a policy of emancipation. Radicals hailed the war as a second American Revolution, one that would abolish slavery. Many subscribed to Pennsylvanian Thaddeus Stevens's urging that the Union "free every slave—slay every traitor—burn every Rebel mansion, if these things be necessary to preserve this temple of freedom." Radicals agreed with black abolitionist Frederick Douglass that "to fight against slaveholders without fighting against slavery, is but a half-hearted business."

With every new northern setback, support for the Radicals' point of view grew. Each Union military defeat reminded northerners that the confederacy, with a slave labor force in place to harvest southern crops and run southern factories, could commit a higher proportion of its white men to battle. As a measure conducive to total war, the idea of emancipation thus gained increasing favor in the North, and in July 1862 Congress passed the second Confiscation Act. This law authorized the seizure of the property of all persons in rebellion and stipulated that slaves who came within Union lines "shall be forever free." Finally, the law opened the door to blacks' military service by authorizing the president to employ blacks as soldiers.

Nevertheless, Lincoln continued to stall, even in the face of rising pressure for emancipation. "My paramount object in this struggle *is* to save the Union, and is *not* either to save or destroy slavery," Lincoln told antislavery journalist Horace Greeley. "If I could save the Union without freeing *any* slave, I would do it, and if I could save it by freeing *all* the slaves, I would do it; and if I could save it by freeing some and leaving others alone, I would also do that." Yet Lincoln had always loathed slavery, and by the spring of 1862, he had come around to the Radical position that the war must lead to the abolition of slavery. He hesitated principally because he did not want to be stampeded by Congress into a measure that might disrupt northern unity and because he feared that a public commitment to emancipation in the summer of 1862, on the heels of the northern defeat at Second Manassas and the collapse of the Peninsula Campaign, might be interpreted as an act of frantic desperation. After failing to persuade the Union slave states to emancipate slaves in return for federal compensation, he drafted a proclamation of emancipation, circulated it within his cabinet, and waited for a right moment to issue it. Finally, after the Union victory in September 1862 at Antietam, Lincoln issued the Preliminary Emancipation Proclamation, which declared all slaves under rebel control free as of January 1, 1863. Announcing the plan in advance softened the surprise, tested public opinion, and gave the states still in rebellion an opportunity to preserve slavery by returning to the Union—an opportunity that none, however, took. The final Emancipation Proclamation, issued on January 1, declared "forever free" all slaves in areas in rebellion.

The proclamation had limited practical impact. Applying only to rebellious areas, where the Union had no authority, it exempted the Union slave states and those parts of the Confederacy then in Union hands (Tennessee, West Virginia, southern Louisiana, and sections of Virginia). Moreover, it mainly restated what the second Confiscation Act had already stipulated: if rebels' slaves fell into Union hands, those slaves would be free. Yet the proclamation was a brilliant political stroke. By issuing it as a military measure, in his role as commander in chief, Lincoln pacified northern conservatives. Its aim, he stressed, was to injure the Confederacy, threaten its property, heighten its dread, sap its morale, and thus hasten its demise. By issuing the proclamation himself, Lincoln stole the initiative from the Radicals in Congress and mobilized support for the Union among European liberals far more dramatically than could any act of Congress. Further, the declaration pushed the border states toward emancipation: by the end of the war, Maryland and Missouri would abolish slavery. Finally, it increased slaves' incentives to escape as northern troops approached. Fulfilling the worst of Confederate fears, it enabled blacks to join the Union army.

Clearly, the Emancipation Proclamation did not end slavery everywhere or free "*all* the slaves." But it changed the nature of the war. From 1863 on, the war for the Union would also be a war against slavery.

Crossing Union Lines

The attacks and counterattacks of the opposing armies turned many slaves into pawns of war. Some slaves became free when Union troops overran their plantations. Others fled their plantations at the approach of federal troops to take refuge behind Union lines. A few were freed by northern assaults, only to be reenslaved by Confederate counterthrusts. One North Carolina slave celebrated liberation on twelve occasions, the number of times that Union soldiers marched through his area. By 1865 about half a million slaves were in Union hands.

In the first year of the war, when the Union had not yet established a policy toward contrabands (fugitive slaves), masters were able to retrieve them from the Union army. After 1862, however, the thousands of slaves who crossed Union lines were considered free. The continual influx of freedmen created a huge refugee problem for army

The Sea Island Experiments, 1861–1865

In November 1861 a Union fleet sailed into Port Royal Sound, an inlet among the South Carolina Sea Islands, and bombarded the port's defenses. Before Union troops could occupy the islands, the white residents, many of them slaveowning planters, fled to the mainland. Left behind were elegant mansions, sprawling cotton plantations, and ten thousand slaves, who would remember the invasion as the "gun shoot at Bay Point."

The Sea Islands

The island chain, famous for the production of what had come to be called sea-island cotton, was the site of unique wartime experiments in new social policies.

Lying just off the southern coast between Charleston and Savannah, the conquered islands—including Port Royal, Hilton Head, and St. Helena—provided an operating base for the Union blockade fleet. They were of potential value to the Treasury Department, too. The Sea Islands were known for their high-grade cotton, which could be used to feed northern textile mills and to bolster the Union economy. But the takeover of the islands presented the Union with a challenge as well as a triumph.

Before the invasion, slaves had composed 83 percent of the Sea Island population. Long isolated from the mainland, they retained a distinctive culture and perpetuated many African customs. Their syntax and vocabulary were West Indian, and their Gullah dialect was almost incomprehensible to outsiders. Since the late eighteenth century, they had endured a harsh slave system similar to that of the West Indies. To the northerners who now arrived on the Sea Islands—army personnel, treasury agents, plantation managers, teachers, and missionaries—the very numbers of the black inhabitants seemed overwhelming. "Negroes, negroes, negroes," wrote Elizabeth Botume, a Boston teacher. "They hovered around like bees in a swarm. . . . Every doorstep, box, or barrel was covered with them." With the war barely under way and victory still a vision on the distant horizon, the Union suddenly had to forge a policy toward these thousands of "contrabands." While warfare occupied the rest of the nation, Sea Island administrators embarked on a series of experiments in emancipation.

These experiments revealed deep divisions in northerners' thinking about the future of blacks. Some northerners on the scene focused on blacks' potential as soldiers. In May 1862 General David Hunter, who commanded the Union forces occupying the Sea Islands, formed a black army regiment; by August Sea Island men were being impressed into the First South Carolina "Volunteers," commanded by Massachusetts minister Thomas Wentworth Higginson. The drafting of blacks infuriated idealistic teachers and missionaries, who saw education as the blacks' primary need. "The negroes . . . will do anything for us, if we will only teach them," another teacher from Boston claimed. "The majority learn with wonderful rapidity," reported the free black Charlotte Forten of Philadelphia, "and they are said to be among the most degraded negroes of the South."

Equally sharp disagreements swirled around the question of economic opportunity for blacks. Edward Philbrick of Boston, an engineer who worked as a plantation superintendent on the islands, embodied one approach to the issue. Philbrick hoped to make the islands a showcase for free labor by turning the freedmen into wage earners on the large cotton plantations there. For blacks to produce more cotton as wage earners than they had as slaves, Philbrick reasoned, would squelch northern "gabble about the danger of immediate emancipa-

Sea Island School *Thousands of liberated slaves enrolled in the schools established by northern missionaries and teachers after the capture of the Sea Islands. This school was in Beaufort on Port Royal Island.*

tion" and buttress the position of those northerners who wanted emancipation to become the Union's main war goal. But the freedmen themselves had little enthusiasm for working in gangs on plantations, even if for wages. The practice smacked too much of their conditions under slavery. Instead, most Sea Island blacks would have preferred to plant food for themselves rather than cotton for northern factories, and many dreamed of owning their own land. "I should like to buy the very spot on which I live," an elderly freedman wrote to President Abraham Lincoln in a dictated letter. "I had rather work for myself . . . than work for a gentleman for wages."

Union administrators made some concessions to blacks' wishes. When, in the fall of 1863, Sea Island officials sold sixty thousand acres of confiscated rebel estates, only sixteen thousand acres were reserved for freedmen. The rest of the land was open to purchase by northern investors and speculators. Protesting the injustice of reserving a mere quarter of the acreage for those who composed the vast majority of the Sea Island residents, General Rufus Saxton, the islands' military governor and a "thoroughgoing Abolitionist, of the radical sort," secured approval in Washington to a plan to allow blacks to claim unsold land merely by squatting on it (a practice called preemption). Pressured by Saxton's rivals, however, the federal government reversed itself early in 1864 and forbade squatter claims.

Sea Islands Enterprise

Garbed in castoff Union army uniforms, these newly liberated slaves cultivate a sweet-potato patch on a Hilton Head Island plantation.

The policy shifts continued. In December 1864 General William T. Sherman, fresh from his sweep across Georgia, arrived on the Sea Islands in the company of thousands of black camp followers who had gathered around his army during its march to the sea. To provide for these people, Sherman took steps to establish a class of black freeholders. General Sherman's Order No. 15 granted blacks the right to preempt unsold land not only on the Sea Islands but for thirty miles inland, on the mainland. By 1865 the islands had become a haven for black refugees from all over the South.

The new land policy would yet again be reversed: in August 1865 President Andrew Johnson would order all Sea Island lands returned to their original owners, thus dispossessing most of the blacks anew and leaving them no better or worse off than emancipated slaves elsewhere in the South. But during the Civil War, the islands had fulfilled a unique function. They had provided an arena wherein the Union first supervised emancipation and abolitionists first confronted large numbers of slaves. The scene of pioneer ventures in freedmen's education, black wage labor, and land redistribution, the Sea Islands had served as a testing ground for new social policies.

commanders. "What shall I do about the negroes?" wrote a Union general in Louisiana to army headquarters in 1862:

> *You can form no idea of . . . the appearance of my brigade as it marched down the Bayou. . . . Every soldier had a negro marching in the flanks, carrying his knapsack. Plantation carts, filled with negro women and children, with their effects; and of course compelled to pillage for their subsistence, as I have no rations to issue them. I have a great many more negroes in my camp now than I have whites.*

As 1862 drew to a close, Union commanders in the South were appointing superintendents of freedmen to supervise large contraband camps. Many freedmen served in army camps as cooks, teamsters, and laborers. Some were paid to work on abandoned plantations or were leased out to planters who swore allegiance to the Union and who paid them wages stipulated by the army. Whether confined to contraband camps or working outside of them, many freedmen had reason to question the value of their liberation. Deductions for clothing, rations, and medicine ate up most, if not all, of their earnings. Labor contracts frequently tied them to individual employers for prolonged periods. Moreover, freedmen encountered fierce prejudice among Yankee soldiers, many of whom feared that emancipation would propel blacks north after the war. The best solution to the "question of what to do with the darkies," wrote one northern soldier, "would be to shoot them."

But this was not the whole story. Contrabands who aided the Union army as spies and scouts helped to break down ingrained bigotry. "The sooner we get rid of our foolish prejudice the better for us," a Massachusetts soldier wrote home. Before the end of the war, northern missionary groups and freedmen's aid societies sent agents into the South to work among the freedmen, distribute relief, and organize schools. In March 1865, just before the hostilities ceased, Congress created the Freedmen's Bureau, which had responsibility for the relief, education, and employment of former slaves. The Freedmen's Bureau law also provided that forty acres of abandoned or confiscated land could be leased to each freedman or southern Unionist, with an option to buy after three years. This was the first and only time that Congress provided for the redistribution of confiscated Confederate property.

Black Soldiers in the Union Army

During the first year of war, the Union had rejected black soldiers. Black applicants at northern recruiting offices were sent home, and black companies that had been formed in the occupied South were disbanded. After the second Confiscation Act, Union generals formed black regiments in occupied New Orleans and on the Sea Islands off the coasts of South Carolina and Georgia. Only after the Emancipation Proclamation, however, did large-scale enlistment begin. Leading blacks such as Frederick Douglass and Harvard-educated physician Martin Delany now worked as recruiting agents in northern cities. Douglass grasped the connection between recruiting blacks as soldiers and advancing their claims to citizenship. "Once let the black man get upon his person the brass letters, U.S.; let him get an eagle on his button, and a musket on his shoulder and bullets in his pocket, and there is no power on earth which can deny that he has earned the right to citizenship." Blacks were included in Union drafts, recruiting offices were set up in the loyal border states, and freedmen residing in refugee camps throughout the occupied South were enlisted. By the end of the war, 186,000 blacks had served in the Union army, one-tenth of all Union soldiers. Fully half came from the Confederate states.

White Union soldiers commonly objected to the new recruits on racial grounds. But some, including Colonel Thomas Wentworth Higginson, a liberal minister and former John Brown supporter who headed a black regiment, genuinely welcomed the black soldiers. "Nobody knows anything about these men who has not seen them in battle," Higginson exulted after a successful raid in Florida in 1863. "There is a fierce energy about them beyond anything of which I have ever read, except it be the French Zouaves [French troops in North Africa]." Even Union soldiers who held blacks in contempt pragmatically came to approve of "anything that will kill a rebel." Further, black recruitment offered new opportunities for whites to secure commissions, for blacks served in separate regiments under white officers.

Black soldiers suffered a far higher mortality rate than white troops. Typically assigned to labor detachments or garrison duty, blacks were less likely than whites to be killed in action but more likely to die of disease in the bacteria-ridden garrisons.

Flag of the Second Regiment of U.S. Colored Troops; Black Artillerymen

Black troops were organized late in the war and fought under flags such as these rare colors. The blacks in the photograph belonged to the Second U.S. Colored Light Artillery, which took part in the Battle of Nashville in 1864.

In addition, the Confederacy refused to treat captured black soldiers as prisoners of war, a policy that denied captured blacks the opportunity to be exchanged for Confederate prisoners. Instead, Jefferson Davis ordered all blacks taken in battle to be sent back to the states from which they came, where they were reenslaved or executed. In an especially gruesome incident, when Confederate troops captured Fort Pillow, Tennessee, in 1864, they massacred 262 blacks—an action that provoked outcries but no retaliation from the North.

Well into the war, black soldiers faced inequities in their pay. In contrast to white soldiers, who earned $13.00 a month plus a $3.50 clothing allowance, black privates received only $10.00 a month, with clothing deducted. "We have come out Like men and we Expected to be Treated as men but we have bin Treated more Like Dogs then men," a black soldier complained to Secretary of War Edwin Stanton. In June 1864 Congress belatedly equalized the pay of black and white soldiers.

Although fraught with hardships and inequities, military service was a symbol of citizenship for blacks. It proved that "black men can give blows as well as take them," Frederick Douglass declared. "Liberty won by white men would lose half its lustre." A black private explained: "If we hadn't become sojers, all might have gone back as it was

before. But now things can never go back because we have showed our energy and our courage . . . and our natural manhood." Above all, the use of black soldiers, especially former slaves, was seen by northern generals as a major strike at the Confederacy. "They will make good soldiers," General Grant wrote to Lincoln in 1863, "and taking them from the enemy weakens him in the same proportion they strengthen us."

Slavery in Wartime

Anxious white southerners on the home front felt as if they were perched on a volcano. "We should be practically helpless should the negroes rise," declared a Louisiana planter's daughter, "since there are so few men left at home." When Mary Boykin Chesnut of South Carolina learned that her cousin had been murdered in bed by two trusted house slaves, she became almost frantic. "The murder," Chesnut wrote, "has clearly driven us all wild." To maintain control over their 3 million black slaves, white southerners resorted to a variety of measures. They tightened slave patrols, at times moved entire plantations to relative safety in Texas or in the upland regions of the coastal South, and spread scare stories among the slaves. "The whites would tell the colored people not to go to the Yankees, for they would harness them to carts . . . in place of horses," reported Susie King Taylor, a black fugitive from Savannah.

Wartime developments had a mixed effect on the slaves. Some remained faithful to their masters and mistresses and helped hide treasured family belongings from marauding Union soldiers. Others were torn between loyalty and lust for freedom: one body servant, for example, accompanied his master to war, rescued him when he was wounded, and then escaped on his master's horse. Given a clear choice between freedom and bondage, slaves usually chose freedom. Few slaves helped the northern cause as dramatically as Robert Smalls, a hired-out slave boatman who turned over a Confederate steamer to the Union navy, but most slaves who had a chance to flee to Union lines did so. The idea of freedom had an irresistible attraction. Upon learning from a Union soldier that he was free, a Virginia coachman dressed in his master's clothes, "put on his best watch and chain, took his stick, and . . . told him that he might for the future drive his own coach."

The majority of slaves, however, had no escape and remained on their plantations under the nominal control of their masters. Despite the fears of southern whites, no general uprising of slaves occurred; and the Confederate war effort continued to depend heavily on slave labor. The Confederacy impressed thousands of slaves to work in war plants, to toil as teamsters and cooks in army camps, and to serve as nurses in field hospitals. But wartime conditions reduced the slaves' productivity. With most of the white men off at war, the master-slave relationship weakened on plantations. The women and boys who remained on plantations complained of their difficulty in controlling slaves, who commonly refused to work, performed their labors inefficiently, or spitefully destroyed property. A Texas wife contended that her slaves were "trying all they can, it seems to me, to aggravate me" by neglecting the stock, breaking plows, and tearing down fences. "You may give your Negroes away," she finally wrote despairingly to her husband in 1864.

Whether southern slaves fled to freedom or merely stopped working, they effectively undermined the plantation system. Thus southern slavery was disintegrating even as the Confederacy fought to preserve it. Hard pressed by Union armies, short of manpower, and deeply unsettled by the erosion of plantation slavery, the Confederate Congress in 1864 considered the drastic step of impressing slaves into its army as soldiers in exchange for their freedom at the war's end. Robert E. Lee favored the use of slaves as soldiers on the grounds that if the Confederacy did not arm its slaves, the Union would. Others, however, were adamantly opposed. "If slaves will make good soldiers," a Georgia general argued, "our whole theory of slavery is wrong." Originally hostile to the idea of arming slaves, Jefferson Davis changed his mind in 1865. In March 1865 the Confederate Congress narrowly passed a bill to arm three hundred thousand slave soldiers, although it omitted any mention of emancipation. With the end of the war a few weeks later, however, the plan was never put into effect.

Although the Confederacy's decision to arm the slaves came too late to affect the war, the debate over arming them damaged southern morale by revealing deep internal disagreements concerning war goals. Even before these conflicts had become obvious, the South's military position had started to deteriorate.

The Turning Point of 1863

In the summer and fall of 1863, Union fortunes dramatically improved in every theater of the war. Yet the year began badly for the North. The slide, which had started with Burnside's defeat at Fredericksburg, Virginia, in December 1862, continued into the spring of 1863. Burnside's successor, General Joseph "Fighting Joe" Hooker, a windbag fond of issuing grandiloquent proclamations to his troops, devised a plan to dislodge the Confederates from Fredericksburg by crossing the Rappahannock River north of the town and descending on the rebel rear. But Lee and Stonewall Jackson beat Hooker to the punch by attacking and routing him at Chancellorsville, Virginia, early in May 1863. The battle proved costly for the South, because Jackson was accidentally shot by Confederate pickets and died a few days later. Because Hooker had twice as many men as Lee, however, the Union defeat at Chancellorsville was especially humiliating for the North. "What will the country say?" Lincoln moaned. News from the West was no more

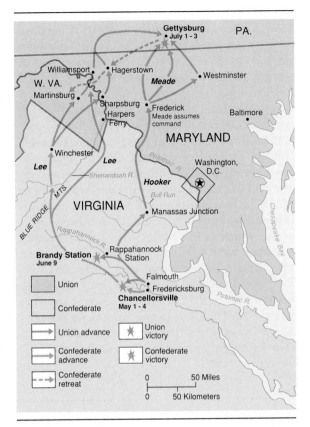

The War in the East, 1863

Victorious at Chancellorsville in May 1863, Lee again invaded Union territory but was decisively stopped at Gettysburg.

heartening for the Union. Although repulsed at Shiloh in western Tennessee, the Confederates still had a powerful army in central Tennessee under General Braxton Bragg. Further, despite repeated efforts, Grant was unable to take Vicksburg; the two-hundred-mile stretch of the Mississippi between Vicksburg and Port Hudson remained in rebel hands.

The upswing in Union fortunes began with Lee's decision after Chancellorsville to invade the North. The decision provoked dissent within the Confederate government, and Lincoln suspected that Lee was making a big mistake, but Lee had his reasons. He needed supplies that war-wracked Virginia could no longer provide, he hoped to panic Lincoln into moving troops from besieged Vicksburg to the eastern theater, and he thought that a major Confederate victory on northern soil would tip the balance in northern politics to the pro-peace Demo-

crats and gain European recognition of the Confederacy. Moving his seventy-five thousand men down the Shenandoah Valley, Lee crossed the Potomac into Maryland and pressed forward into southern Pennsylvania. At this point, with Lee's army now far to the west of Richmond, Hooker recommended a Union stab at the Confederate capital. But Lincoln brushed aside Hooker's advice. "Lee's *army,* and not *Richmond,* is your true objective," Lincoln shot back, and then the president replaced Hooker with the more reliable General George G. Meade.

Early in July 1863, Lee's offensive ground to a halt at a Pennsylvania road junction, Gettysburg. Confederates foraging for shoes in the town encountered some Union cavalry. Soon both sides called for reinforcements, and the war's greatest battle commenced. On July 1 Meade's troops installed themselves in hills south of town along a line that resembled a fishhook: the shank ran along Cemetery Ridge and a northern hook encircled Culp's Hill. By the end of the first day of fighting, most of the troops on both sides had arrived: Meade's army outnumbered the Confederates ninety thousand to seventy-five thousand. On July 2 Lee rejected advice to plant the Confederate army in a defensive position between Meade's forces and Washington and instead attacked the Union flanks, with some success. But because the Confederate assaults were uncoordinated, and some southern generals disregarded orders and struck where they chose, the Union was able to move in reinforcements and regain its earlier losses.

By the afternoon of July 3, believing that the Union flanks had been weakened, Lee attacked Cemetery Ridge in the center of the North's defensive line. After southern cannon shelled the line, a massive infantry force of fifteen thousand Confederates, Pickett's charge, moved in. But as the Confederate cannon sank into the ground and fired a shade too high, and as Union fire wiped out the rebel charge, rifled weapons proved their deadly effectiveness. At the end of the day, Confederate bodies littered the field. "The dead and the dying were lying by the thousands between the two lines," a dazed Louisiana soldier wrote. "The enemy seemed to be launching his cavalry to sweep the remaining handful of men from the face of the earth." A little more than half of Pickett's troops were dead, wounded, or captured in the horrible encounter.

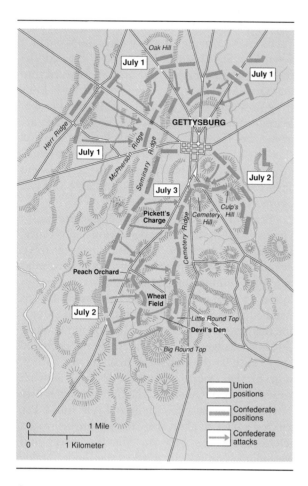

Gettysburg, 1863

The failure of Pickett's charge against the Union center on July 3 was the decisive action in the war's greatest battle.

When Lee withdrew to Virginia on July 4, he had lost seventeen generals and over one-third of his army. Total Union and Confederate casualties numbered almost fifty thousand. Despite the Confederate defeat, Gettysburg was not an exemplary Union victory, since Meade failed to pursue and destroy the retreating southern army. Still, because he had halted Lee's foray into the North, the Union was jubilant.

Almost simultaneously, the North won a less bloody but more strategic victory in the West, where Grant finally solved the puzzle posed by Vicksburg's defenses. Situated on a bluff on the east bank of the Mississippi, Vicksburg was protected on the west by the river and on the north by hills, forests, and swamps. Vicksburg could be attacked only over a thin strip of dry land to its east and south. Positioned to the north of Vicksburg, Grant had to find a way to get his army south of the city and onto the Mississippi's east bank. His solution lay in moving his troops far to the west of the city and down to a point on the river south of Vicksburg. Meanwhile, Union gunboats and supply ships ran past the Confederate batteries overlooking the river at Vicksburg (not without sustaining considerable damage) to rendezvous with Grant's army and transport it across to the east bank. Grant then swung in a large semicircle, first northeastward to capture Jackson, the capital of Mississippi, and then westward back to Vicksburg. After a six-week siege, during which famished soldiers and civilians in Vicksburg were reduced to eating mules and even rats, General John C. Pemberton surrendered his thirty-thousand-man garrison to Grant on July 4, the day after Pickett's charge at Gettysburg. Port Hudson, the last Confederate holdout on the Mississippi, soon surrendered to another Union army. "The Father of Waters flows unvexed to the sea," Lincoln declared.

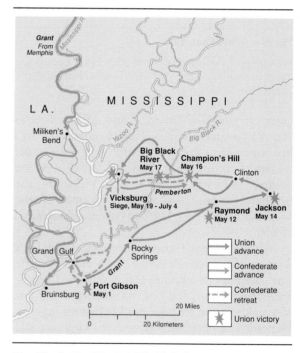

The War in the West, 1863: Vicksburg

Grant first moved his army west of Vicksburg to a point on the Mississippi south of the town. Then he marched northeast, taking Jackson, and finally west to Vicksburg.

Confederate Private James C. Gill

Gill fought at First Bull Run in 1861 and was wounded in 1862. With the help of his brother, who was killed pulling Gill from the field, Gill survived and was promoted to sergeant major. In the vanguard of Pickett's charge at Gettysburg, he was wounded again and died a few days after the battle.

Before the year was out, the Union won another crucial victory in the West. General William S. Rosecrans fought and maneuvered Braxton Bragg's Confederate army out of central Tennessee and into Chattanooga, in the southeastern tip of the state, and then forced Bragg to evacuate Chattanooga. Bragg defeated the pursuing Rosecrans at the Battle of Chickamauga (September 19–20, 1863), one of the bloodiest of the war, and drove him back into Chattanooga. But the arrival of Grant and of reinforcements from the Army of the Potomac enabled the North to break Bragg's siege of Chattanooga in November. With Chattanooga secure, the way lay open for a Union strike into Georgia.

Coming on the heels of reverses that had dri-

ven northern morale to its lowest point of the war, Union successes in the second half of 1863 stiffened the North's will to keep fighting and plunged some rebel leaders into despair. After hearing of the fall of Vicksburg, the Confederacy's ordnance chief, Josiah Gorgas, wrote in his diary: "Yesterday we rode the pinnacle of success—today absolute ruin seems our portion. The Confederacy totters to its destruction."

Totter it might, but the South was fa · from beaten. Although the outcome at Gettysburg quashed southerners' hopes for victory on northern soil, it did not significantly impair Lee's ability to defend Virginia. The loss of Vicksburg and the Mississippi cut the Confederate states west of the river—Arkansas, Louisiana, and Texas—off from those to the east; but these western states could still provide soldiers. Even with the loss of Chattanooga, the Confederacy continued to hold most of the Carolinas, Georgia, Florida, and Mississippi. Few contemporaries thought that the fate of the Confederacy had been sealed.

War and Society, North and South

Extending beyond the battlefields of Gettysburg and Vicksburg, the Civil War engulfed two economies and societies. By 1863 the progress of the war provided stark contrasts: with its superior resources, the Union could meet wartime demands as the imperiled Confederacy could not. But both regions experienced labor shortages and inflation. As the conflict dragged on, both societies confronted problems of disunity and dissent, for war issues opened fissures between social classes. In both regions war encroached on everyday life. Families were disrupted and dislocated, especially in the South. Women on both sides took on new roles at home, in the workplace, and in relief efforts.

The War's Economic Impact: The North

The war had an uneven effect on the Union's economy. Some industries fared poorly. For instance, the loss of southern markets damaged the shoe industry in Massachusetts, where output declined from 45 million pairs in 1855 to 32 million pairs in 1865. A shortage of raw cotton sent the cotton-textile industry into a tailspin that was only partly offset by a rise in the production of woolens. On the other hand, industries directly related to the war effort, such as the manufacture of arms and ready-made clothing, benefited from huge government contracts. By 1865, for example, the ready-made clothing industry was receiving orders for more than a million uniforms a year. Military demand also provided abundant business for the railroads. Some privately owned lines, which had suffered from excess capacity before the war, doubled the volume of their traffic during the war. In 1862 the federal government itself went into the railroad business by establishing the United States Military Railroads (USMRR) to carry troops and supplies to the front. "The quicker you build the railroad," Union general William T. Sherman told his troops, "the quicker you'll get something to eat." By 1865 the USMRR was the world's largest railroad.

The Republicans in Congress actively promoted business development during the war. Holding 102 of 146 House seats and 29 of 36 Senate seats in 1861, they overrode Democratic opposition and hiked the tariff in 1862 and again in 1864 to protect domestic industries. The Republican-sponsored Pacific Railroad Act of 1862 provided for the development of a transcontinental railroad, an idea that had foundered before the war on disagreements over which route such a railroad should follow. With the South out of the picture and no longer able to demand a southern route from New Orleans across the Southwest, Congress chose a northern route from Omaha to San Francisco. Chartering the Union Pacific and Central Railroad corporations, Congress then gave to each large land grants and generous loans. These two corporations combined received more than 60 million acres in land grants and $20 million in loans from the government. The issuance of greenbacks and the creation of a national banking system brought a measure of uniformity to the nation's financial system and facilitated the emergence of a truly national economy.

By raising the federal government's profile in the North's economy, the Republicans hoped to benefit a wide variety of social classes. To a degree, they succeeded. Republican measures like the Homestead Act, passed in 1862, embodied the party's ideal of "free soil, free labor, free men" by

granting 160 acres of public land to settlers after five years of residence on the land. By 1865 twenty thousand homesteaders occupied new land in the West under the Homestead Act. To bring higher education within the reach of the common people, the Republicans secured passage in 1862 of the Morrill Land Grant Act. This law donated to the states proceeds from the sale of public lands—monies that would fund the establishment of universities emphasizing "such branches of learning as are related to agriculture and mechanic arts." The Morrill Act spurred the growth of large state universities, mainly in the Midwest and West. Michigan State, Iowa State, and Purdue universities, among many others, profited from its provisions.

Despite the idealistic goals behind some Republican laws, the war benefited the wealthy more than the average worker. Corrupt contractors grew fat by selling the government substandard merchandise such as the notorious "shoddy," clothing made from compressed rags, which quickly fell apart. Speculators who locked their patriotism in the closet made millions in the gold market. Because the price of gold in relation to greenbacks rose whenever public confidence in the government declined, those who bought gold in the hope that its price would rise actually benefited from Union defeats, and even more from Union disasters. Businessmen with access to scarce commodities also reaped astounding profits. For example, manpower shortages stimulated wartime demand for the mechanical reaper that Cyrus McCormick had patented in 1834. McCormick profited in addition from his distrust of the greenbacks. When paid in greenbacks for reapers, he immediately reinvested greenbacks in pig iron and then watched in glee as wartime demand drove the price of pig iron from twenty-three dollars to forty dollars a ton.

The war had a far less happy impact on ordinary workers. Protected from foreign competition by higher tariffs, northern manufacturers hoisted the prices of finished goods. Wartime excise taxes and inflation combined to push prices still higher. At the same time, wages lagged 20 percent or more behind cost increases for most of the war. This lag in wages, common in most periods of rapid inflation, became especially severe during the war because boys and women poured into government offices and factories as replacements for adult male workers who had joined the army. The proportion of women in the work force in manufacturing rose from one-quarter before the war to one-third during the war. Not only did boys and women draw lower pay than the men whom they had replaced, but employers' mere threats of hiring more youths and females undercut the bargaining power of the men who remained in the work force.

Some workers organized to decry their low wages. "We are unable to sustain life for the price offered by contractors who fatten on their contracts," Cincinnati seamstresses declared in a petition to President Lincoln. Cigar makers and locomotive engineers formed national unions, a process that would accelerate after the war. But organized protests had little impact on wages; employers often denounced worker protests as unpatriotic hindrances to the war effort. In 1864 army troops were diverted from combat to put down protests in war industries from New York to the Midwest.

The War's Economic Impact: The South

While stimulating some sectors of the North's economy, the war shattered the South's. Indeed, if the North and the South are considered together, the overall impact of the war was to retard *American* economic growth. For example, the commodity output of the American economy, which had registered huge increases of 51 percent and 62 percent in the 1840s and 1850s, respectively, rose only 22 percent during the 1860s. Even this modest gain depended wholly on the North, for in the 1860s commodity output in the South actually *declined* 39 percent.

Substantial wartime industrial growth by the South was more than offset by other factors. For example, the war wrecked the South's railroads; in 1864 Union troops, marching through Georgia under General William T. Sherman, tore up railroad tracks, heated them in giant ovens, and twisted them into "Sherman neckties." Cotton production, the foundation of the South's antebellum prosperity, sank from more than 4 million bales in 1861 to 300,000 bales four years later as Union invasions took their toll on production, particularly in Tennessee and Louisiana.

Invading Union troops also occupied the South's food-growing as well as cotton-producing regions.

Moreover, in agricultural areas under Confederate control, the drain of manpower into the army decreased the yields per acre of commodities like wheat and corn. Even the loss of a few carpenters and blacksmiths could disrupt the agricultural economy of rural districts. For example, the drafting of certain of their craftsmen, complained some Alabama petitioners to the federal government in 1863, had left their county "entirely Destitute of any man that is able to keep in order any kind of Farming Tules." Food shortages abounded late in the war. "The people are subsisting on the ungathered crops and nine families out of ten are left without meat," a Mississippi citizen lamented in 1864.

Agricultural shortages worsened the South's already severe inflation. By 1863 salt selling for $1.25 a sack in New York City cost $60.00 in the Confederacy. Food riots erupted in 1863 in Mobile, Atlanta, and Richmond; in Richmond the wives of ironworkers paraded to demand lower food prices.

Part of the blame for the South's food shortages rested with the planter class itself. While some planters heeded government pleas to shift from cotton to food production, many clung to the belief that cotton would never fail them. Although cotton production declined sharply overall, some individual planters still raised more cotton than they could market abroad. The consequences were far-reaching. Slave labor, which could have been diverted to army camps, where slaves might have relieved southern soldiers of menial tasks, remained essential on the labor-intensive cotton plantations, a circumstance that increased the Confederacy's reliance on its unpopular conscription laws. Moreover, cotton continued to sprout from land that could have been used for food production. To feed its hungry armies, the Confederacy had to resort to impressing food from civilians. This policy not only increased popular resentment of planters but also contributed to the South's mounting military desertions. Food-impressment agents usually concentrated on the easiest targets—farms run by the wives of active soldiers. Soldiers found it hard to resist the desperate pleas of their loved ones to return home. The wife of an Alabama soldier wrote to him: "We haven't got nothing in the house to eat but a little bit o meal. I don't want you to stop fighting them Yankees . . . but try and get off and come home and fix us all up some and then you can go back." By the end of 1864, half of the Confederacy's soldiers were absent from their units.

In one respect, the persistence of cotton growing did aid the South, because cotton became the basis for the Confederacy's flourishing trade with the enemy. The United States Congress virtually legalized this trade in July 1861 by allowing northern commerce with southerners loyal to the Union. In practice, of course, it proved impossible to tell whether receipts had fallen into the hands of loyalists or disloyalists, and for most traders it hardly mattered. As long as Union textile mills stood idle for lack of cotton, northern traders happily swapped bacon, salt, blankets, and other necessaries for southern cotton. The Union's penetration of the Confederate heartland both increased the need for trade and eased business dealings between the two sides; after its capture by the Union in 1862, Memphis became a major entrepôt for commerce that filled northern pockets and southern bellies. By 1864 traffic through the lines was providing the South with enough food daily to feed the entire Army of Northern Virginia. To a northern congressman, it seemed that the Union's policy was "to feed an army and fight it at the same time."

Trading with the enemy alleviated the South's food shortages but intensified its morale problems. The prospect of traffic with the Yankees gave planters an incentive to keep growing cotton, a decision that contributed to their unpopularity, and it fattened merchants and middlemen. "Oh! the extortioners," complained a Confederate war-office clerk in Richmond. "Our patriotism is mainly in the army and among the ladies of the South. The avarice and cupidity of men at home could only be exceeded by ravenous wolves."

Dealing with Dissent

Both wartime governments faced mounting dissent and disloyalty. Within the Confederacy, dissent took two basic forms. First, a vocal group of states' rights activists, notably Vice President Alexander Stephens and governors Zebulon Vance of North Carolina and Joseph Brown of Georgia, spent much of the war attacking Jefferson Davis's government as a despotism. Second, loyalty to the Union flourished among a segment of the Confederacy's common people, particularly those living in the Appalachian Mountain region that ran from western

North Carolina through eastern Tennessee and into northern Georgia and Alabama. The nonslaveholding small farmers who predominated here saw the Confederate rebellion as a slaveowners' conspiracy. Resentful of such measures as the "20-Negro" exemption from conscription, they were reluctant to fight for what a North Carolinian defined as "an adored trinity, cotton, niggers, and chivalry." "All they want," an Alabama farmer complained of the planters, "is to get you pupt up and to fight for their infurnal negroes and after you do there fighting you may kiss there hine parts for o they care." On the whole, the Confederate government responded mildly to popular disaffection from the war effort. In 1862 the Congress of the Confederacy gave Jefferson Davis the power to suspend the writ of habeas corpus, but Davis used his power only sparingly, by occasionally and briefly putting areas under martial law, mainly to aid tax collectors.

Lincoln faced similar challenges in the North, where the Democratic minority opposed both emancipation and the wartime growth of centralized power. Although "War Democrats" conceded that war was necessary to preserve the Union, "Peace Democrats" (called Copperheads by their opponents, to suggest a resemblance to a species of easily concealed poisonous snakes) disagreed. Demanding a truce and a peace conference, they charged that administration war policy was intended to "exterminate the South," make reconciliation impossible, and spark "terrible social change and revolution" nationwide.

Strongest in the border states, the Midwest, and the northeastern cities, the Democrats mobilized the support of farmers of southern background in the Ohio Valley and of members of the urban working class, especially recent immigrants, who feared losing their jobs to an influx of free blacks. In 1863 this volatile brew of political, ethnic, racial, and class antagonisms in northern society exploded into antidraft protests in several cities. By far the most violent eruption occurred in July in New York City. Catalyzed by the first drawing of names under the Enrollment Act, and by a longshoremen's strike in which blacks had been used as strikebreakers, mobs of Irish working-class men and women roamed the streets for four days until suppressed by federal troops. The city's laboring Irish loathed the idea of being drafted to fight a war on behalf of the slaves, who, once emancipated, might migrate north to compete with them for low-paying jobs. Too, they bitterly resented the provision of the draft law that allowed the rich to purchase substitutes. The Irish mobs' targets revealed the scope of their grievances. The rioters lynched at least a dozen blacks, injured hundreds more, and burned draft offices, the homes of wealthy Republicans, and the Colored Orphan Asylum.

President Lincoln's speedy dispatch of federal troops to quash these riots typified his forceful approach to dealing with dissent. Throughout the war, Lincoln imposed martial law with far less hesitancy than Davis. After suspending the writ of habeas corpus in Maryland in 1861, he barred it nationwide in 1863 and authorized the arrest of rebels, draft resisters, and those engaged in "any disloyal practice." The differing responses of Davis and Lincoln to dissent underscored the differences between the Confederacy's and the Union's wartime political systems. As we have seen, Davis lacked the institutionalization of dissent provided by party conflict and thus had to tread warily, lest his opponents brand him a despot. In contrast, Lincoln and other Republicans used dissent to rally patriotic fervor against the Democrats. After the New York City draft riots, for example, the Republicans blamed the violence on New York's antidraft Democratic governor, Horatio Seymour. When Seymour, rushing to the city to quell the disturbances, addressed a crowd of rioters as "my friends," the Republican press had a field day in branding the Democrats as disloyal.

Forceful as he was, Lincoln did not unleash a reign of terror against dissent. In general, the North preserved freedom of the press, speech, and assembly. In 1864 the Union became the first warring nation in history to hold a contested national election. Moreover, although some fifteen thousand civilians were arrested during the war, most were quickly released. A few cases, however, aroused widespread concern. In 1864 a military commission sentenced an Indiana man to be hanged for an alleged plot to free Confederate prisoners. The Supreme Court reversed his conviction two years later when it ruled that civilians could not be tried by military courts when the civil courts were open (*Ex parte* Milligan, 1866). Of more concern were the arrests of politicians, notably Clement L. Vallandigham, an Ohio Peace Democrat. Courting

arrest, Vallandigham challenged the administration, denounced the suspension of habeas corpus, proposed an armistice, and in 1863 was sentenced to jail for the rest of the war by a military commission. When Ohio Democrats then nominated him for governor, Lincoln changed the sentence to banishment. Escorted to enemy lines in Tennessee, Vallandigham was left in the hands of bewildered Confederates and eventually escaped to Canada. The Supreme Court refused to review his case.

The Medical War

Despite the discontent and disloyalty of some citizens, both the Union and the Confederacy witnessed a remarkable wartime patriotism that propelled civilians, especially women, to work tirelessly toward alleviating the suffering of soldiers. The United States Sanitary Commission, organized early in the war by civilians to assist the Union's medical bureau, consisted mainly of women volunteers. Described by one woman as a "great artery that bears the people's love to the army," the commission raised funds at "sanitary fairs," bought and distributed supplies, ran special kitchens to supplement army rations, tracked down the missing, and inspected army camps. The volunteers' exploits became legendary. One poor widow, Mary Ann "Mother" Bickerdyke, served sick and wounded Union soldiers as both nurse and surrogate mother. When asked by a doctor by what authority she demanded medical supplies for the wounded, she shot back: "From the Lord God Almighty. Do you have anything that ranks higher than that?"

The nursing corps also exemplifies how women on the home front reached out to aid the battlefront. Before the war ended, some thirty-two hundred women served the Union and the Confederacy as nurses. Already famed for her tireless campaigns on behalf of the insane, Dorothea Dix became the head of the Union's nursing corps. Clara Barton began the war as an obscure clerk in the United States Patent Office, but she, too, greatly aided the medical effort, in finding ingenious ways of channeling medicine to the sick and wounded. Catching wind of Union movements before Antietam, Barton showed up at the battlefield on the eve of the clash with a wagonload of supplies. When army surgeons ran out of bandages and started to dress wounds with corn husks, she raced forward with

Aiding the Sick and Wounded, North and South

Clean and gaily festooned, Carver Hospital in Washington, D.C., was a vast improvement over fetid field hospitals. Belle Boyd served the Confederacy as a nurse and a spy. Twice imprisoned by the Yankees, she later married a Union officer.

lint and bandages. "With what joy," she wrote, "I laid my precious burden down among them." After the war, in 1881, she would found the American Red Cross. The Confederacy, too, had its nurses extraordinary. One, Sally Tompkins, was commissioned a captain for her hospital work; another, Belle Boyd, served the Confederacy as both a nurse and a spy and once dashed through a field, waving her bonnet, to give Stonewall Jackson information. Few nurses got as close to the fighting as Clara Barton, who discovered a bullet hole in her sleeve after Antietam, and Belle Boyd, but danger stalked nurses even in hospitals far from the front. Author Louisa May Alcott, a nurse at the Union Hotel Hospital in Washington, D.C., contracted typhoid. Wherever they worked, nurses witnessed haunting, unforgettable sights. "About the amputating table," one reported, "lay large piles of human flesh— legs, arms, feet, and hands ... the stiffened membrances seemed to be clutching oftentimes at our clothing."

Pioneered by British reformer Florence Nightingale in the 1850s, nursing was a new vocation for women and, in the eyes of many, a brazen departure from women's proper sphere. Male doctors were unsure about how to react to female nurses

and sanitary workers. Some saw the potential for mischief in attractive women's roaming around male hospital wards. But other doctors viewed nursing and sanitary work as potentially useful. The miasm theory of disease (see Chapter 11) commanded wide respect among physicians and stimulated some valuable sanitary measures, particularly in hospitals behind the lines. In partial consequence, the ratio of disease to battle deaths was much lower in the Civil War than in the Mexican War.

Despite improvements, for every soldier killed during the Civil War, two died of disease. "These Big Battles is not as Bad as the fever," a North Carolina soldier wrote. The scientific investigations that would lead to the germ theory of disease were only commencing in Europe during the 1860s. Arm and leg wounds frequently led to gangrene or tetanus, and typhoid, malaria, diarrhea, and dysentery raged through army camps.

Prison camps posed a special problem. Prisoner exchanges between the North and the South, common early in the war, collapsed by the middle of the war, partly because the South refused to exchange the black prisoners that it held and partly because the North gradually concluded that exchanges benefited the manpower-short Confederacy more than the Union. As a result, the two sides had far more prisoners than either could handle. Prisoners on both sides suffered gravely from camp conditions. "This cold weather is not just suited to Southern Constitutions," a Mississippian imprisoned in the Union camp at Rock Island, Illinois, wrote home. As much as southerners suffered in northern camps, the worst conditions plagued southern camps. Squalor and insufficient rations turned the Confederate prison camp at Andersonville, Georgia, into a virtual death camp; three thousand prisoners a month (out of a total of thirty-two thousand) were dying there by August 1864. After the war an outraged northern public demanded and secured the execution of Andersonville's commandant. Although the commandant was partly to blame for camp conditions, the deterioration of the southern economy contributed massively to the wretched state of southern prison camps. The Union camps were not much better, but the fatality rate among northerners held by the South exceeded that of southerners imprisoned by the North.

The War and Women's Rights

Female nurses and Sanitary Commission workers were not the only women to serve society in wartime. In both northern and southern government offices and mills, thousands of women took over jobs vacated by men. Moreover, home industry revived at all levels of society. "Old spinning wheels and handlooms were brought out from dusty corners," a Kentucky woman recalled. "Every scrap of leather was saved for the manufacture of rough shoes." In rural areas, where manpower shortages were most acute, women often did the plowing, planting, and harvesting.

Few women worked more effectively for their region's cause than Philadelphia-born Anna E. Dickinson. After losing her job in the federal mint (for denouncing General George McClellan as a traitor), Dickinson threw herself into hospital volunteer work and public lecturing. Her lecture "Hospital Life," recounting the soldiers' sufferings that she had witnessed, entranced audiences and brought her to the attention of Republican politicians. In 1863, hard pressed by the Democrats, these politicians invited Dickinson to campaign on

behalf of the Republican tickets in New Hampshire and Connecticut. This decision involved considerable risk, for Dickinson was a woman and scarcely twenty-one years old, but it paid handsome dividends for the party. Articulate and poised, Dickinson captured the hearts and votes of her listeners. Soon Republican candidates who had dismissed the offer of aid from a woman were begging her to campaign in their districts.

Mindful of the contributions of Dickinson and others to the Union cause, northern feminists hoped that the war would yield equality for women as well as for slaves. Not only should a grateful North reward women for their wartime services, these women reasoned, but it should recognize the intimate connection between equality for blacks and for women. In 1863 feminists Elizabeth Cady Stanton and Susan B. Anthony organized the National Woman's Loyal League. Although the league's main activity was to gather four hundred thousand signatures on a petition calling for a constitutional amendment to abolish slavery, Stanton and Anthony used the organization to promote woman suffrage as well as equality for blacks.

Despite high expectations, the war did not bring women significantly closer to economic or political equality. Women in government offices and factories continued to be paid less than men. Sanitary Commission workers and most wartime nurses, as volunteers, were paid nothing. Nor did the war produce a major change in the prevailing definition of woman's sphere. In 1860 that sphere already included charitable and benevolent activities; during the war the scope of benevolence was extended to embrace organized care for the wounded. But it was men who continued to dominate the medical profession, and for the remainder of the nineteenth century, nurses would be classified in the census as domestic help.

Feminists' keenest disappointment lay in their failure to capitalize on rising sentiment for the abolition of slavery to secure the vote for women. While the North had compelling reasons to abolish slavery in the rebellious areas of the South, northern politicians could see little practical value in woman suffrage. The *New York Herald,* which supported the Loyal League's attack on slavery, dismissed its call for woman suffrage as "nonsense and tomfoolery." Stanton wrote bitterly, "So long as woman

Southern Women Sewing, Cedar Mountain, Virginia

With their men off to war, southern women ran farms and sewed clothing for the soldiers at the front.

labors to second man's endeavors and exalt his sex above her own, her virtues pass unquestioned; but when she dares to demand rights and privileges for herself, her motives, manners, dress, personal appearance, and character are subjects for ridicule and detraction."

The Union Victorious, 1864–1865

Despite successes at Gettysburg and Vicksburg in 1863, the Union stood no closer to taking Richmond at the start of 1864 than in 1861, and most of the Lower South still remained under Confederate control. The constant press of Union invasion had taken its toll on the South's home front, but the North's persistent inability to destroy the main Confederate armies had eroded the Union's will to keep attacking. Northern war weariness strengthened the Democrats and jeopardized Lincoln's prospects for reelection in 1864.

The year 1864 proved to be crucial for the North. While Grant occupied Lee in the East, a Union army under General William T. Sherman attacked from Tennessee into northwestern Geor-

gia and took Atlanta in early September. The fall of Atlanta not only boosted northern morale but contributed to Lincoln's reelection. Now the curtain began to rise on the last act of the war. After taking Atlanta, Sherman marched unimpeded across Georgia to Savannah, devastated the state's resources, and cracked its morale. Pivoting north from Savannah, Sherman then moved into South Carolina. Meanwhile, having backed Lee into trenches around Petersburg and Richmond, Grant finally forced the evacuation of both cities and brought on the final collapse of the Confederacy.

The Eastern Theater in 1864

Early in 1864 Lincoln made Grant commander of all Union armies and promoted him to lieutenant general. At first glance, the stony-faced Grant seemed an unlikely candidate for so exalted a rank, held previously only by George Washington. Grant, a contemporary noted, "padlocks his mouth, while his countenance in battle or repose . . . indicates nothing." Grant's only distinguishing characteristics were his ever-present cigars and a penchant for whittling sticks into chips. "There is no glitter, no parade about him." But Grant's success in the West had made him the Union's most popular general, perhaps even the Union's most popular person. With his promotion, Grant moved his headquarters to the Army of the Potomac in the East and mapped a strategy for final northern victory.

Like Lincoln, Grant believed that the Union had to coordinate its attacks on all fronts in order to exploit its numerical advantage and prevent the South from shifting troops back and forth between the eastern and western theaters. (The South's victory at Chickamauga in September 1863, for example, had depended in part on reinforcements sent by Lee to Braxton Bragg in the West.) Accordingly, Grant planned a sustained offensive against Lee in the East while ordering William T. Sherman to move against the rebel army in Georgia commanded by Bragg's replacement, General Joseph Johnston. Sherman's mission was "to break it [the Confederate army] up, and to get into the interior of the enemy's country . . . inflicting all the damage you can."

In early May 1864, Grant led 118,000 men against Lee's 64,000 in a forested area near Fredericksburg, Virginia, called the Wilderness. After being checked by Lee in a series of bloody engagements (the Battle of the Wilderness, May 5–7), Grant tried to swing around Lee's right flank, only to suffer new reverses at Spotsylvania on May 12 and Cold Harbor on June 3. These engagements were among the fiercest of the entire war; at Cold Harbor, Grant lost 7,000 men in a single hour. Oliver Wendell Holmes, Jr., a young Union lieutenant and later a Supreme Court justice, wrote home how "immense the butcher's bill has been." But Grant refused to interpret repulses as defeats. Rather, he viewed the engagements at the Wilderness, Spotsylvania, and Cold Harbor merely as less than complete victories. Pressing on, he forced Lee to pull back to the trenches guarding Petersburg and Richmond.

Grant had accomplished a major objective, because once entrenched, Lee could no longer swing around to the Union rear, cut Yankee supply lines, or as at Chancellorsville, surprise the Union's main force. Lee did dispatch General Jubal A. Early on raids down the Shenandoah Valley, which the Confederacy had long used both as a granary and as an indirect way to menace Washington. But Grant countered by ordering General Philip Sheridan to march up the valley from the north and so devastate it that a crow flying over would have to carry its own provisions. The time had come, a Union chaplain wrote, "to peel this land." After defeating Early at Winchester, Virginia, in September 1864, Sheridan controlled the valley.

Sherman in Georgia

While Grant and Lee grappled in the Wilderness, Sherman advanced into Georgia at the head of 98,000 men. Opposing him with 53,000 Confederate troops (soon reinforced to 65,000), General Joseph Johnston retreated slowly toward Atlanta. Johnston's plan was to conserve his strength for a final defense of Atlanta while forcing Sherman to extend his supply lines. But Jefferson Davis, dismayed by Johnston's defensive strategy, replaced him with the more adventurous John B. Hood. Hood, having lost the use of an arm at Gettysburg and a leg at Chickamauga, had to be strapped to his saddle, but for all his physical impairments, he liked to take risks. During a prewar poker game,

he had bet $2,500 with "nary a pair in his hand." Hood promptly gave Davis what he wanted, a series of attacks on Sherman's army. These attacks, however, failed to dislodge Sherman and severely depleted Hood's own army. No longer able to defend Atlanta's supply lines, Hood evacuated his army from the city, which Sherman took on September 2, 1864.

The Election of 1864

Atlanta's fall came at a timely moment for Lincoln, who was in the thick of a tough campaign for reelection. Indeed, Lincoln had secured the Republican renomination with great difficulty. The Radicals, who had earlier flayed Lincoln for delay in adopting emancipation as a war goal, now dismissed his plans to restore the occupied parts of Tennessee, Louisiana, and Arkansas to the Union. The Radicals insisted that Congress, not the president, could alone set the requirements for the readmission of conquered states and criticized Lincoln's reconstruction standards as too lenient. While the Radicals rallied around Secretary of the Treasury Salmon P. Chase for the nomination, the Democrats attacked from a different direction. They had never forgiven Lincoln for making emancipation a war goal, and now the Copperheads, or Peace Democrats, demanded an immediate armistice, followed by negotiations between the North and the South to settle outstanding issues.

Although facing formidable challenges, Lincoln benefited from both his own resourcefulness and that of his political enemies. Playing his hand too quickly and openly, Chase turned the early boom for his nomination into a bust. By the time of the Republican convention in July, Lincoln's managers were firmly in control. Moreover, to isolate the Peace Democrats and attract prowar Democrats, the Republicans formed a temporary organization, the National Union party, and replaced Lincoln's vice president, Hannibal Hamlin, with a prowar southern Unionist, Democratic senator Andrew Johnson of Tennessee. This tactic helped exploit the widening division among the Democrats, who nominated George B. McClellan, the former commander of the Army of the Potomac and an advocate of continuing the war until the Confederacy's collapse, and then ran him on a platform written by the Peace Democrats. McClellan had to spend

The Election of 1864

Candidates	Parties	Electoral Vote	Popular Vote	Percentage of Popular Vote
ABRAHAM LINCOLN	Republican	212	2,206,938	55.0
George B. McClellan	Democratic	21	1,803,787	45.0

much of his campaign trying to distance himself from his party's peace-without-victory platform.

Despite the Democrats' disarray, as late as August 1864, Lincoln seriously doubted that he would be reelected. Leaving little to chance, he arranged for furloughs so that Union soldiers, most of whom supported Lincoln, could vote in states lacking absentee ballots. But in the end it was chance, the timely fall of Atlanta, that immeasurably aided him. Although Hood's army had escaped from the city, a Richmond newspaper conceded that the "disaster at Atlanta" had punctured the antiwar movement in the North and saved Lincoln's presidency. With 55 percent of the popular vote and 212 out of 233 electoral votes, Lincoln swept to victory.

Sherman's March Through Georgia

Meanwhile, Sherman gave the South a new lesson in total war. After evacuating Atlanta, Hood led his Confederate army north toward Tennessee in the hope of luring Sherman out of Georgia. But Sherman did not rise to the bait. The war would never be won, he concluded, by chasing Hood around Tennessee and stretching his own supply lines to the breaking point. Rather, Sherman proposed to abandon his supply lines altogether, march his army across Georgia to Savannah, and live off the countryside as he moved along. He would break the South's will to fight, terrify its people, and "make war so terrible . . . that generations would pass before they could appeal again to it."

Sherman began by burning much of Atlanta and forcing the evacuation of most of its civilian population. This harsh measure relieved him of the need to feed and garrison the city. Then, sending enough troops north to ensure the futility of Hood's campaign in Tennessee, he led the bulk of his army, sixty-two thousand men, out of Atlanta to start the 285-mile trek to Savannah. Soon thousands of slaves were following the army. "Dar's de man dat rules the world," a slave cried on seeing Sherman. Sherman's four columns of infantry, augmented by

Sherman and His Generals

Sherman, shown here seated at center, was a moody and restless man, much like Grant. More than any other Union general, Sherman recognized that the best way to destroy the Confederacy was to undermine its ability to supply southern troops. Ruthless in his march through Georgia and the Carolinas, he nevertheless sought generous terms for the South after the war.

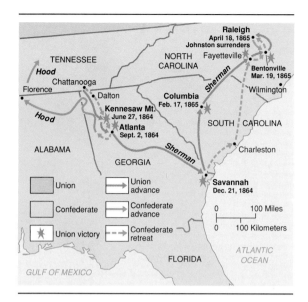

Sherman's March Through the South, 1864–1865

cavalry screens, moved on a front sixty miles wide and at a pace of ten miles a day. They destroyed everything that could aid southern resistance—arsenals, railroads, munitions plants, cotton gins, cotton stores, crops, and livestock. The ruin far exceeded Sherman's orders. Moreover, although Sherman's troops were told not to destroy civilian property, foragers carried out their own version of total war, ransacking and sometimes demolishing homes. Indeed, the havoc seemed a vital part of Sherman's own strategy. By the time that he occupied Savannah and made contact with the Union navy, he estimated that his army had destroyed about a hundred million dollars worth of property. After taking Savannah in December 1864, Sherman's army wheeled north toward South Carolina, the first state to secede and, in the general's view, one "that deserves all that seems in store for her." Sherman's columns advanced unimpeded to Columbia, South Carolina's capital. After fires set by looters, slaves, soldiers of both sides, and liberated Union prisoners gutted much of the city, Sherman headed for North Carolina. By the spring of 1865, his army had left over four hundred miles of ruin. Other Union armies moved into Alabama and Georgia and took thousands of prisoners. Northern forces had penetrated the entire Confederacy, except for Texas and Florida, and crushed much of its wealth. "War is cruelty and you cannot

refine it," Sherman wrote. "Those who brought war into our country deserve all the curses and maledictions a people can pour out."

Toward Appomattox

While Sherman headed north, Grant renewed his assault on the entrenched Army of Northern Virginia. Grant's main objective was Petersburg, a city south of Richmond through which most of the rail lines to the Confederate capital passed. Although Grant had failed on several occasions to overwhelm the Confederate defenses in front of Petersburg, the fall of Atlanta and Sherman's subsequent march through Georgia and into the Carolinas had taken their toll on Confederate morale. Rebel soldiers were accustomed to shortages of food, shoes, and clothing, but now they were burdened as well by a growing feeling of hopelessness. Rebel desertions, proportionally about the same as Union desertions until 1864, reached epidemic proportions in the winter of 1864–1865. Lee reported that hundreds of his men were deserting every night. Reinforced by Sheridan's army, triumphant from its campaign in the Shenandoah Valley, Grant late in March 1865 swung his forces around the western flank of Petersburg's defenders. Lee could not stop him. On April 2 Sheridan smashed the rebel flank at the Battle of Five Forks. A courier bore the grim news to Jefferson Davis, attending church in Richmond: "General Lee telegraphs that he can hold his position no longer."

Davis quickly left his pew, gathered his government, and fled the city. In the morning of April 3, Union troops entered Richmond, pulled down the Confederate flag, and ran up the Stars and Stripes over the capitol. As regiments of white and black troops entered in triumph, explosions set by retreating Confederates left the city "a sea of flames." "Over all," wrote a Union officer, "hung a canopy of dense smoke lighted up now and then by the bursting shells from the numerous arsenals throughout the city." Fires damaged the Tredegar Iron Works. Union troops liberated the town jail, which housed slaves awaiting sale, and its rejoicing inmates poured into the streets. On April 4 Lincoln toured the smoldering city and, for a few minutes, sat at Jefferson Davis's desk with a dreamy expression on his face.

Meanwhile, Lee was making a last-ditch effort to escape from Grant and from Sheridan's envel-

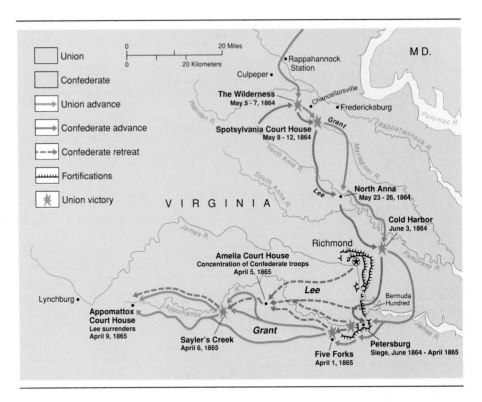

The Final Virginia Campaign, 1864–1865

Grant turned tactical reverses at the Wilderness, Spotsylvania, and Cold Harbor into strategic victories by refusing to abandon his campaign in the face of enormous casualties. He finally succeeded in pushing Lee into defensive fortifications around Petersburg, whose fall doomed Richmond. When Lee tried to escape to the west, Grant cut him off and forced his surrender at Appomattox Court House.

oping movements. Lee's destination was Lynchburg, sixty miles west of Petersburg. He planned to use the rail connections at Lynchburg to join General Joseph Johnston's army, which Sherman had pushed into North Carolina. But Grant and Sheridan swiftly choked off Lee's escape route, and on April 9 Lee bowed to the inevitable. He asked for terms of surrender and met Grant in a private home in the village of Appomattox Courthouse, Virginia, east of Lynchburg. While stunned troops gathered outside, Lee appeared in full dress uniform, with a sword. Grant entered in his customary disarray, smoking a cigar. When Union troops began to fire celebratory salutes, Grant put a stop to it. The final surrender of Lee's army occurred four days later. Lee's troops laid down their arms between federal ranks. "On our part," wrote a Union officer, "not a sound of trumpet . . . nor roll of drum; not a cheer . . . but an awed stillness rather." Grant paroled Lee's twenty-six thousand men and sent them home with their horses and mules "to work their little farms." The remnants of Confederate resistance collapsed within a month of Appomattox. Johnston surrendered to Sherman on April 18. While jubilation swept the North, Jefferson Davis was captured in Georgia on May 10.

Robert E. Lee

Posing in his uniform a few days after the war ended, Lee, as one historian has written, "looked like a perfect soldier, and was."

Grant headed back to Washington. On April 14 he turned down a theater date with the Lincolns, because Julia Grant found first lady Mary Lincoln overbearing. During an English comedy that night at Ford's Theater, an unemployed pro-Confederate actor, John Wilkes Booth, entered Lincoln's box and shot him in the head. Waving a knife, Booth leaped onto the stage shouting the Virginia state motto, *"Sic semper tyrannis"* ("Such is always the fate of tyrants") and then escaped, despite having broken his leg. That same night, one of Booth's accomplices stabbed Secretary of State Seward, who later recovered, while a third conspirator, who had been assigned to Vice President Johnson, failed to attack. Union troops hunted down Booth and shot him within two weeks, or else he shot himself. Of eight accused accomplices, including a woman boarding-house keeper, four were hanged and the rest imprisoned. On April 15, when Lincoln died, Andrew Johnson became president. Six days later Lincoln's funeral train departed on a mournful journey from Washington to Springfield, Illinois, with crowds of thousands gathering at stations to weep as it passed.

Conclusion

The Civil War took a larger human toll than any other war in American history. The death count stood at 360,000 Union soldiers and 260,000 Confederates. Most families in the nation suffered losses. Vivid reminders of the human toll remained to the end of the century and beyond. For many years armless and legless veterans gathered at regimental reunions. Citizens erected monuments to the dead in front of town halls and on village greens. Soldiers' widows collected pensions well into the twentieth century.

The economic costs were staggering, but the war did not ruin the national economy, only the southern part of it. The vast Confederate losses, about 60 percent of southern wealth, were offset by northern advances. At the war's end, the North had almost all of the nation's wealth and capacity for production. Spurring economic modernization, the war provided a hospitable climate for industrial development and capital investment. "The truth is," wrote Ohio senator John Sherman to his brother, General William T. Sherman, "the close of the war with our resources unimpaired gives an elevation, a scope to the ideas of leading capitalists, far higher than anything undertaken in this country before." No longer the largest slaveowning power in the world, the United States would now become a major industrial nation.

The war had political as well as economic ramifications. It created a "more perfect Union" in place of the prewar federation of states. The doctrine of states' rights did not disappear, but it was shorn of its extreme features. There would be no further talk of secession, nor would states ever again exercise their antebellum range of powers. The national banking system, created in 1863, gradually supplanted state banks. The greenbacks provided a national currency. The federal government had exercised powers that many in 1860 doubted that it possessed. By abolishing slavery and imposing an income tax, it asserted power over kinds of private property once thought untouchable. The war also promoted large-scale organization in both the business world and public life. The giant railroad corporation, with its thousands of employees, and the huge Sanitary Commission, with its thousands of auxiliaries and volunteers, pointed out the road that the nation increasingly would take.

Finally, the Civil War fulfilled abolitionist prophecies as well as Unionist goals. The war produced the very sort of radical upheaval within southern society that Lincoln originally said that it would not induce. Beaten Confederates had no idea of what to expect. Some wondered whether blacks and Yankees would permanently take over the South. The same thought occurred to the freedmen. "Hello, massa," a black Union soldier called out when he spotted his former owner among a group of Confederate prisoners whom he was guarding. "Bottom rail top dis time." The nation now turned its attention to the reconstruction of the conquered South and to the fate of 3.5 million newly freed slaves.

CHRONOLOGY

1861 President Abraham Lincoln calls for volunteers to suppress the rebellion (April).

Virginia, Arkansas, Tennessee, and North Carolina join the Confederacy (April–May).

Lincoln imposes a blockade on the South (April).

First Battle of Bull Run (July).

First Confiscation Act (August).

1862 Legal Tender Act (February).

George B. McClellan's Peninsula Campaign (March–July).

Battle of Shiloh (April).

Confederate Congress passes the Conscription Act (April).

David G. Farragut captures New Orleans (April).

Homestead Act (May).

Seven Days' Battles (June–July).

Pacific Railroad Act (July).

Morrill Land Grant Act (July).

Second Confiscation Act (July).

Second Battle of Bull Run (August).

Battle of Antietam (September).

Preliminary Emancipation Proclamation (September).

Battle of Fredericksburg (December).

1863 Emancipation Proclamation issued (January).

Lincoln suspends writ of habeas corpus nationwide (January).

National Bank Act (February).

Congress passes the Enrollment Act (March).

Battle of Chancellorsville (May).

Battle of Gettysburg (July).

Surrender of Vicksburg (July).

New York City draft riots (July).

Battle of Chickamauga (September).

1864 Ulysses S. Grant given command of all Union armies (March).

Battle of the Wilderness (May).

Battle of Spotsylvania (May).

Battle of Cold Harbor (June).

Surrender of Atlanta (September).

Lincoln reelected (November).

William T. Sherman's march to the sea (November–December).

1865 Sherman moves through South Carolina (January–March).

Grant takes Richmond (April).

Robert E. Lee surrenders at Appomattox (April).

Lincoln dies (April).

Joseph Johnston surrenders to Sherman (April).

For Further Reading

David Donald, *Lincoln Reconsidered: Essays on the Civil War Era,* 2d ed. (1956). Explorations of the gamut of Civil War topics, from Lincoln folklore to military history.

David Donald, ed., *Why the North Won the Civil War* (1960). Essays by major historians, analyzing the military, political, diplomatic, and economic reasons for Union victory.

Leon Litwack, *Been in the Storm So Long: The Aftermath of Slavery* (1979). A prizewinning examination of slaves' responses to the process of emancipation, continuing into the Reconstruction era.

James M. McPherson, *Battle Cry of Freedom: The Civil War Era* (1988). An award-winning study of the war years, skillfully integrating political, military, and social history.

Stephen B. Oates, *With Malice Toward None: The Life of Abraham Lincoln* (1977). The most recent one-volume study of Lincoln; an invaluable biography.

James G. Randall and David Donald, *The Civil War and Reconstruction,* 2d ed. (1961). The basic Civil War textbook for decades, notable for clarity and readability.

Emory M. Thomas, *The Confederate Nation, 1861–1865* (1979). An engaging narrative history, emphasizing the rise and fall of southern nationalism, with a complete bibliography.

Additional Bibliography

General

Daniel Aaron, *The Unwritten War* (1973); William L. Barney, *Flawed Victory: A New Perspective on the Civil War* (1975); William R. Brock, ed., *The Civil War* (1969); David P. Crook, *Diplomacy During the Civil War* (1975); Eric Foner, *Politics and Ideology in the Age of the Civil War* (1980); Paul G. Gates, *Agriculture and the Civil War* (1965); Harold Hyman, *A More Perfect Union: The Impact of the Civil War and Reconstruction on the Constitution* (1975); Eric L. McKitrick, "Party Politics in the Union and Confederate War Efforts," in William N. Chambers and Walter D. Burnham, eds., *The American Party System* (1975); James M. McPherson, *Ordeal by Fire: The Civil War and Reconstruction* (1982); Mary Elizabeth Massey, *Bonnet Brigades: American Women and the Civil War* (1966); Allan Nevins, *The War for the Union,* 4 vols. (1959–1971); Edmund Wilson, *Patriotic Gore* (1961).

The Military Experience

Michael Barton, *Good Men: The Character of Civil War Soldiers* (1981); Richard G. Beringer et al., *Why the South Lost the Civil War* (1986); Bruce Catton, *Mr. Lincoln's Army* (1951), *Glory Road* (1952), *A Stillness at Appomattox* (1953), and "Prison Camps of the Civil War," *American Heritage* 10 (August 1959): 4–13; Shelby Foote, *The Civil War: A Narrative,* 3 vols. (1958–1974); Herman Hattaway and Archer Jones, *How the North Won: A Military History of the Civil War* (1984); John T. Hubbell, *Battles Lost and Won: Essays from Civil War History* (1975); Gerald E. Linderman; *Embattled Courage: The Experience of Combat in the American Civil War* (1987).

The Black Experience

Dudley Cornish, *The Sable Arm: Negro Troops in the Union Army* (1956); John Hope Franklin, *The Emancipation Proclamation* (1963); Louis S. Gerteis, *From Contraband to Freedman: Federal Policy Toward Southern Blacks, 1861–1865* (1973); James M. McPherson, ed., *The Negro's Civil War* (1965) and *The Struggle for Equality: Abolitionists and the Negro in the Civil War and Reconstruction* (1964); Benjamin Quarles, *The Negro in the Civil War* (1953); Willie Lee Rose, *Rehearsal for Reconstruction: The Port Royal Experiment* (1964).

The Southern Experience

Thomas B. Alexander and Richard E. Beringer, *The Anatomy of the Confederate Congress* (1972); Paul D. Escott, *After Secession: Jefferson Davis and the Failure of Southern Nationalism* (1978); Douglas Southall Freeman, *R. E. Lee: A Biography,* 4 vols. (1934–1935); Clarence Mohr, *On the Threshold of Freedom: Masters and Slaves in Civil War Georgia* (1986); Robert M. Myers, ed., *The Children of Pride: A True Story of Georgia and the Civil War* (1972); James L. Roark, *Masters Without Slaves: Southern Planters in the Civil War and Reconstruction* (1978); Emory M. Thomas, *The Confederacy as a Revolutionary Experience* (1971); Bell I. Wiley, *The Plain People of the Confederacy* (1943) and *Road to Appomattox* (1956).

The Northern Experience

Adrian Cook, *The Army of the Streets: The New York City Draft Riots of 1863* (1974); Ann Douglas, "The War Within a War: Women Nurses in the Union Army," *Civil War History* 18 (1972), 197–212; George M. Fredrickson, *The Inner Civil War: Northern Intellectuals and the Crisis of the Union* (1965); David Gilchrist and W. David Lewis, eds., *Economic Change in the Civil War Era* (1965); Frank L. Klement, *The Copperheads of the Middle West* (1960) and *Dark Lanterns: Secret Political Societies, Conspiracies, and Treason Trials in the Civil War* (1984); William S. McFeely, *Grant: A Biography* (1981); James H. Moorhead, *American Apocalypse: Yankee Protestants and the Civil War* (1978); Joel Silbey, *A Respectable Minority: The Democratic Party in the Civil War Era, 1860–1868* (1977); George W. Smith and Charles Judah, eds., *Life in the North During the Civil War* (1968); Benjamin Thomas, *Abraham Lincoln* (1952); Hans L. Trefousse, *The Radical Republicans* (1968); T. Harry Williams, *Lincoln and the Radicals* (1942).

Personal Narratives

Eliza Frances Andrews, *Wartime Journal of a Georgia Girl* (1908); David Donald, ed., *Inside Lincoln's Cabinet: The Civil War Diaries of Salmon P. Chase* (1959); Rupert S. Hallard, ed., *The Letters and Diaries of Laura M. Towne* (1970); T. W. Higginson, *Army Life in a Black Regiment* (1867); John B. Jones, *A Rebel War Clerk's Diary* (1935); Mary Ashton Livermore, *My Story of the War* (1881); W. T. Sherman, *Memoirs,* 2 vols. (1886); C. Vann Woodward, ed., *Mary Chesnut's Civil War* (1982).

CHAPTER 15

The Crises of Reconstruction, 1865–1877

When the Civil War ended, parts of the South resembled a wasteland. The landscape "looked for many miles like a broad black streak of ruin and desolation," wrote a Union general, "the fences all gone; lonesome smoke stacks, surrounded by dark heaps of ashes and cinders." Homes, crops, and railroads had been destroyed; farming and business had come to a standstill; and uprooted southerners wandered about. As the Confederate armies dispersed, remnants of regiments made their way home. White refugees who had fled Union armies and burned-out plantations traveled the roads. So did black refugees. Some former slaves returned to areas where they had once lived, in search of relatives from whom they had been separated. Others moved off plantations to test their freedom, to look for work, or to seek relief. "Right off colored folks started on the move," a Texas freedman recalled. "They seemed to want to get closer to freedom—so they'd know what it was—like a place or a city."

The mood of the ex-Confederates was often as grim as the landscape. "The South lies prostrate—their foot is on us—there is no help," a Virginia woman lamented in her diary. Unable to face "southern Yankeedom," some planters considered emigrating to the American West or to Europe, Mexico, or Brazil, and a few hundred did. A large northern presence increased the rebels' dismay: two hundred thousand federal troops occupied the former Confederacy. Northern journalists and government officials also ventured south to investigate conditions and assess rebel attitudes. Their conclusions varied. Chief Justice Salmon P. Chase, on a self-appointed fact-finding mission, insisted that southerners were conciliatory and flexible. "The people are now in a mood to accept almost anything which promises of a definite settlement," he wrote from North Carolina in May 1865. A few days later, a *New York Tribune* reporter, also in North Carolina, sent his editor a harsher view of the ex-Confederates. "They are haughty, exacting, unsubdued, and if possible, *more* devilish than they ever were," he contended. "One would think that we were the subjugated and conquered people and not the rebels."

The mood of the vanquished had rarely, if ever, concerned victorious powers in previous wars. But the Civil War was a special case, for the Union had sought not merely victory but the return of national unity. The questions that the federal government faced in 1865 were therefore unprecedented. First, how could the Union be restored and the defeated South reintegrated into the nation? Would the Confederate states be treated as conquered territories, or would they quickly be readmitted to the Union with the same rights as other states? Who would set requirements for readmission—Congress or the president? Would Confederate leaders be punished for treason? Would their property be confiscated and their political rights curtailed? Most important, what would happen to the more than 3.5 million former slaves? The future of the freedmen constituted *the* crucial issue of the postwar era, for emancipation had set in motion the most profound upheaval in the nation's history. Before the war slavery had been the distinguishing feature of southern society. Both a labor system and a means of racial control, it had determined the South's social, economic, and political structure. What would replace slavery in the postwar South? The end of the Civil War, in short, posed two problems that had to be solved simultaneously: how to readmit the South to the Union and what status the free blacks would enjoy in American society.

Between 1865 and 1877, the drama of Reconstruction unfolded in several theaters. In Washington a conflict between President Andrew Johnson and Congress led to the enactment of a stringent Republican plan for restoring the South to the Union. In the defeated Confederate states, which were first readmitted to the Union under presidential directives, governments were reorganized according to the new congressional measures, and Republicans took power. Throughout the localities of the South, the Reconstruction years spawned far-reaching social and economic changes. Emancipation reshaped black communities, where former slaves sought new identities as free people, and it transformed the southern economy as a new labor system replaced slavery. The North, meanwhile, hurtled headlong into an era of industrial expansion, labor unrest, and financial crises. By the mid-1870s northern politicians of both parties were ready to discard the Reconstruction policies that Congress had initiated in the 1860s. Simultaneously, the southern states were rapidly returning to "home rule," or Democratic control, as Republican regimes toppled one by one. In 1877 Reconstruction collapsed. But the nature and causes of its failure have engaged historians ever since.

Reconstruction Politics

At the end of the Civil War, President Johnson might have exiled, imprisoned, or executed Confederate leaders and imposed martial law indefinitely. Demobilized Confederate soldiers might have continued armed resistance to federal occupation forces. Freedmen might have taken revenge on former owners and the rest of the white community. But none of these drastic possibilities occurred. Instead, intense *political* conflict dominated the three years immediately after the war. In national politics unparalleled disputes produced two new constitutional amendments, a presidential impeachment crisis, and some of the most ambitious domestic legislation ever enacted by Congress, the Reconstruction Acts of 1867–1868. The major outcome of Reconstruction politics was the enfranchisement of black men, a development that few had expected when Lee surrendered.

That black suffrage became the pivot of federal Reconstruction policy proved a major surprise, for in 1865 only a small group of politicians supported such a controversial change. These advocates were all Radical Republicans, a minority faction that had emerged during the war. Led by Senator Charles Sumner of Massachusetts and Congressman Thaddeus Stevens of Pennsylvania, the Radicals had clamored for the abolition of slavery, just as they supported a demanding reconstruction policy, both in wartime and after. Any valid plan to restore the Union, Stevens contended, must "revolutionize Southern institutions, habits, and manners . . . or all our blood and treasure have been spent in vain." But the Radicals, outnumbered by moderate and conservative Republicans in the Thirty-ninth Congress, and opposed by the Democratic minority, seemingly had little chance of success. Nonetheless, in the complex political battles of 1865–1868, the Radicals managed to win the support of a majority of Republicans for parts of their Reconstruction program, including black male enfranchisement. Just as civil war had led to emancipation, a goal once supported by only a minority of Americans, so Reconstruction policy became bound to black suffrage, a momentous change that originally had only narrow political backing.

Lincoln's Plan

Conflict over Reconstruction began even before the war ended. In December 1863 President Lincoln issued the Proclamation of Amnesty and Reconstruction, which outlined a path by which each southern state could rejoin the Union. Under Lincoln's plan a minority of voters (equal to at least 10 percent of those who had cast ballots in the election of 1860) would have to take an oath of allegiance to the Union and accept emancipation. This minority could then create a loyal state government. But Lincoln's plan excluded some southerners from taking the oath: Confederate government officials, army and naval officers, as well as those military or civil officers who had resigned from Congress or from U.S. commissions in 1861. All such persons would have to apply for presidential pardons. Also excluded, of course, were blacks, who had not been voters in 1860. Lincoln hoped through his wartime "10 percent plan" to undermine the Confederacy by establishing pro-Union governments within it. Characteristically, the Republican Lincoln had partisan goals, too. He wanted to win the allegiance of southern Unionists (those who had opposed secession), especially former Whigs, and to build a southern Republican party.

Radical Republicans in Congress, however, envisioned a slower, more exacting readmission process that would exclude even more ex-Confederates from political life. Their plan won the backing of almost all Republicans, who agreed that Lincoln's program was too weak. Thus in July 1864 Congress enacted the Wade-Davis bill, which provided that each former Confederate state would be ruled by a military governor. Under the Wade-Davis plan, after at least half the eligible voters took an oath of allegiance to the Union, delegates could be elected to a state convention that would repeal secession and abolish slavery. But to qualify as a voter or delegate, a southerner would have to take a second, "ironclad" oath, swearing that he had never voluntarily supported the Confederacy. Like the 10 percent plan, the congressional plan did not provide for black suffrage, a measure then supported by only some of the Radicals. Unlike Lincoln's plan, however, the Wade-Davis scheme would have delayed the readmission process almost indefinitely.

Claiming that he did not want to bind himself to any single restoration policy, Lincoln pocket-vetoed* the Wade-Davis bill. The bill's sponsors, Senator Benjamin Wade of Ohio and Congressman Henry Winter Davis of Maryland, blasted Lin-

---

*Pocket veto: failure to sign a bill within ten days of the adjournment of Congress.

coln's act as an outrage. By the end of the war, the president and Congress had reached an impasse. Arkansas, Louisiana, Tennessee, and parts of Virginia under Union army control moved toward readmission under variants of Lincoln's plan. But Congress refused to seat their delegates, as it had a right to do. Lincoln, meanwhile, gave hints that a more rigorous Reconstruction policy might be in store. In his last speech (April 1865), he revealed that he favored some form of black suffrage, perhaps for blacks who had served in the Union army. He also entertained Secretary of War Stanton's proposal for temporary military occupation of the South. What Lincoln's ultimate policy would have been remains unknown. But at the time of his death, Radical Republicans turned with hope toward his successor, Andrew Johnson of Tennessee, in whom they felt that they had an ally.

Presidential Reconstruction Under Johnson

The only southern senator to remain in Congress when his state seceded, Andrew Johnson had worked amicably with Radical Republicans in wartime and had served as military governor of Tennessee from 1862 to 1864. He had taken a strong anti-Confederate stand, declaring, for example, that "treason is a crime and must be made odious," and had urged punishment of active Confederates. Above all, Johnson had long sought the destruction of the planter aristocracy, a goal that dominated his political career. A self-educated man of humble North Carolina origins, Johnson had moved to Greenville, Tennessee in 1826 and become a tailor. His wife, Eliza McCardle, had taught him how to write. An ardent Jacksonian, he had entered politics in the 1830s as a spokesman for nonslaveowning whites and risen rapidly from local official to congressman to governor to senator. Once the owner of eight slaves, Johnson reversed his position on slavery during the war. When emancipation became Union policy, he supported it, and as military governor, he assured Tennessee blacks that he would be their "Moses." But Johnson neither adopted abolitionist ideals nor challenged racist sentiments. He hoped mainly that the fall of slavery would injure southern aristocrats. Andrew Johnson, in short, had his own political agenda, which, as Republicans would soon learn, did not coincide

Andrew Johnson

When Vice President Johnson became president at Lincoln's death in April 1865, many Republicans expected him to impose "harsh terms" upon the defeated South.

with theirs. Moreover, he was a lifelong Democrat who had been added to the Republican, or National Union, ticket in 1864 to broaden its appeal and who had become president by accident.

Many Republicans voiced shock when Johnson announced a new plan for the restoration of the South in May 1865—with Congress out of session and not due to convene until December. The president presented his program as a continuation of Lincoln's plan, but in fact, it was very much his own. He explained in two proclamations how the seven southern states still without reconstruction governments could return to the Union. Almost all southerners who took an oath of allegiance would receive a pardon and amnesty, and all their property except slaves would be restored. Oath takers could elect delegates to state conventions, which would provide for regular elections. Each state convention, Johnson later added, would have to proclaim the illegality of secession, repudiate state debts incurred when the state belonged to the Confederacy, and ratify the Thirteenth Amendment,

which abolished slavery. (Proposed by an enthusiastic wartime Congress early in 1865, the amendment would be ratified in December of that year.) As under Lincoln's plan, all Confederate civil and military officers would be excluded from the oath needed for voting. But Johnson added a new disqualification. All well-off ex-Confederates, those with taxable property worth $20,000 or more, would also be barred from political life. Such an exclusion, said Johnson, would benefit "humble men, the peasantry and yeomen of the South, who have been decoyed . . . into rebellion." Johnson seemed to be planning a purge of aristocratic leadership. Poorer white southerners would now be in control.

Presidential Reconstruction took effect in the summer of 1865, supervised by provisional governors. But it had unforeseen consequences. Those southerners disqualified on the basis of wealth or high Confederate position applied for pardons in droves. Either gratified by their supplications or seeking support for reelection in 1868, Johnson handed out pardons liberally—some thirteen thousand of them. He also dropped plans for the punishment of treason. By the end of 1865, all seven states had created new civil governments to replace military rule, but in other ways the states had almost returned to the status quo ante bellum. Confederate army officers and large planters assumed state offices. Former Confederate congressmen, state officials, and generals were elected to serve in Congress. (Most of these new representatives were former Whigs who had not supported secession; southerners thought that they were electing "Union" men.) Georgia sent Alexander Stephens, the former Confederate vice president and a onetime Unionist, back to Congress as a senator. Some states refused to ratify the Thirteenth Amendment or to repudiate their Confederate debts.

Most important, all states took steps to ensure a landless, dependent black labor force—in one Alabamian's words, to "secure the services of the negroes, teach them their place." This goal was achieved through the "black codes," which replaced the slave codes, the state laws that had regulated slavery. Because the ratification of the Thirteenth Amendment was assured by the terms of Johnson's Reconstruction plan, all states guaranteed the freedmen some basic rights. They could marry, own property, make contracts, and testify in court against other blacks. But the important parts of the black codes were their restrictions, which varied from state to state. Some codes established racial segregation in public places; most prohibited racial intermarriage, jury service by blacks, and court testimony by blacks against whites. All codes included economic restrictions that would prevent former slaves from leaving the plantations. South Carolina required special licenses for blacks who wished to enter nonagricultural employment. Mississippi prohibited blacks from buying and selling farmland. Most states required annual contracts between landowners and black agricultural workers and provided that blacks without lawful employment would be arrested as vagrants and auctioned off to employers who would pay their fines.

The black codes established a halfway status for the southern freedmen, who, while no longer slaves, were not really liberated either. Although "free" to sign labor contracts, for instance, those who failed to sign them would be considered in violation of the law and swept back into involuntary servitude. The black codes thus solidified the alliance between planters and local law-enforcement agents—a white power structure with control over black labor. In practice, many clauses in the codes never took effect: the Union army and the Freedmen's Bureau swiftly suspended the enforcement of racially discriminatory provisions of the new laws. But the black codes were important indicators of white southern intentions. They showed what "home rule" would have been like without federal interference.

When former abolitionists and Radical Republicans decried the black codes, Johnson defended the codes and his restoration program. Ex-Confederates, he contended, should not be forced back into the Union as "a degraded and debased people." Many northerners, however, perceived signs of southern defiance: voters had elected ex-rebels to public office; southern conventions had been reluctant to repudiate secession or slow to pronounce slavery dead; and new laws had robbed freedmen of basic rights. "What can be hatched from such an egg but another rebellion?" asked a Boston newspaper. Republicans in Congress agreed. When the Thirty-ninth Congress convened in December 1865, it refused to seat the delegates of the ex-Confederate states. Establishing the Joint (House-Senate) Committee on Reconstruction,

Republicans prepared to dismantle the black codes and lock ex-Confederates out of power.

Congress Versus Johnson

The status of the southern blacks now became the major issue in Congress. "This is not a 'white man's government,'" exclaimed Republican congressman Thaddeus Stevens. "To say so is political blasphemy." But Radical Republicans like Stevens—who hoped to impose black suffrage on the former Confederacy, delay the readmission of the southern states into the Union, and transform the South into a biracial democracy—still constituted a congressional minority. Conservative Republicans, who tended to favor the Johnson plan, formed a minority too, as did the Democrats, who also supported the president. Moderate Republicans, the largest congressional bloc, agreed with the Radicals that Johnson's plan was too feeble. But they did not believe that northern voters would support black suffrage, and they wanted to avoid a dispute with the president. Since none of the four congressional blocs even approached the two-thirds majority required to overturn a presidential veto, Johnson's program would stay in place unless the moderates and the Radicals joined forces. The impetus for creating this alliance came from an unexpected source—Andrew Johnson himself, who soon alienated a majority of moderates and pushed them into the Radicals' arms.

The moderate Republicans supported two proposals drafted by one of their own, Senator Lyman Trumbull of Illinois, to invalidate the black codes. These measures won wide Republican support. In the first, Congress voted to continue the Freedmen's Bureau, established in 1865, whose term was coming to an end. This agency, headed by former Union general O. O. Howard and staffed mainly by army officers, was a major federal arm in the South. It provided relief, rations, and medical care; built schools for the freedmen; put them to work on abandoned or confiscated lands; and tried to protect their rights as laborers. Congress voted not only to extend the bureau's life for three years but to give it new power: it could run special military courts to settle labor disputes and could invalidate labor contracts forced on freedmen by the black codes. In February 1866 Johnson vetoed the Freedmen's Bureau bill. The Constitution, he declared, did not sanction military trials of civilians in peacetime, nor did it support a system to care for "indigent persons."

In March 1866 Congress passed a second measure proposed by Trumbull, a bill that made blacks U.S. citizens with the same civil rights as other citizens and gave the federal government the right to intervene in the states to ensure black rights in court. Johnson vetoed the civil-rights bill also. He argued that it would "operate in favor of the colored and against the white race." But in April Congress overrode his veto; the Civil Rights Act of 1866 was the first major law ever passed over a presidential veto. Then in July Congress enacted the Supplementary Freedmen's Bureau Act over Johnson's veto as well.

Johnson's vetoes bewildered many Republicans because the new laws did not undercut the basic structure of presidential Reconstruction. The president insisted, however, that both bills were illegitimate because southerners had been shut out of the Congress that passed them. His stance won support not only from the South but from northern Democrats, who were fast becoming the president's constituency. After the civil-rights veto, one New England Democrat praised Johnson for his opposition to "compounding our race with niggers, gypsies, and baboons." But the president had alienated the moderate Republicans, who rejected his arguments and began to work with the Radicals against him. Johnson had lost "every friend he has," one moderate legislator declared.

Some historians view Andrew Johnson as a political incompetent who, at this crucial turning point, bungled both his readmission scheme and his political future. Others contend that he was merely trying to forge a coalition of the center, made up of Democrats and non-Radical Republicans. In either case, Johnson underestimated the possibility of Republican unity. Once united, the Republicans moved on to a third step: the passage of a constitutional amendment that would prevent the Supreme Court from invalidating the new Civil Rights Act and would block Democrats in Congress from repealing it.

The Fourteenth Amendment

In April 1866 Congress adopted the Fourteenth Amendment, which had been proposed by the Joint Committee on Reconstruction. To protect blacks' rights, the amendment declared in its first clause that all persons born or naturalized in the United States were citizens of the nation and citizens of their states and that no state could abridge their rights without due process of law or deny them equal protection of the law. This section nullified the *Dred Scott* decision of 1857 (see Chapter 13), which had declared that blacks were not citizens. Second, the amendment guaranteed that if a state denied suffrage to any of its male citizens, its representation in Congress would be proportionally reduced. This provision did not guarantee black suffrage, but it threatened to deprive southern states of some of their legislators if black men were denied the vote. Third, the amendment disqualified from state and national office *all* prewar officeholders—civil and military, state and federal—who had supported the Confederacy, unless Congress removed their disqualifications by a two-thirds vote. In so providing, Congress intended to invalidate Johnson's wholesale distribution of amnesties and pardons. Finally, the amendment repudiated the Confederate debt and maintained the validity of the federal debt.

The Fourteenth Amendment was the most ambitious step that Congress had yet taken. It revealed the growing receptivity among Republican legislators to the Radicals' demands, including black enfranchisement. It reflected the Republican consensus that southern states would not deal fairly with blacks unless forced to do so. Most important, it was the first national effort to limit state control of civil and political rights. With its passage a huge controversy erupted. Abolitionists decried the second clause as a "swindle" because it did not explicitly ensure black suffrage. Southerners and northern Democrats condemned the third clause as vengeful. Southern legislatures, except for Tennessee's, refused to ratify the amendment, and President Johnson denounced it. His intransigence solidified the new alliance between the moderate and Radical Republicans. It also turned the congressional elections of 1866 into a referendum on the Fourteenth Amendment.

Over the summer Johnson set off on a whistle-stop train tour from Washington to St. Louis and Chicago and back, speaking to the public at railroad stations along the way. But this innovative campaign tactic—the "swing around the circle," as Johnson called it—was a debacle. Humorless and defensive, the president argued with his audiences and made fresh enemies. His hope of creating a new National Union party, composed of Democrats and conservative Republicans who opposed the Fourteenth Amendment, thus made little headway. Moderate and Radical Republicans, meanwhile, defended the amendment, condemned the president, and branded the Democratic party "a common sewer . . . into which is emptied every element of treason, North and South."

When the votes in the congressional elections were tallied, Republican candidates won in a landslide, often with even greater margins of victory than in 1864. In the Fortieth Congress, which would convene in March 1867, Republicans would outnumber Democrats almost two to one in the House and almost four to one in the Senate. In the interim the Republicans had secured a mandate to overcome southern resistance to the Fourteenth Amendment and to enact their own Reconstruction program, even if the president vetoed every part of it.

Congressional Reconstruction

The congressional debate over how to reconstruct the South began in December 1866 and lasted three months. To stifle a resurgence of Confederate power, Radical Republican leaders called for black suffrage, federal support for public schools, confiscation of Confederate estates, and an extended period of military occupation in the South. Reducing the ex-Confederate states to the status of territories, they believed, would enable Republicans to make the South over in the image of an idealized North, with "small farms, thrifty tillage, free schools . . . respect for honest labor and for equality of political rights." Moderate Republicans, who once would have rejected such a plan as too extreme, were now willing to accept parts of it. Legislators debated every ramification, including the constitutional question of whether the southern states had in fact seceded from the Union during the war; many issues grew so involved that one senator, who had lost the thread of a debate, complained that "the arguments seem to be drawn so fine that it [the subject at hand] has almost passed from my perception." In February 1867 after complex legislative maneuvers and many late-night sessions, Congress passed the Reconstruction Act of 1867, and, after Johnson vetoed it, repassed the law on March 2. Later that year and in 1868, Congress passed three further Reconstruction acts, all enacted over presidential vetoes, to refine and enforce the first.

The Reconstruction Act of 1867 invalidated the state governments formed under the Lincoln and Johnson plans and all the legal decisions made by those governments. Only Tennessee, which had ratified the Fourteenth Amendment and had been readmitted to the Union, escaped further reconstruction. The new law divided the other ten former Confederate states into five temporary military districts, each run by a Union general. Voters—all black men, plus those white men who had not been disqualified by the Fourteenth Amendment—

King Andrew

This Thomas Nast cartoon published in Harper's Weekly *just before the 1866 congressional elections conveyed Republican antipathy to Andrew Johnson. The president is depicted as an autocratic tyrant. Radical Republican Thaddeus Stevens, upper right, has his head on the block and is about to lose it. The Republic sits in chains.*

Major Reconstruction Legislation

Law	Provisions	Date of Congressional Passage	Purpose
Civil Rights Act of 1866	Declared blacks citizens and guaranteed them equal protection of the laws.	April 1866*	To invalidate the black codes.
Supplementary Freedmen's Bureau Act	Extended the life of the Freedmen's Aid Bureau and expanded its powers.	July 1866*	To invalidate the black codes.
Reconstruction Act of 1867	Invalidated state governments formed under Lincoln and Johnson. Divided the former Confederacy into five military districts. Set forth requirements for readmission of ex-Confederate states to the Union.	March 1867*	To replace presidential Reconstruction with a more stringent plan.
Supplementary Reconstruction Acts			To enforce the First Reconstruction Act.
Second Reconstruction Act	Required military commanders to initiate voter enrollment.	March 1867*	
Third Reconstruction Act	Expanded the powers of military commanders.	July 1867*	
Fourth Reconstruction Act	Provided that a majority of voters, however few, could put a new state constitution into force.	March 1868*	
Army Appropriations Act	Declared (in a rider to the main law) that military orders could be issued only by the general of the army.	March 1867*	To prevent President Johnson from obstructing Reconstruction.

(continued)

*Passed over Johnsons's veto.

Law	Provisions	Date of Congressional Passage	Purpose
Tenure of Office Act	Prohibited the president from removing any federal official without consent of the Senate.	March 1867*	To prevent President Johnson from obstructing Reconstruction.
Omnibus Act	Readmitted seven ex-Confederate states to the Union.	June 1868†	To restore the Union, under the terms of the First Reconstruction Act.
Enforcement Act of 1870	Provided for the protection of black voters.	May 1870‡	To enforce the Fifteenth Amendment.
Second Enforcement Act	Provided for federal supervision of southern elections.	February 1871	To enforce the Fifteenth Amendment.
Third Enforcement Act (Ku Klux Klan Act)	Strengthened sanctions against those who prevented blacks from voting.	April 1871	To combat the Ku Klux Klan and enforce the Fourteenth Amendment.
Amnesty Act	Restored the franchise to almost all ex-Confederates.	May 1872	Effort by Grant Republicans to deprive Liberal Republicans of a campaign issue.
Civil Rights Act of 1875	Outlawed racial segregation in transportation and public accommodations and prevented exclusion of blacks from jury service.	March 1875§	To honor the late senator Charles Sumner.

*Passed over Johnson's veto.
†Georgia was soon returned to military rule. The last four states were readmitted in 1870.
‡Sections of the law declared unconstitutional in 1876.
§Invalidated by the Supreme Court in 1883.

could elect delegates to a state convention that would write a new state constitution granting black suffrage. When eligible voters ratified the new constitution, elections could be held for state officers. Once Congress approved the state constitution, once the state legislature ratified the Fourteenth Amendment, and once the amendment became part of the federal Constitution, Congress would readmit the state into the Union—and Reconstruction, in a constitutional sense, would be complete.

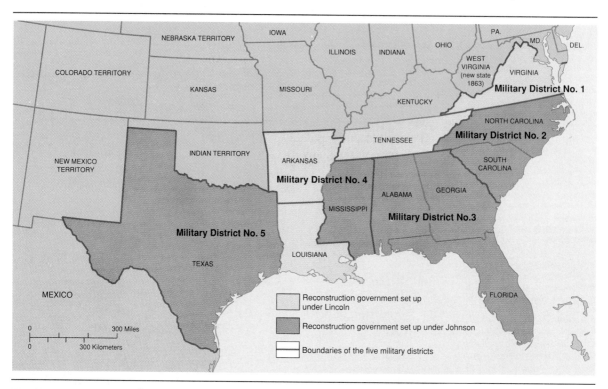

The Reconstruction of the South

The Reconstruction Act of 1867 divided the former Confederate states, except Tennessee, into five military districts and set forth the steps by which new state governments could be created.

The Reconstruction Act of 1867 was far more radical than the Johnson program because it enfranchised blacks and disfranchised many ex-Confederates. It fulfilled a central goal of the Radical Republicans: delaying the readmission of former Confederate states until Republican governments could be established and thereby preventing an immediate rebel resurgence. But the new law was not as severe toward former Confederates as it might have been. It provided for only temporary military rule. It did not prosecute Confederate leaders for treason or permanently exclude them from politics. Most important, it made no provision for the confiscation or redistribution of property.

During the congressional debates, Radical Republican congressman Thaddeus Stevens had argued for the confiscation of large Confederate estates to "humble the proud traitors" and to provide for the former slaves. In March 1867 he had proposed subdividing such confiscated property into forty-acre tracts to be distributed among the freedmen. The remainder of the confiscated land, some 90 percent of it, would be sold to pay off war debts.

Stevens wanted to crush the planter aristocracy and create a new class of self-sufficient black yeoman farmers. Political independence rested on economic independence, he contended; land grants would be more valuable to the freedmen than the right of suffrage, although both were deserved. Stevens's land-reform bill won the support of other Radicals, but it never made progress, for most Republicans held property rights sacred. Tampering with such rights in the South, they feared, would jeopardize them in the North. Moreover, Stevens's proposal would alienate southern ex-Whigs from the Republican cause, antagonize other white southerners, and thereby endanger the rest of Reconstruction. Thus land reform never came about. The "radical" Reconstruction acts were a compromise.

Congressional Reconstruction took effect in the spring of 1867. But it could not be enforced without military power, and Johnson, as commander in chief, controlled the army. When he impeded the congressional plan by replacing military officers sympathetic to the Radical cause with conservative ones, Republicans seethed. More suspicious than ever of the president and frustrated by his roadblocks, congressional moderates and Radicals once again joined forces to block Johnson from obstructing Reconstruction.

The Impeachment Crisis

In March 1867 Republicans in Congress passed two laws to limit presidential power. The Tenure of Office Act prohibited the president from removing civil officers without Senate consent. Cabinet members, the law stated, were to hold office "during the term of the president by whom they may have been appointed" and could be fired only with the Senate's approval. The goal was to bar Johnson from dismissing Secretary of War Stanton, the Radicals' ally, whose support Congress needed to enforce the Reconstruction acts. The second law, a rider to an army appropriations bill, prohibited the president from issuing military orders except through the commanding general, Ulysses S. Grant, who could not be removed without the Senate's consent.

The Radicals' enmity to Johnson, however, would not die until he was out of office. They began to look for grounds on which to impeach him and convict him and thereby remove all potential obstacles to congressional Reconstruction. The House Judiciary Committee, aided by private detectives, could at first uncover no valid charges against Johnson. On a second try, they produced some charges, but the House found them inade-quate. Just as impeachment efforts seemed a lost cause, Johnson again came to his opponents' rescue by providing the charges that they needed.

In August 1867, with Congress out of session, Johnson suspended Secretary of War Stanton and replaced him with General Grant. In early 1868 the reconvened Senate refused to approve Stanton's suspension, and Grant, sensing the Republican mood, vacated the office. Johnson then removed Stanton and replaced him with another general, the aged Lorenzo Thomas. Johnson's defiance forced Republican moderates, who had at first resisted impeachment, into yet another alliance with the Radicals: the president had "thrown down the gauntlet," a moderate charged. The House approved eleven charges of impeachment, nine of them based on violation of the Tenure of Office Act. The other charges accused Johnson of being "unmindful of the high duties of office," of seeking to disgrace Congress, and of failing to enforce the Reconstruction acts.

Johnson's trial, which began in the Senate in March 1868, riveted public attention for eleven weeks. Seven congressmen, including leading Radical Republicans, served as prosecutors or "managers," while prominent attorneys represented the president. Johnson's lawyers maintained that he was merely seeking a court test by violating the Tenure of Office Act, which he thought was unconstitutional. They also contended, somewhat inconsistently, that the law did not protect Secretary Stanton, an appointee of Lincoln, not Johnson. Finally,

The Impeachment Managers

Seven Radical Republicans, chosen by the House of Representatives, served as impeachment "managers" at President Johnson's Senate trial in 1868. Benjamin F. Butler of Massachusetts, seated, far left, a criminal lawyer, assumed the role of chief prosecutor. Thaddeus Stevens, gaunt and haggard, seated next to Butler, spoke less but still dominated the proceedings. "If you don't kill the beast, it will kill you," he told Republican colleagues. Civil War photographer Mathew B. Brady captured the seven managers with his camera.

they asserted, Johnson was guilty of no crime indictable in a regular court.

The congressional "managers" countered that impeachment was a political process, not a criminal trial, and that Johnson's "abuse of discretionary power" constituted an impeachable offense. Although Senate opinion split along party lines and Republicans outnumbered Democrats, some Republicans wavered, fearing that the removal of a president would destroy the balance of power among the three branches of the federal government. They also distrusted Radical Republican Benjamin Wade, the president pro tempore of the Senate, who, because there was no vice president, would accede to the presidency if Johnson were thrown out.

Intense pressure from colleagues and constituents bombarded the wavering Republican senators, whose votes would prove crucial. Late in May 1868, the suspenseful trial reached its climax. The Senate voted against Johnson 35 to 19, one vote short of the two-thirds majority needed for conviction. Seven Republicans had risked political suicide and sided with the twelve Senate Democrats in voting against removal. In so doing, they set a precedent. Future presidents would not be impeached solely on political grounds or because two-thirds of Congress disagreed with them. But the anti-Johnson forces had also achieved their goal: Andrew Johnson had no future as president. After serving out his term, he returned to Tennessee, where he was reelected to the Senate five years later. Republicans in Congress, meanwhile, pursued their last major Reconstruction objective: to guarantee black suffrage.

The Fifteenth Amendment

Black suffrage was the linchpin of congressional Reconstruction. Only with the support of black voters could Republicans secure control of the ex-Confederate states, and only with the vote could southern blacks protect their own rights. The Fourteenth Amendment had promoted black suffrage indirectly, by threatening a penalty where it was denied. The Reconstruction Act of 1867, however, forced every southern state legislature to enfranchise black men as a prerequisite for readmission to the Union. But while black voting had begun in the South, much of the North had rejected it. At the end of the Civil War, only five New England states enfranchised black men; so did New York, on the condition that they owned property. Between 1867 and 1869, nine referenda in northern states defeated proposals for black suffrage. Iowa voters alone extended the franchise to blacks. Congressional Republicans therefore had two aims. They sought to protect black suffrage in the South against future repeal by Congress or the states and to enfranchise northern and border-state blacks, who would presumably vote Republican. To achieve these goals, Congress in 1869 proposed the Fifteenth Amendment, which prohibited the denial of suffrage by the states to any citizen on account of race, color, or previous condition of servitude.

Democrats argued that the proposed amendment violated states' rights by denying each state the power to determine who would vote. But Democrats did not control enough states to defeat the amendment and it was ratified in 1870. Four votes came from those ex-Confederate states—Mississippi, Virginia, Georgia, and Texas—that had delayed the Reconstruction process and were therefore forced to approve the Fifteenth Amendment, as well as the Fourteenth, in order to rejoin the Union. Some southerners contended that the new amendment's omissions made it acceptable, for it had, as a Richmond newspaper pointed out, "loopholes through which a coach and four horses can be driven." What were these loopholes? The Fifteenth Amendment did not guarantee black officeholding, nor did it prohibit voting restrictions such as property requirements and literacy tests. Such restrictions might be used to deny blacks the vote, and indeed, ultimately they were so used.

The controversy over black suffrage not only permeated national politics but drew new participants into the political debate. Since the end of the war, a small contingent of abolitionists, male and female, had sought to revive the cause of women's rights. In 1866, when Congress adopted the Fourteenth Amendment, women's rights advocates tried to join forces with their old abolitionist allies to campaign for both black suffrage and woman suffrage. Most Radical Republicans, however, did not want to be saddled with the woman-suffrage plank, for they feared that it would impede their primary goal, black enfranchisement.

This defection provoked disputes among women's rights advocates. Some, who continued

The Reconstruction Amendments

Amendment	Provisions	Date of Congressional Passage	Ratification
Thirteenth	Prohibited slavery in the United States.	January 1865	December 1865
Fourteenth	Defined citizenship to include all persons born or naturalized in the United States. Provided proportional loss of congressional representation for any state that denied suffrage to any of its male citizens. Disqualified prewar officeholders who supported the Confederacy from state or national office. Repudiated the Confederate debt.	June 1866	July 1868, after Congress made ratification a prerequisite for readmission of ex-Confederate states to the Union.
Fifteenth	Prohibited the denial of suffrage because of race, color, or previous condition of servitude.	February 1869	March 1870. Ratification required of Virginia, Texas, Mississippi, and Georgia for readmission to the Union.

to support black suffrage, contended that it would pave the way for the women's vote and that black men deserved priority. "If the elective franchise is not extended to the Negro, he is dead," explained Frederick Douglass, a longtime women's rights supporter. "Woman has a thousand ways by which she can attach herself to the ruling power of the land that we have not." But the women's rights leaders Elizabeth Cady Stanton and Susan B. Anthony, who repudiated black suffrage without attendant woman suffrage, decried the Fifteenth Amendment and denounced the Republicans for supporting it. The amendment, insisted Stanton, would establish an "aristocracy of sex." Moreover, she argued, if suffrage were extended without including women, their disabilities would merely increase. The battle over black suffrage and the Fifteenth Amendment divided women's rights

advocates into two rival suffrage associations, both formed in 1869. It also severed reformers such as Stanton and Anthony from the abolitionist tradition in which they had matured politically and inspired the development of an independent women's rights movement.

By the time that the Fifteenth Amendment was ratified in 1870, Congress could look back on five years of momentous achievement. Since the start of 1865, federal legislators had broadened the scope of American democracy by passing three constitutional amendments. The Thirteenth Amendment abolished slavery, the Fourteenth affirmed the rights of federal citizens, and the Fifteenth prohibited the denial of suffrage on the basis of race. Congress had also readmitted the former Confederate states into the Union. But after 1868 congressional momentum slowed. And in 1869, when Ulysses S.

Grant became president, the fierce battle between Congress and the executive ceased. The theater of action now shifted to the South, where an era of tumultuous change was under way.

Reconstruction Governments

During the unstable years of presidential Reconstruction, 1865–1867, the southern states had to create new governments, revive the war-torn economy, and face the impact of emancipation. Social and economic problems abounded. War costs had cut into southern wealth, cities and factories lay in rubble, plantation-labor systems disintegrated, and racial tensions flared. No sooner did legislatures enact the black codes than their impact was muted by the army, the Freedmen's Bureau, and a new civil-rights law. Beginning in 1865, freedmen organized black conventions, political meetings at which they protested ill treatment and demanded equal rights. These meetings took place in a climate of violence. Race riots erupted in major southern cities. In Memphis in May 1866, white crowds attacked black veterans, charged through black neighborhoods, and killed forty-six people; in New Orleans two months later, a white mob and police assaulted black delegates on their way to a political convention and left forty people dead. Even when Congress reimposed military rule in 1867, ex-Confederates did not feel defeated. "Having reached bottom, there is hope now that we may rise again to the surface in the course of time," a South Carolina planter wrote in his diary.

Congressional Reconstruction, supervised by federal troops, took effect in the spring of 1867. Despite efforts to stall it—many southern whites preferred military rule to the prospect of new civil governments based on black suffrage—the process moved forward. The Johnson regimes were dismantled, state constitutional conventions met, and voters elected new state governments, which Republicans dominated. In 1868 a majority of the former Confederate states rejoined the Union, and two years later, the last four states—Virginia, Mississippi, Georgia and Texas—followed.

Readmission to the Union did not end the *process* of Reconstruction, for Republicans still held power in the South. Republican rule was very brief, lasting less than a decade in all southern states, far less in most of them, and on average under five years. Opposition from southern Democrats, the landowning elite, thousands of vigilantes, and indeed, the majority of white voters proved insurmountable. But although short-lived, the governments formed under congressional Reconstruction marked a unique achievement, because black men, including former slaves, participated in them. In no other society where slaves had been liberated—neither Haiti, where slaves had revolted in the 1790s, nor the British Caribbean islands, where Parliament had ended slavery in 1833—had freedmen gained democratic political rights.

A New Electorate

The Reconstruction laws of 1867–1868 transformed the southern electorate by temporarily disfranchising 10 percent to 15 percent of potential white voters and by enfranchising more than seven hundred thousand freedmen. Outnumbering registered white voters by one hundred thousand, blacks gained voting majorities in five states.

The new electorate provided a base for the Republican party, which had never existed in the South. To their Democratic opponents, southern Republicans comprised three types of scoundrels: northern "carpetbaggers," who had allegedly come south seeking wealth and power (with so few possessions that they could be stuffed into traveling bags made of carpet material); southern "scalawags," predominantly poor and ignorant, who sought to profit from Republican rule; and hordes of uneducated freedmen, who where ready prey for Republican manipulators. Although the "carpetbag" and "scalawag" labels were derogatory and the stereotypes that they conveyed inaccurate, they remain in use as a form of shorthand. Crossing class and racial lines, the hastily established Republican party was in fact a loose coalition of factions with varied and often contradictory goals.

To northerners who moved south after the Civil War, the former Confederacy was an undeveloped region, ripe with possibility. The carpetbaggers' ranks included many former Union soldiers who hoped to buy land, open factories, build railroads, or simply enjoy the warmer southern climate. Albion Tourgee, a young lawyer who had served with the New York and Ohio volunteers, for example, relocated in North Carolina after the war to improve his health. There he worked as a journalist, poli-

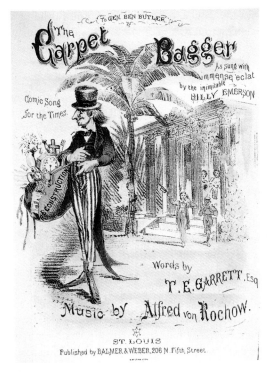

The Carpetbaggers

Southern Democrats disparaged carpetbaggers as inter-lopers who hoped to "fatten on our misfortunes." In reality, most were Union army officers, businessmen, and professionals with capital and energy to invest in the South. This 1869 sheet-music cover caricatures the carpetbaggers by depicting a rather hungry-looking northern migrant casting a greedy eye upon the defeated Confederacy.

tician, and Republican judge, until Republican rule collapsed. Perhaps no more than twenty thousand northern migrants like Tourgee—including veterans, missionaries, teachers, and Freedmen's Bureau

agents—headed south immediately after the war, and many returned north by 1867. But those who remained played a disproportionate part in Reconstruction politics, for they held almost one out of three state offices. Carpetbaggers recruited black support through a patriotic society called the Union League, which held meetings and rallies, urged blacks to vote, and escorted them to the polls.

Scalawags, white southerners who supported the Republicans, included some entrepreneurs who applauded party policies such as the national banking system and high protective tariffs as well as some prosperous planters, former Whigs who had opposed secession. They also comprised a few prominent politicians, among them James Orr of South Carolina and Mississippi's governor James Alcorn, who became Republicans for practical reasons: they wanted to retain influence and limit Republican radicalism. Republicans appreciated such important recruits and hoped to attract more of them. Most scalawags, however, were small farmers from the mountain regions of North Carolina, Georgia, Alabama, and Arkansas. Former Unionists who had owned no slaves and had no allegiance to the landowning elite, they sought to improve their economic position. Unlike carpetbaggers, they lacked commitment to black rights and black suffrage; most came from regions with small black populations and cared little whether blacks voted or not. Scalawags held the most political offices during Reconstruction, but they proved the least stable element of the southern Republican coalition: eventually, many drifted back to the Democratic fold.

Freedmen, the backbone of southern Republicanism, provided eight out of ten Republican votes. Republican rule lasted longest in states with the

American Citizens at the Polls,
by Thomas Waterman Wood, 1867

Black southerners voted for the first time in 1867, when the former Confederate states organized constitutional conventions. This painting conveys the enthusiasm that led up to 90 percent of eligible black voters to cast ballots. "The negroes voted their entire walking strength," an Alabama Republican reported, ". . . no one staying at home that was able to come to the polls."

The South Carolina Legislature

Although blacks served in all Reconstruction legisla-
tures, only in South Carolina did they assume control.
Forming a majority in the state House of Representa-
tives, black legislators elected black speakers and ran
major committees throughout Reconstruction. This
scene depicts South Carolina lawmakers voting on an
appropriations bill in 1873.

largest black populations, such as South Carolina, Mississippi, Alabama, and Louisiana. Introduced to politics in the black conventions of 1865–1867, the freedmen sought land, education, civil rights, and political equality. Even when land was not forthcoming, they continued to vote Republican. As an elderly freedman announced at a Georgia political convention in 1867, "We know our friends."

Although Reconstruction governments would have collapsed without black votes, freedmen held at most one in five political offices. Blacks served in all southern legislatures and filled many high posts in Louisiana, Mississippi, and South Carolina. They constituted a majority, however, only in the legislature of South Carolina, a state in which more than 60 percent of the population was black. No blacks won the office of governor, and only two served in the U.S. Senate, Hiram Revels and

Blanche K. Bruce, both of Mississippi. In the House of Representatives, a mere 6 percent of southern members were black, and almost half of these came from South Carolina.

Black officeholders on the state level, most of whom had risen to leadership roles in the black conventions, formed a political elite. They often differed from their black constituents in background, education, wealth, and complexion. A disproportionate number were literate blacks who had been free before the Civil War. (Many more former slaves held office on the local level than on the state level.) South Carolina's roster of elected officials illustrates some distinctions between high-level black officeholders and the freedmen who voted for them. Among those blacks sent to Congress, almost all claimed some secondary education, and some had attained advanced degrees. In South Carolina's state legislature, most black members, unlike the majority of their constituents, came from large towns and cities; many had spent time in the North; and some were well-off property owners or even former slaveowners. Color differences were evident, too: 43 percent of South Carolina's black state legislators, but only 7 percent of the state's black population, were mulattos.

The status gap between high-level black officials and black voters was significant. Most freedmen cared mainly about their economic future, especially about acquiring land, whereas black officeholders cared most about attaining equal rights. Still, both groups shared high expectations, and both prized enfranchisement. "We are not prepared for this suffrage," averred William Beverly Nash, an uneducated former slave, at the South Carolina constitutional convention. "But we can learn. Give a man tools and let him commence to use them and in time he will learn a trade. So it is with voting. We may not understand it at the start, but in time we shall learn to do our duty."

Republican Rule

Large numbers of blacks participated in American government for the first time in the state constitutional conventions of 1867–1868. The South Carolina convention had a black majority, and in Louisiana half the delegates were freedmen. The conventions forged democratic changes in their state constitutions. Delegates abolished property qualifications for officeholding, made many appointive offices elective, and redistricted state legislatures more equitably. All states established universal manhood suffrage, and some conventions offered further innovations: the new constitutions of Louisiana and South Carolina opened public schools to both races. These provisions integrated the New Orleans public schools as well as the University of South Carolina, from which whites withdrew. But most states did not provide for integrated education. Further, no state instituted land reform. When proposals for land confiscation and redistribution came up at the state conventions, they went down to defeat, as they had in Congress. Hoping to attract northern investment to the reconstructed South, southern Republicans hesitated to threaten property rights or to adopt land-reform measures that northern Republicans had rejected. South Carolina did set up a commission to buy land and make it available to freedmen, and several states changed their tax structures to force uncultivated land onto the market, but in no case was ex-Confederate land confiscated.

Once civil power shifted from the federal army to the newly formed state governments, the Republican administrations began ambitious programs of public works. They built roads, bridges, and public buildings; repaired broken-down facilities; promoted railroad development by endorsing railroad bonds; and funded institutions to care for orphans, the insane, and the disabled. The Republican regimes also expanded state bureaucracies, raised salaries for government employees, and formed state militia, in which blacks were often heavily represented. Finally, they created public-school systems, almost nonexistent in the South until then. In South Carolina prior to 1867, only one in eight white children, and hardly any blacks, had attended any school; but by 1875, with the advent of public schools, half the state's white children and 41 percent of its black children were enrolled.

Because rebuilding the devastated South and expanding the state governments cost millions, state debts and taxes skyrocketed. During the 1860s the southern tax burden rose 400 percent. State legislatures increased poll taxes or "head" taxes (levies on individuals); enacted luxury, sales, and occupation taxes; and imposed new property taxes. Before the war southern states had taxed property

in slaves but had barely taxed landed property at all. Now for the first time, state governments assessed even small farmers' holdings, and big planters paid what they considered an excessive burden. Although northern tax rates still exceeded southern rates, southern landowners resented the new levies. In their view, Reconstruction strained the pocketbooks of the propertied, who were already beset by labor problems and falling land values, in order to finance the vast expenditures of Republican legislators, or what one Alabamian called the "no property herd."

Landowners complained about more than rising taxes. To Reconstruction's opponents, Republican rule was wasteful and corrupt, if not the "most stupendous system of organized robbery in history." A state like Mississippi, which had an honest government, provided little basis for such charges. But critics could justifiably point to Louisiana, where the governor pocketed thousands of dollars of state funds and corruption permeated all government transactions (as indeed it had before the war). Or they could cite South Carolina, where bribery ran rampant. The main postwar profiteers, besides the government officials who took bribes, were the railroad promoters who doled them out, and these were not necessarily Republicans. Nor did the Republican regimes in the South hold a monopoly on big spending or corruption. After the war bribery pervaded government transactions North and South, and far more money changed hands in the North. But Reconstruction's critics assailed Republican rule for additional reasons.

Counterattacks

Vexed as they were by northern interference, scalawag "treachery," and high taxes, ex-Confederates especially chafed at black enfranchisement and black officeholding and spoke with dread about the "horror of Negro domination." As soon as congressional Reconstruction took effect, a clamorous Democratic campaign began to undermine it. When the state constitutional conventions met, the Democratic press stood ready. Newspapers assailed North Carolina's delegates as an "Ethiopian minstrelsy . . . baboons, monkeys, mules . . . and other jackasses." They demeaned Louisiana's constitution as "the work of ignorant Negroes cooperating with a gang of white adventurers." A

Little Rock newspaper denigrated the Arkansas convention as "a foul gathering whose putridity stinks in the nostrils of all decency."

The Democrats delayed political mobilization until the southern states were readmitted to the Union. "The duty of the hour is to provide for our familys [sic] and avoid *politics*," declared Ella Thomas, the wife and daughter of Georgia planters, in 1868. Sharing such sentiments, perhaps one out of four eligible white voters abstained from voting. After readmission, however, the Democrats swung into action, calling themselves Conservatives so as not to repel those former Whigs who might join them. At first they sought to win the votes of blacks; but when that effort failed, they tried other tactics. In 1868–1869 Georgia Democrats challenged the eligibility of black legislators and expelled them from office. In response, the federal government reestablished military rule in Georgia, but determined Democrats still undercut Republican power. In every southern state, they contested elections, backed dissident Republican factions, and elected some Democratic legislators. They also made steady inroads among the scalawags, siphoning some of their votes from the Republicans.

Vigilante efforts to reduce black votes bolstered the Democrats' campaigns to win white ones. Antagonism toward free blacks, long a prominent motif in southern life, again flourished after the war. During presidential Reconstruction, when the white South sought to control freedmen's mobility, antiblack violence often erupted. Freedmen's Bureau agents in 1865 itemized a variety of outrages against blacks, including shooting, murder, rape, arson, roasting, and "severe and inhuman beating." Vigilante groups sprang up spontaneously in all parts of the former Confederacy under names like moderators, regulators, and in Louisiana, Knights of the White Camelia. A new group soon rose to dominance. In the spring of 1866, when the Johnson governments were still in power, six young Confederate war veterans in Tennessee formed a social club, the Ku Klux Klan, distinguished by elaborate rituals, hooded costumes, and secret passwords. New Klan dens spread through the state, and within a year Democratic politicians and former Confederate officers took control of them. By the election of 1868, when black suffrage had become a reality, Klan dens existed in all the southern states, and Klansmen embarked on night raids

to intimidate black voters. One of its founders now denounced the Klan as "perverted" and "pernicious," and indeed, it was no longer a social club but a widespread terrorist movement. Reminiscent of the antebellum slave patrols, the Ku Klux Klan became a violent arm of the Democratic party.

The Klan's goals were to suppress black voting, reestablish white supremacy, and topple the Reconstruction governments. Its members attacked Union League officers, Freedmen's Bureau officials, white Republicans, black militia units, economically successful blacks, and black voters. Concentrated in areas where the black and white populations were most evenly balanced and racial tensions greatest, Klan dens adapted their strategies and timing to local conditions. In Mississippi the Klan targeted black schools; in Alabama it concentrated on Republican officeholders. In Arkansas terror reigned in 1868; in Georgia and Florida Klan strength surged in 1870. Some Democrats denounced Klan members as "cut-throats and riffraff." But prominent ex-Confederates were also known to be active Klansmen, among them General Nathan Bedford Forrest, the leader of the 1864 Fort Pillow massacre (see Chapter 14). Vigilantism united southern whites of different social classes and drew on the energy of many a Confederate veteran. In areas where the Klan was inactive, other vigilante groups took its place.

Republican legislatures outlawed vigilantism through laws providing for fines and imprisonment of offenders. But the state militia could not enforce the laws, and state officials turned to the federal government for help. In May 1870 Congress passed the Enforcement Act to protect black voters. Even this law was unenforceable, because witnesses to violations were afraid to testify against vigilantes, and local juries refused to convict them. The Second Enforcement Act, which provided for federal supervision of southern elections, followed in February 1871. Two months later Congress passed the Third Enforcement Act, or Ku Klux Klan Act, which strengthened the sanctions against those who prevented blacks from voting. It also empowered the president to use federal troops to enforce the law and to suspend the writ of habeas corpus in areas that he declared in insurrection. President Grant suspended the writ in nine South Carolina counties that had been devastated by Klan attacks.

After Congress enacted the three laws, a joint congressional committee launched a full-scale

The Ku Klux Klan

Disguised in long white gowns and hoods, Ku Klux Klansmen sometimes claimed to be the ghosts of Confederate soldiers. The Klan, which spread rapidly after 1867, hoped to end Republican rule, restore white supremacy, and obliterate, in one southern editor's words, "the preposterous and wicked dogma of Negro equality."

investigation of Klan activities. Victimized blacks and southern politicians of both parties testified. "I have heard of any quantity of horrible deeds," Henry M. Turner, a black minister, politician, and former Union army chaplain told government investigators. "Every man in Georgia who has got any brains must be satisfied, that there are organized bands of night assassins, murderous villains, who have banded themselves together and roam about and kill Republicans, kill any man who has got the name of radical attached to him." While Turner and others testified, the Ku Klux Klan Act generated thousands of arrests; most terrorists, however, escaped conviction.

By 1872 the federal government had effectively suppressed the Klan, but vigilantism had served its purpose. Only a large military presence in the South could have protected black rights, and the government in Washington never provided it. Instead, federal power in the former Confederacy diminished. President Grant steadily reduced troop levels in the South; Congress allowed the Freedmen's Bureau to die in 1869; and the Enforcement acts became dead letters. White southerners, a Georgia politician explained to congressional investigators in 1871, could not discard "a feeling

of bitterness, a feeling that the Negro is a sort of instinctual enemy of ours." The battle over Reconstruction was in essence a battle over the implications of emancipation, and it had begun as soon as the war ended.

The Impact of Emancipation

"The master he says we are all free," a South Carolina slave declared in 1865. "But it don't mean we is white. And it don't mean we is equal." Emancipated slaves faced extreme handicaps. They had no property, tools, or capital and usually possessed meager skills. Only a minority had been trained as artisans, and more than 95 percent were illiterate. Still, the exhilaration of freedom was overwhelming, as slaves realized, "Now I am for myself" and "All that I make is my own." At emancipation they gained the right to their own labor and a new sense of autonomy. Under Reconstruction the freedmen asserted their independence by seeking to cast off white control and shed the vestiges of slavery.

Confronting Freedom

For the former slaves, mobility was often the first perquisite of liberty. Some moved out of the slave quarters and set up dwellings elsewhere on their plantations; others left their plantations entirely. Landowners found that one freedman after another vanished, with house servants and artisans leading the way. "I have never in my life met with such ingratitude," a South Carolina mistress exclaimed when a former slave ran off. Field-workers, who had less contact with whites, were more likely to stay behind or more reluctant to leave. Still, flight remained tempting. "The moment they see an opportunity to improve themselves, they will move on," diarist Mary Chesnut observed.

Emancipation stirred waves of migration within the former Confederacy. Some freedmen left the Upper South for the Deep South and the Southwest—Florida, Mississippi, Arkansas, and Texas—where planters desperately needed labor and paid higher wages. Even more left the countryside for towns and cities, traditional havens of independence for blacks. Urban black populations sometimes doubled or tripled after emancipation; by 1866 Charleston had a black majority, and by 1870 almost equal numbers of blacks and whites lived in Atlanta, Richmond, Montgomery, and Raleigh. Overall during the 1860s, the urban black population increased by 75 percent, and the number of blacks in small rural towns grew as well. Many migrants eventually returned to their old locales, in search of their families or out of an attachment to the land. But they tended to settle on neighboring plantations rather than with their former owners. Freedom was the major goal. "I's wants to be a free man, cum when I please, and nobody say nuffin to me, nor order me roun'," an Alabama freedman declared to a northern journalist.

Freedmen's yearnings to find lost family members prompted considerable movement. "They had a passion, not so much for wandering as for getting together," a Freedmen's Bureau official commented. Parents sought children who had been sold; husbands and wives who had been separated by sale, or who lived on different plantations, reunited; and families reclaimed youngsters who were being raised in masters' homes. The Freedmen's Bureau helped former slaves get information about missing relatives and travel to find them. Bureau agents also tried to resolve entanglements over the multiple alliances of spouses who had been separated under slavery.

Reunification efforts often failed. Some fugitive slaves had died during the war or were untraceable. Other ex-slaves had formed new partnerships and could not revive old ones. "I am married," one husband wrote to a former wife (probably in a dictated letter), "and my wife [and I] have two children, and if you and I meet it would make a very dissatisfied family." But there were success stories, too. "I's hunted an' hunted till I track you up here," one freedman told his wife, whom he found in a refugee camp twenty years after their separation by sale.

Once reunited, freedmen quickly legalized unions formed under slavery, sometimes in mass ceremonies of up to seventy couples. Legal marriage had a tangible impact on family life. Men asserted themselves as household heads; wives and children of able-bodied men often withdrew from the labor force. "When I married my wife, I married her to wait on me and she has got all she can do right here for me and the children," a Tennessee freedman explained. Black women's desire to "play the lady," as southern whites described it, caused planters severe labor shortages. Before the war at least half of field-workers had been women; in 1866, a southern journal claimed, men performed almost all the field labor. Nevertheless, by the end of Reconstruction, many black women had returned to agricultural work as part of sharecropper families. Others took paid work in cities, as laundresses, cooks, and domestic servants. (Many white women sought employment as well, for the war had incapacitated white breadwinners, reduced the supply of future husbands, and left families destitute or in diminished circumstances.) Still, former slaves continued to view stable, independent domestic life, especially the right to bring up their own children, as a major blessing of freedom. In 1870 eight out of ten black families in the cotton-producing South were two-parent families, about the same proportion as among whites.

Black Institutions

The freedmen's desire for independence also led to the postwar growth of black churches. During the late 1860s, while some freedmen congregated at churches operated by northern missionaries in the

Freedmen's Schoolhouse

The establishment of freedmen's schools in the South represented the greatest triumph of the Freedmen's Bureau. Although underfunded and unable to reach many rural areas, the schools evoked tremendous support among blacks and laid a foundation for public-education systems in the southern states.

South, others withdrew from white-run churches and formed their own. The African Methodist Episcopal church, founded by Philadelphia blacks in the 1790s, gained thousands of new southern members. Negro Baptist churches sprouted everywhere, often growing out of plantation "praise meetings," religious gatherings organized by slaves.

The black churches, which offered a fervent, participatory experience, served many purposes. Beyond affording a closer communion among freedmen, they provided relief, raised funds for schools, and supported Republican policies. From the outset black ministers assumed leading political roles, first in the black conventions of 1865–1866 and later in the Reconstruction governments. After southern Democrats excluded most freedmen from political life at Reconstruction's end, ministers remained the main pillars of authority within black communities.

Black schools played a crucial role for freedmen as well. The ex-slaves eagerly sought literacy for themselves and above all for their children. At emancipation blacks organized their own schools, which the Freedmen's Bureau soon supervised. Northern philanthropic societies paid the wages of instructors, about half of whom were women. These teachers sometimes felt like pioneers in a foreign land. "Our work is just as much missionary work as if we were in India or China," a Sea Islands teacher commented. In 1869, just before it expired, the bureau reported more than four thousand black

schools in the former Confederacy. Within three years each southern state had a public-school system, at least in principle, generally with separate schools for blacks and whites. Advanced schools for blacks opened as well, to train tradespeople, teachers, and ministers. The Freedmen's Bureau and northern organizations like the American Missionary Association helped to found Howard, Atlanta, and Fisk universities (all started in 1866–1867) and Hampton Institute (1868).

Despite these advances, black education remained limited. Located in towns, most freedmen's schools could not reach the large black rural population. Black public schools, similarly inaccessible to most rural black children, held classes only for very short seasons. Underfunded and inferior, they were sometimes the targets of vigilante attacks. At the end of Reconstruction, illiteracy claimed more than 80 percent of the black population. Still, the proportion of youngsters who did not know how to read and write had declined and would continue to decline (see table on the following page). "Perhaps some *will* get an education in a little while. I *knows* de *next generation will*," a freedman told a missionary in 1865. "But . . . we has been kep down *a hundred years* and I think it will take *a hundred years to get us back again*."

School segregation and other forms of racial separation were taken for granted. Some black codes of 1865–1866 had segregated public-transit conveyances and public accommodations. Even after

Howard University

Founded by the Freedmen's Bureau in 1867, Howard University in Washington, D.C., was named after its first president, O. O. Howard, Union general and Freedmen's Bureau head. In 1870, the year this picture was taken, the pioneer black institution offered preparatory and collegiate programs, as well as training in law, pharmacy, and medicine.

the invalidation of the codes, the custom of segregation had continued on streetcars, steamboats, and trains as well as in churches, theaters, inns, and restaurants. On railroads, for example, whites could ride in the "ladies' car" or first-class car, while blacks had to stay in smoking cars or boxcars

Percentage of Persons Unable to Write, by Age Group, 1870–1890, in South Carolina, Georgia, Alabama, Mississippi, and Louisiana			
	1870	*1880*	*1890*
10–14			
black	78.9	74.1	49.2
white	33.2	34.5	18.7
15–20			
black	85.3	73.0	54.1
white	24.2	21.0	14.3
Over 20			
black	90.4	82.3	75.5
white	19.8	17.9	17.1

SOURCE: Roger Ransom and Richard Sutch, *One Kind of Freedom* (Cambridge: Cambridge University Press, 1978), 30.

with benches. In 1870 Senator Charles Sumner began campaigning in Congress for a bill that would desegregate schools, transportation facilities, juries, and public accommodations. After Sumner's death in 1874, Congress honored him by enacting a new law, the Civil Rights Act of 1875, which encompassed his program, except for the extremely controversial school-integration provision. But the law was largely unenforced, and in 1883 the Supreme Court invalidated it. The Fourteenth Amendment did not prohibit discrimination by individuals, the Court ruled, only that perpetrated by the state.

White southerners adamantly rejected the prospect of racial integration, which they insisted would lead to racial amalgamation. "If we have social equality, we shall have intermarriage," one white southerner contended, "and if we have intermarriage, we shall degenerate." Urban blacks, the most likely to be affected by segregation practices, sometimes challenged them, and black legislators promoted bills to desegregate public transit. Some black officeholders decried all forms of racial separatism. "The sooner we as a people forget our sable complexion," said a Mobile official, "the better it will be for us as a race." But most freedmen were less interested in "social equality," in the sense of interracial mingling, than in black liberty and community. The newly formed postwar elite—teachers, ministers, and politicians—served black constituencies and therefore had a vested interest in separate black institutions. Rural blacks, too, widely preferred all-black institutions. They had little desire to mix with whites. On the contrary, they sought freedom from white control. Above all else, they wanted to secure personal independence by acquiring land.

Land, Labor, and Sharecropping

"The sole ambition of the freedman," a New Englander wrote from South Carolina in 1865, "appears to be to become the owner of a little piece of land, there to erect a humble home, and to dwell in peace and security, at his own free will and pleasure." Indeed, to freedmen everywhere, "forty acres and a mule" promised emancipation from plantation labor, from white domination, and from cotton, the "slave crop." Just as garden plots provided a measure of autonomy under slavery, so did landownership signify economic independence afterward. "We want to be placed on land until we are able to buy it and make it our own," a black minister had told General Sherman in Georgia during the war. Some freedmen defended their right to the land on which they lived, by pointing out that they and their forebears had worked on it for decades without pay.

But freedmen's visions of landownership failed to materialize, for, as we have seen, large-scale land reform never occurred. Proposals to confiscate or redistribute Confederate property failed in Congress as well as in the southern state legislatures. Some freedmen did obtain land with the help of the Union army or the Freedmen's Bureau, and black soldiers sometimes pooled resources to buy land, as on the Sea Islands (see Chapter 14). The federal government also attempted to provide ex-slaves with land. In 1866 Congress passed the Southern Homestead Act, which set aside 44 million acres of land in five southern states for freedmen and loyal whites. Not only did this acreage contain poor soil, but few former slaves had the resources to survive even until their first harvest. Thus although about four thousand blacks were resettled on homesteads under the law, most were unable to establish farms. (White southern homesteaders fared little better.) By the end of Reconstruction, only a small minority of former slaves in each state owned working farms. In Georgia in 1876, for instance, blacks controlled a mere 1.3 percent of total acreage. Without large-scale land reform, the obstacles to black landownership remained overwhelming.

What were these obstacles? First, most freedmen lacked the capital to buy land and the equipment needed to work it. Further, white southerners on the whole opposed selling land to blacks. Most important, planters sought to preserve a black labor force. They insisted that freedmen would work only under coercion, and not at all if the possibility of landownership arose. As soon as the war ended, therefore, the white South took steps to make sure that black labor would remain available where it was needed, on the plantations.

During presidential Reconstruction, southern state legislatures tried to limit black mobility and to preserve a captive labor force through the black codes. Under labor contracts in effect in 1865–1866, freedmen received wages, housing, food, and clothing in exchange for fieldwork. With cash so short, wages usually took the form of a very small share of the crop, often one-eighth or less, divided among the entire plantation work force. Serving as mediators between former slaves and landowners, Freedmen's Bureau agents actively promoted the new labor system; they encouraged freedmen to sign labor contracts and tried to ensure adequate wages. Imbued with the northern free-labor ideology, which held that wage workers could rise to the status of self-supporting tradesmen and property owners, bureau officials and agents endorsed black wage labor as an interim arrangement that would lead to economic independence. "You must begin at the bottom of the ladder and climb up," Freedmen's Bureau head O. O. Howard exhorted a group of Louisiana freedmen in 1865.

But the freedmen disliked the new wage system, especially the use of gang labor, which resembled the work pattern under slavery. Planters had complaints, too. In some regions the black labor force had shrunk to half its prewar size or less, due to the migration of freedmen and to black women's withdrawal from fieldwork. Once united in defense of slavery, planters now competed for black workers. Moreover, their labor problems mounted, for the freedmen, whom planters often scorned as lazy

A Georgia Plantation, 1865–1881

The transformation of the Barrow plantation in Oglethorpe County, Georgia, illustrates in microcosm the striking changes that occurred in southern agriculture during Reconstruction. Before the Civil War, David Crenshaw Barrow had been the absentee owner of a two-thousand-acre plantation long known as the Pope Place. He had inherited the land through his first wife, Sarah Elizabeth Pope. The owner of several other plantations as well, Barrow had possessed some 400 slaves, about 135 of whom had lived on the "Pope Place." Assisted by slave foremen, an overseer had run the plantation. The overseer had lived in the main plantation house, from where he had kept a watchful eye on the slave quarters.

After the war the plantation changed in so many ways that by 1881, according to Barrow's son, David Crenshaw Barrow, Jr., "the place would now hardly be recognized." But the changes had occurred in stages.

The critical period immediately followed the war. At emancipation some of Barrow's former slaves had left the plantation, probably for nearby towns or other plantations. Those remaining had signed annual labor contracts with Barrow. Divided into two competing squads and supervised by a hired foreman, the freedmen grew cotton under the gang system. They received wages in the form of a share of the crop, with a reward going to the squad that worked more efficiently. Barrow liked the new system, but the freedmen did not. Within a few years, they rebelled against the hired foreman, "each man feeling the very natural desire to be his own 'boss' and farm to himself," Barrow's son wrote. The squads split into smaller groups and spread over the plantation. Still working for a small share of the crop, they continued to use the owner's mules and equipment. Now Barrow found the system unsatisfactory. He claimed that the freedmen mistreated the mules and failed to deliver his full share of the crop.

In the late 1860s, life on the Barrow plantation entered a third phase. One of the first planters in his area to subdivide his land, Barrow transformed the plantation into tenant farms of twenty-five to thirty acres. With this change, the freedmen moved their households from the old slave quarters to their own farms. They typically set up their log cabins at springs around the plantation and then added outhouses, stables, corncribs, and fodderhouses. Each head of family signed an annual contract, agreeing to pay a rent of 500 to 750 pounds of cotton plus varied amounts of other crops. As tenant farmers, the freedmen raised cotton (about half their crop), corn, and vegetables; the men did the plowing, and women and children the hoeing. Using uncultivated land for pasture, the tenants also raised hogs, chickens, and a few cattle. Barrow sold each farmer a mule on credit, and he set aside an acre on the edge of the plantation for a church and a school, which was open three months a year.

In 1881 David Crenshaw Barrow lived in the main house with two family members, probably his second wife (a former New Englander) and an unmarried daughter, Clara. The plantation's tenants

Tenants on the Barrow Plantation

Children pick cotton on the Barrow plantation in this late-nineteenth-century scene.

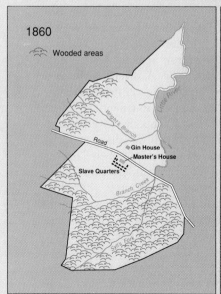

1860

~~ Wooded areas

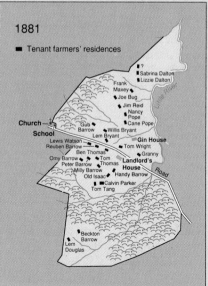

1881

■ Tenant farmers' residences

The Barrow Plantation, 1860 and 1881

These maps show the changes that transformed the Barrow plantation after the Civil War.

numbered 162, at least half of them children. One out of four families was named Barrow. When David Crenshaw Barrow, Jr., summed up plantation life in 1881 for the readers of *Scribner's Monthly,* he emphasized "how completely the relations between the races at the South have changed." For instance, his father's tenants needed little supervision. "Very many negro farmers are capable of directing the working of their own crops," he explained, "and not a few object to directions." The younger Barrow expressed pride that no tenant on his father's land had joined the "exodus" movement that had drawn blacks out of the South in the late 1870s. He also took pleasure in the fact that the most troublesome slave, Lem Bryant, once beyond the overseer's control, had become the most industrious tenant—a transformation Barrow, Jr., attributed to the impact of freedom.

Claiming satisfaction with the changes that he and his father had seen, planter Barrow's son assured

David Crenshaw Barrow, Jr.

The young Barrow, posed for this photograph around the time that his article in Scribner's Monthly *appeared.*

his readers that southern freedmen were content with their lives as tenant farmers. "In Georgia, the negro has adapted himself to his new circumstances, and freedom fits him

as if it had been cut out and made for him," he reported. "As a people, they are happy; they have become suited to their new estate and it to them." The younger Barrow's positive view of postwar farming arrangements might well have been challenged by the growing number of southerners, black and white, who had become mired in debt as sharecroppers. His article in *Scribner's,* however, written for a northern audience, was intended to convey a political message. Not only had the one-time slaves adjusted to emancipation, Barrow, Jr., suggested, but so had their former owners. This concession was part of the national celebration of reunion that followed the Compromise of 1877 (see below).

Few if any of David Crenshaw Barrow's nine offspring, all born on the "Pope Place," found a vocation in southern agriculture. Two sons had died as young men, and another in a Civil War battle. By 1881 the surviving Barrow children, save Clara, had moved away from their father's home and chosen a variety of occupations. Pope Barrow, the oldest, became a lawyer and a judge and would later serve as U.S. senator from Georgia. Thomas Barrow, who had fought with the Confederate army, first turned to business and then became a Baptist minister. Lucy Barrow married the son of a prominent Georgian, Howell Cobb, who had once been considered for the post of president of the Confederacy. Nellie Barrow also married and moved to Sapelo Island off the coast of Georgia. David Crenshaw Barrow, Jr., began his career as a lawyer but in 1879 became a mathematics teacher at the University of Georgia in Athens, not far from the Oglethorpe County plantation. Barrow, Jr., retained an avid interest in farming, which he later practiced in partnership with the son of his father's former overseer.

and incorrigible, did not intend to work as long or as hard as they had labored under slavery. One planter estimated that workers accomplished only "two-fifths of what they did under the old system"; and as productivity fell, so did land values. Some planters considered importing white immigrant labor, but they doubted that whites would perform black fieldwork for long. To top off the planters' problems, cotton prices plummeted, for during the war northern and foreign buyers had found new sources of cotton in Egypt and India, and the world supply had vastly increased. Finally, the harvests of 1866 and 1867 were extremely poor. By then an agricultural impasse had been reached: landowners lacked labor and freedmen lacked land. But free blacks, unlike slaves, had the right to enter into contracts—or to refuse to do so—and thereby gained some leverage.

Planters and freedmen began experimenting with new labor schemes, including the division of plantations into small tenancies (see "A Place in Time"). Sharecropping, the most widespread arrangement, evolved as a compromise. Under the sharecropping system, landowners subdivided large plantations into farms of thirty to fifty acres, which they rented to freedmen under annual leases for a share of the crop, usually half. Freedmen preferred this system to wage labor because it represented a step toward independence. The decentralized plan enabled heads of households to use the labor of family members. Moreover, a half-share of the crop far exceeded the fraction that freedmen had received as wages under the black codes. Planters often spoke of sharecropping as a capitulation, but they gained as well. Landowners retained power over tenants, because annual leases did not have to be renewed; they could expel undesirable tenants at the end of the year. Planters also shared the risk of planting with tenants: if a crop failed, both suffered the loss. Most important, planters retained control of their land and in some cases extended their holdings. The most productive land, therefore, remained in the hands of a small group of owners, as before the war. Sharecropping forced planters to relinquish day-to-day control over the labor of freedmen, but it helped to preserve the planter elite.

Sharecropping arrangements varied widely and were not universal. On sugar and rice plantations, the wage system continued. Some freedmen remained independent renters. Some landowners

leased areas to white tenants who then subcontracted with black labor. But by the end of the 1860s, the plantation tradition had given way to sharecropping in the cotton South, and the new system continued to expand. A severe depression in 1873 drove many black renters into sharecropping. By then thousands of independent white farmers had become sharecroppers as well. Stung by wartime losses and by the dismal postwar economy, they sank into debt and lost their land to creditors. Many backcountry residents, no longer able to get by on subsistence farming, shifted to cash crops like cotton and suffered the same fate. At the end of Reconstruction, one-third of the white farmers in Mississippi, for instance, worked as sharecroppers.

By 1880, 80 percent of the land in the cotton-producing states had been subdivided into tenancies, most of it farmed by sharecroppers, white and black. Indeed, white sharecroppers now outnumbered black ones, although a higher proportion of southern blacks, about 75 percent, were involved in the system. Changes in marketing and finance, meanwhile, made the sharecroppers' lot increasingly precarious.

Toward a Crop-Lien Economy

Before the Civil War, planters had depended on factors, or middlemen, who sold them supplies, extended credit, and marketed their crops through urban merchants. These long-distance credit arrangements were backed by the high value and liquidity of slave property. When slavery ended, the factorage system collapsed. The postwar South, with hundreds of thousands of tenants and sharecroppers, needed a far more localized network of credit.

Into the gap stepped the rural merchants (often themselves planters), who advanced supplies to tenants and sharecroppers on credit and sold their crops to wholesalers or textile manufacturers. Since renters had no property to use as collateral, the merchants secured their loans with a lien, or claim, on each farmer's next crop. They charged exorbitant interest of 50 percent or 60 percent or more and quickly drew many tenants and sharecroppers into a cycle of indebtedness. Owing part of the crop to a landowner for rent, a sharecropper also owed his rural merchant a large sum (perhaps

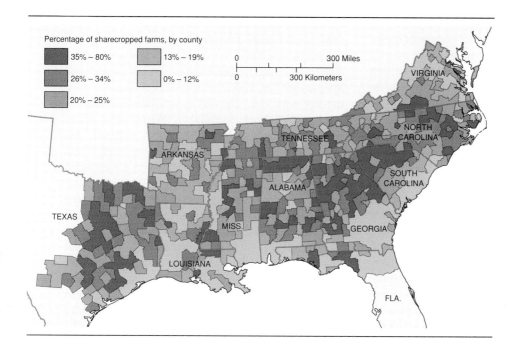

Percentage of sharecropped farms, by county

- 35% – 80%
- 26% – 34%
- 20% – 25%
- 13% – 19%
- 0% – 12%

0   300 Miles

0   300 Kilometers

VIRGINIA
TENNESSEE
NORTH CAROLINA
ARKANSAS
SOUTH CAROLINA
ALABAMA
TEXAS
MISS.
GEORGIA
LOUISIANA
FLA.

Southern Sharecropping, 1880

The depressed economy of the late 1870s caused poverty and debt, increased tenancy among white farmers, and forced many renters, black and white, into sharecropping. By 1880 the sharecropping system pervaded most southern counties, with highest concentrations in the cotton belt from South Carolina to eastern Texas.

SOURCE: U.S. Census Office, Tenth Census, 1880, *Report of the Production of Agriculture* (Washington, D.C.: Government Printing Office, 1883) Table 5.

amounting to the rest of his crop, if not more) for supplies. Moreover, an illiterate tenant often could not keep track of his financial arrangements, and a merchant could easily take advantage of him. "A man that didn't know how to count would always lose," an Arkansas freedman later explained. Once a tenant's debts or alleged debts exceeded the value of his crop, he was tied to the land, to cotton, and to sharecropping.

By the end of Reconstruction, sharecropping and crop liens had transformed southern agriculture. They bound the entire region to staple production and prevented crop diversification, for despite plunging cotton prices, creditors—landowners and merchants—insisted that tenants raise only easily marketable cash crops. Short of capital, planters could no longer invest in new equipment or improve their land by such techniques as crop rotation and contour plowing. Soil depletion, land erosion, and agricultural backwardness soon locked much of the South into a cycle of poverty. Overall, postwar changes in southern agriculture left the region with extremely bleak economic prospects.

But the major victims of the new agricultural arrangements were the indebted tenant farmers, who had been trapped in a system of what has been called debt peonage. Raising cotton for distant markets, for prices over which they had no control, remained the only survival route open to poor farmers, regardless of race. But the low income thus derived often forced them into sharecropping and crop liens, from which escape was difficult. Black tenants, for whom neither landownership nor economic independence ever materialized, suffered further handicaps. Not only were their rights as workers limited, but when Reconstruction ended, their political rights dwindled too. As one southern regime after another returned to Democratic control, freedmen could no longer look to the state governments for protection. Nor could they turn to the federal government, for northern politicians were preoccupied with their own problems.

New Concerns in the North

The nomination of Ulysses S. Grant for president in 1868 launched a chaotic era in national politics. Grant's two terms in office featured political scandals, a party revolt, a massive depression, and a steady retreat from Reconstruction policies. By the mid-1870s, northern voters cared more about the economic climate, unemployment, labor unrest, and currency problems than about the "southern question." Responsive to the shift in popular mood, Republicans became eager to end sectional conflict and consequently turned their backs on the freedmen of the South.

Grantism

Republicans had good reason to pass over longtime party leaders and nominate the popular Grant. A war hero, Grant was endorsed by Union veterans and admired throughout the North. Although identified with Radical Republican views by 1867, he had nonetheless escaped the bitter feuds of Reconstruction politics. At first a Johnson adviser, Grant had broken with Johnson during the tenure-of-office crisis and had become his competitor. Even before Grant's nomination, important visitors to Washington were sure to call on him as well as on the president.

To oppose Grant in the 1868 election, the Democrats nominated New York governor Horatio Seymour, archcritic of the Lincoln administration during the war. Seymour opposed Reconstruction and advocated "sound money," or the withdrawal of greenbacks from circulation, a policy begun by Hugh McCulloch, Johnson's treasury secretary. Grant, who defended Reconstruction, ran on his personal popularity more than on issues. Although he carried all but eight states in the election, the popular vote was very close; in the South, the votes of newly enfranchised freedmen provided the margin of victory. When he was inaugurated, Grant vowed to execute all the laws whether he agreed with them or not, to support sound money, and to follow a humane policy toward the Indians.

A strong leader in war, Grant proved a passive president. Although he lacked Johnson's instinct for disaster, he had little skill at politics. Many of his cabinet appointees—business executives, army men, and family friends—were mediocre if not unscrupulous, and a string of scandals plagued his administration. In 1869 financier Jay Gould and his partner Jim Fisk attempted to corner the gold market with the help of Grant's new brother-in-law, a New York speculator. When gold prices tumbled, Gould salvaged his own fortune, but investors were ruined and Grant's reputation was tarnished. Then before the president's first term ended, his vice president, Schuyler Colfax, was found to be linked to the Crédit Mobilier, a fraudulent construction company created to skim off the profits of the Union Pacific Railroad. Using government funds granted to the railroad, the Union Pacific directors awarded padded construction contracts to the Crédit Mobilier, of which they were also the directors. Discredited, Colfax was dropped from the Grant ticket in the election of 1872. More trouble lay ahead. Grant's private secretary, Orville Babcock, was unmasked in 1875 after taking money from the "whiskey ring," a group of distillers who bribed federal agents to avoid paying millions in whiskey taxes. And in 1876 voters learned that Grant's secretary of war, William E. Belknap, had taken bribes to sell lucrative Indian trading posts in Oklahoma. Impeached and disgraced, Belknap resigned.

Although Grant was not personally involved in the scandals, he loyally defended his subordinates. To his critics, "Grantism" came to stand for fraud, bribery, and corruption in office. Such evils spread far beyond Washington. In Pennsylvania, for example, the Standard Oil Company and the Pennsylvania Railroad controlled the legislature. Urban politics also provided rich opportunities for graft and swindles. The New York City press revealed in 1872 that Democratic boss William M. Tweed, the "Grand Sachem" of Tammany Hall, led a ring that looted the city treasury and collected

The Election of 1868				
Candidates	Parties	Electoral Vote	Popular Vote	Percentage of Popular Vote
ULYSSES S. GRANT	Republican	214	3,013,421	52.7
Horatio Seymour	Democratic	80	2,706,829	47.3

Boss Tweed

Thomas Nast's cartoons in Harper's Weekly *helped topple New York Democratic boss William M. Tweed, who, with his associates, embodied corruption on a large scale. Known among reformers as the forty thieves, the Tweed Ring had granted lucrative franchises to companies they controlled, padded construction bills, practiced graft and extortion, and exploited every opportunity to plunder the city's funds.*

an estimated $200 million in kickbacks and payoffs. When Mark Twain and coauthor Charles Dudley Warner published their satiric novel *The Gilded Age** (1873), readers recognized the book's speculators, self-promoters, and maniacal opportunists as familiar types in public life.

Grant had some success in foreign policy. In 1872 his competent secretary of state, Hamilton Fish, engineered the settlement of the *Alabama* claims with England. To compensate for damage done by British-built raiders sold to the Confederacy during the war, an international tribunal awarded the United States $15.5 million. But the

---

*The name Gilded Age was subsequently used to refer to the decades from the 1870s to the 1890s.

Grant administration undercut this success with a fiasco when it tried to add nonadjacent territory to the United States, as the Johnson administration had done. In 1867 Johnson's secretary of state, William H. Seward, had negotiated a treaty in which the United States bought Alaska from Russia at the bargain price of $7.2 million. Although the press mocked "Seward's Ice Box," the purchase kindled expansionists' hopes. In 1870 Grant decided to annex the Caribbean island nation of Santo Domingo. Formerly known as Hispaniola and today called the Dominican Republic, Santo Domingo had been passed back and forth since the late eighteenth century among France, Spain, and Haiti. Annexation, Grant believed, would promote Caribbean trade and provide a haven for persecuted southern blacks, who might settle among the Dominicans. American speculators, meanwhile, anticipated windfalls from land sales, commerce, and mining in Santo Domingo. But Congress disliked Grant's annexation plan. Senator Charles Sumner denounced the Santo Domingo scheme as an imperialist "dance of blood." The Senate killed the annexation treaty and further diminished Grant's reputation.

As the election of 1872 approached, dissident Republicans expressed fears that "Grantism" at home and abroad would ruin the party. Even Grant's new running mate, Henry Wilson, referred to the president privately as a millstone, or burden, on his fellow Republicans. The dissidents took action. Led by a combination of former Radicals—including Sumner (now Grant's enemy), Senator Carl Schurz of Missouri, and Congressman George Julian of Indiana—and Republicans left out of Grant's "Great Barbecue," the president's critics formed their own party, the Liberal Republicans.

The Liberals' Revolt

The Liberal Republican revolt marked a turning point in Reconstruction history. By splitting the Republican party, it undermined support for Republican southern policy. The Liberals attacked the "regular" Republicans on several key issues. Denouncing "Grantism" and "spoilsmen" (political hacks who gained party office), they demanded civil-service reform to bring the "best men" into government. Rejecting the usual Republican high-tariff policy, they espoused free trade. Most important, the Liberals condemned "bayonet rule" in the South. Even some Republicans once known for radicalism did a turnabout, claiming that Reconstruction had achieved its goal: blacks had been enfranchised and could henceforth manage for themselves. Corruption in government, North and South, they asserted, now posed a greater danger than Confederate resurgence. In the South, indeed, corrupt Republican regimes were *kept* in power, the Liberals said, because the "best men"—the most capable and experienced politicians—were ex-Confederates who had been barred from officeholding.

For president the new party bypassed Charles Sumner and nominated *New York Tribune* editor Horace Greeley, who had inconsistently supported both a stringent reconstruction policy and leniency toward former rebels. The Democrats endorsed Greeley as well, despite his longtime condemnation of them. Their campaign slogan explained their support: "Anything to Beat Grant." Republican reformers were suddenly allied with the Democratic party that they had recently castigated as a "sewer" of treasonous sentiments.

Horace Greeley proved so diligent a campaigner that he worked himself to death making speeches from the back of a campaign train. He died a few weeks after the election. Grant, who won 56 percent of the popular vote, carried all the northern states as well as a majority of the sixteen southern and border states. But the division among Republicans affected Reconstruction. To deprive the Liberals of a campaign issue, Grant Republicans in Congress, the "regulars," passed an amnesty act that effectively allowed all but a few hundred ex-Confederate officials to hold office. The flood of private amnesty acts that followed convinced white southerners that any ex-Confederate save Jefferson Davis could rise to power. During Grant's second term, Republican desires to discard the "southern question" mounted as a depression of unprecedented scope gripped the nation.

The Panic of 1873

With the postwar years came accelerated industrialization, rapid economic expansion, and frantic speculation. Investors rushed to take advantage of rising prices, new markets, high tariffs, and seemingly boundless opportunities. Railroads provided the biggest lure. In May 1869 railroad executives drove a golden spike into the ground at Promontory Point, Utah, joining the Union Pacific and Central Pacific lines (see Chapter 16). The first transcontinental railroad heralded a new era. By 1873 almost four hundred railroad corporations crisscrossed the Northeast, consuming tons of coal and miles of steel rail from the mines and mills of Pennsylvania and neighboring states. Transforming the northern economy, the railroad boom led entrepreneurs to overspeculate, with drastic results.

Philadelphia banker Jay Cooke, who had helped finance the Union effort with his bond campaign during the Civil War, had taken over a new transcontinental line, the Northern Pacific, in 1869. Northern Pacific securities sold briskly for several years, but in 1873 the line's construction costs outran new investments. In September of that year, his vaults full of bonds that he could no longer sell, Cooke failed to meet his obligations, and his bank, the largest in the nation, shut down. Smaller firms collapsed as well, and so did the stock market. This Panic of 1873 triggered a shattering five-year depression that spread quickly, wreaking widespread devastation. Banks closed, farm prices plummeted, steel furnaces stood idle, and one out of four railroads failed. Within two years eighteen thousand businesses went bankrupt, and by 1878 3 million employees were out of jobs. Those still

The Election of 1872				
Candidates	Parties	Electoral Vote	Popular Vote	Percentage of Popular Vote
ULYSSES S. GRANT	Republican	286	3,596,745	55.6
Horace Greeley*	Democratic		2,843,446	43.9

*Upon Greeley's death shortly after the election, the electors supporting him divided their votes among minor candidates.

at work suffered repeated wage cuts, labor protests mounted, and industrial violence spread (see Chapter 17). The depression of the 1870s revealed the conflicts that would characterize a new, industrial America.

The depression also fed a dispute over currency that had begun in 1865. The Civil War had created fiscal chaos. During the war, Americans had used both national bank notes, yellow in color, which would eventually be converted into gold, and greenbacks, a paper currency not "backed" by a particular weight in gold. To stabilize the postwar currency, greenbacks would have to be withdrawn from circulation. This "sound-money" policy, favored by investors, was implemented by Treasury Secretary Hugh McCulloch with the backing of Congress. But those who depended on easy credit, both indebted farmers and manufacturers, wanted an expanding currency; that is, more greenbacks. Once the depression began, demands for such "easy money" rose. The issue divided both major parties and was compounded by another one: how to repay the federal debt.

During the war the Union government had borrowed what were then astronomical sums, on whatever terms it could get, mainly through the sale of war bonds—in effect, short-term federal IOUs—to private citizens. By 1869 the issue of war-debt repayment was straining the Republican party, whose support came from voters with diverse financial interests. To pacify bondholders, Senator John Sherman of Ohio and other Republican leaders obtained passage of the Public Credit Act of 1869, which promised to pay the war debt in "coin." Holders of war bonds expected no less; in fact, they expected payment in coin, although many had bought their bonds with greenbacks!

With investors reassured by the Public Credit Act, Sherman guided legislation through Congress that swapped the old short-term bonds for new ones payable over the next generation. In 1872 another bill in effect defined "coin" as "gold coin" by dropping the traditional silver dollar from the official coinage. Through a feat of ingenious compromise, which placated investors and debtors, Sherman preserved the public credit, the currency, and Republican unity. In 1875 he engineered the Specie Resumption Act, which promised to put the nation effectively on the gold standard in 1879, while tossing a few more immediate but less impor-

tant bones to Republican voters who wanted "easy money." Grant, no financial theorist, signed this act.

The Republican leadership acted not a moment too soon, because when the Democrats gained control of the House in 1875, with the depression in full force, a verbal storm broke out. Many Democrats and some Republicans passionately demanded that the silver dollar be restored in order to expand the currency and relieve the depression. These "free-silver" advocates secured passage of the Bland-Allison Act of 1878, which partially restored silver coinage. The law required the Treasury to buy $2 million to $4 million worth of silver each month and turn it into coin but did not revive the silver standard. In 1876 other expansionists formed the Greenback party, which adopted the debtors' cause and fought to keep greenbacks in circulation. But despite the election of fourteen Greenback congressmen, they did not get even as far as the free-silver people had. As the nation emerged from depression in 1879, the clamor for "easy money" subsided, only to resurge in the 1890s (see Chapter 20). The controversial "money question" of the 1870s, never permanently solved, gave politicians and voters another reason to focus on new northern issues and forget about the South.

Reconstruction and the Constitution

The Supreme Court of the 1870s also played a role in weakening northern support for Reconstruction. In the wartime crisis, few cases of note had come before the Court. After the war, however, constitutional questions surged into prominence.

First, would the Court support congressional laws to protect freedmen's rights? The decision in *Ex parte* Milligan (1866) suggested not. In this case, the Court declared that a military commission established by the president or Congress could not try civilians in areas remote from war where the civil courts were functioning. Thus special military courts to enforce the Supplementary Freedmen's Bureau Act were doomed. Second, would the Court sabotage the congressional Reconstruction plan, as Republicans feared? Their qualms were valid, for if the Union was indissoluble, as the North had claimed during the war, then the concept of *restoring* states to the Union would be meaningless. In *Texas* v. *White* (1869), the Court took a stand on this question, ruling that, although the

Union was indissoluble and secession was legally impossible, the process of Reconstruction was still constitutional. It was grounded in Congress's power to ensure each state a republican form of government and to recognize the legitimate government in any state.

The 1869 decision protected the Republicans' Reconstruction program. But during the 1870s, when faced with cases involving the Fourteenth and Fifteenth amendments, the Court backed away from Reconstruction policy. Significantly, most of the justices at this time were Republicans who had been appointed to the Supreme Court by Lincoln and Grant.

In the *Slaughterhouse* cases of 1873, the Supreme Court began to chip away at the Fourteenth Amendment. Although the cases involved a business monopoly rather than freedmen's rights, they provided the opportunity for a narrow interpretation of the amendment. In 1869 the Louisiana legislature had granted a monopoly over the New Orleans slaughterhouse business to one firm and had closed down all other slaughterhouses in the interest of public health. The excluded butchers brought suit. The state had deprived them of their lawful occupation without due process of law, they claimed, and such action violated the Fourteenth Amendment, which guaranteed that no state could "abridge the privileges or immunities" of U.S. citizens. The Supreme Court upheld the Louisiana legislature by putting forth a doctrine of "dual citizenship." The Fourteenth Amendment, declared the Court, protected only the rights of *national* citizenship, such as the right of interstate travel or the right to federal protection when on the high seas. It did not protect those basic civil rights that fell to citizens by virtue of their *state* citizenship. Therefore, the federal government was not obliged to protect such rights against violation by the states. The *Slaughterhouse* decision came close to nullifying the intent of the Fourteenth Amendment—to secure freedmen's rights against state encroachment.

The Supreme Court again backed away from Reconstruction in two cases involving the Enforcement Act of 1870. The case of *U.S.* v. *Reese* (1876) centered on Kentucky officials who, after barring blacks from voting, had been indicted in 1873 by a Kentucky federal court under the First Enforcement Act. In its decision in favor of the officials,

the Supreme Court stated that the Fifteenth Amendment did not "confer the right of suffrage upon anyone." It merely prohibited the hindrance of voting on the basis of race, color, or previous condition of servitude. Since the Enforcement Act prohibited the hindrance of *anyone* from voting for *any* reason (that is, since it did not repeat the exact wording of the amendment), the Court declared its crucial sections, and the Kentucky indictment, invalid. Another 1876 case, *U.S.* v. *Cruikshank,* concerned the indictment under the 1870 Enforcement Act of white Louisianians after the Colfax massacre, a battle between armed whites and black state militiamen in which seventy blacks had surrendered, half of whom were then murdered. The Fourteenth Amendment, contended the Court, prohibited only the encroachment on individual rights by a *state,* not by other individuals; "ordinary crime" was not the target of federal law. The decision threw out the indictments and, with them, the effectiveness of the Enforcement Act.

Continuing its retreat from Reconstruction, the Supreme Court in 1883 invalidated both the Civil Rights Act of 1875 and the Ku Klux Klan Act of 1871 and later upheld segregation laws (see Chapter 20). These decisions cumulatively dismantled the Reconstruction policies that Republicans had sponsored after the war. The 1870s rulings that initiated the judicial retreat had a more immediate impact as well. They confirmed rising northern sentiment that Reconstruction's egalitarian goals could not be enforced.

Republicans in Retreat

The Republicans did not reject Reconstruction suddenly but rather disengaged from it gradually. The withdrawal process began with Grant's election to the presidency in 1868. Although not an architect of Reconstruction policy, Grant defended that policy and tried to enforce the laws. But he shared with most Americans a belief in decentralized government and a reluctance to assert federal authority in local and state affairs.

During the 1870s, as the northern military presence shrank in the South, Republican idealism waned in the North. The Liberal Republican revolt of 1872 eroded what remained of radicalism. Although the "regular" Republicans, who backed Grant, continued to defend Reconstruction in the

1872 election, many held ambivalent views. Commercial and industrial interests now dominated both wings of the party, and Grant supporters had greater zeal for doing business in and with the South than for rekindling sectional strife. After the Democrats showed renewed strength by winning control of the House in the 1874 elections, in a nationwide sweep, Reconstruction became a political liability.

By 1875 the Radical Republicans, so prominent in the 1860s, had vanished from the political scene. Chase, Stevens, and Sumner were dead. Other Radicals had lost office or had abandoned their former convictions. "Waving the Bloody Shirt," or defaming Democratic opponents by reviving wartime animosity, now struck many Republicans, including former Radicals, as counterproductive. Party leaders reported that voters were "sick of carpet-bag government" and tiring of both the "southern question" and the "Negro question." Under such circumstances, it seemed pointless to continue the unpopular and expensive policy of military intervention in the South to prop up Republican regimes that even President Grant found corrupt. Finally, few Republicans shared the egalitarian spirit that had animated Stevens and Sumner. Politics aside, Republican leaders and voters generally agreed with southern Democrats that blacks, although deserving of freedom, were inferior to whites. To insist on black equality would be a thankless, divisive, and politically suicidal undertaking. Moreover, it would quash any hope of reunion between the regions. The Republicans' retreat from Reconstruction set the stage for its demise in 1877.

Reconstruction Abandoned

"We are in a very hot political contest just now," a Mississippi planter wrote to his daughter in 1875, "with a good prospect of turning out the carpet-bag thieves by whom we have been robbed for the past six to ten years." Similar contests raged through the South in the 1870s, as the resentment of white majorities grew and Democratic influence surged. By the end of 1872, the Democrats had regained power in Tennessee, Virginia, Georgia, and North Carolina. Within three years they won control in Texas, Alabama, Arkansas, and Mississippi. As the 1876 elections approached, Republican rule survived in only three states—South Carolina, Florida, and Louisiana. Democratic victories in the state elections of 1876 and political bargaining in Washington in 1877 abruptly ended what little remained of Reconstruction.

Redeeming the South

After 1872 the Republicans' collapse in the South accelerated. Congressional amnesty enabled almost all ex-Confederate officials to regain office, divisions among the Republicans loosened their party's weak grip on the southern electorate, and attrition diminished Republican ranks. Some carpetbaggers gave up and returned North, while others, including supporters of Liberal Republicans in the divisive 1872 election, shifted to the Democratic party. Scalawags deserted in even larger numbers. Southerners who had joined the Republicans to moderate rampant radicalism tired of northern interference; once "home rule" by Democrats became a possibility, staying Republican meant going down with a sinking ship. As a Mississippian explained, *not* being a Democrat would condemn his family to "social isolation" and "political oblivion." Scalawag defections ruined Republican prospects for survival. In some states, as white southerners fled the Republican party, blacks became more powerful within it, thus polarizing voters into white and black camps. Unable to win new white votes or retain the old ones, the always precarious Republican coalition fell apart.

Meanwhile, the Democrats mobilized grassroots support and overcame the white voter apathy that had plagued the early days of Reconstruction. The resurrected southern Democratic party was not a pillar of unity. Within it, businessmen who envisioned an industrialized "New South" opposed an agrarian faction called the Bourbons, who represented the old planter elite. But all Democrats shared a major goal: to oust the Republicans from office. Their tactics varied from state to state. Alabama Democrats won by promising to cut taxes and by getting out the white vote. In Louisiana the "White League," a vigilante organization formed in 1874, undermined the Republicans' hold. Intimidation also proved effective in Mississippi, where violent incidents—like the 1874 slaughter in Vicksburg of

The White League

Alabama's White League, formed in 1874, strove to oust Republicans from office by intimidating black voters. To political cartoonist Thomas Nast, such vigilante tactics suggested an alliance between the White League and the outlawed Ku Klux Klan.

about three hundred blacks by rampaging whites— terrorized black voters. In 1875 the "Mississippi plan" took effect: local Democratic clubs armed their members, dispersed Republican meetings, patrolled voter-registration places, and marched through black areas. "Even in counties where there is no actual killing, the Republicans are paralyzed through fear and will not act," the anguished carpetbag governor of Mississippi wrote to his wife. "Why should I fight a hopeless battle . . . when no possible good to the Negro or anybody else would result?" In 1876, South Carolina's "Rifle Clubs" and "Red Shirts," armed groups that threatened Republicans, continued the scare tactics that had worked so well in Mississippi.

New outbursts of intimidation did not completely squelch black voting. Many blacks throughout the South continued to vote until the end of Reconstruction and after. But the Democrats deprived the Republicans of enough black votes to win state elections. In some counties they encouraged freedmen to vote Democratic at supervised polls where voters cast their ballots in public by placing a card with a party label in a box. In other instances white employers and landowners prevented blacks from voting. Labor contracts included clauses forbidding attendance at political meetings; planters used the threat of eviction to keep sharecroppers in line. Since the Enforcement acts could not be enforced, intimidation and economic pressure succeeded.

Redemption, the word that Democrats used to describe their return to power, meant more than a mere rotation in personnel. When the Democrats took office, they made changes as sweeping as those imposed by the Republicans in 1867–1868. Some

The Duration of Republican Rule in the Ex-Confederate States			
Former Confederate States	*Readmission to the Union Under Congressional Reconstruction*	*Democrats (Conservatives) Gain Control*	*Duration of Republican Rule*
Alabama	June 25, 1868	November 14, 1874	6½ years
Arkansas	June 22, 1868	November 10, 1874	6½ years
Florida	June 25, 1868	January 2, 1877	8½ years
Georgia	July 15, 1870	November 1, 1871	1 year
Louisiana	June 25, 1868	January 2, 1877	8½ years
Mississippi	February 23, 1870	November 3, 1875	5½ years
North Carolina	June 25, 1868	November 3, 1870	2 years
South Carolina	June 25, 1868	November 12, 1876	8 years
Tennessee	July 24, 1866*	October 4, 1869	3 years
Texas	March 30, 1870	January 14, 1873	3 years
Virginia	January 26, 1870	October 5, 1869†	0 years

*Admitted before start of Congressional Reconstruction.
†Democrats gained control before readmission.
SOURCE: John Hope Franklin, *Reconstruction After the Civil War* (Chicago: University of Chicago Press, 1962), 231.

Ho for Kansas!

Benjamin "Pap" Singleton, a one-time fugitive slave from Tennessee, returned there to promote the "exodus" movement of the late 1870s. Forming a real-estate company, Singleton traveled the South recruiting parties of freedmen who were disillusioned with the outcome of Reconstruction to settle the "fine rolling prairies" of Kansas. These emigrants, awaiting a Mississippi River boat, looked forward to midwestern homesteads, freedom from violence, and political equality.

states called constitutional conventions to reverse Republican policies. All cut back expenses, wiped out social programs, lowered taxes, and revised their tax systems to relieve landowners of large burdens. State courts limited the rights of tenants and sharecroppers. Most important, the Democrats used the law to ensure a stable black labor force. Legislatures restored vagrancy laws and revised crop-lien statutes to make landowners' claims superior to those of merchants. The redeemers extended their inventiveness to criminal law. Local ordinances in heavily black counties might restrict hunting, fishing, gun carrying, and ownership of dogs and thereby curtail the everyday activities of freedmen who lived off the land. States passed severe laws against trespassing and theft; stealing livestock or wrongly taking part of a crop became grand larceny with a penalty of up to five years at hard labor. By the end of Reconstruction, a large black convict work force had been leased out to private contractors, who profited from their labor.

For the freedmen, whose aspirations had been raised by Republican rule, the impact of redemption was dispiriting if not demoralizing. The new laws, Tennessee blacks contended at an 1875 convention, would "place the race in a condition of servitude scarcely less degrading than that endured before the late civil war." During the late 1870s, as the political climate grew more oppressive, an "exodus" movement spread through Mississippi, Tennessee, Texas, and Louisiana. "We looked around and we seed that there was no way on earth that we could better our condition," a Louisiana "colonization council" declared in 1877. Seeking a way out of the South, some freedmen decided to become homesteaders in Kansas. After a major outbreak of "Kansas fever" in 1879, four thousand "exodusters" from Mississippi and Louisiana joined about ten thousand who had reached Kansas in smaller groups earlier in the decade. But the vast majority of freedmen, devoid of resources, had no migration options or escape route. Mass movement of southern blacks to the North and Midwest would not gain momentum until the twentieth century.

The Election of 1876

By the autumn of 1876, with redemption almost complete, both parties moved to discard the heritage of animosity left by the war and Reconstruction. The Republicans nominated Rutherford B. Hayes, three times Ohio's governor, for president. Untainted by the scandals of the Grant administration and popular with all factions in his party, Hayes presented himself as a "moderate" on southern policy. He favored "home rule" in the South and a guarantee of civil and political rights for all—two planks that were by now clearly contradictory. The Democrats nominated Governor Samuel B. Tilden of New York, a millionaire corporate lawyer and political reformer. Known for his assaults on the rapacious Tweed Ring that had plundered New York City's treasury, Tilden campaigned against governmental fraud and waste. The candidates had much in common. As fiscal conservatives, both favored sound money. Both endorsed civil-service reform and decried corruption, an irony since the 1876 election would prove extremely corrupt.

Tilden won the popular vote by a small margin and seemed destined to capture the 185 electoral votes needed for victory. But the Republicans challenged the pro-Tilden returns from South Carolina, Florida, and Louisiana. If they could deprive the Democrats of these nineteen electoral votes, Hayes would become president. The Democrats, who needed only one of the disputed electoral votes for victory, challenged the validity of Oregon's single electoral vote, which the Republicans had won, on a technicality. Twenty electoral votes, therefore, were in contention. Republicans, however, still controlled the electoral machinery in the three unredeemed southern states, where they threw out enough Democratic ballots to declare Hayes the winner.

The nation now faced an unprecedented dilemma: each party claimed victory in the contested states, and each accused the other of fraud. In fact, both sets of southern results had been obtained by fraud: the Republicans had discarded legitimate Democratic ballots, while the Democrats had illegally prevented freedmen from voting. To resolve the conflict, Congress in January 1877 created a special electoral commission to determine which party would get the contested electoral votes. Made up of senators, representatives, and Supreme Court justices, the commission included seven Democrats, seven Republicans, and one independent, justice David Davis of Illinois. When

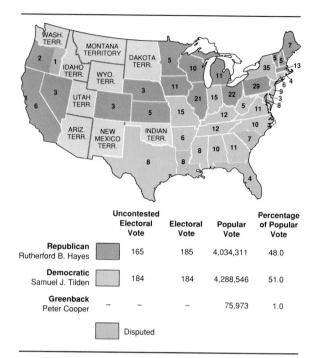

	Uncontested Electoral Vote	Electoral Vote	Popular Vote	Percentage of Popular Vote
Republican Rutherford B. Hayes	165	185	4,034,311	48.0
Democratic Samuel J. Tilden	184	184	4,288,546	51.0
Greenback Peter Cooper	–	–	75,973	1.0
Disputed				

The Disputed Election of 1876

Davis resigned to run for the Senate, Congress replaced him with a Republican, and the commission handed the election to Hayes by an 8 to 7 vote.

Congress now had to certify the new electoral vote. But since the Democrats controlled the House, a new obstacle loomed. Some Democrats planned a filibuster to forestall approval of the electoral vote. Had they carried out their scheme, the nation would have been without a president on inauguration day. But there remained room for compromise, for many southern Democrats accepted Hayes's election. Among them were former scalawags with commercial interests, who still favored Republican financial policies, and railroad investors, who hoped that a Republican administration would help them build a southern transcontinental line. Other southerners cared mainly about Democratic state victories and did not mind conceding the presidency as long as the new Republican administration would leave the South alone. Republican leaders, although sure of eventual triumph, were willing to bargain as well, for candidate Hayes desired not merely victory but southern approval.

A series of informal negotiations ensued, at which politicians of both parties exchanged promises. Ohio Republicans and southern Democrats who met at the Wormley House, a Washington hotel, reached an agreement that if Hayes won the election, he would remove federal troops from South Carolina and Louisiana, and Democrats could gain control of those states. In other bargaining sessions, southern politicians asked for federal patronage, federal aid to railroads, and federal support for internal improvements. In return, they promised to drop the filibuster, to accept Hayes as president, and to treat freedmen fairly.

With the threatened filibuster broken, Congress ratified Hayes's election. Once in office, Hayes fulfilled some of the promises that his Republican colleagues had made. He appointed a former Confederate as postmaster general and ordered federal troops who guarded the South Carolina and Louisiana statehouses back to their barracks. Although federal soldiers remained in the South after 1877,

they no longer served a political function. The Democrats, meanwhile, took control of state governments in Louisiana, South Carolina, and Florida. When Republican rule toppled in these states, the era of Reconstruction finally ended, though more with a whimper than with a resounding crash.

But some of the bargains struck in the Compromise of 1877, such as the Democrats' promises to treat southern blacks fairly, were forgotten, as were Hayes's campaign pledges to ensure the freedmen's rights. "When you turned us loose, you turned us loose to the sky, to the storm, to the whirlwind, and worst of all . . . to the wrath of our infuriated masters," Frederick Douglass had charged at the Republican convention in 1876. "The question now is, do you mean to make good to us the promises in your Constitution?" The answer provided by the 1876 election and the 1877 compromises was "No."

Conclusion

The end of Reconstruction brought benefits to both political parties. Although unable to retain a southern constituency, the Republican party was no longer burdened by the unpopular "southern question." And it had firm support in New England, the Middle Atlantic states, and the Great Lakes states. The Democrats, who had regained power in the ex-Confederate states, would remain entrenched there for almost a century. To be sure, the South was now tied to sharecropping and economic backwardness as securely as it had once been tied to slavery. But "home rule," or Democratic control, was firmly in place.

Reconstruction's end also signaled a triumph for nationalism and the spirit of reunion. In the fall of 1877, President Hayes made a rousing goodwill tour of the South to champion reconciliation, and similar celebrations continued through the 1880s and 1890s. When former president Grant died in 1885, veterans of both Civil War armies served as pallbearers. Jefferson Davis, imprisoned for two years after the war but never brought to trial, urged young men to "lay aside all rancor, all bitter sectional feeling." The federal government turned battlefields into national parks where veterans of both armies could gather for reunions. As the nation applauded reconciliation, the reputation of Reconstruction sank. Looking back on the 1860s and 1870s, most late-nineteenth-century Americans dismissed the congressional effort to reconstruct the South as a fiasco—a tragic interlude of "radical rule" or "black reconstruction," fashioned by carpetbaggers, scalawags, and Radical Republicans.

With the hindsight of a century, recent historians continue to regard Reconstruction as a failure, though of a different kind. No longer viewed as a misguided scheme that collapsed because of radical excess, Reconstruction is now widely seen as a democratic experiment that did not go far enough. Historians cite two main causes. First, Congress did not promote freedmen's independence through land reform; without property of their own, southern blacks lacked the economic power to defend their interests as free citizens. Property ownership, however, does not necessarily ensure political rights, nor does it invariably provide economic security. Considering the depressed state of southern agriculture in the postwar decades, the freedmen's fate as independent farmers would likely have been perilous. Thus the land-reform question, like much else about Reconstruction, remains a subject of debate. A second cause of Reconstruction's collapse is less open to dispute: the federal government neglected to back congressional Reconstruction with military force. Given the choice between protecting blacks' rights at whatever cost and promoting reunion, the government opted for reunion. Reconstruction's failure, therefore, was the federal government's failure to fulfill its own goals and create a biracial democracy in the South. As a result, the nation's adjustment to the consequences of emancipation would continue into the twentieth century.

The Reconstruction era left some significant legacies, including the Fourteenth and Fifteenth amendments, both products of an extraordinary chain of postwar political crises. Although neither amendment would be used to protect minority rights for almost a century, they remain monuments to the democratic zeal that swept Congress in the 1860s. The Reconstruction years also hold a significant place in black history. During this brief respite between slavery and repression, southern blacks reconstituted their families, created new institutions, took part in the transformation of southern agriculture, and participated in government, for the first time in American history. The aspirations and achievements of the Reconstruction era left an indelible mark on black citizens, as is vividly conveyed in an excerpt from a federal document. In the 1880s a congressional committee investigating southern labor conditions solicited the testimony of James K. Green of Montgomery, Alabama, a black politician during Reconstruction and subsequently a carpenter and contractor. At the end of the war, Green reported,

I knew nothing more than to obey my master, and there were thousands of us in the same attitude, that didn't know the Lord's prayer, but the tocsin of freedom sounded and knocked at the door and we walked out like free men and we met the exigencies as they grew up, and shouldered the responsibilities.

Green's proud memory of blacks' achievements reflected one kind of postwar experience. Consigning the Reconstruction era to history, other Americans of the 1880s turned their energies to their economic futures—to their railroads, factories, and mills, and to the exploitation of their bountiful natural resources.

CHRONOLOGY

1863 President Abraham Lincoln issues Proclamation of Amnesty and Reconstruction.

1864 Wade-Davis bill passed by Congress and pocket-vetoed by Lincoln.

1865 Freedmen's Bureau established.

Civil War ends.

Lincoln assassinated; Andrew Johnson becomes president.

1865 Johnson issues Proclamation of Amnesty and
(cont.) Reconstruction.

Ex-Confederate states hold constitutional conventions (May–December).

Black conventions begin in the ex-Confederate states.

Thirteenth Amendment added to the Constitution.

Presidential Reconstruction completed.

1866 Congress enacts the Civil Rights Act of 1866 and the Supplementary Freedmen's Bureau Act over Johnson's vetoes.

Ku Klux Klan founded in Tennessee.

Congress proposes the Fourteenth Amendment.

Tennessee readmitted to the Union.

Race riots in southern cities.

Republicans win congressional elections.

Thirty-ninth Congress begins debates over Reconstruction policy.

1867 Reconstruction Act of 1867.

William Seward negotiates the purchase of Alaska.

Constitutional conventions meet in the ex-Confederate states.

Howard University founded.

1868 President Johnson is impeached, tried, and acquitted.

Omnibus Act.

Fourteenth Amendment added to the Constitution.

Ulysses S. Grant elected president.

1869 Transcontinental railroad completed.

1870 Congress readmits the four remaining southern states to the Union.

Fifteenth Amendment added to the Constitution.

Enforcement Act of 1870.

1871 Second Enforcement Act.

Ku Klux Klan Act.

1872 Liberal Republican party formed.

Amnesty Act.

Alabama claims settled.

Grant reelected president.

1873 Panic of 1873 begins (September–October), setting off a five-year depression.

1874 Democrats gain control of the House of Representatives.

1875 Civil Rights Act of 1875.

Specie Resumption Act.

1876 Disputed presidential election: Rutherford B. Hayes versus Samuel B. Tilden.

GRAND NATIONAL REPUBLICAN BANNER.

1877 Electoral commission decides election in favor of Hayes.

The last Republican-controlled governments overthrown in Florida, Louisiana, and South Carolina.

1879 "Exodus" movement spreads through several southern states.

For Further Reading

Eric Foner, *Reconstruction: America's Unfinished Revolution, 1863–1877* (1988). A thorough exploration of Reconstruction that draws on recent scholarship and stresses the centrality of the black experience.

John Hope Franklin, *Reconstruction After the Civil War* (1961). An overview that dismantles the traditional view of Reconstruction as a disastrous experiment in radical rule.

William Gillette, *Retreat from Reconstruction, 1869–1879* (1979). A survey of the era's national politics, indicting Republican policy makers for vacillation and lack of commitment to racial equality.

Leon Litwack, *Been in the Storm So Long: The Aftermath of Slavery* (1979). A comprehensive study of the black response to emancipation in 1865–1866.

Michael Perman, *The Road to Redemption: Southern Politics, 1869–1879* (1984). Analysis of how the Democratic party gained power in the South and toppled the Reconstruction governments.

Roger L. Ransom and Richard Sutch, *One Kind of Freedom: The Economic Consequences of Emancipation* (1977). Two economists' assessment of the impact of free black labor on the South and explanation of the development of sharecropping and the crop-lien system.

Kenneth M. Stampp, *The Era of Reconstruction, 1865–1877* (1965). A classic recent interpretation of Reconstruction, focusing on the establishment and fall of Republican governments.

Allen W. Trelease, *White Terror: The Ku Klux Klan Conspiracy and Southern Reconstruction* (1971). An examination of postwar vigilantism in the southern states until the suppression of the Ku Klux Klan by the federal government in 1871–1872.

Joel Williamson, *The Negro in South Carolina During Reconstruction, 1861–1877* (1965). A pioneer study of black life and institutions after emancipation.

Additional Bibliography

Reconstruction Politics

Richard H. Abbott, *The Republican Party and the South, 1855–1877* (1986); Herman Belz, *Emancipation and Equal Rights: Politics and Constitutionalism in the Civil War Era* (1978); Michael Les Benedict, *A Compromise of Principle: Congressional Republicans and Reconstruction, 1863–1869* (1974) and *The Impeachment and Trial of Andrew Johnson* (1973); W. R. Brock, *An American Crisis: Congress and Reconstruction, 1865–1867* (1963); Fawn Brodie, *Thaddeus Stevens: Scourge of the South* (1959); LaWanda Cox and John H. Cox, *Politics, Principles, and Prejudice: Dilemma of Reconstruction in America* (1963); Richard O. Curry, ed., *Radicalism, Racism, and Party Realignment: The Border States During Reconstruction* (1969); David Donald, *Charles Sumner and the Rights of Man* (1970) and *The Politics of Reconstruction, 1863–1867* (1965); Ellen Carol DuBois, *Feminism and Suffrage: The Emergence of an Independent Women's Movement in America, 1848–1869* (1978), Chapters 2–6; William Gillette, *The Right to Vote: Politics and Passage of the Fifteenth Amendment* (1969); Harold Hyman, *A More Perfect Union: The Impact of the Civil War and Reconstruction on the Constitution* (1973); Stanley I. Kutler, *Judicial Power and Reconstruction* (1968); Eric McKitrick, *Andrew Johnson and Reconstruction* (1960); James M. McPherson, *Ordeal by Fire: The Civil War and Reconstruction* (1982); James C. Mohr, *Radical Republicans in the North: State Politics During Reconstruction* (1976).

The South

Dan C. Carter, *When the War Was Over: Self-Reconstruction in the South, 1865–1867* (1985); Richard Nelson Current, *Those Terrible Carpetbaggers* (1988); Stephen Hahn, *The Roots of Southern Populism: Yeoman Farmers and the Transformation of the Georgia Upcountry, 1850–1890* (1983); William C. Harris, *The Day of the Carpetbagger: Republican Reconstruction in Mississippi* (1979); Otto Olsen, ed., *Reconstruction and Redemption in the South* (1980); Michael Perman, *Reunion Without Compromise: The South and Reconstruction, 1865–1868* (1973); Mark W. Summers, *Railroads, Reconstruction, and the Gospel of Prosperity: Aid Under the Radical Republicans, 1865–1877* (1984); Ted Tunnell, *Crucible of Reconstruction: War, Radicalism, and Race in Louisiana, 1862–1877* (1984); Jonathan M. Wiener, *Social Origins of the New South: Alabama, 1860–1885* (1978).

Emancipation and the Freedmen

Ira Berlin et al., eds., *Freedom: A Documentary History of Emancipation*, No. 1 (1986) and No. 2 (1983); Carol Rothrock Bleser, *The Promised Land: The History of the South Carolina Land Commission, 1869–1890* (1969); LaWanda Cox, "The Promise of Land for the Freedmen," *Mississippi Valley Historical Review* 45 (1958): 413–440; W. E. B. Du Bois, *Black Reconstruction in America, 1860–1880* (1935); Barbara Jeanne Fields, *Slavery and Freedom on the Middle Ground: Maryland During the Nineteenth Century* (1985); Eric Foner, *Nothing but Freedom: Emancipation and Its Legacies* (1983) and *Politics and Ideology in the Age of the Civil War* (1980), Chapters 6–7; Herbert G. Gutman, *The Black Family in Slavery and Freedom, 1750–1925* (1976); Robert Higgs, *Competition and Coercion: Blacks in the American Economy, 1865–1914* (1977); Thomas Holt, *Black over White: Negro Political Leadership in South Carolina During Reconstruction* (1977); Jacqueline Jones, *Soldiers of Light and Love: Northern Teachers and Georgia Blacks, 1865–1873* (1980) and *Labor of Love, Labor of Sorrow: Black Women, Work, and the Family from Slavery to the Present* (1985), Chapter 2; Peter Kolchin, *First Freedom: The Responses of Alabama's Blacks to Emancipation and Reconstruction* (1972); Lawrence W. Levine, *Black Culture and Black Consciousness: Afro-American Folk*

Thought from Slavery to Freedom (1977); William S. McFeely, *Yankee Stepfather: General O. O. Howard and the Freedmen* (1966); Nell Irvin Painter, *Exodusters* (1977); James Roark, *Masters Without Slaves: Southern Planters in the Civil War and Reconstruction* (1978); William Preston Vaughan, *Schools for All: The Blacks and Public Education in the South, 1865–1877* (1974); Joel Williamson, *The Crucible of Race: Black-White Relations in the American South Since Emancipation* (1984).

National Trends

Paul H. Buck, *The Road to Reunion, 1865–1900* (1937); Adrian Cook, *The Alabama Claims* (1975); Ari M. Hoogenboom, *Outlawing the Spoils: A History of the Civil Service Reform Movement* (1961); William S. McFeely, *Grant: A Biography* (1981); David Montgomery, *Beyond Equality: Labor and the Radical Republicans, 1862–1872* (1967); Walter T. K. Nugent, *The Money Question During Reconstruction* (1967) and *Money and American Society, 1865–1880* (1968); Keith I. Polakoff, *The Politics of Inertia: The Election of 1876 and the End of Reconstruction* (1973); John C. Sproat, *"The Best Men": Liberal Reformers in the Gilded Age* (1968); Irwin Unger, *The Greenback Era: A Social and Political History of American Finance* (1964); Allen Weinstein, *Prelude to Populism: Origins of the Silver Issue, 1867–1878* (1970); C. Vann Woodward, *Reunion and Reaction: The Compromise of 1877 and the End of Reconstruction* (rev. ed., 1956).

APPENDIX

Declaration of Independence

IN CONGRESS, JULY 4, 1776

THE UNANIMOUS DECLARATION OF THE THIRTEEN UNITED STATES OF AMERICA

When, in the course of human events, it becomes necessary for one people to dissolve the political bands which have connected them with another, and to assume, among the powers of the earth, the separate and equal station to which the laws of nature and of nature's God entitle them, a decent respect to the opinions of mankind requires that they should declare the causes which impel them to the separation.

We hold these truths to be self-evident: That all men are created equal; that they are endowed by their Creator with certain unalienable rights; that among these are life, liberty, and the pursuit of happiness; that, to secure these rights, governments are instituted among men, deriving their just powers from the consent of the governed; that whenever any form of government becomes destructive of these ends, it is the right of the people to alter or to abolish it, and to institute new government, laying its foundation on such principles, and organizing its powers in such form, as to them shall seem most likely to effect their safety and happiness. Prudence, indeed, will dictate that governments long established should not be changed for light and transient causes; and accordingly all experience hath shown that mankind are more disposed to suffer, while evils are sufferable, than to right themselves by abolishing the forms to which they are accustomed. But when a long train of abuses and usurpations, pursuing invariably the same object, evinces a design to reduce them under absolute despotism, it is their right, it is their duty, to throw off such government, and to provide new guards for their future security. Such has been the patient sufferance of these colonies; and such is now the necessity which constrains them to alter their former systems of government. The history of the present King of Great Britain is a history of repeated injuries and usurpations, all having in direct object the establishment of an absolute tyranny over these states. To prove this, let facts be submitted to a candid world.

He has refused his assent to laws, the most wholesome and necessary for the public good.

He has forbidden his governors to pass laws of immediate and pressing importance, unless suspended in their operation till his assent should be obtained; and, when so suspended, he has utterly neglected to attend to them.

He has refused to pass other laws for the accommodation of large districts of people, unless those people would relinquish the right of representation in the legislature, a right inestimable to them, and formidable to tyrants only.

He has called together legislative bodies at places unusual, uncomfortable, and distant from the depository of their public records, for the sole purpose of fatiguing them into compliance with his measures.

He has dissolved representative houses repeatedly, for opposing, with manly firmness, his invasions on the rights of the people.

He has refused for a long time, after such dissolutions, to cause others to be elected; whereby the legislative powers, incapable of annihilation, have returned to the people at large for their exercise; the state remaining, in the mean time, exposed to all the dangers of invasions from without and convulsions within.

He has endeavored to prevent the population of these states; for that purpose obstructing the laws of naturalization of foreigners; refusing to pass others to encourage their migration hither, and raising the conditions of new appropriation of lands.

He has obstructed the administration of justice, by refusing his assent to laws for establishing judiciary powers.

He has made judges dependent on his will alone, for the tenure of their offices, and the amount and payment of their salaries.

He has erected a multitude of new offices, and sent hither swarms of officers to harass our people and eat out their substance.

He has kept among us, in times of peace, standing armies, without the consent of our legislatures.

He has affected to render the military independent of, and superior to, the civil power.

He has combined with others to subject us to a jurisdiction foreign to our constitution, and unacknowledged by our laws, giving his assent to their acts of pretended legislation:

For quartering large bodies of armed troops among us;

For protecting them, by a mock trial, from punishment for any murders which they should commit on the inhabitants of these states;

For cutting off our trade with all parts of the world;

For imposing taxes on us without our consent;

For depriving us, in many cases, of the benefits of trial by jury;

For transporting us beyond seas, to be tried for pretended offenses;

For abolishing the free system of English laws in a neighboring province, establishing therein an arbitrary government, and enlarging its boundaries, so as to render it at once an example and fit instrument for introducing the same absolute rule into these colonies;

For taking away our charters, abolishing our most valuable laws, and altering fundamentally the forms of our governments;

For suspending our own legislatures, and declaring themselves invested with power to legislate for us in all cases whatsoever.

He has abdicated government here, by declaring us out of his protection and waging war against us.

He has plundered our seas, ravaged our coasts, burned our towns, and destroyed the lives of our people.

He is at this time transporting large armies of foreign mercenaries to complete the works of death, desolation, and tyranny already begun with circumstances of cruelty and perfidy scarcely paralleled in the most barbarous ages, and totally unworthy of the head of a civilized nation.

He has constrained our fellow-citizens, taken captive on the high seas, to bear arms against their country, to become the executioners of their friends and brethren, or to fall themselves by their hands.

He has excited domestic insurrection among us, and has endeavored to bring on the inhabitants of our frontiers the merciless Indian savages, whose known rule of warfare is an undistinguished destruction of all ages, sexes, and conditions.

In every stage of these oppressions we have petitioned for redress in the most humble terms; our repeated petitions have been answered only by repeated injury. A prince, whose character is thus marked by every act which may define a tyrant, is unfit to be the ruler of a free people.

Nor have we been wanting in our attentions to our British brethren. We have warned them, from time to time, of attempts by their legislature to extend an unwarrantable jurisdiction over us. We have reminded them of the circumstances of our emigration and settlement here. We have appealed to their native justice and magnanimity; and we have conjured them by the ties of our common kindred, to disavow these usurpations, which would inevitably interrupt our connections and correspondence. They, too, have been deaf to the voice of justice and of consanguinity. We must, therefore, acquiesce in the necessity which denounces our separation, and hold them, as we hold the rest of mankind, enemies in war, in peace friends.

We, therefore, the representatives of the United States of America, in General Congress assembled, appealing to the Supreme Judge of the world for the rectitude of our intentions, do, in the name and by the authority of the good people of these colonies, solemnly publish and declare, that these United Colonies are, and of right ought to be, FREE AND INDEPENDENT STATES; that they are absolved from all allegiance to the British crown, and that all political connection between them and the state of Great Britain is, and ought to be, totally dissolved; and that, as free and independent states, they have full power to levy war, conclude peace, contract alliances, establish commerce, and do all other acts and things which independent states may of right do. And for the support of this declaration, with a firm reliance on the protection of Divine Providence, we mutually pledge to each other our lives, our fortunes, and our sacred honor.

JOHN HANCOCK [*President*]
[*and fifty-five others*]

The Articles of Confederation and Perpetual Union

BETWEEN THE STATES OF NEW HAMPSHIRE, MASSACHUSETTS BAY, RHODE ISLAND AND PROVIDENCE PLANTATIONS, CONNECTICUT, NEW YORK, NEW JERSEY, PENNSYLVANIA, DELAWARE, MARYLAND, VIRGINIA, NORTH CAROLINA, SOUTH CAROLINA, GEORGIA.*

Article 1.

The stile of this confederacy shall be "The United States of America."

Article 2.

Each State retains its sovereignty, freedom and independence, and every power, jurisdiction, and right, which is not by this confederation expressly delegated to the United States, in Congress assembled.

Article 3.

The said states hereby severally enter into a firm league of friendship with each other for their common defence, the security of their liberties and their mutual and general welfare; binding themselves to assist each other against all force offered to, or attacks made upon them, or any of them, on account of religion, sovereignty, trade, or any other pretence whatever.

Article 4.

The better to secure and perpetuate mutual friendship and intercourse among the people of the different states in this union, the free inhabitants of each of these states, paupers, vagabonds, and fugitives from justice excepted, shall be entitled to all privileges and immunities of free citizens in the several states; and the people of each State shall have free ingress and regress to and from any other State, and shall enjoy therein all the privileges of trade and commerce, subject to the same duties, impositions, and restrictions, as the inhabitants thereof respectively; provided, that such restrictions shall not extend so far as to prevent the removal of property, imported into any State, to any other State of which the owner is an inhabitant; provided also, that no imposition, duties, or restriction, shall be laid by any State on the property of the United States, or either of them.

If any person guilty of, or charged with treason, felony, or other high misdemeanor in any State, shall flee from justice and be found in any of the United States, he shall, upon demand of the governor or executive power of the State from which he fled, be delivered up and removed to the State having jurisdiction of his offence.

Full faith and credit shall be given in each of these states to the records, acts, and judicial proceedings of the courts and magistrates of every other State.

Article 5.

For the more convenient management of the general interests of the United States, delegates shall be annually appointed, in such manner as the legislature of each State shall direct, to meet in Congress, on the 1st Monday in November in every year, with a power reserved to each State to recall its delegates, or any of them, at any time within the year, and to send others in their stead for the remainder of the year.

No State shall be represented in Congress by less than two, nor by more than seven members; and no person shall be capable of being a delegate for more than three years in any term of six years; nor shall any person, being a delegate, be capable of holding any office under the United States, for which he, or any other for his benefit, receives any salary, fees, or emolument of any kind.

Each State shall maintain its own delegates in a meeting of the states, and while they act as members of the committee of the states.

In determining questions in the United States, in Congress assembled, each State shall have one vote.

---

*This copy of the final draft of the Articles of Confederation is taken from the *Journals*, 9:907–925, November 15, 1777.

Freedom of speech and debate in Congress shall not be impeached or questioned in any court or place out of Congress: and the members of Congress shall be protected in their persons from arrests and imprisonments, during the time of their going to and from, and attendance on Congress, *except for treason,* felony, or breach of the peace.

Article 6.

No State, without the consent of the United States, in Congress assembled, shall send any embassy to, or receive any embassy from, or enter into any conference, agreement, alliance, or treaty with any king, prince, or state; nor shall any person, holding any office of profit or trust under the United States, or any of them, accept of any present, emolument, office or title, of any kind whatever, from any king, prince, or foreign state; nor shall the United States, in Congress assembled, or any of them, grant any title of nobility.

No two or more states shall enter into any treaty, confederation, or alliance, whatever, between them, without the consent of the United States, in Congress assembled, specifying accurately the purposes for which the same is to be entered into, and how long it shall continue.

No State shall lay any imposts or duties which may interfere with any stipulations in treaties entered into by the United States, in Congress assembled, with any king, prince, or state, in pursuance of any treaties already proposed by Congress to the courts of France and Spain.

No vessels of war shall be kept up in time of peace by any State, except such number only as shall be deemed necessary by the United States, in Congress assembled, for the defence of such State or its trade; nor shall any body of forces be kept up by any State, in time of peace, except such number only as, in the judgment of the United States, in Congress assembled, shall be deemed requisite to garrison the forts necessary for the defence of such State; but every State shall always keep up a well regulated and disciplined militia, sufficiently armed and accoutred, and shall provide, and constantly have ready for use, in public stores, a due number of field pieces and tents, and a proper quantity of arms, ammunition and camp equipage.

No State shall engage in any war without the consent of the United States, in Congress assembled, unless such State be actually invaded by enemies, or shall have received certain advice of a resolution being formed by some nation of Indians to invade such State, and the danger is so imminent as not to admit of a delay till the United States, in Congress assembled, can be consulted; nor shall any State grant commissions to any ships or vessels of war, nor letters of marque or reprisal, except it be after a declaration of war by the United States, in Congress assembled, and then only against the kingdom or state, and the subjects thereof, against which war has been so declared, and under such regulations as shall be established by the United States, in Congress assembled, unless such States be infested by pirates, in which case vessels of war may be fitted out for that occasion, and kept so long as the danger shall continue, or until the United States, in Congress assembled, shall determine otherwise.

Article 7.

When land forces are raised by any State for the common defence, all officers of or under the rank of colonel, shall be appointed by the legislature of each State respectively, by whom such forces shall be raised, or in such manner as such State shall direct; and all vacancies shall be filled up by the State which first made the appointment.

Article 8.

All charges of war and all other expences, that shall be incurred for the common defence or general welfare, and allowed by the United States, in Congress assembled, shall be defrayed out of a common treasury, which shall be supplied by the several states, in proportion to the value of all land within each State, granted to or surveyed for any person, as such land and the buildings and improvements thereon shall be estimated according to such mode as the United States, in Congress assembled, shall, from time to time, direct and appoint.

The taxes for paying that proportion shall be laid and levied by the authority and direction of the legislatures of the several states, within the time agreed upon by the United States, in Congress assembled.

Article 9.

The United States, in Congress assembled, shall have the sole and exclusive right and power of determining on peace and war, except in the cases mentioned in the 6th article; of sending and receiving ambassadors; entering into treaties and alliances, provided that no treaty of commerce shall be made, whereby the legislative power of the respective states shall be restrained from imposing such imposts and duties on foreigners as their own people are subjected to, or from prohibiting the exportation or importation of any species of goods or commodities whatsoever; of establishing rules for deciding, in all cases, what captures on land or water shall be legal, and in what manner prizes, taken by land or naval forces in the service of the United States, shall be divided or appropriated; of granting letters of marque and reprisal in times of peace; appointing courts for the trial of piracies and felonies committed on the high seas, and establishing courts for receiving and determining, finally, appeals in all cases of captures; provided, that no member of Congress shall be appointed a judge of any of the said courts.

The United States, in Congress assembled, shall also be the last resort on appeal in all disputes and differences now subsisting, or that hereafter may arise between two or more states concerning boundary, jurisdiction or any other cause whatever; which authority shall always be exercised in the manner following: whenever the legislative or executive authority, or lawful agent of any State, in controversy with another, shall present a petition to Congress, stating the matter in question, and praying for a hearing, notice thereof shall be given, by order of Congress, to the legislative or executive authority of the other State in controversy, and a day assigned for the appearance of the parties by their lawful agents, who shall then be directed to appoint, by joint consent, commissioners or judges to constitute a court for hearing and determining the matter in question; but, if they cannot agree, Congress shall name three persons out of each of the United States, and from the list of such persons each party shall alternately strike out one, in the petitioners beginning, until the number shall be reduced to thirteen; and from that number not less than seven, nor more than nine names, as Congress shall direct, shall, in the presence of Congress, be drawn out by lot; and the persons whose names shall be drawn, or any five of them, shall be commissioners or judges to hear and finally determine the controversy, so always

as a major part of the judges who shall hear the cause shall agree in the determination; and if either party shall neglect to attend at the day appointed, without shewing reasons which Congress shall judge sufficient, or, being present, shall refuse to strike, the Congress shall proceed to nominate three persons out of each State, and the secretary of Congress shall strike in behalf of such party absent or refusing; and the judgment and sentence of the court to be appointed, in the manner before prescribed, shall be final and conclusive; and if any of the parties shall refuse to submit to the authority of such court, or to appear or defend their claim or cause, the court shall nevertheless proceed to pronounce sentence or judgment, which shall, in like manner, be final and decisive, the judgment or sentence and other proceedings being, in either case, transmitted to Congress, and lodged among the acts of Congress for the security of the parties concerned: provided, that every commissioner, before he sits in judgment, shall take an oath, to be administered by one of the judges of the supreme or superior court of the State where the cause shall be tried, "well and truly to hear and determine the matter in question, according to the best of his judgment, without favour, affection, or hope of reward": provided, also, that no State shall be deprived of territory for the benefit of the United States.

All controversies concerning the private right of soil, claimed under different grants of two or more states, whose jurisdictions, as they may respect such lands and the states which passed such grants, are adjusted, the said grants, or either of them, being at the same time claimed to have originated antecedent to such settlement of jurisdiction, shall, on the petition of either party to the Congress of the United States, be finally determined, as near as may be, in the same manner as is before prescribed for deciding disputes respecting territorial jurisdiction between different states.

The United States, in Congress assembled, shall also have the sole and exclusive right and power of regulating the alloy and value of coin struck by their own authority, or by that of the respective states; fixing the standard of weights and measures throughout the United States; regulating the trade and managing all affairs with the Indians not members of any of the states; provided that the legislative right of any State within its own limits be not infringed or violated; establishing and regulating post offices from one State to another throughout all the United States, and exacting such postage on the papers passing through the same as may be requisite to defray the expences of the said office; appointing all officers of the land forces in the service of the United States, excepting regimental officers; appointing all the officers of the naval forces, and commissioning all officers whatever in the service of the United States; making rules for the government and regulation of the said land and naval forces, and directing their operations.

The United States, in Congress assembled, shall have authority to appoint a committee to sit in the recess of Congress, to be denominated "a Committee of the States," and to consist of one delegate from each State, and to appoint such other committees and civil officers as may be necessary for managing the general affairs of the United States, under their direction; to appoint one of their number to preside; provided that no person be allowed to serve in the office of president more than one year in any term of three years; to ascertain the necessary sums of money to be raised for the service of the United States, and to appropriate and apply the same for defraying the public expences; to borrow money or emit bills on the credit of the United States, transmitting, every half year, to the respective states, an account of the sums of money so borrowed or emitted; to build and equip a navy; to agree upon the number of land forces, and to make requisitions from each State for its quota, in proportion to the number of white inhabitants in such State; which requisitions shall be binding; and, thereupon, the legislature of each State shall appoint the regimental officers, raise the men, and cloathe, arm, and equip them in a soldier-like manner, at the expence of the United States; and the officers and men so cloathed, armed, and equipped, shall march to the place appointed and within the time agreed on by the United States, in Congress assembled; but if the United States, in Congress assembled, shall, on consideration of circumstances, judge proper that any State should not raise men, or should raise a smaller number than its quota, and that any other State should raise a greater number of men than the quota thereof, such extra number shall be raised, officered, cloathed, armed, and equipped in the same manner as the quota of such State, unless the legislature of such State shall judge that such

extra number cannot be safely spared out of the same, in which case they shall raise, officer, cloathe, arm, and equip as many of such extra number as they judge can be safely spared. And the officers and men so cloathed, armed, and equipped, shall march to the place appointed and within the time agreed on by the United States, in Congress assembled.

The United States, in Congress assembled, shall never engage in a war, nor grant letters of marque and reprisal in time of peace, nor enter into any treaties or alliances, nor coin money, nor regulate the value thereof, nor ascertain the sums and expences necessary for the defence and welfare of the United States, or any of them: nor emit bills, nor borrow money on the credit of the United States, nor appropriate money, nor agree upon the number of vessels of war to be built or purchased, or the number of land or sea forces to be raised, nor appoint a commander in chief of the army or navy, unless nine states assent to the same; nor shall a question on any other point, except for adjourning from day to day, be determined, unless by the votes of a majority of the United States, in Congress assembled.

The Congress of the United States shall have power to adjourn to any time within the year, and to any place within the United States, so that no period of adjournment be for a longer duration than the space of six months, and shall publish the journal of their proceedings monthly, except such parts thereof, relating to treaties, alliances or military operations, as, in their judgment, require secrecy; and the yeas and nays of the delegates of each State on any question shall be entered on the journal, when it is desired by any delegate; and the delegates of a State, or any of them, at his, or their request, shall be furnished with a transcript of the said journal, except such parts as are above excepted, to lay before the legislatures of the several states.

Article 10.

The committee of the states, or any nine of them, shall be authorized to execute, in the recess of Congress, such of the powers of Congress as the United States, in Congress assembled, by the consent of nine states, shall, from time to time, think expedient to vest them with; provided, that no power be delegated to the said committee for the exercise of which, by the articles of confederation, the voice of nine states, in the Congress of the United States assembled, is requisite.

Article 11.

Canada acceding to this confederation, and joining in the measures of the United States, shall be admitted into and entitled to all the advantages of this union; but no other colony shall be admitted into the same, unless such admission be agreed to by nine states.

Article 12.

All bills of credit emitted, monies borrowed and debts contracted by, or under the authority of Congress before the assembling of the United States, in pursuance of the present confederation, shall be deemed and considered as a charge against the United States, for payment and satisfaction whereof the said United States and the public faith are hereby solemnly pledged.

Article 13.

Every State shall abide by the determinations of the United States, in Congress assembled, on all questions which, by this confederation, are submitted to them. And the articles of this confederation shall be inviolably observed by every State, and the union shall be perpetual; nor shall any alteration at any time hereafter be made in any of them, unless such alteration be agreed to in a Congress of the United States, and be afterwards confirmed by the legislatures of every State.

These articles shall be proposed to the legislatures of all the United States, to be considered, and if approved of by them, they are advised to authorize their delegates to ratify the same in the Congress of the United States; which being done, the same shall become conclusive.

Constitution of the United States of America

PREAMBLE

We the people of the United States, in order to form a more perfect union, establish justice, insure domestic tranquillity, provide for the common defense, promote the general welfare, and secure the blessings of liberty to ourselves and our posterity, do ordain and establish this CONSTITUTION for the United States of America.

Article I

Section 1. All legislative powers herein granted shall be vested in a Congress of the United States, which shall consist of a Senate and a House of Representatives.

Section 2. The House of Representatives shall be composed of members chosen every second year by the people of the several States, and the electors in each State shall have the qualifications requisite for electors of the most numerous branch of the State Legislature.

No person shall be a Representative who shall not have attained to the age of twenty-five years, and been seven years a citizen of the United States, and who shall not, when elected, be an inhabitant of that State in which he shall be chosen.

Representatives and direct taxes shall be apportioned among the several States which may be included within this Union, according to their respective numbers, *which shall be determined by adding to the whole number of free persons, including those bound to service for a term of years and excluding Indians not taxed, three-fifths of all other persons.* The actual enumeration shall be made within three years after the first meeting of the Congress of the United States, and within every subsequent term of ten years, in such manner as they shall by law direct. The number of Representatives shall not exceed one for every thirty thousand, but each State shall have at least one Representative; *and until such enumeration shall be made, the State of New Hampshire shall be entitled to choose three, Massachusetts eight, Rhode Island and Providence Plantations one, Connecticut five, New York six, New Jersey four, Pennsylvania eight, Delaware one, Maryland six, Virginia ten, North Carolina five, South Carolina five, and Georgia three.*

When vacancies happen in the representation from any State, the Executive authority thereof shall issue writs of election to fill such vacancies.

The House of Representatives shall choose their Speaker and other officers; and shall have the sole power of impeachment.

Section 3. The Senate of the United States shall be composed of two Senators from each State, *chosen by the legislature thereof,* for six years; and each Senator shall have one vote.

Immediately after they shall be assembled in consequence of the first election, they shall be divided as equally as may be into three classes. The seats of the Senators of the first class shall be vacated at the expiration of the second year, of the second class at the expiration of the fourth year, and of the third class at the expiration of the sixth year, so that one-third may be chosen every second year; *and if vacancies happen by resignation or otherwise, during the recess of the legislature of any State, the Executive thereof may make temporary appointments until the next meeting of the legislature, which shall then fill such vacancies.*

No person shall be a Senator who shall not have attained to the age of thirty years, and been nine years a citizen of the United States, and who shall not, when elected, be an inhabitant of that State for which he shall be chosen.

The Vice President of the United States shall be President of the Senate, but shall have no vote, unless they be equally divided.

Note: Passages that are no longer in effect are printed in italic type.

The Senate shall choose their other officers, and also a President *pro tempore*, in the absence of the Vice President, or when he shall exercise the office of the President of the United States.

The Senate shall have the sole power to try all impeachments. When sitting for that purpose, they shall be on oath or affirmation. When the President of the United States is tried, the Chief Justice shall preside: and no person shall be convicted without the concurrence of two-thirds of the members present.

Judgment in cases of impeachment shall not extend further than to removal from the office, and disqualification to hold and enjoy any office of honor, trust or profit under the United States; but the party convicted shall nevertheless be liable and subject to indictment, trial, judgment and punishment, according to law.

Section 4. The times, places and manner of holding elections for Senators and Representatives shall be prescribed in each State by the legislature thereof; but the Congress may at any time by law make or alter such regulations, except as to the places of choosing Senators.

The Congress shall assemble at least once in every year, and such meeting *shall be on the first Monday in December, unless they shall by law appoint a different day.*

Section 5. Each house shall be the judge of the elections, returns and qualifications of its own members, and a majority of each shall constitute a quorum to do business; but a smaller number may adjourn from day to day, and may be authorized to compel the attendance of absent members, in such manner, and under such penalties, as each house may provide.

Each house may determine the rules of its proceedings, punish its members for disorderly behavior, and with the concurrence of two-thirds, expel a member.

Each house shall keep a journal of its proceedings, and from time to time publish the same, excepting such parts as may in their judgment require secrecy; and the yeas and nays of the members of either house on any question shall, at the desire of one-fifth of those present, be entered on the journal.

Neither house, during the session of Congress, shall, without the consent of the other, adjourn for more than three days, nor to any other place than that in which the two houses shall be sitting.

Section 6. The Senators and Representatives shall receive a compensation for their services, to be ascertained by law and paid out of the treasury of the United States. They shall in all cases except treason, felony and breach of the peace, be privileged from arrest during their attendance at the session of their respective houses, and in going to and returning from the same; and for any speech or debate in either house, they shall not be questioned in any other place.

No Senator or Representative shall, during the time for which he was elected, be appointed to any civil office under the authority of the United States, which shall have been created, or the emoluments whereof shall have been increased, during such time; and no person holding any office under the United States shall be a member of either house during his continuance in office.

Section 7. All bills for raising revenue shall originate in the House of Representatives; but the Senate may propose or concur with amendments as on other bills.

Every bill which shall have passed the House of Representatives and the Senate, shall, before it become a law, be presented to the President of the United States; if he approve he shall sign it, but if not he shall return it with objections to that house in which it originated, who shall enter the objections at large on their journal, and proceed to reconsider it. If after such reconsideration two-thirds of that house shall agree to pass the bill, it shall be sent, together with the objections, to the other house, by which it shall likewise be reconsidered, and, if approved by two-thirds of that house, it shall become a law. But in all such cases the votes of both houses shall be determined by yeas and nays, and the names of the persons voting for and against the bill shall be entered on the journal of each house respectively. If any bill shall not be returned by the President within ten days (Sundays excepted) after it shall have been presented to him, the same shall be a law, in like manner as if he had signed it, unless the Congress by their adjournment prevent its return, in which case it shall not be a law.

Every order, resolution, or vote to which the concurrence of the Senate and House of Representatives may be necessary (except on a question of adjournment) shall be presented to the President of the United States; and before the same shall take effect, shall be approved by him, or being disapproved by him, shall be repassed by two-thirds of the Senate and House of Representatives, according to the rules and limitations prescribed in the case of a bill.

Section 8. The Congress shall have power

To lay and collect taxes, duties, imposts, and excises, to pay the debts and provide for the common defense and general welfare of the United States; but all duties, imposts and excises shall be uniform throughout the United States;

To borrow money on the credit of the United States;

To regulate commerce with foreign nations, and among the several States, and with the Indian tribes;

To establish an uniform rule of naturalization, and uniform laws on the subject of bankruptcies throughout the United States;

To coin money, regulate the value thereof, and of foreign coin, and fix the standard of weights and measures;

To provide for the punishment of counterfeiting the securities and current coin of the United States;

To establish post offices and post roads;

To promote the progress of science and useful arts by securing for limited times to authors and inventors the exclusive right to their respective writings and discoveries;

To constitute tribunals inferior to the Supreme Court;

To define and punish piracies and felonies committed on the high seas and offenses against the law of nations;

To declare war, grant letters of marque and reprisal, and make rules concerning captures on land and water;

To raise and support armies, but no appropriation of money to that use shall be for a longer term than two years;

To provide and maintain a navy;

To make rules for the government and regulation of the land and naval forces;

To provide for calling forth the militia to execute the laws of the Union, suppress insurrections, and repel invasions;

To provide for organizing, arming, and disciplining the militia, and for governing such part of them as may be employed in the service of the United States, reserving to the States respectively the appointment of the officers, and the authority of training the militia according to the discipline prescribed by Congress;

To exercise exclusive legislation in all cases whatsoever, over such district (not exceeding ten miles square) as may, by cession of particular States, and the acceptance of Congress, become the seat of government of the United States, and to exercise like authority over all places purchased by the consent of the legislature of the State, in which the same shall be, for erection of forts, magazines, arsenals, dock-yards, and other needful buildings;—and

To make all laws which shall be necessary and proper for carrying into execution the foregoing powers, and all other powers vested by this Constitution in the government of the United States, or in any department or officer thereof.

Section 9. *The migration or importation of such persons as any of the States now existing shall think proper to admit shall not be prohibited by the Congress prior to the year 1808; but a tax or duty may be imposed on such importation, not exceeding $10 for each person.*

The privilege of the writ of habeas corpus shall not be suspended, unless when in cases of rebellion or invasion the public safety may require it.

No bill of attainder or ex post facto law shall be passed.

No capitation, or other direct, tax shall be laid, unless in proportion to the census or enumeration herein before directed to be taken.

No tax or duty shall be laid on articles exported from any State.

No preference shall be given by any regulation of commerce or revenue to the ports of one State over those of another; nor shall vessels bound to, or from, one State, be obliged to enter, clear, or pay duties in another.

No money shall be drawn from the treasury, but in consequence of appropriations made by law; and a regular statement and account of the receipts and expenditures of all public money shall be published from time to time.

No title of nobility shall be granted by the United States: and no person holding any office of profit or trust under them, shall, without the consent of the Congress, accept of any present, emolument, office, or title, of any kind whatever, from any king, prince, or foreign state.

Section 10. No State shall enter into any treaty, alliance, or confederation; grant letters of marque and reprisal; coin money; emit bills of credit; make anything but gold and silver coin a tender in payment of debts; pass any bill of attainder, ex post facto law, or law impairing the obligation of contracts, or grant any title of nobility.

No State shall, without the consent of Congress, lay any imposts or duties on imports or exports, except what may be absolutely necessary for executing its inspection laws: and the net produce of all duties and imposts, laid by any State on imports or exports, shall be for the use of the treasury of the United States; and all such laws shall be subject to the revision and control of the Congress.

No State shall, without the consent of Congress, lay any duty of tonnage, keep troops or ships of war in time of peace, enter into any agreement or compact with another State, or with a foreign power, or engage in war, unless actually invaded, or in such imminent danger as will not admit of delay.

Article II

Section 1. The executive power shall be vested in a President of the United States of America. He shall hold his office during the term of four years, and, together with the Vice President, chosen for the same term, be elected as follows:

Each state shall appoint, in such manner as the legislature thereof may direct, a number of electors, equal to the whole number of Senators and Representatives to which the State may be entitled in the Congress; but no Senator or Representative, or person holding an office of trust or profit under the United States, shall be appointed an elector.

The electors shall meet in their respective States, and vote by ballot for two persons, of whom one at least shall not be an inhabitant of the same State with themselves. And they shall make a list of all the persons voted for, and of the number of votes for each; which list they shall sign and certify, and transmit sealed to the seat of government of the United States, directed to the President of the Senate. The President of the Senate shall, in the presence of the Senate and the House of Representatives, open all the certificates, and the votes shall then be counted. The person having the greatest number of votes shall be the President, if such number be a majority of the whole number of electors appointed; and if there be more than one who have such majority, and have an equal number of votes, then the House of Representatives shall immediately choose by ballot one of them for President; and if no person have a majority, then from the five highest on the list said house shall in like manner choose the President. But in choosing the President the votes shall be taken by States, the representation from each State having one vote; a quorum for this purpose shall consist of a member or members from two-thirds of the States, and a majority of all the States shall be necessary to a choice. In every case, after the choice of the President, the person having the greatest number of votes of the electors shall be the Vice President. But if there should remain two or more who have equal votes, the Senate shall choose from them by ballot the Vice President.

The Congress may determine the time of choosing the electors and the day on which they shall give their votes; which day shall be the same throughout the United States.

No person except a natural-born citizen, *or a citizen of the United States at the time of the adoption of this Constitution,* shall be eligible to the office of President; neither shall any person be eligible to that office who shall not have attained to the age of thirty-five years, and been fourteen years a resident within the United States.

In case of the removal of the President from office or of his death, resignation, or inability to discharge the powers and duties of the said office, the same shall devolve on the Vice President, and the Congress may by law provide for the case of removal, death, resignation, or inability, both of the President and Vice President, declaring what officer shall then act as President, and such officer shall act accordingly, until the disability be removed, or a President shall be elected.

The President shall, at stated times, receive for his services a compensation, which shall neither be increased nor diminished during the period for which he shall have been elected, and he shall not receive within that period any other emolument from the United States, or any of them.

Before he enter on the execution of his office, he shall take the following oath or affirmation:— "I do solemnly swear (or affirm) that I will faithfully execute the office of the President of the United States, and will to the best of my ability preserve, protect and defend the Constitution of the United States."

Section 2. The President shall be commander in chief of the army and navy of the United States, and of the militia of the several States, when called into the actual service of the United States; he may require the opinion, in writing, of the principal officer in each of the executive departments, upon any subject relating to the duties of their respective offices, and he shall have power to grant reprieves and pardons for offenses against the United States, except in cases of impeachment.

He shall have power, by and with the advice and consent of the Senate, to make treaties, provided two-thirds of the Senators present concur; and he shall nominate, and by and with the advice and consent of the Senate, shall appoint ambassadors, other public ministers and consuls, judges of the Supreme Court, and all other officers of the United States, whose appointments are not herein otherwise provided for, and which shall be established by law: but Congress may by law vest the appointment of such inferior officers, as they think proper, in the President alone, in the courts of law, or in the heads of departments.

The President shall have power to fill up all vacancies that may happen during the recess of the Senate, by granting commissions which shall expire at the end of their next session.

Section 3. He shall from time to time give to the Congress information of the state of the Union, and recommend to their consideration such mea-

sures as he shall judge necessary and expedient; he may, on extraordinary occasions, convene both houses, or either of them, and in case of disagreement between them, with respect to the time of adjournment, he may adjourn them to such time as he shall think proper; he shall receive ambassadors and other public ministers; he shall take care that the laws be faithfully executed, and shall commission all the officers of the United States.

Section 4. The President, Vice President and all civil officers of the United States shall be removed from office on impeachment for, and on conviction of, treason, bribery, or other high crimes and misdemeanors.

Article III

Section 1. The judicial power of the United States shall be vested in one Supreme Court, and in such inferior courts as the Congress may from time to time ordain and establish. The judges, both of the Supreme and inferior courts, shall hold their offices during good behavior, and shall, at stated times, receive for their services a compensation which shall not be diminished during their continuance in office.

Section 2. The judicial power shall extend to all cases, in law and equity, arising under this Constitution, the laws of the United States, and treaties made, or which shall be made, under their authority;—to all cases affecting ambassadors, other public ministers and consuls;—to all cases of admiralty and maritime jurisdiction;—to controversies to which the United States shall be a party;—to controversies between two or more States; —*between a State and citizens of another State;*—between citizens of different States;—between citizens of the same State claiming lands under grants of different States, and between a State, or the citizens thereof, and foreign states, citizens or subjects.

In all cases affecting ambassadors, other public ministers and consuls, and those in which a State shall be party, the Supreme Court shall have original jurisdiction. In all the other cases before mentioned, the Supreme Court shall have appellate jurisdiction, both as to law and fact, with such exceptions, and under such regulations, as the Congress shall make.

The trial of all crimes, except in cases of impeachment, shall be by jury; and such trial shall be held in the State where said crimes shall have been committed; but when not committed within any State, the trial shall be at such place or places as the Congress may by law have directed.

Section 3.   Treason against the United States shall consist only in levying war against them, or in adhering to their enemies, giving them aid and comfort. No person shall be convicted of treason unless on the testimony of two witnesses to the same overt act, or on confession in open court.

The Congress shall have power to declare the punishment of treason, but no attainder of treason shall work corruption of blood, or forfeiture except during the life of the person attainted.

Article IV

Section 1.   Full faith and credit shall be given in each State to the public acts, records, and judicial proceedings of every other State. And the Congress may by general laws prescribe the manner in which such acts, records, and proceedings shall be proved, and the effect thereof.

Section 2.   The citizens of each State shall be entitled to all privileges and immunities of citizens in the several States.

A person charged in any State with treason, felony, or other crime, who shall flee from justice, and be found in another State, shall on demand of the executive authority of the State from which he fled, be delivered up, to be removed to the State having jurisdiction of the crime.

No person held to service or labor in one State, under the laws thereof, escaping into another, shall, in consequence of any law or regulation therein, be discharged from such service or labor, but shall be delivered up on claim of the party to whom such service or labor may be due.

Section 3.   New States may be admitted by the Congress into this Union; but no new State shall be formed or erected within the jurisdiction of any other State; nor any State be formed by the junction of two or more States, or parts of States, without the consent of the legislatures of the States concerned as well as of the Congress.

The Congress shall have power to dispose of and make all needful rules and regulations respecting the territory or other property belonging to the United States; and nothing in this Constitution shall be so construed as to prejudice any claims of the United States, or of any particular State.

Section 4.   The United States shall guarantee to every State in this Union a republican form of government, and shall protect each of them against invasion; and on application of the legislature, or of the executive (when the legislature cannot be convened), against domestic violence.

Article V

The Congress, whenever two-thirds of both houses shall deem it necessary, shall propose amendments to this Constitution, or, on the application of the legislatures of two-thirds of the several States, shall call a convention for proposing amendments, which, in either case, shall be valid to all intents and purposes, as part of this Constitution, when ratified by the legislatures of three-fourths of the several States, or by conventions in three-fourths thereof, as the one or the other mode of ratification may be proposed by the Congress; provided *that no amendments which may be made prior to the year one thousand eight hundred and eight shall in any manner affect the first and fourth clauses in the ninth section of the first article;* and that no State, without its consent, shall be deprived of its equal suffrage in the Senate.

Article VI

All debts contracted and engagements entered into, before the adoption of this Constitution, shall be as valid against the United States under this Constitution, as under the Confederation.

This Constitution, and the laws of the United States which shall be made in pursuance thereof; and all treaties made, or which shall be made, under the authority of the United States, shall be the supreme law of the land; and the judges in every State shall be bound thereby, anything in the Constitution or laws of any State to the contrary notwithstanding.

The Senators and Representatives before mentioned, and the members of the several State legislatures, and all executive and judicial officers, both of the United States and of the several States, shall be bound by oath or affirmation to support this Constitution; but no religious test shall ever be required as a qualification to any office or public trust under the United States.

Article VII

The ratification of the conventions of nine States shall be sufficient for the establishment of this Constitution between the States so ratifying the same.

Done in Convention by the unanimous consent of the States present, the seventeenth day of September in the year of our Lord one thousand seven hundred and eighty-seven and of the Independence of the United States of America the twelfth. In witness whereof we have hereunto subscribed our names.

[Signed by]
G° WASHINGTON
Presidt and Deputy from Virginia
[*and thirty-eight others*]

Amendments to the Constitution

Article I*

Congress shall make no law respecting an establishment of religion, or prohibiting the free exercise thereof; or abridging the freedom of speech, or of the press; or the right of the people peaceably to assemble, and to petition the government for a redress of grievances.

Article II

A well-regulated militia being necessary to the security of a free State, the right of the people to keep and bear arms shall not be infringed.

Article III

No soldier shall, in time of peace, be quartered in any house without the consent of the owner, nor in time of war, but in a manner to be prescribed by law.

Article IV

The right of the people to be secure in their persons, houses, papers, and effects, against unreasonable searches and seizures, shall not be violated, and no warrants shall issue but upon probable cause, supported by oath or affirmation, and particularly describing the place to be searched, and the persons or things to be seized.

*The first ten Amendments (Bill of Rights) were adopted in 1791.

Article V

No person shall be held to answer for a capital, or otherwise infamous crime, unless on a presentment or indictment of a grand jury, except in cases arising in the land or naval forces, or in the militia, when in actual service in time of war or public danger; nor shall any person be subject for the same offense to be twice put in jeopardy of life or limb; nor shall be compelled in any criminal case to be a witness against himself, nor be deprived of life, liberty, or property, without due process of law; nor shall private property be taken for public use without just compensation.

Article VI

In all criminal prosecutions, the accused shall enjoy the right to a speedy and public trial, by an impartial jury of the State and district wherein the crime shall have been committed, which district shall have been previously ascertained by law, and to be informed of the nature and cause of the accusation; to be confronted with the witnesses against him; to have compulsory process for obtaining witnesses in his favor, and to have the assistance of counsel for his defense.

Article VII

In suits at common law, where the value in controversy shall exceed twenty dollars, the right of trial by jury shall be preserved, and no fact tried by a jury shall be otherwise reexamined in any court of the United States, than according to the rules of the common law.

Article VIII

Excessive bail shall not be required, nor excessive fines imposed, nor cruel and unusual punishments inflicted.

Article IX

The enumeration in the Constitution, of certain rights, shall not be construed to deny or disparage others retained by the people.

Article X

The powers not delegated to the United States by the Constitution, nor prohibited by it to the States, are reserved to the States respectively, or to the people.

Article XI

[Adopted 1798]

The judicial power of the United States shall not be construed to extend to any suit in law or equity, commenced or prosecuted against one of the United States by citizens of another State, or by citizens or subjects of any foreign state.

Article XII

[Adopted 1804]

The electors shall meet in their respective States, and vote by ballot for President and Vice President, one of whom, at least, shall not be an inhabitant of the same State with themselves; they shall name in their ballots the person voted for as President, and in distinct ballots the person voted for as Vice President, and they shall make distinct lists of all persons voted for as President, and of all persons voted for as Vice President, and of the number of votes for each, which lists they shall sign and certify, and transmit sealed to the seat of government of the United States, directed to the President of the Senate;—the President of the Senate shall, in the presence of the Senate and House of Representatives, open all the certificates and the votes shall then be counted;—the person having the greatest number of votes for President shall be the President, if such number be a majority of the whole number of electors appointed; and if no person have such majority, then from the persons having

the highest numbers not exceeding three on the list of those voted for as President, the House of Representatives shall choose immediately, by ballot, the President. But in choosing the President, the votes shall be taken by States, the representation from each State having one vote; a quorum for this purpose shall consist of a member or members from two-thirds of the States, and a majority of all the States shall be necessary to a choice. And if the House of Representatives shall not choose a President whenever the right of choice shall devolve upon them, before *the fourth day of March* next following, then the Vice President shall act as President, as in the case of the death or other constitutional disability of the President.

The person having the greatest number of votes as Vice President shall be the Vice President, if such a number be a majority of the whole number of electors appointed; and if no person have a majority, then from the two highest numbers on the list the Senate shall choose the Vice President; a quorum for the purpose shall consist of two-thirds of the whole number of Senators, and a majority of the whole number shall be necessary to a choice. But no person constitutionally ineligible to the office of President shall be eligible to that of Vice President of the United States.

Article XIII

[Adopted 1865]

Section 1.   Neither slavery nor involuntary servitude, except as a punishment for crime whereof the party shall have been duly convicted, shall exist within the United States, or any place subject to their jurisdiction.

Section 2.   Congress shall have power to enforce this article by appropriate legislation.

Article XIV

[Adopted 1868]

Section 1.   All persons born or naturalized in the United States, and subject to the jurisdiction thereof, are citizens of the United States and of the State wherein they reside. No State shall make or enforce any law which shall abridge the privileges or immunities of citizens of the United States; nor shall any State deprive any person of life, liberty, or property, without due process of law; nor deny to any person within its jurisdiction the equal protection of the laws.

Section 2. Representatives shall be apportioned among the several States according to their respective numbers, counting the whole number of persons in each State, excluding Indians not taxed. But when the right to vote at any election for the choice of Electors for President and Vice President of the United States, Representatives in Congress, the executive and judicial officers of a State, or the members of the legislature thereof, is denied to any of the male inhabitants of such State, being twenty-one years of age and citizens of the United States, or in any way abridged, except for participation in rebellion, or other crime, the basis of representation therein shall be reduced in the proportion which the number of such male citizens shall bear to the whole number of male citizens twenty-one years of age in such State.

Section 3. No person shall be a Senator or Representative in Congress or Elector of President and Vice President, or hold any office, civil or military, under the United States, or under any State, who, having previously taken an oath, as a member of Congress, or as an officer of the United States, or as a member of any State legislature, or as an executive or judicial officer of any State, to support the Constitution of the United States, shall have engaged in insurrection or rebellion against the same, or given aid and comfort to the enemies thereof. Congress may, by a vote of two-thirds of each house, remove such disability.

Section 4. The validity of the public debt of the United States, authorized by law, including debts incurred for payment of pensions and bounties for services in suppressing insurrection or rebellion, shall not be questioned. But neither the United States nor any State shall assume or pay any debt or obligation incurred in aid of insurrection or rebellion against the United States, or any claim for the loss or emancipation of any slave; but all such debts, obligations, and claims shall be held illegal and void.

Section 5. The Congress shall have the power to enforce, by appropriate legislation, the provisions of this article.

Article XV
[*Adopted 1870*]

Section 1. The right of citizens of the United States to vote shall not be denied or abridged by the United States or by any State on account of race, color, or previous condition of servitude.

Section 2. The Congress shall have power to enforce this article by appropriate legislation.

Article XVI
[*Adopted 1913*]

The Congress shall have power to lay and collect taxes on incomes, from whatever source derived, without apportionment among the several States, and without regard to any census or enumeration.

Article XVII
[*Adopted 1913*]

Section 1. The Senate of the United States shall be composed of two Senators from each State, elected by the people thereof, for six years; and each Senator shall have one vote. The electors in each State shall have the qualifications requisite for electors of [voters for] the most numerous branch of the State legislatures.

Section 2. When vacancies happen in the representation of any State in the Senate, the executive authority of such State shall issue writs of election to fill such vacancies: Provided, that the Legislature of any State may empower the executive thereof to make temporary appointments until the people fill the vacancies by election as the Legislature may direct.

Section 3. This amendment shall not be so construed as to affect the election or term of any Senator chosen before it becomes valid as part of the Constitution.

Article XVIII
[*Adopted 1919; repealed 1933*]

Section 1. *After one year from the ratification of this article the manufacture, sale, or transportation of intoxicating liquors within, the importation* *thereof into, or the exportation thereof from the United States and all territory subject to the jurisdiction thereof, for beverage purposes, is hereby prohibited.*

Section 2.   *The Congress and the several States shall have concurrent power to enforce this article by appropriate legislation.*

Section 3.   *This article shall be inoperative unless it shall have been ratified as an amendment to the Constitution by the legislatures of the several States, as provided by the Constitution, within seven years from the date of the submission thereof to the States by the Congress.*

Article XIX
[*Adopted 1920*]

Section 1.   The right of citizens of the United States to vote shall not be denied or abridged by the United States or by any State on account of sex.

Section 2.   The Congress shall have the power to enforce this article by appropriate legislation.

Article XX
[*Adopted 1933*]

Section 1.   The terms of the President and Vice President shall end at noon on the 20th day of January, and the terms of Senators and Representatives at noon on the 3d day of January, of the years in which such terms would have ended if this article had not been ratified; and the terms of their successors shall then begin.

Section 2.   The Congress shall assemble at least once in every year, and such meeting shall begin at noon on the 3d of January, unless they shall by law appoint a different day.

Section 3.   If, at the time fixed for the beginning of the term of the President, the President-elect shall have died, the Vice President-elect shall become President. If a President shall not have been chosen before the time fixed for the beginning of his term, or if the President-elect shall have failed to qualify, then the Vice President-elect shall act as President until a President shall have qualified; and the Congress may by law provide for the case wherein neither a President-elect nor a Vice President-elect shall

have qualified, declaring who shall then act as President, or the manner in which one who is to act shall be selected, and such persons shall act accordingly until a President or Vice President shall have qualified.

Section 4.   The Congress may by law provide for the case of the death of any of the persons from whom the House of Representatives may choose a President whenever the right of choice shall have devolved upon them, and for the case of the death of any of the persons from whom the Senate may choose a Vice President whenever the right of choice shall have devolved upon them.

Section 5.   Sections 1 and 2 shall take effect on the 15th day of October following the ratification of this article.

Section 6.   This article shall be inoperative unless it shall have been ratified as an amendment to the Constitution by the Legislatures of three-fourths of the several States within seven years from the date of its submission.

Article XXI
[*Adopted 1933*]

Section 1.   The eighteenth article of amendment to the Constitution of the United States is hereby repealed.

Section 2.   The transportation or importation into any State, Territory, or Possession of the United States for delivery or use therein of intoxicating liquors, in violation of the laws thereof, is hereby prohibited.

Section 3.   This article shall be inoperative unless it shall have been ratified as an amendment to the Constitution by conventions in the several States, as provided in the Constitution, within seven years from the date of submission thereof to the States by the Congress.

Article XXII
[*Adopted 1951*]

Section 1.   No person shall be elected to the office of President more than twice, and no person who has held the office of President, or acted as President, for more than two years of a term to which some other person was elected President shall be elected to the office of President more than once. But this article shall not apply to any person holding the office of President when this article was proposed by the Congress, and shall not prevent any person who may be holding the office of President, or acting as President, during the term within which this article becomes operative from holding the office of President or acting as President during the remainder of such term.

Section 2. This article shall be inoperative unless it shall have been ratified as an amendment to the Constitution by the legislatures of three-fourths of the several States within seven years from the date of its submission to the States by the Congress.

Article XXIII
[*Adopted 1961*]

Section 1. The District constituting the seat of Government of the United States shall appoint in such manner as the Congress may direct:

A number of electors of President and Vice President equal to the whole number of Senators and Representatives in Congress to which the District would be entitled if it were a State, but in no event more than the least populous State; they shall be in addition to those appointed by the States, but they shall be considered for the purposes of the election of President and Vice President, to be electors appointed by a State; and they shall meet in the District and perform such duties as provided by the twelfth article of amendment.

Section 2. The Congress shall have the power to enforce this article by appropriate legislation.

Article XXIV
[*Adopted 1964*]

Section 1. The right of citizens of the United States to vote in any primary or other election for President or Vice President, for electors for President or Vice President, or for Senator or Representative in Congress, shall not be denied or abridged by the United States or any State by reason of failure to pay any poll tax or other tax.

Section 2. The Congress shall have the power to enforce this article by appropriate legislation.

Article XXV
[*Adopted 1967*]

Section 1. In case of the removal of the President from office or of his death or resignation, the Vice President shall become President.

Section 2. Whenever there is a vacancy in the office of the Vice President, the President shall nominate a Vice President who shall take office upon confirmation by a majority vote of both Houses of Congress.

Section 3. Whenever the President transmits to the President pro tempore of the Senate and the Speaker of the House of Representatives his written declaration that he is unable to discharge the powers and duties of his office, and until he transmits to them a written declaration to the contrary, such powers and duties shall be discharged by the Vice President as Acting President.

Section 4. Whenever the Vice President and a majority of either the principal officers of the executive departments or of such other body as Congress may by law provide, transmit to the President pro tempore of the Senate and the Speaker of the House of Representatives their written declaration that the President is unable to discharge the powers and duties of his office, the Vice President shall immediately assume the powers and duties of the office as Acting President.

Thereafter, when the President transmits to the President pro tempore of the Senate and the Speaker of the House of Representatives his written declaration that no inability exists, he shall resume the powers and duties of his office unless the Vice President and a majority of either the principal officers of the executive department[s] or of such other body as Congress may by law provide, transmit within four days to the President pro tempore of the Senate and the Speaker of the House of Representatives their written declaration that the President is unable to discharge the powers and duties of his office. Thereupon Congress shall decide the issue, assembling within forty-eight hours for that purpose if not in session. If the Congress, within twenty-one days after receipt of the latter written declaration, or, if Congress is not in session, within twenty-one days after Congress is required to assemble, determines by two-thirds vote of both

Houses that the President is unable to discharge the powers and duties of his office, the Vice President shall continue to discharge the same as Acting President; otherwise, the President shall resume the powers and duties of his office.

Article XXVI

[Adopted 1971]

Section 1.   The right of citizens of the United States, who are eighteen years of age or older, to vote shall not be denied or abridged by the United States or by any State on account of age.

Section 2.   The Congress shall have power to enforce this article by appropriate legislation.

Growth of U.S. Population and Area

Census	Population	Percentage of Increase over Preceding Census	Land Area, Square Miles	Population per Square Mile
1790	3,929,214		867,980	4.5
1800	5,308,483	35.1	867,980	6.1
1810	7,239,881	36.4	1,685,865	4.3
1820	9,638,453	33.1	1,753,588	5.5
1830	12,866,020	33.5	1,753,588	7.3
1840	17,069,453	32.7	1,753,588	9.7
1850	23,191,876	35.9	2,944,337	7.9
1860	31,443,321	35.6	2,973,965	10.6
1870	39,818,449	26.6	2,973,965	13.4
1880	50,155,783	26.0	2,973,965	16.9
1890	62,947,714	25.5	2,973,965	21.2
1900	75,994,575	20.7	2,974,159	25.6
1910	91,972,266	21.0	2,973,890	30.9
1920	105,710,620	14.9	2,973,776	35.5
1930	122,775,046	16.1	2,977,128	41.2
1940	131,669,275	7.2	2,977,128	44.2
1950	150,697,361	14.5	2,974,726*	50.7
†1960	178,464,236	18.4	2,974,726	59.9
1970	204,765,770	14.7	2,974,726	68.8
1980	226,504,825	10.6	2,974,726	76.1
‡1987	243,396,000	7.5	2,974,726	81.8

* As remeasured in 1940.
† Not including Alaska (pop. 226,167) and Hawaii (632,772).
‡ As of July 1, 1987.

Admission of States into the Union

State	Date of Admission	State	Date of Admission
1. Delaware	December 7, 1787	26. Michigan	January 26, 1837
2. Pennsylvania	December 12, 1787	27. Florida	March 3, 1845
3. New Jersey	December 18, 1787	28. Texas	December 29, 1845
4. Georgia	January 2, 1788	29. Iowa	December 28, 1846
5. Connecticut	January 9, 1788	30. Wisconsin	May 29, 1848
6. Massachusetts	February 6, 1788	31. California	September 9, 1850
7. Maryland	April 28, 1788	32. Minnesota	May 11, 1858
8. South Carolina	May 23, 1788	33. Oregon	February 14, 1859
9. New Hampshire	June 21, 1788	34. Kansas	January 29, 1861
10. Virginia	June 25, 1788	35. West Virginia	June 20, 1863
11. New York	July 26, 1788	36. Nevada	October 31, 1864
12. North Carolina	November 21, 1789	37. Nebraska	March 1, 1867
13. Rhode Island	May 29, 1790	38. Colorado	August 1, 1876
14. Vermont	March 4, 1791	39. North Dakota	November 2, 1889
15. Kentucky	June 1, 1792	40. South Dakota	November 2, 1889
16. Tennessee	June 1, 1796	41. Montana	November 8, 1889
17. Ohio	March 1, 1803	42. Washington	November 11, 1889
18. Louisiana	April 30, 1812	43. Idaho	July 3, 1890
19. Indiana	December 11, 1816	44. Wyoming	July 10, 1890
20. Mississippi	December 10, 1817	45. Utah	January 4, 1896
21. Illinois	December 3, 1818	46. Oklahoma	November 16, 1907
22. Alabama	December 14, 1819	47. New Mexico	January 6, 1912
23. Maine	March 15, 1820	48. Arizona	February 14, 1912
24. Missouri	August 10, 1821	49. Alaska	January 3, 1959
25. Arkansas	June 15, 1836	50. Hawaii	August 21, 1959

Presidential Elections, 1789–1988

Year	States in the Union	Candidates	Parties	Electoral Vote	Popular Vote	Percentage of Popular Vote
1789	11	GEORGE WASHINGTON	No party designations	69		
		John Adams		34		
		Minor candidates		35		
1792	15	GEORGE WASHINGTON	No party designations	132		
		John Adams		77		
		George Clinton		50		
		Minor candidates		5		
1796	16	JOHN ADAMS	Federalist	71		
		Thomas Jefferson	Democratic-Republican	68		
		Thomas Pinckney	Federalist	59		
		Aaron Burr	Democratic-Republican	30		
		Minor candidates		48		
1800	16	THOMAS JEFFERSON	Democratic-Republican	73		
		Aaron Burr	Democratic-Republican	73		
		John Adams	Federalist	65		
		Charles C. Pinckney	Federalist	64		
		John Jay	Federalist	1		
1804	17	THOMAS JEFFERSON	Democratic-Republican	162		
		Charles C. Pinckney	Federalist	14		
1808	17	JAMES MADISON	Democratic-Republican	122		
		Charles C. Pinckney	Federalist	47		
		George Clinton	Democratic-Republican	6		
1812	18	JAMES MADISON	Democratic-Republican	128		
		DeWitt Clinton	Federalist	89		
1816	19	JAMES MONROE	Democratic-Republican	183		
		Rufus King	Federalist	34		
1820	24	JAMES MONROE	Democratic-Republican	231		
		John Quincy Adams	Independent Republican	1		
1824	24	JOHN QUINCY ADAMS	Democratic-Republican	84	108,740	30.5
		Andrew Jackson	Democratic-Republican	99	153,544	43.1
		William H. Crawford	Democratic-Republican	41	46,618	13.1
		Henry Clay	Democratic-Republican	37	47,136	13.2
1828	24	ANDREW JACKSON	Democratic	178	642,553	56.0
		John Quincy Adams	National Republican	83	500,897	44.0
1832	24	ANDREW JACKSON	Democratic	219	687,502	55.0
		Henry Clay	National Republican	49	530,189	42.4
		William Wirt	Anti-Masonic	7 ⎤	33,108	2.6
		John Floyd	National Republican	11 ⎦		
1836	26	MARTIN VAN BUREN	Democratic	170	765,483	50.9
		William H. Harrison	Whig	73 ⎤		
		Hugh L. White	Whig	26 ⎬	739,795	49.1
		Daniel Webster	Whig	14		
		W. P. Mangum	Whig	11 ⎦		
1840	26	WILLIAM H. HARRISON	Whig	234	1,274,624	53.1
		Martin Van Buren	Democratic	60	1,127,781	46.9
1844	26	JAMES K. POLK	Democratic	170	1,338,464	49.6
		Henry Clay	Whig	105	1,300,097	48.1
		James G. Birney	Liberty		62,300	2.3
1848	30	ZACHARY TAYLOR	Whig	163	1,360,967	47.4
		Lewis Cass	Democratic	127	1,222,342	42.5
		Martin Van Buren	Free Soil		291,263	10.1

Because candidates receiving less than 1 percent of the popular vote are omitted, the percentage of popular vote may not total 100 percent. Before the Twelfth Amendment was passed in 1804, the electoral college voted for two presidential candidates; the runner-up became vice president.

Year	States in the Union	Candidates	Parties	Electoral Vote	Popular Vote	Percentage of Popular Vote
1852	31	FRANKLIN PIERCE	Democratic	254	1,601,117	50.9
		Winfield Scott	Whig	42	1,385,453	44.1
		John P. Hale	Free Soil		155,825	5.0
1856	31	JAMES BUCHANAN	Democratic	174	1,832,955	45.3
		John C. Frémont	Republican	114	1,339,932	33.1
		Millard Fillmore	American	8	871,731	21.6
1860	33	ABRAHAM LINCOLN	Republican	180	1,865,593	39.8
		Stephen A. Douglas	Democratic	12	1,382,713	29.5
		John C. Breckinridge	Democratic	72	848,356	18.1
		John Bell	Constitutional Union	39	592,906	12.6
1864	36	ABRAHAM LINCOLN	Republican	212	2,206,938	55.0
		George B. McClellan	Democratic	21	1,803,787	45.0
1868	37	ULYSSES S. GRANT	Republican	214	3,013,421	52.7
		Horatio Seymour	Democratic	80	2,706,829	47.3
1872	37	ULYSSES S. GRANT	Republican	286	3,596,745	55.6
		Horace Greeley	Democratic	*	2,843,446	43.9
1876	38	RUTHERFORD B. HAYES	Republican	185	4,034,311	48.0
		Samuel J. Tilden	Democratic	184	4,288,546	51.0
		Peter Cooper	Greenback		75,973	1.0
1880	38	JAMES A. GARFIELD	Republican	214	4,453,295	48.5
		Winfield S. Hancock	Democratic	155	4,414,082	48.1
		James B. Weaver	Greenback-Labor		308,578	3.4
1884	38	GROVER CLEVELAND	Democratic	219	4,879,507	48.5
		James G. Blaine	Republican	182	4,850,293	48.2
		Benjamin F. Butler	Greenback-Labor		175,370	1.8
		John P. St. John	Prohibition		150,369	1.5
1888	38	BENJAMIN HARRISON	Republican	233	5,477,129	47.9
		Grover Cleveland	Democratic	168	5,537,857	48.6
		Clinton B. Fisk	Prohibition		249,506	2.2
		Anson J. Streeter	Union Labor		146,935	1.3
1892	44	GROVER CLEVELAND	Democratic	277	5,555,426	46.1
		Benjamin Harrison	Republican	145	5,182,690	43.0
		James B. Weaver	People's	22	1,029,846	8.5
		John Bidwell	Prohibition		264,133	2.2
1896	45	WILLIAM McKINLEY	Republican	271	7,102,246	51.1
		William J. Bryan	Democratic	176	6,492,559	47.7
1900	45	WILLIAM McKINLEY	Republican	292	7,218,491	51.7
		William J. Bryan	Democratic; Populist	155	6,356,734	45.5
		John C. Wooley	Prohibition		208,914	1.5
1904	45	THEODORE ROOSEVELT	Republican	336	7,628,461	57.4
		Alton B. Parker	Democratic	140	5,084,223	37.6
		Eugene V. Debs	Socialist		402,283	3.0
		Silas C. Swallow	Prohibition		258,536	1.9
1908	46	WILLIAM H. TAFT	Republican	321	7,675,320	51.6
		William J. Bryan	Democratic	162	6,412,294	43.1
		Eugene V. Debs	Socialist		420,793	2.8
		Eugene W. Chafin	Prohibition		253,840	1.7
1912	48	WOODROW WILSON	Democratic	435	6,296,547	41.9
		Theodore Roosevelt	Progressive	88	4,118,571	27.4
		William H. Taft	Republican	8	3,486,720	23.2
		Eugene V. Debs	Socialist		900,672	6.0
		Eugene W. Chafin	Prohibition		206,275	1.4

*When Greeley died shortly after the election, his supporters divided their votes among the minor candidates.

Because candidates receiving less than 1 percent of the popular vote are omitted, the percentage of popular vote may not total 100 percent.

Year	States in the Union	Candidates	Parties	Electoral Vote	Popular Vote	Percentage of Popular Vote
1916	48	WOODROW WILSON	Democratic	277	9,127,695	49.4
		Charles E. Hughes	Republican	254	8,533,507	46.2
		A. L. Benson	Socialist		585,113	3.2
		J. Frank Hanly	Prohibition		220,506	1.2
1920	48	WARREN G. HARDING	Republican	404	16,143,407	60.4
		James N. Cox	Democratic	127	9,130,328	34.2
		Eugene V. Debs	Socialist		919,799	3.4
		P. P. Christensen	Farmer-Labor		265,411	1.0
1924	48	CALVIN COOLIDGE	Republican	382	15,718,211	54.0
		John W. Davis	Democratic	136	8,385,283	28.8
		Robert M. La Follette	Progressive	13	4,831,289	16.6
1928	48	HERBERT C. HOOVER	Republican	444	21,391,993	58.2
		Alfred E. Smith	Democratic	87	15,016,169	40.9
1932	48	FRANKLIN D. ROOSEVELT	Democratic	472	22,809,638	57.4
		Herbert C. Hoover	Republican	59	15,758,901	39.7
		Norman Thomas	Socialist		881,951	2.2
1936	48	FRANKLIN D. ROOSEVELT	Democratic	523	27,752,869	60.8
		Alfred M. Landon	Republican	8	16,674,665	36.5
		William Lemke	Union		882,479	1.9
1940	48	FRANKLIN D. ROOSEVELT	Democratic	449	27,307,819	54.8
		Wendell L. Willkie	Republican	82	22,321,018	44.8
1944	48	FRANKLIN D. ROOSEVELT	Democratic	432	25,606,585	53.5
		Thomas E. Dewey	Republican	99	22,014,745	46.0
1948	48	HARRY S TRUMAN	Democratic	303	24,105,812	49.5
		Thomas E. Dewey	Republican	189	21,970,065	45.1
		Strom Thurmond	States' Rights	39	1,169,063	2.4
		Henry A. Wallace	Progressive		1,157,172	2.4
1952	48	DWIGHT D. EISENHOWER	Republican	442	33,936,234	55.1
		Adlai E. Stevenson	Democratic	89	27,314,992	44.4
1956	48	DWIGHT D. EISENHOWER	Republican	457	35,590,472	57.6
		Adlai E. Stevenson	Democratic	73	26,022,752	42.1
1960	50	JOHN F. KENNEDY	Democratic	303	34,227,096	49.7
		Richard M. Nixon	Republican	219	34,108,546	49.5
		Harry F. Byrd	Independent	15	502,363	.7
1964	50	LYNDON B. JOHNSON	Democratic	486	43,126,506	61.1
		Barry M. Goldwater	Republican	52	27,176,799	38.5
1968	50	RICHARD M. NIXON	Republican	301	31,770,237	43.4
		Hubert H. Humphrey	Democratic	191	31,270,533	42.7
		George C. Wallace	American Independent	46	9,906,141	13.5
1972	50	RICHARD M. NIXON	Republican	520	47,169,911	60.7
		George S. McGovern	Democratic	17	29,170,383	37.5
1976	50	JIMMY CARTER	Democratic	297	40,827,394	49.9
		Gerald R. Ford	Republican	240	39,145,977	47.9
1980	50	RONALD W. REAGAN	Republican	489	43,899,248	50.8
		Jimmy Carter	Democratic	49	35,481,435	41.0
		John B. Anderson	Independent		5,719,437	6.6
		Ed Clark	Libertarian		920,859	1.0
1984	50	RONALD W. REAGAN	Republican	525	54,451,521	58.8
		Walter F. Mondale	Democratic	13	37,565,334	40.5
1988	50	GEORGE H. W. BUSH	Republican	426	47,946,422	54.0
		Michael S. Dukakis	Democratic	112	41,016,429	46.0

Because candidates receiving less than 1 percent of the popular vote are omitted, the percentage of popular vote may not total 100 percent.

Vice Presidents and Cabinet Members, 1789–1989

The Washington Administration (1789–1797)

Vice President	John Adams	1789–1797
Secretary of State	Thomas Jefferson	1789–1793
	Edmund Randolph	1794–1795
	Timothy Pickering	1795–1797
Secretary of Treasury	Alexander Hamilton	1789–1795
	Oliver Wolcott	1795–1797
Secretary of War	Henry Knox	1789–1794
	Timothy Pickering	1795–1796
	James McHenry	1796–1797
Attorney General	Edmund Randolph	1789–1793
	William Bradford	1794–1795
	Charles Lee	1795–1797
Postmaster General	Samuel Osgood	1789–1791
	Timothy Pickering	1791–1794
	Joseph Habersham	1795–1797

The John Adams Administration (1797–1801)

Vice President	Thomas Jefferson	1797–1801
Secretary of State	Timothy Pickering	1797–1800
	John Marshall	1800–1801
Secretary of Treasury	Oliver Wolcott	1797–1800
	Samuel Dexter	1800–1801
Secretary of War	James McHenry	1797–1800
	Samuel Dexter	1800–1801
Attorney General	Charles Lee	1797–1801
Postmaster General	Joseph Habersham	1797–1801
Secretary of Navy	Benjamin Stoddert	1798–1801

The Jefferson Administration (1801–1809)

Vice President	Aaron Burr	1801–1805
	George Clinton	1805–1809
Secretary of State	James Madison	1801–1809
Secretary of Treasury	Samuel Dexter	1801
	Albert Gallatin	1801–1809
Secretary of War	Henry Dearborn	1801–1809
Attorney General	Levi Lincoln	1801–1805
	Robert Smith	1805
	John Breckinridge	1805–1806
	Caesar Rodney	1807–1809
Postmaster General	Joseph Habersham	1801
	Gideon Granger	1801–1809
Secretary of Navy	Robert Smith	1801–1809

The Madison Administration (1809–1817)

Vice President	George Clinton	1809–1813
	Elbridge Gerry	1813–1817
Secretary of State	Robert Smith	1809–1811
	James Monroe	1811–1817
Secretary of Treasury	Albert Gallatin	1809–1813
	George Campbell	1814
	Alexander Dallas	1814–1816
	William Crawford	1816–1817

Secretary of War	William Eustis	1809–1812
	John Armstrong	1813–1814
	James Monroe	1814–1815
	William Crawford	1815–1817
Attorney General	Caesar Rodney	1809–1811
	William Pinkney	1811–1814
	Richard Rush	1814–1817
Postmaster General	Gideon Granger	1809–1814
	Return Meigs	1814–1817
Secretary of Navy	Paul Hamilton	1809–1813
	William Jones	1813–1814
	Benjamin Crowninshield	1814–1817

The Monroe Administration (1817–1825)

Vice President	Daniel Tompkins	1817–1825
Secretary of State	John Quincy Adams	1817–1825
Secretary of Treasury	William Crawford	1817–1825
Secretary of War	George Graham	1817
	John C. Calhoun	1817–1825
Attorney General	Richard Rush	1817
	William Wirt	1817–1825
Postmaster General	Return Meigs	1817–1823
	John McLean	1823–1825
Secretary of Navy	Benjamin Crowninshield	1817–1818
	Smith Thompson	1818–1823
	Samuel Southard	1823–1825

The John Quincy Adams Administration (1825–1829)

Vice President	John C. Calhoun	1825–1829
Secretary of State	Henry Clay	1825–1829
Secretary of Treasury	Richard Rush	1825–1829
Secretary of War	James Barbour	1825–1828
	Peter Porter	1828–1829
Attorney General	William Wirt	1825–1829
Postmaster General	John McLean	1825–1829
Secretary of Navy	Samuel Southard	1825–1829

The Jackson Administration (1829–1837)

Vice President	John C. Calhoun	1829–1833
	Martin Van Buren	1833–1837
Secretary of State	Martin Van Buren	1829–1831
	Edward Livingston	1831–1833
	Louis McLane	1833–1834
	John Forsyth	1834–1837
Secretary of Treasury	Samuel Ingham	1829–1831
	Louis McLane	1831–1833
	William Duane	1833
	Roger B. Taney	1833–1834
	Levi Woodbury	1834–1837
Secretary of War	John H. Eaton	1829–1831
	Lewis Cass	1831–1837
	Benjamin Butler	1837
Attorney General	John M. Berrien	1829–1831
	Roger B. Taney	1831–1833
	Benjamin Butler	1833–1837
Postmaster General	William Barry	1829–1835
	Amos Kendall	1835–1837

Secretary of Navy	John Branch	1829–1831
	Levi Woodbury	1831–1834
	Mahlon Dickerson	1834–1837

The Van Buren Administration (1837–1841)

Vice President	Richard M. Johnson	1837–1841
Secretary of State	John Forsyth	1837–1841
Secretary of Treasury	Levi Woodbury	1837–1841
Secretary of War	Joel Poinsett	1837–1841
Attorney General	Benjamin Butler	1837–1838
	Felix Grundy	1838–1840
	Henry D. Gilpin	1840–1841
Postmaster General	Amos Kendall	1837–1840
	John M. Niles	1840–1841
Secretary of Navy	Mahlon Dickerson	1837–1838
	James Paulding	1838–1841

The William Harrison Administration (1841)

Vice President	John Tyler	1841
Secretary of State	Daniel Webster	1841
Secretary of Treasury	Thomas Ewing	1841
Secretary of War	John Bell	1841
Attorney General	John J. Crittenden	1841
Postmaster General	Francis Granger	1841
Secretary of Navy	George Badger	1841

The Tyler Administration (1841–1845)

Vice President	None	
Secretary of State	Daniel Webster	1841–1843
	Hugh S. Legaré	1843
	Abel P. Upshur	1843–1844
	John C. Calhoun	1844–1845
Secretary of Treasury	Thomas Ewing	1841
	Walter Forward	1841–1843
	John C. Spencer	1843–1844
	George Bibb	1844–1845
Secretary of War	John Bell	1841
	John C. Spencer	1841–1843
	James M. Porter	1843–1844
	William Wilkins	1844–1845
Attorney General	John J. Crittenden	1841
	Hugh S. Legaré	1841–1843
	John Nelson	1843–1845
Postmaster General	Francis Granger	1841
	Charles Wickliffe	1841
Secretary of Navy	George Badger	1841
	Abel P. Upshur	1841
	David Henshaw	1843–1844
	Thomas Gilmer	1844
	John Y. Mason	1844–1845

The Polk Administration (1845–1849)

Vice President	George M. Dallas	1845–1849
Secretary of State	James Buchanan	1845–1849
Secretary of Treasury	Robert J. Walker	1845–1849
Secretary of War	William L. Marcy	1845–1849

Attorney General	John Y. Mason	1845–1846
	Nathan Clifford	1846–1848
	Isaac Toucey	1848–1849
Postmaster General	Cave Johnson	1845–1849
Secretary of Navy	George Bancroft	1845–1846
	John Y. Mason	1846–1849

The Taylor Administration (1849–1850)

Vice President	Millard Fillmore	1849–1850
Secretary of State	John M. Clayton	1849–1850
Secretary of Treasury	William Meredith	1849–1850
Secretary of War	George Crawford	1849–1850
Attorney General	Reverdy Johnson	1849–1850
Postmaster General	Jacob Collamer	1849–1850
Secretary of Navy	William Preston	1849–1850
Secretary of Interior	Thomas Ewing	1849–1850

The Fillmore Administration (1850–1853)

Vice President	None	
Secretary of State	Daniel Webster	1850–1852
	Edward Everett	1852–1853
Secretary of Treasury	Thomas Corwin	1850–1853
Secretary of War	Charles Conrad	1850–1853
Attorney General	John J. Crittenden	1850–1853
Postmaster General	Nathan Hall	1850–1852
	Sam D. Hubbard	1852–1853
Secretary of Navy	William A. Graham	1850–1852
	John P. Kennedy	1852–1853
Secretary of Interior	Thomas McKennan	1850
	Alexander Stuart	1850–1853

The Pierce Administration (1853–1857)

Vice President	William R. King	1853–1857
Secretary of State	William L. Marcy	1853–1857
Secretary of Treasury	James Guthrie	1853–1857
Secretary of War	Jefferson Davis	1853–1857
Attorney General	Caleb Cushing	1853–1857
Postmaster General	James Campbell	1853–1857
Secretary of Navy	James C. Dobbin	1853–1857
Secretary of Interior	Robert McClelland	1853–1857

The Buchanan Administration (1857–1861)

Vice President	John C. Breckinridge	1857–1861
Secretary of State	Lewis Cass	1857–1860
	Jeremiah S. Black	1860–1861
Secretary of Treasury	Howell Cobb	1857–1860
	Philip Thomas	1860–1861
	John A. Dix	1861
Secretary of War	John B. Floyd	1857–1861
	Joseph Holt	1861
Attorney General	Jeremiah S. Black	1857–1860
	Edwin M. Stanton	1860–1861
Postmaster General	Aaron V. Brown	1857–1859
	Joseph Holt	1859–1861
	Horatio King	1861
Secretary of Navy	Isaac Toucey	1857–1861
Secretary of Interior	Jacob Thompson	1857–1861

The Lincoln Administration (1861–1865)

Vice President	Hannibal Hamlin	1861–1865
	Andrew Johnson	1865
Secretary of State	William H. Seward	1861–1865
Secretary of Treasury	Samuel P. Chase	1861–1864
	William P. Fessenden	1864–1865
	Hugh McCulloch	1865
Secretary of War	Simon Cameron	1861–1862
	Edwin M. Stanton	1862–1865
Attorney General	Edward Bates	1861–1864
	James Speed	1864–1865
Postmaster General	Horatio King	1861
	Montgomery Blair	1861–1864
	William Dennison	1864–1865
Secretary of Navy	Gideon Welles	1861–1865
Secretary of Interior	Caleb B. Smith	1861–1863
	John P. Usher	1863–1865

The Andrew Johnson Administration (1865–1869)

Vice President	None	
Secretary of State	William H. Seward	1865–1869
Secretary of Treasury	Hugh McCulloch	1865–1869
Secretary of War	Edwin M. Stanton	1865–1867
	Ulysses S. Grant	1867–1868
	Lorenzo Thomas	1868
	John M. Schofield	1868–1869
Attorney General	James Speed	1865–1866
	Henry Stanbery	1866–1868
	William M. Evarts	1868–1869
Postmaster General	William Dennison	1865–1866
	Alexander Randall	1866–1869
Secretary of Navy	Gideon Welles	1865–1869
Secretary of Interior	John P. Usher	1865
	James Harlan	1865–1866
	Orville H. Browning	1866–1869

The Grant Administration (1869–1877)

Vice President	Schuyler Colfax	1869–1873
	Henry Wilson	1873–1877
Secretary of State	Elihu B. Washburne	1869
	Hamilton Fish	1869–1877
Secretary of Treasury	George S. Boutwell	1869–1873
	William Richardson	1873–1874
	Benjamin Bristow	1874–1876
	Lot M. Morrill	1876–1877
Secretary of War	John A. Rawlins	1869
	William T. Sherman	1869
	William W. Belknap	1869–1876
	Alphonso Taft	1876
	James D. Cameron	1876–1877
Attorney General	Ebenezer Hoar	1869–1870
	Amos T. Ackerman	1870–1871
	G. H. Williams	1871–1875
	Edwards Pierrepont	1875–1876
	Alphonso Taft	1876–1877

Postmaster General	John A. J. Creswell	1869–1874
	James W. Marshall	1874
	Marshall Jewell	1874–1876
	James N. Tyner	1876–1877
Secretary of Navy	Adolph E. Borie	1869
	George M. Robeson	1869–1877
Secretary of Interior	Jacob D. Cox	1869–1870
	Columbus Delano	1870–1875
	Zachariah Chandler	1875–1877

The Hayes Administration (1877–1881)

Vice President	William A. Wheeler	1877–1881
Secretary of State	William M. Evarts	1877–1881
Secretary of Treasury	John Sherman	1877–1881
Secretary of War	George W. McCrary	1877–1879
	Alex Ramsey	1879–1881
Attorney General	Charles Devens	1877–1881
Postmaster General	David M. Key	1877–1880
	Horace Maynard	1880–1881
Secretary of Navy	Richard W. Thompson	1877–1880
	Nathan Goff, Jr.	1881
Secretary of Interior	Carl Schurz	1877–1881

The Garfield Administration (1881)

Vice President	Chester A. Arthur	1881
Secretary of State	James G. Blaine	1881
Secretary of Treasury	William Windom	1881
Secretary of War	Robert T. Lincoln	1881
Attorney General	Wayne MacVeagh	1881
Postmaster General	Thomas L. James	1881
Secretary of Navy	William H. Hunt	1881
Secretary of Interior	Samuel J. Kirkwood	1881

The Arthur Administration (1881–1885)

Vice President	None	
Secretary of State	F. T. Frelinghuysen	1881–1885
Secretary of Treasury	Charles J. Folger	1881–1884
	Walter Q. Gresham	1884
	Hugh McCulloch	1884–1885
Secretary of War	Robert T. Lincoln	1881–1885
Attorney General	Benjamin H. Brewster	1881–1885
Postmaster General	Timothy O. Howe	1881–1883
	Walter Q. Gresham	1883–1884
	Frank Hatton	1884–1885
Secretary of Navy	William H. Hunt	1881–1882
	William E. Chandler	1882–1885
Secretary of Interior	Samuel J. Kirkwood	1881–1882
	Henry M. Teller	1882–1885

The Cleveland Administration (1885–1889)

Vice President	Thomas A. Hendricks	1885–1889
Secretary of State	Thomas F. Bayard	1885–1889
Secretary of Treasury	Daniel Manning	1885–1887
	Charles S. Fairchild	1887–1889

Secretary of War	William C. Endicott	1885–1889
Attorney General	Augustus H. Garland	1885–1889
Postmaster General	William F. Vilas	1885–1888
	Don M. Dickinson	1888–1889
Secretary of Navy	William C. Whitney	1885–1889
Secretary of Interior	Lucius Q. C. Lamar	1885–1888
	William F. Vilas	1888–1889
Secretary of Agriculture	Norman J. Colman	1889

The Benjamin Harrison Administration (1889–1893)

Vice President	Levi P. Morton	1889–1893
Secretary of State	James G. Blaine	1889–1892
	John W. Foster	1892–1893
Secretary of Treasury	William Windom	1889–1891
	Charles Foster	1891–1893
Secretary of War	Redfield Proctor	1889–1891
	Stephen B. Elkins	1891–1893
Attorney General	William H. H. Miller	1889–1891
Postmaster General	John Wanamaker	1889–1893
Secretary of Navy	Benjamin F. Tracy	1889–1893
Secretary of Interior	John W. Noble	1889–1893
Secretary of Agriculture	Jeremiah M. Rusk	1889–1893

The Cleveland Administration (1893–1897)

Vice President	Adlai E. Stevenson	1893–1897
Secretary of State	Walter Q. Gresham	1893–1895
	Richard Olney	1895–1897
Secretary of Treasury	John G. Carlisle	1893–1897
Secretary of War	Daniel S. Lamont	1893–1897
Attorney General	Richard Olney	1893–1895
	James Harmon	1895–1897
Postmaster General	Wilson S. Bissell	1893–1895
	William L. Wilson	1895–1897
Secretary of Navy	Hilary A. Herbert	1893–1897
Secretary of Interior	Hoke Smith	1893–1896
	David R. Francis	1896–1897
Secretary of Agriculture	Julius S. Morton	1893–1897

The McKinley Administration (1897–1901)

Vice President	Garret A. Hobart	1897–1901
	Theodore Roosevelt	1901
Secretary of State	John Sherman	1897–1898
	William R. Day	1898
	John Hay	1898–1901
Secretary of Treasury	Lyman J. Gage	1897–1901
Secretary of War	Russell A. Alger	1897–1899
	Elihu Root	1899–1901
Attorney General	Joseph McKenna	1897–1898
	John W. Griggs	1898–1901
	Philander C. Knox	1901
Postmaster General	James A. Gary	1897–1898
	Charles E. Smith	1898–1901
Secretary of Navy	John D. Long	1897–1901
Secretary of Interior	Cornelius N. Bliss	1897–1899
	Ethan A. Hitchcock	1899–1901
Secretary of Agriculture	James Wilson	1897–1901

The Theodore Roosevelt Administration (1901–1909)

Vice President	Charles Fairbanks	1905–1909
Secretary of State	John Hay	1901–1905
	Elihu Root	1905–1909
	Robert Bacon	1909
Secretary of Treasury	Lyman J. Gage	1901–1902
	Leslie M. Shaw	1902–1907
	George B. Cortelyou	1907–1909
Secretary of War	Elihu Root	1901–1904
	William H. Taft	1904–1908
	Luke E. Wright	1908–1909
Attorney General	Philander C. Knox	1901–1904
	William H. Moody	1904–1906
	Charles J. Bonaparte	1906–1909
Postmaster General	Charles E. Smith	1901–1902
	Henry C. Payne	1902–1904
	Robert J. Wynne	1904–1905
	George B. Cortelyou	1905–1907
	George von L. Meyer	1907–1909
Secretary of Navy	John D. Long	1901–1902
	William H. Moody	1902–1904
	Paul Morton	1904–1905
	Charles J. Bonaparte	1905–1906
	Victor H. Metcalf	1906–1908
	Truman H. Newberry	1908–1909
Secretary of Interior	Ethan A. Hitchcock	1901–1907
	James R. Garfield	1907–1909
Secretary of Agriculture	James Wilson	1901–1909
Secretary of Labor and Commerce	George B. Cortelyou	1903–1904
	Victor H. Metcalf	1904–1906
	Oscar S. Straus	1906–1909
	Charles Nagel	1909

The Taft Administration (1909–1913)

Vice President	James S. Sherman	1909–1913
Secretary of State	Philander C. Knox	1909–1913
Secretary of Treasury	Franklin MacVeagh	1909–1913
Secretary of War	Jacob M. Dickinson	1909–1911
	Henry L. Stimson	1911–1913
Attorney General	George W. Wickersham	1909–1913
Postmaster General	Frank H. Hitchcock	1909–1913
Secretary of Navy	George von L. Meyer	1909–1913
Secretary of Interior	Richard A. Ballinger	1909–1911
	Walter L. Fisher	1911–1913
Secretary of Agriculture	James Wilson	1909–1913
Secretary of Labor and Commerce	Charles Nagel	1909–1913

The Wilson Administration (1913–1921)

Vice President	Thomas R. Marshall	1913–1921
Secretary of State	William J. Bryan	1913–1915
	Robert Lansing	1915–1920
	Bainbridge Colby	1920–1921
Secretary of Treasury	William G. McAdoo	1913–1918
	Carter Glass	1918–1920
	David F. Houston	1920–1921
Secretary of War	Lindley M. Garrison	1913–1916
	Newton D. Baker	1916–1921

Attorney General	James C. McReynolds	1913–1914
	Thomas W. Gregory	1914–1919
	A. Mitchell Palmer	1919–1921
Postmaster General	Albert S. Burleson	1913–1921
Secretary of Navy	Josephus Daniels	1913–1921
Secretary of Interior	Franklin K. Lane	1913–1920
	John B. Payne	1920–1921
Secretary of Agriculture	David F. Houston	1913–1920
	Edwin T. Meredith	1920–1921
Secretary of Commerce	William C. Redfield	1913–1919
	Joshua W. Alexander	1919–1921
Secretary of Labor	William B. Wilson	1913–1921

The Harding Administration (1921–1923)

Vice President	Calvin Coolidge	1921–1923
Secretary of State	Charles E. Hughes	1921–1923
Secretary of Treasury	Andrew Mellon	1921–1923
Secretary of War	John W. Weeks	1921–1923
Attorney General	Harry M. Daugherty	1921–1923
Postmaster General	Will H. Hays	1921–1922
	Hubert Work	1922–1923
	Harry S. New	1923
Secretary of Navy	Edwin Denby	1921–1923
Secretary of Interior	Albert B. Fall	1921–1923
	Hubert Work	1923
Secretary of Agriculture	Henry C. Wallace	1921–1923
Secretary of Commerce	Herbert C. Hoover	1921–1923
Secretary of Labor	James J. Davis	1921–1923

The Coolidge Administration (1923–1929)

Vice President	Charles G. Dawes	1925–1929
Secretary of State	Charles E. Hughes	1923–1925
	Frank B. Kellogg	1925–1929
Secretary of Treasury	Andrew Mellon	1923–1929
Secretary of War	John W. Weeks	1923–1925
	Dwight F. Davis	1925–1929
Attorney General	Henry M. Daugherty	1923–1924
	Harlan F. Stone	1924–1925
	John G. Sargent	1925–1929
Postmaster General	Harry S. New	1923–1929
Secretary of Navy	Edwin Denby	1923–1924
	Curtis D. Wilbur	1924–1929
Secretary of Interior	Hubert Work	1923–1928
	Roy O. West	1928–1929
Secretary of Agriculture	Henry C. Wallace	1923–1924
	Howard M. Gore	1924–1925
	William M. Jardine	1925–1929
Secretary of Commerce	Herbert C. Hoover	1923–1928
	William F. Whiting	1928–1929
Secretary of Labor	James J. Davis	1923–1929

The Hoover Administration (1929–1933)

Vice President	Charles Curtis	1929–1933
Secretary of State	Henry L. Stimson	1929–1933
Secretary of Treasury	Andrew Mellon	1929–1932
	Ogden L. Mills	1932–1933

Secretary of War	James W. Good	1929
	Patrick J. Hurley	1929–1933
Attorney General	William D. Mitchell	1929–1933
Postmaster General	Walter F. Brown	1929–1933
Secretary of Navy	Charles F. Adams	1929–1933
Secretary of Interior	Ray L. Wilbur	1929–1933
Secretary of Agriculture	Arthur M. Hyde	1929–1933
Secretary of Commerce	Robert P. Lamont	1929–1932
	Roy D. Chapin	1932–1933
Secretary of Labor	James J. Davis	1929–1930
	William N. Doak	1930–1933

The Franklin D. Roosevelt Administration (1933–1945)

Vice President	John Nance Garner	1933–1941
	Henry A. Wallace	1941–1945
	Harry S Truman	1945
Secretary of State	Cordell Hull	1933–1944
	Edward R. Stettinius, Jr.	1944–1945
Secretary of Treasury	William H. Woodin	1933–1934
	Henry Morgenthau, Jr.	1934–1945
Secretary of War	George H. Dern	1933–1936
	Henry A. Woodring	1936–1940
	Henry L. Stimson	1940–1945
Attorney General	Homer S. Cummings	1933–1939
	Frank Murphy	1939–1940
	Robert H. Jackson	1940–1941
	Francis Biddle	1941–1945
Postmaster General	James A. Farley	1933–1940
	Frank C. Walker	1940–1945
Secretary of Navy	Claude A. Swanson	1933–1940
	Charles Edison	1940
	Frank Knox	1940–1944
	James V. Forrestal	1944–1945
Secretary of Interior	Harold L. Ickes	1933–1945
Secretary of Agriculture	Henry A. Wallace	1933–1940
	Claude R. Wickard	1940–1945
Secretary of Commerce	Daniel C. Roper	1933–1939
	Harry L. Hopkins	1939–1940
	Jesse Jones	1940–1945
	Henry A. Wallace	1945
Secretary of Labor	Frances Perkins	1933–1945

The Truman Administration (1945–1953)

Vice President	Alben W. Barkley	1949–1953
Secretary of State	Edward R. Stettinius, Jr.	1945
	James F. Byrnes	1945–1947
	George C. Marshall	1947–1949
	Dean G. Acheson	1949–1953
Secretary of Treasury	Fred M. Vinson	1945–1946
	John W. Snyder	1946–1953
Secretary of War	Robert P. Patterson	1945–1947
	Kenneth C. Royall	1947
Attorney General	Tom C. Clark	1945–1949
	J. Howard McGrath	1949–1952
	James P. McGranery	1952–1953
Postmaster General	Frank C. Walker	1945
	Robert E. Hannegan	1945–1947
	Jesse M. Donaldson	1947–1953

Secretary of Navy	James V. Forrestal	1945–1947
Secretary of Interior	Harold L. Ickes	1945–1946
	Julius A. Krug	1946–1949
	Oscar L. Chapman	1949–1953
Secretary of Agriculture	Clinton P. Anderson	1945–1948
	Charles F. Brannan	1948–1953
Secretary of Commerce	Henry A. Wallace	1945–1946
	W. Averell Harriman	1946–1948
	Charles W. Sawyer	1948–1953
Secretary of Labor	Lewis B. Schwellenbach	1945–1948
	Maurice J. Tobin	1948–1953
Secretary of Defense	James V. Forrestal	1947–1949
	Louis A. Johnson	1949–1950
	George C. Marshall	1950–1951
	Robert A. Lovett	1951–1953

The Eisenhower Administration (1953–1961)

Vice President	Richard M. Nixon	1953–1961
Secretary of State	John Foster Dulles	1953–1959
	Christian A. Herter	1959–1961
Secretary of Treasury	George M. Humphrey	1953–1957
	Robert B. Anderson	1957–1961
Attorney General	Herbert Brownell, Jr.	1953–1958
	William P. Rogers	1958–1961
Postmaster General	Arthur E. Summerfield	1953–1961
Secretary of Interior	Douglas McKay	1953–1956
	Fred A. Seaton	1956–1961
Secretary of Agriculture	Ezra T. Benson	1953–1961
Secretary of Commerce	Sinclair Weeks	1953–1958
	Lewis L. Strauss	1958–1959
	Frederick H. Mueller	1959–1961
Secretary of Labor	Martin P. Durkin	1953
	James P. Mitchell	1953–1961
Secretary of Defense	Charles E. Wilson	1953–1957
	Neil H. McElroy	1957–1959
	Thomas S. Gates, Jr.	1959–1961
Secretary of Health, Education, and Welfare	Oveta Culp Hobby	1953–1955
	Marion B. Folsom	1955–1958
	Arthur S. Flemming	1958–1961

The Kennedy Administration (1961–1963)

Vice President	Lyndon B. Johnson	1961–1963
Secretary of State	Dean Rusk	1961–1963
Secretary of Treasury	C. Douglas Dillon	1961–1963
Attorney General	Robert F. Kennedy	1961–1963
Postmaster General	J. Edward Day	1961–1963
	John A. Gronouski	1963
Secretary of Interior	Stewart L. Udall	1961–1963
Secretary of Agriculture	Orville L. Freeman	1961–1963
Secretary of Commerce	Luther H. Hodges	1961–1963
Secretary of Labor	Arthur J. Goldberg	1961–1962
	W. Willard Wirtz	1962–1963
Secretary of Defense	Robert S. McNamara	1961–1963
Secretary of Health, Education, and Welfare	Abraham A. Ribicoff	1961–1962
	Anthony J. Celebrezze	1962–1963

The Lyndon Johnson Administration (1963–1969)

Vice President	Hubert H. Humphrey	1965–1969

Secretary of State	Dean Rusk	1963–1969
Secretary of Treasury	C. Douglas Dillon	1963–1965
	Henry H. Fowler	1965–1969
Attorney General	Robert F. Kennedy	1963–1964
	Nicholas Katzenbach	1965–1966
	Ramsey Clark	1967–1969
Postmaster General	John A. Gronouski	1963–1965
	Lawrence F. O'Brien	1965–1968
	Marvin Watson	1968–1969
Secretary of Interior	Stewart L. Udall	1963–1969
Secretary of Agriculture	Orville L. Freeman	1963–1969
Secretary of Commerce	Luther H. Hodges	1963–1964
	John T. Connor	1964–1967
	Alexander B. Trowbridge	1967–1968
	Cyrus R. Smith	1968–1969
Secretary of Labor	W. Willard Wirtz	1963–1969
Secretary of Defense	Robert F. McNamara	1963–1968
	Clark Clifford	1968–1969
Secretary of Health, Education, and Welfare	Anthony J. Celebrezze	1963–1965
	John W. Gardner	1965–1968
	Wilbur J. Cohen	1968–1969
Secretary of Housing and Urban Development	Robert C. Weaver	1966–1969
	Robert C. Wood	1969
Secretary of Transportation	Alan S. Boyd	1967–1969

The Nixon Administration (1969–1974)

Vice President	Spiro T. Agnew	1969–1973
	Gerald R. Ford	1973–1974
Secretary of State	William P. Rogers	1969–1973
	Henry A. Kissinger	1973–1974
Secretary of Treasury	David M. Kennedy	1969–1970
	John B. Connally	1971–1972
	George P. Shultz	1972–1974
	William E. Simon	1974
Attorney General	John N. Mitchell	1969–1972
	Richard G. Kleindienst	1972–1973
	Elliot L. Richardson	1973
	William B. Saxbe	1973–1974
Postmaster General	Winton M. Blount	1969–1971
Secretary of Interior	Walter J. Hickel	1969–1970
	Rogers Morton	1971–1974
Secretary of Agriculture	Clifford M. Hardin	1969–1971
	Earl L. Butz	1971–1974
Secretary of Commerce	Maurice H. Stans	1969–1972
	Peter G. Peterson	1972–1973
	Frederick B. Dent	1973–1974
Secretary of Labor	George P. Shultz	1969–1970
	James D. Hodgson	1970–1973
	Peter J. Brennan	1973–1974
Secretary of Defense	Melvin R. Laird	1969–1973
	Elliot L. Richardson	1973
	James R. Schlesinger	1973–1974
Secretary of Health, Education, and Welfare	Robert H. Finch	1969–1970
	Elliot L. Richardson	1970–1973
	Caspar W. Weinberger	1973–1974
Secretary of Housing and Urban Development	George Romney	1969–1973
	James T. Lynn	1973–1974
Secretary of Transportation	John A. Volpe	1969–1973
	Claude S. Brinegar	1973–1974

The Ford Administration (1974–1977)

Vice President	Nelson A. Rockefeller	1974–1977
Secretary of State	Henry A. Kissinger	1974–1977
Secretary of Treasury	William E. Simon	1974–1977
Attorney General	William Saxbe	1974–1975
	Edward Levi	1975–1977
Secretary of Interior	Rogers Morton	1974–1975
	Stanley K. Hathaway	1975
	Thomas Kleppe	1975–1977
Secretary of Agriculture	Earl L. Butz	1974–1976
	John A. Knebel	1976–1977
Secretary of Commerce	Frederick B. Dent	1974–1975
	Rogers Morton	1975–1976
	Elliott L. Richardson	1976–1977
Secretary of Labor	Peter J. Brennan	1974–1975
	John T. Dunlop	1975–1976
	W. J. Usery	1976–1977
Secretary of Defense	James R. Schlesinger	1974–1975
	Donald Rumsfeld	1975–1977
Secretary of Health, Education, and Welfare	Caspar Weinberger	1974–1975
	Forrest D. Mathews	1975–1977
Secretary of Housing and Urban Development	James T. Lynn	1974–1975
	Carla A. Hills	1975–1977
Secretary of Transportation	Claude Brinegar	1974–1975
	William T. Coleman	1975–1977

The Carter Administration (1977–1981)

Vice President	Walter F. Mondale	1977–1981
Secretary of State	Cyrus R. Vance	1977–1980
	Edmund Muskie	1980–1981
Secretary of Treasury	W. Michael Blumenthal	1977–1979
	G. William Miller	1979–1981
Attorney General	Griffin Bell	1977–1979
	Benjamin R. Civiletti	1979–1981
Secretary of Interior	Cecil D. Andrus	1977–1981
Secretary of Agriculture	Robert Bergland	1977–1981
Secretary of Commerce	Juanita M. Kreps	1977–1979
	Philip M. Klutznick	1979–1981
Secretary of Labor	Ray F. Marshall	1977–1981
Secretary of Defense	Harold Brown	1977–1981
Secretary of Health, Education, and Welfare	Joseph A. Califano	1977–1979
	Patricia R. Harris	1979
Secretary of Health and Human Services	Patricia R. Harris	1979–1981
Secretary of Education	Shirley M. Hufstedler	1979–1981
Secretary of Housing and Urban Development	Patricia R. Harris	1977–1979
	Moon Landrieu	1979–1981
Secretary of Transportation	Brock Adams	1977–1979
	Neil E. Goldschmidt	1979–1981
Secretary of Energy	James R. Schlesinger	1977–1979
	Charles W. Duncan	1979–1981

The Reagan Administration (1981–1989)

Vice President	George Bush	1981–1989
Secretary of State	Alexander M. Haig	1981–1982
	George P. Shultz	1982–1989
Secretary of Treasury	Donald Regan	1981–1985
	James A. Baker III	1985–1988
	Nicholas Brady	1988–1989

Attorney General	William F. Smith	1981–1985
	Edwin A. Meese III	1985–1988
	Richard Thornburgh	1988–1989
Secretary of Interior	James Watt	1981–1983
	William P. Clark, Jr.	1983–1985
	Donald P. Hodel	1985–1989
Secretary of Agriculture	John Block	1981–1986
	Richard E. Lyng	1986–1989
Secretary of Commerce	Malcolm Baldridge	1981–1987
	C. William Verity, Jr.	1987–1989
Secretary of Labor	Raymond Donovan	1981–1985
	William E. Brock	1985–1988
	Ann Dore McLaughlin	1988–1989
Secretary of Defense	Caspar Weinberger	1981–1988
	Frank Carlucci	1988–1989
Secretary of Health and Human Services	Richard Schweiker	1981–1983
	Margaret Heckler	1983–1985
	Otis R. Bowen	1985–1989
Secretary of Education	Terrel H. Bell	1981–1985
	William J. Bennett	1985–1988
	Lauro F. Cavazos	1988–1989
Secretary of Housing and Urban Development	Samuel Pierce	1981–1989
Secretary of Transportation	Drew Lewis	1981–1983
	Elizabeth Dole	1983–1987
	James L. Burnley IV	1987–1989
Secretary of Energy	James Edwards	1981–1982
	Donald P. Hodel	1982–1985
	John S. Herrington	1985–1989

The Bush Administration (1989–   )

Vice President	J. Danforth Quayle III	1989–
Secretary of State	James Baker III	1989–
Secretary of Treasury	Nicholas Brady	1989–
Attorney General	Richard Thornburgh	1989–
Secretary of Interior	Manuel Lujan	1989–
Secretary of Agriculture	Clayton Yeutter	1989–
Secretary of Commerce	Robert Mosbacher	1989–
Secretary of Labor	Elizabeth Dole	1989–
Secretary of Defense	Richard Cheney	1989–
Secretary of Health and Human Services	Louis W. Sullivan	1989–
Secretary of Education	Lauro Cavazos	1989–
Secretary of Housing and Urban Development	Jack Kemp	1989–
Secretary of Transportation	Samuel Skinner	1989–
Secretary of Energy	James Watkins	1989–
Secretary of Veterans' Affairs	Edward Derwinski	1989–

Supreme Court Justices

Name	Terms of Service	Appointed By
JOHN JAY	1789–1795	Washington
James Wilson	1789–1798	Washington
John Rutledge	1790–1791	Washington
William Cushing	1790–1810	Washington
John Blair	1790–1796	Washington
James Iredell	1790–1799	Washington
Thomas Johnson	1792–1793	Washington
William Paterson	1793–1806	Washington
JOHN RUTLEDGE*	1795	Washington
Samuel Chase	1796–1811	Washington
OLIVER ELLSWORTH	1796–1800	Washington
Bushrod Washington	1799–1829	J. Adams
Alfred Moore	1800–1804	J. Adams
JOHN MARSHALL	1801–1835	J. Adams
William Johnson	1804–1834	Jefferson
Brockholst Livingston	1807–1823	Jefferson
Thomas Todd	1807–1826	Jefferson
Gabriel Duvall	1811–1835	Madison
Joseph Story	1812–1845	Madison
Smith Thompson	1823–1843	Monroe
Robert Trimble	1826–1828	J. Q. Adams
John McLean	1830–1861	Jackson
Henry Baldwin	1830–1844	Jackson
James M. Wayne	1835–1867	Jackson
ROGER B. TANEY	1836–1864	Jackson
Philip P. Barbour	1836–1841	Jackson
John Cartron	1837–1865	Van Buren
John McKinley	1838–1852	Van Buren
Peter V. Daniel	1842–1860	Van Buren
Samuel Nelson	1845–1872	Tyler
Levi Woodbury	1845–1851	Polk
Robert C. Grier	1846–1870	Polk
Benjamin R. Curtis	1851–1857	Fillmore
John A. Campbell	1853–1861	Pierce
Nathan Clifford	1858–1881	Buchanan
Noah H. Swayne	1862–1881	Lincoln
Samuel F. Miller	1862–1890	Lincoln
David Davis	1862–1877	Lincoln
Stephen J. Field	1863–1897	Lincoln
SALMON P. CHASE	1864–1873	Lincoln
William Strong	1870–1880	Grant
Joseph P. Bradley	1870–1892	Grant
Ward Hunt	1873–1882	Grant
MORRISON R. WAITE	1874–1888	Grant
John M. Harlan	1877–1911	Hayes
William B. Woods	1881–1887	Hayes
Stanley Matthews	1881–1889	Garfield
Horace Gray	1882–1902	Arthur
Samuel Blatchford	1882–1893	Arthur
Lucious Q. C. Lamar	1888–1893	Cleveland
MELVILLE W. FULLER	1888–1910	Cleveland

NOTE: The names of Chief Justices are printed in capital letters.
* Although Rutledge acted as Chief Justice, the Senate refused to confirm his appointment.

Name	Terms of Service	Appointed By
David J. Brewer	1890–1910	B. Harrison
Henry B. Brown	1891–1906	B. Harrison
George Shiras, Jr.	1892–1903	B. Harrison
Howell E. Jackson	1893–1895	B. Harrison
Edward D. White	1894–1910	Cleveland
Rufus W. Peckham	1896–1909	Cleveland
Joseph McKenna	1898–1925	McKinley
Oliver W. Holmes	1902–1932	T. Roosevelt
William R. Day	1903–1922	T. Roosevelt
William H. Moody	1906–1910	T. Roosevelt
Horace H. Lurton	1910–1914	Taft
Charles E. Hughes	1910–1916	Taft
EDWARD D. WHITE	1910–1921	Taft
Willis Van Devanter	1911–1937	Taft
Joseph R. Lamar	1911–1916	Taft
Mahlon Pitney	1912–1922	Taft
James C. McReynolds	1914–1941	Wilson
Louis D. Brandeis	1916–1939	Wilson
John H. Clarke	1916–1922	Wilson
WILLIAM H. TAFT	1921–1930	Harding
George Sutherland	1922–1938	Harding
Pierce Butler	1923–1939	Harding
Edward T. Sanford	1923–1930	Harding
Harlan F. Stone	1925–1941	Coolidge
CHARLES E. HUGHES	1930–1941	Hoover
Owen J. Roberts	1930–1945	Hoover
Benjamin N. Cardozo	1932–1938	Hoover
Hugo L. Black	1937–1971	F. Roosevelt
Stanley F. Reed	1938–1957	F. Roosevelt
Felix Frankfurter	1939–1962	F. Roosevelt
William O. Douglas	1939–1975	F. Roosevelt
Frank Murphy	1940–1949	F. Roosevelt
HARLAN F. STONE	1941–1946	F. Roosevelt
James F. Byrnes	1941–1942	F. Roosevelt
Robert H. Jackson	1941–1954	F. Roosevelt
Wiley B. Rutledge	1943–1949	F. Roosevelt
Harold H. Burton	1945–1958	Truman
FREDERICK M. VINSON	1946–1953	Truman
Tom C. Clark	1949–1967	Truman
Sherman Minton	1949–1956	Truman
EARL WARREN	1953–1969	Eisenhower
John Marshall Harlan	1955–1971	Eisenhower
William J. Brennan, Jr.	1956–	Eisenhower
Charles E. Whittaker	1957–1962	Eisenhower
Potter Stewart	1958–1981	Eisenhower
Byron R. White	1962–	Kennedy
Arthur J. Goldberg	1962–1965	Kennedy
Abe Fortas	1965–1970	L. Johnson
Thurgood Marshall	1967–	L. Johnson
WARREN E. BURGER	1969–1986	Nixon
Harry A. Blackmun	1970–	Nixon
Lewis F. Powell, Jr.	1971–	Nixon
William H. Rehnquist	1971–1986	Nixon
John Paul Stevens	1975–	Ford
Sandra Day O'Connor	1981–	Reagan
WILLIAM H. REHNQUIST	1986–	Reagan
Antonin Scalia	1986–	Reagan
Anthony Kennedy	1988–	Reagan

PHOTOGRAPH CREDITS

The following abbreviations are used for some sources from which several illustrations were obtained:
A—Bettmann Archive. CHS—Chicago Historical Society. CP—Culver Pictures. GC—Granger Collection. HSP—Historical Society of Pennsylvania. LC—Library of Congress. MMA—Metropolitan Museum of Art. NA—National Archive. NPG—National Portrait Gallery. NYHS—New-York Historical Society. NYPL—New York Public Library. SI—Smithsonian Institution. UPI/Bettmann—UPI Bettmann Newsphotos. WW—Wide World. YU—Yale University.

Prologue p. xxxiii, Frank Whitney/The Image Bank; p. xxxv, Eric Meola/The Image Bank; p. xxxix(top), Cara Moore/The Image Bank; p. xxxix(bottom), Steve Proehl/The Image Bank; p. xl, Mike Malyszko/Stock, Boston; p. xli, Alan Becker/The Image Bank; p. xliii(top), Nathan Benn/Stock, Boston, p. xliii(bottom), Gary S. Chapman/The Image Bank; p. xliiia(top), Allen Russell/Profiles West; p. xliiia(bottom), Tim Haske/Profiles West; p. xliiib(top), Tim Haske/Profiles West; p. xliiib(bottom), Jerry Jacka Photography; p. xliv(top), Denver Museum of Natural History; pp. xliv–xlv, Eric Meola/The Image Bank; p. xlv(top), Georg Gerster/Comstock; p. xlv(bottom), Mound City Group National Monument, National Park Service, Michael Bitsko; p. xlvii(top), Don Landwehrle/The Image Bank; p. xlvii(center), Al Satterwhite/The Image Bank; xlvii(bottom), H. Wendler/The Image Bank; p. xlviii(top), John Aldridge/The Picture Cube; p. xlviii(bottom), Peter Cole/New England Stock Photo; p. il, Steve Dunwell/The Image Bank; p. l, Ken Dequaine/Third Coast Stock Source.

Chapter 1 p. liv, St. Louis Science Center, Photo: Dirk Bakker, Detroit Institute of Arts; p. 1, MMA, Gift of J. P. Morgan; p. 5(top), National Gallery of Art; p. 5(bottom left, center, and right), Jerry Jacka Photography; p. 8(left), Werner Foreman Archive; p. 8(right), Werner Foreman Archive/Museum of Anthropology with British Columbia; p. 11, Lee Boltin; p. 13, The Marquess of Salisbury at Hatfield House/The Fotomas Index; p. 14, GC; p. 15, GC; p. 18, GC; p. 19, GC; p. 21, Lee Boltin; p. 22, Lee Boltin; p. 25, Bodleian Library; p. 26, GC; p. 29, National Maritime Museum, Greenwich, England; p. 31a, GC; p. 31b(all), GC; p. 33(all) Flowerdew Hundred Foundation; p. 35, CP; p. 37, Massachusetts Historical Society; p. 39, GC.

Chapter 2 p. 42, Massachusetts Historical Society; p. 43, GC; p. 46, American Antiquarian Society; p. 48(left), Pilgrim Society, Boston; p. 48(right), Eliot Elisofon/Life Picture Service; p. 49, Massachusetts Historical Society; p. 53(both), Mick Heles; p. 55, Frank Siteman/Stock Boston; p. 56(left), Massachusetts Historical Society; p. 56(bottom right), Museum of Fine Arts, Boston, Gift of Leverett Saltonstall; p. 56(top right), Pilgrim Society, Plymouth, MA; p. 59, Huntington Library; p. 62, Essex Institute, Salem, MA; pp. 66–67, John Carter Brown Library; p. 71, GC; p. 74, Trustees of British Museum; p. 75, GC; pp. 75a–75b(all), Photos courtesy of Louise E. Gray, The Middlesex County Historical Society; Sarah Streetman, photographer; p. 77(both), GC.

Chapter 3 p. 80, Brookline Historical Society; p. 81, GC; p. 87, Collection Albany Institute of History and Art, Gift of Governor and Mrs. Averell Harriman and Three Anonymous Owners; p. 89(left), Library Company of Philadelphia; p. 89(right), HSP; p. 91, Peabody Museum, Harvard University; p. 93, Bob Daenmrich/Stock Boston; p. 94(both), NYPL Manuscript Division; p. 97(both), GC; p. 99, Colonial Williamsburg; p. 103a, Museum of the American Indian; p. 103b(top), Public Archives of Canada; p. 103b(bottom), Rochester Museum and Science Center; p. 104, GC; p. 105, Henry du Pont Winterthur Collection of Earl of Shaftsbury; p. 107, NYHS MacDonald/Aldus Archive; p. 110, GC; p. 111, MMA, Edward W. C. Arnold Collection of New York Prints, Maps, and Pictures. Bequest of Edward W. C. Arnold, 1954. p. 113, Newport Historical Society; p. 115(both), David R. White/Stockfile; p. 119(left), YU Bequest of Eugene Phelps Edwards, 1938; p. 119(right), NYPL Rare Book Division; p. 121, The Princeton University Library; p. 123, GC.

Chapter 4 p. 126, HSP(detail); p. 127, GC; p. 128, HSP; p. 130, Collection Brown University, MacDonald/Aldus Archive; p. 134, GC; p. 137(left), NYPL Emmett Collection; p. 137(right), Massachusetts Historical Society; p. 141, North Wind Picture Archives; p. 145, Museum of Fine Arts, Boston, Deposited by City of Boston, 1876; p. 147, GC; p. 149 Corcoran Gallery, Washington, D.C.; p. 150, GC; p. 151, GC; p. 155, GC; p. 156, GC; p. 159(left), HSP; p. 159(right), Robert Llewellyn;

p. 159a, American Antiquarian Society; p. 159b(top), GC; p. 159b(bottom), John Carter Brown Library; p. 160, LC; p. 161(left), HSP; p. 161(right), GC.

Chapter 5 p. 164, MMA Bequest of Charles Allen Munn, 1924; p. 165, Museum of Fine Arts, Boston, Deposited by City of Boston, 1876; p. 168, NYHS; p. 169, NYPL Print Collection, Astor, Lenox and Tilden Foundations; p. 171, HSP; p. 174, Independence National Historical Park, Philadelphia; p. 175a, The Filson Club, Louisville, KY; p. 175b, Kentucky Military History Museum; p. 177, Detroit Public Library, Burton Historical Collection, Photo: Thomas Featherstone; p. 182, Virginia Museum of Fine Arts, Boston, Gift of Miss Dorothy Payne; p. 184(right), The Friends Historical Library of Swarthmore College; p. 184(center), Frick Art Reserve Library; p. 184(left), YU, Bequest of Mrs. Katherine Rankin Wolcott Verplanck; p. 186, HSP; p. 192, National Gallery of Canada, Ottawa; p. 193, New Orleans Museum of Art, Museum Purchase, Art Acquisition Fund Drive; p. 195, Anne van der Vaeren/Image Bank; p. 196, Colonial Williamsburg; p. 198, Virginia Museum of Fine Arts, Boston; p. 201(left), Museum of Fine Arts, Boston, Boston, Bequest of Winslow Warren, 1931; p. 201(right), GC.

Chapter 6 p. 204, National Gallery of Art, Washington, Gift of Edgar William and Bernice Chester Garbisch; p. 205, BA; p. 208, Maryland Historical Society; p. 209a, Mr. and Mrs. Karolik Collection, Museum of Fine Arts, Boston; p. 209b, Maryland Historical Society; p. 209(left), Worcester Art Museum, Worcester, MA; p. 209(right), Maryland Historical Society; p. 210, HSP; p. 215, NYHS; p. 216, Donaldson, Lufkin & Jenrette Collection of Americana; p. 221, Boston Public Library; p. 223, NYPL, Print Collection; p. 224, CHS; p. 226, Brooklyn Museum, Gift of the Crescent Hamilton Athletic Club; p. 227, Winterthur Museum; p. 229, Robert Llewellyn; p. 231(left), Adams National Historical Site, Jeffrey Dunn Photographer; p. 231(right), SI, National Museum of American Art, Adams-Clement Collection, gift of Mary Louisa Adams in memory of her mother, Louisa Catherine Adams Clement; p. 235, Henry Francis du Winterthur Museum; p. 239(left), HSP; p. 239(right), Museum of Fine Arts, Boston, George Nixon Black Fund.

Chapter 7 p. 242, Minneapolis Institute of Arts, William Hood Dunwoody Fund; p. 243, GC; p. 245, Maryland Historical Society; p. 245(both), Robert Llewellyn; p. 246, Franklin D. Roosevelt Library; p. 248, Boston Atheneum; p. 252(both), Independence National Historical Park Collection; p. 253, Peabody Museum, Harvard University. Photo by Hillel Berger;

p. 258, Peabody Museum; p. 260, GC; p. 264, The New Haven Historical Society, Gift of Mrs. Philip Galpin, 1886; p. 266, The Pennsylvania Academy of Fine Arts, Harrison Earl Fund; p. 267a, Charles Bulfinch by Mather Brown, 1786, Harvard University Art Museums, Gift of Francis V. Bulfinch, 1933; p. 267b(top), plan of State House by Bulfinch, 1787, Phelps Stokes Collection, NYPL; p. 267b(bottom), Gift of Mrs. Horatio A. Lamb in memory of Mr. and Mrs. Winthrop Lamb, Museum of Fine Arts, Boston, Boston; p. 268, BA; p. 274(left), Harvard University Portrait Collection, Bequest Ward Nicholas; p. 274(right), Anne S. K. Brown Military Collection, Brown University Library.

Chapter 8 p. 276, The St. Louis Art Museum Purchase, Ezra H. Lilly Fund (detail); p. 277, GC; p. 279(left) Walters Art Gallery; p. 279(top), Buffalo Bill Historical Center; p. 279(bottom), Missouri Historical Center; p. 280, MMA, Rogers Fund 1942; p. 281a, NYHS; p. 281b(top), State Historical Society of Wisconsin; p. 281b(bottom), National Museum of American Art, SI, Gift of the Misses Henry; p. 286, National Museum of American Art, SI, Harriet Cane Johnston Collection; p. 288, Museum of Natural History, Le Havre, France; p. 290, NYHS; p. 296, Rhode Island Historical Society; p. 297, University of Lowell; p. 300, St. Louis Art Museum, Loan from Collection of Arthur Ziern, Jr.; p. 302, New York State Historical Association, Cooperstown; p. 307, Cheekwood Botanical Gardens and Fine Arts Center, Nashville, TN; p. 310, YU, Gift of George Hoadley.

Chapter 9 p. 312, Walters Art Gallery; p. 313, Cornell University Library, Department of Rare Books; p. 316, MMA; p. 320(both), GC; p. 325, NYHS; p. 328, NYHS; p. 329, SI, Division of Political History; p. 331, SI; p. 334, Church Museum, Brigham Young University; p. 335, Lightfoot Collection; p. 337, New York State Historical Association; p. 337a, Museum of Art, Rhode Island School of Design, Jesse Metcalf Fund; p. 337b(top), NYPL, Stokes Collection; p. 337b(bottom), Memorial Art Gallery of the University of Rochester, Gift of Thomas J. Watson, photo, James Via; p. 340, Collection of the Museum of American Folk Art, New York City, Promised Bequest of Dorothy and Leo Rabkin; p. 343(both), GC; p. 344, Free Library of Philadelphia; p. 347, GC; p. 348, LC.

Chapter 10 p. 350, The Historic New Orleans Collection(detail); p. 351, GC; p. 357, The Historic New Orleans Collection; p. 360, Helga Photo Studio; p. 361, Louisiana State Museum; p. 364, Everson Museum of Art of Syracuse and Onondaga County, Gift of Hon. Andrew D. White; p. 367,

NYHS; p. 369a(both), South Caroliniana Library; p. 369b, South Caroliniana Library; p. 371(top), Historical Society of New York City; p. 371(bottom), Peabody Museum, Harvard University; p. 372, from The Whitney Museum of American Arts, exhibit "The Painter's America," Collection of Hon. and Mrs. John Heinz, III, Washington, DC/Laurie Platt Winfrey, Inc.; p. 373, LC; p. 377, NYPL; p. 380, Virginia State Library; p. 382, Hampton University Museum; p. 383, BA; p. 384(right), Collection of Glenbow Museum, Calgary, Alberta, Canada; p. 384(left), Virginia State Library.

Chapter 11 p. 386, Edison Institute, Henry Ford Museum & Greenfield Village; p. 387, State Historical Society of Wisconsin; p. 388, WW; p. 390, BA; p. 392, GC; p. 396, International Museum of Photography at George Eastman House; p. 398, Clarence Davies Collection, Museum of the City of New York; p. 399, BA; p. 402, National Museum of American Art, SI, Gift of Frederick Weingeroff; p. 405, BA; p. 406, CP; p. 409(left), YU; p. 409(right), National Gallery of Art, Andrew W. Mellon Collection; p. 411, National Portrait Gallery; p. 413, Cleveland Museum of Art; p. 413a, GC; p. 413b(top), Olmstead Office Portfolio; p. 413b(bottom), J. Clarence Davies Collection, Museum of the City of New York; p. 416, NPG, SI, transfer from National Gallery of Art, Gift of Andrew W. Mellon, 1942.

Chapter 12 p. 418, Museum of Fine Arts, Boston, Boston(detail); p. 419, LC; p. 422, Levi Stauss; p. 424, GC; p. 427, GC; p. 431, GC; p. 432, NPG, SI; p. 433, National Park Service, Scotts Bluff National Monument; p. 434, CHS; p. 437, SI, Division of Political History; p. 443, Amon Carter Museum, Fort Worth; p. 444(left), National Academy of Design; p. 444, GC; p. 447a, International Museum of Photography at George Eastman House; p. 447b, Bancroft Library, University of California, Berkeley, CA; p. 450, Oakland Museum, Gift of Concours d'Antiques Art Guild, Oakland, CA/Laurie Platt Winfrey, Inc.

Chapter 13 p. 452, MMA, Arthur Hoppock Hearn Fund, 1950, Courtesy of Kathleen Curry; p. 453, LC; p. 455, LC; p. 458, SI, Division of Political History; p. 459, Detroit Institute of the Arts, Gift of Mrs. Jefferson Butler and Miss Grace R. Conover; p. 466, SI, Division of Political History; p. 471, NPG, SI, transfer from the National Gallery of Art; p. 474(left), GC; p. 474(right), NPG, SI; p. 476, MMA Gift of Mr. and Mrs. Carl Stoeckel, 1897; p. 479a, Charlestown Museum; p. 479b(top), GC; p. 479b(bottom), Gibbes Museum of Art; p. 480, Museum of the Confederacy; p. 482, GC; p. 484(top),

Missouri Historical Society; p. 484(bottom), SI, Division of Political History.

Chapter 14 p. 486, Meed Art Gallery, Amherst College, Museum Purchase; p. 487, Index of American Design, National Gallery of Art; p. 488, NYHS; p. 490, Cook Collection, Valentine Museum; p. 493, Lincoln Collection, John Hay Library, Brown University; p. 496, Meserve Collection; p. 497(right), Bill Dekker, photo by Henry Groskinsky; p. 497(center left), Russ Pritchard, photo by Larry Sherer; p. 497(bottom left), Confederate Memorial Hall; p. 497(top left), Historical Collections, National Museum of Health and Medicine, Armed Forces Institute of Pathology; p. 500, LC; p. 502, BA; p. 505b(top), Historical Pictures Service, Inc.; p. 505b(bottom), Western Reserve Historical Society; p. 507(left), National Infantry Museum; p. 507(right), CHS; p. 511, Dale C. Wheary; p. 516(left), NA; p. 516(right), GC; p. 518, LC; p. 520, Brady Collection, NA; p. 522, GC.

Chapter 15 p. 526, YU, Gift of William W. Garretson; p. 527, The Museum of the Confederacy; p. 530, NPG, SI; p. 533, GC; p. 537, GC; p. 541(top), GC; p. 541(bottom), Wood Art Gallery, Montpelier, VT; p. 542, North Wind Picture Archives; p. 545, Tennessee State Library and Archives; p. 547, LC; p. 548, Moorland Spingarn Research Center, Howard University; p. 549a, Georgia Department of Archives and History; p. 549b, Hargrett Rare Book and Manuscript Library, University of Georgia Libraries; p. 558, GC; 559(left), Kansas State Historical Society; p. 559(right), LC; p. 563, GC.

Table of Contents p. xvi(top), The Huntington Library; p. xvi(bottom), New-York Historical Society/MacDonald Aldus Archive; p. xvii, GC; p. xviii(top), Historical Society of Pennsylvania; p. xviii(bottom), Metropolitan Museum of Art, Bequest of Charles Allen Munn, 1924; p. xix(top), Historical Society of Pennsylvania; p. xix(bottom), Henry Francis du Pont Winterthur Museum; p. xx(top), Anne S.K. Brown Military Collection, Brown University Library; p. xx(bottom left), New York Public Library, Phelps Stokes Collection; p. xx(bottom right), Museum of Fine Arts, Gift of Mrs. Horatio A. Lamb in memory of Mr. and Mrs. Winthrop Lamb; p. xxi(top), New-York Historical Society; p. xxi(bottom), State Historical Society of Wisconsin; p. xxii(top), GC; p. xxii(center), Lightfoot Collection; p. xxii(bottom) New York Public Library, Stokes Collection; p. xxiii(left), LC; p. xxiii(right), Louisiana State Museum; p. xxiv, GC; p. xxv, Bancroft Library, University of California Berkeley, CA; p. xxvi(top), BA; p. xxvi(bottom), Dale C. Wheary.